2008
Deskbook Encyclopedia of
American School Law

Center for
Education & Employment Law

Center for Education & Employment Law
P.O. Box 3008
Malvern, Pennsylvania 19355

> "This publication is designed to provide accurate and authoritative information in regard to
> the subject matter covered. It is sold with the understanding that the publisher is not engaged
> in rendering legal, accounting or other professional service. If legal advice or other expert
> assistance is required, the services of a competent professional person should be sought."—
> *from a Declaration of Principles jointly adopted by a Committee of the American Bar
> Association and a Committee of Publishers and Associations.*

ISBN 978-1-933043-23-4
ISSN 1058-4919

The Library of Congress has cataloged this serial title as follows:
Deskbook Encyclopedia of American School Law.—1980/81—Rosemount, Minn.:
Informational Research Systems, 1981-

v.; 23 cm.

Annual.
Published 2007   by: Center for Education & Employment Law
Prepared by the editors of: Legal Notes for Education,
1980/81-
1. Educational law and legislation—United States—Digests. 2. Educational law and legislation—
United States—Periodicals. I. Informational Research Systems (Washington, D.C.) II. Oakstone Legal
& Business Publishing III. Center for Education & Employment Law IV. Legal Notes for Education.
V. Title: Encyclopedia of American School Law.
KF4114.D46   92-054912
                                          344.73'07'02638—dc19
                                          [347.304702638]
                                                        AACR 2#M#MARC-S

Library of Congress   [8704r86]rev

Cover Design by Patricia Jacoby

Other Titles Published By
Center for Education & Employment Law:

Students with Disabilities and Special Education
Private School Law in America
Higher Education Law in America
U.S. Supreme Court Education Cases
Deskbook Encyclopedia of Public Employment Law
U.S. Supreme Court Employment Cases
Deskbook Encyclopedia of Employment Law
Statutes, Regulations and Case Law Protecting Individuals with Disabilities
Federal Laws Prohibiting Employment Discrimination

TABLE OF CONTENTS

Page

INTRODUCTION i

ABOUT THE EDITORS iii

HOW TO USE YOUR DESKBOOK v

TABLE OF CASES ix

TABLE OF CASES BY STATE xxvii

CHAPTER ONE
Accidents, Injuries and Deaths

I. NEGLIGENCE...2
   A. Elements 2
   B. Defenses 3
      1. Immunity 3
      2. Comparative and Contributory Negligence...................6

II. SCHOOL ATHLETICS..8
   A. Participants 8
      1. Duty of Care 8
      2. Governmental Immunity 10
      3. Assumption of Risk and Waiver 12
   B. Spectators, Employees and Parents..............................13

III. OTHER SCHOOL ACTIVITIES 14
   A. Physical Education Class Accidents 14
      1. Duty of Care 14
      2. Governmental Immunity 17
   B. Shop Class Injuries...19
      1. Duty of Care 19
      2. Governmental Immunity 20
   C. Other Supervised Activities..21
      1. Duty of Care 21
      2. Governmental Immunity 23

IV. UNSUPERVISED ACCIDENTS 25
   A. On School Grounds 25
      1. Duty of Care 25
      2. Governmental Immunity 26
   B. Off School Grounds 26
      1. Duty of Care 26
      2. Governmental Immunity 28

TABLE OF CONTENTS

V. LIABILITY FOR INTENTIONAL CONDUCT 29
    A. Employee Misconduct.......................................29
        1. Types of Misconduct 29
        2. Governmental Immunity 32
    B. Student Misconduct 34
        1. Types of Misconduct 34
        2. Governmental Immunity 38
    C. Parent Misconduct 41
    D. Suicide 43
    E. Defamation 45

VI. SCHOOL BUS ACCIDENTS..51
    A. Duty of Care 51
    B. Governmental Immunity 52

CHAPTER TWO
Religion and the Public Schools

I. RELIGIOUS ESTABLISHMENT 55
    A. Prayer and Religious Activity 56
    B. Instruction of Students 60
        1. Curriculum...60
        2. Textbooks 64
    C. Commencement Ceremonies 65
    D. School Policies 67
        1. The Pledge of Allegiance 67
        2. Other Policies 70
        3. Immunization.....................................72

II. USE OF SCHOOL FACILITIES...74
    A. Assemblies and School-Sponsored Events 74
    B. Student Groups...75
    C. The Equal Access Act.......................................78
    D. Non-Student Use 81
    E. Religious Literature and Symbols 85

III. LIMITATIONS ON EMPLOYEE RELIGIOUS ACTIVITY 90

IV. FINANCIAL ASSISTANCE AND VOUCHER PROGRAMS......93

CHAPTER THREE
Freedom of Speech and Association

I. STUDENTS..97
    A. Protected Speech 98
        1. Disciplinary Cases 98
        2. Threats and Bullying..............................101
        3. Internet Cases 106

    4. Confederate Flags 108
B. Student Publications 111
C. Non-School Publications.......................................113
D. Personal Appearance and Dress Codes.........................114
    1. Dress Codes 114
    2. Hair Length and Appearance 120
    3. Gang Affiliation 122

II.   EMPLOYEES 123
A. Protected Speech 124
B. Personal Appearance and Dress Codes.........................130
C. Association Rights 131

III. ACADEMIC FREEDOM 134
A. Library Materials 134
B. Textbook Selection 136
C. School Productions...137

IV. PARENTAL SPEECH AND ASSOCIATION RIGHTS 138
A. Access to School Campuses 139
B. Curriculum..141

V.   USE OF SCHOOL FACILITIES..................................143
A. Student Organizations and Demonstrations 143
B. Non-Student Groups...146

<h3 style="text-align:center">CHAPTER FOUR
Student Rights</h3>

I.   ADMISSIONS AND ATTENDANCE 149
A. Race, Admission and School Assignment 149
B   Age and Residency Requirements 154

II.   COMPULSORY ATTENDANCE 160
A. Compulsory Attendance and Truancy............................160
B. Home Study Programs 162
C. Attendance Policies..164

III. CORPORAL PUNISHMENT 165
A. Student Due Process Rights...................................165
B   Teacher Liability Protection 168

IV. RACE AND NATIONAL ORIGIN DISCRIMINATION.............172

V.   SEX DISCRIMINATION..176
A. Sexual Harassment by Students................................176
B. Sexual Harassment by Staff 180
C. Sexual Orientation 185

TABLE OF CONTENTS

CHAPTER FIVE
Student Discipline

I. EXPULSIONS AND SUSPENSIONS 187
    A. Due Process 187
        1. Notice and Procedural Protections 188
        2. Alternative Placements 193
        3. Zero-Tolerance Policies.......................................197
    B. Misconduct 200
        1. Sexual Harassment..200
        2. Drugs, Alcohol and Weapons Possession 202
        3. Extracurricular and Co-Curricular Events.................207
        4. Fighting and Violence 209
        5. Cell Phones and Electronic Devices.......................212
    C. Academic Expulsions or Suspensions 213

II. STUDENT SEARCH AND SEIZURE 215
    A. Fourth Amendment "Reasonable Suspicion" 215
        1. Searches Based on Individualized Suspicion...........215
        2. Off-Campus Searches 220
        3. Locker Searches 222
        4. Strip Searches 222
    B. Random Testing Policies 225
    C. Police Involvement 228
        1. *Miranda* Warnings 229
        2. Police-Assisted Searches 232
        3. Drug-Sniffing Dogs 234
        4. Liability Issues 235

CHAPTER SIX
Employment Practices

I. EMPLOYEE PRIVACY 239
    A. Employee Search and Seizure 239
        1. Drug Testing 240
        2. Individualized Searches 241
        3. Employee Examinations 243
    B. Technology and Surveillance 244
    C. Personnel Records 246
        1. Media Access 246
        2. Disclosure to Third Parties 250
        3. Electronic Communications 253

II. EMPLOYEE QUALIFICATIONS 254
    A. Certification and Licensure 254
    B. Testing and Reform Legislation 259
    C. Residency, Anti-Nepotism and Patronage Policies.........261

TABLE OF CONTENTS

III. VOLUNTARY EMPLOYEE LEAVE 264
  A. Family and Maternity Leave 264
  B. Compensatory, Vacation and Sick Leave 270

IV. REASSIGNMENTS, TRANSFERS AND SUSPENSIONS 272

V. REPORTING ABUSE AND NEGLECT................................275

CHAPTER SEVEN
Employment Discrimination

I. OVERVIEW 279

II. SEX DISCRIMINATION...280
  A. Title VII of the Civil Rights Act 280
  B. Pregnancy Discrimination 285
  C. Equal Pay and Gender 287
  D. Sexual Harassment..290
  E. Sexual Orientation 292

III. RACE AND NATIONAL ORIGIN DISCRIMINATION..............294
  A. Race Discrimination 294
  B. National Origin 297
  C. Affirmative Action 300

IV. RELIGIOUS DISCRIMINATION 302

V. AGE DISCRIMINATION 307

VI. DISABILITY DISCRIMINATION 311
  A. Rehabilitation Act of 1973................................311
  B. Americans with Disabilities Act............................314
  C. State Statutes 320

VII. DISCRIMINATION AGAINST VETERANS 322

CHAPTER EIGHT
Employment Termination, Resignation and Retirement

I. BUDGET REDUCTIONS AND REDUCTIONS IN FORCE....325

II. IMMORALITY AND OTHER MISCONDUCT........................328
  A. Sexual Misconduct 328
  B. Immoral Conduct..330
  C. Criminal Conduct 333
  D. Neglect of Duty 336
  E. Misuse of Technology 338

TABLE OF CONTENTS

III.   INCOMPETENCE 341
       A. Teaching Deficiencies 341
       B. Procedural Problems...344

IV.   INSUBORDINATION AND OTHER GOOD CAUSE 346

V.   RESIGNATION AND RETIREMENT....................................350
       A. Resignation 350
       B. Retirement..353
       C. Retirement Benefits 355

VI.   UNEMPLOYMENT BENEFITS 358
       A. Eligibility Requirements..358
       B. Misconduct 360

VII. WRONGFUL DISCHARGE..362

VIII. WORKERS' COMPENSATION 366

CHAPTER NINE
Tenure and Due Process

I.   STATE TENURE STATUTES..369
       A. Tenure Status 369
       B. Tenure Rights 376
            1. Reductions in Force 376
            2. Other Substantive Rights 380
       C. Collective Bargaining Agreements 381
       D. State Regulatory Authority 383

II.   DUE PROCESS REQUIREMENTS 385
       A. Property Interest 386
       B. Notice 390
       C. Hearing 393
            1. Minimum Requirements 393
            2. Hearing Procedures 396
            3. Impartiality 399

CHAPTER TEN
Labor Relations

I.   PROFESSIONAL ASSOCIATIONS.....................................401
       A. Representation 401
       B. Agency Fees 404

II.   COLLECTIVE BARGAINING AGREEMENTS 407
       A. Compensation..407
       B. Positions 413

TABLE OF CONTENTS

C. Other Terms and Conditions 416

III. GRIEVANCES AND ARBITRATION 419
    A. Arbitrability 419
    B. Procedures 423
    C. Standard of Review...424
    D. Association Duties and Rights 427

IV. STRIKES...428

CHAPTER ELEVEN
School Operations

I. BUDGET AND FINANCE 431
    A. Educational Finance and Equal Opportunity 431
    B. Property Taxes and Other Local Funding Issues 440
    C. Federal Funding 442
    D. School Expenditures and State Appropriations 443
    E. Student Fees and Tuition 448
        1. Transportation Fees 448
        2. Tuition and Other Fees 449
    F. Private Contractors 452
    G. Insurance Cases 455

II. DESEGREGATION 458
    A. Release from Federal Court Supervision 458
    B. Compliance with Desegregation Orders 461
    C. Liability Issues...463
        1. Government Liability 463
        2. Inter-District Remedies 465
        3. Budget Issues 466

III. SCHOOL DISTRICT OPERATIONS 469
    A. School Closing and District Dissolution Issues..............469
    B. Redistricting and Zoning 470

IV. SCHOOL BOARDS..472
    A. Membership 472
        1. Appointments, Elections, Residency and Recall........472
        2. Misconduct, Conflict of Interest and Nepotism 475
    B. School Board Powers and Duties 477
    C. Open Meeting Laws 483

CHAPTER TWELVE
Academic Practices

I. REFORM LEGISLATION 487
    A. The No Child Left Behind Act of 2001 487

B. State Reform Acts 493
C. Charter Schools 496
   1. Legislation..496
   2. Applications...498
   3. Operations and Finance 500

II. CURRICULUM AND GRADING 505
A. Curriculum..505
B. Bilingual Education 507
C. Grading 509

III. STUDENT RECORDS 513
A. Student and Parental Rights.................................513
B. Media Requests 520
C. Electronic and Video Records..............................523

IV. TESTING...526

V. EDUCATIONAL MALPRACTICE...............................531

CHAPTER THIRTEEN
Students with Disabilities

I. THE IDEA 534
A. IDEA Substantive Requirements 534
B. Procedural Protections 536
   1. IEPs and Team Meetings 537
   2. Notice and Hearing Requirements 541

II. DISCIPLINE OF STUDENTS WITH DISABILITIES 545
A. Discipline as a Change in Placement....................545
B. Manifestation Determinations 546
C. Delinquency and Juvenile Justice........................548

III. PLACEMENT OF STUDENTS WITH DISABILITIES 550
A. Identification and Evaluation 550
B. Child Find Obligation...553
C. Least Restrictive Environment 556
D. Change in Placement and the 'Stay-Put' Provision..........559
E. Other Placement Issues 562
   1. Behavior Problems 562
   2. Extended School Year Services 564
   3. Transfer Students 565

IV. RELATED SERVICES...567
A. Medical Services..567
B. Level or Location of Services 568
C. Provision of Related Services at Private Schools..........571

TABLE OF CONTENTS

V. TUITION REIMBURSEMENT 572
   A. Private School Tuition Claims 572
   B. Parental Conduct 575

VI. TRANSITION AND GRADUATION 578
   A. Transition Plans..578
   B. Graduation 579
   C. Compensatory Education 582

VII. SECTION 504 AND THE ADA 584
   A. Section 504 Accommodation Plans 584
   B. Discrimination Claims 586
   C. Standardized Testing..590

CHAPTER FOURTEEN
Private Schools

I. PRIVATE SCHOOL EMPLOYMENT 593
   A. Employment Discrimination...............................594
   B. Labor Relations...596
   C. Termination from Employment 598

II. STATE AND FEDERAL REGULATION 601
   A. Accreditation 601
   B. Sex Abuse and Mandatory Reporting...............602
   C. Taxation...604
      1. Federal Income Taxation.............................604
      2. State and Local Taxation 605

III. PRIVATE SCHOOL STUDENT RIGHTS....................609
   A. Admissions and Other School Policies 609
   B. Athletics and Extracurricular Activities 611
   C. Breach of Contract 612
      1. Educational Programs.................................612
      2. Tuition 614
   D. Discipline, Suspension, and Expulsion 615
   E. Students with Disabilities 618

IV. PUBLIC AND PRIVATE SCHOOL COOPERATION 622
   A. Dual Enrollment 622
   B Textbook Loans and Other Materials 623
   C. Transportation 625
   D. Personnel Sharing..627
   E. School Facilities and Property 628
   F. Release Time Programs 631

V. STUDENT FINANCIAL ASSISTANCE 632

TABLE OF CONTENTS

CHAPTER FIFTEEN
Interscholastic Athletics

I.   HIGH SCHOOL ATHLETICS..637
     A. Drug Testing 637
     B. Athletic and Extracurricular Suspensions 639
     C. Eligibility Rules and Restrictions..................................641
         1. Transfer Students 641
         2. Other Rules..644

II. DISCRIMINATION AND EQUITY 647
     A. Gender Equity...647
     B. Race Discrimination 651
         1. Secondary Schools...651
         2. Intercollegiate Athletics..653
     C. Students with Disabilities 655

III. ISSUES IN COACHING 659
     A. Employment 659
     B   Defamation 662
     C. Liability 665
     D. Misconduct 668

REFERENCE SECTION

APPENDIX A
     United States Constitution:
     Provisions of Interest to Educators..................................671

APPENDIX B
     Table of Supreme Court Education Cases 677

THE JUDICIAL SYSTEM 689

HOW TO READ A CASE CITATION.......................................693

GLOSSARY..695

INDEX 701

INTRODUCTION

The *2008 Deskbook Encyclopedia of American School Law* is a completely updated encyclopedic compilation of state and federal appellate court decisions that affect education. These decisions have been selected and edited by the editorial staff of Center for Education & Employment Law, publishers of *Legal Notes for Education*. Topical classifications have been revised and edited to reflect rapid changes in education law, and many cases reported in previous editions have been re-edited or reclassified.

This edition contains a brief introductory note on the American judicial system and an updated appendix of recent U.S. Supreme Court cases. Also included are portions of the U.S. Constitution that are most frequently cited in education cases. This publication is intended to provide educators and lawyers with access to the most current available cases in education. We believe that you will find this edition even more readable and easier to use than previous editions.

ABOUT THE EDITORS

James A. Roth is the editor of *Legal Notes for Education* and *Special Education Law Update*. He is a co-author of *Students with Disabilities* and *Special Education Law* and an adjunct program assistant professor at St. Mary's University in Minnesota. Mr. Roth is a graduate of the University of Minnesota and William Mitchell College of Law. He is admitted to the Minnesota Bar.

Thomas D'Agostino is a managing editor at the Center for Education & Employment Law. He graduated from the Duquesne University School of Law and received his undergraduate degree from Ramapo College of New Jersey. He is a past member of the American Bar Association's Section of Individual Rights and Responsibilities as well as the Pennsylvania Bar Association's Legal Services to Persons with Disabilities Committee. Mr. D'Agostino is admitted to the Pennsylvania bar.

Curt J. Brown is the Group Publisher of the Center for Education & Employment Law. Prior to assuming his present position, he gained extensive experience in business-to-business publishing, including management of well-known publications such as *What's Working in Human Resources, What's New in Benefits & Compensation, Keep Up to Date with Payroll, Supervisors Legal Update,* and *Facility Manager's Alert.* Mr. Brown graduated from Villanova School of Law and graduated magna cum laude from Bloomsburg University with a B.S. in Business Administration. He is admitted to the Pennsylvania Bar.

HOW TO USE YOUR DESKBOOK

We have designed the *2008 Deskbook Encyclopedia of American School Law* in an accessible format for both attorneys and non-attorneys to use as a research and reference tool toward prevention of legal problems.

Research Tool

As a research tool, our deskbook allows you to conduct your research on two different levels – by topics or cases.

Topic Research

♦ If you have a general interest in a particular **topic** area, our **table of contents** provides descriptive chapter headings containing detailed subheadings from each chapter.

   ➤ For your convenience, we also include the chapter table of contents at the beginning of each chapter.

Example:
For more information on alternative placements, the table of contents indicates that a discussion of this topic begins in Chapter Five on page 193:

CHAPTER FIVE
Student Discipline

I. EXPULSIONS AND SUSPENSIONS 187
  A. Due Process...187
    1. Notice and Procedural Protections 187
    2. Alternative Placements 193
    3. Zero-Tolerance Policies..............................197
  B. Misconduct..200
    1. Sexual Harassment...................................200
    2. Drugs, Alcohol and Weapons Possession 202
    3. Extracurricular and Co-Curricular Events 207
    4. Fighting and Violence 209
    5. Cell Phones and Electronic Devices................212
  C. Academic Expulsions or Suspensions....................213

HOW TO USE YOUR DESKBOOK

◆ If you have a specific interest in a particular **issue**, our comprehensive **index** collects all of the relevant page references to particular issues.

Example:
For more information on misconduct by coaches, the index provides references to all of the cases dealing with coaches instead of only those cases dealing with misconduct:

Coaches
defamation, 662-665
employment, 659-662
liability, 665-668
➡ misconduct, 668-670

Case Research

◆ If you know the **name** of a particular case, our **table of cases** will allow you to quickly reference the location of the case.

Example:
If someone mentioned a case named *Zelman v. Simmons-Harris,* looking in the table of cases, which has been arranged alphabetically, the case would be located under the "Z" section.

Z

Zellman v. Independent School Dist. No. 2758, 214
Zellner v. Cedarburg School Dist., 339
➡ Zelman v. Simmons-Harris, 93, 94, 95, 633
Zobrest v. Catalina Foothills School Dist., 571, 624, 628
Zorach v. Clauson, 71, 631, 632

✓ Each of the cases summarized in the deskbook also contains the case citation, which will allow you to access the full text of the case if you would like to learn more about it. *See How to Read a Case Citation, p. 693.*

♦ If your interest lies in cases from a **particular state**, our **table of cases by state** will identify the cases from your state and direct you to their page numbers.

Example:
    If cases from Texas were of interest, the table of cases by state, arranged alphabetically, would list all of the case summaries contained in the deskbook from Texas.

➡ **TEXAS**

Adams v. Groesbeck Independent School Dist., 281, 363, 660
Amaral-Whittenberg v. Alanis, 268
Barrow v. Greenville Independent School Dist., 262, 263
Bates v. Dallas Independent School Dist., 512

✓ Remember, the judicial system has two court systems—state and federal court—which generally function independently from each other. *See The Judicial System, p. 689.* We have included the federal court cases in the table of cases by state according to the state in which the court resides. However, federal court decisions often impact other federal courts within that particular circuit. Therefore, it may be helpful to review cases from all of the states contained in a particular circuit.

Reference Tool

As a reference tool, we have highlighted important resources that provide the framework for many legal issues.

♦ If you would like to see specific wording of the **U.S. Constitution**, refer to **Appendix A**, which includes relevant provisions of the U.S. Constitution such as the First Amendment (freedom of speech and religion).

♦ If you would like to review **U.S. Supreme Court decisions** in a particular subject matter area, our topical list of U.S. Supreme Court case citations located in **Appendix B** will be helpful.

We hope you benefit from the use of the *2008 Deskbook Encyclopedia of American School Law.* If you have any questions about how to use the deskbook, please contact Jim Roth at jroth@pbp.com.

TABLE OF CASES

A

A.B. v. Slippery Rock Area School Dist., 102
A.M.J. v. Royalton Public Schools, 177
A.P. v. Pemberton Township Board
of Educ., 547
A.W. v. Fairfax County School Board, 560
Aaron M. v. Yomtoob, 570
Abbott by Abbott v. Burke, 437
Abbott v. Burke, 437
Abbott v. North East Independent School
Dist., 251
Abington School Dist. v. Schempp, 57
Abood v. Detroit Board of Educ., 405
Ackerman v. Quilcene School Dist.
No. 48, 286
Adair v. State of Michigan, 445
Adams v. Baker, 651
Adams v. Groesbeck Independent School
Dist., 281, 363, 660
Adler v. Duval County School Board, 67
Agostini v. Felton, 624, 628
Aguilar v. Felton, 627
Aguilera v. Board of Educ. of Hatch Valley
Schools, 327
Akuluze v. Oakland Unified School Dist., 302
Albers v. Breen, 40
Albright v. Columbia Board of Educ., 317
Alex G. v. Board of Trustees of Davis Unified
School Dist., 563
Alex K. v. Wissahickon School Dist., 621
Alex R. v. Forrestville Community Unit
School Dist. #221, 563
Alexis v. Board of Educ., Baltimore Public
Schools, 541
Aliffi v. Liberty County School Dist., 24
Allen v. Wright, 605
Allison C. v. Advanced Educ. Services, 45
Amanda J. v. Clark County School Dist., 544
Amaral-Whittenberg v. Alanis, 268
Ambach v. Norwick, 264
Anderson v. Anoka Hennepin Independent
School Dist. 11, 20
Anderson v. City of Boston, 153
Anderson v. Independent School Dist.
No. 97, 49
Anderson v. Town of Durham, 95
Angstadt v. Midd-West School Dist., 646
Ansonia Board of Educ. v. Philbrook, 303
Appeal of Laconia School Dist., 421
Appeal of White Mountain Regional School
Dist., 425
Argueta v. Government of District
of Columbia, 582
Arizona State Board for Charter Schools v.
U.S. Dep't of Educ., 501
Arline v. School Board of Nassau County, 312

Arlington Cent. School Dist. Board
of Educ. v. Murphy, 535
Arteman v. Clinton Community Unit School
Dist. No. 15, 19
Ashby v. Hesperia Union School Dist., 669
Ashford v. Culver City Unified School
Dist., 396
Ashong v. Independent School Dist. #625, 361
Ass'n of Catholic Teachers v. PLRB, 598
Ass'n of Community Organizations
for Reform Now v. New York City Dep't
of Educ., 490, 493
Ass'n of Mexican-American Educators v.
State of California, 261
Aubrey v. School Board of Lafayette
Parish, 241
Auguster v. Vermilion Parish School
Board, 297
Avila v. Citrus Community College Dist., 9
Azure v. Belcourt Public School Dist., 23

B

B.C. through Powers v. Plumas Unified
School Dist., 235
B.W.S. v. Livingston Parish School Board, 189
Babb v. Hamilton County Board of Educ., 24
Back v. Hastings on Hudson Union Free
School Dist., 284
Bacus v. Palo Verde Unified School Dist.
Board of Educ., 60
Badger v. Greater Clark County Schools, 397
Bagley v. Raymond School Dep't, 95
Bajjani v. Gwinnett County School
Dist., 39, 489
Baker v. Adams County/Ohio Valley School
Board, 87
Bakersfield Elementary Teachers Ass'n v.
Bakersfield City School Dist., 257
Ballard v. Independent School Dist. No. 4
of Bryan County, Oklahoma, 332
Baltimore City Board of School
Commissioners v. Taylorch, 620
Baltimore Teachers Union v. Maryland State
Board of Educ., 494
Bannon v. School Dist. of Palm Beach
County, 88
Barber v. Dearborn Public Schools, 101
Bar-Navon v. School Board of Brevard
County, Florida, 116
Barnes v. Spearfish School Dist.
No. 40-2, 346
Barnett v. Memphis City School, 583
Barnica v. Kenai Peninsula Borough School
Dist., 424
Barrett v. Steubenville City Schools, 264
Barrett v. Unified School Dist. No. 259, 12

TABLE OF CASES

Barrino v. East Baton Rouge Parish School Board, 512

Barrow v. Greenville Independent School Dist., 262, 263

Bartell v. Aurora Public Schools, 274

Barton v. Independent School Dist. No. I-99, Custer County, 380

Bates v. Dallas Independent School Dist., 512

Bates v. U.S., 635

Batson v. Pinckneyville Elementary School Dist. No. 50, 26

Battles v. Anne Arundel County Board of Educ., 164

Baynard v. Malone, 184

Beard v. Whitmore Lake School Dist., 224

Beaufort County Board of Educ. v. Lighthouse Charter School Committee, 500

Behymer-Smith v. Coral Academy of Science, 138

Bell v. New Jersey, 442

Bell v. West Haven Board of Educ., 506

Bellevue John Does 1-11 v. Bellevue School Dist. #405, 246

Ben Bolt-Palito Blanco Consolidated Independent School Dist. v. Texas Political Subdivisions Property/Casualty Joint Self-Insurance Fund, 456

Benjamin G. v. Special Educ. Hearing Office, 553

Benjamin v. Metropolitan School Dist., 180

Bennett v. Kentucky Dep't of Educ., 442

Bennett v. New Jersey, 442

Berger v. Medina City School Dist., 576

Bergerson v. Salem-Keizer School Dist., 331

Berkshire School v. Town of Reading, 607

Beshears v. Unified School Dist. No. 305, 38

Beth B. v. Van Clay, 558

Bethel School Dist. No. 403 v. Fraser, 99

Billings v. Madison Metropolitan School Dist., 154

Bitting v. Lee, 165

Blaine v. Savannah Country Day School, 614

Bland v. Candioto, 41, 42

Blau v. Ft. Thomas Public School Dist., 116

Block v. Rockford Public School Dist., 589

Board of County Commissioners of Shelby County, Tennessee v. Burson, 474

Board of Educ. of Borough of Englewood Cliffs v. Board of Educ. of City of Englewood, 465

Board of Educ. of City of Millville v. New Jersey Dep't of Educ., 438, 442

Board of Educ. of City of New York v. Tom F., 619

Board of Educ. of City of Passaic v. New Jersey Dep't of Educ., 442

Board of Educ. of Independent School Dist. 92, Pottawatomie County v. Earls, 226, 638

Board of Educ. of Kiryas Joel Village School Dist. v. Grumet, 471

Board of Educ. of Monticello Cent. School Dist. v. Commissioner of Educ., 114

Board of Educ. of Oklahoma City Public Schools v. Dowell, 458, 459

Board of Educ. of Ottawa Township High School Dist. No. 140 v. U.S. Dep't of Educ., 491

Board of Educ. of Sacramento City Unified School Dist. v. Sacramento County Board of Educ., 193

Board of Educ. of Talbot County v. Heister, 351

Board of Educ. of Thornton Township High School Dist. 205 v. Board of Educ. of Argo Community High School Dist. 217, 652

Board of Educ. of West Windsor-Plainsboro Regional School Dist. v. Board of Educ. of Township of Delran, 570

Board of Educ. of Westside Community School v. Mergens, 79

Board of Educ. v. Allen, 625

Board of Educ. v. McCluskey, 202

Board of Educ. v. Pico, 135

Board of Educ. v. Rowley, 534, 536

Board of Regents v. Roth, 385

Board of Trustees of Bastrop Independent School Dist. v. Toungate, 121

Board of Trustees of Fremont County School Dist. #25 v. BM, 189

Board of Trustees of Univ. of Alabama v. Garrett, 315, 318

Bob Jones Univ. v. U.S., 604

Bogle-Assegai v. Bloomfield Board of Educ., 189

Bojarczuk v. Mills, 381

Boles-El v. Cleveland Municipal School Dist., 258

Boone v. Boozeman, 73

Boone v. Reese, 170

Boring v. Buncombe County Board of Educ., 138

Boroff v. Van Wert City Board of Educ., 116

Boss v. Peninsula School Dist., 483

Bowalick v. Comwlth. of Pennsylvania, 334

Bowers v. NCAA, 657

Boy Scouts of America v. Dale, 146

Boy Scouts of America v. Till, 146

Boyd County High School Gay Straight Alliance v. Board of Educ. of Boyd County, 145

Bradshaw v. Cherry Creek School Dist. No. 5, 158

Bragdon v. Abbott, 314

Bragg v. Swanson, 110

Brennan v. Giles County Board of Educ., 254

TABLE OF CASES

Brentwood Academy v. Tennessee Secondary School Athletic Ass'n, 611, 612, 664

Brigham v. State, 437

Briseno v. State of Texas, 218

Bristol Warren Regional School Committee v. Rhode Island Dep't of Educ., 572

Brooks v. Logan, 44

Brosch v. Mariemont City School Dist. Board of Educ., 207

Brouillette v. Dep't of Employment and Training Board of Review, 359

Brown v. Board of Educ., 153, 458, 463, 466, 652

Brown v. State of Washington, 409

Brubaker v. Hardy, 371

Brunswick School v. Hutter, 615

BRV v. Superior Court, 248

Bryant v. Independent School Dist. No. I-38, Garvin County, Oklahoma, 175

Buchna v. Illinois State Board of Educ., 345

Budworth v. Los Angeles Unified School Dist., 238

Bukowski v. Wisconsin Interscholastic Ass'n, 648

Buncombe County, North Carolina, Board of Educ. v. Roberts, 192

Burch v. Barker, 114

Burger v. Board of School Directors of McGuffey School Dist., 273

Burkybile v. Board of Educ. of Hastings-On-Hudson Union Free School Dist., 244

Burlington Industries, Inc. v. Ellerth, 282, 290

Burlington Northern & Santa Fe Railway Co. v. White, 281

Burlington School Committee v. Dep't of Educ., 573

Burns v. Warwick Valley Cent. School Dist., 306

Burr and Burton Seminary v. Town of Manchester, 607

Bush v. Holmes, 94

Butler v. Rio Rancho Public Schools Board of Educ., 205

Butler v. South, 274

Byrd v. Irmo High School, 192

C

C.N. v. Ridgewood Board of Educ., 515

Cabouli v. Chappaqua Cent. School Dist., 557

Cagle v. St. Johns County School Dist., 413

Caitlin W. v. Rose Tree Media School Dist., 621

California Teachers Ass'n v. Governing Board of Golden Valley Unified School Dist., 391

California Teachers Ass'n v. Governing Board of San Diego Unified School Dist., 131

Californians For Justice Educ. Fund v. State Board of Educ., 529

Campaign for Fiscal Equity Inc. v. State of New York, 164, 432

Campbell v. Board of Educ. of the Centerline School Dist., 588

Camps Newfound/Owatonna, Inc. v. Town of Harrison, Maine, 606

Cannon County Board of Educ. v. Wade, 420

Carbajal v. Albuquerque Public School Dist., 508

Carbondale Area School Dist. v. Fell Charter School, 504

Carestio v. School Board of Broward County, 172

Carmel Cent. School Dist. v. V.P., 575

Carpenito v. Board of Educ. of Borough of Rumson, 379

Carpenter v. Dillon Elementary School Dist. 10, 147

Carrier v. Lake Pend Oreille School Dist., 44

Carriveau v. Davison School Dist. #25140, 54

Carroll v. Ringgold Educ. Ass'n, 430

Cartwright v. District of Columbia, 553

Case v. Unified School Dist. No. 233, 136

Cason v. Cook, 237

Cassimy v. Board of Educ. of Rockford Public Schools, Dist. 205, 317

Cassise v. Walled Lake Consolidated Schools, 663

Catherine G. v. County of Essex, 275, 276

Caudillo v. Lubbock Independent School Dist., 144

Cedar Rapids Community School Dist. v. Garret F. by Charlene F., 568

Cent. Dauphin School Dist. v. Founding Coalition of Infinity Charter School, 500

Cerny v. Cedar Bluffs Junior/Senior Public School, 667, 668

Cerra v. Pawling Cent. School Dist., 542

Chapel Hill-Carrboro City Schools System v. Chavioux, 452

Chavez v. Martinez, 235, 238

Chicago Board of Educ. v. Substance, Inc., 530

Chicago Teachers Union v. Hudson, 406

Chicago Teachers Union, Local 1 v. Board of Educ. of City of Chicago, 482

Chicago Tribune Co. v. Board of Educ. of City of Chicago, 521

Child Evangelism Fellowship of Maryland v. Montgomery County Schools, 82, 83

Child Evangelism Fellowship of New Jersey v. Stafford Township School Dist., 83

Child Evangelism Fellowship of South Carolina v. Anderson School Dist. Five, 77

Chiras v. Miller, 137

Chittenden Town School Dist. v. Vermont Dep't of Educ., 96

Chiu v. Plano Independent School Dist., 143

Christensen v. Harris County, 270

Christensen v. Royal School Dist. #160, 6, 7

Cigan v. Chippewa Falls School Dist., 319

Cioffi v. Averill Park Cent. School Dist. Board of Educ., 126

Circle School v. Pappert, 70

Citizens Concerned for Kids v. Yellow Medicine East Independent School Dist., 480

Citizens for Responsible Curriculum v. Montgomery County Public Schools, 63

City of Rancho Palos Verdes v. Abrams, 648

Civil Service Employees Ass'n, Local 1000 v. New York State Public Employment Relations Board, 403

CJN v. Minneapolis Public Schools, Special School Dist. No. 1, 564

Claar v. Auburn School Dist. No. 408, 52

Claremont School Dist. v. Governor, 433

Clark County Educ. Ass'n v. Clark County School Dist., 342

Clark County School Dist. v. Breeden, 291

Clark County School Dist. v. Buchanan, 322

Clark County School Dist. v. Bundley, 360

Clark County School Dist. v. Riley, 375

Clark v. Banks, 565

Clear Creek Independent School Dist. v. J.K., 582

Cleveland Board of Educ. v. LaFleur, 269

Cleveland Board of Educ. v. Loudermill, 395

Coachella Valley Unified School Dist. v. State of California, 490

Cochran v. Louisiana State Board of Educ., 623

Coggin v. Longview Independent School Dist., 387

Cohn v. New Paltz Cent. School Dist., 203

Cole v. Montague Board of Educ., 139

Coleman v. Newburgh Enlarged City School Dist., 547

Colin v. Orange Unified School Dist., 145

Collette v. Tolleson Unified School Dist. No. 214, 3

Columbia Falls Elementary School Dist. No. 6 v. State of Montana, 438

Columbus Board of Educ. v. Penick, 465

Combs v. Homer Center School Dist., 62

Comfort v. Lynn School Committee, 151

Committee for Public Educ. & Religious Liberty v. Nyquist, 93, 94, 636

Communications Workers of America, Local 3180 v. Indian River County School Board, 418

Communities for Equity v. Michigan High School Athletic Ass'n, 648

Comprehensive Community Solutions v. Rockford School Dist., 498

Comwlth. of Massachusetts v. Buccella, 519

Comwlth. of Massachusetts v. Damian D., 220

Connecticut v. Spellings, 488

Connick v. Myers, 123, 140

Connolly v. Rye School Dist., 156

Cooksey v. San Bernardino City Unified School Dist., 345

Coolidge v. Riegle, 43, 539

Copley Press v. Board of Educ. for Peoria School Dist. No. 150, 248

Corbett v. Scranton School Dist., 275

Corley v. Detroit Board of Educ., 292

Cornfield v. Consolidated High School Dist., 223

Corp. of the Presiding Bishop of the Church of Jesus Christ of Latter-Day Saints v. Amos, 595

Cortez v. Calumet Public School Dist. No. 132, 509

County School Board of York County v. A.L., 542

Courson v. Danville School Dist. No. 118, 21

Cox v. Zanesville City School Dist. Board of Educ., 343

Coy v. Board of Educ. of North Canton City Schools, 108

Crager v. Board of Educ. of Knott County, 240

Crawford v. Huntington Beach Union High School Dist., 465

Cresskill Board of Educ. v. Cresskill Educ. Ass'n, 381

Crete Educ. Ass'n v. Saline County School Dist., 413

Creusere v. Board of Educ. of City School Dist. of Cincinnati, 305

Crist v. Alpine Union School Dist., 245

Critchelow v. Breckinridge County Board of Educ., 208, 640

Crocker v. Tennessee Secondary School Athletic Ass'n, 658

Cross County School Dist. v. Spencer, 210

Crowe v. School Dist. of Pittsburgh, 626

Crowley v. McKinney, 141

Cruz v. Pennsylvania Interscholastic Athletic Ass'n, 656

Csorny v. Shoreham-Wading River Cent. School Dist., 484

Cuesta v. School Board of Miami-Dade County, Florida, 199

Culbertson v. San Gabriel Unified School Dist., 391

Curcio v. Collingswood Board of Educ., 266

Cureton v. NCAA, 653, 654, 655

Cypress-Fairbanks Independent School Dist v. Michael F., 536

TABLE OF CASES

D

D.B. v. Lafon, 109

D.C. v. School Dist. of Philadelphia, 194

D.E.R. v. Board of Educ. of Borough of Ramsey, 557

D.F. v. Board of Educ. of Syosset Cent. School Dist., 103

D.F. v. Codell, 511

D.L. and Z.Y., on Behalf of T.L. and K.L. v. Board of Educ. of Princeton Regional School Dist., 451

D.L. v. Warsaw Community Schools, 523

D.N. v. Penn Harris Madison School Corp., 640

D.O.F. v. Lewisburg Area School Dist., 203

D.P. v. School Board of Broward County, Florida, 557

Dale M. v. Board of Educ. of Bradley Bourbonnais High School Dist. No. 307, 550

Daleiden v. Jefferson County Joint School Dist. No. 251, 367

Daniels v. Woodside, 195

Davenport v. Washington Educ. Ass'n, 131

Davis v. Chester Upland School Dist., 423

Davis v. Greenwood School Dist. 50, 409

Davis v. Macon County Board of Educ., 346

Davis v. Monroe County Board of Educ., 174, 176, 177, 178, 586

Daw v. School Dist. 91 Board of Trustees, 193

Day v. Ouachita Parish School Board, 9

Daye v. School Board of City of Norfolk, 319

Dean v. Utica Community Schools, 112

DeCesare v. Niles City School Dist. Board of Educ., 268

DeKalb County School Dist. v. M.T.V., 569

Delekta v. Memphis Community Schools, 510

Demmon v. Loudoun County Public Schools, 89

Denver Parents Ass'n v. Denver Board of Educ., 532

Dep't of Finance v. Comm'n on State Mandates, 446

DeRolph v. State, 496

DiRusso v. Aspen School Dist., 310

Dobrich v. Walls, 59

Dodgeland Educ. Ass'n v. Wisconsin Employment Relations Comm'n, 422

Doe v. Kamehameha Schools, 610

Doe v. Little Rock School Dist., 227

Doe v. Lutheran High School of Greater Minneapolis, 594

Doe v. Metropolitan Nashville Public Schools, 555

Doe v. North Panola School Dist., 37

Doe v. Paris Union School Dist. No. 95, 139

Doe v. Perry Community School Dist., 185

Doe v. Porter, 64

Doe v. Rohan, 31

Doe v. San Antonio Independent School Dist., 38

Doe v. School Dist. of City of Norfolk, 66

Doe v. State of Hawaii, 167

Doe v. Superintendent of Schools of Stoughton, 202

Doe v. Tangipahoa Parish School Board, 59

Doe v. Woodford County Board of Educ., 658

Dombrowski v. Wissahickon School Dist., 584

Dominic J. v. Wyoming Valley West High School, 513, 639

Donovan v. Punxsutawney Area School Board, 80

Doria v. Stulting, 172

Douglas v. Londonderry School Board, 112

Dowell v. Board of Educ. of Oklahoma City Public Schools, 460

Downing v. City of Lowell, 385

Downing v. West Haven Board of Educ., 92

Doyle v. Rondout Valley Cent. School Dist., 237

Dragonis v. School Committee of Melrose, 47

Draudt v. Wooster City School Dist. Board of Educ., 113

Duck v. Isle of Wight County School Board, 587

Duitch v. Canton City Schools, 37

Dupuis v. Board of Trustees, Ronan School Dist. No. 30, 477

Durant v. Michigan, 444

E

E.D. v. Enterprise City Board of Educ., 578

Eason v. Clark County School Dist., 33

East Penn School Dist. v. Scott B., 579

Ecklund v. Byron Union School Dist., 62

Edelson v. Uniondale Union Free School Dist., 13

Eden v. Oblates of St. Francis de Sales, 603

Educ. Minnesota – Chisholm v. Independent School Dist. No. 695, 403

Educ. Minnesota – Greenway, Local 1330 v. Independent School Dist. No. 316, 412

Educ. Minnesota Lakeville v. Independent School Dist. No. 194, 134

Edwards v. Aguillard, 60

Ekalaka Unified Board of Trustees v. Ekalaka Teachers' Ass'n, MEA-MFT, NEA, 408

Elgin Independent School Dist. v. R.N., 53

Elk Grove Unified School Dist. v. Newdow, 68

Ellis v. Cleveland Municipal School Dist., 166

Embry v. O'Bannon, 622

Emery v. Roanoke City School Board, 568

Engel v. Vitale, 57

TABLE OF CASES

Environmental Charter High School v. Centinela Valley Union High School Dist., 503

Eric H. v. Methacton School Dist., 559

Erich D. v. New Milford Board of Educ., 160, 549

Erik V. by and through Catherine V. v. Causby, 531

Escambia County Board of Educ. v. Benton, 538

Etheredge v. Richland School Dist. One, 6

Eulitt v. State of Maine, 95

Evanston Community Consolidated School Dist. No. 65 v. Michael M., 569

Everett v. Santa Barbara High School Dist., 584

Everson v. Board of Educ. of School Dist. of City of Highland Park, 128

Everson v. Board of Educ., 626

Ex Parte Dunn, 659

Ex Parte Jackson, 397

Ex Parte McCord-Baugh, 289

F

Fankhauser v. Cobb, 347

Faragher v. City of Boca Raton, 290

Farner v. Idaho Falls School Dist. No. 91, 390

Farrin v. Maine School Administrative Dist. No. 59, 548

Fauconier v. Committee on Special Educ., 543

Fauconier v. Committee on Special Educ., Dist. 3, New York Board of Educ., 543

Febres v. Camden Board of Educ., 267

Fenceroy v. Morehouse Parish School Board, 121

Fick v. Sioux Falls School Dist. 49-5, 571

Fielder v. Board of Directors of Carroll Community School Dist., 335

Fields v. Palmdale School Dist., 142

Finch v. Fort Bend Independent School Dist., 393

Flaskamp v. Dearborn Public Schools, 133

Flatt v. Tennessee Secondary Schools Athletic Ass'n, 665

Fleenor v. Darby School Dist., 478

Fleischfresser v. Directors of School Dist. 200, 137

Flint v. Manchester Public Schools, 163

Florence County School Dist. Four v. Carter, 573

Flores v. Morgan Hill Unified School Dist., 186

Flores v. Rzeslawski, 527

Florida Dep't of Educ. v. Cooper, 517

Florida Dep't of Educ. v. NYT Management Services, 249

Florida High School Athletic Ass'n v. Marazzito, 646

Flour Bluff Independent School Dist. v. R.S., 193

Floyd v. Horry County School Dist., 192

Folkers v. Lincoln County School Dist., 408

Foote v. Manchester School Dist., 479

Foote v. Pine Bluff School Dist., 17

Foreman School Dist. No. 25 v. Steele, 392

Fort Stewart Schools v. Federal Labor Relations Authority, 411

Foster v. Mahdesian, 407

Fowler v. Williamson, 195

Francine Delany New School for Children Inc. v. Asheville City Board of Educ., 505

Franklin v. St. Louis Board of Educ., 272

Fratus v. Marion Community Schools Board of Trustees, 355

Frazer v. St. Tammany Parish School Board, 8

Frazier v. Alexandre, 68

Frederick v. Morse, 99

Freedom From Religion Foundation, Inc. v. Bugher, 625

Freeman v. Pitts, 458, 459

Fresh Start Academy v. Toledo Board of Educ., 492

Friery v. Los Angeles Unified School Dist., 301

Frugis v. Bracigliano, 278

Fuentes v. Board of Educ. of City of New York, 543

Fuhr v. School Dist. of City of Hazel Park, 285

Fuller v. Decatur Public School Board of Educ., Dist. 61, 211

Fuller v. Lakeview Academy, 614

Funston v. School Town of Munster, 7

G

Gabrielle M. v. Park Forest-Chicago Heights School Dist., 179

Gabrilson v. Flynn, 476

Garcetti v. Ceballos, 123, 124

Garcia v. Board of Educ. of Albuquerque Public Schools, 173

Garcia v. Puccio, 46

Gary S. v. Manchester School Dist., 620

Gatto v. St. Richard School, 600

Gebser v. Lago Vista Independent School Dist., 181, 183

Gedney v. Board of Educ. of Town of Groton, 314

Gee v. Professional Practices Comm'n, 399

General Star Indemnity Co. v. Lake Bluff School Dist. No. 65, 457

Gernetzke v. Kenosha Unified School Dist. No. 1, 81

Gettysburg School Dist. 53-1 v. Larson, 382

GI Forum v. Texas Educ. Agency, 592

TABLE OF CASES

Giacomucci v. Southeast Delco School Dist., 451

Gibson v. Caruthersville School Dist. No. 8, 394

Gikas v. Washington School Dist., 324

Gilbert v. Homar, 395

Gilder-Lucas v. Elmore County Board of Educ., 660

Globe Newspaper Co. v. Commissioner of Educ., 521

Golden Christian Academy v. Zelman, 602

Golden ex rel. Balch v. Anders, 168

Golden v. Rossford Exempted Village School Dist., 75

Gonzaga Univ. v. Doe, 493, 518

Good News Club v. Milford Cent. School, 76

Gooding Public Joint School Dist. No. 231, 206

Goss v. Lopez, 187, 188, 192, 194, 201, 506, 617

Graham v. Mock, 158

Graham v. Springfield Vermont School Dist., 132

Granowitz v. Redlands Unified School Dist., 201

Granville v. Minneapolis School Dist., 174

Gratz v. Bollinger, 150, 151

Green v. County School Board of New Kent County, 458, 460

Green v. Jersey City Board of Educ., 32

Greendale Educ. Ass'n v. Greendale School Dist., 330

Greene v. Plano Independent School Dist., 3

Greenshields v. Independent School Dist. I-1016, 126

Grendysa v. Evesham Township Board of Educ., 329

Grieb v. Unemployment Compensation Board of Review, 362

Griggs v. Ft. Wayne School Board, 117

Grim v. Rhinebeck Cent. School Dist., 540

Gruenke v. Seip, 670

Grumet v. Cuomo, 471

Grumet v. Pataki, 471

Grutter v. Bollinger, 150, 151

Gumm v. Nevada Dep't of Educ., 583

Guy v. New York State Public High School Athletic Ass'n, 645

H

Hale v. Poplar Bluff R-I School Dist., 561

Halter v. Iowa Board of Educ. Examiners, 258

Hamilton County Dep't of Educ. v. Deal, 535

Hamilton Roofing Co. of Carlsbad, Inc. v. Carlsbad Municipal Schools Board of Educ., 455

Hammond v. Board of Educ. of Carroll County, 10

Hamrick by Hamrick v. Affton School Dist. Board of Educ., 211

Hancock v. Commissioner of Educ., 436

Hanes v. Board of Educ. of City of Bridgeport, 332

Haney v. Bradley County Board of Educ., 43

Hansen v. Ann Arbor Public Schools, 72

Hanson v. Vermillion School Dist. No. 13-1, 376

Hardin County Schools v. Foster, 523

Harper v. Poway Unified School Dist., 115

Harrah Independent School Dist. v. Martin, 255

Harris v. Forklift Systems, Inc., 290

Harris v. McCray, 666

Harrisburg School Dist. v. Hickok, 495

Harrisburg School Dist. v. Zogby, 495

Harris-Thomas v. Christina School Dist., 175

Harry A. v. Duncan, 36

Hassberger v. Board of Educ., Cent. Community Unit School Dist., 623

Haugerud v. Amery School Dist., 285

Hawkins v. Sarasota County School Board, 180

Hayenga v. Nampa School Dist. No. 131, 236

Hayes v. State Teacher Certification Board, 331

Hazelwood School Dist. v. Kuhlmeier, 61, 88, 111, 112

Hearn v. Board of Public Educ., 241

Hearn v. Muskogee Public School Dist., 119

Hedges v. Musco, 220

Heinkel v. School Board of Lee County, Florida, 144

Hellmann v. Union R-XI School Dist., 343

Hemady v. Long Beach Unified School Dist., 16

Hemstad v. Jefferson Parish School Board, 456

Henderson v. Chartiers Valley School, 288

Henderson v. Independent School Dist. No. 706, 378

Henderson v. Simpson County Public School Dist., 41

Henderson v. Walled Lake Consolidated Schools, 181

Henney v. Shelby City School Dist., 11

Hernandez v. Don Bosco Preparatory High School, 618

Hibbs v. Winn, 605

Hildebrant v. Educational Testing Service, 528

Hill v. Board of Educ., Dist. I-009, Jones, Oklahoma, 483

Hills v. Scottsdale Unified School Dist. No. 48, 85

Hines v. Caston School Corp., 122

Hinkle v. Shepherd School Dist. #37, 22

Hiram College v. Courtad, 614

Hoffman v. East Troy Community School Dist., 556

TABLE OF CASES

Hoke County Board of Educ. v. State of North Carolina, 439

Hoke v. Elizabethtown Area School Dist., 191

Holloman v. Harland, 70

Holmes v. Board of Educ. of West Harvey-Dixmoor School Dist. No. 147, 265

Holmes v. Macon County Board of Educ., 369

Holton v. City of Thomasville School Dist., 464

Honig v. Doe, 546, 562

Hood v. The Illinois High School Ass'n, 662

Hope v. Pelzer, 224

Hornstine v. Township of Moorestown, 588

Hortonville Joint School Dist. No. 1 v. Hortonville Educ. Ass'n, 429

Houston Independent School Dist. v. Bobby R., 536

Houston v. Nelson, 371

Howard v. West Baton Rouge Parish School Board, 337

Howard v. Yakovac, 236

Hudon v. West Valley School Dist., 290

Hudson v. C.F. Vigor High School, 19

Hugger v. Rutherford Institute, 49

Hughes v. Stanley County School Dist., 278

Hull v. Albrecht, 446

Hunt v. McNair, 635, 636

Huntsman v. Perry Local School Dist. Board of Educ., 339

I

Ianicelli v. McNeely, 476

Idaho Schools For Equal Educational Opportunity v. State, 434

Immaculate Conception Corp. and Don Bosco High School v. Iowa Dep't of Transportation, 630

In re Amir X.S., 101, 102

In re Chisago Lakes School Dist., 552

In re D.D., 549

In re Dissolution of Union County Regional High School Dist. No. 1, 470

In re Expulsion of B.M. from Independent School Dist. No. 2142, 191

In re Expulsion of G.H., 202

In re Expulsion of I.A.L., 190

In re Expulsion of Rogers, 206

In re G.S.P., 232

In re Grant of Charter School Application of Englewood on Palisades Charter School, 498

In re Ivan, 163

In re Johnny F., 219

In re Maine-Endwell Teachers' Ass'n v. Board of Educ. of Maine-Endwell Cent. School Dist., 305

In re Maison Scahill v. Greece Cent. School Dist., 335

In re O.E., 218

In re Patrick Y., 222

In re Petition of Billings High School Dist. No. 2, 247

In re R.H., 231

In re R.M., 195

In re Randy G., 219

In re Recall of Young, 473

In re Roberts, 192

In re V.P., 232

In re: Removal of Kuehnle, 484

Indiana High School Athletic Ass'n v. Martin, 643

Indiana State Board of Educ. v. Brownsburg Community School Corp., 478

Ingraham v. Wright, 165, 166, 670

Irving Independent School Dist. v. Tatro, 568

J

J.H. v. Henrico County School Board, 565

J.S. v. Bethlehem Area School Dist., 107

J.S.W. v. Lee County Board of Educ., 203

Jackson v. Benson, 96

Jackson v. Birmingham Board of Educ., 662

Jackson v. State of Alabama State Tenure Comm'n, 127

Jacobs v. Clark County School Dist., 118

James v. Jackson, 16

James v. Sevre-Duszynska, 348

Jankovitz v. Des Moines Independent Community School Dist., 309

Jasa v. Millard Public School Dist. No. 17, 577

Jaynes v. Newport News School Board, 545

Jeffrey v. Board of Trustees of Bells Independent School Dist., 507

Jenkins by Jenkins v. State of Missouri, 468

Jennings v. Wentzville R-IV School Dist., 208

Jensen v. Reeves, 520

Jerideau v. Huntingdon Union Free School Dist., 14

Joel R. v. Board of Educ. of Mannheim School Dist. 83, Cook County, Illinois, 452

Johansen v. Louisiana High School Athletic Ass'n, 642

Johnson v. Deluz, 516

Johnson v. North Union Local School Dist. Board of Educ., 271

Johnson v. Paradise Valley Unified School Dist., 320

Johnson v. School Union No. 107, 287

Johnson v. Special Educ. Hearing Office, 566

Johnston School Committee v. Rhode Island State Labor Relations Board, 417

Johnstone v. Thompson, 441

Jones v. Indiana Area School Dist., 178, 562

Jones v. Miami-Dade County Public Schools, 374

Jones v. West Virginia State Board of Educ., 645
Jordan v. Smyrna School Dist. Board of Educ., 213
Joye v. Hunterdon Cent. Regional High School Board of Educ., 228

K

K.D. v. Fillmore Cent. School Dist., 117
K.M. v. Hyde Park Cent. School Dist., 586
Kadrmas v. Dickinson Public Schools, 449
Kahn v. East Side Union High School Dist., 15, 667
Kansas State Board of Educ. v. Marsh, 338
Karr v. Schmidt, 120
Katherine G. v. Kentfield School Dist., 559
Katruska v. Bethlehem Center School Dist., 400
Keeling v. Jefferson County Board of Educ., 353
Kelly v. Board of Educ. of McHenry Community High School Dist., 122
Kelso v. Southfield Public Schools Board of Educ., 246
Kenton County School Dist. v. Hunt, 565
Kentucky Dep't of Educ. v. Risner, 477
Kentucky Educ. Professional Standards Board v. Gambrel, 260
Kern v. Saydel Community School Dist., 324
Kerr v. Valdez, 299
Ketchersid v. Rhea County Board of Educ., 349
Kevin T. v. Elmhurst Community School Dist. No. 205, 581
Kilgore v. Jasper City Board of Educ., 371
Kimball v. Keystone Local School Dist., 647
Kimel v. Florida Board of Regents, 308
Kings Local School Dist. v. Zelazny, 540
Kinman v. Omaha Public School Dist., 185
Kirkland v. Greene County Board of Educ., 167
Kitzmiller v. Dover Area School Dist., 63
Kleczek v. Rhode Island Interscholastic League, 651
Klinger v. Adams County School Dist. No. 50, 351
Kloberdanz v. Swan Valley School Dist., 200
Klump v. Nazareth Area School Dist., 213
Knight v. Hayward Unified School Dist., 321
Knox County Educ. Ass'n v. Knox County Board of Educ., 240
Knubbe v. Detroit Board of Educ., 344
Koenick v. Felton, 72
Kotterman v. Killian, 605
Kozlowski v. Hampton School Board, 310
Kozura v. Tulpehocken Area School Dist., 428

Kristin National Inc. v. Board of Educ. of the City of Marietta, 507
Kurtz v. Unified School Dist. No. 308, 32
Kuszewski v. Chippewa Valley School Dist., 561

L

L.M. v. Evesham Township Board of Educ., 574
L.T. on Behalf of N.B. v. Warwick School Committee, 566
L.W. v. Knox County Board of Educ., 56
Lafayette Parish School Board v. Cormier, 42
Lafferty v. Board of Educ. of Floyd County, 398
Laiche v. Kohen, 668
Laidlaw Transit Inc. v. Alabama Educ. Ass'n, 483
Lake Ridge Academy v. Carney, 614
Lake View School Dist. No. 25 v. Huckabee, 433
Lakin v. Birmingham Public Schools, 541
Lamb's Chapel v. Center Moriches Union Free School Dist., 82
Lancaster School Dist. Support Ass'n, OEA/NEA v. Board of Educ., Lancaster City School Dist., 426
Land v. Board of Educ. of City of Chicago, 328
Lannom v. Board of Educ. for Metropolitan Government, Nashville and Davidson County, 336
Las Virgenes Educators Ass'n v. Las Virgenes Unified School Dist., 511
Lassonde v. Pleasanton Unified School Dist., 66
Latour v. Riverside Beaver School Dist., 103
Lautermilch v. Findlay City Schools, 388
Lawrence County School Dist. v. Bowden, 380
Layshock v. Hermitage School Dist., 107
Leandro v. State, 439
Lee v. Pine Bluff School Dist., 30
Lee v. Weisman, 58, 65
Lehman v. Zumbrota-Mazeppa Public Schools, 252
Lehnert v. Ferris Faculty Ass'n, 405
LeLeaux v. Hampshire-Fannett Independent School Dist., 53
Lemon v. Kurtzman, 58, 73, 82, 85, 624, 628
LeVake v. Independent School Dist. No. 656, 93
Leventhal v. Knapek, 242
Lewis Jorge Construction Management v. Pomona Unified School Dist., 455
Lewis v. Keegan, 47

Liedtke v. Carrington, 603
Lightfoot v. School Administrative Dist. No. 35, 11
Lindeman v. Kelso School Dist., 524
Linhart v. Lawson, 54
Linke v. Northwestern School Corp., 228
Little Rock School Dist. v. North Little Rock School Dist., 462
Littlefield v. Forney Independent School Dist., 118, 120
Livingston v. DeSoto Independent School Dist., 665
Livingston v. Wausau Underwriters Insurance Co., 18
Locke v. Davey, 95, 634
Lockhart v. U.S., 633
Loeffelman v. Board of Educ. of Crystal City School Dist., 350
Logiodice v. Trustees of Maine Cent. Institute, 616
Londonderry School Dist. SAU #12 v. State, 434
Long v. Board of Educ. of Jefferson County, Kentucky, 123
Longwood Cent. School Dist. v. Springs Union Free School Dist., 156
Loren F. v. Atlanta Independent School System, 576
Lott v. Strang, 41
Love v. Kansas State High School Activities Ass'n, 643
Love-Lane v. Martin, 129
Lovern v. Edwards, 141
Lowe v. State of Georgia, 634
Lower Merion School Dist. v. Doe, 571
Loy v. Dodgeville School Dist., 170
Lyons v. School Committee of Dedham, 373

M

M.E. and P.E. v. Buncombe County Board of Educ., 543
M.H. v. Nassau County School Board, 552
M.K. v. School Board of Brevard County, 206
M.K.J. v. Bourbon County Board of Educ., 204
M.L. v. Federal Way School Dist., 539
M.P. v. Independent School Dist. No. 721, 585
M.W. v. Panama Buena Union School Dist., 28
Madison-Oneida Board of Cooperative Educational Services v. Mills, 377
Magaw v. Middletown Board of Educ., 368
Mahaffey v. Aldrich, 108
Maimonis v. Urbanski, 217
Malone v. Special School Dist. No. 1, 40, 293
Mark H. v. Lemahieu, 587
Marner v. Eufala City School Board, 196

Mars Area School Dist. v. Laurie L., 553
Marsh v. Chambers, 58, 59, 60
Marshall v. Sisters of Holy Family of Nazareth, 619
Martin Engineering v. Lexington County School Dist. One, 453
Martinez v. Bynum 157, 158
Martone v. Johnston School Committee, 273
Mason v. Load King Manufacturing Co., 360
Mason v. Minnesota State High School League, 650
Massachusetts Federation of Teachers, AFT, AFL-CIO v. Board of Educ., 261
Massey v. Banning Unified School Dist., 186
Matter of Arbitration Between Binghamton City School Dist. and Peacock, 425
McAlpine v. Reese. 102
McCardle v. Mitchell School Dist., 283
McCarthy v. Boozeman, 73
McCarthy v. Ozark School Dist., 73
McCollum v. Board of Educ., 631
McCormick v. School Dist. of Mamaroneck, 649
McCracken v. Lockwood School Dist. #26, 355
McCrary v. Aurora Public Schools, 311
McCreary County v. American Civil Liberties Union of Kentucky, 85
McDermott v. Town of Windham Public Schools, 300
McDuffy v. Secretary of Executive Office of Educ., 435, 529
McEuen v. Missouri State Board of Educ., 535
McGowan v. State of Washington, 448
McGreevy v. Stroup, 127
McGurl v. Friends School Inc., 613
McKinney v. Irving Independent School Dist., 52
McLaughlin v. Holt Public Schools Board of Educ., 558
McMorrow v. Benson, 159
McQueen v. Beecher Community Schools, 34
McQuinn v. Douglas County School Dist. No. 66, 393
Medley v. Board of Educ. of Shelby County, 525
Meek v. Pittenger, 624
Mellen v. Congress of the U.S., 70
Mellin v. Flood Brook Union School Dist., 416
Memphis Community School Dist. v. Stachura, 136
Menke v. Broward County School Board, 253, 340
Merrell v. Chartiers Valley School Dist., 323
Metropolitan Nashville Educ. Ass'n v. Metropolitan Board of Public Educ., 414

TABLE OF CASES

Meyer v. Nebraska, 263

Michael C. v. Radnor Township School Dist., 567

Michigan Dep't of Educ. v. Grosse Pointe Public Schools, 620

Milliken v. Bradley, 465

Mills v. Freeman, 459

Minnesota Community College Ass'n v. Knight, 402

Mirand v. City of New York, 36

Miranda v. Arizona, 231

Mississippi Employment Security Comm'n v. Harris, 362

Missouri v. Jenkins, 458, 467

Mitchell v. Helms, 624

Moe v. Independent School Dist. No. 696, Ely, Minnesota, 378

Mohammed v. Racine Unified School Dist., 303

Mohammed v. School Dist. of Philadelphia, 35

Molly L. v. Lower Merion School Dist., 586

Montanye v. Wissahickon School Dist., 363

Montgomery County Board of Educ. v. Horace Mann Insurance Co., 457

Montgomery v. Carr, 134

Montgomery v. Jefferson County School Dist. No. 0008, 344

Montoy v. State of Kansas, 444

Montrose Christian School Corp. v. Walsh, 595

Moore v. Board of Educ. of City of Chicago, 33

Moore v. Detroit School Reform Board, 496

Moore v. Fennville Public Schools Board of Educ., 486

Moore v. New York City Dep't of Educ., 50

Moore v. Willis Independent School Dist., 168

Morris-Hayes v. Board of Educ. of Chester Union Free School Dist., 124, 322

Morse v. Frederick, 99

Mosaica Academy Charter School v. Comwlth. Dep't of Educ., 504

Moss v. Enlarged City of School Dist. of City of Amsterdam, 296

Mr. and Mrs. I. v. Maine School Administrative Dist. No. 55, 552

Ms. S. and her Daughter G. v. Vashon Island School Dist., 566

Mt. Adams School Dist. v. Cook, 421

Mt. Healthy City School Dist. v. Doyle, 127

Mudrovich v. D.C. Everest Area School Dist., 47

Mueller v. Allen, 636

Mullen v. Thompson, 470

Murdock v. Mingus Union High School Dist., 386

Murphy v. United Parcel Service, Inc., 315

Murray v. Chicago Youth Center, 4

Myers v. Indiana, 216

Myers v. Loudoun County Public Schools, 69

N

N.L. v. Knox County Schools, 539

NAACP, Jacksonville Branch v. Duval County School Board, 461

Nack v. Orange City School Dist., 537

Nagel v. Green Bay Area Public School Dist., 23

Nagy v. Evansville-Vanderburgh School Corp., 450

Nalepa v. Plymouth-Canton Community School Dist., 532

Nampa Charter School v. DeLaPaz, 48

Natay v. Murray School Dist., 298

Nathan v. Richland County School Dist. Two, 294

National Educ. Ass'n – South Bend v. South Bend Community School Corp., 430

National Law Center on Homelessness and Poverty, R.I. v. State of New York, 155

Navarre v. South Washington County Schools, 250

Neal v. Fulton County Board of Educ., 670

Neeley v. West Orange-Cove Consolidated Independent School Dist., 435

Neosho R-V School Dist. v. Clark, 564

New Jersey v. T.L.O., 215, 216, 217, 218, 221, 223, 224, 233, 237

New York State Employment Relations Board v. Christ the King Regional High School, 597

New York State Employment Relations Board v. Christian Brothers Academy, 598

Newport-Mesa Unified School Dist. v. State of California Dep't of Educ., 590

Newsom v. Albemarle County School Board, 119

Nichol v. ARIN Intermediate Unit 28, 92

Nichols v. DeStefano, 190

Nichols v. Western Local Board of Educ., 481

Nieshe v. Concrete School Dist., 580

Nix v. Franklin County School Dist., 20

NLRB v. Catholic Bishop of Chicago, 596, 597, 598

NLRB v. Yeshiva Univ., 598

Norristown Area School Dist. v. Norristown Educ. Support Personnel Ass'n, 420

Norton v. Deuel School Dist. #19-4, 367

Norwood v. Harrison, 625

O

O'Connell v. Superior Court of Alameda County, 527

O'Connor v. Ortega, 239, 241

O'Connor v. Pierson, 243

Oak Hills Educ. Ass'n v. Oak Hills Local School Dist. Board of Educ., 416

Oakes v. Massena Cent. School Dist., 16

Oberti v. Board of Educ. of Borough of Clementon School Dist., 556

Ohio Ass'n of Independent Schools v. Goff, 611

Ohio Congress of Parents and Teachers v. State Board of Educ., 497

Oleske v. Hilliard City School Dist. Board of Educ., 341

Olson v. Robbinsdale Area School Dist., 581

Oncale v. Sundowner Offshore Services, Inc., 292

Orlando v. Broward County, Florida, 28

Ortega v. Bibb County School Dist., 535

Oswald v. Waterloo Board of Educ., 389

Ott v. Edinburgh Community School Corp., 661

Owasso Independent School Dist. No. I-011 v. Falvo, 518

Owens v. Colorado Congress of Parents, Teachers and Students, 96

P

Pace v. Bogalusa City School Board, 536

Pachl v. School Board of Independent School Dist. No. 11, 565

Packer v. Orange County School Board, 349

Paige v. Tangipahoa Parish School Board, 663

Pajaro Valley Unified School Dist. v. J.S., 551

Palmer v. Louisiana State Board of Elementary and Secondary Educ., 392

Parents Involved in Community Schools v. Seattle School Dist. No. 1, 152

Parizek v. Roncalli Catholic High School of Omaha, 600

Parker-Bigback v. St. Labre School, 595

Pascagoula Municipal Separate School Dist. v. Barton, 482

Patton v. Indianapolis Public School Board, 296

Pauley v. Anchorage School Dist., 25

Payne v. Worthington Schools, 176

Peck v. Baldwinsville Cent. School Dist., 61

Peck v. Upshur County Board of Educ., 85

Pell v. Board of Educ. of Union Free School Dist., 334

Pelletier v. Maine Principals' Ass'n, 612

Peninsula School Dist. No. 401 v. Public School Employees of Peninsula, 382

Pennsylvania School Boards Ass'n v. Comwlth. of Pennsylvania, 356

Pentagon Academy v. Independent School Dist. No. 1 of Tulsa County, Oklahoma, 497

People Who Care v. Rockford Board of Educ., 461

Peoples v. San Diego Unified School Dist., 255

Perry Educ. Ass'n v. Perry Local Educators' Ass'n, 401

Perry v. Sindermann, 385, 386

Peters v. Baldwin Union Free School Dist., 313

Peters v. Jenney, 365

Peterson v. Independent School Dist. No. 272, 257

Petho v. Wakeman, 24

PGA Tour, Inc. v. Martin, 656

Phaneuf v. Fraikin, 223

Philbrook v. Ansonia Board of Educ., 303

Phillips v. Anderson County Board of Educ., 182

Phoenix Newspapers Inc. v. Keegan, 522

Pickering v. Board of Educ., 90, 123, 124

Pierce v. Sullivan West Cent. School Dist., 71, 632

Pigue v. Christian County Board of Educ., 328

Pike Township Educ. Foundation v. Rubenstein, 390

Pinard v. Clatskanie School Dist. 6J, 100

Pisacane v. Desjardins, 142

Piscataway Township Educ. Ass'n v. Piscataway Township Board of Educ., 419

Plyler v. Doe, 157

Pointer v. Beacon Educ. Management, 384

Polk County Board of Educ. v. Polk County Educ. Ass'n, 418

Polmanteer v. Bobo, 441

Pony Lake School Dist. 30 v. State Committee for Reorganization of School Districts, 469

Port Washington Teachers' Ass'n v. Board of Educ. of Port Washington Union Free School Dist., 514

Porter v. Ascension Parish School Board, 104

Porter v. Grant County Board of Educ., 14

Pottstown School Dist. v. Hill School, 608

Powell v. Bunn, 78

Powell v. Cascade School Dist. No. 228, 391

Power v. School Board of City of Virginia Beach, 589

Prejean v. Cypress-Fairbanks Independent School Dist., 312

Prescott v. Northlake Christian School, 599

Price v. Boyceville Community School Dist., 35

Price Waterhouse v. Hopkins, 284

Priester v. Lowndes County, 653

Priester v. Starkville School Dist., 653

Prince v. Jacoby, 81

Prince v. Louisville Municipal School Dist., 666

Proud v. San Pasqual Union School Dist. No. D037921, 485

TABLE OF CASES

Providence Catholic School v. Bristol School Dist. No. 1, 627

Pryor v. NCAA, 654

R

R.D. Brown Contractors v. Board of Educ. of Columbia County, 453

Raad v. Fairbanks North Star Borough School Dist., 299

Racine Charter One v. Racine Unified School Dist., 502

Ragsdale v. Wolverine World Wide Inc., 269

Raleigh County Board of Educ. v. Gatson, 359

Ramos v. Lee County School Board, 410

Ratner v. Loudon County Public Schools, 200

Reading School Dist. v. Dep't of Educ., 491

Reed v. Vermilion Local School Dist., 215

Reeves v. Rocklin Unified School Dist., 148

Regan v. Governing Board of Sonora Union High School Dist., 400

Regents of the Univ. of California v. Bakke, 150

Regents of Univ. of Michigan v. Ewing, 214, 509

Reid v. District of Columbia, 554

Reis v. Biggs Unified School Dist., 370

Remus v. Board of Educ. for Tonawanda City School Dist., 375

Rendell-Baker v. Kohn, 609

Rene v. Reed, 591

Reno v. Bossier Parish School Board, 474

Renzi v. Connelly School of the Holy Child Inc., 631

Reynolds v. Board of Educ. of Wappingers Cent. School Dist., 365

Rhoads v. Board of Educ. of Mad River Local School Dist., 321

Rhodes v. Guarricino, 222

Richardson v. Dietrich, 323

Ridgecrest Charter School v. Sierra Sands Unified School Dist., 503

Riley v. St. Ann Catholic School, 618

Rim of the World Unified School Dist. v. Superior Court, 520

Rivera v. Houston Independent School Dist., 26

Robert B. v. West Chester Area School Dist., 620

Roberts v. Burke County School Dist., 54

Robinson v. Racine Unified School Dist., 249

Rocci v. Ecole Secondaire MacDonald-Cartier, 50

Rogers v. Duncanville Independent School Dist., 140

Rolle v. Worth County School Dist., 309

Rome City School Dist. Disciplinary Hearing v. Grifasi, 524

Rome School Committee v. Mrs. B., 575

Romer v. Evans, 186

Roosevelt Elementary School Dist. No. 66 v. State of Arizona, 447

Rosario v. Does 1-10, 91

Roslyn Union Free School Dist. v. Geoffrey W., 561

Rossi v. Salinas City Elementary School Dist., 372

Rubio v. Turner Unified School Dist., 173

Rudolph v. Lowndes County Board of Educ., 235

Rumsfeld v. Forum for Academic and Institutional Rights, 146, 147

Runkle v. Gonzales, 513

Runyon v. McCrary, 609

Rusk v. Crestview Local Schools, 84

Russell v. State of Texas, 233

RV v. New York City Dep't of Educ., 164

Ryan v. California Interscholastic Federation, 644

Ry-Tan Construction v. Washington Elementary School Dist. No. 6, 454

S

S.B. v. St. James School, 615

S.G., as Guardian of A.G. v. Sayreville Board of Educ., 106

S.H. v. State of Alabama, 161

S.H. v. State-Operated School Dist. of City of Newark, 560

S.H.B. v. State of Florida, 101

S.I. v. Sennott, 276

S.M. v. Weast, 577

S.W. v. Holbrook Public Schools, 548

Sain v. Cedar Rapids Community School Dist., 5

Sammons v. Polk County School Board, 580

Sample v. Rend Lake College, 267

Samuels v. Independent School Dist. 279, 238

Samuels v. Kansas City Missouri School Dist., 316

San Antonio School Dist. v. Rodriguez, 432

San Diego Unified School Dist. v. Comm'n on State Mandates, 446

Santa Fe Independent School Dist. v. Doe, 58, 67

Sauls v. Pierce County School Dist., 183

Save Our Schools v. Board of Educ. of Salt Lake City, 479

Saxon v. Chapman, 30

Scalise v. Boy Scouts of America, 77

Scarbrough v. Morgan County Board of Educ., 132

Schaffer v. Weast, 542

Scheer v. Independent School Dist. No. I-26, Ottawa County, 376

Scherzinger v. Portland Custodians Civil Service Board, 424

Schilling v. Sheboygan Area School Dist., 18

Schnee v. Alameda Unified School Dist., 372

Schneider v. Corvallis School Dist. 509J, 214

School Board of Independent School Dist.
No. 11 v. Renollett, 562

School Board of Miami-Dade County, Florida
v. Trujillo, 51

School Board of Nassau County v. Arline, 312

School Board of Osceola County v. UPC
of Cent. Florida, 499

School Committee of Pittsfield v. United
Educators of Pittsfield, 414

School Dist. of Beverly v. Geller, 427

School Dist. of City of Pontiac v.
Spellings, 489

School Dist. of Wisconsin Dells v. Z.S., 563

Schroeder v. Hamilton School Dist., 293

Schumacher v. Argosy Educ. Group, 616

Schumacher v. Lisbon School Board, 486

Scobey School Dist. v. Radakovich, 326

Scott v. Minneapolis Public Schools, Special
Dist. No. 1, 514

Scott v. Pasadena Unified School Dist., 463

Scott v. Savers Property and Casualty
Insurance Co., 5

Scott v. School Board of Alachua County, 110

Scott v. Stewart, 396

Seidman v. Paradise Valley Unified School
Dist., 89

Selapack v. Iroquois Cent. School Dist., 276

Selman v. Cobb County School Dist., 65

Setliff v. Rapides Parish School Board, 169

Settlegoode v. Portland Public Schools, 129

Shade v. City of Farmington, Minnesota, 221

Shanklin v. Fitzgerald, 295

Shapiro v. Paradise Valley Unified School
Dist. No. 69, 540

Sharon v. City of Newton, 12, 13

Shaul v. Cherry Valley-Springfield Cent.
School Dist., 242

Shaw v. Sargent School Dist. No. RE-33-J, 357

Sheikh v. Independent School Dist. 535, 307

Shelby S. v. Conroe Independent School
Dist., 551

Shell v. Richland County School Dist.
One, 334

Sherer v. Pocatello School Dist. #25, 21

Sherrell v. Northern Community School Corp.
of Tipton County, 209

Sherrod v. Palm Beach County School
Board, 342

Shinaberger v. LaPine, 34

Shively v. Santa Fe Preparatory School, 601

Shohadaee v. Metropolitan Government of
Nashville and Davidson County, 282

Shuman v. Penn Manor School Dist., 216

Silvestris v. Tantasqua Regional School
Dist., 288

Simmons v. New Public School Dist.
No. Eight, 290

Simon v. Celebration Co., 531

Simpson v. Alanis, 337

Skinner v. Ogallala Public School Dist.
No. 1, 368

Skoros v. City of New York, 86

Sloan v. Lemon, 451

Smiley v. California Dep't of Educ., 591

Smith v. Board of Educ. of School Dist.
Fremont RE-1, 292

Smith v. City of Jackson, 308

Smith v. East Baton Rouge Parish School
Board, 265

Smith v. Estate of Reverend P. Kelly, 604

Smith v. Half Hollow Hills Cent. School
Dist., 36

Smith v. Jackson County Board of Educ., 31

Smith v. Lincoln Park Public School, 45

Smith v. Petal School Dist., 661

Smith v. Revere Local School Dist. Board
of Educ., 511

Soirez v. Vermilion Parish School Board, 587

Sonkowsky v. Board of Educ. for Independent
School Dist. No. 721, 590

South Gibson School Board v. Sollman, 199

South Jersey Catholic School Teachers
Organization v. St. Teresa of the Infant
Jesus Church Elementary School, 597

Southgate Community School Dist. v. County
of Wayne, 251

Spencer v. Lakeview School Dist., 15

Spencer v. Unified School Dist. No. 501, 207

Squire v. Board of Educ. of Red Clay
Consolidated School Dist., 256

St. Francis College v. Al-Khazraji, 297

St. Mary's Honor Center v. Hicks, 280

Stacy v. Batavia Local School Dist. Board
of Educ., 411

Stancourt v. Worthington City School Dist.
Board of Educ., 559

Standefer v. Missouri Division of Labor and
Industrial Relations Comm'n, 359

Stanley v. Darlington County School
Dist., 468

State ex rel. Antonucci v. Youngstown City
School Dist. Board of Educ., 379

State ex rel. Boggs v. Springfield Local
School Dist., 429

State ex rel. Burch v. Sheffield-Sheffield Lake
City School Dist. Board of Educ., 383

State ex rel. Consumer News Services Inc. v.
Worthington City Board of Educ., 249

State ex rel. Estes v. Egnor, 162

State ex rel. Lecklider v. SERS, 357

State ex rel. Liberty School Dist. v.
Holden, 448

TABLE OF CASES

State ex rel. Ohio Ass'n of Public School Employees/AFSCME, Local 4, AFL-CIO v. Batavia Local School Dist., 410

State of Florida v. N.G.B., 232

State of New Hampshire v. Heirtzler, 234

State of Ohio, ex rel. Stacy v. Batavia Local School Dist. Board of Educ., 354

State of Pennsylvania v. Riley, 443

State of Washington, ex rel. Washington State P.D.C. v. Washington State Educ. Ass'n, 406

State of West Virginia v. Board of Educ. of Summers County, 627

State v. Smrekar, 161

State v. Tywayne H., 237

State v. White, 162

Steele v. Industrial Development Board of Metropolitan Government of Nashville, 630

Stein v. Asheville City Board of Educ., 27

Stewart v. Bibb County Board of Educ., 641

Stinson v. Winn, 256, 528

Stockbridge School Dist. v. Dep't of Public Instruction School Dist. Boundary Appeal Board, 472

Stone v. Graham, 85, 86

Stone v. State of Hawaii, Dep't of Educ., 296

Stowers v. Clinton Cent. School Corp., 12

Straights and Gays for Equality v. Osseo Area Schools-Dist. No. 279, 80

Stratechuk v. Board of Educ., South Orange-Maplewood School Dist., 61

Stratham School Dist. v. Beth, 570

Student No. 9 v. Board of Educ., 436, 529

Studier v. Michigan Public School Employees' Retirement Board, 356

Stueber v. Gallagher, 398

Susquehanna Township School Dist. v. Frances J., 578

Sutton v. United Airlines, Inc., 314

Sutton v. West Chester Area School Dist., 585

Swenson v. Lincoln County School Dist., 588

Swift Lake Park High School Dist. 108, 513

Swift v. Breckinridge County Board of Educ., 449

Swisher v. Darden, 326

T

T.B. v. Board of Trustees of Vicksburg Warren School Dist., 189

T.H. v. San Diego Unified School Dist., 198

T.J. v. Hargrove, 509

T.M.M. v. Lake Oswego School Dist., 230

T.W. v. School Dist. of Philadelphia, 210

T.W. v. Unified School Dist. No. 259, Wichita, Kansas, 557

Taetle v. Atlanta Independent School System, 629

Tarkington Independent School Dist. v. Ellis, 197

Tarter v. Raybuck, 224

Tave v. Alanis, 340

Taylor Board of Educ. v. SEIU Local 26M, 426

Taylor v. Enumclaw School Dist. No. 216, 641

Taylor v. School Board of Brevard County, 367

Taylor v. Vermont Dep't of Educ., 517

Tazewell County School Board v. Brown, 423

Tennessee Small School Systems v. McWherter, 440

Tesmer v. Colorado High School Activities Ass'n, 655

Tesoriero v. Syosset Cent. School Dist., 183

Texas Educ. Agency v. Goodrich Independent School Dist., 472

Texas v. U.S., 473

Theodore v. Delaware Valley School Dist., 227

Thomas More High School v. Burmaster, 629

Thomas v. Independent School Dist. No. 2142, 354

Thomas v. Roberts, 224

Thompson v. Carthage School Dist., 218

Thompson v. Mt. Diablo Unified School Dist., 130

Times Publishing Co. v. City of Clearwater, 254

Tindley v. Williamsport Area School Dist., 4

Tinker v. Des Moines Independent Community School Dist., 56, 97, 98, 100, 106, 114, 115, 116, 117

Todd v. Duneland School Corp., 574

Todd v. Natchez-Adams School Dist., 295

Toney v. Bower, 608

Townsend v. Board of Educ. of Robeson County, 130

Toyota Motor Manufacturing v. Williams, 315

Tracy Educators Ass'n v. Superior Court of San Joaquin County, 404

Travis v. Bohannon, 27

Tun v. Whitticker, 209

Turley v. Sauquoit Valley School Dist., 196

Turlock Joint Elementary School Dist. v. PERB, 131

Turnbough v. Mammoth Spring School Dist. No. 2, 271

Turner v. Liverpool Cent. School, 74

Turton v. Frenchtown Elementary School Dist. Board of Educ., 75

U

U.S. v. American Library Ass'n Inc., 135

U.S. v. Board of Educ. of Consolidated High School Dist. 230, 287

U.S. v. Board of School Commissioners of City of Indianapolis, 466

TABLE OF CASES

U.S. v. State of Texas, 467

Ulichny v. Merton Community School Dist., 389

Ullmo v. Gilmour Academy, 621

Unified School Dist. No. 233, Johnson County, Kansas v. Kansas Ass'n of American Educators, 402

Unified School Dist. No. 501, Shawnee County, Kansas v. Baker, 475

United Public Workers, AFSCME, Local 646, AFL-CIO v. Yogi, 412

United Steelworkers of America v. Weber, 300

Upsher v. Grosse Pointe Public School System, 368

Urofsky v. Gilmore, 125

V

Valentino C. v. School Dist. of Philadelphia, 549

Valeria v. Davis, 507

Vallandigham v. Clover Park School Dist. No. 400, 366

Van Orden v. Perry, 85

Vance v. Spencer County Public School Dist., 562

Veazey v. Ascension Parish School Board, 560

Vernonia School Dist. 47J v. Acton, 224, 225, 226, 227, 638

Vibert v. Board of Educ. of Regional School Dist. No. 10, 481

Village of Willowbrook v. Olech, 289

W

W.E.R. v. School Board of Polk County, 212

Wade-Lemee v. Board of Educ. for City of St. Louis, 318

Wagner v. Ft. Wayne Community Schools, 205

Wakefield Teachers Ass'n v. School Committee of Wakefield, 252

Walker v. Elmore County Board of Educ., 269

Walker-Serrano v. Leonard, 101

Wallace v. Jaffree, 58

Wallmuth v. Rapides Parish School Board, 17

Walthart v. Board of Directors of Edgewood-Colesburg Community School Dist., 399

Walz v. Egg Harbor Township Board of Educ., 90

Warnock v. Archer, 304

Washington v. Davis, 294

Washington v. Illinois Dep't of Revenue, 294

Watkins v. Millenium School, 225

Watson v. Beckel, 617

Watson v. North Panola School Dist., 387

Webster Educ. Ass'n v. Webster School Dist., 415

Webster v. Public School Employees of Washington Inc., 270

Weems v. North Franklin School Dist., 333

Weinbaum v. Las Cruces Public Schools, 87

Weinberger v. Maplewood Review, 664

Weisberg v. Riverside Township Board of Educ., 251, 317

Weiss v. Williamsport Area School Dist., 515

Weixel v. Board of Educ. of City of New York, 590

Wells v. One2One Learning Foundation, 501

West Cent. Educ. Ass'n v. West Cent. School Dist. 49-4, 419

West v. Derby Unified School Dist. No. 260, 111

West Virginia State Board of Educ. v. Barnette, 67, 69

WFTV, Inc. v. School Board of Seminole, 526

White v. Ascension Parish School Board, 569

Widder v. Durango School Dist. No. 9-R, 171

Wigg v. Sioux Falls School Dist. 49-5, 91

Wilder v. Grant County School Dist. No. 0001, 327

Wilkins v. Penns Grove-Carneys Point Regional School Dist., 118

Williams v. Augusta County School Board, 477

Williams v. Cambridge Board of Educ., 105

Williams v. Ellington, 224

Williams v. Lafayette Parish School Board, 371

Williams v. Little Rock School Dist., 353

Williams v. School Dist. of Bethlehem, 651

Wilson ex rel. Geiger v. Hinsdale Elementary School Dist., 105

Winkelman v. Parma City School Dist., 537

Winters v. Arizona Board of Educ., 259

Winters v. Pasadena Independent School Dist., 318

Winzer v. School Dist. for City of Pontiac, 179

Wirt v. Parker School Dist. #60-04, 352, 371

Wise v. Bossier Parish School Board, 336

Witters v. State Comm'n for the Blind, 635

Witters v. Washington Dep't of Services for the Blind, 635

Wittman v. Nelson, 374

Wofford v. Evans, 229

Wolfe v. Taconic-Hills Cent. School Dist., 556

Wolman v. Walter, 624, 625

Wood v. Battle Ground School Dist., 486

Wood v. Omaha School Dist., 314

Woodbury Heights Board of Educ. v. Starr, 159

Woodland Hills School Dist. v. S.F., 582

Woodruff v. Georgia State Univ., 613

Woonsocket Teachers' Guild, Local Union 951, AFT v. Woonsocket School Committee, 358, 427

Worthington v. Elmore County Board of Educ., 53

Wowkun v. Closter Board of Educ., 262, 304
Wright v. Ashe, 29
Wright v. Richland County School Dist. Two, 358
Wygant v. Jackson Board of Educ., 300, 301

Y

Yates v. Mansfield Board of Educ., 277
York v. Wahkiakum School Dist. No. 200, 639
Young v. Hammond, 494
Youren v. Tintic School Dist., 364
Ysleta Independent School Dist. v. Griego, 383
Ysleta Independent School Dist. v. Monarrez, 283

Z

Z.W. v. Smith, 573
Zellman v. Independent School Dist. No. 2758, 214
Zellner v. Cedarburg School Dist., 339
Zelman v. Simmons-Harris, 93, 94, 95, 633
Zobrest v. Catalina Foothills School Dist., 571, 624, 628
Zorach v. Clauson, 71, 631, 632
Zottola v. Three Rivers School Dist., 361
Zuni Public School Dist. No. 89 v. Dep't of Educ., 443

TABLE OF CASES BY STATE

ALABAMA

Board of Trustees of Univ. of Alabama v.
Garrett, 315, 318
E.D. v. Enterprise City Board of Educ., 578
Escambia County Board of Educ. v.
Benton, 538
Ex Parte Dunn, 659
Ex Parte Jackson, 397
Ex Parte McCord-Baugh, 289
Frederick v. Morse, 99
Gilder-Lucas v. Elmore County Board
of Educ., 660
Holloman v. Harland, 70
Holmes v. Macon County Board of Educ., 369
Hope v. Pelzer, 224
Hudson v. C.F. Vigor High School, 19
Jackson v. Birmingham Board of Educ., 662
Jackson v. State of Alabama State Tenure
Comm'n, 127
Kilgore v. Jasper City Board of Educ., 371
Kirkland v. Greene County Board
of Educ., 167
Laidlaw Transit Inc. v. Alabama Educ.
Ass'n, 483
Marner v. Eufala City School Board, 196
Morse v. Frederick, 99
Rudolph v. Lowndes County Board
of Educ., 235
S.B. v. St. James School, 615
S.H. v. State of Alabama, 161
Walker v. Elmore County Board of Educ., 269
Wallace v. Jaffree, 58
Worthington v. Elmore County Board
of Educ., 53

ALASKA

Barnica v. Kenai Peninsula Borough
School Dist., 424
Pauley v. Anchorage School Dist., 25
Raad v. Fairbanks North Star Borough
School Dist., 299

ARIZONA

Arizona State Board for Charter Schools v.
U.S. Dep't of Educ., 501
Collette v. Tolleson Unified School
Dist. No. 214, 3
Flores v. Rzeslawski, 527
Hibbs v. Winn, 605
Hills v. Scottsdale Unified School
Dist. No. 48, 85
Hull v. Albrecht, 446
Johnson v. Paradise Valley Unified
School Dist., 320
Kotterman v. Killian, 605

Miranda v. Arizona, 231
Murdock v. Mingus Union High School
Dist., 386
Phoenix Newspapers Inc. v. Keegan, 522
Roosevelt Elementary School Dist. No. 66 v.
State of Arizona, 447
Ry-Tan Construction v. Washington
Elementary School Dist. No. 6, 454
Seidman v. Paradise Valley Unified School
Dist., 89
Shapiro v. Paradise Valley Unified
School Dist. No. 69, 540
Winters v. Arizona Board of Educ., 259
Zobrest v. Catalina Foothills School
Dist., 571, 624, 628

ARKANSAS

Board of Educ. v. McCluskey, 202
Boone v. Boozeman, 73
Cross County School Dist. v. Spencer, 210
Doe v. Little Rock School Dist., 227
Foote v. Pine Bluff School Dist., 17
Foreman School Dist. No. 25 v. Steele, 392
Golden ex rel. Balch v. Anders, 168
Lake View School Dist. No. 25 v.
Huckabee, 433
Lee v. Pine Bluff School Dist., 30
Little Rock School Dist. v. North Little Rock
School Dist., 462
McCarthy v. Boozeman, 73
McCarthy v. Ozark School Dist., 73
Ragsdale v. Wolverine World Wide Inc., 269
T.J. v. Hargrove, 509
Thompson v. Carthage School Dist., 218
Turnbough v. Mammoth Spring School
Dist. No. 2, 271
Warnock v. Archer, 304
Williams v. Little Rock School Dist., 353

CALIFORNIA

Alex G. v. Board of Trustees of Davis Unified
School Dist., 563
Allison C. v. Advanced Educ. Services, 45
Akuluze v. Oakland Unified School Dist., 302
Ashby v. Hesperia Union School Dist., 669
Ashford v. Culver City Unified School
Dist., 396
Ass'n of Mexican-American Educators v. State
of California, 261
Avila v. Citrus Community College Dist., 9
B.C. through Powers v. Plumas Unified
School Dist., 235
Benjamin G. v. Special Educ. Hearing
Office, 553
Bacus v. Palo Verde Unified School Dist.
Board of Educ., 60

TABLE OF CASES BY STATE

Bakersfield Elementary Teachers Ass'n v. Bakersfield City School Dist., 257

Board of Educ. of Sacramento City Unified School Dist. v. Sacramento County Board of Educ., 193

BRV v. Superior Court, 248

Budworth v. Los Angeles Unified School Dist., 238

California Teachers Ass'n v. Governing Board of Golden Valley Unified School Dist., 391

California Teachers Ass'n v. Governing Board of San Diego Unified School Dist., 131

Californians For Justice Educ. Fund v. State Board of Educ., 529

Chavez v. Martinez, 235, 238

City of Rancho Palos Verdes v. Abrams, 648

Coachella Valley Unified School Dist. v. State of California, 490

Colin v. Orange Unified School Dist., 145

Cooksey v. San Bernardino City Unified School Dist., 345

Crawford v. Huntington Beach Union High School Dist., 465

Crist v. Alpine Union School Dist., 245

Culbertson v. San Gabriel Unified School Dist., 391

Dep't of Finance v. Comm'n on State Mandates, 446

Ecklund v. Byron Union School Dist., 62

Elk Grove Unified School Dist. v. Newdow, 68

Environmental Charter High School v. Centinela Valley Union High School Dist., 503

Everett v. Santa Barbara High School Dist., 584

Fields v. Palmdale School Dist., 142

Flores v. Morgan Hill Unified School Dist., 186

Foster v. Mahdesian, 407

Friery v. Los Angeles Unified School Dist., 301

Garcetti v. Ceballos, 123, 124

Granowitz v. Redlands Unified School Dist., 201

Harper v. Poway Unified School Dist., 115

Hemady v. Long Beach Unified School Dist., 16

Honig v. Doe, 546, 562

In re Johnny F., 219

In re Randy G., 219

Johnson v. Special Educ. Hearing Office, 566

Kahn v. East Side Union High School Dist., 15, 667

Katherine G. v. Kentfield School Dist., 559

Knight v. Hayward Unified School Dist., 321

Las Virgenes Educators Ass'n v. Las Virgenes Unified School Dist., 511

Lassonde v. Pleasanton Unified School Dist., 66

Lewis Jorge Construction Management v. Pomona Unified School Dist., 455

M.W. v. Panama Buena Union School Dist., 28

Massey v. Banning Unified School Dist., 186

Newport-Mesa Unified School Dist. v. State of California Dep't of Educ., 590

O'Connell v. Superior Court of Alameda County, 527

O'Connor v. Ortega, 239, 241

Pajaro Valley Unified School Dist. v. J.S., 551

Peoples v. San Diego Unified School Dist., 255

Proud v. San Pasqual Union School Dist. No. D037921, 485

Reeves v. Rocklin Unified School Dist., 148

Regan v. Governing Board of Sonora Union High School Dist., 400

Regents of the Univ. of California v. Bakke, 150

Reis v. Biggs Unified School Dist., 370

Ridgecrest Charter School v. Sierra Sands Unified School Dist., 503

Rim of the World Unified School Dist. v. Superior Court, 520

Rossi v. Salinas City Elementary School Dist., 372

Ryan v. California Interscholastic Federation, 644

San Diego Unified School Dist. v. Comm'n on State Mandates, 446

Schnee v. Alameda Unified School Dist., 372

Scott v. Pasadena Unified School Dist., 463

Smiley v. California Dep't of Educ., 591

T.H. v. San Diego Unified School Dist., 198

Thompson v. Mt. Diablo Unified School Dist., 130

Tracy Educators Ass'n v. Superior Court of San Joaquin County, 404

Turlock Joint Elementary School Dist. v. PERB, 131

Valeria v. Davis, 507

COLORADO

Bartell v. Aurora Public Schools, 274

Bradshaw v. Cherry Creek School Dist. No. 5, 158

Denver Parents Ass'n v. Denver Board of Educ., 532

DiRusso v. Aspen School Dist., 310

Klinger v. Adams County School Dist. No. 50, 351

McCrary v. Aurora Public Schools, 311

Nichols v. DeStefano, 190

Owens v. Colorado Congress of Parents, Teachers and Students, 96

Romer v. Evans, 186

TABLE OF CASES BY STATE

Shaw v. Sargent School Dist.
No. RE-33-J, 357
Smith v. Board of Educ. of School Dist.
Fremont RE-1, 292
Sutton v. United Airlines, Inc., 314
Tesmer v. Colorado High School Activities
Ass'n, 655
Widder v. Durango School Dist. No. 9-R, 171

CONNECTICUT

Ansonia Board of Educ. v. Philbrook, 303
Bell v. West Haven Board of Educ., 506
Bogle-Assegai v. Bloomfield Board
of Educ., 189
Brunswick School v. Hutter, 615
Connecticut v. Spellings, 488
Downing v. West Haven Board of Educ., 92
Gedney v. Board of Educ. of Town
of Groton, 314
Hanes v. Board of Educ. of City
of Bridgeport, 332
McDermott v. Town of Windham Public
Schools, 300
O'Connor v. Pierson, 243
Phaneuf v. Fraikin, 223
Philbrook v. Ansonia Board of Educ., 303
Vibert v. Board of Educ. of Regional School
Dist. No. 10, 481

DELAWARE

Dobrich v. Walls, 59
Eden v. Oblates of St. Francis de Sales, 603
Harris-Thomas v. Christina School Dist., 175
Jordan v. Smyrna School Dist. Board
of Educ., 213

DISTRICT OF COLUMBIA

Allen v. Wright, 605
Argueta v. Government of District
of Columbia, 582
Cartwright v. District of Columbia, 553
Price Waterhouse v. Hopkins, 284
Reid v. District of Columbia, 554
Runkle v. Gonzales, 513
Squire v. Board of Educ. of Red Clay
Consolidated School Dist., 256
Washington v. Davis, 294

FLORIDA

Adler v. Duval County School Board, 67
Arline v. School Board of Nassau County, 312
Bannon v. School Dist. of Palm Beach
County, 88

Bar-Navon v. School Board of Brevard
County, Florida, 116
Boy Scouts of America v. Till, 146
Bush v. Holmes, 94
Cagle v. St. Johns County School Dist., 413
Carestio v. School Board of Broward
County, 172
Communications Workers of America, Local
3180 v. Indian River County School
Board, 418
Cuesta v. School Board of Miami-Dade
County, Florida, 199
D.P. v. School Board of Broward County,
Florida, 557
Faragher v. City of Boca Raton, 290
Florida Dep't of Educ. v. Cooper, 517
Florida Dep't of Educ. v. NYT Management
Services, 249
Florida High School Athletic Ass'n v.
Marazzito, 646
Frazier v. Alexandre, 68
Hawkins v. Sarasota County School Board, 180
Heinkel v. School Board of Lee County,
Florida, 144
Ingraham v. Wright, 165, 166, 670
Johnson v. Deluz, 516
Jones v. Miami-Dade County Public
Schools, 374
Kimel v. Florida Board of Regents, 308
M.H. v. Nassau County School Board, 552
M.K. v. School Board of Brevard County, 206
Mason v. Load King Manufacturing Co., 360
Menke v. Broward County School
Board, 253, 340
NAACP, Jacksonville Branch v. Duval County
School Board, 461
Orlando v. Broward County, Florida, 28
Packer v. Orange County School Board, 349
Ramos v. Lee County School Board, 410
Sammons v. Polk County School Board, 580
School Board of Miami-Dade County, Florida
v. Trujillo, 51
School Board of Nassau County v. Arline, 312
School Board of Osceola County v. UPC
of Cent. Florida, 499
Scott v. School Board of Alachua County, 110
S.H.B. v. State of Florida, 101
Sherrod v. Palm Beach County School
Board, 342
Simon v. Celebration Co., 531
State of Florida v. N.G.B., 232
Stinson v. Winn, 256, 528
Stueber v. Gallagher, 398
Taylor v. School Board of Brevard
County, 367
Times Publishing Co. v. City
of Clearwater, 254
W.E.R. v. School Board of Polk County, 212
WFTV, Inc. v. School Board of Seminole, 526

GEORGIA

Albright v. Columbia Board of Educ., 317
Aliffi v. Liberty County School Dist., 24
Bajjani v. Gwinnett County School
    Dist., 39, 489
Blaine v. Savannah Country Day School, 614
Davis v. Monroe County Board of
    Educ., 174, 176, 177, 178, 586
DeKalb County School Dist. v. M.T.V., 569
Fort Stewart Schools v. Federal Labor
    Relations Authority, 411
Freeman v. Pitts, 458, 459
Fuller v. Lakeview Academy, 614
Gee v. Professional Practices Comm'n, 399
Hearn v. Board of Public Educ., 241
Holton v. City of Thomasville School
    Dist., 464
Ianicelli v. McNeely, 476
Johnstone v. Thompson, 441
Kristin National Inc. v. Board of Educ.
    of the City of Marietta, 507
Loren F. v. Atlanta Independent School
    System, 576
Lowe v. State of Georgia, 634
Mills v. Freeman, 459
Neal v. Fulton County Board of Educ., 670
Nix v. Franklin County School Dist., 20
Ortega v. Bibb County School Dist., 535
R.D. Brown Contractors v. Board of Educ.
    of Columbia County, 453
Roberts v. Burke County School Dist., 54
Rolle v. Worth County School Dist., 309
Sauls v. Pierce County School Dist., 183
Selman v. Cobb County School Dist., 65
Stewart v. Bibb County Board of Educ., 641
Taetle v. Atlanta Independent School
    System, 629
Thomas v. Roberts, 224
Woodruff v. Georgia State Univ., 613
Wright v. Ashe, 29

HAWAII

Doe v. Kamehameha Schools, 610
Doe v. State of Hawaii, 167
Mark H. v. Lemahieu, 587
Stone v. State of Hawaii, Dep't of Educ., 296
United Public Workers, AFSCME, Local 646,
    AFL-CIO v. Yogi, 412

IDAHO

Brooks v. Logan, 44
Carrier v. Lake Pend Oreille School Dist., 44
Daw v. School Dist. 91 Board of Trustees, 193
Daleiden v. Jefferson County Joint School
    Dist. No. 251, 367

Farner v. Idaho Falls School Dist. No. 91, 390
Gooding Public Joint School Dist. No. 231, 206
Hayenga v. Nampa School Dist. No. 131, 236
Howard v. Yakovac, 236
Idaho Schools For Equal Educational
    Opportunity v. State, 434
In re Expulsion of Rogers, 206
Nampa Charter School v. DeLaPaz, 48
Sherer v. Pocatello School Dist. #25, 21

ILLINOIS

Aaron M. v. Yomtoob, 570
Albers v. Breen, 40
Alex R. v. Forrestville Community Unit
    School Dist. #221, 563
Arteman v. Clinton Community Unit School
    Dist. No. 15, 19
Batson v. Pinckneyville Elementary School
    Dist. No. 50, 26
Beth B. v. Van Clay, 558
Bland v. Candioto, 41, 42
Block v. Rockford Public School Dist., 589
Board of Educ. of Ottawa Township High
    School Dist. No. 140 v. U.S. Dep't
    of Educ., 491
Board of Educ. of Thornton Township
    High School Dist. 205 v. Board of Educ.
    of Argo Community High School
    Dist. 217, 652
Buchna v. Illinois State Board of Educ., 345
Burlington Industries, Inc. v. Ellerth, 282, 290
Cassimy v. Board of Educ. of Rockford Public
    Schools, Dist. 205, 317
Chicago Board of Educ. v. Substance, Inc., 530
Chicago Teachers Union v. Hudson, 406
Chicago Teachers Union, Local 1 v. Board
    of Educ. of City of Chicago, 482
Chicago Tribune Co. v. Board of Educ.
    of City of Chicago, 521
Comprehensive Community Solutions v.
    Rockford School Dist., 498
Copley Press v. Board of Educ. for Peoria
    School Dist. No. 150, 248
Cornfield v. Consolidated High School
    Dist., 223
Cortez v. Calumet Public School Dist.
    No. 132, 509
Courson v. Danville School Dist. No. 118, 21
Crowley v. McKinney, 141
Dale M. v. Board of Educ. of Bradley
    Bourbonnais High School Dist.
    No. 307, 550
Doe v. Paris Union School Dist. No. 95, 139
Evanston Community Consolidated School
    Dist. No. 65 v. Michael M., 569
Fleischfresser v. Directors of School
    Dist. 200, 137

Fuller v. Decatur Public School Board of Educ., Dist. 61, 211

Gabrielle M. v. Park Forest-Chicago Heights School Dist., 179

General Star Indemnity Co. v. Lake Bluff School Dist. No. 65, 457

Hassberger v. Board of Educ., Cent. Community Unit School Dist., 623

Hayes v. State Teacher Certification Board, 331

Holmes v. Board of Educ. of West Harvey-Dixmoor School Dist. No. 147, 265

Hood v. The Illinois High School Ass'n, 662

In re D.D., 549

Joel R. v. Board of Educ. of Mannheim School Dist. 83, Cook County, Illinois, 452

Kelly v. Board of Educ. of McHenry Community High School Dist., 122

Kevin T. v. Elmhurst Community School Dist. No. 205, 581

Land v. Board of Educ. of City of Chicago, 328

Lott v. Strang, 41

Maimonis v. Urbanski, 217

McCollum v. Board of Educ., 631

Moore v. Board of Educ. of City of Chicago, 33

Murray v. Chicago Youth Center, 4

NLRB v. Catholic Bishop of Chicago, 596, 597, 598

People Who Care v. Rockford Board of Educ., 461

Pickering v. Board of Educ., 90, 123, 124

Sample v. Rend Lake College, 267

Swift Lake Park High School Dist. 108, 513

Toney v. Bower, 608

Washington v. Illinois Dep't of Revenue, 294

Wilson ex rel. Geiger v. Hinsdale Elementary School Dist., 105

U.S. v. Board of Educ. of Consolidated High School Dist. 230, 287

Village of Willowbrook v. Olech, 289

INDIANA

Badger v. Greater Clark County Schools, 397

Bates v. U.S., 635

Benjamin v. Metropolitan School Dist., 180

D.L. v. Warsaw Community Schools, 523

D.N. v. Penn Harris Madison School Corp., 640

Embry v. O'Bannon, 622

Fratus v. Marion Community Schools Board of Trustees, 355

Funston v. School Town of Munster, 7

Gatto v. St. Richard School, 600

Griggs v. Ft. Wayne School Board, 117

Hines v. Caston School Corp., 122

Indiana High School Athletic Ass'n v. Martin, 643

Indiana State Board of Educ. v. Brownsburg Community School Corp., 478

Linke v. Northwestern School Corp., 228

Myers v. Indiana, 216

Nagy v. Evansville-Vanderburgh School Corp., 450

National Educ. Ass'n – South Bend v. South Bend Community School Corp., 430

Ott v. Edinburgh Community School Corp., 661

Patton v. Indianapolis Public School Board, 296

Perry Educ. Ass'n v. Perry Local Educators' Ass'n, 401

Pike Township Educ. Foundation v. Rubenstein, 390

Rene v. Reed, 591

Sherrell v. Northern Community School Corp. of Tipton County, 209

South Gibson School Board v. Sollman, 199

Stowers v. Clinton Cent. School Corp., 12

Todd v. Duneland School Corp., 574

Tun v. Whitticker, 209

U.S. v. Board of School Commissioners of City of Indianapolis, 466

Wagner v. Ft. Wayne Community Schools, 205

IOWA

Cason v. Cook, 237

Cedar Rapids Community School Dist. v. Garret F. by Charlene F., 568

Doe v. Perry Community School Dist., 185

Fielder v. Board of Directors of Carroll Community School Dist., 335

Gabrilson v. Flynn, 476

Halter v. Iowa Board of Educ. Examiners, 258

Immaculate Conception Corp. and Don Bosco High School v. Iowa Dep't of Transportation, 630

Jankovitz v. Des Moines Independent Community School Dist., 309

Kern v. Saydel Community School Dist., 324

Oswald v. Waterloo Board of Educ., 389

Sain v. Cedar Rapids Community School Dist., 5

Schumacher v. Lisbon School Board, 486

Tinker v. Des Moines Independent Community School Dist., 56, 97, 98, 100, 106, 114, 115, 116, 117

Walthart v. Board of Directors of Edgewood-Colesburg Community School Dist., 399

KANSAS

Adams v. Baker, 651
Barrett v. Unified School Dist. No. 259, 12
Beshears v. Unified School Dist. No. 305, 38
Brown v. Board of Educ., 153, 458, 463, 466, 652
Case v. Unified School Dist. No. 233, 136
Kansas State Board of Educ. v. Marsh, 338
Kurtz v. Unified School Dist. No. 308, 32
Love v. Kansas State High School Activities Ass'n, 643
Montoy v. State of Kansas, 444
Murphy v. United Parcel Service, Inc., 315
Richardson v. Dietrich, 323
Rubio v. Turner Unified School Dist., 173
Spencer v. Unified School Dist. No. 501, 207
T.W. v. Unified School Dist. No. 259, Wichita, Kansas, 557
Unified School Dist. No. 233, Johnson County, Kansas v. Kansas Ass'n of American Educators, 402
Unified School Dist. No. 501, Shawnee County, Kansas v. Baker, 475
West v. Derby Unified School Dist. No. 260, 111

KENTUCKY

Bennett v. Kentucky Dep't of Educ., 442
Blau v. Ft. Thomas Public School Dist., 116
Boyd County High School Gay Straight Alliance v. Board of Educ. of Boyd County, 145
Butler v. South, 274
Crager v. Board of Educ. of Knott County, 240
Critchelow v. Breckinridge County Board of Educ., 208, 640
D.F. v. Codell, 511
Doe v. Woodford County Board of Educ., 658
Fankhauser v. Cobb, 347
Hardin County Schools v. Foster, 523
James v. Sevre-Duszynska, 348
Kentucky Dep't of Educ. v. Risner, 477
Keeling v. Jefferson County Board of Educ., 353
Kenton County School Dist. v. Hunt, 565
Kentucky Educ. Professional Standards Board v. Gambrel, 260
Lafferty v. Board of Educ. of Floyd County, 398
Long v. Board of Educ. of Jefferson County, Kentucky, 123
M.K.J. v. Bourbon County Board of Educ., 204
McCreary County v. American Civil Liberties Union of Kentucky, 85

McGurl v. Friends School Inc., 613
Medley v. Board of Educ. of Shelby County, 525
Pigue v. Christian County Board of Educ., 328
Stone v. Graham, 85, 86
Swift v. Breckinridge County Board of Educ., 449
Toyota Motor Manufacturing v. Williams, 315
Vance v. Spencer County Public School Dist., 562
Williams v. Ellington, 224
Young v. Hammond, 494

LOUISIANA

Aubrey v. School Board of Lafayette Parish, 241
Auguster v. Vermilion Parish School Board, 297
Barrino v. East Baton Rouge Parish School Board, 512
Boone v. Reese, 170
B.W.S. v. Livingston Parish School Board, 189
Cochran v. Louisiana State Board of Educ., 623
Connick v. Myers, 123, 140
Day v. Ouachita Parish School Board, 9
Doe v. Tangipahoa Parish School Board, 59
Edwards v. Aguillard, 60
Fenceroy v. Morehouse Parish School Board, 121
Frazer v. St. Tammany Parish School Board, 8
Hemstad v. Jefferson Parish School Board, 456
Howard v. West Baton Rouge Parish School Board, 337
James v. Jackson, 16
Johansen v. Louisiana High School Athletic Ass'n, 642
Lafayette Parish School Board v. Cormier, 42
Laiche v. Kohen, 668
Mitchell v. Helms, 624
Oncale v. Sundowner Offshore Services, Inc., 292
Pace v. Bogalusa City School Board, 536
Paige v. Tangipahoa Parish School Board, 663
Palmer v. Louisiana State Board of Elementary and Secondary Educ., 392
Porter v. Ascension Parish School Board, 104
Prescott v. Northlake Christian School, 599
Reno v. Bossier Parish School Board, 474
Setliff v. Rapides Parish School Board, 169
Smith v. East Baton Rouge Parish School Board, 265
Soirez v. Vermilion Parish School Board, 587
United Steelworkers of America v. Weber, 300
Veazey v. Ascension Parish School Board, 560

Wallmuth v. Rapides Parish School Board, 17
White v. Ascension Parish School Board, 569
Williams v. Lafayette Parish School
    Board, 371
Wise v. Bossier Parish School Board, 336

MAINE

Anderson v. Town of Durham, 95
Bagley v. Raymond School Dep't, 95
Bragdon v. Abbott, 314
Camps Newfound/Owatonna, Inc. v. Town
    of Harrison, Maine, 606
Eulitt v. State of Maine, 95
Farrin v. Maine School Administrative Dist.
    No. 59, 548
Johnson v. School Union No. 107, 287
Lewis v. Keegan, 47
Lightfoot v. School Administrative Dist.
    No. 35, 11
Logiodice v. Trustees of Maine Cent.
    Institute, 616
Mr. and Mrs. I. v. Maine School
    Administrative Dist. No. 55, 552
Pelletier v. Maine Principals' Ass'n, 612
Rome School Committee v. Mrs. B., 575

MARYLAND

Alexis v. Board of Educ., Baltimore Public
    Schools, 541
Baltimore City Board of School
    Commissioners v. Taylorch, 620
Baltimore Teachers Union v. Maryland State
    Board of Educ., 494
Battles v. Anne Arundel County Board
    of Educ., 164
Board of Educ. of Talbot County v.
    Heister, 351
Child Evangelism Fellowship of Maryland v.
    Montgomery County Schools, 82, 83
Citizens for Responsible Curriculum v.
    Montgomery County Public Schools, 63
Hammond v. Board of Educ. of Carroll
    County, 10
Hildebrant v. Educational Testing Service, 528
In re Patrick Y., 222
Koenick v. Felton, 72
Montgomery County Board of Educ. v.
    Horace Mann Insurance Co., 457
Montrose Christian School Corp. v.
    Walsh, 595
Renzi v. Connelly School of the Holy
    Child Inc., 631
S.M. v. Weast, 577
Schaffer v. Weast, 542
Z.W. v. Smith, 573

MASSACHUSETTS

Anderson v. City of Boston, 153
Comfort v. Lynn School Committee, 151
Comwlth. of Massachusetts v. Buccella, 519
Comwlth. of Massachusetts v.
    Damian D., 220
Doe v. Superintendent of Schools
    of Stoughton, 202
Downing v. City of Lowell, 385
Dragonis v. School Committee of Melrose, 47
Globe Newspaper Co. v. Commissioner
    of Educ., 521
Hancock v. Commissioner of Educ., 436
In re Ivan, 163
Lyons v. School Committee of Dedham, 373
Massachusetts Federation of Teachers,
    AFT, AFL-CIO v. Board of Educ., 261
McDuffy v. Secretary of Executive Office
    of Educ., 435, 529
Pisacane v. Desjardins, 142
Rendell-Baker v. Kohn, 609
S.I. v. Sennott, 276
S.W. v. Holbrook Public Schools, 548
School Committee of Pittsfield v. United
    Educators of Pittsfield, 414
School Dist. of Beverly v. Geller, 427
Sharon v. City of Newton, 12, 13
Silvestris v. Tantasqua Regional School
    Dist., 288
Student No. 9 v. Board of Educ., 436, 529
Wakefield Teachers Ass'n v. School
    Committee of Wakefield, 252

MICHIGAN

Abood v. Detroit Board of Educ., 405
Adair v. State of Michigan, 445
Barber v. Dearborn Public Schools, 101
Beard v. Whitmore Lake School Dist., 224
Campbell v. Board of Educ. of the Centerline
    School Dist., 588
Carriveau v. Davison School Dist. #25140, 54
Cassise v. Walled Lake Consolidated
    Schools, 663
Clark v. Banks, 565
Communities for Equity v. Michigan High
    School Athletic Ass'n, 648
Corley v. Detroit Board of Educ., 292
Daniels v. Woodside, 195
Dean v. Utica Community Schools, 112
Delekta v. Memphis Community Schools, 510
Durant v. Michigan, 444
Everson v. Board of Educ. of School Dist.
    of City of Highland Park, 128
Flaskamp v. Dearborn Public Schools, 133
Flint v. Manchester Public Schools, 163

Fuhr v. School Dist. of City of Hazel Park, 285
Gratz v. Bollinger, 150, 151
Grutter v. Bollinger, 150, 151
Hansen v. Ann Arbor Public Schools, 72
Henderson v. Walled Lake Consolidated Schools, 181
Kelso v. Southfield Public Schools Board of Educ., 246
Kloberdanz v. Swan Valley School Dist., 200
Knubbe v. Detroit Board of Educ., 344
Kuszewski v. Chippewa Valley School Dist., 561
Lakin v. Birmingham Public Schools, 541
Lehnert v. Ferris Faculty Ass'n, 405
Mahaffey v. Aldrich, 108
McAlpine v. Reese. 102
McLaughlin v. Holt Public Schools Board of Educ., 558
McQueen v. Beecher Community Schools, 34
Memphis Community School Dist. v. Stachura, 136
Michigan Dep't of Educ. v. Grosse Pointe Public Schools, 620
Milliken v. Bradley, 465
Moore v. Detroit School Reform Board, 496
Moore v. Fennville Public Schools Board of Educ., 486
Nalepa v. Plymouth-Canton Community School Dist., 532
Regents of Univ. of Michigan v. Ewing, 214, 509
Saxon v. Chapman, 30
Scalise v. Boy Scouts of America, 77
School Dist. of City of Pontiac v. Spellings, 489
Smith v. Lincoln Park Public School, 45
Southgate Community School Dist. v. County of Wayne, 251
Studier v. Michigan Public School Employees' Retirement Board, 356
Taylor Board of Educ. v. SEIU Local 26M, 426
Upsher v. Grosse Pointe Public School System, 368
Winzer v. School Dist. for City of Pontiac, 179
Wygant v. Jackson Board of Educ., 300, 301

MINNESOTA

A.M.J. v. Royalton Public Schools, 177
Anderson v. Anoka Hennepin Independent School Dist. 11, 20
Anderson v. Independent School Dist. No. 97, 49
Ashong v. Independent School Dist. #625, 361

Citizens Concerned for Kids v. Yellow Medicine East Independent School Dist., 480
CJN v. Minneapolis Public Schools, Special School Dist. No. 1, 564
Doe v. Lutheran High School of Greater Minneapolis, 594
Educ. Minnesota – Chisholm v. Independent School Dist. No. 695, 403
Educ. Minnesota – Greenway, Local 1330 v. Independent School Dist. No. 316, 412
Educ. Minnesota Lakeville v. Independent School Dist. No. 194, 134
Granville v. Minneapolis School Dist., 174
Henderson v. Independent School Dist. No. 706, 378
In re Chisago Lakes School Dist., 552
In re Expulsion of B.M. from Independent School Dist. No. 2142, 191
In re Expulsion of G.H., 202
In re Expulsion of I.A.L., 190
In re G.S.P., 232
Lehman v. Zumbrota-Mazeppa Public Schools, 252
LeVake v. Independent School Dist. No. 656, 93
M.P. v. Independent School Dist. No. 721, 585
Malone v. Special School Dist. No. 1, 40, 293
Mason v. Minnesota State High School League, 650
Minnesota Community College Ass'n v. Knight, 402
Moe v. Independent School Dist. No. 696, Ely, Minnesota, 378
Mueller v. Allen, 636
Navarre v. South Washington County Schools, 250
Olson v. Robbinsdale Area School Dist., 581
Pachl v. School Board of Independent School Dist. No. 11, 565
Peterson v. Independent School Dist. No. 272, 257
Samuels v. Independent School Dist. 279, 238
School Board of Independent School Dist. No. 11 v. Renollett, 562
Schumacher v. Argosy Educ. Group, 616
Scott v. Minneapolis Public Schools, Special Dist. No. 1, 514
Shade v. City of Farmington, Minnesota, 221
Sheikh v. Independent School Dist. 535, 307
Sonkowsky v. Board of Educ. for Independent School Dist. No. 721, 590
Straights and Gays for Equality v. Osseo Area Schools-Dist. No. 279, 80
Thomas v. Independent School Dist. No. 2142, 354

Weinberger v. Maplewood Review, 664
Zellman v. Independent School Dist.
    No. 2758, 214

MISSISSIPPI

Doe v. North Panola School Dist., 37
Harris v. McCray, 666
Henderson v. Simpson County Public School
    Dist., 41
Lawrence County School Dist. v.
    Bowden, 380
Mississippi Employment Security Comm'n v.
    Harris, 362
Norwood v. Harrison, 625
Pascagoula Municipal Separate School Dist. v.
    Barton, 482
Priester v. Lowndes County, 653
Prince v. Louisville Municipal School
    Dist., 666
Priester v. Starkville School Dist., 653
Smith v. City of Jackson, 308
Smith v. Petal School Dist., 661
T.B. v. Board of Trustees of Vicksburg Warren
    School Dist., 189
Todd v. Natchez-Adams School Dist., 295
Watson v. North Panola School Dist., 387

MISSOURI

Franklin v. St. Louis Board of Educ., 272
Gibson v. Caruthersville School Dist.
    No. 8, 394
Hale v. Poplar Bluff R-I School Dist., 561
Hamrick by Hamrick v. Affton School Dist.
    Board of Educ., 211
Hazelwood School Dist. v. Kuhlmeier, 61, 88,
    111, 112
Hellmann v. Union R-XI School Dist., 343
Neosho R-V School Dist. v. Clark, 564
Jenkins by Jenkins v. State of Missouri, 468
Jennings v. Wentzville R-IV School Dist., 208
Loeffelman v. Board of Educ. of Crystal City
    School Dist., 350
McEuen v. Missouri State Board of Educ., 535
Missouri v. Jenkins, 458, 467
Pointer v. Beacon Educ. Management, 384
Samuels v. Kansas City Missouri School
    Dist., 316
Shanklin v. Fitzgerald, 295
St. Mary's Honor Center v. Hicks, 280
Standefer v. Missouri Division of Labor
    and Industrial Relations Comm'n, 359
State ex rel. Liberty School Dist. v.
    Holden, 448
Wade-Lemee v. Board of Educ. for City
    of St. Louis, 318

MONTANA

Carpenter v. Dillon Elementary School
    Dist. 10, 147
Columbia Falls Elementary School Dist. No. 6
    v. State of Montana, 438
Dupuis v. Board of Trustees, Ronan School
    Dist. No. 30, 477
Ekalaka Unified Board of Trustees v. Ekalaka
    Teachers' Ass'n, MEA-MFT, NEA, 408
Fleenor v. Darby School Dist., 478
Harry A. v. Duncan, 36
Hinkle v. Shepherd School Dist. #37, 22
In re Petition of Billings High School Dist.
    No. 2, 247
McCracken v. Lockwood School Dist.
    #26, 355
Parker-Bigback v. St. Labre School, 595
Scobey School Dist. v. Radakovich, 326

NEBRASKA

Board of Educ. of Westside Community
    School v. Mergens, 79
Cerny v. Cedar Bluffs Junior/Senior Public
    School, 667, 668
Crete Educ. Ass'n v. Saline County School
    Dist., 413
Doe v. School Dist. of City of Norfolk, 66
Jasa v. Millard Public School Dist.
    No. 17, 577
Kinman v. Omaha Public School Dist., 185
Marsh v. Chambers, 58, 59, 60
McQuinn v. Douglas County School Dist.
    No. 66, 393
Meyer v. Nebraska, 263
Montgomery v. Jefferson County School Dist.
    No. 0008, 344
Parizek v. Roncalli Catholic High School
    of Omaha, 600
Pony Lake School Dist. 30 v. State
    Committee for Reorganization
    of School Districts, 469
Skinner v. Ogallala Public School Dist.
    No. 1, 368
Wilder v. Grant County School Dist.
    No. 0001, 327
Wood v. Omaha School Dist., 314

NEVADA

Amanda J. v. Clark County School Dist., 544
Behymer-Smith v. Coral Academy
    of Science, 138
Clark County Educ. Ass'n v. Clark County
    School Dist., 342
Clark County School Dist. v. Breeden, 291

Clark County School Dist. v. Buchanan, 322
Clark County School Dist. v. Bundley, 360
Clark County School Dist. v. Riley, 375
Eason v. Clark County School Dist., 33
Gumm v. Nevada Dep't of Educ., 583
Jacobs v. Clark County School Dist., 118

NEW HAMPSHIRE

Appeal of Laconia School Dist., 421
Appeal of White Mountain Regional School Dist., 425
Claremont School Dist. v. Governor, 433
Douglas v. Londonderry School Board, 112
Foote v. Manchester School Dist., 479
Gary S. v. Manchester School Dist., 620
Londonderry School Dist. SAU #12 v. State, 434
State of New Hampshire v. Heirtzler, 234
Stratham School Dist. v. Beth, 570

NEW JERSEY

Abbott by Abbott v. Burke, 437
Abbott v. Burke, 437
A.P. v. Pemberton Township Board of Educ., 547
Bell v. New Jersey, 442
Bennett v. New Jersey, 442
Board of Educ. of Borough of Englewood Cliffs v. Board of Educ. of City of Englewood, 465
Board of Educ. of City of Millville v. New Jersey Dep't of Educ., 438, 442
Board of Educ. of City of Passaic v. New Jersey Dep't of Educ., 442
Board of Educ. of West Windsor-Plainsboro Regional School Dist. v. Board of Educ. of Township of Delran, 570
Bowers v. NCAA, 657
Boy Scouts of America v. Dale, 146
C.N. v. Ridgewood Board of Educ., 515
Carpenito v. Board of Educ. of Borough of Rumson, 379
Child Evangelism Fellowship of New Jersey v. Stafford Township School Dist., 83
Cole v. Montague Board of Educ., 139
Cresskill Board of Educ. v. Cresskill Educ. Ass'n, 381
Curcio v. Collingswood Board of Educ., 266
D.E.R. v. Board of Educ. of Borough of Ramsey, 557
D.L. and Z.Y., on Behalf of T.L. and K.L. v. Board of Educ. of Princeton Regional School Dist., 451
Everson v. Board of Educ., 626
Febres v. Camden Board of Educ., 267

Frugis v. Bracigliano, 278
Green v. Jersey City Board of Educ., 32
Grendysa v. Evesham Township Board of Educ., 329
Hedges v. Musco, 220
Hernandez v. Don Bosco Preparatory High School, 618
Hornstine v. Township of Moorestown, 588
In re Dissolution of Union County Regional High School Dist. No. 1, 470
In re Grant of Charter School Application of Englewood on Palisades Charter School, 498
Joye v. Hunterdon Cent. Regional High School Board of Educ., 228
L.M. v. Evesham Township Board of Educ., 574
Magaw v. Middletown Board of Educ., 368
New Jersey v. T.L.O., 215, 216, 217, 218, 221, 223, 224, 233, 237
Oberti v. Board of Educ. of Borough of Clementon School Dist., 556
Piscataway Township Educ. Ass'n v. Piscataway Township Board of Educ., 419
Rocci v. Ecole Secondaire MacDonald-Cartier, 50
Rumsfeld v. Forum for Academic and Institutional Rights, 146, 147
S.G., as Guardian of A.G. v. Sayreville Board of Educ., 106
S.H. v. State-Operated School Dist. of City of Newark, 560
Smith v. Estate of Reverend P. Kelly, 604
South Jersey Catholic School Teachers Organization v. St. Teresa of the Infant Jesus Church Elementary School, 597
Stratechuk v. Board of Educ., South Orange-Maplewood School Dist., 61
Turton v. Frenchtown Elementary School Dist. Board of Educ., 75
Walz v. Egg Harbor Township Board of Educ., 90
Weisberg v. Riverside Township Board of Educ., 251, 317
Wilkins v. Penns Grove-Carneys Point Regional School Dist., 118
Woodbury Heights Board of Educ. v. Starr, 159
Wowkun v. Closter Board of Educ., 262, 304

NEW MEXICO

Aguilera v. Board of Educ. of Hatch Valley Schools, 327
Butler v. Rio Rancho Public Schools Board of Educ., 205
Carbajal v. Albuquerque Public School Dist., 508

Garcia v. Board of Educ. of Albuquerque Public Schools, 173

Hamilton Roofing Co. of Carlsbad, Inc. v. Carlsbad Municipal Schools Board of Educ., 455

Kerr v. Valdez, 299

Santa Fe Independent School Dist. v. Doe, 58, 67

Shively v. Santa Fe Preparatory School, 601

State v. Tywayne H., 237

Swisher v. Darden, 326

Watson v. Beckel, 617

Weinbaum v. Las Cruces Public Schools, 87

Zuni Public School Dist. No. 89 v. Dep't of Educ., 443

NEW YORK

Agostini v. Felton, 624, 628

Aguilar v. Felton, 627

Ambach v. Norwick, 264

Arlington Cent. School Dist. Board of Educ. v. Murphy, 535

Ass'n of Community Organizations for Reform Now v. New York City Dep't of Educ., 490, 493

Back v. Hastings on Hudson Union Free School Dist., 284

Bitting v. Lee, 165

Board of Educ. of City of New York v. Tom F., 619

Board of Educ. of Kiryas Joel Village School Dist. v. Grumet, 471

Board of Educ. of Monticello Cent. School Dist. v. Commissioner of Educ., 114

Board of Educ. v. Allen, 625

Board of Educ. v. Pico, 135

Board of Educ. v. Rowley, 534, 536

Bojarczuk v. Mills, 381

Burkybile v. Board of Educ. of Hastings-On-Hudson Union Free School Dist., 244

Burns v. Warwick Valley Cent. School Dist., 306

Cabouli v. Chappaqua Cent. School Dist., 557

Campaign for Fiscal Equity Inc. v. State of New York, 164, 432

Carmel Cent. School Dist. v. V.P., 575

Catherine G. v. County of Essex, 275, 276

Cerra v. Pawling Cent. School Dist., 542

Cioffi v. Averill Park Cent. School Dist. Board of Educ., 126

Civil Service Employees Ass'n, Local 1000 v. New York State Public Employment Relations Board, 403

Cohn v. New Paltz Cent. School Dist., 203

Coleman v. Newburgh Enlarged City School Dist., 547

Committee for Public Educ. & Religious Liberty v. Nyquist, 93, 94, 636

Connolly v. Rye School Dist., 156

Csorny v. Shoreham-Wading River Cent. School Dist., 484

D.F. v. Board of Educ. of Syosset Cent. School Dist., 103

Doe v. Rohan, 31

Doyle v. Rondout Valley Cent. School Dist., 237

Edelson v. Uniondale Union Free School Dist., 13

Engel v. Vitale, 57

Erich D. v. New Milford Board of Educ., 160, 549

Fauconier v. Committee on Special Educ., 543

Fauconier v. Committee on Special Educ., Dist. 3, New York Board of Educ., 543

Fuentes v. Board of Educ. of City of New York, 543

Garcia v. Puccio, 46

Good News Club v. Milford Cent. School, 76

Grim v. Rhinebeck Cent. School Dist., 540

Grumet v. Cuomo, 471

Grumet v. Pataki, 471

Guy v. New York State Public High School Athletic Ass'n, 645

In re Maine-Endwell Teachers' Ass'n v. Board of Educ. of Maine-Endwell Cent. School Dist., 305

In re Maison Scahill v. Greece Cent. School Dist., 335

Jerideau v. Huntingdon Union Free School Dist., 14

K.D. v. Fillmore Cent. School Dist., 117

K.M. v. Hyde Park Cent. School Dist., 586

Lamb's Chapel v. Center Moriches Union Free School Dist., 82

Leventhal v. Knapek, 242

Longwood Cent. School Dist. v. Springs Union Free School Dist., 156

Madison-Oneida Board of Cooperative Educational Services v. Mills, 377

Matter of Arbitration Between Binghamton City School Dist. and Peacock, 425

McCormick v. School Dist. of Mamaroneck, 649

Mirand v. City of New York, 36

Moore v. New York City Dep't of Educ., 50

Morris-Hayes v. Board of Educ. of Chester Union Free School Dist., 124, 322

Moss v. Enlarged City of School Dist. of City of Amsterdam, 296

National Law Center on Homelessness and Poverty, R.I. v. State of New York, 155

New York State Employment Relations Board v. Christ the King Regional High School, 597

New York State Employment Relations Board v. Christian Brothers Academy, 598
NLRB v. Yeshiva Univ., 598
Oakes v. Massena Cent. School Dist., 16
Peck v. Baldwinsville Cent. School Dist., 61
Pell v. Board of Educ. of Union Free School Dist., 334
Peters v. Baldwin Union Free School Dist., 313
Pierce v. Sullivan West Cent. School Dist., 71, 632
Polmanteer v. Bobo, 441
Port Washington Teachers' Ass'n v. Board of Educ. of Port Washington Union Free School Dist., 514
Remus v. Board of Educ. for Tonawanda City School Dist., 375
Reynolds v. Board of Educ. of Wappingers Cent. School Dist., 365
Rhodes v. Guarricino, 222
Rome City School Dist. Disciplinary Hearing v. Grifasi, 524
Rosario v. Does 1-10, 91
Roslyn Union Free School Dist. v. Geoffrey W., 561
RV v. New York City Dep't of Educ., 164
Selapack v. Iroquois Cent. School Dist., 276
Shaul v. Cherry Valley-Springfield Cent. School Dist., 242
Skoros v. City of New York, 86
Smith v. Half Hollow Hills Cent. School Dist., 36
Tesoriero v. Syosset Cent. School Dist., 183
Turley v. Sauquoit Valley School Dist., 196
Turner v. Liverpool Cent. School, 74
Weixel v. Board of Educ. of City of New York, 590
Wolfe v. Taconic-Hills Cent. School Dist., 556
Zorach v. Clauson, 71, 631, 632

NORTH CAROLINA

Boring v. Buncombe County Board of Educ., 138
Buncombe County, North Carolina, Board of Educ. v. Roberts, 192
Chapel Hill-Carrboro City Schools System v. Chavioux, 452
Davis v. Macon County Board of Educ., 346
Erik V. by and through Catherine V. v. Causby, 531
Francine Delany New School for Children Inc. v. Asheville City Board of Educ., 505
Graham v. Mock, 158
Hoke County Board of Educ. v. State of North Carolina, 439
Hugger v. Rutherford Institute, 49
In re Roberts, 192

J.S.W. v. Lee County Board of Educ., 203
Leandro v. State, 439
Love-Lane v. Martin, 129
M.E. and P.E. v. Buncombe County Board of Educ., 543
Petho v. Wakeman, 24
Smith v. Jackson County Board of Educ., 31
Stein v. Asheville City Board of Educ., 27
Townsend v. Board of Educ. of Robeson County, 513

NORTH DAKOTA

Azure v. Belcourt Public School Dist., 23
Kadrmas v. Dickinson Public Schools, 449
Simmons v. New Public School Dist. No. Eight, 290

OHIO

Baker v. Adams County/Ohio Valley School Board, 87
Barrett v. Steubenville City Schools, 264
Berger v. Medina City School Dist., 576
Boles-El v. Cleveland Municipal School Dist., 258
Boroff v. Van Wert City Board of Educ., 116
Brosch v. Mariemont City School Dist. Board of Educ., 207
Brubaker v. Hardy, 371
Cleveland Board of Educ. v. LaFleur, 269
Cleveland Board of Educ. v. Loudermill, 395
Columbus Board of Educ. v. Penick, 465
Coolidge v. Riegle, 43, 539
Cox v. Zanesville City School Dist. Board of Educ., 343
Coy v. Board of Educ. of North Canton City Schools, 108
Creusere v. Board of Educ. of City School Dist. of Cincinnati, 305
DeCesare v. Niles City School Dist. Board of Educ., 268
DeRolph v. State, 496
Draudt v. Wooster City School Dist. Board of Educ., 113
Duitch v. Canton City Schools, 37
Ellis v. Cleveland Municipal School Dist., 166
Fresh Start Academy v. Toledo Board of Educ., 492
Golden Christian Academy v. Zelman, 602
Golden v. Rossford Exempted Village School Dist., 75
Goss v. Lopez, 187, 188, 192, 194, 201, 506, 617
Henney v. Shelby City School Dist., 11
Hiram College v. Courtad, 614
Huntsman v. Perry Local School Dist. Board of Educ., 339

In re: Removal of Kuehnle, 484
Johnson v. North Union Local School Dist. Board of Educ., 271
Kimball v. Keystone Local School Dist., 647
Kings Local School Dist. v. Zelazny, 540
Lake Ridge Academy v. Carney, 614
Lancaster School Dist. Support Ass'n, OEA/NEA v. Board of Educ., Lancaster City School Dist., 426
Lautermilch v. Findlay City Schools, 388
Liedtke v. Carrington, 603
Montgomery v. Carr, 134
Mt. Healthy City School Dist. v. Doyle, 127
Nack v. Orange City School Dist., 537
Nichols v. Western Local Board of Educ., 481
Oak Hills Educ. Ass'n v. Oak Hills Local School Dist. Board of Educ., 416
Ohio Ass'n of Independent Schools v. Goff, 611
Ohio Congress of Parents and Teachers v. State Board of Educ., 497
Oleske v. Hilliard City School Dist. Board of Educ., 341
Payne v. Worthington Schools, 176
Reed v. Vermilion Local School Dist., 215
Rhoads v. Board of Educ. of Mad River Local School Dist., 321
Riley v. St. Ann Catholic School, 618
Rusk v. Crestview Local Schools, 84
Smith v. Revere Local School Dist. Board of Educ., 511
Spencer v. Lakeview School Dist., 15
Stacy v. Batavia Local School Dist. Board of Educ., 411
Stancourt v. Worthington City School Dist. Board of Educ., 559
State ex rel. Antonucci v. Youngstown City School Dist. Board of Educ., 379
State ex rel. Boggs v. Springfield Local School Dist., 429
State ex rel. Burch v. Sheffield-Sheffield Lake City School Dist. Board of Educ., 383
State ex rel. Consumer News Services Inc. v. Worthington City Board of Educ., 249
State ex rel. Lecklider v. SERS, 357
State ex rel. Ohio Ass'n of Public School Employees/AFSCME, Local 4, AFL-CIO v. Batavia Local School Dist., 410
State of Ohio, ex rel. Stacy v. Batavia Local School Dist. Board of Educ., 354
State v. Smrekar, 161
Tarter v. Raybuck, 224
Ullmo v. Gilmour Academy, 621
Watkins v. Millenium School, 225
Williams v. Cambridge Board of Educ., 105
Winkelman v. Parma City School Dist., 537
Wolman v. Walter, 624, 625
Yates v. Mansfield Board of Educ., 277
Zelman v. Simmons-Harris, 93, 94, 95, 633

OKLAHOMA

Ballard v. Independent School Dist. No. 4 of Bryan County, Oklahoma, 332
Barton v. Independent School Dist. No. I-99, Custer County, 380
Board of Educ. of Oklahoma City Public Schools v. Dowell, 458, 459
Board of Educ. of Independent School Dist. 92, Pottawatomie County v. Earls, 226, 638
Bryant v. Independent School Dist. No. I-38, Garvin County, Oklahoma, 175
Dowell v. Board of Educ. of Oklahoma City Public Schools, 460
Greenshields v. Independent School Dist. I-1016, 126
Harrah Independent School Dist. v. Martin, 255
Hearn v. Muskogee Public School Dist., 119
Hill v. Board of Educ., Dist. I–009, Jones, Oklahoma, 483
Owasso Independent School Dist. No. I-011 v. Falvo, 518
Pentagon Academy v. Independent School Dist. No. 1 of Tulsa County, Oklahoma, 497
Scheer v. Independent School Dist. No. I-26, Ottawa County, 376

OREGON

Bergerson v. Salem-Keizer School Dist., 331
Folkers v. Lincoln County School Dist., 408
PGA Tour, Inc. v. Martin, 656
Pinard v. Clatskanie School Dist. 6J, 100
Powell v. Bunn, 78
Scherzinger v. Portland Custodians Civil Service Board, 424
Schneider v. Corvallis School Dist. 509J, 214
Settlegoode v. Portland Public Schools, 129
T.M.M. v. Lake Oswego School Dist., 230
Vernonia School Dist. 47J v. Acton, 224, 225, 226, 227, 638
Zottola v. Three Rivers School Dist., 361

PENNSYLVANIA

A.B. v. Slippery Rock Area School Dist., 102
Abington School Dist. v. Schempp, 57
Alex K. v. Wissahickon School Dist., 621
Angstadt v. Midd-West School Dist., 646
Ass'n of Catholic Teachers v. PLRB, 598
Bowalick v. Comwlth. of Pennsylvania, 334
Burger v. Board of School Directors of McGuffey School Dist., 273
Caitlin W. v. Rose Tree Media School Dist., 621

TABLE OF CASES BY STATE

Carbondale Area School Dist. v. Fell Charter School, 504
Carroll v. Ringgold Educ. Ass'n, 430
Cent. Dauphin School Dist. v. Founding Coalition of Infinity Charter School, 500
Circle School v. Pappert, 70
Combs v. Homer Center School Dist., 62
Corbett v. Scranton School Dist., 275
Crowe v. School Dist. of Pittsburgh, 626
Cruz v. Pennsylvania Interscholastic Athletic Ass'n, 656
Cureton v. NCAA, 653, 654, 655
D.C. v. School Dist. of Philadelphia, 194
D.O.F. v. Lewisburg Area School Dist., 203
Davis v. Chester Upland School Dist., 423
Dombrowski v. Wissahickon School Dist., 584
Dominic J. v. Wyoming Valley West High School, 513, 639
Donovan v. Punxsutawney Area School Board, 80
East Penn School Dist. v. Scott B., 579
Eric H. v. Methacton School Dist., 559
Giacomucci v. Southeast Delco School Dist., 451
Gikas v. Washington School Dist., 324
Gilbert v. Homar, 395
Grieb v. Unemployment Compensation Board of Review, 362
Gruenke v. Seip, 670
Harrisburg School Dist. v. Hickok, 495
Harrisburg School Dist. v. Zogby, 495
Henderson v. Chartiers Valley School, 288
Hoke v. Elizabethtown Area School Dist., 191
In re R.H., 231
Jones v. Indiana Area School Dist., 178, 562
J.S. v. Bethlehem Area School Dist., 107
Katruska v. Bethlehem Center School Dist., 400
Kitzmiller v. Dover Area School Dist., 63
Klump v. Nazareth Area School Dist., 213
Kozura v. Tulpehocken Area School Dist., 428
Latour v. Riverside Beaver School Dist., 103
Layshock v. Hermitage School Dist., 107
Lemon v. Kurtzman, 58, 73, 82, 85, 624, 628
Lower Merion School Dist. v. Doe, 571
Mars Area School Dist. v. Laurie L., 553
Marshall v. Sisters of Holy Family of Nazareth, 619
McGreevy v. Stroup, 127
Meek v. Pittenger, 624
Merrell v. Chartiers Valley School Dist., 323
Michael C. v. Radnor Township School Dist., 567
Mohammed v. School Dist. of Philadelphia, 35
Molly L. v. Lower Merion School Dist., 586

Montanye v. Wissahickon School Dist., 363
Mosaica Academy Charter School v. Comwlth. Dep't of Educ., 504
Mullen v. Thompson, 470
Nichol v. ARIN Intermediate Unit 28, 92
Norristown Area School Dist. v. Norristown Educ. Support Personnel Ass'n, 420
Pennsylvania School Boards Ass'n v. Comwlth. of Pennsylvania, 356
Pottstown School Dist. v. Hill School, 608
Pryor v. NCAA, 654
Reading School Dist. v. Dep't of Educ., 491
Robert B. v. West Chester Area School Dist., 620
Shuman v. Penn Manor School Dist., 216
Sloan v. Lemon, 451
St. Francis College v. Al-Khazraji, 297
Susquehanna Township School Dist. v. Frances J., 578
State of Pennsylvania v. Riley, 443
Sutton v. West Chester Area School Dist., 585
Theodore v. Delaware Valley School Dist., 227
T.W. v. School Dist. of Philadelphia, 210
U.S. v. American Library Ass'n Inc., 135
Valentino C. v. School Dist. of Philadelphia, 549
Walker-Serrano v. Leonard, 101
Weiss v. Williamsport Area School Dist., 515
Williams v. School Dist. of Bethlehem, 651
Woodland Hills School Dist. v. S.F., 582

RHODE ISLAND

Bristol Warren Regional School Committee v. Rhode Island Dep't of Educ., 572
Brouillette v. Dep't of Employment and Training Board of Review, 359
Johnston School Committee v. Rhode Island State Labor Relations Board, 417
Kleczek v. Rhode Island Interscholastic League, 651
L.T. on Behalf of N.B. v. Warwick School Committee, 566
Lee v. Weisman, 58, 65
Lemon v. Kurtzman, 58, 73, 82, 85, 624, 628
Martone v. Johnston School Committee, 273
Woonsocket Teachers' Guild, Local Union 951, AFT v. Woonsocket School Committee, 358, 427

SOUTH CAROLINA

Beaufort County Board of Educ. v. Lighthouse Charter School Committee, 500
Bob Jones Univ. v. U.S., 604
Byrd v. Irmo High School, 192
Child Evangelism Fellowship of South Carolina v. Anderson School Dist. Five, 77

Davis v. Greenwood School Dist. 50, 409
Etheredge v. Richland School Dist. One, 6
Florence County School Dist. Four v.
    Carter, 573
Floyd v. Horry County School Dist., 192
Hunt v. McNair, 635, 636
In re Amir X.S., 101, 102
Martin Engineering v. Lexington County
    School Dist. One, 453
Nathan v. Richland County School Dist.
    Two, 294
Shell v. Richland County School Dist.
    One, 334
Stanley v. Darlington County School
    Dist., 468
Wright v. Richland County School Dist.
    Two, 358

SOUTH DAKOTA

Barnes v. Spearfish School Dist. No. 40-2, 346
Fick v. Sioux Falls School Dist. 49-5, 571
Gettysburg School Dist. 53-1 v. Larson, 382
Hanson v. Vermillion School Dist.
    No. 13-1, 376
Hughes v. Stanley County School Dist., 278
McCardle v. Mitchell School Dist., 283
Norton v. Deuel School Dist. #19-4, 367
Webster Educ. Ass'n v. Webster School
    Dist., 415
West Cent. Educ. Ass'n v. West Cent. School
    Dist. 49-4, 419
Wigg v. Sioux Falls School Dist. 49-5, 91
Wirt v. Parker School Dist. #60-04, 352, 371

TENNESSEE

Babb v. Hamilton County Board of Educ., 24
Barnett v. Memphis City School, 583
Board of County Commissioners of Shelby
    County, Tennessee v. Burson, 474
Brennan v. Giles County Board of Educ., 254
Brentwood Academy v. Tennessee Secondary
    School Athletic Ass'n, 611, 612, 664
Burlington Northern & Santa Fe Railway Co.
    v. White, 281
Cannon County Board of Educ. v. Wade, 420
Crocker v. Tennessee Secondary School
    Athletic Ass'n, 658
D.B. v. Lafon, 109
Doe v. Metropolitan Nashville Public
    Schools, 555
Doe v. Porter, 64
Flatt v. Tennessee Secondary Schools Athletic
    Ass'n, 665
Hamilton County Dep't of Educ. v. Deal, 535
Haney v. Bradley County Board of Educ., 43

Harris v. Forklift Systems, Inc., 290
Ketchersid v. Rhea County Board
    of Educ., 349
Knox County Educ. Ass'n v. Knox County
    Board of Educ., 240
Lannom v. Board of Educ. for Metropolitan
    Government, Nashville and Davidson
    County, 336
L.W. v. Knox County Board of Educ., 56
Metropolitan Nashville Educ. Ass'n v.
    Metropolitan Board of Public Educ., 414
N.L. v. Knox County Schools, 539
Phillips v. Anderson County Board
    of Educ., 182
Polk County Board of Educ. v. Polk County
    Educ. Ass'n, 418
Scarbrough v. Morgan County Board
    of Educ., 132
Shohadaee v. Metropolitan Government of
    Nashville and Davidson County, 282
Steele v. Industrial Development Board
    of Metropolitan Government
    of Nashville, 630
Tennessee Small School Systems v.
    McWherter, 440

TEXAS

Abbott v. North East Independent School
    Dist., 251
Adams v. Groesbeck Independent School
    Dist., 281, 363, 660
Amaral-Whittenberg v. Alanis, 268
Barrow v. Greenville Independent School
    Dist., 262, 263
Bates v. Dallas Independent School Dist., 512
Ben Bolt-Palito Blanco Consolidated
    Independent School Dist. v. Texas
    Political Subdivisions Property/Casualty
    Joint Self-Insurance Fund, 456
Board of Trustees of Bastrop Independent
    School Dist. v. Toungate, 121
Briseno v. State of Texas, 218
Caudillo v. Lubbock Independent School
    Dist., 144
Chiras v. Miller, 137
Chiu v. Plano Independent School Dist., 143
Christensen v. Harris County, 270
Clear Creek Independent School Dist. v.
    J.K., 582
Coggin v. Longview Independent School
    Dist., 387
Cypress-Fairbanks Independent School Dist v.
    Michael F., 536
Doe v. San Antonio Independent School
    Dist., 38
Doria v. Stulting, 172
Elgin Independent School Dist. v. R.N., 53

Finch v. Fort Bend Independent School Dist., 393

Flour Bluff Independent School Dist. v. R.S., 193

Gebser v. Lago Vista Independent School Dist., 181, 183

GI Forum v. Texas Educ. Agency, 592

Greene v. Plano Independent School Dist., 3

Houston Independent School Dist. v. Bobby R., 536

Houston v. Nelson, 371

In re O.E., 218

In re V.P., 232

Irving Independent School Dist. v. Tatro, 568

Jeffrey v. Board of Trustees of Bells Independent School Dist., 507

Karr v. Schmidt, 120

LeLeaux v. Hampshire-Fannett Independent School Dist., 53

Littlefield v. Forney Independent School Dist., 118, 120

Livingston v. DeSoto Independent School Dist., 665

Martinez v. Bynum 157, 158

McKinney v. Irving Independent School Dist., 52

Mellen v. Congress of the U.S., 70

Moore v. Willis Independent School Dist., 168

Neeley v. West Orange-Cove Consolidated Independent School Dist., 435

Perry v. Sindermann, 385, 386

Plyler v. Doe, 157

Prejean v. Cypress-Fairbanks Independent School Dist., 312

Rivera v. Houston Independent School Dist., 26

Rogers v. Duncanville Independent School Dist., 140

Russell v. State of Texas, 233

San Antonio School Dist. v. Rodriguez, 432

Santa Fe Independent School Dist. v. Doe, 58, 67

Shelby S. v. Conroe Independent School Dist., 551

Simpson v. Alanis, 337

Tarkington Independent School Dist. v. Ellis, 197

Tave v. Alanis, 340

Texas Educ. Agency v. Goodrich Independent School Dist., 472

Texas v. U.S., 473

U.S. v. State of Texas, 467

Van Orden v. Perry, 85

Wells v. One2One Learning Foundation, 501

Winters v. Pasadena Independent School Dist., 318

Wittman v. Nelson, 374

Ysleta Independent School Dist. v. Griego, 383

Ysleta Independent School Dist. v. Monarrez, 283

UTAH

Corp. of the Presiding Bishop of the Church of Jesus Christ of Latter-Day Saints v. Amos, 595

Jensen v. Reeves, 520

Natay v. Murray School Dist., 298

Save Our Schools v. Board of Educ. of Salt Lake City, 479

Tindley v. Williamsport Area School Dist., 4

Youren v. Tintic School Dist., 364

VERMONT

Berkshire School v. Town of Reading, 607

Brigham v. State, 437

Burlington School Committee v. Dep't of Educ., 573

Burr and Burton Seminary v. Town of Manchester, 607

Chittenden Town School Dist. v. Vermont Dep't of Educ., 96

Graham v. Springfield Vermont School Dist., 132

Mellin v. Flood Brook Union School Dist., 416

Taylor v. Vermont Dep't of Educ., 517

VIRGINIA

A.W. v. Fairfax County School Board, 560

Baynard v. Malone, 184

County School Board of York County v. A.L., 542

Daye v. School Board of City of Norfolk, 319

Demmon v. Loudoun County Public Schools, 89

Duck v. Isle of Wight County School Board, 587

Emery v. Roanoke City School Board, 568

Green v. County School Board of New Kent County, 458, 460

J.H. v. Henrico County School Board, 565

Jaynes v. Newport News School Board, 545

Kozlowski v. Hampton School Board, 310

Linhart v. Lawson, 54

Lovern v. Edwards, 141

Myers v. Loudoun County Public Schools, 69

Newsom v. Albemarle County School Board, 119

Peters v. Jenney, 365

Power v. School Board of City of Virginia Beach, 589

Ratner v. Loudon County Public Schools, 200
Runyon v. McCrary, 609
Tazewell County School Board v. Brown, 423
Urofsky v. Gilmore, 125
Clark County School Dist. v. Bundley, 360
Williams v. Augusta County School
Board, 477
Wofford v. Evans, 229

WASHINGTON

Ackerman v. Quilcene School Dist. No. 48, 286
Bellevue John Does 1-11 v. Bellevue School
Dist. #405, 246
Bethel School Dist. No. 403 v. Fraser, 99
Boss v. Peninsula School Dist., 483
Brown v. State of Washington, 409
Burch v. Barker, 114
Christensen v. Royal School Dist. #160, 6, 7
Claar v. Auburn School Dist. No. 408, 52
Davenport v. Washington Educ. Ass'n, 131
Gonzaga Univ. v. Doe, 493, 518
Hudon v. West Valley School Dist., 290
In re Recall of Young, 473
Lindeman v. Kelso School Dist., 524
Locke v. Davey, 95, 634
Lockhart v. U.S., 633
M.L. v. Federal Way School Dist., 539
McGowan v. State of Washington, 448
Ms. S. and her Daughter G. v. Vashon Island
School Dist., 566
Mt. Adams School Dist. v. Cook, 421
Nieshe v. Concrete School Dist., 580
Parents Involved in Community Schools v.
Seattle School Dist. No. 1, 152
Peninsula School Dist. No. 401 v. Public
School Employees of Peninsula, 382
Powell v. Cascade School Dist. No. 228, 391
Prince v. Jacoby, 81
Shinaberger v. LaPine, 34
State of Washington, ex rel. Washington State
P.D.C. v. Washington State Educ.
Ass'n, 406
Taylor v. Enumclaw School Dist.
No. 216, 641
Travis v. Bohannon, 27
Vallandigham v. Clover Park School Dist.
No. 400, 366
Webster v. Public School Employees
of Washington Inc., 270
Weems v. North Franklin School
Dist., 333
Witters v. State Comm'n for the Blind, 635
Witters v. Washington Dep't of Services
for the Blind, 635
Wood v. Battle Ground School Dist., 486
York v. Wahkiakum School Dist.
No. 200, 639

WEST VIRGINIA

Bragg v. Swanson, 110
Jones v. West Virginia State Board of
Educ., 645
Peck v. Upshur County Board of Educ., 85
Porter v. Grant County Board of Educ., 14
Raleigh County Board of Educ. v.
Gatson, 359
Scott v. Stewart, 396
State ex rel. Estes v. Egnor, 162
State of West Virginia v. Board of Educ.
of Summers County, 627
West Virginia State Board of Educ. v.
Barnette, 67, 69

WISCONSIN

Billings v. Madison Metropolitan School
Dist., 154
Board of Regents v. Roth, 385
Bukowski v. Wisconsin Interscholastic
Ass'n, 648
Cigan v. Chippewa Falls School Dist., 319
Dodgeland Educ. Ass'n v. Wisconsin
Employment Relations Comm'n, 422
Freedom From Religion Foundation, Inc. v.
Bugher, 625
Gernetzke v. Kenosha Unified School
Dist. No. 1, 81
Greendale Educ. Ass'n v.
Greendale School Dist., 330
Haugerud v. Amery School Dist., 285
Hoffman v. East Troy Community School
Dist., 556
Hortonville Joint School Dist. No. 1 v.
Hortonville Educ. Ass'n, 429
Jackson v. Benson, 96
Livingston v. Wausau Underwriters
Insurance Co., 18
Loy v. Dodgeville School Dist., 170
McMorrow v. Benson, 159
Mohammed v. Racine Unified School
Dist., 303
Mudrovich v. D.C. Everest Area School
Dist., 47
Nagel v. Green Bay Area Public School
Dist., 23
Price v. Boyceville Community School
Dist., 35
Providence Catholic School v. Bristol School
Dist. No. 1, 627
Racine Charter One v. Racine Unified School
Dist., 502
Robinson v. Racine Unified School Dist., 249
Schilling v. Sheboygan Area School Dist., 18
School Dist. of Wisconsin Dells v. Z.S., 563

Schroeder v. Hamilton School Dist., 293
Scott v. Savers Property and Casualty
     Insurance Co., 5
State v. White, 162
Stockbridge School Dist. v. Dep't of Public
     Instruction School Dist. Boundary
     Appeal Board, 472
Thomas More High School v. Burmaster, 629
Ulichny v. Merton Community School
     Dist., 389
Zellner v. Cedarburg School Dist., 339

WYOMING

Board of Trustees of Fremont County School
     Dist. #25 v. BM, 189
Fowler v. Williamson, 195
In re R.M., 195
Swenson v. Lincoln County School Dist., 588

CHAPTER ONE

Accidents, Injuries and Deaths

Page

I. NEGLIGENCE..2
   A. Elements 2
   B. Defenses 3
      1. Immunity 3
      2. Comparative and Contributory Negligence..................6

II. SCHOOL ATHLETICS..8
   A. Participants 8
      1. Duty of Care 8
      2. Governmental Immunity 10
      3. Assumption of Risk and Waiver 12
   B. Spectators, Employees and Parents...............................13

III. OTHER SCHOOL ACTIVITIES..14
   A. Physical Education Class Accidents............................14
      1. Duty of Care 14
      2. Governmental Immunity 17
   B. Shop Class Injuries..19
      1. Duty of Care 19
      2. Governmental Immunity 20
   C. Other Supervised Activities..21
      1. Duty of Care 21
      2. Governmental Immunity 23

IV. UNSUPERVISED ACCIDENTS 25
   A. On School Grounds 25
      1. Duty of Care 25
      2. Governmental Immunity 26
   B. Off School Grounds 26
      1. Duty of Care 26
      2. Governmental Immunity 28

V. LIABILITY FOR INTENTIONAL CONDUCT 29
   A. Employee Misconduct..29
      1. Types of Misconduct 29
      2. Governmental Immunity 32
   B. Student Misconduct 34
      1. Types of Misconduct 34
      2. Governmental Immunity 38
   C. Parent Misconduct 41

    D.   Suicide 43
    E.   Defamation 45

VI.   SCHOOL BUS ACCIDENTS...51
    A.   Duty of Care 51
    B.   Governmental Immunity 52

I.   NEGLIGENCE

Negligence is the failure to use reasonable or ordinary care under the circumstances. In order for a school district to be liable for negligence, it must have a duty to the person claiming negligence, and there must be some failure to prevent foreseeable harm. A district may be held vicariously liable for the acts or omissions of a negligent employee. There is some overlap in the cases between negligence and intentional misconduct. A pattern of negligence by school districts showing a conscious disregard for safety may be deemed "willful or wanton misconduct," which is a form of intentional conduct.

A. Elements

The elements of a negligence lawsuit are: 1) the existence of a **legal duty** *to conform conduct to a specific standard in order to protect others from unreasonable risks of injury, 2) the* **breach** *of that duty that is, 3) the direct* **cause of the injury***, and 4)* **damages***. In short, negligence consists of a duty of care, followed by a breach of that duty which causes injury and damages. If these elements are satisfied, a court may proceed to the question of whether the harm was foreseeable by the district.*

◆   An Arizona school district policy allowed some students to check out during lunch periods if certain conditions, including obtaining parental permission, were met. A student informed a security guard that he was going off campus to retrieve books from his car. Although the student did not have permission to leave, the guard did not attempt to stop him and he drove to a shopping mall. On the return trip to school, he drove his vehicle into oncoming traffic and collided with another vehicle. The driver and passengers of the other vehicle sued the school district in a state trial court. They asserted the district had a duty to protect the public from the risk of negligent driving by students who left campus and that the policy of allowing students to leave created an unreasonable risk of harm. The court awarded judgment to the district.

The driver and passengers appealed to the Arizona Court of Appeals. It held **a negligence action cannot be maintained in the absence of a recognized legal duty. Such a duty could be found only if reasonable persons would recognize it and agree it exists.** The district did not directly cause injury to the driver and passengers, and there was no legal relationship among the parties. The court rejected the argument that the district had a special relationship with the student that imposed a duty upon it to control his conduct and prevent injury to others. While a district has a statutory and common-law duty to its students, and state law holds districts to strict account for disorderly conduct on school property, this did not extend to the general public. The district had no knowledge of any dangerous propensity of the student, and his off-campus driving was for his own purposes. The district had no power to control the student off campus, and the court refused to impose a duty on it to keep him from driving his car at the time of the accident. **School officials are not authorized to physically restrain students, and districts do not breach their duty to supervise students by failing to enforce a closed-campus policy.** The court affirmed the judgment for the district. *Collette v. Tolleson Unified School Dist. No. 214*, 54 P.3d 828 (Ariz. Ct. App. 2002).

◆ A Texas teacher asserted water leaked into her school building for years, allowing mold to form and exposing her to toxic mold accumulations. She claimed that despite knowledge of the school's poor design, the district failed to warn employees and students of the dangers, inadequately maintained the building and failed to take adequate remedial measures. The teacher sued the district and its superintendent in a federal district court, asserting due process violations through 42 U.S.C. § 1983. The district moved for dismissal, arguing the complaint asserted failure to provide a safe, healthy work environment, which is not a right guaranteed by the Constitution. The teacher contended the district created the risk of harm to her from toxic mold through its customs, practices, policies and procedures. The court disagreed, stating the government typically has no affirmative duty to protect individuals from the acts of private citizens. Liability under the "state-created danger" theory exists only if the government has created or increased an individual's danger from third persons.

On appeal, the U.S. Court of Appeals, Fifth Circuit, held **a government employer's failure to warn employees about known workplace hazards does not violate the Due Process Clause, even if this may be actionable under state law.** The court held the teacher's claims did not rise to the level of a constitutional violation. **Failure to maintain a safe workplace was not a due process violation under the state-created danger theory or any other theory.** As the teacher alleged nothing more than negligence, the court found no basis for her due process claim. *Greene v. Plano Independent School Dist.*, 103 Fed.Appx. 542 (5th Cir. 2004).

B. Defenses

1. Immunity

Immunity is an exemption from a legal duty or liability that protects school districts and employees from liability in many cases. "Discretionary" or "official" immunity protects school employees and officials from liability where they perform "discretionary" as opposed to "ministerial" duties. The distinction between discretionary and ministerial is difficult to apply, but is usually construed as protecting decision-makers.

Public officials whose duties require them to exercise judgment or discretion are not personally liable for damages unless they act willfully or maliciously. A "ministerial act" is one that leaves nothing to discretion and is a simple or definite duty. Discretionary or official immunity ensures that public officials who are charged by law with duties calling for the exercise of judgment or discretion are not held personally liable for damages unless they commit a willful or malicious wrong.

◆   An Illinois eighth grader participated in an extracurricular tumbling class held during lunch periods in his school gymnasium. The teacher who supervised the class had a physical education degree, but little mini-trampoline experience. The student seriously injured his neck and became quadriplegic after taking a forward flip off the mini-trampoline. He had done forward flips from the mini-trampoline five or six times before the injury. The student and his mother sued the school board and teacher in a state circuit court. They claimed the teacher failed to provide any spotters and did not watch students while they used the mini-trampoline. The complaint also named the Chicago Youth Centers (CYC), which ran the tumbling class. The family asserted that use of a mini-trampoline was a hazardous recreational activity, and that the CYC and the teacher could not claim state law immunity because they acted willfully and wantonly. The trial court granted immunity to the teacher, the CYC and board.

The Appellate Court of Illinois reversed in part, finding no immunity for injuries caused by any willful and wanton misconduct. The parties appealed to the Supreme Court of Illinois, which noted that under ordinary circumstances, state law would immunize the board, CYC and teacher for discretionary and supervisory conduct. However, this immunity was limited by state law exceptions for hazardous recreational activity. It was clear to the court that the legislature did not intend for government immunity to be absolute in all cases. The use of a trampoline was listed as a "hazardous recreational activity." The legislature intended to hold government entities and employees to a higher standard of care, and the immunity exceptions of state law applied. The teacher, CYC and board would be liable for any willful and wanton misconduct. However, the court found no evidence of willful or wanton misconduct in this case. **These terms required "a course of action which shows an actual or deliberate intention to cause harm" or "utter indifference to or conscious disregard for the safety of others or their property." This was far more than simple negligence.** Use of a trampoline was a hazardous activity in which accidents could occur even with spotters and safety equipment. As the family only alleged negligence, not willful and wanton misconduct, the trial court had properly awarded judgment to the teacher, board and CYC. *Murray v. Chicago Youth Center*, No. 99457, 2006 WL 1822656 (Ill. 2006).

◆   **The Supreme Court of Utah upheld the state Governmental Immunity Act, which places an aggregate cap of $500,000 on claims for two or more persons in any one occurrence.** The court held the act's limitations did not violate the Due Process or Uniform Operation of Laws clauses of the Utah Constitution. As a result, the families of students who died or were injured in a van crash after a debate tournament could receive no more than the statutory cap. *Tindley v. Williamsport Area School Dist.*, 116 P.3d 295 (Utah 2005).

◆   A Wisconsin school guidance counselor agreed to help select appropriate courses for a student who expected to receive a National Collegiate Athletic Association (NCAA) Division I hockey scholarship. During the student's senior year, the counselor incorrectly advised the family that a course titled "Broadcast Communications" satisfied NCAA "core course" requirements. The student completed the course prior to graduation. He then accepted a hockey scholarship from an NCAA Division I college. The scholarship was rescinded when the college learned the course was not NCAA-approved. The student sued the district and its insurers in a state court for negligence and breach of an alleged contract with the counselor for advice. The court dismissed the case, declaring the district immune from liability on the negligence claim and finding no contract existed. The state court of appeals affirmed the decision.

On appeal, the Wisconsin Supreme Court explained that state law provides immunity to political subdivisions and public officials for acts involving the exercise of discretion. Previous court decisions recognized limits to governmental immunity when their acts were "ministerial duties imposed by law" or involved known dangers, and when official conduct was intentional, malicious and willful. The court rejected the family's characterization of the counselor's advice as "ministerial." His guidance and counseling services to students were "inherently discretionary," because each student's case involved an interpretive process. No laws or regulations defined the provision of guidance services. The counselor's failure to provide correct advice despite his ready access to the information indicated he was negligent, but it did not change the inherently discretionary nature of his job. **The doctrine of government immunity was developed to protect officials from being intimidated by the threat of lawsuits in the exercise of their discretion.** The lower courts had properly held the district was entitled to immunity. The family's contract-based claims had no merit, and the court affirmed the judgment. *Scott v. Savers Property and Casualty Insurance Co.*, 663 N.W.2d 715 (Wis. 2003).

◆   In a similar case involving an all-state Iowa basketball player, the Iowa Supreme Court noted that the courts must refrain from rejecting "all claims that arise out of a school environment under the umbrella of educational malpractice." The case instead arose under a tort cause of action for negligent misrepresentation. **Guidance counselors assumed an advisory role and were aware that students would rely on the information they provided. They owed students a duty of reasonable care when supplying information.** The school district was not entitled to summary judgment on a claim for negligent misrepresentation. However, the trial court had correctly held the school had no duty to submit information about a course to the NCAA for approval. *Sain v. Cedar Rapids Community School Dist.*, 626 N.W.2d 115 (Iowa 2001).

◆   A South Carolina high school student was shot and killed by another student in the hallway of their school during a class change. His estate sued the district in a state court for wrongful death. A campus security monitor, who formerly worked at the school, submitted an affidavit stating he had received no training from the district, was not properly equipped to conduct his duties and lacked authority to perform personal or locker searches of students.

The court awarded summary judgment to the district, finding insufficient evidence it had acted in a grossly negligent manner. The state court of appeals reversed, and the district appealed to the South Carolina Supreme Court. The court noted that under state law, **a governmental entity is not liable for a loss resulting from the responsibility or duty to take custody of a student or to confine, supervise, protect or control a student, except where the supervision is grossly negligent**. Gross negligence is defined as the intentional, conscious failure to do something that is incumbent upon one to do, or the intentional doing of a thing that one ought not do. In this case, there was no link between the deficiencies identified by the former employee and the incident leading to the student's death. The district had no direct knowledge or notice of any problems between the two students and at the very least exercised "slight care" to ensure student safety by maintaining hallway supervisors and an intervention system to help resolve student conflicts. The fact that the district might have taken stronger security measures did not negate the efforts that it actually took. The court reinstated the trial court's decision. *Etheredge v. Richland School Dist. One*, 341 S.C. 307, 534 S.E.2d 275 (S.C. 2000).

2. Comparative and Contributory Negligence

Under comparative negligence principles, courts may apportion negligence among parties by their degree of fault. For example, a jury may find a student who slipped on a bar of soap in a school locker room 40% negligent, and the district whose employee left out the bar of soap 60% negligent. If the damages were $10,000, the student would recover $6,000 from the district.

In Christensen v. Royal School Dist. #160, *below, the Supreme Court of Washington held a 13-year-old middle school student had no "duty to protect herself from sexual abuse at school by her teacher," and denied an attempt by her school district and principal to show she consented to sexual relations with a teacher. This result was consistent with cases from Indiana, South Carolina, Colorado and Oregon, and a Pennsylvania decision which held* **"a defense of contributory fault should not be available to the perpetrator of sexual abuse or to a third party that is in a position to control the perpetrator."**

◆   A Washington student and her family sued a teacher, district and principal in federal court for alleged sexual abuse by the teacher. The claims included negligent supervision and hiring of the teacher. The principal and district sought to have part of any damage award reduced because of the student's alleged misconduct. They asserted she consented to have sexual relations four times with the 26-year-old teacher in his classroom. The court found the issue required an authoritative interpretation of state law, and certified it to the Supreme Court of Washington. The supreme court noted the state Tort Reform Act required comparing the fault of parties in negligence cases. Under the act, a claimant's negligence related to the failure to use due care for his or her own protection. **The court held the societal interest in protecting children from sexual abuse, as carried forward in criminal laws, applied in civil actions for harm caused by adult perpetrators of sexual abuse.** This interest applied when contribution was sought by a third party in a position to control the abuse.

The court held contributory fault did not apply as a matter of public policy. The student had no duty to protect herself against sexual abuse by her teacher. **Washington schools have a "special relationship with students" and a duty to protect them from reasonably anticipated dangers. Because of the vulnerability of students, they had no duty to protect themselves from sexual abuse by teachers, and there could be no contributory fault assessed against the student in her negligence case.** The district and principal had a clear duty to protect the student. The court advised the federal district court that the school district could not rely on the defense of contributory negligence by the student. However, this finding should not prevent the district from asserting it was careful in its hiring and supervision of the teacher. *Christensen v. Royal School Dist. #160*, 156 Wash.2d 62, 124 P.3d 283 (Wash. 2005).

◆ An Indiana parent watched his son play in an Amateur Athletic Union basketball game at a high school gym. He sat on portable bleachers that were not pushed against a wall and had no back support. The parent watched two games on lower seats, before moving to the top row for a third game. He leaned back and fell off the bleachers, injuring himself. The parent filed a state court action against the school system. Without allowing the case to go before a jury, the court found he was contributorily negligent and held for the school system.

The state court of appeals reversed the decision, and the Supreme Court of Indiana agreed to review the case. **The court explained that the defense of contributory negligence operates as a complete bar to negligence claims against Indiana public schools and other government entities. Even a slight degree of negligence on the part of the parent would bar a negligence action against the school system, if his conduct was a legal cause of the injury.** The court held "contributory negligence is the failure of a person to exercise for his own safety that degree of care and caution which an ordinary, reasonable and prudent person in a similar situation would exercise." While contributory negligence was normally a question for a jury to consider, summary judgment was appropriate if facts were undisputed. In this case, it was undisputed that the parent fell when he leaned backwards on the bleacher. He had been at the gym for about four hours. It was clearly visible that there was no back rail for spectators to lean upon on the top row, but the parent did so anyway. The court found the parent was negligent to some degree, and this was enough to establish contributory negligence. As the trial court had properly applied the defense of contributory negligence, the supreme court reinstated the judgment for the school system. *Funston v. School Town of Munster*, 849 N.E.2d 595 (Ind. 2006).

◆ A Louisiana high school student was harassed and threatened by three classmates after he came to the defense of a new student while on their school bus. He got off the bus at a stop where he believed that he would be safer than if he disembarked at his regular stop. However, he was followed by the three classmates. While attempting to intervene, the student was thrown to the ground and beaten by the three students. He suffered personal injuries including tremors, loss of memory and post-traumatic stress disorder. His mother sued the other students, their parents, the school board and school officials, including the bus driver, in a Louisiana trial court. The assaulting students, their parents and insurers were voluntarily dismissed. The court held the school board alone was liable for a general damage award of $75,000 for the student and $5,000 for his mother. It also awarded the student special damages.

The Court of Appeal of Louisiana held the trial court had erroneously failed to compare the fault of the parties in this case, as required by state law. **While the school board was responsible for the reasonable supervision of students, it was not the insurer of student safety. In a personal injury case involving negligent supervision, it is necessary to show an unreasonable risk of injury is foreseeable to the board that is known and preventable in the exercise of proper supervision.** Evidence indicated school administrators did not follow board policies regarding the prevention of fights among students despite receiving advance notice of a potential fight. The school disciplinarian failed to inform the bus driver about the harassment of the new student. The driver failed to note unauthorized bus riders and other problems on the bus. **The court held the board 20% at fault and each of the assaulting students 25% at fault for the injuries.** The student was 5% at fault for failing to report the strong possibility of a fight. *Frazer v. St. Tammany Parish School Board*, 774 So.2d 1227 (La. Ct. App. 2000).

II. SCHOOL ATHLETICS

Student athletes assume the risks incidental to sports participation and, absent a showing of gross negligence or intentional conduct by a coach, league or school, may not recover damages for their injuries. For cases attempting to hold coaches personally liable for student injuries, please see Chapter Fifteen, Section III.C.

A. Participants

1. Duty of Care

State laws require a showing that the school or its staff acted recklessly or intentionally to overcome the defense of governmental immunity.

◆   A California community college student played on a visiting baseball team in a preseason game against a host college. The host team's pitcher hit him in the head with a pitch, cracking his batting helmet. The student claimed he was intentionally hit in retaliation for a pitch thrown by his teammate at a batter from the host team in the previous inning. After being hit, the student staggered, felt dizzy, and was in pain. His manager told him to go to first base. The student did so, but complained to his first-base coach, who told him to stay in the game. Soon after that, the student was told to sit on the bench. He claimed no one tended to his injuries. The student sued the host college in a state superior court for breaching its duty of care by failing to supervise or control its pitcher and failing to provide umpires or medical care. The court dismissed the case, but the state court of appeal reversed the judgment. The Supreme Court of California agreed to review the case. It held Section 831.7 of the California Government Code did not extend to injuries suffered during supervised school sports.

Section 831.7 was intended to be a premises liability provision for public entities. The court found no intent by the legislature to limit a public entity's liability for supervision of sporting activities. **When an athletic participant is injured, the court must determine the required duty of care and whether the student has assumed the risk of injury. In sports, the doctrine of assumption of risk precludes any liability for injuries deemed "inherent in a sport." Previous court decisions established that athletic participants have a duty not to act recklessly or outside the bounds of the sport. Coaches and instructors have a duty not to increase the risks inherent in sports participation.** The court found no reason intercollegiate athletics would be harmed by extending a limited duty to a host school not to increase the risk of participation to visiting players and necessary co-participants. The college did not fail to adequately supervise and control the pitcher. Being hit by a pitch is an inherent risk of baseball. Colleges are not liable for the actions of their student-athletes during competition. The failure to provide umpires did not increase risks inherent in the game. The student's own coaches, not the host college, had the responsibility to remove him from the game for medical attention. The court reversed the judgment. *Avila v. Citrus Community College Dist.*, 38 Cal.4th 148, 41 Cal.Rptr. 299, 131 P.3d 383 (Cal. 2006).

◆   A Louisiana freshman football player injured his back in a weight training session. His physician diagnosed him with a lumbar strain and dehydrated disc, and gave him a medical excuse excluding him from football for one week with instructions for "no weightlifting, squats or power cleans." The coaching staff interpreted the weightlifting limitation to be for only one week, and a coach instructed the student to do a particular lift. He did the lift and suffered severe back pain. The student was diagnosed with a disc protrusion and a herniated disc. He lost interest in school, failed classes and transferred to an alternative school. The student sued the school board for personal injury. A state trial court awarded him less than $7,500 for medical expenses, but awarded him $275,500 for pain and suffering, future medical expenses and loss of enjoyment of life.

The school board appealed to a Louisiana Circuit Court of Appeal, which reviewed testimony that the student continued to experience severe back pain and often could not sleep. **The evidence supported the trial court's finding that he had been severely injured and would experience recurring pain that would limit his daily activities indefinitely.** The trial court did not commit error in awarding the student damages for pain and suffering. The court affirmed the damage award for loss of enjoyment of life, based on evidence that the student lost the opportunity to play varsity baseball and football. There was further evidence he suffered depression and emotional anguish. *Day v. Ouachita Parish School Board*, 823 So.2d 1039 (La. Ct. App. 2002).

◆   A Maryland high school junior was the first female football player in her county's history. She participated in weightlifting, strength-training exercises and contact drills. In the first scrimmage with another team, the student was tackled while carrying the football and suffered multiple internal injuries. Three years later, the student and her mother sued the school board, claiming it had a duty to warn them of the risk of serious, disabling and catastrophic injuries.

A Maryland trial court granted the board's motion for summary judgment, finding no such duty to warn of the risk of varsity football participation. The student and her mother appealed to the Court of Special Appeals of Maryland. There they argued the lower court had erroneously held the board had no duty to warn of catastrophic risks and that the student had assumed the risk of injury by participating. **The court found no case from any jurisdiction holding that a school board had a duty to warn varsity high school football players that severe injuries might result. The dangers of varsity football participation were self-evident, and there was no duty to warn of such an obvious danger.** The court affirmed the order for summary judgment. *Hammond v. Board of Educ. of Carroll County*, 639 A.2d 223 (Md. Ct. Spec. App. 1994).

2. Governmental Immunity

The doctrine of governmental immunity (sometimes called discretionary or official immunity) precludes school or individual liability when employees are performing "discretionary duties" within the scope of their employment. By contrast, employees performing "ministerial duties" are unprotected by immunity, as are those who do not act in the scope of their employment.

◆   An Ohio student injured his forehead and wrist during a pole vault at a high school track meet. He landed on improper padding near the landing pad. The padding was later identified as in violation of National Federation of State High School Associations rules. The student sued the school district, coach and other officials in the state court system for negligence. The court awarded summary judgment to the district and school officials. The student appealed to the Court of Appeals of Ohio, which held the trial court had improperly granted immunity under the state recreational user statute. The student was not a "recreational user." The statute relied on by the trial court applied to defects in state-owned lands or buildings, not to negligence from the setting up of equipment for a track meet. The trial court also committed error by finding the student had assumed the risk of injury by inherent dangers in pole vaulting. He did not assume the risk of being provided inadequate safety equipment for pole vaulting. **The court held the sponsor of a sporting event has a duty not to increase the risk of harm over and above any inherent risks of the sport.**

While the Ohio Political Subdivision Tort Liability Act generally grants immunity to government entities, an exception applied when an injury was caused by employee negligence occurring on school grounds in connection with a governmental function. **The court rejected the district's claim to immunity, as there was no discretionary, policy-making, planning or enforcement activity in this case.** The Tort Liability Act protected employees unless they acted with a malicious purpose, in bad faith, or in a wanton or reckless manner. **The track coach was entitled to immunity, because there was no evidence he acted with malice, bad faith or reckless or wanton conduct.** The court affirmed the judgment in the coach's favor, but held the action could proceed against the school district. *Henney v. Shelby City School Dist.*, No. 2005 CA 0064, 2006 WL 747475 (Ohio Ct. App. 2006).

◆ A Maine high school wrestling team ran timed drills in school hallways as part of its warm-up routine. A wrestler was seriously injured after being bumped into a window by a teammate during a drill. The school had no policy prohibiting athletic training in school hallways at the time. The student sued the school district in a state court for personal injury, asserting officials negligently allowed the team to competitively race through the hallways. The court held the district and officials were protected by discretionary immunity. The student appealed to the Maine Supreme Judicial Court, which stated that **governmental entities are generally entitled to absolute immunity from suit for any tort action for damages**. One of four state law exceptions to this rule imposes liability on government entities for the negligent operation of a public building.

The court held that allowing relay races in the school hallway was not the "operation of a public building." The focus of this case was the manner in which the team was required to run through the halls, not the operation of a high school building. To impose liability under the "public building" exception to immunity, the claim must implicate the physical structure of the building. Decisions such as wrestling team rules focused on the supervision of students, not the maintenance or operation of the building. **Since the failure to prohibit racing in the halls was not related to the operation of a public building, the district and officials were protected by discretionary immunity.** *Lightfoot v. School Administrative Dist. No. 35*, 816 A.2d 63 (Me. 2003).

◆ A Kansas school football team held its first practice on an August day when the temperature reached 83 degrees by 8:00 a.m. Players practiced from then until 12:50 p.m. with a 45-minute break at 10:15 and five-minute water breaks every 20 minutes. The team then began circuit conditioning. Players spent four minutes at various stations, then rested for two minutes before rotating to another. A student reported feeling ill after completing the first two stations. An assistant coach instructed him to drink some water, which he did. He asked to sit out further drills and was told again to get water. As the team left practice, the student collapsed and was taken to a hospital, where he died the next day. His estate sued the school district and head coach for negligence. A state court granted the estate's motion to prevent the district and coach from relying on the "recreational use" exception to the Kansas Tort Claims Act (KTCA), which precludes liability for injury claims arising from the use of any public property used for recreational purposes, except in cases of gross and wanton negligence.

The district and coach appealed to the state supreme court, which observed the trial court did not take into account the KTCA's legitimate purpose to encourage construction of public recreational facilities. The court found a rational basis for distinguishing between injuries occurring on public recreational property and those occurring elsewhere. The trial court committed error by refusing to apply the discretionary function exception to the KTCA. **The discretionary function exception protects government entities and employees from claims based on the exercise of discretion or the failure to exercise it.** The recreational use exception eliminated any liability for ordinary negligence and barred all the claims. The court reversed and remanded the case for a determination of whether the district or coach acted with gross or wanton negligence. *Barrett v. Unified School Dist. No. 259*, 32 P.3d 1156 (Kan. 2001).

3. Assumption of Risk and Waiver

Many courts have determined that when a participant has assumed the risks of playing sports, a school district should not be held liable for resulting injuries. One way to guard against liability is through the use of releases. Cases involving parental releases are uncommon, but the Supreme Judicial Court of Massachusetts upheld the use of one in Sharon v. City of Newton, *below.*

◆ **Indiana parents received a new trial in a lawsuit based on the death of their son from heatstroke after a school football practice. The release forms they signed did not specifically waive claims based on negligence.** The student, who weighed over 250 pounds, had "dry heaves" early in a morning practice session. He stopped his activity for a minute, then told two coaches he felt better. The student ate lunch during a team rest period, and kept it down. He spent time lying on the locker room floor. The head coach asked the student how he felt, and the student again said he was okay. Near the end of the afternoon session, the student told a coach he did not feel well. The coach told him to get water, but he soon collapsed. The coaches took him to the locker room and placed him in a cool shower. The student lost consciousness and the coaches called for an ambulance. He died at a hospital the following day.

The student's parents sued the school district in a state court for negligence. After a trial, a jury returned a verdict for the school district. The parents appealed to the Court of Appeals of Indiana, which held they did not submit sufficient evidence to find the district negligent as a matter of law. **The head coach had responded to hot weather by shortening parts of the schedule and adding more frequent water breaks. The coaching staff emphasized the importance of drinking fluids, and several of them checked on the student.** Coaches had no indication that the student was ill until he collapsed. They responded to his collapse and called 911. The trial court did not improperly allow the case to go before a jury. **The court noted the release forms signed by the parents and students did not refer to "negligence." It held that in order to negate a legal duty of care and avoid any finding of negligence, a participant must have "actual knowledge and appreciation of the specific risk involved and voluntarily acceptance of that risk."** The court agreed with the parents that as the release forms did not contain the word "negligence," the district was not effectively released from negligence claims. The trial court should have granted the parents' request for a jury instruction stating they had not released the district from negligence. As their proposal correctly stated the law, the court reversed and remanded the case for a new trial at which their jury instruction was to be used. *Stowers v. Clinton Cent. School Corp.*, 855 N.E.2d 739 (Ind. Ct. App. 2006).

◆ A Massachusetts school district required a signed parental release for all students seeking to participate in extracurricular activities. For four years, the father of a high school cheerleader signed a release form before each season. During her fourth year, she was injured during a practice. When the cheerleader reached age 18, she sued the city in a state superior court for negligence and negligent hiring and retention of the cheerleading coach. The court awarded summary judgment to the city on the basis of the parental release, agreeing that **the father had forever released the city from any and all actions and claims**.

The cheerleader appealed to the Massachusetts Supreme Judicial Court, asserting the release was invalid. The court held the trial court properly allowed the city to amend its answer by asserting release. **Enforcement of a parental release was consistent with Massachusetts law and public policy.** There was undisputed evidence that the father read and understood the release before signing it, and that the form was not misleading, since it required two signatures and clearly ensured parental permission was granted. It was not contrary to public policy to require parents to sign releases as a condition for student participation in extracurricular activities. The father had signed the release because he wanted the student to benefit from cheerleading. The court found that to hold the release unenforceable would expose public schools to financial costs and risks that would lead to the reduction of extracurricular activities. *Sharon v. City of Newton*, 437 Mass. 99, 769 N.E.2d 738 (Mass. 2002).

◆   A New York student participated on his high school wrestling team and was instructed before a match to wrestle an opponent in the next higher weight class. The student agreed to do so and was injured when the opponent hit his jaw during a take-down maneuver. The student voluntarily continued participating in the match after a medical time-out. He later filed a personal injury lawsuit against the school district in a New York trial court, which denied the district's dismissal motion. On appeal, the New York Supreme Court, Appellate Division, stated that **the student had assumed the risk of incurring a blow to the jaw and that the injury was reasonably foreseeable in a wrestling match.** There was evidence that the size of the opponent had not caused the injury and that the student was aware of the risks involved in wrestling. **The district's duty of care was limited to protecting the student from unassumed, concealed or unreasonable risks.** The trial court judgment was reversed. *Edelson v. Uniondale Union Free School Dist.*, 631 N.Y.S.2d 391 (N.Y. App. Div. 1995).

B. Spectators, Employees and Parents

◆   A West Virginia spectator slipped and fell on ice and snow on school grounds while trying to reach a high school basketball game. On the day of the injury, the superintendent of schools cancelled all classes in county schools due to the effects of a major snow storm. Despite this action, the high school principal and athletic director decided not to cancel the basketball game. The spectator sued the board in the state court system, arguing it was negligent to hold the basketball game on a day when the entire school system was closed.

The school board claimed immunity under the state Governmental Tort Claims and Insurance Reform Act. Provisions of the Act create immunity from claims resulting from snow or ice conditions or from temporary or natural conditions on any public way, "unless the condition is affirmatively caused by the negligent act of a political subdivision." The court denied the board's motion to dismiss the case, and the board appealed. The Supreme Court of Appeals of West Virginia, the state's highest court, agreed with the school board that the language of the act was plain. **A political subdivision was not immune from suit if it acted to place snow or ice on a public way.** There were several ways this could happen. An employee might move snow from a roadway onto the sidewalk, or cause ice to form by letting water leak on a sidewalk during cold weather. **The court rejected the spectator's argument that the decision to hold the basketball game was an affirmative act that was not immunized. While the act of holding the game may have encouraged her to venture out into the snow, it did not cause the conditions at the school.** The Tort Claims and Insurance Reform Act provided immunity for losses or claims resulting from snow or ice on public ways resulting from the weather. As there was no merit to the spectator's arguments, the court reversed the decision of the lower court. *Porter v. Grant County Board of Educ.*, 633 S.E.2d 38 (W.Va. 2006).

◆ A spectator at a high school football game in New York was stabbed during a fight that occurred on school grounds following the game. The spectator sued the school district and school officials in a New York trial court. The court held for the spectator, and the school appealed to a New York appellate division court. The spectator claimed the school was negligent when it failed to properly supervise the crowd. The court disagreed, holding **the district could not be found negligent because it did not have a duty to supervise non-student spectators at the game**. The court reversed the judgment and held for the district. *Jerideau v. Huntingdon Union Free School Dist.*, 21 A.D.3d 992, 801 N.Y.S.2d 394 (N.Y. App. Div. 2005).

III. OTHER SCHOOL ACTIVITIES

Courts have held schools liable for injuries during school events which resulted from the failure to provide a reasonably safe environment, failure to warn participants of known hazards (or to remove known dangers), failure to properly instruct participants in the activity, and failure to provide supervision adequate for the type of activity and the ages of the participants involved.

A. Physical Education Class Accidents

1. Duty of Care

Courts have held that schools and staff members are not liable for injuries that are unforeseeable. It has long been recognized that schools are not the insurers of student safety. The fact that each student is not personally supervised at all times does not itself constitute grounds for liability.

◆ **The Court of Appeals of Ohio agreed with a school board that the death of a student who had a history of mild asthma was unforeseeable.** The student was a 14-year-old eighth grader. During a gym class, he obtained his teacher's permission to retrieve his prescription inhaler from his locker. Minutes later, another teacher found the student unconscious and not breathing on the locker room floor. Despite the administration of medical treatment, he died. The school board maintained a policy requiring parents or guardians to bring prescription medications to the school office. Students were not allowed to bring medicine to school themselves, but the school principal let students carry inhalers once they were at school. The student's estate sued the school board in the state court system for wrongful death. The case went before a jury in two phases; one on the question of liability for negligence, the other on the question of damages. The jury found for the school board, and the estate appealed.

The court of appeals found the trial court did not have to exclude evidence of procedures used by the parents in the event of an asthma attack. These facts were not prejudicial to the estate and were relevant in establishing the standard of care for the school board. The trial court did not commit error by failing to instruct the jury that the school board could be held liable if it found the student's possession of prescription medication at school violated school policy. This would have misinterpreted the policy, which did not prevent students from possessing prescriptions at school. State rules of civil procedure allowed courts to separate issues of liability and damages, and they were more inclined to do this in emotionally charged cases, such as this one. The trial court allowed a physician to testify that the death of a student previously recognized as having only "mild asthma" was "one in a million." **According to the physician, not even medical professionals could have foreseen the death.** The court rejected the estate's additional arguments and affirmed the judgment for the school board. *Spencer v. Lakeview School Dist.*, No. 2005-T-0083, 2006 WL 1816452 (Ohio Ct. App. 2006).

◆ A California school district was not liable for injuries to a student who was hit by a golf club swung by a classmate in their physical education class. The golf class teacher was relatively new. His only golf training was an hour-and-a-half seminar. During the sixth day of golf class, the teacher showed students how to do a full golf swing. Before students could try the full swings, he advised them of certain safety precautions. The teacher's practice was to whistle commands and signal when to hit balls and when to rotate positions. According to the student, the class was disorganized and the instructions confusing. She claimed at times students had to decide when to hit and when to change positions. A classmate who was in front of the student swung her club and hit the student in the mouth. According to the student, the teacher did not give a whistle command for the classmate to hit the ball. She sued the school district in a state superior court for negligence. The court applied the standard of care announced by the Supreme Court of California for cases of dangerous conditions or conduct considered integral to a sport. See *Kahn v. East Side Union High School Dist.*, 31 Cal.4th 990 (2003), which is summarized in Chapter 15, Section III.C. of this volume. The *Kahn* standard is an exception to the usual standard of care in negligence cases, which generally creates liability for failure to use due care. The court found the district did not breach the limited duty described in *Kahn* and awarded summary judgment to the district.

The student appealed to a California District Court of Appeal. The court found the policies in *Kahn* did not apply to a seventh-grade golf class. **The state supreme court has applied the "prudent person" standard of care to decide liability in cases of students injured during school hours. This simply required persons to avoid injuring others by using due care.** Applying the prudent person standard in this case would not deter vigorous athletic participation. *Kahn* was inapplicable because being hit by a golf club is not an inherent risk in the sport. As the superior court should have applied the prudent person standard of care, the court reversed the judgment. *Hemady v. Long Beach Unified School Dist.*, 143 Cal.App.4th 566, 49 Cal. Rptr.3d 464 (Cal. Ct. App. 2006). The Supreme Court of California denied review in this case in 2007.

◆   A 16-year-old Louisiana student who weighed 327 pounds collapsed and began having seizures during a PE class. The class was conducted by a substitute art teacher in a gym that was not air-conditioned. The temperature was at least 90 degrees. The student collapsed after playing basketball for 20 minutes and died at a hospital. The substitute teacher had played in the game instead of monitoring students. The student's parent sued the board and its insurer in a state court for wrongful death, and the court awarded her $500,000.

The Court of Appeal of Louisiana found no error in trial court findings that the board breached its duty to exercise reasonable care and supervision. The lower court was also entitled to hear the testimony of a physical education professor and allow medical testimony as reliable. The court held **teachers have a duty to exercise reasonable care and supervision over students in their custody, and to avoid exposing them to an unreasonable risk of injury. As physical education classes may involve dangerous activities, due care must be used in them to minimize the risk of student injury.** *James v. Jackson*, 898 So.2d 596 (La. Ct. App. 2005). The state supreme court denied the board's appeal. *James v. Jackson*, 902 So.2d 1005 (La. 2005).

◆   A New York student was playing football in a physical education class when a classmate threw a football tee that hit her in the eye. A state trial court denied the school district's motion for summary judgment, and the district appealed. A state appellate division court held school districts have a duty to adequately supervise and instruct students, and are liable for foreseeable injuries proximately caused by their negligence. **However, school districts are not insurers of student safety and will not be held liable for every spontaneous, thoughtless or careless act by which one student injures another. The degree of care required is what a reasonably prudent parent would exercise under similar circumstances.** The court found the teacher had not instructed students on how to properly handle the tee and never told them not to throw it. The evidence differed as to whether the students had previously thrown the tee or seen the teacher throw it. **In affirming the judgment for the student, the court held a trial court must determine if the injury causing conduct was reasonably foreseeable and preventable.** *Oakes v. Massena Cent. School Dist.*, 19 A.D.3d 981, 797 N.Y.S.2d 640 (N.Y. App. Div. 2005).

◆   Three Louisiana students assaulted a classmate in their locker room after a PE class, causing serious injuries. The classmate sued the school board, the parents of the students and their insurers in a Louisiana court for personal injuries. A jury found the students were not at fault, and the court found the board 100% at fault. It held the coach caused the injuries by failing to supervise the students. According to the court, an atmosphere of roughhousing and lack of supervision invited the attack, and the board failed to conform to the required standard of care. On appeal, the state court of appeal apportioned 70% of the fault to the board and 30% to one of the students.

The state supreme court held **school boards have a duty of reasonable supervision over students. Boards are not insurers of student safety, and constant supervision of all students is not required. To hold a school board liable for negligence, it must be shown that a risk of unreasonable injury was foreseeable and could have been prevented with the required degree of supervision.** In this case, the attack happened suddenly and without warning. Because it was unforeseeable to the classmate himself, there was no way for the coach to foresee and prevent it. The trial court had erroneously imposed liability on the board independent of the students. As the incident could not have been prevented with a reasonable degree of supervision, the court reversed the judgment. *Wallmuth v. Rapides Parish School Board*, 813 So.2d 341 (La. 2002).

◆   Arkansas parents claimed their son's school district did not administer his Ritalin prescription for five consecutive school days, despite knowledge that failure to do so placed him in jeopardy of physical and psychological injury. The student fell from a slide on school grounds and fractured his right wrist. The parents sued the district in the state court system for outrageous conduct causing injury. The court dismissed the case, and the parents appealed.

The state court of appeals held the parents could not prevail unless they showed the district intended to inflict emotional distress on the student. They were further required to demonstrate extreme and outrageous conduct by the district, and to prove its conduct caused emotional distress so severe that no reasonable person could endure it. **The court found no evidence of knowledge by the district that failure to administer the student's medication would result in emotional distress.** The parents did not show his suffering was so great that no reasonable person could be expected to endure it. The court affirmed the judgment for the district. *Foote v. Pine Bluff School Dist.*, No. CA 02-806, 2003 WL 1827282 (Ark. Ct. App. 2003).

2. Governmental Immunity

◆   A Wisconsin student gashed his knee while diving after a volleyball in his freshman PE class. He collided with the sharp metal edge of a volleyball net stand and had to undergo surgery. His family sued the school district in a state court for negligence, alleging other students had previously been injured when coming into contact with the net stand. The court held the district was entitled to state law immunity. The family appealed to the state court of appeals, arguing the district was liable under the "known danger" exception to the immunity rule, in view of the previous injuries involving the same equipment.

The court explained that immunity will not apply in a negligence case if it involves a ministerial duty and is the result of a known and compelling

danger. The known danger exception applied when a public officer's duty to act was absolute, certain and imperative. The court held the net stand was not so hazardous that the district was required to take some protective measure for students. As the danger was not so compelling that action was necessary, the known danger exception to immunity did not apply. The court affirmed the judgment for the school district. *Schilling v. Sheboygan Area School Dist.*, 705 N.W.2d 906 (Table) (Wis. Ct. App. 2005).

◆   A Wisconsin physical education teacher divided a class into two groups to practice golf. One group practiced driving while the other group practiced chipping. The teacher instructed the drivers to stand in line while waiting to hit and not to swing their clubs in the waiting area. While she was working with the chippers, the drivers practiced about 40 to 50 feet away. A student in the drivers' group was hit in the face by a club swung by a classmate. He sued the district in a state circuit court for personal injuries, but the case was dismissed.

The state court of appeals held Wis. Stat. § 893.80(4) bars actions against government entities and employees for acts done in the exercise of legislative, judicial and similar functions. The law allowed liability for the negligent performance of ministerial duties. **Ministerial duties were "absolute, certain and imperative," leaving nothing for judgment or discretion.** The teacher had a ministerial duty to conduct and supervise her class in a particular manner. **Her decision to provide students with safety instructions was discretionary and did not subject the district to liability.** The court affirmed the judgment, finding the danger created by swinging golf clubs was not so obvious and predictable as to be a compelling or known danger. *Livingston v. Wausau Underwriters Insurance Co.*, 260 Wis.2d 602, 658 N.W.2d 88 (Table) (Wis. Ct. App. 2003), *review denied*, 266 Wis.2d 62, 671 N.W.2d 849 (Wis. 2003).

◆   An Alabama purchasing foreman drafted bid specifications and made recommendations to his school board on bids for movable bleachers for a high school. After the board contracted for the bleachers, the foreman's office issued purchase orders, and the bleachers were installed. A student was severely injured when the bleachers collapsed on him as he and a classmate tried to close them at their teacher's request. The student filed a state court action against the district and school officials, including the purchasing foreman, for negligent inspection and maintenance of the bleachers. The trial court entered summary judgment for all the officials except the foreman, and he appealed.

The Alabama Supreme Court considered the foreman's claim to state-agent immunity based on the discretionary nature of his activities. The student argued the foreman did not deserve immunity, as he was not engaged in discretionary functions. The court held the question of immunity was not properly addressed in the framework of discretionary or ministerial functions. Instead, it had devised an analysis based on categories of state-agent functions under which government employees are immune from liability in the exercise of judgment. One category was the negotiation of contracts, so the foreman was entitled to summary judgment for the claims that he had failed to properly evaluate bids for the bleachers and inspect them after installation. However, the court found **the act of passing along a maintenance brochure to other employees did not require judgment. The foreman was not entitled to state agent immunity** with respect to this claim, and the case was remanded for further proceedings. *Hudson v. C.F. Vigor High School*, 866 So.2d 1115 (Ala. 2003).

◆ Students in an Illinois PE class had to run laps or rollerblade around a wooden gym floor. Rollerbladers paid a $7 fee to use rollerblades with "experimental" toe brakes, and they were not furnished with helmets, gloves or shin, elbow and knee guards. A student who chose to rollerblade fell and broke two bones in his right leg. He sued the school district in a state court for negligence and willful and wanton failure to provide safety equipment. The court held the district was entitled to immunity under Sections 2-201 and 3-108(a) of the state governmental tort immunity act, which affords immunity to government entities and their employees for failing to supervise students except in cases of willful and wanton misconduct. The state appellate court reversed the judgment, and the district appealed to the Supreme Court of Illinois.

The supreme court observed that the immunity act did not create duties for government entities, but accorded them certain immunities based on specific government functions. The district's failure to provide necessary equipment did not involve supervision. The tort immunity act shielded any decision by district employees that involved a determination of policy or the exercise of discretion. **"Policy decisions" were those requiring the balancing of competing interests so that a government entity had to make a "judgment call." The court agreed with the school district that its decision not to provide safety equipment was discretionary and thus entitled to immunity.** *Arteman v. Clinton Community Unit School Dist. No. 15*, 763 N.E.2d 756 (Ill. 2002).

B. Shop Class Injuries

1. Duty of Care

Schools are required to provide their students with a safe environment. Known shop class dangers must be minimized, and safety devices are to be in place and working. Failure to supervise, warn students of known dangers, or maintain safety devices can result in school liability.

◆ A Minnesota student amputated a finger in a wood shop class accident. He had experience using the saw, which was equipped with a blade guard. Before students could use the saw, they had to pass a test on a protocol for its use. The protocol stated the best practice for cutting small strips of wood was to disengage the blade guard and use a push stick to guide the strips through the saw. On the day of the accident, the teacher instructed the student to cut small wood strips using a push stick with the blade guard disengaged. After watching the student cut some strips, he moved to another part of the room. The student then reached over the blade to remove a piece of scrap wood and lost one of his fingers. The student sued the teacher and school district in a state court for negligence. The court denied the teacher's claim to official immunity, and the school district's motion for statutory immunity. After the state court of appeals affirmed the decision, the district and teacher appealed.

The Supreme Court of Minnesota explained that common law official immunity did not protect an official who was executing a "ministerial duty," which was defined as one that is "absolute, certain, and imperative." In distinguishing "discretionary" from "ministerial" duties, the focus was on the nature of the act at issue. The specific conduct in this case was the decision to instruct the student to cut wood with the blade guard disengaged. The decision was ministerial, as it only complied with the protocol. **The court held that a challenge to official conduct in compliance with an established policy is a challenge to the policy itself.** Teachers did not forfeit official immunity because their conduct was "ministerial," if that conduct was established by a policy or protocol that was established though the exercise of discretionary judgment. Both the decision to establish a protocol and the protocol itself involved the exercise of professional judgment. **The teacher was entitled to common law official immunity because his liability was based on compliance with the protocol.** The court reversed the judgment against the teacher and held the district was entitled to vicarious immunity. *Anderson v. Anoka Hennepin Independent School Dist. 11*, 678 N.W.2d 651 (Minn. 2004).

◆   A Georgia shop teacher demonstrated a volt meter by stretching insulated wire across student desks. Parts of the wire were exposed so that students could attach probes to measure voltage. The teacher explained that touching the wire with both hands could cause death. After turning on a transformer that sent 700 volts of electricity through the wire, the teacher noticed a student slumping over with both hands on the wire. Staff performed CPR on the student and called emergency personnel, but he died from electrical shock. A federal district court dismissed an action against the school district, teacher, school principal and superintendent for constitutional rights violations. The parents appealed to the U.S. Court of Appeals, Eleventh Circuit, which explained that a governmental agency or employee may be liable for substantive due process violations only if official conduct is so extreme that it "shocks the conscience."

The U.S. Supreme Court has admonished lower courts to refrain from making the Due Process Clause a "surrogate for more conventional tort principles." Deliberate indifference by officials and unsafe working conditions do not implicate due process rights. **The student's death did not result from intentional conduct by the teacher and did not shock the conscience.** The district court had correctly awarded summary judgment to the teacher and district. *Nix v. Franklin County School Dist.*, 311 F.3d 1373 (11th Cir. 2002).

2. Governmental Immunity

◆   An Illinois student sued his shop teacher and school district in the state court system for personal injuries suffered while operating a table saw in shop class. At the time of the student's injury, a safety shield was not in place on the saw because the teacher had previously removed it. The court held the teacher and district were entitled to immunity under the state Local Governmental and Governmental Employees Tort Immunity Act. On appeal, the Illinois Appellate Court reversed the judgment, holding the student was entitled to gather further information, including statements from the teacher and other school employees, before the action could be dismissed. The case returned to the trial court, and the teacher stated in a deposition that he removed the safety shield because it was not functioning properly and the saw would be safer without it. The trial court again entered judgment for the district and officials. The student appealed.

The state appellate court observed that the immunity act was a complex law due to its conflicting provisions. The Illinois Supreme Court has held the key question under the act was whether an employee's decision was a "discretionary policy determination." The appellate court noted that "discretionary acts" are those unique to a particular public office. In this case, the teacher's decision to remove the safety shield was unique to his particular office. He was charged with balancing the various interests that might compete for the time and resources of his shop class, including the interests of safety and efficiency. **A shop teacher's warning to students, and the provision of safety equipment, was a discretionary policy determination to which the immunity act applied.** The court affirmed the decision for the district and teacher. *Courson v. Danville School Dist. No. 118*, 775 N.E.2d 1022 (Ill. App. Ct. 2002).

C. Other Supervised Activities

1. Duty of Care

School districts have a duty to use reasonable care to supervise and protect students against hazards on school property that create an unreasonable risk of harm. Liability may also exist if supervision is negligently performed.

◆ An Idaho school district held a carnival to celebrate the last day of the school year. A contractor provided the activities. Participants in a "bungee run" wore harnesses tethered to a fixed object by a bungee cord. They raced over an inflated rubberized surface until the cord snapped them backward. A student was injured on the bungee run. She sued the school district and contractor in a state court for negligence. The court found the school's conduct was not reckless and was therefore immune from liability under the Idaho Tort Claims Act. On appeal, **the Supreme Court of Idaho held the Idaho Tort Claims Act generally makes governmental entities liable for monetary damages to the same extent that a private person would be under the circumstances. Schools generally have a duty to supervise student activities, including extracurricular and school-sponsored events, and a duty to protect students in their custody from reasonably foreseeable risks.**

The court found the student had stated valid claims based on allowing her to participate in an unreasonably hazardous activity, failing to supervise her during the activity, and failing to supervise the contractor to ensure it provided adequate instruction and supervision. She would have the opportunity to establish these claims for damages in further proceedings. The district court had correctly found the school district was immune from liability for negligent supervision and failing to inspect the bungee equipment. The student should have been allowed to pursue her theory of direct liability for planning and sponsoring an unreasonably dangerous activity. The fact that a contractor may have actually caused her injury did not absolve the district of its duty, if she could prove her injury was caused by the school's acts or omissions. The court reversed the judgment and returned the case to the trial court. *Sherer v. Pocatello School Dist. #25*, 143 Idaho 486, 148 P.3d 1232 (Idaho 2006).

◆   A Montana high school freshman rode home from an out-of-town school basketball game on a pep band bus. The driver teased students by pumping the brakes and jarring the bus. The student asked for a restroom break, but the band instructor denied the request. Many students threw food and candy during the trip. As the bus neared the school, the band instructor announced that no one could leave the bus until it was cleaned up. The student told the instructor twice "you let me off this fucking bus." The driver pumped the brakes while stopping the bus, and the student wet himself. The school suspended the student for using profanity and placed him on detention for three days. Eight days after the bus incident, the student was hospitalized with ketoacidosis. After remaining in a life-threatening condition for several days, he recovered but was diagnosed with Type I diabetes and post-traumatic stress disorder (PTSD). The student and his parents sued the district, band instructor and driver in a state court for causing or accelerating his diabetes and PTSD. The court awarded summary judgment to the district, and the family appealed to the Supreme Court of Montana.

The court explained that **to impose liability on a school district in a negligence case, it must first be shown the district had a duty of care. The existence of a duty depended on the foreseeability of the harm and the policy considerations involved in imposing liability. The district could be held liable only for injuries that were reasonably foreseeable.** The supreme court held the trial court had erroneously found the district owed no duty to the student. The trial court improperly focused on the nature of his injuries instead of the possibility that the conduct of school employees might result in injury. The trial court had been unable to determine if the student's diabetes was caused or accelerated by the chain of events resulting from the bus trip. Even his doctor could not establish that diabetes was a likely result of the bus trip or its aftermath. Since the family could not prove the injuries were caused by the district's conduct, the court affirmed the judgment. *Hinkle v. Shepherd School Dist. #37*, 322 Mont. 80, 93 P.3d 1239, 2004 MT 175 (Mont. 2004).

◆   A North Dakota school district operated a middle school in a building owned by the U.S. Bureau of Indian Affairs (BIA). The district and BIA had an agreement to jointly operate the school, which was primarily attended by American Indian students. The principal was a BIA employee who supervised both BIA and district staff. BIA teachers supervised the lunchroom under a plan created through a collective bargaining agreement. A BIA teacher tried to break up a fight between two students during her lunchroom supervision period and suffered a disabling, traumatic brain injury. The teacher sued the district in a state court for personal injury, alleging negligent failure to maintain a safe environment. The court held for the district, finding it did not own, supervise or control the building at the time of the injury, and thus owed the teacher no duty of care. The teacher appealed to the Supreme Court of North Dakota.

The court found **the conclusive issue was whether the district had a duty to provide the teacher a safe environment**. The teacher had to establish the existence of a relationship through supervisory and operation controls that created a duty. The court found no evidence establishing district control over the lunchroom, lunchroom supervision plan or the teacher. This was true even assuming the district maintained some control over the school through state funding, accreditation and the arrangement with the BIA. The teacher was a BIA employee performing her lunchroom duties under the collective bargaining agreement. **As the teacher did not show a relationship between herself and the district that imposed a legal duty to provide her with a safe working environment, the trial court had correctly held for the district.** *Azure v. Belcourt Public School Dist.*, 681 N.W.2d 816, 2004 ND 128 (N.D. 2004).

2. Governmental Immunity

◆ The Court of Appeals of Wisconsin affirmed a trial court order granting immunity to a school district in a preschool student's negligence action. The parents sued the district after their child fell from play equipment in her classroom. The court held the district was not required to transfer her to a new room based on a special education evaluation indicating she required speech/language services. **The classroom teacher had exercised her discretion and judgment in creating classroom safety rules. State law conferred immunity on political subdivisions and school officials for their discretionary acts.** *Nagel v. Green Bay Area Public School Dist.*, 293 Wis.2d 362, 715 N.W.2d 240 (Table) (Wis. Ct. App. 2006).

◆ A Tennessee student had a history of aggressive behavior and fighting in classes, but was not identified as having a disability. Soon after an assessment team evaluated him, he struck his teacher. The school principal suspended him for 10 days and prepared to expel him. She then arranged an individualized education program (IEP) team meeting. The IEP team found the student was ineligible for special education based on a specific learning disability. However, its report stated "be careful to not touch this student," and "this student is protected under IDEA" (the Individuals with Disabilities Education Act). The report concluded "this student has a suspected disability," and "re-open the case for Health Impaired." The principal decided to return the student to his classroom and to assign a teacher's aide to him. On his first day back, he assaulted his teacher and the aide. The teacher sued the school board in a state court for negligently returning the student to her classroom. The court held the board was entitled to immunity under the state Governmental Tort Liability Act (GTLA). The teacher appealed to the Court of Appeals of Tennessee.

The court noted **a school official's decision deserved immunity if it was based on a discretionary function. Decisions that involved consideration or debate were "planning decisions."** The court rejected the teacher's assertion that the principal was bound by state and local zero-tolerance policies. She had to balance these mandates against conflicting IDEA requirements. The IDEA required a manifestation determination review by the IEP team if the school sought to suspend a student with a suspected disability for over 10 days. While the student had not yet been declared eligible for special education, the IEP team indicated further evaluation was warranted. The manifestation determination review had not concluded with the IEP team's report. **The IDEA's "stay-put" provision did not allow the principal to expel the student. Her testimony demonstrated she exercised discretion in balancing the zero-tolerance policies against federal law requirements.** As the principal's decision to reinstate the student to his classroom was a discretionary decision, the judgment was affirmed. *Babb v. Hamilton County Board of Educ.*, No. E2004-00782-COA-R3-CV, 2004 WL 2094538 (Tenn. Ct. App. 2004).

◆   A North Carolina student had Down syndrome and severe behavioral problems. While under the supervision of a teacher, he choked on a hot dog in the school cafeteria. The teacher helped the school nurse administer first aid, and another teacher called 911. Although an ambulance arrived within seven minutes, rescue personnel were unable to revive the student. His estate sued the school board and the teachers in their individual capacities for wrongful death. A state trial court denied summary judgment to the teachers and considered evidence of the board's insurance coverage. It found the board immune from any claims of less than $1 million, but it denied immunity for amounts in excess of that amount because there was no evidence it lacked coverage for such a loss.

The teachers and board appealed to the Court of Appeals of North Carolina, which stated **N.C. Gen. Stat. § 115C-42 authorizes local boards to waive their immunity by purchasing insurance. Immunity is waived only to the extent of the amount of insurance coverage.** Although the board argued its insurance would not cover the estate's claims, the only evidence of this was an affidavit by an insurance manager describing the board's self-insured retention limit of $1 million. The limit prevented the board from seeking coverage until it paid a claimant the self-insured retention limit. The court held the manager's statement did not demonstrate the board lacked insurance coverage for claims in excess of $1 million, and the board had not waived immunity. The teachers were board employees and not officers entitled to governmental immunity. **Teachers may be held personally liable for negligent acts in the performance of their duties, as their duties are "ministerial" and do not involve the exercise of sovereign power.** The teachers were not entitled to governmental immunity in their individual capacities, and the court affirmed the judgment. *Petho v. Wakeman*, 583 S.E.2d 427 (N.C. Ct. App. 2003).

◆   A 10-year-old Georgia student was killed when she tried to retrieve paper from a large roll stored in a school garage. Her teacher instructed her to get the paper with a classmate from heavy, eight-foot-high rolls standing upright in a storage garage. The student was killed when the roll fell on her as she tried to get paper from it. Her parents sued the district, its board and the teacher in a state trial court for wrongful death and intentional misconduct. A state trial court awarded summary judgment against the parents, finding the teacher and board were entitled to immunity. On appeal, the Georgia Court of Appeals stated that **the Georgia Supreme Court has previously held that supervising and disciplining students involves discretionary acts.** The teacher was exercising her discretionary authority to monitor, control and supervise students when she sent the fourth-graders to the garage. Because she was entitled to immunity, she could be liable only if her actions were motivated by actual malice or intent to cause injury. As there was no evidence of malice or intentional conduct, the court affirmed the judgment. *Aliffi v. Liberty County School Dist.*, 578 S.E.2d 146 (Ga. Ct. App. 2003).

◆   An Alaska father had legal custody of his son, and the child's mother had visitation during the Christmas and summer vacations. The father warned the principal that the mother would attempt an abduction. A state court stayed enforcement of the parties' custody order pending investigations in Alaska and Washington. Just before Christmas vacation, the mother arrived at school to pick up the student, accompanied by a police officer. The principal noted the custody order provided by the father did not specify visitation terms. The mother produced her copy of a previous order granting her visitation rights. The principal called the father, who objected to releasing the student. However, the principal released the student to the mother after a discussion with the police officer. The mother refused to return the student to the father after the Christmas break and he was unable to regain custody for over five months, when he obtained a Washington court order. The father sued the district and principal in a state superior court for interference with his custodial rights. The court held the principal and district were entitled to qualified immunity.

The father appealed to the state supreme court, which noted that Alaska law prevents actions against municipalities and their employees based on the exercise of, or the failure to perform, a discretionary function or duty. **The law established official immunity for "discretionary actions," which require personal deliberation, decision and judgment. The principal's actions were discretionary, since he acted with deliberation and made a considered judgment** after speaking with the father, verifying the mother's identification, reviewing legal documents and consulting with the police. His actions were not malicious, corrupt or in bad faith and were not subject to any exception to qualified immunity. The principal and district were protected against any lawsuit, and the case was properly dismissed. *Pauley v. Anchorage School Dist.,* 31 P.3d 1284 (Alaska 2001).

IV. UNSUPERVISED ACCIDENTS

Schools are required to exercise reasonable care in maintaining safe buildings, grounds and facilities. They can be found liable for negligently maintaining buildings or tolerating hazardous structures, fixtures or grounds.

A. On School Grounds

1. Duty of Care

◆   In an apparent gang-related fight, a Texas student killed another student with a screwdriver. Several teachers tried to break up the fight but were unable to prevent the stabbing. Although the students had previously fought off school grounds and after school, the murder was the first indication to school staff of their conflict. The deceased student's parents sued the school district in a federal district court, alleging it created the danger that led to their son's death in violation of his due process rights. The parents relied on a theory of state-created danger, which holds states accountable for the actions of employees who increase the risk of a danger and act with deliberate indifference to it.

The court granted summary judgment to the district, ruling the Fourteenth Amendment's Due Process Clause does not obligate the states to protect individuals from private violence. The parents appealed to the U.S. Court of Appeals, Fifth Circuit, which stated that even if it accepted the state-created danger theory, there was no showing school officials put the student in danger. **To hold the district liable for constitutional violations, the parents had to show an official policy or custom was the "moving force" in a constitutional violation.** Only the school board had final policymaking authority on issues of security. The court explained that even if there was a board custom of tolerating gang activity, the parents could not show the board had any knowledge of gang activity in this case. Any allegation that teachers failed to respond to gang activity or students in gang attire only proved a violation of board policy. As the board's lack of diligence did not demonstrate deliberate indifference to a danger of gang activity, the court affirmed the judgment. *Rivera v. Houston Independent School Dist.*, 349 F.3d 244 (5th Cir. 2003).

2. Governmental Immunity

◆ **An Illinois craft fair patron who slipped on a sidewalk adjoining a junior high school gymnasium sued the school district for negligence.** A state circuit court granted summary judgment to the school district, finding the district was entitled to immunity under the Illinois Tort Immunity Act's recreational purposes exclusion. The court denied the patron's motion to amend her claim to incorporate willful and wanton conduct as the cause of her injuries. On appeal, the Appellate Court of Illinois discussed whether the sidewalk was public property intended or permitted to be used for recreational purposes within the meaning of the exclusion. A case-by-case analysis was appropriate to determine whether property was used for recreational purposes and thus subject to exclusion from liability under the act. **The court rejected the school's claim that use of the sidewalk for gymnasium access and occasional student recreation precluded a factual inquiry by a jury.** It reversed and remanded the circuit court decision. *Batson v. Pinckneyville Elementary School Dist. No. 50*, 690 N.E.2d 1077 (Ill. App. Ct. 1998).

B. Off School Grounds

1. Duty of Care

◆ A Washington high school sponsored a "Workday" event, in which community members donated $15 for three hours of student work to raise funds for a student association. A student's mother agreed to let her daughter split and stack firewood with a classmate's father. She learned on the day of the event that the classmate's father planned to have the students split logs with a hydraulic log splitter. The mother cautioned the student, but apparently did not turn in a parental permission slip to perform the work. While the students were operating the log splitter, they were distracted by a car, and the student lost three fingers.

The student sued the school district and classmate's father in a state court for negligence. The court found the student's mother had consented to the activity and awarded judgment to the school district. The student appealed. The Court of Appeals of Washington stated **the general rule that schools have a duty to protect students from reasonably foreseeable harm. School districts are not insurers of student safety, but are liable for foreseeable wrongful acts of third parties.** Harm is foreseeable if the risk was known or should have been known in the exercise of reasonable care. Liability may result if a school supervises and exercises control over extracurricular activities. **Students are under the control and protection of their schools, and are unable to protect themselves. This supervisory duty extends to off-campus activities under district supervision.** As the student was in the district's custody, it owed her a duty of reasonable care. A jury could have found the district should have taken appropriate steps to find out what was planned for each Workday location and identify any obvious safety problems. The court held the student had presented enough evidence to receive a jury trial to decide whether her mother's consent superseded the district's duty. The court reversed and remanded the case for a trial. *Travis v. Bohannon*, 115 P.3d 342 (Wash. Ct. App. 2005).

◆ Two emotionally disturbed North Carolina students rode a public school bus to a program for violent students. A bus attendant overheard them speak about committing robbery and murder with a gun one of them had at home. The attendant reported their conversation to the bus driver, but neither employee informed school officials, the school board or the police department. A week later, the students and two other youths stopped cars at an intersection between 7:00 p.m. and 8:15 p.m. A student shot a driver in the head and severely injured her. The students and their accomplices pleaded guilty to assault charges in criminal court proceedings. The victim sued city and county education officials in a state court for personal injuries. The court awarded summary judgment to the county board, and the victim appealed. The Court of Appeals of North Carolina held there might be a connection between the failure to report the conversation and the victim's injuries. It reversed and remanded the case to the trial court.

On appeal, the Supreme Court of North Carolina stated school personnel who overheard students planning criminal conduct had a moral and civic obligation to report this information. However, this did not create a legal duty which could afford a remedy for the victim. **The court held no legal duty exists unless an injury "was foreseeable and avoidable through due care." The school board could not be held liable for actions by students unless it had some "special relationship" with them.** The victim was attempting to hold the board liable for the actions of students who were outside its control at 8:15 p.m. and not on school property. The appeals court had improperly held the board liable for failing to control them, and the judgment was reversed. *Stein v. Asheville City Board of Educ.*, 626 S.E.2d 263 (N.C. 2005).

◆ A California school opened its campus at 7:00 a.m., but trouble spots such as restrooms were unsupervised before 7:45 a.m. School administrators knew that one eighth-grade special education student was usually dropped off at 7:15 a.m. A classmate who also had disabilities teased and ridiculed the student daily before classes began. The student sometimes went to the office to escape this, and he complained to the staff. He was told to stay away from the classmate, even after he told the vice principal this did not work. The classmate twice isolated the student and sexually assaulted him. The district learned of the incidents and expelled the classmate, who was also arrested. The student was hospitalized with depression, and he attempted suicide. He filed a state court action against the school district and the classmate's family. A jury trial resulted in a verdict of over $2.5 million for the student, and the district appealed.

The Court of Appeal of California observed that **schools have a special relationship with students which imposes an affirmative duty on school districts to "take all reasonable steps to protect students."** The duty arose from the compulsory nature of education and a state constitutional declaration of each student's inalienable right to attend safe, secure and peaceful campuses. **School districts have a well-established duty to supervise students at all times while on school grounds and to enforce necessary rules and regulations for their protection. This duty included supervision during recess and before or after school.** The district was liable for injuries resulting from the failure of school staff to use ordinary care to protect students. The district unlocked its gates at 7:00 a.m. each day, but did not provide supervision until 7:45 a.m. **It could have simply precluded students from arriving early or kept them in particular areas of the school.** The district's claim to immunity failed because there was no exercise of discretion by the principal, and evidence that he knew of the classmate's violent behavior. The damage award was not excessive, and the court affirmed the judgment. *M.W. v. Panama Buena Union School Dist.*, 1 Cal. Rptr. 3d 673 (Cal. Ct. App. 2003).

2. Governmental Immunity

◆ The Court of Appeals of Florida held a school board had sovereign immunity in a negligence lawsuit filed by a parent whose 13-year-old son was killed while walking home from school. The death occurred at an intersection with no crossing guard. The student was the fourth child to die in transit to or from the school in a seven-year period. The mother asserted the decision to operate the school from 9:00 a.m. to 4:00 p.m. negligently exposed students to rush-hour traffic. **The court found the scheduling of school hours was a planning-level decision that deserved immunity. The board did not create a hidden or dangerous condition for which there was no proper warning. Traffic hazards at the site were readily apparent, and the board had no authority over the regulation of traffic.** *Orlando v. Broward County, Florida*, No. 04-3445, 2005 WL 3478364 (Fla. Dist. Ct. App. 2005).

◆ A Georgia student attended summer school and skipped class several times with his parent's knowledge. He left school and was killed in a traffic accident while riding in a vehicle driven by a classmate who was later convicted of vehicular homicide. The student's estate sued school officials in a Georgia superior court for negligently failing to enforce school attendance rules. The court held for the officials, and the estate appealed. The Court of Appeals of Georgia **held that the supervision of students is a protected discretionary activity for which school employees could not be held liable.** The court also observed that **the student's death had been caused by the criminal act of the classmate and would have been an unforeseeable circumstance even if school employees had been negligent**. The court affirmed the judgment. *Wright v. Ashe*, 220 Ga. App. 91, 469 S.E.2d 268 (Ga. Ct. App. 1996).

V. LIABILITY FOR INTENTIONAL CONDUCT

"Willful or wanton misconduct" refers to intentional conduct. A finding of willful or wanton misconduct typically defeats immunity. Courts have found school districts liable for intentional acts of third parties on or near school grounds. In those cases, a court must find the district should have foreseen the potential for misconduct. For intentional misconduct cases involving coaches, please see Chapter Fifteen, Section III.D. For corporal punishment cases, see Chapter Four, Section III. Additional cases involving sexual harassment and abuse appear in Section II.D. of Chapter Seven, and in Chapter Four, Section V.

A. Employee Misconduct

1. Types of Misconduct

◆   An Arkansas student attended a band competition in Atlanta with his school band. He became ill after arriving and missed the entire competition while remaining in his hotel room. Shortly after the student returned home, his mother took him to a medical center. However, he suffered a cardiac arrest and died the next day. The death was attributed to undiagnosed diabetes. The mother sued the school district and officials in a federal district court for negligence and deliberate indifference to her son's medical needs. The court dismissed her federal constitutional claims. It held federal jurisdiction should be rejected in cases that involved common law torts incidentally involving action by a government employee. The mother appealed to the U.S. Court of Appeals, Eighth Circuit. The court echoed the district court's opinion, noting **"the Due Process Clause of the Fourteenth Amendment is not a 'font of tort law.'"** Neither the text nor the history of the clause indicated state entities must guarantee minimal safety and security to individuals. **The Due Process Clause generally does not confer affirmative rights to government aid, even if this may be necessary to secure individual life, liberty or property interests.**

A state assumes a constitutional duty to protect an individual's safety only when it has restrained the individual's liberty through incarceration, institutionalization or some other form of restraint that renders the individual incapable of self care. The district court had correctly dismissed the due process claim against the school district, because there was no district policy of violating student constitutional rights. There was also no evidence that the band director had restrained the student's ability to care for himself. **School officials have no duty to care for students who participate in voluntary school-related activities such as school band trips.** There was no claim that the student could not leave the band activity at any time, and his family was not prevented from arranging for him to leave Atlanta. The court found no evidence that the student's "voluntary participation evolved into an involuntary commitment" during the trip. While a tort remedy might still be available in the state courts, the judgment for the school district on the mother's federal claims was affirmed. *Lee v. Pine Bluff School Dist.*, 472 F.3d 1026 (8th Cir. 2007).

♦   A Michigan student took a coupon cutter with him to his middle school and used it to make red marks on his arms and hands. Other students asked to use it or had him create marks on them. A teacher saw the marks and the student was suspended. The local media ran stories about the incident. The student claimed that during his suspension, a teacher told his classmates he was dangerous, that his father was an alcoholic who was in prison, that his mother had died giving birth and that he had problems at home. The student also claimed the teacher told the class he could be infected by AIDS and could pass the disease to others who used the coupon cutter. He sued the teacher, school district, school officials and a television station in a Michigan trial court for intentional infliction of emotional distress and invasion of his privacy rights.

The court denied the teacher's motion for pretrial disposition, and she appealed. The Court of Appeals of Michigan rejected her claim to state law immunity under MCL Section 691.1407(2). This provision did not apply to claims based on intentional harm by government employees. However, **emotional distress liability is imposed only where conduct is so outrageous and so extreme as to go beyond all possible bounds of decency and be regarded as atrocious and utterly intolerable.** The court held the teacher was entitled to warn other students of the potentially dangerous effects of the student's actions. While her alleged comments "were unfortunately neither sensitive nor discrete," they were not sufficiently extreme or outrageous to create liability. The student did not show the teacher improperly intruded upon his seclusion, as he only speculated that she had viewed his file. As speculation was insufficient to proceed with the claim, the court reversed the judgment and remanded the case for entry of judgment for the teacher. *Saxon v. Chapman*, No. 266077, 2006 WL 1237036 (Mich. Ct. App. 2006).

♦   A North Carolina PE and health teacher encouraged an 18-year-old student-athlete to have sexual relations with a 14-year-old student and allowed him to use his office, home and car to facilitate their relationship. The student's parent claimed the teacher offered them $500 to let him watch them have sex in her home. The students refused and returned to school. According to the parent, the resource officer escorted the student to the teacher's officer, where the teacher sought to obtain her silence about his conduct. The parent sued the student-athlete, teacher, board of education, principal, resource officer and county sheriff in a state court for negligence and intentional misconduct. The court denied motions to dismiss the complaint and cross-claims by the principal and board against the officer and sheriff. It allowed the parent to sue the sheriff in his individual and his official capacity. The officer and sheriff appealed.

The North Carolina Court of Appeals explained the "public duty doctrine" precludes any municipal or police liability for failing to protect specific individuals. The court refused to expand the public duty doctrine to the claims against the resource officer for conspiracy, interference with civil rights and intentional infliction of emotional distress. These claims were based on his affirmative conduct, not negligence. **The negligence claims against the resource officer for failing to report the teacher's conduct and notify the administration of the student's absence from school were not protected by the public immunity doctrine.** State law required any person suspecting abuse of a juvenile to report it to the county director of social services, and it explicitly prevented a person from asserting any privilege for not reporting when a juvenile may have been abused. Resource officers have a "special relationship" to students, and act to preserve student safety, not in a general law enforcement capacity. The trial court had properly denied the officer's motion to dismiss the case under the public duty doctrine. The cross-motion of the board and principal alleging a special duty was properly granted. **The duty to report child abuse is not a discretionary law enforcement function that is shielded by the public duty doctrine.** The court affirmed the judgment for the parent. *Smith v. Jackson County Board of Educ.*, 608 S.E.2d 399 (N.C. Ct. App. 2005).

◆ A New York elementary student alleged a school bus driver sexually molested her several times on her bus. Only one other student was on the bus when the incidents occurred. At the end of the school year, the other student told her father about the molestations, and the driver was charged with sexual abuse. The student sued the school district and officials in a state trial court for negligent hiring, retention and supervision of the driver, and for negligent supervision of the student. The court granted the district's motion for summary judgment on all claims except the one for negligently supervising the student.

The student appealed to a state appellate division court, which noted **New York courts have held school districts have a duty to adequately supervise students in their care, and may be held liable for foreseeable injuries proximately related to inadequate supervision.** Courts must compare a school's level of supervision and protection to what "a parent of ordinary prudence would observe in comparable circumstances." The district presented evidence that the bus driver had no prior criminal history and that no one had accused him of acting improperly in 27 years of prior work. The district had no reason to know he had a propensity to commit sexual misconduct. The court held for the school district on the student's claim for negligent supervision. *Doe v. Rohan*, 17 A.D.3d 509, 793 N.Y.S.2d 170 (N.Y. App. Div. 2005).

◆ A New Jersey teacher participated in student mediation workshops. Her principal asked her to accept a check for another employee who supervised an after-school program for which she lacked adequate credentials. The principal submitted the teacher's name to ensure the other employee would be paid. The teacher told the principal she would not participate in the scheme, as she believed it was fraudulent or illegal. Two months later, she cashed a check she believed was her pay for the workshops. When the principal demanded payment for the amount of the check, the teacher realized it involved the other employee's pay. She notified a payroll supervisor and followed her instructions to send a check for the same amount to the board with a letter of explanation.

The teacher claimed the principal retaliated against her by suspending her from the mediation program, giving her poor evaluations and other unfair treatment. The teacher sued the school board, school officials and the principal in a state superior court, alleging continuous harassment and violation of the New Jersey Conscientious Employee Protection Act (CEPA). The court dismissed the principal and other school officials from the case and conducted a trial on the teacher's CEPA claim. A jury returned a verdict against the school board for $565,000, including $300,000 in punitive damages. A state appellate division court upheld the jury verdict, and the board appealed. The state supreme court held the CEPA protects employees from retaliation for disclosing conduct, if the employee reasonably believes the conduct violates a law, rule or regulation. It allows punitive damage awards and is not limited by the general immunity provisions of the New Jersey Tort Claims Act. The CEPA is a civil rights statute intended to protect employees and encourage the reporting of illegal and unethical workplace activities. **The court upheld the punitive damage award, as the teacher alleged a continual pattern of wrongful conduct.** *Green v. Jersey City Board of Educ.*, 828 A.2d 883 (N.J. 2003).

◆ A Kansas paraprofessional worked with a learning disabled 12-year-old student who had behavior problems and had threatened to commit suicide. The school principal became concerned about her numerous requests to see the student. Teachers stated that the paraprofessional interfered with the student's classroom work, but no staff member had concerns about sexual contact between the paraprofessional and student. Near the end of the school year, she admitted having sexual contact with the student, and she ultimately pled no contest to criminal charges. The student sued the district and officials in a federal district court for negligently retaining and supervising the paraprofessional. The court held for the district, and the family appealed.

The Tenth Circuit noted evidence that school officials had been unaware of the paraprofessional's misconduct. The Kansas Supreme Court has stated that **employers are liable for negligent hiring and retention only if they know or should have known of an employee's unfitness or incompetence**. It has also stated that **employers do not need to be "clairvoyant" to avoid liability for unforeseen risks created by their employees**. District employees had no suspicions about the relationship between the student and paraprofessional, who appeared to be a "model employee." As there was no basis to suspect she presented a risk to any student, and the sexual molestation was not foreseeable, the court affirmed the judgment for the district. *Kurtz v. Unified School Dist. No. 308*, 65 Fed.Appx. 257 (10th Cir. 2003).

2. Governmental Immunity

◆ A Chicago student had spinal abnormalities and visible scars from surgery. His chemistry teacher frequently commented about his part African-American, part Caucasian ancestry in class. When the student's mother complained, school officials admitted the comments were improper and removed the student from the class. The next year, the chemistry teacher attended one of the student's history classes. The student claimed the teacher distracted him and stated that the student felt superior due to his part Caucasian blood. He alleged the chemistry teacher then grabbed him and put him in a "choking headlock." The student later sued the school board, school officials and teacher.

A federal district court considered a dismissal motion by the board and officials based on the state Tort Immunity Act. They stated they were not liable for the student's injuries because their handling of his complaints involved policy-making and the exercise of discretion. The court held that **"policy decisions" are those requiring a municipality to "balance competing interests and make judgment calls as to what solution will best serve each of those interests."** The handling of the chemistry teacher's action, as well as the decision to retain him as an employee, were policy decisions and were discretionary in nature. The court awarded judgment to the board and officials for the personal injury and federal civil rights claims. The student failed to show any deprivation of civil rights due to an official custom or policy. *Moore v. Board of Educ. of City of Chicago*, 300 F.Supp.2d 641 (N.D. Ill. 2004).

◆ Two Nevada students with disabilities sued their school district and staff for severe abuse and corporal punishment. One student alleged staff members repeatedly abused him by force-feeding him oatmeal, despite his allergy to oats, and by using a "take down procedure" in which he was forcibly pinned to the ground while a teacher applied pressure. The other student asserted that school staff severely abused him by, among other things, subjecting him to the "take down procedure," spraying him in the face with cold water and forcing him to run on a treadmill with ankle weights. A federal district court awarded summary judgment to the defendants on Eleventh Amendment immunity grounds.

The families appealed to the Ninth Circuit, which explained that the Eleventh Amendment precludes lawsuits by citizens against the states. However, it does not protect counties, municipalities and state political subdivisions, even if they "exercise a slice of state power." **While California school districts have been held to be arms of the state that are entitled to immunity, Nevada districts have different characteristics that make them closer to county and municipal entities.** Nevada does not treat the operation of public schools as a statewide or central government function, and each school district has the power to sue and be sued. The Ninth Circuit reversed the judgment, finding the district had no Eleventh Amendment immunity. *Eason v. Clark County School Dist.*, 303 F.3d 1137 (9th Cir. 2002).

◆ A Washington sixth-grade special education student claimed the paraeducator assigned to assist her was impatient and rude and taunted her when she complained. She accused the paraeducator of blocking her path in a school hallway and refusing to get out of her way. The student's mother requested a new paraeducator and petitioned a state superior court for an anti-harassment order against the paraeducator. **The court granted the petition, ordering the paraeducator to have no contact with the student for one year, except in an emergency.** The court denied the paraeducator's motion for reconsideration and denied a motion by the school district to join the action on her behalf. The paraeducator and district appealed to the state Court of Appeals.

The court rejected the paraeducator's argument that the anti-harassment law provided public employees with immunity for actions within the scope of their employment. Instead, the law directed courts to consider several factors to determine whether there was a lawful purpose for a public employee's conduct.

The factors were only guidelines, and did not establish a rule of public employee immunity. By requiring courts to consider whether conduct was reasonably necessary to "meet specific statutory duties or requirements," **the state legislature had indicated conduct that was not "reasonably necessary" to fulfill an educator's statutory duties could be deemed harassment**. Courts were required to examine each case to determine whether a person accused under the law had a legitimate or lawful purpose for acting. As school employees could be subject to anti-harassment orders, the court affirmed the judgment. *Shinaberger v. LaPine*, 34 P.3d 1253 (Wash. Ct. App. 2001).

B. Student Misconduct

1. Types of Misconduct

◆   A Michigan teacher lined up most of her students in a hallway and led them to a computer class. She left five students in the classroom because they had not completed their work. A student took a pistol out of his desk, put bullets into it and shot a classmate to death. The teacher was in the hallway at the time. The classmate's parent claimed the student had been involved in several behavior incidents in the months before the shooting, including beating up other students and stabbing another student with a pencil. The parent sued the teacher, principal and school district in a federal district court, asserting a variety of civil rights violations claims. The court held for the district and school employees, and the parent appealed to the U.S. Court of Appeals, Sixth Circuit.

The court stated that **generally, a state's failure to protect an individual against violent acts by a private party is not a violation of the Due Process Clause**. Federal courts have recognized an exception to the general rule known as the "state-created danger" theory. Under it, there may be liability for a due process violation if the state takes some affirmative act that creates or increases the risk of a special danger to the victim, as distinguished from the public at large. **The teacher's act of leaving five students unsupervised in the classroom was not an "affirmative act" creating a specific risk to the classmate. She would have been in about the same degree of danger had the teacher remained.** The danger was the student's possession of the gun, not the teacher's positioning. A court or jury could not conclude the teacher knew the student would use a gun to kill another student if she left him unsupervised for a few minutes. He had never brought a weapon to school or threatened anyone before. The parent did not show the principal approved of any unconstitutional conduct by the teacher. **To hold the district liable for a civil rights violation, there had to be evidence of a district policy or custom of depriving persons of their constitutional rights.** There was no such evidence in this case. As the parent could not show the teacher violated her daughter's civil rights, the claims against the district and principal failed, and the court affirmed the judgment. *McQueen v. Beecher Community Schools*, 433 F.3d 460 (6th Cir. 2006).

◆   Philadelphia's Olney High School experienced increasing attacks on students and staff from 1999 to 2003. An Olney student was punched by an unknown attacker who was trying to hit someone else. On the day of the incident, the student took the only available stairs to his classroom. The intended victim ducked, and the attacker hit the student in the eye, severely injuring him. Neither the attacker nor the intended victim was ever identified. The student's mother sued the school district and school officials in a federal district court, asserting due process violations and willful misconduct.

The court rejected the claims, including one alleging that school officials had created the danger leading to the injury. On appeal, the U.S. Court of Appeals, Third Circuit, considered the mother's arguments that there were no surveillance cameras or security staff in the stairwell at the time of the attack. The school was short four security officers that day, and had been short of a full security staff on 83 of the previous 85 school days. The school's principal admitted "the building basically was out of control." The court stated that to impose liability under the Due Process Clause for creating a danger, **the harm must have been foreseeable and fairly direct. The entity must have acted with a degree of culpability that "shocks the conscience." There must be a "special relationship" between the victim and the state, and the authority must be used in a way that created the danger to the victim. The court held that the injury to the student was not foreseeable to the district. The atmosphere of violence at the school did not make it foreseeable that he would be attacked.** School officials had no knowledge that the student was in any more danger than anyone else at Olney High School. He was not an intended victim of the assault, and only one prior violent incident had taken place in the stairwell. The court found that additional surveillance or security might have helped apprehend the attacker, but it was speculation to say this would have prevented the attack. As the school did not place the student in a position of increased danger, there was no basis for a state-created danger claim. The court affirmed the judgment. *Mohammed v. School Dist. of Philadelphia,* 196 Fed.Appx. 79 (3d Cir. 2006).

◆   The Court of Appeals of Wisconsin held a student could not proceed with emotional distress and defamation claims against her district after her name was replaced with a vulgarity in a yearbook supplement. She claimed the district did not proofread the supplement and did not recall it for 10 days after it was released. **The court of appeals affirmed a trial court decision finding the district's handling of the proofreading and recall of the supplement were discretionary acts or omissions.** As the district's actions were protected by immunity, the case was properly dismissed. *Price v. Boyceville Community School Dist.,* 281 Wis.2d 273, 695 N.W.2d 904 (Table) (Wis. Ct. App. 2005).

◆   Montana high school boys secretly watched and videotaped female students undressing in the school locker room for almost two years. They worked as towel boys and found ways to enter the school during non-school hours to carry out their plan. They showed the tapes to classmates during school hours. Students referred to locker room videotaping in the school yearbook, but the yearbook advisor did not investigate further. A teacher and the superintendent heard reports of possible videotaping, but took limited action. After the scheme had gone on for almost two years, a janitor discovered the boys' activity. Several criminal and civil claims were filed in the state court system as a result of the scheme. One of these was a federal district court action by the female students' parents for violating privacy rights and interfering with family relationships.

The court stated the Ninth Circuit has recognized an action for government interference with parent-child relationships in cases involving the death of a child or the loss of certain parental rights. **Being viewed in stages of undress was not the kind of injury due constitutional protection. The students did not claim any district policy of deliberate indifference to their rights. District practices that allowed male students into the school did not foreseeably cause injury.** The court held that for municipal liability to exist, there must be a policy of inaction that is more than simple negligence. The hiring of towel boys to serve in locker rooms for females did not cause a "state-created danger." No official could be held liable for hiring the towel boys, overlooking yearbook references to videotaping, or failing to detect the scheme. **The failure to be more attentive or to supervise the boys may have been negligent but did not create any constitutional liability.** The superintendent was not told of any obvious risk to constitutional rights. As the officials were not deliberately indifferent to any constitutional rights, they were entitled to summary judgment. *Harry A. v. Duncan*, 351 F.Supp.2d 1060 (D. Mont. 2005).

◆   A New York student and a classmate fought in their school cafeteria about some money. The district suspended the classmate from school for a day, with a day of in-school suspension. The classmate had been disciplined six times in sixth and seventh grades, including suspensions for fighting, but this was his first discipline for grade eight. He was not involved in any prior cafeteria incidents and had no prior encounters with the student. The student sued the district and school officials in a federal district court, claiming they did nothing to protect him even though the classmate's record of fighting and discipline put the district on notice of his "propensity for violence." The court dismissed the federal claims, and the district moved for summary judgment on his state law claims.

In *Mirand v. City of New York*, 84 N.Y. 44, 637 N.E.2d 263 (N.Y. 1994), the state's highest court held a school is liable for student-on-student violence only if it had "specific, prior knowledge of the danger that caused the injury." **A student's acts must have been foreseeable by the district to impose liability. New York courts have held there is no school liability for injuries caused by sudden, impulsive acts that are not preceded by prior misconduct. If an assault occurs so suddenly that it could not be prevented by any amount of supervision, there is no school liability.** Prior unrelated incidents of student discipline do not put a school on notice of a specific threat of danger requiring supervision. **While New York courts hold schools have a duty to adequately supervise students, "this duty does not make schools insurers of the safety of their students, for they cannot be reasonably expected to continuously supervise and control all movements and activities of students."** The student had never seen the classmate before the incident. The classmate's disciplinary record did not put the district on notice of a possible attack on the student. As there was no specific threat to the student, and the district was not required to constantly supervise the classmate, it was not liable for negligence. *Smith v. Half Hollow Hills Cent. School Dist.*, 349 F.Supp.2d 521 (E.D.N.Y. 2004).

◆   An Ohio student claimed two older students invited him to a "jazz band meeting" early in a school year. He followed them into a lavatory, where he was punched and kicked by a group of students. The student said he received numerous bruises and neck and back injuries and was threatened with more beatings. He sued the board and school officials in a state court, asserting the school board and administration knew of and tolerated a "Freshman Beating Day." The court held for the board and administrators, and the student appealed.

State law authorized civil actions against student organizations, schools and school employees, if the school knew or should have known of hazing and made no reasonable attempt to prevent it. The Court of Appeals of Ohio held "student organization" meant a specific organization, not an entire student body. The "jazz band meeting" reference did not make the beating an initiation into a student organization. "Initiation" implied voluntary membership and consent by the victim to be hazed. The student did not agree to be beaten and would probably not have entered the lavatory had he known it was planned. **The court held that even if the school officials were aware of and tolerated "Freshman Friday," the beating did not constitute "hazing" under state law.** It affirmed the judgment for the board and officials. *Duitch v. Canton City Schools*, 157 Ohio App.3d 80, 809 N.E.2d 62 (Ohio Ct. App. 2004).

◆   An educably mentally retarded Mississippi middle school student attended a special education math classroom. Two boys repeatedly took her behind bookshelves at the back of the classroom and took turns sexually assaulting her as the other stood watch. The student sued the school district, teacher, district superintendent and others in a state court for improper supervision. The court found there was some sexual conduct among the students, but it rejected the student's request to hold the district liable for $5.2 million for permanent institutionalization. She had qualified for this placement before the assaults occurred and was receiving Medicaid and Social Security benefits. The court credited evidence that the student should remain in public school as long as possible. It awarded her only $20,197, with nothing for pain and suffering.

The state court of appeals upheld the trial court's refusal to consider the student's preexisting mental condition. The failure to award her damages for pain and suffering was also appropriate. The evidence at trial was insufficient to support an award of damages for pain and suffering, based on her inability to clearly communicate. **The evidence did not show the student required institutionalization due to the assaults, and· she had qualified for the private facility before the assaults.** Public benefits would cover her private expenses. The court affirmed the trial court's comprehensive decision. *Doe v. North Panola School Dist.*, 906 So.2d 57 (Miss. App. 2004).

◆   Two Kansas students arranged to meet after school and fight in a rural area. One of the students had an extensive disciplinary record that did not involve fighting. He seriously injured the other student in the off-campus fight. The other student sued the student and his parents and the school district in a state court, alleging negligent supervision. The court granted the district's summary judgment motion, and the victim appealed to the Supreme Court of Kansas. He argued that certain district officials had knowledge of the other student's disruptive nature and that injury was foreseeable. The supreme court observed that **the students had taken great care to avoid any detection by school authorities when they planned the off-campus fight. The school district owed the student no legal duty to prevent an off-campus injury,** even though the fight had been arranged at school. The district had no special relationship that created a duty to protect students from unknown off-campus fights, and the injuries were not foreseeable. The district was not required to expel or otherwise discipline the other student and had the discretion to refrain from doing so. The court affirmed the summary judgment order for the district. *Beshears v. Unified School Dist. No. 305,* 930 P.2d 1376 (Kan. 1997).

2. Governmental Immunity

◆ A 14-year-old Texas student attended a special education program due to emotional disturbance and attention span problems. Her teacher brought her to the school office for tardiness. The school's assistant principal gave the student a permission slip, allowing her to return to class. However, he soon found her walking in the hallways and suspended her for truancy and insubordination. The assistant principal later contended she did not identify herself and claimed not to know her home address, phone number or student identification number. The student provided him with the phone number of a man she identified as "an uncle," and allegedly stated her father was always drunk and her mother was never at home. The assistant principal could not find her name in the school's electronic database, so he allowed her to call the "uncle." This was contrary to the school's non-discretionary release policy. The assistant principal left the student alone in the lobby of the school office to attend to other duties, and the student left school with the man identified as her uncle. Her parents reported she did not come home after school, and the city police were contacted.

The student alleged the man sexually abused her, and she sued the school district, assistant principal and others in a federal district court. The court awarded summary judgment to the district and school officials, finding the assistant principal was immune from suit. The student appealed to the Fifth Circuit, claiming he violated her right to be free from unjustified intrusion on her personal security. **The court held states are not liable for acts of private violence, unless they have undertaken to protect the victim based on a "special relationship" or have themselves created the danger. The court rejected the student's claim that school officials had a duty to protect her when she was suspended.** Her liberty was not restrained, and she was able to leave the school with relative ease. The assistant principal's behavior was not "deliberate indifference," and there no basis for imposing a duty on him based on any special relationship. He did not know of any danger presented by the man identified as the uncle. The assistant principal was entitled to qualified immunity on the federal claims. The court held he deserved professional immunity from the state law claims under the Texas Education Code. He had ordered her to stay in the office until he could meet the person she identified as her uncle, and never released her to him. *Doe v. San Antonio Independent School Dist.*, 197 Fed.Appx. 296 (5th Cir. 2006).

◆ Georgia parents claimed a classmate severely beat their son outside a classroom. They said the principal and vice principal found him unconscious and bleeding profusely in the hallway. According to the parents, a nurse cleaned the student's wounds but offered him no other treatment. They claimed that nobody called 911 for 40 minutes after their son was found in the hall, even though he was vomiting blood. The parents sued the school district in a state court, asserting officials knew of the classmate's extensive history of violence and that a teacher ignored his threats against their son. They claimed the district under-reported student disciplinary data to avoid a "persistently dangerous" designation. They stated only 4,258 of 70,138 school disciplinary incidents were reported. The court held for the school district and the parents appealed.

The Court of Appeals of Georgia explained that **Georgia law makes public officers or employees liable only for "ministerial acts negligently performed or acts performed with malice or an intent to injure."** The state School Safety and Juvenile Justice Reform Act, OCGA § 20-2-1185, required schools to prepare a safety plan. The court held that although the preparation of a school safety plan was a "mandatory ministerial duty under OCGA § 1185, the development of its contents embraces discretionary functions." While the school had a safety plan, the parents asserted it did not address security issues mandated by OCGA § 20-2-1185. The court reversed the trial court's judgment for the school district on this issue. The family's claims against the school principal, assistant principal and school nurse also should have been presented to a jury. **State law required any school employee with reasonable cause to believe a student had committed a prohibited act, such as aggravated battery, to "immediately report the act and the name of the student to the principal."** Claims based on failure to comply with statutory reporting requirements and failure to immediately obtain medical care for the student had been improperly dismissed. A jury might find the school failed to provide him with adequate medical care in breach of a ministerial duty to do so. **The No Child Left Behind Act requires each state to develop a definition of "persistently dangerous" schools. Local school systems must report criminal offenses at schools to the state education department.** The court held the parents alleged the school had an official policy of discouraging accurate reporting of incidents of school violence to avoid a "persistently dangerous" designation. While official immunity protects public officials and employees from lawsuits in their personal capacities, a jury could find the intentional conduct of officials in this case defeated any claim for immunity. The court reversed and remanded the case to the trial court. *Bajjani v. Gwinnett County School Dist.*, 278 Ga.App. 866, 630 S.E.2d 103 (Ga. Ct. App. 2006).

◆ A Minnesota science teacher was put on administrative leave near the end of his probationary period, then discharged. He sued his school district in a state court, asserting he had reported many incidents of bad behavior by students during his employment with the district. He claimed teachers have a right to be free from any abuse or harassment in the school environment under Minnesota Statutes Section 121A.03 and the district's own policies.

The court awarded summary judgment to the district, and the teacher appealed. The Court of Appeals of Minnesota rejected the teacher's argument that Section 121A.03 created an absolute legal duty for school districts. The section required the state commissioner of education to maintain a model policy on discrimination, harassment and violence. School boards were required to adopt and conspicuously post their policies and verify they conformed to state requirements. **The teacher did not show the district failed to investigate three incidents of student harassment, two of which involved students who implied he was homosexual. In each case, the district responded by disciplining the students and informing their parents.** School district policymaking and enforcement were protected by discretionary immunity, and the judgment for the district was affirmed. *Malone v. Special School Dist. No. 1*, No. 2004 CA 00347, 2005 WL 3289468 (Minn. Ct. App. 2005). The Supreme Court of Minnesota declined to review the case in 2006.

◆   An Illinois student was reluctant to go to school after being bullied, shoved and kicked. His mother complained to the school principal but did not identify the bullies. She later called a school social worker to obtain counseling for her son. The mother told the social worker the names of the bullies and said her son did not wish them to be revealed. The social worker agreed not to disclose their names but soon provided them to the principal. The principal then met with the bullies and revealed the student's name before assigning them to detention. The student claimed to suffer emotional distress from the disclosure of his name to the bullies. He transferred schools and filed a state court privacy rights violation action against the principal, social worker, school board and the rural special education cooperative that employed the social worker. The court held the social worker and cooperative were immune from suit under the Illinois Confidentiality Act, 740 ILCS § 110/11(ii). The principal and board had immunity under the state Tort Immunity Act, 745 ILCS § 10/2-201.

On appeal, the Appellate Court of Illinois stated the Confidentiality Act was implicated whenever a communication was made to a therapist. The social worker was protected under Section 11 of the act, which **permits a good-faith disclosure to protect a person against a clear, imminent risk of serious injury. The trial court correctly held the social worker had sole discretion to decide whether disclosing confidential information was necessary to protect the student.** He relayed this information to the principal in the belief there was a risk of further harm. **The principal's actions involved disciplinary matters and were policy determinations** under Section 2-201. **The principal's handling of bullying fell within the definition of "discretionary," as principals had broad discretion to handle these situations.** The principal and school board were immune from suit under Section 2-201. *Albers v. Breen*, 346 Ill.App.3d 799, 806 N.E.2d 667 (Ill. App. Ct. 2004).

◆   A Mississippi honor student was helping another student during their math class. Their teacher was about five feet away, assisting a third student. A classmate began to loudly taunt and bother the student from across the room. The student asked the classmate to leave him alone, but the classmate walked over to his desk and made repeated threatening gestures. He taunted the student for at least a minute, then struck him so hard the student and his desk were thrown to the floor. The student suffered a fractured tooth, broken facial bone and a concussion. He sued the school district under the Mississippi Tort Claims Act, alleging it failed to use ordinary care to discipline students and provide a safe school environment. The court awarded summary judgment to the district and the student appealed to the Supreme Court of Mississippi.

The court explained **the general duty in school negligence cases is for schools "to use ordinary care and to take reasonable steps to minimize foreseeable risks to students thereby providing a safe school environment." There is no school liability unless a risk of injury is reasonably foreseeable.** While the district asserted injury to the student was not foreseeable because the classmate had no known previous record of violence, the court found several questions of fact made summary judgment improper. The student claimed the classmate's taunts were audible from across the room, yet the teacher did nothing. The reasonableness of her response had a bearing on whether she used ordinary care in supervising her class. Teachers and administrators have immunity only if they use ordinary care in controlling and disciplining students. As this question required a factual inquiry, the case was remanded for a trial. *Henderson v. Simpson County Public School Dist.*, 847 So.2d 856 (Miss. 2003).

C. Parent Misconduct

Section 316 of the Restatement of Torts (a legal encyclopedia) states there is no legal duty for parents to prevent harm by their children unless "they are in a position to exercise immediate control over their children to prevent some foreseeable harm." By contrast, there is no duty on parents "to take precautionary disciplinary measures or to regulate their children's behavior on an ongoing basis." Courts followed Section 316 in Lott v. Strang, 312 Ill.App.3d 521, 727 N.E.2d 407 (Ill. Ct. App. 2000), and Bland v. Candioto, No. 3:05-CV-716RM, 2006 WL 2735501 (N.D. Ill. 2006), summarized below.

◆ An Illinois teacher claimed a student charged at her with scissors and threatened to stab her while screaming obscenities. She was able to disarm the student, who ran out of the room, kicked the door, and slammed it shut on her finger. Without the assistance of an attorney, the teacher filed a state court action against the school district and board, Chicago Teachers Union, school principal and other school officials. She alleged discrimination, defamation, infliction of emotional distress and federal civil rights violations, and added a negligence claim against the student's mother. The teacher claimed the parent should have insisted he receive special education and had prior knowledge of his arrest record, mental illness, conduct disorder, character, and history of outbursts in class. The case was removed to a federal court, which appointed a lawyer for the teacher, then considered the parent's motion to dismiss the negligence claim. She could not be held liable simply because she was the student's mother.

Liability required proof that the parent did not adequately control or supervise her son. **To state a claim for negligent supervision, the teacher had to show the parent was aware of specific prior conduct that put her on notice that the assault was likely to occur, and had the opportunity to control the student. Parents have a duty to exercise "reasonable care" to control their minor children and prevent them from intentionally harming**

others. The court found no duty on parents to "take precautionary disciplinary measures or to regulate their children's behavior on an ongoing basis." **Illinois courts have held parents are not liable for harm caused by their children merely based on the parent-child relationship.** The court stated parents have a duty to exercise reasonable care to control minor children to prevent intentionally harming others or from creating an unreasonable risk of bodily harm. To impose liability, a parent must perceive the ability to control the child, and know of the necessity and opportunity for exercising such control. Since parental liability may result only if parents are in position to exercise immediate control over their children to prevent some foreseeable harm, the court granted the parent's motion to dismiss the teacher's claim against her. *Bland v. Candioto*, No. 3:05-CV-716RM, 2006 WL 2735501 (N.D. Ill. 2006).

◆   Under Louisiana law, parents are legally accountable for the acts of their children. An 11-year-old student with impulsivity and aggression problems pointed a toy gun at a teaching assistant (TA). The TA did not know the gun was a toy and claimed to be emotionally and mentally traumatized. The TA received workers' compensation benefits for psychological injuries. In an effort to recover what was paid to her in workers' compensation benefits, the school board sued the student's mother in a state court. The board claimed the student was negligent and argued the mother was personally liable for his actions.

The court held for the mother, and the board appealed. The Court of Appeal of Louisiana stated that **Louisiana courts have held the parents of minor children liable for harm caused by a child's conduct under Civil Code Article 2318, even where a parent is not personally negligent.** The student could be deemed negligent only if a court found he violated the applicable standard of care. The court affirmed the judgment, finding that given his maturity level, lack of awareness of risks and his inclination to be impulsive and aggressive, he did not breach the standard of care. Because the student was not negligent, his mother could not be held liable for his actions. *Lafayette Parish School Board v. Cormier*, 901 So. 2d 1197 (La. Ct. App. 2005).

◆   A Tennessee father of two children sought to divorce his wife. She obtained a temporary restraining order splitting custody of the children. A school policy allowed students to leave with their parents, with the principal's approval. The date and time of student departure and return was to be recorded with the reason for leaving school. The father became upset when he came to school and learned his mother-in-law had taken the children to their mother. The mother told staff not to release the children to their father, but a staff member said that would require a court order. The next day, the father came to school for both children. The reasons he gave for signing them out were "keeping promise by mother" for the daughter and "pay back" for the son. The son's teacher read the reasons after he left and notified the principal. However, the father had already left with both children. Police arrived at his house to find it ablaze. The father brandished a knife and the police shot him to death. The children's bodies were found inside. The mother sued the school board in a state court for negligence.

The court held for the board, and the mother appealed. The state court of appeals held **schools, teachers and school administrators have a duty to**

exercise ordinary care for student safety. The board was not liable for negligently violating its own sign-out policy. There was no evidence that staff knew of a dispute until the mother called the day before the murders. The trial court correctly held a **school has no legal duty to follow the instruction of one parent not to release a child to the other parent without a court order to this effect**. The court affirmed judgment on a claim based on the father's violent nature. However, **failure to read his reasons for signing out the children was evidence of breach of the duty to exercise ordinary care for the children's safety. The court rejected the board's claim that it had no legal duty to examine a parent's reason for signing out a child**. The reasons the father wrote for signing out the children might cause a reasonable person to suspect he intended harm. The state Governmental Tort Liability Act did not protect the board, since the decision to release the children involved no planning. The case was reversed and remanded for further consideration. *Haney v. Bradley County Board of Educ.*, 160 S.W.3d 886 (Tenn. Ct. App. 2004).

◆   An Ohio student with autism and pervasive disability disorder exhibited violent, disruptive behavior in kindergarten and first grade. His second grade individualized education program (IEP) placed him in regular classes with a full-time aide. Days after the IEP team met to address his increasingly violent and disruptive behavior, the student disrupted a math test, flew into a rage and repeatedly struck his teacher. She took him to the hallway and restrained him, but he kicked her in the face and neck. The teacher sued the student's parents and the school district in a state court. The court found nothing in the student's behavioral history indicated he would cause injuries of the kind alleged by the teacher. It held for the parents and the school district, and the teacher appealed.

The Court of Appeals of Ohio held parents may be found liable for the wrongful conduct of their children when the injury is a foreseeable consequence of their negligence. **Parents may be held liable for failing to exercise reasonable control over a child, despite knowledge that injury to another person is a probable consequence**. The student frequently hit and kicked students, teachers and aides, lashing out when frustrated in his classes or when touched or bumped by classmates. The case was complicated by special education law purposes and procedures. Merely advocating for the placement of the student in regular education settings could not make the parents liable. While they were IEP team members, the placement decision was not theirs alone. The court reversed the judgment for the parents, but held the trial court had correctly found the district was entitled to sovereign immunity under the state code. The judgment for the district was affirmed. *Coolidge v. Riegle*, No. 5-02-59, 2004 WL 170319 (Ohio Ct. App. 2004).

D. Suicide

◆   **The Idaho Supreme Court held a school district and a teacher were not liable for the suicide of a student who formerly attended a district high school**. The student wrote a journal entry as part of an assignment on Hamlet as a high school junior. He wrote "I believe my most difficult decision of all time was not to kill myself," but added "now I've turned my life around," after earlier considering suicide. He stated his brother's move from the family home would stop household conflicts and allow him to "enjoy life and all its little pleasures without any guilt." The student's English teacher returned the essay with a note to talk to someone if such feelings returned. However, the teacher did not tell the student's parents about the essay. The family moved to Washington, where he later committed suicide. The parents sued the teacher and school district in an Idaho court, asserting failure to comply with provisions of the Idaho code requiring school officials to notify parents of a student's suicidal tendencies.

The court held for the parents, and the district appealed to the Supreme Court of Idaho. The court noted the state legislature had enacted Idaho Code Section 33-512B in response to *Brooks v. Logan*, 127 Idaho 484, 903 P.2d 73 (1995). In *Brooks*, the court held a teacher and school district owed a duty to warn parents or otherwise act when confronted with evidence of a student's suicidal tendencies. **The amended code now stated that neither a district nor a teacher had a duty to warn of a student's suicidal tendencies "absent the teacher's knowledge of direct evidence of such suicidal tendencies."** The code stated that "direct evidence" included "unequivocal and unambiguous oral or written statements by a student" that would not cause doubts in a reasonable teacher. **The court held the legislature adopted the new provision specifically to narrow the duty of a teacher to warn of a student's suicidal tendencies.** According to the court, the term "suicidal tendencies" in Section 33-512B meant "a present aim, direction or trend toward taking one's own life." The court observed that the student's essay showed he had contemplated suicide in the past. However, he also stated that he had "turned his life around" and was currently happy. The student's words provided an opposite conclusion to the one urged by his parents. The court held the teacher could not have determined he was currently contemplating suicide without speculating. A reasonable teacher reading the essay could conclude the student's suicidal thoughts were in the past and were now presently resolved. As the student's essay did not create a duty to warn his parents, the court reversed the judgment. *Carrier v. Lake Pend Oreille School Dist. No. 84*, 142 Idaho 804, 134 P.3d 655 (Idaho 2006).

◆ A California student was hospitalized for out-of-control behavior and suicide attempts. He was found eligible for special education for his emotional/behavioral condition, and his parents placed him in a residential non-public school for almost 18 months. At the school, he fought with classmates, put a tack through his ear, cut himself intentionally, carried cigarettes and a lighter on a bus, destroyed property and gave a classmate poison. The student twice left campus without permission. His mother met with staff to discuss ways to keep him on campus. Staff would "shadow" him, try to persuade him to remain, and notify the mother if he left. Restraint was not allowed, except to prevent immediate danger. The student left the campus and was missing for three days. During this time, an adult sexually assaulted him. Three months later, he committed suicide at his grandparents' home. The mother sued the school in a state court for negligence and emotional distress. A jury found for the mother and the court awarded her $5 million for breach of a duty of care to the student and $1 million for her emotional distress. The school was held 60% liable for the damages, resulting in an award of $3.6 million. The school appealed.

The California Court of Appeal held the student's suicide almost four months after the day he left campus was unforeseeable. **Schools have a duty to supervise students and take reasonable steps for their safety, but they are not guarantors of student safety.** The law did not impose a duty on a school to guard students from unforeseeable events. **The court found the risk to a student of falling victim to a child molester during truancy was not foreseeable.** The school had no knowledge of any specific risk if the student left campus and was not liable for the assault or the mother's emotional distress. The court reversed the judgment. *Allison C. v. Advanced Educ. Services*, 129 Cal.App.4th 636, 28 Cal.Rptr.3d 605 (Cal. Ct. App. 2005).

◆ A Michigan student committed suicide at home. Her estate sued her school district and school officials in a state court for negligence, gross negligence and violations of the Michigan Constitution and Civil Rights Act (CRA). The estate claimed the student had been continuously harassed and bullied in school because of her sex and Wiccan religious affiliation. The court awarded summary judgment to the district and officials on the negligence and constitutional rights claims, but denied it regarding the CRA and gross negligence claims. The district appealed to the state court of appeals, which considered only the question of immunity for the gross negligence claim.

The court held the **district was immune under MCL § 691.1407(1) because providing for student safety and welfare was within its powers.** The district superintendent was entitled to absolute immunity for any gross negligence. The court held the direct cause of harm was the teasing and harassment of peers, not official failure to intercede. School officials were entitled to summary judgment, because the estate did not show their conduct amounted to gross negligence that directly caused injury or damage. **As there was no evidence school officials had any advance notice that the student was contemplating suicide, they were entitled to immunity.** The court reversed and remanded the case. *Smith v. Lincoln Park Public School*, No. 245204, 2004 WL 1124467 (Mich. Ct. App. 2004).

E. Defamation

Since teachers are considered "public officials," they must show a false statement has been published to a third party with "actual malice" in order to recover damages in a defamation case. The actual malice standard is difficult to meet. A person seeking recovery in a defamation suit must also prove the publication has caused damage to his or her reputation. For defamation cases involving coaches, please see Chapter Fifteen, Section III.B. of this volume.

Privilege is a defense to certain defamation claims. Persons with a common interest in the subject matter of speech, for instance, a teacher's performance, may enjoy a privilege to discuss their common interest in protecting students.

◆ A New York teacher claimed a principal defamed him by telling a parent about a corporal punishment charge for which the teacher had been discharged from a previous assignment. The action was based on alleged verbal and physical abuse of several students. However, the teacher's unsatisfactory rating was reversed on administrative appeal and the accusations of corporal punishment were expunged from the record. Two years later, the teacher accused the principal of requiring a parent to come to school to discuss allegations of corporal punishment against the teacher. He claimed the parent had already written a letter stating he had done nothing to her son. The teacher stated the principal told the parent she had to come to school "because Mr. Garcia has been accused of corporal punishment before." The teacher sued the principal and school district for defamation. A state court denied a motion to dismiss the case, finding if the teacher could prove his version of the facts, he would establish a case of defamation based on false suggestions, implications and impressions from otherwise truthful statements.

The school district and principal appealed to the state appellate division, arguing the truth of the principal's statement about the previous corporal punishment incident was undisputed. The principal argued her failure to explain that the prior charge was expunged did not convey any defamatory impressions, because truth is a complete defense to a defamation claim. **The court noted the need to protect "substantially truthful speech" has led courts to use different standards for testing the sufficiency of claims for defamation by implication. However, the defamatory implication must be clear and inescapable.** The trial court had expressly delayed determining whether there were false statements, and the resulting inferences this would create. The court affirmed the judgment for the teacher, finding dismissal was premature. The trial court would have to consider whether the principal was privileged to speak to the mother about the teacher, and whether the principal actually made the statements. *Garcia v. Puccio*, 793 N.Y.S.2d 382 (N.Y. App. Div. 2005).

◆   An industrial arts teacher named Lewis taught at a Maine high school for 23 years. The local police chief informed the school principal of a criminal trespass charge against one "Fredric Lewis," and an unrelated claim that this person had improper sexual contact with a former student. The principal told the teacher of these allegations and placed him on administrative leave pending an investigation. The police chief then told the principal that the sexual contact charges were actually against another district employee named Lewis. The investigation continued, but the principal and district superintendent did not tell the teacher what they had learned from the police chief. The teacher retired and signed a letter of resignation. The principal e-mailed other school employees that "I would like to share with you as much information as I can. [Lewis] has retired/resigned and will not be teaching for the remainder of the year. ... There are lots of rumors out there but I would caution that much of what is being said is rumor and should be treated as such." The teacher sued the school district, principal and superintendent in a state court for defamation and related claims. He also brought claims against the municipality and the police chief, including punitive damage claims. The court denied summary judgment to the school district and officials, based on disputed factual issues. While the court acknowledged that immunity had been raised, it did not rule on the question.

The principal and superintendent appealed to the Supreme Judicial Court of Maine, asserting state law immunity. The court stated that a final judgment is generally required before an appeal is proper. Immediate review is only allowed if substantial rights will be lost when review is delayed until the entry of a final judgment. **The court held government employees are entitled to absolute immunity from suit if they perform a discretionary act. If the employee's actions exceed the scope of their discretion, immunity may be lost.** The trial court had denied summary judgment based on factual disputes about the claims. It did not rule on immunity issues. Since there was no final judgment, and no evidence that the officials would suffer irreparable loss of rights, the court dismissed the appeal. *Lewis v. Keegan*, 903 A.2d 342 (Me. 2006).

◆   A 74-year-old Massachusetts foreign language teacher filed a defamation and discrimination lawsuit against her principal. The principal had criticized the teacher's handling of a class trip to Germany, alleging she left a sick child unattended while she visited another town. A state trial court dismissed the case, but the court of appeals held the teacher raised valid concerns about the principal's statements to a group of parents concerning her performance. **His statements and his "ongoing antagonistic relationship" with her were enough to allow the defamation claim to proceed. While the principal was entitled to discuss the teacher's performance with parents, this privilege would be lost if the teacher showed he spoke with malice.** *Dragonis v. School Committee of Melrose*, 64 Mass. App. Ct. 429, 833 N.E.2d 679 (Mass. App. Ct. 2005). The Supreme Judicial Court of Massachusetts denied further review.

◆   A Wisconsin French teacher claimed two Spanish teachers were angry with him for his attempts to turn one of four dedicated Spanish classrooms into a dedicated French classroom. The French teacher sued the Spanish teachers in a state circuit court for defamation. The court held the lawsuit did not involve the public concern, and it awarded summary judgment to the Spanish teachers. The Court of Appeals of Wisconsin affirmed the judgment. The school district then terminated the French teacher's employment. He claimed this came in retaliation for filing the defamation lawsuit against the Spanish teachers.

The French teacher filed a new action in a federal district court against the district, school employees and others, claiming constitutional rights violations. The court found the "true reason" behind the French teacher's state court action had been to clear his name. While the French teacher argued the public would be interested to know about the Spanish teachers' "discrimination against the French program," the court disagreed. He did not show the defamation lawsuit would have revealed discrimination against the French program, or any matter of public concern. **As the action involved only the teacher's employment situation, the district did not violate the First Amendment by terminating his employment. The court agreed with the state courts that there was no possibility that the case involved the public concern.** It awarded summary judgment against the French teacher. *Mudrovich v. D.C. Everest Area School Dist.*, No. 04-C-398-C, 2005 WL 956988 (W.D. Wis. 2005).

◆   The parent of an Idaho child with Down syndrome worked at a charter school and enrolled her child in the school's special education program. The school administrator soon insisted she improve her performance. The school claimed the parent made a series of complaints to discredit the administrator and the special education program. The parent said the administrator was unhappy with many teachers and was intending to leave the school and "take the charter down." The school stated she falsely implied the administrator engaged in illegal conduct, improperly commented about teachers and misused grant funds. The school discharged the parent for refusing to follow directions and poor performance. A teacher at the school stated the parent resisted attempts to discuss her child's individual education program, ignored letters and made harassing calls. The parent complained to the U.S. Department of Education Office for Civil Rights and the state education agency. The school sued the parent in a state court, claiming she used her child's participation in its special education program in a manner calculated to harm the school.

The court denied the school's request to prevent the parent from making further comment, then dismissed the case. The school appealed to the state supreme court, which held **the parent's letters and statements to the board and district concerned a public issue**. For this reason, an injunction would be an impermissible prior restraint on speech. The court rejected the school's argument that it was a nonprofit corporation with the right to sue and be sued under state nonprofit law. The trial court had correctly held **the school was a governmental entity, as it operated within the public school system and was part of the state's program of public education. A governmental entity cannot maintain an action for libel and slander against a person whose speech is related to the public concern.** This would unconstitutionally silence or dampen public debate. **The school could not maintain a libel and slander action against the parent,** and the trial court had properly dismissed the case. *Nampa Charter School v. DeLaPaz*, 89 P.3d 863 (Idaho 2004).

♦ A Minnesota school district maintained a random controlled substance testing program. It required bus drivers to give sufficient urine specimens to provide a "split sample" as required by federal transportation safety regulations. A driver did not provide a sufficient sample to split. Although his sample tested negative for controlled substances, the district superintendent suspended him for refusing to provide an adequate sample. The suspension letter explained the failure to provide an adequate sample was deemed a positive test result. The driver refused to submit to a second urine test and filed a grievance against the district. The district transportation supervisor told a former district employee the driver had been suspended for refusing to take a drug test, and the driver became a topic of conversation in his rural community. The parties settled the grievance, but the driver sued the district in a federal district court for violating state and federal anti-discrimination laws, a federal transportation employee testing law, and the Minnesota Government Data Practices Act (MGDPA).

The court dismissed most of the claims, but held a jury trial on the MGDPA claim. The jury found for the driver in an amount exceeding $120,000, including $108,000 for loss of reputation, $10,000 for lost earnings and $2,000 for future medical expenses. The court then granted the district's motion for judgment as a matter of law. It stated that to prevail in an MGDPA action, the driver had to prove not only an unlawful disclosure, but actual damages as a direct result. The driver appealed to the U.S. Court of Appeals, Eighth Circuit, which agreed with the district court that **none of the statements alleged by the**

driver supported a defamation claim. He did not show any loss of reputation and contributed to his own damages by speaking to others about the incident. There was insufficient evidence of causation between the disclosure of information and any harm to the driver. The statement by the transportation director about his refusal to take a drug test was not false. There was no evidence that any district employee stated the driver was "a drug user." **The district court correctly held he could not prevail on his MGDPA claim, as he did not prove damage as the direct result of an unlawful disclosure.** *Anderson v. Independent School Dist. No. 97*, 357 F.3d 806 (8th Cir. 2004).

◆ A North Carolina student told her mother that her teacher made her read the word "damn" aloud to her class from an assigned book. She said the teacher made her erase an acronym for "what would Jesus do" from an assignment. The mother reported this to the Rutherford Institute (RI), a religious civil liberties organization. The RI interviewed the mother and student and verified that the book contained the word "damn." It demanded a written apology and reprimands of the teacher and principal. The school district's lawyer responded that the matter was being investigated and expressed doubt about the student's account. The RI interviewed the mother and student again, and they affirmed their account. It also attempted to contact other potential witnesses. The RI issued a press release identifying the school and presenting the student's version of the incident. A few days later, the student admitted she had been lying. The RI issued a press release acknowledging the student had lied and apologizing for the earlier press release. The teacher and principal sued the RI for defamation. A federal district court awarded the RI summary judgment.

The U.S. Court of Appeals, Fourth Circuit, held the district court should have decided the case under state law instead of the U.S. Constitution. As the teacher and principal were public officials, the First Amendment barred them from recovering any damages. The court held for the RI, and the teacher and principal brought a second appeal to the Fourth Circuit. The court explained **the First Amendment limits the ability of states to recover damages by victims of defamation. Damages are available for officials only if the defamer publishes a statement with actual malice on a matter of purely private concern.** The press releases certainly involved the public concern, requiring the imposition of the actual malice standard. The court held a "finding of actual malice requires at a minimum that the statements were made with a reckless disregard for the truth." The RI did not act with actual malice because it further investigated the student's allegations when the school's attorney raised the issue of truthfulness. As the principal and teacher did not present enough evidence to avoid summary judgment, the judgment was affirmed. *Hugger v. Rutherford Institute*, 94 Fed.Appx. 162 (4th Cir. 2004).

◆ Two students reported their teacher grabbed, pushed or choked them after they tried to fast-forward a videotape being viewed by the class. A New York City Board of Education investigative report substantiated the allegations. The board proposed terminating the teacher's employment and shared the investigative report with his union representative in advance of a hearing. The teacher appeared at the hearing with a union representative. The board discharged the teacher, and he pursued a grievance and sued the board in a federal district court for defamation and other claims. The court considered the board's dismissal motion and held the investigative report was not "published" by the board when it provided a copy to the teacher's union representative. This was done to allow him to respond to the allegations in the report.

The court stated the internal dissemination of the report to the board's deputy director was not actionable in a defamation case. This was a "privileged communication among persons who have a common interest in the subject matter." **As the education department had a common interest in protecting students and in investigating and reporting corporal punishment allegations, the defamation claim was dismissed.** The court held the teacher failed to comply with state law notice of claim requirements for the defamation and other tort claims he advanced. There was no private right of action under the state Penal Law and no merit to the teacher's due process violation claim. The board provided him with a hearing prior to discharging him, which was all the process he was due. **As a probationary employee, the teacher had no property interest in continued employment under the Due Process Clause.** No federal claims were available as he had state law remedies, including the arbitration he was still pursuing. The court dismissed the case. *Moore v. New York City Dep't of Educ.*, No. 03 Civ. 2034 (LAP) (S.D.N.Y. 2004).

◆ A Canadian teacher wrote a letter to the principal of a New Jersey high school complaining about the behavior of a teacher during a trip to Spain. The principal showed the letter to the teacher, who was not fired or suspended from her teaching position and was permitted to chaperone other student trips. The teacher sued the Canadian teacher and his school in a New Jersey court for defamation, asserting she had suffered a loss of earnings and grievous mental injury. The court awarded summary judgment to the Canadian teacher and school, finding the letter was not defamatory and that the New Jersey teacher failed to allege damages. A state appellate court affirmed the judgment.

The teacher appealed to the New Jersey Supreme Court, where she argued that even if the letter involved the public interest, she had been improperly deprived of the opportunity to demonstrate that it had been motivated by malice. The court observed that **defamation law requires balancing the competing interests in reputation and the protection of free speech.** When allegedly defamatory remarks involve the public interest, there is a high burden of proof to show actionable defamation. Damages will not be presumed in such cases, and **the complaining party must demonstrate that the defendant published the statement with knowledge of its falsity and reckless disregard for whether it was false or not. There is a strong public interest in the behavior of teachers, especially regarding their conduct with students.** The letter was addressed to this subject and the court held that in view of the teacher's role, she was required to allege monetary damage or loss of reputation, not just embarrassment. The New Jersey teacher failed to allege any specific harm to her reputation and incurred no medical expenses. She had also communicated the contents of the letter to students and others. The court affirmed the judgment for the Canadian teacher and school. *Rocci v. Ecole Secondaire MacDonald-Cartier*, 165 N.J. 149, 755 A.2d 583 (N.J. 2000).

VI. SCHOOL BUS ACCIDENTS

Courts have found school bus drivers and districts liable for injuries to students resulting from the failure to exercise reasonable care in the operation of a vehicle or the design of a bus route. Districts are not liable for injuries caused by sudden and unforeseeable attacks of students on school buses.

A. Duty of Care

◆ A four-year-old Florida child with disabilities endured a four-hour bus ride on his first day of school because the driver lost his way. The driver picked up the child almost an hour late, then drove around in an unsuccessful attempt to pick up other students and find the school. The driver finally got directions and arrived at the school at 12:50 p.m. By then, the child had urinated on himself and appeared to be dehydrated. The child's father took him to a pediatrician, who found no signs of abuse or physical injury. The child began having nightmares and wetting his bed. His parents decided to keep him off school buses and began providing their own transportation. They sued the school board in a state court for negligence and false imprisonment of their son.

The court awarded the board summary judgment on the false imprisonment claim, but allowed a jury to consider the negligence claim. The jury found negligence and the court awarded the child emotional distress damages, despite the lack of any physical injury. On appeal, a Florida district court of appeal held **the "impact rule" requires a personal injury plaintiff to show that any emotional distress must "flow from the physical injuries" suffered from an impact**. Without a physical impact requirement, courts would face a barrage of speculative claims. Neither the pediatrician nor the psychologist who examined the child had found any physical or emotional injury. Since the impact rule barred recovery for emotional injury, the court reversed the judgment on the negligence claim. It affirmed the appeal on the false imprisonment claim. There was no evidence of any intent to confine the child or keep him on the bus. Instead, the bus driver had simply gotten lost. *School Board of Miami-Dade County, Florida v. Trujillo*, 906 So.2d 1109 (Fla. Dist. Ct. App. 2005).

◆ A Washington school bus driver dropped a student off past her usual stop, but closer to her home and on the same side of the street as her house. After the bus pulled away, the student started walking across the street to get her mail and was severely injured when struck by another vehicle. She sued the school district and bus driver in a Washington trial court for negligence. The court held for the district and driver, and the student appealed. The state court of appeals held the accident was not caused by the drop-off location. An expert had testified that any point between where the student was dropped off and her driveway would have been safe. The only proof offered to show the drop-off point was dangerous was the accident itself. The driver did not violate a legal duty towards the student. **State rules governing school bus drivers required drivers to take reasonable action to assure a student crosses a road safely, but only if the student must cross the road.** The student did not need to cross the street to get home, and the driver was unaware that she intended to cross it. As the driver was not negligent, the court affirmed the judgment. *Claar v. Auburn School Dist. No. 408*, 125 Wash. App. 1048 (Wash. Ct. App. 2005).

◆   A Texas special education teacher worked at a school for students with severe behavioral problems, emotional disturbance and learning disabilities. He agreed to drive a special education bus, and soon documented frequent and serious behavioral incidents on his bus. The teacher unsuccessfully sought the district's permission to use a monitor to supervise students. A student sprayed him with a fire extinguisher while he was driving, causing permanent injuries that rendered him unable to teach or drive a bus. The teacher sued the school district in a federal court for knowingly creating a dangerous environment and acting with deliberate indifference to his safety. He claimed the district created a risk of foreseeable injury by segregating students with behavior problems into one school. The court held for the district, and the teacher appealed.

The Fifth Circuit held that with limited exceptions, **the Due Process Clause of the Fourteenth Amendment does not require the government to protect citizens from private parties.** Even if the teacher had a viable claim under this theory, he failed to show the district increased any danger he faced. The conduct of students created the dangers on the bus, and the attack might have occurred with a monitor in place. The court agreed with the district court that **the school district did not create or increase the danger** to the teacher and that the district officials were not deliberately indifferent to known dangers. *McKinney v. Irving Independent School Dist.*, 309 F.3d 308 (5th Cir. 2002).

B. Governmental Immunity

◆   A seven-year-old Alabama student with disabilities attended an intensive therapeutic placement center for students with behavioral and emotional problems. Each day, he rode a five-seat special education bus about 30 miles to the center. According to the student, a classmate sexually assaulted him on a day when a substitute driver drove the bus. The classmate denied the claim, stating the two boys had only exposed themselves to each other. The student's parents sued the board and school officials in a federal court for negligence and civil rights violations. The court held the assault did not result from a school board policy. The substitute driver was entitled to immunity, as driving the bus was a discretionary duty. The parents appealed to the Eleventh Circuit.

The court held the Constitution did not require state entities to protect citizens from private misconduct. Public schools do not generally have the required level of control over students to have any constitutional duty to protect them from violent acts by third parties. The court held the student's special education status did not form a "special relationship" creating a duty by the board to protect him from the classmate. Even if the parents could show deliberate indifference to a known threat, there was no constitutional violation. The decision to place an aide on a special education bus was made by an individualized education committee, not the school board. The parents did not show any board policy was the "moving force" behind the incident. There was no evidence that the classmate had previously committed sexual assault or was a known threat to do so. **The Alabama Supreme Court has repeatedly held**

the supervision of students involves discretion and judgment. Persons who supervise students are entitled to immunity in negligence cases. In any case, the evidence did not show the driver was negligent, and the judgment was affirmed. *Worthington v. Elmore County Board of Educ.*, 160 Fed.Appx. 877 (11th Cir. 2005).

◆ A five-year-old Texas pre-kindergarten child fell asleep on her school bus and was locked inside it for a full afternoon. She apparently fell asleep during the ride to school. After arriving at school, the driver and bus monitor failed to check the bus before locking it. The child's parents sued the school district for negligence in a Texas circuit court. The district claimed sovereign immunity under the Texas Code, but the court denied its motion for pretrial judgment.

The parents appealed to the Court of Appeals of Texas, which explained that **sovereign immunity deprives a court of jurisdiction in actions against the state and school districts. The Texas Code waives immunity for property damage, personal injury and death that "arises from the operation or use of a motor-driven vehicle."** The court found *LeLeaux v. Hampshire-Fannett Independent School Dist.*, 835 S.W.2d 49 (Tex. 1992) lent support to the family's claims. In that case, **the Supreme Court of Texas found the unloading of a school bus was part of the transportation process. Texas case law indicated sovereign immunity is waived when an injury is caused by the negligent use or operation of a bus, but not when injury results from supervision.** The family's claim was based on the "use of the bus." Since the locking of bus door was distinguished from negligent supervision, sovereign immunity was waived. The district court did not commit error in denying the school district's appeal, and the appeals court affirmed this result. *Elgin Independent School Dist. v. R.N.*, 191 S.W.3d 263 (Tex. Ct. App. 2006).

◆ After an accident between a school bus and a car, the driver of the car commenced a personal injury suit against the board and school bus driver in a Virginia trial court. The car driver moved for judgment against the bus driver and the board, and they asserted the defense of sovereign immunity. The court granted their request and dismissed the car driver's motion for judgment, ruling the bus driver was entitled to sovereign immunity for simple negligence and the board's liability was entirely dependent upon and derived from the bus driver's negligence. Because the car driver did not allege gross negligence against the bus driver and the board, the court held that the board was entitled to judgment.

The car driver appealed to the state supreme court, which observed that state law abrogated school board immunity for acts of simple negligence to the amount of a board's insurance coverage. **When the conditions of the statute are met, sovereign immunity will not bar recovery up to the board's policy limits.** The court held the common law principle of coterminous liability among principles and agents was inapplicable when altered by statute. The legislature had subjected school boards to limited liability for injuries caused by the acts of employees and did not require that boards and employees be jointly sued. The statute imposed liability on school boards for simple negligence, even where their employees were liable only for gross negligence. The court reversed the judgment dismissing the car driver's motion for judgment against the board.

The court held the transportation of students on school buses was a governmental function over which the district exercised significant control. **The transportation of students involved discretion and judgment by bus drivers, and the court rejected the car driver's argument that the bus driver had no immunity.** *Linhart v. Lawson*, 540 S.E.2d 875 (Va. 2001).

◆ A student who was stuck by lightning after exiting a bus filed a lawsuit in a Michigan trial court against her school district. A state trial court denied summary judgment to the district on grounds that it was not protected by state law immunity. Although the operation of a bus is a governmental function, and a governmental entity normally enjoys immunity from liability, the court applied an exception for negligent operation of a motor vehicle.

The district appealed to the Michigan Court of Appeals, which observed that the exception claimed by the student applied only to the negligent operation of a motor vehicle owned by the government. **There was no evidence of negligence by the driver in this case, and he was not in violation of any duty imposed by statute, ordinance or school rules and regulations.** The bus stop at which the student exited was reasonably safe, and there were no obvious dangers apart from the temporary hazard of the lightning. **The district did not have a general duty to protect its students from the remote risk of a lightning strike.** Since the student's injuries did not result from the negligent operation of a bus, there was no exception to governmental immunity and the district was entitled to summary judgment. *Carriveau v. Davison School Dist. #25140*, No. 222194, 2001 WL 620145 (Mich. Ct. App. 2001).

◆ A Georgia school district permitted its bus drivers to drop students off at unapproved bus stops where requested by parents. **A five-year-old kindergartner was struck and killed by a van shortly after being dropped off at an unapproved stop on a heavily traveled highway with no sidewalk.** His parents sued the district in a Georgia trial court for wrongful death, seeking the $1 million policy limit under the district's comprehensive liability insurance policy. The court held that because the incident had occurred after the student exited the bus, the injury was not excluded from coverage under the board's comprehensive liability policy. Because sovereign immunity was waived to the extent of insurance coverage, the parents were entitled to receive the policy limit. Coverage did not exist under the board's motor vehicle policy.

The district appealed to the state court of appeals, which dismissed the case. It held any causal connection or relationship between the death and the use of a school bus arose out of the use of the bus, defeating the parents' claim that sovereign immunity had been waived. The parents appealed to the Supreme Court of Georgia, which held the analysis by the court of appeals strained the meaning of "use" of a school bus as contemplated by the policy and improperly disturbed the trial court findings. **As the trial court had correctly determined the death could not have arisen from the use of the bus within the meaning of the liability policy, the court reversed and remanded the case.** *Roberts v. Burke County School Dist.*, 482 S.E.2d 283 (Ga. 1997).

CHAPTER TWO

Religion and the Public Schools

		Page
I.	RELIGIOUS ESTABLISHMENT	55
	A. Prayer and Religious Activity	56
	B. Instruction of Students	60
	1. Curriculum	60
	2. Textbooks	64
	C. Commencement Ceremonies	65
	D. School Policies	67
	1. The Pledge of Allegiance	67
	2. Other Policies	70
	3. Immunization	72
II.	USE OF SCHOOL FACILITIES	74
	A. Assemblies and School-Sponsored Events	74
	B. Student Groups	75
	C. The Equal Access Act	78
	D. Non-Student Use	81
	E. Religious Literature and Symbols	85
III.	LIMITATIONS ON EMPLOYEE RELIGIOUS ACTIVITY	90
IV.	FINANCIAL ASSISTANCE AND VOUCHER PROGRAMS	93

I. RELIGIOUS ESTABLISHMENT

*The Establishment Clause of the First Amendment to the U.S. Constitution prohibits Congress from making any law respecting the establishment of a religion. Because public schools and administrators are subject to this mandate by operation of the Fourteenth Amendment, the courts have struck down practices that improperly entangle public schools with religion. The U.S. Supreme Court has set forth various tests in Establishment Clause cases, but has held **"the touchstone for our Establishment Clause analysis is the principle that the First Amendment mandates government neutrality between religion and religion, and between religion and non-religion."***

The No Child Left Behind (NCLB) Act created a new obligation for school districts to certify in writing to their state educational agencies "that no policy of the local educational agency prevents, or otherwise denies participation in, constitutionally protected prayer in public elementary schools and secondary schools." The requirement is a condition of receiving federal funds. The NCLB section, codified at 20 U.S.C. § 7904, requires the U.S. Education Secretary to provide and revise guidance each two years to state and local educational agencies and the public on "constitutionally protected" prayer in public schools. The Secretary was further directed to issue and secure compliance with rules or orders regarding local agencies that fail to certify, or are "found to have certified in bad faith," that their policies prevent or deny student participation in constitutionally protected prayer in public schools. Federal NCLB Act guidance became a factor in the following Tennessee case.

◆   A Tennessee elementary school student and some of his friends began informally discussing the Bible in a corner of the school playground during recess. Their discussions did not involve any parents, teachers or other adults. A parent complained about Bible discussions at school and the principal stopped the meetings. She later stated she did so because she believed the students had requested formal group meetings during school hours. She felt this would violate the Constitution. The student's family sued the school board and several officials in a federal district court for constitutional violations. **The court found the student's religious expression was entirely private.** The case was governed by *Tinker v. Des Moines Independent Community School Dist.*, 393 U.S. 503 (1969). *Tinker* emphasized that **First Amendment protections for students extend to the cafeteria, playing field or "simply being on the campus during the authorized hours."** The court disagreed with the board's assertion that recess remained instructional time. A trial was necessary to resolve whether the Bible discussions were stopped due to a misunderstanding, or in pursuit of an unconstitutional policy. School officials had repeatedly defended the principal's action and stated that students could only read or discuss the Bible "during their free time, which does not include recess."

The court denied pretrial judgment motions by the school district, principal and superintendent. **The student's constitutional right to read and study his Bible was clearly established.** *Tinker* **established that student speech restrictions are unconstitutional unless there is a showing that speech would materially and substantially interfere with appropriate discipline or collide with the rights of others.** The court held the principal should have been aware of U.S. Department of Education guidelines issued under the No Child Left Behind Act. **The guidelines state that "students may read their Bibles or other scriptures, say grace before meals and pray or study religious materials with fellow students during recess, the lunch hour or other non-instructional time to the same extent that they may engage in nonreligious activities."** The court denied the principal's motion for summary judgment, but held she could renew her motion at trial. *L.W. v. Knox County Board of Educ.*, No. 3:05-CV-274, 2006 WL 2583151 (E.D. Tenn. 2006).

A. Prayer and Religious Activity

◆   A New York school board directed a principal to have a prayer read aloud by each class in the presence of a teacher at the beginning of the school day. This procedure was adopted on the recommendation of the state board of regents. State officials had composed the prayer and published it as part of their "Statement on Moral and Spiritual Training in the Schools." The parents of 10 students sued the board in a state court, insisting that use of this official prayer in public schools violated the Establishment Clause of the First Amendment. The New York Court of Appeals upheld the use of the prayer as long as the schools did not compel any pupil to join in the prayer over the parents' objections. On appeal, the U.S. Supreme Court held the practice was wholly inconsistent with the Establishment Clause. **The Court stated that there could be no doubt that the classroom invocation was a religious activity.** Neither the fact that the prayer was denominationally neutral nor that its observance was voluntary served to free it from the Establishment Clause. *Engel v. Vitale*, 370 U.S. 421, 82 S.Ct. 1261, 8 L.Ed.2d 601 (1962).

◆   Pennsylvania law required that "[a]t least ten verses from the Holy Bible shall be read, without comment, at the opening of each public school on each school day. Any child shall be excused from such Bible reading, or attending such Bible reading, upon written request of his parents or guardian." A family sued school officials to enjoin enforcement of the laws as violative of the First Amendment. A three-judge federal district court panel held that the statutes violated the Establishment Clause, and it granted injunctive relief. The school commissioner of Baltimore had also adopted a rule that mandated the reading of a chapter of the Bible or the Lord's Prayer at the start of each school day without comment. The rule was challenged in the Maryland state court system, which upheld the rule under the First Amendment.

The Supreme Court consolidated the cases and held that both rules violated the Establishment Clause. The Court reiterated the premise of *Engel v. Vitale*, above, that **neither the state nor the federal government can constitutionally force a person to profess a belief or disbelief in any religion. Nor can it pass laws that aid all religions as against nonbelievers.** The Court stated that the primary purpose of the statutes and rule was religious. The Court also noted that it was intended by school officials to be a religious ceremony. The compulsory nature of the ceremonies was not mitigated by the fact that students could excuse themselves. *Abington School Dist. v. Schempp*, 374 U.S. 203, 83 S.Ct. 1560, 10 L.Ed.2d 844 (1963).

◆   **The U.S. Supreme Court invalidated an Alabama statute allowing meditation or voluntary prayer in public school classrooms.** The case was initiated in 1982 by the father of three elementary students who filed a lawsuit in a U.S. district court challenging the validity of two Alabama statutes: a 1981 statute that allowed a period of silence for "meditation or voluntary prayer," and a 1982 statute authorizing teachers to lead "willing students" in a nonsectarian prayer composed by the state legislature. The district court held the First Amendment did not prohibit Alabama from establishing a state religion.

The father appealed to the Eleventh Circuit, which reversed the district court's ruling and held both statutes unconstitutional. The state of Alabama then appealed to the U.S. Supreme Court, which agreed to review only the portion of the court of appeals' decision invalidating the 1981 statute that allowed "meditation or voluntary prayer." The Supreme Court reviewed the legislative history of the 1981 statute and concluded the intent of the Alabama legislature was to affirmatively reestablish prayer in the public schools. **The inclusion of** the words "or voluntary prayer" in the statute indicated that it had been enacted to convey state approval of a religious activity and violated the First Amendment Establishment Clause. *Wallace v. Jaffree*, 472 U.S. 38, 105 S.Ct. 2479, 96 L.Ed.2d 29 (1985).

◆   Two Texas students challenged a number of their school district's practices, including one allowing overtly Christian prayers at graduation ceremonies and football games. The district also permitted nondenominational prayers at graduation ceremonies, read by students selected by vote of the graduating class. In response to the complaint, the district revised its policies for prayer at school functions, subjecting pre-game invocations to the same controls applying to graduation prayers, which required them to be nonsectarian and non-proselytizing. Shortly thereafter, the district enacted new policies deleting the nonsectarian, non-proselytizing requirements for pre-game invocations and graduation prayers. A federal district court issued an order precluding enforcement of the open-ended policy under *Lee v. Weisman*, 505 U.S. 577 (1992), finding the graduation prayers and pre-game invocations coerced student participation in religious events. The parties appealed to the Fifth Circuit, which upheld the validity of the district policy allowing nonsectarian and non-proselytizing high school graduation prayers. The court further held that the district could not extend the graduation prayer policy to athletic events.

The U.S. Supreme Court rejected arguments by the school district that the student invocations could be characterized as private speech. Although the district asserted that students determined the content of the pre-game message without review by school officials and with approval by the student body, the Court found school officials regulated the forum. **The majoritarian process for selecting speakers guaranteed that minority candidates would never prevail and that their views would be effectively silenced. Fundamental rights such as freedom of religion cannot be subjected to a vote. The degree of school involvement in the pre-game prayers created the perception and actual endorsement of religion by school officials.** Finding the district policy created the perception of official encouragement of religion, the Supreme Court affirmed the Fifth Circuit's decision. *Santa Fe Independent School Dist. v. Doe*, 530 U.S. 290, 120 S.Ct. 2266, 147 L.Ed.2d 295 (2000).

◆   A Louisiana parent claimed his children's school permitted prayers to be said over the PA systems at sporting events and in schools. Student-athletes prayed before and after games, and the school board opened its meetings with a prayer. The parent sued the school board in a federal district court for Establishment Clause violations. The parties resolved challenges to most of the practices by consent judgment, but could not agree on the issue of prayers before board meetings. The court then held these prayers violated the Establishment Clause under the traditional analysis of *Lemon v. Kurtzman*, 403 U.S. 602 (1971). The prayers fell outside a limited exception allowing prayers before legislative sessions found in *Marsh v. Chambers*, 463 U.S. 783 (1983). The court permanently enjoined the board from saying prayers at its meetings.

The board appealed to the Fifth Circuit, which found board members, students, school administrators or teachers said most of the prayers at board meetings over a two-year period. Each of the prayers reviewed by the court had a reference to Jesus Christ, God and the Lord. **The court held the Establishment Clause prohibits state or federal governments from promoting any religious doctrine or organization. Government entities cannot discriminate on the basis of religion, nor become too deeply involved with religious institutions.** In *Marsh*, the Supreme Court held the Nebraska state legislature's practice of opening sessions with a prayer did not violate the Establishment Clause, as there is a "unique history" of prayer at legislative sessions dating to 1789. The unwritten practice of selecting speakers to say prayers of their choosing remained in effect after the filing of the lawsuit. The court found the board had violated the Establishment Clause because it allowed explicit references to Jesus Christ, selected persons to offer prayers who referred exclusively to the Christian deity, and did not modify its policy even after the lawsuit was filed. **A reasonable observer at board meetings would perceive the prayers as affiliating the board with Christianity, making them impermissible under the Establishment Clause.** Other federal courts had limited *Marsh* to non-sectarian prayers. The court took no position on whether another form of prayer might be permissible at board meetings. It held only that allowing the Christian prayers in evidence was unconstitutional. *Doe v. Tangipahoa Parish School Board*, 473 F.3d 188 (5th Cir. 2006).

◆ A group of Delaware families claimed their school board and district established religion and prohibited them from exercising their own religious freedom by sponsoring prayers and failing to train school personnel to avoid Establishment Clause violations. Prayers allegedly took place at graduation ceremonies, athletic events, holiday festivals, award presentations, potluck dinners, ice cream socials and other events. The families claimed several teachers referred to religion in classes and awarded students special privileges for participating in school Bible clubs. They asserted board members devised policies on school prayers at graduation and board meetings, but "gave these policies token readings" and refused to distribute copies of the policies or invite public comment. The court found the allegations against the board members involved the development, adoption and implementation of school policies.

The court noted the U.S. Supreme Court's decision in *Marsh v. Chambers*, 463 U.S. 783 (1983). The *Marsh* case held that opening a legislative session or deliberative public body with a prayer did not violate the Establishment Clause. Opening a school board meeting with a prayer was "simply a tolerable acknowledgment of beliefs widely held among the people of this country." **The Delaware court held the practice of opening school board meetings with a prayer was acceptable. Board members were absolutely immune from the claims based on the development, adoption or implementation of policies, practices and customs dealing with religion and prayer.** The court dismissed an additional claim by one parent attempting to hold school board members responsible as supervisors for the actions of teachers in the district. There was no evidence that any board member directed teachers to violate constitutional rights, or that board members knew of and acquiesced to any violations. *Dobrich v. Walls*, 380 F.Supp.2d 366 (D. Del. 2005).

♦   A California school board member recited prayers or invocations at board meetings that made references to Jesus. Teachers brought a federal district court action against the board and its members on behalf of students in the district, asserting violation of the Establishment Clause. The court denied their petition for relief, and the teachers appealed to the U.S. Court of Appeals, Ninth Circuit.

The court noted that while prayers in state legislatures were approved in *Marsh v. Chambers*, 463 U.S. 781 (1983), **the repeated references to Jesus Christ in this case made the prayers and invocations unconstitutional**. Despite the teachers' objections, the references were not removed. The same board member typically said the invocation or prayer, and no other individual of any other faith ever said a prayer or invocation. This advanced Christianity by providing it with a special endorsed or privileged status. **Solemnizing board meetings "in the Name of Jesus" displayed government allegiance to a particular sect or creed.** The court rejected the board's argument that any restriction on the invocations infringed on the First Amendment rights of board members. While individual board members were not prohibited from praying, **the board was not entitled to incorporate regular prayers into its agenda that gave a privileged status to one faith**. *Bacus v. Palo Verde Unified School Dist. Board of Educ.*, 52 Fed.Appx. 355 (9th Cir. 2002).

B. Instruction of Students

1. Curriculum

♦   In 1981, the Louisiana legislature enacted "Balanced Treatment for Creation Science and Evolution Science in Public School Instruction," an act providing that any school offering instruction in evolution must include equal time for instruction in "creation science." The act required that curriculum guides be developed and research services supplied for creation science but not for evolution. The stated purpose of the act was to protect academic freedom. A group of parents, teachers, and religious leaders challenged the law's constitutionality. A federal district court and the Fifth Circuit both held that the act was an unconstitutional establishment of religion, and Louisiana state officials appealed to the U.S. Supreme Court. The Court addressed the issue of whether the Creationism Act was enacted for a clear secular purpose. It noted that **because the act provided for sanctions against teachers who chose not to teach creation science, it did not promote its avowed purpose of furthering academic freedom. The Court ruled that "[b]ecause the primary purpose of the Creationism Act is to advance a particular religious belief, the Act endorses religion in violation of the First Amendment."** The Creationism Act was therefore declared unconstitutional. *Edwards v. Aguillard*, 482 U.S. 578, 107 S.Ct. 2573, 96 L.Ed.2d 510 (1987).

♦   A New York parent helped her child with an environmental poster assignment for his kindergarten class. The child could not yet read, and the parent wrote religious statements on the poster such as "prayer changes things" and "Jesus loves children." The teacher said she did not think she could hang the poster for religious reasons, and because it did not show any learning of the environmental lessons. The school principal told her to have the child make a new poster. The child's mother helped her son select images and arrange them on a new poster. This one had a church, a cross, and a robed, praying figure. The teacher and principal decided to display the second poster, but they folded part of it over to obscure its religious content. The mother sued the district, principal and district superintendent in a federal district court for violations of the child's speech and religious rights. The court held for the district, but in 2001, the Second Circuit vacated the judgment and returned the case to the district court to further develop the evidence. The court again entered judgment for the district, and the case returned to the Second Circuit.

The court found that as the poster was for a class assignment given under specific parameters, the school could regulate its content in a reasonable manner. *Hazelwood School Dist. v. Kuhlmeier*, 484 U.S. 260 (1988) applied to activities that "may fairly be characterized as part of the school curriculum." This included school-sponsored publications, theatrical productions and other expression that the public might reasonably perceive to bear a school's imprimatur. The court held the Establishment Clause claim had been properly dismissed. No evidence indicated the district had acted to inhibit religion. However, as there was a possibility that the principal and teacher were disposed to religious censorship, the mother should have an opportunity to show viewpoint discrimination. Her speech rights claim was returned to the district court. *Peck v. Baldwinsville Cent. School Dist.*, 432 F.3d 617 (2d Cir. 2005).

◆ **A New Jersey parent did not show his children were subjected to a message of disapproval of religion based on an alleged school ban on religious music.** The parent claimed his children's school district had an unwritten policy preventing students from playing traditional Christmas music. He alleged the district conveyed a message that Christianity is disfavored, and sued the district in a federal district court. The school district moved to dismiss the case and submitted a copy of its official policy on religion. The parent objected to consideration of the official policy, asserting it did not reflect the district's actual policy during the 2004-05 school year. He claimed the actual policy more strictly restricted religious music than the official one. The court dismissed the case on the basis of the official policy, and the parent appealed.

The U.S. Court of Appeals, Third Circuit, noted the official policy permitted the use of religious music at religious holidays and concerts, "if it achieves specific goals of the music curriculum." The court rejected the district court's decision not to consider the unofficial policy alleged by the parent. The policy he alleged was significantly more restrictive of religious music than the one officially published by the district. Even if the school's written policy was a public record, the district court had committed error by ruling on it. The court vacated and remanded the case for further proceedings concerning the unofficial policy. *Stratechuk v. Board of Educ., South Orange-Maplewood School Dist.*, 200 Fed.Appx. 91 (3d Cir. 2006).

◆ A federal district court held Pennsylvania's Home Schooling Act did not violate the rights of families who claimed it burdened their religious rights. The families home-schooled their children for five to 13 years before challenging the act. Each of the families was then threatened with prosecution for truancy if they did not comply with the act. The families claimed "education is religious" and asserted that allowing the state to have final authority over the education of their children was sinful. They claimed Act 169 reporting requirements were burdensome and violated the state Religious Freedom Protection Act (RFPA).

A federal district court noted the U.S. Supreme Court has never held an individual may be excused from complying with an otherwise valid law on the grounds of personal religious beliefs. **Religious free exercise does not relieve individuals of the obligation to comply with valid and neutral laws that incidentally forbid or require an act that may be contrary to the individual's religious beliefs.** The court rejected the families' claims that Act 169 requirements were burdensome and violated their rights under the RFPA or the U.S. Constitution. None of the families showed how the filing of an affidavit or the submission of educational logs with samples of student work burdened their right to freely exercise religion or their privacy rights. Nothing in Act 169 restricted the practice of religion. The families only had secular concerns such as health and the expense of extra time and energy. **Parents do not have an absolute or unqualified right to control the upbringing and education of their children.** The court denied each of the families' challenges. *Combs v. Homer Center School Dist.*, No. 04CV 599, 04CV1670, 04CV1932, 04CV1936, 05VC 0070 (ERIE), 05CV203, 2005 WL 3338885 (W.D. Pa. 2005).

◆ **The U.S. Supreme Court let stand a decision by lower courts that held a school district's Islam program did not violate the Establishment Clause of the First Amendment.** Prior to the Court's order denying review, the U.S. Court of Appeals, Ninth Circuit, held the program activities were not "overt religious exercises that raise Establishment Clause concerns." The action was brought by two families who alleged a middle school world history teacher asked them to choose Muslim names, learn prayers, simulate Muslim rituals and engage in other role-playing exercises. The Ninth Circuit held the school district and individual school employees were entitled to qualified immunity "because they did not violate any constitutional right, let alone a clearly-established one." *Ecklund v. Byron Union School Dist.*, No. 05-1539, 74 USLW 3687, 2006 WL 1522671 (U.S. cert. denied 10/2/06).

◆ Dover (Pennsylvania) area residents elected two Fundamentalist Christians to their school board. One became the board's president. He sought to include creationism and prayer in the district curriculum and recommended purchasing a text book advocating "intelligent design." The board accepted 60 copies and forced teachers to use it as a reference text. The board president met with an attorney from a Christian organization to discuss the legality of teaching "intelligent design." The board then voted to change the district's ninth-grade biology curriculum so that "students will be made aware of gaps/problems in Darwin's theory and of other theories of evolution, including but not limited to intelligent design. Note: Origins of Life is not taught." The board issued a press release acknowledging that state academic standards required students to learn Darwin's theory, but stating the theory "was not fact." The press release stated intelligent design was an alternative explanation of the origin of life, and referred students to the intelligent design text book. Resident parents sued the board in a federal district court, asserting Establishment Clause violations.

The court denied several pretrial motions, then conducted a six-week trial. **It held the government violates the Establishment Clause if it fails to be religiously neutral or shows religious favoritism or sponsorship. The government may not convey a message that religion or a particular belief is favored. The court held the intelligent design policy conveyed a message of religious endorsement.** None of the experts who testified at trial could explain how intelligent design "could be anything other than an inherently religious proposition." The disclaimer singled out evolution from everything else being taught in the district, suggesting evolution was a "highly questionable opinion or hunch." While evolution was "overwhelmingly accepted" by the scientific community, intelligent design had been refuted in peer-reviewed research papers. **The conduct of the board members conveyed a strong message of religious endorsement.** The court entered a permanent order preventing the district from maintaining the intelligent design policy and from requiring teachers to denigrate or disparage evolutionary theory. *Kitzmiller v. Dover Area School Dist.*, 400 F.Supp.2d 707 (M.D. Pa. 2005).

◆ A Maryland school board citizens advisory committee recommended health education curriculum changes to address "sexual variation." The board voted to approve the committee's recommendations as a pilot "revised curriculum" at six middle and high schools. The revised curriculum said fundamentalists were more likely to have negative attitudes about gay people than others, and identified Christian sects, notably Baptists, that opposed homosexuality as "unenlightened and Biblically misguided." The revised curriculum asserted the Baptist Church's position on homosexuality was theologically flawed. The revised curriculum stated "it is unreasonable to say a gay, lesbian, bisexual or transgender parent is of lesser moral fiber than a heterosexual parent," and compared religious ostracism of homosexuality with the practice of certain churches that had formerly defended racial segregation.

Opponents of the new curriculum sued the board in a federal district court, seeking to stop implementation of the pilot program. **The court observed the "clearest command" of the Establishment Clause is that one religion cannot be officially preferred.** The revised curriculum violated this mandate by favoring religious sects that were "friendly to the homosexual lifestyle" over others. The court expressed concern that the curriculum proclaimed the Baptist Church intolerant, while lauding churches that were friendly to homosexuals. **The groups had presented a valid First Amendment claim based on a revised curriculum that declared a single view of "the moral rightness of the homosexual lifestyle," to the exclusion of all other perspectives.** The court found there would be no harm to the board if it simply kept its original curriculum in place at the six pilot schools through the end of the school year. As the Establishment Clause and First Amendment claims deserved further consideration, the court issued a temporary order for the community groups. *Citizens for Responsible Curriculum v. Montgomery County Public Schools*, No. Civ.A. AW-05-1194, 2005 WL 1075634 (D. Md. 2005).

◆ A Tennessee school district conducted a Bible education program in three elementary schools, using student volunteers from a private Christian college as instructors. The district did not obtain parental consent for student participation, and there was no evidence any student had ever opted out. A nonprofit organization and some parents filed a federal district court action against the district. The court analyzed the case under tests devised by the U.S. Supreme Court. **While the Supreme Court has never banned all religious activity from public schools, the government may not teach, or allow the teaching of, a particular religious viewpoint. The district violated the Establishment Clause by allowing biblical teaching in elementary schools. The program had the purpose and effect of endorsing and advancing religion.** While biblical literature, history and social customs may be taught in public schools by trained educators in a nondevotional manner, the district did not meet these criteria. The involvement of the Christian college was a constitutionally impermissible entanglement of government and religion. It was doubtful that the program was truly voluntary. The court granted the parents' motion for summary judgment. *Doe v. Porter*, 188 F.Supp.2d 904 (E.D. Tenn. 2002).

On appeal, the U.S. Court of Appeals, Sixth Circuit, held the district had abdicated its supervisory authority over the teaching program. The practices being challenged in this case "resemble paradigmatic cases of unconstitutional entanglement." As the board violated the Establishment Clause, the court affirmed the judgment. *Doe v. Porter*, 370 F.3d 558 (6th Cir. 2004).

2. Textbooks

◆ A Georgia school district's textbook review committee recommended purchasing *Biology* by Miller and Levine as the best available text. School board members were concerned that their constituents wanted texts with "alternate theories of the origin of life." The board adopted a new policy and regulation providing that evolution would be taught in county science classes, and that religion would not be taught. A school attorney drafted a statement that was eventually used on stickers placed on each textbook. The stickers informed students that: "This textbook contains material on evolution. Evolution is a theory, not a fact, regarding the origin of living things. This material should be approached with an open mind, studied carefully, and critically considered." Parents who believed the stickers endorsed religion sued the school board in a federal district court for constitutional rights violations. **The court held that an informed, reasonable observer would believe the stickers sent a message of approval to creationists who opposed the teaching of evolution in public schools. As the board impermissibly entangled itself with religion, the court ordered it to remove the stickers.** The board appealed to the Eleventh Circuit.

The appeals court found the district court had improperly relied on a letter from a parent who objected to the teaching of evolution and a petition that she allegedly submitted to the board prior to its vote to place the stickers on the new textbooks. The district court had specifically relied on the timing of events in finding the stickers had the effect of endorsing religion. However, the record did not establish that the letter and petition were submitted to the board before the vote. The parties had submitted 94 documents to supplement the record, but only two of these were part of the district court's record. None of the documents could have caused the board's decision, as they were all dated after the vote. The court recommended that the district court issue new findings of fact and conclusions of law. Of particular importance would be what petition, if any, was submitted prior to the board's vote. The court vacated and remanded the decision for further proceedings. *Selman v. Cobb County School Dist.*, 449 F.3d 1320 (11th Cir. 2006). In late 2006, the board voluntarily agreed to refrain from placing any stickers or labels disclaiming evolutionary theory in textbooks.

C. Commencement Ceremonies

◆ A Rhode Island student and her father sued their school district in a federal district court to prevent an annual graduation prayer performed by clergy members of various faiths. The court held the clergy-led prayers violated the Establishment Clause of the First Amendment. The defendants appealed to the U.S. Court of Appeals, First Circuit, which also held the prayers violated the Establishment Clause. The First Circuit affirmed the judgment.

On appeal, the U.S. Supreme Court **held the district violated the Establishment Clause by selecting clergy members to say prayers as part of an official public school graduation ceremony. The government may not coerce anyone to support or participate in religion, or otherwise act in any way that establishes a state religion or religious faith, or tends to do so.** In this case, state officials directed the performance of a formal religious exercise. The principal decided that a prayer should be given, selected the clergy participant, and directed and controlled the prayer's content. The district's supervision and control of the graduation ceremony placed subtle and indirect public and peer pressure on attending students to stand as a group or maintain respectful silence during the invocation and benediction. The state may not force a student dissenter to participate or protest. The argument that the ceremony was voluntary was unpersuasive. The Court affirmed the judgment. *Lee v. Weisman*, 505 U.S. 577, 112 S.Ct. 2649, 120 L.Ed.2d 467 (1992).

No Child Left Behind (NCLB) Act guidance from the U.S. Department of Education states that expression is not attributable to the school and may not be restricted because of its religious (or anti-religious) content when students or other private graduation speakers are selected on the basis of genuinely neutral, evenhanded criteria and they retain primary control over their expression. The guidance states that to "avoid any mistaken perception that a school endorses student or other private speech that is not in fact attributable to the school, school officials may make appropriate, neutral disclaimers."

The guidance must be construed in light of Lee v. Weisman, *above. The Ninth Circuit's decision in a California case,* Lassonde v. Pleasanton Unified School Dist. *below, is in apparent conflict with this guidance.*

◆ A California high school principal reviewed a draft of the class salutatorian's graduation speech, which included several proselytizing sentences. The principal decided that allowing the salutatorian to give these remarks at graduation would violate the Establishment Clause. The parties agreed on a modified version of the speech, which the salutatorian delivered. He later sued the district and school officials in a federal district court for constitutional rights violations and for violating a state law prohibiting districts from sponsoring activities that adversely reflect upon persons because of their creed. The court agreed with the officials that their actions were necessary to avoid the appearance of state sponsorship of a proselytizing speech that would violate the Establishment Clause. The Ninth Circuit affirmed the judgment. The officials exercised "plenary control" over graduation exercises, including the principal's review of proposed speeches. **Allowing the salutatorian to go forward with a religiously proselytizing speech would have violated the rights of other students who attended the ceremony. This violated the Establishment Clause**, since a reasonable dissenter would have felt compelled to remain silent and participate in a school-sponsored religious exercise. *Lassonde v. Pleasanton Unified School Dist.*, 320 F.3d 979 (9th Cir. 2003).

◆ Graduating Nebraska seniors voted to follow a district tradition of including an invocation and benediction in commencement ceremonies. The family of one senior contacted the American Civil Liberties Union, which threatened to sue the district if it included prayers in the graduation ceremony. The school board responded by agreeing to remove the prayers from the ceremony. The superintendent of schools opened the ceremony by advising attendees of the need to remove prayers, and the event went on without them. Later in the ceremony, a school board member spoke in accordance with an unwritten tradition allowing board members who were also parents of graduating seniors to make remarks. The board member then asked others to join him in reciting the Lord's Prayer, and concluded by saying "may God be with you always." Although no school official attempted to interrupt him, there was no evidence anyone else knew of his intentions prior to his speech.

The student sued the school district, principal and board member in a federal district court for Establishment Clause violations. The court denied relief to the student, and he appealed. The U.S. Court of Appeals, Eighth Circuit, found the board had agreed to cancel the prayers prior to the graduation ceremony. **The board member's prayer was "private speech," even though he used the graduation ceremony to deliver it. His remarks were not sponsored or approved by the board, and they were constitutionally protected.** The unwritten district policy permitted parent/board members to address graduation ceremonies, and his remarks were in his capacity as a private parent. The court held **private speech remains constitutionally protected, even if it occurs at a school-related function**. As there was no affirmative school sponsorship of prayers by the district, there was no constitutional rights violation. The board member's speech was a one-time action that did not create a district "custom or policy." There could be no liability based on the district's failure to disclaim a single religious exercise. The court affirmed the judgment. *Doe v. School Dist. of City of Norfolk*, 340 F.3d 605 (8th Cir. 2003).

◆ A Florida school district permitted a brief opening and/or closing message by a student volunteer at graduation, if the senior class voted for a message. The policy mandated "the content of that message shall be prepared by the student volunteer and shall not be monitored or otherwise reviewed by Duval County School Board, its officers or employees." A group of objecting students sued the board in federal district court. The court upheld the policy, and the Eleventh Circuit held the case was mooted by the students' graduation. A new group of student objectors sued the district, and the court again upheld the policy. The U.S. Court of Appeals, Eleventh Circuit, initially reversed the decision, but a majority of the Eleventh Circuit later held the absence of state involvement in the student vote, the nomination of a student speaker, and the content of the speech insulated the policy from any finding of facial unconstitutionality.

The U.S. Supreme Court remanded the case to the Eleventh Circuit for reconsideration in view of *Santa Fe Independent School Dist. v. Doe*. The Eleventh Circuit reiterated its finding that **the policy divorced school officials from the decision-making process**. Control over this aspect of the graduation ceremony rested with students, and schools did not adopt or endorse private religious speech by failing to censor messages. The court refused to assume that seniors would interpret the failure to censor student messages as an endorsement of religion. It pointed to numerous factual distinctions between the Duval County case and the Texas school district policy at issue in *Santa Fe*. The Duval County policy referred only to graduation "messages," and it did not encourage prayers, affirmatively forbidding school officials from reviewing student messages. By contrast, the Santa Fe policy subjected student messages to regulation by the high school principal, and therefore, the state. **The Duval County policy did not preordain that a prayer would be delivered**, as the Supreme Court had found in *Santa Fe*. The court reinstated its decision for the county. *Adler v. Duval County School Board*, 250 F.3d 1330 (11th Cir. 2001).

D. School Policies

1. The Pledge of Allegiance

Over 60 years ago, the U.S. Supreme Court held the states cannot compel citizens to recite the Pledge of Allegiance in West Virginia State Board of Educ. v. Barnette, *319 U.S. 624 (1943). The Court held the First Amendment protects both the right to speak freely and the right to refrain from speaking at all. The terrorist attacks of September 11, 2001 prompted many new laws and policies providing for the recitation of the Pledge in public schools.*

◆ The non-custodial father of a California student sued state, local and federal officials in a federal district court, claiming a 1954 Act of Congress adding the words "under God" to the Pledge violated the Establishment Clause. He also claimed a state law requiring elementary schools to open the day with patriotic exercises and the school district's use of daily Pledge recitations violated the Constitution. The court dismissed the case, but the U.S. Court of Appeals, Ninth Circuit, held the father had standing to challenge a practice that interfered with his right to direct his daughter's religious education. It held the 1954 Act and district policy violated the Establishment Clause. The court denied a motion by the child's mother to intervene in the case, even though a state family court order granted her the child's exclusive legal custody. She alleged her daughter was a Christian who did not object to recitation of the Pledge. The Ninth Circuit reconsidered the standing issue and noted the father no longer claimed to represent his daughter. It held he retained a state law right to expose her to his particular religious views, even if they contradicted those of the mother.

The U.S. Supreme Court granted the district's petition for review. It stated that domestic relations was an area in which the Court had customarily declined to intervene. The family court order was the controlling document at the time of the Ninth Circuit's standing decision. It gave the mother the final decision in the event the parents disagreed about the child's education. The Court rejected the father's claim to unrestricted rights to inculcate his daughter in his atheistic beliefs. His rights could not be viewed in isolation from the mother's parental rights. The father could not litigate the case as his daughter's next friend. Nothing done by the mother or the school board impaired his right to instruct the child in his religious views. **The Court held state law did not authorize the father to dictate what others could say or not say to his daughter about religion. It was improper for federal courts to accept a claim by a person whose standing was based on family law rights that were in dispute, when the lawsuit might adversely affect the person who was the very source of the claim to standing.** The Court reversed the judgment. *Elk Grove Unified School Dist. v. Newdow*, 542 U.S. 1, 124 S.Ct. 2301, 159 L.Ed.2d 98 (2004).

◆ Florida Statutes Section 1003.44(1) required students to obtain their parents' written permission to be excused from reciting the Pledge of Allegiance. A school district patterned its policy after the law. Like the statute, the policy stated that "when a parent requests in writing, the student must be excused from reciting the pledge." It provided that each student had the right not to participate in daily Pledge recitations, but stated that "any student who is excused from reciting the pledge must still show full respect for the flag by standing at attention while the pledge is recited." A fourth-grade student was removed from class after he remained seated during a Pledge recitation. He sued the school and state and local education officials in a federal district court.

The court noted "a longstanding rule of constitutional law that a student may remain quietly seated during the pledge on grounds of personal or political belief." Many federal courts recognized the right of students to remain silent and seated during the Pledge, including the Eleventh Circuit. Parental rights to direct a child's education did not create a parental approval requirement for the exercise of a child's speech rights. The court held unconstitutional the parts of the state law requiring students to obtain a parent's excuse from reciting the Pledge and requiring students to stand during the Pledge. School officials could not require students to stand or obtain parental permission to be excused from reciting the Pledge. The board had to rescind its policy and was also ordered to pay the student $32,500. *Frazier v. Alexandre*, 434 F.Supp.2d 1350 (S.D. Fla. 2006).

◆ Virginia law provides for the daily, voluntary recitation of the Pledge and placement of the U.S. flag in each public school classroom. Loudoun County Public Schools implemented the provision through a policy allowing students to remain seated quietly during Pledge recitation if their parents objected on religious, philosophical or other grounds. An Anabaptist Mennonite parent asserted the Pledge indoctrinated his children with a "'God and Country' religious worldview" and violated the Mennonite Confession of Faith. He sued the school system in a federal district court, asserting the inclusion of the words "under God" in the Pledge made it a religious exercise that violated the Establishment Clause. The Commonwealth of Virginia intervened in the case.

The court dismissed the action, finding recitation of the Pledge was a secular activity that neither advanced nor inhibited religion. The parent appealed to the U.S. Court of Appeals, Fourth Circuit. **The court stated that the Establishment Clause bars state and federal governments from aiding one religion, all religions, or preferring one religion, but does not require separation of church and state "in every and all aspects."** It rejected the parent's assertion that Pledge recitation amounted to a daily prayer. **The Supreme Court has indicated "fleeting references to God in the class-room [are] not unconstitutional."** The Pledge recognized only the fact that the founding fathers considered the nation to be one under God. Former Supreme Court Justice Sandra Day O'Connor characterized the words "under God" as an "acknowledgment of religion with the legitimate secular purposes of solemnizing public occasions, and expressing confidence in the future." The court held Pledge recitation was a patriotic exercise to foster national unity and pride. As the Pledge was a statement of loyalty to the U.S. and its flag, prayer cases were irrelevant. The court held the Establishment Clause "does not extend so far as to make unconstitutional the daily recitation of the Pledge in public school," and it affirmed the judgment for the school system and commonwealth. *Myers v. Loudoun County Public Schools*, 418 F.3d 395 (4th Cir. 2005).

◆ A few days before graduating, an Alabama student raised his fist and remained silent while the rest of his class recited the Pledge. He did this to protest the treatment of a classmate who had previously objected to reciting the Pledge. The principal told the student he could not receive a diploma unless he served three days of detention and apologized to the class. As there was not enough time left in the school year for the student to serve the detention and still receive a diploma, he accepted the alternative punishment of a paddling. The student sued the teacher, principal and school board in a federal district court, claiming First Amendment violations. He then added a claim based on a teacher's practice of beginning each school day by asking students for prayer requests and holding a moment of silence. The court held the teacher, principal and school board were all entitled to immunity, and the student appealed.

The U.S. Court of Appeals, Eleventh Circuit, noted that *West Virginia State Board of Educ. v. Barnette*, **319 U.S. 624 (1943) established a clear right for students to refuse to say the Pledge.** Any reasonable person would have known that disciplining the student for refusing to recite the Pledge violated his First Amendment rights. **School officials may reasonably restrict the time, place and manner of student expression, but cannot discriminate on the basis of viewpoint. Officials may only regulate student expression that materially and substantially interferes with school activities or discipline.** The court found the student was being punished for his unpatriotic views, not for being disruptive. As this violated his clearly established rights to free expression and freedom from compelled speech, the officials were not entitled to immunity. **The school board was liable for violating the student's speech rights, as it had an official policy of requiring students to say the Pledge.** *Holloman v. Harland*, 370 F.3d 1252 (11th Cir. 2004).

◆ Pennsylvania Act 157 of 2002 required all public and private schools to display the U.S. flag in each classroom, and to conduct daily recitations of the Pledge of Allegiance or the National Anthem. Although students could opt out of daily recitations for personal or religious reasons, school officials had to report any such refusal to parents in writing. The law exempted religious and parochial schools from displaying the flag and conducting Pledge or Anthem recitations. No similar exception applied to nonreligious private schools. A federal district court held the parental notification requirement deterred public school students from their right to abstain from recitations. The law violated a fundamental liberty interest of parents to direct the education of their children and interfered with private school educational missions and association rights.

On appeal, the Third Circuit struck down **the parental notification requirement as viewpoint discrimination**. It was only triggered when a student exercised the right to refrain from a Pledge or Anthem recitation. This supported a finding that **the clause was drafted to deter students from opting out**. The court also held **the daily Pledge or Anthem recitations substantially burdened freedom of choice for private schools**. The notion that schools could overcome this burden through disclaimers did not erase the law's First Amendment infringement. The government interest in teaching patriotism could be satisfied in other ways besides rote recitation. The court held the law violated private school free association rights, and affirmed the judgment. *Circle School v. Pappert*, 381 F.3d 172 (3d Cir. 2004).

◆ The U.S. Court of Appeals, Fifth Circuit, affirmed the dismissal of an action filed by a Texas parent who claimed several practices of a school district violated the Constitution. These included the Pledge of Allegiance, the use of certain symbols, and its observance of school holidays and celebrations. A federal district court properly dismissed the case because no reasonable observer would find the disputed phrases, symbols and actions indicated government approval of religion. *Mellen v. Congress of the U.S.*, 105 Fed.Appx. 566 (5th Cir. 2004).

2. Other Policies

◆ A New York school district released Catholic and Protestant students to nearby programs at designated times during the school day. Others remained in classrooms with nothing to do until released students returned. A family claimed the program led to "abusive religious invective directed against those who did not participate and that the district did not adequately train teachers and principals to protect non-participants from the taunts of program participants." The family sued the district in a federal district court, asserting the "released time" program violated the Establishment Clause by promoting Christianity over other religions and non-religion. The court held for the district, ruling it did not implement the released-time provision of state Education Law Section 3210(2)(b) in a way that advanced Christianity over other religions and non-religion. The family appealed to the U.S. Court of Appeals, Second Circuit.

The court explained the released-time program authorized by New York Education Law Section 3210(2)(b) and state regulations permitted districts to release students, with parental permission, for one hour per week for religious instruction. The U.S. Supreme Court upheld this law in *Zorach v. Clauson*, 343 U.S. 306 (1952). The family insisted the district's implementation of the program violated the Establishment Clause by favoring Christianity over other religions and non-religion. The court disagreed, finding nothing in this case suggested a different result than *Zorach*. **The program used no public funds and involved no on-site religious instruction. Schools simply adjusted their schedules to accommodate student religious needs. The court rejected the argument that the school's imprimatur was placed on a program of religious instruction** and that churches used the schools in support of their religious missions. Nothing in this case suggested the released time program was administered in a coercive manner. Because the district implemented the law consistently with *Zorach*, the court affirmed the judgment. *Pierce v. Sullivan West Cent. School Dist.*, 379 F.3d 56 (2d Cir. 2004).

◆ A Michigan high school student council invited student organizations to help with panel discussions for its 2002 Diversity Week. The faculty advisor agreed to turn over a panel on sexual orientation to the Gay/Straight Alliance (GSA) and its two faculty co-sponsors, both of whom were openly gay teachers at the school. The GSA Club invited religious leaders to speak and expanded the panel discussion to "homosexuality and religion." The club arranged for six speakers, including a "very gay friendly" minister. A member of the "Pioneers for Christ" student club was denied permission to include clergy members with opposing viewpoints on the panel. An e-mail sent by the advisor acknowledged the Pioneer Club's legal right to be on the panel and recited the available options of canceling the panel or allowing the Club to speak. The principal rejected the student's request for her club to appear on the panel, because she failed to attend a "mandatory" student council meeting. The faculty advisor offered to let the student speak about "what diversity means to me." She accepted the offer, but changed her mind when the principal disapproved parts of her message. During the panel discussion, panelists stated biblical passages had been misconstrued by others to mean homosexuality was incompatible with Christianity.

The student and her mother sued the school district, principal and staff in a federal district court for violating her constitutional rights. The court explained that educators must remain neutral to the viewpoint of student speech in school-sponsored forums. **The decisions to restrict the student's speech and exclude her club from the panel were not viewpoint neutral. They were motivated by the school's disagreement with her message. The administrators suppressed the student's speech in violation of the First Amendment.** Their decision was made despite full knowledge of her club's speech rights, as the advisor's e-mail indicated. The school's stated reasons for excluding the student, particularly her absence from the "mandatory" meeting, were pretextual. **The administration violated the Establishment Clause by** creating a panel with an overtly religious message. **The panel was created to convey only a religious viewpoint that homosexuality is not condemned in the Bible.** The court described this as "one-way diversity." The administration's actions discriminated against the student in violation of the Equal Protection Clause. The court denied immunity to the administrators, as they had violated the student's clearly established fundamental rights. *Hansen v. Ann Arbor Public Schools,* 293 F.Supp.2d 780 (E.D. Mich. 2003).

◆ Maryland law established a public school holiday from the Friday before Easter through the Monday after Easter. A Maryland teacher asserted the law violated the Establishment and Equal Protection Clauses of the U.S. Constitution because she was required to use personal leave or leave without pay to observe Jewish holidays. She filed a federal district court action against state education officials, seeking a declaration that the school holiday was unconstitutional. The court considered the parties' cross motions for summary judgment and observed that Easter is now highly secularized. The statutory vacation period surrounded Easter and did not mention Good Friday. The Monday after Easter has no religious significance. The school officials advanced a secular purpose for the statute. Many students and teachers would be absent on the Friday and Monday surrounding Easter, which might disrupt effective instruction and cause monetary outlays for substitute teachers.

The court held the law did not violate the Establishment or Equal Protection Clauses, and it granted summary judgment to the school officials. The teacher appealed to the U.S. Court of Appeals, Fourth Circuit, which stated **the law was not facially unconstitutional because it provided an annual holiday to all students and teachers, regardless of religious affiliation**. The law passed the *Lemon* test because it had the legitimate secular purpose of economizing scarce educational resources that would otherwise be wasted on days when many students and teachers would be absent. The holiday did not advance or endorse Christianity over other religions. Entanglement between the state and religion also did not occur. The district court decision was upheld. *Koenick v. Felton,* 190 F.3d 259 (4th Cir. 1999).

3. Immunization

School districts and state educational agencies have a compelling state interest in requiring the immunization of all students in an effort to prevent and control communicable diseases.

◆ Arkansas Code Section 6-18-702(a) prevented schools from admitting students without certification of immunization for specified diseases. It made an exemption available to parents who objected to immunization on religious grounds if they were members of a "recognized church or religious denomination." Four Arkansas students filed separate federal district court actions against state and local officials, asserting Section 6-18-702(a) violated the Establishment Clause by limiting the exemption from immunization to those who objected on religious tenets and practices of a "recognized" church or denomination. In two cases, the students claimed they had sincere religious beliefs even though they did not belong to a religion "recognized" by the state. The courts held the exemption violated the Establishment Clause, agreeing with the students that the exemption had a discriminatory impact on religious groups not officially recognized by the state. One of the decisions held state education department regulations improperly entangled the state with religion by requiring officials to inquire into the sincerity of student religious beliefs. Although the courts found the exclusion unconstitutional, it was severable from the rest of the immunization law. As a result, the students still had to be immunized. *McCarthy v. Boozeman*, 212 F.Supp.2d 934 (W.D. Ark. 2002), and *Boone v. Boozeman*, 217 F.Supp.2d 938 (E.D. Ark. 2002).

The students appealed to the Eighth Circuit, which observed the Arkansas legislature had by then amended Section 6-18-702 to omit the references to "recognized religions." The exemption was now available to any student whose family had religious or philosophical objections to immunization. The state health department passed regulations implementing the law. The court observed that none of the students were denied the benefit of the new exemption under the amended law or regulations. **The legislative amendment made the exemption to immunity available to each of the students. As the legislature had provided them even greater relief than they sought by bringing the litigation, the case was now moot.** The court rejected the students' speculative arguments that the legislature might repeal the new legislation or that the amendment discriminated against religious objectors. The legislature had acted to protect students and other citizens, and the health department had acted quickly to pass new regulations. The state had powers to exclude nonimmunized students from school during an outbreak or other emergency. Neither the amended law nor the regulations allowed officials to assess the merits of a student's religious beliefs. As the case was now moot, the court dismissed it. *McCarthy v. Ozark School Dist.*, 359 F.3d 1029 (8th Cir. 2004).

◆ Members of "the Congregation of Universal Wisdom" objected to the introduction of any foreign material into the body on religious grounds. A New York student and her mother, who were members of the congregation, notified their school district of their religious objection to New York Public Health Law Section 2164, which requires immunization before admission to public school. The district determined the congregation was not a genuine religion and denied the mother's objection. The district found her objection was based on personal philosophy, not a legitimate religion. The school board denied the mother's appeal, and she sued the board and district in a federal district court, alleging violation of the Constitution and Section 2164. The court allowed the student to attend school pending consideration of the case. While it found her religious affiliation "questionable," the court said she was likely to prevail on the merits of the case because her objection was apparently based on religion, not philosophical or scientific reasons. The board moved to dismiss the case.

The court observed Section 2164 exempts children from the immunization requirement if their parents hold genuine and sincere religious beliefs that are contrary to immunization. The court applied the three-part Establishment Clause analysis from *Lemon v. Kurtzman*, 403 U.S. 602 (1971). It found the exemption was sufficiently neutral to satisfy the secular purpose test, because it did not favor one religion over another. Instead, it exempted all religious believers from immunization if their faith required it. The law did not violate the religious effect part of the test because it did not confer any financial benefit on religious believers. It only permitted those with genuine and sincere beliefs to live in conformity with their beliefs. The exemption did not have the effect of advancing or inhibiting religion because it did not promote religion or favor one religious group over another. The court held **the exemption did not create religious entanglement because it did not directly subsidize or benefit religious organizations. School officials were not required to assess the validity of parental beliefs when determining whether they were genuine or sincere.** The court denied the board's motion for summary judgment. *Turner v. Liverpool Cent. School*, 186 F.Supp.2d 187 (N.D.N.Y. 2002).

II. USE OF SCHOOL FACILITIES

Courts use the "forum analysis" when considering the use of school facilities and the types of expression that have been approved by a school. A "limited public forum" exists whenever a government agency voluntarily opens up its facilities or programs for public use. The "forum" may be a bulletin board, public address system, or the use of classrooms for meetings during noninstructional time. Once a district makes the decision to open a limited public forum, any restriction it places on speech must be reasonable in view of the purposes of the forum. There can be no discrimination on the basis of viewpoint. The nature of the forum determines the limits that may be placed on speech by intended users. The forum analysis applies in both religious and secular speech cases. Groups including Gay/Straight Alliance Clubs have relied on court precedents discussing the access rights of religious groups in their efforts to gain official recognition. For additional cases involving the forum analysis and secular speech, see Chapter Three, Section V.

A. Assemblies and School-Sponsored Events

◆ A New Jersey school district hosted after-school talent shows called "Frenchtown Idol." The shows were held at 7:00 p.m. in the school auditorium and were entirely voluntary. Students were invited to develop their own performances at home and received no school credit for participating. Three teachers reviewed all song lyrics, skits, and acts. A student submitted "Awesome God" as her talent show selection. The district superintendent found this inappropriate for the show because of its "overtly religious message and proselytizing nature." She found the song was "the musical equivalent of a spoken prayer." The music teacher informed the student she could not sing "Awesome God" at the show and offered her two songbooks to select a replacement. She suggested the selection of another song, even if it was a religious one. The student sued the board in a federal district court.

The court noted that elementary schools are not traditional public forums that are open to all speech. The talent show was not a "school-sponsored production," as the school invited students to display their own

talent, not to convey its own message. Speech taking place in the show "was the private speech of a student and not a message conveyed by the school itself." The board could not engage in viewpoint discrimination. Any restrictions on speech had to be viewpoint neutral and reasonable in view of the purposes served by the forum. The court held the exclusion of speech simply because it is controversial or divisive is "viewpoint discrimination." The board engaged in viewpoint discrimination. The song was banned based on the belief that it "would likely be offensive to some in the audience." The court rejected the school board's argument that it had to exclude the song to avoid an Establishment Clause violation. It was unlikely an audience would perceive the student's song to be the expression of anyone's view but her own. The court awarded summary judgment to the student. *Turton v. Frenchtown Elementary School Dist. Board of Educ.*, 465 F.Supp.2d 369 (D.N.J. 2006).

◆ A group of Ohio high school students had a band that performed mostly Christian songs. The father of one student was a school board member and the band's manager. He sought approval for a band performance at a school-wide assembly during school hours. The district superintendent initially consented to the performance but cancelled it after a school attorney warned her of Establishment Clause problems. The news media reported cancellation of the event, and the board member appeared in a television interview. He said "together we can bring religion back into the schools." The board then asked another band that performed secular music to perform at the assembly.

The Christian band members sued the school district in a federal district court, asserting their appearance had been cancelled because of disapproval of their Christian message. The court rejected the band members' claim that the assembly was a public forum in which the district had to maintain viewpoint neutrality. **The assembly was not a "forum" of any kind, and for that reason, the district was not subject to any neutrality requirement.** The school district "was entitled to exercise editorial control" over it. When the school itself was the speaker, educators were entitled to exercise greater control to assure the views of speakers were not erroneously attributed to the school. **The school district was entitled to discriminate against the band members because of their Christian religious identity precisely because an audience might associate that identity with the school. The district was entitled to select whom it wished to represent the school, and it had a compelling state interest in avoiding a potential Establishment Clause violation.** The court awarded pretrial judgment to the school district. *Golden v. Rossford Exempted Village School Dist.*, 445 F.Supp.2d 820 (N.D. Ohio 2006).

B. Student Groups

◆ A New York student submitted a request to use school facilities for private religious club meetings after school hours. The superintendent denied the request, stating this use of facilities amounted to school support of religious worship. The club commenced a federal district court action against the school under 42 U.S.C. § 1983 for violation of its speech, equal protection and other federal rights. The court issued an order preventing the school from prohibiting the club's use of school facilities, but it later awarded judgment to the school. The club appealed to the Second Circuit, which held the school's denial of access was permissible because it was based on content rather than viewpoint.

The club appealed to the U.S. Supreme Court, which observed **the nature of the forum determines the limits that a school may place on speech taking place in the forum.** The school had established a limited public forum in which it could reasonably seek to avoid identification with a particular religion. **While the school was not required to allow all speech, limits on speech could not be based upon viewpoint and had to be reasonable in light of the purpose of the forum.** The Court held the school's policy broadly permitted speech about the moral and character development of children. **The school had excluded the club from school facilities solely because of its religious viewpoint. This resulted in unconstitutional viewpoint discrimination.** The Court found no difference between the club and other student organizations that were not excluded. It held "speech discussing otherwise permissible subjects cannot be excluded from a limited public forum on the ground that the subject is discussed from a religious viewpoint." Club meetings took place after school hours and were not sponsored by the school. No risk of coercion was present, because students had to obtain permission from their parents before attending meetings. The district failed to show any risk of school endorsement of religion. The Court reversed the judgment. *Good News Club v. Milford Cent. School*, 533 U.S. 98, 121 S.Ct. 2093, 150 L.Ed.2d 151 (2001).

◆ A South Carolina school district charged the Child Evangelism Fellowship of South Carolina fees to use its facilities for Good News Club meetings after school. Many other users had free access to school facilities, including parent-teacher and district organizations, booster clubs, political parties, the SADD, 4-H, FFA and FHA. After paying the district over $1,500 during a two-year period, the Good News Club sought a waiver from the fee. The district denied the request, and the club sued the school board in a federal district court. The board eliminated a "best interest" waiver provision from the policy. A new provision waived fees for organizations that had used its facilities for at least 20 years. The only organizations meeting this definition were scouting groups.

The court found the waiver provision "left a conspicuous door open" for school administrators to deny free access to facilities based on viewpoint. However, it rejected the club's challenge, finding the board had applied its policy neutrally. The club appealed to the U.S. Court of Appeals, Fourth Circuit. **The court explained that the government may not regulate speech based on its content or the message it conveys. Once government facilities are opened for private speech, an agency may not discriminate based upon the viewpoint of the speaker.** Recent Supreme Court cases indicate "any tension between the Establishment and Free Speech Clauses that may have motivated past exclusion of religious groups from government forums is more apparent than real." The court held that school administrators do not possess "unfettered discretion to burden or ban speech." The fee waiver did exactly that. **The "best interest of the district" provision was subjective and "a virtual prescription for unconstitutional decision making."** The fee waiver policy violated the First Amendment, since nothing prevented officials from encouraging some views and discouraging others through the arbitrary application of fees. The Good News Club was the only group that had ever been denied a request for a "best interest waiver." The court reversed the judgment, as there was a threat of viewpoint discrimination. *Child Evangelism Fellowship of South Carolina v. Anderson School Dist. Five*, 470 F.3d 1062 (4th Cir. 2006).

◆   A Michigan school district allowed the Boy Scouts to make recruiting visits in its schools during school hours and to use school facilities during non-school hours. The Scouts and other community groups were allowed to distribute and post literature in public schools. A parent enrolled his third-grade son in the Scouts. He volunteered to be a den leader, but stated the Scouts' religious declaration was contrary to his beliefs. The Scouts rejected the parent's request to be exempt from the declaration and revoked his membership. The district complied with the parent's request to put a disclaimer on Scouting literature "informing parents of the religious character of the Boy Scouts." The parent was dissatisfied with the disclaimer, and sued the district and local Scouting affiliate in a state court under the Michigan Constitution and state law. The court held for the Scouts, and the parent appealed to the Court of Appeals of Michigan.

   The court found the district's facilities use policy had the secular purpose of encouraging public use of school facilities for worthwhile purposes that did not interfere with school. While Scouts and other "school-related" groups had free use of facilities and priority over non-school groups, this was not a district preference for religion. The policy was secular, neutral, and did not advance religion over non-religion. **There was no Establishment or Equal Protection Clause violation in the district's decision to allow the Scouts to meet in its facilities after school.** The district did not grant a special privilege to the Scouts. There had been no religious aspect in Scout literature until the parent demanded inclusion of a religious disclaimer. In-school recruiting visits by Scouts during school hours did not violate the Constitution. **The Scouting affiliate was not a primarily religious organization, and the district's decision to allow informational meetings did not have a primary effect of advancing religion.** Recitation of the Scout Promise or Oath took place at voluntary private meetings. A private organization such as the Scouts was not subject to the restrictions of the Michigan Constitution. **The district's acquiescence in the use of neutral school policies did not create "state action" by the Scouts.** The court affirmed the judgment. *Scalise v. Boy Scouts of America*, 265 Mich. App. 1, 692 N.W.2d 858 (Mich. Ct. App. 2005). The Supreme Court of Michigan denied further reconsideration of the case. *Scalise v. Boy Scouts of America*, 474 Mich. 1065, 713 N.W.2d 252 (Mich. 2006).

◆   An Oregon school district let Boy Scout representatives make presentations during school lunch periods when students were required to be present. School employees helped the Scouts by quieting children, directing attention to the Scout representative and helping fasten hospital-style bracelets on students with information on Scout meetings. Staff also distributed Scout flyers in classes and put Scout information in school newsletters. An atheist parent objected to these practices and claimed that a religious membership criterion of the Scouts made her son ineligible to join. She filed a discrimination complaint against the district under Oregon Statutes Section 659.850. "Discrimination" under the statute included intentional and unintentional acts, and could result from "any act that is fair in form but discriminatory in operation." The state superintendent of public instruction investigated the complaint, but did not find substantial evidence of discrimination. A state circuit court reversed the superintendent's ruling, and the Court of Appeals of Oregon affirmed the decision.

The Supreme Court of Oregon reviewed the case, and noted there was no challenge to district policies under the Establishment Clause. The parent did not challenge the decision to allow Boy Scout recruiting at school, but only sought to determine whether the district had discriminated under Section 659.850. **The court held it was clear that there can be no discrimination on the basis of religion or other protected grounds in any public school program, service or school activity**. Class time and lunch periods were "school activities." However, handing out Boy Scout flyers and making presentations did not transform all Scout activities into a public school activity. The district would discriminate against the student if it treated him differently, or permitted the Boy Scouts to treat him differently than others because of religion. **The court found no different treatment in this case, because the flyers and other information were distributed to all students, with no mention of a religious affiliation**. The court found the lunchroom presentations were neutral in content, making no mention of religion or a religious requirement for joining the Scouts. The use of wristbands did not introduce any religious element into the presentations. The court rejected the argument that simply exposing the student to a message about the Boy Scouts subjected him to different treatment. Scout recruiting at school was not discriminatory, and any enrollment of students in the organization took place away from school. The court reversed the judgment. *Powell v. Bunn*, 341 Or. 306, 142 P.3d 1054 (Or. 2006).

C. The Equal Access Act

The federal Equal Access Act (EAA), 20 U.S.C. §§ 4071-4074, governs student use of secondary school facilities during noninstructional time. It makes it unlawful for a public secondary school to deny equal access to facilities, if the school maintains a "limited open forum." A limited open forum exists where student groups have been accorded the right to meet in non-curricular groups on school grounds during noninstructional time.

Congress selected the term "limited open forum" in the EAA to describe a school district's opening of school programs or facilities for non-curricular uses during noninstructional time. U.S. Supreme Court First Amendment cases employ the term "limited public forum," not "limited open forum." Courts have noted the terms are not identical, so districts must comply with both standards.

◆   A Nebraska high school student wanted permission to begin a Christian Club. The school permitted its students to join, on a voluntary basis, a number of groups and clubs that met after school. Each of these clubs had faculty sponsors. However, the student who wished to start the Christian Club did not have a faculty sponsor. School administrators denied her request because she did not have a sponsor and because they believed a religious club at the school would violate the Establishment Clause. The student sued the school board and administrators in a federal district court. She alleged a violation of the EAA. The district court ruled in favor of the school, holding that the other clubs at the school related to the school's curriculum and thus, the school did not have a "limited open forum" as defined by the EAA.

The student appealed to the Eighth Circuit, which ruled in her favor. The school then appealed to the U.S. Supreme Court, which stated the other clubs did not relate to the school's curriculum. **The school had to provide a limited open forum to all students wishing to participate in groups.** The EAA provided that schools could limit activities that substantially interfered with their orderly conduct. The Court also stated **the EAA did not violate the Establishment Clause because it had a secular purpose and limited the role of teachers who work with religious clubs**. The Court affirmed the decision, holding the school violated the EAA. *Board of Educ. of Westside Community School v. Mergens*, 496 U.S. 226, 110 S.Ct. 2356, 110 L.Ed.2d 191 (1990).

In the following case, the U.S. Court of Appeals, Eighth Circuit, suggested ways for schools to limit EAA claims by decreasing the number of curriculum-related student groups. The court held a Minnesota school district could legitimately categorize cheerleading and synchronized swimming classes as "curriculum related" by awarding P.E. credits to participating students. A more drastic option would be to "wipe out all of its noncurriculum related student groups and totally close its forum."

◆ A Minnesota school district recognized about 60 student groups. "Curricular groups" related to the school curriculum and were school-sponsored. These groups could use school PA systems and other school facilities and participate in yearbook, fundraisers and field trips. "Noncurricular groups" could not use the same facilities and could not fundraise or take school field trips. The district classified a gay tolerance organization as "noncurricular." The organization claimed the district violated the EAA by denying it access to school facilities enjoyed by other noncurricular groups like cheerleading and a synchronized swimming club. A federal district court granted the organization's request for a preliminary order, finding cheerleading and synchronized swimming, like the tolerance group, were "noncurricular."

The district appealed to the U.S. Court of Appeals, Eighth Circuit, where it argued that cheerleading and synchronized swimming related to the physical education curriculum and were thus "curricular." **The court explained that the EAA prohibits public secondary schools from discriminating against students on the basis of speech, where the school has opened a "limited open forum."** A limited open forum exists when one or more noncurriculum related group is allowed to meet on school grounds during non-instructional time. The court noted the EAA is triggered even if a school permits only one noncurriculum group. A curriculum-related group is one that directly relates to a school curriculum. The court agreed with the gay tolerance group that cheerleading and the synchronized swimming club were not curriculum-related. The school offered no courses for these activities, and they were not required for a particular course. As cheerleading and synchronized swimming were not curriculum-related, the gay tolerance group was on the same ground as they were and could use the facilities they enjoyed. The court affirmed the district court's preliminary order for the gay tolerance group. *Straights and Gays for Equality v. Osseo Area Schools-Dist. No. 279*, 471 F.3d 908 (8th Cir. 2006).

◆ A Pennsylvania school district established an "activity period" after homeroom and prior to the first class of the day. During this time, students had to remain on school grounds but could participate in club meetings, go to study hall, attend student activities or relax. The district recognized three student groups as "curriculum-related" and allowed them to meet during the activity period, post signs and use the public address system. A student Bible Club was not allowed to meet during the activity period. A club member sued the school board in a federal district court for violating the EAA and her First Amendment speech rights. The court denied her request for a preliminary order, finding the activity period was not "noninstructional time" under the EAA.

The student appealed to the Third Circuit, which explained that a limited open forum is created whenever a school allows at least one non-curriculum-related student group to meet on school grounds during noninstructional time. "Noninstructional time" could include the activity period, even though it was neither before the start of the school day, nor after its conclusion. The district had set aside the activity period as noninstructional time. **The court rejected an interpretation of the EAA that would allow districts to evade application of the Act by describing an otherwise "limited open forum" as time that counted toward student instruction.** The court held the district violated the EAA by forbidding Bible club meetings during the activity period. Its action could not be justified as necessary to avoid an Establishment Clause violation. The government may not discriminate against speech based on viewpoint when it has created a limited open forum. The court reversed the order dismissing the damage claims and remanded the case to determine damages and attorneys' fees. *Donovan v. Punxsutawney Area School Board*, 336 F.3d 211 (3d Cir. 2003).

◆ Washington students established a religious club. Their district rejected a request by the club's student organizer to gain official recognition as an "associated student body" (ASB) club, stating that religious organizations could only be formed as "Policy 5525 clubs." The ASB designation allowed student organizations many benefits, including access to funding, school facilities, and use of school public address systems. The student sued the district and officials in a federal district court action for EAA and First Amendment violations. The court awarded judgment to the district, finding the school was a nonpublic forum and the distinction between types of student clubs did not violate the Free Speech or Free Exercise Clauses of the First Amendment.

The student appealed to the Ninth Circuit, which rejected the district's argument that the EAA only required that student religious groups receive a "fair opportunity" for access to school facilities. The EAA's legislative history indicated "equal access" meant that **once a school established a limited open forum, religious clubs must receive the same terms and conditions as other extracurricular groups**. Religious speech is entitled to the same protection as nonreligious speech. The court rejected the district's assertion that Washington education regulations prevented it from granting the club ASB status. The district unlawfully discriminated against the club by preventing it from participating on the same basis as other ASB groups in fund-raising activities, yearbook appearances, use of the public address system and posting messages on bulletin boards. **The district violated the First Amendment by allowing only ASB clubs to use school-funded facilities, and it discriminated against the religious club on the basis of its speech.** The restriction on access to facilities was based purely on viewpoint, which violated the Free Exercise and Establishment Clauses. The court reversed and remanded the judgment. *Prince v. Jacoby*, 303 F.3d 1074 (9th Cir. 2002).

◆ A Wisconsin school invited all student groups to paint murals in a school hallway. The student Bible Club's submission included a heart, two doves, an open Bible depicting the text of John 3:16, and a large cross. The principal approved the submission with the exception of the cross, which he believed might create an Establishment Clause violation and require him to approve satanic or neo-Nazi materials from active white supremacists enrolled in the school. The club's mural was later defaced with a witchcraft symbol, and a group of skinheads unsuccessfully petitioned to paint a mural containing a swastika. The principal also forbade one group from including the name of a brand of beer in its mural. Bible Club members sued the district, principal and district superintendent in a federal district court for EAA and constitutional rights violations under 42 U.S.C. § 1983. The court held for the district and administrators, and club members appealed to the Seventh Circuit.

The court explained the EAA forbids schools from denying equal access to student groups on the basis of the content of speech at group meetings. The school was prohibited from discriminating against the Bible Club because it was a religious, rather than secular, organization. There was no evidence of discrimination in this case, as the principal refused to allow the depiction of the cross due to his fear of a lawsuit and the prospect of student confrontations. His reaction to the cross, the swastika and the beer brand demonstrated **he was not discriminating against religion but was acting reasonably to prevent school disruption**. In any event, his action to forbid the cross display was insulated from liability under the EAA, which cannot be construed to limit the authority of school officials to maintain order and discipline on school premises. The exclusion of the cross from the mural also did not violate student rights under the First Amendment. The court affirmed the judgment. *Gernetzke v. Kenosha Unified School Dist. No. 1*, 274 F.3d 464 (7th Cir. 2001).

D. Non-Student Use

◆ A New York school district issued regulations allowing social, civic, or recreational uses of its property as well as limited use by political organizations, but provided that the school not be used for religious purposes. An evangelical church sought permission to use school facilities to show a film series on traditional Christian family values. The district denied permission to use its facilities because the film was religious. The church filed a lawsuit in a federal court alleging the district violated the First Amendment. The court found the district's action "viewpoint neutral," and the U.S. Court of Appeals, Second Circuit, agreed. The church appealed to the U.S. Supreme Court, which **held the exclusion of subject matter based on its religious content would impermissibly favor some viewpoints or ideas at the expense of others. Therefore, the regulation discriminated on the basis of viewpoint.**

The exclusion of the church from using school property was not viewpoint neutral. Next, the Court determined that since the film series was not to be shown during school hours and was to be open to those outside the church, the public would not perceive the district to be endorsing religion. Since use of school facilities by the church did not violate the test from *Lemon v. Kurtzman*, permission by the district would not violate the Establishment Clause. The film had a secular purpose, its primary effect did not advance religion, and the showing of the film would not "foster excessive state entanglement with religion." Thus, speech about "family and child related issues" from a religious perspective could be aired on public school grounds. The Court reversed the lower court decisions. *Lamb's Chapel v. Center Moriches Union Free School Dist.*, 508 U.S. 384, 113 S.Ct. 2141, 124 L.Ed.2d 352 (1993).

◆   A Maryland school district allowed many nonprofit groups to distribute flyers to teachers, who then placed them in student cubbies. The district did not let the Child Evangelism Fellowship distribute flyers for student meetings of the Good News Club through this forum. The group sued the district in a federal district court. The court granted the club's request for preliminary relief concerning bulletin boards, open houses and other events, but denied its request to distribute flyers based on the risk of an Establishment Clause violation.

On appeal, the U.S. Court of Appeals, Fourth Circuit, reviewed evidence that the district had allowed over 225 groups to distribute flyers in 18 months. Only 32 requests to distribute flyers had been turned down, many because they were profit-motivated. Other religious groups, such as the Salvation Army, Jewish Community Center and YMCA were allowed to circulate flyers. The court held that **when the district opened a forum to various groups, it could not constitutionally exclude speech on the basis of viewpoint.** There was no reason to treat the group's use of religion as "something other than viewpoint" because of its evangelical message. **The role of teachers in placing the materials in student cubbies during school hours did not create an Establishment Clause risk.** The court found the risk of religious endorsement was no greater than the risk of a perception of hostility toward religion if the group was not allowed to distribute its flyers. Students were not being forced to pray or engage in a formal religious exercise. The court reversed the order denying preliminary relief to the group. *Child Evangelism Fellowship of Maryland v. Montgomery County Schools*, 373 F.3d 589 (4th Cir. 2004).

On remand from the Fourth Circuit, the district court found the board had materially revised its take-home mail policy. Under the revised policy, materials and announcements of five organizations could be approved for display or direct distribution to students. The club now enjoyed access to back-to-school nights, open houses and school bulletin boards, making any request for a permanent injunction moot. The revised take-home policy treated the club the same as all other community organizations. **Schools were entitled to limit access to their**

facilities, also called "forums," by non-school groups, so long as they did so reasonably and not on the basis of speech. The club was not denied access to the mailboxes, as it was sponsored by one the five approved organizations. The policy did not unlawfully regulate speech or discourage a particular viewpoint, and the court upheld it. *Child Evangelism Fellowship of Maryland v. Montgomery County Public Schools*, 368 F.Supp.2d 416 (D. Md. 2005).

◆ A New Jersey school district policy reserved the superintendent's right to approve materials from community groups to be sent home with students. Teachers placed approved materials from community organizations in student mailboxes at the close of the school day. Community materials had to meet five requirements, including approval by the superintendent and some relationship to the school or its students. Partisan and election materials were not allowed, nor could students "be exploited" by profit-makers. The policy applied to requests by community groups to post information on school walls, and to "Back to School nights." The district rarely excluded groups from these events. An evangelical organization sponsored weekly Good News Club meetings after school. The meetings included activities such as Bible lessons and learning games. The superintendent approved the club's request to meet in an elementary school classroom after school hours but rejected its request to distribute flyers and parent permission slips through student mailboxes, citing Establishment Clause concerns. The organization sued the district and its officials in a federal district court for constitutional violations. The court granted the organization's request for a preliminary injunction, and the district appealed.

The Third Circuit held **the district created "limited open public forums" by allowing community groups to use school channels for communication on particular topics. It was bound to respect the boundaries it set, and it could not exclude speech unreasonably or discriminate based on viewpoint.** The club's materials satisfied all five district requirements. The court held the district's rejection of religious groups who attempted to recruit members was viewpoint discrimination. **Since the district permitted discussion of topics from a secular perspective, it could not shut out speech on the same topics with a religious perspective.** The court stated the district could not prohibit the group's message as inconsistent with its obligation to teach diversity and tolerance. Suppressing speech on that ground was viewpoint-based. The court rejected the claim that allowing the club to use school facilities would violate the Establishment Clause. **Equal access to educational facilities is not an impermissible endorsement of religion.** Distribution of club literature would not pressure students into religious activity. As the district committed viewpoint discrimination, the judgment was affirmed. *Child Evangelism Fellowship of New Jersey v. Stafford Township School Dist.*, 386 F.3d 514 (3d Cir. 2004).

◆ An Ohio elementary school let community groups place flyers in student mailboxes advertising activities sponsored by the American Red Cross, 4-H Club, sports leagues and local churches. Some of the flyers described religious activities. The principal reviewed the flyers to ensure sponsoring organizations were nonprofit groups serving children in the community, did not advocate any particular religion and did not seek to use flyers as a recruiting tool. Approved flyers were distributed to teachers, who then placed them in student mailboxes with official school papers. Teachers did not discuss the flyers with students. A parent claimed the distribution of flyers advertising religious activities violated the Establishment Clause. He sued the school in a federal district court for an order halting any distribution of flyers that advertised religious activities. The court awarded partial relief to the parent, ordering the school to stop distributing flyers that advertised activities at which proselytization would occur.

The school appealed to the Sixth Circuit, which noted that because elementary school students could not participate in any advertised activity without parental permission, the "relevant observers" in this case were parents, not students. **The court held no reasonable parent observing the flyers would perceive any religious endorsement by the school. Possible misperceptions of endorsement were not sufficient to find an Establishment Clause violation. There was no risk of any religious coercion in this case, because the activities advertised in the flyers were not school-sponsored events and they did not take place on school grounds.** The court explained that if the school refused to distribute flyers advertising religious activities while continuing to distribute other flyers, students might conclude that the school disapproved of religion. **The school's practice was neutral toward religion** and did not send a message of disfavor to students who did not want to attend the advertised activities. The court reversed the district court's judgment. *Rusk v. Crestview Local School Dist.*, 379 F.3d 418 (6th Cir. 2004).

◆   An Arizona school district had a policy and practice of allowing certain outside groups to distribute or display promotional literature to students. The policy allowed only nonprofit groups and government entities to distribute literature, and it clearly stated that "commercial, political or religious" material could not be distributed or displayed. Acceptable flyers included those promoting summer camps, art classes, sports leagues, artistic performances or exhibits, the YMCA, boys and girls clubs, and scouting activities. When the president of a nonprofit religious corporation decided to offer a summer camp, he sought to advertise it by distributing a multi-page brochure in nine district elementary schools. Ultimately, **the district decided to allow the brochures to be distributed with a waiver and the stipulation that two descriptions of Bible classes be removed.** The president sued the school district in a federal district court, which granted judgment to the district.

On appeal, the Ninth Circuit noted the district had created a limited public forum. Limited public forums occur when the government opens a nonpublic forum to certain groups or topics. Where a school district creates a limited public forum with the broad purpose of providing a community service to parents and students, as was the case here, it cannot discriminate against speech that falls within that umbrella simply because the speech is religious in nature. **Since the district allowed brochures on summer camps and YMCA activities, the court held it could not disallow the distribution of brochures from the nonprofit camp because the camp had a religious sponsor.** The Ninth Circuit rejected the district's assertion that allowing distribution of the brochures would violate the Establishment Clause, since it could disclaim any school sponsorship of the camp. Because the district had created a limited public forum, it could require the deletion of proselytizing language. The district later agreed to pay the camp director $150,000 to settle the lawsuit. *Hills v. Scottsdale Unified School Dist. No. 48*, 329 F.3d 1044 (9th Cir. 2003).

◆ A West Virginia school board allowed community members to make Bibles available to students in public schools by placing them on unattended tables with a sign stating "please feel free to take one." A group of individuals sued the board in a federal district court. The court granted a preliminary order for the group and later held the board policy did not create a public forum that opened the schools to all forms of communication. Bible distribution opponents appealed to the Fourth Circuit, which held that the board's policy was neutral and did not create the impression of official sponsorship of religious speech. Students were not coerced to accept a Bible. Prior to adopting the challenged policy, the board had unconstitutionally denied private religious speech on the same basis as that afforded to private nonreligious speech. **Withholding access to the Bible group would have created the impression that religious speech was disfavored. However, the policy was invalid at the elementary school level in view of the greater potential for coercing younger students and the difficulty they might have distinguishing between official and private speech.** The court otherwise affirmed the district court judgment. *Peck v. Upshur County Board of Educ.*, 155 F.3d 274 (4th Cir. 1998).

E. Religious Literature and Symbols

Stone v. Graham, *below, remains the legal benchmark for evaluating the constitutionality of government displays of the Ten Commandments. In* McCreary County v. American Civil Liberties Union of Kentucky, *545 U.S. 844 (2005), the U.S. Supreme Court stuck down the display of the Ten Commandments at county courthouses in Kentucky. In* McCreary County, *the Supreme Court held it would look to the events leading up to a Ten Commandments display to assess its constitutionality. It found substantially religious objectives by both the Kentucky counties. In another 2005 case,* Van Orden v. Perry, *545 S.Ct. 677 (2005), the Supreme Court allowed a display of the Ten Commandments on a monument at the Texas Capitol. The Court explained the display was "a far more passable use of those texts than was the case in* Stone, *where the text confronted elementary school students every day."*

◆ A Kentucky statute required the posting of the Ten Commandments on the wall of each public school classroom in the state. A group of citizens sought an injunction against the statute's enforcement, claiming it violated the First Amendment's Establishment and Free Exercise Clauses. The Kentucky state courts upheld the statute, finding it was secular and did not advance or inhibit any religion and did not entangle the state with religion. Utilizing the test from *Lemon v. Kurtzman*, **the U.S. Supreme Court struck down the statute. The Court held the posting of the Ten Commandments had no secular purpose.**
Kentucky state education officials insisted the statute served the secular purpose of teaching students the foundation of western civilization and the common law. The Court stated, however, the pre-eminent purpose was plainly

religious in nature. **The Ten Commandments undeniably came from a religious text**, despite the legislative recitation of a secular purpose. The Court noted the text of the Commandments was not integrated into a course or study of history, civilization, ethics, or comparative religion, but simply posted to induce children to read, meditate upon, and perhaps, to venerate and obey them. The Court held it made no difference that the cost of posting the commandments was paid for through private funds and that they were not read aloud. *Stone v. Graham*, 449 U.S. 39, 101 S.Ct. 192, 66 L.Ed.2d 199 (1981).

◆ New York City's holiday display policy did not permit creches (nativity scenes). The policy allowed the display of secular holiday symbols, including "Christmas trees, Menorahs, and the Star and Crescent." Displays could not "appear to promote or celebrate any single religion or holiday." Significantly, the policy stated "any symbol or decoration which may be used must be displayed simultaneously with other symbols or decorations reflecting different beliefs or customs." The policy recited that "the primary purpose of all displays shall be to promote the goal of fostering understanding and respect for the rights of all individuals regarding their beliefs, values and customs. The Catholic League for Religious and Civil Rights protested the absence of creches from holiday displays in city schools. After the city refused to change the policy, a Catholic parent of two elementary students sued the city and school officials in a federal district court. She claimed the policy promoted Judaism and Islam and disapproved of Christianity. The court held a trial and upheld the policy.

On appeal, the U.S. Court of Appeals, Second Circuit, found over 125,000 of New York City's million-plus public school students attended English learner programs. The student population, like the city, "represents virtually every race, nationality, ethnicity, and religious and cultural tradition in the world." School displays depicted Santa, reindeer, Christmas trees, gifts and wreaths, menorahs, dreidels, the star and crescent, a Kwanzaa kinara, snowflakes, snowmen, stockings, candy canes, and cards describing Kwanzaa, Christmas, Chanukah and Ramadan. **The Supreme Court has allowed "passive religious displays, whether of a creche or a menorah" with secular holiday symbols. The decision to represent Christmas with secular symbols, rather than creches, did not show hostility to Christianity. The menorah and the star and crescent were religious symbols, but they did not depict a deity while a nativity scene did.** The court found the policy had a secular purpose. It supported a strong public interest "to teach the lesson of pluralism." Promoting tolerance and respect for diverse customs did not violate the Religion Clauses of the First Amendment. **The critical inquiry is whether religious texts or symbols have been sufficiently integrated into a secular scheme to avoid a clearly religious message.** The city policy did so by requiring any symbol or decoration to be displayed simultaneously with others reflecting different beliefs or customs. Objective observers would perceive the promotion of pluralism, not religion. The policy did not violate the parent's right to control the upbringing and education of her children. **There is no constitutional right for a parent to dictate a public school curriculum.** The court affirmed the judgment for the city. *Skoros v. City of New York*, 437 F.3d 1 (2d Cir. 2006).

◆ A federal district court denied a taxpayer challenge to the use of three crosses incorporated into insignia used by the Las Cruces Public Schools. The court noted "Las Cruces" is Spanish for "the crosses." The most reliable theory on the derivation of the name "Las Cruces" was that during the Spanish colonial and Mexican period, groups of crosses were used to mark graves and massacre sites. The city had long used crosses in its official insignia, as did non-religious and private entities in the area. There was evidence that the insignia had been adopted in the 1960s to make school district vehicles more readily identifiable. The crosses were in a part of the insignia that was less than two inches wide.

The court held the district did not use the insignia on school maintenance vehicles to proselytize the taxpayer's daughter or anyone else. No evidence indicated the district's stated purpose for using the insignia on school maintenance vehicles was insincere. **The crosses were recognized in the area as having a secular purpose, and they did not advance any particular religion or entangle the government with religion. No reasonable observer of the insignia would find an establishment of religion. The court held the district did not violate the Establishment Clause.** *Weinbaum v. Las Cruces Public Schools*, 465 F.Supp.2d 1182 (D.N.M. 2006).

◆ A ministerial association donated monuments inscribed with the Ten Commandments to an Ohio school board and agreed to indemnify the board for any resulting litigation costs. The board's president spoke informally with board members before accepting the donation, but the board made no resolution. Once the monuments were accepted, the board resolved to dedicate the grounds on which they stood as areas for structures of symbolic history. It erected the monuments at four new high schools and installed signs reciting that the board had incurred no costs and intended no endorsement of religion.

Two county residents sued the board in a federal district court to prohibit the display. The board modified the display to add excerpts from the Justinian Code, the Preamble to the U.S. Constitution, the Declaration of Independence and the Magna Carta. The board stated the Ten Commandments provided the "moral background of the Declaration of Independence and the foundation of our legal tradition." The court held the display violated the Establishment Clause, and the board appealed. The U.S. Court of Appeals, Sixth Circuit, **held the original display had no secular purpose. Acceptance of the monuments from a religious organization implied the opposite.** The board declared no secular purpose until after the litigation began. **The modified display was overtly religious,** stating "The Commandments remind us of our obligation to one another and to the Creator." As the display had no secular purpose, the court affirmed the judgment. *Baker v. Adams County/Ohio Valley School Board*, 86 Fed.Appx. 104 (6th Cir. 2004).

◆ A Florida student painted murals with religious messages or symbols for a school project, without informing the teacher who supervised the project. The student placed them in conspicuous locations in the school, where they caused a commotion. The teacher instructed the student to paint over the overt religious words and sectarian symbols, but allowed other images and messages to remain. Other students were also instructed to edit their murals due to profanity, gang symbols or satanic images. The student complied with the instructions, but sued the district in a federal district court for First Amendment violations. The court held the school did not create a public forum when it invited students and staff to paint murals. It found the restrictions placed on the murals were reasonable.

The student appealed to the U.S. Court of Appeals, Eleventh Circuit. It held the project was a nonpublic forum. Schools may create open public forums by intentionally opening their facilities for use, but cannot do so through inaction. The school did not display an intent to open the project for indiscriminate use. **The principal explicitly forbade profane or offensive content, and the teacher maintained supervision of the project. The district court correctly found the mural project was a nonpublic forum, over which the school could exert editorial control**. Schools can regulate expression in nonpublic forums, so long as their regulations are viewpoint neutral and reasonable in light of the purpose of the forum. **The court held the murals were made in a curricular context and were "school-sponsored speech"** under *Hazelwood School Dist. v. Kuhlmeier*, 484 U.S. 260 (1988). Curricular expression did not have to occur in a classroom. The court found parents, students and others might reasonably believe the murals bore the school's imprimatur. They were displayed prominently near the school office, and a reasonable observer would likely perceive the school had a role in setting their guidelines. The school refused to allow the student, or anyone else, design murals that were explicitly religious or offensive. It did not discriminate on the basis of viewpoint. The school had a legitimate pedagogical concern in avoiding disruption, and the court affirmed the judgment. *Bannon v. School Dist. of Palm Beach County*, 387 F.3d 1208 (11th Cir. 2004).

◆   A Virginia high school approved of a "walk of fame" as a parent group's fundraiser. The walk was in a prominent area near the school entrance. Bricks could be engraved with names, emblems or slogans, and could be personalized to honor students and staff. Some families selected bricks with a Latin cross. After the school principal received a letter complaining about the crosses, he told brick purchasers the crosses had to be removed due to legal problems. He offered them replacement bricks and a refund of the extra $5 they paid for crosses. A new school board policy limited inscriptions on bricks to the names of students and staff, and their class, grade or year. Objectors to the policy sued the district, superintendent, school board, principal and others in a federal district court. The court dismissed the religious free exercise claim, but denied judgment to the board on the Speech and Establishment Clause claims.

The court explained **government entities have inherent rights to control their property for the use to which it is dedicated**. The degree of government control over speech depends on the nature of the "forum" for expression. The court agreed with the parents that **the walkway was a "limited public forum," which was opened for student expression.** The school demonstrated the intent to create a public forum for limited expression by encouraging brick purchasers to state their feelings. As the school had established a limited public forum for expression, it was not allowed to discriminate against any viewpoint. **The school engaged in impermissible viewpoint discrimination when it removed only bricks with Latin crosses from the walkway.** The U.S. Supreme Court has held a school "may not deny benefits to a group solely on account of their religious viewpoint." **Schools need not open their facilities up to private**

speech, but once they do, they cannot discriminate against speakers with a religious viewpoint. School policies must be neutral. The court held for the parents, finding the district had no compelling interest in excluding the crosses based on the need to avoid an Establishment Clause violation. *Demmon v. Loudoun County Public Schools*, 342 F.Supp.2d 474 (E.D. Va. 2004).

◆   An Arizona parent-teacher group planned a fundraiser to sell personalized tiles for an interior wall of an elementary school. The school authorized the project, reserving the right to modify tiles under an unwritten policy precluding "any and all controversial messages." The school rejected a family's requests to submit tiles with messages such as "God Bless Quinn, We Love You Mom & Dad," and "God Bless Haley, We Love You Mom & Dad." It also rejected submissions from other parents with religious messages. The district eventually approved the submission "In God We Trust, the Seidman Family" and installed it. However, the family sued the school district in a federal district court for Speech, Free Exercise, Equal Protection and Establishment Clause violations.

   The court noted the extent to which schools may limit speech depended largely on the nature of the forum. Schools may exercise editorial control over school-sponsored speech, so long as this is reasonably related to legitimate pedagogical concerns. But even school-sponsored speech is subject to the requirement of viewpoint neutrality, and discrimination against speech based on viewpoint is impermissible. The district allowed others to buy tiles with personalized messages, statements of personal belief and even business advertisements. The family's messages appeared to be within the range of the subject matter allowed by the tile forum. **The decision to exclude the use of the word "God" was unconstitutional viewpoint discrimination.** The court rejected the claim that the Establishment Clause required the school to exclude religious messages. The words "God bless" referred to religion in only a general sense, not to any particular faith. Acceptance of the family's tiles would not have created an Establishment Clause violation. The tiles would have been scattered through a display of over 360 tiles. The court awarded summary judgment to the family on its speech and equal protection claims. **The speech rights questions raised in this case were complex and unclear.** For this reason, **the individual school officials were entitled to qualified immunity and were not liable for damages.** *Seidman v. Paradise Valley Unified School Dist.*, 327 F.Supp.2d 1098 (D. Ariz. 2004).

◆   A New Jersey preschool student tried to distribute pencils stamped with the message "Jesus [heart symbol] The Little Children" at a class party. His teacher confiscated them because of their religious message. The next year, a teacher stopped him from handing out candy canes with an attached religious story. After the student's mother contacted the school, officials allowed him to distribute candy canes at recess or after school. When the student reached first grade, he again tried to distribute candy canes with the religious story at a holiday party. Officials halted the distribution but let him distribute the canes during non-class time. The student sued the school board and superintendent in a federal district court for constitutional and state law violations.

   The court held for the board and superintendent, and the student appealed. The U.S. Court of Appeals, Third Circuit, held **age and context are key**

considerations in school speech cases. A student's age bore an inverse relationship to the degree and kind of control a school could exercise. Schools had authority to restrict student expression that contradicted or interfered with curricular activity. **Classroom parties were part of the curriculum, not a place for student advocacy. In an elementary school classroom, the line between school-endorsed speech could be blurred for young, impressionable students and their parents.** It was appropriate to allow school officials to set these boundaries, and for the courts to afford them leeway to create an appropriate learning environment and to restrict student messages intending to promote religion. A religious message was in conflict with the holiday parties. The student was the only person to bring a non-generic gift, and it was within the school's authority to stop the distribution. In any event, the school had allowed him to distribute the message outside class time. *Walz v. Egg Harbor Township Board of Educ.*, 342 F.3d 271 (3d Cir. 2003).

III. LIMITATIONS ON EMPLOYEE RELIGIOUS ACTIVITY

The Free Exercise Clause of the First Amendment provides that Congress shall make no law prohibiting the free exercise of religion. Courts examining the rights of school employees to engage in religious speech follow the First Amendment analysis from Pickering v. Board of Educ., *discussed in Chapter Three, Section II, with the additional consideration of the employee's right to freely exercise religion. For cases involving religious discrimination against employees, see Chapter Seven, Section IV.*

◆ A South Dakota school district let the Good News Club hold meetings on school grounds under its community use policy. A teacher attended the club's first meeting at her school. The principal told her she could not attend future meetings, warning that her participation might be perceived as an establishment of religion. The teacher proposed a disclaimer stating her participation was in the capacity of private citizen. After unsuccessfully arguing she should be allowed to attend meetings under district religion and facilities use policies, she sued the district in a federal district court. The court denied the teacher's request for a preliminary order allowing her to participate in club meetings. However, it later held the district had engaged in viewpoint regulation by excluding her from meetings. While the district could bar the teacher from club meetings at her own school, no Establishment Clause concerns applied to meetings at other schools. The court issued a permanent order allowing the teacher to attend meetings at schools other than her own. It ruled for the district on her religious free exercise and free association claims, and the parties appealed.

The U.S. Court of Appeals, Eighth Circuit, **held the government may reserve a forum for certain groups or to discuss certain topics, but it must abstain from regulations based on viewpoint**. The Supreme Court has held the government must follow neutral criteria and evenhanded policies toward various ideologies and viewpoints. The district discriminated on the basis of viewpoint by restricting employees from meetings based on the subject matter of speech anticipated at those meetings, and from engaging in religious speech on their own time. The relevant inquiry was "whether an objective observer, acquainted with the text, legislative history, and implementation of the statute, would perceive it as a state endorsement of prayer in public schools." **The teacher's participation in after-school club meetings was private speech that did not put the district at risk of violating the Establishment Clause.** Nonparticipants left the building by the time meetings were held, and student participants had parental permission. The court found no reasonable observer would perceive the teacher's presence at club meetings in her own school or any other school to be a state endorsement of religion. It reversed the decision in part and affirmed it in part, holding for the teacher on all issues appealed. *Wigg v. Sioux Falls School Dist. 49-5*, 382 F.3d 807 (8th Cir. 2004).

◆   A New York student's death was announced over a school intercom. Those in the school were asked to observe a moment of silence. Students in a substitute teacher's classroom began to cry and hug each other, and the teacher tried to comfort them by speaking about her religious beliefs. She told students they did not have to participate in the discussion and could instead go to their computers or open their books. The teacher said, "Jesus was the son of God" and "one must come through Jesus to get to God." She touched each student on the forehead and "asked God to protect them and their families." The teacher asked a student if she wanted her to pray for her, despite knowledge that the student was a Jehovah's witness. The student's parent complained to the school, and the district discharged the teacher, who then sued the school board in a federal district court for speech rights violations.

The court granted the board's motion for a directed verdict on certain claims, but it allowed a jury to consider her claims for equal protection violations based on religion or national origin. The jury found against the teacher, and the court denied her post-trial motions and dismissed the case. She appealed to the U.S. Court of Appeals, Second Circuit, which found no error in the judgment. The teacher had no property right in continued employment as a non-tenured substitute. **Even if her speech had addressed a matter of public concern, the board had a strong interest in avoiding an Establishment Clause violation.** There was ample evidence in support of the jury's findings and the court affirmed the judgment. *Rosario v. Does 1–10*, 36 Fed. Appx. 25 (2d Cir. 2002).

◆   A Pennsylvania instructional assistant often wore a small crucifix to work over a six-year period without disruption or controversy. Her supervisor saw her a few times each week but did not notice the crucifix until "someone in the teachers union" reported it. The district suspended the assistant for violating its policy and 24 Pa. Stat. Ann. Section 11-1112, which prohibits public school teachers from wearing religious dress, marks, emblems or insignia while performing their duties. The law calls for "permanent disqualification" from employment and exposes school directors to potential liability for noncompliance. The assistant declined her supervisor's instruction to remove or hide the crucifix. The district suspended her with pay, and she filed a federal district court action for reinstatement and a declaration that the policy was unconstitutional. The court noted the crucifix caused no dissension, controversy or complaints. Although district policy forbade employees from wearing religious symbols, it allowed them to wear nonreligious decorative jewelry.

The court held the district's policy was overtly averse to religion, because it punished religious content or viewpoint while "permitting its employees to wear jewelry containing secular messages or no messages at all." **The U.S. Supreme Court has declared a "neutrality principle, synthesized from the Free Speech, Free Exercise and Establishment Clauses of the First Amendment." The affiliations policy constituted impermissible viewpoint discrimination because it was directed only at religious speech. It had a discriminatory purpose and effect** that was not justified by any countervailing government interest. The court rejected the district's arguments based on potential criminal liability under Section 11-1112 and threatened violations of the Establishment Clause. The section did not apply to the instructional assistant, since she was not a certificated teacher. No reasonable observer would perceive the district as endorsing religion if it allowed employees to wear unobtrusive crucifixes or similar jewelry. The court upheld the assistant's religious and speech rights claims. She was entitled to an order preventing the district from enforcing its religious affiliations policy and reinstating her. *Nichol v. ARIN Intermediate Unit 28*, 268 F.Supp.2d 536 (W.D. Pa. 2003).

◆   A Connecticut teacher reported for work one day wearing a shirt that had the words "Jesus 2000 – J2K" prominently displayed. Administrators instructed her to cover the shirt or change her clothes. The teacher agreed to wear a lab coat, but later sued the school board, individual board members and other school officials in a federal district court. See asserted violations of her speech and religious rights, and state law violations. The court observed that the board members were entitled to qualified immunity if they showed restraining the teacher's expression was necessary to avoid an Establishment Clause violation. Not all restrictions on employee expression are invalid restraints on the free exercise of speech and religion. The school's interest in avoiding an Establishment Clause violation may be so compelling that it justifies restraining expression that might otherwise enjoy First Amendment protection.

Because school officials cannot be expected to resolve with precision the tension between conflicting articles of the Constitution, the protection given to employees must sometimes yield to the legitimate government interest in avoiding Establishment Clause litigation. **The administrators were entitled to summary judgment because their conduct did not impermissibly infringe on the teacher's speech rights. If they had permitted her to wear the shirt, the school could have been viewed as endorsing religion.** The teacher's Free Exercise Clause argument failed because she did not show officials impeded her practice of religion. She was not subjected to any adverse employment action or retaliation in violation of the Constitution or state law. School officials were entitled to qualified immunity because they acted reasonably in view of established law. The court's analysis applied with equal force to the teacher's state constitutional claims, and it awarded judgment to the board and officials. *Downing v. West Haven Board of Educ.*, 162 F.Supp.2d 19 (D. Conn. 2001).

◆   A teacher worked for a Minnesota school district for 13 years before being assigned to teach a tenth-grade biology class that included a discussion of evolution. When the teacher arrived at the course's evolution component, he spent only one day on the topic and told the science department co-chair that he could not teach in accordance with the standard curriculum. The teacher stated he did not regard evolution as a viable scientific concept. The principal reassigned the teacher to a ninth-grade natural science class the following year, based on concerns that he would dilute the theory of evolution. The teacher sued the district and school administrators in a state trial court for violation of his religious free exercise, free speech and due process rights. The court awarded summary judgment to the district defendants, and the teacher appealed.

The Court of Appeals of Minnesota stated the teacher **failed to explain how the reassignment equated to a violation of his right to freely exercise religion. The district had an important pedagogical interest in establishing a curriculum and a legitimate concern for ensuring that its schools were religiously neutral.** The teacher did not find evolution theory credible, and his proposed manner of teaching it directly conflicted with curricular requirements. The district had well-founded concerns about his inability to teach the curriculum, and there was no merit to his speech rights claims. The due process claim failed because a school board may regulate a teacher's classroom speech if teachers are provided specific notice of what conduct is prohibited. As the teacher failed to show that his reassignment violated any of his constitutional rights, the court affirmed the judgment for the district and officials. *LeVake v. Independent School Dist. No. 656*, 625 N.W.2d 502 (Minn. Ct. App. 2001).

IV. FINANCIAL ASSISTANCE AND VOUCHER PROGRAMS

The U.S. Supreme Court upheld an Ohio law authorizing public funding of a private school voucher program in Zelman v. Simmons-Harris. *The case may be contrasted to 1970s cases like* Committee for Public Educ. and Religious Liberty v. Nyquist, *413 U.S. 756 (1973), where the Court held direct aid from states to sectarian schools "in whatever form is invalid." While* Zelman *found no Establishment Clause violation in the Ohio program, it did not resolve the constitutionality of voucher programs under state constitutional provisions.*

◆ The Ohio General Assembly adopted the Ohio Pilot Scholarship Program in 1995 in response to a federal district court order to remedy problems in the Cleveland School District. The program made vouchers of up to $2,500 available for Cleveland students to attend public or private schools, including schools with religious affiliations. The Supreme Court of Ohio struck down the program on state constitutional grounds in 1999. The general assembly cured the state constitutional deficiencies and reauthorized the program for 1999-2000. A new lawsuit was commenced against state officials in a federal district court, which permanently enjoined the state from administering the program. The Sixth Circuit affirmed the judgment, and state officials appealed.

The U.S. Supreme Court considered whether the Cleveland program had the unconstitutional effect of advancing or inhibiting religion. The program allowed government aid to reach religious institutions only because of the deliberate choices of the individual recipients. Any incidental advancement of religion, or perceived endorsement of a religious message, was attributable to the individual recipients, not to the government, avoiding an Establishment Clause violation. The Court held the New York program struck down in *Committee for Public Educ. and Religious Liberty v. Nyquist* gave benefits exclusively to private schools and the parents of private school enrollees. Ohio's program offered aid directly to a broad class of individual recipients defined without regard to religion. **The Court held where government aid is religiously neutral and provides direct assistance to a broad class of citizens that in turn directs funds to religious schools through genuine and independent private choices, the program is not readily subject to an Establishment Clause challenge.** As the Ohio program did not violate the Establishment Clause, the Court reversed the judgment. *Zelman v. Simmons-Harris*, 536 U.S. 639, 122 S.Ct. 2460, 153 L.Ed.2d 604 (2002).

◆   Opponents of Florida's Opportunity Scholarship Program (OSP) sued state officials in a Florida court for violating three state constitutional provisions. The court held the OSP was unconstitutional under the "no aid" provision, Article I, Section Three of the Florida Constitution. The Supreme Court of Florida noted the OSP permitted students who were assigned to a public school that did not meet minimum standards for specific time periods to attend a better public school or receive a state scholarship to attend a private school. Article IX, Section 1(a) of the state constitution imposed a "maximum duty on the state to provide for public education that is uniform and of high quality."

   The court held the OSP violated the state constitution's uniformity requirement by diverting public funds into "separate private systems parallel to and in competition with the free public schools that are the sole means set out in the Constitution for the state to provide for the education of Florida's children." The court found paying tuition for students to attend private schools was a substantially different manner than the one prescribed in the state constitution. OSP funding was taken directly from each school district's appropriated funds, reducing the funds available to the district. **No OSP provision ensured private schools were "uniform."** While public schools were held accountable for teaching certain state standards and to teach all basic subjects, private schools were not required to do so. Private schools could even hire teachers who did not possess bachelor's degrees. **The court held "because voucher payments reduce funding for the public education system, the OSP by its very nature undermines the system of 'high quality' free public schools."** The diversion of funds reduced available money for public schools and funded private schools that were not "uniform." The court found a "clear intent that public funds be used to support the public school system, not to support a duplicative, competitive private system." It struck down the OSP program. *Bush v. Holmes*, 919 So.2d 392 (Fla. 2006).

◆   Maine law authorizes public funding to pay private school tuition on behalf of students living in school districts that do not operate their own high schools. Districts may operate their own high schools or contract with other school districts or private schools meeting state criteria to satisfy their obligation to educate resident high school students. In 1980, the state added MRSA Section

2951(2), a provision limiting public funding to nonsectarian schools for school districts that contracted with private schools to educate their high school students. The Supreme Court of Maine upheld Section 2951(2) against a challenge by parents who sought public funding for their children to attend religious schools. *Bagley v. Raymond School Dep't*, 782 A.2d 172 (Me. 1999).

After the U.S. Supreme Court upheld the Ohio voucher program in *Zelman v. Simmons-Harris*, a bill to repeal Section 2951(2) was introduced in the Maine Legislature. The bill failed, and another group of parents seeking public funding for their children to attend religious schools filed a federal court challenge. **The U.S. Court of Appeals, First Circuit, held that even after *Zelman*, the Constitution did not require Maine to fund tuition at sectarian schools.** *Eulitt v. State of Maine*, 386 F.3d 344 (1st Cir. 2004).

Yet another group of parents filed a challenge to Section 2951(2) in a state court. They sent their children to private schools that did not qualify as "nonsectarian schools" under the law. A Maine superior court held Section 2951(2) did not violate the Constitution, and the parents appealed. The Supreme Court of Maine noted the state had decided to exclude sectarian schools from the tuition program based on a 1980 attorney general's opinion.

The court explained that in the 1970s and 1980s, the U.S. Supreme Court "strongly disfavored use of public funds for direct or indirect payments to religious institutions." Had Maine continued to fund religious schools after 1980, it "faced a high risk of a successful challenge." **The court found the state had acted prudently and responsibly in taking the attorney general's advice and enacting Section 2951(2). The state was not motivated by religious discrimination.** In *Locke v. Davey*, 540 U.S. 712 (2004), the U.S. Supreme Court rejected a claim that a state college scholarship restriction was "presumptively unconstitutional" because it was allegedly not neutral with respect to religion. **Section 2951(2) merely prohibited the state from funding a school of choice and did not burden or inhibit the free exercise of religion in any constitutionally significant way.** Maine's failure to extend tuition funding to sectarian schools did not prove religious hostility. Even after *Zelman*, avoiding religious entanglement remained a valid reason for excluding sectarian schools from the program. The court affirmed the judgment for the state and school officials, upholding Section 2951(2). *Anderson v. Town of Durham*, 2006 ME 39, 895 A.2d 944 (Me. 2006).

◆   The Colorado Opportunity Contract Pilot Program was enacted to meet the educational needs of low-achieving students in the state's highest poverty areas. Participation was mandatory for any district that had at least eight schools with low or unsatisfactory academic performance ratings. Districts in the eligible categories made assistance payments to parents, who then endorsed checks to a nonpublic school. Voucher opponents sued the governor and state in a Colorado district court. The court upheld a claim based on Article IX, Section 15 of the Colorado Constitution, which requires school boards to have control of instruction in their districts. State officials appealed to the Supreme Court of Colorado. The court noted Colorado was one of only six states with an express constitutional mandate for control by school boards. Colorado cases dating to 1915 held **"local control" required school districts to maintain discretion**

over any instruction paid for with locally raised funds. Allowing districts to raise and spend their own funds enabled them to determine their educational policies, free from state restriction. Local boards retained no authority under the pilot program to determine which students were eligible to participate or how much funding to devote to the program.

The court held the program deprived school districts of all local control over instruction. The program violated the local control provision by requiring districts to pay funds, including some locally raised tax revenues, to parents who paid them to nonpublic schools in the form of vouchers. The state's argument was based only on the theory that public schools had failed, and the court affirmed the judgment for the voucher opponents. *Owens v. Colorado Congress of Parents, Teachers and Students*, 92 P.3d 933 (Colo. 2004).

◆ Vermont law requires school districts that do not maintain schools to pay the tuition for resident students to attend approved public schools in other districts or approved independent schools selected by parents. Until 1997, one district with no high school authorized tuition payments only for nonsectarian schools. It then adopted a policy allowing tuition reimbursement for the costs of sectarian schools. The parents of 15 students residing in the district selected a parochial school that required instruction in theology prior to graduation and attendance at mass on some occasions. The state terminated assistance to the district when it voted to reimburse the parents. The district sued the commissioner and state education department in a Vermont superior court, which held that the payments violated the Establishment Clause of the First Amendment and the Compelled Support Clause of the Vermont Constitution.

The district appealed to the Supreme Court of Vermont, which declined to evaluate the case under the U.S. Constitution, instead focusing on the Compelled Support Clause of the Vermont Constitution. The court observed that no state law or department rule discussed payment for sectarian education. **The method for tuition payment selected by the district would result in the impermissible commingling of public and private funds and the expenditure of public funds for religious education.** The Compelled Support Clause prohibits compelled worship, church attendance or support of any place of worship contrary to the dictates of a person's conscience. The court stated the Clause also pertained to "any place of worship," which could include a school. The Vermont Supreme Court criticized the Supreme Court of Wisconsin's opinion upholding the constitutionality of the Milwaukee School Choice Program in *Jackson v. Benson*, 578 N.W.2d 602 (Wis. 1998), and refused to apply it. **Allowing the district to pay tuition for parochial school students would result in a direct state payment for religious instruction that violated the state constitution.** This was primarily because of the lack of any restriction on the schools' expenditure of public funds once they were received. The court affirmed the judgment for the commissioner and department. *Chittenden Town School Dist. v. Vermont Dep't of Educ.*, 169 Vt. 310, 738 A.2d 539 (Vt. 1999).

CHAPTER THREE

Freedom of Speech and Association

	Page
I. STUDENTS...97	
A. Protected Speech 98	
1. Disciplinary Cases 98	
2. Threats and Bullying...................................101	
3. Internet Cases 106	
4. Confederate Flags 108	
B. Student Publications 111	
C. Non-School Publications.....................................113	
D. Personal Appearance and Dress Codes...................114	
1. Dress Codes..114	
2. Hair Length and Appearance 120	
3. Gang Affiliation 122	
II. EMPLOYEES 123	
A. Protected Speech 124	
B. Personal Appearance and Dress Codes...................130	
C. Association Rights 131	
III. ACADEMIC FREEDOM 134	
A. Library Materials 134	
B. Textbook Selection 136	
C. School Productions...137	
IV. PARENTAL SPEECH AND ASSOCIATION RIGHTS 138	
A. Access to School Campuses 139	
B. Curriculum..141	
V. USE OF SCHOOL FACILITIES....................................143	
A. Student Organizations and Demonstrations 143	
B. Non-Student Groups 146	

I. STUDENTS

The courts balance student First Amendment speech rights against the strong school interest in maintaining an appropriate educational environment. Schools have a legitimate interest in restricting obscene or disruptive student speech and have considerable discretion in determining what speech is permissible in school. In Tinker v. Des Moines Independent Community School Dist., *the Supreme Court recognized that students and teachers do not shed their speech rights at the schoolhouse gate. Under* Tinker *and later cases, school officials may prohibit expression if they can show it would "materially and substantially interfere" with the requirements of appropriate discipline in the operation of the school, or if the speech "intrudes upon the rights of other students," or collides with the right of others to be secure and let alone.*

A. Protected Speech

1. Disciplinary Cases

◆   In 1965, a group of Iowa adults and high school students publicized their objections to the hostilities in Vietnam by wearing black armbands during the holiday season. Three students and their parents had previously engaged in similar activities, and they decided to participate in this program. The principals of Des Moines schools became aware of the plan and adopted a policy that **any student wearing an armband to school would be asked to remove it or face suspension.** The three students wore their armbands and were all suspended until they agreed to come back without the armbands. The students did not return to their school until the planned protest period had ended.

The students sued the school district for First Amendment violations under 42 U.S.C. § 1983, seeking to prevent school officials from disciplining them, plus their nominal damages. A federal district court dismissed the complaint and the Eighth Circuit summarily affirmed the decision. On appeal, the Supreme Court stated neither students nor teachers shed their constitutional rights to freedom of speech or expression at the schoolhouse gate. **In order for school officials to justify prohibition of a particular expression of opinion, they must show something more than a mere desire to avoid the discomfort and unpleasantness associated with unpopular viewpoints.** Where there was no evidence that student expression would materially interfere with the requirements of appropriate discipline in the operation of the school, or collide with the rights of others, the prohibition was improper. The expressive act of wearing black armbands did not interrupt school activities or intrude in school affairs. The Court reversed the lower court decisions. *Tinker v. Des Moines Independent Community School Dist.*, 393 U.S. 503, 89 S.Ct. 733, 21 L.Ed.2d 733 (1969).

◆   A male high school student in Bethel, Washington, delivered a speech nominating a fellow student for elective office before an assembly of over 600 peers. All students were required to attend the assembly as part of the school's self-government program. **In his nominating speech, the student referred to his candidate in terms of an elaborate, explicit sexual metaphor, despite having been warned in advance by teachers not to do so.** Students' reactions during the speech included laughter, graphic sexual gestures, hooting, bewilderment and embarrassment. When the student admitted he had deliberately used sexual innuendo in his speech, he was informed that he would be suspended for three days and that his name would be removed from the list of candidates for student speaker at graduation.

The student sued the school district in a federal district court, claiming his First Amendment right to freedom of speech had been violated. The court agreed and awarded him damages and attorneys' fees. It also ordered the district to allow the student to speak at graduation. The decision was affirmed by the Ninth Circuit, under the authority of *Tinker*. The Supreme Court reversed the decision, holding that **while public school students have the right to advocate unpopular and controversial views in school, that right must be balanced against the school interest in teaching socially appropriate behavior**. The Constitution does not protect obscene language, and a public school, as an instrument of the state, may legitimately establish standards of civil and mature conduct. *Bethel School Dist. No. 403 v. Fraser*, 478 U.S. 675, 106 S.Ct. 3159, 92 L.Ed.2d 549 (1986).

◆   An 18-year-old Alaska student displayed a banner reading "Bong Hits 4 Jesus" at a privately sponsored "Winter Olympics Torch Relay" held near his school. Students had been released from the high school to observe the event on a street near the school. Many of them got into fights, and some threw snowballs and plastic bottles. The student said the banner was "meaningless and funny" and was only meant to get him on television. The school principal crossed the street to confront him when she saw the banner. The student claimed he asked her about freedom of speech. He said the principal then grabbed the banner and crumpled it. School officials later admitted the banner caused no disruption. They stated the banner advocated illegal drug use that was inconsistent with the school's basic education mission. The student sued the principal and school board in a federal district court for speech rights violations. The court awarded summary judgment to the board and principal, and the student appealed.

The Ninth Circuit found the reason the principal had ripped down the banner was that its message would be understood as advocating or promoting illegal drug use. The student was an adult citizen of Alaska, a state that "has had repeated referenda about whether, and to what extent, to criminalize or legalize marijuana." Speech about marijuana might be understood as political. Under *Tinker*, student speech cannot be suppressed based on viewpoint unless there is evidence this is required to avoid material and substantial interference with school discipline. The board could not discipline the student for advocating a position contrary to its message of preventing illegal drugs. The phrase "Bong Hits 4 Jesus" was not "plainly offensive." **Schools may only suppress student speech that is disruptive. No educational function was disrupted in this case and the school board could not control student communication that was not a part of the curriculum.** The principal was not entitled to qualified immunity, since the student's speech rights were clearly established. She could not have reasonably believed she was not violating his rights. The court held the banner raised the same concerns as the armbands in *Tinker*. It vacated and remanded the case. *Frederick v. Morse*, 439 F.3d 1114 (9th Cir. 2006). The U.S. Supreme Court announced it will review the decision. *Morse v. Frederick*, No. 06-278, 2006 WL 2503545 (U.S. cert. granted, 12/1/06).

◆   Most of the boys varsity basketball team at an Oregon high school claimed their head coach used abusive tactics, intimidated them, yelled incessantly and frequently used profanity. After a game, the coach told players that if they wanted him to quit, they should say so, and he would resign. The players drafted a petition requesting his resignation, and all but two players signed it. The coach brought the petition to the school principal, who allowed him to take part of the day off. The school's athletic director and the principal met with the team, offered them mediation and told them they would have to board the team bus for a game that evening or forfeit their privilege to play in the game. The coach stated he would not coach the game that evening, but the players were not informed of this, and eight of them did not board the bus. The principal permanently suspended players who refused to board the bus from the team. They sued the coach, principal, and school district for speech rights violations.

A federal district court upheld the discipline, finding the students' speech and conduct were not constitutionally protected. Moreover, their conduct substantially and materially interfered with a school activity. The students appealed to the Ninth Circuit, which found the petition and grievances against the coach were "a form of pure speech." **The students could not be disciplined unless there was a reasonable forecast of substantial disruption or material interference.** The court held the district court had improperly applied the "public concern" test, which is used to analyze public employment speech rights cases. Student speech cases are properly analyzed under *Tinker v. Des Moines Independent Community School Dist.* The First Amendment protected the petition and the complaints to school administrators. However, the boycott of the game substantially disrupted and materially interfered with a school activity. **If students decide not to participate in an extracurricular activity on the day it is scheduled to take place, "their conduct will inevitably disrupt or interfere with the activity."** This was true even if the event was not cancelled. The case was remanded for further proceedings. The district court would have to consider whether the players were disciplined only for boycotting the game, or if the suspensions also came in retaliation for their speech. *Pinard v. Clatskanie School Dist. 6J*, 446 F.3d 964 (9th Cir. 2006).

◆   A few weeks before U.S. troops were deployed to Iraq in 2003, a Michigan student wore a T-shirt depicting President George Bush over the caption "international terrorist." He received no complaints about the shirt during morning classes, but a student who had a relative in the military noticed the shirt at lunch. He complained about the T-shirt to an assistant school principal, as did a teacher. The assistant principal ordered the student to either remove the shirt or turn it inside out. The student refused and left school. The principal contacted him at home, saying the shirt was inappropriate as it caused disruption or had the potential to do so. The principal told the student he would be disciplined if he wore the shirt to school again. The student sued the district and principal in a federal district court for restraint of his First Amendment rights. He sought a preliminary order to prevent the district from banning his T-shirt.

The court applied the *Tinker* analysis and rejected the district's claim it needed to prohibit the T-shirt or risk the appearance of embracing its view. **The district did not show substantial disruption or a material interference with school activities based on the complaints of one student and a teacher.** There was no showing of a future risk to the school if the student wore the shirt again. To justify prohibiting expression under *Tinker*, officials had to show more than a mere desire to avoid the discomfort and unpleasantness that accompany an unpopular viewpoint. The court rejected testimony by the principal based on her experience at another school during Operation Desert Storm in 1991. Over 30% of the school's students were Arab, but the district did not show they would be offended by the shirt. **Imminent war in Iraq did not create evidence of student disruption.** Any tension between students who might be for or against the action was no greater than what existed during the 1960s over U.S. involvement in Vietnam. The court issued a preliminary injunction preventing the district from absolutely prohibiting the T-shirt at school. **Nothing in its opinion prevented the district from exercising its authority to limit student expression if there was an objective basis for believing it would materially and substantially interfere with school operations.** *Barber v. Dearborn Public Schools*, 286 F.Supp.2d 847 (E.D. Mich. 2003).

◆   **A Pennsylvania third-grader who objected to a school field trip to a circus circulated a petition opposing the trip among her classmates** during a recess period. The next day, she was told to put the petition away during a quiet reading period, and again during a recess period when a classmate was injured. The district did not punish the student for soliciting signatures, and it permitted her to pass out coloring books and stickers about cruelty to animals. The family sued the district in a federal district court for speech rights violations, seeking monetary damages under 42 U.S.C. § 1983. The court awarded summary judgment to the district and its officials.

The family appealed to the Third Circuit, which found that **student age and maturity are relevant considerations in analyzing speech rights.** Moreover, the speech rights of elementary students are diminished in relation to those of older students, as they require a far greater level of guidance from schools. If third-graders had any rights at all under *Tinker*, the court found them very limited. **Elementary officials may regulate much, if not all speech that is protected in the higher grades, and may do so if they have a legitimate educational reason. This could be the need to preserve order, facilitate learning or social development, or protect other students.** There was no evidence of a First Amendment violation, as the district had never disciplined the student. *Walker-Serrano v. Leonard*, 325 F.3d 412 (3d Cir. 2003).

2. Threats and Bullying

In In re Amir X.S., *below, the Supreme Court of Carolina relied on* S.H.B. v. State of Florida, *355 So.2d 1176 (Fla. 1977), to help resolve a challenge to a juvenile prosecution brought under a state law prohibiting school disruption. In* S.H.B., *the Florida Supreme Court held Fla. Stat. § 871.01 only prohibited disturbances of lawful school gatherings. It recognized that "school gatherings are fragile by their nature," and differ from general public forums.*

◆   A South Carolina teacher claimed a student disrupted her classroom for over two hours. He also took a swing at the teacher before being escorted from the class. Officials filed a juvenile delinquency petition against him for violating S.C. Code Ann. Section 16-17-420 "by willingly, unlawfully, and unnecessarily interfering with and disturbing the students and teachers." The student sought to dismiss the petition, asserting Section 16-17-420 was unconstitutionally vague and overbroad in violation of the First Amendment to the U.S. Constitution. The court upheld the statute and committed the student to the custody of the juvenile justice department for 90 days, with one year of probation. The student appealed to the state supreme court. He argued the statute was overly broad because it punished a substantial amount of protected speech and was so vague that persons of common intelligence would have to guess at its meaning.

The court noted that Section 16-17-420 was appropriately analyzed under cases involving statutes that targeted conduct which was termed "disruptive" to schools. Most analogous was *McAlpine v. Reese*, 390 F.Supp. 136 (E.D. Mich 1970) which upheld a similar Michigan ordinance prohibiting any noise, disturbance or improper diversion in schools. The Michigan ordinance applied to the type of conduct that could not be tolerated in any ordered society. **The South Carolina court held Section 16-17-420 did not prohibit any speech that was protected by the First Amendment. By its terms, the statute did not apply to protected speech or broadly regulate conduct. "Instead, Section 16-17-420 criminalizes conduct that 'disturbs' or 'interferes' with schools, or is 'obnoxious.'" Section 16-17-420 was limited and was not a substantial threat to free speech. It dealt specifically with school disturbances, not public forums.** The state had a legitimate interest in maintaining the integrity of its education system by preserving classroom discipline. The court found any conduct interfering with the state's legitimate objectives could be prohibited. Section 16-17-420 drew "the very same constitutional line drawn by *Tinker*" and was not unconstitutionally overbroad. The court vacated the lower court's ruling on vagueness for lack of standing. *In re Amir X.S.*, 371 S.C. 380, 639 S.E.2d 144 (S.C. 2006).

◆ A Pennsylvania sixth-grader had no disciplinary record and was described as a good student. She was excused from class and went to the lavatory. There, she found a note on a toilet that read: "A bomb will go off in the school tomorrow." The student notified her teacher about the note. The teacher called the school principal, who in turn called police. Two officers interviewed the student without anyone else present. After extensive questioning, the student admitted she had written the note as "a joke." The student was immediately suspended for violating the district's policy against terroristic threats. The school board held a hearing at which it credited a police officer's testimony. It did not find testimony by the student's father credible and voted for expulsion.

The student sued the school district in a state court. It held the board's decision was not supported by substantial evidence, because it was not shown that she intentionally communicated a threat or placed the note in the lavatory. The school district appealed to the Commonwealth Court of Pennsylvania, which held there was no need for direct evidence that the student put the note in the lavatory. **Circumstantial evidence was sufficient to establish that she communicated a threat. The court found the state can meet its burden of proof in criminal cases with circumstantial evidence.** Courts may not substitute their judgment for that of a school board. As the evidence was sufficient to support expulsion, the court reinstated it. *A.B. v. Slippery Rock Area School Dist.*, 906 A.2d 674 (Pa. Commw. Ct. 2006).

◆ A Pennsylvania student wrote and recorded four "rap songs" at his home that were thought to represent threats against three classmates. He mentioned classmates in two recordings. Some content was uploaded onto a Web site. One CD track was titled "Murder, He Wrote." Although the expression took place at home and none of the CDs were brought on school grounds, the school board voted to expel the student and ban him from school grounds. The student sought a federal court order preventing the expulsion and the ban from school property.

The court found no evidence of a "true threat" to the classmates. The rap genre used rhymes, metaphors and "violent imagery," but the court found no actual violence was intended. **There was no evidence that the student directly communicated a message to classmates. The "songs" were either published on the internet or sold in the community. The classmates themselves did not indicate they felt threatened.** The school district did not perform its own investigation before acting. According to the court, there was no evidence that copies of the CDs were sold or distributed in school. As there was no evidence of any school disruption due to the student's expression, he was entitled to a preliminary order preventing expulsion. *Latour v. Riverside Beaver School Dist.*, No. Civ.A. 05-1076, 2005 WL 2106562 (W.D. Pa. 2005).

◆ A sixth-grade New York student wrote a violent story about a boy who is bullied at school, stabs a "mean kid" in the head, and later chops off the head of a girl who is having sex with another student. Some characters were named after actual classmates. The student had no prior disciplinary record at the time. The principal suspended him for five days and notified his parents of the suspension. A school psychiatrist conducted a number of psychological tests on the student without informing the parents. After a hearing, the principal imposed a 30-day suspension. The student sued the school district in a federal district court for federal constitutional violations, and for defamation.

The court held schools can prohibit speech that would substantially interfere with the work of the school or impinge upon the rights of others. Speech that constitutes a true threat of violence can be prohibited. It does not matter whether the speaker intends to carry out the threat. The student's speech and due process claims failed. Even though no notice of the harassment charge was provided, he received sufficient notice of the charges forming the basis of the hearing. A 30-day suspension was not excessive. The court dismissed a Fourth Amendment claim for unreasonable search and seizure. **The school was justified in conducting psychological tests on the student because it was reasonable to believe he was capable of violence.** He failed to show that he was defamed, as the principal's statements were truthful. *D.F. v. Board of Educ. of Syosset Cent. School Dist.*, 386 F.Supp.2d 119 (E.D.N.Y. 2005). The U.S. Court of Appeals, Second Circuit, affirmed the judgment in *D.F. v. Board of Educ. of Syosset Cent. School Dist.*, 180 Fed.Appx. 232 (2d Cir. 2006). The U.S. Supreme Court denied further review in 2007.

◆ A Louisiana student drew a sketch of his high school being soaked with gasoline and threatened by a missile launcher, helicopter and armed figures. The sketch included obscenities and racial epithets, and it showed a brick being thrown at the principal. The sketch pad was put in a closet for two years. The student's brother found the pad and drew a picture on it. He brought the pad to school, and a classmate noticed the student's old sketch. He told a school bus driver "look, they're going to blow up EAHS." The driver confiscated the pad and gave it to the principal. School officials questioned the student and searched him after he admitted he drew the sketch. They found a box cutter, notebooks referring to death, drugs, sex and gang symbols, as well as a fake ID. The principal recommended expulsion. Before the hearing, the student's mother signed a waiver form agreeing to enroll the student in an alternative school. After returning to the high school the next year, the student sued the school board in a federal district court.

The court held the sketch was not entitled to First Amendment protection, because it was a "true threat" under standards set by the U.S. Supreme Court. The court found no Fourth Amendment violation in the search, and no due process violation concerning the waiver of a hearing. The family appealed to the U.S. Court of Appeals, Fifth Circuit. It held the sketch was not speech on school grounds. **The fact that the student's brother unwittingly took the sketch to his school did not make it campus-related speech. The district court improperly found the sketch was a "true threat" with no First Amendment protection.** The school lacked authority to discipline the student for its accidental appearance on campus. Despite the First Amendment violation, the court found the line between fully protected "off-campus speech" and less protected "on-campus speech" was unclear. The principal was entitled to qualified immunity, as he had acted reasonably. The court upheld the judgment on the Fourth Amendment and due process claims. The search was appropriate under the circumstances. The mother knowingly waived a hearing so her son could gain the alternative school placement. The student admitted his responsibility for the sketch and his ownership of the box cutter. The district court had correctly awarded summary judgment to the school board and officials. *Porter v. Ascension Parish School Board*, 393 F.3d 608 (5th Cir. 2004).

◆ Two Ohio eighth-grade students with criminal records watched television coverage of the Columbine incident together. One of them called a classmate and told her that they planned to bring a gun or a bomb to school. The student told her he would "kill the preps" first and she would be "one of the first to go." Two days later at school, one of the students wrote a similar threat to another classmate. The classmates told a school guidance counselor, and a vice principal obtained their written statements. After attempting to reach the first student's mother, the vice principal contacted the student's probation officer and showed him the classmates' statements. The probation officer inquired about their credibility and the vice principal verified he believed them. Both students were placed in a detention facility and then appeared in juvenile court. A prosecutor eventually dropped their cases. The first student's mother received no suspension notice, but kept him home from school for over a week to shield him from any backlash by peers. The assistant superintendent told the second student's parent there would be no expulsion unless he was convicted.

The parents sued school and law enforcement officials in a federal district court, which held for the officials. The parents appealed to the Sixth Circuit. The court noted the probation officer investigated the classmates' statements before he acted. The vice principal met with the first student, who confirmed he knew about the note and admitted talking about Columbine. **The court found the probation officer and his supervisor had probable cause to believe the students made threats of aggravated menacing.** The Due Process Clause does not impose formalities on short-term school discipline. **Oral or written notice of the charges and an opportunity for the student to explain his or her side of the story usually satisfies due process.** Neither student was even suspended. The first student's mother admitted she made the choice to keep him home. The second student's mother was advised that suspension papers would not be prepared unless her son was found guilty of the juvenile charges. Both students received all the process they were due, and the court affirmed the judgment on their due process claims. Their state law claims for false arrest and false imprisonment failed because there was probable cause to detain them. *Williams v. Cambridge Board of Educ.*, 370 F.3d 630 (6th Cir. 2004).

◆   An Illinois sixth-grade student earned good grades and had no disciplinary record until he brought CDs to school containing a "song" titled "Gonna Kill Mrs. Cox's Baby." A classmate played the CD twice in the school's computer lab. The school suspended the student and scheduled an expulsion hearing. At the hearing, a police officer testified the student was not dangerous and did not intend to harm the teacher. Many witnesses testified about the student's good character. The principal recommended expelling him for the remaining 50 days of the school year. The school board voted in favor of the recommendation. The student petitioned a state court for a temporary restraining order reinstating him to school. The court held for the student, finding he did not cause any disruption at school and that "the disruption resulted from the investigation."

On appeal, the state appellate court explained **school officials were in a better position than judges to decide what to do with disobedient students**. The court rejected the trial court's findings. The school administration could not turn a blind eye to a CD stating a teacher's baby would be killed. It was not unreasonable to suspend the student for 50 days for a threat that was "gross disobedience" or "misconduct" under state law. School policy prohibited threats or joking about violent acts that might be reasonably interpreted as a threat or plan to engage in violence. The student clearly committed a violation of school rules. **Threats of violence in school were not permitted whether they were serious or not.** A threat like this one was not subject to an immediate determination about whether a student intended to carry it out. The court found the board had reasonably imposed the 50-day expulsion. State law permitted expulsions of up to two calendar years, and the student would be allowed to return for seventh grade. School officials have wide discretion in their disciplinary actions. As the trial court abused its discretion, the appellate court reversed and vacated its decision. *Wilson ex rel. Geiger v. Hinsdale Elementary School Dist. 181*, 349 Ill.App.3d 243, 810 N.E.2d 637 (Ill. App. Ct. 2004).

◆   New Jersey school officials grew concerned about three incidents involving threats by young students to use firearms. The principal visited each class to discuss firearms threats. She wrote letters to parents asking them to discuss the situation with their children. Five days after the principal addressed students and sent home the letter, a student said he was playing cops and robbers with his friends when he said "I'm going to shoot you." However, a teacher reported other students were upset and took the student and three others to the office. The principal suspended them for four days. She was unable to contact the student's parents, but sent them a letter explaining the suspension. The student's father sued the school board, principal and district superintendent in a federal district court for constitutional rights violations. The court held for the board and administrators on immunity grounds. The father appealed to the Third Circuit.

The court explained that "**a school's authority to control student speech in an elementary school is undoubtedly greater than in a high school setting.**" **Officials need not provide students the same latitude afforded to adult speakers and do not have to tolerate student speech that is inconsistent with the school's basic educational mission.** The student did not establish a First Amendment violation. The principal acted within her discretion by determining threats of violence and simulated firearms use were unacceptable. The court dismissed the student's attempt to "ratchet up" his playground speech to the level of a political statement. Unlike *Tinker v. Des Moines Independent Community School Dist.* (this chapter) there was no political speech here. The prohibition on threats of violence and firearms was a legitimate decision related to reasonable pedagogical concerns and was not a First Amendment violation. The school officials were entitled to immunity as they could reasonably believe they were acting within their authority. The student's claims of due process and equal protection violations had no merit, and the court affirmed the judgment. *S.G., as Guardian of A.G. v. Sayreville Board of Educ.*, 333 F.3d 417 (3d Cir. 2003).

3. Internet Cases

Internet communication does not have any more or less protection under the First Amendment than other forms of expression. Tinker v. Des Moines Independent Community School Dist. *(this chapter) has been applied to Internet cases and interpreted to allow schools to prohibit off-campus student expression that materially and substantially interferes with school operations.*

◆ A Pennsylvania high school student posted a parody of his principal on MySpace.com, using his grandmother's computer during non-school hours. The parody stated the principal was "too drunk to remember" his birth date and included a photo of the principal from the school's Web site. Most of the school's students learned of the parody, and so many of them tried to access it at school that the system was closed to student use for several days. Several computer classes were cancelled as a result. The school held an informal hearing, and found the student violated its disciplinary code by causing disruption, harassing the principal, and using obscene and vulgar language. He violated the school computer use policy by using the principal's picture without authorization.

The student was suspended for 10 days, assigned to an alternative school, and banned from his graduation ceremony and other school events. The student and his parents sued the school district in a federal district court, asserting the punishment violated his speech rights. **The court noted considerable evidence that the Web site parody disrupted the day-to-day operations of the high school.** In addition to the computer system shut-down, the district technology coordinator and a co-principal spent at least 25% of their time during the week dealing with the student's disruption. **The student violated the school's computer policy by misappropriating the principal's picture for use in the parody.** The court found he substantially disrupted school operations and interfered with the rights of others. This conduct, along with his violation of school rules, provided a sufficient legal basis for the district's actions. The alternative school placement, while not ideal, was not so onerous as to harm the student. The court held the student did not meet the standard required for preliminary relief, and it denied his motion. *Layshock v. Hermitage School Dist.*, No. 2:06-CV-116, 2006 WL 240655 (W.D. Pa. 2006).

◆   A Pennsylvania middle school student used a home computer to create a Web site called "Teacher Sux." The site included derogatory, profane, offensive and threatening comments about his algebra teacher and principal. One page showed an image of the teacher morphing into Adolf Hitler and a diagram of her with her head cut off and blood dripping from her neck. The site sought contributions "for a hitman" to kill the teacher and directed 136 profanities at her. It also accused the principal of having an extramarital affair with another administrator. Classmates accessed the site at school, and a teacher reported it to the principal. The student voluntarily took down the site. The algebra teacher was so upset by the Web site that she had to take a full year's leave of absence, requiring the district to employ substitutes. The district notified the student of its intent to suspend him, and the board later voted for expulsion.

The student challenged the decision in a state court as a violation of his speech rights. The court affirmed the expulsion order, and the Commonwealth Court of Pennsylvania also upheld it. The student appealed to the Pennsylvania Supreme Court, which held the site did not represent a "true threat," and so was not beyond all First Amendment protection. The inaction of district officials for several months after they learned of the site confirmed they did not consider it a true threat. **Speech that would otherwise enjoy constitutional protection may be subject to restriction and punishment if it materially disrupts the school environment. Officials may determine what speech is inappropriate in school.** While use of the Internet complicated the analysis of school-imposed speech restrictions, there was a sufficient connection between the site and the campus to consider the student's speech as occurring on campus. The disruption created by the site was substantial, and it harmed the entire school community. **As the site created disorder and significantly and adversely affected the school, the court affirmed the expulsion** and held it did not violate the First Amendment. *J.S. v. Bethlehem Area School Dist.*, 807 A.2d 847 (Pa. 2002).

◆   A Michigan student created "Satan's Web Page," which included a list of people he wished would die and statements encouraging murder. The student admitted contributing to the site, and the district held an expulsion hearing. The expulsion was based on three school conduct code violations. The parents withdrew the student from school but then sought his re-enrollment. The district conducted a hearing pursuant to its "discipline hearing protocol" instead of the procedures described in its code of conduct. During the proceeding, the administrator who presided over the hearing apologized to the student's counsel and the recommendation for expulsion was withdrawn. The district notified the parents more than one month later that the student could re-enroll in the district, but they refused to do so. The family sued the district in a federal district court.

The court found the evidence did not establish any misconduct occurred at school. Even had this been the case, **the district could punish the student for his speech only if it substantially interfered with the school or infringed on the rights of other students. There was no evidence the web page caused interference or disruption at school.** Naming other students on the site was not a true threat, as no reasonable person would interpret this as an intent to harm or kill anyone. The student was entitled to summary judgment on his speech and free expression claims. The district violated the student's due process rights by suspending him indefinitely. Use of the discipline hearing protocol denied him an opportunity to cross-examine witnesses or call district employees as witnesses. The student was entitled to code of conduct hearing protections, regardless of whether he was enrolled as a student in the district. As the district had disregarded his due process rights, he was entitled to summary judgment. *Mahaffey v. Aldrich*, 236 F.Supp.2d 779 (E.D. Mich. 2002).

◆   An Ohio student made a Web site at home identifying three classmates as "losers." A teacher reported the site, and the district's technology specialist determined the student had viewed it at school. The district expelled the student for 80 days, but allowed him to stay in school if he did not further violate the student code. He sued the district and officials in a federal district court.

The court noted the district had initially disciplined the student for the site's content, but now argued the discipline was for accessing the site at school. While the site was crude and juvenile, it contained no obscenity. As there was evidence that school officials were attempting to discipline the student for the site's content, the district and officials were not entitled to summary judgment. **The court held the school conduct code might be overbroad, as it had the potential to cover constitutionally protected speech.** The code's prohibition on defiance and disrespect covered some speech that deserved constitutional protection. It was impermissibly vague because it did not inform students of what behavior could lead to discipline. The district and officials were entitled to summary judgment on the claim they had attempted to shut down the site to suppress the student's speech rights. The court denied summary judgment to the district on his speech rights claims under the Ohio Constitution and denied a motion for immunity by the superintendent and principal. *Coy v. Board of Educ. of North Canton City Schools*, 205 F.Supp.2d 791 (N.D. Ohio 2002).

4. Confederate Flags

◆   A Tennessee high school was the site of several racially motivated incidents, including fighting and threats. One incident resulted in the school being locked down with the involvement of law officers. Racial harassment complaints were made to the school board, and a civil rights complaint was filed against the district alleging the school had a racially hostile environment. Based on these complaints, the director of schools determined the wearing of confederate flag symbols had a significant disruptive effect upon the high school. At the end of the school year, students were informed of the flag ban at a school assembly. Three students sued the director, principal and school board in a federal district court, seeking an order to halt the ban on Confederate flags. They claimed the principal threatened to suspend them for wearing shirts depicting Confederate flags. According to the students, other students wore shirts with foreign flags, Malcolm X symbols and political slogans. They alleged violations of their speech, equal protection and due process rights.

The court explained that the Supreme Court has repeatedly emphasized a need for the comprehensive authority of state and school officials. **School officials may "ban racially divisive symbols when there has been actual racially motivated violence, and the policy is enforced without viewpoint discrimination."** However, they may not enforce a viewpoint-specific ban on some racially divisive symbols and not on others. School officials described how racial tensions had resulted in several disruptions during the prior school year. **Officials did not have to prove a direct causal relationship between the shirts and the disruptions. The court found the racially charged atmosphere at the school gave officials reason to believe the display of Confederate flags would cause disruption and interfere with the rights of students to be secure and let alone.** The students were unable to support their claim that the policy was selectively enforced only against Confederate flags. As they did not show a viewpoint-specific ban, and there was evidence of disruption, they were not entitled to an order against enforcing the flag ban. *D.B. v. Lafon*, No. 3:06-CV-75, 2006 WL 1875585 (E.D. Tenn. 2006).

◆   A West Virginia high school with only 14 students of African-American descent enjoyed generally good race relations. The school dress code did not mention Confederate flags, and many students wore flag clothing. A student wore a shirt and a belt buckle depicting the Confederate flag to school almost every day for three years. He received no complaints until a new principal began working at the school. She had worked at other schools that had experienced serious racial violence surrounding use of Confederate flags. After the new principal arrived, the school inserted a ban on "the Rebel flag" in the dress code. The principal confronted the student and told him Confederate flags were banned from school. He was later placed in detention for violating the ban, and he sued the school district, school board and principal in a federal district court. The court held schools may prohibit student speech or conduct that is materially disruptive, involves substantial disorder, or invades the rights of others.

A Confederate flag display was not itself "patently offensive" expression that could be banned. **Schools must show a specific and significant fear of disruption, not just a remote apprehension of disturbance, in order to suppress student speech.** There was evidence that the school did not enforce its ban on prohibited messages related to alcohol and "Malcolm X" t-shirts. About 75% of the school's students had worn flag paraphernalia to school prior to the policy change, without complaints or racial incidents. The court distinguished the case from others involving racially charged school settings. **School boards could ban racially divisive symbols only when there had been actual racially motivated violence and when a policy was enforced without viewpoint discrimination.** The principal's past experiences at other schools did not justify banning the flag at this school. She had acted only with a remote apprehension of disturbance, not a specific and significant fear of disruption. The court held the dress code violated the First Amendment. The student was entitled to an order preventing enforcement of the flag ban and clearing his name from discipline. The court cautioned that its opinion should not be interpreted as a "safe haven" for those would use the flag for disruption or intimidation. Should that occur, the ban it had struck down might then be appropriate. *Bragg v. Swanson*, 371 F.Supp.2d 814 (W.D. W.Va. 2005).

◆ The principal of a Florida high school had an unwritten rule barring the Confederate flag from school grounds. He suspended two students for displaying Confederate flags on school grounds after they were warned against this. They sued the school board in a federal district court for constitutional rights violations. The court awarded summary judgment to the board, finding the principal's action appropriate because of the disruption likely to result from displaying Confederate symbols. There was evidence of racial tension in the school. The court held school officials may limit student speech to halt disruption and to inculcate manners and civility. The students appealed.

The U.S. Court of Appeals, Eleventh Circuit, embraced the district court decision, citing its reasoning at length. The principal did not unconstitutionally restrict student speech. The district court had correctly held **it is a highly appropriate function of public school administrators to prohibit speech that is vulgar and offensive**. The fact that Confederate symbols aroused particularly high emotions made it constitutionally permissible for school administrators to "closely contour the range of expression children are permitted regarding such volatile issues." As the principal and board did not violate the students' constitutional rights, the court affirmed the decision. *Scott v. School Board of Alachua County*, 324 F.3d 1246 (11th Cir. 2003).

◆ A Kansas school board responded to racial incidents in its schools by adopting an anti-harassment policy prohibiting certain clothing and materials, including Confederate flags. A student was disciplined numerous times during the school year and accused of using racial slurs. Later that year, the student drew a Confederate flag during class, which resulted in a three-day suspension for intentionally violating the anti-harassment policy. The student's father filed a federal district court action against the district. The court dismissed the case, holding it involved no fundamental speech rights but was a question of appropriate discipline for willful violation of a school policy. The policy had been adopted to prevent further racial disturbances at district schools, and the district had acted reasonably and within its constitutional authority in doing so. The suspension was upheld because it was clear to the court that the student had intentionally violated the policy. The student appealed.

The U.S. Court of Appeals, Tenth Circuit, rejected the student's due process claim. He was provided with notice of the charges against him and given an opportunity to explain his position. The district was not required to demonstrate he intentionally violated the harassment policy before taking disciplinary action. **The court found no reason to mandate a finding of intent before school districts can impose disciplinary sanctions.** No Equal Protection violation occurred. Because of the district's history of racial tension, the policy was an acceptable way of avoiding disruption. **The district did not violate the student's First Amendment rights, as its interest in avoiding additional racial disputes was enough to trump the student's speech rights.** The court rejected the student's facial challenge to the anti-harassment and intimidation policy, concluding it was neither unconstitutionally vague nor overbroad. *West v. Derby Unified School Dist. No. 260,* 206 F.3d 1358 (10th Cir. 2000).

B. Student Publications

Student publications are not "public forums," so school administrators may exercise editorial control over them if a reasonable basis exists for the belief that a publication would materially disrupt class work, involve substantial disorder or violate the rights of others.

◆ A Missouri high school principal objected to two articles prepared for publication in the school newspaper. Because the principal believed there was no time to edit the articles before the publication deadline, he deleted the two pages on which the articles appeared. Former students who were members of the newspaper staff filed a federal district court lawsuit alleging their First Amendment rights were violated when the pages were removed from the newspaper before publication. The court ruled in favor of the school district. The Eighth Circuit reversed the decision, holding the newspaper was a public forum "intended to be and operated as a conduit for student viewpoint."

The U.S. Supreme Court agreed to hear the case and noted that school facilities, including school-sponsored newspapers, become public forums only if school authorities have intentionally opened those facilities for indiscriminate use by either the general public "or by some segment of the public, such as student organizations." The Court determined that since the district allowed a large amount of control by the journalism teacher and the principal, it had not intentionally opened the newspaper as a public forum for indiscriminate student speech. **The Court held school officials can exercise "editorial control over the style and content of student speech in school-sponsored expressive activities so long as their actions are reasonably related to legitimate pedagogical concerns."** Because the decision to delete two pages from the newspaper was reasonable under the circumstances, the Supreme Court found no violation of the First Amendment. *Hazelwood School Dist. v. Kuhlmeier,* 484 U.S. 260, 108 S.Ct. 562, 98 L.Ed.2d 592 (1988).

◆ New Hampshire school yearbook editors considered publishing a picture of a student holding a shotgun and dressed in trap-shooting attire. The yearbook faculty advisor and the school principal encouraged the editors to make their own decision. The staff voted 8-2 not to publish the student's photograph in the senior portrait section of the yearbook. After the student's parents complained, the staff offered to publish the picture in the community sports section of the yearbook. The school board adopted a new publications policy banning the use of "props" in senior portraits. The student sued the board in a federal district court for an order requiring the publication of the picture as his senior portrait.

The court observed the student editors were not coerced, unduly influenced or pressured in any way by school officials to reject the student's picture. The editors believed the display of a firearm would be inappropriate in a school publication, given school policies and recent tragedies such as Columbine. **The court found the editorial judgment exercised by students was sufficiently independent from the school administration to avoid attribution to the school.** The staff's decision could not be grounds for any constitutional rights violation claim, because the student could not establish "state action." While the revised board policy was state action, it was content neutral and viewpoint neutral. The board was entitled to judgment, as there was no evidence that it selectively enforced the new policy against the student. *Douglas v. Londonderry School Board*, No. Civ. 04-424-SM, 2005 WL 626984 (D.N.H. 2005).

◆   A Michigan student newspaper staff controlled the newspaper's content, and their decisions were not subject to significant administrative intervention. A faculty advisor reviewed news items, but she did not restrict any content. The newspaper was circulated to students and to homes and businesses in the community. A local newspaper reprinted student articles twice annually. Over the years, the school newspaper had covered topics such as teenage sex, suicide, drug and alcohol abuse and sexual orientation. A student wrote an article about a pending lawsuit against the district by a family claiming harm from diesel fumes at a district bus garage. The student interviewed the family and sought to interview district officials. Officials declined to comment, despite the student's repeated efforts. The superintendent reviewed a draft of the article and ordered it deleted. She stated it was inappropriate for a school newspaper to comment on pending litigation. The superintendent did not allow students to revise the article and refused to reconsider her decision. The student sued the district and superintendent in a federal district court for violating the First Amendment.

The court noted the newspaper class was intended to teach students journalism. Journalistic independence often required journalists to question, rather than side with authorities. The court found the speech was "school-sponsored," and thus governed by *Hazelwood School Dist. v. Kuhlmeier* (this chapter). **Administrators may exercise editorial control over school-sponsored speech, so long as this is reasonably related to legitimate pedagogical concerns.** In contrast to the administrators in *Hazelwood*, the administration in this case had opened the newspaper for public speech. In doing so, it created a limited public forum for expression, not just an exclusively educational tool. The paper had covered controversial subjects in the past, and it was circulated to the general public as well as to students. The students ran the newspaper in all relevant ways. Administrators had never previously attempted to regulate its content, and the superintendent's action violated a 25-year district policy of non-intervention in the editorial process. The court held **suppression of the article was unreasonable under *Hazelwood*, unrelated to any pedagogical concern** and based on the superintendent's difference of opinion with it. **A school may not suppress speech based on its viewpoint.** The deletion of the article was not viewpoint neutral, and the student was entitled to judgment. *Dean v. Utica Community Schools*, 345 F.Supp.2d 799 (E.D. Mich. 2004).

◆   Student editors of an Ohio high school newspaper wrote an article about the school board's underage drinking policy that alleged preferential treatment of athletes who had been caught drinking. According to the article, a female student admitted drinking alcohol at a school-sponsored event. The student editors were supervised by a faculty advisor charged with ensuring publications were free of obscene, defamatory or disruptive material. The advisor approved the article, but after copies were printed, the school principal and district superintendent stopped distribution based on their belief that the student who was quoted had denied drinking and was never disciplined by the board. The board later stated the allegations of punishment for any of the six "violators" were untrue and potentially defamatory. The editors sued the board in a federal district court for First Amendment violations. The court denied their motion for a temporary restraining order allowing the immediate release of the publication.

The court held the newspaper was not a public forum where speech rights were at their height. Under *Hazelwood* (this chapter), schools may prohibit speech that substantially interferes with school work or the rights of others, and officials may exercise editorial control over student speech. The board had intended the newspaper to be a "limited public forum." The court held **the board had a reasonable belief that the article was defamatory. Under district policy and relevant case law, the district was permitted to prohibit its publication.** Three board policies gave the district the right to determine what material in the newspaper was defamatory and attempted to protect the rights of the quoted student. The court held defamatory expression is not protected by the First Amendment, and the students were not entitled to preliminary relief. *Draudt v. Wooster City School Dist. Board of Educ.*, 246 F.Supp.2d 820 (N.D. Ohio 2003).

C. Non-School Publications

◆   A New York high school senior produced a publication advocating the destruction of school property and other acts of insubordination. Copies were found throughout the school. The school's assistant principal suspended the student for five days after the student admitted he produced and distributed the publication. A hearing officer held that the student had participated in the publication and distribution on school grounds of an unauthorized publication containing vulgar language and calling for the destruction of school property. The district superintendent adopted the hearing officer's recommendation to add five days to the suspension, and the school board upheld it. The student appealed to the state commissioner of education, who held the student was denied due process, and the finding of guilt was unsupported by the evidence.

A state appellate division court annulled the commissioner's decision, finding the notice adequately advised the student of the subject matter of the hearing and that proof of the student's guilt was overwhelming. The family appealed to the Court of Appeals of New York, which found the notice satisfied due process requirements. **While school officials need not specify every single charge against a student, the notice must be sufficiently specific to advise the student and his or her counsel of the incidents giving rise to discipline.** If students are given a fair opportunity to tell their side of the story and present evidence, due process is served. The district had complied with this requirement, and the court held the commissioner abused his discretion by reversing the suspension. *Board of Educ. of Monticello Cent. School Dist. v. Commissioner of Educ.*, 91 N.Y.2d 133, 667 N.Y.S.2d 671, 690 N.E.2d 480 (N.Y. 1997).

◆ A Washington school district adopted a policy requiring high school students to submit all student-written material to school officials before it could be distributed on school grounds or at school functions. The policy was aimed at student writing that was not contained in official school publications. A group of students published and distributed a newspaper at a school barbecue without submitting it for review. As a result, the students received reprimands on their permanent records. The students sued the district in a federal district court under 42 U.S.C. § 1983, claiming the pre-distribution review policy violated their speech rights. The court held the policy did not violate the students' rights. The students appealed to the U.S. Court of Appeals, Ninth Circuit, which contrasted the case with *Hazelwood* (this chapter). In this case, **the policy was aimed at curtailing communications among students that were not associated with school sponsorship or endorsement. Therefore, the court held the policy violated the students' free speech rights** under the First Amendment. *Burch v. Barker*, 861 F.2d 1149 (9th Cir. 1988).

D. Personal Appearance and Dress Codes

1. Dress Codes

Clothing that contains expressive content may be protected as "speech" under the First Amendment and is subject to the balancing of interests test from Tinker v. Des Moines Independent Community School Dist. *(this chapter). Officials may bar messages that materially disrupt school, involve substantial disorder or violate the rights of others. Dress codes also implicate the Due Process Clause and must be specific enough to notify students of what particular expression is unacceptable, but not so broad as to prohibit protected expression.*

◆ A California school with a history of conflict over sexual orientation let a Gay-Straight Alliance group hold a "Day of Silence" to "teach tolerance." The 2003 event was accompanied by student fights. A group of students held an informal "Straight-Pride Day" and wore T-shirts with anti-gay slogans. Some students were asked to remove these shirts. Others were suspended for fighting. When the school allowed another "Day of Silence" in 2004, one student wore a T-shirt to school stating "I will not accept what God has condemned." The reverse of the shirt stated "homosexuality is shameful 'Romans 1:27.'" A teacher heard others talking about the shirt and told the student to remove it. He refused, and was sent to the office. The student was detained in a school conference room for the rest of the day for refusing to remove the shirt. An assistant principal told him he shared the Christian faith, but that he had to "leave his faith in the car" when he came to work. The student was not further disciplined, and no record of the incident was placed in his file. He sued the district and school officials for violating his speech and religious free exercise rights. A federal district court denied his request for a preliminary order. The student appealed to the Ninth Circuit, which noted there was evidence that school officials could reasonably forecast substantial disruption or material interference with school activities. *Tinker v. Des Moines Independent Community School Dist.* (this chapter) allows schools to **"prohibit speech that intrudes upon the rights of other students," or collides with the rights of others to be secure and to be let alone**. The First Amendment requires balancing "the free speech rights of students and the special need to maintain a safe, secure, and effective learning environment." The T-shirt collided with other students' rights in the most fundamental way. The court held speech that attacked minority-group high school students served to injure and intimidate them, as well as to damage their sense of security and their learning opportunities. **School administrators "need not tolerate verbal assaults that may destroy the self-esteem of our most vulnerable teenagers and interfere with their educational development." Schools had a right to reach civic responsibility and tolerance as part of their basic educational mission. They did not have to permit hateful and injurious speech that ran counter to that message. The court limited its holding to cases of "derogatory and injurious remarks directed at students' minority status such as race, religion, and sexual orientation."** The school did not punish the student, and he was free to express his views off campus. The court affirmed the judgment. *Harper v. Poway Unified School Dist.*, 445 F.3d 1166 (9th Cir. 2006).

◆   A Florida school district's code of conduct stated "[p]ierced jewelry shall be limited to the ears." A student wore pierced jewelry on her body and had piercings on her tongue, nasal septum, lip, navel and chest. On her first day of school, an administrator told her that her body jewelry violated the dress code. The student refused to remove the jewelry and was assigned to lunch detention for four days for violating the school's dress code. She claimed removal of her pierced jewelry during school hours created a significant risk for pain, infection and health problems. The student sued the school board in a federal district court, seeking a preliminary order to suspend the district's prohibition on "non-ear pierced jewelry." She argued the dress code rule limiting pierced jewelry to earrings was unconstitutionally vague and overbroad, in violation of her First Amendment rights. The student sued the school board in a federal district court, seeking a preliminary order to suspend the prohibition on her body jewelry.

The court explained that the First Amendment to the U.S. Constitution protects expressive conduct. However, the U.S. Supreme Court has cautioned against applying the First Amendment to the "apparently limitless variety of conduct" that can be labeled "speech" intending to express an idea. The student in this case did not present any evidence of what message, if any, she sought to convey by her appearance. As she did not show that a reasonable person would interpret her body jewelry as conveying any type of message, the court found the case "analogous to a long line of so-called 'individuality' or 'self-expression' cases holding that school rules limiting a student's rights to dress, style one's hair, or wear jewelry, without more, do not implicate concerns about 'expressive conduct' under the meaning of the First Amendment." The student could not show a likelihood of prevailing on the legal merits of her claim, and she failed to show an imminent risk of harm if the court did not grant relief. *Bar-Navon v. School Board of Brevard County, Florida*, No. 6:06-cv-1434, 2007 WL 121342 (M.D. Fla. 2007).

◆ A Kentucky middle school proposed a dress code to "create unity, strengthen school spirit and pride, and focus attention upon learning and away from distractions." A committee of teachers, parents and students considered, then adopted, a policy generally requiring students to wear solid-colored clothing and restricting tight, baggy, revealing, form-fitting or "distressed" clothing, as well as clothing that was "too long" or not of appropriate size and fit. A parent sued the school district in a federal district court, stating his daughter wanted to "be able to wear clothes that look nice on her, that she feels good in and that express her individuality." After the case was filed, the council modified the code to prohibit blue jeans. The court held for the district, and the parent appealed.

The U.S. Court of Appeals, Sixth Circuit, noted it had allowed an Ohio district to enforce a ban on clothes with "offensive illustrations" in *Boroff v. Van Wert City Board of Educ.*, 220 F.3d 465 (6th Cir. 2000). The court held that if a district could bar Marilyn Manson T-shirts, as it did in *Boroff*, it could enforce a dress code regulating pants and tops where a student did not wish to convey any particular message through her clothing. **The First Amendment does not apply unless there is a "particularized message." The student had no message, wanting only to "wear clothes she feels good in."** *Tinker v. Des Moines Independent Community School Dist.* (this chapter) contrasted the expressive wearing of black armbands with "the permissible regulation of the length of skirts or the type of clothing," hair style, or deportment. The student's First Amendment claim failed, as she only stated "a generalized and vague desire to express her middle-school individuality." The court held a person's choice of clothing "does not possess the communicative elements necessary to be considered speech-like conduct." **The list of fundamental rights is short, and does not include a right to wear blue jeans.** The dress code did not interfere with the parent's rights, as **parents have no fundamental right generally to direct how public schools teach their children.** The court affirmed the judgment. *Blau v. Fort Thomas Public School Dist.*, 401 F.3d 381 (6th Cir. 2005).

◆ About once a week, a New York student wore a shirt to school stating "ABORTION IS HOMICIDE." The school dress code required students to wear clothing that was appropriate and did not disrupt or interfere with the educational process. The principal stated he received complaints from three other students who were upset by the shirt. He told the student his shirt was not appropriate for school and asked him to cover its message or wear a different one. If he refused, he was to go home for the day. The student went home and did not wear the shirt for the rest of the school year. He then sued the school district and principal in a federal district court for speech rights violations.

School officials argued the ban was imposed due to the "aggressive" and "confrontational" tone of the shirt, especially its use of the word "homicide." The school did not prohibit the student from wearing other shirts with pro-life messages. According to the principal, "since abortion is legal, it is not an unlawful taking of life and thus the content of the T-shirt is inaccurate." He also stated the shirt was a "direct attack" on any student who had undergone, or was thinking of undergoing, an abortion. As the district maintained only one school, and elementary students were present, they should not be exposed to the term "abortion." **The court held the school district had to show the T-shirt would "materially and substantially interfere" with school discipline. It found all of the district's objections to the T-shirt were based on its message.** Since the school was attempting to regulate the content of the student's expression, *Tinker v. Des Moines Independent Community School Dist.* (this chapter) applied. The district did not show the shirt disrupted the school. Complaints from other students about the shirt did not rise to the level of "disruption," much less "material and substantial interference" under *Tinker.* The court granted the student's request for an order preventing the district from requiring him to remove the T-shirt, cover up its message, or threaten him with discipline for wearing it until there was a final decision in the case. *K.D. v. Fillmore Cent. School Dist.*, No. 05-CV-0336(E), 2005 WL 2175166 (W.D.N.Y. 2005).

◆   An Indiana school dress code banned symbols of violence. A student wore a T-shirt to school that bore the text of "My Rifle," the Creed of a United States Marine. The Creed states in part "My rifle is my best friend. It is my life," and "I must shoot straighter than my enemy who is trying to kill me. I must shoot him before he shoots me." The shirt depicted an M-16 rifle and the seal of the U.S Marines. Administrators told the student to remove the shirt or turn it inside out and instructed him not to wear it in the future. The school principal sent the student home, and wrote a note stating the shirt was inappropriate. The student stopped wearing the shirt, but sued the school board in a federal district court. The board argued the community was still feeling the effects of the brutal murder of a high school senior. It claimed it had disciplined 274 students for weapons violations in the past three years. However, there was no disruption over student attire, and no student had complained about the student's T-shirt.

The court found the dress code complied with the First Amendment. A prohibition on apparel depicting symbols of violence was "certainly a reasonable way for the board to discourage such violence in its schools." The court found the rule prohibiting symbols of violence primarily regulated attire, not speech. As the student could not show the school rule banned a substantial amount of speech protected by the First Amendment, the rule was upheld. **The court held the school overstepped its authority by banning the student's T-shirt. While the rule on symbols of violence was reasonably related to legitimate pedagogical concerns, the shirt had nothing to do with school violence.** Despite the conspicuous graphic of an M-16, the court found its context was within "a relatively benign message of support for the military." The shirt concerned only a United States Marine's pledge to shoot enemies of the U.S. No reasonable observer of the shirt would view references to military violence as related to Columbine or other school shootings. While the board had a legitimate interest in defusing conflict in school, it did not show how a ban on the T-shirt related to this interest. The court found no evidence of disruption, and held the student was entitled to an order allowing him to wear the shirt to school. *Griggs v. Fort Wayne School Board*, 359 F.Supp.2d 731 (N.D. Ind. 2005).

◆ Nevada law allowed school districts to create mandatory uniform policies with the consultation of parents, employee associations and schools. One district had a regulation requiring schools to survey all families and obtain a favorable response before implementing mandatory uniform policies. A district high school adopted a "dress restriction" requiring students to wear khaki pants and red, white or blue shirts with no printed materials. A group of students sued the district in a federal district court, asserting they were disciplined or threatened with discipline for violating the dress code. Some alleged their schools implemented policies without parental surveys. Two students claimed they had religious objections to wearing school uniforms.

The court reviewed *Littlefield v. Forney Independent School Dist.*, (this chapter) and other cases holding a uniform policy may be upheld if it furthers an important school interest that is unrelated to the suppression of student speech. **The court held that for clothing to be considered expressive, the wearer must have the "intent to convey a particularized message"** that is likely to be understood by observers. The students who sought to wear religious articles were entitled to First Amendment protection. The others, who indicated no intent to convey any particular message, had no such protection. The court held the state law did not violate the First Amendment. The regulation did not impose any greater restrictions on student speech than was necessary, and did not infringe on student expression. **Uniform colors reinforced the school's interest in safety by allowing the ready identification of non-students on campus.** The court held two sections of the policy giving administrators almost unlimited discretion to make exceptions to mandatory uniforms could not survive constitutional scrutiny. The court struck the two offensive provisions from the policy as unconstitutional prior restraints on speech. The rest of the policy was upheld as having a rational basis to improve student achievement, safety and the school environment. *Jacobs v. Clark County School Dist.*, 373 F.Supp.2d 1162 (D. Nev. 2005).

◆ A New Jersey school district adopted a mandatory uniform policy that exempted students with sincerely held religious beliefs, financial hardships, or scouting or school club requirements. A parent sought an exemption to the policy for her children, objecting to the "militarism conveyed by the uniforms." After the district rejected this rationale, she sought an exemption based on her atheism. The district superintendent found no evidence that wearing uniforms was incompatible with atheism and denied the request. The parent sued the district in a federal district court under the Equal Protection Clause and the New Jersey Law Against Discrimination. The court denied her request for an order halting enforcement of the uniform policy. It then awarded summary judgment to the district. The parent appealed to the U.S. Court of Appeals, Third Circuit, which held **the religious exemption furthered the educational goals of the uniform policy while protecting student rights to freely exercise religion.** The court found the exception was rationally drawn to further this legitimate interest, without undermining the pedagogical goals of the policy. The court upheld judgment for the district. *Wilkins v. Penns Grove-Carneys Point Regional School Dist.*, 123 Fed.Appx. 493 (3d Cir. 2005).

◆   An Oklahoma student was suspended for refusing to remove her Muslim hijab. Her school dress code barred students from wearing hats, hoods and bandannas indoors, but did not expressly prohibit hijabs or other religious clothing. The dress code permitted principals to interpret its provisions and make case-by-case exceptions. The student began to wear a hijab to school near the end of her fifth-grade year, without incident. On the second anniversary of the September 11, 2001 terrorist attacks, a teacher told the student to remove her hijab. The district superintendent later advised the student's family she could no longer wear a hijab at school. The student refused, claiming it was a religious requirement, and the school suspended her. After another five-day suspension, the district agreed to allow her to attend school until a ruling could be made about the constitutionality of the district dress code.

The student returned to school and sued the district in a federal district court. **The U.S. government intervened on her behalf, and eventually announced a consent agreement requiring the district to amend its dress code to allow religious headwear.** The agreement allowed the student to remain in district schools and required the district to conduct training for staff on the new dress code. *Hearn v. Muskogee Public School Dist.* 020, No. CIV 03-598-S (E.D. Okla. 2004).

◆   A Virginia middle school dress code prohibited clothes, jewelry or other items with messages relating to drugs, alcohol, tobacco, sex and vulgarity. A student wore a T-shirt to school depicting silhouettes of armed men with the letters "NRA" and the phrase "shooting sports camp." An assistant principal believed the armed figures were reminiscent of Columbine. She believed the T-shirt had the potential for disruption and told the student to either remove it or turn it inside out. The student complied. The school revised its dress code by adding weapons to the list of prohibited messages on student items. The student wore other shirts bearing NRA initials and logos to school and sued the school board in a federal district court for First Amendment and due process violations. The court found censorship of the T-shirt was permissible, as the school sought only to suppress the graphic depiction of gunmen, not the shirt's message.

The student appealed to the U.S. Court of Appeals, Fourth Circuit, where he argued the dress code was unconstitutionally overbroad by reaching too much expression that was protected by the First Amendment. **The court held the *Tinker* decision requires school authorities to identify a well-founded expectation of disruption in order to regulate student speech.** In the school setting, the First Amendment protects the non-disruptive expression of ideas. The dress code in this case reached too much protected expression. The revised code applied to even nonviolent and non-threatening messages related to weapons. The board presented no evidence that weapons-related messages would substantially disrupt school or interfere with the rights of others. The code could ban from school all lawful, nonviolent symbols depicting persons holding weapons, such as the seal of the Commonwealth of Virginia, the University of Virginia's "Cavalier," and the mascot of the district's high school. As the dress code was overbroad, the court vacated and remanded the decision. *Newsom v. Albemarle County School Board*, 354 F.3d 249 (4th Cir. 2003).

◆ A Texas school district approved a dress code forbidding students from wearing denim, leather or suede clothing, except as outerwear, and any clothing suggesting gang affiliation. The policy limited student apparel to khaki or navy pants or skirts and specific kinds of shirts. An opt-out provision allowed parents to apply for an exemption for their children based on philosophical or religious objections or medical necessity. Families who were denied permission to opt out through the district's three-step grievance procedure sued the district in a federal district court for First Amendment violations.

The court held for the district. The students and parents appealed to the Fifth Circuit, which observed that student rights of expression are balanced by the corresponding interest of schools in furthering education. Even assuming students intended to convey messages by wearing particular items of clothing, the uniform policy survived constitutional scrutiny. **The policy was validly implemented pursuant to state law, furthered an important government interest, was unrelated to the suppression of student speech and was no more restrictive of First Amendment activities than necessary.** The court rejected the parents' assertion that the policy violated their due process rights to make decisions about the care, custody and control of their children. While parents maintain fundamental rights to direct the upbringing of their children, these rights are not absolute in the public school context and are subject to reasonable regulation. **The policy was rationally related to legitimate school interests and did not violate any parental rights.** The court also rejected the families' Establishment Clause challenge to the opt-out provision. *Littlefield v. Forney Independent School Dist.*, 268 F.3d 275 (5th Cir. 2001).

2. Hair Length and Appearance

◆ An African-American male student was told to remove braids from his hair, even though no policy prohibited them. The school board revised its dress code to require all students to "wear their hair in a standard, acceptable style." All students were required to wear uniforms. Any hairstyle detrimental to student performance or school activities was prohibited. Male students could not wear their hair in braids, spiked, or in a style distracting to other students. However, females could wear braids. The student claimed the policy had a disparate impact on African-American males and violated his equal protection, free exercise and speech rights. He sued the school board in a federal district court.

The court rejected the student's claim that he had been denied a hairstyle favored by African-American males in violation of the First Amendment. There was also no violation of his equal protection rights. The court denied the board's motion for summary judgment on the gender discrimination claim, but granted it on all other claims. The court later reconsidered the gender discrimination claim, observing that a school committee had revised the dress code in conjunction with a safety policy. **The court held the dress code should be upheld under *Karr v. Schmidt*, 460 F.2d 609 (5th Cir. 1972), in which the Fifth Circuit held "there is no constitutional right to wear one's hair in a public high school in the length and style that suits the wearer."** *Karr* created a *per se* rule that hair and grooming regulations are constitutional, so long as they are not arbitrary. The court found the board's policy advanced legitimate concerns for discipline, avoiding disruption and fostering respect for authority. As the policy was not arbitrary, *Karr* compelled summary judgment for the board. *Fenceroy v. Morehouse Parish School Board*, No. Civ.A. 05-0480, 2006 WL 39255 (W.D. La. 2006).

◆ A Texas school board adopted a student grooming policy prohibiting boys from wearing their hair below the shirt collar. An elementary school principal observed a third-grade boy with a ponytail and advised him and his mother that he was in violation of the grooming policy. The school board suspended the student for three days for refusing to comply, and it placed him on in-school suspension. The student's mother removed him from school and filed a state court action against the board for violation of the Texas Constitution and state law. The court held a jury trial resulting in a decision for the board, but later modified its judgment, ruling the board had violated state law.

The court permanently enjoined the board from enforcing the policy, and the state court of appeals later affirmed the judgment. **The Supreme Court of Texas held school grooming policies do not implicate constitutional issues and should not be reviewed by the courts**. Therefore, there was no violation of the Texas Constitution. The Texas statute relied upon by the trial court was similar to Title VII of the Civil Rights Act of 1964, since both prohibited certain types of discrimination on the basis of sex. Neither was intended to address hair-length regulations in schools. The court noted that seven federal courts of appeals have held that employer grooming regulations do not violate Title VII. **The grooming policy did not deprive male students of equal educational opportunities or impose other improper barriers.** The regulation of hair length and other grooming or dress requirements was not discriminatory on the basis of sex, and the court reversed the judgment. *Board of Trustees of Bastrop Independent School Dist. v. Toungate*, 958 S.W.2d 365 (Tex. 1997).

◆ A fourth-grade Indiana boy wore an earring to school. The school lacked a written dress code, but the district's junior and senior high schools prohibited male students from wearing earrings. The school principal met with the student and his parents and advised them that he would enforce the policy against elementary students. The student continued to wear an earring, even after the school board revised its school handbook to bar the wearing of jewelry by male students. After a five-day suspension, a hearing examiner recommended transferring the student to another school that did not have similar policies. The board adopted the recommendations, but the student refused to transfer. The family sued the school district in a state court, seeking a declaration and order prohibiting enforcement of the policy. The court held for the district, and the family appealed to the Court of Appeals of Indiana.

The court rejected the student's argument that the policy denied him equal protection of the law because girls were permitted to wear earrings. Although the court rejected some of the reasons advanced by the district in justification for the policy, it found evidence that the enforcement of a strict dress code was a factor in improving student attitudes toward school. There was evidence that the local community associated earrings with female attire and that the policy discouraged rebelliousness. **The policy served the valid educational purpose**

of instilling discipline and creating a positive educational environment. Because the dress code was a reasonable exercise of school authority and did not violate constitutional rights, the court affirmed the judgment. *Hines v. Caston School Corp.*, 651 N.E.2d 330 (Ind. Ct. App. 1995).

3. Gang Affiliation

◆   An Illinois school disciplinary code defined "gang activity" as "prohibited student conduct." Gang activity included any act in furtherance of a gang, and use or possession of gang symbols, such as drawings, hand signs and attire. The code stated gangs and their activities substantially disrupted school by their very nature. A student was suspended three times for drawing gang-related symbols, including an inverted pitchfork and crowns with five points. Each time, the student was informed about the code prohibition on gang symbols and warned of its disciplinary implications. After the third incident, the superintendent notified the student's mother of a proposed expulsion, the date of a hearing and the right of the student to counsel. A school resource officer testified at the hearing that the pitchfork and crowns were gang-related signs. She said drawing them could be dangerous if misconstrued as a sign of disrespect by another gang. The school board voted to expel the student for the second half of the school year. His mother sued the board in a state court for constitutional violations. The board removed the case a federal district court.

The court explained that "a school need not tolerate student speech that is inconsistent with the school's basic educational mission," under *Hazelwood School Dist. v. Kuhlmeier*, (this chapter). To claim First Amendment protection, the student had to show he intended to convey a particular message that would be understood by those who viewed it. Although he claimed his drawings were "artistic expression," he did not claim he was attempting to convey any particular message. The court rejected the student's argument that the student code did not sufficiently define "gang symbol." A common-sense interpretation showed the student code was specifically directed at gang affiliations that disrupted the educational process. School disciplinary rules did not have to be as detailed as criminal codes. The court rejected all of the student's First Amendment arguments, and his due process claim fared no better. The board provided him with notice of the charges against him and a hearing with a full opportunity to be heard. Finding no constitutional violations, the court upheld the expulsion. *Kelly v. Board of Educ. of McHenry Community High School Dist.*, No. 06 C 152, 2006 WL 2726231 (N.D. Ill. 2006).

◆   A Kentucky school-based decision-making council devised a student dress code for a school district through a parent/teacher subcommittee. The council adopted the subcommittee's recommended dress code based on the need to address the school's gang problem, promote student safety, prevent violence and disputes over clothing, and enable the identification of non-students and intruders on campus. The dress code limited the clothing available to students as well as the way it could be worn. It prohibited logos, shorts, cargo pants, jeans, the wearing of certain jewelry outside clothes and other specified items.

A number of students who were disciplined for dress code violations sued the school board in a federal district court for First Amendment violations. The court held **school officials had an important and substantial interest in creating an appropriate learning environment by preventing the gang presence and limiting fights**. The regulation of student expression furthered an important government interest without suppressing free speech. The council and subcommittee believed the dress code would help reduce gang activity, ease tension among students who fought over attire and otherwise enhance student safety. The dress code addressed those issues in a manner that was unrelated to the expressive nature of student dress. The court held **school officials may control student speech or expression that is inconsistent with a school's educational mission**. The goal of maintaining a safe and focused educational atmosphere was viewpoint neutral and did not offend the First Amendment. The board had struck a reasonable balance between the need to anticipate problems and the personal rights of students, and it was entitled to judgment. *Long v. Board of Educ. of Jefferson County, Kentucky*, 21 Fed.Appx. 252 (6th Cir. 2001).

II. EMPLOYEES

The Supreme Court's recent decision in Garcetti v. Ceballos, *126 S.Ct. 1951 (2006) reiterated the rule that public employees have certain First Amendment rights to speak as private citizens on matters of public concern. However,* Garcetti *clarified that **a public employee's speech made pursuant to official duties is not protected by the First Amendment. The Court held "when public employees make statements pursuant to their official duties, the employees are not speaking as citizens for First Amendment purposes."***

Prior law held that public employee speech about purely private matters was unprotected by the Constitution. In Pickering v. Board of Education *the Supreme Court held a public employee may not be disciplined for speaking on matters of public concern unless there is proof that the communication was made in reckless disregard for the truth. The Supreme Court refined the* Pickering *analysis in* Connick v. Myers, *461 U.S. 138 (1983). Under* Pickering *and* Connick, *school employees are entitled to First Amendment speech protection if they speak on matters of public concern and their interest in public comment outweighs the government interest in efficient public service.*

◆   *Garcetti* involved a deputy district attorney in California who examined a search warrant affidavit presented by a defense attorney. He determined that it contained serious misrepresentations and recommended dismissing the case. At a subsequent meeting, a heated discussion ensued. The DA's office decided to proceed with the prosecution, and the deputy district attorney was reassigned, then transferred to another courthouse and denied a promotion. He sued county officials under 42 U.S.C. § 1983, claiming First Amendment violations. On appeal, the U.S. Supreme Court held that **public employees who make statements pursuant to their official duties are not speaking as citizens for First Amendment purposes, and are not insulated from employer discipline when they do so**. It was part of the deputy district attorney's job to advise his supervisors about the affidavit, and if his supervisors thought his speech was inflammatory or misguided, they had the authority to take corrective action against him. *Garcetti v. Ceballos*, 126 S.Ct. 1951, 164 L.Ed.2d 689 (2006).

◆ **The U.S. Court of Appeals, Second Circuit, held a New York elementary principal's retaliation case depended upon whether the speech for which she claimed protection occurred as part of her official duties.** The principal claimed she was fired for refusing a school board member's request to place his child in a particular classroom. A federal district court would have to reconsider the case under *Garcetti v. Ceballos*, 126 S.Ct. 1951 (2006). **In** *Garcetti*, **the U.S. Supreme Court held that First Amendment protection is unavailable for public employee speech that is made pursuant to official job duties.** *Morris-Hayes v. Board of Educ. of Chester Union Free School Dist.*, No. 06-1446-cv, 2007 WL 28317 (2d Cir. 2007).

A. Protected Speech

◆ *Pickering v. Board of Educ.* involved an Illinois school district that fired a teacher for sending a letter to the editor of the local newspaper. The letter criticized the board and district superintendent for their handling of school funding methods. Voters in the district had voted down a tax rate increase to fund a bond issue for two new schools. The teacher also charged the superintendent with attempting to stifle opposing views on the subject. **The board held a hearing at which it charged the teacher with publishing a defamatory letter. After deeming the teacher's statements to be false, the board fired the teacher.** An Illinois trial court affirmed the board's action, finding substantial evidence that publication of the letter was detrimental to the school district's interest. The Illinois Supreme Court affirmed the dismissal, ruling the teacher was unprotected by the First Amendment, as he had accepted a position that required him to refrain from speaking about school operations.

The U.S. Supreme Court reversed and remanded the case, finding no support for the state supreme court's view that public employment subjected the teacher to deprivation of his constitutional rights. The state interest in regulating employee speech was to be balanced with individual rights. The Court outlined a general analysis for evaluating public employee speech, ruling that **employees are entitled to First Amendment protection to comment on matters of public concern. The public interest in free speech and debate on matters of public concern was so great that it barred public officials from recovering damages for defamatory statements unless they were made with reckless disregard for their truth.** Because there was no evidence that the letter damaged any board member's professional reputation, the teacher's comments were not detrimental to the school system, but only constituted a difference of opinion. Since there was no proof of reckless disregard for the truth by the teacher and the matter concerned the public interest, the board could not constitutionally terminate his employment. The Supreme Court reversed and remanded the state court decision. *Pickering v. Board of Educ*, 391 U.S. 563, 88 S.Ct. 1731, 20 L.Ed.2d 811 (1968).

◆   The U.S. Court of Appeals, Fourth Circuit, shed light on what the Supreme Court meant by "matters of public concern" in *Pickering* and *Connick*. In a case brought by Virginia public university professors who challenged a state law restricting their use of university owned or leased computers, the Fourth Circuit explained "[s]peech involves a matter of public concern when it involves an issue of social, political, or other interest to a community." An inquiry into whether a matter is of public concern does not involve a determination of how interesting or important the subject of an employee's speech is. Further, the place where the speech occurs is irrelevant; an employee may speak as a citizen on a matter of public concern at the workplace, and may speak as an employee away from the workplace. The court added "[t]he Supreme Court has made clear that the concern is to maintain for the government employee the same right enjoyed by his privately employed counterpart. To this end, in its decisions determining speech to be entitled to First Amendment protection the Court has emphasized the lack of relation of the speech at issue to the speaker's employment duties." **The critical determination for whether employee speech is entitled to First Amendment protection is whether the speech is made primarily in the employee' role as citizen or primarily in the role of employee.** *Urofsky v. Gilmore*, 216 F.3d 401 (4th Cir. 2000).

◆   A New York school athletic director (AD) complained to the school board and district superintendent that the high school football coach improperly supervised students and encouraged them to use a dangerous muscle enhancer. A parent of one team member wrote to the school board president that she heard stories of severe misconduct in the locker room, including shoving a bottle up a student's rectum. During a subsequent school investigation, a 14-year-old freshman football player told the AD that some teammates had rubbed their genitals in his face, a form of hazing called "tea-bagging." The district changed its supervision protocols in football locker rooms. It also sought involvement by the state police and advised parents that unspecified sexual harassment and/or hazing had been discovered. The AD sent the superintendent a letter repeating his criticisms of the football coach. He further expressed concern about the district's handling of the tea-bagging investigation. A number of students and teachers were arrested, and the entire high school football coaching staff was suspended. The school board met in an executive session and reached "informal consensus" to abolish the AD position from the district budget. He called a press conference, where he stated that the decision to abolish his position was in retribution for his criticism of the coach and the district's investigation. After being demoted to a social studies teaching position at a lower salary, the AD sued the board and administrators in a federal district court for retaliation.

The court held for the board, finding no causal connection between the AD's speech and the elimination of his position. On appeal, the U.S. Court of Appeals, Second Circuit, stated **"the First Amendment protects any matter of political, social or other concern to the community."** The AD's speech arose from an incident of obvious public concern – the sexual assault of a student on school property. The fact that the letter was private did not make its content a purely private grievance. Having a personal stake in the speech did not destroy any public concern the speech contained. The court held a reasonable jury could reject the board's argument that the AD's position would have been eliminated even if not for his protected speech. The decision on the retaliation claim was vacated and remanded. *Cioffi v. Averill Park Cent. School Dist. Board of Educ.*, 444 F.3d 158 (2d Cir. 2006).

◆ An Oklahoma teacher had worked in public schools for over 30 years when her school board approved a comprehensive education plan setting curriculum and standards for district schools. The plan required elementary teachers to adopt an inquiry-based approach using learning modules. The teacher rejected the approach, believing it was inferior to traditional methods and materials. She wrote letters to an assistant superintendent and the school board president, voicing concerns about the use of learning modules for science instruction. The school principal issued the teacher several Admonishment and Plan for Improvement (API) letters over the next two years, but she did not use the learning modules. The school board held a hearing and found the teacher should not be reemployed due to willful neglect of duty, incompetency and unsatisfactory teaching performance. She filed several unsuccessful grievances, then sued the school district. A state court ordered the board to reinstate the teacher. She filed a federal court action for retaliation by the board for engaging in protected speech. The federal court found no evidence of retaliation, and held she was discharged for refusing directives and failing to comply with APIs.

On appeal, the Tenth Circuit stated a teacher's interest in public comment must be balanced by the employer's interest in workplace efficiency. Speech must be a substantial or motivating factor in the adverse employment action. In this case, the district court found no evidence to support the teacher's claim. The board presented evidence that her speech played no role in its decision not to renew her contract. The board documented the teacher's unprofessional conduct, violation of school policies and insubordinate behavior, and it did not reference her protected activities. While the state court held the teacher could select her own teaching methodology, it did not find the board's reasons for not rehiring her were a pretext. The Tenth Circuit stated that even if she "excelled in front of her students," this did not overcome evidence that she refused to use learning modules, violated school policies and failed to follow directives. Since the teacher did not prove the decision not to rehire her was based on speech, the court affirmed the judgment. *Greenshields v. Independent School Dist. I-1016*, No. 04-6195, 2006 WL 856213 (10th Cir. 2006).

◆ An Alabama teacher wrote numerous insulting letters to members of his school board, including one accusing a board member of being grand wizard of the Ku Klux Klan. He released information on special education students in his classes, and one of his students burned his hand while working without safety gloves. The board voted to terminate the teacher's contract, and he filed a federal district court action for discrimination, speech rights violations and retaliation. The court found his speech was protected by the First Amendment, but held the board would have discharged him regardless of his speech.

The U.S. Court of Appeals, Eleventh Circuit, held the board did not offer any legitimate nondiscriminatory reason for the action. The case was remanded to the district court, which held a trial. The jury returned a $186,000 verdict for the teacher, but the court ordered a new trial when it was learned a jury member lied about her criminal history. The case was reassigned to a different judge, who awarded judgment to the board. The teacher appealed again to the Eleventh Circuit, which considered his speech claim under *Pickering*, and *Mt. Healthy City School Dist. v. Doyle*, 429 U.S. 274 (1977). **Mt. Healthy permits a school district to discharge a teacher who brings speech rights claims, if the district shows it would have done so regardless of speech.** The Eleventh Circuit held the evidence before the judge at the trial was far different than what the first judge had encountered. In contrast to the limited record on the first appeal, there were now two trial transcripts of evidence about the teacher's "acerbic and demeaning letter-writing campaign" and its effect on the school. Since new evidence indicated he could cause discipline problems, undermine morale and impair workplace harmony, the trial court had permissibly held in the board's favor on remand. The teacher's inflammatory letter-writing campaign was itself a legitimate basis for termination. The board had abundant, non-racial reasons for its action, and the court affirmed the judgment. *Jackson v. State of Alabama State Tenure Comm'n*, 405 F.3d 1276 (11th Cir. 2005).

◆ A Pennsylvania school nurse enjoyed outstanding employment ratings for five years. She then began advocating on behalf of two disabled students and criticized the district's employment of an unlicensed person to spray pesticides, after spraying caused students and staff to become ill. The nurse communicated with the state health department and filed two complaints with the state office for civil rights. Following these complaints, her employment ratings fell. The complaints led to an investigation by a state agency and the withholding of state reimbursement for school nurse services. The nurse asserted that the school principal, assistant principal and district superintendent began to harass her, compelling her to take a leave and ultimately resign. The nurse sued the district and school administrators in a federal district court for First Amendment violations. She added state law claims including defamation, conspiracy and infliction of emotional distress. The court awarded pretrial judgment to the district and administrators on all the claims except one based on retaliatory evaluations. After a trial, the court awarded judgment to the district and administrators on the retaliation claim, and the nurse appealed.

The U.S. Court of Appeals, Third Circuit, held the nurse's reporting was "speech involving government impropriety," which occupied "the highest rung of First Amendment protection." There was no evidence that her speech disrupted the functioning of her elementary school. The court rejected the district court's finding that school administrators were entitled to qualified immunity. **The unlawfulness of their conduct was sufficiently clear that they were on notice of their own misconduct.** The court also denied qualified immunity to the school district. The superintendent was a final policymaker, and his conduct could create official district policy. The court upheld the judgment for the district and school administrators on the nurse's state law, conspiracy and emotional distress claims, but remanded her speech rights claims to the district court for further consideration. *McGreevy v. Stroup*, 413 F.3d 359 (3d Cir. 2005).

◆ A Michigan school board hired a principal after the district superintendent recommended her for employment. The board did not offer the principal a written contact. The superintendent later reduced certain perks for board members. The board placed him on administrative leave and appointed an interim superintendent. The principal spoke on behalf of the superintendent at the same time. A month later, the interim superintendent moved the board to discharge the principal for alleged problems dealing with parents. Immediately before discharging her, the interim superintendent presented her with a written contract. The principal claimed she signed it without reading it carefully and did so under duress. She sued the board in a federal district court, asserting a right to receive written notice of non-renewal and retaliation for voicing support for the superintendent. The court held for the board, and the principal appealed.

The U.S. Court of Appeals, Sixth Circuit, analyzed the speech claims under *Pickering*, which required balancing the public employee's interest in speech against the government interest in promoting efficient services. **The court held the principal's speech in opposition to the action against the superintendent was protected by the First Amendment.** The board did not show her comments harmed workplace efficiency, undermined a legitimate board interest, created disharmony among co-workers, or destroyed relationships of loyalty or trust. The court found "a serious issue" concerning the truth of the board's assertion that it actually relied on parental complaints in discharging the principal. The board did not document any performance problems and had never previously disciplined her. The suspect sequence of events, the fact that the discharge followed the principal's speech, and the lack of documentation raised an issue about the board's motive. The court remanded her speech rights claim. *Everson v. Board of Educ. of School Dist. of City of Highland Park*, 123 Fed.Appx. 221 (6th Cir. 2005).

◆ An Oregon district hired an adapted physical education teacher for a one-year probationary term. Her initial performance evaluations were good. The teacher wrote a 10-page letter to a district administrator, alleging systematic discrimination against disabled students, poor administration, curricular problems and denial of access that "greatly compromised federal law." She also criticized her supervisor. The administrator instructed a supervisor to respond to the letter and investigate the accusations. The supervisor told the teacher to stop writing letters and gave her evaluations stating she did not meet performance standards in several areas, including writing IEPs. The teacher wrote a 15-page letter to the district superintendent, asserting retaliation. Her next evaluation indicated deficient IEPs, communications problems and performance below district standards. The school board voted not to rehire the teacher. She sued the district, supervisor and administrator in a federal district court for civil rights violations. A jury awarded her $902,000 in damages, plus $50,000 in punitive damages against the administrator and supervisor. A federal magistrate judge awarded the district judgment as a matter of law. She held school officials were entitled to qualified immunity and a new trial due to misconduct by the teacher's attorney. The teacher appealed to the U.S. Court of Appeals, Ninth Circuit.

The court noted the only evidence that the teacher's IEPs were inadequate consisted of the supervisor's evaluations, which were written after the teacher's first critical letter. While a teacher might draft parts of an IEP, "no single teacher writes an IEP alone." The magistrate improperly held the supervisor and administrator were entitled to qualified immunity. **Public employees have a clearly established right to speak about matters of public concern, so long as it does not disrupt the workplace.** The verdict reflected the jury's finding that any disruption caused by the teacher's comments was outweighed by her interest in free speech. The teacher had a strong interest in expression, as her letters "may have had important effects for the disabled students in the district." By contrast, the district presented very little evidence of disruption. The letters went through proper channels, and the teacher made no public statements. The magistrate judge erroneously found the teacher's attorney made improper statements to the jury, and the court reversed the judgment. *Settlegoode v. Portland Public Schools*, 371 F.3d 503 (9th Cir. 2004).

◆   A North Carolina administrator of African-American descent worked as an assistant principal at an elementary school with a history of racial tension. She believed some teachers were disciplining disproportionate numbers of African-American students in a time-out room to avoid handling minor problems that could be addressed in class. The administrator did not comment on the practice in her first year at the school, and she received a superior evaluation. In her second year, she brought her concerns to the superintendent. He allegedly told her not to make waves and to avoid actions that might cause conflict. The administrator's evaluations remained excellent, but her communication ratings dropped. She continued to raise concerns about discrimination during her third year, and she received low scores for communications skills. After the administrator was demoted to a teaching position, she sued the board and superintendent in a federal district court for race discrimination, retaliation, and speech rights violations.

The court awarded summary judgment to the board and superintendent, and the administrator appealed. The Fourth Circuit held **speech about race discrimination is of great public concern and is protected by the First Amendment. The public concern is implicated when employee speech involves matters of social, political or other interest to the community.** The administrator raised serious, substantial issues that outweighed the district's interest in efficient operations. Despite the adverse effect the speech had on working relationships, it did not diminish the quality of education at the school. The administrator's speech was a substantial factor in her demotion. The court reversed the judgment on the speech claim and denied the superintendent's claim to immunity. **The law is clearly established that employees cannot be demoted in retaliation for protected speech.** However, the board could not be held liable for this, as it was not aware of any constitutional violation. The court affirmed the judgment on the race discrimination claim. While the administrator had shown her demotion was a violation of her speech rights, she could not prove it was based on race. *Love-Lane v. Martin*, 355 F.3d 766 (4th Cir. 2004).

◆   A California school employee entered a locked classroom and saw two co-workers under a table, apparently trying to have sex. The district investigated the incident and informed school staff that "appropriate action had been taken" against the co-workers. District administrators told staff "all speculation and talking about the improper conduct must stop immediately," to avoid morale problems and damaging rumors. The principal met privately with the employee to emphasize the "importance of the school moving forward." He warned her not to discuss the co-workers' conduct "with any person for any reason." However, the employee discussed the incident with a former district employee at a holiday party. Another employee discussed the incident with a co-worker at school. The district reprimanded both employees for disobeying its directives.

The employees sued the district in a state court for defamation, infliction of emotional distress and speech rights violations. The court held for the district, and the employees appealed to the California Court of Appeal. The court held **the employees were not speaking on matters of public concern but were only discussing private gossip. Public employee speech that does not touch on a public concern is unprotected by the First Amendment.** The employees' speech was not constitutionally protected under *Pickering*. This was not a "whistleblower" case involving criticism of a public employer. Instead, the employees sought constitutional protection to rehash the salacious details of the co-workers' encounter. They were not reprimanded for exposing misconduct, but for continuing to gossip about it after the district's investigation ended. Even had there been some public concern in the employees' speech, it would not have outweighed the district's interest in restoring efficient operations. School administrators had a legitimate interest in curtailing discussion of the incident and were entitled to qualified immunity. *Thompson v. Mt. Diablo Unified School Dist.*, No. A097629, 2003 WL 22049568 (Cal. Ct. App. 2003).

B. Personal Appearance and Dress Codes

◆ A California school district and the association representing its teachers could not reach a new agreement as their contract neared expiration. The association called for teachers to wear buttons supporting its bargaining position. Most of the teachers taught in self-contained classrooms in which only teachers and students were present. The district superintendent advised teachers of a district policy preventing them from engaging in any political activity during work time. Teachers complied with the directive, but the association filed an unfair practice charge against the district. The state Public Employee Relations Board (PERB) found the wearing of buttons was not political activity and held the district had interfered in the teachers' rights. The district appealed to the state court of appeal, which considered the case under the California Educational Employment Relations Act (EERA) and the state Education Code.

The EERA gave public school employees the right to form and join unions and participate in collective bargaining. Employee organizations had rights of access "at reasonable times" to use bulletin boards, mailboxes and other means of communication to exercise their rights. The court held the wearing of buttons by teachers was protected by the EERA. **Case law interpreting the National Labor Relations Act recognized the right of employees to wear union buttons in the workplace. But the court held button-wearing was "political activity" that could be barred under the Education Code.** The Code authorized restricting political activities during work hours and on the premises of a local agency. Public school teachers acted with the imprimatur of their employing districts. It was reasonable to prohibit them from political advocacy during instructional activities. The wearing of union buttons during instructional time was "inherently political." The court held keeping the labor relations dispute from spilling into the classroom was a proper restriction of political activity and reversed the PERB's decision. *Turlock Joint Elementary School Dist. v. PERB*, 5 Cal.Rptr.3d 308 (Cal. Ct. App. 2003).

◆   *Turlock Joint Elementary School Dist. v. PERB*, above, is limited to instructional time. **A ban on political advocacy could not be enforced in noninstructional settings.** Another California district prohibited employees from distributing partisan election materials on school grounds and from campaigning during work hours. The teachers association objected to the policy and demanded its rescission so that teachers could wear buttons expressing their opposition to a state education finance voter initiative. A state superior court held the policy violated the First Amendment speech rights of teachers.

The Court of Appeal of California held state law allows schools to restrict the political speech of teachers during work hours. **Because public school teachers have considerable power and influence in classroom situations and their speech may be reasonably interpreted as reflecting the official view of their school districts, it was reasonable to prohibit them from wearing political buttons in classrooms.** This restriction did not violate the First Amendment or the state constitution, as school authorities must have the power to disassociate themselves from political controversy and the appearance of approval of political messages. However, it was unreasonable for the district to restrict political speech by teachers outside their classrooms. The court modified the decision so that teachers were prohibited from wearing political buttons only in the classroom. *California Teachers Ass'n v. Governing Board of San Diego Unified School Dist.*, 53 Cal.Rptr.2d 474 (Cal. Ct. App. 1996).

C. Association Rights

◆   The U.S. Supreme Court agreed to review a decision by the Supreme Court of Washington which held unconstitutional a state law governing the ability of employee associations to use agency or "fair share" fees for political purposes. The action was filed against two employee associations by union non-members who claimed violation of their First Amendment rights based on use of their agency fees to support political and ideological causes without affirmative authorization. *Davenport v. Washington Educ. Ass'n*, No. 05-1589, 2006 WL 1646515 (U.S. cert. granted 9/26/06).

◆   A Tennessee school superintendent was invited to say a breakfast prayer at a convention held by a religious congregation. He initially agreed, but declined after learning of a scheduling conflict. The superintendent declined a later request to speak at the same convention. He did not know the congregation was primarily gay and lesbian. Meanwhile, the congregation informed the media he would be a speaker. A newspaper incorrectly reported the superintendent would address the convention. He submitted statements to two newspapers, informing them he had declined the speaking invitations, and declared "that he did not endorse, uphold or understand homosexuality, but that he would not refuse to associate with gay people or refuse the opportunity to share with them his beliefs." Several board members believed the article called his judgment into question, undermined public confidence in him, and impaired his functioning. The board did not hire the superintendent to become the director of schools, which is the state's current designation for chief executive of a school district.

The superintendent sued the board and its members in a federal district court. The court held for the board and board members. The U.S. Court of Appeals, Sixth Circuit, held the First Amendment does not permit public employers to retaliate against employees on the basis of protected speech. The superintendent's intended prayer or speech touched on the public concern. The speech concerned religion and perhaps homosexuality, and would occur on his own time. **The superintendent sought to share his religious beliefs with the congregation and the community. This conduct was protected. The court held "it would contravene the intent of the First Amendment to permit the Board effectively to terminate [the superintendent] for his speech and religious beliefs in this way."** The court reversed the judgment for three school board members who had apparently changed their view of the superintendent on the basis of his intended speech. The superintendent also stated claims for relief under the Equal Protection Clause. The board members were not entitled to qualified immunity, as he had a clearly established right to express his religious beliefs. The case was returned to the district court for further proceedings. *Scarbrough v. Morgan County Board of Educ.*, 470 F.3d 250 (6th Cir. 2006).

◆   A Vermont school district fired a maintenance worker for misappropriating school equipment. He claimed the action was instead based on retaliation for union activities during his 25 years of employment. The worker sued the district for a variety of claims in a state court. The court granted the district's motion to dismiss all claims except one brought directly under the U.S. and Vermont Constitutions. After a trial resulted in a hung jury, the district moved the court to dismiss the direct constitutional claims. The court denied the motions and held another trial. This time, the jury awarded the worker $257,728.

After the court denied the district's motion to set aside or reduce the jury verdict, it appealed to the Supreme Court of Vermont. **The court found little evidence that the worker had engaged in constitutionally protected speech. It agreed with the district that the worker did not have a direct cause of action under the state or U.S. constitutions.** The worker failed to plead the case under 42 U.S.C. § 1983 or bring an unfair labor practice claim under state law. The trial court should have granted the district's motions and the case should never have gone before the jury. As all the claims should have been dismissed, the supreme court vacated the judgment. *Graham v. Springfield Vermont School Dist.*, 2005 VT 32, 872 A.2d 351 (Vt. 2005).

◆   A Michigan high school senior and a teacher began communicating outside class through e-mails and instant messages. As the student neared graduation, the teacher told her she was gay. The student's mother found an e-mail from the teacher to the student with sexual innuendoes. The teacher told the principal the e-mail was sent to all her e-mail address book recipients and was mistakenly sent to the student. She denied any inappropriate relationship with the student. However, the two continued to correspond after the student enrolled in college. The principal recommended the teacher for tenure. Days later, the mother told the principal the explicit e-mail was sent to her daughter alone, not each address in the teacher's book. She revealed an instant-messaging session between the teacher and student with explicit sexual and romantic content. The principal suspended the teacher and recommended denying her tenure for her lack of candor. The school board upheld his recommendation, and the teacher sued the district, its board and district officials in a federal district court for due process violations relating to rights to privacy and intimate associations, and to be free from arbitrary state action. The court held the Constitution did not protect the teacher's relationship with the student, and the teacher appealed.

The U.S. Court of Appeals, Sixth Circuit, **held that schools can act to prevent teachers from having intimate relationships with students**. While the Due Process Clause protects personal decisions relating to marriage, family and intimate relationships, only rules prohibiting all personal relationships violated due process rights. The court had previously upheld an anti-nepotism rule barring school employees from marrying. Just as that rule did not directly burden an employee's right to marry, the board's action in this case did not directly and substantially affect the teacher's intimate association rights. The principal's assessment of the teacher's candor was alone a legitimate explanation for denying her tenure. **A policy against relationships between teachers and recent graduates would prevent high school seniors from being perceived as prospective dates after graduating.** As the board did not violate the teacher's due process or privacy rights, the judgment was affirmed. *Flaskamp v. Dearborn Public Schools*, 385 F.3d 935 (6th Cir. 2004).

◆ A Minnesota school district policy reserved the use of employee mailboxes, internal mail, voice mail and e-mail systems for school-related business. The policy allowed "nonschool persons or organizations that engage in activities of interest and educational relevance to students" to use these systems. While the policy opened district mail systems to employee representatives for official business, the policy forbade distribution of literature endorsing political candidates in district mail systems. A few weeks before the 2004 elections, associations representing district teachers and instructional assistants sought to place John Kerry brochures in the employee mailboxes. When the district denied the request, the associations sought relief from a state district court.

The school district removed the case to a federal district court, which stated the First Amendment applied to teacher mailboxes, as well as elsewhere in a school. **The Supreme Court has noted the Constitution does not require the government to grant access to all those who wish to speak on government property. The extent to which schools may control access to their property depends on the nature of the forum. The mailbox systems were a nonpublic forum, not an open forum**, as the associations argued. The district did not open its mail systems for public discourse. It had reserved them for school district related business. The district could restrict access to this forum, so long as the restrictions were reasonable and were not intended to suppress speech. The restriction of mailbox access was both reasonable and viewpoint neutral. The district's justification for the mailbox policy was to "minimize disruption in the educational setting." The associations had substantial alternative channels for communications, including direct mail, Web site and in-person solicitation outside the mailbox system. As the associations did not show their interest in distributing political literature outweighed the district interest in promoting efficient public services, the court denied relief. *Educ. Minnesota Lakeville v. Independent School Dist. No. 194*, 341 F.Supp.2d 1070 (D. Minn. 2004).

◆ An Ohio secondary vocational education system maintained an unwritten anti-nepotism policy for over 20 years. Although the policy prohibited teachers who were married to each other from working at the same facility, the policy was not applied to employees who were cohabiting or dating. Two instructors, each employed by the system for over nine years, got married without telling system officials. When a human resources officer learned of the marriage, she arranged for the transfer of the wife to a different campus. The transferred teacher was required to commute an extra hour each day and began to suffer psychiatric problems. The couple filed a complaint against the school system in a federal district court, asserting the anti-nepotism policy violated their First Amendment associational rights. The court granted summary judgment to the school system, and the couple appealed to the Sixth Circuit.

The court agreed with the couple that marriage is a constitutionally protected fundamental right. However, the policy did not directly and substantially burden that right. The policy only prohibited employees who were married to each other from teaching at the same facility, and it did not require the couple to end their marriage. The stated reasons for maintaining the policy represented legitimate educational concerns of avoiding workplace friction in the event of a marital breakdown and minimizing other identified employment problems. The teachers failed to meet the system's evidence that allowing married teachers to work together may lead to problems, and the court affirmed the judgment. *Montgomery v. Carr*, 101 F.3d 1117 (6th Cir. 1996).

III. ACADEMIC FREEDOM

Schools have broad discretion in curricular matters and courts are unwilling to closely scrutinize the reasonable exercise of a board's discretion in this area. However, the same level of discretion does not apply to decisions involving school library books.

A. Library Materials

◆ The U.S. Supreme Court held the right to receive information and ideas is "an inherent corollary of the rights of free speech and press" embodied in the First Amendment. The case arose when a New York school board rejected the recommendations of a committee of parents and school staff it had appointed and ordered that certain books be removed from school libraries. The board characterized the books as "anti-American, anti-Christian, anti-Semitic, and just plain filthy." Students brought an action for declaratory and injunctive relief against the board and its individual members, alleging the board's actions violated their rights under the First Amendment. The Supreme Court noted that while school boards have broad discretion in the management of curriculum, they do not have absolute discretion to censor libraries and are required to comply with the First Amendment. **A decision to remove books from a school library is unconstitutional if it is motivated by an intent to deny students access to ideas with which school officials disagree.** *Board of Educ. v. Pico,* 457 U.S. 853, 102 S.Ct. 2799, 73 L.Ed.2d 435 (1982).

◆   The U.S. Supreme Court upheld the Children's Internet Protection Act (CIPA), finding **public libraries can be required to install filters on Internet computers as a condition of receiving federal technology grants and e-rate discounts.** The case consolidated two actions challenging the CIPA, which requires public schools and libraries receiving federal technology grants or e-rate discounts to install filtering systems on computers used by children 17 or younger to block out obscenity, child pornography and other harmful material. Local boards or agencies can decide what software to install and what to block. The complaints alleged the CIPA violated the First and Fifth Amendments and sought to permanently bar the Federal Communications Commission from implementing the law. A three-judge federal panel agreed with the complaining parties that the CIPA's unblocking provisions did not save the law, because a library patron might wish to remain anonymous or might be too embarrassed to ask for the filters to be removed in order to view sensitive materials.

On appeal, the Supreme Court held that Internet access in public libraries is neither a traditional nor a designated public forum. For this reason, **libraries have discretion to choose what parts of the Internet they will offer patrons, in the same way they choose which books to put on the shelves.** "A public library does not acquire Internet terminals in order to create a public forum for Web publishers to express themselves, any more than it collects books in order to provide a public forum for the authors of books to speak." The Court found any concerns about innocuous Web sites being wrongly blocked were addressed by CIPA provisions allowing librarians to disable filters when asked by adult patrons. The Court rejected the contention that people seeking medical, sexual or other sensitive information would be reluctant to ask for unblocking. It concluded "the Constitution does not guarantee the right to acquire information at a public library without any risk of embarrassment." *U.S. v. American Library Ass'n Inc.,* 539 U.S. 194, 123 S.Ct. 2297, 156 L.E.2d 221 (2003).

◆   A gay and lesbian organization donated two books with homosexual themes to a Kansas school district. The district conducted a review for their acceptability. One of the books was already on the library shelves of several district schools, but no one had ever checked out a copy. However, the media publicized the donation and individuals opposed to it burned copies of the book on district property. **The district superintendent recommended removing existing copies from the libraries and rejecting the donation.** The school board voted to remove the books and refuse the donation, and a teacher and some students sued the district in the U.S. District Court for the District of Kansas.

The court granted a temporary order to the complaining parties and then considered a motion to make the order permanent. It observed the book contained no vulgarity or explicit sexual language and had won numerous literary awards. The district had failed to abide by its own rules in rejecting the donation and removing existing copies from its shelves. Testimony of board members indicated they disapproved of the book's subject matter and had voted to remove it because of their disagreement with it. The failure of the board to follow its own procedures for library procurement affirmed the court's belief that **board members had been motivated to remove the book based on their personal disagreement with ideas expressed in it**. Removal of the book violated the constitutional rights of students presently attending district schools. The court issued an order requiring school officials to return copies to district libraries. *Case v. Unified School Dist. No. 233*, 908 F.Supp. 864 (D. Kan. 1995).

B. Textbook Selection

◆ A teacher in a Michigan public school taught a life science course using a textbook approved by the district's school board. He showed films to his class regarding human reproduction (*From Boy to Man* and *From Girl to Woman*) after obtaining approval from his principal. The films were shown to his seventh-grade classes with girls and boys in separate rooms, and only students with parental permission slips were allowed to attend. Both films had traditionally been shown to seventh-grade students in the school. However, **after a school board meeting where community residents demanded that the teacher be tarred and feathered for showing the films, the superintendent of schools suspended the teacher with pay pending "administrative evaluation."** The board approved this action.

The teacher then sued the district in a U.S. district court for violation of his First Amendment and other civil rights. The jury awarded the teacher $321,000 in compensatory and punitive damages. The U.S. Supreme Court reversed the decision and remanded the case to the district court. According to the Supreme Court, an award of money damages may be made only to compensate a person for actual injuries that are caused by the deprivation of a constitutional right. **The Court held that damages for abstract violations of the U.S. Constitution were not allowed.** *Memphis Community School Dist. v. Stachura*, 477 U.S. 299, 106 S.Ct. 2537, 91 L.Ed.2d 249 (1986).

◆ A Texas student and the author of an environmental textbook had no constitutional right to compel the state board of education to select a textbook, according to the U.S. Court of Appeals, Fifth Circuit. It held **textbook selection was "government speech" that did not involve a "forum," so the forum analysis applied by courts in student speech cases did not apply**. The Supreme Court has stated that the government can, without violating the constitution, selectively fund programs to encourage activities it believes to be in the public interest, and may discriminate on the basis of viewpoint by choosing to fund one activity over another. The Supreme Court has also carefully distinguished a school's decision to expend funds to encourage diversity of the views of private speakers from the school's choice regarding its own message. Schools could thus promote policies and values of their own choosing, free from the forum analysis and the viewpoint-neutrality requirement. The court held when the school board set the curriculum and selected textbooks, "it is the state speaking, and not the textbook author."

Devising the curriculum and selecting textbooks were core functions of the board, which needed to keep editorial judgment over the content of instructional materials for public school classrooms. **The court agreed with the board that its selection of curricular materials was government speech, and it rejected the student's claim to a right to receive information in the textbook. Students have no constitutional right to compel the selection of classroom materials of their choosing.** *Chiras v. Miller*, 432 F.3d 606 (5th Cir. 2005).

◆ A group of parents whose children attended grade school in an Illinois school district filed a lawsuit in the U.S. District Court for the Northern District of Illinois, seeking an order to prevent use of the Impressions Reading Series as the main supplemental reading program for grades kindergarten through five. **The parents alleged the series "foster[ed] a religious belief in the existence of superior beings exercising power over human beings" and focused on "supernatural beings"** including "wizards, sorcerers, giants and unspecified creatures with supernatural powers." The court granted a motion to dismiss the lawsuit. The parents appealed to the Seventh Circuit.

The court found the parents' argument that use of the textbook series established a religion was speculative. Although the series contained some stories involving fantasy and make-believe, their presence in the series did not establish a coherent religion. The intent of the series was to stimulate imagination and improve reading skills by using the works of C.S. Lewis, A.A. Milne, Dr. Suess and other fiction writers. **The primary effect of using the series was not to endorse any religion, but to improve reading skills.** Use of the series did not impermissibly endorse religion under the Establishment Clause or the Free Exercise Clause. The parents failed to show the use of the series had a coercive effect that prevented the parents from exercising their religion. The school directors were entitled to judgment as a matter of law. *Fleischfresser v. Directors of School Dist. 200*, 15 F.3d 680 (7th Cir. 1994).

C. School Productions

◆ A Nevada high school student selected a W.H. Auden poem containing the words "hell" and "damn" for recital at a statewide poetry reading competition. He practiced the poem twice a day for over two months. When the student recited the poem at a competition in the school, the dean of students e-mailed the English chair that it was objectionable due to inappropriate language. The student recited the poem again at a district-wide competition held off campus.

A school dean formally reprimanded English department members for not prohibiting the recitation. The student learned he would have to choose a new poem for the state competition because the Auden poem had profanity. He filed an emergency motion in a federal district court, seeking a temporary restraining order to prevent the school from interfering with his recitation. The court found the recitation of the Auden poem could not be considered vulgar, lewd, obscene or offensive. The state competition was a non-curricular activity that was only partly supervised by school officials. **Off-campus poetry recitation at a state competition sponsored by national organizations was not school-sponsored speech and was not a part of the curriculum or any regular classroom activity. Where there was no showing that student speech would materially and substantially interfere with appropriate discipline, the court could not uphold speech restraint by school officials.** A poem by a recognized poet, recited at an off-campus student competition authorized by the school, did not present even a remote risk of disruption. As there was a "total absence of evidence" that the school could constitutionally prohibit the recitation of the poem, the student was entitled to a temporary order restraining the school from prohibiting his selection of poetry for recitation. *Behymer-Smith v. Coral Academy of Science*, 427 F.Supp.2d 969 (D. Nev. 2006).

◆   A North Carolina high school English and drama instructor won numerous awards for directing and producing student plays. She selected a play for a state competition that depicted a divorced mother with a lesbian daughter and a daughter who was pregnant with an illegitimate child. Her advanced acting class won 17 of 21 possible awards at a regional competition for performing the play. However, when a scene from the play was performed before an English class, a parent objected and the principal forbade students from performing the play at the state finals. He later allowed the performance with the deletion of certain scenes. The school board approved a transfer of the teacher to a middle school for violating the district's controversial materials policy. She filed a state court retaliatory discharge action against the board and school officials. The case was removed to a federal district court.

The court dismissed the action, and the teacher appealed to the U.S. Court of Appeals, Fourth Circuit. A three-judge panel of the court rejected the board's argument that the First Amendment protects only original expression and not the selection of a play by a teacher. The panel held that because of the important role that teachers play in society, the First Amendment extended to the selection of plays for high school drama classes. The full court then agreed to rehear the panel decision and vacated its prior decision. **The court held the selection of a school play is part of a public school curriculum, and it does not constitute a matter of public concern for which a teacher might enjoy constitutional protection.** The court vacated the panel decision and upheld the transfer. *Boring v. Buncombe County Board of Educ.*, 136 F.3d 364 (4th Cir. 1998).

IV. PARENTAL SPEECH AND ASSOCIATION RIGHTS

The U.S. Supreme Court has recognized a fundamental right of parents to direct and control the upbringing of their children. This does not include a parental right to direct and control public school curriculums. Federal courts have approved many state actions that intrude on parental liberty, such as mandatory sex and health education programs, school uniforms, community service and attendance requirements, and condom distribution programs. Parents have no unrestricted right to enter school campuses.

A. Access to School Campuses

◆   An Illinois parent was convicted of a crime which defined him as a child sex offender. However, he was not required to register under the Illinois Sex Offender Registration Act. He brought his children to school activities, games and practices, and picked them up for medical appointments and emergencies. A 2005 legislative amendment prohibited child sex offenders from being on or within 500 feet of school grounds when children were present, unless the offender was a parent or guardian of a student attending the school, and was there to meet or confer with school staff about the child's performance and adjustment in school. The amendment further required a child sex offender to notify the school principal of his or her presence at a school. School officials denied the parent's requests to come to school for his own children's activities. He claimed the amended law violated his due process and equal protection rights, and he sued the district. The parent asked the court for a preliminary order to allow him to attend school events, concerts and games with his family. He also sought to proceed under the fictitious name "John Doe."

The court found the parent's interests in privacy did not outweigh the public interest in the open nature of court proceedings, and it ordered him to proceed under his true name. The court denied his motion for permission to attend school events during the litigation. The potential harm to the district and to society could not be ignored. Illinois law sought to avoid further child predation by requiring those convicted of sex abuse to identify themselves and be supervised when near children. **The court found the parent was asking it "to negate the declared social policy requirements of identification and supervision." As the potential harm to others was much stronger than the parent's need to attend school events, the court denied his motion for preliminary relief.** *Doe v. Paris Union School Dist. No. 95*, No. 05-2249, 2006 WL 44304 (C.D. Ill. 2006).

◆   The U.S. Court of Appeals, Third Circuit, rejected an action by New Jersey parents who claimed they were wrongfully escorted from a school campus by a sheriff's deputy. **There was no evidence of physical force by the deputy, so no "seizure" occurred to support a constitutional claim. The school board did not violate the parents' rights by "illegally banning" them from school property. There is no due process right for parents to enter school property.** Even if the No Child Left Behind Act created a private cause of action as the parents claimed, they did not substantiate such a claim by alleging the board did not meet state education standards for five years. The superintendent had immunity, and the remaining claims had no merit. *Cole v. Montague Board of Educ.*, 145 Fed.Appx. 760 (3d Cir. 2005).

◆   A Texas parent yelled at his son's first-grade teacher and followed her into a parking lot. He spanked his son and a classmate while they walked in a school hallway, and he used profanity when speaking to administrators. The school restricted him from classrooms and instructed him to schedule a formal conference with the principal if he wanted to speak to teachers. When the parent ignored these directives, the school banned him from campus, and twice called the police to have him removed from school property. The parent picketed in front of the school and confronted a teacher during a class field trip, shouting and swearing in front of students. He sued the district in a federal district court, claiming a constitutional right to be on school grounds, and alleging speech violations and infliction of emotional distress by the district.

A federal magistrate judge found **no court has ever construed the Due Process Clause as creating a parental right of access to school facilities. Courts have "consistently upheld the authority of school officials to control activities on school property."** The magistrate judge held **this included the authority to bar parents from campus when necessary to maintain order.** There was an escalating pattern of threatening, abusive and disruptive conduct by the parent toward the school faculty and administration, defeating his due process claim. **Under *Connick v. Myers*, 461 U.S. 138 (1983), speech is only protected by the Constitution if it addresses a "matter of public concern."** The parent's speech claim was based on private communications about his own children, and did not involve the public concern. There was no evidence that the school was motivated by retaliation. It banned him from campus as a result of his threatening, abusive and disruptive behavior. The magistrate judge recommended that the court award summary judgment to the district on all the parent's claims. *Rogers v. Duncanville Independent School Dist.*, No. 3-04-CV-0365-D, 2005 WL 770712 (N.D. Tex. 2005).

The district court reviewed the magistrate judge's findings and recommendations, found them correct and adopted them. It awarded summary judgment to the district. *Rogers v. Duncanville Independent School Dist.*, No. 3:04CV0365D, 2005 WL 991287 (N.D. Tex. 2005).

◆ An Illinois mother had sole custody of her two children, but her divorce decree specified the children's father had joint, equal access rights to school records. The parents were required to cooperate to ensure authorities sent them dual notices of their children's school progress and activities. The father criticized a school principal at public meetings, complained that nothing was done when his son was bullied, and claimed the school did not provide him notices, records, correspondence and other documents sent to custodial parents. He wrote letters to the principal about these matters, then stated the principal excluded him from the playground when he sought to observe his son during recess, and turned him down as a volunteer playground monitor. The father sued the principal and school district in a federal district court for constitutional and state law violations. The court dismissed the case, and he appealed.

The U.S. Court of Appeals, Seventh Circuit, noted the difficulty for schools to accommodate demands by divorced parents. **School officials could not know a parent's rights until they consulted the divorce decree, but did not have to be dragged into fights between divorced parents over their children.** The father's rights concerning his children's records were no greater than the school's interest in keeping as free as possible from divorce matters. **The only constitutional right concerning the education of one's child was the right to choose the child's school. The court held this was not a right to participate in the school's management. Schools also have a valid interest in limiting a parent's presence on campus.** The court rejected the father's claim to a constitutional right to participate in his children's education in the degree he sought. However, he should receive a chance to show that the principal had deliberately treated him differently than custodial parents, and had violated his speech rights. While most of the father's criticisms of administrators were "personal," he also alleged being critical of them in public meetings and questioned their inadequate responses to bullying. The district and the principal prevailed on the father's due process claims, but the equal protection and speech rights claims were remanded to the district court for further consideration. *Crowley v. McKinney*, 400 F.3d 965 (7th Cir. 2005).

◆ The non-custodial parent of a Virginia high school student complained repeatedly to school employees that his son was not selected for the varsity basketball team. The student's mother had previously requested notice from the school so that she could be present for discussions involving her children. The school principal notified the father that such meetings had to be scheduled in advance to accommodate the mother's request, and that he should otherwise limit his presence on school property to public events. The father asserted that these limitations violated his constitutional rights. The superintendent sent him a letter barring him from school property due to continuing inappropriate behavior toward school officials, staff, and board members. The father sued the district in a federal district court for constitutional rights violations. The case was dismissed, and he appealed to the U.S. Court of Appeals, Fourth Circuit.

The court held "school officials have the authority and responsibility for assuring that parents and third parties conduct themselves appropriately while on school property." While the specific contours of this authority and responsibility were defined by state law, **"officials should never be intimidated into compromising the safety of those who utilize school property."** In this case, the school district gave the father ample opportunity to complain about the conduct of school board members and officials before the superintendent's letter. **The superintendent found the father's conduct was a threat and appropriately requested that he not enter school property.** The right to communicate is not limitless, and the letter banning the father from school property did not implicate any constitutional rights. The court held the claims against the superintendent for money damages were frivolous. *Lovern v. Edwards*, 190 F.3d 648 (4th Cir. 1999).

B. Curriculum

◆ A California volunteer mental health counselor developed a psychological assessment questionnaire as part of her master's degree program in psychology. The district agreed to survey first-, third- and fifth-graders and use the results for an intervention program to help children reduce barriers to learning created by anxiety, depression, aggression and verbal abuse. The counselor sought the consent of parents in a letter stating the nature and purpose of the questionnaire. She did not mention that 10 of the 79 questions involved sexual topics. After the survey was administered, parents learned of the survey questions about sex. Students were asked if they felt they touched their private parts too much, could not stop thinking about sex, thought of touching others' private parts, had "sex feelings in my body," or washed themselves because of feeling "dirty on the inside." Parents claimed they would not have consented to the survey had they known of these questions. They sued the school district in a federal district court for constitutional privacy rights violations, and included a state law negligence claim. The court dismissed the case, and the parents appealed.

The U.S. Court of Appeals, Ninth Circuit, rejected the parents' claim to a fundamental right to control the upbringing of their children by "introducing them to matters of and relating to sex in accordance with their personal religious values and beliefs," and to exclusively determine when and how their children were exposed to sexually explicit subjects. While the Supreme Court has held parents have a fundamental liberty interest to make decisions about the care, custody and control of their children that is protected by the Due Process Clause, this right was limited. Supreme Court cases on private schools did not support the claim that parents may "replace state educational requirements with their own idiosyncratic views of what knowledge a child needs" to be a productive, happy member of society. **Parents could not dictate the public school curriculum.** The school district did not violate any parental privacy rights. The protection of children's mental health was well within the state's broad interest, and the court affirmed the judgment. *Fields v. Palmdale School Dist.*, 427 F.3d 1197 (9th Cir. 2005).

◆   A Massachusetts father claimed his daughter's school district retaliated against him after he complained about its use of a science textbook. He asserted she was excluded from a journalism class and that school officials had police escort him from school after he came there to pick up records. According to the father, this was based on the superintendent's misrepresentations of disruption. He claimed a school committee member had the police remove his wife from a committee meeting based on her speech. The father alleged the superintendent said his daughter's safety could not be guaranteed if his wife filed a formal complaint. The family sued school officials in a federal district court. The wife and daughter settled their claims. The court awarded summary judgment to the school officials on the father's claims, and he appealed to the First Circuit.

The court stated the constitutional liberty interest of parents to direct the upbringing and education of their children has only been construed as a right to choose a child's school. This limited right does not permit parents to dictate a public school curriculum. The father did not show any interference with the right to enroll his daughter at the school of his choice. The school committee allowed him to remove her from school for home schooling. The committee did not violate any due process rights by refusing to let the father dictate what science text to use or allegedly excluding his daughter from the journalism class. The district court properly held for school officials on all of the claims, and its judgment was affirmed. *Pisacane v. Desjardins*, No. 02-1694, 115 Fed. Appx. 446, 2004 WL 2339204 (1st Cir. 2004).

◆   Texas school administrators introduced a Connected Math Program (CMP) through a "Parents' Math Nights" series held in district schools. Some parents objected to the CMP as an unproven alternative to the traditional curriculum. A parent brought flyers to a math night criticizing the CMP and placed them on a table with district materials. He brought a petition requesting an independent evaluation of the CMP and more parental input. A school official asked the parent to remove the flyers from the table, and another asked him to leave. An assistant superintendent allegedly e-mailed district employees the next day, warning them not to allow anyone to circulate a petition or pass out material related to the CMP. The parent tried to display a poster at a Math Night and was told by the assistant superintendent to turn it face-down. Another parent distributed copies of a state education agency report about CMP at a Math Night meeting. The school's principal told him he could not distribute material on school property without prior approval.

The parents sued the district and officials in a federal district court for First Amendment violations. The court denied summary judgment to the principal and assistant superintendent, and they appealed to the U.S. Court of Appeals, Fifth Circuit. The court stated **qualified immunity protects officials if their conduct does not violate clearly established statutory or constitutional rights of which a reasonable person would know.** Government regulation of speech is unconstitutional, if the regulation depends on the will of an official. There was evidence of viewpoint discrimination in this case, particularly in the assistant superintendent's e-mail. The parents' speech involved the public concern and there was no evidence it disrupted the schools. Because the principal and assistant superintendent unconstitutionally applied school policies, the court denied their request for qualified immunity. *Chiu v. Plano Independent School Dist.*, 339 F.3d 273 (5th Cir. 2003).

V. USE OF SCHOOL FACILITIES

Schools may establish reasonable rules governing the time, place and manner of speech on school property, as discussed in Chapter Two, Section II. As in religious speech cases, the reasonableness of these rules depends upon the type of forum established by the school. A "limited public forum" exists on property that is generally open for use by the public. Time, manner and place regulations regarding a limited public forum must be content-neutral and narrowly tailored to serve a significant governmental interest. They must also provide for ample alternative channels of communication.

A. Student Organizations and Demonstrations

Student First Amendment rights are not coextensive with those of adults. School demonstrations may be enjoined if they are materially disruptive or invade the rights of others. Many student group access cases interpret the federal Equal Access Act (EAA), 20 U.S.C. §§ 4071-4074, which is more fully discussed in Chapter Two, Section II.C.

◆   A Florida school board policy required all individuals to obtain prior approval from the superintendent to distribute written material to students. Materials also had to include a bold disclaimer stating they were not school-sponsored. The superintendent turned down a middle school student's request to distribute pro-life literature at schools, based on the threat of substantial disruption and her failure to include a disclaimer. The student sued the school board in a federal district court for speech rights violations. **The court stated that the rights of students in public schools are not coextensive with those of adults.** The board had not opened up the middle school to the general public to distribute literature. The school was a non-public forum, in which administrators could impose reasonable, viewpoint-neutral restrictions on student speech. Despite viewpoint restrictions in the policy, the court found the board did not violate the student's speech rights by denying her request.

The court held the **"school need not wait for the disruption to occur, but instead may prohibit conduct when it reasonably concludes student expression would materially and substantially interfere with the discipline in the school or would interfere with others' rights."** The court found the distribution of pro-life materials at school without allowing pro-choice materials would be unconstitutional and that "permitting pro-life and pro-choice literature to be distributed by students in the school hallways would turn the school hallways into a battlefield." Given the divisive nature of the topic, school officials could reasonably forecast substantial disruption if the student distributed anti-abortion literature. Their decision to deny her request to distribute literature was upheld. *Heinkel v. School Board of Lee County, Florida*, No. 2:04-CV-184-FTM-33-SPC, 2005 WL 1571077 (M.D. Fla. 2005).

◆ A Texas school board adopted a policy allowing non-curriculum related student clubs to meet and use school bulletin boards and public address systems. It also had an "abstinence-only policy" banning all speech about sexual activity. A gay/straight club sought permission to post notices about its meetings and to distribute flyers at school and use the school's PA system. Club members addressed the board and stated their goals were to educate and help the community, improve relations between heterosexuals and homosexuals, and "educate willing youth about safe sex, AIDS, hatred, etc." The board did not act on the club's request, and the club was not allowed to post advertisements in school. Administrators turned down further requests to use school facilities, and club members sued the district and superintendent in a federal district court for First Amendment and Equal Access Act (EAA) violations.

The court **held the district had a compelling interest in protecting student health and well-being and preventing recognition of groups based on sexual activity.** There was obscene material on the club's Web site. **As club members failed to show any other groups intended to discuss sexual content, they could not show discrimination against their viewpoint. The district was entitled to summary judgment on the First Amendment and EAA claims.** The EAA bars discrimination against the "religious, political, philosophical content" of student speech, but allows officials to exclude speech on sexual topics and disruptive speech. **The EAA does not limit a school's authority to maintain order and discipline on school grounds.** The club's stated goals contradicted the district curriculum, and the district did not violate the EAA. The superintendent was entitled to qualified immunity. *Caudillo v. Lubbock Independent School Dist.*, 311 F.Supp.2d 550 (N.D. Tex. 2004).

◆   A Kentucky high school's site-based decision-making council approved a proposal for a gay straight alliance (GSA) club. Students who opposed the GSA club protested, and many parents threatened to remove their children from the school system. The school board then voted to ban all non-curricular clubs. The principal let the GSA club use school facilities as an outside organization, but did not allow the club to meet in homerooms or before school in a classroom. Four other non-curriculum-related student organizations continued to enjoy access to school facilities during this time. The GSA club and its members filed a federal district court action, seeking an order requiring the board to afford it the same opportunity to use school facilities as other student clubs enjoyed.

The court rejected the board's argument that the other organizations were "curriculum related." **A school opens up a "limited open forum" if it allows even one non-curriculum-related student group to use its facilities. A club cannot be denied permission to meet at school during noninstructional time if others may do so**. When a limited open forum has been created, a school may prohibit only meetings that materially and substantially interfere with school activities. The court found the school's treatment of the GSA club was content-based restriction that was forbidden by the EAA. The **board could not deny access to its facilities based on the uproar caused by recognition of the GSA club.** *Boyd County High School Gay Straight Alliance v. Board of Educ. of Boyd County*, 258 F.Supp.2d 667 (E.D. Ky. 2003).

◆   A California school board denied an application to recognize a Gay-Straight Alliance Club on the grounds that the club was curriculum-related. The board found the club's subject matter related to sexual conduct and that the district offered courses addressing sex, abstinence and disease prevention. The students rejected an offer by the principal to edit the name of the group and to declare that sex would not be discussed at meetings. They sued the school district and board in a federal district court for violating the EAA and U.S. Constitution. The court held **the board established a limited open forum by allowing non-curriculum-related student groups to meet on school grounds during noninstructional time. The board was precluded from discriminating against groups seeking access to the open forum on the basis of content.** There was no merit to the board's assertion that the club was unprotected by the EAA on grounds that it was "related to the curriculum." The club intended to discuss tolerance, issues related to sexual orientation and homophobia, and the need to treat persons with respect, not human sexuality. Even if there was some overlap between the curriculum and club discussions, the Gay-Straight Alliance, like other clubs, was unrelated to the curriculum. No other group had to submit to a name change or declare its meetings would include no discussion of sex. The students were entitled to a preliminary order. *Colin v. Orange Unified School Dist.*, 83 F.Supp.2d 1135 (C.D. Cal. 2000).

◆   A Florida school board let organizations such as the Boy Scouts use school facilities under leases or partnership agreements. In 1998, the board authorized a five-year agreement allowing the Scouts to use school facilities and buses. The agreement required school administrators to make school announcements and distribute Scout literature. Board members took note of the U.S. Supreme

Court's decision in *Boy Scouts of America v. Dale*, 530 U.S. 640 (2000), in which the organization was allowed to bar an avowed homosexual from serving as a Scout leader. The board voted to terminate the agreement, because the Scouts discriminated on the basis of sexual orientation. The Scouts sued the school board and superintendent in a federal district court for First Amendment and equal protection violations. The parties agreed that the board had created a limited public forum for many organizations and groups to use district facilities after school. The board argued it had a compelling interest in enforcing its anti-discrimination policy so students could learn respect and tolerance.

The court held the board was entitled to disapprove of intolerance and did not have to assist the Boy Scouts in solicitation efforts under the agreement. **The board was not allowed to punish any group for its message. The government must abstain from regulating speech based on a group's ideology or opinion.** Once the board created a limited public forum, it could not exclude groups based on unreasonable distinctions. The board allowed many other student groups to use its facilities, despite their exclusive policies, without interference by the board. Speech that the board had found objectionable did not take place during school hours. The court held the board could not prevent the Scouts from using school facilities and buses during non-school hours pending further consideration of the case. *Boy Scouts of America v. Till*, 136 F.Supp.2d 1295 (S.D. Fla. 2001).

B. Non-Student Groups

A section of the No Child Left Behind Act requires each local educational agency that receives assistance under the Act to provide military recruiters access to secondary student names, addresses and telephone numbers. The section, 20 U.S.C. § 7908, has a parental notification requirement. In Rumsfeld v. Forum for Academic and Institutional Rights, *below, the Supreme Court considered the Solomon Amendment, which has no such provision.*

◆ Congress enacted the Solomon Amendment to address restrictions put on military recruiting by some law schools that disagreed with the U.S. government's policy on homosexuals in the military. The Solomon Amendment disqualified institutions of higher learning from receiving certain federal funds, if any part of an institution denied access to military recruiters that was equal to that provided other recruiters. An association of law schools and faculties sued the U.S. government in a federal district court, asserting the Solomon Amendment violated the schools' First Amendment speech and association rights. The association claimed the Solomon Amendment unconstitutionally required law schools to choose between federal funding and their First Amendment speech and association rights, and made them unable to enforce campus non-discrimination policies. The court denied the association's request for a preliminary order against enforcement of the Solomon Amendment. Congress took note of the court's decision and amended the law to require "equal access" for military recruiters. Meanwhile, the association appealed to the U.S. Court of Appeals, Third Circuit. The court held the amendment regulated speech, and it reversed and remanded the decision.

The U.S. Supreme Court found the Solomon Amendment forbade higher education institutions from applying their general non-discrimination policies to military recruiters. Law schools had to provide the military the same access they provided to all other employment recruiters. **The Court stated the broad and sweeping power of Congress to provide for defense included the authority to require campus access for military recruiters. Congress was free to attach reasonable conditions to federal funding. The Solomon Amendment regulated conduct, not speech. As there was no restriction on speech, the amendment did not place unconstitutional conditions on receiving federal funds.** The Court held the presence of military recruiters on campus did not violate law school association rights. Students and faculty remained free to associate and voice disapproval of the military's message. The association had exaggerated the reach of prior First Amendment cases. The Court reversed the judgment. *Rumsfeld v. Forum for Academic and Institutional Rights*, 547 U.S. 47 (2006).

◆   A Montana speaker received $1,000 from a ministerial association to serve as the master of ceremonies at a religious rally held the evening after a school assembly. He claimed the board reversed a decision to allow him to speak at the assembly in violation of the First Amendment. The U.S. Court of Appeals, Ninth Circuit, **held the speaker had no protected interest in addressing a public school assembly**. He was not being paid by the board, and was thus not deprived of any valuable government benefit. The speaker later gave his speech off school grounds, and was paid by the ministerial association. No other federal circuit court had found that permission to speak at a school assembly was a valuable government benefit. *Carpenter v. Dillon Elementary School Dist. 10*, 149 Fed.Appx. 645 (9th Cir. 2005).

◆   Members of an anti-abortion group planned to distribute leaflets and speak to students at a California high school. The school principal stated they had no legitimate business on campus and did not allow them to register as visitors. He instructed them to leave, expressing concerns about disruption of the school's routine and student safety. The group demonstrated across the street from school, carrying signs and distributing leaflets to drivers and students. Traffic was backed up for almost two miles because a group member repeatedly pushed a walk signal to stop cars. Another member blocked the sidewalk with a poster so that some students had to walk in the street. Police diverted students from the demonstrators, and many were late for classes. Group members sued the district and school officials in a California trial court, asserting speech rights violations. The court held the officials acted reasonably and to avoid disruption. The group appealed to the Court of Appeal of California.

The court held California laws on school access recognized the risk of violent crimes on school grounds by unauthorized outsiders. One law prohibited outsiders from entering or remaining on school campuses without registration, and another permitted officials to refuse registration based on a reasonable belief the outsider would disrupt school. Other state laws sought to prevent disruption or interference with classes and school activities, and district policies addressed these concerns. **Nothing in state law permitted** unrestricted access by outsiders to a school campus. High schools are not public forums to which rights of access are guaranteed. School officials have authority to monitor campus access and determine who is likely to be disruptive. They are entitled to make decisions based on subject matter and the speaker's identity that cannot be made in an open forum. School administrators have inherent authority to prescribe and control conduct in the schools. The First Amendment does not require them to wait for actual disruption before acting to stop it. Since the school administrators had acted reasonably and did not open a public forum on school grounds, the court affirmed the judgment. *Reeves v. Rocklin Unified School Dist.*, 109 Cal.App.4th 652 (Cal. Ct. App. 2003).

CHAPTER FOUR

Student Rights

                                                                    Page

I.   ADMISSIONS AND ATTENDANCE 149
     A. Race, Admission and School Assignment 149
     B   Age and Residency Requirements 154

II. COMPULSORY ATTENDANCE 160
     A. Compulsory Attendance and Truancy...........................160
     B. Home Study Programs 162
     C. Attendance Policies..164

III. CORPORAL PUNISHMENT 165
     A. Student Due Process Rights...................................165
     B   Teacher Liability Protection 168

IV. RACE AND NATIONAL ORIGIN DISCRIMINATION.............172

V.   SEX DISCRIMINATION..176
     A. Sexual Harassment by Students................................176
     B. Sexual Harassment by Staff 180
     C. Sexual Orientation 185

I. ADMISSIONS AND ATTENDANCE

The U.S. Constitution does not make a free public education a fundamental right, but the education clauses of state constitutions do. The Equal Protection Clause of the Fourteenth Amendment requires that once a program of free public education has been established, the law must be applied equally to all persons. Thus, children of illegal aliens, children with disabilities, and minority students are entitled to equal protection of the laws.

School districts may, within certain limits, establish health regulations, set minimum age requirements for all students beginning school, require immunization, adopt a curriculum and require that all students meet certain graduation requirements. For cases involving religious challenges to immunization requirements, please see Chapter Two, Section I.D.3.

A. Race, Admission and School Assignment

◆   In two cases involving the University of Michigan, **the Supreme Court considered the use of race in higher education admissions**. In the first case, the U.S. Court of Appeals, Sixth Circuit, upheld the University of Michigan Law School's admissions policy. The appeals court upheld the policy under

Regents of the Univ. of California v. Bakke, 438 U.S. 265 (1978), finding the law school had a compelling interest in achieving a diverse student body.

The Supreme Court noted the university asserted the policy's purpose was to ensure a diverse student body. Any governmental distinction based on race must be examined under the strict scrutiny standard. Under this standard, the classification must be "narrowly tailored to further compelling governmental interests" to be deemed constitutional. The Court concluded, based on *Bakke,* that the goal of having a diverse student body is a compelling governmental interest. **The law school admissions policy utilized a narrowly tailored method of achieving that interest through its consideration of race as a "plus" factor.** The policy was flexible, and it did not create an impermissible quota system. One of the most important factors supporting the decision was the individualized review of applicants that considered several race-neutral factors. *Grutter v. Bollinger,* 539 U.S. 306, 123 S.Ct. 2325, 156 L.E.2d 304 (2003).

The second Michigan case involved the undergraduate admissions policy for the university's College of Literature, Science and the Arts. During the course of the litigation, the policy was changed several times. The policy being considered by the Court awarded applicants from underrepresented minority groups 20 points. Applicants were awarded points for a variety of factors, and they needed at least 100 points for admission. The Court applied the strict scrutiny analysis to the policy and held it was not narrowly tailored to achieve the compelling state interest in diversity declared by the university. **The policy impermissibly gave underrepresented minority students an advantage or preference** by automatically awarding them 20 points. **The policy was also deficient because it failed to require an individualized review of each applicant, which is essential when race is a consideration.** *Gratz v. Bollinger,* 539 U.S. 244, 123 S.Ct. 2411, 156 L.Ed.2d 257 (2003).

◆   Schools in Lynn, Massachusetts became racially imbalanced in the mid-1970s. Schools identified as mostly non-white had resource shortages, overcrowding, disciplinary problems, high absentee rates, teacher apathy, racial tension, and low test scores. In 1989, the school committee responded with a voluntary plan to improve schools and eliminate the isolation of minority students. Each child was entitled to attend a neighborhood school, but race was taken into account in transfer cases. The plan prohibited "segregative transfers," which would increase racial imbalance in the sending or receiving school. Appeals were typically granted for medical or safety concerns, daycare issues, hardship or to keep siblings in the same school. After implementation of the plan, Lynn public school students increased their test scores, and racial tensions and absenteeism decreased. Parents of students who were denied transfers challenged the plan in a federal district court. They asserted claims under the Equal Protection Clause, and state and federal laws. The court upheld the plan. A three-judge panel of the U.S. Court of Appeals, First Circuit, reversed the judgment, finding the plan was not narrowly tailored to achieve educational diversity. The full First Circuit voted to rehear the case. The court reviewed the Equal Protection claim under *Gratz v. Bollinger* and *Grutter v. Bollinger,* above.

The court rejected the parents' assertion that the plan was not narrowly tailored to achieve its goal. The plan sought to keep elementary schools within

15% of the total minority percentage of 58%, and other schools within 10% of the total minority attendance rate. **The *Grutter* decision held diversity can be a "compelling interest in the educational context." The benefits of diversity included reducing minority isolation, promoting a positive racial climate, fostering tolerance and ensuring an equal, quality education for all. The court held *Grutter* applied in the K-12 context.** There was evidence that the benefits of a racially diverse school were even more compelling at younger ages than in higher education settings. The Michigan decisions held that admission policies cannot institutionalize a quota or otherwise insulate a category of applicants from competition based on race. Schools must consider viable, race-neutral alternatives, apply time limits to racial distinctions and not unduly burden the members of any racial group. The Lynn transfer policy was not tied to merit and did not risk the fueling of stereotypes. The court found no reason to impose a blanket prohibition on the use of race as a decisive factor in a student transfer plan. The plan applied only to transfers, not initial student assignments, and it preserved neighborhood schools. The school committee showed it seriously considered race-neutral alternatives. The court held the parents did not prove any violation of the U.S. Constitution, federal law or the Massachusetts Constitution. *Comfort v. Lynn School Committee*, 418 F.3d 1 (1st Cir. 2005).

◆   Seattle public schools were never legally segregated, but the city's racially segregated housing patterns led to school segregation. The district adopted an "open choice plan," applying only to ninth-graders. Students were assigned to their school of choice, if possible. However, as four high schools were highly desirable and greatly "over-subscribed," the assignment plan relied on a four-part tie-breaker. Race was the second tie-breaker, accounting for 10% of ninth-grade admissions. The race-based tie-breaker was triggered only if a school was "racially imbalanced," defined as a deviation of 15% or more from the district's racial makeup. A group of parents sued the school district in a federal district court, asserting the race-based tie-breaker violated the Equal Protection Clause and the Washington Civil Rights Act, which precludes racial preferences. The court upheld the use of the tie-breaker under both state and federal law. A three-judge panel of the U.S. Court of Appeals, Ninth Circuit, reversed the decision in 2002, but withdrew its opinion and sought a ruling on the state Civil Rights Act by the Washington Supreme Court. The state court found that without the tie-breaker, city schools would resegregate. Schools had the power to address segregation, and Seattle's race-neutral plan was not an affirmative action program. The Ninth Circuit panel then held the tie-breaker was indistinguishable from a racial quota and not sufficiently narrowly-tailored to meet its goals under *Grutter v. Bollinger* and *Gratz v. Bollinger*.

The majority of the judges of the Ninth Circuit voted to rehear the Equal Protection Clause claim, and found that while all governmental uses of race are subject to strict scrutiny, not all race-based policies are invalidated by it. ***Grutter* recognized the educational and social benefits that flow from diversity were compelling reasons to consider race** in selective admissions to higher educational institutions. The Supreme Court had found a diverse student body provided the advantage of having many viewpoints represented, and promoted greater societal legitimacy to higher educational institutions. **Seattle school officials found that diverse classrooms had important educational advantages, and ensured students had access to schools which enabled them to reach their full potential. Experts agreed that diversity encouraged students to think critically and democratically.** The court held public secondary schools may have an even greater role than higher educational institutions in preparing students for work and citizenship in a racially diverse society. The district demonstrated a compelling interest for using the race-based tie-breaker. The court rejected the parents' assertion that the plan was not sufficiently narrowly tailored. The race-based tie-breaker did not uniformly benefit the members of one race. The court found the plan imposed a minimal burden that was shared equally among all the district's students. Students had no right to attend a local school or their school of choice. As the plan was a narrowly tailored, constitutional means of achieving compelling school interests, the court affirmed the judgment for the district. *Parents Involved in Community Schools v. Seattle School Dist. No. 1*, 426 F.3d 1162 (9th Cir. 2005).

◆   A federal district court held Boston Public Schools (BPS) were unlawfully segregated in 1974. The court supervised BPS until 1987, when the system was declared fully integrated. BPS adopted a controlled choice student assignment plan in 1989. The plan used the attendance zones from the desegregation orders to keep neighborhoods intact. The controlled choice plan allowed students to attend any school in their own attendance zone, using four considerations for assignments. One of these was whether an assignment would cause a deviation of over 15% from the assigned school's "ideal racial percentage." The BPS abandoned this criterion in 1999, when the First Circuit struck down a racial set-aside in the city's three competitive examination schools. An advocacy group and several parents sued the BPS and its officials in a federal district court, asserting the controlled choice plan violated state and federal law. Near this time, the Boston School Committee voted to eliminate race from the controlled choice plan. The committee adopted a new plan for the 2000-2001 school year that was free of any racial considerations. The plan reduced the allocation of available seats for students within a school's walk zone from 100 to 50%. Students who did not live in the walk zone of any school were treated as though they had a walk zone preference for their first two school choices. The district court denied the parents' request for an order requiring BPS to quit using race in any phase of school assignment. It also denied a request to reassign first-graders, kindergartners and students who had tried to transfer schools under the controlled choice plan. The court rejected the parents' argument that city attendance zones were "racially gerrymandered" and found no evidence of discrimination in the new plan. The reduction in the walk zone preference was race neutral. Two students received nominal damages for being denied assignments under the controlled choice plan.

The parents appealed to the First Circuit, which reviewed evidence of substantial inequities among city schools. Some 1,772 Boston students did not live in the walk zone of any school. While some schools had excess capacity, others had significant space shortages. High demand schools were over-chosen, while others lacked enough applicants for available seats. The strong disparities among neighborhood school quality and capacity, the number of resident students and walk zone choices were significant considerations in the reduction of the walk zone preference to 50%. **The court found the committee had adopted the 50% reduction in walk zone seats primarily out of concern for limited choice and equity for students with an insufficient number of walk-zone schools. The parents did not show the new plan was discriminatory. There was no merit to their argument that the stated goal of diversity made the new plan discriminatory. Diversity is not a suspect goal.** The committee adopted the new plan without racial criteria, despite strong pressure to comply with the state Racial Imbalance Law. The parents presented evidence on only three of the city's 85 elementary schools, and they did not attempt to show a district-wide impact. They only showed 20 white students out of 25,000 elementary students in BPS did not receive their first choice of schools. The new plan did not violate the Equal Protection Clause, Title VI or other state and federal laws. There was no error in refusing to enjoin the BPS from ever using race in its student assignment system. The court affirmed the judgment. *Anderson v. City of Boston*, 375 F.3d 71 (1st Cir. 2004).

◆   A Wisconsin school district had no formal policy or practice for elementary school class assignments, but a principal issued a memorandum to staff, urging the balancing of classes according to student gender, ethnicity, academic ability, special needs and parental input. The parents of an African-American student requested their daughter learn from a teacher with high expectations. They also expressed concerns about some negative incidents she had experienced with special education students. After the start of the school year, the student's teacher divided her class into five small groups and put two African-American students in each group, so that they sat together in pairs. She justified this because she believed "African-American students need a buddy, and sometimes it works well if they have someone else working with them because they view things in a global manner." She also seated Hispanic students in pairs.

The student's family sued the district, teacher and other staff members in a federal district court, alleging the assignment and seating policies violated the Equal Protection Clause. The court awarded summary judgment to the district and officials, finding the decision to place the student was the result of race-neutral factors, and that there was no evidence that the teacher's seating policy resulted in different treatment of the student. The family appealed to the U.S. Court of Appeals, Seventh Circuit, which affirmed the decision concerning the school assignment policy. The student's assignment took into consideration her parents' race-neutral concerns. The court held the district court should not have awarded summary judgment to the teacher on the Equal Protection claim. **Racial and ethnic distinctions in schools are subject to the highest judicial scrutiny, and school officials have a constitutional obligation to assign students without regard to race.** *Brown v. Board of Educ.* **established that state-imposed racial classifications of students can significantly affect a student's ability to learn.** Even if the teacher believed she was acting in the best interests of minority students by seating them in pairs, her action was based purely on race and was justified only by stereotypical notions. **The Supreme Court condemned race-based seating as early as 1950 and has reinforced**

this finding on numerous occasions since then. Because the law in this area was well established, the teacher was not entitled to qualified immunity on the equal protection claim arising from the seating policy. She should have known of the well-established restrictions on the use of race as a seating criterion. The student was unable to show the seating policy was an express policy of the district or a widespread practice that had the force of law or custom. The district was thus not liable for the teacher's race-based seating arrangement. The court reversed in part and remanded the district court decision. *Billings v. Madison Metropolitan School Dist.*, 259 F.3d 807 (7th Cir. 2001).

B. Age and Residency Requirements

The No Child Left Behind (NCLB) Act reauthorized the McKinney-Vento Homeless Assistance Act. It states homeless children should not be stigmatized or segregated from the "mainstream school environment on the basis of their being homeless." Schools must continue the education of a homeless student in the student's "school of origin," or enroll the student in a public school that non-homeless students in the same attendance area are eligible to attend. NCLB section 722(g), which is codified at 42 U.S.C. § 11432, defines "school of origin" as "the school that the child or youth attended when permanently housed or the school in which the child or youth was last enrolled."

If a homeless student's school enrollment is disputed, the NCLB Act requires a district to immediately admit the student to the school in which enrollment is sought, pending resolution of the dispute. Schools must provide homeless students with access to the same free, appropriate public education as other children. This includes transportation, special education, English learner, gifted and talented programs and school lunch programs for which students meet eligibility requirements. Schools must also notify the parents of homeless children about the NCLB Act's school choice provisions. In the following case, a federal district court recognized a cause of action under the McKinney-Vento Act, allowing New York families to bring a class action suit against state officials for violating the Act and their equal protection rights.

◆ Six New York families claimed homeless children in Suffolk County missed significant amounts of school time due to a systematic failure to provide them with access to education and transportation. The families sued state education officials in a federal district court for failing to locate and ensure the enrollment of homeless children, provide them immediate enrollment, or furnish the services provided to non-homeless children. The court considered a dismissal motion by state and local officials, along with the families' motion to certify a class action. It explained the McKinney-Vento Act was enacted in 1987 to require states to assure homeless children had access to a free and appropriate public education. **The McKinney Act, at 42 U.S.C. § 11432(g)(3)(A), directed local education agencies to immediately enroll homeless students, even if they were unable to produce the records normally required for enrollment. Enrolling schools are required to immediately contact the school last attended by a homeless student to obtain necessary records, and they must help parents of homeless students obtain necessary immunizations or medical records.** The No Child

Left Behind Act reauthorized the McKinney Act, retaining the purpose of ensuring equal access to public education for homeless students and allowing them to meet the standards to which all students are held.

The court held Congress intended to create a private right of action to enforce the McKinney-Vento Act. The act had no comprehensive administrative enforcement scheme, and Congress showed a clear intent to confer individual rights on homeless children. The act provided specific entitlements, conferring on parents the right to choose their children's "school of origin" or school of enrollment, the right to immediate enrollment in the school in which enrollment was sought, and a right to "comparable transportation services." The act directed local educational agencies to continue a student's education in a school of origin for the duration of homelessness. Schools were required to provide an education for the rest of the academic year if the student became permanently housed, or to enroll the student in a school attended by non-homeless students in the area where the student was actually living. As these entitlements were directed at specific individuals, the court found Congress intended the act to confer individually enforceable rights. The families could proceed with their Equal Protection Clause claims. The court found the families were appropriate representatives of homeless students in Suffolk County, and it certified the case as a class action. *National Law Center on Homelessness and Poverty, R.I. v. State of New York*, 224 F.R.D. 314 (E.D.N.Y. 2004).

The New York Court of Appeals applied state law consistently with the No Child Left Behind Act in the following case, in which a homeless student's last permanent residence counted, not his brief stay in a homeless shelter.

◆   A New York family rented a house in Springs School District for parts of two school years. The family was evicted, and the children moved to temporary homes, including stays in motels and with relatives. The mother was jailed for part of this time, and the family moved into a homeless shelter in the Longwood School District. The county Department of Social Services (DSS) placed the children in foster care, and they then began attending Longwood schools. DSS forms indicated Springs as the "district of origin" for the children. Longwood filed a claim against Springs for tuition reimbursement for the children. When Springs refused, Longwood sued it in a state court. The court awarded summary judgment to Longwood, ruling Springs was the mother's last permanent home. It interpreted the term "resided" from state Education Law Section 3202(4)(a) to include an intention to remain in a place permanently. The New York Supreme Court, Appellate Division, held the mother's temporary stay in the homeless shelter obligated Longwood to pay for the children's education. It reversed the decision, and Longwood appealed to the Court of Appeals of New York.

The court recited Section 3202(4)(a) language requiring the district in which a child resided at the time of a social services placement to bear the child's instructional costs. The court agreed with Longwood that **"resided" included both physical presence and an intention to remain permanently. The family's last permanent residence was what counted, not the brief stay in a shelter.** The court's interpretation was consistent with state education department rulings construing "residence" to mean "domicile." An existing domicile was assumed to continue until a new one was acquired. Education Code Section 3202 created a presumption that children share the domicile of their parent. That section was designed to allocate costs sensibly between districts and avoid burdening a district with the cost of educating nonresident children. **Residence was established by physical presence as an inhabitant within the district, combined with an intent to remain.** Districts were required to provide tuition-free education only to students whose parents or guardians resided in the district. The "temporary stayovers" following the eviction, including time in the homeless shelter, did not change the family residence. Rejecting Springs' argument that the mother was "domiciled" at the shelter, the court reversed the judgment. *Longwood Cent. School Dist. v. Springs Union Free School Dist.*, 1 N.Y.3d 385, 774 N.Y.S.2d 857, 806 N.E.2d 970 (N.Y. 2004).

◆   New York parents enrolled their son in a public school as a non-resident student. The principal later suspended the student based on information that he had threatened others on a Web site. The parents sought a state court order to prevent the expulsion, asserting he did not create the Web site entries. The parents argued the district violated New York Education Law Section 3214 by removing their son from school without proper notice or a hearing. They agreed to dismiss the court action and the district agreed to end the suspension and to expunge all related records under a written agreement. The parents attempted to reenroll their son in a district high school, but the district superintendent informed them he was not in good standing in the district based on the Web site threats. The parents filed another state court action against the district, arguing the superintendent's action was barred by their agreement. The court dismissed the case because they did not first appeal to the state education commissioner.

On appeal, the New York Supreme Court, Appellate Division, held the agreement was binding. **The superintendent had based his decision at least partly on material he was foreclosed from considering by the terms of the agreement.** The interpretation of a contract did not involve educational expertise and was best resolved by a court. For this reason, the parents did not have to exhaust their administrative remedies by applying to the commissioner. **The court held the parents were entitled to have the superintendent determine if their son remained a student in good standing in the district.** He could not consider any records that the district had agreed to expunge. *Connolly v. Rye School Dist.*, 817 N.Y.S.2d 663 (N.Y. Ct. App. 2006).

◆   In May 1975, the Texas legislature revised its education laws to withhold from school districts any state funds for the education of children who were not legally admitted into the U.S. It authorized school districts to deny enrollment to these children. A group filed a class action on behalf of school-age children of Mexican origin who could not establish they had been legally admitted into the U.S. The action complained of the exclusion of the children from public school. A federal district court enjoined the school district from denying a free education to the children, and the U.S. Court of Appeals, Fifth Circuit, upheld the decision. The legislation was also challenged by numerous other plaintiffs whose cases were consolidated by the district court. The district court held the law violated the Equal Protection Clause, and the Fifth Circuit affirmed the decision. The Supreme Court consolidated the cases and granted review.

The state claimed that undocumented aliens were not "persons" within the jurisdiction of Texas, and so were not entitled to equal protection of its laws. The Court rejected this argument, stating that whatever an alien's status under the immigration laws, an alien is a "person" in any sense of the term. The term "within its jurisdiction" was meant as a term of geographic location, and the Equal Protection Clause extended its protection to all persons within a state, whether citizen or stranger. **The statute could not be upheld because it did not advance any substantial state interest.** The Court stated that **the Texas statute imposed a lifetime hardship on a discrete class of children not accountable for their disabling status.** There was no evidence to show the exclusion of the children would improve the overall quality of education in the state. *Plyler v. Doe*, 457 U.S. 202, 102 S.Ct. 2382, 72 L.Ed.2d 786 (1982).

◆ The Texas Education Code permitted school districts to deny free admission to public schools for minors who lived apart from a "parent, guardian, or the person having lawful control of him" if the minor's primary purpose in being in the district was to attend local public schools. A minor left his parent's home in Mexico to live with his sister in a Texas town for the purpose of attending school there. When the school district denied his application for tuition-free admission, his sister sued the state in federal court, alleging the law was unconstitutional. The district court held for the state, and the Fifth Circuit Court of Appeals affirmed. The U.S. Supreme Court upheld the residency requirement. **The Court held a bona fide residence requirement, appropriately defined and uniformly applied, furthered a substantial state interest in assuring that services provided for its residents were enjoyed only by residents.** Such a requirement with respect to attendance in public free schools did not violate the Equal Protection Clause. **Residence generally requires both physical presence and intention to remain.** The code stated that as long as the child was not living in the district for the sole purpose of attending school, he satisfied the statutory test. The Court held this was a bona fide residency requirement and that the Constitution permits a state to restrict eligibility for tuition-free education to its bona fide residents. *Martinez v. Bynum*, 461 U.S. 321, 103 S.Ct. 1838, 75 L.Ed.2d 879 (1983).

◆ A disabled Colorado student and her family moved out of her school district when she was in second grade. The district permitted her to stay in her school for the rest of the year. It readmitted her to the school for third and fourth grade under the state's school choice law. However, the district denied her application to re-enroll for grade five, stating its special education program had exceeded its capacity. A special education due process hearing officer held for the district, and an administrative law judge affirmed the decision. The parents moved back into the school district and re-enrolled their daughter into the school she had formerly attended. They sued the district in a state court for violating the state school choice law, the Individuals with Disabilities Education Act (IDEA), the Due Process Clause, Section 504 of the Rehabilitation Act and the Americans with Disabilities Act (ADA). The court awarded summary judgment to the district, and the parents appealed to the state court of appeals.

The court held the school choice law allowed elementary students who became district "nonresidents" during a school year or between school years to remain in their schools. **This right extended only to the following school year and did not entitle a nonresident student to return for subsequent school years, as the parents argued.** The court noted the district's special education programs exceeded nonresident enrollment limits. **The school choice statute authorized the district to deny re-enrollment based on nonresident status.** The IDEA claim failed, as it was derivative of the state school choice claim. The parents failed to show they were denied due process. There was no merit to the disability discrimination claims under Section 504 and the ADA because the decision to limit the number of nonresident students requesting special education was not an illegal quota. **The district had a "potentially limitless" obligation to provide special education to disabled resident students, but this obligation was distinguished from any obligation to accept nonresident students under the school choice law.** The court affirmed the judgment. *Bradshaw v. Cherry Creek School Dist. No. 5*, 98 P.3d 886 (Colo. Ct. App. 2003).

◆   A parent who lived in Chicago sent her daughter to North Carolina after the girl was threatened with assault. The student's uncle attempted to enroll her in a local school, but the district superintendent denied admission because she was not domiciled in a county school administrative unit. The family sued the superintendent and school board in a county superior court, which awarded summary judgment to school officials. The family appealed to the North Carolina Court of Appeals, which observed that **under North Carolina law, a child who is not domiciled in a local administrative unit may attend its schools without paying tuition if the child resides with an adult in the unit as the result of a parent or guardian's death, serious illness, incapacity or incarceration.** A non-domiciliary student may also enroll in school in another administrative unit in cases of abandonment, child abuse or natural disaster. In these cases, the student must present an affidavit including a statement that the claim to residency is not primarily related to attendance at a particular school and that an adult with whom the child resides accepts responsibility for the child's educational decisions.

The court held the law was based on sound public policy and that any change in it would have to be addressed by the legislature. It rejected the family's argument that the law violated due process and equal protection rights. The U.S. Supreme Court upheld a Texas law conditioning public school enrollment on residency within a school district or proof that enrollment was not being sought for the sole purpose of attending school within the district in *Martinez v. Bynum* (this chapter). **The North Carolina statute, like the Texas law, was a reasonable standard for determining the residential status of public school students.** State law definitions of domicile were based on traditional legal criteria and granted the benefit of a free public education to those who satisfied them. The law did not create an irrebuttable presumption or a durational residency requirement. The court affirmed the judgment for school officials. *Graham v. Mock*, 545 S.E.2d 263 (N.C. Ct. App. 2001).

◆   A Wisconsin student attended school in a district from kindergarten through middle school, when his family moved. After attending school in another district for two years, he sought to return under **the state open enrollment law,** which **provides students with the opportunity to attend any public school of their choice, even if residing in another district**. The district denied the application on the basis of a priority assignment for three students transferring under another program. The student appealed to the state superintendent of public instruction, who upheld the district action based on lack of class space. The student appealed to a Wisconsin circuit court. The court found the district's action arbitrary, because it had accepted the other three students.

The superintendent appealed to the Wisconsin Court of Appeals, which agreed with the student and circuit court that the district's decision had been arbitrary and could not be upheld. The district had permitted three other nonresident students to enroll in its schools, despite the fact that no space was available in two core courses. The preference cited by the district and superintendent in favor of particular classes of students, such as siblings, had no application where no class space was available. The court agreed with the circuit court that the district's decision had been based on priority, not class space. **There was no rational explanation for admitting three students who would push average class sizes over the acceptable limit, while excluding one whose presence would increase class size by less than one percentage point.** The court affirmed the judgment for the student. *McMorrow v. Benson,* 238 Wis.2d 329, 617 N.W.2d 247 (Wis. Ct. App. 2000).

◆   A New Jersey student attended school in the district where his grandfather resided. His mother rented an apartment outside the district. **At the start of the student's third year in the district, the district notified the mother of its intent to deny him admission, based on the lack of appropriate residency documents.** The grandfather appealed to the state commissioner of education. At a hearing, the board presented evidence indicating the student actually resided in his mother's apartment. An administrative law judge agreed, and the grandfather appealed to the state education commissioner, who upheld the decision. The school board commenced a state court action against the grandfather for $18,000 in tuition. The court awarded judgment to the board, and the grandfather appealed.

The Superior Court of New Jersey, Appellate Division, noted that the commissioner's residency determination became final when the grandfather failed to timely appeal the education commissioner's decision. Prior to the third year in which residency was at issue, the school board had not contacted the grandfather for the collection of tuition, and he had made no assertion on behalf of the student's residency until the third year. **There was a valid basis for charging one year of tuition to the grandfather, since he had actively pursued the residency contest.** However, there was no basis for a tuition award for the first two years. The commissioner's order did not clearly indicate an intent to charge the grandfather for these two years, when the mother alone had communicated with the board and superintendent. The court reduced his liability to $6,190, the tuition for one year. *Woodbury Heights Board of Educ. v. Starr,* 319 N.J.Super. 528, 725 A.2d 1180 (N.J. Super. Ct. App. Div. 1999).

II. COMPULSORY ATTENDANCE

States have a compelling interest in providing public education and may establish and enforce reasonable school attendance laws.

A. Compulsory Attendance and Truancy

◆   A New York Appellate Division court held the adjudication of a 16-year-old student as a child in need of supervision did not constitute a change in placement under the Individuals with Disabilities Education Act. A high school principal initiated a family court proceeding to determine the student was in need of supervision based on 16 unexcused absences from school during a two-month period. The student admitted the absences, and the family court ordered the school's committee on special education (CSE) to conduct an evaluation. The CSE found he was emotionally disturbed and had a disability. The student renewed his objection to the child protection proceeding, but the court rejected it, placing him on probation for a year. He appealed to the appellate division, which affirmed the family court order. It observed that not every petition for supervision of a child contemplated a change in educational placement. There was no change in placement in this case. **The family court had simply ordered the student to attend school and participate in his individualized education program.** The court affirmed the family court's order. *Erich D. v. New Milford Board of Educ.*, 767 N.Y.S.2d 488 (N.Y. App. Div. 2003).

◆   An Alabama high school handbook required the referral of tardy students first into parent conferences, then for discipline or alternative programs. After a student's third unexcused absence in a semester, the handbook provided for referral to an "early warning program" conducted by the county juvenile court system. After a student's tenth tardy in one semester, the school principal reported her to the school truant officer. The principal did not refer her to the early warning program or contact her parents, as specified in the school handbook. The truant officer filed a child in need of supervision petition in the juvenile court. After a trial, the court adjudicated the student a child in need of supervision and placed her on probation for the rest of the school year. The student appealed to the Alabama Court of Civil Appeals.

The court reviewed testimony by the principal, who allowed the student to accumulate 10 tardies before notifying the truant officer and never sought an explanation from the student about the reasons for her tardiness. The principal stated he did not attempt to contact the student's father or provide an in-school conference as required by the school handbook. The student asserted the principal violated the Compulsory School Attendance Law and school policy by failing to investigate the causes of her tardiness before referring her to the truant officer. The student admitted being tardy on 10 occasions, but explained she had a medical condition that made it difficult for her to be on time to school. **The court found nothing in state law requiring the principal to investigate the causes of a student's tardiness.** The law stated parents will not be convicted if they can establish one of five defenses, including sickness or other "good cause or valid excuse." The principal did not violate the student's due process rights by failing to follow the student handbook's progressive discipline policies before submitting her name to the truant officer. The handbook placed a duty on students to provide a timely excuse for their absences. The student was unable to show the school selectively enforced the prosecution of truancy cases. The compulsory attendance law applied after a child reached the age of 16, when parents were no longer accountable for truancy by their children. The juvenile court petition correctly named the student as the subject of the proceeding, excluding her parents from it. The court affirmed the judgment. *S.H. v. State of Alabama*, 868 So.2d 1110 (Ala. Civ. App. 2003).

◆   An Ohio school policy required the school to provide parents with written notification of state compulsory education laws upon a student's third unexcused absence. After the fifth absence, the school was required to hold an informal conference with the parents, student and a probation officer, and upon the tenth absence, a formal hearing was mandated. **A student was absent without excuse approximately 20 days during a four-month period.** On some occasions the parents explained there was a medical problem. The school accepted these explanations until the parents applied to the county educational service center for permission to home-school the student. They did not tell the school about the pending home-school application, and the school did not send them any notices concerning truancy proceedings. The service center advised the school principal that the student's home school application was being denied, and the principal filed a complaint against the parents in an Ohio county court on charges of contributing to the delinquency of a minor.

The trial court conducted a jury trial and sentenced the parents to seven days in jail and fines of $250. They appealed to a state appeals court, which found that to uphold the conviction, the state was required to prove the student was actually delinquent or unruly. The definition of "unruly child" included one who was habitually truant. Reference to the school policy was a crucial factor in determining whether habitual truancy occurred. The state presented the school's policy on unexcused absences as contained in its parent/student handbook. It was required to show under local standards that the student was habitually truant, but it failed to make this showing. **Because truancy involved more than absenteeism, the state was required to show a lack of excuse or permission as established by school policy.** It was therefore required to show evidence that it sent the parents written notices that their daughter was absent without an excuse for three or more days. Without this proof, the state could not satisfy the essential element of habitual truancy. As the school was bound to follow its own policies and abide by them, the court reversed the judgment. *State v. Smrekar*, No. 99 CO 35, 2000 Ohio App. Lexis 5381, 2000 WL 1726518 (Ohio Ct. App. 2000).

◆   An 18-year-old West Virginia student missed five days of school without an excuse. He was warned that continued absences could result in criminal prosecution. **After continuing unexcused absences, the county prosecutor's office filed a criminal complaint against the student.** After he was convicted of violating a state compulsory attendance statute, he petitioned the Supreme Court of Appeals of West Virginia for review. The court observed that the compulsory attendance statute mandated school attendance for children between the ages of six and 16 and provided enforcement sanctions against parents, guardians or custodians, but not against individual students. **There was no possibility of liability under the statute for a non-attending student, regardless of age.** A different statute applied to cases involving students who were 18 or older, and school boards were allowed to suspend students for improper conduct. For students under the age of 18, the possibility of a delinquency adjudication also existed. The court granted the writ as requested. *State ex rel. Estes v. Egnor*, 443 S.E.2d 193 (W. Va. 1994).

◆ **Wisconsin's compulsory school attendance statute requires any person having control of a school-aged child to "cause the child to attend school regularly. ..."** The statute cross-references other Wisconsin statutes detailing state procedures for truancy, including a statute that requires each school board to establish written attendance policies. The parent of a student who was absent without excuse eight times during a three-month period failed to respond to repeated notices from the school to meet with officials. The district attorney's office brought charges against the student's parent, resulting in a misdemeanor conviction. The parent appealed to the Court of Appeals of Wisconsin.

On appeal, the parent argued the compulsory attendance statute was unconstitutionally vague because it failed to describe the word "regularly." The court held the statute was sufficiently definite and understandable to a person of average intelligence to preclude a finding of unconstitutional vagueness. It sufficiently cross-referenced other statutes so that the full statutory scheme of mandatory attendance was clear. The court rejected the parent's defense that the student was uncontrollable, because evidence in the record indicated she had a consistent pattern of unexcused absences dating from her kindergarten year. The court affirmed the conviction and found the statute constitutional. *State v. White*, 509 N.W.2d 434 (Wis. Ct. App. 1993).

B. Home Study Programs

◆ The Court of Appeals of Michigan upheld an order by a family court to exercise jurisdiction over a student with disabilities whose mother claimed she was home-schooling him. The court found evidence she was not even at home during most of the school day. The family court assumed jurisdiction over the student based on the mother's failure to ensure he would receive a proper education. It found the student had missed 111 out of the 134 days of the current school year. Nothing indicated the mother was ensuring his educational needs were being met. The mother appealed to the court of appeals, stating she had gone to great efforts to get the student to attend school. She also expressed disagreement with the school district's educational intervention. The court expressed sympathy with the challenge presented to a single parent with a full-time job who was attempting to raise a child with special needs. However, it was troubled by the mother's responses to school intervention.

The court noted the mother's reluctance to use negative consequences for improper conduct by the student. Although there might be clinical support for her approach, it had been clearly ineffective. Since the mother's methods did not succeed, it was appropriate for her to try something new. It appeared she had been resistant to the school's methods, and her response was contrary to the student's best interests. The court found the student's best interests would be better served by her full cooperation with the district. It was not in the student's best interests to be home-schooled, especially where this required him to be unsupervised for most of the day. **The court found the mother's home schooling plan "painfully neglectful" of his educational needs. Although this was not a severe case of educational neglect, it was proper for the trial court to assume jurisdiction over the student.** *Flint v. Manchester Public Schools*, No. 240251, 2003 WL 22244692 (Mich. Ct. App. 2003).

◆ Two Massachusetts children were not enrolled in school and lacked approved home schooling plans. The parents contended that school committee approval of their home schooling activities would conflict with their learner-led approach to education, and that the Constitution prohibited infringement on their privacy and family rights. The school committee initiated a state district court proceeding for the care and protection of the children. The court found the parents had failed over a two-year period to show the children's educational needs were being met, effectively preventing any evaluation of their educational level and instructional methods. The parents did not comply with a court order to file educational plans, resulting in adjudication of the children as in need of care and protection. The court transferred legal custody of the children to the social services department, although they remained in their parents' physical custody. The parents appealed to the Appellate Court of Massachusetts.

The court noted that the trial court order had required the parents to submit a detailed home schooling plan to the school committee to allow assessment of the program and the children's progress. **This was a legitimate educational condition that a school committee could impose on a home school proposal without infringing on the constitutional rights of a family.** The U.S. Supreme Court has recognized a degree of parental autonomy to direct the education of children, but state laws effectively incorporated this requirement by allowing for flexibility in the evaluation of private instruction in homes and private schools. The parents had rejected accommodations proposed by the school committee, and the custody order was entered only after they had received a final opportunity to comply with the committee's requests. The court affirmed the order for temporary care and protection of the children. *In re Ivan*, 717 N.E.2d 1020 (Mass. App. Ct. 1999).

◆ Maryland education law permits parents to educate their children at home but requires them to maintain a portfolio of instructional materials with examples of coursework. The law also requires observation of teaching methods and up to three annual portfolio reviews. Parents must sign a consent form indicating their intent to comply with state regulations. A parent who selected home schooling for her child for religious reasons came under scrutiny by local authorities for possible child neglect. She alleged that this suspicion arose from her disagreement with her compliance obligations under the home schooling regulations. The neglect charges were not substantiated, but the parent's name remained on a county registry of potential child neglecters.

The parent sued the county education board in the U.S. District Court for the District of Maryland, seeking a declaration that her religious free exercise rights exempted her from state home schooling laws. She claimed the county's retention of her name on a list of possible child neglecters justified a permanent order and monetary damages. The district moved to dismiss the case. The parent argued public schools indoctrinated children in atheism and sought to suppress their religious upbringing. The court found no support for this argument under the First Amendment or the Religious Freedom Restoration Act. **The home schooling regulations did not substantially burden her exercise of religion. The parent and her child were not compelled to affirm beliefs they did not hold, and the state law and regulations did not discriminate against them.** The court stated Maryland was not required to subsidize the family's religious beliefs by eliminating items from the state's required curriculum. It denied the parent's demand to remove her name from the list of potential child neglecters, as the information was confidential and already shielded from public release. *Battles v. Anne Arundel County Board of Educ.*, 904 F.Supp. 471 (D. Md. 1995).

C. Attendance Policies

◆   A federal district court approved settlements in three cases involving the alleged "pushing out" of difficult-to-educate students in New York City schools. The city agreed to provide services for students in different categories while avoiding a finding of liability. Students claimed illegal exclusion, expulsion and discharge from three public high schools in New York City. They filed three separate federal district court actions against the city education department, advancing claims on behalf of students in various categories who had attended Franklin K. Lane, Martin Luther King, Jr. (MLK) and Bushwick High Schools.

The parties settled the actions under separate agreements, by which the department denied liability but agreed to provide more services and support to allow the students to complete high school. The Bushwick settlement addressed a claim that the school unlawfully excluded or "pushed out" 30% of its students from 1998 to 2001. The court approved an agreement allowing students who were discharged, transferred or absent for long terms to re-enroll at Bushwick. Each student would attend a guidance conference before re-enrolling. Most students would be entitled to a planning interview prior to being discharged or transferred. The MLK and Lane High School actions were settled under similar terms. The MLK agreement protected the rights of separated students, including those who had missed 20 or more consecutive days of school and those who were discharged or transferred from school due to their age, lack of credits, Regents' exam failure, bad grades, truancy or pregnancy. Separated students would be given re-enrollment rights after attending a guidance conference. Lane agreed to establish a young adult success center to operate with existing support services. The agreements protected the rights of currently enrolled students facing transfer, discharge or separation. The court emphasized the importance of the actions and similar cases brought to ensure students are not deprived of educational opportunities. See *Campaign for Fiscal Equity, Inc. v. State of New York*, 100 N.Y.2d 893, 801 N.E.2d 326, 769 N.Y.S.2d 106 (2003), Chapter 11, Section I.A. Some provisions of the agreements remain in effect until 2008. Students over age 21 at the time of a request for readmission will be allowed to enter GED, evening, or adult education programs. *RV v. New York City Dep't of Educ.*, 321 F.Supp.2d 538 (E.D.N.Y. 2004).

◆   A New York school's attendance policy required students to attend 90% of all classes in each course to receive credit and dropped students from any course from which they were deliberately absent. **A group of students brought** a state court **challenge to the attendance policy**. The students argued that the denial of credit for a class is equivalent to dropping a student from enrollment, which is contrary to New York law. The school district's motion for summary judgment was granted. The students appealed to the New York Supreme Court, Appellate Division. **The court** rejected the students' arguments and **held the denial of credit was not equivalent to dropping a student from enrollment, since it did not bar a student from attending classes or make-up classes**. The court upheld the lower court's entry of summary judgment on behalf of the school. *Bitting v. Lee*, 564 N.Y.S.2d 791 (N.Y. App. Div. 1990).

III. CORPORAL PUNISHMENT

The U.S. Supreme Court held in Ingraham v. Wright, *below, that the infliction of corporal punishment implicates student liberty interests under the Due Process Clause of the Fourteenth Amendment. However, as corporal punishment was authorized by common law, the Court refused to create any procedural safeguards for students beyond those offered by state law. Corporal punishment is distinguishable from "reasonable physical force" to restrain unruly students, maintain order and prevent injury, as permitted by state law.*

A. Student Due Process Rights

◆   The U.S. Supreme Court held the use of corporal punishment is a matter of state law. Two Florida students were paddled by school administrators. One was beaten so severely he missed 11 days of school. The other suffered a hematoma and lost the use of his arm for a week. The parents sued school authorities, alleging cruel and unusual punishment and due process violations. **The Supreme Court held the Eighth Amendment prohibition against cruel and unusual punishment did not apply to corporal punishment in schools.** The Court's reasoning for this decision lay in the relative openness of the school system and its surveillance by the community. The Eighth Amendment was intended to protect the rights of incarcerated persons, not students. State civil and criminal penalties restrained school employees from issuing unreasonable punishment. **While corporal punishment implicated the Due Process Clause, state law vested the decision to issue it with school officials. The Court found corporal punishment served important educational interests. There was no requirement for notice and a hearing prior to imposing corporal punishment as the practice was authorized and limited by state law.** *Ingraham v. Wright*, 430 U.S. 651, 97 S.Ct. 1401, 51 L.Ed.2d 711 (1977).

◆   An Ohio school district banned corporal punishment in its schools in 1987. Substitute teachers had to undergo training on the subject before becoming eligible for hire. During orientation, they were informed of the district policy prohibiting corporal punishment and told how to handle student misconduct.

The policy for substitutes prohibited corporal punishment in any form. Substitutes had to seek assistance from the principal or assistant principal if a student disciplinary situation occurred. One substitute worked for the school district for four years and had no criminal record or history of hitting students. A third grader claimed the substitute "slammed her into a chalkboard, threw her on the ground, and choked her" for a minute because she did not have a pencil with her. Her parent sued the school district for state and federal law violations.

The case reached the U.S. Court of Appeals, Sixth Circuit, which rejected the parent's claim that the state Tort Liability Act violated the Ohio Constitution. It had not been improper for the district court to exclude reports describing 10 prior incidents of corporal punishment, because they were irrelevant and inadmissible under federal rules. **To show corporal punishment violates the Constitution, a student must show "the force applied caused injury so severe, was so disproportionate to the need presented, and was so inspired by malice or sadism rather than a merely careless or unwise excess of zeal that it amounted to a brutal and inhumane abuse of official power literally shocking to the conscience."** The court found no reasonable jury could have found the district was deliberately indifferent to complaints of abuse by substitutes. To find a municipality liable for violations of constitutional rights by employees, it must be proven that an injury was caused by a municipal policy or custom. **The student did not show the district was deliberately indifferent to student abuse by substitute teachers.** Only two of the 10 prior incident reports were severe enough to give the school district notice of possible constitutional violations. Two incidents in a two-year period in a school district with 127 schools serving over 69,000 students did not create "notice" of constitutional problems. The court affirmed the judgment for the school district. *Ellis v. Cleveland Municipal School Dist.*, 455 F.3d 690 (8th Cir. 2006).

◆ The U.S. Court of Appeals, Eleventh Circuit, upheld a federal district court order denying qualified immunity to an Alabama principal accused of beating a student. The student claimed the principal called him into his office for disciplinary reasons and hit him in the head, ribs and back with a metal cane. His mother filed a federal district court action on his behalf against the district and principal for violating his federal civil rights. The principal moved for summary judgment, asserting he was entitled to qualified immunity. He alleged the student had previously been disciplined for bringing a weapon to school, justifying his use of force. The court denied the request for immunity, and the principal appealed to the Eleventh Circuit. The court stated **excessive corporal punishment may create a due process violation if it involves "arbitrary, egregious, and conscience-shocking behavior."** A student complaint meets this standard by alleging excessive force by an official that presents a reasonably foreseeable risk of serious bodily injury.

The court held that repeatedly striking a 13-year-old with a metal cane was an obvious constitutional violation. It rejected the principal's assertion that any prior incident involving weapons possession allowed him to beat the student. There was also no merit to the principal's claim that the right to be free from corporal punishment was not clearly established at the time of the incident. ***Ingraham v. Wright* held the deliberate infliction of physical pain by school**

authorities as punishment implicated student due process rights. The Alabama Supreme Court has held corporal punishment deprives students of their substantive due process rights when it is arbitrary, capricious or unrelated to the legitimate goal of maintaining an atmosphere conducive to learning. The principal was not entitled to qualified immunity, and the district court would have to consider whether he violated principles established by the U.S. and Alabama courts. *Kirkland v. Greene County Board of Educ.*, 347 F.3d 903 (11th Cir. 2003).

♦   A Hawaii elementary school teacher sent a student to the school office to be disciplined for fighting. Once there, the student refused to stand still against a wall for time-out punishment. The school's vice principal warned the student he would take him outside and tape him to a tree if he did not stand still. He then made good on his threat by taping the student to the tree with masking tape. After about five minutes, a fifth-grade student told the vice principal "she did not think he should be doing that." The vice principal allowed her to remove the tape from the student. The student's family sued the state education department and vice principal in a federal district court for constitutional rights violations.

The court denied the vice principal's motion for summary judgment, and he appealed to the Ninth Circuit. It held the case involved the Fourth Amendment right to be free from unreasonable searches and seizures, not the more general Due Process Clause of the Fourteenth Amendment. School seizures violated the Fourth Amendment if they were objectively unreasonable under the circumstances. There was no suggestion in this case that the student was a danger to others. **Taping an eight-year-old to a tree was objectively unreasonable conduct. Students have a clearly established right to be free from excessive force by their teachers.** The district court had properly found a violation of the student's rights, and the court affirmed the judgment. *Doe v. State of Hawaii*, 334 F.3d 906 (9th Cir. 2003).

♦   When a teacher observed an Arkansas ninth-grader violently kicking a vending machine, she attempted to stop him. The student initially ignored the teacher, but stopped kicking the machine when she began to shake him by the arms. The principal of the adjacent high school grabbed the student's neck and shirt collar, led him from the school and "threw" him on a bench, where he landed on his shoulder. The principal instructed the school's resource officer to handcuff the student, and he was taken to the county jail. The student's mother then took him to an emergency room, where he was diagnosed with a strained neck and treated. The student's mother sued the principal in a federal district court. The court awarded summary judgment to the principal, and the mother appealed to the U.S. Court of Appeals, Eighth Circuit.

The court stated that courts have limited substantive due process claims to violations of personal rights that are so severe, disproportionate and inspired by malice or sadism as to amount to a "brutal and inhumane abuse of official power that is literally shocking to the conscience." The U.S. Supreme Court has rejected a single standard for excessive force claims under 42 U.S.C. § 1983. Courts do not impose Section 1983 liability in actions caused by unforeseen circumstances where immediate action is required. The court held the principal's conduct could not be considered shocking to the conscience unless it was malicious and sadistic. There was no evidence that he disliked the student or had even met him prior to the incident. **School administrators are entitled to substantial deference in their efforts to maintain order and discipline. The principal responded quickly and decisively to an incident of serious student misbehavior,** and the court affirmed the judgment in his favor. *Golden ex rel. Balch v. Anders,* 324 F.3d 650 (8th Cir. 2003).

◆ A Texas middle school student was singled out for talking by his teacher and ordered to do 100 squat-thrusts. He was later diagnosed with a degenerative skeletal-muscular disease, renal failure and esophagitis/gastritis. After his return to school, he was unable to participate in school athletics and physical education classes. His mother claimed the teacher told her that squat-thrusts were a necessary form of punishment. The family sued the teacher and district in a federal district court for constitutional violations under 42 U.S.C. § 1983, adding state law negligence and intentional infliction of emotional distress claims. The court awarded summary judgment to the teacher and district. The family appealed to the U.S. Court of Appeals, Fifth Circuit.

The court held a Section 1983 claim must allege the violation of a right secured by the Constitution or laws of the United States and demonstrate the violation was "committed by a person acting under color of state law." The family failed to meet the threshold requirement of demonstrating a constitutional violation. **The Fifth Circuit has consistently held that if a state remedy is present to redress the denial of substantive due process through excessive corporal punishment, there can be no federal claim based on denial of due process rights against a school system, administrator or school employee. Corporal punishment violates due process only where it is arbitrary, capricious or wholly unrelated to educational goals. Excessive corporal punishment in the discipline of a student does not implicate due process, irrespective of the severity, if state law civil or criminal remedies are available to a student.** There were adequate common law remedies for the vindication of the student's claim. The federal claim was properly dismissed, but the district court should have declined jurisdiction over the state law claims. *Moore v. Willis Independent School Dist.,* 248 F.3d 1145 (5th Cir. 2000).

B. Teacher Liability Protection

Subpart Five of the No Child Left Behind (NCLB) Act (20 U.S.C. §§ 6731-38) is the Paul D. Coverdell Teacher Protection Act, which parallels state law provisions protecting school employees from liability when they restrain students in order to preserve order in the school or to prevent injury.

The NCLB provision protects school staff from liability if they act on behalf of the school, within the scope of their employment, in conformity with law and "in furtherance of efforts to control, discipline, expel, or suspend a student or maintain order or control in the classroom or school.;" ... and there is no willful or criminal misconduct, gross negligence or reckless misconduct or flagrant disregard for rights. The NCLB prohibits punitive damage awards against teachers unless there is "clear and convincing evidence that the harm was proximately caused by an act or omission of such teacher that constitutes willful or criminal misconduct" or flagrant indifference to rights.

◆ A Louisiana student was enrolled in special education and took medication for attention deficit hyperactivity disorder. He was frequently disciplined for misconduct including fighting, kicking, cursing, taking things from others and "flipping people off." The student's parents agreed to a behavior management plan. A week later, he severely bit a classmate during recess. The school's assistant principal paddled the student three times in the presence of a teacher, in conformity with the school's corporal punishment policy. The parents sued the school board and assistant principal in a state court for negligence. The court held for the parents, even though the paddling was authorized by Louisiana law and school board policy. It awarded the family $45,000, and the board appealed.

The Louisiana Court of Appeal recited **provisions of state law authorizing teachers to hold each student "to a strict account for any disorderly conduct" in school, on a school playground, or on any school bus**. Corporal punishment was expressly allowed in Louisiana by school boards that adopted rules governing its use. The board in this case adopted rules allowing corporal punishment only after other methods had failed. The rules protected student due process rights, required a staff witness, and specified the type of paddle and the number of strokes to be used. The assistant principal testified he administered the paddlings because of the severity of the student's misconduct and only after other methods failed. He complied with board rules and felt the student needed immediate negative reinforcement. The student had a longstanding pattern of continual misbehavior, and other methods failed. His parents had complained of these other methods and refused counseling for him. **The legislature recognized the need for corporal punishment in some cases, and the law did not require advance parental consent.** The court reversed the judgment. *Setliff v. Rapides Parish School Board*, 888 So.2d 1156 (La. Ct. App. 2004).

The Supreme Court of Louisiana denied further appeal. *Setliff v. Rapides Parish School Board*, 896 So.2d 1011 (La., writ denied, 2005).

◆ A Wisconsin student with mild autism had difficulty concentrating and became easily frustrated. His individualized education program (IEP) called for teachers to take him to a particular room when he became anxious and frustrated. The student began to cry and left his table after a disagreement with classmates. The teacher instructed him several times to report to the room specified in his IEP, but he refused. According to the student, the teacher then removed him from class and pushed him into a wall. The student sued the district and teacher in a state trial court, which denied his motion for a restraining order preventing any further contact between himself and the teacher. The court awarded judgment to the district, teacher, superintendent and principal on claims for battery and negligence, and additional claims such as violation of the Americans with Disabilities Act (ADA). The student appealed.

The Wisconsin Court of Appeals stated the teacher had used only minor and reasonable physical contact to maintain classroom order, as allowed by Wisconsin Statutes Section 118.31(3)(h). **Section 118.31 provided a complete defense to battery claims.** Nothing indicated the teacher slammed or shoved the student. The court found no reasonable jury could find a battery in this case. The student argued Wis. Stat. Section 118.31 imposed a duty on the district and its employees to refrain from using corporal punishment. The court disagreed, noting the statute authorized corporal punishment for several purposes. **Actions consistent with an IEP or athletic training were not corporal punishment. The statute defined "corporal punishment" as the intentional infliction of physical pain for discipline. School staff could use incidental, minor or reasonable physical force to maintain classroom order and control.** The law required each school board to adopt policies allowing reasonable force to maintain school order. It also provided for deference to reasonable, good-faith judgments made by school employees when acting in accordance with the statutory purposes. The court affirmed the judgment for the district. *Loy v. Dodgeville School Dist.*, 688 N.W.2d 783 (Wis. Ct. App. 2004).

◆   A Louisiana student with a congenital heart condition claimed his PE teacher normally called him "heart man" or "heart attack." Midway through the year, the teacher instructed him to run around the gym with his class. The student claimed the teacher grabbed his shirt and pushed him into a wall. The teacher admitted some contact but denied pushing the student and said he had only told the student to walk. The student's mother took him to an emergency room and contacted the police, but declined to file criminal charges. She sued the school board and teacher in the state court system, claiming the incident damaged the student's heart further and would require treatment.

The court dismissed the mother's slander claim, then held a trial on the assault and battery claims. Based on testimony from the student, teacher and others, the court found the contact "was necessary to maintain control of the classroom" and was not a battery. The mother appealed to the Court of Appeal of Louisiana, arguing the name-calling was slander and intentional infliction of emotional harm on her son. The court upheld dismissal of the slander claim. It appeared there was a school custom of assigning nicknames to all freshmen. The teacher did not use names to "specifically defame or cast a personal reflection" on the student. The trial court credited testimony that the teacher had grabbed or pushed the student, but not forcefully. **The evidence indicated the student was disrespectful, and that the confrontation resulted from his behavior. The court noted there are occasions when staff must administer discipline. The teacher had a duty to maintain discipline when the student confronted him and ignored requests to walk around the gym.** The court affirmed the judgment for the teacher and board, finding the attempt to maintain order was reasonable. *Boone v. Reese*, 889 So.2d 435 (La. Ct. App. 2004).

◆   A Colorado school custodian broke up a fight between two students in a school hallway. He "head-butted" the student he perceived to be the aggressor and told him "there's always someone bigger than you. Now get out of here." The district investigated the incident and proposed discharging the custodian for inappropriate contact with a student. It afforded him a hearing before the superintendent under the applicable collective bargaining agreement. The custodian appeared with counsel, who submitted documents and argued on his behalf. The superintendent issued a one-page memorandum outlining the hearing evidence and recommending discharge for deliberate or inappropriate conduct. The school board approved the recommendation and the custodian sued the district in a state court. He alleged breach of contract and violation of C.R.S. § 22-32-110(4)(c), a state law that protects employees from discipline for good faith compliance with a school disciplinary code.

The court held the discharge violated Section 22-32-110(4)(c) and ordered the district to reinstate the custodian to his job with back wages. In doing so, the court conducted a new hearing, described by courts as *"de novo* review." The state court of appeals vacated the order, holding the trial court should have deferred to the board's findings instead of performing a *de novo* review. On appeal, the Supreme Court of Colorado explained C.R.S. § 22-32-110(4)(c) requires school districts to adopt disciplinary codes to deal with disorderly students. **Districts must have policies and procedures for using reasonable and appropriate physical intervention or force when dealing with disruptive students. A teacher or other person acting in good-faith compliance with a disciplinary code is not subject to discipline for acting lawfully under Section 22-32-110(4)(c). The court found the clear public policy of Section 22-32-110(4)(c) was to encourage educators to intervene in cases of disruption, violence and bullying.** However, a court was to review the school board record to determine if there had been an abuse of discretion, and the trial court committed error by conducting a *de novo* review. The district provided the custodian a hearing as required by the collective bargaining agreement. The court affirmed the appellate court decision that *de novo* court review was inappropriate. It expressed no opinion on whether the custodian should be reinstated and ordered the case remanded to the board to correct the deficient, one-page record. School boards, not courts, retained discretion over employees and the enforcement of their own conduct and discipline codes. *Widder v. Durango School Dist. No. 9-R*, 85 P.3d 518 (Colo. 2004).

◆   A Florida teacher called school security to escort a student from class for disruptive behavior. A security officer brought the student to a detention room. The two "got into a disagreement," and the student claimed the officer began to beat him. Two more security officers then arrived at the room and allegedly kicked and punched the student. The student and his family sued the school board and officers in a state trial court for constitutional rights violations and battery. The constitutional claims were removed to a federal district court, where they were dismissed. The state court granted summary judgment to the board on the claim of vicarious liability for battery, and the family appealed.

The Florida District Court of Appeal noted the state's vicarious liability was limited by Florida Statutes Section 768.28(9)(a). In general, **state subdivisions were not liable for the acts or omissions of employees who acted outside the scope of their employment.** The state supreme court has held an employing agency is immune from liability as a matter of law when an employee's acts are so extreme as to be "a clearly unlawful usurpation of authority." In this case, **the security officers had the authority to escort the student from class and restrain him. They acted within the scope of their authority, and the trial court should have considered whether their actions were within the scope of Section 768.28(9)(a).** The court reversed the decision and remanded the case to determine if the board had immunity under that section. *Carestio v. School Board of Broward County,* 866 So.2d 754 (Fla. Dist. Ct. App. 2004).

◆   A Texas high school student threw an object at another student and used profanity in the classroom. The teacher removed him from class by holding on to his hair and arm and took him to the vice principal's office for discipline. The student was sent to the district opportunity center as punishment. **The student's parents sued the teacher in a Texas court, claiming he suffered injuries in being removed from the classroom.** The court granted summary judgment to the teacher, and the parents appealed to the Court of Appeals of Texas. **The court observed that Texas teachers were protected by absolute immunity from personal liability for any act involving the exercise of discretion with only limited exceptions, including excessive force or negligence during student discipline. It held the teacher had not been engaged in disciplinary action but was merely transporting the student to the vice principal's office for discipline.** The teacher was entitled to absolute immunity. *Doria v. Stulting,* 888 S.W.2d 563 (Tex. Ct. App. 1994).

IV. RACE AND NATIONAL ORIGIN DISCRIMINATION

Title VI of the Civil Rights Act of 1964 prohibits race discrimination in any program that receives federal funds. Title VI is based on the principles of the Equal Protection Clause, and many discrimination complaints allege violations of Title VI, the Equal Protection Clause, and analogous state law provisions. Courts require proof of intentional discrimination in Title VI cases. School officials may be held liable if they are deliberately indifferent to clearly established student rights. This occurs where a pattern or practice of civil rights violations is proven to exist that is attributable to policy-making employees.

◆   A Kansas student claimed the principal and teachers at his alternative school repeatedly forbade him and other students of Hispanic origin from speaking Spanish on school grounds. According to the student, the principal suspended him after telling him "he was not in Mexico" and that "he should speak only English on school premises." The suspension notice she wrote indicated he was not to speak Spanish on school grounds. The student's father brought the notice to the superintendent, who overturned the suspension. The family sued the superintendent, principal, teachers, school board and district, and members of the school board in a federal district court. The complaint alleged race and national origin discrimination in violation of Title VI of the Civil Rights Act of 1964, as well as equal protection violations. The court noted the Equal Opportunity Commission has stated that rigid English-only workplace rules may violate Title VII of the Civil Rights Act of 1964.

By claiming school officials singled out students of Hispanic origin and targeted them for attributes based upon race or national origin, the student made out a valid equal protection claim. He did not allege a district-wide custom of prohibiting Spanish on school property. Principals lack policymaking authority and typically do not create district-wide liability for constitutional claims. The court denied pretrial dismissal of the constitutional claims against the principal and teacher, as the student had alleged intentional discrimination based on membership in a protected class. However, the principal and teacher were entitled to qualified immunity because he could not show they violated a clearly established federal right. **The court found no case establishing a right to speak a foreign language at a public school. In the employment context, some English-only rules were permissible.** There was enough evidence of intentional discrimination to avoid pretrial dismissal of the Title VI discrimination claim. The district could be held liable for the principal's acts, because she had authority to take corrective action to end the discrimination. The court allowed the student to amend his complaint by adding a Title VI claim for retaliation, and denied other pre-trial motions. *Rubio v. Turner Unified School Dist.*, 453 F.Supp.2d 1295 (D. Kan. 2006).

◆ A student of African-American and Hispanic heritage received special education for a specific learning disability. In eighth grade, she stopped coming to school, due in part to family problems. She enrolled in an intensive phonics program for grade nine, but never attended class. The student was charged with aggravated battery and assault of her mother and brother with a deadly weapon. After serving time in juvenile facilities, she was placed in a residential treatment center. Upon returning to school, the student used drugs and alcohol at school and received numerous disciplinary referrals for truancy. She skipped school to provoke her mother's boyfriend into leaving their home. The student became pregnant and was sent to a day shelter. The school suspended her for fighting. The student's mother claimed the district denied her access to the Wilson Reading System. She filed a special education due process complaint, where the district prevailed. The student transferred to a neighboring district, where she enrolled in a Wilson class. She initially earned a 4.0 grade average but later dropped out due to more family turmoil and drug use. The parent sued her residence school board and officials in a federal district court for equal protection and Title VI violations. The court found the Wilson system was one of several Orton-Gillingham-based programs available for schools. Both Wilson and Corrective Reading met the requirements of the No Child Left Behind Act.

The court found no merit to the student's claim that she did not benefit from her education. **A party claiming Title VI violations may only prevail by proving a school acted with a discriminatory intent or motive.** The court found that when she chose to attend class, seek help from teachers and apply herself, she could achieve a 4.0 grade average. There was no evidence that any district decision was tainted by discrimination. **There is no constitutional right for a student to attend a preferred reading program. School staff have the right to select services or programming, not students, parents, or even the courts.** The court found the curricular choices made for the student were undermined by factors under her control. The "absurdity" of her position was demonstrated when she again dropped out of school, while still in a Wilson program. The court awarded summary judgment to the district. *Garcia v. Board of Educ. of Albuquerque Public Schools*, 436 F.Supp.2d 1181 (D.N.M. 2006).

◆ Two African-American students collided in a dark gymnasium during a game of flashlight tag held in their physical education class. Their parents sued the school district for personal injury. The district claimed immunity under Minn. Stat. § 466.12, subd. 3a, which provides immunity to school districts that are unable to obtain liability insurance for an average rate of $1.50 or less per student. The students claimed the classification in the statute was arbitrary and violated the equal protection rights of Minneapolis students. They based this on the relatively high number of African-American students attending Minneapolis schools, and the district's status as the only one in the state that was unable to obtain certification of its inability to buy insurance at the $1.50/student rate.

The court held the $1.50 per student classification was arbitrary and violated equal protection guarantees. The students appealed, arguing the statute created a class of African-American students that was prevented from exercising rights to sue a school district. The state court of appeals disagreed, noting the statute afforded all Minnesota school districts immunity, treating similarly situated entities the same. The effect of Section 466.12, subd. 3a was to allow any Minnesota school district to apply for and receive immunity from tort liability. While the Minneapolis school district was the only one in the state to obtain immunity by certification, it was not treated differently from those districts that obtained immunity by purchasing insurance. The court found the $1.50 classification resulted in the equal treatment of all school districts, and of all their potential student tort victims. **As the classification did not result in any different treatment, there was no equal protection violation.** *Granville v. Minneapolis School Dist.*, 716 N.W.2d 387 (Minn Ct. App. 2006).

◆ An Oklahoma school district maintained a "fight policy" subjecting second-time offenders to expulsion for a semester. After the district expelled two African-American students for violating the fight policy, they alleged white students were not expelled despite similar conduct. They claimed the principal tolerated racial slurs and epithets by white students and allowed swastikas and the letters "KKK" to be inscribed in desks and placed in the lockers or notebooks of African-American students. The students sued the district in a federal district court for violating Title VI. The court awarded summary judgment to the district, and the students appealed to the Tenth Circuit.

The court noted that the U.S. Supreme Court has not allowed a private right of action under Title VI to remedy non-intentional discrimination arising from neutral policies with an unintentional discriminatory effect. Since the students could not disprove the school's legitimate reasons for discipline, summary judgment was appropriate on the intentional discrimination claim. The court examined the students' hostile educational environment claims, which arose from events occurring before the fight leading to their discipline. They were entitled to an opportunity to prove their assertions of the principal's inaction in the face of a racist environment. The court held **school administrators could be liable under Title VI for remaining "deliberately indifferent" to known acts of student-on-student harassment.** The hostile race environment claim was remanded to the district court, with instructions to apply the standard of liability for peer sexual harassment claims from *Davis v. Monroe County Board of Educ.*, 526 U.S. 629 (1999), summarized in Section V of this chapter. The district court was to determine if the harassment was so severe, pervasive and objectively offensive that it deprived the victims of access to educational benefits or opportunities. **The court held school administrators "are not simply bystanders in the school. They are the leaders of the educational environment."** *Bryant v. Independent School Dist. No. I-38, Garvin County, Oklahoma*, 334 F.3d 928 (10th Cir. 2003).

◆ Two Delaware students, one African-American, the other white, fought each other until a teacher stepped between them. The teacher reported the African-American student hit her as she tried to separate them. The school principal spoke to the African-American student immediately after the fight and asked him to write down his version of the incident. In this written description, the student admitted hitting the teacher. The principal suspended him for five days for "assaulting" the teacher, while suspending the white student for three days for "fighting" under separate provisions of the student code. The district's alternative placement committee assigned the African-American student to an alternative program for the rest of the school year. The district reported the incident to the police and after a family court trial, the African-American student was adjudicated delinquent for assault and disorderly conduct. Although he returned to his middle school for grade eight, his mother filed a complaint against the district with federal officials. An investigation determined the African-American student was disciplined more severely than his classmate due to his conduct, not his race. His mother sued the district in a federal district court for violations of Title VI, the Due Process Clause and state law.

The court observed that **private claims under Title VI must allege intentional discrimination**. To prove a facially neutral policy was intentionally discriminatory, a party had to show it was adopted because of its adverse effect on an identifiable group. As the school code of conduct did not discriminate against any identifiable group or minority, the district was entitled to summary judgment on the Title VI claim. There was no merit to the due process claim because the student received notice of the charges against him and an opportunity to present his side of the story. The principal spoke to the student immediately after the fight and asked him for his written version of the facts. The student code clearly defined "assault" and specified a five-day suspension as discipline for this offense. There was no evidence that criminal charges were brought to embarrass, humiliate or inflict severe emotional distress upon the student. As the principal reported the incident pursuant to state law, the district was entitled to summary judgment. *Harris-Thomas v. Christina School Dist.*, No. Civ.A. 02-253-KAJ, 2003 WL 22999541 (D. Del. 2003).

◆ Two Ohio brothers of African-American descent claimed they were disciplined for fighting back against white students who harassed them. They stated the white students repeatedly called them racist names and used racial slurs but were not punished by their school. The brothers said that in at least two cases, references to the use of racial epithets were omitted from school disciplinary records. The brothers sued the school district and officials in a federal district court for civil rights violations.

The court found evidence that racial comments by the white students were not officially recorded and sometimes went unpunished. Although only two of the eight incidents indicated disparate discipline, the court refused to dismiss the claim that racial harassment went virtually unreported and unpunished. The court found the failure to record the use of racial epithets was strong evidence of an equal protection violation. Because the brothers presented evidence that school officials were deliberately indifferent to their reports of harassment, the court denied summary judgment to the school board. **According to the court, inaction by the officials created an atmosphere that allowed harassment. Since the board had a custom and practice of failing to discipline racial harassment, liability could be imposed on it for racial harassment under the Equal Protection Clause.** The court denied summary judgment to the principal and district superintendent, based on their acquiescence to the reported harassment and failure to impose discipline. The district and officials were entitled to judgment on the due process and retaliation claims. The court held any claim the brothers might have for punitive damages based on violations of their federal civil rights was not barred by Ohio law. *Payne v. Worthington Schools*, No. C2-99-830, 2001 WL 506509 (S.D. Ohio 2001).

V.   SEX DISCRIMINATION

A.   Sexual Harassment by Students

Sexual harassment has been recognized by the courts as a form of sex discrimination. Title IX of the Education Amendments of 1972 prohibits sex discrimination by all recipients of federal funding. In Davis v. Monroe County Board of Educ., *below, the U.S. Supreme Court first held schools could be liable under Title IX for student-on-student harassment. The court established a three-part test for school liability in* Davis *for peer sexual harassment. Students must show (1) sexual harassment by peers; (2) deliberate indifference by school officials with actual knowledge of the harassment; and (3) harassment so severe, pervasive and objectively offensive it deprived the student of access to educational opportunities. A teacher's knowledge of peer harassment is sufficient to create "actual knowledge" that may trigger liability for a district.*

◆   A Georgia fifth-grader complained to her teacher of sexual harassment by a male student. The teacher did not immediately notify the principal about it. **Although the harasser was eventually charged with sexual battery, school officials took no action against him.** The student sued the school board in a federal district court for Title IX violations. The court dismissed the case and the student appealed to the U.S. Court of Appeals, Eleventh Circuit. The court reversed the judgment but granted the board's petition for rehearing. On rehearing, the court observed that if it adopted the student's argument, a school board must immediately isolate an alleged harasser to avoid a Title IX lawsuit. It affirmed the dismissal of the student's claims and she appealed.

The U.S. Supreme Court reversed the judgment, holding **school districts may be held liable under Title IX for deliberate indifference to known acts**

of peer sexual harassment, where the school's response is clearly unreasonable under the circumstances. A recipient of federal funds may be liable for student-on-student sexual harassment where the funding recipient is deliberately indifferent to known sexual harassment and the harasser is under the recipient's disciplinary authority. To create Title IX liability, the harassment must be so severe, pervasive and objectively offensive that it deprives the victim of access to educational opportunities or benefits. The Court held the harassment alleged by the student was sufficiently severe enough to avoid pretrial dismissal. It reversed and remanded the case. *Davis v. Monroe County Board of Educ.*, 526 U.S. 629, 119 S.Ct. 1661, 143 L.Ed.2d 839 (1999).

◆   A Native American student claimed ongoing race and sex harassment over a six-year period in her Minnesota school. She claimed students made daily derogatory statements and physically attacked her, and that the conduct was so severe she stopped going to school for extended time periods. The student further claimed that some behavior and comments occurred in the presence of school staff, but that no action was taken. She asserted school administrators blamed her for the misconduct, accused her of lying and retaliated against her.

The student sued the district and school officials in a federal district court for Equal Protection and Due Process violations, and discrimination under Title IX and Title VI. She added state law claims for discrimination, negligence and infliction of emotional distress, and sought $5 million in damages. The court refused to limit any damages for her federal claims under a state law limiting compensatory damages to a district's insurance policy liability limits. The law applied only to tort claims. The student could not recover punitive damages against the district under state law, Title VI, Title IX, or the Constitution. However, she could recover up to $8,500 in punitive damages from the district under the state Human Rights Act. The court held that the case required an expert opinion to define the standard of care for school administrators in the exercise of their judgment. The student failed to identify an expert to define the duty of care within the specified time frame. As this was fatal to her negligence claims, the court dismissed them. **Her remaining tort claims would be limited to $1 million in compensatory damages, with $8,500 available for any human rights act violation.** *A.M.J. v. Royalton Public Schools*, Civil No. 05-2541 (PAM/RLE), 2006 WL 3626979 (D. Minn. 2006).

◆   A Pennsylvania general education student claimed her school did nothing to address repeated sexual harassment by a disabled classmate for over four years. The classmate's individualized education program (IEP) had a behavior plan for grade seven, but no mention was made of his harassing behavior toward the student and no services were provided to address it. The student continued to report unwanted attention from the classmate over the next four years, such as notes, drawings, and offers to be her boyfriend. In grade eleven, she reported the classmate began to stalk her, but the IEP team removed his behavior plan and recommended no discipline. In their senior year, the classmate found the student alone in a school weight room and prevented her from leaving for half an hour. School administrators met with the student's family and a state trooper. Criminal charges were not filed because the trooper found the classmate "was too low functioning to understand the nature of the offenses." The school district advised staff that the classmate was to have no contact with the student, and a behavior plan was placed in his IEP. The student's mother had worked for 26 years as a vision specialist for an education agency that served the school district. She asked to address the district's board, but the superintendent told her to write a letter instead. The mother wrote a letter reviewing the situation and asking the board to take steps to prepare and train district administrators and staff on handling students with noncompliant behavior. Her complaint to the state department of education was dismissed. The district superintendent asked the education agency's director to reassign the mother. She filed an unsuccessful grievance to challenge the transfer, then sued the school district, education agency, superintendent and others in a federal district court.

The court held liability for sexual harassment exists under Title IX if a school official with control over a harasser had actual knowledge of sexual harassment, but was deliberately indifferent to it. The student and her mother had reported the classmate's conduct to teachers, guidance counselors and vice principals, who should have informed the principal. Officials with control over school discipline had actual knowledge of the harassment, beginning in grade eight. While a "district is not required to purge its schools of actionable peer harassment," officials must "respond to known peer harassment in a manner that is not clearly unreasonable." The district's response was unreasonable. It removed a behavior plan from the classmate's IEP, and he had no behavior plan for much of his high school career. The court denied a motion to dismiss the student's Title IX claim. The mother's claims were not dismissed either, as she raised issues of public concern about school safety and sexual harassment. Public agencies cannot retaliate against employees based on their speech. *Jones v. Indiana Area School Dist.*, 397 F.Supp.2d 628 (W.D. Pa. 2005).

◆ A Michigan student claimed a classmate raped her in a school lavatory during school hours. She sued the district, its board and two administrators in a federal district court for violations of state and federal law. The student claimed the principal and an assistant principal knew the classmate was sexually active, warranting liability for the district. The court awarded summary judgment to the district, finding no evidence that the district knew of sexual harassment by the classmate prior to the rape. The court declined jurisdiction over the state law claims, and the student appealed to the U.S. Court of Appeals, Sixth Circuit.

The court noted the Supreme Court recognized a private cause of action under Title IX for peer sexual harassment in *Davis v. Monroe County Board of Educ.* The *Davis* standard imposes liability on a district for harassment so severe, pervasive and objectively offensive it deprives the victim of educational benefits. The court noted **the district could be found to have subjected the student to harassment by the classmate only if it acted with "deliberate indifference to known acts of student-on-student harassment." The student could not meet this standard, as there was no evidence the district knew of even one incident of student-on-student harassment before the reported rape.** Evidence that the principal knew students engaged in sexual activity on campus was irrelevant. Harassment claims involve only "unwelcome" sexual advances. As there was no evidence of any student-on-student sexual harassment prior to the reported rape, the student could not show the district "subjected" her to sexual harassment. The court affirmed the judgment for the district. *Winzer v. School Dist. for City of Pontiac*, 105 Fed.Appx. 679 (6th Cir. 2004).

◆   An Illinois kindergartner reported a male classmate jumped on her back during a recess period near the start of the school year. He continued to exhibit inappropriate behavior, including repeatedly unzipping his pants. The school assigned the classmate to detention and sent him to the school psychologist's office. Several female students were also sent to the psychologist, and they reported the classmate had been jumping on them and kissing them during recess. Later in the year, the kindergartner's mother informed the school that the kindergartner had experienced nightmares, bedwetting and a growing fear of school. The principal suspended the classmate for two days and reassigned him to a new classroom, lunch and recess period. However, the classmate and kindergartner were later returned to the same lunch and recess periods, and the mother alleged he continued to bother her. A counselor diagnosed the kindergartner as having acute stress disorder and separation anxiety, and she received therapy. The district granted the parents' request to transfer her to a different school for first grade, and they sued the district for sexual harassment under Title IX. A federal district court awarded the district summary judgment.

The parents appealed to the Seventh Circuit, which applied the *Davis* deliberate indifference standard. While common sense weighed against a finding that kindergartners could engage in sexual harassment, the case could be decided without answering that question. As noted in *Davis*, young students are still learning how to act appropriately, and they "regularly interact in a manner that would be unacceptable among adults." For this reason, **"simple acts of teasing and name calling among children" do not create Title IX liability**. The kindergartner was unable to report conduct other than "vague and unspecific" allegations that the classmate "bothered her by doing nasty stuff." This did not provide the court with necessary details to evaluate its severity and pervasiveness. There was evidence kindergartners were unaware of the sexual nature of the conduct. The kindergartner was not denied access to an education, as neither her grades nor her attendance suffered. The court affirmed the judgment, because the district's response to the harassment was not clearly unreasonable and did not amount to deliberate indifference. *Gabrielle M. v. Park Forest-Chicago Heights School Dist. 163*, 315 F.3d 817 (7th Cir. 2003).

◆   Two female second-graders claimed a boy repeatedly chased, touched and grabbed them and often made sexual remarks and gestures. This conduct continued for several months, but the girls did not communicate the sexual nature of it, telling the teacher that the boy was "annoying," "gross," "nasty" or "disgusting." While staff members observed the boy's behavior and disciplined him for it, no adult saw him engage in overtly sexual behavior. Near the end of the school year, a third girl began attending the school and promptly complained to her teacher that the boy had told her to "suck his dick." The third girl's mother contacted the school principal and teacher and was told that the school was working with the boy's parents to resolve his problems. After meeting with the third girl's mother, the principal suspended the boy for one week, followed by an in-school suspension. The principal instructed the teacher to keep the boy away from the third girl. When the girls' attorney notified the principal that the boy's misconduct was continuing, the school suspended him for the rest of the school year. The families sued the school board in a federal district court, asserting Title IX violations. The court awarded summary judgment to the board, and the parents appealed to the Eleventh Circuit.

The court stated **whether conduct amounts to harassment depends on the circumstances, expectations and relationships of the people involved. This includes consideration of the ages of the harasser and victims. Damages are not available for** "simple acts of teasing and mere name-calling" among children even when comments target differences in gender. Although the conduct alleged by the first two girls persisted for months and was sexually explicit and vulgar, it was not so severe, pervasive or offensive that it denied them access to their education. They suffered no physical exclusion from school facilities. While the third girl's complaints were more explicit, the school responded to them and was not deliberately indifferent. **To create liability, discrimination must be more widespread than a single instance of peer harassment.** The effects of the harassment must touch the whole of an educational program or activity. **As the girls were not denied access to their educational programs or activities and did not suffer any decline in grades or participation, the board could not be held liable for harassment.** *Hawkins v. Sarasota County School Board*, 322 F.3d 1279 (11th Cir. 2003).

◆   An Indiana student alleged an ex-boyfriend and some of his friends, both male and female, began calling her names such as "bitch, slut and whore" at school. Although school administrators spoke with the perpetrators on several occasions, the student alleged their efforts were insufficient, as the abusive language continued. When the student accused a female student of hitting her car with a purse, the police were summoned. The student transferred to another school and sued the district in a federal district court for Title IX violations.

The court explained that Title IX requires a showing of sexual harassment by peers that is so severe, pervasive and objectively offensive that it undermines the educational experience by denying equal access to education. To become actionable, **the harassment must be based on sex, rather than a personal reason such as a failed romantic relationship.** Although the terms used by the perpetrators had some sexual connotations, this was not necessarily proof of discrimination. The name-calling started as the result of the break-up, and **the slurs were based on personal hostility to the student, not sexual desire or gender bias. The Supreme Court cautioned in** *Davis* **that Title IX damages are not available for simple name-calling and teasing.** The student was not subjected to any actionable peer harassment, and the court entered judgment for the district. *Benjamin v. Metropolitan School Dist.*, No. IP 00-0891-C-T/K, 2002 WL 977661 (S.D. Ind. 2002).

B. Sexual Harassment by Staff

◆   In 1998, the U.S. Supreme Court examined the liability of school districts for sexual harassment of students by teachers and other staff under Title IX. The case involved a Texas student who had a sexual relationship with a teacher. The

Court rejected the liability standard advocated by the student and by the U.S. government, which resembled *respondeat superior* liability under Title VII. Title IX contains an administrative enforcement mechanism that assumes actual notice has been provided to officials prior to the imposition of enforcement remedies. **An award of damages would be inappropriate in a Title IX case unless an official with the authority to address the discrimination failed to act despite actual knowledge of it, in a manner amounting to deliberate indifference to discrimination.** Here, there was insufficient evidence that a school official should have known about the relationship to impose Title IX liability. Accordingly, the district could not be held liable for the teacher's misconduct. *Gebser v. Lago Vista Independent School Dist.*, 524 U.S. 274, 118 S.Ct. 1989, 141 L.Ed.2d 277 (1998).

◆ A Michigan high school soccer coach addressed players with obscenities, engaged them in "flirtatious conversations," and made suggestive remarks. He called players and sent them e-mails at unusual hours. He told one student on the team that he had "a special interest" in a particular teammate. The student said that when she discouraged the coach from pursuing the teammate, he threatened the entire team with consequences. The assistant principal, principal and athletic director met with him to address complaints by parents about his late-evening communications. The administrators composed a memo prohibiting him from late calls and from e-mailing players unless he copied the assistant principal. The coach was prohibited from counseling players about personal matters, conducting activities off-campus without parents present, and from inappropriate relationships. The teammate later informed the student she had broken off her relationship with the coach. According to the student, the coach blamed her for this and threatened to "break her nose and take out her knees so she would never play soccer again." The coach then threatened suicide. Police arrived at his residence, recovered a pistol, and took him to a hospital.

The coach resigned and was prohibited from entering school property. The student transferred to a different school and sued the district, coach and school officials in a federal district court. The case reached the U.S. Court of Appeals, Sixth Circuit, which held **the state civil rights act required her to show she was subjected to unwelcome sexual advances, requests for sexual favors, or sexual conduct or communication. The coach's threats to harm the student did not involve any sexual communication. While the threats were an abuse of authority, they did not pertain to sex. The district court correctly applied Michigan law, which holds that verbal or physical conduct or communications that are not sexual in nature cannot be considered sexual harassment.** The court noted that liability can be imposed for creating hostile environment harassment only if there is reasonable notice and failure to take action by officials. The meeting with administrators and the subsequent memo were evidence of a prompt and reasonable response. The student's claims for retaliation, negligence, sexual harassment and discrimination under Title IX and other federal laws failed for many of the same reasons as her state law claims. The extent of the coach's misconduct did not become known until he resigned. The judgment for the district and officials was affirmed. *Henderson v. Walled Lake Consolidated Schools*, 469 F.3d 479 (6th Cir. 2006).

◆   A Tennessee student enrolled in a weightlifting/conditioning class as a high
school senior. Only one other girl enrolled in the class, along with 35 boys. The
principal removed the student from the class, stating concern for inappropriate
behavior by males. According to the student, a staff member informed her and
the other girl they were being removed from the class due to lack of other
females, and said they were to report to the guidance office to work as helpers.
The student's parent claimed the principal said "he was not concerned about
Title IX, that this was 'our' school," and that he would not allow her into the
class. The principal agreed to a television interview where he repeatedly
acknowledged he had removed the student from the class based on her gender
and because of safety concerns. He expressed fear "that she may be raped or
sexually assaulted." A state official contacted the district's director of schools,
and within a few days, the principal permitted the student to return to the class.
She missed only three days of class, earned an A grade, and graduated.
However, the student claimed the stress of being removed from the class made
her unable to eat and that she contracted mononucleosis as a result.

The student and her parent sued the school board and officials in a federal
district court for violating the Equal Protection Clause and Title IX. The court
stated that the board could not be held liable for the actions of employees for a
constitutional rights violation, unless it resulted from an official board policy or
custom. **The principal was not a policymaker for the board. Once the board
became aware of his actions, it investigated and reversed his decision. The
court held the board could not be liable for the principal's actions.** The high
school had offered weightlifting/conditioning to both males and females for
years. While the principal apparently removed the student from the class based
on gender, the court rejected her invitation to hold the board liable for this
action. His conduct did not involve an official board policy. The court applied
the standard for sexual harassment cases under Title IX. The school board acted
reasonably and promptly to address the student's complaint. It was not
deliberately indifferent to gender discrimination, and the court dismissed the
Equal Protection and Title IX claims. *Phillips v. Anderson County Board of
Educ.*, No. 3:06-CV-35, 2006 WL 3759893 (E.D. Tenn. 2006).

◆   A Georgia teacher socialized with a troubled student's family, befriending
his mother and promising to "look after" both him and his sister. An assistant
school superintendent received an anonymous e-mail during the school year,
accusing the teacher of having inappropriate relationships with a list of students
who had graduated or dropped out of school. She learned of a similar complaint
against the teacher three years earlier, but the student involved in that incident
vehemently denied anything inappropriate. The teacher denied both the report
and the e-mail accusation. The assistant superintendent warned her, both orally
and in writing, to avoid any appearance of impropriety with students and
situations where she would be alone with male students. Vehicles owned by the
teacher and the troubled student were later seen parked together in some woods.
The superintendent promptly notified the school board and the police, and asked
the state Professional Standards Commission (PSC) to investigate the incident.
She told the school principal to monitor the two, prevent unnecessary contact
between them and to report suspicious behavior to her. The teacher resigned and

surrendered her teaching certificate after a substitute teacher discovered a note written by the student that threatened to expose their relationship if she did not comply with certain demands. The parents sued the district in a federal district court for Title IX and civil rights violations under 42 U.S.C. § 1983. The court awarded summary judgment to the district, and the parents appealed.

The U.S. Court of Appeals, Eleventh Circuit, reviewed *Gebser v. Lago Vista Independent School Dist.* **A district is not liable under *Gebser* unless a school official with authority to institute corrective measures has actual notice of misconduct, but is deliberately indifferent to it. "Deliberate indifference" was defined as an official decision by the school district not to remedy a violation.** The court held the parents could not demonstrate school officials acted with deliberate indifference at any time. They responded to each report of misconduct by investigating the charges and interviewing relevant persons. The officials consistently monitored the teacher and warned her about her interaction with students. They requested a PSC investigation after they received the first report specifically linking the teacher and student, monitored her and confronted her when the explicit note was discovered. In light of the many corrective measures taken by district officials, the court held they were not deliberately indifferent. **A district is not deliberately indifferent because the measures it takes are ultimately ineffective in stopping the harassment.** The court affirmed the judgment for the district. *Sauls v. Pierce County School Dist.*, 399 F.3d 1279 (11th Cir. 2005).

◆ New York twins claimed their history teacher sexually harassed them. One of them claimed the teacher confided to her about his personal life. According to one of the twins, a school psychologist dismissed her report about the teacher and implied the relationship between her and the teacher was a good one. The psychologist later dismissed reports by the twins' mother and one of the twins. The psychologist did not investigate or report the teacher's conduct, which included improper touching and the giving of gifts and cards. Many incidents occurred before the principal met with the teacher and told him he was to have no more contact with the twins than he would with any other student. The following summer, the teacher spoke with one of the twins several times on her cell phone and left her a romantic message. Their parents gave the recorded message to the principal. The school reassigned the teacher the next day and told him not to report to the high school until further notice.

The twins sued the school district in a federal district court for sexual harassment in violation of Title IX. **The court held that even though the case did not involve allegations of an official policy of sex discrimination, there could be district liability for sexual harassment under Title IX. The twins only had to show "an official of the school district – who at a minimum has authority to institute corrective measures on the district's behalf – had actual notice of, and was deliberately indifferent to, the teacher's misconduct."** The court rejected the district's claim that the principal had no actual notice that the teacher was harassing the twins until he heard the phone message. It denied the district's motion for summary judgment. *Tesoriero v. Syosset Cent. School Dist.*, 382 F.Supp.2d 387 (E.D.N.Y. 2005).

◆ A Virginia elementary school principal learned a teacher had sexually molested a student, but took no action. Fifteen years later, a librarian observed a student sitting in the teacher's lap. The principal instructed the teacher to limit his physical contact with students. Another teacher told the principal that the teacher had a reputation for abusing children. The principal reported these accusations to a district personnel director, who began an investigation. The teacher resigned after the investigation. Another former student reported the teacher had sexually abused him. This student sued the teacher, principal, director, school board, school district, superintendent and other officials in a federal district court under 42 U.S.C. § 1983 for constitutional rights violations and violations of Title IX. A federal district court conducted a trial and awarded judgment to the director and superintendent. A jury returned verdicts against the school district for $700,000 and the principal for $350,000.

The parties appealed to the U.S. Court of Appeals, Fourth Circuit, which held that to establish supervisory liability under Section 1983, a supervisor must have knowledge that a subordinate's conduct poses a pervasive and unreasonable risk of constitutional injury, yet shows deliberate indifference to the risk. There must also be a causal link between the inaction and a constitutional injury. **A reasonable jury could find the principal knew the teacher created an unreasonable risk of injury to students and that her response was deliberately indifferent to this risk.** The court affirmed the judgment against the principal. A different liability standard applied to the district and administrators on the Title IX claims. **A district can be held liable under Title IX only where it intentionally remains indifferent to student-teacher harassment of which it has actual knowledge.** Although the principal's awareness of the teacher's potential for abuse created personal liability for her under Section 1983, she had no power to hire or fire employees. There was no Title IX liability for the district, as no reasonable juror could have found the director, superintendent or district deliberately indifferent to the student's rights. *Baynard v. Malone*, 268 F.3d 228 (4th Cir. 2001).

◆ A Nebraska student alleged she attempted suicide for reasons including a teacher's attempts to convince her she was gay. The district investigated their relationship and determined the teacher had engaged her in sexual relations over a four-year period. The teacher was fired for violating a district policy prohibiting such relationships for up to two years after a student's graduation. She also had her teaching license revoked. The student sued the teacher, school district and school officials in a federal district court for violations of Title IX. The court approved a jury verdict against the school officials in their official capacities, and they appealed to the Eighth Circuit. The court held that under Title IX, a school district may be held liable for sexual harassment of a student if its officials knew or should have known of harassing behavior.

The U.S. Supreme Court held in *Gebser* (this chapter), that a school district may not be held liable for Title IX violations unless the complaining party shows that a school official with authority to remedy the violation had actual notice of harassing conduct, yet failed to adequately respond. The Eighth Circuit then reconsidered the case and reversed the judgment, observing that **school officials had investigated her complaint and fired the teacher upon proof of**

the sexual relationship. The district and officials were entitled to judgment. However, the student was entitled to a default judgment against her former teacher. *Kinman v. Omaha Public School Dist.*, 171 F.3d 607 (8th Cir. 1999).

C. Sexual Orientation

◆   An Iowa student claimed he endured years of severe harassment at school due to a perception that he was homosexual. He stated school administrators failed to provide a safe environment after dozens of incidents of vandalization and physical assault. The student said the school resource officer advised him to either ignore a harassing classmate or confront him. When the student confronted the classmate, the two got into a fight. The school suspended both students, and they were arrested for disorderly conduct. The student sued the district and several school and police officials in a federal district court for civil rights violations. He claimed he was unable to return to school during his senior year since he did not feel safe there. The court considered the student's motion for a preliminary order to prevent school officials from suspending him.

The court upheld the school's anti-fighting policy as content and viewpoint neutral. The school had a strong interest in maintaining order to promote its learning environment, and the anti-fighting policy helped promote this interest. There was no evidence that the district interfered with the student's expression. **To prevail on his Title IX claim, the student had to show the district intentionally failed to intervene to stop the harassment. The district could not be held liable for "negligent" failure to stop harassment.** The court held the student showed a likelihood of success on his Title IX claim by alleging repeated harassment resulting in a hostile environment that forced him to leave school. He also claimed administrators knew of the harassment but were deliberately indifferent to it. Despite the student's strong showing on his Title IX claim, he was not entitled to a preliminary order preventing his suspension. *Doe v. Perry Community School Dist.*, 316 F.Supp.2d 809 (S.D. Iowa 2004).

◆   A group of California students who were or were perceived by peers to be gay, lesbian or bisexual claimed harassment by classmates over a seven-year period. The students stated school officials took little or no action to protect them and sued the school district, its board and several school administrators in a federal district court. The court held the administrators were not entitled to qualified immunity for the claims. The officials appealed to the Ninth Circuit, which ordered the district court to reconsider the case. On remand, the district court held the students presented evidence of official failure to remedy peer harassment and that this failure was based on sexual orientation. As the students' right to be free from sexual orientation discrimination was clearly established, the officials were not entitled to immunity.

The officials appealed again to the Ninth Circuit, which stated the general rule that officials enjoy qualified immunity in a Section 1983 action if their conduct does not violate clearly established statutory or constitutional rights of which a reasonable person would know. To establish an equal protection violation, the students had to show intentional discrimination. The students were members of an "identifiable class" under the Equal Protection Clause because they asserted unequal treatment on the basis of sexual orientation. The court found evidence of years of harassment during which school administrators failed to enforce policies to protect the students. **There was evidence administrators were motivated by intentional discrimination or acted with deliberate indifference despite many complaints.** The court explained "deliberate indifference" is found if school administrators are clearly unreasonable in response to harassment complaints. The students presented sufficient evidence of deliberate indifference to avoid summary judgment. This included failure to respond or inadequate response to at least two assault incidents, as well as repeated verbal harassment and pornography given to the students or placed in lockers. The district court had properly denied immunity to the administrators. *Flores v. Morgan Hill Unified School Dist.*, 324 F.3d 1130 (9th Cir. 2003).

◆ A lesbian student was allowed to proceed with discrimination claims against California school administrators who barred her from taking a physical education class based on her sexual orientation. The student told a friend she was lesbian after their physical education class. The next day, she was barred from attending the class and sent to the school principal's office. No school official met with the student or her mother to discuss the situation, and she continued to sit in the principal's office during school hours for the next week and a half, apparently as "discipline." The student sued the school district and officials in a federal district court for violations of the Equal Protection Clause through 42 U.S.C. § 1983, also asserting state law claims.

The court denied the school officials' motion for summary judgment based on Eleventh Amendment immunity. The student was not barred from seeking damages against them in their individual and personal capacities, including punitive damages. The court stated **the U.S. Supreme Court held in *Romer v. Evans*, 517 U.S. 620 (1996) that arbitrary sexual orientation discrimination violates the Establishment Clause**. The court explained that several cases have held sexual orientation discrimination gives rise to an equal protection claim. The student made out an adequate showing of a constitutional rights deprivation. The officials could not immunize themselves from liability simply because there was no other Ninth Circuit case with nearly identical facts. The court also denied their claim to state tort law immunity, as immunity applied only to "basic policy decisions." *Massey v. Banning Unified School Dist.*, 256 F.Supp.2d 1090 (C.D. Cal. 2003).

CHAPTER FIVE

Student Discipline

Page

I. EXPULSIONS AND SUSPENSIONS 187
  A. Due Process 187
    1. Notice and Procedural Protections 188
    2. Alternative Placements 193
    3. Zero-Tolerance Policies...197
  B. Misconduct 200
    1. Sexual Harassment..200
    2. Drugs, Alcohol and Weapons Possession 202
    3. Extracurricular and Co-Curricular Events.................207
    4. Fighting and Violence 209
    5. Cell Phones and Electronic Devices.........................212
  C. Academic Expulsions or Suspensions 213

II. STUDENT SEARCH AND SEIZURE 215
  A. Fourth Amendment "Reasonable Suspicion" 215
    1. Searches Based on Individualized Suspicion...........215
    2. Off-Campus Searches 220
    3. Locker Searches 222
    4. Strip Searches 222
  B. Random Testing Policies...225
  C. Police Involvement 228
    1. *Miranda* Warnings..229
    2. Police-Assisted Searches 232
    3. Drug-Sniffing Dogs 234
    4. Liability Issues 235

I. EXPULSIONS AND SUSPENSIONS

A. Due Process

The Due Process Clause of the Fourteenth Amendment prohibits the states from depriving any person of life, liberty or property without due process of law. "Due process" requires school districts to provide students all the notices and procedural protections to which they are entitled under state law or school policies when they are faced with school discipline.

The U.S. Supreme Court did not recognize due process rights in a student disciplinary case until 1975, when it decided Goss v. Lopez. *Students facing short-term suspensions and other minor school discipline have minimal due process rights. An informal discussion between the student and administrator typically satisfies due process for suspensions of up to 10 days. The student must be advised of the charges supporting the suspension and receive an opportunity to tell his or her side of the story. When a suspension is for a longer term, greater procedural protections apply, such as a formal hearing.*

◆   In *Goss v. Lopez*, the U.S. Supreme Court recognized a due process right to receive notice and a hearing in student disciplinary actions. In *Goss*, Ohio students had been suspended from school for up to 10 days for participating in demonstrations and other school disturbances. Their suspensions were handed down without a hearing either before or after the school board's ruling. The Supreme Court held that students facing temporary suspensions from a public school have property and liberty interests in their education that are protected by the Due Process Clause of the Fourteenth Amendment. **Students faced with suspension or expulsion must be given oral or written notice of the charges against them along with some opportunity to present their version of what happened.** Recognizing that situations often do not allow time to follow adequate procedures prior to the suspensions, such as in cases where there is a danger to students or property, the Court stated that, at the very least, **proper notice and a hearing should be given as soon after the suspension as is practicable.** The Court also stated that if a student is threatened with a suspension longer than 10 days, more elaborate procedural safeguards may be necessary. *Goss v. Lopez*, 419 U.S. 565, 95 S.Ct. 729, 42 L.Ed.2d 725 (1975).

1.   Notice and Procedural Protections

◆   According to witness statements, a female Connecticut student pushed a male student, then "rushed" him and put him in a headlock. He did not retaliate against her and was taken to the school nurse for a small cut. A police officer interviewed school security guards, determined the female student was the sole aggressor, and arrested her for breach of the peace and assault. The school suspended her for 10 days pending an expulsion hearing. Her parents were notified of the suspension and of the date, time and place of the expulsion hearing. They appeared at the hearing with their daughter and an attorney, who cross-examined a witness for the board. The hearing officer then expelled the student for 180 days. Her parents sued the board in a federal district court for due process and equal protection violations. The board argued the student received all the process she was due, and that she had not been treated differently than other students who were disciplined for similar misconduct.

The court held the student had a property interest in her education that was protected by the Fourteenth Amendment. However, **she received notice of the charges against her and a hearing, where she had an opportunity to cross examine the board's witness. This was sufficient process to meet the demands of the Constitution.** The parents argued the hearing was invalid because no students were at the hearing to testify. The court found no authority for the parents' position and noted their attorney got to question the board's witness. The parents claimed the district violated the Equal Protection Clause because the male student was not expelled. The court found all the evidence indicated he was injured, while the female student was not. Thus, there was no equal protection violation. The court granted pretrial judgment to the school board. *Bogle-Assegai v. Bloomfield Board of Educ.*, 467 F.Supp.2d 236 (D. Conn. 2006).

◆ **A Mississippi school board did not deprive a student of due process by failing to provide him with a list of witnesses in advance of his expulsion hearing for selling drugs at school.** The state court of appeals rejected his claim that he was not informed of the charges against him because a key witness had changed his story. The witness had only changed the date of one alleged drug purchase. As the charges were based on continuous incidents, this change was insignificant. *T.B. v. Board of Trustees of Vicksburg Warren School Dist.*, 931 So.2d 634 (Miss. Ct. App. 2006).

◆ **The Louisiana Supreme Court held the state court of appeal should not have considered new evidence in an appeal from an expulsion order.** A school board expelled a student for 12 months during her eighth-grade year. Near the end of the school year, her parents petitioned a trial court for an order requiring the board to evaluate her for placement in ninth grade. The court denied the request, as the 12-month expulsion period was not yet complete. The court of appeal directed the board to answer seven questions, then granted the family's request. The supreme court vacated the court of appeal's decision. It held **appellate courts are prohibited from receiving new evidence**. The case was returned to the trial court for an expedited hearing to consider whether the board was obligated to provide the student with any alternative education. *B.W.S. v. Livingston Parish School Board*, 936 So.2d 181 (La. 2006).

◆ The Wyoming Supreme Court held a school board's appeal from a lower court decision reversing a student suspension was moot, as the student had already graduated. The board had expelled the student for violating a state law prohibiting the possession, use, transfer, carrying or selling of a deadly weapon on school property or grounds. The expulsion was modified to a 10-day in-school suspension and the student was required to abide by a behavior contract.

The student appealed to a state district court, which held the board violated the notice and hearing requirements of Wyoming Statutes Section 16-3-107. The court also found insufficient evidence to support the discipline. The appeal to the supreme court was moot, as the student had already served his suspension and graduated. The case did not present any constitutional issues, and the court affirmed the judgment. *Board of Trustees of Fremont County School Dist. #25 v. BM*, 129 P.3d 317 (Wyo. 2006).

◆ A Minnesota student fought with another student in their junior high school cafeteria. Although school employees repeatedly directed them to stop fighting they did not. One employee intervened, and the student hit him and pulled out some of his hair. The district suspended the student for five days, then notified her parents of a second five-day suspension pending expulsion. A school attorney contacted the parents to make a settlement offer. The student's mother said she would accept the agreement, but two weeks later, her attorney served a restraining order on the district and rejected the agreement. The district scheduled a hearing 29 days after the initial suspension. This exceeded the 15-day time frame specified by Minnesota law. The hearing went forward, and the school board adopted the hearing officer's recommendation to expel the student.

The case reached the Court of Appeals of Minnesota, which noted the state Pupil Fair Dismissal Act limited suspensions to a 15-day period pending an expulsion proceeding. The 17-day delay between the second suspension and the initiation of expulsion proceedings was due to the mother's reconsideration of the settlement offer. **There was no fault in district procedures. The reason for delay was to honor the request for time to consult with an attorney.** Had the district initiated expulsion proceedings immediately, it would have risked interfering with the student's ability to obtain counsel and the possibility of a settlement. **The court held the delay did not violate the student's due process rights, and noted decisions from courts in Colorado, Wisconsin and Mississippi approving similar delays.** It rejected the student's challenge to the sufficiency of the evidence, as she willfully violated reasonable school rules, endangered others and caused significant disruption. The court rejected the claim that her conduct could not be "willful" because she acted in self-defense. **A self-defense claim would undercut school authority to discipline students. The school's student handbook put her on notice that assault could lead to expulsion.** The court affirmed the expulsion decision. *In re Expulsion of I.A.L.*, 674 N.W.2d 741 (Minn. Ct. App. 2004).

◆   **The Supreme Court of Colorado affirmed a state appellate decision vacating a student expulsion order, because the student's school board refused to allow her to call witnesses to provide evidence of her good character at her expulsion hearing.** The district expelled the student for fighting, but it denied her request to present positive statements from her teachers at her expulsion hearing. A state trial court held the district violated her due process rights and made it "as difficult as possible" to present evidence in her favor. The court of appeals agreed that the student did not receive a fair hearing, and the supreme court affirmed its decision in a brief memorandum. *Nichols v. DeStefano*, 84 P.3d 496 (Colo. 2004).

◆   A Minnesota student was suspended for five days for "verbally assaulting" a teacher. Two months later, he pushed his teacher, threatened and swore at her, and called her names. The principal indefinitely suspended the student and notified him of an expulsion hearing. The district did not provide him a tutor for over a month. The student requested the class roster to prepare for a hearing. The district instead gave him a list of all seventh- and eighth-graders, and notice of the witnesses it intended to call at the hearing. The hearing was held within 15 days of the notice of expulsion. The teacher did not appear at the hearing, but the hearing officer accepted her notarized statement as evidence and recommended expulsion. The state education commissioner held the admission of a notarized statement into evidence did not violate due process.

The state court of appeals held the **absence of the teacher from the expulsion hearing did not violate the student's due process rights because the principal was available for cross-examination, and the student had the opportunity to present his own evidence.** The Minnesota Pupil Fair Dismissal

Act (PFDA) did not guarantee students facing expulsion the right to obtain class rosters. The student cross-examined the school's witnesses and did not show what additional evidence was available from a class roster. The court found no violation of PFDA limitations on "indefinite" suspensions. **The district substantially complied with PFDA alternative education requirements. While the student did not have a tutor for one month, he did not show this caused any harm.** The district conduct code defined "verbal assault" as words that "arouse alarm in others through the use of language that is discriminatory, abusive, threatening, or obscene." The student used this kind of language during the second incident. As substantial evidence supported the expulsion and there was no due process violation, the court affirmed the school's decision. *In re Expulsion of B.M. from Independent School Dist. No. 2142*, No. A04-421, 2004 WL 1834270 (Minn. Ct. App. 2004).

◆ **The Commonwealth Court of Pennsylvania held a school district could not prevent a student from enrolling in its schools based on his conduct at a parochial school.** The student sold prescription medication to another student at a parochial school. School officials searched his book bag and found a pocketknife, which violated diocese and school policy. The principal advised the student's parents that this conduct required expulsion without a hearing. The parents withdrew the student from the parochial school in lieu of a permanent expulsion, and attempted to enroll him in a public high school. District officials informed the family of a district policy denying admission to students seeking to transfer into district schools when they were subject to an incomplete suspension or expulsion imposed by another school entity. The policy also required students who withdrew from schools other than its own to attend an "expulsion hearing" to determine whether an expulsion should be implemented. The student refused to participate in a district hearing and was denied admission. He sued the district in a state court for a declaration that the policy was unlawful and an order admitting him to regular classes in district schools. The court declared the policy unlawful and awarded judgment to the student.

The district appealed to the commonwealth court, which considered the assertion that the student should have participated in district hearing procedures before going to court. **The court rejected the district's claim to inherent powers to implement the policy in the name of school safety. School authority was limited to statutory powers. The policy granting "full faith and credit" to the disciplinary actions of other school entities was neither expressly nor impliedly permitted under the state school code.** The code allowed districts to discipline only those students who were enrolled in the district at the time of an incident. A school's power to discipline its own students did not support the imposition of expulsion proceedings for students expelled from other schools. **State law permitted districts receiving transfer students from another school during a period of expulsion to assign them to an alternative placement during that period.** As there was no authority for the district's argument that it could discipline a student who was not enrolled in its schools at the time of an incident, the court affirmed the judgment. *Hoke v. Elizabethtown Area School Dist.*, 833 A.2d 304 (Pa. Commw. Ct. 2003).

◆   The Court of Appeals of North Carolina held **a school district denied a student due process by refusing to allow him to be represented by an attorney at a disciplinary hearing**. The district imposed discipline on the student for violation of its sexual harassment policy. Its policy specifically forbade attorneys from appearing at hearings on behalf of students. The court of appeals affirmed a trial court judgment for the student, ruling the district denied him due process. The facts were in dispute and **the student was entitled to full hearing rights for a long-term suspension, including the right to be represented by counsel**. *In re Roberts*, 563 S.E.2d 37 (N.C. Ct. App. 2002). The state supreme court dismissed the board's appeal, as did the U.S. Supreme Court. *Buncombe County, North Carolina, Board of Educ. v. Roberts*, 540 U.S. 820, 124 S.Ct. 103, 157 L.Ed.2d 38 (2003).

◆   **The South Carolina Supreme Court reversed a state appellate decision denying any judicial review to several students who were suspended for three days. While it was improper to disallow any review of short-term suspensions, judicial review was limited** to consideration of due process violations. The suspended students were high school seniors who vandalized a high school they did not attend. A state trial court granted their request for a temporary injunction, but the South Carolina Court of Appeals held the trial court had no jurisdiction to hear any case involving a short-term student suspension under *Byrd v. Irmo High School*, 321 S.C. 426, 468 S.E.2d 861 (1996). The students appealed to the state supreme court, which noted it had explained in *Byrd* that **state law did not permit judicial review of student suspensions of 10 days or less**. Otherwise, students and parents might burden the court system and strain school resources with a flood of appeals from short-term suspensions. While public policy weighed against judicial review, the court said limited review was necessary to meet the due process rights of students recognized in *Goss v. Lopez* (this chapter). **The students received notice, an explanation and an opportunity to respond, which was all the process they were due under *Goss*.** The court affirmed the appeals court's decision. *Floyd v. Horry County School Dist.*, 569 S.E.2d 343 (S.C. 2002).

◆   A California student was suspended by his school principal for possession of a pipe bomb. The school board granted his parents' request to postpone an expulsion hearing for 15 days. An administrative panel met and recommended expulsion, but the board adjourned for the summer before acting on the recommendation. Upon its return, the board voted to expel the student, 51 days after it received the recommendation. The student appealed to the county board of education, which held the summer recess did not extend the 40-day period for such decisions. The school board appealed to a California trial court, which affirmed the county board's decision for the student.

    The state court of appeal observed that **while the California Education Code required school boards to decide whether to expel a pupil within 40 school days after removal from school, it contained no penalty for failing to meet this deadline**. The absence of a statutory penalty for failing to comply with the deadline indicated only that the remedy against a noncomplying school board was a court order requiring it to make a decision. The overall purpose of the Education Code indicated the time limit did not impose an absolute jurisdictional deadline. Otherwise, proceedings that had already occurred would be nullified and a student who had made serious rules violations would be reinstated. **As it was unlikely the legislature intended to allow a dangerous student back into school due to a technicality, the judgment was reversed.** *Board of Educ. of Sacramento City Unified School Dist. v. Sacramento County Board of Educ.*, 85 Cal.App.4th 1321, 102 Cal.Rptr.2d 872 (Cal. Ct. App. 2001).

◆   **The Idaho Supreme Court rejected a student's argument that he had a right to judicial review of a school board order expelling him.** Idaho law does not specify such review, and the state supreme court refused to create one by implication from other laws. The student allegedly brought a gun with him to a school choir concert on the grounds of a district junior high school. The school board expelled him from school for at least one year for carrying a weapon to school and threatening another student with it. Although the board later allowed the student to enroll in another district school, he sued the board in a state trial court. The court granted the board's dismissal motion. The student appealed to the state supreme court, which held **no Idaho statute provided for appellate review of school board decisions**. The court affirmed the judgment and awarded the board its attorneys' fees on appeal. *Daw v. School Dist. 91 Board of Trustees*, 41 P.3d 234 (Idaho 2001).

2. Alternative Placements

◆   A Texas school security officer opened a purse found on school property to help determine who owned it. A cheerleader's school athletic pass and what was later identified as a hydrocodone pill were found inside the purse. The school district held a hearing to consider expelling the cheerleader for violating its zero tolerance anti-drug policy. After a hearing, a school hearing officer determined the pill most likely belonged to the parent of another student and not the cheerleader. The district placed the cheerleader in an alternative education program for 36 days and excluded her from the cheerleading squad for the 2005-06 school year, as specified by the school's "cheerleader constitution."

The school board upheld the decision, and the cheerleader completed the alternative assignment. She obtained a Texas trial court order reinstating her to the cheerleading squad, and the school district appealed. The Court of Appeals of Texas held **Texas Education Code Section 37.009(b) expressly stated a board's decision regarding an alternative education program was final and unappealable. As the trial court had no power to review the assignment of a student to an alternative program, the court upheld the placement and the district's decision to keep incident records.** The court could address the cheerleader's constitutional claims, including one for unlawful search and seizure, but the 2005-06 cheerleading season was over. While the cheerleader had not yet graduated, the incident would not affect her eligibility for the 2006-07 season or any other extracurricular activity. The court dismissed the district's appeal relating to the temporary injunction as moot. *Flour Bluff Independent School Dist. v. R.S.*, No. 13-05-623-CV, 2006 WL 949968 (Tex. Ct. App. 2006).

◆   Section 2134 of the Pennsylvania Public School Code required the School District of Philadelphia to make a transitional placement for up to four weeks for each student who was returning from juvenile placement, probation, or conviction in an adult proceeding. The law was amended to allow students to directly return to regular classes under a transition plan, except where the juvenile or criminal offense involved a weapon, controlled substance, use or sale of alcohol or tobacco on school property, or violence. Three students who were assigned to alternative placements after their delinquency adjudications sued the school district in a state court for constitutional rights violations. They claimed Section 2134 was local or special legislation in violation of Article III, Section 32 of the Pennsylvania Constitution, and violated their equal protection and due process rights. The court held for the district, and the students appealed.

The Commonwealth Court of Pennsylvania held Philadelphia was reasonably classified as the only "first class" school district in the state. Even though two other districts had higher delinquency rates than Philadelphia's, the court held the legislature did not violate Article III, Section 32. The district received from 1,200 to 1,500 students from juvenile placements each year. The high number of returning students made a formal transition program to assess their status reasonable. However, the court rejected the district's assertion that Section 2134 was not disciplinary in nature and did not involve a protected due process right. The placement of students returning from juvenile or criminal proceedings was based on a determination that they were not currently fit for regular classrooms. This automatic exclusion of students from regular classes resulted from an "irrebuttable presumption that they are not fit to return." The students were entitled to minimal notice and some type of informal hearing as described by the Supreme Court in *Goss v. Lopez*, 419 U.S. 565 (1975). **The absence of some opportunity for returning students to challenge transfers to alternative education settings violated their due process rights.** *D.C. v. School Dist. of Philadelphia*, 879 A.2d 408 (Pa. Commw. Ct. 2005).

◆   A Michigan student dropped out of high school but was admitted to an alternative education program called "Skills Quest." Enrollment in the program was discretionary with the district superintendent and required students to comply with its attendance policy and the district's student code of conduct. The student was charged with murder and jailed in an adult correctional facility. A state court ordered the county sheriff to segregate him from adult prisoners as required by state law. The student expressed suicidal thoughts and was placed on "suicide watch." The student was later released from jail after a preliminary hearing, based on lack of admissible evidence. The superintendent rejected his request to reenter Skills Quest, but reversed himself after another individual confessed to the murder. The student reenrolled in Skills Quest but dropped out after only a month. He then sued state, county and school officials in a federal district court for civil rights violations. The court granted summary judgment to the sheriff and district but denied it to the superintendent. The parties appealed.

The U.S. Court of Appeals, Sixth Circuit, noted Michigan law permits detention of juveniles in a jail, if the juvenile is "a menace to other children," or "may not otherwise be safely detained." As the jail staff had a legitimate, non-punitive purpose of preventing his suicide or injury, the court affirmed the judgment for the sheriff. **The student chose to forgo his right to a free public education when he dropped out of high school. Neither the Michigan Constitution nor state law mandated alternative education programs.** The student could not show a legitimate claim of entitlement to participate in Skills Quest, since participation was "entirely at the discretion of the superintendent and continues only so long as the participant abides by the program's rules and policies." **As the student had no property right to an alternative education, he could not show a due process violation by the district or superintendent.** The court affirmed the judgment for the sheriff and school district, and reversed it for the superintendent. *Daniels v. Woodside*, 396 F.3d 730 (6th Cir. 2005).

◆   A Wyoming school district expelled three students for marijuana violations. One was enrolled in special education programs and continued receiving the educational services described in his individualized education program. The others were adjudicated delinquent in juvenile court proceedings. The court held the Wyoming Constitution imposed a duty on the school district to provide the students a free appropriate education during their expulsion periods. The school district and the Wyoming School Boards Association intervened in the case and asked the Supreme Court of Wyoming to rule on the constitutional question. **The court held that while education is a fundamental right under the Wyoming Constitution, the state interest in student safety and welfare was compelling enough to temporarily interfere with this right.**

The court noted with approval *Fowler v. Williamson*, 39 N.C. App. 715, 251 S.E.2d 889 (N.C. Ct. App. 1979), a North Carolina case recognizing that educational services are contingent upon appropriate conduct. The school district in this case had offered students an education system that conformed to its constitutional obligation to provide an equal opportunity for a quality education. **Reasonable suspension rules did not deny the right to an education; they only denied students an opportunity to misbehave.** The court held the students could be temporarily denied educational services if their conduct threatened the safety and welfare of others and interfered with the district's obligation to provide equal opportunities to all its students. State law limited expulsions to one year. After this term expired, students could return to school and receive educational services until the age of 21. School districts were in the best position to judge student actions in view of the circumstances and to issue appropriate punishment. **The school district was not required to provide lawfully expelled students with an alternate education under the circumstances of this case. The court rejected the claim that the expulsions violated the non-disabled students' equal protection rights. Special education students must receive services under the Individuals with Disabilities Education Act (IDEA), even after discipline is imposed.** The IDEA's history demonstrated a compelling interest in treating disabled students differently than non-disabled students. *In re R.M.*, 102 P.3d 868 (Wyo. 2004).

◆   A federal district court held a New York student had no viable federal constitutional claims arising from her assignment to an alternative school. The student had substantial academic and behavioral problems. During her freshman year of high school, the student and her mother agreed to placement in an alternative school for students with similar problems. During the student's sophomore year at the alternative school, she was involved in an incident in which she chased a male student into a room. He broke window glass out of the door to escape, causing serious and permanent injuries to the student. She sued the school district and agency that operated the alternative school, asserting personal injury and constitutional claims.

The court noted the **only basis for a constitutional claim arising from an alternative school placement was that the decision to segregate certain students from their peers was not rationally related to a legitimate state objective**. The student could not make this showing. **It was clearly rational to take some action for students with behavioral and academic problems who were in danger of failing to graduate from a traditional school.** The student had graduated on time and though she was entitled to an education, this did not mean the best education possible. The student's claim did not involve any basic federal constitutional right such as freedom from discrimination. **Her transfer to the alternative school did not violate any constitutional right.** A state court was the more appropriate forum for her personal injury claims, and the court declined to take jurisdiction over them. *Turley v. Sauquoit Valley School Dist.*, 307 F.Supp.2d 403 (N.D.N.Y. 2003).

◆   An Alabama school policy made possession of a weapon a major offense, and it defined knives, razors and fingernail files as "weapons" regardless of blade length. Sanctions for major offenses included suspension, referral to law enforcement, expulsion, and alternative school placement. The school allowed law officers to conduct drug searches in a school parking lot with dogs. A dog alerted on an honor student's car. Officials called him to unlock it, then found a pocketknife and utility knife. The school principal suspended the student for three days and placed him in an alternative school for 45 days at the beginning of the next school year. He did not recommend expelling the student, as there was no evidence he intended to harm anyone. The student sued the school board, principal and others in a federal district court, alleging deprivation of his rights to due process and freedom from unreasonable searches and seizures.

The court held **assignment to the alternative school was an "executive act" that did not implicate any fundamental student rights**. A suspension of less than 10 days requires only oral or written notice of the charges, an explanation of the evidence, and an opportunity for the student to explain his or her side of the story. The court rejected the student's assertion that 45 days spent in the alternative school should be combined with his three days of suspension for a total disciplinary time of 48 days. He failed to show the alternative school was so inferior that it amounted to expulsion. The student did not show any educational detriment, and the court dismissed his due process claims. School officials do not need search warrants or probable cause to search students. **The Eleventh Circuit has held the alerting of a drug-sniffing dog to personal property supplies both reasonable suspicion and probable cause to search the property.** An immediate search may then be performed without a warrant. The court held for the school officials on the Fourth Amendment claim. *Marner v. Eufala City School Board,* 204 F.Supp.2d 1318 (M.D. Ala. 2002).

3. Zero-Tolerance Policies

◆   A drug dog alerted on a student's truck during a routine check of a Texas school parking lot. The student consented to a search by the police, who found brass knuckles in the glove box of the truck. The school board held a hearing. The principal testified that under the board's policy, students were responsible for the contents of their vehicles, whether or not they knew a weapon might be present. The student testified that the brass knuckles belonged to a friend. He claimed he did not know they were still there when he drove the truck to school. The student also submitted a statement from the friend, polygraph test results indicating he did not know the knuckles were in the truck, and evidence that he was an honor student with an A average. Board policy tracked Texas Education Code language stating that students would be expelled for using, exhibiting or possessing prohibited weapons. A hearing officer found the student was "in possession of an illegal weapon" on campus. The board voted to expel the student for one day and to assign him to an alternative school for the rest of the school year. After a state trial court granted the student's request for a preliminary order halting the expulsion, the school board appealed.

The Court of Appeals of Texas **found a 2005 Texas Education Code amendment required school districts to specify whether they considered intent or lack of intent as a factor in student expulsions**. The legislative history of the 2005 amendment indicated "the intent of the amendment is to give discretion to principals to allow them not to expel students when expulsion was not warranted, such as cases where the student accidentally possesses a prohibited weapon." **The amendment indicated the legislature intended to allow school districts to choose between adopting zero-tolerance policies, or allowing alternatives for involuntary possession of prohibited weapons.** The court held state law permitted school districts to decline expelling students for unknowing possession of weapons, if they have adopted intent as a factor in expulsion decisions. In this case, the district policy allowed it to consider intent, and it could decline to expel the student if possession of a weapon was involuntary. The trial court found the hearing officer incorrectly interpreted the Education Code as requiring expulsion, even if possession of a prohibited weapon was unknowing. The appeals court held the trial court did not abuse its discretion in granting the student a temporary injunction to halt his expulsion. *Tarkington Independent School Dist. v. Ellis*, 200 S.W.3d 794 (Tex. Ct. App. 2006).

◆   A California school district regulation required an immediate suspension with a recommended expulsion for three or more fighting incidents in a year. A 12-year-old student was involved in three fights in one school year. A hearing panel upheld the principal's recommendation for expulsion, and the student was placed in an alternative program. The student was suspended there for physically confronting a staff member. The district placed her in a community school, where she claimed older male students sexually harassed and physically assaulted her. The student sued the district in a state court for personal injury and violation of her statutory and due process rights. The court dismissed her personal injury claim, but it held the district's policy requiring the principal to recommend expulsion violated state law and the Due Process Clause.

The district appealed to the Court of Appeal of California, which noted the state Education Code permitted suspension or expulsion of a student for committing one of 18 offenses. Section 48918 permitted an impartial hearing panel to conduct expulsion hearings. **Expulsion was permitted for serious physical injury or possession of a dangerous object or controlled substance, if a school board found other means were not feasible or repeatedly failed to bring about proper conduct, or the student was a continuing danger.** District regulations had a zero-tolerance provision requiring the principal to immediately suspend and recommend the expulsion of a student for serious offenses, including three or more fighting incidents within one year. **The court found the district's zero-tolerance provision consistent with the education code. The policy did not require expulsion for specified offenses. It only put these cases before an impartial hearing panel. The elimination of a principal's discretion to refrain from referring a case to an expulsion hearing did not deprive students of due process rights. Students who committed a zero-tolerance expulsion offense remained entitled to the expansive protections of Education Code Section 48915.** The hearing panel retained discretion to order an expulsion or other suitable discipline. District procedures required principals to consult with legal specialists and attempt to handle discipline at the school level. The court reversed the judgment, as the trial court incorrectly held the district had unlawfully diminished the principal's role in evaluating these situations. *T.H. v. San Diego Unified School Dist.*, 122 Cal.App.4th 1267, 19 Cal.Rptr.3d 532 (Cal. Ct. App. 2004).

◆   Nine Florida high school students distributed an anonymous pamphlet on school grounds that depicted the school's African-American principal with a dart through his head. The pamphlet contained vulgar and offensive language as well as cartoons depicting violence and sexual activity. The principal learned who distributed the pamphlet and summoned the police. Each of the students admitted being involved, and the police determined they had violated a state misdemeanor law criminalizing anonymous distribution of a publication exposing any individual or religious group to "hatred, contempt, ridicule or obloquy." Police also found the racially motivated content could enhance the crime to a felony. Because one student was 18, she was taken to an adult correctional facility, where she was criminally charged and subjected to a strip search. However, she was not prosecuted. The student sued the school board and county law enforcement officials in a federal district court for constitutional rights violations. The court held the police officer was entitled to qualified immunity and awarded summary judgment to the county and school board.

The student appealed to the Eleventh Circuit, asserting the county's express policy and custom deprived her of her constitutional rights. She asserted that the board's zero-tolerance policy was the "moving force" behind her arrest. The court found that the policy consisted of three provisions in the board's rules and student code of conduct. The rules required school police to act to prevent and detect crime on school grounds. The board endorsed a zero-tolerance policy against school-related violent crime. The code of conduct required the district to invoke serious consequences when dealing with students who engaged in violent crime, including contacting the police. **The court held the board's zero-tolerance rules and code were not the "moving force" behind the**

arrest. They only required that school officials report criminal behavior, which the principal had done. The principal had no final policy-making authority to make an arrest. For this reason, the board could not be held liable for any constitutional rights violation. The county officers had reasonable suspicion to search the student based on the violent and threatening language and imagery of the pamphlet. The court affirmed the judgment. *Cuesta v. School Board of Miami-Dade County, Florida*, 285 F.3d 962 (11th Cir. 2002).

◆ All students who attended an Indiana school received notice of the school's zero-tolerance drug possession policy and were informed that any student in possession of marijuana would be expelled. With three days left in a fall semester, **a drug-sniffing dog located marijuana in a student's truck.** The school principal suspended the student pending an expulsion hearing. A hearing examiner held the student should be expelled for the rest of the school year, plus summer school and fall semester of the next year. The student appealed to the school board, which upheld the discipline. **The school denied him all credit for the semester during which he was expelled.** The student and his parents appealed to an Indiana trial court, which held the board's action was arbitrary and capricious. It ordered the board to assign the student zeros for course work he missed as the result of the expulsion, but to award him credit for courses in which he earned passing grades after taking the zeros into account. The board appealed to the Indiana Court of Appeals, which affirmed the decision.

The state supreme court granted the board's petition for review. It explained the Indiana code limits expulsions for misconduct occurring in a fall semester to the rest of the school year. The lower courts had properly reversed the board's decision expelling the student through the following school year. **The court held a school board decision should be upheld unless it is arbitrary and capricious.** While the trial court expressed concern about the harshness of the zero-tolerance policy, **it was not the role of the courts to set aside the decisions of school administrators. A consistently applied policy weighed against a finding of arbitrariness.** State law authorized school staff "to take any disciplinary action necessary to promote student conduct that conforms with an orderly and effective educational system." The board expelled the student in conformity with the law and had discretion to impose the additional sanction of loss of credit. It was reasonable for the board to conclude that expulsion without the loss of credit was an insufficient deterrent. The court reversed the order requiring the board to award the student credit for his fall classes. *South Gibson School Board v. Sollman*, 768 N.E.2d 437 (Ind. 2002).

◆ A Virginia student took a knife from a classmate for her safety after she told him she had been suicidal the previous evening and had inadvertently brought the knife to school. The student put the knife in his locker, but he did not tell school authorities about it. He then admitted possession of the knife to a school administrator, but he explained he was acting in the classmate's best interest. An assistant principal suspended the student for 10 days under the school board's zero-tolerance weapons possession policy. The district superintendent extended the suspension indefinitely pending board action and recommended that the board suspend the student for the rest of the semester. After a hearing, the board affirmed the suspension and excluded him from school for four months.

The student sued the school district and four employees in a federal district court. The court dismissed the case, and the student appealed to the Fourth Circuit. **The court expressed concern over the harsh result of enforcing the board's zero-tolerance of weapons policy, but it found no constitutional violation. It stated that federal courts are not properly called on to judge the wisdom of zero-tolerance policies or their application.** The student's claim was essentially one for due process violations, but the district had complied with all required notices and provided a hearing, in satisfaction of its due process obligations. The court affirmed the judgment. *Ratner v. Loudon County Public Schools*, 16 Fed.Appx. 140 (4th Cir. 2001).

B. Misconduct

1. Sexual Harassment

◆   A Michigan school counselor made a presentation to a language arts class. She saw a student place his fingers in his mouth and believed he was making a sexual gesture about her. The school suspended the student and he appealed to the district superintendent, who interviewed the counselor, student and a classmate who saw the gesture. The students asserted the gesture simply indicated boredom. The superintendent found the counselor more reliable and upheld the suspension for "indecency," as defined in the high school's student handbook. A state trial court affirmed the discipline, and the student appealed.

The Court of Appeals of Michigan found the superintendent's findings were supported by material and substantial evidence. **Courts are bound by school administrators' findings when there is any evidence in the record to support them.** The court rejected the student's claim that his behavior was not a "gross misdemeanor" as defined by MCL § 380.1311(1). **A student must be guilty of some willful or malicious act of detriment to a school before being suspended or expelled. This is "something more than a petty or trivial offense" against school rules. The court found the student's gesture qualified as "gross misbehavior and misconduct," as it was both willful and malicious.** He had an opportunity to deny his misconduct and was not entitled to trial-type procedures. The school complied with due process requirements for a short-term suspension by giving the student oral notice of the general nature of the charges and a chance to be heard. Allowing him to go unpunished for embarrassing a school employee would welcome more disrespect. As schools have a clear right and duty to protect their basic educational mission and promote mature conduct, the court affirmed the discipline. *Kloberdanz v. Swan Valley School Dist.*, No. 256208, 2006 WL 234880 (Mich. Ct. App. 2006). The state supreme court refused to review the decision. *Kloberdanz v. Swan Valley School Dist.*, 476 Mich. 863, 720 N.W.2d 306 (Mich. 2006).

◆   A California student was accused of sexually related misconduct, including grabbing a girl by the buttocks, groping other boys, making inappropriate comments or gestures, and simulating masturbation or sex. He denied most of the allegations, explaining he had accidentally touched the girl. The student's father, an attorney, attended a meeting to consider discipline. The school principal said he had interviewed several credible witnesses and issued a five-day suspension. The student served his suspension, then graduated. He sued the school district in a state court under 42 U.S.C. § 1983. The court held the district violated his due process rights and awarded him general damages of $45,000, punitive damages of $50,000 and attorneys' fees of $72,268.

The district appealed to the California Court of Appeal, which discussed the U.S. Supreme Court's decision in *Goss v. Lopez* (this chapter), the leading case on student due process rights. Under *Goss*, **students faced with short-term suspensions are entitled to due process in the form of oral or written notice of the charges, and an opportunity to state the student's side of the story. The principal had complied with these "rudimentary precautions" of student due process during the pre-suspension meeting** with the student and his parents. He adequately explained the reasons for the suspension and was not required to give the student any further procedural protections to comply with *Goss*. The student was not entitled to learn the identities of his accusers, and had the principal done so, the district might be exposed to further lawsuits. The different reasons stated for suspension by the principal at the meeting and in his written notice of suspension involved specific statutory language. The use of statutory language in the notice of suspension did not violate the student's due process rights, and there was no substantive due process violation. **The court found the district had issued a proper suspension for the grounds stated in the notice of suspension, and it reversed the judgment.** *Granowitz v. Redlands Unified School Dist.*, 129 Cal.Rptr.2d 410 (Cal. Ct. App. 2003).

◆ A Massachusetts high school student sodomized a six-year-old and was charged with various felonies. His school principal obtained a police report describing the student's description of the incident as "a joke." The principal suspended the student, finding he posed a threat to the safety, security and welfare of students at the high school. School officials notified the student's parents by letter of the disciplinary action, and they appealed to the superintendent of schools. After a hearing, the superintendent upheld the suspension and the parents sought a preliminary order from a state superior court. The court denied the request for preliminary relief but later reversed the suspension, finding the superintendent's action was an abuse of discretion. According to the court, Massachusetts General Laws Chapter 71, § 37H 1/2 requires more than criminal charges alone to justify a student suspension. The Massachusetts Supreme Judicial Court accepted the superintendent's appeal.

The court observed that Section 37H 1/2 authorizes the suspension of students who have been charged with felonies. School principals or headmasters must provide students with written notice and a hearing before any suspension takes effect. As the trial court had found, a felony charge against a student is an insufficient basis for suspension. **There must be a finding that the student's continued presence in school would have a substantial detrimental effect** on the general welfare of the school. A suspension may be overturned only if it is so arbitrary and capricious that it constitutes an abuse of discretion and lacks any rational explanation. **The superintendent's decision was within his discretion because it was fully supported by the evidence.** The principal was permitted to draw inferences from the nature of the crime and the student's lack of remorse. **Given the seriousness of the charges, the principal reasonably concluded there was a danger the student would attempt similar behavior at school. The principal met the procedural requirements of Section 37H 1/2.** As the superintendent acted within his discretion by suspending the student, the court reversed and remanded the case. *Doe v. Superintendent of Schools of Stoughton*, 437 Mass. 1, 767 N.E.2d 1054 (Mass. 2002).

◆   A Minnesota student was suspended pending an expulsion hearing after he was accused of sexually assaulting a female classmate. The student weighed 210 pounds and was active in football, wrestling and track. The classmate was five feet tall, weighed 93 pounds and had a mild form of cerebral palsy. The expulsion hearing was delayed for four months. When a hearing was finally held, the district failed to employ an independent hearing examiner. The school board voted to expel the student for sexual assault, based on evidence that his semen was found at the scene of the incident. The student appealed to the state education commissioner, who affirmed the expulsion decision.

The student appealed to the Minnesota Court of Appeals, which found no error in the findings of the board and commissioner. **The student was twice the size of the classmate and capable of controlling the circumstances. He failed to show he was prejudiced by the delay in his expulsion hearing or by the board's failure to timely disclose certain evidence. The provision of an audio tape and transcript of the hearing afforded him with procedural due process.** The dual roles played by the district's attorney as prosecutor and decision maker did not violate the state Pupil Fair Dismissal Act, which allows school boards to make their own findings in expulsion proceedings. The court affirmed the expulsion decision. *In re Expulsion of G.H.*, No. C1-00-2201, 2001 WL 799972 (Minn. Ct. App. 2001).

2.   Drugs, Alcohol and Weapons Possession

In a case involving off-campus alcohol consumption by an Arkansas student, the U.S. Supreme Court limited the role of federal courts to construe school regulations differently than a school board. The Court held it was not within the purview of federal court judges to substitute their own view of the facts for that of a school board. An Arkansas school board had authority to expel a student for drinking alcohol off campus and returning to school. Board of Educ. v. McCluskey, *458 U.S. 966, 102 S.Ct. 3469, 73 L.Ed.2d 1273 (1982).*

◆   A New York school board suspended a student for possessing a handgun off campus after learning he had talked about the gun while in the school cafeteria. The police decided to lock the school down, and the guns were found off school grounds. The student was suspended for the rest of the school year. The state education commissioner affirmed the suspension, but a New York court held the hearing officer denied the student a fair hearing and vacated the discipline. The student sued the board and hearing officer in a federal district court for civil rights violations. The court dismissed the student's due process claim, since he had already received notice and a hearing to consider his suspension. This was all the process to which he was entitled under state law. The state court had vacated the discipline, curing any procedural defects.

The court held that talking with students about handguns was a material and substantial disruption of the educational process. The suspension did not violate the student's substantive due process rights. **The court agreed with the board that public school students may be disciplined for conduct off school grounds. It was within the board's discretion to punish conduct "outside the school situation, so long as there exists a nexus between the behavior and the school."** Misconduct occurring off campus could adversely affect the educational process or endanger students. However, a lock-down incident, occurring three months after the student's gun possession, was not "definitive proof" that his speech and actions were a "substantial disruption." The court refused to dismiss the student's speech rights claim. He raised a valid equal protection claim by asserting the other students implicated in the conversation were only suspended for three weeks, while he was suspended for the rest of the school year. The court refused to dismiss the equal protection claims against the board and hearing officer, and held they were not entitled to qualified immunity. *Cohn v. New Paltz Cent. School Dist.*, 363 F.Supp.2d 421 (N.D. N.Y. 2005). The Second Circuit affirmed the decision in a brief memorandum. *Cohn v. New Paltz Cent. School Dist.*, 171 Fed.Appx. 877 (2d Cir. 2006).

◆ **A Pennsylvania court held a school district had no power to expel an honor student for using drugs on a school playground after school hours, when no school activity was taking place.** A trial court properly found the student was not under school supervision at the time of the incident and had exceeded its statutory powers by expelling him. The school board had voluntarily reinstated the student to school prior to the trial court decision, and the court's order required it to expunge the expulsion from his record. *D.O.F. v. Lewisburg Area School Dist.*, 868 A.2d 28 (Pa. Commw. Ct. 2004).

◆ A North Carolina school district's conduct code imposed long-term suspensions or expulsions on students for drug offenses. It allowed first-time offenders to avoid long-term suspension if they agreed to enroll in approved drug education programs. The high school handbook permitted the principal to modify disciplinary action, if parents agreed. Teachers discovered two bags of cocaine in a student's possession. An assistant principal suspended him for 10 days and recommended suspending him for the rest of the school year. The student signed an agreement to enroll in an approved drug education program, but the district superintendent recommended suspending him for the rest of the school year. The school board then voted to accept the recommendation. The student and his parents appealed, and a state trial court reversed the decision.

The board appealed to the Court of Appeals of North Carolina. The case did not reach the court until over a year after completion of the school year at issue. The court held the case was now moot and review was inappropriate. **State law allowed suspensions "in excess of 10 school days but not exceeding the time remaining in the school year." Even if the court were to reverse the decision, the board could not "re-suspend" the student.** As the case was moot, the court did not review whether the evidence supported the suspension. *J.S.W. v. Lee County Board of Educ.*, 604 S.E.2d 336 (N.C. Ct. App. 2004).

◆ A Kentucky high school received a bomb threat. The administration contacted a private company under contract with the district to provide canine detection services. The search revealed no explosives, but a dog alerted to a car parked in the school parking lot that was identified as belonging to the student. The principal called the student from his class but did not accompany him to the parking lot, despite a board policy requiring principals or their designees to be present when any student search was conducted. A dog handler said "he could handle the situation," but advised the principal to send somebody to the parking lot as soon as possible. The handler went with the student to the car and found marijuana inside it. A school liaison officer and an assistant principal promptly arrived, and the student was suspended pending an expulsion hearing. The board voted to expel the student, and a state court affirmed the decision.

The student appealed to the Court of Appeals of Kentucky. It held **the board could expel students for bringing drugs to school, but its policy mandated that the school principal or designee be present during any student search. Because the evidence for the expulsion was obtained in violation of the board's own policy, the decision to expel the student was arbitrarily based on incompetent evidence. The board had to comply with its own policy.** The principal knew of the search and declined to accompany the dog handler. The presence of the dog handler did not satisfy the board's requirement, as this would have made the board's express policy superfluous. The court held the evidence used against the student was incompetent and inadmissible. Since it was the only evidence upon which the board had relied, the expulsion decision was clearly erroneous. The court reversed the decision as arbitrary. *M.K.J. v. Bourbon County Board of Educ.*, No.2003-CA-0003520MN, 2004 WL 1948461 (Ky. Ct. App. 2004).

◆ A New Mexico school security guard noticed a car parked in a faculty lot without a required permit. He contacted a law enforcement agency to check its registration and then observed a knife in plain view between the passenger seat and console. The guard called the student who had driven the car from his class and had him open the car. He found a sheathed hunting knife, handgun, ammunition and drug paraphernalia. The student claimed he did not know the items were in the car, which belonged to his brother. He was then suspended pending a hearing. A hearing officer held the student should be suspended for a year. The school board upheld the decision, and the student sued the board in a federal district court for civil rights violations. He added claims against school and law enforcement officers for violating his due process rights. **The court found the board could not suspend a student who unknowingly brought drugs or weapons to school.** It granted the student a preliminary injunction that allowed him to return to school and graduate. The board appealed.

The U.S. Court of Appeals, Tenth Circuit, held the appeal was moot because the student had graduated. The district court then partially dismissed the student's civil rights claims. The board appealed again to the Tenth Circuit, which held **a school suspension decision is to be upheld unless it is arbitrary, lacking a rational basis or shocking to the conscience.** The board did not suspend the student for "unknowingly" bringing a knife to school. Instead, it found he should have known he was in possession of a knife, since it was in plain view to persons standing outside the car. The board also found the student should have known he was responsible for the vehicle and its contents after driving the car to school. The court found the board had a legitimate interest in maintaining a safe school environment. **It was not unreasonable for it to conclude the possession of weapons on school property threatened this interest, and there was a rational basis for the one-year suspension.** The decision was not arbitrary or shocking to the conscience, and there was no substantive due process violation. The court reversed and remanded the district court decision, finding the board was entitled to qualified immunity. *Butler v. Rio Rancho Public Schools Board of Educ.*, 341 F.3d 1197 (10th Cir. 2003).

◆ An Indiana middle school student gave caffeine pills to eight classmates. One classmate was taken to the emergency room for a rapid heartbeat and other symptoms. An assistant principal confiscated the pills from the student's locker. The school suspended the student for five days, pending expulsion for violating the district's behavior code. At the expulsion hearing, the assistant principal summarized a district investigation and read into the record statements by six students who took pills. The hearing officer upheld the expulsion and ordered the student to complete a substance abuse assessment, enroll in counseling and perform 15 hours of community service. The students who accepted pills were barred from extracurricular activities and field trips for the semester. The student sued the district and school officials in a federal district court.

The court found the student had endangered the lives of two classmates and disrupted the educational environment. The district did not arbitrarily interpret its behavior code, and she admitted distributing the pills. **The court held the code was not impermissibly vague. A reasonably intelligent 13-year-old would understand the distribution of caffeine pills at school was improper.** The presentation of student testimony through the assistant principal did not violate the student's due process rights. She had no constitutional right to cross-examine these students. School administrators had reason to trust the other students and could rely on their "hearsay" evidence. **The district was relieved of more formal procedures because the need to protect student witnesses greatly outweighed the slight value of providing the student their names.** The student's equal protection claims failed, despite her claim the expulsion was "grossly unfair" in comparison with the discipline imposed on other students. As there was a rational basis for distinguishing her conduct from the others, the court awarded judgment to the district and officials. *Wagner v. Fort Wayne Community Schools*, 255 F.Supp.2d 915 (N.D. Ind. 2003).

◆ An Idaho student left a pellet gun in a car parked on school grounds. Another student took the gun and superficially wounded a third student with it. The first two students admitted possessing the gun, and the principal suspended them. The superintendent and principal met with the students and their parents to discuss the suspensions and inform them of a hearing. Letters from the principal and superintendent confirmed the hearing. The board suspended both students for 13 days after their hearing, then voted to expel them for over three months. The students were notified of their expulsions for violating Idaho law. At a second hearing, the board again voted for expulsion, and they petitioned a state court for review. The court found the board acted arbitrarily and abused its discretion. On appeal, the Idaho Supreme Court stated it became involved in school cases only if they directly implicated basic constitutional values.

While procedural errors during a suspension may justify judicial relief, there were none in this case. By the time the students had requested a court order, their suspensions had been over for two months. As any procedural errors pertained only to the suspensions, it was error for the trial court to issue relief. State procedures for student discipline are not as strict as criminal or juvenile protections. In school disciplinary cases, notice of the incidents giving rise to discipline is generally sufficient. **The board had properly invoked Idaho Code Section 33-205 as authority for the expulsions for carrying weapons on school property.** The students understood they had harmed another student, and the board could reasonably find their presence was detrimental to others at the school. *Gooding Public Joint School Dist. No. 231, In re Expulsion of Rogers*, 20 P.3d 16 (Idaho 2001).

♦   A Florida middle school had a disciplinary policy prohibiting students from disrupting classes, distracting others, defacing school property or endangering the safety of self or others. The only items expressly prohibited by the policy were telephone pagers, weapons and firearms. Students were prohibited from carrying knives, weapons or any item that could be used as a weapon, and the policy declared the use or possession of a weapon on school property or while attending school functions cause for expulsion and referral to law enforcement agencies. The school board expelled a student for possessing eight bullets on a school bus. At an expulsion hearing, an assistant principal acknowledged the student had not been disruptive on the bus, while the school's principal testified the incident had constituted a major disruption on the school campus. The board voted to expel the student, and he appealed to the state court of appeal.

The student argued on appeal that he could not be found guilty of violating the school disciplinary policy because bullets are not weapons. He also argued that any item could be dangerous under the policy and denied that any person had been placed at risk by his conduct. The court agreed, finding the policy did not prohibit possession of any item except paging devices and items that could be used as weapons. **The policy forbidding dangerous and disruptive items could not be relied upon in this case because there was no evidence the student used the bullets in any way.** The court reversed the expulsion order. *M.K. v. School Board of Brevard County*, 708 So.2d 340 (Fla. Dist. Ct. App. 1998).

♦   A Kansas high school student brought to school a pellet pistol that resembled a real gun. He displayed the gun to friends during the school day, and no student who observed the gun believed it was a threat to their safety. However, a parent who saw the gun reported the student to school security officials. The principal imposed an extended suspension on the student for possession of a look-alike handgun in violation of a student handbook code section prohibiting unruly conduct that disrupts school, and another code section broadly extending to other matters covered by state law. The suspension was affirmed by both the school board and a Kansas district court.

The student appealed to the Court of Appeals of Kansas, which found that

the board and principal had not exceeded their authority by issuing the suspension, despite the lack of specific language in the student code prohibiting possession of look-alike handguns. The U.S. Supreme Court has recognized that the need for school discipline requires the ability to impose discipline for a wide range of conduct. The court held that the suspension was supported by substantial evidence, and it affirmed the district court decision. *Spencer v. Unified School Dist. No. 501*, 935 P.2d 242 (Kan. Ct. App. 1997).

3. Extracurricular and Co-Curricular Events

◆ A group of Ohio students attended a school-sponsored student exchange program in Germany. Before the trip, a teacher explained to students that they would stay with a "host family" for two weeks. They would have some supervised field trips, but would spend a great deal of time with host families without any direct supervision by school staff or the host school. While in Germany, a number of students consumed alcoholic beverages at biergartens with their "host parents." They were of legal drinking age in Germany and believed they were permitted to drink without supervision. Upon returning home, the school suspended the students for three to five days for violating student code prohibitions on consuming or possessing alcohol while in the school's control and custody. The students asked for a hearing before the school board, arguing the teacher had "verbally created an exception to the school's code of conduct regarding the consumption of alcohol." Students and parents understood the exception as allowing the parents and host parents to determine whether students could drink alcohol. The board overturned the suspensions but required the students to perform community service.

An Ohio trial court vacated the discipline, and the board appealed to the Court of Appeals of Ohio. **The court stated Ohio Rev. Code § 3313.661 gives school districts and boards the authority to devise codes of conduct, adopt a policy for suspension, expulsion, removal and permanent exclusion of students, and to specify the types of misconduct resulting in discipline.** There was undisputed evidence that the teacher had "engrafted an exception on the disciplinary code's provisions concerning alcohol consumption." Only the teacher and another employee had testified that the "exception" required direct supervision of host parents for any student drinking. The exception was not written. The students and parents had all stated their understanding of the policy allowed parents and host parents to determine the circumstances for alcohol consumption by students. The court upheld the trial court's decision to vacate any discipline. *Brosch v. Mariemont City School Dist. Board of Educ.*, No. C-050283, 2006 WL 250947, 2006-Ohio-453 (Ohio Ct. App. 2006).

◆ A Kentucky student admitted drinking off school property, and the school board excluded him from playing basketball and other extracurricular activities. He sued the board and principal in a state court, asserting the discipline was arbitrary and capricious. He further alleged discrimination and due process violations. The court dismissed the complaint, and the student appealed to the Court of Appeals of Kentucky. **The court first noted that students have no fundamental or vested property right to participate in interscholastic**

athletics. For that reason, the student's constitutional claims were not viable, and had been properly dismissed. The court stated a school board may suspend or expel a student for violating lawful school regulations. Courts may not interfere with a board's exercise of discretion, unless it acted arbitrarily or maliciously. The student claimed the board acted arbitrarily and capriciously in denying his opportunity to participate in interscholastic athletics. **The court held he stated a viable claim for arbitrary and capricious action by the board and principal, and the trial court should not have dismissed it on the summary basis of the record.** The court reversed this part of the judgment and returned it to the trial court. *Critchelow v. Breckinridge County Board of Educ.*, No. 2005-CA-001194-MR, 2006 WL 3456658 (Ky. Ct. App. 2006).

◆   Missouri cheerleading squad members reported two cheerleaders were drinking alcohol before a school football jamboree. A late-night, off-campus investigation by the squad's faculty advisor was inconclusive. The school principal later began a new investigation, but the parents of the cheerleaders did not cooperate, and one of them removed her daughter from school. The parents then sued the school district and school officials in a federal district court. The principal continued his investigation and obtained statements from several students who said they had seen the two cheerleaders drinking alcohol. The principal suspended both cheerleaders for 10 days based on "overwhelming evidence" they had violated school policy by being under the influence of alcohol at a school event. He advised the parents of the decision, and the district sent them written confirmations of the suspensions, informing them of the reason for the action and their right to school board review. The parents did not respond. The court held for the district and officials, and the parents appealed.

The U.S. Court of Appeals, Eighth Circuit, noted there was evidence that the cheerleaders knew drinking alcohol before a school event violated the school disciplinary code. The court rejected the parents' claim that the district "patently failed to train" its employees. The district provided coaches with triennial training sessions for responding to student misconduct. To establish school liability for failing to train staff, the parents would have to prove the district showed deliberate indifference to student rights. The court found no deliberate indifference by the district in this case. The cheerleaders received proper notice they were being charged with a violation of the school code. Although the parents complained that the district had deprived their daughters of due process, they themselves had terminated contact with the principal. Their suggestion that the principal was biased because he suspended the students shortly after the filing of the lawsuit was frivolous. Administrators must be free to pursue discipline without fear of "the threats and acts of litigious parents and students." The students had the opportunity to present their side of the story, satisfying due process requirements. As the suspensions were based on violations of a longstanding, published policy, the judgment was affirmed. *Jennings v. Wentzville R-IV School Dist.*, 397 F.3d 1118 (8th Cir. 2005).

◆   An Indiana wrestling coach confiscated some negatives from a student who was a member of the school wrestling team. A school administrator instructed the coach to develop the negatives, which revealed the student and three other wrestlers naked in the boys' shower room. The school principal recommended expelling the student for "possessing or distributing pornographic material." The student's attorney argued at an expulsion hearing that the district code did not specify this offense. The hearing officer upheld the recommendation for expulsion, but the decision was reversed after a school administrative review. The student returned to school after six weeks and made up his work. He sued school officials in a federal district court. The court held the principal and hearing officer were entitled to qualified immunity in the case.

The student appealed to the U.S. Court of Appeals, Seventh Circuit, which held **the conduct of the principal and hearing officer did not meet the high threshold for proving a substantive due process violation**. The court explained qualified immunity is not simply a defense to liability. It provides immunity from being sued. **School officials are entitled to qualified immunity for federal civil rights violations, unless the unlawfulness of their conduct is apparent in light of preexisting law.** It was not the role of a federal court to void school decisions which the court viewed as lacking in wisdom or compassion. According to the court, 42 U.S.C. § 1983 actions alleging civil rights violations did not create a right to relitigate in federal court questions of evidence arising in school disciplinary cases. The public education system relied on the discretion and judgment of school administrators and board members. While the administrators "exercised questionable judgment," they were entitled to qualified immunity. The case demonstrated the importance of due process rights, as the administrative review had set the expulsion aside and cleared the student's school record. The court found no due process violation, and reversed the judgment. *Tun v. Whitticker*, 398 F.3d 899 (7th Cir. 2005).

4. Fighting and Violence

◆ An Indiana student told friends he was going to get his father's gun, "bring it to school, start with the seventh grade, and work his way up." The threat was made off school grounds, but school officials learned of it. The student admitted making a threat and admitted "what he had done was wrong and against school rules." The student's locker was searched, but no gun was found. Police officers did not find "an unlawful act" and did not file charges against him. The school suspended the student for 10 days for violating its student code of conduct, which adopted Section 20-8.15.7(a)(1) of the Indiana Code. The superintendent held a hearing and expelled the student for three months. The school board upheld the expulsion after a hearing, and a state court upheld the action.

On appeal, the Court of Appeals of Indiana explained that **Section 20-8.1-5.1-9 permits student discipline for unlawful activity on or off school grounds if it may reasonably be considered an interference with school purposes or an educational function**. Removal of a student is authorized if necessary to restore order or protect persons on school property. The court found it was not necessary for law officers to determine whether the student engaged in unlawful activity for school officials to expel him. The board had found his threat was an unlawful act of intimidation. *Sherrell v. Northern Community School Corp. of Tipton County*, 801 N.E.2d 693 (Ind. Ct. App. 2004).

◆ **A federal district court denied a Pennsylvania student's request for a preliminary order preventing her expulsion for fighting at the home of a classmate. It held that her magnet school's "24/7" disciplinary policy permitted an expulsion for off-campus conduct that could be reasonably expected to cause disruption at school.** The student went to a party at the classmate's home, to which she had not been invited. When she was asked to leave, she assaulted the classmate's mother and the police were summoned. The magnet school principal received information about the fight and took written statements from student witnesses. The principal suspended the student for five days and then convened a hearing. A hearing officer upheld the expulsion under the school's disciplinary policy, which applied to any conduct "off school grounds when the conduct may reasonably be expected to undermine the proper disciplinary authority of the school, safety of students or staff," or disrupt the school. As a result, the student was reassigned to her neighborhood school, which did not offer a comparable curriculum to the magnet school.

The student sought a federal district court order seeking her readmission to the magnet school pending further consideration of her case, and a declaration that the school district violated her due process rights by expelling her for off-campus activity. The court issued a brief memorandum and order denying the student's request, finding that she was unlikely to prevail on her due process or state law claims. Even if she did prevail on the merits of her case, allowing her to return to the magnet school would undermine the district's strong interest in protecting students from violence. *T.W. v. School Dist. of Philadelphia*, Civil No. 02-8862, 2003 WL 735095 (E.D. Pa. 2003).

◆ An Arkansas student shouted at a classmate near their school cafeteria and approached her until a teacher intervened. The school principal received a handwritten note from the student in which she threatened the classmate's life and described her plan to initiate a fight. The principal suspended the student pending a recommended expulsion. The school board accepted the expulsion recommendation. The student obtained a temporary order from an Arkansas county court allowing her to return to school a few days later. The court converted the order to a permanent injunction, and the district appealed.

The Arkansas Court of Appeals agreed with the district that the county court had ignored its proper role by substituting its judgment for that of the school board. **The Arkansas Code requires school boards to hold students strictly accountable for disorderly conduct in school**, and there is a general policy against court intervention in matters that are properly before school authorities. The board expelled the student for violating a school handbook provision prohibiting student threats. The handbook cross-referenced an Arkansas law prohibiting terroristic threats. The county court had no power to substitute its judgment for that of the school board, and the appeals court reversed its judgment. *Cross County School Dist. v. Spencer*, 58 S.W.3d 406 (Ark. Ct. App. 2001).

◆ An Illinois school board's anti-gang rule specifically prohibited students from representing gang affiliation, recruiting others for gang membership and threatening or intimidating others to further gang purposes. The board voted to expel six African-American students for two years because of their involvement in a fight. The board reviewed a videotape of the incident and found the students were members of rival street gangs. The videotape revealed that each of the students actively participated in the fight. After twice voting to expel each student for two years, the board met with an advocacy group led by the Reverend Jesse Jackson and representatives of the state governor. One student withdrew from school, but the board agreed to reduce the expulsions to one year and allow the others to immediately attend alternative education programs. Despite the board's concessions, the students sued the board in a federal district court for civil rights violations, alleging that the anti-gang provision violated the Due Process Clause of the U.S. Constitution.

The court awarded judgment to the board, and the students appealed to the Seventh Circuit, arguing the anti-gang rule was unconstitutionally vague due to its lack of clear definitions. According to the court, **the anti-gang rule clearly defined what conduct it prohibited and was not unconstitutionally vague. The rule did not involve speech rights**, and fighting by the students in support of their gang was clearly within its definitions. It was reasonable for school officials to see the fight as gang-like activity, and the rule was sufficiently definite to avoid a constitutional challenge. The court affirmed the judgment for the school board. *Fuller v. Decatur Public School Board of Educ., Dist. 61*, 251 F.3d 662 (7th Cir. 2001).

◆   Missouri's Safe Schools Act permits school districts to apply an expulsion or suspension from another school district where the underlying offense would be grounds for excluding the student from the district where enrollment is sought. A student committed burglary, theft and property damage when he attended a parochial school. After being expelled, he sought enrollment in the school district in which he resided. The school board held a hearing under the Safe Schools Act and denied the student's application on grounds that if he had committed the same acts on school district property, he would have been expelled. A state trial court affirmed the board's decision to make the parochial school expulsion effective in the district. The Missouri Court of Appeals held the act applied only to school districts, not parochial schools. While the act did not define "school district," the term was defined in state law and connoted a public school system. Accordingly, **a school district in which a student is attempting to enroll may make an expulsion effective from another school district, but not a nonpublic school**. Because the school board and trial court had erroneously applied state law, the court reversed the judgment. *Hamrick by Hamrick v. Affton School Dist. Board of Educ.*, 13 S.W.3d 678 (Mo. Ct. App. 2000).

◆   A hearing officer considered the discipline of two Florida students charged with battering a school employee. He found they were unaware of her official position and should not be punished under a section of the school's student code that enhanced penalties for harming a school employee. The school board held the section imposed strict liability on any student involved in a confrontation with a school employee and that lack of knowledge of official status was immaterial. It held both students violated the student code and expelled them for the remainder of the current school year and the next school year. The students appealed to the Florida District Court of Appeal.

The court stated that a student must know or have reason to know the identity or position of employment of a victim to be convicted under a state law pertaining to offenses against school employees. School boards are required to adopt rules providing that violators be expelled or placed in alternative settings as appropriate, with immediate removal from the classroom. The court rejected the claim that the board and superintendent had inherent rights to issue student disciplinary rules. While they had significant authority in this respect, school officials were powerless to issue rules at variance with state legislation. **The board's strict liability interpretation of the student code was inconsistent with a state law requirement that a student have knowledge of a victim's official status to suffer increased penalties applying to crimes against school board employees.** The students should not have been disciplined under the school code section governing harm against a school employee. *W.E.R. v. School Board of Polk County*, 749 So.2d 540 (Fla. Dist. Ct. App. 2000).

5. Cell Phones and Electronic Devices

◆ A Pennsylvania student had his cell phone on, in violation of a school policy. A teacher confiscated the phone and stated that while she was in possession of it, a text message appeared on its screen from another student requesting marijuana. The teacher and an assistant principal then called nine students listed in the cell phone's directory to see if their phones were turned on in violation of school policy. They accessed the student's text messages and voice mail and used the cell phone's instant messaging feature. The student stated the district superintendent later told the press that the student was a drug user or peddler. The student and his parents sued the teacher, assistant principal, superintendent and school district for violations of state and federal law.

A federal district court held the student and his parents had no standing to assert a claim under the Pennsylvania Wiretapping and Electronic Surveillance Control Act. A claim under that section could only be advanced by a caller, not by a recipient. The cell phone directory and call log were not "communications" as defined by the act. **The court held the superintendent could not assert absolute immunity for the student's invasion of privacy, defamation and slander claims based on his statements to the press. This was because the family claimed he knew his statements were false at the time he made them.** In further proceedings, the family would receive an opportunity to show the superintendent acted outside his authority. The teacher and assistant principal also had no immunity on the invasion of privacy claims. The court agreed with the family that accessing the phone directory, voice mail and text messages, and use of the phone to call persons who were listed in the directory amounted to a search or seizure under the Fourth Amendment. While school officials are not held to the warrant and probable cause standard of the Fourth Amendment, they must have some reasonable grounds for a search or seizure at school. **The court found no basis for the "search," as it was not done to find evidence of wrongdoing by the student,** but instead to obtain evidence of possible misconduct by others. The student could pursue his Fourth Amendment claim in further court proceedings, but could not seek compensatory or punitive damages from the district under the Pennsylvania Constitution. However, the punitive damage claims against the teacher, assistant principal and superintendent would be considered in future court activity. The state law negligence claims deserved further consideration and would not be dismissed. *Klump v. Nazareth Area School Dist.*, 425 F.Supp.2d 622 (E.D. Pa. 2006).

◆   A Delaware student used his cell phone at a school assembly, in violation of the school code of conduct. He refused to surrender his phone to a staff member, and the principal asked him four times to hand it over. The principal told the student he would have to come with him to the office. The student still refused to move, and the principal tried to escort him from the assembly by the elbow. The student struggled, pushed the principal and stepped on his foot. After being removed from the assembly, he continued to use his cell phone. The student remained disruptive in the school office and told the principal "you can't touch me," and "just wait till I call my mom. She'll sue you." He also threatened other students and teachers. The police arrived at the school and took the student into custody. The school board expelled the student for the rest of the school year and assigned him to an alternative school. The state board of education affirmed the action, and the student appealed to a state superior court.

The court held the state board could overturn a local board decision only if it was contrary to state law or state regulations, was not supported by substantial evidence, or was arbitrary and capricious. **The court found sufficient evidence that the student had pushed the principal and stepped on his foot. The student had intentionally and offensively touched the principal in violation of the school code. Expulsion with referral to an alternative program was not disproportionate to the misconduct.** The court affirmed the decision, as it was supported by substantial evidence. *Jordan v. Smyrna School Dist. Board of Educ.*, No. 05A-02-004, 2006 WL 1149149 (Del. Super. Ct. 2006).

C. Academic Expulsions or Suspensions

◆   An Oregon student had Attention Deficit Hyperactivity Disorder. With the help of the school football team's quarterback, he created counterfeit money. Both students were caught passing counterfeit bills at the student store. The student was charged with forgery and suspended for ongoing disciplinary issues, including a minor-in-possession charge, two harassment and misconduct complaints, and at least one athletic code violation. The school informed the student that since he intended to finish his course load outside of the classroom, the district was recommending expulsion for the rest of the year. The actual proceedings would be stayed if certain conditions were met. The quarterback received an in-school suspension for four days, along with a three-week suspension from athletic activity and community service/grounds work at the high school. He was unable to compete in football playoffs as well as the first two weeks of wrestling. The student transferred to another high school, where he succeeded academically. He sued the school district in a federal court.

The student claimed equal protection violations, asserting that the greater punishment inflicted on him was because of behavior issues arising from his learning disabilities. **The court noted that as long as there was a rational** basis for the difference in the way the students were treated, the district was entitled to judgment. **This was because disabled students are not a "protected class" under the Equal Protection Clause.** The court noted the student's prior disciplinary record and the fact that the quarterback had no disciplinary history. The distinction between their situations allowed for the rational decision to treat the learning disabled student more harshly. The court granted pretrial judgment to the school district. *Schneider v. Corvallis School Dist. 509J,* No. CIV 05-6375-TC, 2006 WL 3827457 (D. Or. 2006).

◆   A student enrolled in the University of Michigan's "Inteflex" program – a special six-year course of study leading to both an undergraduate and medical degree. He struggled with the curriculum and failed the NBME Part I, receiving the lowest score in the brief history of the Inteflex program. **The university's medical school executive board reviewed the student's academic career and decided to drop him from registration in the program.** It denied his request to retake the NBME Part I. The student sued the university in a U.S. district court, claiming due process violations. At trial, the evidence showed the university had a practice of allowing students who had failed the NBME Part I to retake the test up to four times. The student was the only person ever refused permission to retake the test. Nonetheless, the district court held his dismissal did not violate the Due Process Clause. The U.S. Supreme Court agreed, ruling **the Due Process Clause was not offended because "the University's liberal retesting custom gave rise to no state law entitlement to retake NBME Part I."** *Regents of Univ. of Michigan v. Ewing,* 474 U.S. 214, 106 S.Ct. 507, 88 L.Ed.2d 523 (1985).

◆   Four Minnesota students submitted work for a history project that included significant portions copied verbatim from reference sources. Each of the students received a zero grade. The parents of one of the students believed he was treated unfairly, claiming the teacher's instructions were unclear. The parents argued their cause twice before the school principal, who refused to change the student's grade. The district superintendent affirmed the grade after a hearing, which found the teacher had clearly explained plagiarism.

The parents appealed to the Court of Appeals of Minnesota, which rejected their argument that a plagiarism provision in the student handbook formed a contract between the school and its students. It also rejected the claim that the district had violated the student's property and liberty rights when charging him with plagiarism. In this case, there was no protected property or liberty interest of which the student could claim to have been deprived. He was not entitled to a hearing before an impartial hearing officer, and the informal meetings held by the principal and superintendent were sufficient to protect any due process interest. **The process afforded the student had been fair and reasonable, and the grade was fair and supported by the record.** *Zellman v. Independent School Dist. No. 2758,* 594 N.W.2d 216 (Minn. Ct. App. 1999).

◆   Three Ohio high school students stole copies of an algebra test from their teacher's file cabinet. They distributed copies to two other students. After they took the test, the teacher noted their identical answers. The school held a disciplinary hearing at which witnesses testified that one of the students acted as a lookout while the other two stole the copies. **The five students who had cheated on the test were given Fs for the class. The three students who participated in the theft were suspended for 10 days in addition to receiving Fs.** One of the students who was suspended sued the school district in an Ohio trial court, which abated the suspension, finding it unreasonable. The Court of Appeals of Ohio, Erie County, reinstated the suspension, finding that it was both rational and reasonable. **The school had appropriately imposed separate penalties for the separate offenses of cheating and theft.** *Reed v. Vermilion Local School Dist.*, 614 N.E.2d 1101 (Ohio Ct. App. 1992).

II.   STUDENT SEARCH AND SEIZURE

The U.S. Supreme Court has held the Fourth Amendment warrant and probable cause standard does not apply to school officials who search students suspected of violating a law or school rules. Instead, the legality of a student search depends upon the reasonableness of the search in light of all the circumstances. Under the test established in New Jersey v. T.L.O., *below, a search performed by school officials must be reasonable at its inception and not overly intrusive under all the circumstances. A student's age and sex are relevant considerations when evaluating the intrusiveness of a search.*

A.   Fourth Amendment "Reasonable Suspicion"

1.   Searches Based on Individualized Suspicion

◆   A teacher at a New Jersey high school found two girls smoking in a school lavatory in violation of school rules. She brought them to the assistant vice principal's office, where one of the girls admitted to smoking in the lavatory. However, the other girl denied even being a smoker. The assistant vice principal then asked the latter girl to come to his private office, where he opened her purse and found a pack of cigarettes. As he reached for them, he noticed rolling papers and decided to thoroughly search the entire purse. He found marijuana, a pipe, empty plastic bags, a substantial number of one dollar bills and a list of "people who owe me money." The matter was then turned over to the police. A juvenile court hearing was held, and the girl was adjudicated delinquent. She appealed the juvenile court's determination, contending that her constitutional rights had been violated by the search of her purse. She argued that the evidence against her should have been excluded from the juvenile court proceeding.

The U.S. Supreme Court held that the search did not violate the Fourth Amendment's prohibition on unreasonable searches and seizures. Stated the Court: "The legality of a search of a student should depend simply on the reasonableness, under all the circumstances, of the search." Two considerations are relevant in determining the reasonableness of a search. First, **the search must be justified initially by reasonable suspicion of a violation.** Second, **the scope and conduct of the search must be reasonably related to the circumstances which gave rise to the search, and school officials must take into account the student's age, sex and the nature of the offense.** The Court upheld the search of the student in this case because the initial search for cigarettes was supported by reasonable suspicion. The discovery of rolling papers then justified the further searching of the purse, since such papers are commonly used to roll marijuana cigarettes. The Court affirmed the delinquency adjudication, ruling the "reasonableness" standard was met by school officials in these circumstances and the evidence was properly obtained. *New Jersey v. T.L.O.*, 469 U.S. 325, 105 S.Ct. 733, 83 L.Ed.2d 720 (1985).

◆   The U.S. Supreme Court will not review an order allowing the state of Indiana to use as evidence a firearm seized by school officials in a drug dog sweep search to support firearms possession charges against a student. The Supreme Court of Indiana held school officials who conducted the search should not be held to the "probable cause" standard to which police are held. The officials decided when and where the search was to be conducted, and there was no evidence that police directed them. As school officials could conduct the search without a warrant, the state supreme court held the firearm they seized could be used as evidence in the proceeding against the student. *Myers v. Indiana*, No. 05-1202, 126 S.Ct. 2295 (U.S. cert. denied 5/22/06).

◆   A Pennsylvania assistant principal detained a student for nearly four hours while investigating a classmate's claim that the student touched her in a sexual manner without her consent in a class. The student denied unwanted touching. He instead claimed the incident was consensual and named some witnesses. The assistant principal told the student to remain in a conference room while he interviewed the witnesses. The student remained there and did school work for several hours. The student was allowed to leave for lunch and get a drink of water, but otherwise remained in the room from 10:15 a.m. until 2:00 p.m. The school principal suspended him for four days for inappropriate conduct. The student sued the school district, board and administrators in a federal district court for due process, equal protection and Fourth Amendment violations. The court held for the district, and he appealed to the U.S. Court of Appeals, Third Circuit. The court held confinement in a conference room was a "seizure" under the Fourth Amendment. The student was not free to go for nearly four hours.

The court explained that public school searches are governed by the "reasonableness standard" of *New Jersey v. T.L.O.*, above. **What is reasonable depends on the context of the search. In school cases, the courts balance the need for a search against the personal invasion which the search entails.** The court noted the detention was to investigate the incident, and to determine appropriate punishment. **In light of the serious nature of the charge, it was reasonable for the school to detain the student.** The court rejected his due process claim, as the assistant principal had allowed him to present his side of the story before discipline was administered. He claimed the district denied him equal protection by disciplining him and ignoring his evidence that any sexual misconduct was consensual. However, the student had admitted misconduct, while the classmate did not. The court held the student and classmate were not similarly situated, defeating his equal protection claim. The judgment was affirmed. *Shuman v. Penn Manor School Dist.*, 422 F.3d 141 (3d Cir. 2005).

◆   An Illinois high school dean suspected a student of marijuana possession after he saw her younger sister smoking marijuana inside her car. He searched the car and found several marijuana cigarettes there. The dean removed the student from class for further searching and questioning. The student refused the dean's request to search her personal property or face a one-week suspension. Her request for a hearing before the board was denied. The student and her father sued the dean and school district in a federal district court for violating her state and federal constitutional rights.

The court held the Fifth Amendment does not apply to school discipline. Consent to be searched is not a "self-incriminating statement" and does not amount to an interrogation. The student incorrectly argued the dean needed probable cause to search her. The court held school officials do not require probable cause to search a student suspected of violating rules. **A school search is permissible if it is both justified at its inception and reasonably related in scope to the circumstances that initially justified searching a student.** The court found reasonable grounds for a search and dismissed the Fourth Amendment claim. The student's remaining claim based on the alleged violation of her due process rights was also without merit. **The Supreme Court has held a school suspension of 10 days or less only requires that a student receive oral or written notice of the charges and an opportunity to explain his or her conduct. In most suspension cases of 10 days or less, due process is satisfied by an informal discussion between the student and disciplinarian within minutes of the misconduct.** As this requirement was met, the student did not state a valid due process violation claim. She was not entitled to a hearing before the board, and the court dismissed the case. *Maimonis v. Urbanski*, No. 04 C 1557, 2004 WL 1557657 (N.D. Ill. 2004).

◆   A Texas assistant principal saw a student in a school hallway and asked him why he was not in class. The student gave evasive answers, lied about the location of his class and said he needed to go to his locker to get class materials. The two eventually went to the student's class. The student dropped his backpack under a table by another student upon arriving. The teacher told the assistant principal that no materials were required for that day's class. The assistant principal believed the teacher's information, coupled with the student's behavior, indicated he was hiding contraband. The assistant principal took the student into a library office and asked to search the backpack. The two argued, and the principal alleged the student eventually gave him permission to search the backpack. The search revealed marijuana, and the assistant principal summoned a school liaison officer. The officer asked the student to empty his pockets and found cocaine there. The student was arrested and charged with possession of cocaine in a drug-free zone. In juvenile court proceedings, the student claimed the cocaine evidence was unlawfully seized and moved for a suppression order. The court denied the motion and placed him on community supervision. The student appealed to the Court of Appeals of Texas.

The court reviewed *New Jersey v. T.L.O.*, in which the Supreme Court held school officials do not need probable cause when searching students. Student searches need only be reasonable under all the circumstances and **will be upheld if they are reasonable at the inception and reasonably related to the** circumstances giving rise to the search. **A student search is "justified at its inception" when reasonable grounds exist that a search will reveal evidence of a violation of the law or school rules.** The assistant principal was justified in approaching the student because he was late for class, in violation of school policy and possibly state truancy law. **His evasiveness and insistence on going to his locker for supplies he did not need created a reasonable basis to suspect he was concealing contraband.** As the search was justified at its inception and reasonably related to the circumstances giving rise to it, the court held the search of the backpack was proper, and the cocaine evidence could be used in the juvenile court prosecution. *Briseno v. State of Texas*, No. 05-02-01630-CR, 2003 WL 22020800 (Tex. Ct. App. 2003).

◆ Students at a Texas alternative learning center had to submit to a daily inspection routine before proceeding to class. All students and their parents were advised about the daily screening procedure during orientation. A student entered a security station, emptied his pockets, passed through a metal detector and put his shoes on the table. A school official discovered a marijuana cigarette in his shoe. The student was arrested and adjudicated delinquent for drug possession. He pled guilty and was sentenced to six months probation.

The student appealed to the Court of Appeals of Texas, which held administrative searches do not require probable cause, because student privacy interests are outweighed by the school interest in maintaining order. Since the states are public school custodians, students are subject to a greater degree of supervision than adults. Searches that require students to empty their pockets and have their backpacks checked have previously been upheld. The court relied on *Thompson v. Carthage School Dist.*, 87 F.3d 979 (8th Cir. 1996), an Arkansas case finding the removal of a pupil's shoes during a weapons search was "minimally intrusive." **The search was designed to meet security needs in a setting highly susceptible to drug and weapons-related disciplinary problems.** As the search was an "administrative search" permitted by the Fourth Amendment, the court affirmed the delinquency adjudication. *In re O.E.*, No. 03-02-00516-CV, 2003 WL 22669014 (Tex. Ct. App. 2003).

◆ A California high school security aide and counselor entered a classroom to investigate incidents of defacing school property. They told students they were looking for markers and instructed them to take their belongings from pockets and backpacks and put them on their desks. As they walked around the room searching for markers, they observed a lighter on a student's desk. They detected the odor of marijuana and brought him to the principal's office, where they asked him to empty his pockets. The employees observed a baggie in the student's jacket and after the principal ordered the security aide to conduct a pat-down search, the student admitted that it contained marijuana. The state initiated juvenile court proceedings against the student. The court denied his motion to suppress the marijuana and declared him a ward of the state.

The state court of appeal observed that *New Jersey v. T.L.O.* relieved schools of the warrant and "probable cause" requirements of the Fourth Amendment. School officials need only act reasonably under all the circumstances when searching students. The state supreme court has required "articulable facts supporting reasonable suspicion" of a rules violation in order to justify a student search. However, individual suspicion is not an absolute prerequisite for "reasonableness," which is determined by balancing the need to search against the invasion of privacy that the search entails. In this case, **the search was justified at its inception because of reported markings in the classroom. There were "articulable facts" to support an objectively reasonable suspicion** that someone was marking school property. The scope of the search was not excessively intrusive, as students were initially told only to place their possessions on their desks. As the government interest in education outweighed the minimal intrusiveness of the search, and the search was based on reports that someone was marking school property, the court affirmed the decision. *In re Johnny F.*, No. B149430, 2002 WL 397046 (Cal. Ct. App. 2002).

◆ A California high school security officer observed a student in an area that was off limits to students. When she approached him, she noticed that he "fixed his pocket very nervously" and became "very paranoid and nervous." After the student entered a classroom, **the officer and a colleague summoned him to the hallway and performed a pat-down search that yielded a knife with a locking blade.** The state commenced judicial proceedings against the student and placed him on probation, declaring him a ward of the court.

On appeal, the Supreme Court of California explained that schools may perform their primary duty of educating students by enacting disciplinary rules and regulations and enforcing them through police or security officers. The school environment calls for immediate, effective action, and school officials are allowed to exercise the same degree of physical control over students as parents are privileged to exercise. **While at school, students may be stopped, told to remain in or leave a classroom, sent to the office and held after school.** They are deprived of liberty from the moment they enter school, and detention by a school official for questioning does not increase the limitations already in effect simply by being in school. **Although individualized suspicion is usually required to perform a search or seizure, special needs exist in the school environment that relax this requirement.** The governmental interest at stake is of the highest order, since school personnel need to send students in and out of classrooms, set schedules, send them to offices and question them in hallways. Detentions of minor students on school grounds did not violate the Constitution, so long as they were not arbitrary, capricious or for the purposes of harassment. Reasonable suspicion did not have to be shown in such cases. Since the student in this case did not allege that the officer acted arbitrarily, capriciously or in a harassing manner, the court affirmed the judgment. *In re Randy G.*, 26 Cal. 4th 556, 110 Cal. Rptr. 2d 516, 28 P. 3d 239 (Cal. 2001).

◆ A Massachusetts school administrator saw three students in a parking lot when they should have been in class. One student's mother did not come to school to discuss the incident as requested. When the student came to the office, **school administrators and a school police officer searched him and found a small bag of marijuana** concealed in his socks. A juvenile court denied his motion to suppress the marijuana evidence and found him delinquent. On appeal, the Supreme Judicial Court of Massachusetts stated the general rule that school searches need only to be reasonable under all the circumstances.

The court explained that reasonable suspicion is not a hunch or "unparticularized suspicion," but instead requires common-sense conclusions about human behavior. In this case, there was evidence that the student had recently been truant and failed to bring his mother to a meeting to discuss it. School officials had no evidence he possessed contraband or had violated a law or school rule. The court rejected the argument that the search was appropriate based on the student's truancy. He was not searched for evidence of truancy, but instead for contraband. School searches should be limited to occasions when administrators have reasonable grounds to believe a search would yield evidence of a violation of law or school rules. **A violation of school rules, standing alone, would not provide reasonable grounds for a search unless the specific facts of the violation created a reasonable suspicion of wrongdoing.** Because administrators had no information of an individualized nature that he might possess contraband, their search had been unreasonable at its inception. The court vacated the juvenile court order. *Comwlth. of Massachusetts v. Damian D.*, 752 N.E. 2d 679 (Mass. 2001).

◆ A New Jersey teacher observed a high school student was acting strangely and had a flushed face, red eyes and dilated pupils. The school nurse found the student "looked high," and a school security guard searched the student's locker and book bag. After he found two kinds of pills there, the principal suspended the student and advised her father she would have to complete a physical examination before she could return to school. A blood test performed on the student was negative for drugs and alcohol. The school promptly readmitted her and she sued the principal, school board and other officials in a federal district court for civil rights violations. The court awarded summary judgment to the officials, and the family appealed to the Third Circuit.

The court held **the testing was supported by reasonable suspicion that the student was under the influence of illegal substances.** The actions against the teacher and school nurse were properly dismissed, as their observations were not excessively intrusive, given the student's age, sex and the nature of the suspected violation. The possession of pills was a violation of school policy, and **the principal acted reasonably in requiring the student to undergo testing before returning to school. Requiring the student to submit to testing in a medical clinic was reasonable** under the circumstances, and summary judgment for the school officials was appropriate. The court rejected the student's assertion that school officials violated her privacy rights by inadvertently disclosing the results of the drug tests to other students. It found no connection between the injury she claimed and the nurse's inadvertent release of the test results. Because there was no link between the release of information about the negative test results by the nurse, the court affirmed the district court's judgment. *Hedges v. Musco*, 204 F.3d 109 (3d Cir. 2000).

2. Off-Campus Searches

◆ Minnesota students attending an auto shop class were bused to a body shop for class instruction. En route, the teacher observed a student holding a knife that was passed to him from a classmate. When the bus arrived at the body shop, the teacher called a school coordinator to report the knife. The coordinator and principal decided each student should be searched, and the principal called a school liaison officer. Before the search began, the classmate voluntarily handed over the knife. The liaison officer found a collapsible baton in the student's pocket, and he was charged with violating a state law prohibiting possession of a dangerous weapon on school property. The district brought an expulsion proceeding against the student for violating its ban on weapons and look-alikes. The student pursued civil rights claims against the liaison officer and his municipality in a state court. Municipal officials removed the case to a federal district court, where they obtained summary judgment.

The student appealed to the Eighth Circuit, which recited the general rule that school and municipal officers are entitled to qualified immunity when their conduct does not violate clearly established federal statutory or constitutional rights of which a reasonable officer would have knowledge. While law officers are normally required to have probable cause of wrongdoing to support a search or seizure of persons or property, the more lenient standard of "reasonable suspicion" applies to searches and seizures in the context of public schools. There is a special need to ensure safety in schools, and officials may conduct a search that is "justified at its inception" and reasonable in scope. The court held **the *New Jersey v. T.L.O.* standard applies to law enforcement officers who conduct student searches away from traditional school grounds.** School administrators initiated the search, and one of them played a substantial role in it. **The fact that the search took place off school grounds did not call for imposing the stricter probable cause standard.** The liaison officer's conduct was reasonable, as he did not know whether other students might also have weapons. He had reasonable grounds to believe that the student possessed a knife and was not required to use the least intrusive means of performing a search. As the search was justified and reasonable in scope, the officer was entitled to immunity and the court affirmed the judgment. *Shade v. City of Farmington, Minnesota*, 309 F.3d 1054 (8th Cir. 2002).

◆ Before leaving for a school-sponsored trip, New York students were informed that drugs and alcohol were banned and that participants would be subject to room searches. Each student signed a pledge to avoid alcohol and drugs. The pledge recited that a violation would result in disqualification from senior activities and graduation ceremonies. During the trip, the school principal smelled marijuana where many of the students had congregated in the hallway of their motel. He then obtained a hotel security pass key and searched most of their rooms. The principal found marijuana in the safe of one room. He sent two students home early and suspended them from school for three days.

The students sued the principal and school district in a federal district court. The court held **students who are under supervision in school activities, including field trips, are subject to the reasonable cause standard for student searches first announced by the U.S. Supreme Court in *New Jersey v. T.L.O.*,** not the more stringent Fourth Amendment probable cause standard. **The students had no legitimate reason to expect complete privacy in their rooms, and it was reasonable for the principal to search the rooms** based on his detection of marijuana smoke and the gathering of students. This was true even though he was without individualized suspicion that any one student possessed drugs. The court upheld the search, noting the existence of specific evidence that students were using drugs. Even if the principal had committed a constitutional violation, he would still be entitled to immunity, since there was no clearly established law on the subject at the time of the alleged violation. The court granted summary judgment to the principal and school district. *Rhodes v. Guarricino*, 54 F.Supp.2d 186 (S.D.N.Y. 1999).

3. Locker Searches

◆ A Maryland student attended a school for students with emotional, learning and behavioral difficulties. The county school system's search and seizure policy permitted school administrators to search students or their lockers if there was probable cause to believe that a student had items whose possession would constitute a Maryland criminal offense, including weapons, drugs and drug paraphernalia, alcohol or pagers. The principal pursued an anonymous tip that there were drugs or weapons at the middle school and authorized a search of all middle school lockers. **A school security officer opened the student's locker in the student's absence and found a book bag containing a folding knife and pager.** The student was detained and admitted the items belonged to him. In juvenile court proceedings, he admitted possessing the items but moved to suppress them as evidence, claiming the policy created a reasonable expectation of privacy in his locker. The juvenile court disagreed, and its decision was affirmed by the state court of special appeals. The appeals court observed that school searches must be justified at their inception and reasonably related in scope to the circumstances that justified the search.

Whether a student's legitimate privacy interests were violated by a locker search required a factual inquiry by the court. The only evidence indicating the student had a legitimate privacy expectation in his locker was the school policy statement. The policy statement purported to limit searches to cases in which school authorities had probable cause of contraband items that gave rise to violations of state criminal laws. However, Maryland law, not the local policy, defined and controlled the authority of school officials to conduct public school locker searches. **Section 7-308 of the Maryland Education Article permitted reasonable searches of students based on a reasonable belief that a student possessed an item whose possession would create a criminal offense. School lockers are designated school property and subject to search by school officials in the same manner as other school property.** Accordingly, the school policy was invalid and could not serve as the basis for a student's reasonable expectation of privacy in a school locker. Since the student had no reasonable expectation of privacy in the school locker temporarily assigned to him, the court affirmed the judgment of the lower courts. *In re Patrick Y.*, 358 Md. 50, 746 A.2d 405 (Md. 2000).

4. Strip Searches

◆ Connecticut school officials held a security search prior to the boarding of buses to a senior class picnic. A student was found with a pack of cigarettes, but no action was taken against her. A classmate then reported to a teacher that the student said she planned to hide marijuana in her pants after the security check. The principal instructed the nurse to search the student's underpants. The nurse expressed apprehension, and the student's mother was called. While waiting for her, the principal searched the student's purse and found cigarettes and a lighter inside it. The mother arrived and agreed to help with the search after being told the police would be called otherwise. The nurse and mother then performed the search behind a curtain. The student was required to raise her shirt, pull down her bra and skirt, and pull her underpants away from her body. The search revealed no marijuana, and she was allowed to attend the picnic. The student sued the principal and other officials for constitutional violations. A federal district court upheld the search under *New Jersey v. T.L.O.* (this chapter).

The student appealed to the U.S. Court of Appeals, Second Circuit, which **joined other federal circuit courts that have held the flexible "reasonableness" standard of *T.L.O.* should govern strip searches in the school context**. It stated that as the intrusiveness of a student search intensified, so did the reasonableness requirement. The court agreed with *Cornfield v. Consolidated High School Dist.*, 991 F.2d 1316 (7th Cir. 1993), an Illinois case that found an intrusive strip search required such a high level of suspicion that it approached probable cause. **The Second Circuit held the factors relied on by the school officials were insufficient to create reasonable suspicion for a strip search. While the teacher may have been entitled to rely on the classmate as a reliable informant, the principal was not.** After receiving the tip, the principal did not investigate or try to corroborate the classmate's account. **The court held a student's past history of drug use could be a factor justifying a school search. However, the student in this case was not previously disciplined for any drug offense. Disciplinary problems did not by themselves indicate drug abuse.** The "discovery" of cigarettes and a lighter had only a tenuous connection to the report of marijuana possession. School officials had already seen this contraband during the security check and did not confiscate any items or express concern. As the court was not persuaded by any of the stated reasons for performing the strip search, it reversed the decision and remanded the case. *Phaneuf v. Fraikin*, 448 F.3d 591 (2d Cir. 2006).

◆ A Michigan student told her gym teacher that money had been stolen from her during class. The principal was absent, and a teacher who was assigned as acting principal called the police. The gym teacher searched backpacks of male students in the class, without success. A male teacher searched the boys in their locker room, instructing them to lower their pants and underwear and remove their shirts. A police officer arrived and told the teacher to continue searching, and said the girls should be checked in the same way as the boys "to prevent any claims of gender discrimination." The acting principal and another female teacher then searched the girls in their locker room, requiring them to pull up their shirts and pull down their pants. About 25 students were searched, but the stolen money was not discovered. The students sued the school district, teachers and police officer in a federal district court for Fourth Amendment violations.

The case reached the U.S. Court of Appeals, Sixth Circuit, which stated that qualified immunity protects school officials from liability if they are performing discretionary functions and do not violate clearly established rights of which a reasonable person would have known. **School searches are justified at their inception when reasonable grounds exist for suspecting they will turn up evidence of a violation of law or school rules.** A search is generally permitted if it is limited in scope and not excessively intrusive to the student. **A search for missing money served a less important governmental interest than a search for drugs or weapons. This interest was further diluted when a school searched over 20 students without reason to suspect any one in particular was responsible.** The search was unlikely to succeed and was unlawful. The court noted two Sixth Circuit decisions, *Williams v. Ellington*, 936 F.2d 881 (6th Cir. 1991) and *Tarter v. Raybuck*, 742 F.2d 977 (6th Cir. 1984), had upheld strip searches of students. The *T.L.O.* decision itself (this chapter) did not discuss strip searches. **These cases did not establish that strip searches were clearly unreasonable.** Accordingly, the teachers and officer were entitled to qualified immunity. *Beard v. Whitmore Lake School Dist.*, 402 F.3d 598 (6th Cir. 2005).

◆ A teacher, assistant principal and school police officer strip-searched an entire Georgia fifth-grade class after the teacher reported $26 in cash was missing. The students were divided by sex and searched in school lavatories by same-sex officials. Some boys were asked to drop their pants and some girls were asked to lift their brassieres and dresses or to lower their pants. Thirteen of the students sued the officials, school district and county in a federal district court for constitutional rights violations. The court dismissed the action and the U.S. Court of Appeals, Eleventh Circuit, awarded judgment to the school officials. It ruled that while the search was unreasonable due to a lack of individualized suspicion, and thus violated the Fourth Amendment, the officials were entitled to qualified immunity. The U.S. Supreme Court vacated and remanded the case with instructions to reconsider it under *Hope v. Pelzer*, 536 U.S. 730 (2002), in which Alabama prison guards were denied immunity in a case filed by an inmate who was allegedly handcuffed without water or lavatory breaks. The *Hope* Court held the obvious cruelty of the guards' conduct put them on notice that they were violating the inmate's constitutional rights.

On remand to the Eleventh Circuit, the students argued school officials were on notice of the clearly established right to be free from a mass strip search under *New Jersey v. T.L.O.* and *Vernonia School Dist. 47J v. Acton*, this chapter. The court noted that neither of these cases involved a strip search. **In order to hold school officials liable for a constitutional rights violation, the asserted right must be clearly established by case law** or be such an obvious violation of law that its unconstitutionality is readily apparent to the official. The court held that *Hope* did not change the outcome of its prior decision. **No case law put school officials on notice that a strip search was unlawful, and their conduct was not so egregious as to alert them that the search was unconstitutional.** *Thomas v. Roberts*, 323 F.3d 950 (11th Cir. 2003).

◆ An Ohio community school teacher agreed to hold $10 for a student. She later discovered the money was missing from her desk. Three students were present in the classroom at the time. The school's policy required the teacher to call the school's chief executive officer to conduct any search. However, she asked the girls to empty out their pockets. When no money was discovered, the teacher had them pull out the waistbands of their pants. This caused two of the girls to cry. The teacher asked the student who did not cry to accompany her to a supply closet, where she continued searching and viewed her private parts. The student's parents sued the school and teacher in a federal district court.

The court noted no quick or urgent response was required in this case. **The teacher did not need individualized suspicion for the initial search of the three girls, since they were the only ones present when she learned of the missing cash. However, the supply closet search required individualized suspicion.** Such a search was not contemplated by *T.L.O.*, as it was secluded and there were no witnesses. The search would not have been jeopardized had the teacher complied with school policy. **A reasonable jury might find she acted unreasonably in requesting a third-grader to accompany her alone into a supply closet to perform a second search with no apparent basis. A jury might also conclude the school's policy put her on notice that her actions were unreasonable.** The teacher was not entitled to qualified immunity. *Watkins v. Millennium School*, 290 F.Supp.2d 890 (S.D. Ohio 2003).

B. Random Testing Policies

The U.S. Supreme Court has upheld random testing programs for students seeking to participate in extracurricular activities and use school parking facilities. According to the Court, students participating in extracurricular programs have a reduced expectation of privacy when compared to the general student population, justifying random testing. See Chapter Fifteen for more cases concerning random searches of students in interscholastic athletics.

◆ An Oregon school district responded to increased student drug use by instituting a random drug-testing policy for all students wishing to participate in varsity athletics. A student who wanted to play football refused to sign the drug-testing consent form and was suspended from sports for the season. His parents sued the district in a federal district court. The court upheld the policy, but the Ninth Circuit held it violated the U.S. and Oregon Constitutions. On appeal, the Supreme Court noted **students have a lesser expectation of privacy than the general populace, and that student-athletes had an even lower expectation of privacy in the locker room.** The invasion of privacy in this case was no worse than what was typically encountered in public restrooms. Positive test results were disclosed to only a limited number of school employees. **The insignificant invasion of student privacy was outweighed by the district's important interest in addressing drug use by students who risked physical harm while playing sports.** The Court vacated the judgment and remanded the case. *Vernonia School Dist. 47J v. Acton*, 515 U.S. 646, 115 S.Ct. 2386, 132 L.Ed.2d 564 (1995).

◆ An Oklahoma school district adopted a policy requiring all students who sought to participate in extracurricular activities to submit to random drug testing. A student challenged the policy in a federal district court, which awarded summary judgment to the board. On appeal, the Tenth Circuit examined the "special needs" exception to the Fourth Amendment. This exception allows drug testing in the absence of probable cause of drug use when the government identifies a special need that makes adherence to the normal warrant and probable cause requirements of the Fourth Amendment improper. The existence of a drug problem led by student-athletes was held to justify a random testing program of student-athletes in *Vernonia School Dist. 47J v. Acton*. The court held student drug use in the Oklahoma district was far from epidemic or an immediate crisis and reversed the judgment.

The board appealed to the U.S. Supreme Court, which noted the testing policy was adopted to protect students and that their privacy interests in the school environment were limited. **The Court found no reason to limit testing to student-athletes, extending** *Vernonia* **to cover all extracurricular activities participants.** Participants in these activities had limited privacy rights, as they voluntarily subjected themselves to certain intrusions on their privacy. They also agreed to abide by extracurricular club rules and requirements that did not apply to the student body at large. The policy's intrusion on student privacy was minimal. Test results could have no impact on student discipline or academics, but could only lead to the limitation of extracurricular activities participation. By contrast, the district and board had an important interest in preventing student drug use. The Court found sufficient evidence of drug use by students to justify the policy. **It deemed the policy a reasonably effective means of addressing legitimate concerns in preventing, deterring and detecting student drug use**, and it reversed the appeals court decision. *Board of Educ. of Independent School Dist. 92, Pottawatomie County v. Earls*, No. 536 U.S. 822, 122 S.Ct. 2559, 153 L.Ed.2d 735 (2002).

◆ An Arkansas district handbook permitted random searches of book bags, backpacks, purses and other containers at all times when they were brought on school property. A staff member found some marijuana in a student's purse after all the students in her classroom were ordered to wait in the hall during a search. The student sued the district in a federal district court for constitutional rights violations. The court awarded summary judgment to the district, and the student appealed. The Eighth Circuit held **students have a legitimate, though limited, privacy expectation in their personal belongings while in school. Subjecting them to full-scale searches without any suspicion of wrongdoing virtually eliminated their privacy interests.** There was no evidence of any special circumstances that would justify the intrusiveness of the district policy.

Public school students were entitled to some degree of privacy in personal items brought to school. Student searches in sports and other extracurricular activities involved separate systems of rules and an agreement by students to sacrifice some personal privacy in return for the privilege of participation. The district could not claim that students made any voluntary tradeoff of privacy in exchange for a benefit in this case. Students were required to attend school by state law, and the handbook did not resemble an employment contract with elements of mutual consent. The court held the search invaded student privacy in a major way. Many students would feel uncomfortable or embarrassed about the search, regardless of whether they had contraband. **Searches involving "people rummaging through personal belongings" were much more**

intrusive than searches involving metal detectors or police dogs. The contraband was made available to the police in criminal proceedings. As the policy was highly intrusive and not justified by any significant school interest, the court held it violated the Fourth Amendment. The judgment was reversed. *Doe v. Little Rock School Dist.*, 380 F.3d 349 (8th Cir. 2004).

◆ A Pennsylvania school district required all students who sought to participate in extracurricular activities or obtain a school parking permit to agree to random urinalysis testing. The policy was intended to deter drug use, prevent physical harm and require students to serve as role models for their peers. Two students sued the district in a state court for violating Article I, Section 8 of the Pennsylvania Constitution, which prohibits unreasonable searches and seizures. The court held for the district, but the Commonwealth Court of Pennsylvania reversed the decision. The district appealed to the Supreme Court of Pennsylvania, which held Article I, Section 8 recognized stronger privacy interests than those recognized by the Fourth Amendment. **There was no reason to rewrite the state's heightened rights of privacy in view of the uncertainty created by recent federal cases.**

Under *Vernonia School Dist. 47J v. Acton* and Pennsylvania decisions, the district policy could not survive the Article I, Section 8 challenge. The policy was not a trivial incursion on student privacy. Students had a reasonable expectation their excretory functions would only be modestly diminished at school. **The district did not suggest it had a specialized need to test students for drugs and alcohol based on an existing problem, and there was no showing the group targeted for testing presented a drug problem. The district singled out these involved students for the symbolic purpose of setting an example for others.** The policy unconstitutionally authorized a direct invasion on student privacy, with no suspicion that targeted students used drugs or alcohol in greater numbers than those who were exempt. **The court held random testing of all students in extracurricular activities was unreasonable, and it affirmed the judgment.** *Theodore v. Delaware Valley School Dist.*, 575 Pa. 321, 836 A.2d 76 (Pa. 2003).

◆ A New Jersey school district implemented a series of policies to deter students from using drugs and alcohol, and to refer those with abuse problems into counseling. The school board implemented a random drug and alcohol testing program for all interscholastic sports participants. It later accepted a task force recommendation to expand the testing to all extracurricular participants and those who held school parking permits. Test results were confidential and those who tested positive for drug or alcohol use did not face other school penalties or criminal prosecution. Parents sued the board and superintendent in a state court for violating Article I, Paragraph 7 of the New Jersey Constitution.

The court invalidated the entire program, and the board appealed. The Supreme Court of New Jersey commented that Article I, Paragraph 7 was nearly identical to the Fourth Amendment. The court employed the *Vernonia* factors for evaluating the constitutionality of testing programs for interscholastic sports participants. It found the program less obtrusive than the one upheld in *Earls* (this chapter). **The court embraced U.S. Supreme Court language approving** of the use of minimally obtrusive drug testing to address the nationwide drug epidemic. The court held the testing program was justified by the special need to maintain school order and safety. **Participants in extracurricular activities and those seeking parking privileges subjected themselves to additional regulation that did not apply to the entire student body.** The collection process afforded students privacy and protected personal dignity. The board reasonably tailored the program to address the drug problem in its high school. **The court rejected the invitation to interpret the state constitution as providing greater protection of individual rights than the Fourth Amendment.** It affirmed the decision, cautioning other districts not to interpret its holding as "an automatic green light" to replicate the district's program. *Joye v. Hunterdon Cent. Regional High School Board of Educ.*, 176 N.J. 568, 826 A.2d 624 (N.J. 2003).

◆ After an Indiana student overdosed on drugs he acquired at school, his school district adopted a random drug-testing policy that applied to all students in grades seven through 12 who participated in school athletics, extracurricular and co-curricular activities, and those who wished to park vehicles on campus. Students who sought to participate in the specified activities had to submit a form consenting to testing and obtain the consent of their parents. Positive tests did not result in academic penalties, were not documented and were not disclosed to legal authorities. Those who submitted negative retests had their privileges reinstated, while those who submitted positive retests could be retested and barred from returning to activities for up to a year until they had a negative test. Two students who participated in extracurricular activities sued the district for violations of the Indiana Constitution. A state trial court held for the district, but the Indiana Court of Appeals reversed the decision.

The Supreme Court of Indiana rejected the students' claim that the policy should be analyzed under the "individualized suspicion standard" applicable to police. School searches were substantively different from law enforcement searches because the relationship between school officials and students was not adversarial. School officials did not offer test results to law enforcement agencies or use them for school discipline, undercutting the rationale for use of an individualized suspicion standard. The court adopted the analysis used by the U.S. Supreme Court in *Vernonia*. Students enjoy less privacy at school than do adults in comparable situations. The voluntary decision to submit to drug testing further decreased student privacy expectations. The policy only deprived students of participation in the extracurricular part of an activity and was less intrusive than the one upheld in *Vernonia*. **The court held the policy did not violate the Indiana Constitution. It was reasonably related to the school's purposes of providing for student health and safety, undermining peer pressure and encouraging users to participate in treatment programs.** *Linke v. Northwestern School Corp.*, 763 N.E.2d 972 (Ind. 2002).

C. Police Involvement

School officials are not agents of the police, as they act to ensure student safety and maintain school order, not combat crime. For this reason, the courts have held school officials do not need to advise students of their Fifth Amendment rights or have probable cause to conduct student searches. However, the presence of municipal police during a school search may complicate the correct constitutional standard to apply.

◆   Several Virginia elementary school students reported to their teacher that a 10-year-old student brought a gun to school. An assistant principal questioned the student repeatedly in her office and searched her book bag and desk. After no weapon was found, the assistant principal allowed the student to leave. The following Monday, the assistant principal and principal interviewed some of the student witnesses. One of them said the student had thrown a handgun into the woods adjoining the school. School officials called police and brought the student to the office. They resumed the interrogation, despite her complaints of illness and requests to see her mother. The police continued interrogating the student, with school administrators present. The student repeatedly asked for her mother, but officials denied her requests. She claimed they detained her for over one hour and refused to let her go to the lavatory. The officers found no weapon and did not call the student's mother until after they left. The student and her mother sued school and police officials in a federal district court for due process and Fourth Amendment violations. The court dismissed the case.

The student appealed to the U.S. Court of Appeals, Fourth Circuit. **The court refused to adopt a general rule requiring school administrators to notify parents during school investigations, or to forbid student detentions of a particular length.** A contrary rule would subject administrators to the threat of lawsuits and a variety of new questions involving the extent of the efforts necessary to contact parents in such cases. Virginia law and the school board's rules required a principal to make reasonable efforts to contact parents or guardians before police interrogations. The balance of rights and interests implicated in this case should be achieved in local district disciplinary processes. Board policies and police regulations derived their authority from state law. **The Constitution imposed no parental notification duty while a student was detained.** The court explained school officials do not require probable cause to conduct student searches. Board rules and the state code prohibited the carrying of guns onto school grounds. While police are normally bound by Fourth Amendment warrant and probable cause requirements, a student suspected of a crime presented a unique case. **When school officials seize a student in a constitutional manner and tell police the basis for their suspicion, the detention is justified at its inception. The court held when a student detention justifies police involvement, no Fourth Amendment violation occurs when the police detain a student.** The officers detained the student only until they determined no guns were on school grounds. The court found no fault with the efforts of the school officials to protect school safety. As their actions reflected a concern to avert a greater tragedy, the judgment was affirmed. *Wofford v. Evans*, 390 F.3d 318 (4th Cir. 2004).

1. *Miranda* Warnings

When persons are taken into police custody, they must be advised of their Fifth and Sixth Amendment rights. Otherwise, any statement may not be used in *juvenile or criminal proceedings. The advisory includes the right to remain silent, to know that any statement can be used against the person in court, and the right to have assistance of counsel. This is known as a "*Miranda *warning." Courts in Texas, Rhode Island, New Jersey, Massachusetts, Florida and California have held school liaison officers need not issue* Miranda *warnings when questioning students about school rules violations, but the Supreme Court of Pennsylvania has held they must. The Oregon Court of Appeals refused to apply the* Miranda *requirement in a civil action to reverse a school expulsion.*

◆   An Oregon student was suspended from school and subjected to a juvenile court adjudication early in his freshman year of high school. A vice principal called the student's mother several weeks later, and told her the student was again in the school office. The mother told the vice principal she was very uncomfortable with him talking to her son without his lawyer present. The next month, school officials questioned the student for two hours after a teacher smelled marijuana smoke coming from a restroom while the student and a classmate were there. The student first denied using marijuana, but later admitted it to the vice principal and other officials. As required by school policy, they reported this admission to municipal police. The school held a hearing, and the school board voted for expulsion. The student appealed to an Oregon trial court, claiming he was entitled to *Miranda* warnings when he was questioned by school officials. The court dismissed the case because no police officers were involved and the matter was not a criminal prosecution.

The student appealed to the Court of Appeals of Oregon, claiming he was unlawfully subjected to a custodial interrogation without receiving his *Miranda* warnings. He argued the district policy requiring school officials to refer information to the police made them agents of the police and the state. **The court found no authority in Oregon or elsewhere in which a court suppressed evidence in a school disciplinary hearing on grounds of failure to administer *Miranda* warnings.** A school expulsion did not resemble the deprivation of liberty present in criminal cases. The court observed the student was excluded from a public high school for a maximum of five months, with the ability to cut this in half by complying with school rules. The differences between a school expulsion and a juvenile proceeding required affirming the judgment for the school officials. **The exclusionary rule from criminal proceedings did not apply in the school context, as it would prevent the discipline of students who disrupted school or threatened classmates.** Since this would frustrate the governmental function of educating and protecting children, the court affirmed the judgment. *T.M.M. v. Lake Oswego School Dist.,* 198 Or.App. 572, 108 P.3d 1211 (Or. Ct. App. 2005).

◆   Pennsylvania school police officers were notified by a county sheriff's department that someone had broken into a high school and vandalized a classroom. School police discovered graffiti, overturned desks and residue from a fire extinguisher. They found footprints, distinctive because of their small size, in fire extinguisher residue on classroom floors and desks. The police began to suspect a student who attended one class in the classroom, as he was of small stature and had a poor disciplinary record. After determining the student's shoe matched the footprints in the fire extinguisher residue, one officer advised him he was keeping the shoe as evidence and began questioning him about the break-in. The officer did not administer *Miranda* warnings before questioning the student about the break-in and did not allow him to leave the room. During the questioning, the student admitted involvement in the break-in. He was charged with burglary, criminal trespass, vandalism and other offenses. A juvenile court denied the student's motion to suppress his statements during the school police officer's questioning and adjudicated him delinquent.

The state supreme court agreed to review the decision, based on the student's argument that the questioning violated the Fifth Amendment. **In** *Miranda v. Arizona*, **384 U.S. 436 (1966), the Supreme Court held criminal suspects who are detained for custodial interrogation must be clearly advised of their constitutional rights to remain silent, to know that any statement may be used against them in court, and to have an attorney present.** Evidence obtained in violation of these rights cannot be used in a later criminal or juvenile proceeding. Persons are "in custody" for *Miranda* purposes if the police physically deny their freedom in any significant way, or if they are placed in a situation in which they reasonably believe that freedom of action or movement is restricted by the interrogation. **The court agreed with the student that school police were indistinguishable from municipal police. They have the same powers as municipal police to issue citations and detain suspects on school property.** The court observed the school police in this case were judicially appointed officers. Their questioning had led to sanctions by a juvenile court against the student, not to punishment by school officials under school rules. **As the school police were law enforcement officers under** *Miranda* **and were required to read the student his rights before questioning him,** the juvenile court decision was reversed. *In re R.H.*, 568 Pa. 1, 791 A.2d 331 (Pa. 2002).

◆   A 14-year-old Texas student brought a gun to school, claiming that a group of bullies had been harassing him. School administrators and a school police officer escorted him to a school office for questioning. The officer left the office during the questioning, and the student asked to speak to his mother and his lawyer. He first denied, then admitted bringing the gun to school. A Texas district court adjudicated the student delinquent and placed him in a treatment facility for 14 months. The student appealed to the Texas Court of Appeals, arguing that his confession and the seized gun evidence should have been suppressed because he had not received *Miranda* warnings.

The court stated that minors have the same constitutional privilege against self-incrimination that adults enjoy. Minors taken into custody for questioning must be informed that anything said may be used in court, and that they enjoy the right to remain silent and have an attorney present during questioning. The questioning of a minor who is "in custody" must stop upon a request to speak to an attorney. However, **the student in this case was not considered to be in police custody, even if school officials were serving as agents of the state.** The court agreed with the courts in cases from Rhode Island, New Jersey, Massachusetts, Florida and California holding that **school officials are not required to meet the strict requirements of probable cause and need not** issue *Miranda* **warnings when questioning students about school rules violations. School officials do not act as agents of the police when asking students about violations of school rules.** The court affirmed the district court judgment. *In re V.P.*, 55 S.W.3d 25 (Tex. Ct. App. 2001).

◆   The Minnesota Court of Appeals held that the questioning of a seventh-grade student in a middle school principal's office with the participation of a police officer was a custodial interrogation requiring the reading of the student's criminal rights. **The officer's presence made the *Miranda* warning necessary. As a result, the student's admissions could not be used in juvenile court proceedings.** According to the court, juveniles are entitled to receive *Miranda* warnings. Although school officials had the right to reasonably inquire about the student's conduct on school grounds, *Miranda* warnings were required in this case. The court reversed and remanded a juvenile court delinquency adjudication, holding **where a peace officer interrogates a student in custody in a manner likely to elicit criminally incriminating responses, the student must be afforded Fifth Amendment protection.** *In re G.S.P.*, 610 N.W.2d 651 (Minn. Ct. App. 2000).

2.   Police-Assisted Searches

◆   A classmate of a Florida middle school student saw a baggie that appeared to contain marijuana on the floor of their alternative behavior class. An assistant principal and a school resource officer – who was a county sheriff's deputy – questioned several students and searched their belongings. They found a note indicating the student planned to smoke marijuana with others. The classmate told the resource officer she believed the marijuana had fallen out of the student's pocket. The resource officer searched the student's person and discovered another baggie containing marijuana in his pants pocket. The state prosecuted the student for marijuana possession in a state court. He moved to suppress the marijuana as illegally obtained evidence.

The court held that probable cause, not reasonable suspicion, was the appropriate legal standard in this case. It found insufficient grounds to permit a sheriff's deputy to perform the search without the student's consent. Because the resource officer was employed by a law enforcement agency, he was not a school official entitled to the benefit of the less exacting reasonable suspicion standard described by the U.S. Supreme Court in *T.L.O.* The state appealed to the Florida Second District Court of Appeal, which observed that in *T.L.O.*, the Supreme Court held that the legality of a search performed by school officials upon a student depended upon the reasonableness of the search under all the circumstances. **Courts have applied the *T.L.O.* reasonable suspicion standard to cases in which school officials initiate searches and where the involvement of law enforcement officers is minimal. The court held that the reasonable suspicion standard applied in this case because the investigation was initiated by the assistant principal.** The trial court's suppression order was reversed. *State of Florida v. N.G.B.*, 806 So.2d 567 (Fla. Dist. Ct. App. 2002).

◆ A Texas school parking lot attendant told the school principal that three students were smoking in a car parked in a school lot. The principal encountered the students returning to the school and directed them to her office. She noted one of them wore baggy shorts and believed he might have a weapon concealed in them. The student refused the principal's request to empty his pockets and she obtained the assistance of a municipal police officer assigned to the high school. **The officer patted down the student and found him in possession of marijuana.** The state prosecuted the student in juvenile court for possession of marijuana in drug-free zone. The court denied the student's pretrial motion to suppress the marijuana seized by the officer. He pleaded no contest to drug possession and was fined and placed under community supervision for one year.

The student appealed to the Texas Court of Appeals, where he argued the officer lacked reasonable suspicion to conduct a pat-down search. The court noted in *New Jersey v. T.L.O.*, the U.S. Supreme Court did not determine the standard to apply to school searches when a law enforcement officer is involved. The court said **where school officials initiate a search, or police involvement is minimal, the "reasonable suspicion" test applies**, not the more exacting **"probable cause" standard applicable to traditional law enforcement searches**. Because the student was smoking in the parking lot, wore baggy shorts and refused to empty his pockets, reasonable grounds existed for suspecting a search would turn up evidence of a rules violation. Facts known to the officer gave him reasonable suspicion to believe the student possessed a weapon or other contraband, and the pat-down search was justified at its inception. The search was reasonably related to the objectives of the search and not excessively intrusive in view of the student's age and sex. The court held the search did not violate the Fourth Amendment and affirmed the judgment. *Russell v. State of Texas*, 74 S.W.3d 887 (Tex. Ct. App. 2002).

◆ A resource officer was assigned to work at a New Hampshire school by the municipal police department. Due to the many searches there, administrators agreed to investigate less serious matters, including drug possession, and refer those involving weapons or a threat to school safety to the officer. If the officer felt he lacked probable cause for an arrest, he would deem the case a "school issue" and let administrators handle it. A science teacher observed a student passing tinfoil to a classmate and reported it to the resource officer. The officer referred the student to an assistant principal. The assistant principal and another administrator questioned the student and asked if they could search him. The student agreed to be searched and they discovered tinfoil that the student admitted "might be LSD." The administrators contacted the resource officer and returned the case to him. A state court granted the student's motion to suppress evidence found by the administrators, finding they acted as agents of the police and had to provide him the safeguards afforded to criminal suspects.

The state appealed to the New Hampshire Supreme Court, which found an "agreement" between the officer and administrators that the officer would inform school officials of suspicious behavior for which he lacked probable cause to investigate. Warrantless searches or seizures are presumed to be illegal, and **evidence acquired by an agent of the police must be reviewed by the same constitutional standard that governs the police**. This prevents the government from circumventing a suspect's rights. The court held school officials are responsible for school administration and discipline and must regularly conduct inquiries concerning both violations of school rules and violations of the law. Their duties do not include law enforcement and they should not be charged with knowing the intricacies of criminal law. However, **school officials may take on the mantle of criminal investigators if they assume police duties. This is what had occurred in this case,** as there was an understanding between the resource officer and school officials on how violations would be investigated. The court cautioned school administrators to "be vigilant not to assume responsibilities beyond the scope of their administrative duties" when establishing working relationships with police. Because an agency relationship existed between the police and school officials, the court affirmed the trial court order granting the student's motion to suppress the evidence. *State of New Hampshire v. Heirtzler*, 789 A.2d 634 (N.H. 2001).

3. Drug-Sniffing Dogs

◆   An Alabama county sheriff's department conducted a drug-sweep search using drug-sniffing dogs at a school. A small package of drugs was found under a table where a student had been sitting with classmates. Law officers patted him down and asked him to empty his pockets. After a classmate said the drugs belonged to the student, two male officers took him to a teachers' lounge, where a strip search yielded no further drugs. A second student was asked to empty his pockets onto a table in the cafeteria where all vocational students had been taken. The officers then led their dogs through the cafeteria and patted down students, even though no dogs alerted. A third student was called to the school parking lot when dogs alerted on his car. He then attempted to swallow a small package, and officers tried to make him spit it out. The third student admitted the package contained marijuana seeds, and the officers made him strip to his underwear while in the parking lot. The students sued the school board, school officials and law enforcement officers for violating their constitutional rights.

The court found that since the searches in this case were initiated by school officials, *T.L.O.* applied. The strip search of the first student was reasonable at its inception. Drugs were found at his table, and a classmate stated that he had placed them there. While the student claimed the police had no reason to believe a strip search would yield further evidence, they had "individualized suspicion" of a violation. The second student failed to show any constitutional violation occurred when he was required to empty his pockets. The court held **a search may be conducted without individualized suspicion when student privacy interests are minimal and important governmental interests exist.** Students have a reduced expectation of privacy in comparison to the general public, and there was evidence that school officials were concerned about drug use in the school. As the search was reasonably related to the objective of finding illegal drugs, it met the *T.L.O.* reasonableness standard. **The search of the third student was supported by individualized suspicion, as sniffing dogs had alerted to his car. However, the court held the search excessively intrusive, because the police officers required him to strip to his underwear while in a public parking lot.** The school officials were entitled to judgment, as there was no evidence that they participated in any constitutional rights violation. There was no evidence of deliberate indifference to his rights, and the court awarded summary judgment to the officials. *Rudolph v. Lowndes County Board of Educ.*, 242 F.Supp.2d 1107 (M.D. Ala. 2003).

◆ **A sheriff's drug-sniffing dog sniffed California high school students as they left a classroom. A deputy then accompanied the dog while it sniffed student belongings left in the classroom.** The search yielded no drugs. One student asserted that the incident was an unlawful search and seizure, and he sued the school district, sheriff's department, and several of their employees and officers in a federal district court for injunctive relief and monetary damages. The court agreed with the student that the search was unreasonable, but dismissed his request for a preliminary injunction as moot, since he was by then no longer a student in the district. It denied his request for class certification and ruled in favor of school and sheriff's department officials.

The student appealed to the Ninth Circuit, which affirmed the mootness issue on the alternate ground that he lacked standing to seek injunctive relief. The court affirmed the judgment for school officials as barred by the Eleventh Amendment, and for the sheriff's department officials, because department policy allowed dog sniff searches of objects, not persons. The Ninth Circuit stated the school officials had admitted the lack of individualized suspicion of wrongdoing by any student. It found the dog sniff search of the students as they left the room was highly intrusive. Even though there is an important government interest in deterring drug use, **the random, suspicionless search of students by dog sniffing was unreasonable under the circumstances, especially since there was no evidence of a drug problem in the school**. The officials were entitled to immunity because there was no clearly established law that the use of a dog sniff search of students in a school setting constituted a search. There was no merit to the student's suggestion that his removal from the classroom was a seizure of his person. The court affirmed the judgment. *B.C. through Powers v. Plumas Unified School Dist.*, 192 F.3d 1260 (9th Cir. 1999).

4. Liability Issues

In Chavez v. Martinez, *538 U.S. 760 (2003), the U.S. Supreme Court held courts cannot award damages against police investigators who wrongly induce suspects to provide incriminating information that is never used in a criminal prosecution. Until compelled statements are used in a criminal case, there is no potential violation of the self-incrimination clause of the Fifth Amendment.*

◆ An Idaho high school custodian discovered a stack of flyers in a school parking lot alleging sexual activities by a local judge's daughter. The principal investigated the incident and learned who made the documents. She also found the documents were not produced at school. About two months later, the judge came to the school and sought to interview some students about a note he had received concerning his daughter's conduct. The principal allowed the judge and a staff member to interview three students without notice to their parents. This violated a school policy allowing parents to refuse or limit interviews of their children that were not held by school or law enforcement officials.

The three students sued the principal and school district in a federal district court, asserting civil rights and tort claims. The court held there was no "search" under the Fourth Amendment. However, it was possible that the students were "seized" and underwent due process violations. They stated they did not feel free to leave the school office, and were aware of the judge's position. It appeared he had threatened at least one student with prosecution for failing to answer a question. Some of the questions had nothing to do with the note and might have been beyond the scope of the school's interest or authority. **At the time of the interview, the principal already knew who had written the note. The court denied her request for qualified immunity, as she allowed the interviews without first contacting parents, in violation of district policies and due process guidelines. There was no reasonable educational interest in asking students about their off-campus sexual activities or their interpersonal relationships.** The district was entitled to summary judgment on the unlawful seizure and invasion of privacy claims, as there was no evidence that it regularly disregarded its interview permission policy. The claims for simple negligence and negligent infliction of emotional distress were for a jury. *Howard v. Yakovac*, No. CV 04-202-S-ELJ, 2006 WL 1207615 (D. Idaho 2006).

◆   An Idaho student was developmentally disabled and had a form of autism. His school called a police officer to his class twice to observe his aggressive behavior with school staff. During one episode, the student hit the officer while she was trying to calm him. On another day, the student continuously tapped on his desk and was "verbally aggressive" toward teachers. School staff called the officer, who attempted to block the student from exiting, then took him to the floor, handcuffed him and hobbled his legs. After being restrained, the student was sent to hospital on "mental hold," while he struggled against confinement and remained verbally aggressive. The student later sued the school district and the police officer in a federal district court, claiming the district was negligent and the officer used excessive force in violation of the Fourth Amendment. The court held the district was immune from suit under the Idaho Code and the officer was entitled to qualified immunity. The student appealed to the U.S. Court of Appeals, Ninth Circuit, arguing the district breached a duty to protect him by calling the police officer, creating an unreasonable risk of harm.

The court observed the district did not employ the officer and had no real or apparent authority over her. **The district did not breach an asserted duty to intervene in her handling of the incident. The student did not show the district could have foreseen the officer would harm or endanger him.** She knew of non-invasive techniques and had been able to calm him during past episodes. The court held the type and amount of force the officer used was excessive. However, she was entitled to qualified immunity. There was no clearly established right to be free of the kind of force used in this case. As the officer's conduct "fell into the hazy border between excessive and acceptable force," the court affirmed the order for summary judgment. *Hayenga v. Nampa School Dist. No. 131*, No. 03-35197, 2005 WL 375731 (9th Cir. 2005).

◆   A New York school employee told a middle school principal two high school students regularly sold marijuana at their high school. The principal accompanied the employee to the high school principal's office to report this. The employee learned from students that the high school students were planning to bring marijuana to school. She reported this to a state police officer, who came to the high school and asked the principal to search the students. The principal agreed, and the students were searched separately by the principal, school dean and officer. They were asked to empty their pockets and book bags, to raise pants legs to expose their socks, and finally to drop their pants and turn around. Neither student was touched at any time, and no drugs were found.

One of the students alleged other students saw him through the window of the principal's office in only his underwear. His father sued the district, principal and officer in a state court for civil rights violations. The court noted *New Jersey v. T.L.O.* does not explain the legal standard to apply when police and school officials combine to conduct a school search. The Eighth Circuit held *T.L.O.*'s reasonable suspicion standard insulated school and law officials who combined to search an Iowa student in *Cason v. Cook*, 810 F.2d 188 (8th Cir. 1987). A New Mexico court held police-initiated and police-controlled searches involving minimal school involvement require probable cause in *State v. Tywayne H.*, 933 P.2d 251 (N.M. 1997). The New York court applied the *T.L.O.* standard, and held for the district, principal and officer. On appeal, a state appellate division court held officials who perform discretionary functions are entitled to qualified immunity if their conduct does not violate clearly established rights of which a reasonable person would have known. To receive immunity, the officer had to show it was objectively reasonable for him to believe his conduct was appropriate under the circumstances. **The court acknowledged the ambiguous state of the law in mixed police/school searches. Given this ambiguity, police officers of reasonable competence could have disagreed about whether probable cause was required for a search conducted by school officials.** The complaint against the officer had been correctly dismissed. *Doyle v. Rondout Valley Cent. School Dist.*, 770 N.Y.S.2d 480 (N.Y. App. Div. 2004).

◆   A Minnesota school employee's job was to handle disciplinary referrals at the school. He responded to a distress call from a teacher who reported a verbal dispute between two ninth-graders he feared would become a physical fight. The employee found the student standing in the classroom in an agitated state and escorted him away. The employee instructed the liaison officer to handcuff the student. There was evidence of another disturbance in the school that required the employee's attention, but the student asserted the handcuffing was performed only to "teach him a lesson about the possible consequences of getting into fights at school." The officer released the student from the handcuffs after 30 to 40 seconds, when he realized the employee's intent.

The student's family sued the employee, officer, school district and municipality for federal civil rights violations, adding a state law claim of false imprisonment. The court noted evidence indicating the **handcuffing was done to teach the student a lesson, not to maintain school safety. The employee might have been justified in issuing some discipline, but under the**

circumstances, the handcuffing violated the student's Fourth Amendment right to be free from unreasonable searches and seizures. The officer carried out the employee's instructions and was not liable for any civil rights violations. As soon as he learned the reason for handcuffing, he released the student. The officer and municipality were entitled to qualified immunity against the student's claims. The employee was not entitled to qualified immunity because his conduct violated well-established constitutional principles. Both he and the district were barred from claiming immunity. *Samuels v. Independent School Dist. 279*, No. Civ. 02-474 (JRT/SRN), 2003 WL 23109698 (D. Minn. 2003).

◆   A California teacher discovered a note sent by a student to a classmate complaining that others had accused him of being homosexual since grade six. The note stated: "I'm gonna kill everyone one day. I'll bring a gun, and bodies will be flying around like burning rag dolls." The teacher turned the note over to the school dean, who contacted the police. The next school day, the police department instructed a school police officer to arrest the student and take him into custody. The school officer interviewed the student in the dean's office with the dean and assistant principal. The officer was uniformed and wore a holstered gun. The student twice denied writing the note, but when the officer and assistant principal left the room, he admitted to the dean he wrote it. He asked to speak to his parents, but the dean refused. The officer read him his *Miranda* rights and asked him about the harassment he experienced, but twice refused to allow him to call his parents. After completing his report on the incident about an hour and one half later, the officer called the student's mother to advise her that her son was under arrest. The student was booked for making terrorist/criminal threats, but no criminal charges were ever filed against him.

The student sued the district, officer and school principal in a state court for civil rights violations, claiming they continued the interrogation after he invoked his right to counsel. The court granted summary judgment to the district and officials, ruling the officials were not required to give *Miranda* warnings prior to questioning students. **A minor's request to speak to parents during a custodial interrogation was not deemed an invocation of the Fifth Amendment right to remain silent.** The student appealed to the state court of appeal, which noted the U.S. Supreme Court's recent decision in *Chavez v. Martinez*, 538 U.S. 760 (2003). In *Chavez*, the Court invalidated a civil rights action based on claimed Fifth Amendment violations because no criminal charges were ever filed by the party asserting violations. As no criminal charges were filed against the student in this case, and his admissions were never used in a prosecution, there could be no civil rights liability for the district or its officials. The court commented in the post-Columbine context, the teacher and administrators were fully justified in bringing the note to the police. The district and officials were entitled to judgment. *Budworth v. Los Angeles Unified School Dist.*, No. B161467, 2003 WL 22138018 (Cal. Ct. App. 2003).

CHAPTER SIX

Employment Practices

		Page
I.	EMPLOYEE PRIVACY	239
	A. Employee Search and Seizure	239
	1. Drug Testing	240
	2. Individualized Searches	241
	3. Employee Examinations	243
	B. Technology and Surveillance	244
	C. Personnel Records	246
	1. Media Access	246
	2. Disclosure to Third Parties	250
	3. Electronic Communications	253
II.	EMPLOYEE QUALIFICATIONS	254
	A. Certification and Licensure	254
	B. Testing and Reform Legislation	259
	C. Residency, Anti-Nepotism and Patronage Policies	261
III.	VOLUNTARY EMPLOYEE LEAVE	264
	A. Family and Maternity Leave	264
	B. Compensatory, Vacation and Sick Leave	270
IV.	REASSIGNMENTS, TRANSFERS AND SUSPENSIONS	272
V.	REPORTING ABUSE AND NEGLECT	275

I. EMPLOYEE PRIVACY

Courts reviewing employee privacy cases balance legitimate personal interests against the government employer's interest in supervision, control and workplace efficiency. In O'Connor v. Ortega, 480 U.S. 709 (1987), the U.S. Supreme Court held public employees have a reasonable expectation of privacy in their personal workspaces, desks and file cabinets. Security cameras create new issues of privacy for staff who may be recorded during surveillance activity. School personnel data are the subject of state privacy law protections.

A. Employee Search and Seizure

Searches and seizures conducted by school authorities implicate the Fourth Amendment. Because these searches are not carried out to enforce criminal laws, the courts consider them "administrative searches," which may be justified by the need to protect student safety and ensure order in schools.

1. Drug Testing

◆ In *Knox County Educ. Ass'n v. Knox County Board of Educ.*, 158 F.3d 361 (6th Cir. 1998), the U.S. Court of Appeals, Sixth Circuit, found a compelling public policy supported a Tennessee school district's employee drug testing program. The court noted there are "few governmental interests more important to a community than that of insuring the safety and security of its children while they are entrusted to the care of teachers and administrators." The court relied in part on its finding that Tennessee teachers were "heavily regulated" by state law. Teachers enter the profession knowing it is highly regulated, and they are charged by law to secure order and protect students in their custody.

◆ A Kentucky district randomly tested 25% of its employees in "safety-sensitive" positions, including teachers. A tenured teacher with 14 years of experience in district schools sued the district in a federal district court, arguing the policy violated her Fourth Amendment rights and the Americans with Disabilities Act (ADA). The court considered her motion for a preliminary order to halt the testing and noted the Fourth Amendment generally requires "individualized suspicion" of a violation before drug testing is permitted. **An exception to the individualized suspicion requirement arises when there are "special needs" beyond crime detection. Special needs can arise when a job is safety-sensitive.** In these cases, courts balance individual privacy interests against the government interest in preventing accidents or injuries. The court relied on *Knox County Educ. Ass'n v. Knox County Board of Educ.*, above. Kentucky law required teachers to submit to certain duties, responsibilities and licensing requirements. Those entering the profession understand it is heavily regulated and have a reduced expectation of privacy in comparison with others.
    The Sixth Circuit approved of a suspicionless drug testing program in *Knox* **where there was little evidence of a drug problem. By contrast, the Kentucky district was in a location experiencing extensive drug problems.** Given the high concentration of drugs in the area, it was reasonable to assume drug use was an imminent threat to students and faculty. The court found the program adequately ensured reliability and privacy. Test results were forwarded to the state Educational Professional Standards Board but not law enforcement agencies. The district was already required to report teacher misconduct, and this part of the policy did not implicate additional privacy concerns. While the Sixth Circuit and Supreme Court had never approved a random testing program of the kind at issue in this case, the court found significant public policy reasons justifying the program. Random testing would significantly enhance the board's ability to ensure teachers remained drug free. **The court held drug testing was not a "medical examination" as defined by the ADA.** As the claims were without merit, the court denied the teacher's request for injunctive relief. *Crager v. Board of Educ. of Knott County*, 313 F.Supp.2d 690 (E.D. Ky. 2004).

◆ Police conducted a random drug search on the campus of a Georgia high school. A drug-sniffing dog alerted on a teacher's unlocked vehicle, which was parked in a school lot. A campus officer opened the door and found marijuana in the vehicle. The school had a zero-tolerance policy providing for testing of employees based on reasonable suspicion of drug and alcohol use. Refusal to consent to testing or a search of personal property was grounds for termination, as was a positive test for alcohol or illegal drugs. The teacher refused to undergo urinalysis testing within two hours, as required by the policy. She received written notice of potential disciplinary action and was recommended for termination. After a hearing, the school board terminated the teacher for insubordination. This decision was affirmed by the state board of education.

A federal district court affirmed the action, and the teacher appealed to the Eleventh Circuit. She argued she could not be discharged for refusing to take a test because there was no reasonable suspicion of a violation of board policy. The court rejected the teacher's assertion that the board's policy applied to the search of her vehicle. The policy did not apply to a drug sweep of the school parking lot by law enforcement officers. The presence of a campus police officer did not alter this fact, and **the police were not bound by the board's policy. Dog sniff searches of personal property located in public places are not protected by the Fourth Amendment. The Constitution permits the immediate, warrantless search of a vehicle when a dog alerts to the vehicle.** There was reasonable suspicion that the teacher violated board policy, and her refusal to undergo testing was a proper reason for terminating her employment. *Hearn v. Board of Public Educ.,* 191 F.3d 1329 (11th Cir. 1999).

◆   A Louisiana school board adopted an employee drug testing policy that required employees in safety-sensitive positions to submit to random drug testing. An elementary school custodian submitted a urine sample that tested positive for marijuana, and the board ordered him into a substance abuse program. The custodian denied drug use and obtained a federal district court order allowing him to attend individual, rather than group, therapy sessions, with periodic drug testing. The court then granted summary judgment to the school board, holding that the drug testing was proper.

The Fifth Circuit reversed and remanded the case, finding insufficient evidence of the board's interest in protecting students and the custodian's Fourth Amendment rights. On remand, the district court again awarded summary judgment to the board, and the custodian brought a second appeal to the Fifth Circuit. This time, the court found the board had properly identified the custodian as a safety-sensitive employee whose performance affected almost 900 students and could place them at significant risk. It agreed with the board that **the interest in protecting students was compelling, that the custodian had received adequate notice that he would be subject to testing, and that the intrusiveness of the testing was minimal.** Because the board's need to conduct suspicionless searches outweighed the custodian's privacy interests, the court affirmed the judgment for the board. *Aubrey v. School Board of Lafayette Parish,* 148 F.3d 559 (5th Cir. 1998).

2. Individualized Searches

The special need of public employers to protect the public safety allows them to avoid the Fourth Amendment warrant and probable cause requirement. In O'Connor v. Ortega, 480 U.S. 709 (1987), the Supreme Court held the search of a public employee's office was reasonable when the measures adopted were reasonably related to the objectives of the search and not excessively intrusive.

♦ A longtime New York teacher was found guilty of having an inappropriate relationship with a female student in 1990. In 1998, he was accused of sexually harassing a student, and was later arrested for stalking the student from the 1990 incident. The district suspended the teacher without pay and reassigned him to an administrative job. He was instructed to remove his personal belongings from his classroom so it could be used by another teacher. The teacher refused to appear at the designated time, but turned in his classroom keys. Administrators and custodians cleaned out the classroom. They drilled out the lock of a filing cabinet and found a picture of the student from the 1990 incident. When the teacher came to retrieve his property, he claimed some items were missing, including tests, quizzes and other teaching materials. A hearing officer found the teacher guilty of misconduct. He was allowed to resume teaching the next year, but sued the district in a federal district court for constitutional rights violations.

The court dismissed the case, and the teacher appealed. **The U.S. Court of Appeals, Second Circuit held he had to show an expectation of privacy that society was willing to consider "reasonable" in order to prove the search violated the Fourth Amendment**. Many persons had access to the classroom, and the teacher acknowledged his property was commingled with school materials. The discharge or suspension of an employee greatly reduced, if not eliminated, any reasonable expectation of workplace privacy. The demand to remove personal items put the teacher on notice he had no remaining expectation of privacy in the classroom. It was reasonable for school officials to remove items so the classroom could be used by his successor. **The government interest in efficient operation of the school justified some intrusion on employee privacy.** Tests, quizzes and homework problems stored in the classroom and file cabinet were the district's property. Federal copyright law considers an employer the "author" of a work, if it is prepared by an employee in the course of employment. Failure to return the teacher's items did not implicate his constitutional rights, and the court upheld the judgment. *Shaul v. Cherry Valley Springfield Cent. School Dist.*, 363 F.3d 177 (2d Cir. 2004).

♦ **The Second Circuit upheld discipline against a New York state employee for downloading personal tax programs on the state-owned computer he used in his office.** The state had a policy prohibiting use of state equipment for personal business. The employee came under suspicion of neglecting his duties, and the state authorized an investigation of his computer usage. A list of file names revealed nonstandard software was loaded on the computer, and additional searches determined the employee loaded a personal tax preparation program on it. The employee challenged the search of his computer in a federal district court. The court awarded summary judgment to the state, and on appeal, the Second Circuit found no Fourth Amendment violation. Although the employee had a reasonable expectation of privacy in his office computer, the investigatory searches were reasonably related to the objectives of the search and not excessively intrusive in light of the nature of his suspected misconduct. *Leventhal v. Knapek*, 266 F.3d 74 (2d Cir. 2001).

3. Employee Examinations

◆ Students, parents and colleagues complained that a Connecticut teacher used foul language, made sexual remarks to students, yelled and "breached school security." The district placed him on paid administrative leave, pending an investigation. His cardiologist advised him to take an indefinite leave for chest pains, anxiety and depression. The board later found the teacher violated its standards of conduct, but could return to work under a remediation plan. The district superintendent advised the teacher he should submit to an independent psychiatric evaluation and sign an unrestricted medical records release. The board's psychiatrist examined the teacher, then requested more interviews and tests, and sought to review his treatment records from 13 years earlier. These records included his written responses to highly personal questions of a sexual nature. School attorneys wrote the teacher he would have to submit to the evaluations and release the records to keep his job. The teacher obtained three medical and psychiatric opinions stating he was able to return to work. He sued the board for a court order allowing his return. The board advised the teacher he could not return to work until he saw the board's psychiatrist and signed the unrestricted release. A federal district court held for the school board, and the teacher agreed to examination by a board psychiatrist. He released medical records to the psychiatrist, but not to the board. The psychiatrist examined him and determined he had no psychiatric disability. The teacher returned to his job.

On appeal, the U.S. Court of Appeals, Second Circuit, affirmed the district court decision on the due process claims. **The board made no false statements about him and did not stigmatize him by seeking his medical records.** The teacher received a grievance hearing under his collective bargaining agreement. He raised an issue regarding his due process rights to privacy. **The court held a person's psychiatric health data and substance abuse history is intimate information that is protected by a right of confidentiality. The teacher had a protected privacy right in his medical records and did not have to disclose them without sufficient justification.** The board conditioned his return to work on an examination by its own psychiatrist and the release of medical information that was 13 years old. The board and its superintendent were not qualified to assess these records and should have left this to the psychiatrist. The court found the board's demand for medical records was arbitrary. The teacher was entitled to further develop his case before the district court. *O'Connor v. Pierson*, 426 F.3d 197 (2d Cir. 2005).

◆ A New York school administrator won numerous awards for her job performance over a 10-year period. However, she had a history of conflict with her supervisor, who gave her a poor performance evaluation. The school board appointed a special counsel to investigate the administrator's claims of improper actions by the supervisor. The administrator was placed on administrative leave due to concerns for her mental health. An investigation cleared the supervisor of fault, while questioning the administrator's performance and professional judgment. **The board ordered the administrator to undergo medical examinations as permitted by New York Education Law Section 913.** Board-appointed doctors found the administrator had several disorders and indications of a degenerative brain disease. She obtained evaluations to contest this, but the board discharged her for mental disability, insubordination and incompetence in a proceeding filed under Education Law Section 3020-a. A state court later upheld her discharge.

The administrator sued the board in a federal district court for violation of her First Amendment speech rights. The court held the lawsuit was precluded by the state Section 3020-a proceeding. The administrator appealed to the U.S. Court of Appeals, Second Circuit, which **held the "arbitration like features" of Section 3020-a proceedings did not negate them as administrative adjudications**. Federal courts must give state court judgments preclusive effect. The Second Circuit found the administrator's retaliation claim failed. **There was no connection between her accusations to the board and the initiation of her discharge over a year later.** The board appointed special counsel upon receiving the administrator's charges about the supervisor, and took a variety of actions indicating its good faith. The Section 3020-a proceeding was begun only after the board received a final medical report about the administrator. The court affirmed the judgment for the board. *Burkybile v. Board of Educ. of Hastings-On-Hudson Union Free School Dist.*, 411 F.3d 306 (2d Cir. 2005).

B. Technology and Surveillance

A California school district did not violate employee rights by secretly installing a video surveillance camera in a computer lab office. A federal district court found the surveillance was justified by the district's strong, legitimate need to obtain evidence of misconduct by a custodial employee.

◆ A California technology resource specialist worked at two school sites. She considered a small office in a computer lab her "home office," and kept personal items there. The door had no lock, but a part-time computer aide also stored her personal items in the office. The resource specialist notified her supervisors of her suspicion that a school custodian was using a computer after hours. Without informing the computer employees, the supervisors began after-hours surveillance of the office with a hidden video camera and VCR. The district had no policy prohibiting the use of surveillance equipment for security purposes. The surveillance was not immediately discontinued after the custodian was videotaped using the computer without authorization. The computer employees discovered the surveillance equipment after about three weeks and were greatly upset. The aide stated she had changed her clothes in the office on several occasions, but this was not videotaped. One tape showed the resource specialist working at her computer for almost an hour, and another showed a brief office visit by the specialist, a man and two dogs. The computer employees sued the school district in a state superior court for invasion of privacy. The court held the employees had a reasonable expectation of privacy, but held the surveillance was reasonable and furthered district goals. The employees appealed.

The Court of Appeal of California observed that the right to be free from an invasion of privacy is not absolute. A party seeking to recover tort damages for intrusion must show a party has "intruded into a place, conversation or matter where the plaintiff had an objectively reasonable

expectation of privacy," and did so in a highly offensive manner. The California Constitution recognized a right to privacy for government and private entities. The court held the employees had a reasonable expectation of privacy in the computer office. An unlocked office would not normally be subject to secret video surveillance by an employer. However, the intrusion on privacy in this case was not highly offensive. Surveillance occurred only after school hours, when the only person expected to be present was the custodian suspected of misconduct. **The videotaping was confined to the precise area where misconduct was occurring and did not include audio surveillance.** The court found the district had a strong, legitimate reason for conducting surveillance. The expectation of privacy for bodily exposure was more limited in an office with no lock than it would in a locking office. The computer office was not a place employees would ordinarily attend to bodily matters. **While the better practice would have been for the school district to notify the computer employees about the surveillance, their privacy rights were not absolute.** The court found no privacy violation under either a constitutional or tort theory and affirmed the judgment for the district. *Crist v. Alpine Union School Dist.,* No. D044775, 2005 WL 2362729 (Cal. Ct. App. 2005).

◆ A Michigan high school athletic director (AD) was responsible for school athletic ticket sales and volunteered to handle concession sales. He stopped complying with a district policy requiring him to turn over concession sales proceeds to the school bookkeeper on the first business day after games. When athletic funds disappeared, the AD was instructed to immediately turn over all ticket and concession proceeds to the bookkeeper. He failed to do this and disregarded instructions not to staff concession stands with his family members. **The district placed hidden cameras on campus and hired an employee to follow the AD with a hand-held video recorder. Although hours of tape were compiled, neither the AD nor his family were seen directly taking school funds.** The AD denied keeping concession proceeds, but officials found $370 in change and small bills in his office. The school suspended the AD, then held a hearing where several hours of videotape were reviewed. An employee testified that the AD removed cash from the ticket booth and concession stand and kept tickets for resale. There was evidence that the AD sold tickets after the end of first quarters and used relatives to staff the concession stand. The hearing referee held the AD was insubordinate by employing relatives and not stopping ticket sales when required. The referee held the AD misappropriated concession proceeds by failing to disclose them, but did not misappropriate ticket proceeds.

The state tenure commission affirmed the referee's findings of insubordination, but rejected the finding of misappropriation of ticket proceeds. **The parties appealed to the Court of Appeals of Michigan, which found the commission had improperly reweighed the testimony of district employees.** The school board did not show the AD engaged in a scheme to misappropriate ticket revenue, as he had turned this money in. **The referee's decision included a painstaking review of the video evidence, and he found the number of actual ticket transactions consistent with the sum of money the AD had turned in.** The court held the referee's decision was supported by competent, material and substantial evidence. The commission had impermissibly reassessed the credibility of witnesses. The court remanded the case for reinstatement of the hearing referee's findings. *Kelso v. Southfield Public Schools Board of Educ.*, No. 256161, 2005 WL 2758571 (Mich. Ct. App. 2005).

The state supreme court will not review the case. *Kelso v. Southfield Public Schools Board of Educ.*, 475 Mich. 884, 715 N.W.3d 872 (Mich. 2006).

C. Personnel Records

State data privacy acts protect the confidentiality of public employee personnel files. Common law rules of defamation may also provide a basis for legal action against a school district or its officers for wrongful disclosure of private facts or erroneous factual statements. For additional cases involving open meeting laws, see Chapter Eleven, Section IV. C., of this volume.

1. Media Access

◆ A Washington newspaper publisher asked three school districts for records identifying teachers accused of, investigated for, or disciplined for sexual misconduct in the previous 10 years. Thirty-seven of the 55 current and former teachers whose records were being sought objected and sued the districts in a state superior court. They claimed the records could be withheld under the Public Records Act, RCW §§ 42.17.250 - .348. The court held teacher identities were not a matter of legitimate public concern when an investigation was inadequate or uncovered no significant misconduct and resulted in no restrictions or punishment. Teacher identities had to be withheld unless allegations were substantiated or a teacher was disciplined with "more than a letter of direction." Under this ruling, the districts were ordered to release the names of 22 teachers. Three of these teachers appealed, and the publisher appealed to gain disclosure of the 15 teachers who avoided disclosure.

The Court of Appeals of Washington held the districts had to disclose the names of the teachers who were accused of sexual misconduct, even if their investigations were unsubstantiated or too minor to justify discipline. The districts could withhold identities only if an accusation was "patently false," since the public has a legitimate interest in the performance of public employees. **The Public Records Act required public agencies to disclose public records upon request, unless a specific exemption applied. Privacy rights were invaded only if disclosure would be highly offensive to a reasonable person, and not of legitimate public concern.** Teachers who were the subject of unsubstantiated but not patently false accusations were not entitled to have their names withheld. The court reversed the nondisclosure order pertaining to them. Those who received letters of direction were not categorically exempt from disclosure. The three teachers who appealed argued that they were entitled to exemption because charges against them were either unsubstantiated or did not lead to serious discipline. The court disagreed, as they were not covered by any exception to the Pubic Records Act. *Bellevue John Does 1-11 v. Bellevue School Dist. #405*, 129 Wash.App. 832, 120 P.3d 616 (Wash. Ct. App. 2005).

◆ **Montana's Supreme Court held the employment records of two teachers who were undergoing disciplinary investigations had to be disclosed to a newspaper.** The newspaper sought documents relating to the disciplinary actions under the "right to know" provisions of the Montana Constitution and state law. A state trial court held the employees had no reasonable expectation of privacy in their conduct as public employees and that any interest was exceeded by the interest in disclosure. The employees requested a stay of the trial court order and appealed. The Supreme Court of Montana dismissed the appeal as premature. The trial court then dissolved the stay and ordered the district to release designated documents to the newspaper.

The district released the documents, and the teachers appealed to the supreme court a second time. They did not request a stay and the documents were released to the newspaper, which published them. **The supreme court refused to consider the teachers' claim that they had reasonable expectations of privacy in the documents. The issue was moot in view of the publication of the documents by the newspaper.** The court held no decision it made could grant the teachers the relief they sought because "once the bell is rung, it cannot be un-rung." The teachers had made no attempt to preserve the status quo during their appeal by requesting a stay, as they had done the first time. The court rejected the teachers' additional arguments, but affirmed the trial court's decision to deny an award of attorneys' fees to the newspaper. There was no evidence of wrongdoing by the district, which had not "lost" the action. The court affirmed the trial court's decision. *In re Petition of Billings High School Dist. No. 2*, 335 Mont. 94, 149 P.3d 565 (Mont. 2006).

◆ Thirteen people complained about verbal abuse and sexual harassment by a California school superintendent. The school board hired an investigator to draft a report on the complaints. She interviewed students, parents, employees and former students, prepared summaries of the interviews and presented them to the board. The board shared copies of interview summaries with some of the complaining parties. Although they were marked "confidential," they were leaked to a newspaper. The board accepted the superintendent's resignation in return for a financial settlement and a promise to keep the report confidential. The report exonerated him of all serious misconduct, but 40 tort claims were filed regarding his conduct. The public and media demanded release of the report and related documents. The board declined most of the request, and media corporations sued to obtain them. A state superior court upheld the decision not to release the report, and the media corporations appealed.

The state court of appeal explained that California Education Code Section 49076 is based on the Family Educational Rights and Privacy Act (FERPA), which requires written parental consent prior to releasing student records. State law defined "pupil records" as any information directly related to an identifiable pupil that was maintained by a school district. FERPA defined "education records" in nearly the same way. **The Supreme Court has held "education records" are institutional records maintained by a single custodian, not individual assignments handed in by students in separate classes.** The investigatory report filed in this case was not an institutional record maintained in the normal course of business by a single records custodian. It did not directly relate to student educational interests. The report was not a "pupil record" under state law. The public interest in the board's actions far outweighed the superintendent's interest in keeping them quiet. The court ordered the board to release the report, with the names of students and others blocked. *BRV, Inc. v. Superior Court*, 143 Cal.App.4th 742, 49 Cal.Rptr.3d 519 (Cal. Ct. App. 2006).

◆　An Illinois school board put its superintendent on paid administrative leave, with the intention of buying out the remainder of her contract due to poor evaluations. The board sent her a letter explaining the reasons for her dismissal. A newspaper publisher requested copies of two evaluations and the dismissal letter, citing the state Freedom of Information Act (FOIA). The board denied the request, asserting the documents were exempt from disclosure because they were part of the superintendent's personnel file. A state court held the documents were not exempt under the FOIA, and noted the board could not "make a non-exempt document exempt merely by placing it in a personnel file."

The board appealed to the Appellate Court of Illinois, which stated public records are presumed to be open and accessible under the state FOIA. **The Illinois FOIA exempted from public inspection and copying "information that, if disclosed, would constitute a clearly unwarranted invasion of personal privacy." The FOIA also exempted personnel files and personal data maintained with respect to employees, appointees, elected officials or applicants. A document fitting one of the FOIA exemptions was absolutely exempt from disclosure.** Since the documents sought by the publisher were within the "personnel file exemption" of FOIA Section 7(b)(ii), the court held they were exempt from FOIA and did not have to be disclosed. The FOIA had to be construed with the state Open Meetings Act, which permitted the school board to meet in closed session to consider the superintendent's performance. The evaluations and letter clearly belonged in the superintendent's personnel file. The lower court's judgment had to be reversed, as it would nullify an exception to the open meetings act concerning any writing produced in closed sessions of a public body. *Copley Press v. Board of Educ. for Peoria School Dist. No. 150*, 359 Ill.App.3d 321, 834 N.E.2d 558 (Ill. App. Ct. 2005).

◆　The Florida education department maintained "staff" and "certification" databases containing teacher social security numbers (SSNs). A newspaper publisher made a verified request for teacher SSNs from both databases. The department complied with the staff database request, but omitted information on teachers from two counties and did not supply SSNs from the certification database. The department denied a formal request for the information, and the publisher sued it in a state court. The court held the department had to comply with the request, as the information pertained to "public records."

The Florida District Court of Appeal noted all SSNs held by an agency or its employees are confidential and exempt from disclosure as public records under Florida Statutes Section 119.07(1). However, a statutory exception existed for commercial entities using SSNs "for a legitimate business purpose," if a verified written request is made. **The court found the publisher had failed to properly verify the requests for SSNs from the certification database and for the two counties from which SSNs were omitted.** Verification required a party to state under oath the specific purposes for which SSNs were needed, and how they would be used in the normal course of business for legitimate business purposes. The production of SSNs from the certification database was limited to the administration of the Social Security Act for child support enforcement. **Federal law safeguards controlled over any contrary state authority.** As the request did not further a program of enforcing child support obligations, the department had properly denied it. The court reversed the trial court's judgment, except the part requiring the department to furnish properly verified information requested from the staff database. *Florida Dep't of Educ. v. NYT Management Services*, 895 So.2d 1151 (Fla. Dist. Ct. App. 2005).

◆   A Wisconsin newspaper sought the records of a special education teacher for a series of articles about charges based on sexual misconduct. The Court of Appeals of Wisconsin held the state open records law presumed records were open to the public. **The teacher's records were not exempt from the law, as they were unrelated to the current proceedings against him.** Even if they would be used against him and might make it hard for him to get a fair trial, they were not covered by any statutory exception. *Robinson v. Racine Unified School Dist.*, 690 N.W.2d 886 (Wis. Ct. App. 2004).

◆   When an Ohio school district sought to hire a new treasurer, it held two executive sessions to interview five finalists for the position. A third meeting was scheduled to reduce the field, and **a local newspaper reporter sought the names and résumés of the finalists for the district treasurer position**. The district supplied only two résumés and delayed releasing the others, stating the other three candidates were no longer under consideration and had been promised confidentiality. The newspaper sued the district in the state court system for an order requiring immediate disclosure of the requested records. The district complied with the request, but the newspaper continued to pursue the lawsuit, arguing that the district's lack of diligence in honoring past records requests justified a broader order providing access to district documents in future cases. The case reached the Supreme Court of Ohio, which observed that timeliness is an important consideration in cases involving the state public records law.

The information sought by the reporter was a public record under the act, regardless of whether the district had assured job candidates they could expect confidentiality. **The district could not withhold or delay records requests because of disagreement with the policies behind state law.** The six-day delay in responding to the reporter's request was unreasonable, since the records she requested were readily available, not voluminous and clearly identified. The district had not yet reduced the field of candidates at the time of the request, and **the reporter was entitled to inspect each resume within a reasonable time of her request**. As the district violated its duty to comply with the record requests in a reasonable time, and there was no good reason for delay, the newspaper was entitled to an order providing access to them. Despite the district's history of delay, the court refused the request for an order requiring it to respond to future records requests "without delay." *State ex rel. Consumer News Services Inc. v. Worthington City Board of Educ.*, 97 Ohio St.3d 58, 776 N.E.2d 82 (Ohio 2002).

◆ A Minnesota principal investigated a teacher's classroom management problems, then advised parents by letter that he was placing her on medical leave. An assistant superintendent sent another letter to parents stating their children would be taking a standardized test. A parent faxed a copy of this letter to a newspaper reporter, who interviewed the assistant superintendent. The newspaper published an article under the headline "100 kids who learn 'nothing' face summer school." The article identified the teacher and discussed concerns about her teaching. The district superintendent issued a press release about the teacher. He appeared in a televised news report, during which he agreed with a reporter that the teacher "wasn't teaching." The teacher sued the newspaper for defamation in a state court, adding claims against the district and administrators for defamation, lost wages, infliction of emotional distress, constructive discharge and violating the state Government Data Practice Act (GDPA). A jury held for the teacher on her data Practice claim, and the court awarded her $520,000 for loss of reputation, emotional distress and lost income.

The state court of appeals reversed the judgment, and the teacher appealed. The Supreme Court of Minnesota held the existence and status of any complaint or charge against an employee are "public data" under the GDPA, as is the final disposition of a disciplinary action. **A disclosure during an investigation that describes any quality or characteristic of the complaint goes beyond the existence and status of the complaint and violates the GDPA.** The principal's letter to parents did not violate the act, as it only revealed the teacher was on medical leave. The assistant superintendent's letter went beyond disclosure of "the existence and status of a complaint" by revealing personally identifiable information about her. Several communications to the media by district officials also violated the GDPA, including statements by the assistant principal to the newspaper. Pending final disposition of any disciplinary action, the disclosure of "mental impressions" derived from recorded district personnel data was private. The superintendent's press release and the televised interview stated his opinions and violated the GDPA because they were made before the final disposition of a disciplinary action. The court remanded the case for a new trial. *Navarre v. South Washington County Schools*, 652 N.W.2d 9 (Minn. 2002).

2. Disclosure to Third Parties

◆ A New Jersey school employee suffered a concussive brain injury after a speaker fell off a wall and struck him on the head. He began having "profound, incapacitating fatigue" and difficulty with concentration and memory. An incident report describing his injury was accidentally stuffed into an envelope with another teacher's contract. Later, the employee walked into a meeting and found some teachers laughing. One of them joked that he had gotten the results of the employee's CAT scan and said "and as we all knew, there was nothing there." The employee sued the school board in a federal district court, asserting it had failed to accommodate his disability and unlawfully disclosed medical information. The court held that below-average comprehension and mental functioning alone could not confer federal disability law protection. The accidental disclosure of the medical report and CAT scan joke did not violate any constitutional rights.

The employee appealed to the U.S. Court of Appeals, Third Circuit. The court stated the Americans with Disabilities Act protects individuals with impairments that substantially limit one or more major life activities. It was insufficient for individuals attempting to prove disability status to merely submit medical evidence of an impairment. There must be evidence that the extent of the limitation caused by the impairment, in terms of the individual's own experience, is substantial. **The court stated the Due Process Clause of the Fourteenth Amendment protects individual privacy interests. Medical information is entitled to privacy protection against disclosure. However, the Due Process Clause was simply not implicated by the negligent act of an official causing an accidental disclosure of data.** The court held the CAT scan joke did not create a constitutional violation. The comment did not reveal anything about the employee's medical condition. As no person could take the CAT scan joke at face value, the judgment for the school board was affirmed. *Weisberg v. Riverside Township Board of Educ.*, 180 Fed.Appx. 357 (3d Cir. 2006).

◆ A Texas school district received a request for all records on a teacher. The district provided some documents but withheld others, including one memorializing a meeting with the principal. The district sought a ruling from the state attorney general, who found the memorandum was not a document evaluating the performance of a teacher and thus not "confidential" under the state Public Information Act. The district then asked for the opinion of a Texas district court, which found the memorandum was confidential and exempt from disclosure. The attorney general appealed to the Court of Appeals of Texas.

The court stated that to withhold information under the Texas Public Information Act, the government entity must show the requested information is either not subject to the act or is exempt under one of the act's exceptions. **Teacher evaluations are exempt from public disclosure under Section 21.355 of the act.** The attorney general claimed the memorandum was a "reprimand" containing no evaluative information. The court found the memorandum touched on the performance issues discussed at the meeting. It gave the teacher corrective direction and referred her to school board policies. The memorandum "evaluated" the teacher because it reflected the principal's judgment, gave her correction and provided for further review. The judgment for the school district was affirmed. *Abbott v. North East Independent School Dist.*, 212 S.W.3d 364 (Tex. Ct. App. 2006).

◆ **The Court of Appeals of Michigan upheld a trial court's decision to delay the release of a teacher's criminal records for sexual misconduct involving a student** under the Michigan Freedom of Information Act. A school board had sought the records for the teacher's tenure hearing, but the trial court held releasing them before the conclusion of the criminal prosecution would deprive him of a fair trial. The appeals court held the trial court properly weighed the risk of denial of a fair criminal trial against the risk of harm by delaying the tenure hearing. *Southgate Community School Dist. v. County of Wayne*, No. 254717, 2005 WL 3481435 (Mich. Ct. App. 2005).

◆   A Minnesota principal obtained a doctor's authorization excusing him from work for three months and referring him to a psychologist at the Mayo Clinic. The psychologist diagnosed the principal with work-related depression. The principal obtained authorizations excusing him from work for the next sixth months, when his sick leave was exhausted. A newspaper published a letter to the editor from the principal, which acknowledged he had "struggled with some issues," and that he was "confident that the Mayo Clinic will help to correct the problems that are medically related." Three newspapers reported the principal had taken leave and was being treated for job stress. The district sought a statement to support the principal's request for unpaid medical leave. He obtained one from the psychologist, which he sent to the board. The board considered the principal's leave request at a regular meeting. The psychologist's letter was included in a packet distributed to all attendees, including the press.

The principal sued the board in a state court for violating his privacy and for disclosing his medical condition in violation of the state Government Data Practice Act (GDPA). The court dismissed the case, and the principal appealed. The Court of Appeals of Minnesota upheld the trial court's decision on the privacy claim. The principal had voluntarily provided information to the board, and it did not invade his privacy by distributing the psychologist's letter at the meeting. **There was no liability for giving further publicity to what the public already knew.** The GDPA claim had been properly dismissed. "Medical data" was defined as data collected on patients or clients by a state agency or political subdivision, or data provided to such an agency. The fact that the principal was on paid medical leave was public data. **The GDPA classified as "public" any data used to account for employee work time for payroll purposes, except if it would reveal the purpose for using medical leave. The letter did not reveal the principal's reason for taking leave.** As there was no GDPA violation, and he did not show he was injured by the release of information, the court affirmed the judgment. *Lehman v. Zumbrota-Mazeppa Public Schools*, No. A04-1226, 2005 WL 894756 (Minn. Ct. App. 2005).

◆   A Massachusetts superintendent compiled an investigative summary of an incident involving a teacher's inappropriate message to two seventh-graders. The teacher was suspended for four weeks. A member of the public requested information from the superintendent about the suspension. The supervisor of public records concluded disclosure was mandated by the state public records act, without the names of the students. The local teacher's association challenged the report's release. A state superior court judge held the report was a public record requiring disclosure with the exception of writings identifying students. He prohibited disclosure of the report pending appeal to the Massachusetts Court of Appeals. The court remanded the case for *in camera* (private) inspection of the report by the superior court judge. The judge again ordered disclosure of the report, without some of the student information. The case reached the Supreme Judicial Court of Massachusetts. **According to the court, personnel records were statutorily exempt from disclosure under any circumstances.** Since disciplinary reports are part of an individual's personnel records, the disputed report could not be released. *Wakefield Teachers Ass'n v. School Committee of Wakefield*, 431 Mass. 792, 731 N.E.2d 63 (Mass. 2000).

3. Electronic Communications

◆ **The Court of Appeals of Florida held a high school teacher accused of exchanging sexually explicit e-mails with students did not have to turn over all his home computers for inspection by his school board for use in his formal employment termination hearing.** The board suspended the teacher for misconduct for exchanging e-mails and instant messages with students that were sexually explicit and made derogatory comments about staff members and school operations. An administrative law judge issued an order allowing a board expert to inspect the hard drives of the teacher's home computers to discover if they had relevant data for use against him in a formal termination hearing.

The teacher appealed, arguing production of the home computer records would violate his Fifth Amendment right against self-incrimination and his privacy rights. He argued the production of "every byte, every word, every sentence, every data fragment, and every document," including those that were privileged, substantially invaded his privacy and that of his family. The court noted that computers store bytes of information in an "electronic filing cabinet." It agreed with the teacher that **the request for wholesale access to his personal computers would expose confidential communications and extraneous personal information such as banking records**. There might also be privileged communications with his wife and his attorney. The only Florida decision discussing the production of electronic records in pretrial discovery held **a request to examine a computer hard drive was permitted "in only limited or strictly controlled circumstances," such as where a party was suspected of trying to purge data. Other courts had permitted access to a computer when there was evidence of intentional deletion of data.** There was no evidence that the teacher was attempting to thwart the production of evidence in this case. The court held the broad discovery request violated the teacher's Fifth Amendment rights and his personal privacy, as well as the privacy of his family. It reversed the administrative order allowing the board to have unlimited access to the teacher's home computers. *Menke v. Broward County School Board*, 916 So.2d 8 (Fla. Dist. Ct. App. 2005).

◆ **A Tennessee citizen made a written request to a county education board to view and inspect digital records of Internet activity, including e-mails sent and received, Web sites visited, and the identity of Internet service providers conducted during school hours or stored on school-owned computers.** A trial court judge reviewed the requested records privately, and found they were not accessible under the state Public Records Act (PRA).

The citizen appealed to the Court of Appeals of Tennessee, asserting the digital records or documents were open to public inspection because they had been made during business hours or were stored on the school's computers. The court found the PRA had a clear legislative purpose favoring disclosure of public records. The PRA defined "public record" to include documents, papers, electronic data processing files and other material "made or received pursuant to law or ordinance or in connection with the transaction of official business by any governmental agency." **The PRA did not limit access to records based on the time a record was created or the place the record was produced or** stored. **The citizen's argument that the material he sought was produced during business hours and on school-owned computers was not relevant.** The court held the trial court judge had properly inspected documents in private to decide if they were "made or received pursuant to law or ordinance or in connection with the transaction of official business." The Tennessee PRA definition of "public records" is almost verbatim to that of Florida law. **The Supreme Court of Florida has rejected arguments that placement of a document in a public employee's file made the document a "public record." The Tennessee court stated that while it was not bound by Florida decisions on public records, it found them well-reasoned and applicable to this case.** The trial court did not commit error in privately reviewing the records, and the judgment was affirmed. *Brennan v. Giles County Board of Educ.*, No. M2004-00998-COA-R3-CV, 2005 WL 1996625 (Tenn. Ct. App. 2005).

◆   In a case involving a newspaper's request for e-mails sent from or received by municipal employees on government-owned computers, a Florida District Court of Appeal held **personal e-mail falls outside the current definition of public records.** The court held personal e-mail was not "made or received pursuant to law or ordinance." **Although digital in nature, "there was little to distinguish a personal e-mail from personal letters delivered to public employees through a government post office box and stored in a government-owned desk."** The court noted the state supreme court has held "only materials prepared 'with the intent of perpetuating and formalizing knowledge' fit the definition of a public record." The court denied a publisher's request to compel a municipality to release all e-mail sent from or received by two employees on their government-owned computers. *Times Publishing Co. v. City of Clearwater*, 830 So.2d 844 (Fla. Dist. Ct. App. 2002).

II. EMPLOYEE QUALIFICATIONS

A. Certification and Licensure

State laws grant broad powers to state education agencies to regulate professional teaching standards through licensure and continuing education requirements. Courts in Arizona and Pennsylvania have recently upheld state agency decisions to revoke professional licenses based on misconduct that relates to a teacher's fitness to teach, even if the misconduct does not result in a criminal conviction or occurs off campus.

◆   **The U.S. Supreme Court held the non-renewal of a tenured teacher's contract because of her failure to earn certain continuing education credits was not a deprivation of her due process and equal protection rights.** The teacher persistently refused to comply with her district's continuing education requirements. After several years, the Oklahoma Legislature mandated certain salary increases for teachers regardless of compliance with the continuing education requirements. The district then threatened the teacher with dismissal unless she fulfilled the requirements. The teacher failed to do so, and the district fired her. The Supreme Court held in favor of the school board, noting the desire of the district to provide well-qualified teachers was not arbitrary, especially when it made every effort to give the teacher a chance to meet the requirements. There was no deprivation of equal protection since all teachers were obligated to obtain the credits, and the sanction of contract non-renewal was rationally related to the district's objective of enforcing the continuing education obligation of its teachers. *Harrah Independent School Dist. v. Martin*, 440 U.S. 194, 99 S.Ct. 1062, 59 L.Ed.2d 248 (1979).

◆   A teacher worked for the San Diego Unified School District for a year under a pre-intern certificate, then obtained a university intern credential. She continued teaching for the district in a job requiring certification qualifications. After two years, the teacher obtained her clear (non-internship) teaching credential. The district rehired her for a teaching position requiring certification qualifications. At the end of the year, the district issued a summary performance evaluation stating the teacher met her employment objectives and was an asset to her school. However, a letter dated May 27 stated she would not be rehired. The teacher sued the district in a state superior court, asserting the district had to give her notice of non-reelection by March 15. The district stated she had only worked as a probationary employee for one year, and her employment under an internship credential did not count toward the consecutive two-year requirement of state Education Code Section 44929.21. The court ordered the district to reinstate the teacher as a permanent, certificated teacher.

The Court of Appeal of California stated Education Code Section 44929.21 deems a probationary teacher reelected for the next year, if she is employed for two consecutive years under a position requiring certification qualifications and is not given a contrary notice by March 15 of the school year. The teacher was not denied probationary employee status by virtue of her final year of internship work. The court rejected the district's assertion that work under a university intern credential did not count toward the two-year tenure requirement. The teacher had finished her second complete consecutive school year of employment by the district in a position requiring certification qualifications at the time she received the late non-reelection notice. The legislature had amended Education Code Section 44466 in 1997 to allow one year of employment under a university internship credential to count toward tenure. The change was intended to eliminate the inconsistency between requirements for attaining permanent status by district and university interns. The court affirmed the judgment for the teacher. *Peoples v. San Diego Unified School Dist.*, 41 Cal.Rptr.3d 383 (Cal. Ct. App. 2006).

◆   A Florida district court of appeal upheld an administrative ruling rejecting charges that a teacher provided inappropriate assistance to her students during the Florida Comprehensive Assessment Test. The state education Practice commission filed a complaint against the teacher for providing answers and other help to her students on the test. However, after a hearing, an administrative law judge found all of the commission's student witnesses not credible. The judge accepted the testimony of the lone student who testified for the teacher. The commission held another hearing and issued a final order suspending the teacher's certification. The court of appeal held the commission had improperly modified the judge's findings. As substantial evidence supported the judge's decision, the complaint was dismissed. *Stinson v. Winn*, 938 So.2d 554 (Fla. Dist. Ct. App. 2006).

◆ A Delaware school district employed a media specialist who had originally worked as an elementary school librarian. Her position changed over the years, and by the year 2000, her duties came to include teaching reading and language skills to students. Five different observers conducted eight formal evaluations of the specialist's classroom performance. She did not dispute findings that her instructional planning and strategies were unsatisfactory. District officials held post-evaluation conferences but later notified her she would be discharged. The specialist contested the action and sought a hearing, noting the district stated no grounds. The district withdrew the notice and reissued one. It stated the specialist was being fired for incompetence and neglect of duty. After a hearing, the board discharged her. The specialist appealed to a state superior court, which found the board action was supported by substantial evidence.

The court found it proper to evaluate the specialist using the Lesson Analysis Form based on the Delaware Performance Appraisal Standards (DPAS I) for teachers. The evaluations were properly conducted during appraisal periods, and she declined opportunities to suggest changes to her improvement plan. The court found the specialist remained uncooperative while superficially complying with her improvement plan. **On appeal, the Supreme Court of Delaware found that library functions had changed from an emphasis on cataloging to providing complementary teaching of reading and language skills. The district required its librarians to teach, and it was reasonable to evaluate the specialist in instructional situations.** As the August 2004 notice gave her the statutorily required 30 days notice of termination, the judgment for the school board was affirmed. *Squire v. Board of Educ. of Red Clay Consolidated School Dist.*, 911 A.2d 804 (Table) (Del. 2006).

◆ A California school district classified all teachers and counselors holding less than a regular teaching credential as "temporary employees." The school board voted to lay off 225 certificated employees who were classified as either probationary or temporary before the 2003-04 school year for budget reasons. Most of the probationary employees pursued their state law hearing rights. An administrative law judge (ALJ) found the layoffs were reasonable. The district teachers association sued the school district in a state court, which held invalid the policy of classifying teachers and counselors solely on the basis of their certification. The district was ordered to reinstate misclassified employees.

The school district appealed. The Court of Appeal of California held that a provision in district contracts purporting to waive the protections of the state Education Code was void. Employees cannot bargain away statutory rights. **Employees who were qualified to teach were not "temporary employees" simply because they were not yet fully accredited. Education Code Section 44915 required school boards to classify as probationary employees those persons who were employed in positions requiring certification**

qualifications for the school year, if they have not been classified as permanent or substitute employees. The court rejected the district's claim that it had the discretion to classify employees as "temporary," based on their certification status. The district had to classify as "probationary employees" all teachers who were employed in positions requiring certification qualifications, unless they had been classified as permanent employees or substitutes. **The court held that teachers holding emergency permits and satisfying the other conditions of state law could be classified as probationary employees.** Probationary employees working under emergency or specialist permits accrued no credit toward permanent status. The Education Code required interns who were reemployed in a succeeding school year to be classified as permanent. The court affirmed the judgment for the employees, and remanded the case to the superior court for further consideration of their claims for back wages and benefits. *Bakersfield Elementary Teachers Ass'n v. Bakersfield City School Dist.*, 145 Cal.App.4th 1260, 52 Cal.Rptr.3d 486 (Cal. Ct. App. 2006).

◆   A Minnesota school psychologist was suspended with pay when Internet use logs revealed his computer had been used to access pornographic Web sites. He denied intentionally accessing pornographic sites, stating they invaded his computer due to a virus. A Minnesota Board of Teaching committee recommended suspending his teaching licenses for a year, but accepted an administrative law judge's recommendation to take no action due to lack of proof he intentionally attempted to access pornography.

The case reached the state court of appeals, which observed that Minnesota Statutes Section 122A.20, subd. 2 required the district to report the suspension or resignation of a teacher to the board of teaching within 10 days. The board was required to investigate the report, and the district had to cooperate with the board. **School boards and district employees are immune from civil or criminal liability under Section 122A.20 for reporting or cooperating with the licensing board if they act in good faith and with due care.** The court rejected the psychologist's claim that a district human resources director did not act in good faith by going outside the school's filtering system and printing an image from a Web site she knew he did not access. **The reporting of suspected teacher misconduct was based on an "unassailable public policy" to protect students.** The report to the Board of Teaching was not made with ill will or improper motive, and the court affirmed the judgment. *Peterson v. Independent School Dist. No. 272*, No. A04-1213, 2005 WL 757694 (Minn. Ct. App. 2005).

◆   A Cleveland teacher received a notice that her four-year teaching certificate would expire before the next school year. During the summer, the district notified her that her certificate had expired and that she had to immediately seek renewal from the state board of education. The state board denied the teacher's application for an eight-year teaching certificate, but the district rehired her, unaware of the board's action. She taught for several months, then requested a leave of absence. The district learned the teacher lacked a teaching certificate and did not let her resume her job. She submitted a professional development plan, but resigned prior to a committee meeting. The board accepted the teacher's resignation, and she sought a court order, called a writ of mandamus.

The Court of Appeals of Ohio explained that the mandamus procedure was not a substitute for an appeal. The teacher argued the district did not help her with new state law requirements and failed to inform her of the appeals process. **The court found neither the district nor its employees had any authority to issue a teaching certificate. This duty belonged to the education department. Maintaining teacher certification fell squarely on the shoulders of the teacher seeking recertification.** The district had no duty to consider the teacher's individual professional development plan, since she resigned before the local professional development committee meeting. A state education regulation allowed her to apply directly to the department to renew a teaching certificate or educator's license. The teacher could have also asked for grievance arbitration, and the case was dismissed. *Boles-El v. Cleveland Municipal School Dist.*, No. 86136, 2005 WL 1994501 (Ohio Ct. App. 2005).

◆   The Iowa Department of Human Services (DHS) determined a child abuse complaint against a teacher was well-founded, based on her 11-year-old daughter's statement that she had instructed her to help avoid an auto interlock ignition device. The DHS reported the complaint to the Iowa Board of Educational Examiners, which found probable cause for a hearing. The teacher denied ordering her daughter to blow into her car's interlock ignition device so that she could drive the vehicle while intoxicated. She admitted asking her daughter to blow into the device to avoid a false reading after she had smoked cigarettes or used mouthwash. The teacher admitted using marijuana, but not in her daughter's presence. The board suspended her certification for not less than three years. A state court affirmed the judgment, and the teacher appealed.

   The Court of Appeals of Iowa held the board only needed proof of a founded child abuse report to suspend or revoke a teaching certificate. The board did not have to determine if a teacher actually committed the acts substantiating a founded report. The teacher admitted the existence of the report and some of its findings, and there was substantial evidence of a violation. The court rejected her assertion that the abuse complaint was unrelated to her fitness to teach because it only involved her own child. **The board found the abuse report against the teacher involved illegal activities that threatened the health and safety of a child and set an extremely poor example of behavior.** The court held any founded child abuse report against a teacher had some relevance to licensure. The willing exposure of illegal activities by the teacher to her daughter demonstrated poor judgment that could adversely affect her classroom decisions. Her behavior undermined public trust and confidence that parents and administrators needed. It was reasonable for the board to determine the abuse of any child related to a teacher's fitness to teach. The court affirmed the judgment. *Halter v. Iowa Board of Educ. Examiners*, 698 N.W.2d 337 (Table) (Iowa Ct. App. 2005).

◆   An Arizona teacher was arrested once and charged with disorderly conduct three times in his first two years of teaching. He was charged with threatening and intimidating an 18-year-old former student at a convenience store and also fired a .357 revolver into a neighbor's air-conditioning unit. Four of the five incidents involved neighbors, with the last resulting in charges of aggravated harassment, threatening and intimidating, interfering with a judicial proceeding, and obstructing a criminal investigation. The teacher violated an order for protection held by a neighbor, and he threatened the neighbor's children that they "had better sleep with one eye open." He pled guilty to misdemeanor charges of aggravated harassment and was sentenced to a year of probation and anger-management counseling. The state board of education sought to censure, suspend or revoke the teacher's teaching certificate. The board's professional Practice advisory committee conducted a hearing and then recommended the revocation of his certification. The board adopted the recommendation.

The state court of appeals held the finding of immoral or unprofessional conduct was implicit in numerous charges of disorderly conduct, threats, intimidation, criminal damage, and the guilty plea for aggravated harassment. The court refused to limit "immoral or unprofessional conduct" to teacher-student interactions. **Teachers could be disciplined for off-campus conduct that related to their fitness to teach and had an adverse effect on or within the school community. The board could consider all three incidents for which the teacher was not criminally prosecuted.** He admitted his conduct, even for those incidents. **The teacher's conduct related to his fitness to teach**, and the evidence established his tendency to react with violence and aggression. One conviction involved threatening children and two involved young adults about the age of high school seniors. As these incidents gave the board reasonable cause for concern and a basis to act to prevent or control future harm, the court affirmed the board's decision. *Winters v. Arizona Board of Educ.*, 207 Ariz. 173, 83 P.3d 1114 (Ariz. Ct. App. 2004).

B. Testing and Reform Legislation

The No Child Left Behind Act required all teachers of "core academic subjects" to be "highly qualified" by the end of the 2005-2006 school year. A "highly qualified" teacher holds a bachelor's degree, is fully licensed by the state, and demonstrates knowledge in the subject area taught. The "full state certification" requirement does not include emergency, temporary or provisional licenses. The states are responsible for devising rigorous tests for current teachers in their academic subject areas, and subject knowledge and teaching skills for basic curriculum areas for new elementary teachers.

◆ The Kentucky Instructional Results Information System (KIRIS) is a statewide examination administered to students in certain grades. Some Bell County High School employees reported cheating on a KIRIS administration, and a state education department office found violations of KIRIS practices. The Kentucky Education Professional Standards Board charged individuals, including a county secondary supervisor and a high school principal, with misconduct, willful neglect of duty, and incompetence under state law and the state professional ethics code for school-certified personnel. Most individuals settled the charges, but the supervisor and principal demanded hearings. After the hearings, the Professional Standards Board found the supervisor and principal guilty of encouraging teachers to clarify KIRIS test questions, allowing a "student accountability scale" that rewarded students for asking questions, and inappropriately extending test times. The board suspended the supervisor's teaching certificate and endorsements for a year, and the principal's certificate and endorsements for 18 months. The administrators appealed to a state court, which dismissed the charges against the supervisor and remanded the principal's case to the Professional Standards Board. The board appealed.

The Kentucky Court of Appeals found the principal had assigned building coordinator duties to the supervisor without officially conferring this designation on her. KIRIS assessment materials clearly detailed appropriate assessment practices for test administrations. The supervisor testified she did not read KIRIS materials and was unaware of prohibited testing practices such as using an accountability scale, allowing extended test times, allowing students to leave testing areas with test materials, and encouraging teachers to assist students. The principal said he read KIRIS instruction manuals, was familiar with the appropriate assessment practices form, and had a good-faith belief that the school conformed to KIRIS rules. The court agreed with the Professional Standards Board that the supervisor was guilty of misconduct. **The court reinstated the misconduct findings against the principal and harshly criticized his failure to ensure proper administration of the KIRIS. There was evidence that teachers reported improper practices during the test and that he allowed the violations to continue.** The court reinstated the board's findings against both school administrators. *Kentucky Educ. Professional Standards Board v. Gambrel*, 104 S.W.3d 767 (Ky. Ct. App. 2002).

◆   The 1993 Massachusetts Education Reform Act created the Massachusetts Comprehensive Assessment System for assessing individual student academic performance. The Reform Act required the state board to establish ways to improve schools designated as under-performing or chronically under-performing. As part of the reforms, the board established regulations governing review of mathematics programs. The board identified circumstances under which it could declare a school's mathematics program "low-performing" and require math teachers to take a diagnostic mathematics content assessment. The results were to be used to develop or revise individual professional development plans for teachers seeking license renewal. The act required teachers to complete individual professional development plans in order to renew their licenses, and the corresponding regulations required teachers in low-performing mathematics programs to take the assessment before supervisors could approve their professional development plans. The Massachusetts Federation of Teachers and the Massachusetts Teachers Association/NEA sued the state board, asserting the regulations were unconstitutional and exceeded the board's authority. A Massachusetts superior court entered judgment in the board's favor.

The associations appealed to the Massachusetts Supreme Judicial Court, which held the regulations were within the board's authority and were consistent with Reform Act accountability provisions. **Agencies have broad authority to effectuate legislation through regulations when the statutory focus is on reform.** The Reform Act sought to establish and achieve specific educational performance goals and hold educators responsible for student achievement. The Reform Act gave the board the power to include the assessment in teacher professional development plans, which were a recertification condition. **The regulations were reasonably related to the purposes of the act and were a valid exercise of board authority, since assessment of teacher knowledge and subject matter proficiency was a critical component of the board's ability to comply** with the legislation. The regulations did not violate the Constitution, as they did not infringe upon the teachers' fundamental personal rights. The judgment for the board was affirmed. *Massachusetts Federation of Teachers, AFT, AFL-CIO v. Board of Educ.*, 436 Mass. 763, 767 N.E.2d 549 (Mass. 2002).

◆   State law prohibited the California Commission for Teacher Preparation and Licensing (CTPL) from issuing credentials, permits or certificates to applicants who were unable to demonstrate reading, writing and mathematics skills in English. The CTPL used a basic skills proficiency test, the California Basic Education Skills Test (CBEST), to make this assessment. Groups representing minority educators asserted that they had historically failed the test at a higher rate than Caucasians, and that the test violated Titles VI and VII because it had a disproportionately adverse impact on minorities. A federal district court awarded summary judgment to the state. The Ninth Circuit held Title VI did not apply to the state commission's administration of the test. The decision was withdrawn, and the Ninth Circuit voted to rehear the case. It then observed Title VII may apply to an entity that is not the complaining party's "direct employer," if it interferes with the party's employment opportunities with another employer.

The court found the control exerted over local school districts by the state of California was particularly strong. Districts were considered state agencies in other legal contexts, so the state was in a practical position to "interfere with" local employment decisions. This brought the state within the reach of Title VII. No decision on the Title VI question was necessary to resolve the case. The complaining parties showed the CBEST requirement had a disparate impact upon minority applicants. However, the court upheld the finding that **the test was properly validated. It had a manifest relationship to school employment, adequately identified specific job duties to which the CBEST could be correlated and established a minimum level of competence in three areas of basic education skills.** The skills it measured were important, and the state did not set passing scores at an impermissible level. For these reasons, the court held the CBEST requirement did not violate Title VII. *Ass'n of Mexican-American Educators v. State of California*, 231 F.3d 572 (9th Cir. 2000).

C. Residency, Anti-Nepotism and Patronage Policies

◆   A New Jersey school board's anti-nepotism policy applied to the immediate families of school board members, school administrators and board employees. However, the policy stated it "shall have no effect on tenured employees." The board notified an untenured teacher that her one-year teaching contract would not be renewed after she married a tenured teacher in the district. Both teachers sued the board, asserting violations of the state Law Against Discrimination (LAD). They added federal claims for due process and equal protection violations. The board presented evidence that the policy had a negligible effect on its workforce, and had the legitimate purpose of eliminating conflicts of interest that could arise when employees were married to each other. A state court agreed with the board, and the teachers appealed.

A New Jersey appellate division court held the untenured teacher's contract was not renewed because of her relationship to a tenured teacher, not on the basis of her marital status. The LAD was not designed to prohibit discrimination based on specific family relationships, even though the relationship itself existed by reason of a marriage. The teacher's due process claim failed. She was not tenured and had no right to continued employment beyond her current contract. The court held the policy was not unconstitutionally vague, as persons of common intelligence could discern its meaning and application. While the teacher asserted her contract was not renewed due to her religious beliefs, the policy did not even mention religion. **There was a rational basis for the policy, and it was reasonably related to avoiding conflicts of interest, discord and favoritism.** There was no Equal Protection Clause violation, because the policy did not directly and substantially burden the fundamental right to marry. *Wowkun v. Closter Board of Educ.*, 2006 WL 1933475 (N.J. Super. Ct. App. Div. 2006).

◆　A Texas school employee enrolled her children in private religious schools. She sought to be promoted from her teaching position to a middle school principalship. The superintendent refused to consider her application, stating the district required the children of all administrators to attend public schools. The employee sued the district and superintendent in a federal district court for civil rights violations. The court held the superintendent deserved qualified immunity, ruling the rights asserted by the employee were not clearly established. The Fifth Circuit Court of Appeals reversed the decision in 2003. *Barrow v. Greenville Independent School Dist.*, 332 F.3d 844 (5th Cir. 2003).

As the case was pending in the courts, the employee was promoted to high school assistant principal. She became a high school principal in 2004. The case returned to the district court, which found the delayed promotions deprived the employee of future salary increases, since she would have earned a higher salary in future years had her administrative career begun earlier. She might also establish a loss of future pension benefits. The court denied the motion to dismiss the employee's claims for punitive damages and mental anguish damages. Since the claims against the superintendent had been revived by the Fifth Circuit, the employee could amend her original complaint to seek these damages. **There was evidence that the superintendent refused to consider her for any promotion despite being subjectively conscious he was enforcing an illegal patronage policy.** *Barrow v. Greenville Independent School Dist.*, No. Civ.A.3:00CV0913-D, 2005 WL 39086 (N.D. Tex. 2005).

The court then held a jury trial. The jury found the employee did not prove any of her claims against the district, but did prove her parental rights claim against the superintendent. It returned a verdict against the superintendent for $15,455 in compensatory damages and $20,000 in punitive damages. The court rejected motions by both the employee and the superintendent regarding the jury's decision not to base any damage award on the exercise of religious rights. **The Fifth Circuit had found either the employee's parental or religious rights were sufficient to find the superintendent had violated a clearly**

established constitutional right. The superintendent did not deserve qualified immunity concerning the parental rights claim. The court refused to set aside the jury's decision to award punitive damages, as the superintendent testified he understood he should not make employment decisions based on where a person educated her children. The judgment could not be altered to hold the district liable under 42 U.S.C. § 1983. District liability resulted only if a decision-maker had final authority to set school policy. The district's board, not the superintendent, established school policy. *Barrow v. Greenville Independent School Dist.*, No. Civ.A.3:00CV0913-D, 2005 WL 1867292 (N.D. Tex. 2005).

    The case returned to the Fifth Circuit, which agreed with the district court that under Texas law, a school board retains the ultimate policymaking authority for hiring and promotion. School districts have no vicarious liability for federal civil rights violations under 42 U.S.C. § 1983. Districts are liable for the unconstitutional conduct of policymakers. The superintendent was not such a policymaker, and the court affirmed the judgment for the school district. There was no evidence that the superintendent's decision was based on religious discrimination, and the court also affirmed the judgment for the district on the employee's discrimination claim. *Barrow v. Greenville Independent School Dist.*, 480 F.3d 777 (5th Cir. 2007).

◆   An Ohio principal told a substitute teacher the district's new superintendent would not allow him to work full-time unless his son attended a district school. During the teacher's interview for full-time work, the superintendent asked him where his son would attend school. The teacher responded his son would remain at the Catholic school he had attended since kindergarten. The teacher was not hired full time, and he substituted for another year. The principal often repeated the superintendent's statement that the teacher would not receive a full-time contract unless he placed his son in district schools. The teacher turned down an opportunity for full-time employment with a former employer and enrolled his son in a district high school. The superintendent told him the school board wanted teachers to enroll their children in public schools because it "looked good to parents." The teacher claimed the superintendent then promised him a full-time contract. He began another year as a substitute and then reenrolled his son in a Catholic school. The superintendent discharged the teacher, stating he was "disloyal." The teacher sued the district, school board and superintendent in a federal district court for civil rights violations, religious discrimination and contract claims. The court awarded pretrial judgment to the district and board on several claims, but it denied qualified immunity to the superintendent.

    The superintendent appealed to the Sixth Circuit. **The court stated qualified immunity shields school officials from civil liability, unless a complaining party alleges a deprivation of a federal right that is "clearly established" at the time of the claimed violation.** The complaint stated the superintendent conditioned the teacher's employment on where his son attended school and discharged him based on the removal of his son from public school. These facts stated a claim for violation of the constitutional right of parents to direct the education of their children. The district court had correctly found the right of parents to direct the education of their children is clearly established. The Supreme Court recognized this right 81 years earlier in *Meyer v. Nebraska,*

262 U.S. 390 (1923). The teacher could not be denied public employment for exercising a fundamental right. **Since preexisting law clearly established the unlawfulness of denying employment based on constitutionally protected conduct, the superintendent was not entitled to qualified immunity.** *Barrett v. Steubenville City Schools*, 388 F.3d 967 (6th Cir. 2004).

◆ The U.S. Supreme Court addressed the issue of citizenship requirements for certification of non-U.S. citizens lacking a manifest intent to apply for citizenship. Two teachers who consistently refused to seek citizenship despite their eligibility to do so challenged the law under the Due Process Clause of the Fourteenth Amendment to the U.S. Constitution. In upholding the state law, **the U.S. Supreme Court held that teaching in the public schools is a state function so bound up with the operation of the state as a governmental entity as to permit exclusion from that function of those who have not become part of the process of self-government.** The Constitution requires only that a citizenship requirement applicable to teaching in the public schools bear a rational relationship to a legitimate state interest. Here, a rational relationship existed between the educational goals of the state and its desire that citizenship be a qualification to teach in the state. *Ambach v. Norwick*, 441 U.S. 68, 99 S.Ct. 1589, 60 L.Ed.2d 49 (1979).

III. VOLUNTARY EMPLOYEE LEAVE

A. Family and Maternity Leave

The Family and Medical Leave Act (FMLA), 29 U.S.C. §§ 2601–2654, grants eligible employees 12 weeks of leave in a one-year period for specific disabling health problems of employees and their families, including a family member's serious illness or a childbirth. It requires employers to issue two forms of notice to employees: (1) a generalized notice posted in the employer's premises; and (2) a customized notice of FMLA rights and procedures for employees who indicate a need to take leave for an FMLA purpose.

The federal Pregnancy Discrimination Act, 42 U.S.C. § 2000e(k), prohibits employers from discriminating against employees on the basis of pregnancy and requires them to treat pregnancy the same as any other disabling illness for all employment-related purposes, including health benefits.

◆ A Louisiana school employee worked as an assistant supervisor of school accounts. She helped school principals and staff with bookkeeping, working directly with school staff at various school sites. The employee took maternity leave. While she was on leave, the school board reorganized her department and revised her job description. Upon her return to work, she was no longer required to travel to various schools or to work directly with principals and staff. Instead, she audited the books of schools from a central office location. The employee claimed the change in her job title and her duties violated the FMLA and sued the school board in a federal district court. The court found her new position was equivalent to her former one and held for the school board.

On appeal, the U.S. Court of Appeals, Fifth Circuit, stated that employees returning from FMLA leave must be restored to their same job, or a comparable one with equivalent pay, benefits and working conditions. An "equivalent" new position must be "virtually identical to the employee's former position in terms of pay, benefits and working conditions, including privileges, perquisites and status. It must involve the same or substantially similar duties and responsibilities, which must entail substantially equivalent skill, effort, responsibility and authority." A new position must also have similar opportunities for promotion and salary increases as the former job. The court held that minimal, intangible changes in an employee's position do not violate the FMLA. In this case, the employee's duties before and after her leave both involved school accounting responsibilities. The court held the board offered her an equivalent position upon her return to work and affirmed the judgment for the school board. *Smith v. East Baton Rouge Parish School Board*, 453 F.3d 650 (5th Cir. 2006).

◆ An Illinois teacher stopped reporting for work and submitted a doctor's note stating she should not work until her blood pressure was controlled. The district notified her in writing when her available sick leave was exhausted. She was directed to request a medical leave of absence and to submit a physician's note explaining her illness, certifying her inability to work and stating her estimated return date. However, the district lacked a formal FMLA policy and did not supply her with any FMLA notice. The teacher claimed she submitted a doctor's statement indicating she could not perform her present job due to hypertension and the side effects of her medication. The district denied receiving any verification, and the superintendent warned her that the school board would consider discharging her for job abandonment. The teacher submitted a physician's statement indicating she had hypertension and fatigue resulting from her medication. Within a week, the board voted to dismiss her.

The teacher sued the board in a federal district court for violating her rights under the FMLA, and for due process violations. **The court held employees only need to provide an employer with enough information to place it on notice that FMLA-qualifying leave is needed and submit medical certification establishing a qualifying condition.** There was evidence that the superintendent received a note from the teacher's physician describing her hypertension before the board made its first attempt to discharge her. This was enough to demonstrate she had a "serious health condition" qualifying for FMLA protection. The school district had made no genuine effort to determine whether the teacher qualified for leave. The board did not show she violated any policy or failed to cooperate. The teacher could prevail if she provided medical evidence that she would have been able to return to work at the end of her leave. **Employers are required to provide employees both general and individualized notice of their FMLA rights. The FMLA imposes fines for failure to conspicuously post FMLA notices, but does not allow private lawsuits for not doing so.** The board was awarded judgment on this claim. *Holmes v. Board of Educ. of West Harvey-Dixmoor School Dist. No. 147*, No. 03 C 6897, 2006 WL 1843393 (N.D. Ill. 2006).

◆   An untenured New Jersey teacher told his class about his homosexuality to
address rumors circulating in his school. He then claimed he was targeted for
harassment by teachers and administrators. The superintendent of schools
placed the teacher on administrative leave for refusing to speak with him about
the harassment. The teacher fought with another teacher and reported regular
harassment. The superintendent reprimanded him three times for using class
time to discuss his homosexuality. The teacher accused the superintendent of
being homophobic, stopped coming to work and stated that he had been
hospitalized. He submitted a doctor's statement excusing him from work for at
least four weeks due to severe anxiety and stress. The school district informed
the teacher his paid sick leave had been exhausted and that he was "entitled to
protect his health benefits under the FMLA." However, a school attorney wrote
that he could not return to work without first providing doctors' "diagnoses,
prognoses and medical opinions" regarding his fitness for duty. The teacher met
with school officials and showed them a doctor's note clearing him to return to
work. The superintendent rejected the note as too "generic." The teacher sued
the board and superintendent in a federal district court for FMLA violations,
adding state discrimination and wrongful discharge claims.

     **The court stated federal regulations create a lenient standard for what
constitutes FMLA notice. Employees do not have to mention the FMLA to
obtain protection. They need only state a qualifying reason for leave.** The
doctor's note complied with FMLA notice requirements. The court rejected the
board's claim that it could require additional psychiatric or physical
examinations of any employee who deviated from normal, physical or mental
health. The court awarded judgment to the teacher on his FMLA claim for
retaliation. The board violated the act by requiring him to provide additional
medical reports as a condition of returning to work. The teacher complied with
FMLA regulations by presenting certification from his health care provider that
he could return to work. As there was evidence of unlawful discrimination, the
board was denied judgment on the state law claims. *Curcio v. Collingswood
Board of Educ.*, No. Civ.A. 04-5100 (JBS), 2006 WL 1806455 (D.N.J. 2006).

◆   A financially distressed New Jersey school board fired several custodians
and mechanics for excessive absenteeism. They sued the board in a federal
district court for violating the Family and Medical Leave Act. The court held the
board was "an arm of the state" and was therefore entitled to claim Eleventh
Amendment immunity. The employees appealed to the Third Circuit, which
explained that **the Eleventh Amendment provides the states immunity from
federal lawsuits by private parties, unless the state has consented to be
sued**. School boards and districts are usually considered political subdivisions
of a state, which are not entitled to claim immunity. A school board or district
may claim Eleventh Amendment immunity in limited circumstances.

     **The court found the most important consideration in this case was
whether payment of a judgment would come from the state.** The district
court had found this would occur, because 85% to 90% of the board's funds
came from the state. However, once state funds were deposited in the board's
account, they belonged to the board. Any judgment it paid was satisfied with its
own funds. The district had a poor tax base and was more financially dependent

upon the state than other entities, but it did not prove a judgment would come from the state. **New Jersey law generally treated school boards as separate political subdivisions from the state.** The district court incorrectly held the board was an arm of the state that could claim immunity, and its decision was reversed. *Febres v. Camden Board of Educ.*, 445 F.3d 227 (3d Cir. 2006).

◆   An Illinois college instituted a new dress code that prohibited employees from wearing shorts. An employee arrived at work wearing maternity shorts and refused to change after being instructed to do so. The college denied her request to be exempt from the dress code policy based on her pregnancy. The employee was suspended, then fired, for not complying with the dress code. She sued the college in a federal district court, alleging it denied her FMLA leave by firing her before she became entitled to exercise that right. **The court stated the FMLA requires an employee to provide sufficient notice to qualify for leave. For leave that is foreseeable, such as for the birth of a child, the employee must give at least 30 days advance notice.** The employee argued she had told the college she was pregnant and intended to take leave months before the dress code incident. The court found the employee gave sufficient notice. However, she did not show she would not have been terminated had she not requested FMLA leave. The evidence supported other reasons for the termination. **The court held the school did not retaliate because of the employee's request for FMLA leave and dismissed the case.** *Sample v. Rend Lake College*, No. 04-CV-4161-JPG, 2005 WL 2465905 (S.D. Ill. 2005).

◆   An Ohio teacher became ill with leukemia and asked to be excused from teaching her first period classes. Her school board denied the request, and she resigned. The teacher sued the board in a state court for FMLA violations, adding state law disability discrimination claims under Ohio Revised Code Section 4112.02. The court held for the board on the disability discrimination claims, but held for the teacher on her FMLA claims. The board appealed to the Court of Appeals of Ohio, which noted the teacher had asserted two FMLA violations. One involved failure to grant her request for leave. The other asserted failure to provide proper FMLA notice. The court held **the district did not satisfy the FMLA's "customized posting requirement" with general contract language about the FMLA in its collective bargaining agreement** with the teacher's union. **The district had to specifically notify the teacher about the FMLA when she requested leave.** Even if she did not qualify for FMLA leave, the district had a duty to discuss her rights under the FMLA.

The district's duty to discuss the FMLA arose when the teacher asked to reduce her workload. The trial court should not have awarded summary judgment to the teacher on her FMLA claim, as she did not specifically request FMLA leave. This claim was remanded for further proceedings. The court explained disability discrimination claims are allowed under Section 4112 for adverse employment action or failure to reasonably accommodate an employee's disability. The state administrative code placed a duty on employers to reasonably accommodate disabled employees. **Employers must offer their employees reasonable accommodations unless it causes an undue hardship. The court stated an employer must participate in an "interactive process"**

with employees who request an accommodation. Employers must make a good-faith effort to assist an employee requesting accommodation. There was evidence that the teacher had requested job restructuring or realignment as an accommodation. There was a factual dispute about the board's good-faith efforts to reasonably accommodate her disability. The trial court should not have entered summary judgment for the board on the disability discrimination claims, and the case was reversed and remanded. *DeCesare v. Niles City School Dist. Board of Educ.*, 798 N.E.2d 655 (Ohio Ct. App. 2003).

◆ A Texas district policy required employees to give at least two days notice for discretionary leave, which was granted on a first-come, first-served basis. Only two employees from any campus could take leave at the same time, and leave was limited to two consecutive days. The policy prevented employees from taking leave the day before or after a school holiday, at the end of the semester, on exam days, staff development days, or on the first and last days of a school semester. A teacher requested five days of leave immediately before a spring break to spend time with a grandchild. The school principal granted her two days of leave, and she took the remaining three days off without pay. The district denied the teacher's grievance, and she appealed. The state education commissioner held that **under the Texas Education Code, a personal leave policy must be neutral regarding the purpose for which leave is taken, cannot distinguish between uses for leave, and must have a rational basis.**

The commissioner held for the district, finding its policy was neutral and implemented for rational reasons such as continuity of instruction and minimizing the difficulty of obtaining substitutes. Nothing indicated the policy made it difficult for teachers to use their annual allocation of leave. On appeal, the Court of Appeals of Texas held the standard used by the commissioner reasonably interpreted legislative intent. It ensured districts would not distinguish between uses of leave, and it required policies to have a rational basis. **The commissioner's standard focused on the legislative intent to prevent policies that made it difficult for employees to take their leave. The policy had a rational basis and did not interfere with the use of leave. It reasonably limited leave, provided for classroom continuity and minimized disruption.** There was no evidence the principal had inquired into the teacher's reasons for taking leave. Substantial evidence supported the commissioner's decision, and the court affirmed it. *Amaral-Whittenberg v. Alanis*, 123 S.W.3d 714 (Tex. Ct. App. 2003).

◆ An Alabama school district hired an untenured third-grade teacher on August 9, 1999. Her contract was not approved until the end of the month, and not signed until September 8, 1999. She informed her principal three months later that she was pregnant and mentioned it again after another four months. The school board did not rehire the teacher at the end of the year, noting she failed to maintain proper relationships with students and parents, did not turn in data in a timely manner and did not maintain proper classroom control. She continued to receive paychecks and benefits from the district until August 30, 2000, more than a month after her child was born. The teacher sued the school board in a federal district court, asserting FMLA violations and retaliation.

The court rejected the teacher's argument that she met the FMLA's definition of "eligible employee." **FMLA eligibility required employment for at least 12 months by the employer from which leave is sought.** The teacher was not employed by the board for 12 months by virtue of her receipt of benefits and wages over a 12-month period. **The FMLA prohibits employers from interfering with employee rights under the act and does not require employees to be FMLA-eligible to file a retaliation claim.** However, **the teacher was unable to counter the board's evidence that non-renewal of her contract was based on her deficiencies as an employee, and the board was entitled to summary judgment.** *Walker v. Elmore County Board of Educ.*, 223 F.Supp.2d 1255 (M.D. Ala. 2002).

◆ An Arkansas employer exceeded FMLA minimum requirements by allowing employees to take 30 weeks of unpaid leave. It denied an employee's request for additional time off for treatment of Hodgkin's disease. **The employer never notified the employee that 12 of her 30 weeks of leave were considered "FMLA leave."** The employer discharged her when she did not return to work after she exhausted her 30 weeks of leave. The employee sued the employer in a federal district court, alleging violations of 29 C.F.R. Part 825.700(a), a U.S. Department of Labor regulation that does not count leave taken against an employee's FMLA entitlement if the employer does not designate it as "FMLA leave." The court agreed with the employer that it complied with the FMLA by allowing the employee to take 30 weeks of leave.

Appeal reached the U.S. Supreme Court, which stated the FMLA grants eligible employees 12 weeks of leave in a one-year period in the event of a disabling health problem, family member's serious illness or birth of a child. During these 12 weeks, the employer must maintain an employee's group health coverage. Upon return, the employee is entitled to reinstatement to the same position or an equivalent one. The Court held the regulation imposed a penalty on employers that was contrary to the law's remedial design, without regard to harm the employee might suffer from lack of notice. **A "categorical penalty" was incompatible with the FMLA and invalid because it fundamentally altered the law. Because administrative agencies are not allowed to exercise their authority inconsistently with the law, the court struck down the regulation** and affirmed the judgment for the employer. *Ragsdale v. Wolverine World Wide Inc.*, 535 U.S. 81, 122 S.Ct. 1155, 152 L.Ed.2d 167 (2002).

◆ **The U.S. Supreme Court held a school board rule requiring maternity leaves at mandatory and fixed time periods violated the Due Process Clause.** Two cases were involved in this appeal to the Supreme Court. In both cases school district rules required mandatory leaves at a fixed time early in pregnancy. The Court said that the rules were unconstitutional. The test in this case and other similar cases is that the maternity policy, in order to be valid, must bear a rational relationship to legitimate school interests. If there is a relationship, the rules pass constitutional examination; if not, they are unconstitutional and cannot be enforced. *Cleveland Board of Educ. v. LaFleur,* 414 U.S. 632, 94 S.Ct. 791, 39 L.Ed.2d 52 (1974).

B. Compensatory, Vacation and Sick Leave

◆ A group of Texas county deputy sheriffs agreed individually to accept compensatory time off in lieu of cash compensation for working overtime. The county implemented a budgetary protection policy under which supervisors set a maximum number of hours that could be accumulated by an employee. Employees were advised of the maximum and asked to take voluntary steps to reduce compensatory time accumulations. Supervisors could require employees to take their compensatory time at scheduled times. The deputies sued the county in a federal district court, alleging the compelled use of compensatory time violated the Fair Labor Standards Act (FLSA).

The case reached the U.S. Supreme Court, where the deputies claimed the FLSA prohibited public employers from compelling employees to take accrued compensatory time. The Court noted that Congress had amended the FLSA in 1985 to permit states and political subdivisions to pay employees one and one-half times their rate of pay for every hour in excess of 40 per week. The FLSA guaranteed that an employee could make some use of compensatory time upon request. However, **the FLSA did not expressly or impliedly limit a public employer from scheduling employees to take time off work with full pay**. Because the FLSA was silent on employer-compelled compensatory time use, the Court affirmed the judgment for the county. *Christensen v. Harris County*, 529 U.S. 576, 120 S.Ct. 1655, 146 L.Ed.2d 621 (2000).

◆ A Washington education employees' union required field representatives to use sick leave and vacation time in partial-day increments for any absence during a regular work week of 9 a.m. to 5 p.m., Monday through Friday. After the union deducted leave from one field representative's employee leave bank 79 times, he commenced a state court action against it under the Washington Minimum Wage Act (MWA) and the FLSA for failure to pay him time-and-one-half of his wage for overtime hours. The union removed the case to a federal district court, which held the representative was exempt from the MWA and FLSA as an administrative employee. He appealed to the Ninth Circuit, which affirmed the decision concerning the FLSA claim but remanded the case for reconsideration of the state law claim under the MWA. The district court asked the Washington Supreme Court to answer certain state law questions.

The supreme court held the MWA exempted executive, administrative and professional employees from its overtime pay requirements by allowing the payment of fixed salaries. To qualify as an exempt employee under both state and federal law, employees must meet both a "duties test" and a "salary basis test." The court stated employees must show their pay is "subject to improper deductions" to prove they are not paid on a salary basis. An employer's single improper salary deduction did not prevent a finding that an employee was paid on a salary basis. **The partial-day deductions from accrued leave banks did not create an automatic violation of the MWA**, but could be considered by the district court in determining whether the representative was exempt from its requirements as an administrative employee. *Webster v. Public School Employees of Washington Inc.*, 60 P.3d 1183 (Wash. 2003).

◆   After working for an Arkansas school district for almost 20 years, a teacher quit to work as a school counselor in Missouri. She sought payment for 90 days of unused sick leave, but the district refused because she did not meet either of the criteria for such a payment – retirement or being hired by another Arkansas school district. The teacher sued the district in a state court, asserting the law and her collective bargaining agreement required payment for accumulated, unused sick leave. The court dismissed the complaint, and the teacher appealed. The Arkansas Court of Appeals held state law allowed teachers to take unused sick leave as pay only when they retired or as a credit upon their employment by another Arkansas district. The teacher appealed to the state supreme court.

The court held the teacher's interpretation of state law could devastate school budgets with "a sudden onslaught of requests for cash payments." The terms of the teacher's employment provided for payment for unused sick leave only in the two circumstances identified by the lower courts. While the Arkansas legislature amended state law in 1979 to allow payments for unused sick leave, **such a payment was not required in this case, as the teacher was ineligible for retirement and had not been reemployed by another Arkansas district**. The court rejected her alternative argument that she had a vested contractual right to be paid for the sick leave. It affirmed the judgment. *Turnbough v. Mammoth Spring School Dist. No. 2*, 78 S.W.2d 89 (Ark. 2002).

◆   A bus mechanic worked for an Ohio district for more than 10 years and routinely requested to use part of his vacation time during hunting season. After generally approving these requests for years, the school superintendent began denying them. On one occasion, she approved only three days of the mechanic's request for 17 nonconsecutive vacation days during a two-month period. The superintendent relied on a district policy giving her the responsibility to see that vacations were scheduled in a way that caused the least interference with school operations. The mechanic then sued the school board in a state trial court for a declaration that he was entitled to vacation time under state law. The court dismissed the action and the mechanic appealed to the state court of appeals, which remanded the case. The trial court issued the declaratory relief sought by the mechanic, and the district appealed again.

The appeals court held the trial court decision did not grant the mechanic unfettered rights to use his vacation time, but rather declared the board policy an abuse of discretion under Ohio Rev. Code Section 3319.084. The trial court had found the board acted arbitrarily by summarily rejecting the mechanic's requests for time off when school was in session. The court found it was not convenient for the board if the mechanic took his vacation either during the summer or during the school year. This resulted in a situation in which the mechanic could not use his accrued vacation time. The trial court had properly interpreted Section 3319.084 as creating an employee right to accrue vacation time, while vesting school boards with the discretion to schedule use of the time. **The court affirmed the judgment, as the board abused its discretion by applying its rules in a way that deprived the mechanic of the use of his vacation time.** *Johnson v. North Union Local School Dist. Board of Educ.*, 750 N.E.2d 1233 (Ohio Ct. App. 2001).

◆   Missouri law prohibits public school teachers from striking. However, when St. Louis teachers reached a collective bargaining impasse with the school board, about 1,200 teachers, almost a third of the force, called in sick on the same day. The superintendent retroactively required the teachers to furnish physician statements to document their absences, and withheld their pay for the day. The teachers' union filed a grievance that was denied, but a Missouri trial court held school board regulations prohibited the compelled submission of physician statements, except for those employees who had been absent for five consecutive days or for 10 days during a school year. The union appealed.

The Missouri Court of Appeals affirmed the trial court's ruling that the superintendent was not authorized to order medical documentation for most of the absent employees. However, the trial court had inappropriately ordered the board to pay the absent employees. Although the superintendent was powerless to demand medical verification from most of the employees for taking leave, he still had the authority to seek non-medical verification for the absences. A separate issue of fact existed for each employee who had missed work on that day, and **each employee had the burden to establish that the absence resulted from a legitimate reason**. The court reversed and remanded this aspect of the case to the trial court for further consideration. *Franklin v. St. Louis Board of Educ.*, 904 S.W.2d 433 (Mo. Ct. App. 1995).

IV. REASSIGNMENTS, TRANSFERS AND SUSPENSIONS

Subject to state laws and the terms of any applicable collective bargaining agreement, courts have evaluated reassignment, transfer and suspension cases on the basis of whether the action violates the law or contract, or is arbitrary and capricious or an abuse of discretion.

◆   A Pennsylvania school board hired a superintendent under a five-year contract. Within two years, an administrative assistant formally complained to the school board president of a pattern of inappropriate sexual behavior. She claimed the superintendent retaliated against her for refusing his advances by demoting her, increasing her workload, imposing unreasonable deadlines, interfering with her duties and treating her differently than other employees.

The district suspended the superintendent with pay and hired an attorney to investigate the complaint. The attorney interviewed witnesses and then held an informal hearing, where he questioned the superintendent about the allegations in the presence of his counsel. The attorney advised the board there was sufficient evidence for termination. The board suspended the superintendent without pay or benefits. He filed a state court action for reinstatement with salary and benefits. The case reached the state supreme court, which held **the Pennsylvania School Code's removal provision did not divest school boards of their implied authority to suspend superintendents accused of serious misconduct**. Action could be taken against superintendents without pay and benefits, within the constraints of procedural due process. Section 211 of the School Code reflected the General Assembly's "explicit and open-ended confirmation of implied powers in furtherance of school districts' essential functions." The court affirmed the judgment. *Burger v. Board of School Directors of McGuffey School Dist.*, 839 A.2d 1055 (Pa. 2003).

◆ **The Supreme Court of Rhode Island held a teacher placed on paid administrative leave for sexual harassment had no right to a hearing as a "suspended" employee because he initiated a grievance concerning the harassment and resulting discipline.** The superintendent of schools placed the teacher on paid leave near the end of a school year, pending an investigation into the harassment charge. Over three months later, the superintendent issued the teacher a reprimand letter stating the language he used had been "highly unprofessional and in violation of the department's harassment policy." The teacher was allowed to resume his teaching duties upon completing a course. His teachers' association requested a grievance on his behalf. The grievance was intended to have the reprimand letter declared void and removed from district records. The school committee agreed to the association's request to bypass initial grievance steps and prepared to hear the case in its next executive session. The session was delayed because of the September 11, 2001 terrorist attacks, and the teacher sought to delay the hearing on two later occasions.

The teacher then petitioned a state superior court for an order requiring the school committee to conduct a hearing. The court disagreed with the district's argument that the teacher was barred from a hearing because he had elected instead to file a grievance under the collective bargaining agreement (CBA). It held the committee had suspended him under Rhode Island G.L. § 16-13-5 and was required to hold a hearing. The supreme court agreed to review the district's appeal. It discussed the "doctrine of election of remedies," which prevents a party to a collective bargaining agreement from using a CBA's grievance procedure and then pursuing the same dispute in a lawsuit. The teacher was not entitled to a Section 16-13-5 hearing as a "suspended" employee. The continuation of his pay after the disciplinary letter required finding that he was not "suspended." The use of paid administrative leave was a "reasonable means of immediately neutralizing a potentially contentious situation while minimally affecting the teacher." **Continuation of pay while pursing an investigation provided sufficient incentive to the district for a prompt investigation, reinstatement of the teacher or other appropriate action.** While the better practice was to provide a tenured teacher with the reasons for imposing leave, Section 16-13-5 did not require it. The court vacated the judgment and returned the case to the superior court. *Martone v. Johnston School Committee*, 824 A.2d 426 (R.I. 2003).

◆ Several female students at a Kentucky middle school alleged inappropriate sexual contact by a teacher, prompting an investigation by state police. The teacher took a voluntary leave after being indicted on 19 misdemeanor charges of third-degree sexual abuse. The school board rejected his request to grant a paid leave. The teacher's sexual abuse case was not tried until four years later, when he was acquitted of the charges. He then sought reinstatement and compensation for the intervening four years. The teacher was reinstated, but after two weeks, he was granted disability retirement based on posttraumatic stress syndrome related to the sexual abuse allegations. The board denied the teacher's request for back wages, and he sued it in a state court for back wages, sick pay, retirement benefits and personal days related to his four-year absence.

A state trial court granted summary judgment to the board, and the teacher appealed. The Court of Appeals of Kentucky considered his claim based on Section Three of the Kentucky Constitution, which prohibits payments by the state "except in consideration of public services." In a 1980 case, the appeals court construed this section as prohibiting the payment of public funds except for the actual performance of public services. The teacher argued there was consideration for the payment of back wages in his waiver of a hearing to consider his employment status. He also claimed the district agreed to rehire him following the eventual favorable outcome of his criminal prosecution. The court disagreed, ruling **a teacher cannot be paid for time spent on leave of absence**. The superintendent lacked authority to grant the teacher a leave of absence, as the board maintained this exclusive authority under state law. The court held the board was "not accountable for the failure of a superintendent to properly apply a statute," and affirmed the judgment. *Butler v. South*, No. 2002-CA-001343-MR, 2003 WL 21991570 (Ky. Ct. App. 2003).

◆ A Colorado administrator had worked for a school district for almost 20 years when an employee complained about an outburst during a meeting. She complained to the administrator's supervisor that he treated women less favorably than men, was abusive to all employees and had physically bumped her. The district superintendent for human resources began an investigation. The administrator admitted some of the allegations, and the district placed him on administrative leave with full pay and benefits, pending completion of the investigation. Although district policies did not mention "administrative leave," they permitted the suspension of an employee pending an investigation. Six months after the incident, the district placed the administrator on paid sick leave. The Colorado Public Employees' Retirement Association found him eligible for permanent disability retirement benefits.

The administrator sued the district in a federal district court for due process and equal protection violations through 42 U.S.C. § 1983. The court awarded summary judgment to the district, and the administrator appealed. The Tenth Circuit observed the administrator had voluntarily retired. **There was no due process violation by placing him on "administrative leave," despite the absence of such a classification in district policies. The policy allowed suspension during an investigation, and there was no distinction between "suspension" and "administrative leave."** The administrator received ample opportunity to present his version of the facts and respond to the allegations. There were no grounds for an equal protection violation, since he could not show that he was singled out for persecution. The court affirmed the judgment. *Bartell v. Aurora Public Schools*, 263 F.3d 1143 (10th Cir. 2001).

◆ Pennsylvania intermediate unit employees who provided services to disabled students requested suspension so they could be transferred to other duties under the state Transfer Between Entities Act. Even though each had more than seven years of experience with the intermediate unit, the school district they were being transferred to allowed only seven years of service to be counted toward salary steps, citing a limit of seven years that applied to newly appointed teachers under the parties' collective bargaining agreement. It also claimed that the agreement superseded contrary language contained in the transfer act. The employees filed a state court action seeking a declaration of their rights. The court agreed with the employees, and the district appealed.

The Commonwealth Court of Pennsylvania reversed the trial court decision, and the state supreme court agreed to review the case. It agreed with the employees that the transfer act had been enacted with recognition for the unique situation present in the state special education system. **The transfer act contained the legislative intent to distinguish between employee transfers and new hire situations to ensure that intermediate unit employees retained their benefits** within the education system. The court reversed the judgment, holding the employees were entitled to credit for all years of service. *Corbett v. Scranton School Dist.*, 557 Pa. 118, 731 A.2d 1287 (Pa. 1999).

V. REPORTING ABUSE AND NEGLECT

State laws require the reporting of suspected child abuse or neglect by teachers and other mandatory reporters and afford immunity for good-faith reports. In Catherine G. v. County of Essex, *below, New York's highest court suggested that teachers and other state-mandated reporters of child abuse and neglect "ought to err on the side of caution and make a report" if they reasonably suspect the abuse or neglect of a child.*

◆ A New York parent believed her son was inappropriately touching one of her three daughters. The parent told a pediatrician and called the state Central Register of Child Abuse and Maltreatment hotline, but the agency did not act because the son was not "a person legally responsible" for his sister under Section 412(3) of the New York Social Services Law. The parent then told a school principal and psychologist about the problem. The psychologist referred the sister to a crisis center for counseling. The pediatrician, psychologist, principal and a crisis center counselor did not make a report to the central register. Several months later, a third party reported incidents involving the two children. An investigation found only "an isolated incident of touching" and determined "no further threat existed." The parent later learned her son had repeatedly raped and sodomized all three girls. She sued the county and school district in a state court, claiming they breached their duties as mandatory child abuse reporters by failing to call the state hotline to report her son's conduct.

The case reached the Court of Appeals of New York, which noted the state Family Court Act's definition of "abused child" applied to a child harmed by a "parent or other person responsible for his care." **The boy was not a parent or guardian and he was not a "person legally responsible" for his sisters' care.** The parent did not leave them in his charge. There was no legislative intent to uniformly include minor siblings in the statutory definition. The court noted "ordinarily, the state would not need to intervene when a minor is abusing a sibling. Parents would usually be the ones to take action." The parent never suggested she could not stop her own son from harming her daughters. No mandatory reporter or any person answering the state hotline considered a parent's report about her own child's misconduct to be within the reporting statute. The court found no reason to believe a report by the school psychologist would have changed anything. **The legislature excluded mandatory reporting requirements for suspected abuse among siblings.** As the parent's claims were without merit, the court denied all of them. *Catherine G. v. County of Essex*, 3 N.Y.3d 175, 785 N.Y.S.2d 369, 818 N.E.2d 1110 (N.Y. 2004).

◆ A student who attended a private school in Massachusetts claimed the 22-year-old brother of a classmate forced her to have sex with him when she was 15. The incident occurred off school grounds. The brother had previously sexually abused another student and his own sister. The student sued the school in a Massachusetts court for negligently failing to report the brother's history of sexually abusing other students to the state Department of Social Services. The court held for the school, and the student appealed. The Court of Appeals of Massachusetts held that to prove the school was negligent, the student had to first show it had a duty to protect her. She was not on school property and was under her parents' control at the time of the assault. **The state child abuse reporting statute created no duty for the school to protect unnamed, potentially at-risk children in the abstract. It was instead intended to protect specific children that a reporter had reasonable cause to believe were at risk.** The court affirmed the judgment for the school. *S.I. v. Sennott*, 65 Mass. App. Ct. 1102, 836 N.E.2d 350 (Table) (Mass. App. Ct. 2005).

◆ New York parents sought the names of school employees who reported them for suspected child abuse and maltreatment to the statewide central register. In response to the report, the parents sued the school district and an employee in a state court, asserting claims for defamation and intentional infliction of emotional distress. They sought to compel the disclosure of the names of the persons who reported the incidents. The court granted the motion and the district appealed. The New York Supreme Court, Appellate Division, stated **Social Services Law Section 422 makes reports to the central register confidential and available only to persons and agencies listed by statute. The court stated the parents, as the subjects of the report, were entitled to see the report, but not the names of the reporters.** It rejected the trial court's reasoning that because a court could obtain these names, it had an implied right to release them to the subject. While the parents might encounter difficulty in bringing their civil action against the reporters, **Social Services Laws Sections 419 and 422 did not permit the release of reporter names based on allegations that the reporters acted with wilful misconduct or gross negligence**. This holding was consistent with the intent of Section 422 to protect the confidentiality of reporters of suspected child abuse. **Disclosure of the names might have a chilling effect on reporting and hamper agency efforts to help families.** The court reversed the trial court order. *Selapack v. Iroquois Cent. School Dist.*, 794 N.Y.S.2d 547 (N.Y. App. Div. 2005).

◆ An Ohio teacher was investigated for inappropriately touching and making sexual remarks to a ninth-grader. The principal determined the student was lying and took no action. The allegation was not reported to the police or a child services agency. Three years later, the teacher sexually assaulted another ninth-grader in a school athletic equipment room. He admitted the incident, resigned and was convicted of sexual battery. The student and her parents sued the school board, alleging its failure to report the first incident violated mandatory state abuse and neglect reporting requirements. The court held the board was entitled to sovereign immunity. The Court of Appeals of Ohio affirmed the sovereign immunity ruling and determined Ohio R.C. Section 2151.421 created a duty only to a specific child. Failure to report the 1996-97 incident could result in liability to that child, but not a different one. The Supreme Court of Ohio reversed the sovereign immunity ruling. After further proceedings, the case returned to the court for consideration of the abuse reporting issue.

The court found the legislation was enacted to protect children from abuse and neglect, not to protect political subdivisions and their employees. **Section 2151.421 encouraged teachers and others in special relationships with children to report known or suspected child abuse. It imposed criminal penalties for failure to report abuse and imposed liability on state political subdivisions if they failed to report abuse.** The General Assembly did not intend to withhold protection from children until they were actually injured. **Section 2151.421 required designated persons to immediately report their knowledge or suspicion that a child has suffered or faced the threat of any injury indicating abuse or neglect.** When circumstances indicated a danger existed to a child from a suspected perpetrator of another victim, and the reporter stood in an official relationship with the child, the law did not withhold its protection. The court held **teachers and school officials have a special responsibility to protect students committed to their care and control. They should appreciate that all students are in danger when an abuse report is received about a teacher.** A school board could be held liable for failing to report sexual abuse of a minor student by a teacher, when the failure caused the abuse of another minor student by the same teacher. *Yates v. Mansfield Board of Educ.*, 102 Ohio St.3d 205, 808 N.E.2d 861 (Ohio 2004).

◆ A New Jersey principal covered his school office windows in violation of a state law and always kept the door locked. The district superintendent did not monitor this and other violations, and the school board took no action to ensure he complied with the law. A school secretary frequently heard the principal taking pictures of students in his office but failed to report it because he was her "superior." Other staff observed many questionable incidents involving the principal and male students, but no one reported him. Law enforcement investigators arrested the principal for suspected child abuse and found 176 photographs in his office of male students with their legs spread in a chair. The parents of two student victims sued him in a state court for intentional conduct and civil rights violations under 42 U.S.C. § 1983. The jury returned a verdict of $275,000 for each student, adding over $100,000 for their parents.

The court entered a judgment of over $775,000 against the board, and the parties appealed. The case reached the Supreme Court of New Jersey, which held **school boards have a duty to protect students from foreseeable dangers**. It upheld the trial court's liability finding against the board, finding the **board did not fulfill its most basic obligation of protecting students and did not implement even rudimentary reporting procedures**. The board "grossly disregarded critical information" requiring scrutiny of the principal's activities. **School nurses and others breached their independent state law obligation to report child abuse to the appropriate state agency.** The trial court's liability decision was correct, but the supreme court upheld an appellate court's decision on apportionment of fault between the board and the principal. New Jersey law required public entities to contribute their percentage of liability to a joint defendant such as the principal. This rule applied even if the apportionment involved both negligent and intentional acts. The court affirmed the decision to direct a verdict against the board and remanded the case to the trial court. *Frugis v. Bracigliano*, 827 A.2d 1040 (N.J. 2003).

◆ A South Dakota elementary school counselor met several times with a third-grader. The child said her father had engaged in questionable behavior on several occasions and had asked her to touch his penis. The counselor discussed these statements with a high school guidance counselor and decided the third-grader's reports were probably untrue, based on the student's tendency to fabricate or exaggerate. District policy forbade employees from speaking with parents about abuse allegations, but the counselor discussed the child's statements with the parents. Over a year later, the father was investigated by the county sheriff's office for sexual assault of a neighbor child. The sheriff's office questioned the counselor about her conversations with the student. In a written report to school officials about the assertions, the teacher explained she did not believe them but admitted contacting the parents. The father pleaded guilty to sexually assaulting the neighbor child. The state then brought criminal charges against the counselor for failing to report child abuse. The charges were eventually dismissed, but the district notified the counselor of its intent to terminate her employment. A state circuit court affirmed the decision.

The Supreme Court of South Dakota found no evidence to support the district's conclusion that the failure to report child abuse was a breach of the counselor's contract. The court remanded the case to the board for a determination of whether the counselor violated school policy by talking to the parents, implicitly requiring the board to apply a subjective standard on the issue of whether she suspected child abuse. The board made no additional findings of fact and again voted to discharge the counselor. The supreme court found the case involved procedures used by the district when discharging an employee and had nothing to do with the interpretation of child abuse reporting statutes. The counselor's actions in speaking to the parents were in no way excused. However, the board was required to make findings of fact in support of its decision and had failed to do so. **In the absence of a finding in the record that the counselor suspected child abuse, the board action was arbitrary, capricious and an abuse of discretion.** The court affirmed the judgment. *Hughes v. Stanley County School Dist.*, 638 N.W.2d 50 (S.D. 2001).

CHAPTER SEVEN

Employment Discrimination

	Page
I. OVERVIEW	279
II. SEX DISCRIMINATION	280
A. Title VII of the Civil Rights Act	280
B. Pregnancy Discrimination	285
C. Equal Pay and Gender	287
D. Sexual Harassment	290
E. Sexual Orientation	292
III. RACE AND NATIONAL ORIGIN DISCRIMINATION	294
A. Race Discrimination	294
B. National Origin	297
C. Affirmative Action	300
IV. RELIGIOUS DISCRIMINATION	302
V. AGE DISCRIMINATION	307
VI. DISABILITY DISCRIMINATION	311
A. Rehabilitation Act of 1973	311
B. Americans with Disabilities Act	314
C. State Statutes	320
VII. DISCRIMINATION AGAINST VETERANS	322

I. OVERVIEW

Title VII of the Civil Rights Act of 1964 prohibits employment discrimination based upon race, color, sex, religion or national origin. It applies to any employer with 15 or more employees. In addition, every state has enacted anti-discrimination statutes.

The federal Civil Rights Act, 42 U.S.C. § 1983, is also used in employment discrimination cases. It prohibits any "person" (including a school district) from depriving any other person of rights protected by the U.S. Constitution or laws. Section 1981 of the federal Civil Rights Act provides that all persons have the same right to make and enforce contracts as "white citizens."

The constitutional prohibition against employment discrimination is found in the Equal Protection Clause of the Fourteenth Amendment, which commands that no state shall "deny to any person within its jurisdiction the equal protection of the laws."

The U.S. Equal Employment Opportunity Commission (EEOC) is empowered to enforce Title VII. Persons alleging discrimination must pursue their remedies within the EEOC before they are allowed to file suit against employers under Title VII. Plaintiffs who prevail in employment discrimination lawsuits are entitled, where appropriate, to back pay, front pay, accumulated seniority and other benefits, and attorneys' fees. Punitive and compensatory damages are available where discrimination has been shown to be intentional.

As the Supreme Court noted in *St. Mary's Honor Center v. Hicks*, 509 U.S. 502, 113 S.Ct. 2742, 125 L.Ed.2d 407 (1993), intentional discrimination can be inferred from a disbelief of the employer's stated reason for the adverse employment action. Title VII's bona fide occupational qualification (BFOQ) exception allows employers (especially religiously affiliated private schools) to use sex, religion or national origin as a hiring criteria if one of those characteristics is a "bona fide occupational qualification necessary to the normal operation of that particular business or enterprise." A BFOQ defense will fail unless the qualification at issue is a matter of "necessity," not merely employer convenience. Successful assertion of a BFOQ defense will result in dismissal of a discrimination claim. Race can never be a BFOQ.

II. SEX DISCRIMINATION

A. Title VII of the Civil Rights Act

In the following case, the U.S. Supreme Court held the anti-retaliation provision of Title VII is not limited to employment-related activity. The provision covers any employer action that could discourage a reasonable employee from filing a discrimination claim.

◆   A Tennessee railway employee was the only woman in her department. Her primary job duty was to operate a forklift. The employee complained that her immediate supervisor told her that women should not be working in the department. The company disciplined the supervisor but also transferred the employee from her forklift duties to standard track laborer tasks. A supervisor said her reassignment reflected complaints by co-workers that a "more senior man" should have the "less arduous and cleaner job of forklift operator." The employee filed a federal Title VII complaint against the railway. The company suspended her without pay for insubordination. The employee then filed a second retaliation complaint with a federal agency, alleging the company placed her under surveillance in response to her complaints.

The case reached the Supreme Court, which explained that **the core anti-discrimination provision of Title VII of the Civil Rights Act of 1964, 42 U.S.C. § 2000e-2(a), forbids employment discrimination based on race, religion, sex, or national origin. By contrast, the anti-retaliation provision of Title VII prohibits discrimination against an employee or job applicant who has made a charge, testified, assisted, or participated in a Title VII proceeding or investigation.** The Court held it was not improper to read Title

VII's anti-retaliation provision more broadly than its anti-discrimination provision. The anti-retaliation provision was created to prohibit a wide variety of employer conduct intended to restrain employees in the exercise of protected activities. This included the retaliatory filing of a lawsuit against an employee. **The Court had previously held Title VII does not create "a general civility code for the American workplace." Petty slights, minor annoyances, and lack of good manners did not create actionable retaliation.** In this case, there was sufficient evidence to support the jury verdict finding the reassignment and suspension amounted to retaliation. The reassignment was "materially adverse" to the employee, who went unpaid for 37 days during which she was uncertain of her employment status. The Court affirmed the judgment in her favor. *Burlington Northern & Santa Fe Railway Co. v. White*, 126 S.Ct. 2405 (2006).

◆   A teacher/coach and his wife worked for a Texas school district. He sued the district in 1999, claiming Title VII violations. The action was settled, but the district did not rehire him for 2000-01, based on complaints about his coaching abilities. The district did not fill his position. As a result, the girls' coaching staff was made up of the teacher/coach's wife and a male employee. The district later placed the male employee on administrative leave and brought in high school coaches to help coach the middle school girls' teams. When the male employee resigned, the district decided to delay hiring a replacement. The district did not post any job announcement, review applications or interview anyone for the male employee's position, but the teacher/coach submitted an application for it. The teacher/coach's wife complained to the district athletic director that another coach should be hired. The athletic director allegedly stated that he could not hire her husband because of his previous lawsuit.

The teacher/coach sued the school district in a federal district court for not rehiring him. He asserted retaliation by the district based on his prior lawsuit. A jury agreed with the teacher/coach and found he should receive $5,400. The parties appealed to the U.S. Court of Appeals, Fifth Circuit. The court found the teacher/coach did not suffer "adverse employment action." The district did not fill the male employee's position. **The court held an employer does not discriminate or retaliate against an employee if there is no job vacancy.** The athletic director was not responsible for deciding if an available position existed at the middle school at the time of his statements. The district had determined that teaching duties could be covered by a long-term substitute. The teacher/coach submitted an unsolicited application for full-time work. **The fact that a position had become vacant did not make it "available."** The jury verdict was not supported by the evidence, and the court reversed the decision. *Adams v. Groesbeck Independent School Dist.*, 475 F.3d 688 (5th Cir. 2007).

◆   After teaching high school Spanish for three years, a Tennessee teacher expected to gain tenure. She claimed her principal sexually harassed her, and she filed a complaint against him with the U.S. Equal Employment Opportunity Commission (EEOC). Shortly after the teacher filed her EEOC charge, the district notified her of her employment termination. With the assistance of her union, the teacher appealed the action to a school district administrator. The administrator found the election to non-renew the teacher's contract would stand. However, she would be rehired for the next school year. If the teacher met evaluation requirements, she would receive tenure at the end of the next school year. The teacher sued the school district in a federal district court for sex discrimination under Title VII. After a trial, a jury found the delay in granting tenure did not amount to an "adverse employment action." Since adverse employment action is a necessary element of a Title VII claim, the court awarded judgment to the district. The teacher appealed to the Sixth Circuit.

The court found the teacher did not lose any tangible benefits or income as a result of the initial denial of tenure. After teaching another school year, she received tenure. **To prevent lawsuits involving "trivial workplace dissatisfaction," a Title VII plaintiff must show discrimination has resulted in some "adverse employment action." This occurs if there is "a materially adverse change in the terms of employment." Mere inconvenience or alteration of job responsibilities is insufficient to prevail in a Title VII case.** Job reassignments without salary or work hour changes do not ordinarily constitute adverse employment decisions. According to the U.S. Supreme Court in *Burlington Industries v. Ellerth*, 524 U.S. 742 (1998), "tangible employment action constitutes a significant change in employment status," such as hiring, firing, failure to promote, reassignment to significantly different duties or a change in benefits. The court found that while the teacher had been initially denied tenure, she received another opportunity to prove herself. She was no worse off with respect to seniority, income or benefits despite being granted tenure after her fourth year, rather than her third. As the teacher lost no income or benefits and did not claim her job had been materially changed, the court affirmed the judgment. *Shohadaee v. Metropolitan Government of Nashville and Davidson County*, 150 Fed.Appx. 402 (6th Cir. 2005).

◆ A Texas bus driver asked another driver to punch his time card in at work the morning after the two had been drinking at a bar. The other driver did so, but the driver later called in sick and never showed up for work. The school board accepted a review committee's recommendation to discharge both drivers for misconduct. They sued the school district in a state court for gender discrimination, claiming the district did not fire female employees who had also clocked in for their co-workers. After a trial, the court awarded the drivers lost wages and $175,000 each for mental anguish. The state court of appeals affirmed the judgment, and the district appealed to the Supreme Court of Texas.

The court stated the Texas Commission on Human Rights Act prohibits employment discrimination based on race, color, disability, religion, sex, national origin or age. The act was based on Title VII of the Civil Rights Act of 1964, and as the legislature intended it to parallel federal law, the court reviewed federal cases for guidance. **The court found federal case law deemed employees "similarly situated if their circumstances are comparable in all material respects."** To prove the discipline was discrimination based on sex, the drivers had to show time clock violations by female employees of comparable seriousness to their own. **The U.S. Court of Appeals, Fifth Circuit, has held that to show discrimination based on disparate discipline, an employee must show the misconduct for which he or she was discharged was nearly identical to that engaged in by the employee with whom** comparison is sought. The court found that while female employees had been reprimanded for time card violations, and some incidents went unpunished, there was no incident in which a female employee did not show up for work. In no case had female employees conspired to conceal an absence. The nature and degree of the time card violations by the female employees could not be compared with the bus drivers' conspiracy to conceal an absence. The court refused to find the male and female employees were "similarly situated," as their misconduct was not of comparable seriousness. The court reversed the judgment and held the drivers should take nothing. *Ysleta Independent School Dist. v. Monarrez*, 177 S.W.3d 915 (Tex. 2005).

◆   A female South Dakota physical education teacher applied for a full-time middle school PE teaching position. She had previously supervised both male and female students and had helped a physically challenged male student change into a swimsuit for an adaptive PE course. The job notice for the full-time position did not specify a gender preference or limit applicants by gender. The school district had no other written requirements or policies documenting gender as a qualification for the job. The district interviewed only male candidates and did not consider the teacher's application. It then hired a male who was not currently teaching, did not have a valid teaching certificate, and was not certified to teach swimming, perform CPR or administer first aid. The teacher had the certifications and qualifications the male teacher lacked. She sued the school district in a federal district court for violating Title VII of the Civil Rights Act of 1964 and Title IX of the Education Amendments of 1972.

The court agreed with the district that gender-based discrimination is permitted if it is reasonably necessary to the normal operation of a school. However, an employer must have some basis in fact for believing no members of one sex could perform the job. The employer was required to show it could not reasonably arrange job responsibilities to minimize the clash between the privacy interests of students and the non-discrimination rule of Title VII. The court noted a factual dispute over whether locker room supervision was a bona fide occupational qualification of the full-time PE teaching position. The job description was silent concerning gender, and the district admitted it did not communicate a male-only job requirement until after it hired a male. The court held there was a factual dispute concerning the district's ability to rearrange job duties if it hired a female PE teacher. As the evidence indicated a balance of male and female PE teachers was necessary and that opposite-sex staff occasionally supervised locker rooms, the court denied the district's motion for pre-trial judgment. *McCardle v. Mitchell School Dist.*, No. Civ. 03-4092-KES, 2005 WL 1118154 (D.S.D. 2005).

◆   A New York school psychologist earned excellent performance reviews in her first two years of employment. During her third year, she took a three-month maternity leave. As the psychologist's tenure review approached, the principal and a district personnel director questioned her commitment to her job and suggested she wait until her son was in kindergarten to have another child. She claimed the director and principal said if she received tenure, she would reduce her work hours and could not be a good mother and employee. The principal and director wrote the district superintendent a formal memo recommending she not receive tenure due to serious issues with parents and teachers, persistent organizational difficulties, inaccuracies in her reports and failing to show improvement. The superintendent accepted the recommendation, and the school board terminated her probationary appointment. The psychologist sued the board, superintendent, principal and director in a federal district court under the Equal Protection Clause and state law. The court held for the board and administrators, and she appealed to the U.S. Court of Appeals, Second Circuit.

The court stated the psychologist had to prove intentional discrimination to prevail in a sex discrimination claim under the Equal Protection Clause. The district court had erroneously found statements attributed to the director and principal were "stray remarks." The court held **stereotyped comments about a woman's perceived inability to combine work and motherhood were direct evidence of sex discrimination**. The Supreme Court held in *Price Waterhouse v. Hopkins*, 490 U.S. 228 (1989) that stereotyped remarks may be evidence of gender discrimination. Though the psychologist had no evidence that the district treated "similarly situated men differently," the court held she could proceed with her case. The principal and director were personally involved in the alleged deprivation of rights. **A reasonable jury could find they gave false reasons for denying the psychologist tenure, and that discrimination was a motivating reason for their action.** The principal and director were not entitled to qualified immunity, as **the constitutional right to be free from unlawful gender discrimination was clearly established** at the time they denied tenure. The court vacated and remanded the judgment concerning the principal and director, but it affirmed the judgment for the superintendent and school board. They were not personally involved in the decision to deny tenure, and the board had no policy or custom of gender discrimination. *Back v. Hastings on Hudson Union Free School Dist.*, 365 F.3d 107 (2d Cir. 2004).

◆   A female Michigan coach served for 10 years as a girls' varsity basketball coach. She also coached the boys' junior varsity for eight years and was an assistant coach of the boys' varsity team for eight years. The coach applied for the boys' varsity head coaching position when the incumbent retired. The only other applicant was a less experienced male teacher who had coached the boys' freshman team for two years. The superintendent walked out of the coach's interview, and district hiring committee members expressed concerns about complaints from the community if it hired her for the boys' varsity job. The school board president voiced similar concerns, and the male teacher was hired for the job. The coach sued the school district in a federal district court for sex discrimination under Title VII and the state's Elliott-Larsen Civil Rights Act. A jury returned a verdict of $455,000 for the coach. The court ordered the district to name her coach of the boys' varsity basketball team, but it reduced the award by $210,000 – the amount the jury awarded her for future damages.

On appeal, the Sixth Circuit Court of Appeals rejected the district's argument that she did not suffer adverse employment action. As she would have received a pay raise with the promotion, denial of the boys' varsity coaching job was an adverse employment action. **The court rejected the district's assertion that it had legitimate, nondiscriminatory reasons for not hiring the coach.**

It found direct evidence that gender was a factor in its decision. The board president and the superintendent made similar comments about hiring a female coach, and the superintendent admitted board members opposed her application. The district court was entitled to reduce the jury verdict by the amount of future damages, and the court affirmed the judgment. *Fuhr v. School Dist. of City of Hazel Park*, 364 F.3d 753 (6th Cir. 2004).

◆   A Wisconsin custodian twice used her seniority rights to bump a male co-worker from a daytime custodial position. She claimed the co-worker then enlisted the help of the district human resources administrator to get his daytime position back. The custodian stated she became the target of numerous discriminatory and harassing remarks and incidents, including being given an impossible workload. The school board took no action when she complained by letter, and the principal and district human rights administrator imposed an extended period of probation upon her in excess of that required by the collective bargaining agreement. The custodian filed administrative complaints alleging discrimination by the board with state and federal civil rights agencies, and she then sued the district in a federal district court for violating Title VII.

The court awarded summary judgment to the district, and the custodian appealed. **The Seventh Circuit held the custodian met the threshold requirement for a hostile work environment claim with a number of factual allegations she was exposed to disadvantageous terms or conditions of employment to which members of the other sex were not exposed.** She had been required to perform many tasks traditionally performed by outside contractors or the maintenance department, and she presented evidence of harassment by the male superintendent, principal, supervisor and male custodians. The frequency of their misconduct supported a finding of objective hostility, and there was no evidence that men were treated similarly. **The district could be liable for allowing the hostile work environment because it never took corrective, preventive or investigatory action in response to her complaints.** The court vacated the judgment on this claim. *Haugerud v. Amery School Dist.*, 259 F.3d 678 (7th Cir. 2001).

B. Pregnancy Discrimination

The Pregnancy Discrimination Act, 42 U.S.C. § 2000e(k), is an amendment to Title VII prohibiting employment discrimination on the basis of pregnancy. The act requires employers to treat pregnancy the same as disabling illnesses for purposes of health benefits programs and all other employment-related purposes. For example, if an employer's policy is to allow two months unpaid leave to employees with disabling illnesses, a pregnant employee must be granted two months unpaid leave. For more cases involving health-related leaves of absence, please see Chapter Six, Section III.

◆   A Washington custodian who was her district's only full-time custodial employee took maternity leave in 1998. The district's family leave policy stated employees need not be reinstated to a specific job if the job was eliminated by a restructuring or reduction in force. The custodian took maternity leave again in 1999, when she experienced complications with twins. The district superintendent allowed her to structure a leave of over nine months through the use of sick days, family leave, holidays and unpaid leave time. The district demolished some buildings and built new ones during the custodian's second maternity leave. It then reduced daily custodial hours from 13 to nine district-wide and reallocated this time between the two part-time custodians. The district later hired a full-time custodial employee from another school system.

The custodian sued the district in a state court for discrimination on the basis of gender, pregnancy and family status. She added claims for retaliation, wrongful discharge and breach of the reduction-in-force policy. The court awarded summary judgment to the district, and the custodian appealed. The Court of Appeals of Washington held **the district was not required to reinstate an employee whose job was eliminated by a restructuring or reduction in force caused by a lack of funding or work**. Family status was "conspicuously absent" from the list of unfair discriminatory employment practices in Section 46.60.180 of the Revised Washington Code. **Because the state had no clear public policy against family status discrimination, the wrongful discharge claim failed.** The district showed its decision not to rehire the custodian was the result of a major construction project, not discrimination. The court found no significance in comments by the superintendent indicating the custodian would benefit by staying home with her children while receiving unemployment benefits. **Stray remarks that are unrelated to the decision-making process do not prove discrimination.** The trial court properly held for the district and the court affirmed its judgment. *Ackerman v. Quilcene School Dist. No. 48*, No. 29300-5-II, 2003 WL 21744331 (Wash. Ct. App. 2003).

◆   A Maine school district hired a teacher on a probationary basis after she served as a long-term substitute for most of one year. Although she experienced classroom management issues, her performance improved during the year and she received a second probationary contract. At the time the teacher received the second contract, she was pregnant. She missed the first weeks of her second probationary year due to her pregnancy. Upon resuming her duties, she received a poor evaluation due to her messy and disorganized classroom. The teacher showed improvement during the year, and she eventually received recommendations for a continuing contract. She became pregnant again during her second probationary year and asserted she was visibly pregnant when the school board voted not to award her a continuing contract. Without explanation, the board replaced her with a teacher who was not pregnant.

The teacher sued the district in a state court. The case was removed to a federal district court, which **applied the same legal standard to the Maine Human Rights Act and pregnancy discrimination claims under Title VII. Title VII prevents an employer from discharging an employee on the "categorical fact of her pregnancy," or in retaliation for taking an authorized maternity leave.** In tenure denial cases involving alleged poor performance, employees may avoid summary judgment by showing an employer's stated reason for denying tenure is a pretext. The board asserted the teacher was not a good enough teacher to deserve tenure. Two board members voting against tenure were allegedly unaware of her pregnancy. The principal and superintendent had given her good evaluations when her case came up for review. However, **a board member who was alleged to be unaware of the teacher's pregnancy saw her frequently at a time when the signs of her advancing pregnancy were unmistakable.** The teacher pointed out inconsistencies and weaknesses in the statements of four board members, and she showed a financial motive for her termination. The court denied summary judgment to the board, finding the teacher produced sufficient evidence that it gave false justifications for denying her tenure to make a trial necessary. *Johnson v. School Union No. 107*, 295 F.Supp.2d 106 (D. Me. 2003).

◆ A high school teachers' association entered into a collective bargaining agreement with an Illinois board of education. The agreement prohibited pregnant teachers from taking sick leave for pregnancy-related disability and then taking maternity leave at the expiration of the sick leave. The collective bargaining agreement excluded maternity benefits from the sick leave bank. The U.S. government sued the board and teachers' association in a federal district court for violation of the Pregnancy Discrimination Act. **The court held the collective bargaining agreement provision allowing teachers to take sick leave in conjunction with any other leave exclusive of maternity leave did not violate the Pregnancy Discrimination Act, as maternity leave was a gratuitous extra option.** However, sick leave bank provisions that automatically excluded maternity benefits discriminated against pregnant teachers who elected to utilize accumulated sick leave for a pregnancy-related disability. This violated the Pregnancy Discrimination Act. *U.S. v. Board of Educ. of Consolidated High School Dist. 230,* 761 F.Supp. 519 (N.D. Ill. 1990).

C. Equal Pay and Gender

The Equal Pay Act requires employers to pay males and females the same wages for jobs involving "equal skill, effort, and responsibility, and which are performed under similar working conditions, except where such payment is made pursuant to (i) a seniority system; (ii) a merit system; (iii) a system which measures earnings by quantity or quality of production; or (iv) a differential based on any other factor other than sex." The act has been interpreted to require only that the jobs under comparison be "substantially" equal. Strict equality of the jobs under comparison is not required. Claimants may also bring sex-based wage claims under the Equal Protection Clause.

◆ A Massachusetts school district hired a female teacher in its technical division for the first time in 1993. She began at a salary level for employees with five years of experience, and she had the highest starting salary of any teacher hired by the division up to that time. Her job duties were essentially the same as those of her male colleagues. Five years later, the district hired a male technology teacher with four years of teaching experience and 18 years of contracting experience. His starting wage was the same as that earned by an employee with seven years of teaching experience. The female employee and a colleague believed the district paid them lower starting wages than males. They filed a complaint with the state commission against discrimination, then sued the district in a state court. The court awarded over $60,000 to the employee and over $115,000 to a female colleague, plus their attorneys' fees and costs.

On appeal, **the Supreme Judicial Court of Massachusetts noted the state equal pay act allowed for variations in rates of pay based on seniority.** The legislature recognized that employers may offer different compensation levels based on prior experience. In this case, **the collective bargaining agreement authorized the superintendent to set the salaries of new teachers. The agreement did not specify how previous experience would be considered in particular cases.** The evidence showed the superintendent employed by the district at the relevant time did not use her discretion in any clear or consistent way to set initial salaries for either men or women. The trial court committed error when it found male teachers were given more credit for prior work experience than females. The evidence did not support a finding that the superintendent's methods were discriminatory. There was evidence that four male technical teachers who were hired before the females all received three years of credit, even though their relevant work experience varied from over six years to 17 years. The court held that when compared with male teachers, the female employees were not subjected to wage discrimination based on gender. The district's allocation of credit for prior work experience did not have a discriminatory impact on women. As the lack of uniformity in starting salaries did not establish wage discrimination, the court reversed the judgment. *Silvestris v. Tantasqua Regional School Dist.*, 446 Mass. 756 (Mass. 2006).

◆   Two female Pennsylvania school employees claimed they were paid less than male teachers with less seniority. Both male teachers received full credit for their past employment history, and one had insisted on a certain starting wage. Although a female teacher had 13 years of experience at the time she was hired, and a female librarian had 12, they did not receive full credit for this time, based on lapses in their employment history. The females sued the school district in a federal district court for violating the Equal Pay Act.

The court assigned a set of questions to the jury. In its deliberations, the jury sought clarification of one question regarding the district's motivation in determining employee wages. The court answered "the [district] must prove that a factor other than sex caused them to set the salaries that they did." The jury unanimously held for the district, and the employees appealed. The U.S. Court of Appeals, Third Circuit, held both the jury question and the court's clarification correctly stated the district's burden to defend the salary policy. **In Equal Pay Act cases, employers must produce evidence that would allow a reasonable jury to find a factor unrelated to gender motivated its salary decisions.** During the trial, the district introduced evidence that the disparity in pay was not caused by gender, but by the particular certification possessed by one male teacher, his salary demand, and the collective bargaining agreement. As the district introduced sufficient evidence to allow a jury to reasonably determine the wage disparity was caused by a factor other than sex, the district court had properly denied the female teachers' motion for a new trial. *Henderson v. Chartiers Valley School*, 136 Fed.Appx. 456 (3d Cir. 2005).

◆   An employee worked for an Alabama school board as a special projects coordinator for three years. She then began to perform the same duties as district community school coordinators, but she was not paid according to their salary schedule. The board turned down the employee's request for a salary adjustment, and she sued it in a state court. The court held for the board, and the Alabama Civil Court of Appeals affirmed. On appeal to the Alabama Supreme Court, the employee argued an equal protection claim may be brought without proof of discrimination under *Village of Willowbrook v. Olech*, 528 U.S. 562 (2000). In *Olech,* the U.S. Supreme Court recognized equal protection claims brought by a "class of one" when there is intentionally different treatment of a person from others who are similarly situated without a rational basis.

The state supreme court explained the intent of the Equal Protection Clause is to protect every person from intentional discrimination. Equal protection claims may be brought when a party alleges intentional treatment that is different from others who are similarly situated, and there is no rational basis for the different treatment. The court allowed the employee to pursue her claim based on different pay for performing community-school coordinator job duties. She satisfied the *Olech* factors by claiming the board intentionally treated her differently from community school coordinators who performed the same work, without having a rational basis. The lower courts improperly found the board had legitimate reasons for the wage differential. As there was no evidence for this holding, the court reversed it. *Ex Parte McCord-Baugh*, 894 So.2d 679 (Ala. 2004).

◆   A Washington school nutrition director earned the same as her district's maintenance and transportation directors, who were males. The maintenance director threatened to leave the district unless he received a raise. The district complied, but it did not grant raises to the nutrition director or the director of transportation. The nutrition director then began to campaign for a matching raise. The district denied her requests, relying on an annual statewide salary survey indicating her pay was competitive with food service supervisors in comparable districts. The survey also showed the maintenance supervisor was overpaid in relation to maintenance supervisors in comparable districts. The nutrition director claimed her job duties were increasing, and she met with two school board members. Her employment evaluations became unfavorable and she was reprimanded for insubordination. The disparity in pay between the nutrition director and the male directors continued to grow under the district's merit pay system. The district stated she made less than the male directors due to budgetary constraints and the maintenance director's previous threat to quit.

The nutrition director sued the district in a state court for violating the state equal pay act, and for sex discrimination and retaliation. The court awarded summary judgment to the district, and the nutrition director appealed. The Court of Appeals of Washington noted the state equal pay act was virtually identical to its federal counterpart. It found the district did not rely on the salary survey, paying the maintenance director a wage higher than the mean for districts with twice the enrollment and more than directors earned in the district where he had once threatened to accept a job. **The court held the nutrition director raised the possibility that the survey simply listed titles and pay rates, and** perpetuated discrimination in traditionally female job designations such as her own. **Market forces could justify a pay disparity, but there had to be some legitimate business reason for the disparity.** The district did not state a rational policy for relying on the survey and selectively withholding raises from employees who had received equal pay for 10 years. The nutrition director was entitled to the opportunity to contest the district's use of the survey and other explanations for the pay disparity. The court reversed the judgment on her equal pay act and retaliation claims. *Hudon v. West Valley School Dist. No. 208*, 97 P.3d 39 (Wash. Ct. App. 2004).

◆ A North Dakota school administrator asserted her school board violated state law by voting not to renew her contract. She claimed the board president stated "a woman can't handle [the administrator's] job," and that she was "a woman in a man's job." Although the administrator was paid $37,200 in her last year of employment, the board hired a male to replace her at a salary of $60,000. It also hired another male employee to help the replacement and paid him $46,500. A state trial court rejected her claims, but the state supreme court reversed its decision. The parties then reached a settlement that preserved the administrator's right to pursue her claims for gender discrimination and unequal pay. She sued the district in a federal district court, which dismissed the claims, ruling they were barred by the state court settlement.

The administrator appealed to the Eighth Circuit, which held she had explicitly reserved her right to bring the claims that formed the basis for her federal lawsuit. The board president's comments provided sufficient evidence of discrimination to allow the case to go to trial. While stray remarks in the workplace do not constitute evidence of discrimination, the president's comments were not stray remarks. Since the remarks were direct evidence of discrimination, the administrator was entitled to the inference that the president influenced other board members to vote against the contract. **Because it was permissible to infer she was paid less than male employees for performing the same work, there was evidence of an equal pay violation** that had to be considered by a jury. The court reversed and remanded the case. *Simmons v. New Public School Dist. No. Eight*, 251 F.3d 1210 (8th Cir. 2001).

D. Sexual Harassment

Sexual harassment is a form of sex discrimination that violates Title VII. Harassment creating a hostile work environment entails discriminatory behavior if a reasonable person would find it hostile, as well as the victim's subjective perspective. See Harris v. Forklift Systems, Inc., *510 U.S. 17 (1993).*

In 1998, the Supreme Court held Title VII is violated if an employee is "exposed to disadvantageous terms or conditions of employment to which members of the other sex are not exposed." In Burlington Industries, Inc. v. Ellerth, *524 U.S. 742 (1998), and* Faragher v. City of Boca Raton, *524 U.S. 775 (1998),* **the Court held Title VII may impose vicarious liability on employers for sexual harassment committed by supervisors.** *However, where no adverse employment action (such as discharge or demotion) occurs, an affirmative defense is available. In such cases, the employer may be able to avoid liability* *by showing that it exercised reasonable care to prevent and promptly correct any sexual harassment, and that the employee unreasonably failed to avail herself of any employer remedies or otherwise avoid harm.*

◆   A Nevada school employee met with two male supervisors to review psychological evaluation reports from job applicants. She alleged that during a meeting, one supervisor read a report that an applicant had commented to a co-worker, "I hear making love to you is like making love to the Grand Canyon." The employee claimed one supervisor then said, "I don't know what that means." According to the complaining employee, the other supervisor responded, "Well, I'll tell you later," and the two males chuckled. The employee was transferred to another job 20 months after this incident. She sued the school district in a federal district court for sexual harassment. The court awarded summary judgment to the district, but the Ninth Circuit reversed the decision.

The U.S. Supreme Court accepted the district's petition for review and held no reasonable person could have believed the single incident giving rise to the lawsuit violated Title VII. **Sexual harassment is actionable only if it is so severe or pervasive as to alter the conditions of the victim's employment and creates an abusive working environment.** In this case, the employee's job required her to review the offensive statement in the applicant's file. She conceded it had not upset her to read the written remark. The supervisor's comment and the other male's response was at worst "an isolated incident" that could not be considered serious. There was "no causality at all" between the job transfer and the employee's complaint. The Court reversed the judgment, stating **there must be a close proximity in time between an employer's knowledge of an employee's protected conduct and an adverse employment action, if this is the employee's only evidence of retaliation.** *Clark County School Dist. v. Breeden*, 532 U.S. 268, 121 S.Ct. 1508, 149 L.Ed.2d 509 (2001).

◆   A Michigan counselor worked full-time for the Detroit Board of Education and part-time at a vocational center. She had a long-term sexual relationship with her supervisor at the vocational center. When it ended, he became involved with another employee. The counselor claimed the supervisor threatened her with adverse employment action if she did anything to interfere with his new relationship. She stated the other employee taunted and embarrassed her. The vocational center discharged the counselor, and she sued the school board in a state court for sexual harassment, breach of contract and intentional infliction of emotional distress. The court granted the board's motion for summary disposition, but the state court of appeals held there were grounds for a sexual harassment claim. The board appealed to the state supreme court.

The court explained **claims for sexual harassment require a showing of unwelcome sexual advances, requests for sexual favors, or other verbal or physical conduct or communications of a sexual nature. When submission to these forms of conduct or communication is used as a factor in decisions affecting a person's employment or education, the person may prevail in a "quid pro quo" harassment action.** Sexual conduct or communication substantially interfering with employment or education may create grounds for a "hostile environment" sexual harassment claim. The court held "sexual harassment requires conduct or communication that inherently pertains to sex." The conduct and communication alleged by the counselor fell short of this definition. The supervisor's threats were not inherently sexual, but were instead based on the consequences of interfering with his new relationship. Conduct or communication that was not sexual in nature was not "sexual harassment." State law did not prohibit personal animosity between romantic rivals, even if it involved sexual competition. Since the counselor could not demonstrate a connection between the conduct or communications she complained about and sex, the court reinstated the trial court's judgment. *Corley v. Detroit Board of Educ.*, 470 Mich. 274, 681 N.W.2d 342 (Mich. 2004).

◆ A Colorado school clerical worker said her supervisor repeatedly pinched her, "hovered over her," and made derogatory gestures and remarks. She complained and sought a job reclassification based on her belief that her duties did not match her job description and salary. After the worker complained, she claimed the supervisor gave her negative evaluations. When the district did not reclassify her, she filed a grievance. Near this time, the worker became an active recruiter and organizer of a union for the district's classified employees. As the district had yet to recognize a union for classified employees, she sought assistance in prosecuting her grievance from a representative of the district's teachers association. The district found this request violated its collective bargaining agreement with the teachers association. It refused to allow the representative to attend meetings related to the worker's grievance.

The worker filed a Title VII lawsuit against the school board in a state court, asserting sexual harassment and retaliation. The court held for the board, and she appealed. The Court of Appeals of Colorado found **pinching violated Title VII and was listed as an example of sexual harassment in the district's employee manual.** The worker was entitled to a trial on the sexual harassment and Title VII retaliation claims. The court held she could proceed with her breach of contract claim, as she showed the district did not follow progressive discipline procedures from its employee handbook. As there was evidence that the district denied the grievance because of anti-union bias, the court reversed the judgment on the retaliation claim based on union association. *Smith v. Board of Educ. of School Dist. Fremont RE-1*, 83 P.3d 1157 (Colo. Ct. App. 2003).

E. Sexual Orientation

In *Oncale v. Sundowner Offshore Services*, 523 U.S. 75 (1998), **the U.S. Supreme Court held that same-sex harassment is a violation of Title VII.** Title VII is not a general code of workplace civility, but covers conduct that is severe or pervasive enough to create an objectively hostile or abusive work environment. No language in Title VII bars a sex discrimination claim when the complaining party and alleged perpetrators are of the same sex.

◆ A Minnesota teacher was placed on administrative leave near the end of his probationary period, then discharged. He sued the school district in a state court, asserting he had reported many incidents of bad behavior by students during his three years with the district, including taunts that he was homosexual.

The teacher claimed a right to be free from any abuse or harassment by students in the school environment under Minnesota Statutes Section 121A.03 and the district's own policies. The court held for the district, and the teacher appealed to the Court of Appeals of Minnesota.

The court rejected the teacher's argument that Section 121A.03 created an absolute legal duty for school districts. **The section required the commissioner of education for the state to maintain a model policy on discrimination, harassment and violence. School boards were required to adopt and conspicuously post their policies and verify they conformed to state requirements.** The teacher did not argue the school district violated a particular part of section 121A.03. He did not show the district failed to investigate three incidents of student harassment, two of which involved students who implied he was homosexual. In each case, the district responded by disciplining the students and informing the parents. The court held district policymaking and enforcement required discretion. The trial court had properly held the school district was protected by discretionary immunity. The court affirmed the judgment. *Malone v. Special School Dist. No. 1*, No. 2004 CA 00347, 2005 WL 3289468 (Minn. Ct. App. 2005). The Supreme Court of Minnesota declined to review the case in 2006.

◆ A middle school teacher worked for a Wisconsin school district for many years before disclosing his homosexuality. After the disclosure, he reported being subjected to derogatory comments, insults, name-calling, lavatory graffiti and obscene or harassing phone calls. The school disciplined students who engaged in offensive behavior, such as using inappropriate or offensive racial and/or gender-related language. It also granted the teacher's request to transfer to an elementary school, where the level of student harassment dropped but parental taunts and threats increased. The teacher experienced a "mental breakdown" and resigned. The district terminated his employment, and he sued the district a federal district court for failing to take effective steps to prevent harassment. The court held for the district, and the teacher appealed.

The Seventh Circuit stated **homosexuals do not enjoy a heightened level of constitutional protection. Title VII does not provide a private right of action based on sexual orientation discrimination, and there is no remedy under 42 U.S.C. § 1983 for sexual orientation discrimination based on rights created under Title VII.** There was no evidence that the district treated the teacher's complaints differently than race or gender complaints. Its decision not to address sexual orientation discrimination was not an equal protection violation. School administrators are primarily required to address and prevent harassment and abuse directed at students, not teachers. The lack of a district policy against sexual orientation discrimination was not evidence of deliberate indifference, and there was no evidence of discrimination against homosexual teachers or students in the district. **The Equal Protection Clause does not require a district to do anything about "parental unpleasantries" that take place off school grounds.** As the district could not have done more without expending a disproportionate share of its resources, it was entitled to summary judgment. *Schroeder v. Hamilton School Dist.*, 282 F.3d 946 (7th Cir. 2002).

III. RACE AND NATIONAL ORIGIN DISCRIMINATION

A. Race Discrimination

The Equal Protection Clause prohibits discrimination by states and state agents, such as school boards. Its coverage, however, is limited both to government bodies and to situations involving intentional discrimination. The latter requirement was imposed by the U.S. Supreme Court in Washington v. Davis, *426 U.S. 229 (1976), which involved a written verbal skills test that was a requirement for employment as a police officer. The test resulted in the rejection of a disproportionately high percentage of African-Americans.*

The Supreme Court held an adverse impact or effect on racial minorities was not sufficient to show a violation of the Equal Protection Clause. Proof of intent to discriminate was required. *Because in most cases it is difficult to prove an intent to discriminate (except in affirmative action cases),* **civil rights statutes such as Title VII provide a more common basis for claims of employment discrimination in the school context.**

◆   The U.S. Court of Appeals, Seventh Circuit, held the removal of an Illinois employee's flex-time schedule was retaliation for the filing of a race discrimination complaint. The flex time schedule was critical to the employee, who had a child with Down syndrome. During her 16 years of employment before her complaint, she had been allowed to work a flexible schedule to care for him. **This is an example of "actionable retaliation" against an employee by an employer.** *Washington v. Illinois Dep't of Revenue,* 420 F.3d 658 (7th Cir. 2005).

◆   A South Carolina teacher of African-American heritage was not subjected to race discrimination when his school district did not provide him with additional time to pass the state Education Entrance Examination. He failed the exam after several attempts, and the district discharged him. **The U.S. Court of Appeals, Fourth Circuit, held the teacher did not produce enough evidence of illegal race discrimination or a hostile work environment to proceed with his case. He did not show the district treated non-African American employees more favorably or that harassment by co-workers created an abusive atmosphere.** *Nathan v. Richland County School Dist. Two,* 180 Fed.Appx. 462 (4th Cir. 2006).

◆   For six years, an African-American teacher received acceptable evaluations as a marketing education teacher at a Missouri alternative high school. An assistant principal expressed concerns about her teaching, communications and classroom management skills. The following year, he reprimanded the teacher for swearing at a student and using a person's income tax form for instructional purposes without consent. The teacher was placed on an improvement plan designed to address her deficiencies. She was again reprimanded for denigrating students and using profanity. The teacher received another performance improvement plan, but was transferred to a newly created business education teacher position. The school board hired a white employee to fill her former position. The teacher filed a grievance to challenge the action, then filed a race discrimination complaint. The assistant principal reprimanded the teacher again for cursing in class and for tape-recording her class after being instructed not to do so. The board issued her a notice of deficiency alleging incompetency, inefficiency and insubordination. The notice also noted the teacher's "conduct reflects a mental condition making it unfit for [her] to instruct or associate with children." The board gave the teacher five months to correct her deficiencies. At her request, a three-member team evaluated her performance. The evaluators all expressed strong concerns, and each recommended discharge. After a hearing, the board discharged the teacher. She sued the district and school officials in a federal district court for employment discrimination and retaliation.

The court awarded summary judgment to the district and officials, and the teacher appealed. The U.S. Court of Appeals, Eighth Circuit, held the teacher's case "quickly unravels because she failed to show she met the Board's legitimate expectations." While she claimed her teaching ability far exceeded that of any other teacher at her school, she did not present any evidence of this. Instead, **there was evidence of poor evaluations and failure to cure serious and repeated deficiencies. Even under known scrutiny and with five additional months to improve, the teacher's performance was unacceptable.** Evaluators found serious deficiencies in her relationships with students and inability to structure lessons. They found her instruction was harming her students due to negativity. One evaluator indicated she was "probably the worst teacher that I've observed." The teacher's denial of this evidence was insufficient to allow her to proceed with her claims. The board had legitimate, nondiscriminatory reasons for discharging her, and the judgment for the district was affirmed. *Shanklin v. Fitzgerald*, 397 F.3d 596 (8th Cir. 2005).

◆   The U.S. Court of Appeals, Fifth Circuit, held a Mississippi school board did not discriminate against a 57-year-old African-American female applicant by hiring a "young white female" for a principal position. **The applicant did not perform well in her interview, and she did not prove the board's use of the interview was discriminatory. The board used standardized questions for the interviews and selected the candidate who received the highest score. The court held the board's decision was based on a legitimate, non-discriminatory reason.** It rejected the applicant's claim that the board ignored all her objective qualifications and relied instead on a subjective interview. *Todd v. Natchez-Adams School Dist.*, 160 Fed.Appx. 377 (5th Cir. 2005).

◆   A New York teacher claimed her school district refused to extend her employment contract because she was female and in an interracial marriage. She argued the district treated her differently from male directors and those not married to someone of another race. She received a poor performance evaluation and was subsequently discharged. She argued the actions were in retaliation for her voicing concerns about discrimination, and she sued the district in a federal district court. The court awarded judgment to the district, and the teacher appealed. **The U.S. Court of Appeals, Second Circuit, found no evidence to support the teacher's claim that she was fired in a** discriminatory manner. **Even had she established discrimination, the district proved she wasn't performing well, and she had personality conflicts with other staff.** As the teacher failed to show the district discharged her because of her activities to improve race relations, the court affirmed the judgment. *Moss v. Enlarged City School Dist. of City of Amsterdam*, 81 Fed.Appx. 389 (2d Cir. 2003).

◆ A Hawaii elementary school teacher applied for several teaching positions, but the state education department did not select her for any of them. She claimed she was not selected because of her race and national origin, and she filed a complaint against the department with the state civil rights and equal opportunity commission. The teacher later sued the department in a federal district court for disparate treatment. The court accepted the department's nondiscriminatory reasons for not selecting her for employment, and she appealed. The U.S. Court of Appeals, Ninth Circuit, held the teacher failed to show disparate treatment because she could not show adverse employment action. It accepted the department's nondiscriminatory reasons for denying her the jobs. The court also rejected the teacher's hostile work environment claim. **A "hostile work environment" requires proof of verbal or physical conduct that is racial in nature.** The teacher offered no evidence of such acts, and the court affirmed the judgment. *Stone v. State of Hawaii, Dep't of Educ.*, 81 Fed.Appx. 159 (9th Cir. 2003).

◆ An Indiana school district promoted two African-American transportation supervisors to implement major changes to the transportation system. When the school year began, there was mass confusion over the system, which resulted in drivers not knowing their routes, children being stranded or delivered to the wrong places, and thousands of students missing school. The district superintendent described the supervisors as being incapable of solving the crisis, hired a consulting firm and demoted them. The supervisors filed a race and sex discrimination complaint in a federal district court against the superintendent and school board. The court awarded summary judgment to the superintendent and board, finding the demotions were nondiscriminatory.

The supervisors appealed, claiming their demotions violated Title VII and 42 U.S.C. §§ 1981 and 1983. The Seventh Circuit found the supervisors did not identify any similarly situated male or white employees who were treated more favorably than they were. **It was not improper to hold the supervisors accountable for their performance.** The restructuring of the department was based on legitimate, nondiscriminatory reasons. There was no merit to the supervisors' assertion that they were entitled to be reinstated to their former positions based on a departmental policy. No other employee was restored to a former position. The court noted that **to prevail in a Title VII or Section 1981 case, claimants must show their employers have singled them out because of race or gender. The supervisors had not done so.** There was evidence that several men and women of various racial backgrounds also suffered adverse employment actions related to the crisis, while others were promoted. *Patton v. Indianapolis Public School Board*, 276 F.3d 334 (7th Cir. 2002).

◆   An African-American teacher was reprimanded for violating a Louisiana school's corporal punishment policy and showing his class an R-rated film. An evaluation outlined his deficiencies, and the board placed him on an intensive assistance plan. The superintendent recommended that his contract not be renewed, but the board did not vote on the recommendation. The superintendent then falsely notified the teacher that the board had voted against renewing his employment, and a white female was hired to take his place. The teacher sued the board in a federal district court for race discrimination under Title VII and 42 U.S.C. § 1981. The court awarded summary judgment to the board.

The teacher appealed to the Fifth Circuit. The board stated a legitimate, nondiscriminatory reason for failing to renew his contract, and the teacher was then required to show that the reason was pretextual. In order to show pretext by an employer in a discrimination case, the complaining party's evidence must be substantial. A subjective belief that discrimination has occurred is insufficient. **The board had given a legitimate, nondiscriminatory reason for not renewing the teacher's contract based on his poor employment evaluation and inappropriate conduct.** The superintendent's unlawful conduct and the board's assumption that he had the unilateral authority to terminate the employment of a non-tenured teacher had no bearing on whether the contract non-renewal was pretextual. Without evidence that the superintendent would be more tolerant of similar conduct by a white teacher, his allegedly racial comments at the time the teacher was hired did not establish a discriminatory motive. The court affirmed the judgment for the school board. *Auguster v. Vermilion Parish School Board,* 249 F.3d 400 (5th Cir. 2001).

B. National Origin

◆   Persons of Arab descent are protected from racial discrimination under 42 U.S.C. § 1981. A Pennsylvania college professor, born in Iraq, was a U.S. citizen and a Muslim. He sued St. Francis College in a U.S. district court under Title VII and Section 1981 after St. Francis denied his tenure request. The district court ruled that Section 1981 did not cover discrimination based on Arab ancestry. On appeal, the U.S. Supreme Court noted Section 1981 states "[a]ll persons ... shall have the same right to make and enforce contracts ... as is enjoyed by white citizens..." In affirming the decision, the Court noted that although Section 1981 does not use the word "race," the statute forbids all racial discrimination in the making of private as well as public contracts. The Court cited several dictionary and encyclopedic sources to support its finding that under Section 1981, Arabs, Englishmen, Germans and certain other ethnic groups are not to be considered a single race. Based on the history of Section 1981, it concluded Congress "intended to protect from discrimination identifiable classes of persons who are subjected to intentional discrimination solely because of their ancestry or ethnic characteristics." The Court affirmed the decision. **If the professor could prove he was subjected to intentional discrimination because he was Arab, rather than solely because of his place of origin or religion, he could proceed under Section 1981.** *St. Francis College v. Al-Khazraji,* 481 U.S. 604, 107 S.Ct. 2022, 97 L.Ed.2d 749 (1987).

◆   A Utah school district hired a Native American teacher on a provisional basis. She claimed the principal discriminated against her, but not others, for returning late from lunch. The teacher stated the principal told her she was "geographically, racially, culturally, and socially out of place" at the school. He gave her bad evaluations and eventually recommended her contract not be renewed. The teacher asked the superintendent to evaluate her performance. He came to the school three times to observe her, but was unable to ever see her actively teaching her class. The superintendent reviewed critical letters from parents and other teachers, and he met with the teacher twice to discuss her effectiveness and her discrimination claims. He decided the teacher should not be rehired. The teacher claimed the principal made a racially derogatory remark to her on her last day, and she sued the district in a federal district court.

The court held for the district. On appeal, **the U.S. Court of Appeals, Tenth Circuit, held a supervisor's statement may show a discriminatory motive in a Title VII case**. Under certain circumstances, the employer may be held liable if a decisionmaker who discharges the employee "merely acted as a rubber stamp, or the 'cat's paw' for a subordinate employee's prejudice," even if the supervisor had no discriminatory motive. The court held the teacher could not rely on the "cat's paw doctrine" to connect the principal's alleged bias to the superintendent's decision. The doctrine did not apply if the decisionmaker made an impartial investigation, as had occurred in this case. The superintendent's meetings with the teacher were important, as they allowed her to state her version of the events. The superintendent's meetings with the teacher and his investigation of her discrimination complaints allowed her to respond to the non-renewal decision. As this was enough "to insulate his decision from any bias of a subordinate," the court affirmed the judgment. *Natay v. Murray School Dist.*, 119 Fed.Appx. 259 (10th Cir. 2005).

◆   An Alaska school district employed a teacher of Lebanese descent as a substitute for three years. It refused to hire her for a full-time position, citing her accent. During the teacher's third year as a substitute, the district's equal employment officer assured her she would be hired to replace a teacher who was leaving the district. However, the district again rejected her for full-time employment, stating her accent was the reason. After the teacher learned the district had hired a health teacher without conducting competitive interviews, she insisted on speaking to the district superintendent. Staff members turned her away, and in a state of extreme frustration, she said she was very angry and did not want to "blow up." Staff interpreted this as a threat to blow up the building. They summoned police, but the police did not prosecute the teacher. The district informed the teacher by letter that she would not be offered any substitute work. She filed a charge against the district with the state human rights commission for discrimination on the basis of national origin and her Muslim religion.

The teacher then sued the school district in a federal district court under Title VII. The case reached the Ninth Circuit, which held the district court had improperly given the district the benefit of certain factual inferences. In pretrial stages of a lawsuit, courts must construe the facts in favor of the party who is not moving for dismissal – in this case, the teacher. She met her initial burden of showing national origin and religious discrimination. Although the district asserted it had legitimately denied her applications based on her qualifications, accent and temperament, the court was required to construe the facts in her favor. **There was evidence that the teacher was substantially more qualified for one position than the person hired, and that her accent was not an impediment to teaching. It also appeared she did not make any bomb threat and that the staff members who kept her from the superintendent's office were influenced by stereotypes about her religion or nationality.** The district court had properly awarded judgment to the district on one of the retaliation claims, but its decision was otherwise reversed and remanded. *Raad v. Fairbanks North Star Borough School Dist.*, 323 F.3d 1185 (9th Cir. 2003).

◆   A New Mexico teacher of Native American descent did not apply for a vacant position as athletic director for her district, since it was only a part-time position and her current job was full time. After the position remained vacant for several weeks, the district combined it with vice principal duties to create a single, full-time position. The new position was advertised in a central office, the high school, a Web site and a local newspaper. The teacher claimed to be unaware that the full-time position had been created until just before the start of the next school year. She asked the school principal if it was still open, but he told her that it had been offered to the only person who had applied for it. A few days before school was to resume, the sole applicant declined the position, and the district re-posted it. The principal interviewed a male Caucasian teacher, and he was hired for the position. The Native American teacher applied for the job a month later. After filing an unsuccessful grievance, she sued the board and school officials in a federal district court for race and sex discrimination.

The district court awarded summary judgment to the school officials, and the teacher appealed to the Tenth Circuit. The court noted that her claims for relief implicated theories of disparate treatment and disparate impact under Title VII. It agreed with school officials that **use of an emergency hiring procedure was not direct evidence of discrimination. The emergency was an example of a nondiscriminatory "business necessity," created by the immediate need to fill a position that had remained open for two months.** With the start of school only one day away, the only applicant for the job had withdrawn his name from consideration and numerous athletic events were underway or about to begin. In the absence of a formal job application, the district had no obligation to follow up on the teacher's inquiry. In any event, she did not apply for the job until after the board had approved the Caucasian teacher's hiring. **The emergency hiring practice did not create a disadvantage to the Native American teacher or have a disparate impact on minority employees.** The court affirmed the judgment for the board and officials. *Kerr v. Valdez*, 55 Fed.Appx. 491 (10th Cir. 2002).

◆   A white Connecticut teacher began dating a Hispanic/Native American man who also taught at her middle school. The school investigated a sexual harassment complaint against him by two other female teachers, one of whom was his former girlfriend. The white teacher discussed the sexual harassment investigation, in direct violation of a directive not to do so, and later tried to intimidate witnesses. The Hispanic/Native American teacher's contract was not renewed, and the white teacher made a false child abuse charge against one of his accusers. The district proposed terminating her contract, and an impartial hearing panel recommended termination for insubordinate and otherwise unacceptable conduct. The teacher resigned. After she did so, the board took the precaution of discharging her. The teacher sued the district in a federal district court for constitutional rights violations, race discrimination based on her association with the Hispanic/Native American teacher, and related claims.

The court stated **the teacher could not prevail unless she could show her termination was motivated by race.** The discrimination claim was not well founded, as a reasonable juror would be bound to agree with the hearing panel's decision rejecting any racial motivation. The court held the district's interest in performing a difficult, sensitive and potentially volatile investigation of a sexual harassment complaint outweighed the teacher's speech interests. Her speech had taken place in the context of the investigation, and **the district was entitled to believe her activities presented a risk of obstructing the investigation and seriously interfering with school functions.** The teacher's due process claim was meritless, as she was not entitled to another hearing after submitting her resignation. The court awarded summary judgment to the district on her federal claims, allowing her to refile any state claims in a state court. *McDermott v. Town of Windham Public Schools,* 225 F.Supp.2d 180 (D. Conn. 2002).

C. Affirmative Action

Government entities, including school districts, must comply with the Equal Protection Clause, as well as Titles VI and VII when devising affirmative action programs. The U.S. Supreme Court struck down a no-minority-layoff (or "affirmative retention") clause in a teacher collective bargaining agreement in Wygant v. Jackson Board of Educ., *below.*

However, in United Steelworkers of America v. Weber, *443 U.S. 193 (1979), the Court held a voluntary affirmative action in employment plan could withstand a Title VII challenge if: 1) there was a statistical disparity between the races or sexes in a job category, or if the institution was guilty of discrimination in the past; 2) the affirmative action plan did not "unnecessarily trammel" the rights of non-minority employees; 3) the plan did not stigmatize non-minority employees; and 4) the plan was temporary in nature and scheduled to terminate upon the achievement of its goals.*

◆ An affirmative action (or "affirmative retention") plan implemented by the Jackson, Michigan, Board of Education called for the layoff of non-minority teachers with greater seniority than some minority teachers. A federal district court held the importance of providing minority teachers as "role models" for minority students as a remedy for past "societal discrimination" justified the layoff provision. The U.S. Court of Appeals, Sixth Circuit, affirmed the decision and the non-minority teachers appealed to the Supreme Court. The Court reversed the decision and held the non-minority teachers had been unfairly discriminated against in violation of the Equal Protection Clause.

The Court rejected the "role model" justification for retaining minority teachers on the ground that such a theory would allow racially based layoffs long after they were needed to cure the ills of past discrimination. Even if the Jackson school board had sufficient justification for engaging in remedial or "benign" racial discrimination, laying off white teachers was too drastic and intrusive a remedy. **While hiring goals and promotion policies favorable to minorities are acceptable under the Equal Protection Clause, the actual laying off of a certain race of employees was held unconstitutional.** "Denial of future employment is not as intrusive as loss of an existing job," observed the Court. The lower court rulings were reversed. *Wygant v. Jackson Board of Educ.,* 476 U.S. 267, 106 S.Ct. 1842, 90 L.Ed.2d 260 (1986).

◆ A Los Angeles high school physical education teacher sought a transfer to a similar position at a magnet school located on the same campus. According to the teacher, the principal of the high school told him he need not apply for the transfer, because the teacher was of "the wrong ethnic origin." The teacher did not formally apply for the transfer, instead relying on this statement. In fact, the district's policy allowed employment transfers that did not cause a school's percentage of minority faculty to deviate more than 15% below or 25% above the overall percentage of minority faculty in Los Angeles Unified School District (LAUSD) schools. The transfer policy did not apply to hiring or firing decisions, and provided that its goals could be modified as a result of the qualifications of available applicants, to meet student instructional needs, or to meet other school requirements. The teacher sued the principal, school district, school board, district superintendent and the union representing LAUSD teachers in a federal district court, asserting equal protection violations.

The court held the policy did not violate the teacher's equal protection rights, and he appealed. The U.S. Court of Appeals, Ninth Circuit, considered LAUSD's claim that the teacher lacked legal standing to proceed with his case because he had never applied for the transfer. The court found it was uncertain if the transfer policy would have affected the teacher. The principal's statement might be "wholly irrelevant" if he lacked decision-making power. He was the principal of the high school, not the magnet school where the teacher sought to work. **The court also noted the transfer policy could be modified based on the qualifications of applicants. LAUSD might have accepted the teacher's application based on need, his qualifications, or any other reason.** Since there were many unanswered questions about the transfer policy and whether the teacher had legal standing to pursue the action, the court returned the case to the district court for more fact-finding. *Friery v. Los Angeles Unified School Dist.,* 448 F.3d 1146 (9th Cir. 2006).

◆ An African-American school administrator sought promotion to one of three program evaluator positions advertised by a California school district. A form relating to the job described "ethnic groups needed to achieve racial balance," with a list of nine ethnic groups. The only group not marked by the department director was "Black not Hispanic." Another form stated individuals whose ethnicity and/or gender reflected the district's affirmative action goals should be hired. The administrator did not have a degree in any of the specified fields sought in the job posting. The director, herself an African-American, filled only two of the three vacancies, finding the administrator did not meet minimum requirements. After exhausting collective bargaining grievance procedures, the administrator sued the district in a state court for discrimination. The court granted some of the district's pretrial motions, but allowed the discrimination claims to go before a jury. The director testified the district's affirmative action policy was no longer implemented due to Proposition 209, a California voter initiative that created a law eliminating racial preferences. Another district official testified the district no longer relied on ethnic balance information and was using outdated forms because it was such a large district.

After the jury heard the evidence, the court presented it with a special verdict form with four questions. Question Two asked jurors whether the district selected anyone less qualified than the administrator for one of the jobs. Question Four asked whether the administrator's race or gender motivated the decision not to hire him. If the answer to Question Two was "no," jurors were not to proceed. The jury's answer to Question Two was "no," so it never reached the question of the district's motivation. The administrator appealed to the California Court of Appeal, arguing he was entitled to a new trial and that substantial evidence supported a verdict in his favor. The court agreed with the administrator's arguments. It noted **the elements of an unlawful employment discrimination claim required him to show an adverse employment decision by the district that was motivated by race or gender. The arrangement of questions on the special verdict form prevented the jury from ever ruling on the question of whether the district had a discriminatory motive.** As this was the ultimate question in the case, the trial court had no basis for deciding liability, and the court of appeal reversed the judgment. *Akuluze v. Oakland Unified School Dist.*, Nos. A097485, A097909, 2003 WL 22026691 (Cal. Ct. App. 2003).

IV. RELIGIOUS DISCRIMINATION

Title VII prohibits employment discrimination on the basis of religion, but exempts religious employers from coverage. The U.S. Supreme Court has held that an employer discharges its duty under Title VII by making a reasonable accommodation of an employee's religious needs, but no duty to accommodate arises where it would work an undue hardship upon the employer.

◆ A Connecticut high school teacher belonged to a church that required members to refrain from secular employment during designated holy days. This required him to miss approximately six school days each year for religious purposes. The district's collective bargaining agreement allowed only three days of paid leave for religious observation. The agreement also allowed three days paid leave for "necessary personal business" which, the district said, could not be used for religious purposes. The teacher repeatedly asked to be granted permission to use three days of his "necessary personal business" leave for religious purposes. He also offered to pay for a substitute teacher if the school board would pay him for the extra days that he missed. The board rejected this offer, and the teacher filed a lawsuit alleging the board's policy regarding "necessary personal business" leave was discriminatory on the basis of religion.

The Second Circuit held the board was bound to accept one of the teacher's proposed solutions unless "that accommodation causes undue hardship on the employer's conduct of his business." On appeal, the U.S. Supreme Court modified the decision. It held the district did not need to accept the teacher's proposals, even if acceptance would not result in "undue hardship." **The board was only bound to offer a fair and reasonable accommodation of the teacher's religious needs.** The collective bargaining agreement policy of allowing three days paid leave for religious purposes, but excluding additional days of "necessary personal business" leave for religious purposes, would not be reasonable, if paid leave was provided "for all purposes *except* religious ones." Because the lower courts had not decided whether the "necessary personal business" leave policy had been administered fairly in the past, the Supreme Court remanded the case for resolution of that question. *Ansonia Board of Educ. v. Philbrook,* 479 U.S. 60, 107 S.Ct 367, 93 L.Ed.2d 305 (1986).

On remand, the Second Circuit held the accommodation was reasonable. *Philbrook v. Ansonia Board of Educ.,* 925 F.2d 47 (2d Cir. 1991).

◆ The U.S. Court of Appeals, Seventh Circuit, held a Wisconsin school district did not retaliate against an employee on the basis of his religion. He was disciplined numerous times and eventually suspended for violating school policies he knew about and had promised to follow. The misconduct included making inappropriate comments, touching female students, offering students rides home and recruiting students for his nonprofit organization. **The court held the discipline was not evidence of discrimination, as the employee was not performing his job satisfactorily.** *Mohammed v. Racine Unified School Dist.,* 206 Fed.Appx. 543 (7th Cir. 2006).

◆ An Arkansas district required a teacher to attend in-service trainings at a Christian college where an opening prayer was said. He objected to mandatory prayers at teacher training meetings and the display of a Bible and scriptural quotes in the superintendent's office. The superintendent refused to remove the displays. The teacher claimed he was harassed because of his opposition to district religious practices. He sued the district, superintendent and other school officials in a federal district court. The court held prayers at mandatory faculty meetings and in-service trainings violated the Establishment Clause. However, the Bible and framed scripture displays, as well as religious jewelry and T-shirts worn by students and staff, were protected by the Speech and Free Exercise Clauses. The court found school officials took appropriate action in each case of claimed harassment. It ordered the district to stop offering prayers at mandatory meetings and to end trainings at religious colleges. The court awarded the teacher $1,000 and his attorneys' fees, and he appealed to the Eighth Circuit.

The court noted that while school-mandated prayer for students is clearly unconstitutional, there is no blanket rule prohibiting prayers at all government-sponsored functions. The teacher's relationship with the district was contractual, not compulsory. The court found "the government can permissibly engage in any number of activities that its citizens find deeply offensive without violating the Constitution." However, the Constitution forbids the government from conveying a message that it endorses a particular religious position. The prayers at mandatory meetings and trainings unconstitutionally conveyed religious endorsement. The court modified the district court order to preclude prayers at mandatory meetings, regardless of whether the teacher was present. Some of the harassment alleged by the teacher involved actions by students and staff that were constitutionally protected. While religious harassment by a government employer might violate the Free Exercise Clause, no harassment occurred in this case. The incidents alleged by the teacher involved his opposition to the district's practices. **Each time he complained, school officials took prompt disciplinary action.** The district responded appropriately by suspending a student for part of a day after he attempted to place a cross outside the teacher's classroom. The court held the teacher heard unconstitutional prayers but did not suffer any harassment. It remanded the case to the district court. *Warnock v. Archer*, 380 F.3d 1076 (8th Cir. 2004).

The teacher later attended a baccalaureate ceremony at a district high school that included an invocation and benediction by ministers. He sought a contempt order from the district court. **The court granted the motion for contempt, finding school district employees had planned and supervised the ceremony where prayers were offered**. The school district appealed to the Eighth Circuit. The court found no abuse of discretion in the district court's finding of contempt. There was ample evidence that school employees were involved in almost every aspect of the event. The court affirmed the judgment, but declined the teacher's invitation to impose more severe sanctions. *Warnock v. Archer*, 443 F.3d 954 (8th Cir. 2006).

◆ **A New Jersey school board's anti-nepotism policy, which applied only to untenured employees, did not violate any state or federal laws**, according to a state appellate court. The provision also did not violate the constitutional rights of untenured teachers. The board presented evidence that the policy had a negligible effect on its work force, and a legitimate purpose of eliminating real or apparent conflicts of interest that could arise when employees were married to each other. The court rejected a teacher's assertion that her contract was not renewed due to her religious beliefs. The policy did not even mention religion and only precluded employment based on certain family relationships. **There was no evidence that the board sought to discriminate against persons who chose marriage over cohabitation for religious reasons.** Nothing indicated the policy resulted in a pattern of unlawful religious discrimination. There was a rational basis for the policy, and it was reasonably related to avoiding conflicts of interest, discord and favoritism. There was no Equal Protection Clause violation, because the policy did not directly and substantially burden the fundamental right to marry. The court held the board policy was rational and affirmed the judgment for the board. *Wowkun v. Closter Board of Educ.*, 2006 WL 1933475 (N.J. Super. Ct. App. Div. 2006).

◆ A New York school board had a collective bargaining agreement with the union representing its teachers containing a clause allowing teachers up to three paid days of leave for religious observance upon written request. The leave was limited to days required by an employee's religion, such as observance of the Sabbath or other holy day, plus reasonable travel time. Any additional time was charged to an employee's personal leave or unpaid leave. The board denied requests by two teachers for paid leave under the religious observance clause and directed them to take personal leave time instead. The union sued the board in a state trial court on their behalf for an order compelling compliance with the leave clause. The court held the clause violated the Establishment Clause.

The union appealed. The New York Supreme Court, Appellate Division, rejected the board's argument that the religious leave clause impermissibly advanced religion. It imposed no requirements on teachers to pick the religious holidays that could be invoked for leave. **The clause was better viewed as a reasonable accommodation of teachers' religious beliefs than an impermissible advancement of religion. The U.S. Constitution mandates religious accommodation, not mere tolerance.** The court reinstated the union's petition and remitted the case for further proceedings. *In re Maine-Endwell Teachers' Ass'n v. Board of Educ. of Maine-Endwell Cent. School Dist.*, 771 N.Y.S.2d 246 (N.Y. App. Div. 2004).

◆　An Ohio school board employed a Sabbatarian carpenter as a temporary for over two years. He did not work from sunset Friday to sunset Saturday, and he observed holidays such as Passover and the Feast of Trumpets. The carpenter declined Saturday work based on his religious convictions several times. The board rejected his offer to work on Sundays as a violation of the collective bargaining agreement (CBA). The board laid off the carpenter due to budget concerns and lack of work. A supervisor then decided he should not be rehired.

The carpenter sued the board and two school administrators in a federal district court for religious discrimination under Title VII and retaliation under Title VII and the Free Exercise Clause. The court ruled for the board, and the carpenter appealed. The U.S. Court of Appeals, Sixth Circuit, explained **Title VII creates liability only if the accommodation of an employee's religious beliefs does not unduly burden the employer. Employers are not required to violate collective bargaining agreements to reasonably accommodate employees.** Had the board granted the carpenter's request for Sunday work, the CBA required it to double his regular wage. The board would have had to pay another employee double time to open the building. **This expense was enough to create an undue burden, defeating the carpenter's Title VII claim.** The carpenter's retaliation claim failed because he did not show a link between the board's refusal to reemploy him and his religious beliefs. The evidence showed the board laid him off for lack of work and did not rehire him because he did not get along with others. The board did not substantially burden the carpenter's religious free exercise rights or retaliate against him based on his religious activity. It met his requests to avoid work on the Sabbath and holy days. The carpenter's state law claim failed because he was employed under the CBA and could assert wrongful discharge in violation of public policy. The court affirmed the judgment. *Creusere v. Board of Educ. of City School Dist. of Cincinnati*, 88 Fed.Appx. 813 (6th Cir. 2003).

◆　The collective bargaining agreement between a New York teachers association and a school district provided for three paid absences per year upon five days' prior approval. No reason was required for two days, but applicants needed to explain the reason for the third day, which had to be for stated reasons, including Title VII accommodation. Two teachers who professed to be devout, practicing Catholics filed a successful grievance against the district to challenge their denial of days off for "Title VII accommodation" on Catholic Holy Days of Obligation. The arbitrator held the district violated the collective bargaining agreement by denying leave. After losing in arbitration, the district eliminated the requirement that teachers demonstrate that an absence from work was mandated by religion. Under a new policy, **the district reserved its right to interview applicants to determine whether they held genuine personal religious beliefs requiring absence from work**. The district processed requests from Catholic, Episcopal and Buddhist teachers for days off based on their answers to inquiries from district administrators.

The teachers sued the district, its superintendent and other administrators in a federal district court, seeking a declaration that the district could not inquire into their religious practices and beliefs to determine whether a conflict existed between the practices and work hours. The district and administrators moved for summary judgment, asserting the teachers had no standing to bring the action since they had never been adversely affected by the new policy. The court explained that Article III of the U.S. Constitution limits federal court jurisdiction to "cases and controversies." This was an essential component of standing to sue. Even though the teachers claimed to be injured by the district's pre-arbitration policy, none of them could show the district's existing policy was likely to cause them recurring injury. **The Constitution permitted the district to make inquiries about the sincerity of employee religious beliefs by determining whether teachers had a good-faith belief in the need to take a day off for religious observance.** The district could not be precluded from questioning the teachers about their religious requirements, and they were unable to show the new policy injured them. The district and administrators were entitled to summary judgment. *Burns v. Warwick Valley Cent. School Dist.*, 166 F.Supp.2d 881 (S.D.N.Y. 2001).

◆ A Minnesota school district hired a Somali Muslim as a hall monitor and allowed him to adjust his schedule to attend religious services. The employee contended staff members ostracized him and fabricated complaints about his performance after he refused on religious grounds to shake the hand of female staff members during introductions. The employee met with the principal and district superintendent to discuss these issues. The principal then noted some performance deficiencies in an evaluation. The district granted the employee's request for a leave of absence and then laid him off with 12 other paraprofessionals. He was soon recalled to a hall monitor position at another school. The principal there initially denied the employee's request to leave work on Fridays to attend religious services. The district later allowed him to take prayer breaks during the school day. The principal suspended the employee for creating a negative work climate, and the district laid him off again for budget reasons.

The employee sued the district in a federal district court. The court found the evidence of tension between the employee and his co-workers did not establish harassment had occurred. Ostracism and workplace unrest do not prove hostile work environment harassment without evidence of some tangible change in duties or working conditions that creates a material disadvantage. The district responded promptly when it became aware of unrest in the school, working with community leaders and consultants to improve the environment. The employee did not substantiate his claim that the district laid him off and failed to immediately recall him because of his religion or national origin. Both of the other positions for which the employee applied were filled by members of a protected class who were objectively more qualified. **His religious discrimination claim failed because the district granted his requests for accommodation with minimal limitations. Employers have no duty to accommodate employees' religious observances if this would cause undue hardship.** There was no evidence the employee was disciplined for requesting religious accommodations. As he failed to show action by the district that was unjustified or that he was treated less favorably than other employees, the district was entitled to summary judgment. *Sheikh v. Independent School Dist. 535*, Civ. No. 00-1896 (DWF/SRN), 2001 WL 1636504 (D. Minn. 2001).

V.   AGE DISCRIMINATION

The federal Age Discrimination in Employment Act of 1967 (ADEA), 29 U.S.C. § 621 et seq., is part of the Fair Labor Standards Act. It prohibits the use of age as a criterion for employment with respect to persons ages 40 and over, and applies to institutions with 20 or more employees that "affect interstate commerce." The ADEA contains an exception allowing the use of age as an employment criterion "where age is a bona fide occupational qualification reasonably necessary to the normal operation of the particular business."

In 2005, the U.S. Supreme Court held employees may bring "disparate impact" actions under the ADEA. Disparate impact actions do not require proof of intentional age discrimination, instead requiring an employee to show an employment policy has the effect of discriminating on the basis of age.

◆   A Mississippi city increased all employee salaries in 1999. Those with under five years of experience received comparatively higher raises than more experienced employees. The city justified the action as a way to remain competitive and "ensure equitable compensation to all employees." A group of veteran police officers, most over 40 years old, claimed the city's action constituted discrimination on the basis of age. The officers sued the city in a federal district court for ADEA violations, alleging disparate treatment and disparate impact. The court held for the city. The U.S. Court of Appeals, Fifth Circuit, affirmed the judgment, finding the ADEA did not recognize disparate impact claims. However, the officers could proceed with intentional discrimination claims. The Supreme Court agreed to review the disparate impact claim. It compared the ADEA with Title VII of the Civil Rights Act of 1964. Except for the substitution of the word "age" for "race, color, religion, sex, or national origin," ADEA and Title VII language was identical. Title VII disparate impact claims have long been recognized by the Court.

The Court stated **the ADEA authorizes potential recovery for disparate impact cases, in a manner comparable to Title VII disparate impact claims** for race, religion or sex discrimination. **Employees who claim an employer practice has a disparate impact on a class of employees need not show the practice is intentional.** While the Court held the officers were entitled to bring a disparate impact claim under the ADEA, they could not show the city violated the ADEA in this case. The Court noted the ADEA's coverage for disparate impact is narrower than that of Title VII. Under the ADEA, an employer can treat workers differently if the employer is motivated by reasonable factors other than age. The Court found Congress had narrowed the ADEA's scope because there is often a connection between age and ability to perform a job. The Court agreed with the city that the decision to make itself competitive in the job market was based on a reasonable factor other than age. As the city's goal was to raise employee salaries to be competitive, the employees could not prove the increase had a disparate impact, and the Court affirmed the judgment for the city. *Smith v. City of Jackson*, 544 U.S. 228 (U.S. 2005).

◆ The U.S. Court of Appeals, Eleventh Circuit, consolidated three Florida cases filed against public employers and held Congress did not effectively abrogate Eleventh Amendment immunity when it amended the ADEA. Two of the cases involved actions by current and former university employees against public universities. The other case involved the Florida Department of Corrections. The Court explained the Eleventh Amendment prohibits federal suits against non-consenting states. Congress may abrogate state immunity only by making its intention unmistakably clear in statutory language, and only then as a valid exercise of constitutional authority. Congress clearly stated its intent to abrogate Eleventh Amendment immunity by subjecting the states to potential liability for monetary damages in suits filed by employees. However, the Court held **Congress exceeded its authority under the Fourteenth Amendment when it included state employees within the coverage of the ADEA.** *Kimel v. Florida Board of Regents*, 528 U.S. 62, 120 S.Ct. 631, 145 L.Ed.2d 522 (2000).

◆ **The U.S. Court of Appeals, Eighth Circuit, held an Iowa school district's early retirement incentive plan (ERIP) violated the ADEA by varying an employee's retirement benefits solely on the basis of age.** The district initially offered its employees ERIP benefits, including the payment of health insurance premiums until the age of 65, plus a one-time cash payment equal to 30% of the employee's annual salary. In 2001, the plan was amended so eligible teachers could receive a $200 credit for each unused sick leave day they had accumulated as of their date of retirement. A teacher who had reached age 65 was denied benefits under the ERIP. He sued the school district in a federal district court for violating the ADEA and Iowa's Wage Payment Collection Law. The court refused to certify a class action, but it let five other teachers join the lawsuit. Two teachers with the same educational background, number of sick days and years of employment in the district could receive different retirement benefits based solely upon their age. The ERIP conflicted with the purposes of the ADEA, and the teachers were entitled to judgment.

The school district appealed to the Eighth Circuit, which stated **the ADEA prohibits discrimination on the basis of age with respect to compensation, terms, conditions or privileges of employment.** Under the district's ERIP, an employee age 65 or older was ineligible for early retirement benefits. The plan was thus discriminatory on its face, and intent to discriminate could be presumed. **The court held it was not unlawful for an employer to offer an ERIP, but it was unlawful to condition or reduce early retirement benefits on the basis of age.** The district had done this by offering the amended ERIP. The amount of an employee's early retirement benefits dropped to zero upon the attainment of age 65, which was an adverse change in benefits based solely on age. The court agreed with the district court's finding that the ERIP violated the ADEA. The judgment for the teachers was affirmed. *Jankovitz v. Des Moines Independent Community School Dist.*, 421 F.3d 649 (8th Cir. 2005).

◆   The Eleventh Circuit Court of Appeals affirmed a judgment for a Georgia school board that did not rehire a 64-year-old African-American teacher. While he accused the board of age, race and sex discrimination, the court agreed with the board that its action was not improperly motivated. **The evidence showed the board did not rehire the teacher because parents and staff complained about his teaching abilities.** There was no showing of pretext. *Rolle v. Worth County School Dist.*, No. 04-15011, 2005 WL 894013 (11th Cir. 2005).

◆   A Colorado school district sought to hire an inclusion facilitator to make curricular modifications for special education students in regular classrooms. The half-time position required effective communication with regular education staff. The district hired a 50-year-old employee for a one-year, probationary term. Her first evaluation stated she needed to improve her performance and meet with regular teachers consistently. Teachers complained she did not establish collegial working relationships and was not available to them. The employee had an ongoing conflict with a paraprofessional and told others about the problem. The district's special education director told her she would not recommend renewing her contract. The district did not offer to place the employee on a remediation plan, even though its policies allowed this and a probationary teacher had been allowed to do so. The district allowed the employee to resign with a letter of recommendation and did not propose non-renewal to the school board. The district replaced the employee with a 51-year-old special education teacher. The employee accepted a higher-paying job elsewhere and sued the district in a federal district court for ADEA violations.

The court awarded summary judgment to the district, and the employee appealed. The U.S. Court of Appeals, Tenth Circuit, held she was entitled to rely on the theory of constructive discharge. However, **the employee could not show she was replaced by a younger person and had no evidence to counter her negative employment evaluations**. The employee was the only person the special education director ever recommended for non-renewal, but this did not prove age discrimination by the district. She had communication and personality conflicts with other staff and failed to attend training sessions. Failure to offer a remediation plan under these circumstances did not prove the district had an intent to discriminate. As the evidence did not raise any issue of discriminatory motive or hiring practices by the district, summary judgment was upheld on the age discrimination claim. The employee's retaliation claim failed because she did not prove she suffered an "adverse employment action" or any injury. The special education director gave the employee an excellent job reference, and her acknowledgement of the employee's pending discrimination complaint was not a "negative statement about her." *DiRusso v. Aspen School Dist.*, 123 Fed.Appx. 826 (10th Cir. 2004).

◆ A Virginia coach served at a high school for 32 years under a series of one-year contracts. The school's principal advised him his contract would not be renewed, based on his use of an ineligible player and failure to attend a meeting. According to the coach, the principal told him the program needed "new blood" and people who could "communicate better with the kids." The school board accepted the principal's recommendation not to renew the coach's contract, and the coach sued the board in a federal district court under the ADEA. The court held a jury trial, and allowed the board to present evidence he had driven under the influence of alcohol. However, the coach was prohibited from introducing evidence that during a previous assignment, the principal replaced the coaching staff at another school with younger coaches. The court also instructed the jury it would have to find age discrimination was the sole reason for discharge.

The jury returned a verdict for the board, and the coach appealed. The Fourth Circuit held **the district court had misstated the legal requirements for an ADEA action by instructing they jury to find for the coach if the board's action had occurred "solely because of age."** The district court also erred by refusing to instruct the jurors that if they disbelieved the principal's testimony, they could infer, but did not have to infer, the real reason for the board's action was age. The court should have permitted the coach to introduce evidence of the principal's age-based staffing change at another school. As the critical issue in this case was the principal's motivation, the driving under the influence charge was irrelevant and improperly prejudiced the jury. The court should have sequestered the principal from the courtroom to prevent him from re-characterizing his testimony in view of contradictory testimony by other witnesses. Since the district court errors were substantial, the court vacated the case for a new trial. *Kozlowski v. Hampton School Board*, 77 Fed.Appx. 133 (4th Cir. 2003).

◆ After years of teaching fourth grade, a Colorado teacher was assigned to teach third grade based on a performance evaluation indicating failure to meet district standards. The teacher stated she suffered from two sleep disorders and requested accommodation. The school principal developed a remediation plan and granted some of her requested accommodations. He then reprimanded the teacher in writing and sought to transfer her to a classroom support teacher (CST) position based on his belief this would accommodate most of her needs. The teacher asked instead to be reassigned to a fourth-grade classroom or to remain in her current position. She filed an age and disability discrimination charge against the district, asserting that in addition to her sleep disorders, she had adult attention deficit disorder, high blood pressure and esophagus irritation. The teacher submitted another written request for accommodation, but instead of accepting the CST position, she sought disability retirement and later resigned. She then sued the district in a federal district court for age and disability discrimination, retaliation, harassment, and related claims.

The court awarded summary judgment to the district, and the teacher appealed to the Tenth Circuit. **The court stated that in order to establish a viable claim under the ADEA, the complaining party must show age was a determining factor in an adverse employment decision.** The court found no evidence that the principal's remarks that "most of the teachers in the school were old white women" were related to the decision-making process or any of the alleged adverse actions. A move to the CST position would be a lateral transfer and would not constitute an adverse employment action. **Placement on remediation or growth plans could not be considered adverse employment action and did not support the age discrimination claims.** The teacher failed to produce evidence of retaliation or harassment based on her age. Since she was not subjected to any adverse employment action because of her age, the court affirmed the district court's conclusion that no discrimination occurred. The teacher's Americans with Disabilities Act (ADA) claims were also rejected, as she failed to establish she was disabled as defined by the ADA. *McCrary v. Aurora Public Schools*, 57 Fed.Appx. 362 (10th Cir. 2003).

VI. DISABILITY DISCRIMINATION

A. Rehabilitation Act of 1973

Section 504 of the Rehabilitation Act of 1973 bars any employer who receives federal funding from discriminating against an "otherwise qualified individual with a disability." Section 504 provides that no otherwise qualified individual with a disability shall, solely by reason of his or her disability, be denied employment. An otherwise qualified person with a disability is one who can perform the "essential functions" of the job "with reasonable accommodation" of the person's disability by the employer. Employers need not reasonably accommodate a disability if to do so would create undue hardship.

◆ **The U.S. Supreme Court held tuberculosis and other contagious diseases may be considered disabilities under Section 504.** The law defines an individual with a disability as "any person who (i) has a physical or mental impairment which substantially limits one or more of such person's major life activities, (ii) has a record of such impairment or (iii) is regarded as having such an impairment." It defines "physical impairment" as disorders affecting, among other things, the respiratory system and defines "major life activities" as "functions such as caring for one's self ... and working."

The case involved a Florida elementary school teacher who was discharged because of the continued recurrence of tuberculosis. She sued the school board under Section 504 but a U.S. district court dismissed her claims. The Eleventh Circuit reversed the judgment and held that persons with contagious diseases fall within Section 504's coverage. The board appealed to the U.S. Supreme Court. **The Court held tuberculosis was a disability under Section 504 because it affected the respiratory system and the ability to work, which is a "major life activity."** The board contended that in defining the term "individual with a disability" under Section 504, the contagious effects of a disease should be distinguished from the disease's physical effects. The Court reasoned the teacher's contagion and her physical impairment both resulted from tuberculosis. It would be unfair to allow an employer to distinguish between a disease's potential effect on others and its effect on the employee to justify discriminatory treatment. Allowing discrimination based on the contagious effects of a physical impairment would be inconsistent with the underlying purpose of Section 504. The Court remanded the case to the district court to determine whether the teacher was "otherwise qualified" for her job and whether the board could reasonably accommodate her as an employee. *School Board of Nassau County v. Arline*, 480 U.S. 273 (1987).

On remand, the district court held the teacher was "otherwise qualified" to teach. **She posed no threat of transmitting tuberculosis** to her students. The court ordered her reinstatement or a front-pay award of $768,724, representing her earnings until retirement. *Arline v. School Board of Nassau County*, 692 F.Supp. 1286 (M.D. Fla. 1988).

◆   A Texas school district employee worked as a buyer. He claimed depression sometimes prevented him from accomplishing simple tasks like mowing the lawn and working on his car. The district placed him on a deficiency plan and granted him a four-month Family and Medical Leave Act (FMLA) leave. Less than one month into his leave, the employee obtained a note from his doctor indicating he could return to work without restrictions. The employee stated he might need additional time off "to balance his medication." Five weeks later, the district discharged him for failing to complete his deficiency plan. The employee stated he could still perform his job duties, if the district granted his request for additional leave. When the district refused, he sued, asserting it violated the Rehabilitation Act by discharging him on the basis of disability and failing to accommodate him by denying him leave under the FMLA. The court awarded summary judgment to the district on both claims, and the employee appealed.

The Fifth Circuit stated **an employee claiming to have a disability must show a significant restriction in the ability to perform either a class of jobs or a broad range of jobs in various classes. The inability to perform a single, particular job is not a substantial limitation on work.** The court held the employee was not an individual with a disability under the Rehabilitation Act, because he did not show his depression limited the major life activity of working. The employee did not prove he was discharged for any other reason than poor job performance. He did not give the district adequate notice of the need to take additional leave before being discharged, and his physician did not indicate he needed additional time. **The FMLA requires employees to provide employers with written notice at least 30 days before taking leave, or as soon as possible if the need for leave is not foreseeable.** The employee did not seek more leave until after his discharge. As his notice was not given as soon as practicable, the court held it was inadequate under the FMLA. The court affirmed the judgment for the district. *Prejean v. Cypress-Fairbanks Independent School Dist.*, 97 Fed.Appx. 480 (5th Cir. 2004).

◆   A New York guidance counselor with serious medical problems received satisfactory performance evaluations and was recommended for tenure. She described pain she had experienced to a colleague and "joked that she could commit suicide with a gun belonging to her husband," who was a police officer. The colleague later described the conversation as "entirely in jest" but still reported it to school officials. The principal called the police department to secure the husband's gun. The counselor was reassigned to administrative duties and instructed to see two psychiatrists and a neurologist. The principal assigned another employee to her caseload. The psychologists and neurologist provided documentation that the counselor could return to her job, but the principal informed her she would not be granted tenure because of performance problems identified during her absence. The counselor sued the district, principal and superintendent in a federal district court for disability discrimination and defamation. The court directed a verdict for the district and officials.

On appeal, the Second Circuit stated **the Rehabilitation Act protects individuals from discrimination not only for actual disabilities, but also if an employer perceives them as having a disability**. The act may apply even if the perception of disability is incorrect. The counselor's evidence was sufficient to show **the district perceived her as having a mental illness that made her suicidal**. Rehabilitation Act regulations, published at 29 CFR Part 32.3(b)(1)(ii), recognize emotional or mental illness as an "impairment" that may bring an individual under the act's protection. The district court had incorrectly dismissed the case on the basis of the counselor's failure to show she was perceived to be incapable of working in a broad range of suitable jobs. **There was sufficient evidence that she was limited in her ability to care for herself**, which is recognized as a major life activity and a requirement for Rehabilitation Act protection. The court reversed the judgment on the Rehabilitation Act and state law claims. It affirmed the judgment for the principal on the counselor's defamation claim. He was privileged to communicate about her performance, and was not motivated by ill will. *Peters v. Baldwin Union Free School Dist.*, 320 F.3d 164 (2d Cir. 2003).

◆   A Connecticut fourth-grade teacher was arrested for possession of cocaine and drug paraphernalia. He avoided felony charges by receiving accelerated rehabilitation. The teacher's school district notified him his contract would be terminated for moral misconduct and conduct that seriously compromised his effectiveness as a role model and employee. He requested a hearing and admitted drug possession. Although the hearing officer recommended reinstatement, the school board voted to terminate his contract for moral misconduct and other good and sufficient cause. The teacher appealed to a state court, which held that he was unprotected by Section 504 because he had not been discharged for a reason solely related to his disability.

The Appellate Court of Connecticut observed that Section 504 requires a complaining party to prove he or she is otherwise qualified for a position and is being rejected solely by reason of a disability. **Although prior substance abuse is recognized as a disability under Section 504 in some cases, having a disability alone is not enough for legal protection.** The teacher could not show his discharge had been solely because of his disability. He had been arrested and charged with felonious activity that would have disqualified him from his employment despite his disability. The school board did not abuse its discretion by characterizing his illegal activities as moral misconduct and by ruling they were unprotected under federal law and the state constitution. The court affirmed the judgment for the board. *Gedney v. Board of Educ. of Town of Groton*, 47 Conn. App. 297, 703 A.2d 804 (Conn. App. Ct. 1997).

◆   The Omaha School District demoted two diabetic school van drivers to van aide positions at lower pay rates. The drivers sued the school district in a federal court, claiming violations of Section 504. The court granted motions to dismiss the lawsuit, and the drivers appealed to the Eighth Circuit. The court held the drivers had shown their disabilities could be reasonably accommodated and that they were at low risk for hypoglycemic episodes. Because they had demonstrated a material fact issue under Section 504, summary judgment was inappropriate. On remand, the district court found the drivers were Type II insulin-using diabetics with an appreciable risk of developing hypoglycemic symptoms without warning. Because this constituted a danger to students and others using public roads, there was no reasonable accommodation to be offered them. Accordingly, the Rehabilitation Act afforded no protection to the drivers. The drivers appealed again to the Eighth Circuit, which affirmed the judgment. **Because hypoglycemia created an increased risk of sudden and unexpected vision loss and loss of consciousness, the finding by the district court that the drivers presented a danger to themselves and others was supported by the evidence.** *Wood v. Omaha School Dist.*, 25 F.3d 667 (8th Cir. 1994).

B. Americans with Disabilities Act

The Americans with Disabilities Act (ADA) expands disability coverage to most employers with at least 15 employees in public and private institutions. The legal analysis used in Rehabilitation Act Section 504 cases applies to ADA cases. In Bragdon v. Abbott, *524 U.S. 624, 118 S.Ct. 2196, 141 L.Ed.2d 540 (1998), the Supreme Court held an HIV-positive individual was entitled to the protections of the ADA, despite the fact that she was not yet symptomatic.*

◆   In two 1999 ADA cases, **the U.S. Supreme Court held the question of whether an impairment is "substantially limiting" as defined by the ADA should be made with reference to any mitigating measures**.
    In the first case, twin sisters with uncorrected vision of 20/200 or worse but corrected vision of 20/20 or better were denied jobs as global airline pilots with a commercial airline because their uncorrected vision did not meet the airline's minimum uncorrected vision standard. The sisters filed an ADA claim against the airline, which was dismissed by a federal district court. The Supreme Court upheld the lower court decisions, finding the sisters had not demonstrated they were disabled under the ADA. The Court stated that mitigating measures had to be taken into account when evaluating whether an individual was disabled, and that, **because glasses or contacts corrected the sisters' vision to 20/20 or better they were not substantially limited in a major life activity**. The sisters were also not regarded as disabled, as there was no evidence that the airline perceived them as substantially limited in a major life activity. *Sutton v. United Airlines, Inc.*, 527 U.S. 471, 119 S.Ct. 2139, 144 L.Ed.2d 450 (1999).
    In the second case, the Supreme Court held a mechanic with high blood

pressure was not disabled under the ADA. **Because the mechanic was able to control his high blood pressure with medication, he was not substantially limited in a major life activity.** The Court did not address the issue of whether the mechanic would be considered disabled while taking his medication. The mechanic was also not regarded as disabled. At most, the employer regarded the mechanic as unable to perform the job of mechanic because it believed his high blood pressure exceeded the U.S. Department of Transportation's requirements for drivers of commercial motor vehicles. *Murphy v. United Parcel Service, Inc.,* 527 U.S. 516, 119 S.Ct. 2133, 144 L.Ed.2d 484 (1999).

◆ Congress exceeded its authority by allowing monetary damage awards against the states in ADA cases, according to a 2001 U.S. Supreme Court decision. The Court held that Congress did not identify a history and pattern of irrational employment discrimination against individuals with disabilities by the states when it enacted the ADA, and therefore, states were entitled to Eleventh Amendment immunity from such claims. As a result, **two state employees were unsuccessful in their attempt to recover money damages under the ADA from their state employer for disability discrimination they claimed to have been subjected to.** *Board of Trustees of Univ. of Alabama v. Garrett,* 531 U.S. 356, 121 S.Ct. 955, 148 L.Ed.2d 866 (2001).

◆ A Kentucky auto worker was restricted from some job duties due to carpal tunnel syndrome. When her employer refused to accommodate her, she sued it in federal court. The court found the employee was not disabled at the time she sought accommodation and held for the employer. The case reached the U.S. Supreme Court, which agreed to consider the standard for determining when an ADA claimant is substantially limited in the major life activity of performing manual tasks. **The Court held the ADA standard was met only where a person has an impairment that prevents or severely restricts activities that are of central importance to most people's daily lives.** The impairment must also be permanent or long-term. The Court held the employee was not disabled simply because she could not perform a class of manual tasks associated with some assembly line jobs. The lower courts had to examine other relevant evidence, such as whether she could perform tasks of "central importance to most people's daily lives," such as those involved in personal hygiene. **As the ADA applies only to persons with impairments that prevent or severely restrict them from activities that are of central importance to daily life, the Court reversed and remanded the case.** *Toyota Motor Manufacturing v. Williams,* 534 U.S. 184, 122 S.Ct. 681, 151 L.Ed.2d 615 (2002).

◆ A Missouri teacher worked as an exceptional education case manager. This required frequent visits to several schools, extensive walking and stair-climbing and repetitive handwriting. She was injured in a car accident and two slip-and-fall incidents, one of which occurred at a high school. The district withdrew a job offer as a vocational resource educator after the teacher went on medical leave. She returned to her case manager position after four months but was unable to perform physical tasks required by the job. The district assigned her to part-time, light-duty clerical work. The teacher made a formal request for a medical assessment and job accommodations. Her own physician determined she was still recovering from her injuries and needed restrictions. A physician selected by the district determined the teacher's impairments were resolved with no lasting effects. An independent medical examiner later found she did not need accommodations. The district transferred the teacher to an alternative middle school for students with mental and behavioral disorders. She objected to the assignment and was soon injured when a student kicked a chair in which she was sitting. The teacher obtained an extended medical leave of absence and did not return to work for nearly a year. After again requesting a long-term leave of absence, the teacher sued the school district in a federal district court. The court held for the district, and the teacher appealed to the Eighth Circuit.

The court held the teacher had to first show she had a condition that qualified as a "disability" in order to prevail on her ADA claim. She further had to show she was qualified to perform the essential functions of her position and had suffered an adverse employment action based on her disability. Evidence of a medical diagnosis of an impairment was insufficient for this purpose. An impairment must be substantial, as indicated by inability to perform basic functions that an average person could perform. Inability to perform a single particular job did not constitute a "substantial limitation in the major life activity of working" under 29 C.F.R. Part 1630.2(j)(3)(i). **Temporary impairments with little or no long-term impact are not disabilities under the ADA. There was no evidence that the teacher had a long-term or permanent disability or could not perform a broad range of jobs in various classes.** The district court had properly held for the district on the ADA claim. *Samuels v. Kansas City Missouri School Dist.*, 437 F.3d 797 (8th Cir. 2006).

◆ A New Jersey school employee suffered a concussive brain injury after a speaker fell off a wall and struck him on the head. He began having "profound, incapacitating fatigue," and difficulty with concentration and memory. The employee was often unable to work more than an eight-hour day, but he said he could still do his job. The employee sued the school board in a federal district court, asserting it had failed to accommodate his disability and unlawfully disclosed medical information. The court held that even though his comprehension and mental functioning were below average, this alone could not confer federal disability law protection. The accidental disclosure of the medical report and a CAT scan joke did not violate any constitutional rights.

On appeal, the U.S. Court of Appeals, Third Circuit, stated the Americans with Disabilities Act (ADA) protects individuals with impairments that substantially limit one or more major life activities. **A person seeking ADA protection must be unable to perform a major life activity that the average person can perform, or be significantly restricted as to the condition, manner or duration under which the activity can be performed.** The court held it is insufficient for individuals attempting to prove disability status to merely submit medical evidence of an impairment. There must be evidence that the extent of the limitation caused by the impairment, in terms of the individual's own experience, is substantial. The employee still ranked high or in the average range on certain measures of cognitive function. His impairments were relatively minor and could not be considered "substantial limitations." The employee said he could still perform his job well, and he was not significantly restricted in his ability to perform a broad range or class of jobs. *Weisberg v. Riverside Township Board of Educ.*, 180 Fed.Appx. 357 (3d Cir. 2006).

◆ An Illinois high school principal received excellent evaluations before being transferred to a communication academy. Once there, parents and teachers accused him of being unavailable to help and mishandling discipline. The principal claimed he got no support from the school board, causing stress and depression. In response, the board sought a performance improvement plan. Before it could be implemented, he took a leave for work-related stress and produced a doctor's note in support of it. The principal sought reduction to six-hour work days, and to be excused from special projects. The board declined these restrictions as unreasonable. After the principal returned from leave, the board reassigned him to a teaching position, citing budgetary reasons. He filed charges against the board with state and federal civil rights agencies, then sued the board. A federal district court held for the board, and the principal appealed.

The U.S. Court of Appeals, Seventh Circuit, found evidence that the principal functioned well in teaching and administrative positions after leaving the academy. **Evidence showed his depression was not permanent or even long term.** He soon returned to public school administration, becoming a principal in Chicago public schools. **Isolated incidents of depression do not qualify an individual for ADA coverage. While the principal's problems with stress and anxiety made him unable to work as the principal of the academy, he could still work as an administrator and teacher elsewhere.** Panic attacks may have slowed him down, but they did not prevent him from working. The school board did not regard the principal as disabled, and he did not tell any board members he was being treated for depression. The court affirmed the judgment for the school board. *Cassimy v. Board of Educ. of Rockford Public Schools, Dist. 205*, 461 F.3d 932 (7th Cir. 2006).

◆ **A Georgia school bus driver who suffered panic attacks was not protected by the Americans with Disabilities Act (ADA). She could be discharged since she could not perform her job without a reasonable accommodation.** The driver claimed her school board had to accommodate her disability, but a federal district court found the board did not commit any discrimination against her. The U.S. Court of Appeals, Eleventh Circuit, upheld the ruling, finding the driver did not have a disability as defined in the ADA. **She could not claim the board regarded her as an individual with a disability under the ADA, because she did not prove she was substantially limited in a major life activity, such as working.** As the driver was not disabled, the board did not have to accommodate her. *Albright v. Columbia Board of Educ.*, 135 Fed.Appx. 344 (11th Cir. 2005).

◆ A Texas teacher was hospitalized for depression in a mental institution during her third year of probationary employment for a school district. She took medical leave for over three months. When the school board voted not to rehire her for the following school year, she asserted ADA violations based on having a record of depression or being regarded by the district as disabled. The teacher sued the district in a federal district court, which awarded summary judgment to the district. On appeal to the U.S. Court of Appeals, Fifth Circuit, she argued her leave and hospitalization proved a record of disability. The court disagreed, ruling hospitalization itself does not establish a record of mental disability.

The court stated a presumption that temporary hospitalization is disabling would be contrary to ADA goals. The district court performed a properly individualized inquiry and held the teacher's condition did not cause a substantial limitation in a major life activity. She was not disabled within the meaning of the ADA. **The evidence showed the teacher's depression was treatable with medication and did not prevent her from working. Her leave and hospitalization did not establish a disability and did not prove the district regarded her depression as preventing her from performing her job.** The court affirmed the judgment. *Winters v. Pasadena Independent School Dist.*, 124 Fed.Appx. 822 (5th Cir. 2005).

◆   A Missouri teacher had seizures and blackouts associated with injuries from a traffic accident. After being hired as a probationary teacher, she had repeated disagreements with the school's principal and assistant principal. The teacher accused the administrators of trying to remove her due to her disability. She stated they used charges of abusiveness toward students as a "pretext" for firing her. The school board upheld the abuse charges and discharged the teacher. She sued the board and school officials in a federal district court under the ADA, and the Missouri Human Rights Act. The court held the board was entitled to sovereign immunity for the ADA claims. The board was a political subdivision of the state. State governments are not subject to private damages in federal courts for violating the ADA. In *Board of Trustees of Univ. of Alabama v. Garrett*, 531 U.S. 356 (2001), this chapter, the Supreme Court held Congress never validly abrogated the states' Eleventh Amendment immunity when it enacted the ADA. The individual board members were entitled to immunity, as they were named in their official capacities. The board had never waived its immunity for state tort liability. The court dismissed the teacher's state and federal claims. *Wade-Lemee v. Board of Educ. for City of St. Louis*, Civil No. 4:05 CV 1198 HEA, 2005 WL 2333890 (E.D. Mo. 2005).

◆   A Wisconsin teacher with 30 years of experience in her school district had arthritis, bursitis, degenerating spinal discs, scoliosis and spondylitis, which compromised her ability to teach. She took increasingly more time off school, arrived late and required others to cover her class while she rested. Several months before the end of a school year, the superintendent of schools recommended not renewing her contract. The teacher retired, which increased her benefits. She then sued the district in a federal district court for violating the ADA, also asserting the district forced her resignation by proposing non-renewal of her contract. The court awarded judgment to the school district.

The teacher appealed to the U.S. Court of Appeals, Seventh Circuit, which rejected her constructive discharge claim, since she was not subjected to "unendurable working conditions." There was no evidence that the district had given the teacher demeaning assignments or otherwise forced her to resign. She maintained her job for six months after the superintendent proposed her contract non-renewal. The teacher had not allowed due process to run its course, since she resigned instead of contesting the non-renewal. The teacher did not have a disability under the ADA. She did not argue her condition was serious. Instead, she claimed to be disabled because the district regarded her as disabled. **Being "regarded as disabled" by an employer may confer the same rights on an individual as a person who is actually disabled. The court rejected the teacher's argument that the district's efforts at accommodating her meant it regarded her as being disabled.** An employer that offered accommodations to an employee for other reasons did not risk being found as regarding the employee as "disabled." As there was no evidence that the district regarded the teacher as disabled, and it did not force her to resign, the judgment was affirmed. *Cigan v. Chippewa Falls School Dist.*, 388 F.3d 331 (7th Cir. 2004).

◆ A Virginia school district employee with a history of strokes and visual impairments gave the district a letter from her physician stating she could not lift over five pounds. After working as a library aide, she was assigned to work as a teacher's assistant. The school board reassigned her to a special education classroom, where she complained of stress and inability to handle the students. The board transferred her to another special education classroom and then to a kindergarten room where she served as a teacher's assistant. The board later eliminated all kindergarten teacher assistant positions on a system-wide basis. The employee sued it in a federal district court for disability discrimination.

The court awarded summary judgment to the board, and the employee appealed. The Fourth Circuit observed that the only medical evidence in the record was an eight-year-old letter from a physician indicating the teacher should not lift objects. **The court could not conclude the employee was disabled within the meaning of the ADA on the basis of her inability to lift objects weighing more than five pounds.** Even if she was properly deemed to have a qualifying disability, her unsatisfactory evaluations supported the decision that she was unqualified to hold her former position as library assistant. The employee failed to prove the board discriminated against her on the basis of disability when it hired another employee as a library assistant. The record indicated the board had promptly attempted to accommodate the employee's condition. The Fourth Circuit affirmed the judgment for the board. *Daye v. School Board of City of Norfolk*, 18 Fed.Appx. 125 (4th Cir. 2001).

◆ An Arizona groundskeeper severely injured her leg while on the job. She obtained a limited return-to-work release. The district's employment director rejected her return to work under these restrictions, stating, "[W]e don't take limited releases." The district allowed the groundskeeper to take unpaid leave, but it declined her request to use 23 days of unused vacation and sick leave, despite a district policy permitting this usage. The director then asked for the groundskeeper's resignation, stating she could apply for reemployment if she obtained a full release. The groundskeeper resigned, and three weeks later she obtained a full work release. The district repeatedly turned her down for open positions. The groundskeeper sued the district in a federal district court under the ADA. The court held for the district on her disability discrimination claim, but it denied the district's motion for judgment on her claim that the district discriminated against her because it regarded her as disabled. A jury awarded the groundskeeper more than $237,000 in damages, but the court granted a post-trial motion by the district for judgment and a new trial.

The groundskeeper appealed to the Ninth Circuit, which found the district court improperly drew inferences in the district's favor and made credibility determinations that only the jury was entitled to make. There was sufficient evidence to support the belief that the district considered the groundskeeper disabled. A verdict must be upheld if it is supported by substantial evidence. There was undisputed evidence that the district turned the groundskeeper down for reemployment 13 times after she obtained a full return-to-work release. **The district's policy against "partial releases" was itself a violation of the ADA and discriminated against individuals with disabilities. A "fully healed" policy permitted employers to avoid the ADA's individual assessment requirement, which requires a determination of whether an applicant is able to perform the essential functions of a job either with or without reasonable accommodation.** The jury was entitled to conclude the director's explanations were a pretext for unlawful discrimination. The court reversed and remanded the case for entry of a judgment consistent with the verdict. *Johnson v. Paradise Valley Unified School Dist.*, 251 F.3d 1222 (9th Cir. 2001).

C. State Statutes

◆ A California school district offered employee health coverage from several group health maintenance organizations, including PacifiCare. Although the PacifiCare plan specifically excluded in vitro fertilization (IVF) treatment from coverage, it covered many other forms of infertility treatment. A teacher's wife was unable to become pregnant due to polycystic ovarian disease. One of her doctors requested pre-authorization for IVF, despite being aware that it was not covered by the teacher's PacifiCare plan. The teacher and his wife began IVF treatment at their own expense and filed a discrimination charge against the district in a state court, alleging violation of the California Fair Employment and Housing Act (FEHA). The court awarded judgment to the district.

The teacher appealed to the state court of appeal. It found the FEHA was similar to federal employment discrimination laws such as the Americans with Disabilities Act (ADA). Federal agency interpretations of the ADA permitted health insurance plans to provide fewer benefits for eye care than for other physical conditions. **Broad distinctions applying to the treatment of dissimilar conditions, and pertaining to individuals with and without disabilities, are not "distinctions based on disability."** While the distinctions might have a greater impact on certain individuals, they were not intentional disability discrimination and did not violate the ADA. **The discrimination alleged by the teacher was not genuinely based on fertility, because the plan covered many other forms of infertility treatment.** IVF was an expensive treatment used only when others failed. The court explained that if the ADA and FEHA prohibited treatment-based distinctions, they would mandate comprehensive health coverage for all job-related disabilities. This was not the intent of FEHA. Federal case law interpreting the ADA did not prohibit treatment-based distinctions. The court noted California's Knox-Keene Health

Care Service Plan Act, Health and Safety Code § 1340, specifically authorized the exclusion of coverage for IVF treatment. The superior court had correctly held for the district. *Knight v. Hayward Unified School Dist.*, 132 Cal.App.4th 121, 33 Cal.Rptr.3d 298 (Cal. Ct. App. 2005).

◆ An Ohio school bus driver who had worked for a district for 22 years tested positive for marijuana use after transporting disabled children to school. A district supervisor met with the driver two days after the test and denied her request for leave to enter a rehabilitation program. He stated school policy required discharge, but he then agreed to allow her to resign. The supervisor rejected the driver's request to retire instead of resign, and she submitted her written resignation the same day. The school board approved the resignation at a special meeting held six days later. The driver's grievance was denied through the first three steps. Her employee association declined to take the grievance to arbitration. The district denied efforts by the driver to withdraw her resignation and later refused to rehire her. She sued the board and supervisor for disability discrimination and due process violations. A federal district court awarded summary judgment to the board and supervisor, and the driver appealed.

The Sixth Circuit held **ascertaining whether a person is "disabled" requires an individualized inquiry into whether a condition affects the person's ability to perform a major life activity, such as working. Under both Ohio law and the ADA, drug addiction may be a "physical or mental impairment."** An individual with a drug addiction that substantially limits the ability to perform a major life activity may be held to have a disability. However, there must be medical evidence to substantiate a claimed disability. **A disease or condition caused by illegal drug use is not a disability unless the individual has successfully completed a supervised rehabilitation program and no longer uses illegal drugs.** The court found the driver presented little medical evidence of drug addiction and failed to show a disability. There was no indication the district regarded her as a drug addict. As she failed to show she was disabled, the court affirmed the judgment on the disability claim. It rejected the driver's due process argument, noting she herself had proposed resigning. The association's decision not to bring the case to arbitration was not a denial of due process. *Rhoads v. Board of Educ. of Mad River Local School Dist.*, 103 Fed.Appx. 888 (6th Cir. 2004).

◆ A Nevada elementary school music instructor volunteered as a helping dog trainer. The volunteer work required her to acclimate a helping dog to its future master's home and public environment. This included having the dog lie down or sleep next to her for extended time periods. The instructor asked her employer for permission to bring a golden retriever she was training to class each day to lie down or sleep under her desk. The school district denied the request, stating that this would create a distraction and that students might be afraid of or allergic to the dog. The teacher filed a complaint against the school district in a state court under a Nevada law making it an unlawful practice for a place of public accommodation to refuse admittance to a person with a service animal. The court granted the instructor's request for a temporary order allowing her to bring the dog to class pending further consideration, subject to any serious difficulties or dangers created by the presence of the dog at school.

The district appealed to the Supreme Court of Nevada. The court noted **the district had refused to negotiate a reasonable compromise with the music instructor, despite the mandatory language of the statute requiring a place of public accommodation to allow a training dog.** The district court had correctly granted the instructor's request for an injunction. There was a high probability that she would succeed on the merits of her claim, since the school was a place of public accommodation and she was a trainer of helping dogs. If a legitimate health concern could be proven, the employer would be entitled to place reasonable restrictions on her right to train the helping dog as necessary to prevent health problems. The court affirmed the trial court order. *Clark County School Dist. v. Buchanan*, 924 P.2d 716 (Nev. 1996).

VII. DISCRIMINATION AGAINST VETERANS

◆ A New York elementary school principal who was a U.S. Army reservist submitted six leave requests for brief periods of military service in one year. During those times, she was unable to perform her duties as principal, and some board members and the superintendent expressed displeasure over her absences. The principal refused to comply with a board member's request to place his child in a "looping class" so the child could remain with the same teacher for the next grade. The superintendent then told her to place the child in the looping class. Later, the superintendent notified the principal he would recommend her employment termination to the board for inaccessibility to staff and parents, failure to meet with clerical staff in her office, and failure to timely complete class lists. The principal disputed these reasons, but the board discharged her. She sued the board, individual board members and the superintendent for violating the Uniformed Services Employment and Reemployment Rights Act (USERRA), the New York Military Law, and her First Amendment rights.

A federal district court dismissed the claims against the board under the USERRA and the New York Military Law. The court held the school officials were not "employers" under either law. However, the principal could amend her complaint to sue the individual officials under 42 U.S.C. § 1983. **On appeal, the U.S. Court of Appeals, Second Circuit, held the principal could not pursue her USERRA action against the individual board members under 42 U.S.C. § 1983.** Congress provided a comprehensive remedial scheme to ensure the employment and reemployment rights of those called upon to serve in the armed forces in the USERRA, and the scheme was incompatible with individual enforcement under Section 1983. The court dismissed the appeal and remanded the case to the district court for further proceedings. *Morris-Hayes v. Board of Educ. of Chester Union Free School Dist.*, 423 F.3d 153 (2d Cir. 2005).

◆ An untenured Kansas teacher was a Vietnam-era veteran who worked for a school district for three years. After learning he would not be rehired due to performance deficiencies, he followed the recommendation of his principal to submit a resignation letter in lieu of non-renewal. He then sued the district and superintendent in a state court for violating the Kansas Veteran's Preference Act

(VPA), his federal due process rights and defamation. The court held for the district on all claims, and the teacher appealed. The Court of Appeals of Kansas stated the VPA did not mention school districts. It pertained to appointments and reductions in force, not resignations. Resignation could not be considered a reduction in force. The teacher did not show he was equally qualified to any employee who was retained by the district.

The teacher admitted the principal's recommendation for non-renewal was based on performance deficiencies. **As the VPA provided no relief for untenured school employees who resigned under the threat of non-renewal, the court affirmed the judgment on the VPA claim.** The court found the teacher did not prove any defamation, as no defamatory information was communicated to a third party. The teacher claimed his contract was not renewed in retaliation for promoting or endorsing his teacher's association, in violation of his First Amendment speech rights. The court disagreed, noting key district officials were not even aware of his advocacy for the association. The trial court had properly disposed of this claim. The teacher claimed he was entitled to relief under 42 U.S.C. § 1983. This law creates no rights itself, but provides a cause of action to vindicate federally created rights. The teacher's VPA claim was created by state law, and as no federal right was implicated, his Section 1983 claim failed. The trial court had correctly held for the district and superintendent. *Richardson v. Dietrich*, 105 P.3d 279 (Kan. Ct. App. 2005).

◆   A Pennsylvania school district twice rejected a veteran for employment. The second time, he advanced to the fourth step of the district's five-step hiring process. A letter sent by the district informed the veteran he was not selected, but did not state a reason. He sued the district in a state court, which held the district was a "local agency" under the Pennsylvania Local Agency Law. The letter informing the veteran of its decision was an "adjudication" by a local agency that had to be appealed within 30 days. Since the veteran did not file suit until almost 90 days after the date of the letter, the court dismissed the case. The Commonwealth Court of Pennsylvania reversed and remanded the case, and the district appealed to the Supreme Court of Pennsylvania.

The court held an adjudication is invalid if a party does not receive reasonable notice of a hearing and an opportunity to be heard. The Veterans' Preference Act created vested rights, **but to enjoy the preference, a veteran had to possess the minimum qualifications for the job. The act did not require the district to hire a preference-eligible veteran who was unqualified.** Since the veteran had no absolute employment preference, he had no property right that might make the letter an "adjudication." The letter was "informatory in nature, not adjudicatory." As no determination had yet been made concerning the veteran's qualifications, the court reversed and remanded the case to the trial court to determine if the district had attempted to circumvent the act. A preference could "ripen" at the final stage in the hiring process, but only if the veteran could establish he was qualified for employment. *Merrell v. Chartiers Valley School Dist.*, 855 A.2d 713 (Pa. 2004).

◆   A Pennsylvania teacher was a veteran who worked as a part-time substitute teacher. He was twice passed over for full-time teaching positions in favor of non-veteran teachers. The veteran sued the school district in a federal district court for civil rights violations under 42 U.S.C. § 1983. He sought appointment to a teaching position with back wages and benefits, alleging violations of due process and the Pennsylvania Veterans' Preference Act. The court held for the district and the veteran appealed to the U.S. Court of Appeals, Third Circuit.

The court found the veteran correctly argued state law created a constitutionally protected property interest. However, this interest was in the employment preference created by the law, not in employment itself. The court rejected the veteran's procedural due process claim based on the district's failure to notify him of the "requisite qualifications" of the teaching positions. It also disagreed with his assertion that a veteran did not need to be the most qualified applicant for a job. Procedural due process did not require the district to notify the veteran in advance of hiring about the requisite job qualifications. **The Veterans' Preference Act was not intended to place veterans in a better position than other applicants simply because they were veterans. The court stated "the applicant veteran must be independently qualified" in order to be entitled to the preference.** The judgment for the school district was upheld. *Gikas v. Washington School Dist.*, 328 F.3d 731 (3d Cir. 2003).

◆   An Iowa school district hired a Navy veteran as a custodian. It soon gave him a poor performance appraisal that was reviewed at two meetings. The second meeting was "step three" of the district disciplinary procedure. The supervisor recommended discharging the custodian. The school board accepted the superintendent's recommendation to discharge the custodian. An arbitrator held the district did not violate the collective bargaining agreement, but found the district had failed to consider the state Veterans Preference Law.

The custodian filed a wrongful termination action against the district in an Iowa court, which entered judgment for the district. On appeal, the Iowa Supreme Court noted the Veterans Preference Law prevents the discharge of a veteran from a public position except for incompetence or misconduct shown after a hearing with due notice, upon stated charges, and with the right of court review under the state administrative procedure act. **The procedures offered by the district complied with constitutional due process requirements by providing the custodian notice of his deficient performance and an opportunity to respond, with a formal post-discharge procedure available, including a complete evidentiary hearing.** The court rejected the custodian's argument that the Veterans Preference Law required more elaborate protections. It found that the type of hearing for a public employee necessarily varies with the circumstances. As the district had fully satisfied the notice and opportunity to respond requirements of the Veterans Preference Law, the court affirmed the judgment. *Kern v. Saydel Community School Dist.*, 637 N.W.2d 157 (Iowa 2001).

CHAPTER EIGHT

Employment Termination, Resignation and Retirement

		Page
I.	BUDGET REDUCTIONS AND REDUCTIONS IN FORCE	325
II.	IMMORALITY AND OTHER MISCONDUCT	328
	A. Sexual Misconduct	328
	B. Immoral Conduct	330
	C. Criminal Conduct	333
	D. Neglect of Duty	336
	E. Misuse of Technology	338
III.	INCOMPETENCE	341
	A. Teaching Deficiencies	341
	B. Procedural Problems	344
IV.	INSUBORDINATION AND OTHER GOOD CAUSE	346
V.	RESIGNATION AND RETIREMENT	350
	A. Resignation	350
	B. Retirement	353
	C. Retirement Benefits	355
VI.	UNEMPLOYMENT BENEFITS	358
	A. Eligibility Requirements	358
	B. Misconduct	360
VII.	WRONGFUL DISCHARGE	362
VIII.	WORKERS' COMPENSATION	366

I. BUDGET REDUCTIONS AND REDUCTIONS IN FORCE

School districts are bound to observe seniority rights and teacher qualifications when selecting employees who will be retained. In the case below, the Supreme Court of Montana held a financially distressed district could discharge a veteran teacher who was endorsed to teach only one subject while retaining less senior teachers who possessed endorsements in multiple subjects.

◆ A Montana school superintendent recommended budget cuts for the district and devised reduction in force (RIF) criteria. The criteria considered seniority and evaluations, but stated a preference for multiple endorsements "due to the versatility of using teachers in more than one area." The school board approved a restructuring of teaching positions based upon staff certifications. It voted to discharge a teacher who was endorsed to teach only social studies, based on his lack of multiple-subject endorsements. He filed for arbitration under the collective bargaining agreement (CBA). The teacher argued that two less experienced teachers were rehired, including one who was untenured. The arbitrator held for the board, and the decision was upheld at administrative levels. A Montana district court held the discharge violated the CBA and the teacher's rights under Section 20-4-203 of the state code. In 2000, the state supreme court found the superintendent had failed to address the Section 20-4-203 issue. It reversed and remanded the case. The district court again held the use of multiple endorsements as a RIF criteria violated the CBA and state law.

The case returned to the Supreme Court of Montana, which noted that teacher tenure rights must be balanced against a school board's authority to manage the district in a financially responsible manner. A reduction in revenue was "good cause" for the RIF. Tenured teachers are protected in RIFs if they are qualified for a position. A district did not have to restructure itself, revise academic programs or realign staff only to accommodate the seniority of tenured staff. The board had considered the alternatives and was not required to take actions that would negatively affect administrative operations and educational programs to preserve a teacher's bumping rights. **Other states, notably New Mexico, have allowed the retention of junior tenured and untenured teachers over senior tenured teachers when "elevating tenure above all other considerations during a reduction in force" would seriously affect educational programs.** "As a matter of practical policy, this case illustrates that a teacher with multiple endorsements is especially valuable to a small rural district which needs teachers to teach in many subjects and to differing age groups." Teachers in rural areas with declining enrollments should broaden their teaching certificates. The court reversed the district court decision, finding the teacher's dismissal did not violate Section 20-4-203. *Scobey School Dist. v. Radakovich*, 332 Mont. 9, 135 P.3d 778 (Mont. 2006).

◆ A New Mexico teacher was in her third year of employment with a school district and had a good record. However, the superintendent of schools notified her that he was recommending her discharge under a reduction in force (RIF) because of shortfalls in state funding and the discontinuation of federal grant money. The school board accepted the recommendation to discharge the teacher, and the case went before an independent arbitrator. The arbitrator found the RIF constituted "just cause" under New Mexico law. The state court of appeals reversed the arbitrator's decision, holding the RIF was not "just cause."

The Supreme Court of New Mexico agreed to review the case. It explained that Section 22-10A-2(F) of the state code defined the term as a "reason that is rationally related to an employee's competence or turpitude or the proper performance of his duties." **Earlier supreme court decisions interpreted "just cause" to mean reasons related to the satisfactory performance of job duties. In *Swisher v. Darden*, 59 N.M. 511, 287 P.2d 73 (1955), the court held that unless there were personal grounds for discharging a teacher, a school board had to affirmatively show no position was available for which the** teacher was qualified to support discharge by RIF. The court held that *Swisher* was still valid. Accordingly, the board had to affirmatively show no position was available for the teacher. The court found the legislature did not intend to tie the hands of a school board faced with a RIF, but also did not intend to place tenured teachers at the mercy of school administrators. Nothing indicated the school board in this case considered whether any other positions were available for the teacher. The discharge of a teacher, unlike contract non-renewal, resulted in job loss during the middle of a school year. **Given the extreme hardship to the teacher, the school board had to show that it could not survive financially for the present school year to justify a mid-year discharge.** The court affirmed the appeals court's decision, and it reversed and remanded the arbitrator's decision. *Aguilera v. Board of Educ. of Hatch Valley Schools*, 139 N.M. 330, 132 P.3d 587 (N.M. 2006).

◆   A Nebraska school district that served only 22 students during the 2000-01 school year sought to eliminate one of its three full-time teachers based on an expected enrollment of 11 students the next year. The board informed a teacher that it would consider terminating her contract because she had the "least amount of tenure among the certified staff." After a hearing, the board voted to terminate the teacher's contract, and she appealed the decision to a Nebraska state court. The court noted the board's reduction-in-force (RIF) policy, while describing notice and procedural requirements, contained no criteria for actually carrying out RIFs. Because state law required boards to adopt RIF policies, the court held the termination had been arbitrary.

The board appealed to the Nebraska Supreme Court, which noted that the legislature had limited school board discretion to achieve RIFs by requiring them to adopt policies. The law stated that every board was required to adopt an RIF policy for a specific class of employees, and to include employee evaluation as a criterion for RIFs if the board policy did so. In this case, **the district's policy lacked any criteria for RIFs, in violation of state law.** The contract termination did not comply with the law and was not excused on the grounds of "change in circumstances" necessitating an RIF. The court affirmed the judgment for the teacher and ordered her reinstatement. *Wilder v. Grant County School Dist. No. 0001*, 658 N.W.2d 923 (Neb. 2003).

◆   The Illinois Legislature amended 105 ILCS 5/34-18 in 1995 to authorize school boards to establish procedures governing layoffs, recall and other reduction-in-force issues. Another law, 105 ILCS 5/34-8.1, allowed principals to make recommendations to boards about employee discharges and layoffs and vested school boards with the right to employ, discharge and lay off employees. The Chicago School Board "honorably terminated" 138 tenured teachers in 1999 under a board policy adopted in 1997. The policy listed events that could trigger a layoff and adopted a strict rule of seniority, but it did not identify the person or office that made seniority determinations and issued layoff notices.

Some principals notified teachers of their layoff, and five teachers sued the board in a state court, arguing the board policy was invalid under the 1995 amendments. The court awarded summary judgment to the board, and the case reached the Supreme Court of Illinois. It rejected the teachers' argument that the

1995 amendments did not give the board authority to lay off tenured teachers. The amendments were intended to broaden school board authority to formulate and implement layoff rules and procedures, not to bind boards to a legislative procedure. **The court held the amended law did not exempt tenured teachers from layoff. It agreed with the teachers that 105 ILCS 5/34-18 did not allow the board to delegate to principals the responsibility for implementing layoff procedures.** The legislature had limited board powers to delegate this responsibility to school superintendents and attorneys. The board was not prohibited from delegating its layoff authority. The case was remanded to determine if the board properly delegated the responsibility for making layoff decisions under its "self-executing" seniority-based policy. *Land v. Board of Educ. of City of Chicago*, 202 Ill.2d 414, 781 N.E.2d 249 (Ill. 2002).

◆ A Kentucky school board reduced the extended employment days for 46 of its 600 certified employees based on a "budget allocation" to allow the funding of an alternative learning center. Several of the teachers sued the school board in a state circuit court for violations of state law. The court held the reduction in extended employment days had been accomplished according to a uniform plan in compliance with the law, and that there had been no violation of the state open meetings law. The teachers appealed to the state court of appeals, which stated that Ky. Rev. Stat. § 161.760 provided teacher salaries shall not be lowered unless the reduction is part of a uniform plan affecting all teachers in the entire district, and there is a reduction in responsibilities. The reduction in extended employment days was a reduction of responsibilities under the law.

The court noted the board's records indicated the plan included only 46 of 600 certified employees and that specific teachers were targeted for reductions. **While a school board was permitted to adjust its budget to meet district needs, the legislature had provided that there be uniformity when making such adjustments** so that no teacher or class of teachers was "sacrificed." All teachers were to be encompassed in such a plan, even though not all were affected by the implementation of the plan in order to prevent arbitrary salary reductions of a targeted class. Because the circuit court did not reach the issue of whether the teachers received a reduction in responsibility or proper notice as required by the law, the court remanded the case for further proceedings. The determination that no violation of the open meetings law occurred was upheld. *Pigue v. Christian County Board of Educ.*, 65 S.W.3d 540 (Ky. Ct. App. 2001).

II. IMMORALITY AND OTHER MISCONDUCT

School employees can be discharged for a wide variety of misconduct, including conduct deemed immoral or inappropriate. State laws provide for discharging teachers for immoral conduct, incompetence and conduct affecting their fitness to teach or the ability to be a good role model.

A. Sexual Misconduct

◆ A New Jersey teacher resigned after completing a one-year teaching contract. The next school year, two students who had been in his class told a school guidance counselor the teacher had accessed pornographic Web sites on his classroom computer. They said the teacher also told them stories involving violence, weapons, sex and a contest to attract overweight women. The district superintendent ordered an investigation. A district technology director found some sites viewed on the teacher's computer might be pornographic. Three students corroborated the earlier reports. A detective obtained arrest warrants for the teacher and took him into custody. The teacher admitted some of the conduct alleged by the students. He admitted viewing adult Web sites on his school computer, but said students did not see any nudity. A grand jury indicted the teacher on four counts of endangering the welfare of a child and one count of official misconduct. He pleaded guilty to reduced charges of unauthorized computer use and was sentenced to a year of probation.

The teacher sued the detective, school board, district superintendent, administrators and families for malicious prosecution and negligence. The court held a reasonable official in the detective's position would have believed there was probable cause to arrest the teacher. **He admitted web logs revealed his computer accessed inappropriate sites on days he was not absent. The court rejected the argument that the detective should have done more to investigate the students.** The fact that the investigation was not the best one possible did not prevent a finding of probable cause. The teacher's plea bargain to a lesser crime did not demonstrate innocence, and the detective was entitled to qualified immunity for the malicious prosecution claim. **The school officials and families were also entitled to qualified immunity for the malicious prosecution claims.** The teacher did not show school officials played any role in a constitutional violation, and their actions were reasonable in response to the allegations. There was no evidence that students lied or their parents consented to lying. The court held the families could pursue their state law claims against the teacher and school board in a state court. *Grendysa v. Evesham Township Board of Educ.*, No. Civ.A. 02-1493 (FLW), 2005 WL 2416983 (D.N.J. 2005).

◆ A Wisconsin school district reassigned a physical education teacher because of conflicts with a principal. Four years later, several female students filed complaints against the teacher for touching them, referring to them as "honey, dear or sweetheart," refusing to let them wear sweat suits over their swimsuits while doing calisthenics, and related conduct. After suspending the teacher with pay, the school board terminated his employment for just cause as defined in the applicable collective bargaining agreement. The association representing the teacher's bargaining unit filed a grievance on his behalf that was directed to binding arbitration. The arbitrator ruled that the district lacked just cause for termination. The teacher's conduct was inappropriate but was not sexual harassment because it was not sexual in nature. The arbitrator reinstated the teacher but opted to suspend him for a year without pay. The association brought a state court action to confirm the arbitration award, and the district moved to vacate the award. The court held the arbitrator exceeded his authority by substituting his judgment for that of the board. Because the teacher's conduct was contrary to a public policy against sexual harassment, the court vacated the arbitration award and reinstated the termination.

The association appealed to the Court of Appeals of Wisconsin, which noted that state law provided for the vacation of an arbitration award in limited and extraordinary circumstances, including an arbitrator's abuse of powers or failure to make a "mutual, final and definite award upon the subject matter." The court rejected the trial court finding that the arbitrator had to defer to the school board's decision. Instead, the court was required to defer to the arbitrator. The parties' collective bargaining agreement permitted the arbitrator to craft an appropriate remedy and gave him the authority to make findings of fact and determine discipline. The arbitrator's findings were not reviewable by the trial court because he did not exceed his authority or violate public policy in making the award. **There was no evidence of any flaw in the arbitrator's finding of no just cause to terminate the teacher's employment.** The trial court had exceeded its powers by vacating the arbitration award and by characterizing the teacher's conduct as sexual harassment. The court reversed the trial court's decision and affirmed the arbitration award. *Greendale Educ. Ass'n v. Greendale School Dist.*, 259 Wis.2d 481, 655 N.W.2d 546 (Wis. Ct. App. 2002).

B. Immoral Conduct

State laws describe other forms of misconduct that may lead to employment termination, including conduct characterized as immoral, criminal conduct, moral turpitude, and neglect of duty.

◆   An Oregon teacher served a school district for 19 years with no disciplinary problems. Her husband left her, moved in with his girlfriend, and sought a divorce. The teacher drove to the girlfriend's house and argued with him. She attempted suicide by taking prescription medications, then rammed her vehicle into her husband's vehicle and damaged the house. The teacher voluntarily committed herself for psychiatric treatment. The incident was reported in local newspapers. Law officials charged the teacher with four crimes, three of which were dropped via plea bargain. She pleaded no contest to a criminal mischief charge, which provided for dismissal with no charges if she completed her term of probation. The school board voted to dismiss the teacher after a hearing, and she appealed to the Oregon Fair Dismissal Appeals Board (FDAB).

An FDAB hearing panel heard testimony from a psychologist who said the teacher's conduct was isolated and unlikely to reoccur. The board had previously let two teachers return to work after suicide attempts, and another had returned after entering into a diversion agreement for domestic violence charges. The FDAB panel found the dismissal had been "unreasonable" under ORS § 342.905. The board overreacted to an isolated incident and had to reinstate the teacher. The Court of Appeals of Oregon reversed the panel's decision, and the teacher appealed. **The Supreme Court of Oregon stated that contract teachers may be dismissed only for immorality or neglect of duty.** The FDAB was authorized to determine whether actions by school boards were "unreasonable" or "clearly an excessive remedy." **In the context of the statute, "unreasonable" meant "acting without rational or logical justification" for an action.** The FDAB panel failed to apply this interpretation, and its decision did not provide a rational connection between the facts and the conclusion. The court returned the case to the panel to address facts such as the suicide attempt, criminal conduct, and publicity, and apply them to the criteria of ORS § 342.905(6). The panel also had to interpret the term "clearly an excessive remedy," and apply it to the facts of the case. *Bergerson v. Salem-Keizer School Dist.*, 341 Or. 401, 144 P.3d 918 (Or. 2006).

◆   A 14-year-old Illinois student gave birth to a child in 1986. Blood tests indicated a 99.99% probability that the assistant principal of her junior high school was the child's father. The school district dismissed him under Section 24-12 of the Illinois School Code. Almost two years later, the assistant principal was acquitted of aggravated criminal sexual assault. The student's paternity action was closed shortly after the acquittal based on "lack of activity." A hearing officer reversed the school board's action dismissing the assistant principal in 1991, finding the district did not prove he had sexual contact with the student. A state court affirmed the assistant principal's reinstatement, as did the Appellate Court of Illinois. In 1997, the paternity case was reopened and a court ordered him to submit to DNA testing. Testing indicated a 99.9% probability that the assistant principal was the child's father. In 1999, the court entered a judgment of paternity and ordered him to pay child support. The state superintendent of education notified the assistant principal of an action to suspend his teaching and administrative certificates for immoral conduct. A hearing officer upheld the action under Section 21-23 of the state school code.

The case reached the Appellate Court of Illinois, which held the action to suspend the assistant principal's certificates was not barred by the district's effort to dismiss him years earlier. The Section 24-12 employment dismissal and Section 21-23 certificate suspension proceedings were distinct and were brought by entirely different entities. **The court held the assistant principal's acquittal from criminal charges did not prevent the state superintendent from suspending his certificates. The code required the superintendent to suspend a holder's certificate for conviction of specified sex or narcotics offenses.** While suspension proceedings were to be terminated if a criminal conviction was reversed, Section 21-23 said nothing about an acquittal. The court held the suspension action was not untimely, as it was commenced soon after the paternity judgment was issued. The 1998 DNA test results were "evidence of immorality" permitting suspension. *Hayes v. State Teacher Certification Board*, 359 Ill.App.3d 1153, 835 N.E.2d 146 (Ill. App. Ct. 2005). The Supreme Court of Illinois denied further appeal.

◆   An Oklahoma school district tried to discharge a teacher. He eventually won reinstatement in settlement of a state court lawsuit. After the school board adopted the district superintendent's recommendation not to renew his contract, a state court ordered his reinstatement. The district reassigned the teacher to an elementary school. Shortly after the court order was issued, the superintendent encountered the teacher in a copy room at an adjacent middle school. The teacher refused an instruction to report to his assigned area, claiming he was "already in his assigned area." When the superintendent stated he would "write him up for not reporting to his assigned area," the teacher said "if you do, I'll beat the shit out of you" in a threatening manner. The teacher repeated the threat, and the superintendent left to obtain a witness. After the superintendent returned with an assistant principal, the teacher again threatened to hit him and complained that the school's new baseball coach was talking about his wife. The teacher threatened to "pick something up and knock his head off," then said he was sick and left school for the rest of the day. The school board voted to terminate the teacher's contract for moral turpitude under 70 Oklahoma Statutes § 6-101.22. He sued the board in a federal district court for civil rights violations. The court affirmed the board's finding that the conduct constituted moral turpitude justifying termination, and the teacher appealed.

The U.S. Court of Appeals, Tenth Circuit, certified a question to the Oklahoma Supreme Court on the interpretation of "moral turpitude" under 70 Oklahoma Statutes § 6-101.22. The supreme court found **"moral turpitude" involved a level of conduct that was more than "mere impropriety." It was not a catch-all for every kind of offensive, inappropriate or unprofessional conduct.** The court reviewed prior decisions construing the term "moral turpitude," including one dismissing a teacher for falsifying disciplinary reports. Another case stated "moral turpitude is anything done contrary to justice, honesty, modesty or good morals." While the teacher's threats in this case were "unprofessional, unwise and unacceptable behavior," they did not constitute moral turpitude. The court found the "unexecuted threat" against the superintendent was not moral turpitude under state law. *Ballard v. Independent School Dist. No. 4 of Bryan County, Oklahoma*, 77 P.3d 1084 (Okla. 2003).

◆ A tenured Connecticut teacher actively sought a promotion after 20 years of teaching. She filled in answers to questions her students left blank on the Connecticut Mastery Test, a state-required student achievement exam. Ninety-six percent of the teacher's class exceeded the state achievement goal. Although 96% of her former students were placed in advanced English classes the following year, they were retested and only 15% exceeded the state goal. A hearing panel held the teacher's actions constituted "moral misconduct."

The school board discharged the teacher for moral misconduct and other due and sufficient cause, and a Connecticut trial court upheld the decision. The Court of Appeals of Connecticut rejected her argument that she was improperly denied the opportunity to supplement the trial transcript on appeal. It agreed with the board that **substantial evidence supported the finding that the teacher had tampered with her students' state proficiency examinations.** Her assertion that students had tampered with the tests was implausible, and the hearing panel had reached a reasonable conclusion. As there was due and sufficient cause to discharge the teacher, the court affirmed the judgment. *Hanes v. Board of Educ. of City of Bridgeport*, 783 A.2d 1 (Conn. App. Ct. 2001).

◆ On the night before a verification review by a Washington state education compliance monitoring agency, a special education director obtained a faxed list of 41 files the agency intended to audit. He reviewed the files with an intern and made significant alterations to a number of them. The director and intern forged and backdated some documents, making changes in an effort to make their program appear to comply with state and federal special education laws. Although the director denied any misconduct, many of the changes were obvious, and the district discharged him. He sought administrative review before a hearing officer, who concluded that documents had been backdated under his participation, direction or approval and that there was probable cause to terminate his employment. A state superior court affirmed the decision.

On appeal, the Washington Court of Appeals observed the director had tried to create records, not merely correct dates. One of the glaring examples of alterations reflected a classroom observation that allegedly took place on a Sunday. Another indicated a date that never existed – February 29, 1995. The court found this conduct established sufficient cause for employment termination under state law. **Sufficient cause existed to terminate a certificated employee where there was an irremediable deficiency that materially and substantially affected performance, or conduct that lacked any positive educational aspect or legitimate professional purpose.** There was no need to consider remediability, as this was a concern only when a discharge followed deficient performance. The director's conduct lacked any positive educational aspect or legitimate professional purpose, and it was unprofessional and dishonest. Since unprofessional conduct was a ground for revocation of a teaching certificate and discharge, the court affirmed the judgment. *Weems v. North Franklin School Dist.*, 37 P.3d 354 (Wash. Ct. App. 2002).

C. Criminal Conduct

◆ A South Carolina teacher was arrested for possessing crack cocaine in 1988, but authorities dismissed his case. In 2000, the teacher was arrested "in his car in a well-known drug area" while his passenger attempted to buy crack. Charges against the teacher were dropped when the passenger pled guilty. After the 2000 incident, the teacher was placed on administrative leave, pending an investigation into the arrest and "similar behavior in the past." The superintendent advised him by letter his contract was being terminated under S.C. Code Ann. § 59-25-430. At the teacher's school board hearing, the superintendent said the termination was based solely on the teacher's unfitness. The superintendent later testified he did not consider negative publicity in making the decision. The board upheld the discharge based on substantial, compelling evidence justifying immediate employment termination and "evident unfitness as manifested by his conduct. Conduct which, after a reasonable time for improvement, 12 years, shows an evident failure to improve." A state circuit court held that being arrested but not convicted for two criminal charges was not substantial evidence of unfitness to teach. The court reversed the board's decision, and the board appealed. The state court of appeals reinstated the board action. It found substantial evidence of the teacher's unfitness to teach, based on the arrests, his dishonesty, the publicity surrounding the 2000 arrest, and the negative response it caused in the community.

The teacher petitioned the Supreme Court of South Carolina to review his case. **The court held the appeals court committed error by failing to confine its decision to the grounds stated in the order terminating his employment.** The appeals court scoured the record and made independent factual findings supporting the action. **The supreme court found two drug arrests, 12 years apart, neither resulting in charges, did not support a finding of unfitness to teach.** This was especially true when the district did not contend the teacher ever used, possessed or sold illegal drugs. The teacher was entitled to reinstatement with back pay and benefits from the date of his suspension. *Shell v. Richland County School Dist. One*, 362 S.C. 408, 608 S.E.2d 428 (S.C. 2005).

◆   After a Pennsylvania teacher pled guilty to simple assault of his wife, the state education department filed a notice of charges and a motion for summary judgment with the state Professional Standards and Practices Commission to revoke his professional teaching certification. The notice informed the teacher that simple assault was a crime involving moral turpitude, requiring revocation. The teacher admitted the assault, but he contended he had pled guilty to avoid embarrassment to himself and his family. He asserted his actions were unrelated to moral turpitude but were the result of his wife's attempt to gain an advantage in divorce proceedings. The commission revoked the teacher's license without a hearing. It held the circumstances surrounding the guilty plea were irrelevant, since simple assault was within the state code's definition of "moral turpitude."

The teacher appealed to the Commonwealth Court of Pennsylvania, arguing the commission denied him due process by refusing to give him a hearing. The court held a teaching certificate is a property right entitled to due process protection. The court agreed with the teacher that **simple assault is not necessarily a crime involving moral turpitude. It found the state code and cases defining the term "crime of moral turpitude" required the assailant to have a "reprehensible state of mind." At minimum, a crime of moral turpitude required knowledge of private impropriety or the potential for social disruption.** Crimes involving dishonesty, such as fraud, theft by deception and specific intent drug trafficking offenses were crimes of moral turpitude. By contrast, the statutory definition of "simple assault" included negligence. A person could lack a "reprehensible state of mind" when engaged in a fight or scuffle by mutual consent. While many forms of simple assault, including spousal battery, were abhorrent, a simple assault was not always a crime of moral turpitude. The court held the commission had erroneously revoked the teacher's certification without a hearing. There was a material issue of fact concerning whether the teacher's guilty plea was for a crime of moral turpitude, and the court reversed and remanded the judgment. *Bowalick v. Comwlth. of Pennsylvania*, 840 A.2d 519 (Pa. Commw. Ct. 2004).

◆   New York's highest court upheld the employment termination of two school mechanics for misconduct. They sold untaxed cigarettes to employees on school grounds while driving a school-owned vehicle. The mechanics also stored the cigarettes in school vehicles. After a hearing, each was found guilty of disciplinary charges and discharged. The mechanics appealed to a state trial court, where they argued there was insufficient evidence to support a finding of misconduct. The court agreed, ruling that employment termination was too severe a penalty for their offenses. The court relied on *Pell v. Board of Educ. of Union Free School Dist.*, 34 N.Y.2d 222 (N.Y. 1974). That case held that **employee discipline cannot be so disproportionate to the offense as to shock one's sense of fairness**. The district appealed to a state appellate division court, which affirmed the decision. The court held that at most, the mechanics acted inappropriately during work hours and misused school facilities. The court reduced their punishment to two years of suspended pay and benefits. On appeal, **the New York Court of Appeals held the district did not abuse its discretion in discharging the mechanics. The misconduct took place over several months, involved misappropriation of work time and violated the district's trust as well as district policy.** *In re Maison Scahill v. Greece Cent. School Dist.*, 2 N.Y.3d 754, 778 N.Y.S.2d 771 (N.Y. 2004).

◆   About 48 hours after the adult son of a veteran Iowa teacher moved into her house, police officers executed a search warrant on the teacher's house. They found drugs and drug paraphernalia in five locations, including the teacher's bedroom. The district proposed terminating her teaching contract for reasons including drug possession, unprofessional conduct, poor role modeling and leadership, and failure to maintain a good reputation. The school board held a hearing and found that just cause existed to immediately terminate the teacher's employment contract. The teacher appealed to an administrative adjudicator, who found that the board's decision was not supported by the evidence.

A state trial court affirmed the decision, and the district appealed. The Court of Appeals of Iowa found "just cause" for teacher termination exists when the teacher has a significant and adverse effect on the high quality education of students. Just cause "relates to job performance, including leadership and role model effectiveness." **The board's findings did not show the teacher's conduct significantly and adversely affected her job performance. There was no evidence that she ever bought, sold or used marijuana** during her 15-year tenure in the district. The board found it likely she did not know that most of the evidence seized by police was in her house, since her son had returned there less than 48 hours before the search. Other items were kept as "mementos of her deceased husband" and as evidence of her son's marijuana use. The teacher presented evidence that she did not condone drug use and regularly instructed students to stay away from drugs. Since there was insufficient evidence of just cause to discharge the teacher, the judgment was affirmed. *Fielder v. Board of Directors of Carroll Community School Dist.*, 662 N.W.2d 371 (Iowa Ct. App. 2003).

◆   Ritalin was reported missing from student prescription bottles at a Tennessee school six times. A surveillance camera caught a teacher reaching into a secretary's drawer and slipping pills from student prescriptions into her pocket. When a police detective asked her if she had taken the pills, she denied doing so. The superintendent recommended dismissing the teacher for conduct unbecoming a member of the teaching profession, namely dishonesty and unreliability. The school board voted to discharge her, and she appealed to a Tennessee chancery court. The court agreed with the board that the teacher had not been deprived of due process, that the discharge was not disproportionate to the offense, and that the finding of guilt was not arbitrary or capricious.

The teacher appealed to the Tennessee Court of Appeals, which rejected her claims that she did not deny taking the pills and that the board could not dismiss her without proving every charge against her. The court held it was sufficient for the board to advise her of the charges and of the possibility that she would be dismissed. The notice she received made her fully aware that her job was at stake.

While a teacher's employment record is a relevant consideration in determining the penalty for a lapse in judgment, the offense was not a minor one. The teacher compounded the offense by destroying evidence. The school board was entitled to discharge her and was not arbitrary and capricious in doing so. The appeals court affirmed the chancery court decision. *Lannom v. Board of Educ. for Metropolitan Government, Nashville and Davidson County*, No. M1999-00137-COA-R3-N, 2000 Tenn. App. Lexis 133 (Tenn. Ct. App. 2000).

D. Neglect of Duty

◆ A Louisiana teacher served her district for 16 years before being assigned to teach social studies and language arts at a middle school. The principal outlined the procedure for sending students to his office for discipline in an orientation meeting held before the opening of the school year. He explained that if disciplinary problems arose that could not be handled in class, teachers were to call him to have the student escorted to the office. The principal reprimanded the teacher twice during the opening weeks of the school year for sending students unescorted to his office for discipline. On the first occasion, the teacher sent six unescorted students to the office in a single day, even though the practice had been reiterated at a faculty meeting the previous day. Less than two weeks later, she sent another student to the office unattended, believing that she had permission to do so from a school secretary. The principal immediately sought to discipline the teacher, who refused to sign reprimand forms related to her policy violations. The school board accepted the district superintendent's recommendation to discharge her. The teacher requested a hearing at which the board found substantial evidence supporting her discharge. A state trial court upheld the board's decision, and the teacher appealed.

The Court of Appeal of Louisiana held the board abused its discretion by discharging the teacher. The Supreme Court of Louisiana agreed to review the case and recited the statutory grounds for dismissal of tenured teachers from La. Rev. Stat. Ann. § 17:443(A). **It explained that judicial review of tenure proceedings is limited to an inquiry into whether the school board has complied with statutory requirements and whether the board's findings are supported by substantial evidence. Section 17:443(A) permits the removal of a tenured teacher for willful neglect of duty.** The court found the principal's warnings to the teacher against sending unescorted students to the office for discipline adequately explained the policy. There was substantial evidence to support the board's decision that her **repeated failure to follow these directions constituted willful neglect of duty**. The court reversed the court of appeal's decision and reinstated the board's action dismissing the teacher. *Wise v. Bossier Parish School Board*, 851 So.2d 1090 (La. 2003).

◆ A Louisiana teacher was a tenured vocational instructor whose only area of certification was shop mechanics. He was suspended with pay after he reported the theft of a loaded gun from his wife's car – which he had parked outside his classroom. A state trial court affirmed the board's decision to fire the teacher for willful neglect of duty, as did the state court of appeal. The Supreme Court of Louisiana reversed the lower courts, finding there was no rational basis supported by substantial evidence to discharge the teacher. It ordered the board to reinstate him to his former position, with all salary and benefits. Instead of rehiring the teacher, the board notified him it had discontinued shop mechanics from the curriculum. As this was his only area of certification, the board terminated his employment, retroactive to a date four years earlier. However, the notice indicated the teacher could request review of the reduction in force.

The teacher moved the trial court to enforce the supreme court's judgment. The court held he was entitled to reinstatement with full compensation and benefits. The court of appeal amended the judgment, requiring the board to pay the teacher for only the part of the school year in which shop mechanics was eliminated from the curriculum. It held the decision to eliminate the course was not made in bad faith. The teacher appealed to the supreme court a second time. It explained the board had been ordered previously to reinstate the teacher to his former position with all salary and benefits. There was no evidence the board had complied with this mandate. **While the board's notice to the teacher stated his discharge was retroactive to the year of the course elimination, it also permitted him 15 days to request review. By allowing the teacher to challenge the action, the board recognized any termination did not become effective until the date of the letter.** The court held the teacher should be considered reinstated as of the date of his last paycheck until the date of the board's notice of reduction in force, when he was formally advised of employment termination. The court amended the judgment to require the board to pay him for this four-year period, with interest. *Howard v. West Baton Rouge Parish School Board,* 865 So.2d 708 (La. 2004).

◆ A Texas teacher checked out a district vehicle to drive to a soccer clinic. Before picking up a colleague who was going to the clinic, the teacher stopped at a dry cleaner and then a grocery store, where he purchased beer and other items. A witness reported seeing him leaving the store with beer and getting into the vehicle. The teacher admitted buying beer while using the vehicle when the school principal confronted him about it. He submitted his resignation after being formally reprimanded, but he later changed his mind and rescinded it. The superintendent recommended not renewing his contract, and the school board voted for non-renewal after a hearing. The state education commissioner affirmed the decision, finding substantial evidence that the teacher was "in the course and scope of his employment while he was in possession of alcohol."

A Texas district court affirmed the decision, and the teacher appealed to the state court of appeals, arguing he was on a purely personal side trip to run errands at the time of the beer purchase. The court held the commissioner's decision had to be affirmed unless it was arbitrary and capricious. **A court could not substitute its judgment for the commissioner's and could only review it to determine if it was supported by substantial evidence.** The teacher had admitted his error and stated buying beer "was a dumb thing to do." He also stated to the board he was acting within the scope of his duties to attend the soccer clinic. The teacher agreed it was reasonable to assume he was acting for the school when the school day began. As the commissioner's decision was supported by substantial evidence, the court affirmed it. *Simpson v. Alanis,* No. 08-03-00110-CV, 2004 WL 309297 (Tex. Ct. App. 2004).

◆   A teacher employed by the Kansas State School for the Deaf (KSSD) asked an assistant football coach to recruit players to help him improve property he owned. The project involved moving discarded railroad ties that weighed 150 pounds. The school's head teacher turned down a written request for a field trip to the property, but later signed the request form. Two students and the assistant football coach accompanied the teacher to the property. When the teacher left to prepare lunch, one of the students was struck and killed by a train. KSSD's board ruled the teacher's conduct did not reflect high standards of professional conduct, especially for the safety needs of deaf students. A KSSD investigation committee adopted a motion terminating the teacher's employment for jeopardizing the health and safety of students, failing to exercise appropriate professional judgment, failing to comply with school policies, and failing to conduct himself "in a manner reflecting positively on the school." However, a KSSD hearing committee held for the teacher, finding the board did not prove he displayed a lack of professional judgment.

The board appealed to a Kansas district court, which reversed the hearing committee's decision. The teacher appealed to the Kansas Supreme Court, which held the KSSD operated under laws similar to those applying to all Kansas teachers. It was appropriate to evaluate the case under the numerous decisions of state courts regarding the discharge of tenured teachers. **The court upheld the hearing committee's finding that no school policy or student safety regulations applied to the case. The board showed no evidence of a loss of confidence in the teacher**, as the testimony of members of the deaf community was "all to the contrary." While the teacher did not inform parents about the nature of the field trip, this was the head teacher's duty. There was evidence that the practice of taking railroad ties from railroad property was common and not inappropriate. The court refused to reweigh the evidence or substitute its judgment for that of the committee. As the board did not show substantial evidence supporting discharge, and the committee did not act fraudulently, arbitrarily or capriciously, the court reversed the judgment. *Kansas State Board of Educ. v. Marsh*, 50 P.3d 9 (Kan. 2002).

E. Misuse of Technology

◆   A Wisconsin school board held a public hearing to consider discharging a teacher for viewing adult Web site images on his work computer. After the board voted for discharge, a Milwaukee newspaper requested access to the exhibits presented at the hearing. The teacher's union filed a grievance to challenge the discharge action. In preparation for the grievance, the district assembled the images viewed on his work computer and put them on a computer CD. The newspaper filed an Open Records Request for the CD and a memorandum. The teacher sought a court order prohibiting release of the requested information.

The court denied the teacher's request, and he appealed to the Court of Appeals of Wisconsin. Meanwhile, an arbitrator ordered his reinstatement. The teacher argued that the materials sought by the newspaper should not be released because they contained copyrighted images that were reproduced in response to his grievance. The court noted the Open Records Law has a presumption of complete public access that is overcome only in exceptional cases. An exception exists for "materials to which access is limited by copyright." The newspaper claimed the teacher could not raise the copyright objection, since he did not own the copyrights. **The court asked the Supreme Court of Wisconsin to consider whether the additional information should be released. The teacher claimed the materials were off limits to the newspaper as part of a current investigation.** The court certified for review the question of how the Open Records Law treated materials created after discharge, but before arbitration was completed. *Zellner v. Cedarburg School Dist.*, No. 2006AP1143-AC, 2006 WL 3020369 (Wis. Ct. App. 2006).

◆ Ohio school administrators placed a junior high school teacher on leave of absence after investigating charges that he accessed sexually oriented Web sites on school computers and viewed them with students. The school board resolved to suspend him without pay or benefits, but agreed to delay his hearing until criminal proceedings were complete. A jury found the teacher guilty of several felony charges, and he was fined $5,000 and jailed for almost one year. When the state education department sought to revoke his teaching certificate, he agreed to have it suspended pending appeal of his criminal convictions. The state court of appeals vacated as untimely charges of sexual abuse of a juvenile that arose from conduct in 1983-84. It otherwise affirmed the teacher's convictions. The school board declined his requests for reemployment, and the education department found he had violated an agreement by seeking to be reemployed. The school board informed the teacher that Ohio law prohibited the district from employing him. He alleged due process violations, and the board offered to resume his termination hearing. The state supreme court denied the teacher's motion to reconsider his criminal appeal, and the state education department appointed a hearing officer to consider his certification.

The hearing officer found the teacher had sexually abused at least two students, provided students with alcohol and sexually explicit books and movies, let at least one student view sexually oriented Web sites on a school computer and "brutalized" at least two students. The teacher's conduct was found criminal, immoral and unbecoming to a teacher under Ohio education law. The state board revoked the teacher's eight-year teaching certificate, as well as his permanent certification. The teacher filed a new action against the local board, including breach of contract and wrongful discharge claims. The court found the board had "substantially complied" with Ohio R.C. Section 3319.16 in terminating his contract, and he appealed again. **The court of appeals stated the teacher could not be employed as a teacher, because he was convicted of one of the crimes listed in R.C. Section 3319.39(B).** After his teaching certificates were revoked, the local board could not maintain a continuing contract to employ him. The court disapproved of the trial court's finding of "substantial compliance" with state law. However, the issue was moot because the teacher was disqualified from employment. He no longer had a property interest in his teaching contract with the board. As a hearing by the local board would have been a futile act, the court affirmed the judgment. *Huntsman v. Perry Local School Dist. Board of Educ.*, No. 2004 CA 00347, 2005 WL 1519344, 2005-Ohio-3294 (Ohio Ct. App. 2005).

◆ **The Court of Appeals of Florida held a high school teacher accused of exchanging sexually explicit e-mails with students did not have to turn over his home computers for inspection by his school board for use in his formal employment termination hearing.** The board suspended the teacher for misconduct in office for exchanging e-mails and instant messages with students that were sexually explicit and made derogatory comments about staff members and school operations. An administrative law judge issued an order allowing a board expert to inspect the hard drives of the teacher's home computers to discover if they had relevant data for use in a formal termination hearing.

The teacher appealed, arguing production of home computer records would violate his Fifth Amendment right against self-incrimination and his privacy rights. The court held a request for broad access to personal computers would expose confidential communications and extraneous personal information about the teacher. It might also reveal privileged communications with his wife and his attorney. A Florida case discussing the production of electronic records in pretrial discovery held **a request to examine a computer hard drive was permitted "in only limited or strictly controlled circumstances," such as where a party was suspected of trying to purge data.** Other courts had permitted access to a computer when there was evidence of intentional deletion of data. There was no evidence of such conduct in this case. The court held the broad discovery request violated the teacher's Fifth Amendment rights and his personal and family privacy rights. It reversed the administrative order. *Menke v. Broward County School Board*, 916 So.2d 8 (Fla. Dist. Ct. App. 2005).

◆ A Texas teacher found an icon labeled "Teacher Evaluations" on a classroom computer. Some of his students later discovered documents involving employee reprimands on the computer's hard drive. The teacher recognized some of the information as confidential and inappropriate for students, but he read it with them. A student saved the personnel documents on floppy disks, and the teacher gave them to his attorney without telling school administrators of the discovery. The district discharged the teacher, and a Texas trial court later affirmed the state commissioner of education's decision upholding the discharge. The teacher appealed to the Court of Appeals of Texas, which dismissed several procedural claims before advancing to the question of whether the discharge was supported by "good cause" – a term that is undefined in the Texas Education Code. **The commissioner defined "good cause" as an employee's failure to perform employment duties that a "person of ordinary prudence would have done under the same or similar circumstances." The court upheld the commissioner's finding of good cause under any definition.** The commissioner did not commit error in finding the teacher's dissemination of teacher reprimands could cause a loss of confidence in the district. The teacher did not dispute that he discovered confidential records and allowed students to review and download them for future use. The court affirmed the commissioner's decision upholding the discharge. *Tave v. Alanis*, 109 S.W.3d 890 (Tex. Ct. App. 2003).

◆ An Ohio music teacher had an exceptional record with no significant disciplinary violations. However, the parent of a former student wrote the district that the teacher was sending his daughter "dirty e-mail jokes." School officials determined the teacher either sent the e-mails or approved of their transmission. She also occasionally told sexually oriented jokes to female middle school students, called a colleague "turd" and called a student an obscene name. A hearing officer found that two of the charges were substantiated and that the teacher had at the least approved of the e-mail transmission. The board adopted a resolution substantially accepting the officer's findings and conclusions and voted to terminate her contract.

The teacher appealed to a state court, which affirmed the board's action. She appealed to the Court of Appeals of Ohio, asserting the board had denied her due process and claiming the evidence did not support discharging her for "good and just cause" under state law. The court found no evidence that the board had made up its mind not to rehire the teacher prior to the hearing. There was no due process violation, as she was afforded a meaningful hearing and opportunity to be heard. **To show good and just cause for employment termination under state law, the level of conduct must be a "fairly serious matter."** The teacher's conduct was "fairly serious" because it was unprofessional and disruptive of school decorum. Despite her prior exemplary record, she engaged in inappropriate conduct that constituted a serious lapse in judgment. The court's role was not to second-guess the school board, and the lower court did not abuse its discretion in affirming its action. *Oleske v. Hilliard City School Dist. Board of Educ.*, 764 N.E.2d 1110 (Ohio Ct. App. 2001).

III. INCOMPETENCE

A. Teaching Deficiencies

◆   A Nevada school district admonished a teacher for failing to follow district procedures for testing English language learners. She was provided training and mentoring, and her caseload was reduced by 50%. After a second admonition, the district provided the teacher one-on-one training and feedback on testing procedures. After a third admonition, the district suspended the teacher and advised her that her contract would not be renewed. She sought arbitration, claiming the district violated NRS § 391.313 by dismissing her only eight days after the last admonishment. The arbitrator upheld the non-renewal, and a state court affirmed the arbitration award. On appeal to the Supreme Court of Nevada, the teacher argued the district had violated NRS § 391.313 because she was not allowed to improve her job performance after the final admonition.

The court found **Section 391.313 required school administrators to notify an employee in writing whenever it was necessary to admonish the employee, state the reasons, and make reasonable efforts to assist the employee to correct the cause for potential demotion, dismissal or non-renewal.** The law required a "reasonable time for improvement, which must not exceed three months for the first admonition." The teacher was admonished numerous times for the same unprofessional conduct. There was no violation of NRS § 391.313 since all the admonishments were for the same type of conduct.

The arbitrator had found the district provided the teacher assistance for over a year to correct her deficient performance, including training, mentoring and reduction of her workload. She received a reasonable time to improve her performance, but was unable to do so. As the lower court had correctly confirmed the arbitration award, the judgment was affirmed. *Clark County Educ. Ass'n v. Clark County School Dist.*, 131 P.3d 5 (Nev. 2006).

♦   A Florida school board brought formal discharge proceedings against a career contract teacher with many classroom and communication problems. There had been complaints about his classroom presentation and learning environment, planning, record-keeping, policies, procedure and ethics, as well as his communications and his working relationships in prior school years. The teacher was then transferred to a different school. There were new complaints about excessive and inappropriate use of R-rated videos, failure to timely post and enter grades into the system, and failure to provide timely instruction on covered materials. The teacher was charged with failing to properly control students and was put on probation. He was transferred to another school, where he failed to follow lesson plans and had no required text for students. After a formal hearing, an administrative law judge recommended discharging the teacher. The school board adopted the recommendation, and the teacher appealed.

A Florida District Court of Appeal explained that under Florida Statutes Section 1012.34(3) the **"assessment procedure for instructional personnel must be primarily based on the performance of students assigned to their classrooms."** Assessment **"must primarily use data and indicators of improvement in student performance assessed annually."** The school board **did not primarily base its decision on the performance of students in the teacher's classroom, as state law required. The court rejected the board's argument that a teacher may be discharged if factors other than student performance are "properly deemed more crucial."** The statute required primary reliance on standardized tests and left no discretion for teacher assessment. While primary reliance on annual tests made it plausible that the system could end up teaching of and for annual tests, this was for the legislature to resolve. As the board did not primarily rely on student performance on annual tests, the court reversed the decision. *Sherrod v. Palm Beach County School Board*, No. 4D06-590, 2006 WL 3207981 (Fla. Ct. App. 2006).

♦   The Court of Appeals of Missouri found a school district complied with each of the state Tenure Act's requirements when it discharged a resource teacher whose individualized education programs (IEPs) were found incomplete. There was evidence that district administrators had worked with her before and after issuing a notice of deficiencies. The district special education director met with the teacher at least once weekly and made additional efforts to assist her. She received extensions for her job target deadlines.

There was no merit to the teacher's claim that her termination had been improperly based on "non-teaching, non-substantive processing of burdensome administrative paperwork." **Missouri case law defines "incompetency and inefficiency" as the "inability to perform professional teaching duties in a manner acceptable to the Board."** Timely completion of special education paperwork was "inextricable from a special education teacher's professional teaching duties." Failure to comply with paperwork requirements could result in the denial of a student's appropriate education. The record supported the board's findings of incompetency, inefficiency, insubordination, and knowing and persistent failure to comply with board policies and state law. The written charges complied with the Tenure Act. The court was not authorized to second-guess the board's conclusion regarding the required level of competency. *Hellmann v. Union R-XI School Dist.*, 170 S.W.3d 52 (Mo. Ct. App. 2005).

◆ The Ohio Supreme Court decided not to review lower court decisions ordering a school board to rehire a teacher. Her evaluations did not give her specific recommendations for improvement and the means to obtain assistance. **The state court of appeals held comments such as "see me before next observation" did not satisfy Ohio R.C. Section 3319.111(B)(D).** The principal found the teacher lost control of one class, and noted many of her students wandered around, slept or otherwise failed to participate in classes. The court of appeals held the board had to rehire her. **Recommendations in teacher evaluations "must be specific enough to alert a reasonable person to the need for change."** *Cox v. Zanesville City School Dist. Board of Educ.*, 105 Ohio St.3d 1466, 824 N.E.2d 93, Table No. 2004-1605 (Ohio 2005).

◆ After serving as a high school principal for three years, a Nebraska principal acquired tenure. Although state law required that probationary employees receive three annual employment evaluations, the district performed only three probationary evaluations. After the principal acquired tenure, he exhibited performance problems and received a "very thorough" evaluation from the district superintendent that included specific suggestions for improvement. The district hired a communications consulting firm and an executive coach to work with the principal, but he failed to cooperate. The superintendent also had repeated informal discussions with the principal, but he responded "with anger and resistance" to suggestions for improvement. The superintendent recommended that his contract not be renewed. After a hearing, the board voted to terminate the principal's contract for "incompetency, neglect of duty, unprofessional conduct, insubordination" and breach of contract.

The principal sued the school district in the Nebraska court system, asserting he was denied due process by the board and that he was unlawfully discharged because he was not evaluated as frequently as specified by state law. The court affirmed the board's decision, and the principal appealed. The Nebraska Court of Appeals rejected his argument concerning the number of evaluations he received. The discharge had occurred after he acquired tenure, and the district had properly evaluated him during the year of this action as a tenured employee. There was evidence that the district had presented the principal with a thorough evaluation and offered him assistance, but that he did not respond professionally. The lower court had properly found the principal was advised of his deficiencies and given an opportunity to correct them. The court found few objective criteria for evaluating performance and defining "just cause" for employment termination. **There were many examples of incompetence and neglect of duty in this case. The court reviewed evidence** that the principal misled the superintendent about an incident that required police intervention. **He was also dishonest to parents, students and police concerning another incident, and he was slow to discipline a teacher for accessing pornographic Web sites during classroom hours.** The court found substantial evidence of incompetence, neglect of duty and numerous performance issues that supported the finding of just cause for termination. It upheld the decision for the school board. *Montgomery v. Jefferson County School Dist. No. 0008*, No. A-01-1018, 2003 WL 1873713 (Neb. App. 2003).

B. Procedural Problems

◆　A Michigan teacher received unsatisfactory performance ratings and was transferred. When her performance was again rated unsatisfactory, she sought help from her teachers union. The union declined the teacher's request to process her grievances against the school board. A hearing officer found the teacher failed to plan, prepare, develop and provide appropriate lessons and educational activities for students and did not effectively control them or maintain a proper learning atmosphere. The board discharged the teacher, and the state court of appeals affirmed the decision. She filed unfair labor practice charges against the union and board with the Michigan Employment Relations Commission (MERC). A MERC hearing officer recommended dismissing the charge against the union. The court of appeals affirmed the MERC decision.

The teacher filed a new action against the district for age discrimination, conspiracy, breach of contract, and discharge against public policy. She included claims against the union for breach of its duty of fair representation and intentional infliction of emotional distress. The court held the action was barred by the prior case and the statute of limitations. It fined the teacher's lawyer $500 for filing a frivolous action. The teacher appealed to the state court of appeals, which found her claims were barred by collateral estoppel, a legal doctrine that prevents parties from re-litigating an issue in a subsequent, different cause of action involving the same parties. **The complaint in this case, like the first, concerned the teacher's claim of wrongful discharge based on her performance. The tenure commission had addressed this issue and found no impropriety by the board in determining her performance was unsatisfactory.** The court agreed with the union that **the teacher's claims for unfair representation also involved her performance and should have been litigated in the prior MERC action**. The court found no error in the imposition of a $500 sanction against her attorney for filing a frivolous action. *Knubbe v. Detroit Board of Educ.*, No. 240076, 2003 WL 22681553 (Mich. Ct. App. 2003).

◆　A California teacher complained of respiratory problems and went on medical leave. The superintendent was unable to confirm an "off-work order" issued by her doctor. Later in the school year, he learned the teacher had activated her teaching credential in another district and served as a substitute for 10 days while still on leave. The district issued the teacher a dismissal notice with charges against her for immoral conduct, dishonesty and unfitness for service. The parties reached a settlement by which the teacher agreed to resign for $14,500. The district reported the teacher's resignation to the California

Commission on Teacher Credentialing, as required by Title Five, Section 80303 of the state Code of Regulations. The district later noted her resignation in response to her application for disability benefits and an inquiry by a vocational rehabilitation consultant. The teacher sued the district and three school administrators in the state court system for numerous state law violations, including breach or rescission of the settlement agreement, fraudulent concealment and misrepresentation, and due process violations.

The court held for the district and officials, and the teacher appealed to the state court of appeal. The court considered the rescission issue, which was based on the district's failure to notify the teacher that her resignation triggered the mandatory report to the commission under Section 80303. **Although Section 80303 required district superintendents to inform teachers of the mandated report, the court found the district had no duty to inform her about Section 80303 requirements prior to the tendering of her resignation.** Nothing in the settlement agreement mentioned Section 80303, and there was no evidence of misrepresentation or fraud by the district regarding its reporting obligation. **The public policy expressed in Section 80303 was to inform teachers of their own duty to report any disciplinary action to the commission, not to make districts liable for a report.** The court affirmed the judgment for the district and officials. *Cooksey v. San Bernardino City Unified School Dist.*, No. E029838, 2003 WL 21665614 (Cal. Ct. App. 2003). The Supreme Court of California denied a petition for further review of the case.

◆ Section 24A-1 of the Illinois Education Code requires school districts to evaluate employees and take remedial action where necessary. **The section establishes three categories for employment ratings: excellent, satisfactory and unsatisfactory.** Despite this mandatory language, a school district negotiated a collective bargaining agreement establishing two evaluation categories: "does not meet district expectations" and "meets or exceeds district expectations." A district found a teacher deficient in 10 areas and placed her on a one-year remediation plan. She then received "does not meet district expectations" ratings in two consecutive quarterly reports. The district fired the teacher, and she was unable to convince a state hearing officer her termination was improper based on the district's failure to use statutory language.

A state circuit court confirmed the administrative decision, and the teacher appealed to the Appellate Court of Illinois. The district asserted its two-tier rating system was required by the collective bargaining agreement and appropriately collapsed the three statutory categories into two. The court disagreed, finding **the statute clearly indicated a three-tiered, mandatory rating system. The legislature used unmistakable language, which the district was not free to ignore.** The remediation and dismissal provisions of 105 ILCS 5/25A-1 applied only to teachers who received "unsatisfactory" ratings. Since the teacher never received that designation, she was not subject to remediation and her discharge was improper. The court reversed the judgment, holding **the language of a collective bargaining agreement could not justify clear disregard for statutory directives**. *Buchna v. Illinois State Board of Educ.*, 795 N.E.2d 1045 (Ill. App. Ct. 2003).

IV. INSUBORDINATION AND OTHER GOOD CAUSE

◆ A South Dakota teacher's first evaluation indicated she was "excellent," but she disagreed with the principal's comments and refused to sign it. She submitted a written response challenging each of the principal's comments, except the observation that she was an excellent teacher. During the next three years, she refused to sign evaluations and responded to them in writing. The school board later deemed these responses "confrontational" and "insolent." The next school year, the principal grew concerned that the teacher was talking about personnel issues with other staff. He informed her this was inappropriate, undermined school authority, had a negative impact on staff morale and had to stop. The teacher responded that the principal "undermines his own authority and imposes a low morale on the teachers by his own inappropriate actions." She also asserted weekly meetings were held to harass her.

The teacher was reprimanded in writing for performance deficiencies and her intentional and willful failure to heed warnings or to follow performance expectations. During her final year of employment for the district, two conferences were held to discuss problems and remedial measures. After the teacher's fourth year in the district, the principal recommended non-renewal of her contract. The reasons were ineffective communication, unsatisfactory response to supervision and suggestions for improvement, and continued insubordination. After a four-day hearing, the school board found the administration had complied with its policy by holding two conferences, and held the teacher was insubordinate.

The teacher appealed to a state circuit court, which affirmed the decision. On appeal, the Supreme Court of South Dakota held the statutory grounds for non-renewal included those stated in this case. The teacher argued the board had improperly defined the term "insubordinate." **The court held instead that insubordination is "a willful disregard of an employer's instructions" or an "act of disobedience to the proper authority," such as "refusal to obey an order that a superior officer is authorized to give."** The hearing had produced a wealth of testimony and documentation supporting the board's action. The board identified 96 findings of fact and supported each of them with exhibits and testimony. The court affirmed the judgment. *Barnes v. Spearfish School Dist. No. 40-2*, 725 N.W.2d 226, 2006 SD 108 (S.D. 2006).

◆ The Supreme Court of North Carolina declined to review lower court decisions that upheld a school board's decision not to rehire a teacher who squirted her principal with a water pistol at a school-sponsored event. The state Court of Appeals found no evidence that the principal was biased against the teacher. The action was based on several instances of misconduct and was not arbitrary. **The court of appeals held the record indicated the teacher's contract was not renewed because she was a counterproductive force to faculty morale at her school.** *Davis v. Macon County Board of Educ.*, 360 N.C. 645, 638 S.E.2d 465 (N.C. 2006).

◆ A Kentucky principal experienced considerable conflict with staff members and a small group of parents. The district superintendent issued charges against her and advised her she was immediately suspended. He proposed terminating her continuing contract. The charges included insubordination, conduct unbecoming a teacher, inefficiency and incompetence, all violations of KRS Section 161.790(1). The principal was cited for her poor interactions with parents and staff, failure to perform an official attendance count to determine the district's annual funding, improper conduct in her job evaluation and carrying a gun onto school property. A three-member tribunal upheld only two of the six charges. It found the principal carried a loaded gun onto school property and failed to accurately report the number of students attending school. The tribunal held the appropriate sanction for the two remaining violations was a reprimand and a two-year suspension without pay. The school board appealed to a Kentucky circuit court, which upheld the decision. The state court of appeals affirmed the judgment, and the board and superintendent appealed.

The Supreme Court of Kentucky explained KRS Section 161.790 had been amended several times since 1990 to remove the authority of school boards and district superintendents to discipline teachers and provide for hearings by tribunals. The administrative tribunals, made up of a teacher, an administrator and a lay person, held hearings for state hearing officers, who presided over procedural matters. The court found KRS Section 161.790 provided tribunals with implied authority to reduce the sanctions proposed by a superintendent. While tribunals could only resolve factual disputes concerning termination, the statute gave them power to control the decision. The court held Section 161.790 could not be read to exclude from the tribunal the power to alter sanctions recommended by the superintendent. The clear intent of the law was to have the tribunal decide all issues of teacher discipline, except for private reprimands. The court rejected the superintendent's additional arguments. The principal was a "teacher" under Section 161.790 since she required certification to hold her position. As the tribunal was entitled to reduce the discipline, the court affirmed the judgment. *Fankhauser v. Cobb*, 163 S.W.3d 389 (Ky. 2005).

◆ A Kentucky teacher had served her district for 11 years and was "an excellent and dedicated" English as a Second Language teacher. She became involved with "School of the Americas Watch," a religious organization which organized political protests. The teacher led a prayer group as part of a protest on federal government property and was arrested for trespassing. After a trial, she was convicted and sentenced to 90 days in a federal prison. The sentence was imposed near the start of a school year. The teacher informed the district's interim superintendent of the sentence. He suspended her with pay for 20 days, pending an investigation. The teacher requested a leave of absence to serve her sentence. The superintendent denied the request without forwarding it to the school board. As the teacher's release from prison approached, he sent her notice that her contract was being terminated for insubordination, conduct unbecoming a teacher, and breach of contract. The teacher appealed her termination under KRS Section 161.790, the state teacher termination statute. She moved for dismissal of the charges against her, based on the superintendent's failure to follow statutory terms by not forwarding her request for leave to the school board, and by failing to make a written record of teacher performance to support the insubordination charge. A hearing officer held statutes, regulations, local board policies and teacher contracts could provide the teacher with the statutory written notice of performance requirement.

A hearing tribunal held the teacher did not violate the teachers' code of ethics or engage in conduct unbecoming a teacher. While she was technically insubordinate by being absent without leave, she did not intend to defy a direct order. The tribunal found the superintendent had improperly failed to consider the teacher's past teaching record. He "acted improperly in thwarting" her request for leave and ignored her record as a valuable teacher. The tribunal reinstated the teacher with back pay. A Kentucky circuit court affirmed the decision, but held the teacher was not entitled to back wages during her incarceration. The parties appealed. The Court of Appeals of Kentucky rejected the board's claim that the case involved a "common law breach of contract" and not KRS Section 161.790. The statute was the sole avenue for terminating a teacher's continuing contract. **Section 161.790 required a school board to support charges of insubordination with a written record of teacher performance. The hearing officer had improperly relieved the board of this statutory requirement.** The court dismissed the insubordination charge, as it was not supported by the required written record of teacher performance. There was no reason the superintendent could not have informed the teacher her continued absence without leave would lead to termination. The court held the tribunal had discretion to review the circumstances and to reinstate her with full back wages. *James v. Sevre-Duszynska*, 173 S.W.3d 250 (Ky. Ct. App. 2005).

◆ A Tennessee teacher did not meet the requirements of an improvement plan while teaching a kindergarten class. She was transferred to another school and assigned to a classroom of third-graders needing remedial education. A few weeks into the school year, a student reported the teacher had "smacked her on the face." The principal and assistant principal met with the teacher, stressing the importance of being positive with children and admonishing her that "she was not, under any circumstances, to put her hands on the students." Later in the school year, the parents of another student reported the teacher had slapped their child. The district conducted an investigation. Students told administrators the teacher had placed her hands on their faces when she was angry and had pinched them and hit them with a soft-cover textbook. When administrators questioned the teacher about the report, she admitted placing her hands on students to get their attention. She admitted slapping five of seven students in the class "when she was angry and when the children were being disrespectful." The district immediately suspended the teacher for "complete insubordination."

The school board upheld the recommendation to discharge the teacher for insubordination, incompetence, and inefficiency. A state trial court upheld the decision, and the teacher appealed. **The Court of Appeals of Tennessee held the term "insubordination" included the refusal to carry out specific assignments made by the principal. The principal and assistant principal had instructed the teacher to refrain from placing her hands on students.** The court found she refused to follow a specific directive. It expressed shock that a teacher with over 10 years of experience felt the need to grab and hit students. Teachers were required to provide leadership and direction for others by appropriate example. The court stated "a teacher with that much experience should be capable of controlling her anger and handling her students in a more professional – and safe – manner." As there was evidence of unfitness, as well as inefficiency and insubordination, the judgment was affirmed. *Ketchersid v. Rhea County Board of Educ.*, 174 S.W.2d 163 (Tenn. Ct. App. 2005).

◆   A Florida teacher had several incidents involving contact with students and was then directed to report physical confrontations and avoid the appearance of intimidating students. He tried to pass candy out to his students in a class, but they became disruptive and rushed toward him. The teacher refused repeated attempts by one student to take more candy. When the student persisted, the teacher struck or shoved him, causing him to fall back or step back against some lockers. The school board filed an administrative complaint against the teacher. An administrative law judge (ALJ) conducted a hearing and determined the student was disruptive and had put his hands on the teacher. The ALJ found the teacher tried to separate himself from the student as he backed away from an onrushing group of students. The teacher did not have an unlawful purpose. The only evidence of excessive force came from a school board member, whose testimony the ALJ found inconsistent and less than credible.

The ALJ found the teacher's instruction for the student to "back off" was not verbal intimidation. The student's persistence left little alternative but to use force, which the ALJ found reasonable and lawful. The board modified the ALJ's findings and rejected the recommendation to reinstate the teacher. The board discharged him, and he filed a state court action for reinstatement. A state district court of appeal observed that a school board may not reject a hearing officer's findings unless it first determines they were not based on competent, substantial evidence or did not comply with essential requirements of law. Several student witnesses provided inconsistent testimony. Evidence indicated students crowded the teacher into a small locker area and that the student persisted in attempting to get more candy after the teacher told him he could have no more. The court held that when reasonable people could differ about the facts, an agency was bound by the hearing officer's resolution of conflicting inferences. **The ALJ found the teacher had little choice but to separate himself from the student, as he was being rushed by "candy-crazed" children. The teacher did not violate the board's previous directive against touching students in a manner that served no educational purpose.** His actions were not misconduct, gross insubordination, willful neglect of duty, or conduct unbecoming a teacher. The court reversed the board's decision. *Packer v. Orange County School Board*, 881 So.2d 1204 (Fla. Dist. Ct. App. 2004).

◆   A Missouri teacher answered a series of questions from one student on controversial subjects including abortion and interracial relationships. The teacher stated that interracial couples "should be fixed" so that they could not have children and said that such children were "mixed" and "racially confused." With two biracial students in attendance in the classroom, the teacher stated "mixed children are dirty" and were teased by others. Later in the day, she told a parent of one of the biracial students her views on interracial relationships and made further disparaging remarks about biracial children. The district superintendent placed the teacher on administrative leave. The school board conducted a hearing and found she made racially discriminatory comments in violation of four board policies and state law. It terminated the teacher's indefinite contract for willfully violating its policies on equal opportunity, anti-discrimination and harassment. A state circuit court affirmed the judgment.

The teacher appealed to the Court of Appeals of Missouri, which found **sufficient evidence in the record to show the teacher willfully violated board policy. Her statements regarding marriage and the ability to have children solely based on race were disparaging and discriminatory.** It was particularly disturbing to the court that the teacher was aware of the presence of at least one of the biracial students at the time she spoke. The court rejected the teacher's claim to First Amendment protection. To gain such protection, speech must address a matter of public concern and not disrupt the school. The comments in this case were personal in nature, as they expressed a private opinion on race. They were made during class time when the teacher was supposed to be conducting a lesson. Even had the comments been deserving of First Amendment protection, they seriously disrupted the school environment. There was evidence that for several weeks, students were agitated, angry, upset and worried about attending the teacher's class. Because the district interest in efficiently operating a school free from racially discriminatory speech outweighed any personal speech rights held by the teacher, the court affirmed the judgment. *Loeffelman v. Board of Educ. of Crystal City School Dist.*, 134 S.W.3d 637 (Mo. Ct. App. 2004).

V. RESIGNATION AND RETIREMENT

An employee's resignation ends contractual and tenure rights. It may not be withdrawn if the school board has relied on it and hired a replacement.

A. Resignation

◆ Professionally certificated public school employees in Maryland are required to execute employment contracts with a provision forfeiting accrued salary for violating contractual conditions. State regulations allowed a party to provide written notice to terminate a first- or second-year contract according to a specified timeline. For most employees, this date was no later than May 1. A teacher hired under a provisional teaching contract and another who was employed under a regular contract submitted written resignations during the summer. This occurred after their May contract deadlines. The school board withheld their last paychecks for violating their contracts. Each teacher was replaced by a substitute. The superintendent upheld the forfeiture provisions, and the board affirmed her decision. The state board upheld the provision as enforceable, finding it was designed to further the legitimate public purpose of deterring late resignations that deprived local boards of the time needed to recruit and hire replacements at the last minute. It also defrayed some recruiting and hiring costs and the costs of hiring substitute teachers.

Appeal reached the Court of Appeals of Maryland, the state's highest court. It noted the contract forfeiture provision had been included in Maryland public school teaching contracts since at least 1921. Contract language was compelled by state regulations. The state board had "the last word on any matter concerning educational policy or the administration of the system of public education," so long as it did not act arbitrarily. **The court held the forfeiture provision in the teaching contracts satisfied each of the requirements for an enforceable liquidated damages provision. It defined a specific sum of money as the amount of damages to be recovered for a breach of contract.** "Salary already accrued" could be readily calculated as a specific sum. The provision reasonably compensated the school system for damages anticipated by an untimely teacher resignation. The forfeiture provision was a reasonable forecast of just compensation, and was binding and could not be altered to correspond to actual damages. As no evidence indicated the enforcement of the forfeiture provision was arbitrary, the court affirmed the action. *Board of Educ. of Talbot County v. Heister*, 392 Md. 140, 896 A.2d 342 (Md. 2006).

◆ A Colorado teacher worked under annually renewing contracts that permitted her school district to recover "all damages provided by law" for job abandonment or breach of contract. The contracts incorporated Section 22-63-202 of the state code, which authorizes the withholding of up to one-twelfth of a teacher's annual pay for the cost of finding a replacement, if the teacher does not provide notice of resignation 30 days prior to a school year. The teacher learned of a personal conflict and advised the district she could not maintain her assignment. The district did not adjust her assignment, and she sent a letter of resignation only 10 days before the school year began. The district withheld the teacher's entire final paycheck of $1,426.50. She sued the district in a state court, which denied her motion to limit "expenses" under Section 22-63-202 to the district's out-of-pocket costs of $47. The court held a jury must determine the district's "ordinary and necessary expenses." The jury awarded the teacher $133.50, the amount of the district's advertising and recruitment costs. It did not reimburse her for the salaries of employees who found a replacement.

The state supreme court agreed to review the case. It found the term "ordinary and necessary" expenses should be interpreted consistently with case law, education policy priorities, and contract law principles. **Section 22-63-202 indicated "ordinary and necessary expenses" was an additional limit on the damage cap of one-twelfth of the amount of a resigned teacher's annual salary.** The court held "overhead" described continuous and indirect costs of running a business. The term "expense" was more commonly used to describe an actual cash outlay. Section 22-63-202 was not intended to be a penalty or disincentive to mobility. **The teacher correctly argued the legislature had intended to reimburse districts for their actual cost outlays, not the cost of salaries they would have had to pay in any event. A prohibitive penalty would penalize hiring districts.** The teacher tried to resolve a personal conflict in good faith, and had tried to comply with district procedures when she resigned. The district was entitled only to its actual cash outlay. *Klinger v. Adams County School Dist. No. 50*, 130 P.3d 1027 (Colo. 2006).

◆ A South Dakota teacher had worked for her district for 39 years when she learned her position would be reduced from full time to half time the next school year. She retired at the end of the year, took pay for her unpaid sick leave and began receiving benefits from the state retirement system. The teacher came out of retirement before the start of the next school year and signed a one-year probationary contract for the half-time position she had previously rejected. Near the end of the school year, the board did not renew her contract and did not provide her a hearing. The teacher claimed she had no break in service and thus retained her continuing contract status. This would include due process protections for a teacher "in or beyond the fourth consecutive term of employment." The teacher sued the board in a state trial court. It rejected her claims and awarded summary judgment to the district. The teacher appealed.

The Supreme Court of South Dakota held the teacher's arguments overlooked her voluntary retirement and her acceptance of a one-year probationary contract. The teacher had also overlooked legal authorities that have held **resignation generally causes a break in service. Resignation was "a complete termination of her employment relationship" with the district. The court cited cases from 11 states, including Louisiana and Alabama, stating that resignation terminates tenure.** Teachers may waive their continuing contract status, as the teacher here had done. Her actions at the time of retirement reflected an intent to abandon her continuing contract status. As no legal authority indicated this status was to be indefinite, the court affirmed the judgment. *Wirt v. Parker School Dist. #60-04*, 689 N.W.2d 901 (S.D. 2004).

◆ A Kentucky principal reprimanded a teacher for physically punishing students. The principal gave her an unfavorable evaluation and a notice of significant deficiency stating failure to comply with its provisions could result in discharge. The teacher soon received a written reprimand for failing to desist from physically contacting students. Her employees association (EA) filed three grievances on her behalf. The district agreed to conditionally reemploy the teacher pending an evaluation early in the next school year. As a compromise, the teacher was required to sign a letter of resignation, effective at the end of the semester. If the evaluation was adequate, the district would rescind the letter. In a meeting, the teacher complained about the compromise. The EA representative questioned some terms and advised her not to sign the agreement. The teacher signed it, stating she could not afford to be without a job. The district conditionally reemployed her under the agreement, but her performance was unsatisfactory and she was reassigned to a non-teaching position until the effective date of her resignation. The district informed the state Educational Professional Standards Board (EPSB) she had resigned. The EPSB revoked the teacher's license for 20 years for incompetency, misconduct and willful neglect of duty. The teacher sued the school board, school officials, EA and EA representatives in a state court. The court entered summary judgment against the teacher, and she appealed.

The state court of appeals found the agreement did not violate state law provisions on voluntary termination of teacher contracts. **Section 161.780(2) of the state code specified that a voluntary resignation "shall become binding on the date specified in the letter of resignation."** The teacher submitted her letter to stop the pending termination as a last chance for her to keep her job. She never rescinded the resignation, and as it complied with Section

161.780(2), summary judgment was proper on her invalid resignation claim. There was no evidence of fraud or conspiracy between the district and EA. The EA representative had counseled the teacher not to sign the agreement and made no misrepresentations. The conspiracy claim was barred by a one-year statute of limitations. The duress claim was meritless because the district had a legal right to begin termination proceedings. **A threat to fire an employee unless the employee resigns does not amount to duress.** The court rejected the teacher's challenge to the EPSB decision, as she received a hearing to litigate the revocation of her certificate. *Keeling v. Jefferson County Board of Educ.*, No. 2002-CA-000528-MR, 2003 WL 1860539 (Ky. Ct. App. 2003).

◆ An Arkansas teacher verbally informed his principal that he intended to resign. She responded that he would have to submit a written resignation. The teacher changed his mind the following day and asked to withdraw his resignation. The principal said the resignation had already been reported to and accepted by the school administration. The district board did not formally approve the teacher's oral resignation until a meeting three weeks later.

The teacher sued the school district nearly two years afterward, arguing that his resignation did not comply with Arkansas' Teacher Fair Dismissal Act (TFDA) requirements, nullifying his resignation and resulting in breach of his employment contract. The court held Section 6-17-1510(d) of the TFDA was the teacher's exclusive remedy and barred the lawsuit due to its 75-day limit on appeals from board decisions. The teacher appealed to the Arkansas Supreme Court, which determined that Section 6-17-1510(d) applied only to termination or non-renewal actions. **It rejected the school board's argument that its vote to accept the teacher's oral resignation converted the action into a vote to terminate or not renew his contract.** This was true because the board was not required to take any action in response to the resignation. The teacher was not required to commence an action within 75 days as specified in Section 6-17-1510(d), and the court reversed that aspect of the judgment. However, it rejected the teacher's assertion that the district's vote to accept his resignation was itself void. *Williams v. Little Rock School Dist.*, 66 S.W.3d 590 (Ark. 2002).

B. Retirement

As in resignation cases, an employee's notice of retirement is typically binding as it cuts off the employee's contractual rights. A school board may not have to rehire an employee who tries to rescind a valid retirement notice.

◆ **The Ohio Supreme Court held a retired bus mechanic was entitled to reinstatement after his school board illegally abolished his position**, laid him off and outsourced his duties to a private company. **Since the board acted illegally, his retirement was considered involuntary.** The mechanic retired because of the board's illegal action to abolish his position and outsource his work to a private company. His conduct in applying for retirement benefits did not indicate an intent to give up his continuing public employment rights, and he reapplied for his position as soon as he became aware of his potential right to reinstatement. The court remanded the case for resolution of the mechanic's claim for back wages and benefits. *State of Ohio, ex rel. Stacy v. Batavia Local School Dist. Board of Educ.*, 779 N.E.2d 216, 97 Ohio St.3d 269 (Ohio 2002).

◆ After 20 years of service, a Minnesota teacher submitted a notice of his retirement, effective on the day before winter vacation. However, he soon decided to apply for the vacancy he created and resumed teaching the first day after winter vacation. The district superintendent advised the teacher in writing he was now considered a probationary teacher and was subject to employment termination on the last day of the current school year. The correspondence also noted that the teacher's seniority date was the first day he resumed teaching and that he was entitled to benefits accorded to new hires as of that date. The teacher signed a document designating him as a long-term substitute teacher, and the district approved his employment as a probationary teacher. Near the end of the year, the school board resolved not to renew his contract. The teacher petitioned the Minnesota Court of Appeals to review the decision.

The court found no reference to any continuing contract rights for teachers who return to service under the law cited by the teacher. It stated the teacher's argument would make it more difficult for districts to recruit new teachers because even if retired teachers returned to the bottom of a seniority list, they would still have superior rights to probationary teachers. The court also rejected the teacher's claim to continuing contract status as a substitute teacher who had completed a probationary period. A substitute teacher cannot attain continuing contract status without first being offered, and then accepting, a continuing contract. The teacher had signed a document advising him that he was a long-term, probationary substitute with no continuing contract rights. He was clearly advised that he did not have continuing contract rights and that he could regain them only if he were hired for the following school year. **As the teacher had terminated his own contractual rights by retiring and did not reactivate them by resuming his duties, the court affirmed the board's action terminating his employment.** *Thomas v. Independent School Dist. No. 2142*, 639 N.W.2d 619 (Minn. Ct. App. 2002).

◆ Three Indiana teachers notified their district in 1997 they would retire the next year and accept early retirement benefits under the 1995-1997 master contract. The board and teachers association negotiated a master contract for 1997-2000 that dramatically reduced early retirement benefits. The retirees brought a state court action against the association for breach of the duty of fair representation, and against the board for breach of contract for failing to pay benefits under the 1995-1997 contract. The court dismissed the complaint, ruling that it should have been filed with the Indiana Education Employment Relations Board (IEERB). The state court of appeals reversed the judgment.

The Indiana Supreme Court held **the retirees needed to exhaust their available administrative remedies by filing their unfair representation claims with the IEERB**. The state Certificated Educational Employee Bargaining Act recognized the right of school employees to organize and collectively bargain through employee associations, creating a method to resolve labor disputes through the IEERB. However, this ruling did not mean that the trial court had no jurisdiction over the breach of contract claim. The

IEERB had no power to consider the breach of contract claim concerning the board's liability for early retirement benefits. By dismissing the breach of contract claim, the trial court had effectively denied the retirees the only forum in which the claim could be heard. The court ordered the trial court to retain the breach of contract claim, suspending any action on it until the IEERB made a final decision on the unfair representation claim. *Fratus v. Marion Community Schools Board of Trustees*, 749 N.E.2d 40 (Ind. 2001).

C. Retirement Benefits

◆ A Montana school superintendent obtained assurances from his school board that he could retire with lifetime health insurance premiums for himself and his wife under a contract addendum. Six years later, a board made up of all new members voted to terminate his premium payments. The former superintendent sued the school district in a federal district court, asserting violations of state law and his protected due process rights. The court submitted a special verdict form to the jury on the superintendent's claims. The jury found constitutional and state law violations, and the district appealed.

The U.S. Court of Appeals, Ninth Circuit, held the district's arguments to void the contract failed. The former superintendent had provided adequate consideration for the contract addendum by continuing to work for the district for six weeks after its execution. **The court held the Fourteenth Amendment to the U.S. Constitution protects individuals from being deprived of liberty or property by the government without due process.** The former superintendent did not show he was deprived of due process, as the school district had denied him any "present entitlement." He only alleged he was owed payments under a contract. The former superintendent's property interest could be fully protected by a breach of contract action. The contract addendum was purely financial, and as state law procedures provided him with adequate process, the district court should have dismissed his constitutional claims. The court upheld the jury verdict on the basis of the state law findings. *McCracken v. Lockwood School Dist. #26*, 208 Fed.Appx. 513 (9th Cir. 2006).

◆ The Michigan Public School Employees' Retirement Board began providing health care benefits for public school retirees in 1975. Over the years, health insurance deductibles and prescription copays were gradually increased through amendments to the health care plan. Six retirees sued the state, the retirement board and state officials in a Michigan trial court, asserting the increases violated the state constitution, and that plan amendments violated state and federal constitutional provisions prohibiting the impairment of existing government contracts. The court held for the state and board, and the retirees appealed. The court of appeals affirmed the judgment, and the Supreme Court of Michigan accepted the case. It noted article Nine, Section 24 of the Michigan Constitution prohibits the state from diminishing or impairing the accrued financial benefits of any state pension plan or retirement system.

The court held the phrase "accrued financial benefits" as used in Article Nine, Section 24 meant deferred compensation in a pension plan. At the time the provision was adopted, there was no health care plan for retired school employees. Moreover, "accrued benefits" were those that increased over time, such as pension or retirement allowances. Health care benefits were not "accrued." Article Nine, Section 24 only protected benefits that increased over time. Since health care benefits did not qualify as "financial benefits," they were not protected by Article Nine, Section 24, and this claim failed. **The state legislature did not create any contractual right of public school retirees to receive health care benefits.** The legislature expressed no intent to be contractually bound by enacting health care plan legislation for public school retirees. Health care benefits legislation reflected only a policy decision, and did not create contractual rights. The legislature did not authorize a plan with specific deductible and copay amounts. As the lower courts correctly held for the state, the court affirmed their judgments. *Studier v. Michigan Public School Employees' Retirement Board*, 472 Mich. 642, 698 N.W.2d 350 (Mich. 2005).

◆ A Pennsylvania Public School Employees' Retirement System (PSERS) policy interpretation allowed PSERS members to purchase credit for part-time service prior to becoming members. From 1975 through 1998, the PSERS did not allow the purchase of credit for prior part-time service unless employees qualified as "members" of the system. This required employees to work at least 80 days as an hourly employee or 500 hours of work in a given fiscal year. In 1992, PSERS directed school districts not to report non-qualifying service by employees of less than 80 days or 500 hours in a year. In 1999, PSERS issued a policy statement reversing its prior practice. It announced PSERS members would be permitted to buy credit for their previous school service without regard to the 80 day/500 hour threshold. The Pennsylvania School Boards Association (PSBA) petitioned the Pennsylvania Commonwealth Court to review the PSERS policy statement, arguing it contravened the Public School Employees' Retirement Code and would financially burden districts.

The court held the PSERS' governing board had no fiduciary duty to the PSBA. After pretrial activity, the court held for the PSERS on the remaining claims. The PSBA appealed to the state supreme court. **The court noted the code did not restrict the amount or type of prior part-time service that could be purchased if a part-time employee became a PSERS member.** The General Assembly could have easily included words to limit purchases of credit by PSERS members. The PSBA's fiscal arguments were beyond the court's authority. The General Assembly, not the court, had the power to make that judgment. The PSBA had no standing to assert violation of a fiduciary duty to its member districts. As the code allowed the purchase of credit for any previous school service, the court affirmed the judgment. *Pennsylvania School Boards Ass'n v. Comwlth. of Pennsylvania*, 863 A.2d 432 (Pa. 2004).

◆ An Ohio school head cook underwent surgery to repair a rectocele, or prolapse herniation of the rectum. After surgery, she had rectal pain and spasms when lifting heavy objects. The cook's physician wrote a letter permitting her to return to work, restricted to four hours per day and lifting of no more than five pounds. The cook applied for disability benefits. Her physician wrote a letter stating she would remain unable to perform her duties for at least 12 months. A physician appointed by the School Employment Retirement System

(SERS) found the cook was not unable to perform her job duties. He stated a 25-pound permanent restriction on lifting was indicated. The SERS denied the cook retirement benefits, and the state appeals court affirmed the decision.

The Supreme Court of Ohio explained that **to obtain disability retirement benefits under Ohio R.C. § 3309.39(C), employees must be mentally or physically incapacitated from performing their job duties by a condition that is permanent or presumed to be permanent for at least 12 months.** The court held SERS decisions are not subject to reversal unless there is an abuse of discretion when a decision is unreasonable, arbitrary or unconscionable. The SERS did not abuse its discretion by relying on the opinion of the physician it appointed. The cook's own physician had established she was not required to lift heavy items herself, but could seek help from co-workers. Since the SERS did not abuse its discretion by denying the cook's application for disability retirement benefits, the court was required to affirm the decision. *State ex rel. Lecklider v. SERS*, 104 Ohio St.3d 271, 819 N.E.2d 289 (Ohio 2004).

◆   A Colorado school custodian applied for early retirement benefits after working for 30 years. The district's early retirement policy provided an explicit formula for calculating benefits, but gave the school board discretion to determine terms of payment and to "phase out" or repeal the policy with two years' prior notice. The board rejected the custodian's application for benefits without stating a reason. It invited him to rescind his resignation and continue working, but he commenced a Colorado trial court action against the district, board and individual board members. The court awarded summary judgment to the custodian, finding the policy created an implied contract that allowed no discretion to deny benefits. The board appealed to the court of appeals, arguing that it had complete discretion to phase out the policy without prior notice.

The court held changing the early retirement policy was a significant district action that could not be done simply by voting against an application for benefits. **The district was required to confer with groups and individuals affected by the phase-out before denying individual applications.** There had been no official announcement until a year after the board denied the employee's application, when it deleted the policy. The court held the board could still avoid making early retirement payments to the employee if paying him would violate its state law obligation to refrain from deficit spending. The court remanded the case to the trial court to determine whether the district had the means to pay the benefits without spending in excess of appropriations. *Shaw v. Sargent School Dist. No. RE-33-J*, 21 P.3d 446 (Colo. Ct. App. 2001).

◆   The South Carolina legislature enacted an appropriations act authorizing a one-time retirement incentive bonus for public employees. The act established certain minimum requirements for service credit and age, and it set mandatory dates for employees to make an irrevocable election to receive the incentive. One school district adopted the retirement incentive plan, with the additional requirement that employees work through the end of the current school year to be eligible. Although the requirement was stated in a memorandum distributed to all employees, one employee retired in October of the current school year but claimed entitlement to the retirement incentive. When the district refused to pay the incentive, she filed a lawsuit against it in a state circuit court. The court held that the employee was not entitled to receive the incentive, and she appealed to the Supreme Court of South Carolina. The court observed state law authorized districts to prescribe necessary rules and regulations. In general, additional regulations by a municipality that are not as broad as state law and are not inconsistent with the law may be reconciled where either is silent as to express or implied conditions. **Because the district regulation did not conflict with state law, the employee was not entitled to the incentive bonus.** *Wright v. Richland County School Dist. Two*, 486 S.E.2d 740 (S.C. 1997).

◆   A Rhode Island statute required the full payment of teacher salaries where teachers were absent because of injuries resulting from an assault at work. The statute, however, required injured teachers to apply to the Rhode Island employees retirement system for appropriate benefits at the conclusion of one year. One teacher injured in a student assault received her full salary under the law for one year, reduced by the amount of workers' compensation benefits she received. At the conclusion of the year, she obtained a declaratory judgment from a Rhode Island superior court that her right to a full salary continued despite her failure to apply to the retirement system for appropriate benefits. The school committee appealed to the Supreme Court of Rhode Island, which held that **the statute required a disabled employee to apply to the Rhode Island employees retirement system for appropriate benefits. The teacher's failure to do so cut off her entitlement to further full salary benefits.** The court reversed and remanded the judgment. *Woonsocket Teachers' Guild Local Union 951, AFT v. Woonsocket School Committee*, 694 A.2d 727 (R.I. 1997).

VI. UNEMPLOYMENT BENEFITS

A school employee must work a specified minimum amount of time to receive unemployment benefits. If the employee has committed misconduct resulting in dismissal or left a job without good cause, benefits will be denied.

A. Eligibility Requirements

◆   A Missouri school district responded to a loss in revenue by assigning a tenured teacher who was certified in music and English to teach two band classes for which she claimed to have no experience or expertise. She resigned after informing the school board by letter that the assignment required considerable time beyond classroom instruction and constituted an excessive teaching load. She filed a claim for unemployment compensation benefits in which she stated that her employment separation was caused by lack of work. Her claim was initially approved, but an appeals board reversed the determination, finding she had voluntarily separated from work without good cause attributable to her work or employer. The state labor and industrial relations commission affirmed the decision, and appeal reached the Missouri

Court of Appeals, Southern District. **The court adopted the commission's order, reasoning that claimants have an affirmative obligation to attempt to resolve work-related problems prior to abandoning employment.** A claimant must act in good faith before a finding of good cause to leave employment may be found. The court rejected the teacher's assertion that the changed working conditions created good cause or established good faith. It affirmed the denial of benefits. *Standefer v. Missouri Division of Labor and Industrial Relations Comm'n*, 959 S.W.2d 479 (Mo. Ct. App. 1998).

◆ A Rhode Island teacher was laid off after three years of employment and began receiving unemployment compensation benefits. She accepted substitute teaching assignments from two school districts, which partially set off some of her unemployment benefits. She filed a claim for additional benefits based on the lack of available work during the school Christmas break, which was denied by the state Department of Employment and Training (DET). Her later claim for additional unemployment benefits for the summer was also denied on the basis of a state law preclusion for the payment of benefits to school employees during holidays and summer breaks. A Rhode Island trial court found that the claims for additional benefits had been properly denied, but it reversed the decision concerning previously awarded benefits. DET appealed to the Supreme Court of Rhode Island, arguing that the acceptance of substitute teaching work resulted in the denial of unemployment benefits, even for benefits previously awarded for prior full-time work. The court disagreed with the DET, finding **the teacher's substitute teaching income had been properly deducted from her unemployment compensation benefits**. She was not precluded from receiving previously awarded benefits based on her prior full-time employment, since she remained eligible for these benefits under state law. *Brouillette v. Dep't of Employment and Training Board of Review*, 677 A.2d 1344 (R.I. 1996).

◆ A West Virginia custodian worked for his school district during the summer months as a painter for several years. The school board did not offer him employment for the summer break one year, and he filed a claim for unemployment compensation benefits. The West Virginia Department of Employment Security declared **the employee disqualified from benefits on the basis of the existence of reasonable assurances that he would be working for the school board that fall** as a custodian. The department's board of review reversed this decision, finding that the employee was entitled to receive benefits since he had worked for the school district in prior summers and was effectively laid off. This decision was affirmed by a West Virginia circuit court, and the education board appealed to the Supreme Court of Appeals of West Virginia. The court held that **service personnel employed by school boards are ineligible for unemployment compensation benefits unless they hold a second, separate contract for the summer months or show the existence of a continuing contractual relationship**. Since the employee failed to show he had a continuing contract for the summer break, he was not entitled to receive benefits. The circuit court decision was reversed. *Raleigh County Board of Educ. v. Gatson*, 468 S.E.2d 923 (W. Va. 1996).

B. Misconduct

The court in Clark County School Dist. v. Bundley, *below, cited* Virginia Employment Comm'n v. Gantt, *7 Va. App. 631, 376 S.E.2d 808 (Va. Ct. App. 1989) in holding "mere absence without leave is not disqualifying misconduct," but the employer may then show the employee "deliberately and unjustifiably violated any school absence policy." The Supreme Court of Florida has found an absence without authorization is "inherently detrimental to the employer's interests."* Mason v. Load King Manufacturing Co., *758 So.2d 649 (Fla. 2000).*

◆ A Nevada school district fired an in-school suspension teacher for being absent without leave eight times in five weeks. She filed an unemployment compensation claim, which was granted by the state economic security division. The district challenged the award of benefits, maintaining that it admonished the teacher and that excessive absences amounted to misconduct. The teacher stated that her absences were required to see a doctor and to take care of a sick child, whose illness was the result of a continuing medical condition that the school knew about. A hearing referee found the principal more credible than the teacher and held the discharge was based on attendance problems and failure to notify the district of her absences, in violation of a district policy. A review board reversed the decision, and appeal reached the Supreme Court of Nevada.

According to the court, an employee's absence will be misconduct in unemployment compensation cases "only if the circumstances indicate that the absence was taken in willful violation or disregard of a reasonable employment policy" or lacked an appropriate notice. The court found the school district had the burden to show the teacher's conduct disqualified her from benefits. She had no responsibility to show her absences were not misconduct, as the district claimed. Employers are in a unique position to know the reasons for discharge and can more easily prove misconduct than employees can disprove it. In view of the system's protective purposes, employers should have to prove misconduct by an employee in unemployment compensation cases. **An absence without leave was not disqualifying misconduct. The district would have to show the teacher's absences were excessive. Whether she was disqualified from benefits required the district to show she willfully violated or disregarded its standards.** However, as the board failed to consider whether the absences were "excessive" and whether the first five absences were justifiable, the case was returned to the board for further activity. *Clark County School Dist. v. Bundley,* 148 P.3d 750 (Nev. 2006).

◆ Oregon's Supreme Court found no authority for a school district to set off an unemployment benefits award to an employee it discharged, and then rehired by order of the state Fair Dismissal Appeals Board. The teacher was discharged for reasons not stated by the court. She appealed her dismissal to the Fair Dismissal Appeals Board. Meanwhile, she applied for and received unemployment benefits. The board held the dismissal was unlawful and ordered the school district to reinstate her with an award of back pay. The district asserted a right to set off unemployment benefits received by the teacher against her back pay award. It claimed the quarterly payments it made to the state employment department for the Unemployment Compensation Trust Fund justified the offset. The board agreed with the district, finding the district's contributions to the trust fund made it a reimbursing employer. Under that theory, the district had paid dollar for dollar for the benefits it sought to set off.

The case reached the Supreme Court of Oregon. It reviewed ORS § 342.905, the statute under which the board had approved the setoff. The court found the board could reinstate teachers if charges were untrue or if there were inadequate grounds for dismissal. **While Section 342.905 authorized back pay awards for wrongfully discharged employees, nothing in the statute, or any other law, permitted the board to set off unemployment compensation against back pay.** The statute did not permit the board to set off an award of back pay with money received by an employee under an unrelated benefit program. The district had not itself paid unemployment compensation benefits to the teacher. Any such issue was between the teacher and the employment department. As the district did not pay the compensation benefits it now sought to set off, the judgment was reversed and the case was returned to the board. *Zottola v. Three Rivers School Dist.*, 342 Or. 118, 149 P.3d 1151 (Or. 2006).

◆ **The Court of Appeals of Minnesota upheld an administrative decision denying unemployment compensation benefits to a custodian who did not lock the exterior doors to his school at least five times.** After being suspended with a written warning, he yelled at a supervisor and threatened her when she complained about him. The court of appeals held the custodian was properly denied unemployment benefits. His repeated failure to lock exterior doors and his insubordination was misconduct showing both a substantial lack of concern for his employment and a violation of reasonable standards of behavior. *Ashong v. Independent School Dist. #625*, No. A04-1623, 2005 WL 1432203 (Minn. Ct. App. 2005).

◆ A Pennsylvania school district employed a part-time health and physical education teacher. The teacher received a call from the district at approximately 6:00 a.m. on a day she was scheduled to work at 11:30 a.m., requesting that she arrive early to serve as a substitute. Near the end of the school day, a custodian noticed three shotguns in her car and reported them to the administration. The teacher claimed she was in the process of moving and had placed the shotguns into her car with her other belongings the night before. According to the teacher, she left the guns and other items in her car overnight because it was raining and forgot to unload them after receiving the early call to work the next morning. The district suspended the teacher without pay for violating its policy prohibiting weapons on school property. She submitted a claim for unemployment benefits that was denied by a state unemployment compensation referee who found no justification for bringing guns to school. The referee found the teacher had engaged in "willful misconduct" and was ineligible for benefits under Section 402(e) of the state Unemployment Compensation Law. The state Unemployment Compensation Board of Review affirmed the decision, as did the Commonwealth Court of Pennsylvania.

The teacher appealed to the Supreme Court of Pennsylvania, which explained that a finding of willful misconduct was necessary to disqualify a claim for unemployment compensation benefits. It rejected the commonwealth court's decision to create a public policy exception to Section 402(e). The court stated the legislature had limited the disqualification for benefits to employees who demonstrated willful misconduct. **Section 402(e) did not define "willful misconduct," but previous state court decisions characterized it as disregard for an employer's interests, deliberate violation of employer rules, or disregard for the employer's standards of behavior.** Employee negligence could result in a finding of willful misconduct only when it showed intentional disregard for the employer's interest or an employee's duties or obligations. Since the district could not show the teacher's actions were intentional or deliberate, she was not disqualified from benefits. *Grieb v. Unemployment Compensation Board of Review*, 827 A.2d 422 (Pa. 2003).

◆ A Mississippi high school teacher showed his anatomy class a movie about alligator control. The school principal warned him that the film was unrelated to the subject matter of the class, in violation of school policy. Several weeks later, the teacher wished to reward his students for working hard by allowing them to vote on a film to watch in class. The students voted to watch *Silence of the Lambs*, an R-rated film. A student brought the film in and the class watched the first 45 minutes of it, with the rest to be seen the following day. However, parents complained, and the teacher resigned under pressure. He filed a claim for unemployment compensation with the state employment security commission. The commission denied the application based on the misconduct section of state law. The teacher appealed to a state trial court, which reversed. The commission appealed to the Supreme Court of Mississippi.

The court commented that the display of an R-rated movie to students under the age of 17 demonstrated poor judgment. The teacher had been warned that any films presented to classes must relate to class subject matter. The film did not relate to any course work. **Because the teacher had intentionally disregarded the principal's warning and failed to preview the movie, there was substantial evidence to uphold the commissioner's determination that he was guilty of misconduct** under the state code. The trial court order awarding unemployment compensation benefits was reversed. *Mississippi Employment Security Comm'n v. Harris*, 672 So.2d 739 (Miss. 1996).

VII. WRONGFUL DISCHARGE

Employees who claim to be discharged for reasons that violate state law or public policy may have recourse under state "whistleblower" protection acts, and they may bring actions for wrongful or retaliatory discharge.

◆ A ninth-grade Pennsylvania student was hospitalized after a suicide attempt. A special education teacher had ongoing talks with the student's mother about the student's problems. The teacher found a note by the student expressing suicidal thoughts and later suggested that the student see a therapist. The student refused to see the therapist unless the teacher went with her. The teacher obtained the mother's permission to arrange for a session. She transported the student to the session and attended it with her. The principal directed the teacher to stop attending therapy sessions with the student. The district superintendent advised the teacher she had engaged in willful neglect of duty, insubordination, incompetency, persistent negligence, willful violation of laws and improper conduct. After a hearing, the superintendent sent the teacher a letter describing district policies and limiting her interaction with at-risk students. The teacher claimed the letter was designed to stifle her protected speech and punish her for helping special education students. She sued the school district, superintendent and school board in a federal district court for First Amendment, equal protection and Rehabilitation Act Section 504 violations. The court held the teacher may have violated special education laws and district policies. The letter was necessary to assure she was in compliance with special education law and district policy. The court held for the district, and the teacher appealed.

The U.S. Court of Appeals, Third Circuit, considered only the teacher's claims to First Amendment and disability law protection. **Her conduct in scheduling therapy sessions, transporting the student to them and attending them was not intended to convey a message, and was not protected by either the First Amendment or the Rehabilitation Act.** To have Rehabilitation Act protection, the teacher had to show she made a charge or assisted another person in any investigation, proceeding or hearing under federal disability law. The court held disability laws do not protect persons who simply provide assistance to special education students. There must be some advocacy for them, or some protest against discrimination or other unlawful conduct. As the teacher's conduct was not expressive or communicative, the court affirmed the judgment. *Montanye v. Wissahickon School Dist.*, No. 05-5286, 2007 WL 541710 (3d Cir. 2007).

◆   A Texas teacher filed three grievances against her district in the same school year. In the first, she claimed it did not timely provide her a performance appraisal and denied her the opportunity to request a second appraisal, as permitted by state education regulations. The other grievances complained of unfair treatment and retaliation for filing her first grievance. The school board held a hearing and voted to deny the third grievance. The teacher appealed to a state district court, which awarded summary judgment to the district.

The teacher appealed to the Court of Appeals of Texas, claiming the district retaliated against her in violation of the state Whistleblower Act. The district asserted it would have voted against renewing the teacher's contract regardless of her whistleblower act claim. The court noted **the district superintendent's recommendation for non-renewal of the teacher's contract stated 10 reasons for the action. At her hearing, the district included 46 specific grounds for not renewing the contract, including the intentional disparagement of a student.** The teacher presented no evidence concerning retaliation during the hearing. The court held the district conclusively proved it would have voted not to renew her contract for reasons unrelated to her whistleblower claim. The district was entitled to assert the act's affirmative defense, and the court affirmed the judgment. *Adams v. Groesbeck Independent School Dist.*, No. 10-02-313-CV, 2003 WL 22708642 (Tex. Ct. App. 2003).

◆ A teacher accepted a job in a rural Utah school district. She claimed the district superintendent retaliated against her for reporting sexual misconduct and favoritism toward polygamist families by her colleagues. According to the teacher, a colleague dated her daughter and then tried to initiate sexual contact with the daughter and several male students. The teacher alleged the superintendent threatened her, wrote adverse employment reports and ordered her to undergo a psychological examination intended to discredit her reports. She claimed the superintendent induced her daughter to fabricate a sex abuse charge against her stepfather. The district refused to renew the teacher's contract, and she sued the district, superintendent and a colleague in a federal district court for constitutional rights violations as secured by 42 U.S.C. § 1983, wrongful termination, and whistleblower claims under the Utah Protection of Public Employees Act (UPPEA). The court dismissed the wrongful termination claim, but it allowed the teacher to proceed with her federal civil rights and state whistleblower claims. A jury awarded her identical sums of $65,000 against the superintendent and district for the whistleblower claims. It also awarded her $55,000 against the district and $32,500 against the superintendent for the civil rights claims. The court denied post-trial motions by the district and superintendent and awarded the teacher attorneys' fees and costs. It denied her claims for punitive damages against the superintendent and district.

On appeal, the Tenth Circuit rejected the superintendent's argument against liability in her official capacity under the whistleblower act. The UPPEA included "an agent of the employer" within its definition of "employer." The teacher did not receive an "impermissible double recovery," as the district and superintendent argued. The district court explicitly instructed the jury not to award duplicate damages and to compensate the teacher if she suffered different injuries attributable to separate claims. The damages were apportioned to publicly sanction the superintendent. The district court properly disallowed the teacher's claim for punitive damages against the district under the UPPEA and Section 1983. However, she was entitled to proceed with her Section 1983 claim for punitive damages against the superintendent. **Punitive damages are available in Section 1983 actions against public officials when an official has an evil motive or intent, or demonstrates reckless or callous indifference to the federally protected rights of others. Since the teacher presented evidence of the superintendent's "contempt, hostility and anger" in response to her reports of sexual abuse and misconduct by school employees, she was entitled to proceed with her Section 1983 punitive damages claim.** The court held for the teacher on each issue on appeal, and it remanded the case for a trial to determine whether punitive damages should be awarded against the superintendent. *Youren v. Tintic School Dist.*, 343 F.3d 1296 (10th Cir. 2003).

◆ A newly hired Virginia gifted education specialist learned the U.S. Department of Education's Office for Civil Rights was considering a race discrimination complaint against her school board. After being instructed by the district superintendent to take appropriate action, she developed an action plan calling for increased efforts to recruit and retain minority students in the gifted program. The specialist began to experience performance and communication problems after her supervisor was replaced. Complaints about her performance continued for the next year. The superintendent recommended suspending the specialist, but parents complained and he allowed her to continue working under another supervisor. The supervisor recommended terminating her contract, and the board ultimately accepted the recommendation. The specialist sued the board, superintendent and other school officials in a federal district court for retaliatory discharge in violation of Title VI. The district court held for the board and officials, and the specialist appealed to the Fourth Circuit.

The court first considered the lower court's ruling that Title VI and its regulations do not create a legal cause of action for retaliation. It explained that while the U.S. Supreme Court has recently made clear there is no Title VI cause of action for disparate impact claims, a private cause of action exists for intentional discrimination under Title VI and its corresponding regulations. After reviewing cases describing federal agency authority to create private legal remedies, **the court held a private cause of action existed for a retaliation complaint under Title VI.** Recognition of a private cause of action for retaliation was not inconsistent with Title VI. The court held that anti-retaliation regulations including 34 C.F.R. Part 100.7(e) were enforceable through a private cause of action, to the extent that they forbade retaliation for opposing practices that constitute unlawful discrimination. The case was vacated and remanded to the lower court for further exploration of whether the specialist reasonably believed the district was engaging in intentional discrimination that violated Title VI. *Peters v. Jenney*, 327 F.3d 307 (4th Cir. 2003).

◆ During her fourth year of employment by a New York school district, a teacher was called on to testify during Individuals with Disabilities Education Act (IDEA) proceedings. She gave testimony that supported the position advocated by a student's parent, who was successful in the IDEA proceeding. Almost five years later, the teacher was notified by letter that she would be terminated from her position as a home instruction teacher. The letter referred to the teacher's "record of instruction" and stated that she had refused to turn in a grade for a student, failed to respond to repeated requests for work samples by the same student and failed to schedule an appointment with the superintendent. The school district discharged the teacher several months later.

Over two years after the receipt of her discharge notice, and over seven years after the teacher testified in the IDEA hearing, she sued the district in a federal district court for retaliatory discharge. She asserted the discharge was because of her testimony at the hearing, in violation of her speech rights. The teacher also advanced state law claims for defamation, intentional infliction of emotional distress, breach of contract and wrongful discharge. **A federal district court held she had failed to state a claim for deprivation of her constitutional rights.** It dismissed her state law claims in conformity with federal rules. The teacher appealed to the Second Circuit, which affirmed the judgment. The teacher failed to make out a claim for retaliation under the First Amendment or show the district deprived her of any due process rights. Her claims of hostile work environment were time-barred. *Reynolds v. Board of Educ. of Wappingers Cent. School Dist.*, 208 F.3d 203 (2d Cir. 2000).

VIII. WORKERS' COMPENSATION

Workers' compensation is typically the exclusive remedy for an employee injured in the course and scope of employment. Litigation in this area tends to focus on whether an injured employee may assert tort claims for more money than what is available under workers' compensation law by showing an injury occurred outside the course and scope of employment or by intentional conduct.

◆   A disabled Washington student inflicted frequent injuries on students and staff. In one school year, he caused over 200 documented injuries. The student pushed his teacher as she tried to intervene during one of his attacks, knocking her unconscious. The next day, he bit an aide on her breast as she tried to distract him from other students. Despite these incidents, the student remained in his class with the same staff for most of the year. Both employees received industrial insurance (workers' compensation) benefits, but sought additional damages from the school district. They sued the district in the state court system, alleging it had deliberately intended their injuries. The court held for the district, and the Court of Appeals of Washington affirmed the judgment.

On appeal, the Supreme Court of Washington stated that **while workers' compensation is typically the exclusive remedy for an injured employee, a limited exception applies to employers who intentionally injure employees**. In those cases, injured employees could obtain damages in excess of workers' compensation benefits. The court held in a previous case that **an employer's gross negligence or failure to observe safety laws and procedures does not constitute deliberate intent to injure**. An act that had a substantial certainty of producing intent also failed to meet this threshold. **Under the state's narrow view of the exception to workers' compensation exclusivity, an employee had to show an employer had actual knowledge injury was certain to occur before the employer could be liable in a tort case.** The behavior of a child with special needs was far from predictable. The district had tried increasingly restrictive strategies to address his behavior. The employees did not show the district was certain its strategies would fail. As there could be no liability for the district based on simple negligence, the court affirmed the judgment. *Vallandigham v. Clover Park School Dist. No. 400*, 109 P.3d 805 (Wash. 2005).

◆   A Florida school bus attendant was injured when a wheelchair lift fell on him. He claimed a maintenance worker negligently repaired or adjusted the lift twice in a four-month period before the accident. He sued the school board in a state court for negligence. The attendant argued that he and the maintenance employee were involved in "unrelated work" under the workers' compensation law, so that the board was not entitled to immunity. The court held the exception for unrelated work did not apply, and it awarded summary judgment to the board.

The Supreme Court of Florida explained that **the workers' compensation law was a comprehensive scheme for providing injured employees benefits without proof of employer fault. It afforded immunity to employers from tort actions based on workplace injuries.** The law created an exception to immunity for cases involving employees of the same employer when each was assigned primarily to "unrelated works." The attendant and mechanics were both employed by the board, worked in the same facility and were involved in the same transportation services. **The workers' compensation system was based on the mutual renunciation of common law rights and defenses by employers and employees alike.** The unrelated works exception applied only if an employee who caused injury was clearly engaged in works unrelated to the injured employee. The trial court had correctly held the employees had the common goal of providing safe transportation and its judgment was affirmed. *Taylor v. School Board of Brevard County*, 888 So.2d 1 (Fla. 2004).

◆   An Idaho school contracted with a physical therapist to supply services to a wheelchair-bound student. She hurt her back while helping the student off the bus and alleged the school was negligent in failing to provide a bus with a wheelchair lift. The therapist sued the school district for negligence in a state trial court. The court agreed with the district that she was covered under the Workers' Compensation Act, even though it had no employer-employee relationship with her. The therapist appealed to the state supreme court, which held the Idaho Code distinguishes between employees and independent contractors in workers' compensation cases. The workers' compensation act prohibited eligible employees from suing under other theories of law. **The court held the act did not cover independent contractors, so the therapist could sue the school for negligence.** However, summary judgment for the district was appropriate, because there were no special circumstances creating a legal duty by the district to prevent her from assisting the student. *Daleiden v. Jefferson County Joint School Dist. No. 251*, 80 P.3d 1067 (Idaho 2003).

◆   The Supreme Court of South Dakota upheld an administrative decision denying workers' compensation benefits to a school bus driver injured while snow skiing on a school field trip. She was receiving "down time" pay during the student activity and was free to do whatever she wanted when she accepted a free lift pass. **The court held the driver's injury was not "work-related" as it did not arise out of her employment.** She was not expected to supervise students after they left the bus. **The driver had "stepped aside from her employment purpose when she went skiing," and she was not entitled to workers' compensation benefits.** *Norton v. Deuel School Dist. #19-4*, 674 N.W.2d 518 (S.D. 2004).

◆   Michigan school **custodians claimed exposure to asbestos from a school carpeting project caused respiratory irritation, post-traumatic stress disorder and other medical and psychological problems.** They sued the district and school officials in a federal district court for violations of federal environmental laws, due process violations and state law negligence. The court awarded summary judgment to the district. On appeal, the U.S. Court of Appeals, Sixth Circuit, rejected the due process claims, as the custodians did not show the carpeting assignment was so punitive or retaliatory it shocked the conscience. The **Michigan workers' compensation act is the exclusive remedy for occupational injuries, except where an employer has actual knowledge that an injury was certain to occur, yet willfully disregards that knowledge.** The custodians did not show the administration intended to injure them or actually knew injury was certain to occur. *Upsher v. Grosse Pointe Public School System*, 285 F.3d 448 (6th Cir. 2002).

◆ A Nebraska special education coordinator was employed by the same school district as her husband, who was a band teacher. The coordinator helped her husband return some borrowed computer equipment to the school. After they entered a darkened room, she fell four feet through an open trapdoor, suffering a broken leg. The coordinator sued the school district in a state court for personal injuries. The court held the suit was not barred by the Nebraska Workers' Compensation Act and awarded the coordinator almost $195,000.

The Nebraska Supreme Court held **the Workers' Compensation Act is the exclusive remedy for employees whose injuries arise out of and in the course of employment**. The act's coverage is particularly complicated when an employee helps a co-worker to the employer's advantage. The coordinator's duties concerned special education and had nothing to do with the school band. **Since helping her husband was not considered part of her job, the injury did not arise in the course of her employment.** The court affirmed the judgment, finding the coordinator was permanently disabled. *Skinner v. Ogallala Public School Dist. No. 1*, 631 N.W.2d 510 (Neb. 2001).

◆ After being diagnosed with tonsil cancer, a New Jersey teacher underwent surgery that included the partial removal of his jaw and mouth, which were later reconstructed. He utilized his available sick time and submitted a workers' compensation claim that was denied by his employing school board. The teacher claimed his cancer was work-related because he shared an office for 26 years with a chain-smoking co-worker. The teacher appealed to the state department of labor, which held a hearing. A worker's compensation judge agreed with the teacher's witness, who testified that secondhand smoke contains the same toxins as inhaled cigarette smoke, but at greater levels. The teacher's small office was poorly ventilated, and no other known cancer cause was identified. **The judge found that the teacher's cancer probably arose out of and in the course of his employment and was peculiar to his place of employment.** The judge awarded benefits along with other relief.

The board appealed to the Superior Court of New Jersey, Appellate Division, denying a causal relationship between the teacher's cancer and his employment. **The court held the teacher met the state workers' compensation act requirement for claimants to demonstrate the link between employment and disease by a material degree.** The smoke exposure had been constant, consistent and pervasive. The court affirmed the compensation judge's finding of a nexus between the teacher's disease and his place of employment. *Magaw v. Middletown Board of Educ.*, 323 N.J. Super. 1, 731 A.2d 1196 (N.J. Super. Ct. App. Div. 1999).

CHAPTER NINE

Tenure and Due Process

                                                                    Page

I.   STATE TENURE STATUTES...369
     A. Tenure Status 369
     B. Tenure Rights 376
         1. Reductions in Force 376
         2. Other Substantive Rights 380
     C. Collective Bargaining Agreements 381
     D. State Regulatory Authority 383

II. DUE PROCESS REQUIREMENTS 385
     A. Property Interest 386
     B. Notice 390
     C. Hearing 393
         1. Minimum Requirements 393
         2. Hearing Procedures 396
         3. Impartiality 399

I. STATE TENURE STATUTES

State tenure statutes are strictly construed, and failure to comply with statutory notices may result in an employee gaining tenure by operation of law. Teachers who earn tenure (also known as continuing contract status) have protected rights to receive proper notice and an opportunity to be heard.

A. Tenure Status

◆ **An Alabama principal employed under a probationary contract was not entitled to an evaluation and 90 days' notice prior to termination of his contract.** The Alabama Court of Civil appeals held the Teacher Accountability Act distinguished between contract principals and probationary principals. As the principal was not entitled to the statutory protections he claimed, the court affirmed a lower court judgment for the school board. *Holmes v. Macon County Board of Educ.*, No. 2050967, 2006 WL 3823271 (Ala. Ct. App. 2006).

◆ A California teacher taught agricultural maintenance in a school district's regular education program as a .57 full-time equivalent (FTE) employee. He also worked as a .43 FTE maintenance employee in a regional occupational program (ROP). The district classified the teacher "Probationary I" in the .57 FTE position. The next year, the district rehired the teacher for both jobs. His employment contract deemed him a "probationary II employee." It indicated "this is considered a temporary assignment," and noted ROP was "funding

369

43%." For the next three years, the district reemployed the teacher in both teaching positions. After five years, the district notified him he was not being rehired, and he petitioned a California superior court for an order that the district had to reelect him for both positions. The teacher claimed he was a regular teacher who was "subsequently assigned" to the ROP position within the meaning of California Education Code Section 44910. The court agreed and ordered the district to reinstate the teacher to both jobs and to pay his attorney's fees. The district appealed to the Court of Appeal of California.

The court upheld the decision concerning the .57 FTE position. The district's conduct in not reelecting the teacher was arbitrary and capricious. **The court stated Section 44910 excludes service as an ROP instructor from the computation of service required for attaining permanent status in a school district.** The teacher was "not assigned out from a regular teaching position into an ROP position," but was assigned to a second, concurrent position in the ROP. **Section 44910 was designed to prevent an ROP teacher from attaining permanent status after three years as a probationary teacher.** As ROPs involved career technical courses, teachers often had only specialized training, creating a risk that districts would have to retain them permanently, even if the ROP was dropped. The legislature intended Section 44910 to allow more flexibility for schools and avoid the prospect of having to retain teachers who were "virtually untransferable" to other assignments. The exception claimed by the teacher was intended to protect credentialed teachers who, unlike himself, were employed in regular programs, then transferred into ROP programs. The court reversed the judgment concerning the .43 FTE ROP assignment, as this service did not count toward permanent status. *Reis v. Biggs Unified School Dist.*, 126 Cal.App.4th 809, 24 Cal.Rptr.3d 393 (Cal. Ct. App. 2005).

◆ Texas Education Code § 21.055(e) authorizes "school district teaching permits," which allow a person to teach only in the district issuing the permit in a particular subject or class. The State Board for Educator Certification (SBEC) plays no role in issuing district permits, but the state education commissioner may veto applications. By contrast, the Texas Term Contract Non-Renewal Act (TCNA) governs teaching certificates issued by the SBEC to "classroom teachers" with no district or class limitations. A music teacher taught choir classes for six consecutive years in a district under one-year Section 21.055 contracts. The district let his final contract lapse due to declining enrollment. Near this time, the teacher received a state principal's credential and challenged the non-renewal of his Section 21.055 contract. The school board adopted a hearing examiner's recommendation for non-renewal, and the decision was upheld by the state education commissioner. A Texas district court affirmed the decision.

The teacher appealed to the Court of Appeals of Texas. It stated **Texas Education Code § 21.201(1) defined "teacher" as a classroom teacher or other full-time professional who was required to hold a certificate issued under that section.** "Classroom teacher" was defined as an "educator" teaching not less than an average of four hours per day in an academic, career or technology instructional setting. Section 21.201(1) definitions required a person classified as a teacher to hold a certificate issued by the SBEC. **The teacher in this case lacked a teaching certificate issued by the SBEC.** The legislature created a distinction between SBEC-certified teachers and those holding district teaching permits. For this reason, the teacher was not a "teacher" as defined by the TCNA. The court rejected his claim to certification as a "teacher" under the TCNA based on his principal's certificate. The teacher had been allowed to teach because he had a district teaching permit, not by virtue of his principal's certificate. The court affirmed the commissioner's decision. *Houston v. Nelson*, 147 S.W.2d 580 (Tex. Ct. App. 2004).

◆ **The Supreme Court of South Dakota held a school district did not have to provide a hearing or other due process protections to a retired teacher who claimed she retained her continuing contract status upon returning to the district under a probationary contract** (see *Wirt v. Parker School Dist. #60-04*, 689 N.W.2d 901 (S.D. 2004), Chapter Eight, Section V.A.).

Faced with a legal issue it had never before considered, the *Wirt* court fully explored decisions from 11 states, including *Kilgore v. Jasper City Board of Educ.*, 624 So.2d 603 (Ala. Ct. Civ. App. 1993). In *Kilgore,* the Court of Civil Appeals of Alabama held a retired teacher who tried to rescind his retirement and later signed a probationary contract had accepted his probationary status. This terminated the property and tenure rights he enjoyed before retiring.

In *Williams v. Lafayette Parish School Board*, 533 So.2d 1359 (La. Ct. App. 1989), the Court of Appeal of Louisiana held **voluntary resignation breaks the continuity of state tenure law** and is not against public policy. In *Brubaker v. Hardy*, 5 Ohio St.2d 103, 214 N.E.2d 79 (Ohio 1966), the Supreme Court of Ohio held **a school board's acceptance of a teacher's resignation, and the teacher's subsequent acceptance of a one-year teaching contract, resulted in waiver of the right to a continuing employment contract**.

◆ A California teacher served eight years in a reading specialist position that was categorically funded under California Education Code § 44909. The district then hired her for a full-time position in its regular education program supported by the district's general funds. The district classified the teacher as a second-year probationary employee. It notified her by March 15 that she would not be rehired and then discharged her at the end of the school year. The teacher claimed she was improperly classified. A state superior court held the district had an unqualified right to discharge her at the end of the school year.

The Court of Appeal of California **stated employees serving a district for two complete consecutive school years in positions requiring certification qualifications become permanent employees at the commencement of the next succeeding school year, if they are reelected to positions requiring certification qualifications**. The reading specialist position required certification qualifications. However, categorically funded positions, like temporary employees, were covered by other provisions of the Education Code. Service under Section 44909 was not "included in computing the service required as a prerequisite to attainment of, or eligibility to, classification as a permanent employee" unless two conditions were met. The first was to perform service for at least 75% of the district's regular school days. The second was the person "be subsequently employed as a probationary employee in a position requiring certification qualifications." **The court held the second requirement** contemplated employment for an entire school year. Otherwise, a teacher serving in a categorically funded program for at least two years would never serve as a probationary employee. Section 44909 was intended to prevent a person from acquiring probationary status solely through work in categorically funded programs. The teacher's interpretation of the law would deprive districts of the opportunity to evaluate performance as a general curriculum teacher. The court affirmed the judgment, holding the teacher was properly classified as a second-year probationary employee. The district could non-renew her contract at the end of the school year without providing her further procedural protections. *Schnee v. Alameda Unified School Dist.*, 125 Cal.App.4th 555, 22 Cal.Rptr.3d 80 (Cal. Ct. App. 2004).

◆   A California school district hired a teacher in the middle of the 1998-99 school year. He held a valid state teaching certificate but needed to complete course work and obtain a Bilingual, Cross-Cultural, Language and Academic Development (BCLAD) certificate. The teacher replaced a certificated employee on leave of absence and was classified as a temporary employee. The district employed him full time during the next two school years under the same terms. At the same time, it employed many more temporary teachers than the number of its permanent teachers on leave. The teacher obtained his BCLAD certificate in 2001, and the district rehired him for 2001-2002. In February 2002, midway through his third full year of employment by the district under a temporary designation, the district notified him he would not be reemployed. The teacher petitioned a state court to grant him permanent status. It held he became a permanent employee before receiving the non-reemployment notice.

The state court of appeal held **a certificated probationary employee who works for two full consecutive school years is deemed to have permanent status by operation of law if he or she is reemployed by the district for the succeeding year**. The first year of employment as a temporary employee is to be deemed probationary. "Temporary teachers" include those employed due to a leave of absence by another certificated employee. If a temporary teacher's duties continue, the teacher is considered a "probationary employee." **State law deemed all certificated teachers who were not classified as permanent or substitute employees to be "probationary employees."** In this case, the teacher completed over a year as a temporary during the 1999-2000 school year. He was then reemployed in a vacant position requiring certification. The teacher had worked for over a full school year as a temporary by the end of the 1999-2000 school year and was then reemployed in 2000-01, when he became a probationary employee. The district failed to notify him he would not be reemployed for 2001-2002. The teacher completed the year in a certificated position and received proper certification. For this reason, when the district rehired him for 2001-02, he became a permanent employee by operation of law. The court affirmed the judgment in his favor. *Rossi v. Salinas City Elementary School Dist.*, No. H024943, 2003 WL 22373464 (Cal. Ct. App. 2003).

◆   Two Massachusetts teachers worked as public school teachers in the 1950s and 1960s, before leaving their jobs to raise families. Both held elementary education teaching certificates from the state education department. The teachers returned to work in the 1980s, taking jobs in a federally funded Chapter I supplemental instruction program. One worked in the program for 15 years and the other for eight years before being laid off due to budget cuts. They claimed to have "professional teacher status," with the right to bump non-tenured teachers from elementary teaching positions. The district superintendent denied their requests, and after holding separate arbitration hearings, arbitrators issued a joint decision for the school committee. The arbitrators held the teachers had no bumping rights because they were not "teachers" as defined by state law.

The teachers appealed to a state superior court, which vacated the arbitration award as a violation of public policy. The school committee appealed to the Supreme Judicial Court of Massachusetts, which noted the strong public policy in favor of arbitration. Courts may vacate arbitration awards only in limited circumstances. An alleged violation of law is not considered a "violation of public policy" and is not a permissible reason for vacating an arbitration award. The court held state law did not prevent the arbitrators from considering whether they had bumping rights. An arbitrator's ruling on bumping rights did not affect the superintendent's decision to reduce the number of teachers in the district. The court found it unnecessary to decide whether the arbitrators had correctly applied the law. They had analyzed the teachers' conditions of employment and job functions in resolving whether they were "teachers" under the state professional teacher status provision. **The Education Reform Act of 1993 replaced the concept of "tenure" with that of "professional teacher status." It did not change the previous rule of law granting significant employment protections to teachers who serve in public schools for three consecutive school years, and it did not alter the definition of "teacher."** Because the arbitrators had fully decided both cases, the decisions were not subject to judicial review. There were no grounds for vacating the arbitration award. The court vacated the judgment, ordering confirmation of the award. *Lyons v. School Committee of Dedham*, 440 Mass. 74, 794 N.E.2d 586 (Mass. 2003).

◆ A Texas school district suspended a continuing contract teacher for verbally harassing a six-year-old student. The teacher agreed to work as a probationary employee under a single-year contract. Before the end of the year, the school board voted to terminate her probationary contract and sent her a timely notice of the action. She filed a grievance, which was dismissed based on lack of jurisdiction and her acceptance of probationary status. The school board approved the hearing examiner's decision, and the teacher appealed to the Texas Commissioner of Education. The commissioner noted that the district failed to give the teacher proper notice of the termination of her continuing contract prior to the change in her status. But because the teacher failed to contest the change in an administrative proceeding, she did not exhaust her administrative remedies, and the hearing examiner properly declined to accept the case.

A state district court affirmed the decision, and the teacher appealed. The Court of Appeals of Texas stated **probationary teachers may be discharged under the Education Code if it is in the best interest of the district. In such cases, the decision of a school board cannot be appealed. The Education Code allowed the re-designation of a continuing contract teacher as a "probationary teacher" in lieu of discharge, after providing written notice**

of a proposed discharge, termination or non-renewal of contract. The teacher agreed to the terms of her probationary contract, despite having a right to file a grievance over the change in her status. By accepting the probationary contract until she received notice that it would be terminated, she waived her right to complain about any lack of notice from the board. As the teacher failed to exhaust administrative remedies by not filing a grievance, the court affirmed the judgment. *Wittman v. Nelson*, 100 S.W.3d 356 (Tex. Ct. App. 2002).

◆ A Florida school administrator with 27 years of experience received continuing contract status as a teacher in 1972. He was promoted to an assistant principal position in 1974 and later became a principal. He was employed under annual employment contracts, and his school board specified that neither he nor the board owed any further obligation to the other party after expiration of the contract. Near the end of the 2000-2001 school year, the board accepted a supervisor's recommendation not to offer the administrator a new contract.

The administrator appealed to the Florida Third District Court of Appeal, which noted that he was entitled to continuing employment as a teacher by virtue of the status he obtained in 1972. However, **the court rejected the administrator's claim that continuing contract status earned as a teacher automatically conferred this status to his subsequent promotions to administrative positions**. He would have to earn continuing contract status in the position of assistant principal or principal to gain that. The plain language of his annual contracts indicated that he had no such entitlement to continued employment beyond the term of each individual contract year. He was not entitled to a hearing under state law or the Due Process Clause. *Jones v. Miami-Dade County Public Schools*, 816 So.2d 824 (Fla. Dist. Ct. App. 2002).

◆ A probationary New York teacher was appointed to a tenured position near the end of her third year. She then admitted violating the school's zero-tolerance policy against consuming alcohol at school-sponsored events. Three days before the teacher was to receive the tenured position, the superintendent offered to extend her probationary period. She declined, and the board rescinded her "conditional tenure appointment." The teacher sued the board in a state court, asserting she received tenure at the end of her third year of probationary employment, not the beginning of the following school year. The court dismissed the case, and a state appellate division court affirmed. The New York Court of Appeals consolidated the case with that of a special education teacher who received an erroneous notice from her school board that she was approved for tenure. The board rescinded the notice after learning of its mistake three months before the end of her probationary period. The special education teacher sued the district in a federal district court. Appeal reached the Second Circuit, which found the case depended upon unsettled questions of state law.

The state court of appeals held Education Law § 2509 distinguished between probationary teachers, who can be terminated without a hearing at any time for any reason, and tenured teachers, who are subject to dismissal only after formal disciplinary hearings. The law authorized boards to award tenure before the end of a teacher's probationary period, allowing superintendents to recommend a teacher for tenure at the end of the period, or up to six months before that time. **The court held that a board resolution granting tenure to a probationary teacher as of a future date confers tenure to the teacher only as of the specified date.** The law contemplated that school boards would await the conclusion of the full three-year probationary period before making a binding tenure decision. This helped ensure only qualified teachers were hired into tenured positions. A conditional tenure award provided teachers and school districts with notice of a board's intention to confer tenure upon completion of the school year. The court affirmed the decision against the foreign language teacher and certified an answer to the Second Circuit in favor of the special education teacher's school district. Neither teacher was entitled to tenure. *Remus v. Board of Educ. for Tonawanda City School Dist. v. Schenectady City School Dist.*, 727 N.Y.S.2d 43, 750 N.E.2d 1091 (N.Y. 2001).

◆ A probationary music teacher worked for a Nevada district for two years after years of teaching in California and being accredited there. During his third year in Nevada, he received a notice he would be discharged unless he remedied a technical defect in his teaching license application in four days. The district discharged the teacher after he failed to remedy the defect in time. It rehired him a few days later, after he provided the necessary documentation and reapplied for his position. The district reclassified the teacher as probationary for the rest of the school year and the next year. He filed a declaratory judgment action in a state district court, asserting his Nevada school employment never terminated and that he was entitled to post-probationary status.

The teacher claimed the district never terminated his employment because it failed to follow state notice and hearing requirements when it gave him only four days to correct the defective certification forms. The court agreed, and the district appealed to the Supreme Court of Nevada. It held the teacher had post-probationary status. Under state law, he was entitled to 15 days' notice prior to employment termination, plus notice of the right to a hearing. The district had given him only four days of notice with no opportunity for a hearing. Without regard to whether the teacher was properly licensed, **the district had employed him as a post-probationary teacher for over a year. The court affirmed the ruling that he was entitled to statutory procedures and protections.** The teacher was not effectively terminated and did not lose his post-probationary teaching status. *Clark County School Dist. v. Riley*, 14 P.3d 22 (Nev. 2000).

◆ An Oklahoma probationary teacher nearing completion of her third year of employment in a district was offered a temporary contract for the next school year. The district did not offer her a permanent contract due to performance concerns. The temporary contract had a resignation clause effective at the end of the school year and waived the teacher's right to further notice for contract termination. At the end of her fourth year, the board decided not to renew the temporary contract and she sued the district in an Oklahoma trial court for an order compelling tenured status. The court granted the district's summary judgment motion, and the case reached the Supreme Court of Oklahoma.

The court held the teacher was not tenured either before or after she completed the temporary contract. As she was not tenured, the district could offer her a temporary contract instead of not rehiring her. **Teachers employed** under temporary contracts are exempt from the state tenure law. The court rejected the teacher's assertion that she was entitled to tenure rights prior to the completion of three years of employment under a written contract. Under Oklahoma law, teachers gain tenure after the completion of three consecutive complete school years under a written teaching contract. The court affirmed the district court judgment. *Scheer v. Independent School Dist. No. I-26, Ottawa County, Oklahoma*, 1997 OK 115, 948 P.2d 275 (Okla. 1997).

B. Tenure Rights

1. Reductions in Force

A tenured teacher may not be laid off and bumped by a non-tenured teacher if the tenured teacher is properly licensed to hold the position. In the following case, the Supreme Court of South Dakota held a teacher's lack of appropriate certification and experience prevented her retention after a reduction in force.

◆ A South Dakota computer science teacher had worked for a school district for 17 years. The district employed three other computer teachers, including one who had taught in the district for over 30 years. Another teacher had 10 years in the district, while another was in his first year there. The collective bargaining agreement (CBA) between the board and teachers had a two-part method for determining if seniority could be used. This included appropriate certification and the courses taught by a teacher in the preceding seven years. The school board determined the 30-year veteran teacher could use her seniority only for the areas in which she had taught during the previous seven years. As a result, she was allowed to bump only into a computer science position. The computer science teacher was the only teacher who taught this subject exclusively. The 30-year veteran could not bump the 10-year veteran, who also taught business classes. The 30-year veteran teacher was also unable to satisfy the seniority requirements for the first-year teacher's teaching assignments. He taught technology modules that were heavily weighted on math and science.

The computer science teacher was unable to bump the 10-year and first-year teachers for the same reasons that the 30-year veteran could not. Her contract was not renewed, and the district denied her grievance. A South Dakota circuit court held for the teacher. It held the relevant certification for purposes of the CBA was the position that was being non-renewed, not the position that a teacher was trying to bump into. **On appeal, the Supreme Court of South Dakota found the teacher lacked the certification and recent experience of the less-senior teachers whose positions she was trying to assume.** The circuit court's interpretation of the CBA would render its terms meaningless. **The parties did not intend to "relegate seniority to a nearly ineffectual status."** The court rejected the teacher's additional claim that prior reductions in force in the district were conducted on a provisional basis. **She could not partially bump other teachers by assuming parts of their job assignments.** The district had properly followed the CBA policy, and its action was upheld. *Hanson v. Vermillion School Dist. No. 13-1*, 727 N.W.2d 459 (S.D. 2007).

◆   A New York board of cooperative educational services (BOCES) provided student occupational programs in several districts. Teaching assistants (TAs) supplemented the services of classroom teachers. The BOCES laid off nine TAs due to declining student enrollment. Layoffs were not in accord with seniority. Five of the laid off TAs sued the BOCES in a state court, which allowed the state education commissioner to determine if TAs were "teachers" as defined by New York Education Law § 3013(2). The TAs claimed they could only be dismissed according to seniority under Section 3013(2), a tenure provision addressing the appointment of "teachers and members of the teaching staff." The BOCES asserted TAs were like vocational teachers, without specific educational, certification, or licensure requirements. The commissioner disagreed and reinstated the TAs with back pay and benefits. He found the TAs were protected by Section 3013(2) and were "in the same special subject area of teaching assistant." A trial court annulled the commissioner's decision.

On appeal, the Court of Appeals of New York observed the commissioner's finding that TAs helped teachers who were trained to instruct specific subjects. **All teaching assistants were "part of the same subject area."** As the legislative history of Section 3013(2) suggested BOCES staff should be laid off by seniority, the TAs were covered by Section 3013(2). **TAs had a separate tenure area from teachers and should not have their rights judged by whether or not they met the qualifications and credentials of teachers.** Their separate credentials were accorded tenure under state regulations, and they had due process rights within that system. The court held Section 3013(2) protected the rights of "professional educators," not just teachers. Whether TAs were employed by a school board or a BOCES, they were professional educators for tenure purposes and were "teachers" in a layoff under Section 3013(2). The court noted the BOCES personnel policy contemplated including TAs in the tenure system and indicated the system was based on seniority. As the BOCES appeared to be going against its own policies, the court affirmed the judgment. *Madison-Oneida Board of Cooperative Educ. Services v. Mills*, 4 N.Y.3d 51, 823 N.E.2d 1265, 790 N.Y.S.2d 619 (N.Y. 2004).

◆   A Minnesota teacher taught for seven years in a district and was licensed to teach French and social studies for grades 7-12. Near the end of a school year, the board voted to place him on unrequested leave of absence (ULA). The board hired a less experienced teacher for a 0.8 full-time equivalency position (FTE) teaching physical science. It recalled the senior teacher to a 0.6 FTE position and increased the less experienced teacher's position to full time. The district placed a licensed health teacher on ULA and hired a temporary teacher to teach health for two hours per day. The district twice chose not to realign positions to recall the senior teacher and avoid hiring less experienced teachers.

The senior teacher challenged the hiring and ULA decisions in an action that reached the state court of appeals. The court noted that the state Teacher Tenure Act, Minn. Stat. § 122A.40, allows school boards to place teachers on ULA when a position is discontinued or subjected to financial limitations. **School boards may not appoint new teachers to fill vacant positions when a teacher who is licensed for the vacancy remains on ULA.** When a senior teacher on ULA is not licensed to teach a vacant position, a district is required to realign positions and reassign teachers to create a vacancy for the senior teacher. However, school boards need not consider every possible realignment configuration and retain substantial discretion to determine whether realignment is practical and reasonable. **The court held the senior teacher's realignment proposal was neither practical nor reasonable because it did not adequately consider licensure requirements.** The tenure act was intended to protect seniority, not unreasonably restrict school district operations. The court upheld the school board's decision. *Henderson v. Independent School Dist. No. 706*, No. C9-01-1758, 2002 WL 857886 (Minn. Ct. App. 2002).

◆ Another Minnesota school board placed a teacher on unrequested leave of absence for 65 minutes per day after eliminating an elementary art section due to declining enrollment and budget. Her only area of certification was art. The teacher requested a hearing, arguing that she had the right to bump less senior teachers from supervisory work during lunch and study hall periods. The hearing officer disagreed, noting the teacher's schedule did not coincide with periods supervised by less senior teachers and would require students to go unsupervised for several minutes each day. The school board adopted the hearing officer's findings, and the teacher appealed to the state court of appeals.

The court found the case required interpretation of state education statutes, since the applicable collective bargaining agreement had no provision governing unrequested leave. State law prohibited a teacher with continuing contract rights from being placed on unrequested leave while probationary employees retained positions for which the continuing contract teacher was licensed. However, **bumping rights did not require districts to make unlimited staffing changes. A teacher had no right to demand that a board create a new position.** The teacher had a right to bump into schedules for her area of certification, but the district had no other art classes available. Seniority rights normally do not apply to the supervision of study halls, but instead depend on the past practices of the school district. The district had allowed licensed teachers to take supervisory assignments from time to time, but the exercise of school management prerogatives was limited by student educational interests. The school board properly found the teacher's seniority and bumping rights did not require scheduling adverse to student interests. There was no existing position for her to bump other employees and the district appropriately placed her on leave. The court affirmed the judgment. *Moe v. Independent School Dist. No. 696, Ely, Minnesota*, 623 N.W.2d 899 (Minn. Ct. App. 2001).

◆ An Ohio school district laid off a teacher with seven years of experience as part of a reduction in force. The board employed her the next year as a substitute for a teacher on sick leave, and she worked in the position for 180 days during the school year. The board compensated the teacher according to the minimum salary under its salary schedule for teachers with a bachelor's degree and zero years of teaching experience. The next school year, the board rehired the teacher for full-time work, crediting her with eight years of experience on the salary scale. The teacher sued the board in a state court, seeking the salary and benefits that would reflect nine years of teaching experience. The trial court held for the school board, and the Court of Appeals of Ohio affirmed the decision.

The teacher appealed to the Supreme Court of Ohio, which held Ohio R.C. § 3319.10 confers certain "local privileges" upon long-term substitutes, including salary not less than the minimum on the current adopted salary schedule. **School boards were required only to pay the minimum amount to substitutes** under the plain language of the statute. The court agreed with the board and Ohio School Boards Association that the legislature would have stated in the law if it intended that long-term substitutes earn additional service credit or be entitled to additional amounts beyond the minimum. The court affirmed the judgment for the board. *State ex rel. Antonucci v. Youngstown City School Dist. Board of Educ.*, 87 Ohio St.3d 564, 722 N.E.2d 69 (Ohio 2000).

◆   A New Jersey teacher was certificated to teach English, social studies and sciences and taught seventh-grade social studies until his position was eliminated. He was reassigned to a computer applications class and other duties during the next two school years, with no reduction in benefits or salary. Within two years, **the board reinstated a seventh-grade social studies teaching position, for which the teacher applied but was not selected**. The teacher petitioned the state commissioner of education, who held that the district had properly transferred the teacher to a position for which he was certified and that no reduction in force took place. The state education board reversed the commissioner's decision, finding a reduction in force had occurred and ordering the local board to reassign the teacher to the social studies position.

The local board appealed to the Superior Court of New Jersey, Appellate Division, where it argued that no reduction in force occurred when the position was abolished, since there had been no layoff of teaching staff and this is a prerequisite to the creation of a preferred eligibility list under state law. **The court agreed with the local board, finding that the teacher's seniority rights were not triggered. Although the board had abolished the position, it had reassigned the teacher to teach different subjects within his certification without any reduction in salary or benefits.** The transfer was not a demotion because the teacher's new duties were within the scope of his certification. The reasons stated by the board for the reassignment were permissible, and abolishment of the position did not trigger the teacher's seniority rights. The court reversed the state board decision. *Carpenito v. Board of Educ. of Borough of Rumson*, 322 N.J.Super. 522, 731 A.2d 538 (N.J. Super. Ct. App. Div. 1999).

◆   An Oklahoma school superintendent advised his school board that the district should eliminate four teaching positions in order to reduce the annual budget by $120,000. The board eliminated a driver education position occupied by a tenured teacher with 19 years of experience. **The district retained some non-tenured, probationary teachers who instructed classes in academic areas in which the tenured teacher was also certified to teach.** He filed a lawsuit against the school district in an Oklahoma district court. The court granted summary judgment to the school district, and the Court of Appeals of Oklahoma affirmed. The teacher appealed to the Supreme Court of Oklahoma.

The court stated that school boards were allowed to exercise discretion when making necessary reductions in force but were required to conform their actions to the state tenure act. **Although boards were allowed to make** necessary economic adjustments, they were required to retain tenured teachers before rehiring non-tenured or probationary teachers pursuant to any reduction in force. Because the tenured teacher presented evidence that he was certified to teach in other areas and also showed that the school district could have accommodated him through minimal efforts, the summary judgment order was improper. The case was reversed and remanded. *Barton v. Independent School Dist. No. I-99, Custer County*, 914 P.2d 1041 (Okla. 1996).

2. Other Substantive Rights

◆   A Mississippi school guidance counselor learned her contract would not be renewed at the end of her first year. She requested the factual basis for non-renewal and a hearing before the school board. The board upheld the action, and the counselor appealed to a state chancery court under the Education Employment Procedures Act of 2001, Mississippi Code Sections 37-9-101 to 37-9-113. The court held the act unconstitutionally conferred jurisdiction on chancery courts. The parties appealed to the Supreme Court of Mississippi.

The court held chancery court jurisdiction was limited. Several decisions prior to enactment of the 2001 act made it clear that school board and other agency decisions were "matters in equity," which the state constitution allowed chancery courts to hear. **The court held Mississippi Code Sections 37-9-111 allowed an aggrieved school employee to appeal a final board decision to a chancery court.** The scope of a chancery court's review was limited to determining if the board action was supported by substantial evidence, was arbitrary or capricious, beyond the board's authority, or in violation of the employee's statutory or constitutional rights. As the chancery court committed error by holding the Education Employment Procedures Act unconstitutional, the court reversed and remanded the case with instructions for the court to decide if the action complied with Mississippi Code Sections 37-9-101 to 37-9-113. *Lawrence County School Dist. v. Bowden*, 912 So.2d 898 (Miss. 2005).

◆   A New York teacher had served a school district for parts of two school years when the district contracted with a board of cooperative educational services (BOCES) to operate its alternative education program. He accepted a full-time job with the BOCES teaching mathematics, but his employment there was terminated prior to the conclusion of his extended probationary period. The district refused to hire the teacher to fill a vacancy created by another teacher's retirement, and he sought review by the state education commissioner. The commissioner held that once the BOCES took over the district's alternative education program, the probationary teacher was automatically considered a BOCES employee with no preferred eligibility rights with the district.

The teacher appealed to a state trial court, which dismissed the case. A state appellate court upheld the commissioner's decision under New York Education Law § 3014-a, which deems each teacher employed in a program at the time of a takeover to be a BOCES employee. On appeal, the state's highest court rejected the conclusion that the teacher was entitled only to the seniority rights of Section 3014-a. That section does not limit other rights created by the Education Law, including recall rights in a district under Sections 2510(3) and

3013(3). The court reversed the decision, holding **a qualified teacher whose position has been abolished during a BOCES takeover of a district program has a right to be placed on a district's preferred eligibility list for seven years under** Sections 2510(3) and 3013(3). *Bojarczuk v. Mills*, 746 N.Y.S.2d 450 (N.Y. 2002).

C. Collective Bargaining Agreements

State law provisions may conflict with a collective bargaining agreement. Some courts permit the parties to determine their own contractual relationship, but others will not allow parties to "contract away" their statutory rights.

◆ A New Jersey school district employed a custodian under one-year employment contracts containing no language granting tenure or guaranteeing reemployment. It sought to discharge him at the beginning of his third year due to his "attitude, inefficiency" and "lack of cooperation." The custodian's employee association filed a grievance on his behalf that was denied by the district superintendent. An arbitrator for the state Public Employment Relations Commission found that no just cause existed for termination because the board did not provide him with progressive discipline. The district reemployed the custodian for the last month of the school year and then notified him it would not renew his contract. He followed district procedures for an informal board hearing and was informed the district would not reemploy him.

The custodian pursued a second grievance, but the board maintained that a custodian does not acquire tenure and may not grieve the non-renewal of an annual contract. The employee association filed a grievance that was denied, and the board petitioned a state court to restrain the association from proceeding to arbitration. The court made a determination of arbitrability, noting the parties' collective bargaining agreement did not delegate this question to an arbitrator. It also observed the Supreme Court of New Jersey has interpreted state law as allowing school boards to deny tenure to custodians. On appeal, a state appellate division court noted a 1997 decision in which it "declined to insert judicially a tenure provision into a contract when it was not negotiated by the parties." It agreed with the trial court's finding that the non-renewal decision was a contractual prerogative of the board, not "discipline." **The trial court had properly found no contractual rights of reemployment or any right to grieve the non-renewal of his employment. The reinstatement of the custodian for the final month of his contract did not give him additional rights to reemployment.** The non-renewal action was an independent matter from the previous arbitration, which was limited to the term of that contract. The court affirmed the judgment for the board. *Cresskill Board of Educ. v. Cresskill Educ. Ass'n*, 826 A.2d 778 (N.J. Super. Ct. App. Div. 2003).

◆ The collective bargaining agreement (CBA) between a South Dakota district and its teachers association set out mandatory procedures for reductions in force. If normal attrition did not succeed in reducing the work force, teachers with less than full certification would be released first, followed by those without continuing contract status, then those with continuing contract status, according to "length of service." The board voted for a work force reduction because of budgetary constraints, and it notified a teacher and a teacher/coach that they were subject to release. The teacher/coach had three years of continuous service to the district, but the teacher had more than five years of overall service. She had worked as a substitute for one school year, taught summer school and worked as a substitute for two years before becoming a full-time contract teacher two years earlier. The board decided as the teacher/coach would reach continuing contract status first, he had seniority over the teacher. The state labor department held the CBA bound the district. The reduction-in-force policy measured seniority by "length of service," not "continuous service." Because the teacher's overall service was greater, the board had to retain her. A state trial court affirmed the decision, and the district appealed.

The South Dakota Supreme Court rejected the district's argument that a state law governing teacher termination allowed the non-renewal of an untenured teacher's contract. **The case was governed by the CBA, not the contract renewal statute. By acting under the agreement, the district had to abide by its terms and could not add words that the parties left out of it.** The agreement enumerated the protocol for implementing a reduction in force, using a principle of seniority measured by length of service within the school system. The board was not permitted to insert or delete contract language. The contract included no language such as "continuous" or "uninterrupted" to define length of service. Since the teacher should have been retained under the plain language of the agreement, the court affirmed the department's decision. *Gettysburg School Dist. 53-1 v. Larson*, 631 N.W.2d 196 (S.D. 2001).

◆ A Washington law limits the employment term of each school employee to one year. Another law allows public employee collective bargaining agreements to remain in effect for up to three years. A district and association representing district bus drivers entered into a collective bargaining agreement limiting the district's right to discipline or discharge employees by requiring justifiable cause. The district refused to renew the contract of an experienced driver at the end of a school year, claiming just cause was not required since the action was for contract non-renewal rather than discharge. The union filed a demand for arbitration, and the district sued the union in a Washington trial court. The court awarded the district summary judgment, and the driver and union appealed.

The Supreme Court of Washington held the one-year term limitation for school employees must be read in conjunction with the law recognizing the right of public employees to enter into collective bargaining agreements that exceed one year. **The collective bargaining law contained a supremacy clause that prevailed over inconsistent laws.** The collective bargaining law did not conflict with the school district employment statute, which only governed individual employment contracts and did not limit the ability of unions and school districts to negotiate just cause terms in collective bargaining agreements. **Since the reason for terminating the driver's employment involved consideration of the collective bargaining agreement, the case was reversed and remanded for arbitration.** *Peninsula School Dist. No. 401 v. Public School Employees of Peninsula*, 924 P.2d 13 (Wash. 1996).

◆   An Ohio school board employed a tutor to instruct small groups of students with learning disabilities for five hours per day. It reduced her workload to two hours per day, and she refused to accept additional work instructing homebound students. The board gave the tutor an unsatisfactory performance evaluation and advised her she would not be reemployed. She sued the board in an Ohio court, claiming entitlement to compensation at the wage rate specified by state law and seeking an order that the reduction in hours was an illegal wage decrease. The court granted summary judgment to the board, and the tutor appealed. The Supreme Court of Ohio stated that **the terms of a collective bargaining agreement supersede the general provisions of state statutes**. Because the tutor was bound by the terms of the applicable collective bargaining agreement, she was not entitled to a higher rate than specified in the agreement. She was not a salaried employee, and the reduction in hours did not violate state law. The trial court judgment was affirmed. *State ex rel. Burch v. Sheffield-Sheffield Lake City School Dist. Board of Educ.*, 75 Ohio St.3d 216, 661 N.E.2d 1086 (Ohio 1996).

D. State Regulatory Authority

◆   A Texas school counselor was accused of violating district policies and Section 261.101 of the Texas Family Code by failing to report suspected child abuse or neglect, and only minimally cooperating with a police investigation. After a hearing, a hearing examiner recommended non-renewal of his contract. The school board voted to accept the recommendation. Instead of appealing to the state commissioner of education under the Texas Term Contract Nonrenewal Act, the counselor sued the district in a state district court for retaliation. He asserted he was discharged in retaliation for cooperating in good faith with a child abuse or neglect investigation. The court denied the district's motion to dismiss the case, and it appealed to the Court of Appeals of Texas.

The court explained that the Term Contract Renewal Act specified procedures for teachers employed under term contracts to obtain review of adverse decisions. Teachers who were aggrieved by a board's decision could appeal to the commissioner of education. Those who were dissatisfied with a ruling by the commissioner could then appeal to a district court. **An aggrieved party had to first exhaust all administrative remedies if the subject matter of an action concerned the administration of school laws and involved questions of fact. The court held that the termination of the counselor involved questions of fact that must be appealed to administrative authorities before resort to the courts.** It rejected his claim that the case was excused from exhaustion as a retaliation suit under the Family Code. The counselor was a term contract employee. The board had properly notified him of its non-renewal decision and his next step was to appeal to the commissioner. The court reversed the judgment, holding the counselor could not maintain a retaliation suit and had to comply with state administrative procedures. *Ysleta Independent School Dist. v. Griego*, 170 S.W.3d 792 (Tex. Ct. App. 2005).

◆   A Missouri charter school teacher claimed the school's principal told him he would be rehired for another year if he finished the school year and promoted his students. At the end of the year, the management corporation that operated the school did not renew the teacher's contract. The teacher sued the management corporation in a federal district court for race discrimination and state law claims. The court awarded summary judgment to the corporation on the race discrimination claims and refused to exercise jurisdiction over the state law claims. The teacher filed a new action against the corporation in the state court system, asserting the school failed to evaluate him as required by state law. He added claims for breach of contract, libel, defamation, misrepresentation, mental anguish and negligence. The corporation removed the case to federal district court, which agreed to hear it because the parties were citizens of different states and the amount in controversy was over $75,000.

The court explained that under Missouri law, charter schools are exempt from the teacher evaluation requirements of Section 168.128 of the state code. The teacher argued the school breached his employment contract because the employee handbook specified three teacher evaluations annually. The court held the school's act of publishing a handbook was not a contractual offer. As an employee, the teacher had no power to "accept" the handbook as a contract, defeating the breach of contract claim. The teacher asserted the school was negligent in "failing to inform him that the students he was hired to teacher were severely undisciplined." He stated the conduct of his students caused him to suffer elevated blood pressure, which required medical treatment. The court found the concealment, libel and defamation claims were untimely filed and had to be dismissed. The court held the state workers' compensation act was the exclusive remedy for this claim, barring any negligence claim by an employee against an employer. As the remaining claims for negligence, mental anguish, and pain and suffering were not properly before the court, the corporation's dismissal motion was granted. *Pointer v. Beacon Educ. Management*, No. 4:05 CV 628 CEJ, 2005 WL 1463479 (E.D. Mo. 2005).

◆   The superintendent of a Massachusetts school system advised a principal in writing he would be dismissed for inefficiency, insubordination and conduct unbecoming a principal. After obtaining advice from counsel, the superintendent revoked his decision and sent the principal another letter stating his contract would not be renewed after the school year. The principal demanded arbitration, asserting he had served in his position for over three years and was a "tenured principal" whose contract required renewal in the absence of good cause. He sued the city in a state court, seeking a declaration that his contract had to be renewed and asserting his entitlement to a hearing. The court awarded summary judgment to the city, and the principal appealed.

The Massachusetts Court of Appeals noted the Massachusetts Education Reform Act of 1993 eliminated the involvement of a school committee in the decision to renew a principal's employment contract and also removed the collective bargaining rights of principals. **Principals, superintendents and other managerial personnel were reclassified as contractual employees and were no longer insulated from contract non-renewals.** It was permissible to simply let a principal's contract expire, as dismissal was not the same as a contract non-renewal. The court explained the Reform Act recognized principals were distinct from teachers and other staff and enjoyed different rights and responsibilities. While the act created specific procedural safeguards for teachers, principals were excluded from the definition of "teacher." Under the act, principals now had a managerial role and they did not enjoy the same procedural protections as teachers. The court affirmed the judgment for the city. *Downing v. City of Lowell*, 741 N.E.2d 469 (Mass. App. Ct. 2001).

II. DUE PROCESS REQUIREMENTS

Due process protects property and liberty interests that arise from state laws, contracts and expectations. For example, a collective bargaining agreement creates a "property interest" in employment for the term of the contract. State tenure and continuing contract laws create property interests in the procedures described in the laws. Teachers have a "property interest" in their employment under these laws. At a minimum, due process means that the government will give an individual notice and an opportunity to be heard when it threatens the individual's liberty or property interests.

Two U.S. Supreme Court decisions, *Board of Regents v. Roth* and *Perry v. Sindermann*, below, help define the due process rights of teachers. The cases emphasize there must be an independent source for a liberty or property interest as such interests are not created by the Constitution, but arise by employment contract or by operation of state tenure laws. If a liberty or property interest is not established, no requirement of due process exists under the Fourteenth Amendment. If a teacher has a liberty or property interest in employment, then due process protections are required. An untenured teacher has an interest only in the term of his or her contract.

◆   A Wisconsin university hired a teacher for a fixed contract term of one year. At the end of the year, he was informed he would not be rehired. No hearing was provided and no reason was given for the decision not to rehire him. In dismissing the teacher's due process claims, the U.S. Supreme Court held no liberty interest was implicated because in declining to rehire him, the university made no charge such as incompetence or immorality. Such a charge would have made it difficult for the teacher to gain employment elsewhere and thus would have deprived him of liberty. **As no reason was given for the non-renewal of his contract, the teacher's liberty interest in future employment was not impaired and he was not entitled to a hearing on these grounds.** The Court stated as he had not acquired tenure, he had no property interest in continued employment at the university. To be sure, the teacher had a property interest in employment during his one-year contract term, but upon its expiration his property interest ceased to exist. The Court held **"to have a property interest in a benefit, a person clearly must have more than an abstract need or desire for it. He must have more than a unilateral expectation of it. He must, instead, have a legitimate claim of entitlement to it."** *Board of Regents v. Roth*, 408 U.S. 564, 92 S.Ct. 2701, 33 L.Ed.2d 548 (1972).

◆   The *Sindermann* case involved a teacher employed at a Texas university for four years under one-year contracts. When he was not rehired for a fifth year, he brought suit contending that due process required a dismissal hearing. The Supreme Court held "a person's interest in a benefit is a 'property' interest for due process purposes if there are such rules and mutually explicit understandings that support his claim of entitlement to the benefit that he may invoke at a hearing." **Because the teacher had been employed at the university for four years, the Court felt that he might have a protectable property interest in continued employment.** The case was remanded to the trial court to determine whether there was an unwritten "common law" of tenure at the university. If so, the teacher would be entitled to a dismissal hearing. *Perry v. Sindermann*, 408 U.S. 593, 92 S.Ct. 2694, 33 L.Ed.2d 570 (1972).

A. Property Interest

A school employee must have a liberty or property interest in employment to have procedural due process rights. A common source for creating a property interest arises from state tenure statutes.

◆ An Arizona school district determined a teacher had improperly taken a college-level Spanish test for another person. The district did not renew his one-year contract after an investigation. The school board met in closed session but did not consider the teacher's statement. He was later allowed to read a prepared statement at a public meeting. The board then voted not to renew the teacher's contract. A non-renewal letter was placed in his file, but it was later removed. The board reported its action to the state board of education. The teacher completed the remainder of his contract, then sued the school district and board for due process violations under the state and federal constitutions. He also asserted breach of contract and related state law claims.

A federal district court noted that **non-tenured teachers do not have a property right in continued employment under Arizona law.** The teacher's contract stated that his employment would end with the conclusion of the school year. The court rejected his claim that he had a "reasonable expectation of future employment" that was protected by the Due Process Clause. There was no evidence that any board member told the teacher he was assured of continued employment. **The teacher's subjective expectation that he would receive tenure due to performance or positive evaluations did not create a property interest.** There was also no deprivation of a constitutionally protected liberty interest in his good name, reputation, honor and dignity, because there had been no publication of such allegations. The district showed it had complied with a state Open Meetings Law requirement to provide the teacher with 24-hour notice of its executive session. The law did not require the board to allow him to present a statement to an executive session or to call and cross-examine witnesses and present evidence to the board. The board complied with state law by voting not to renew the teacher's contract in a public meeting. There was no breach of contract because the board allowed him to serve until the end of the school year. The court rejected his remaining claims and awarded judgment to the school district and board. *Murdock v. Mingus Union High School Dist.*, No. CV 04-2313-PHX-DGC, 2006 WL 1328817 (D. Ariz. 2006).

◆ A Mississippi Junior ROTC instructor worked for a school district for three school years, left for a year, then returned to his job for a week. The U.S. Court of Appeals, Fifth Circuit, held he had no protected property interest in employment. The school board never approved a recommendation by the principal to rehire the instructor. **State law codified the procedures for hiring teachers and limited the role of principals to recommending candidates. Any expectation for reemployment held by the instructor was based on statements allegedly made by the principal. This was not enough to create a property interest in employment**, and the school district was entitled to judgment. *Watson v. North Panola School Dist.*, 188 Fed.Appx. 291 (5th Cir. 2006).

◆ A Texas school administrator served a district for over 30 years with generally good performance appraisals. The district proposed his termination for sexual harassment, using district resources for personal benefit, obstructing an investigation into his behavior and falsifying school asbestos records. The Texas Education Code permitted discharging teachers and other employees under term contracts at any time for "good cause." Employees were entitled to a pre-termination hearing if they filed written requests with the state education commissioner within 15 days of receiving a termination notice. The statutory procedure required the commissioner to assign a hearing officer to consider employee hearing requests. The administrator submitted a written request for a hearing to the commissioner 12 days after receiving notice of the proposed action. The board received the notice in two days, but the commissioner did not receive it for six days – 18 days after the administrator received notice. The commissioner found the hearing request untimely, stating it had to be "received," rather than "filed," within 15 days. Relying on the commissioner's determination, the school board resolved to discharge the administrator.

The administrator sued the district in a federal district court, which found he had filed a timely hearing request. The board knew he did not receive a hearing despite the timely request and violated his due process rights by discharging him without a hearing. The court awarded the administrator over $215,000 in damages, and the district appealed to the Fifth Circuit. A three-judge panel of the court affirmed the decision, but a majority of Fifth Circuit judges voted to rehear the case before the full court. The district argued the commissioner was responsible for any due process deprivation. **The court held the board action discharging the administrator only four business days after the board received notice of the commissioner's action was the sole cause of a due process violation.** The administrator did not waive any rights by filing a federal action rather than appealing the commissioner's decision. **Texas law gave school boards the exclusive authority to discharge school employees. Only boards could make the finding of "good cause" for termination.** As the board was the final decision-maker in this case, the district court had properly held it violated the administrator's due process rights. *Coggin v. Longview Independent School Dist.*, 337 F.3d 459 (5th Cir. 2003).

◆ During an Ohio teacher's second year of substitute teaching, a district staff became concerned about his inappropriate behavior with students, including suggestive comments and classroom jokes. He commented on a female teacher's breasts and made a suggestive remark to a female student. The principal told him that he was "too macho" and then quit calling him for substitute work. The teacher sued the school district in a federal district court for sex discrimination, due process violations and alleged state law violations.

The court awarded summary judgment to the district, and the teacher appealed to the Sixth Circuit. The court stated the Fourteenth Amendment prohibits the deprivation of a liberty or property interest without due process of law. **Ohio law limited the term of employment of substitute teachers to one year. For this reason, substitutes had no property interest in continued employment and were not entitled to any due process protections such as notices or hearings.** Because the teacher was employed at will by the district, his due process claim failed. There was no evidence of any sex discrimination by the district, as this claim was based entirely on the single "too macho" remark. A reasonable jury would find that this offhand remark was critical of the teacher's behavior, not his gender. The court held he did not raise any issue of speech on matters of public concern, and it affirmed the judgment for the district. *Lautermilch v. Findlay City Schools*, 314 F.3d 271 (6th Cir. 2003).

◆   An Iowa assistant principal heard screams and entered a classroom in time to see a teacher pushing students into seats. The assistant principal wrote the teacher a reprimand letter, noting the action was a direct violation of a school board policy. Parents called the school, and two of them filed a police report. The principal met with the teacher, and a district administrator investigated the incident. He wrote a report concluding the teacher had used unreasonable force in violation of board policy. The district suspended the teacher for two days and then held a hearing, where the parties appeared with counsel, introduced exhibits and heard witnesses. The teacher introduced written exhibits, testified on his own behalf and called a student and the assistant principal to testify. The principal testified and answered questions from the board. The board upheld the suspension without pay and denied the teacher's request for reconsideration.

The teacher sued the board in a federal district court. The court commented that **to prevail in a due process action, there must be a protected property interest at stake. This was determined by looking to state law or a contract. Where no such interest existed, there could be no due process violation. If the teacher showed he had a protected property interest, he would then have to show he was denied appropriate procedural protections.** Where an employee has a property interest, there must be a hearing. Other courts have held **an unpaid two-day suspension does not create a measurable due process interest**. For example, the Sixth Circuit held a two-day suspension without pay did not deserve due process consideration. The Eleventh Circuit has held a one-week suspension with pay did not implicate due process. **The court held the loss of two days' pay was minor and did not trigger due process concerns.** The board provided him with a prompt post-suspension hearing, and there was no interruption in his benefits or harm to his reputation. The board satisfied the fundamental requirement of due process, which is to provide an opportunity to be heard at a meaningful time and in a meaningful manner. The teacher received a hearing where he was represented by counsel and presented witnesses, exhibits and arguments. As he received all the process he was due, the court awarded summary judgment to the board. *Oswald v. Waterloo Board of Educ.*, No. C02-2050, 2003 WL 22284654 (N.D. Iowa 2003).

◆ A Wisconsin principal called the police when a group of five or six students violently and aggressively assaulted a student. After she suspended the students, some of their parents began to denounce her. The district administrator initially recommended renewal of the principal's contract. When a complaining parent reported that the closed board vote renewing the principal's contract violated the state open meetings law, the board rescinded its action and held a second meeting. By the time the board met again, it was bound by state law to renew the contract. However, all district employees were notified that the board had revised the principal's title and job description. The principal resigned, stating that the removal of her main job duties amounted to a constructive discharge.

The principal sued the district, board, and district administrator in a federal district court, asserting violation of an asserted constitutional property right in continued employment, constructive discharge, and violation of her liberty interest in her reputation. The court awarded summary judgment to the board and administrator, and the principal appealed. The Seventh Circuit noted that a constitutional property right in employment arises from state laws and contractual relationships, not the Constitution. State law required principals to perform administrative and leadership responsibilities and receive preliminary notices of non-renewal. The law and the principal's contract did not encompass any right to perform particular job duties. The district did not transfer her, and she retained her title and salary. **An expectation of retaining certain job duties did not create a protectable property interest.** The principal's constructive discharge claim failed because she had abruptly resigned and had declined the opportunity to participate in the creation of her new job duties. There was no violation of her liberty interest in reputation because **a charge of mismanagement or incompetence does not rise to a constitutionally protected level**. The court affirmed the judgment. *Ulichny v. Merton Community School Dist.*, 249 F.3d 686 (7th Cir. 2001).

◆ An Idaho district notified two teachers their coaching assignments would not be renewed. They sued the district in an Idaho trial court, claiming violation of their rights to due process under state and federal law and breach of their contracts. The court found that while the teachers had no property interest in extra duty assignments under Idaho law, a clause in the master contract between the district and their education association prohibited termination, discharge or other adverse action in the absence of just cause. The just cause language was incorporated into their individual contracts, creating a property interest in the extra-duty assignments. The court granted judgment to the teachers, finding the district had violated their state and federal due process rights and breached their contract rights under the master and individual contracts. The district appealed. The Idaho Supreme Court held **to have a property interest in employment, a person must have more than an expectation in it. The person must have a legitimate claim of entitlement to the benefit.** The contracts between the district and teachers regarding extra duties created a property interest in those assignments that was constitutionally protected. The contracts covered both classroom and extra-duty assignments, and the same rights applied to the coaching duties as to the classroom duties. The master contract protected the teachers from a reduction in compensation in the absence of just cause. Since the district failed to provide them notice and a hearing prior to the reduction in compensation, it violated their due process rights. The court affirmed the judgment. *Farner v. Idaho Falls School Dist. No. 91*, 17 P.3d 281 (Idaho 2000).

B. Notice

◆ An Indiana school district hired a biology teacher under a one-year contract, even though he lacked a standard teaching license. The principal e-mailed him on May 7 of the school year that he would meet with him the next day to discuss his employment. The principal then orally notified the teacher his teaching contract would not be renewed. The teacher sued the district in a state court for violating Indiana Code Section 20-6.1-4-14. The court granted the teacher's summary judgment motion, and the district appealed.

The Court of Appeals of Indiana rejected the argument that the teacher's limited teaching license relieved the district of the applicable statutory notice requirements. There was no exception for teachers who held limited licenses. Although non-permanent teachers were entitled to only minimal due process protections, the court held school officials were required to comply with statutory procedures when informing them about contract renewal. **Unless a school district notified a teacher in writing by May 1 of a school year that the teacher's contract would not continue for the next term, the contract would continue under the same terms for the next term following the termination date of the contract.** The notice had to be delivered in person or sent by registered or certified mail to the teacher's last known residence. Since the school district did not give the teacher the written notice he was due by May 1 of the school year, and no statutory exception applied for teachers with limited teaching licenses, the court found he was entitled to summary judgment on his statutory claim. *Pike Township Educ. Foundation v. Rubenstein*, 831 N.E.2d 1239 (Ind. Ct. App. 2005).

◆ A California teacher completed a one-year contact under an emergency teaching permit and then received a professional clear teaching credential. The district classified him as a probationary employee. The teacher worked the full school year for the district. On May 23, he was sent a notice of non-reelection of employment for a third year. The teacher sued the district in a state superior court, arguing he had completed two years of service in a teaching position requiring certification qualifications. He alleged Education Code § 44929.21, subd. (b) conferred a right to notice of non-reelection of employment by March 15. The court denied the teacher's petition, finding the May 23 notice of non-reelection was timely and that the district had no duty to reemploy him.

The teacher appealed to the Court of Appeal of California, arguing he was automatically reelected for another school year. The court stated Section 44929.21, subd. (b) provides for reelecting teachers employed by a district for two consecutive school years in positions requiring certification qualifications.

Those reelected for a third school year in a position requiring certification become permanent employees at the beginning of the third year. Notice of non-reelection must be made by March 15 of a teacher's second complete consecutive school year in a position requiring certification qualifications. If the board does not give notice to a permanent employee by March 15, the employee is deemed re-elected. **The court held Section 44929.21(b) tenure and notice provisions were not separable. Notice applied only to those eligible to become permanent employees under the tenure paragraph.** The teacher was ineligible for permanent employment and could not insist on notice. The case was unlike *California Teachers Ass'n v. Governing Board of Golden Valley Unified School Dist.*, 98 Cal.App.4th 369, 119 Cal.Rptr.2d 642 (2002), where a teacher who served under an emergency credential was held to qualify as a probationary employee. That case did not involve a claim to permanent employment. Accordingly, the court affirmed the judgment for the district. *Culbertson v. San Gabriel Unified School Dist.*, 121 Cal.App.4th 1392, 18 Cal. Rptr.3d 234 (Cal. Ct. App. 2004).

◆ A Washington teacher fired for misconduct with a student was not denied due process protections at her discharge hearing, according to the state court of appeals. The district gave her proper notice of misconduct charges including sexual relations with the student, giving him alcohol and staying with him in a hotel. The notice complied with state law and nothing indicated the hearing officer improperly assigned the burden of proof to the district. **The teacher had no constitutional right to counsel, which is limited to cases in which a fundamental liberty interest is at stake.** *Powell v. Cascade School Dist. No. 228*, No. 22831-2-III, 124 Wash.App. 1055 (Wash. Ct. App. 2004).

◆ A Louisiana teacher with 18 years of experience became a probationary special education teacher at a correctional center for youth. She signed two consecutive annual teaching contracts. At the end of the second year, the center's principal recommended her contract not be renewed. The state board of education approved of the recommendation, but the director's summary did not state the reasons for the action, as required by law. The teacher sued the board in a state court, alleging it tried to circumvent the law by disguising her discharge as a non-renewal. The court held she was improperly discharged, but the Louisiana Court of Appeal reversed, ruling that Louisiana Revised Statutes § 17:45 was inapplicable to the non-renewal of a probationary teacher's contract after the completion of the school year in which she was hired to teach.

The teacher appealed to the state supreme court, which explained that **probationary teachers who do not receive written notification of discharge from their school board automatically become regular or permanent teachers if they have completed their three-year probationary terms**. The court agreed with the teacher's assertion that under state law, her employment continued unless and until the board dismissed her in writing. The board had to state the valid reasons for a recommendation of discharge or dismissal at any time during a teacher's probationary period, even at the conclusion of a school year. The decision not to renew a probationary teacher's contract was a discharge or dismissal under state law. The requirement for written, valid reasons for non-renewal from Section 17:45 had been triggered in this case, and the board violated the law by failing to provide the teacher with valid reasons for its action. While probationary teachers had no constitutionally protected interest in being reappointed, the board still had to provide the teacher with valid reasons for the non-renewal of her contract during the probationary period. The court reversed and remanded the case to the trial court. *Palmer v. Louisiana State Board of Elementary and Secondary Educ.*, 842 So.2d 363 (La. 2003).

◆ An Arkansas district superintendent informed a high school principal he was not going to recommend renewal of his contract. Almost one month later, the principal requested a hearing. The board scheduled a hearing more than 10 days after the principal's request, despite the state Teacher Fair Dismissal Act's (TFDA) requirement for a hearing between five and 10 days after a request is made. The principal objected to the delay, arguing it resulted in the automatic renewal of his contract. The board voted not to renew his contract. After a federal district court held for the district on certain federal claims, it dismissed the principal's TFDA claim, allowing him to refile it in the state court system.

A state court awarded summary judgment to the principal, agreeing with his assertion that the district's failure to strictly comply with the act voided its attempted contract non-renewal. The court held the contract was automatically renewed, and the principal was entitled to a year of pay. The district appealed to the Arkansas Supreme Court, which noted **the TFDA required strict compliance and specified that a noncomplying contract non-renewal, termination, suspension or other disciplinary action was void**. It agreed with the trial court that the non-renewal of the principal's contract was void because the district did not comply with the TFDA's timing requirements. There was no merit to the district's argument that the request for a hearing resulted in a waiver of this requirement. Because the attempted non-renewal was void, the trial court had properly found the district in breach of contract and liable for the principal's salary during the next school year. The court affirmed the judgment in his favor. *Foreman School Dist. No. 25 v. Steele*, 61 S.W.3d 801 (Ark. 2001).

◆ During a Nebraska teacher's third year of employment, her principal sent her a letter stating he would not recommend renewing her contract due to classroom management problems. The board granted the teacher's request for an informal hearing, where she appeared with her attorney. The board considered testimony, and the principal recommended non-renewal. It deliberated in a closed session and then recessed. The parties agreed to extend the deadline for a hearing. The teacher and her attorney declined to attend the final board meeting. During the meeting, the board again went into a closed session. It voted against renewal after returning to open session, and the teacher appealed. A state trial court affirmed the action, finding state law required only that formal action for contract non-renewal take place in an open session.

On appeal, the Nebraska Supreme Court found evidence for the board's decision. The principal had evaluated the teacher, provided a written growth plan for the year, and notified her of her classroom management problems. The court found no requirement in state law that a probationary teacher receive notice that a performance deficiency is of such magnitude that failure to remedy it could lead to contract non-renewal. **The board complied with statutory observation and evaluation requirements, and the notice and hearing requirements of state law by providing written notices of both hearings.** Although state law required that a formal vote on contract non-renewal take place in an open session, it did not require that board deliberations take place in open session. Public meeting laws specifically do not apply to a board's judicial functions in employment matters. The court affirmed the judgment. *McQuinn v. Douglas County School Dist. No. 66,* 259 Neb. 720, 612 N.W.2d 198 (Neb. 2000).

C. Hearing

1. Minimum Requirements

Tenured employees must be given a fair and impartial hearing, conducted in accordance with statutory procedures, as they have a property interest in their continuing employment. A liberty interest may exist if the dismissal involves a stigma upon the character of the teacher.

◆   A Texas middle school principal served as a secondary school principal in Houston for 21 years before coming to the Ft. Bend Independent School District at the request of an area superintendent. The superintendent gave the principal an excellent performance review at the end of her first year, and she received a two-year contract. The next year, the district superintendent abruptly sought her termination, stating he did not like her and that she "was not keeping the parents of her students under control." The superintendent reassigned the principal to the maintenance department, then to a staff development position in which she had no contact with parents. The notice reassigning her cited failure to maintain effective working relationships, failure to timely prepare special education documents, failure to follow established procedures and insubordination. The principal pursued an unsuccessful grievance, and the school board granted her another hearing. The board again upheld the decision, and the principal resigned. She sued the board, district superintendent and area superintendent in a federal district court for due process and speech rights violations.

The superintendents sought summary judgment, asserting qualified immunity. The court denied their motion, and they appealed to the U.S. Court of Appeals, Fifth Circuit, which rejected the principal's claim of entitlement to a pre-termination hearing. **Pre-termination hearings were required only when an employee was forced to choose between resignation and discharge. The principal failed to show any due process violation. She received written notice of the reasons for her reassignment, and at least two grievance hearings.** Reassignment to minimize her interaction with parents appeared to be rational. There was no merit to the principal's speech claim. As her speech concerned internal administrative matters, not the public concern, it was not constitutionally protected. The court reversed the judgment, holding the superintendents were entitled to qualified immunity. *Finch v. Fort Bend Independent School Dist.,* 333 F.3d 555 (5th Cir. 2003).

◆   An untenured Missouri teacher was suspended for grabbing a student by the throat, pushing him into a wall and threatening to hit him. He also directed "threatening, intimidating, erratic and/or potentially violent behavior" at district personnel. The district superintendent notified him he would propose the termination of his one-year contract. The teacher requested a public hearing, which began with testimony by eight district witnesses. The teacher's attorney was permitted to cross-examine them, but due to the lateness of the hour, the hearing was adjourned. The teacher later sought two continuances and rejected a settlement offer by the district. When the hearing reconvened, the district sought to close it and hold an executive session to hear testimony from two students, based on perceived intimidation by the teacher. The parties' attorneys disagreed on whether the hearing could occur in closed session, and the teacher sought a state court order requiring the board to keep it open. The board voted not to renew his contract based on failure to follow district purchasing procedures. The teacher sued the district in a federal district court, asserting it violated his liberty interest in reputation and his property interest in employment. The court held he was entitled to a hearing to "clear his name."

The district appealed to the Eighth Circuit, which observed that the teacher's contract was not terminated and he had received his full pay for the school year. **The failure to complete a termination hearing did not implicate a property interest. Under Missouri law, probationary teachers have a property interest in employment for only the duration of the school year.** The teacher completed the school year, and there was no due process violation. The charges of assault and threatening a student implicated the teacher's liberty interests. The teacher received the opportunity to clear his name during the initial hearing, and again when it reconvened. The district was entitled to close the hearing based on its substantial interest in school safety. The board satisfied the teacher's due process liberty interest by conducting most of the hearing in open session. He received an opportunity to clear his name but failed to pursue it by continuing the hearing and dismissing his state law claim. The court affirmed the judgment for the district. *Gibson v. Caruthersville School Dist. No. 8,* 336 F.3d 768 (8th Cir. 2003).

◆   A police officer employed by a Pennsylvania state university was arrested in a drug raid and charged with several felony counts related to marijuana possession and distribution. State police notified the university of the arrest and charges, and the university's human resources director immediately suspended the officer without pay pursuant to a state executive order requiring such action where a state employee is formally charged with a felony. Although the criminal charges were dismissed, university officials demoted the officer because of the felony charges. The university did not inform him it had obtained his confession from police records and he was unable to fully respond to damaging statements in the police reports. He sued university officials a federal district court for failing to provide him with notice and an opportunity to be heard before his suspension without pay. The court granted summary judgment to the officials, but the U.S. Court of Appeals, Third Circuit, reversed and remanded the case.

The U.S. Supreme Court agreed to review the cases and found the court of appeals had improperly held a suspended public employee must always receive a paid suspension. **The university did not violate due process by refusing to pay a suspended employee charged with a felony pending a hearing.** The Court accepted the officials' argument that the Pennsylvania executive order made any pre-suspension hearing useless, since the filing of charges established an independent basis for believing that the officer had committed a felony. The Court noted the officer faced only a temporary suspension without pay, and not employment termination as in *Cleveland Board of Educ. v. Loudermill*, below. The Court reversed and remanded the judgment for consideration of the officer's arguments concerning a post-suspension hearing. *Gilbert v. Homar*, 520 U.S. 924, 117 S.Ct. 1807, 138 L.Ed.2d 120 (1997).

◆ In two consolidated cases, the U.S. Supreme Court considered what pre-termination process must be afforded a public employee who can be discharged only for cause. In the first case, a security guard hired by a school board stated on his job application that he had never been convicted of a felony. Upon discovering that he had in fact been convicted of grand larceny, the school board summarily dismissed him for dishonesty in filling out the job application. He was not afforded an opportunity to respond to the dishonesty charge or to challenge the dismissal until nine months later. In the second case, a school bus mechanic was fired because he had failed an eye examination. The mechanic appealed his dismissal after the fact because he had not been afforded a pre-termination hearing. **The Court held the employees had a property right in their employment and were entitled to a pre-termination opportunity to at least respond to the charges against them.** The pre-termination hearing need not fully resolve the propriety of the discharge, but should be a check against mistaken decisions. The Court held that in this case, the employees were entitled to a pre-termination opportunity to respond, coupled with a full-blown administrative hearing at a later time. *Cleveland Board of Educ. v. Loudermill*, 470 U.S. 532, 105 S.Ct. 1487, 84 L.Ed.2d 494 (1985).

◆ West Virginia's highest court held that nothing in state law authorized the state Professional Practice Panel to conduct hearings to consider the revocation of professional teaching and administration certifications. A teacher whose certification was revoked by the panel was entitled to a hearing before the state superintendent under the state Administrative Procedure Act. The teacher held appropriate certification to serve in the West Virginia school system for over 40 years. The superintendent notified him of revocation proceedings due to "a history of drunkenness," including a felony conviction for a third drunk-driving offense. The teacher and his attorney were unable to attend a hearing scheduled by the panel and it proceeded with the matter in their absence.

The panel recommended revocation of the teacher's certification, and the superintendent adopted the recommendation. A state trial court dismissed the petition as untimely, and he appealed to the West Virginia Supreme Court of Appeals. The court rejected the superintendent's arguments that the teacher's petition had been untimely and that he was not entitled to seek an extraordinary writ. **The teacher correctly asserted that he was entitled to a hearing before the superintendent. The state code authorized hearings by an agency, a member of the body that comprises the agency or a hearing examiner.** The code did not authorize the establishment of a panel to hold hearings on terminating licenses to teach in the state. The court reversed and remanded the case. *Scott v. Stewart,* 560 S.E.2d 260 (W. Va. 2001).

2. Hearing Procedures

If a hearing has been inadequate or unfair, a court may require that procedural problems be corrected prior to dismissal or demotion.

◆ A California school board employee worked for a district as a plumber for over 21 years. The district put him on administrative leave pending an investigation of charges he used paid sick leave on five days when he was not actually sick. The district asserted the employee performed plumbing services in a private home on work days he had claimed to be ill and received sick pay. The board held a hearing to consider discharge. It relied on videotapes of the employee apparently working in private homes on the days he called in sick. The person who made the videotapes did not attend the hearing. The videotapes had time lapses, and dates on them "skipped around." A human resources officer who introduced the videotapes had no knowledge of who made the tapes, did not know if they had been edited, and could not state whether their dates were accurate. The board found the tapes proved the employee was not ill on the days he called in sick, and it dismissed him for dishonesty, falsifying information, and contract violations. The case reached the state court of appeal.

The court stated that while school boards "are not expected to observe meticulously all of the rules of evidence applicable to a court trial, common sense and fair play dictate certain basic requirements for the conduct of any hearing." The board was required to produce testimony from someone with personal knowledge of the matters and circumstances depicted on the videotapes. This person would have seen the events depicted and would be able to testify as to dates and times of events, and to identify the persons depicted. The court held the unauthenticated videotapes were not properly admitted as evidence and were irrelevant. As the employee's lawyer had objected, the tapes should not have been admitted into evidence. The trial court had incorrectly allowed the case to return to the board for a new chance to authenticate the videotapes. The state code did not permit reconsideration of new evidence in this situation. The court vacated the part of a trial court order that would have allowed a second hearing. *Ashford v. Culver City Unified School Dist.,* 29 Cal.Rptr.3d 728 (Cal. Ct. App. 2005).

◆ An Indiana special education aide claimed two 16-year-old students came to a party at his house without being invited and brought alcohol with them. The students stated the aide offered them alcohol and sexually propositioned them. The students' account reached the school, and officials confronted the aide. He claimed he asked the students to leave several times and denied propositioning them or providing them with liquor or illegal drugs. School officials met with the aide and a union representative and told him they discovered he did not furnish liquor to the students, but that "he had engaged in improper conduct with the minors." The aide denied the charges, but the superintendent suspended him and barred him from school grounds. The aide claimed the union representative did nothing to help him, and that he was never told of his hearing or grievance rights. The board adopted the superintendent's recommendation to discharge the aide. The aide did not attend the board meeting, as he had been excluded from school grounds. The aide sued the board in a federal district court for due process and state law negligence claims.

The court rejected the board's assertion that the meetings with the aide and the hearing satisfied his due process rights. **There was no evidence that the school investigated the students' allegations. The aide was not informed of available administrative procedures. He was excluded from school grounds and reasonably believed he could not attend the meeting where discharge was discussed. The aide was not given appropriate notice of the charges he faced. He was never presented with the evidence against him, or allowed to cross-examine the two students or present his own evidence.** The board did not allow the aide to respond to the charges of sexual impropriety, and denied him due process of law. The aide was entitled to further consideration of his contention that "the School's actions bore all the hallmarks of a witch hunt." His negligence and due process claims could proceed. *Badger v. Greater Clark County Schools*, No. 4:03-CV-0101 SEB-WGH, 2005 WL 645152 (S.D. Ind. 2005).

◆ An Alabama school board unanimously voted to fire an elementary teacher. She appealed to the state tenure commission for a hearing and asked the school to send all documents it intended to present at the hearing. It did so in a timely manner. While many documents were retrieved from the teacher's personnel file, some had been kept elsewhere. The teacher did not know before the request that the files outside her personnel file even existed. She argued the board did not give her proper notice of those documents. The commission rejected her argument and ruled in the board's favor. The teacher petitioned a state circuit court to reverse the decision. The court granted her petition, holding the board did not provide adequate notice of the grounds for dismissal. The state civil appeals court found the notice was sufficient and reversed the trial court's decision. The teacher appealed to the state supreme court.

The teacher claimed the documents outside her personnel file were "illegally obtained," and that their admission at the hearing violated her due process rights. **The court held due process requires only notice and a hearing at a relevant time. The board gave the teacher advance notice of all documents it intended to present and provided a hearing.** The court affirmed the judgment, finding that even if it accepted the teacher's argument that the board could not collect and use the information from outside her personnel file, she did not allege any injury from the retention of these documents. *Ex parte Jackson*, No. 1021330, 2003 WL 22753456 (Ala. 2003).

◆ The Florida commissioner of education sought to permanently revoke a high school teacher's teaching certificate based on charges that he battered his wife and frequently used his school computer to access pornography on the Internet. The teacher requested an informal hearing before the state Education Practices Commission (EPC). The commissioner presented evidence that he had accessed "teenage oriented pornography" and that the battery of his wife had adversely affected her ability to work. The teacher admitted accessing inappropriate Internet sites but denied accessing teenage pornography. The EPC permanently revoked his certificate, and he appealed to the Florida Court of Appeal. The teacher asserted the commissioner's EPC evidence amounted to new claims that should have been referred for a formal administrative hearing. The court disagreed with the teacher's assertion that evidence of teenage pornography and adverse impact on his wife's employment were new charges of wrongdoing. These issues were properly presented to the EPC. **The teacher failed to timely raise the request for a formal hearing before the EPC during the administrative hearing and had thus waived his right to this relief** on appeal. The court affirmed the permanent revocation of his certificate. *Stueber v. Gallagher*, 812 So.2d 454 (Fla. Dist. Ct. App. 2002).

◆ A Kentucky teacher served for 12 years prior to the initiation of a discharge action, which was based on evidence that he initiated a conversation with students about circumcision and penis size. The district provided him with an opportunity to respond to the incident, and he acknowledged the conversation. The district notified him of his statutory right to appeal the termination decision within 10 days, and it provided a hearing where he was represented by counsel, called witnesses and presented evidence. He complained one of his witnesses could not appear for medical reasons, but the hearing officer refused to delay the proceedings. The hearing officer upheld the teacher's termination.

The teacher appealed to a federal district court, asserting violation of his due process rights. The court held the employee had a property interest in his position and was protected by state tenure laws. **The district satisfied due process requirements by providing the opportunity to challenge the termination action both before and after it took place.** Although the pre-termination due process had been limited to the opportunity to respond to the charges, the teacher received an elaborate post-termination hearing where he was represented by counsel and had a full opportunity to present evidence in his own behalf. **The Due Process Clause requires only that a hearing be granted at a meaningful time and in a meaningful manner.** The district had a vital and legitimate interest in protecting students from teachers who exposed them to sexually explicit conversations. The court held for the district on the federal claims and remanded the Kentucky law claims to a state court. *Lafferty v. Board of Educ. of Floyd County*, 133 F.Supp.2d 941 (E.D. Ky. 2001).

◆ Georgia school administrators investigated allegations by students that a teacher in the school system had made sexual advances toward them. The school superintendent reported the matter to the Georgia Professional Practices Commission, which conducted an investigation. The commission recommended that the school board immediately place the teacher on administrative leave and begin a dismissal action. The board then voted to terminate his contract. The commission requested a second investigation concerning revocation of the teacher's teaching certificate. The teacher filed a state court lawsuit against the commission, seeking injunctive relief to prevent the taking of any action against his teaching certificate prior to a hearing.

The court granted summary judgment to the commission, and the teacher appealed to the Supreme Court of Georgia. The commission subsequently held an administrative hearing, at which a formal recommendation was made that his certificate be suspended. The supreme court then held the commission had complied with state law by providing the teacher with a hearing prior to the suspension of the certificate. State law authorized investigations for allegations that a teacher violated ethical or professional standards and authorized the commission to recommend warnings, reprimands, suspensions or the termination of teaching certificates. **The court held the statutory scheme satisfied procedural due process since teachers were allowed a hearing before the commission could impose actual sanctions.** It affirmed the judgment. *Gee v. Professional Practices Comm'n*, 491 S.E.2d 375 (Ga. 1997).

◆ An Iowa teacher hosted a party on her property at which high school students consumed alcohol. She claimed she did not know the students were drinking, and she took car keys from some of them. Four students were killed when their car hit a tree on the night of the party. The district superintendent recommended terminating the teacher's contract on grounds of unprofessional conduct, failure to effectively monitor a party where students used alcohol illegally, failure to protect student safety and welfare, ineffective leadership, inability to be effective as a teacher, and being a poor role model. The teacher requested a hearing, which was held in a private special session. The board voted to terminate her contract, and she appealed to an adjudicator. This was the statutory method of appeal contained in Section 279.17 of the state code.

The teacher petitioned a state court to raise issues she could not effectively raise in her appeal to the adjudicator. She sought to introduce additional evidence that was not included in the board's findings of fact. The court held the board did not act illegally and denied the teacher's request for relief. She appealed to the Supreme Court of Iowa. The court agreed with the board that since the adjudicator had yet to consider the teacher's appeal, there was no final decision to review. **While Section 279.17 required the board to meet within five days to make a final decision, it did not require the board to issue a final decision in that time period. The board's actions could not be challenged in court until a final decision.** The court found no merit to the teacher's objection to the Section 279.17 appeal process. The legislature intended the process to be the exclusive means of challenging a board action. Since the teacher was required to complete her appeal to the adjudicator before appealing to a court, the court affirmed the decision. *Walthart v. Board of Directors of Edgewood-Colesburg Community School Dist.*, 667 N.W.2d 873 (Iowa 2003).

3. Impartiality

◆ A California math teacher was hired under the assumption he would learn the nationwide college preparatory mathematics (CPM) curriculum the district used. The teacher participated in CPM training sessions, but shortly after the start of the school year objected to using CPM materials and allegedly pursued a course of argumentative, rude and arrogant behavior with students, staff and supervisors. The principal observed the teacher's classroom, determined he was not following the curriculum, and placed the teacher on administrative leave. The district held a dismissal hearing, appointing an attorney who represented the district to serve as hearing officer. The teacher noted that the attorney's wife worked for the district and asserted this created bias. The attorney declined to recuse himself. The board voted to discharge the teacher for dishonesty, unfitness for service and persistent refusal to obey administrative directions. The board decision was upheld by a state trial court.

The state court of appeal rejected the teacher's assertion that there was insufficient evidence to support his dismissal. The record established his termination was for the stated reasons, not the exercise of his speech concerning the curriculum and teaching methods. The teacher's due process claim was based on alleged bias by the hearing officer/attorney and superior court judge. **Courts have held that there must be more than an appearance of bias to establish a due process violation. There was no showing of any actual bias or dishonesty.** The district did not have to bring in a hearing officer from outside the area to avoid bias or prejudice. The court affirmed the superior court judgment. *Regan v. Governing Board of Sonora Union High School Dist.*, No. F037765, 2002 WL 31009412 (Cal. Ct. App. 2002).

◆ A Pennsylvania high school principal received satisfactory evaluations but was assigned areas of concern during his first three years of employment. The district superintendent issued him an unsatisfactory rating at the end of his fourth year, and the board voted to demote him. After an evidentiary hearing, the board again voted to demote the principal. He petitioned the state secretary of education for review, arguing a board member was married to a district secretary who had testified against him and that potential bias existed because of their relationship. The secretary held the decision was justified and that while allowing the board member to participate in the voting was imprudent, it did not violate the school code. The secretary's *de novo* review of the case cured any potential for bias in the board proceedings. The Commonwealth Court of Pennsylvania vacated the secretary's order, ruling the principal had been denied due process because of the appearance of bias created by the board member's presence in board deliberations.

The district appealed to the Supreme Court of Pennsylvania, which observed that the state secretary of education is vested with the authority to hear appeals by employees who are aggrieved by school board actions. State law gives the secretary the authority to conduct a *de novo* review. Aggrieved employees receive an opportunity to have the facts of their cases reheard in an independent forum. Minimum requirements of due process demand that a case be heard by a neutral fact finder. **Although school board proceedings have an inherent potential for bias because of a board's dual prosecutorial and judicial roles, independent review by the secretary ensured that the requirements of due process were satisfied.** Since the principal received all the process he was due, the court reversed and remanded the commonwealth court's decision. *Katruska v. Bethlehem Center School Dist.*, 767 A.2d 1051 (Pa. 2001).

CHAPTER TEN

Labor Relations

Page

I. PROFESSIONAL ASSOCIATIONS.......................................401
   A. Representation 401
   B. Agency Fees...404

II. COLLECTIVE BARGAINING AGREEMENTS 407
   A. Compensation...407
   B. Positions 413
   C. Other Terms and Conditions 416

III. GRIEVANCES AND ARBITRATION 419
   A. Arbitrability 419
   B. Procedures 423
   C. Standard of Review..424
   D. Association Duties and Rights 427

IV. STRIKES...428

I. PROFESSIONAL ASSOCIATIONS

Once elected, employee associations become the exclusive collective bargaining agent for the bargaining unit, with a duty to fairly represent and bargain for all members in the unit. Associations collect agency fees from both members and nonmembers, but they may not collect agency fees from nonmembers that are unrelated to collective bargaining, such as political activity.

A. Representation

◆ **The U.S. Supreme Court upheld a collective bargaining agreement between an Indiana school board and a teachers union which gave the union exclusive access to the school district's internal mail system.** A rival union challenged the denial of access to the mail system on grounds that the restriction violated free speech rights under the First Amendment and the Equal Protection Clause. The Supreme Court held that since the inter-school mail system was not a public forum generally available for use by the public, access to it could be reasonably restricted without violating either free speech or equal protection rights. The Court noted the special responsibilities of the exclusive bargaining representative and the fact that other channels of communication remained available to the rival union. *Perry Educ. Ass'n v. Perry Local Educators' Ass'n*, 460 U.S. 37, 103 S.Ct. 948, 74 L.Ed.2d 794 (1983).

◆   A Minnesota law required public employers to engage in official exchanges of views only with their professional employees' exclusive representatives on certain policy questions. Under the law, public employers were required to bargain only with the employees' exclusive bargaining representative. The statute gave professional employees, such as college faculty members, the right to "meet and confer" with the employer on matters outside the scope of a collective bargaining agreement. Community college faculty members sued the State Board for Community Colleges, claiming the law violated their First Amendment rights. The faculty members objected to the "meet and confer" provision, saying that rights of professional employees within the bargaining unit who were not members of the exclusive representative were violated.

The U.S. Supreme Court held the "meet and confer" provision did not violate the faculty members' constitutional rights. There was no constitutional right to force public employers to listen to the members' views. The fact that an academic setting was involved did not give the faculty members any special constitutional right to a voice in the employer's policy-making decisions. The state had a legitimate interest in ensuring that public employers heard one voice presenting the majority view of its professional employees on employment-related policy questions. *Minnesota Community College Ass'n v. Knight*, 465 U.S. 271, 104 S.Ct. 1058, 79 L.Ed.2d 299 (1984).

◆   In 1970, a Kansas school district recognized the Olathe National Education Association (ONEA) as the exclusive representative of its professional employees. By the mid-1990s, some district teachers had joined the Association of American Educators (AAE) instead. The district declined several requests by the AAE to use the district's internal mail system to distribute recruiting materials, noting the ONEA had negotiated this exclusive right through collective bargaining. The AAE continued its recruiting efforts, and the district filed an action in the state court system to resolve the dispute. The court held the district did not violate state law by rejecting the AAE's request.

On appeal, the Kansas Supreme Court explained that the state Negotiations Act recognizes teachers' rights to form professional associations to represent their interests in collective bargaining. While the act allowed more than one professional employees' association per district, only one association could be the exclusive representative. Substantial evidence supported the trial court finding that the AAE was a "professional employees' association" as defined by the Negotiations Act. The AAE's membership literature openly solicited ONEA members and proclaimed its interest in replacing the existing seniority-based compensation system with one based on merit. The AAE existed for collective bargaining purposes and sought to communicate on topics that were the subject of collective bargaining. **Since the ONEA had bargained for the privilege of using the district's mail system, the district was legally prohibited from granting the privilege to any other association.** The court affirmed the finding that the district properly limited use of its mail system to the ONEA. It rejected the AAE's argument that denial of access to the system violated the First Amendment. *Unified School Dist. No. 233, Johnson County, Kansas v. Kansas Ass'n of American Educators*, 275 Kan. 313, 64 P.3d 372 (Kan. 2003).

◆ A group of school nurses petitioned the New York State Public Employment Relations Board (SPERB) for fragmentation of their job title from their collective bargaining unit, which was made up of district noninstructional personnel. The SPERB held the nurses had a unique professional community of interest and an inherent conflict of interest with other noninstructional employees in the district. The employee association representing the other noninstructional employees sought to annul the decision. A state appellate division court found that in order to allow the fragmentation of a bargaining unit, the SPERB typically required both a showing of conflict of interest or inadequate representation and the existence of a unique community of interests. **The court found the nurses had a compelling, unique community of interest that was distinguishable from other district noninstructional personnel.** They were licensed health care professionals who had regular and personal contacts with students about health issues. The other district noninstructional personnel, including bus drivers, mechanics, teachers' aides, custodians, cooks and typists, had no comparable student contacts. The court affirmed the SPERB's determination, allowing fragmentation of the bargaining unit. *Civil Service Employees Ass'n, Local 1000 v. New York State Public Employment Relations Board,* 753 N.Y.S.2d 171 (N.Y. App. Div. 2002).

◆ The education association representing a Minnesota school district's teachers sought to include a number of part-time early childhood family education (ECFE) teachers in the bargaining unit. The request was denied by a state hearing officer, who found that ECFE teachers were hired to provide community education on a non-credit basis. Because they were non-credit instructors, their part-time status precluded a finding that they were public employees under the state Public Employment Labor Relations Act (PELRA), and they were properly excluded from the teachers' bargaining unit.

The Minnesota Court of Appeals held "public employee" is a statutory term that normally excludes employees who work the lesser of 14 hours per week or 35% of a normal workweek in the relevant bargaining unit. The court found ECFE programs and courses were optional. It rejected the education association's argument that the PELRA required the inclusion of ECFE teaches in the bargaining unit regardless of the number of hours they worked. **While the PELRA included teachers within the definition of "public employee" without regard to their hours worked, it created an explicit exception for part-time employees who instructed non-credit community education programs and courses.** The bureau did not commit error by concluding ECFE teachers who did not satisfy minimum requirements for hours worked were not "public employees." *Educ. Minnesota – Chisholm v. Independent School Dist. No. 695,* 649 N.W.2d 474 (Minn. Ct. App. 2002).

◆ A California bilingual education teacher who was elected president of her teachers' association requested permission to share her job with another teacher and work half time. Her request cited California Education Code § 44987(a), which requires districts to grant employee leaves of absence without loss of compensation to serve as elected officers of public employee organizations when an organization reimburses the district. The district refused, asserting the parties' master agreement limited such leave to 36 days or 180 periods in a year. It also claimed the leave would adversely affect the school's bilingual program and that Section 44987(a) allowed it to reasonably limit employee leave. The association sought a state court order requiring the district to grant the request. The court held the request was not one for "leave" under Section 44987 and that the parties' master agreement did not conflict with the statute.

The association appealed to the California Court of Appeal, which noted that in Section 44987(a), **the legislature clearly intended to allow elected officers of school employee organizations to take leaves of absence for any period of time for which an organization was willing to reimburse a school district**. In contrast to the district's argument, Section 44987(a) authorized leaves of short or infrequent duration, as well as those of longer or regular duration. If an employee organization found that an officer should take a leave equaling 50% of a work week, Section 44987(a) required a district to grant the request so long as the association reimbursed it for all the employee's compensation paid for the leave. The court rejected the district's assertion that allowing the teacher to take leave would harm bilingual students because of a shortage of qualified bilingual education teachers. The statute had no hardship exception, and the district presented no evidence that it was impossible to obtain a half-time bilingual education teacher. The parties were not authorized to waive the teacher's right to a leave of absence pursuant to Section 44987(a) through their master agreement. The court granted the association's petition and directed the superior court to vacate its decision. *Tracy Educators Ass'n v. Superior Court of San Joaquin County*, 96 Cal.App.4th 530, 116 Cal.Rptr.2d 916 (Cal. Ct. App. 2002).

B. Agency Fees

Expenditures of employee associations fall into two categories: chargeable expenses, which relate directly to collective bargaining and representation; and nonchargeable expenditures, which include funding of political causes. The U.S. Supreme Court has held that employee financial support of collective bargaining representatives implicates the First Amendment.

◆ The exclusive bargaining representative of the faculty at a state college in Michigan entered into an agency-shop arrangement with the college requiring nonunion bargaining unit employees to pay a service or agency fee equivalent to a union member's dues. Employees who objected to particular uses by the unions of their service fee brought suit under 42 U.S.C. § 1983, claiming that using the fees for purposes other than negotiating and administering the collective bargaining agreement violated their First and Fourteenth Amendment rights. A federal district court held that certain collective bargaining expenses were chargeable to the dissenting employees. The U.S. Court of Appeals, Sixth Circuit, affirmed the decision and the U.S. Supreme Court granted certiorari.

The Court first noted that **chargeable activities must be "germane" to collective bargaining activity and be justified by the policy interest of avoiding "free riders" who benefit from union efforts without paying for union services**. It then stated that the local union could charge the objecting employees for their pro rata share of costs associated with chargeable activities of its state and national affiliates, even if those activities did not directly benefit the local bargaining unit. The local could even charge the dissenters for expenses incident to preparation for a strike that would be illegal under Michigan law. However, lobbying activities and public relations efforts were not chargeable to the objecting employees. The Court affirmed in part and reversed in part the lower court decisions and remanded the case. *Lehnert v. Ferris Faculty Ass'n*, 500 U.S. 507, 111 S.Ct. 1950, 114 L.Ed.2d 572 (1991).

◆   Detroit teachers elected a labor association to become their exclusive collective bargaining representative, and it instituted an agency shop agreement. A group of teachers filed a class action lawsuit in a Michigan trial court, stating that they would not pay dues or agency fees because of their opposition to collective bargaining in the public sector. They specifically disapproved of the union's political and social activities, which they claimed were unrelated to the collective bargaining process. The teachers argued that the agency shop agreement violated state law and the First and Fourteenth Amendments. The case was dismissed by the trial court and was eventually appealed to the U.S. Supreme Court on the federal constitutional issues.

The Supreme Court drew on its earlier private sector decisions concerning labor relations and noted that **compelled support of collective bargaining representatives implicated teacher First Amendment rights to free speech and association and religious freedom.** However, some constitutional infringement was justified in the interest of peaceful labor relations. As long as the union acted to promote the cause of its membership, individual members were not free to withdraw their financial support. The Court agreed with the teachers that **compelled agency fees should not be used to support political views and candidates that were unrelated to collective bargaining issues.** Because the state court had dismissed the case without a trial, the teachers had not received the opportunity to make specific allegations that their contributions were being used to support activities with which they disagreed. There was no evidentiary record, and the Court remanded the case. If the teachers could prove a First Amendment violation, they were entitled to relief in the form of an injunction or a *pro rata* refund of fees being used for such purposes. *Abood v. Detroit Board of Educ.*, 431 U.S. 209, 97 S.Ct. 1782, 52 L.Ed.2d 261 (1977).

◆   In a later case, the Supreme Court found that the Chicago Teachers Union had not adequately protected the free speech rights of nonunion teachers. In 1982, the Chicago school board and the teachers' union agreed to deduct "proportionate share payments" from the paychecks of any nonunion employee. The deduction was fixed at 95% of the dues for union members, and no explanation was given as to how that figure was reached. This method of deduction was held to violate First Amendment freedom of speech protections. **To guard against the possibility of nonunion teachers' service fee payments being used for political purposes disagreeable to the nonmembers, the Supreme Court ruled there must be an adequate accounting and explanation of the basis for the deduction.** In case of a challenge, there must be an opportunity for a reasonably prompt decision by an impartial decision-maker as to whether any part of the service fee deduction has gone to fund political causes. Any amount that was reasonably in dispute must be held in escrow during the pendency of the challenge. *Chicago Teachers Union v. Hudson*, 475 U.S. 292, 106 S.Ct. 1066, 89 L.Ed.2d 232 (1986).

◆ Section 42.17.760 of the Washington Code required unions to obtain affirmative authorizations from union nonmembers before using agency fees (also known as "fair share" fees) for political expenditures. The Washington Education Association (WEA), which represents 70,000 public school employees in the state, had a collective bargaining agreement that included an agency shop provision requiring nonunion members to pay agency fees. While the WEA permitted union nonmembers to object to the calculation of the agency fee, they had to object to the use of their fees for political expenditures. If nonmembers failed to object to the payment of fees for costs that were unrelated to collective bargaining, they did not receive a refund of their fees. The state attorney general prosecuted the WEA for violating RCA § 42.17.760. A Washington superior court held the WEA had to obtain the affirmative authorization of nonunion members before it could collect or use agency fees for political purposes. The court denied summary judgment to the WEA and fined it $400,000 for intentionally violating the statute.

The WEA appealed to the state court of appeals, which discussed U.S. Supreme Court precedents on agency fees. The cases held that **while nonunion members cannot be compelled to support political causes with which they disagree, they must make their objections known to the union**. To vindicate their First Amendment rights, nonmembers had to declare their opposition to the union by challenging its agency fee calculations. The court explained that once dissenting bargaining unit members have expressed opposition to the use of their funds for political purposes, a union is required to prove its calculation of the agency fee is accurate by excluding items that are unrelated to collective bargaining. This included the funding of political causes supported by the union. The WEA had followed the U.S. Supreme Court's requirements for escrowing disputed agency fees until the calculation was resolved. Section 42.17.760 improperly relieved dissenting employees of their obligation to object to a fee calculation in the first place. Since this upset the balance of interests between union members and nonmembers, the court held Section 42.17.760 unconstitutional. *State of Washington, ex rel. Washington State P.D.C. v. Washington State Educ. Ass'n*, 71 P.3d 244 (Wash. Ct. App. 2003).

◆ California teachers who were not members of their local unions but were required to pay agency or "fair share" fees claimed the unions failed to provide them with adequate notice of agency fee deductions. They sued the unions and some school superintendents in a federal district court, asserting violations of the financial disclosure requirements described in *Chicago Teachers Union v. Hudson* (this chapter). The court held the financial disclosure provided by the unions was deficient and that the superintendents violated the teachers' rights by withholding or collecting agency fees from them despite the defective notices.

The superintendents appealed to the Ninth Circuit, which explained that agency fee payers could only be charged a *pro rata* share of union expenditures that were germane to collective bargaining. **The protections required by** *Hudson* **were designed to prevent the use of the agency fee payers' funds for political and ideological causes in violation of their speech rights.** While unions often faced *Hudson* violations claims, the teachers in this case also asserted the superintendents had a legal duty to ensure union compliance with *Hudson*. The court held the routine collection of fees by the superintendents did not trigger a duty to ensure that each employee received proper *Hudson* notice from a teachers union. Even if a union had an appropriate plan for providing notice, some employees might still not receive proper notice. This would only be grounds for challenging the union's accounting, not for holding superintendents liable. The court held that **while employers owe nonunion member employees the general duty described in** *Hudson* **to ensure that procedures exist to protect employee rights, they do not owe employees a specific duty to ensure that the proper** *Hudson* **notice is received by each employee before agency fees are deducted.** The court reversed the district court judgment. *Foster v. Mahdesian*, 268 F.3d 689 (9th Cir. 2001).

II. COLLECTIVE BARGAINING AGREEMENTS

Federal labor law imposes a duty on employers to bargain with duly elected collective bargaining representatives over the terms and conditions of employment. School districts and employees become bound by the terms of their agreements, and failure to abide by them constitutes an unfair labor practice. For cases discussing the interaction between state labor and education statutes and collective bargaining agreements, see Chapter Nine, Section I.C.

A. Compensation

◆ A Montana school superintendent agreed to pay a prospective teaching candidate $2,000 as an inducement for him to accept employment and move to the community. The school board adopted a recommendation to offer the candidate a teaching position. Two weeks later, the board voted to hire another teaching candidate who also sought moving expenses. However, her request was denied on grounds that this would exceed the salary specified in the collective bargaining agreement (CBA). The teachers' association filed an unfair labor practice charge with the state Board of Personnel Appeals (BOPA). After a hearing, the BOPA found the incentive was additional compensation and a condition of employment that was the subject of mandatory collective bargaining. Since the board had agreed to the payment without bargaining with the association, the BOPA held the board committed an unfair labor practice.

On appeal, the Supreme Court of Montana stated the Montana Public Employees Collective Bargaining Act imposes a duty on public employers to bargain collectively and in good faith on the subjects of wages, hours, fringe benefits and other conditions of employment. **A refusal to bargain collectively in good faith is an unfair labor practice.** The board argued the payment was made before the candidate accepted employment. **The court held that terms and conditions offered by an employer to a non-employee may still be** subject to mandatory bargaining if they "vitally affect" the terms and conditions of employment for current employees. The $2,000 inducement materially or significantly affected the terms and conditions of employment for association members. **The court held the board circumvented the collective bargaining process by bargaining directly with and agreeing to pay the candidate compensation beyond what was stated in the CBA.** The timing of the decision to issue the check was irrelevant. The facts supported BOPA's decision that the incentive related to an offer of employment. The supreme court affirmed BOPA's decision. *Ekalaka Unified Board of Trustees v. Ekalaka Teachers' Ass'n, MEA-MFT, NEA*, 335 Mont. 149, 149 P.3d 902 (Mont. 2006).

◆   An Oregon assistant principal signed a three-year contract with a school district requiring him to work 220 days each year. During the first year of the contract, the district adopted a new employee compensation plan for the next five school years. Under the plan, the assistant principal's salary remained the same, but his work days were increased from 220 to 230 each year. The assistant principal appealed to the state Fair Dismissal Appeals Board, contending the action amounted to an unauthorized "reduction in pay." The board found he received the same compensation as the prior year.

The assistant principal appealed to the Court of Appeals of Oregon, where he argued the meaning of the term "pay" must include both the rate of pay and the amount of work stated in the contract. **The court held the addition of 10 work days to the administrator's work load was not an "assignment or reassignment" under Oregon law. It agreed with the board and the district that "reduction in pay" meant a decrease in the amount of money paid under a contract. School administrators could be paid on a salary basis and were exempt from overtime laws.** The legislature intended the term "pay" to mean "salary." The administrator did not receive a reduction in pay, as his salary remained the same as before the salary plan. *Folkers v. Lincoln County School Dist.*, 205 Or.App. 619, 135 P.3d 373 (Or. Ct. App. 2006).

◆   In 1993, the Washington Legislature authorized a pilot program allowing school districts to assign educational employees to non-instructional "learning improvement days" for additional training. Learning improvement days were not a part of the "basic education" required by the Washington Constitution. The program became permanent, and most districts took advantage of learning improvement days. For these districts, the state supplemented employee salaries by allocating them 1/180th of their derived base salary for each learning improvement day. Districts retained the discretion to hold learning improvement days. In 2000, Washington voters approved Initiative 732, which mandated an annual cost-of-living increase for all school employees. Each annual raise was recalculated using a consumer price index. The legislature responded to a significant budget deficit in 2002 by reducing the annual learning improvement days from three to two. Educational employees lost about one-half of a percent of their annual pay as a result. A 2002 legislative appropriation bill expressly stated the learning improvement days were not to be considered part of a basic education. A coalition of teachers, districts and others filed a state superior court action to challenge the reduction.

The court held the cost-of-living increase for education workers must be equivalent to the federal cost-of-living increase over the prior year. The parties appealed to the Supreme Court of Washington. The court stated the Basic Education Act (BEA) did not define the scope of the state's duty to provide a basic education. **The pilot program stated learning improvement days were not part of a basic education. The court rejected the coalition's argument that the legislature had impliedly made learning improvement days a part of a basic education in later appropriation bills describing salary schedules.** These bills did not amend the BEA. The learning improvement days were not part of the required basic education, and cost-of living-increases did not apply to learning improvement days. "State-funded salary base" did not mean "last year's take-home pay." The court held Initiative 732 did not require a wage increase based on a 183-day work year, and it reversed the judgment. *Brown v. State of Washington*, 119 P.3d 341 (Wash. 2005).

◆ **The Supreme Court of South Carolina held teachers had no contractual or statutory right to claim a 10% salary increase that had been offered at one time for obtaining national board certification.** The state General Assembly enacted a law to pay teachers a $7,500 annual bonus for obtaining national board certification. One school district supplemented this incentive by offering a 10% salary increase for teachers obtaining the certification. The district superintendent discussed the program at several teachers' meetings. Documentation regarding the district incentive stated a pay increase was subject to board approval each year. The board reduced the incentive to $3,000 per teacher for the 2002-03 school year due to a budget shortfall. Five teachers sued the district in a state court, alleging the reduced incentive was in breach of contract and a violation of the state Payment of Wages Act. They added related claims based on breach of equitable duties.

The court awarded summary judgment to the district, and the teachers appealed. The state supreme court noted the teachers had continuing contract rights and worked under a contract limited to one school year. They entered into new contracts each year that were subject to change. Each annual contract was subject to board approval. **The court rejected the breach of contract claim. The district was not bound to the 10% incentive program as it was initially described.** The teachers had no equitable claim to a 10% pay increase for obtaining national board certification. They did not show they reasonably relied on a promise by the district superintendent. He informed teachers on several occasions that the pay incentive was subject to the board's approval. The court found no evidence of any breach. The board had acted to reduce its budget, and did not act in bad faith or with malice. The board complied with the South Carolina Payment of Wages Act by informing the teachers well in advance of a seven-day statutory notice requirement for any change in wages. The court affirmed the summary judgment for the district. *Davis v. Greenwood School Dist. 50*, 620 S.E.2d 65 (S.C. 2005).

◆ Florida pre-school program instructors in a federal Head Start program claimed they consistently worked in excess of 40 hours per week. The local school board did not pay them overtime for working excess hours, and they sued the board in a federal district court for violating the Fair Labor Standards Act (FLSA). The court considered the board's argument that an FLSA professional exemption for teachers applied to the instructors, exempting them from any overtime pay. It noted **new labor department regulations governing teachers at 29 CFR Part 541.3 specified that the FLSA teacher exemption extends beyond traditional teachers. The new regulation clarified that teachers of students in kindergarten, nursery school and gifted or disabled programs were subject to the teacher exemption.** Since the claims arose prior to the date of the new regulations, the court construed the case under pre-2004 regulations.

The court noted that in exempting teachers from FLSA overtime provisions, Congress and the U.S. Department of Labor realized that a teacher's usual weekly time commitment exceeds 40 hours per week. Unlike other jobs, these excess hours are built into teacher salaries. Since Head Start instructor duties closely paralleled those of regular academic teachers, their weekly workload was likely to exceed 40 hours. The court applied a two-part test from 29 CFR Part 541.3(e). It found Head Start instructors had a primary duty of teaching, tutoring, instructing or lecturing as teachers in their school system. They shared a common job description with regular academic teachers employed by the board. Head Start instructors did everything done by the certified teachers in the district, and so were engaged in the activity of teaching. They were also board employees whose employment required the consistent exercise of discretion and judgment. As the instructors met the regulatory test, the court found they were within the FLSA's professional teacher exemption. The FLSA overtime provision did not apply to the board, and the court granted its motion for summary judgment. *Ramos v. Lee County School Board*, No. 2:04 CV 308FTM-33SPC, 2005 WL 2405832 (M.D. Fla. 2005).

◆   An Ohio bus mechanic worked for a school board for 13 years. The board abolished all driver and mechanic positions and laid off all employees in these job titles. The board contracted with a private transportation service to operate its buses. Its contract required the service to offer employment to laid-off employees with a 3% pay raise and comparable benefits, including continued participation in the School Employees Retirement System (SERS). The mechanic rejected the offer to perform the same or similar duties for the service. He resigned from employment and received retirement and social security benefits for three years. The mechanic did not seek other employment. The union representing the drivers and mechanic sued the school board in a state court. In 2000, **the state supreme court held the board had unlawfully laid off the drivers and outsourced their jobs.** *State ex rel. Ohio Ass'n of Public School Employees/AFSCME, Local 4, AFL-CIO v. Batavia Local School Dist. Board of Educ.*, 89 Ohio St. 191, 729 N.E.2d 743 (Ohio 2000).

The school board denied the mechanic's request for reinstatement, and he filed a separate action in the state court system for reinstatement with back pay and lost benefits. The mechanic's case reached the state supreme court in 2002, and again in 2005. **It held the board had unlawfully abolished the mechanic's position and outsourced his job to the private bus service. While wrongfully discharged public employees may receive back pay, related benefits and reinstatement in the same action,** the mechanic's failure to accept employment by the private service was a failure to mitigate his lost wages. After subtracting for the offsets for SERS payments the mechanic received, the amount he would have made from the transportation service during this time, and the amount he earned from the board prior to being laid off, **he was not entitled to any back pay. The court held the mechanic could not claim sick leave credits or other benefits lost when he was excluded from employment.** The evidence showed he used up most of his sick leave during his 13 years as a board employee. Since vacation and sick leave days cannot be established with certainty, the mechanic could not claim them. He was denied any compensatory or punitive damages. *Stacy v. Batavia Local School Dist. Board of Educ.*, 105 Ohio St.3d 476, 829 N.E.2d 298 (Ohio 2005).

◆   A union collective bargaining agent who represented the employees of two schools owned and operated by the U.S. Army submitted proposals asking for mileage reimbursement, paid leave, and salary increases on behalf of school employees. The schools refused to negotiate, stating that under Title VII of the Civil Service Reform Act of 1978 they were not required to negotiate these matters. The union filed a complaint with the Federal Labor Relations Authority (FLRA), which held that the union's proposals were negotiable. The U.S. Court of Appeals, Eleventh Circuit, upheld the FLRA's decision, and the schools appealed to the U.S. Supreme Court. It noted **Title VII of the Civil Service Reform Act defines conditions of employment as matters "affecting working conditions" but excludes matters relating to prohibited political activities, classification of positions, and those specifically provided for by federal statute**. The Court determined the union's proposals were "conditions of employment," and it affirmed the district court decision. The Court held the schools were required to negotiate salary increases and fringe benefits. *Fort Stewart Schools v. Federal Labor Relations Authority*, 495 U.S. 641, 110 S.Ct. 2043, 109 L.Ed.2d 659 (1990).

◆   A Minnesota school district and the association representing its teachers were unable to agree on a collective bargaining agreement (CBA), and teachers worked for a year under an expired contract. The district proposed a retroactive freeze on wages and benefits already paid during the prior year, with a 5%t cut in salary and benefits for the next school year. The proposal also froze salary steps based on experience, lane changes based on higher educational achievement, and contributions to health insurance premiums. According to the district, the freeze on wages and benefits was necessary because it was in violation of state law by being in "statutory operating debt." The parties continued to negotiate, but the district maintained the wage and benefits freeze. The association demanded bargaining and then sued the district in a state court for unfair labor practices, asserting the unilateral wage and benefits freeze violated its duty to meet and negotiate on the CBA in good faith. The court held for the district, and the association appealed.

The Court of Appeals of Minnesota held **a public employer commits an unfair labor practice by refusing to meet and negotiate in good faith with the exclusive representative of an employee bargaining unit. An employer's unilateral change in the terms and conditions of employment is, on its face,**

a violation of employee collective bargaining rights. The district asserted it was bound to freeze wages and benefits by Minn. Stat. § 123B.749, which required districts to eliminate any statutory debt and assure that a CBA would not cause structural imbalance in a district budget. The district did not present a CBA to its board, and nothing in the structural balance law excused it from its statutory duty to meet and negotiate with the association in good faith. The district could not balance its budget by the means it employed, and it did not comply with the law's procedures. **The district committed an unfair labor practice by unilaterally freezing wages and benefits under the existing contract after meeting only once with the association and continuing negotiations. According to the U.S. Supreme Court, an employer's unilateral change in employment terms and conditions circumvents its duty to bargain collectively.** The court reversed the judgment, ruling the unilateral action, coupled with failure to respond to the union's demand for bargaining, constituted a refusal to bargain and thus an unfair labor practice. *Educ. Minnesota-Greenway, Local 1330 v. Independent School Dist. No. 316,* 673 N.W.2d 843 (Minn. Ct. App. 2004).

◆ **The Hawaii Supreme Court struck down an attempt by the state legislature to prohibit public employers and employee associations from bargaining over "cost items," including wages,** for the 1999-2001 biennium. The framers of the Hawaii Constitution did not intend for the legislature to deny public employees the right to organize and collectively bargain. The decision was the result of a challenge to a law enacted by the Hawaii legislature in 1999 prohibiting state and county governments, including public schools and the state university system, from negotiating over "cost items" during the 1999-2001 biennium. Cost items included wages, hours, contributions to public employee pensions and other terms and conditions of employment that required legislative appropriations. *United Public Workers, AFSCME, Local 646, AFL-CIO v. Yogi,* 62 P.3d 189 (Haw. 2002).

◆ A Nebraska teacher was hired for a district's base salary of $21,650, plus a $2,350 signing bonus. The employee association representing district teachers filed an action against the district with the state commission on industrial relations, alleging it violated the law by refusing to bargain over the bonus. The commission agreed, and the district appealed to the Nebraska Supreme Court. It contended the association acted in bad faith by suggesting in negotiations that it would not oppose the payment of a signing bonus, then filing suit when the district did so. **The court held it is bad faith for a labor association to remain silent on an issue of possible contention, then file suit after an agreement is finalized. However, there was no issue of bad faith or concealment by the association in this case.**

The commission's finding on this issue was upheld, as was the finding that it fully considered the course of negotiations in its decision and order. The court disagreed with the commission's finding that the district improperly undercut the authority of the collective bargaining agreement by bargaining directly with the teacher before he was hired. When the initial offer was made, he was not a district employee and was not covered by the agreement. While this finding was reversed, the court upheld the finding that the district's offer of a signing bonus at the time of his hiring was direct dealing that excluded the association in violation of the law. The bonus was part of the teacher's wages and thus, a mandatory subject of collective bargaining. *Crete Educ. Ass'n v. Saline County School Dist.*, 654 N.W.2d 166 (Neb. 2002).

B. Positions

◆   A Florida teacher qualified for a veterans' preference as the spouse of a disabled veteran. When the district rejected her application for employment in 2001, she filed an administrative complaint with the state Public Employees Relations Commission (PERC). The district hired the teacher under a settlement agreement that ended the 2001 challenge. She signed a one-year contract and began the 2003-04 school year as a fourth-grade teacher. The school's vice principal gave her a good employment evaluation early in the school year but later observed her without prior notice and issued her a poor evaluation. The teacher responded with a 146-page packet that included a transcript of her veterans' preference hearing. The principal advised her she would not be rehired. She called in sick the next day and was placed on administrative leave for the rest of her contract term. The teacher filed a second PERC complaint against the district, claiming it discharged her and retaliated against her through a series of unfair labor practices, including an unlawful suspension.

The PERC dismissed the claims, and the teacher appealed. The Florida District Court of Appeal stated that a claimant has the burden of proving an unfair labor practice charge. **The claimant must show that protected conduct was a substantial or motivating factor in adverse employment action.** PERC hearing examiners were to balance the rights of an employer to promote efficient public services with the rights of teachers to be secure in their employment and free from discrimination based on union activity. The court held the **teacher did not show retaliation by the district. She failed to show a sufficient connection between any protected activity and adverse action.** As the teacher did not demonstrate protected activity was a motivating factor in the adverse employment decisions, the court affirmed the PERC's final order. *Cagle v. St. Johns County School Dist.*, 939 So.2d 1085 (Fl. Dist. Ct. App. 2006).

◆   A Tennessee teacher had worked for a school district for 21 years and was head coach of boys' high school baseball and basketball teams. The school board placed him on administrative leave for allegedly mishandling athletic funds. After being assigned as a roving substitute aide in elementary schools, the teacher filed a grievance. The board denied the grievance at every level, and the matter proceeded to arbitration. The arbitrator found the transfer violated the collective bargaining agreement and school board policy. The arbitrator directed the board to return the teacher to his high school position. The board returned the teacher to his math classes but claimed it did not have to reinstate him to his coaching positions. The arbitrator clarified his order to declare the failure to reinstate the teacher to his coaching duties did not comply with the arbitration award. The board refused to return the teacher to his coaching duties, and the employee association petitioned a state court to enforce the award.

The court awarded summary judgment to the board. **On appeal, the state court of appeals found the case depended upon whether the coaching** assignments were within the scope of the collective bargaining agreement. While courts lack jurisdiction to review the merits of a grievance or arbitration award, an award is legitimate only so long as it draws its essence from the parties' collective bargaining agreement. Courts may determine the "gateway issue" of whether a binding arbitration clause applies to a particular controversy. The agreement listed supplemental coaching positions, including the teacher's posts. The dispute arose from the teacher's alleged mishandling of athletic funds, not his performance as a math teacher. The entire dispute arose under the collective bargaining agreement and was subject to arbitration. The interpretation of the supplemental coaching positions was within the scope of the arbitrator's award, and the court held the case should be returned to the arbitrator to determine an appropriate remedy. *Metropolitan Nashville Educ. Ass'n v. Metropolitan Board of Public Educ.*, No. M2005-00747-COA-R3-CV, 2006 WL 2619982 (Tenn. Ct. App. 2006).

◆ A Massachusetts special education director sought to transfer a teacher to a special-needs class. The transfer would have involved significant changes for the teacher, including teaching older and more severely disabled students, using inferior resources and working different hours. It also required her to give up a $2,500 annual stipend she received for other duties she performed. She rejected the proposal. The director and a supervisor decided to go through with the transfer, and the teacher filed a grievance. An arbitrator held that the applicable collective bargaining agreement contained a provision on involuntary transfers that was not invalidated by the Massachusetts Education Reform Act. Because the teacher was not transferred to a comparable position, the arbitrator held that the school committee violated the collective bargaining agreement and was required to reinstate her and pay her the stipend.

The school committee sought to vacate the arbitration award in the state court system, but a superior court held that involuntary transfers were subject to grievances under the collective bargaining agreement. The Massachusetts Supreme Judicial Court considered the committee's argument that the authority to make involuntary transfers was part of the broad authority granted to principals under the Reform Act. The court explained that Reform Act language increasing the hiring and firing responsibilities of principals was intended to make them more accountable. However, **the act did not grant principals complete discretion and did not allow them to enter into collective bargaining agreements. The court stated the Reform Act carefully balanced school-based management reforms with district-wide needs and employee collective bargaining rights. Involuntary transfers were distinct personnel actions under a collective bargaining agreement.** While the agreement in this case did not define the term "comparable position," it required that each job transfer involve comparable positions. **Transfers were subject to the grievance procedure, and the arbitrator had properly found that language making the committee's decision "final" did not preclude arbitration** over a violation, misinterpretation or misapplication of the agreement. The court held that the dispute was arbitrable and affirmed the judgment for the association. *School Committee of Pittsfield v. United Educators of Pittsfield*, 784 N.E.2d 11 (Mass. 2003).

◆ A South Dakota school district declared an impasse after collective bargaining with an education association. Pursuant to the rules of impasse, the district implemented its "last best offer," which called for replacing the reduction-in-force and recall policy from the previously negotiated agreement in favor of a non-negotiated board policy. The association filed an unfair labor practice charge against the district. The South Dakota Department of Labor held that the unilateral modification of the policy was an unfair labor practice. A state circuit court affirmed the decision, and the district appealed.

The South Dakota Supreme Court explained that **a "negotiable item" for public employees is one that must relate to rates of pay, wages, hours of employment and other conditions of employment**. A subject is negotiable only if it "intimately and directly affects the work and welfare of public employees" and is a matter on which negotiated agreement would not significantly interfere with the exercise of the employer's management prerogatives. On the other hand, an item is not negotiable if it has been preempted by a statute or regulation. In this case, the reduction-in-force and recall policy intimately and directly affected the work and welfare of teachers working under the collective bargaining agreement. There was no state law or regulation preempting the policy, and no statutory basis for preempting the policy from negotiation. The court found that negotiation of the policy did not significantly interfere with the district's inherent management prerogatives. In reaching this conclusion, **the court distinguished between a public employer's substantive decision to transfer or assign employees, which came within the employer's managerial discretion, and procedural processes to be followed after making a decision, which were mandatory subjects of negotiation**. Because the policy in this case involved only procedures, the court affirmed the judgment for the association. *Webster Educ. Ass'n v. Webster School Dist.* 631 N.W.2d 202 (S.D. 2001).

◆ The Vermont Department of Education erroneously issued a teacher an elementary teaching certificate. She was previously certified by the state of New Jersey to teach high school. After the teacher informed the superintendent of the error, he advised her he had obtained a state waiver allowing her to teach elementary grades. The teacher suffered multiple allergic reactions and took two sick leaves. The board denied her request for additional leave and invited her to take unpaid leave. The teacher instead filed a grievance, and the board voted to discharge her. She then filed a second grievance. An arbitrator denied the first grievance, but found the district had violated contractual termination procedures and ordered the district to reinstate her to her former position as a sixth-grade teacher or to an equivalent one. The district instead offered her a kindergarten position. The teacher learned she could not accept the position because, contrary to the superintendent's statement, she had no waiver to teach elementary classes. She appealed the arbitration award to a state superior court, adding claims for constitutional rights violations. The court awarded summary judgment to the district and officials and the teacher appealed.

The state supreme court held **the teacher had received a full and fair opportunity to litigate her claim for additional sick time in arbitration and should not receive a second opportunity in the court system**. Her appeal was an attempt to circumvent the binding effect of the arbitrator's decision that held allowing her to avoid key learning areas would alter the character of her position. According to the court, the denial of the teacher's contractual protections was evidence of retaliation against her for filing grievances and complaints against the district. In addition, the district had offered her a position that it knew she could not accept. The superintendent failed to request a waiver of state licensing requirements, despite his statement to the contrary. The court held that in view of this evidence, the trial court should have held there was a genuine issue for trial. The court dismissed the teacher's remaining claims. *Mellin v. Flood Brook Union School Dist.,* 790 A.2d 408 (Vt. 2001).

C. Other Terms and Conditions

◆ An Ohio school board and the association representing district teachers had a collective bargaining agreement (CBA) with no tuition reimbursement provision. During the term of the CBA, the board offered to reimburse teachers up to $1,200 for 12 credits toward a master's degree at Xavier University. The association did not want the program, and it sought an order from the state employment relations board (SERB) to stop the board from unilaterally approving it. The SERB held the board committed an unfair labor practice, and the board appealed. An Ohio common pleas court found the CBA contained a midterm bargaining clause that required the parties to negotiate new terms. The SERB and the association appealed to the state court of appeals. The court stated the association might have believed it could negotiate a better plan during the next bargaining period and had the right to reject the offered benefit.

The court explained SERB orders must be upheld if they are supported by "substantial evidence." The common pleas court's decision relied on a CBA clause referring to collective bargaining on all matters pertaining to wages, hours, or terms and conditions of employment, "and the continuation, modification or deletion" of existing provisions of the agreement. The provision did not create a midterm dispute-resolution procedure. The reimbursement plan was covered as a wage or a term and condition of employment. As there was no midterm bargaining provision in the CBA, the plan had to be negotiated. **The court held once the CBA was reached, its terms were preserved and neither the board nor the association could unilaterally modify a management right without the other party's consent. Issues affecting wages, hours or terms and conditions of employment could be modified only through collective bargaining.** As the tuition reimbursement was such an issue, the board could not unilaterally change it, and the court reinstated the SERB decision. *Oak Hills Educ. Ass'n v. Oak Hills Local School Dist. Board of Educ.,* 158 Ohio App.3d 662, 821 N.E.2d 616 (Ohio Ct. App. 2004.)

◆ A Rhode Island school committee distributed an Internet access policy to parents, students and teachers. The policy set guidelines for Internet use in support of educational goals and objectives, and it limited staff Internet use to research and/or instructional purposes. Violations could lead to discipline or criminal prosecution under law, school policy or collective bargaining agreements. The state labor relations board determined the policy affected disciplinary practices and was a mandatory subject for collective bargaining. It found the implementation of the policy by the committee without submitting it to collective bargaining constituted direct dealing with employees. The board ordered the committee to suspend use of the policy as applied to teachers and directed it to enter into collective bargaining. The committee appealed.

A state superior court rejected the committee's argument that it unilaterally implemented the policy in the exercise of its statutory duty to safeguard children. The policy's limitations on conditions of employment did not concern the general obligations of state law, but were specifically limited to ensure teacher rights to collective bargaining. The court also rejected the committee's argument that the policy was an attempt to comply with the federal Children's Online Protection Act (COPA). While the COPA required schools to adopt Internet safety policies to qualify for discount internet access, the district policy exceeded these provisions. **The COPA did not restrict casual personal use of the Internet by school employees. The court held implementation of the policy was a mandatory subject of collective bargaining because it affected employee discipline. Employers cannot unilaterally change any collective bargaining provision involving a mandatory subject of bargaining.** The committee directly approached the teachers to accept the policy, unilaterally changing the terms and conditions of employment. This was direct dealing with teachers in violation of state labor law, which required proper representation for any discussion between employers and employees on any subject of mandatory bargaining. The court upheld the board's findings of an unfair labor practice and direct dealing. *Johnston School Committee v. Rhode Island State Labor Relations Board,* No. Civ.A. PC 03-0141, 2004 WL 877619 (R.I. Super. 2004).

◆   A Florida school board believed its employee health insurance plan was in danger of becoming insolvent after running deficits for many years. It notified the association representing its teachers of the financial urgency and approved modifications to address the deficit. The sides failed to coordinate negotiations. The board then unilaterally changed employee health care benefits and notified the state Public Employees Relations Commission (PERC) of an impasse in negotiations under Florida Statutes § 447.403(4)(2). It also requested a bypass of statutory special master proceedings. The board then reached agreement with the association representing district teachers. However, negotiations between the board and the noninstructional employees union were fruitless. The board declared an impasse and notified the union of its intent to skip mediation and special master proceedings. After a hearing, it implemented the proposed changes. Instead of filing an unfair labor practice claim with the PERC, the union filed a grievance, alleging the unilateral modification of health insurance benefits violated the collective bargaining agreement (CBA). An arbitrator held the board violated the CBA by failing to raise health care issues in annual negotiations. It also violated Section 447.403 and other laws by imposing a resolution without negotiation or waiver of the statutory special master proceeding. A state trial court vacated the arbitration award, finding the arbitrator exceeded his powers. The court noted the arbitration award interpreted Section 447.403 and other laws within PERC jurisdiction.

On appeal, the District Court of Appeal of Florida held arbitration awards may not exceed the authority granted to the arbitrator by the parties' contract. **The legislature intended Part II, Chapter 447 of Florida Statutes to be exclusively within the PERC's jurisdiction. Section 447.403 did not mention submission to arbitration.** The board's unilateral modification of the employee health insurance plan was pursuant to statutory law and was not a breach of the collective bargaining agreement. The arbitrator was preempted by the PERC, which had exclusive jurisdiction of matters arguably covered by Chapter 447. The solvency of the employee health insurance plan was a compelling interest. As the PERC had preemptive authority, the board could not bypass its jurisdiction by proceeding directly to arbitration. The fact that the board did not strictly follow the statutory bargaining process did not divest the PERC of its exclusive authority. The court affirmed the trial court decision to vacate the arbitration award. *Communications Workers of America, Local 3180 v. Indian River County School Board*, 888 So.2d 96 (Fla. Dist. Ct. App. 2004).

◆ A Tennessee school board adopted a dress code for all instructional personnel without first negotiating with the association representing district teachers. The association filed a grievance against the board and sought arbitration. The case reached the state court of appeals, which considered a state law amendment defining "working conditions." The amendment defined the term as "those fundamental matters that affect a professional employee financially or the employee's employment relationship with the board."

The court observed that other state courts have struggled to define "working conditions" in public employment that are subject to mandatory bargaining. **The common theme in the tests used by other state courts focused on the public interest in effective and efficient services.** The court found the board's managerial prerogatives had to be balanced with employee rights to negotiate the terms and conditions of their employment. It did not appear that the dress code had fundamentally affected teachers so as to require mandatory bargaining. While the dress code was not so restrictive that teachers would be forced to buy new wardrobes, it was silent regarding sanctions, enforcement and implementation. **The court held the enforcement of the policy could fundamentally impact the teachers' employment relationships which had to be bargained. The court reversed the judgment and declared the dress code policy a "working condition."** *Polk County Board of Educ. v. Polk County Educ. Ass'n*, 139 S.W.3d 304 (Tenn. Ct. App. 2004).

◆ **A South Dakota employee association could not convert the school calendar into a negotiable item for collective bargaining.** The state supreme court held that the calendar was a matter of general public interest that affected the community and an inherently managerial subject that could not be bargained over. The court observed state law mandates that the parties to a collective bargaining agreement negotiate over wages, hours of employment and other conditions of employment. To determine whether an issue was the subject of mandatory negotiation in public employment, the court was required to balance competing interests by considering the extent to which collective bargaining would impair the determination of government policy.

The court held that **requiring the board to negotiate the school calendar**

would significantly interfere with the exercise of its inherent management prerogatives. Most other jurisdictions that have addressed the issue have held that the school calendar is an inherently managerial subject that is not a mandatory topic of negotiation. The school calendar affected teachers, other school employees, students, parents, taxpayers, other school districts and entire communities. The calendar was a matter of general public interest that required basic judgments about how government could best educate students. If the employee association was allowed to bargain the issue, none of the other community interests would be represented. **Determination of the calendar by collective bargaining substantially interfered with an inherent managerial prerogative pertaining to government educational policy.** *West Cent. Educ. Ass'n v. West Cent. School Dist. 49-4*, 655 N.W.2d 916 (S.D. 2002).

◆ A New Jersey school board unilaterally adopted a revised calendar for a school year. The employees' association filed an unfair labor practices complaint, alleging the changes affected terms and conditions of employment that the board could not unilaterally change. A hearing officer dismissed the case, and the state public employment relations commission denied review. The Superior Court of New Jersey, Appellate Division, noted **establishing a school calendar is a traditional management decision that is not a term or condition of employment.** However, nonnegotiable management decisions may have an effect on terms and conditions of employment and be negotiable. **The court held a case-by-case analysis must be applied to nonnegotiable management decisions to determine if negotiating their impact would significantly or substantially encroach upon a management prerogative.** Because the hearing officer had not conducted such an analysis in this case, the court reversed and remanded the case to the employment relations commission. *Piscataway Township Educ. Ass'n v. Piscataway Township Board of Educ.*, 307 N.J.Super. 263, 704 A.2d 981 (N.J. Super. Ct. App. Div. 1998).

III. GRIEVANCES AND ARBITRATION

Collective bargaining agreements contain grievance procedures for the resolution of contractual terms. Where an arbitrator resolves a dispute concerning the interpretation of contract terms and the arbitration award draws its essence from the agreement, a court may not disturb the award.

A. Arbitrability

◆ A Tennessee school board did not renew a probationary teacher's contract after three years as an in-school suspension teacher. The collective bargaining agreement between the board and teachers association applied to all teachers with certificates, including those without tenure. The teacher filed a grievance against the board, alleging the non-renewal was discriminatory. The board sought a state court order to avoid binding arbitration. The court found the teacher had no right to continued employment beyond a one-year term. The collective bargaining agreement extended additional rights to all teachers. This included the right to written notice of any employment deficiencies, a chance to correct them, the right to be represented when being reprimanded, warned or disciplined, and other due process rights. The collective bargaining agreement limited the board's right to lay off teachers to cases in which there was a substantial drop or change in the student population, or unavoidable budget problems. The court held the parties had agreed to submit the case to arbitration.

On appeal, **the Court of Appeals of Tennessee found the teacher, though not tenured, was certificated and entitled to the due process protections of the collective bargaining agreement. The teacher's individual contract was limited to one year, yet the collective bargaining agreement expressly limited the board's authority to lay off teachers.** The trial court should have further considered whether the teacher was entitled to binding arbitration under the grievance procedure to extend his employment term beyond the term expressly indicated in his individual contract. The court found the subject of the dispute was covered by Section 29-14-103 of the state Code. It remanded the case for further consideration. *Cannon County Board of Educ. v. Wade*, No. M2003-02260-COA-R3-CV, 2005 WL 195106 (Tenn. Ct. App. 2005).

◆   A Pennsylvania district fired a custodian for photographing and tape recording co-workers without their permission. Although law officers filed a felony charge of illegal wiretapping against her, she pled guilty to a reduced, misdemeanor charge of disorderly conduct. The custodian's employee association filed a grievance on her behalf. An arbitrator held her misconduct warranted serious discipline, but not termination, because the felony charge was dropped. The wiretap statute was enacted to protect homes, not workplaces. The district had never taken action against the custodian despite similar conduct in the past. The arbitrator ordered the custodian reinstated as of the date the wiretapping charges against her were dropped and awarded her back wages.

A state common pleas court affirmed the award, and appeal reached the Commonwealth Court of Pennsylvania. It held **arbitration awards are final and binding unless they do not draw their essence from the collective bargaining agreement. The arbitrator, not the district, had the authority to determine the appropriate discipline under the collective bargaining agreement.** The court rejected the district's claim that the award condoned criminal behavior. The collective bargaining agreement provided for discipline upon proof of a felony. The custodian was not convicted of a felony and pled to a non-felony charge. The court found the award was internally consistent, because it ordered the custodian suspended until the date the felony charge was dropped. As the award drew its essence from the collective bargaining agreement, the court affirmed it. *Norristown Area School Dist. v. Norristown Educ. Support Personnel Ass'n*, 847 A.2d 795 (Pa. Commw. Ct. 2004).

◆   A Washington teacher's full-time teaching certificate expired at the end of his second year of employment in a district. He earned the academic credits he needed for renewal during the summer, but he did not obtain his certificate by the first day of school. The district superintendent notified the teacher his failure to possess a valid full-time certificate invalidated his employment contract. The collective bargaining agreement (CBA) provided an arbitrator was to decide all issues of substantive arbitrability, but only after hearing the merits of a grievance. The teachers association filed a grievance on the teacher's behalf, which was denied through the first three steps of the procedure. The district notified the teacher of his right to request arbitration as the final step of the grievance process. It then filed a state court action for a declaration that he had no contract and an order prohibiting arbitration. The court held the teacher's contract was invalid due to his lack of certification. It enjoined the association from commencing or continuing arbitration. The state court of appeals affirmed the judgment, and the teacher appealed to Supreme Court of Washington.

The court stated its duty was to determine if the parties had agreed to arbitrate a dispute, not to decide the merits of the controversy. There is a strong presumption of arbitrability in labor disputes, and courts cannot decide the merits of a case unless there is "positive assurance" the arbitration clause cannot be interpreted to cover the dispute. When parties agree to arbitrate their disputes, they are bound to have an arbitrator grant relief. The district and teachers association had clearly agreed to let an arbitrator decide whether a grievance was arbitrable. The teacher was a member of the association at all times, and his grievance alleged the district had terminated his employment in violation of the CBA without due process. The CBA reserved the question of arbitrability for an arbitrator. The district itself had processed the grievance through the first three steps, and arbitration had been scheduled prior to the filing of the court action. It could not be said with "positive assurance" the CBA precluded arbitration, and the case was remanded with directions to arbitrate the grievance. *Mt. Adams School Dist. v. Cook*, 81 P.3d 111 (Wash. 2003).

◆ A New Hampshire school district reassigned a teacher from a middle school to an elementary school. He claimed the action was based on his pro-union activity, and his teachers association filed a grievance on his behalf. The district denied the grievance, and the association demanded arbitration under the procedure of the collective bargaining agreement (CBA). The association also filed an unfair labor practice complaint with the state public employee labor relations board (PELRB). The PELRB ordered the parties into arbitration, unless a party requested an additional hearing within 30 days of an arbitration decision. The arbitrator upheld the grievance and ordered the district to reassign the teacher to his former position. The district requested a new hearing before the PELRB, asserting the arbitration decision was improper and inconsistent with the CBA. The PELRB held it had no authority to review the case.

The district appealed to the Supreme Court of New Hampshire, which **held the PELRB had jurisdiction over an arbitration award that was consistent with the terms of the governing CBA. This authority may be exercised only where a party claims the award reflects a mistake in the law, or where there is a mistaken application of facts that precludes fair consideration of the issues.** The court rejected the district's claim that the PELRB was obligated to consider an appeal from the arbitration award. Once arbitration was concluded, the PELRB lacked authority to review the award unless there was a filing of a subsequent unfair labor practice complaint by the association alleging district failure to implement the award. As there had been no such filing, the arbitration award was final. *Appeal of Laconia School Dist.*, 840 A.2d 800 (N.H. 2004).

◆   A Wisconsin school district notified its teachers association it would disavow a past practice of guaranteeing teacher prep time, based on budgetary concerns. The parties did not agree on a new collective bargaining agreement (CBA), and the district submitted a salary offer intended to satisfy state law requirements as a "qualified economic offer" (QEO). State law required districts to submit valid QEOs providing statutorily required wage and fringe benefit increases prior to the expiration of a CBA. It also required deadlocked parties to initiate interest arbitration over wages, hours and conditions of employment. The district petitioned the Wisconsin Employment Relations Commission (WERC) for an order that its offer qualified as a QEO and a declaration that prep time was not a fringe benefit or economic issue that could proceed to interest arbitration. The WERC concluded the district proposal was a QEO and declared that while the district had no duty to bargain over the prep time issue, it was required to bargain over the impact proposal. It held that as the district's wage offer was a valid QEO and the association's impact proposal was an economic issue, the association could not seek inclusion of the proposal through interest arbitration. A state circuit court affirmed the WERC decision.

The Wisconsin Supreme Court noted the WERC decision had deemed prep time "primarily related to" educational policy, rather than to wages, hours and conditions of employment. As the WERC had consistently held for over 20 years that preparation time is a permissive subject of bargaining, its decision was entitled to great deference. The WERC had found the educational policy implications of allocating teacher workdays outweighed the impact on teacher hours and conditions of employment. Because the WERC properly balanced the impact of teacher prep time on educational policy, the court affirmed the ruling on teacher prep time. It affirmed the WERC's decision that the district had submitted a valid QEO and that the association could not proceed to interest arbitration to seek additional compensation for increased teacher workloads. **Because teacher prep time was a permissive subject of bargaining and not a fringe benefit, the district was not required to continue guaranteeing prep time in order to submit a valid QEO.** The court upheld the WERC's decision that the association could not proceed to interest arbitration over its impact proposal due to the presence of a valid QEO. *Dodgeland Educ. Ass'n v. Wisconsin Employment Relations Comm'n*, 639 N.W.2d 733 (Wis. 2002).

◆   A Pennsylvania school district laid off tenured professional employees after experiencing a decrease in student enrollment. However, student disciplinary problems increased and the district created new professional positions. It did not employ any of the former employees, and they sued the district in a state common pleas court seeking a declaratory ruling that they were qualified for the new positions by virtue of their state law seniority rights. The court held the collective bargaining agreement did not specifically address the rehiring of laid-off employees and rejected the employees' claim to arbitration. The laid-off employees were qualified for the positions and were entitled to them because of their seniority. The replacement employees appealed to the Pennsylvania Commonwealth Court, which found that one of the new positions did not require certification. As a result, the district had no duty to recall a laid-off employee to fill it. The court reversed the decision with regard to that position, but otherwise affirmed the decision. The replacement employees appealed.

The Supreme Court of Pennsylvania held **a strong public policy favors the arbitration of labor disputes. State law required the arbitration of disputes "arising out of the interpretation of the provisions of a collective bargaining agreement."** The agreement had a grievance procedure designed to resolve problems "at the lowest possible level," with levels of resolution leading to arbitration. The agreement defined "grievance" broadly to cover any complaint between a teacher and the school district. **The determination of whether a matter was properly within the scope of arbitration was for an arbitrator to determine, not the court system. The common pleas court had no jurisdiction** to proceed in the matter, and the supreme court reversed its order. *Davis v. Chester Upland School Dist.*, 786 A.2d 186 (Pa. 2001).

B. Procedures

◆   A Virginia superintendent suspended a principal without pay and advised him of his right to a hearing before the school board. The principal instead sought a hearing before a fact-finding panel under a state board grievance procedure, seeking immediate reinstatement. The superintendent advised the principal he would adjust the grievance and recommended reassigning the principal. He later informed the principal that suspension with pay was not grievable. The school board upheld the decision and demoted the principal to a teaching position, with a reduction in pay. He appealed to a Virginia circuit court, arguing the suspension presented a grievable issue under the local board's grievance procedure. The court rejected the board's argument to dismiss the action as moot. The principal was not an employee covered by the local grievance procedure. The court held the principal's suspension was grievable under the state board procedure and had to be timely resolved. The board appealed to the state supreme court, which held the case was not moot.

While the principal had been reinstated, reassigned and had eventually resigned, the action adversely affected his personal reputation and he might still obtain relief by continuing the case. The state code established two separate grievance procedures, one prescribed by the state board of education under Va. Code § 22.1-308 and the other imposed on local boards by Section 22.1-79(6). Section 22.1-79(6) required local boards without policies adopted before January 1, 1991 to establish grievance procedures for dismissal, suspension or other discipline. **The policies were to be consistent with the state board's procedures, but they did not create rights to a hearing before a fact-finding panel.** The school board in this case had adopted both procedures. Its Section 22.1-79(6) procedure was for supervisory and classified employees, and it defined principals as "supervisory employees." **The board's procedure provided the dismissal or probation of a supervisory employee was governed by Section 22.1-308. The trial court incorrectly held the principal was entitled to Section 22.1-79(6) procedures.** His recourse was the very process he had rejected when the superintendent offered him a hearing. As the trial court had erroneously held the principal presented a grievable issue, the supreme court reversed the judgment. *Tazewell County School Board v. Brown*, 591 S.E.2d 671 (Va. 2004).

◆ **The Oregon Court of Appeals held the Portland Public Schools (PPS) could privatize its custodial force**, resolving two conflicting agency decisions. The Employment Relations Board (ERB) upheld a PPS proposal to contract out custodial work due to a budget crisis. The ERB found the proposal was not a prohibited subject of bargaining. The Custodians Civil Service Board then held the PPS violated a state civil service law. The appeals court held the ERB decision precluded the Civil Service Board from later ruling on the same question. *Scherzinger v. Portland Custodians Civil Service Board*, 196 Or.App. 384, 103 P.3d 1122 (Or. Ct. App. 2004).

◆ A male custodian claimed his supervisor let female custodians do less work and showed partiality toward them. He also asserted his supervisor retaliated against him by assigning him more work. The custodian sued the district in an Alaska trial court, which noted the collective bargaining agreement (CBA) prohibited sex discrimination and provided a four-step grievance procedure for employee complaints. Since the custodian did not use the grievance procedures and they were his exclusive contractual remedy, the district was entitled to judgment. On appeal, the state supreme court held the CBA itself prohibited discrimination on the basis of sex. **The agreement complied with the state Public Employee Relations Act, which requires that all labor agreements include grievance procedures with binding arbitration as the final step.**

Collective bargaining agreement grievance procedures are mandatory, and they preclude judicial remedies that would otherwise be available to employees. The state legislature's decision to require the inclusion of grievance procedures in every CBA recognized these procedures were the preferred method for resolving labor disputes. **Arbitrators had complete authority to provide any appropriate remedy under a CBA.** The court affirmed the judgment. *Barnica v. Kenai Peninsula Borough School Dist.*, 46 P.3d 974 (Alaska 2002).

C. Standard of Review

A court may vacate an arbitration award on the basis of fraud, corruption or procedural irregularities, or if the arbitrator exceeds his or her powers. Arbitration awards may be vacated if they do not draw their essence from a collective bargaining agreement, are not based on a plausible interpretation of the agreement, disregard a contract provision or reach an irrational result.

◆ A New York school district filed formal charges against a teacher who engaged in a relationship with a 16-year-old student over the course of her senior year of high school. A hearing officer determined they had been in "virtually constant telephone contact" during the year. The student visited him in his office and they spent time in private. The hearing officer found the teacher had tried to conceal the relationship from the student's family. School administrators informed the family of the relationship and told him to stay away from the student. The teacher continued to carry on the relationship in private and left school early without permission to take her to his house. An investigator observed the two were together for six hours. Despite this evidence, the hearing officer declined to find they had a romantic relationship. The hearing officer found the teacher guilty of insubordination, neglect of duty and conduct unbecoming a teacher. He also showed no remorse for his conduct and was insensitive to the impact of the relationship on the student and his family.

The hearing officer imposed a one-year, unpaid suspension on the teacher. The school district appealed, and a state supreme court vacated the arbitration award, holding the penalty was "shockingly lenient." The teacher appealed to the New York Supreme Court, Appellate Division, Third Department. **The court held state law limited a court's authority to vacate an arbitration award to "acts in excess of the arbitrator's power" and other grounds set forth in state law. The penalty imposed in this case was within statutory limits. However, the award violated a strong public policy to protect children from the harmful conduct of adults, particularly in an educational setting.** This public policy prohibited an award that would not adequately protect students from a teacher in the future. The court held that vacating the award on public policy grounds was further justified by the teacher's insubordination, refusal to admit wrong and lack of remorse. As the award failed to adequately protect students from him, the court agreed it should be vacated. *Matter of Arbitration Between Binghamton City School Dist. and Peacock*, 33 A.D.3d 1074, 823 N.Y.S.2d 231 (N.Y. App. Div. 2006).

◆ A New Hampshire school district issued several teachers renewal letters requiring them to prepare improvement plans before the end of the 2003-04 school year. The teachers' association claimed the letters were a unilateral change to procedures in the collective bargaining agreement concerning teacher evaluation and performance reviews. The agreement specified that tenured teachers would be observed at least once a year and evaluated in writing. The association filed a complaint with the New Hampshire Public Employee Labor Relations Board (PELRB). The PELRB found the district committed an unfair labor practice by using new procedures to communicate teacher deficiencies.

The district appealed to the Supreme Court of New Hampshire, where it argued its action was consistent with the collective bargaining agreement, past district policies and state law. It also stated the letters were within its authority as a managerial prerogative. The court found collective bargaining agreement procedures for evaluating teachers and communicating deficiencies were clear. **When the district issued renewal letters with reservations and required improvement plans, it did not follow the procedures of the agreement. The court held the use of renewal letters with reservations and requirements for teacher improvement plans violated the collective bargaining agreement.** The district had no reserved right to implement different procedures for addressing teacher performance and evaluation than those specified in the agreement. The letters were not an exercise of "managerial policy" that would allow the district to unilaterally implement such procedures. State law did not except teacher evaluation and performance review procedures as managerial policies. The court upheld the PELRB's decision. *Appeal of White Mountain Regional School Dist.*, 908 A.2d 790 (N.H. 2006).

◆ The Court of Appeals of Ohio dismissed an employee challenge to a school district protocol requiring staff members to administer an anti-seizure drug called Diastat to a student. The court noted the parents had removed the student from district schools. It refused to consider whether a non-nurse in a public school setting may administer medication and assess the medical condition of a student having seizures, or any other questions on appeal. **The case was moot because no association member was now required to administer Diastat to the student.** The court found the case did not raise issues of great public or general interest. Only six of 6,000 students in district schools were identified as potential Diastat recipients. The court dismissed the appeal. *Lancaster School Dist. Support Ass'n, OEA/NEA v. Board of Educ., Lancaster City School Dist.*, No. 06AP-305, 2006 WL 3008475, 2006 Ohio 5520 (Ohio Ct. App. 2006).

◆ A Michigan janitor was charged with making a bomb threat. His school board did not discharge him for the threat, but it later voted to discharge him for falsifying his employment application, threatening students, insubordination and retaining used tampons he collected on school grounds. The janitor filed a grievance, and an arbitrator reinstated him with back wages and benefits, conditioning his return on a psychological evaluation. The board appealed to a Michigan trial court. In the meantime, the evaluation was completed and the evaluator found the janitor could return to work. A neutral psychiatric expert stated the janitor had collected the tampons for one month to prove to his supervisor that they were being found throughout the school. The court held the arbitrator properly exercised his powers and found no public policy violation.

The Michigan Court of Appeals rejected the district's assertion that the janitor was a dangerous employee whose collection of used tampons was "ghoulish fetishism." The board abandoned its attempt to discharge him for the bomb threat, and the record indicated no sexual reason for collecting used tampons. **The arbitration award drew its essence from the collective bargaining agreement, and the arbitrator did not exceed his authority.** The district failed to inquire about several glaring aspects of the janitor's employment application, including a 14-year gap in his employment and a brief military service record of eight months. The court held **when a collective bargaining agreement does not specify what acts constitute just cause for discharge, the arbitrator has authority to determine the appropriate remedy or discipline**. The arbitrator had properly exercised his authority, as the janitor was not found to have endangered students or engaged in other misconduct. The award could not be set aside as a violation of any public policy, and the court affirmed the judgment. *Taylor Board of Educ. v. SEIU, Local 26M*, No. 241872, 2003 WL 356432 (Mich. Ct. App. 2003). The state supreme court denied the school board's request for review in a brief memorandum. *Taylor Board of Educ. v. SEIU, Local 26M*, 673 N.W.2d 102 (Mich. 2004).

◆ A Massachusetts teacher admitted yelling at students during his 25th year as a teacher. Later that same school year, he became involved in three separate incidents in which he yelled at students and then pushed, grabbed or poked them. In one case, the teacher slammed a student into a locker. In another, he shoved a student across a desk. The student was so upset that he did not return to the class for the rest of the year. The district discharged the teacher, and he sought arbitration. An arbitrator found the teacher had not used corporal punishment, but was only acting "as a means of getting the students' attention."

On appeal, the Massachusetts Appeals Court considered whether the award should be vacated for violating a state public policy against the unjustified use of force on children. It held that **arbitration awards can only be vacated where there is fraud, corruption or procedural irregularity, or if an arbitrator exceeds his or her powers**. Massachusetts has a public policy to protect children reflected in laws prohibiting the physical and psychological abuse of children and the use of corporal punishment. State law defined "assault and battery" as any intentional and unjustified use of force on another person, "however slight." As the public policy stated in these laws was well defined and dominant, and related directly to the teacher's employment, the arbitration award could not stand. **The award exceeded the arbitrator's powers because the teacher presented a special risk of injury to children.** The court vacated the arbitration award. The Supreme Judicial Court of Massachusetts affirmed the decision. *School Dist. of Beverly v. Geller*, 435 Mass. 223 (Mass. 2001).

◆ A Rhode Island school nurse filed a grievance against her school committee after the principal ordered her to administer medication to a special education student. Her collective bargaining association argued that any increase in her workload was not covered by the collective bargaining agreement (CBA) and that the non-emergency medication of special education students was not permitted. According to the association, the matter had to be negotiated by the parties, and the student's collaborative program was not a party to the CBA.

An arbitrator held that a school administrator could not order the nurse to dispense medication to a student who was not a member of the regular student body. A state superior court confirmed the arbitrator's decision, and the school committee appealed. The Rhode Island Supreme Court held the **courts may vacate arbitration awards that do not draw their essence from an agreement, are not based on a plausible interpretation of a contract, manifestly disregard a contractual provision or reach an irrational result**. The district had a non-delegable managerial duty to provide health services to students attending the collaborative education program. **The arbitrator was powerless to address the issue because a ruling against the district would cause a violation of state law.** The district was bound by state law to operate a school health program and to provide special education programs. These duties were non-delegable and could not be bargained away in a CBA. There was no contract provision limiting the provision of services to students within the exclusive control of the district. As the arbitration award contradicted the CBA, the court vacated and remanded the award. *Woonsocket Teachers' Guild, Local 951, AFT v. Woonsocket School Committee*, 770 A.2d 834 (R.I. 2001).

D. Association Duties and Rights

◆ A Pennsylvania school district suspended and then fired a teacher due to complaints about his teaching style and conduct. An arbitrator issued an award reinstating the teacher, but denying his claim for back wages and benefits because his conduct warranted strong discipline. The association declined the teacher's request to appeal, and he petitioned a state court for review. The court granted the district's motion to quash the petition, finding an employee appeal was allowed by Pennsylvania law but would conflict with relevant parts of the collective bargaining agreement (CBA). The court held the CBA vested the association with the exclusive right to pursue arbitration. On appeal, the Commonwealth Court held the agreement did not vest the association with exclusive rights to pursue arbitration. However, the teacher was precluded from initiating an appeal because he was not a party to the arbitration proceeding.

The Pennsylvania Supreme Court accepted the teacher's appeal and observed that state law favored arbitration to resolve labor disputes. The state Public Employee Relations Act permits the resolution of collective bargaining disputes through the collective bargaining process, and many agreements establish a substantial degree of union control over the pursuit of individual grievances. While unions typically control the dispute resolution procedure established by a CBA, the teacher asserted the agreement in this case was unusual because it authorized employees to initiate grievances in their own right and to appeal from adverse awards. **The court agreed with the teacher, noting that the CBA referred to the employee, not the association, as the entity that initiated each step of the grievance procedure, including referral to arbitration.** The court rejected the district's argument that the teacher waived any right to bring his own appeal by accepting the association's representation. The court reversed and remanded the decision. *Kozura v. Tulpehocken Area School Dist.*, 791 A.2d 1169 (Pa. 2002).

IV. STRIKES

The purpose of state legislation to prohibit or limit strikes by public employees is to protect the public and not to circumvent meaningful collective bargaining. Courts have upheld punitive actions taken against unlawfully striking teachers and their unions.

◆ Wisconsin education law prohibited strikes by teachers, and gave school boards sole authority over hiring and firing decisions. Boards were required to negotiate the terms and conditions of employment with collective bargaining representatives. When contract negotiations between teachers and a local school board became protracted, the teachers called a strike. The board attempted to end the strike, noting it was in direct violation of state law. When the teachers refused to return to work, the board held disciplinary hearings and fired the striking teachers. The teachers appealed to the Wisconsin courts, arguing the board was not an impartial decision-maker and the discharges had violated their due process rights. The Wisconsin Supreme Court held due process required an impartial decision-maker. The board itself was not sufficiently impartial to make the decision to discharge the teachers.

The board appealed to the U.S. Supreme Court. The Court held **there was no evidence that the board could not make an impartial decision in determining to discharge the teachers**. The mere fact that the board was involved in negotiations with the teachers did not support a claim of bias. The board was the only body vested with statutory authority to employ and dismiss teachers and participation in negotiations with the teachers was required by law. This involvement prior to the decision to discharge the teachers was not a sufficient showing of bias to disqualify the board as a decision-maker under the Due Process Clause. *Hortonville Joint School Dist. No. 1 v. Hortonville Educ. Ass'n*, 426 U.S. 482, 96 S.Ct. 2308, 49 L.Ed.2d 1 (1976).

◆   The collective bargaining agreement between an Ohio school board and the union representing its bus drivers expired without a new agreement. The board contracted with a private company for transportation services and abolished its driver and mechanic job classifications. Union members declared a strike, but within days most of them notified the superintendent of their intention to return to work under their continuing contract rights. The Ohio Court of Appeals denied the drivers' complaint for reinstatement, and the board contracted with the company. The company agreed to hire district drivers. The state supreme court reversed the decision, but on remand the appeals court held for the district. The drivers appealed to the Ohio Supreme Court again, which held that **by returning to work, the drivers assented to be governed by the contract.** The court remanded the case for the calculation of back pay awards for the drivers.

The district's treasurer noted that most of the drivers had by then retired. He sent the remaining drivers letters specifying that they were to be reinstated. The company sent the same employees letters requiring them to either resign from the district and continue working for the company, or resign. Eight of the remaining drivers resigned from the district, and the other four reported to work at the district's bus garage. The board assigned them to new positions for which their wages and daily work hours were reduced. The four drivers sought an order compelling the board to recognize their continuing contract rights. The appeals court held they were entitled to reinstatement, but not lost wages and benefits. The drivers made a third appeal to the state supreme court, which held the drivers were entitled to the relief they requested. **State law did not authorize the board to lay them off by abolishing their positions and hiring nonpublic employees.** The contracting out of the drivers' jobs was invalid. The board's attempt to coerce the drivers into choosing employment with the board or the company was contrary to the spirit of prior decisions. **The drivers were entitled to recognition as continuing contract employees of the board and could not be reclassified as general public employees.** The superintendent had no authority to modify a written contract, and the drivers were entitled to be reinstated. The court reversed the portion of the appeals court decision requiring the board merely to offer the drivers their positions, and it ordered the board to reinstate them with back pay. *State ex rel. Boggs v. Springfield Local School Dist. Board of Educ.*, 757 N.E.2d 339 (Ohio 2001).

◆   A Pennsylvania school district and the education association representing its teachers were unable to reach a new agreement upon the expiration of their collective bargaining agreement. After six months, the association called a two-day strike that ended with an agreement to extend the terms of the expired agreement. As the school year reached its end, the association called a second strike. The strike jeopardized the district's ability to provide 180 days of instruction per year, as required by the state public school code. The state secretary of education filed a complaint against the association in a Pennsylvania county court, seeking a preliminary order compelling a return to work because the district had provided only 163 days of instruction.

The court granted the request and ordered the association and school board to engage in court-monitored bargaining. The district and board appealed to the Commonwealth Court of Pennsylvania, which ruled that the trial court had no authority to order the parties to bargain. The secretary appealed to the Supreme Court of Pennsylvania. On appeal, the board and district argued that the state Public Employee Relations Act did not grant state courts the authority to order negotiations between parties to collective bargaining agreements. **The court ruled that the Public Employee Relations Act must be read in conjunction with the state public school code, which empowers the secretary of education to compel a return to work in order to provide at least 180 days of instruction annually.** Because the trial court had correctly construed the statutes together in ordering the parties to resume bargaining, its order was affirmed. *Carroll v. Ringgold Educ. Ass'n*, 680 A.2d 1137 (Pa. 1996).

◆ Indiana law prohibited public school teachers from striking. Unions representing South Bend public school teachers nonetheless elected to strike in February 1994. The local education agency sought temporary and permanent injunctions from an Indiana trial court to prohibit the strike. The court issued the order, but the teachers went out on strike. The education agency sought a trial court order for contempt against the teachers and then requested a contempt order against the unions for violating the temporary restraining order.

The court allowed the unions a one-day continuance and then conducted a hearing on a Sunday and found the unions in contempt for violating the temporary restraining order. It fined the local association $25,000 and the state teachers' association $175,000. The unions appealed to the Indiana Court of Appeals, which held **the trial court had properly exercised its jurisdiction to issue contempt citations**. There was no merit to the unions' argument that the local education agency had violated the state Open Door Law by failing to specify it would discuss filing a lawsuit against them in a notice concerning the executive session. There was also no merit to the argument of the unions that they had not received enough time to respond to the temporary order. The civil contempt orders granted the unions an opportunity to purge themselves of the contempt fines, and it satisfied the requirements for civil contempt. The court affirmed the orders for contempt. *National Educ. Ass'n – South Bend v. South Bend Community School Corp.*, 655 N.E.2d 516 (Ind. Ct. App. 1995).

CHAPTER ELEVEN

School Operations

		Page
I.	BUDGET AND FINANCE	431
	A. Educational Finance and Equal Opportunity	431
	B. Property Taxes and Other Local Funding Issues	440
	C. Federal Funding	442
	D. School Expenditures and State Appropriations	443
	E. Student Fees and Tuition	448
	1. Transportation Fees	448
	2. Tuition and Other Fees	449
	F. Private Contractors	452
	G. Insurance Cases	455
II.	DESEGREGATION	458
	A. Release from Federal Court Supervision	458
	B. Compliance with Desegregation Orders	461
	C. Liability Issues	463
	1. Government Liability	463
	2. Inter-District Remedies	465
	3. Budget Issues	466
III.	SCHOOL DISTRICT OPERATIONS	469
	A. School Closing and District Dissolution Issues	469
	B. Redistricting and Zoning	470
IV.	SCHOOL BOARDS	472
	A. Membership	472
	1. Appointments, Elections, Residency and Recall	472
	2. Misconduct, Conflict of Interest and Nepotism	475
	B. School Board Powers and Duties	477
	C. Open Meeting Laws	483

I. BUDGET AND FINANCE

A. Educational Finance and Equal Opportunity

Education is not a fundamental right under the U.S. Constitution. However, state constitutional education clauses require states to provide an "adequate," "sound basic" or "thorough and efficient" system of public schools.

The U.S. Supreme Court effectively eliminated educational financing claims based on the Equal Protection Clause of the U.S. Constitution by holding education is not a fundamental right in San Antonio School Dist. v. Rodriguez, *411 U.S. 1, 93 S.Ct. 1278, 36 L.Ed.2d 16 (1973). State courts continue to consider financial equity and education adequacy claims under state constitutions. Typical state court challenges to school financing systems involve differing tax bases that result in disparities among school district revenues.*

◆ **In 1995, the New York Court of Appeals held the state constitution requires the state to offer all children the opportunity of a sound basic education. This included basic literacy, calculating and verbal skills to allow children to "function productively as civic participants capable of voting and serving on a jury."** The state constitution required minimally adequate facilities, classrooms, desks, chairs, pencils and textbooks, and "minimally adequate teaching of reasonably up-to-date basic curricula such as reading, writing, mathematics, science and social studies by adequately trained staff." **In 2003, the court clarified that "opportunity of a sound basic education" meant "the opportunity for a meaningful high school education."** It held New York City students were not receiving an opportunity for a sound basic education due to the state's failure to comply with its duty. The court directed the state to determine the actual cost of a sound basic education in the city, reform the system of school funding and management, provide for a sound basic education, and ensure an accountability system for the reforms by July 30, 2004. A trial court adopted the recommendation of a panel of judicial referees for compliance that called for annual expenditures of $5.63 billion, phased in over four years, plus $9.179 billion in capital improvements over five years. These amounts reflected proposals by the group representing the students who filed the lawsuit. In 2004, the governor proposed spending $1.93 billion to close the gap in operating expenses for city schools with an additional $4.7 billion over five years. The legislature increased funding by only $300 million, and the state failed to meet the July 30, 2004 deadline.

The trial court confirmed the referees' report, but a state appellate division court vacated this decision and the case returned to the court of appeals in 2006. The court stated the trial court had erred by essentially recalculating the compliance question. **The job of the courts was not to calculate the cost of a sound basic education in New York City schools, but to review whether the state's proposal for calculating this cost was rational.** The state had found the cost of providing a sound basic education in city schools could be met with $1.93 billion in additional operating funds. The governor's proposal exceeded this constitutional minimum by adding $4.7 billion during the next five years. **The court held the judiciary must defer to policymaking by the political branches of government. Review of the other branches was "to protect rights, not to make policy."** As the governor's proposal was a reasonable estimate of the cost of a sound basic education in city schools, the court approved it. *Campaign for Fiscal Equity v. State of New York*, 8 N.Y.3d 14, 861 N.E.2d 50, 828 N.Y.S.2d 235 (N.Y. 2006).

◆ In 2002, the Supreme Court of Arkansas held the state's school funding effort was insufficient. The General Assembly responded with Act 57 and Act 108 of the Second Extraordinary Session of 2003. Act 57 described the General

Assembly's continuing duty to assess what constitutes an "adequate education." The court agreed to review the case in 2005 and appointed special masters to make factual findings. The masters filed a report, and a school district asked the supreme court to adopt it. The masters found no evidence that the General Assembly had attempted to comply with Act 57. No hearings were held to assess foundation funding for 2005-06, when the General Assembly froze the amount at the prior year's level and increased it by only $97 for 2006-07. No testimony indicated this was adequate. The masters found the state did not live up to its promise to make education the state's priority. The failure to increase foundation funding was difficult to defend in view of state educational needs.

The supreme court agreed with the masters that compliance with Act 57 was "the linchpin for achieving adequacy in public education." By failing to continually assess what constituted an adequate education by examining district expenditures, the General Assembly was "flying blind." The foundation funding question had been thwarted by legislative inaction. **Education needs were not funded first, as required by Act 108.** Foundation funding aid and categorical funding were set by what funds were available, not by what was needed. The court held facilities funding was inadequate. Only half of what was required to correct deficiencies presenting an immediate hazard had been appropriated. **The facilities needs of some school districts might never be met due to the wealth index formula. As the foundation aid was based in part on local revenues, some districts might receive less than the foundation funding amount per student. The court held the General Assembly made no effort to comply with Act 57 and did not comply with Act 108.** The court gave the state until December 1, 2006 to correct the constitutional deficiencies. *Lake View School Dist. No. 25 v. Huckabee*, No. 01-836, 2005 WL 3436660 (Ark. 2006).

A group of school districts claimed the legislature failed to take necessary action by the December 1, 2006 deadline. The supreme court deferred a decision, finding the parties had not provided enough information to the court to address the constitutional questions. *Lake View School Dist. No. 25 v. Huckabee*, No. 01-836, 2006 WL 3456468 (Ark. 2006).

◆ Educational adequacy and funding litigation reached the Supreme Court of New Hampshire in 1993, 1998, and 2002, when the court held the state had a duty of accountability in *Claremont School Dist. v. Governor*, 794 A.2d 744 (N.H. 2002). In 2005, the legislature mandated student opportunities to acquire skills in core subjects including reading, writing, science and math. Two school district administrative units and a nonprofit organization representing 19 other administrative units and towns initiated a new action against the state. The school districts claimed the 2005 legislation did not comply with prior supreme court decisions declaring the state's duty to provide a constitutionally adequate education. A state superior court held the state again failed in its duty to define a "constitutionally adequate education." It also did not determine the cost of a constitutionally adequate education or provide for accountability.

State officials appealed to the supreme court, claiming the definition of "adequacy" complied with similar definitions upheld by courts in West Virginia, Kentucky, Montana and Washington. The court disagreed. Legislation in those states had general definitions of adequate education, but also established a mechanism through which educational content was identified in fulfillment of constitutional duties. **The court stated "there is no way a citizen or a school district in this State can determine the distinct substantive content of a constitutionally adequate education. Consequently, its cost cannot be isolated. Such a system is also impervious to meaningful judicial review."** The legislature had to develop specific criteria for an adequate education. The law did not comply with the state's duty to define the content of a constitutionally adequate education in an understandable manner. The right to a constitutionally adequate education was meaningless without enforceable, reviewable standards. The state's financial obligations could not be shifted to local districts. The court retained jurisdiction over the core definitional issues of adequacy. It stayed activity on the trial court's findings that the legislature did not comply with cost, accountability and uniform tax requirements of state law. *Londonderry School Dist. SAU #12 v. State*, 907 A.2d 988 (N.H. 2006).

◆   An association of Idaho school districts, superintendents and students sued the state in 1990, asserting state funding levels and the funding method violated Article IX, Section One of the Idaho Constitution. The section requires the legislature to "establish and maintain a general, uniform and thorough system of public, free common schools." **In 1993, the Supreme Court of Idaho held the judicial branch had a constitutional duty to interpret the meaning of a "thorough system of public, free schools."** The state legislature responded by increasing appropriations and directing the state education board to develop new rules. The case returned to the supreme court in 1996 and again in 1998, when state board rules for facilities were found to meet constitutional thoroughness requirements. After a trial in 2001, the district court held the legislative system of school funding was insufficient under the state constitution. In 2005, the supreme court reviewed district court findings of myriad structural problems and fire hazards. The court rejected the state's attempts to "refocus this litigation into small, district-by-district battles" instead of addressing the larger issue of the legislature's constitutional duty toward public education in Idaho. The district court had compiled thousands of pages of testimony and exhibits. The overwhelming evidence documented serious facility and funding problems in the state's public education system.

The state itself documented facilities deficiencies in a 1993 assessment that concluded 57% of all Idaho school buildings had serious safety concerns. A 1999 report found the situation had further deteriorated. The "glaring gap" in the funding system was the lack of a mechanism to quickly deal with major, costly and potentially catastrophic conditions in low-population districts with low tax bases in economically depressed areas. The "list of safety concerns and difficulties in getting funds for repairs or replacements is distressingly long." **The funding system was inadequate to meet the state constitutional mandate for a thorough system of education in a safe environment.** While the legislature failed in its constitutional mandate, the court held an appropriate remedy was a task for the legislature, not the court. *Idaho Schools for Equal Educational Opportunity v. State of Idaho*, 129 P.3d 1199 (Idaho 2005).

◆ From 1989 through 2003, the Texas Supreme Court considered the state's educational financing system five times. The legislature amended state law several times to comply with court orders. In 2005, the supreme court reconsidered the school financing scheme. Forty-seven districts claimed state control of the levy, assessment and disbursement of revenue resulted in a statewide property tax. Other districts claimed funding for school operations and facilities was unconstitutional because children in property-poor districts did not have substantially equal access to revenue. The supreme court noted that over half the annual cost of public education in the state was funded by ad valorem taxes imposed by independent school districts on local property. **The legislature's decision to rely heavily on local property taxes did not in itself violate the Texas Constitution, but the disparity between districts in size and wealth made it difficult to achieve efficient education funding.** Some districts had to pay disproportionately high property taxes. School maintenance and operations were funded by a separate tax capped at $1.50 per $100 of valuation. Revenue disparities among districts were reduced by supplementing property-poor district tax revenue with state funds. This was done through the Foundation School Program and "recapture." The court found most Texas school districts were rated "academically acceptable" or higher. If a district was deemed adequate, it would be free to provide enhanced education opportunities.

The court held the school financing system did not violate the efficiency requirement of the constitution. However, the state control of local taxation for education amounted to an unconstitutional state property tax. The number of districts taxing at the maximum "maintenance and operations" rate had risen from 2% of districts to 48%, and 67% of districts were taxing at or above $1.45. The state controlled more than $1 billion in local tax revenues recaptured from 134 districts. Recapture had doubled in less than a decade, and the number of districts and the amount of revenue subject to recapture had almost tripled since 1994. **The court held the school districts had lost any meaningful discretion to tax below maximum rates and still provide students with an accredited education. Districts were inexorably forced by educational requirements and economic necessities to tax at the valuation cap. This violated the state constitutional prohibition on a state property tax.** As removing the cap would only increase the disparity between rich and poor districts, the court held the cap had to be raised or the system had to be changed by June 1, 2006. *Neeley v. West Orange-Cove Consolidated Independent School Dist.*, 176 S.W.3d 746 (Tex. 2005).

◆ The Massachusetts Legislature enacted the Education Reform Act (ERA) a few days after the Supreme Judicial Court declared the state educational funding system unconstitutional in *McDuffy v. Secretary of Executive Office of Educ.*, 415 Mass. 545 (Mass. 1993). The ERA dramatically increased assistance to public schools based on uniform criteria of need, and it established uniform performance and accountability standards for public school students, teachers, school administrators, schools and districts. A few years later, a group of students moved a judge of the Supreme Judicial Court to reopen *McDuffy*, asserting public education in property-poor districts did not show significant improvement since 1993. The judge assigned the case to a superior court judge to make findings and recommendations. The judge considered four "focus districts," Brockton, Lowell, Springfield and Winchendon, where students argued the state was still failing to fulfill its constitutional obligation. The judge held a trial and found significant failings persisted in the focus districts. She recommended the state education department study the actual cost of funding an adequate level of education for students in the districts, and an order requiring the state to implement certain funding and administrative changes.

The Chief Justice of the Supreme Judicial Court accepted the judge's findings but disagreed with her recommendations. The deficiencies in the focus districts were significant, but did not approach the "statewide abandonment of the constitutional duty" identified in *McDuffy*. **The Chief Justice found elected branches of state government had acted to "transform a dismal and fractured public school system into a unified system" yielding impressive results in improvement of overall student performance.** The ERA reduced spending gaps between property-poor and wealthy districts. State education funds were being allocated effectively. **The ERA had remedied the central problem of public school funding in the state by eliminating its principal dependence on local tax revenue that consigned students in property-poor districts to chronically underfunded schools.** The state now made up the difference between mandatory municipal funding obligations and state foundation budget amounts. The ERA established a centralized system of assessment and accountability, requiring graduating seniors to attain competency in core areas. The court had recently upheld a phase-in of testing under the ERA in *Student No. 9 v. Board of Educ.*, 440 Mass. 752 (Mass. 2004), summarized in Chapter 12, Section IV. The ERA helped underperforming students with extensive remedial opportunities and required the state to assist schools and districts that did not improve student performance. **The Chief Justice rejected the recommendation for more study and oversight, as the state was not presently violating the state constitution's education clause. The holding in *McDuffy* was reaffirmed, and the request for relief was denied.** *Hancock v. Commissioner of Educ.*, 443 Mass. 428, 822 N.E.2d 1134 (Mass. 2005).

◆   In 1997, the Supreme Court of Vermont held the state was denying students equal educational opportunities. The legislature responded with Act 60, also known as the Equal Educational Opportunity Act of 1997. A group of students asserted that nondiscretionary expenditures on special education, transportation and facilities resulted in less funding for instruction and curriculum. They claimed their high school was in poor condition and offered such a limited curriculum that many students had taken all course offerings and had to take gym classes to fill their senior year schedules. The taxpayers claimed Act 60 required them to pay disproportionately high state and local education taxes when compared to taxpayers in other Vermont towns. The students and taxpayers sued the state in a Vermont trial court for equal protection violations.

The trial court refused to consider the case, citing the need for "judicial self-restraint, and finding recent legislation remedied the claims. It interpreted the 1997 supreme court decision as requiring the legislature to resolve the state's education funding deficiencies. The taxpayers and students appealed to the state supreme court, which held the trial court had improperly relied on the notion of judicial restraint in dismissing the case. Deciding cases that involved constitutional rights did not undermine the legislative process. The trial court had abdicated its duty to uphold the Vermont Constitution. **The court found the allegations of the taxpayers and students sufficient to proceed with the case. As they alleged recent legislation caused the same fundamental violations as Act 60, the judgment was reversed and the case was remanded for further proceedings.** *Brigham v. State*, 889 A.2d 715, 2005 VT 105 (Vt. 2005).

◆ **The Supreme Court of New Jersey approved the state education commissioner's method of funding preschool programs through supplemental funding, even though the "scheme is both cumbersome and time-consuming."** The supreme court considered state funding equity in a series of decisions from the late 1980s forward known as the "*Abbott* litigation." The court ordered the state to increase funding for a group of poor urban districts with special needs, now called "*Abbott* districts." Among other things, the court's 1998 decision required the *Abbott* districts to provide half-day preschool programs for three and four-year-olds and directed the commissioner to "ensure that such programs are adequately funded. *Abbott by Abbott v. Burke*, 153 N.J. 480, 710 A.2d 450 (N.J. 1998). The case returned to the court several times during the next few years, with the districts claiming the commissioner had reneged on a promise to provide quality preschool education. **In 2002, the court held the education department must make funding decisions based on an assessment of actual need.** *Abbott v. Burke*, 790 A.2d 842 (N.J. 2002).

In response to a budget crisis, the court relaxed remedies it had previously ordered. The state legislature established a Preschool Expansion Aid (PSEA) fund for preschool expansion, which came in addition to Early Childhood Program Aid (ECPA). Four *Abbott* districts claimed large shortfalls for 2003-2004 due to the difference between state funding for preschool and their approved budgets for preschool plans. The districts appealed in separate actions. The administrative law judges in each case held the education department had to arrange for full state funding of the preschool programs for the fiscal year. The state education commissioner rejected these decisions, finding the state was not required to fund *Abbott* preschool programs in their entirety, without regard to other funds in a district budget. The education department could ask the districts to reallocate funds designated for other approved district programs. The state appellate division agreed with the commissioner. The districts appealed to the supreme court, asserting the commissioner's view undermined legislative intent to provide full funding for preschool programs and prior supreme court decisions.

The court stated whole school reform had been the core constitutional remedy of its *Abbott* decisions. Preschool education was part of that remedy. The commissioner was entitled to determine, before seeking new appropriations, if existing school budget funds were sufficient to meet requests for supplemental programs. The court found the commissioner had expressly accepted responsibility to ensure sufficient funds were available to fully fund preschool programs, and to ensure any gap remaining after the receipt of state formula aid would be addressed by the state. **The commissioner was not required to provide full funding for preschool programs. However, he had**

to address any budget shortfalls during the school year, unless he could demonstrate that district funds not needed for other programs were available. The court found it unimportant whether funding for the districts was drawn from formula aid, local levies or savings from efficiency. It affirmed the commissioner's decision. *Board of Educ. of City of Millville v. New Jersey Dep't of Educ.*, 183 N.J. 264, 872 A.2d 1052 (N.J. 2005).

◆ The Montana Legislature created the state's current educational funding system in 1993. House Bill (H.B.) 667 addressed a 1989 Montana Supreme Court decision concluding the spending disparities among the state's school districts denied students equal educational opportunity under Article X, Section 1(1) of the state constitution. H.B. 667 addressed inequities by relying on a regression analysis to address the financial disparities among districts. The bill created a general fund with built-in maximum and minimum amounts computed by a statutory formula. The general fund included a basic entitlement lump sum from the state, an amount for average number of students, local funds and special education funds. A coalition of schools, school districts, parents and educational associations filed a state court action against the state, alleging H.B. 667 violated two provisions of the state constitution. The coalition stated most districts were at or over their maximum budgets. Some districts said they could not provide a quality education unless they could spend more than their general fund maximum. After a trial, the court found serious problems with the current system's funding and "the educational product the schools are delivering." It held the system violated the Public Schools and Indian Education Clauses of the Montana Constitution, but did not violate the Equal Protection Clause.

The state appealed to the Supreme Court of Montana, which found the Legislature had not determined the meaning of the term "quality" in acting on its duty to provide a basic system of free quality public education. The Legislature could best decide the meaning of the term. The court found the legislature had not undertaken a study of what the Public Schools Clause required when it enacted H.B. 667. The spending formula it created was not based on teacher pay, accreditation standards, fixed costs or special education costs. Increases in allowable spending were not tied to increased costs of factors such as accreditation standards or content and performance standards. The Legislature had used dated information when it passed H.B. 667. It did not study disparities in funding between high schools and elementary schools. **The Legislature did not create a school funding system with quality in mind. Unless school funding related to academic standards, teacher pay, fixed costs, special education costs and performance standards, it was "not related to the cornerstones of a quality education." The court held the current system was constitutionally deficient**, based on evidence of budgeting at or near the maximum budget authority, growing accreditation problems, the cutting of programs, teacher flight to other states, deterioration of buildings and increased competition between special and general education programs for general fund dollars. The court upheld the district court decision on the Public Schools Clause issue. *Columbia Falls Elementary School Dist. No. 6 v. State of Montana*, 326 Mont. 304, 109 P.3d 257 (Mont. 2005).

◆ The North Carolina Supreme Court held students had a fundamental right to an opportunity for a sound basic education in *Leandro v. State*, 346 N.C. 336, 488 S.E.2d 249 (N.C. 1997). The court remanded the case to the Superior Court of Wake County. The parties agreed Hoke County would be the representative district. At trial, evidence indicated many Hoke County students were not at grade level in core academic areas. Student test scores were from 11.7 to 15.1% lower than statewide averages. Only 41% of county high school freshmen graduated. Employers found graduates of the system lacked even basic reading and math skills. The court held the state had failed in its constitutional duty to provide Hoke County students the opportunity to receive a sound basic education. State officials appealed to the supreme court, which recited the *Leandro* **definition of a "sound basic education" as one providing sufficient knowledge of fundamental math and science to enable students to function in a complex, rapidly changing society; sufficient knowledge of geography, history, and economic/political systems to make informed choices; and sufficient academic and vocational skills to enable students to succeed in post-secondary or vocational training and to compete on an equal basis in formal education or gainful employment**. The court found the state had violated *Leandro* standards based on Hoke County standardized test scores, graduation rates, employment potential and other post-secondary outcomes, deficiencies in academic offerings and the administration of schools.

The trial court had properly found **students must be performing at least at grade level to obtain a sound basic education**. Hoke County students consistently underperformed in each of the identified areas. Their **poor scores on statewide testing, high dropout rates, need for remedial help, and inability to compete in job markets and college ranks showed failure to receive an opportunity for a sound basic education**. The state was not allocating available resources to provide at-risk students in Hoke County with an equal opportunity to obtain a sound basic education. The court held the state was accountable for the failings of local school boards. While the state's overall funding and allocation of resources was adequate, the method of funding individual school districts did not comply with *Leandro*. The court affirmed the remedial order of the trial court, which informed the state what was wrong with Hoke County schools and directed it to assess educational priorities and correct the deficiencies so students could have the opportunity for a sound basic education. The court reversed the part of the trial court order requiring the provision of pre-kindergarten services to certain students as premature. *Hoke County Board of Educ. v. State of North Carolina*, 599 S.E.2d 365 (N.C. 2004).

◆ In 1988, a group of rural Tennessee school districts sued the state, alleging their students were denied educational opportunities. The Tennessee Supreme Court struck down the state's public education funding system in 1993, ruling the Tennessee Constitution required the state to maintain and support a public school system affording substantially equal opportunities to all students. The legislature enacted the Basic Education Program (BEP), equalizing state funding among districts. In 1995, the supreme court conditionally approved the BEP formula, which was based on 43 components necessary for a basic education. However, the court held the omission of a requirement for equalizing teacher salaries was a significant defect in the BEP. The legislature responded by enacting a salary equity plan to equalize teacher salaries in districts where average salaries were below $28,094 as of 1993, but it excluded salaries as a component of the BEP.

After a state trial court found the state met its constitutional obligation, the supreme court reviewed the case and noted the cost of hiring teachers was "the most important component of any education plan and a major part of every education budget." **The salary equity plan did not comply with the state's constitutional obligation to formulate and maintain a public education system affording substantially equal opportunity to all students.** The plan lacked any mechanism for cost determination or annual review of teacher salaries, and the exclusion of teacher salaries from the BEP equalization formula substantially impaired the objectives of equalization. There was no rational basis for leaving teacher salaries out of the BEP formula. Teacher cost was a necessary component of the success of Tennessee schools, and salary was a significant factor in any teacher's choice of where to work. Disparities in teacher salaries that existed in 1995 were still present, and rural districts continued to suffer from constitutional inequities present when the suit began in 1988. The court reversed and remanded the case for further proceedings. *Tennessee Small School Systems v. McWherter*, 91 S.W.3d 232 (Tenn. 2002).

B. Property Taxes and Other Local Funding Issues

◆   The Cobb County (Georgia) School Board improperly bought laptop computers for its middle and high school students with proceeds from a special purpose local option sales tax (SPLOST) that had been authorized for a different purpose. The board resolved to impose the tax for educational purposes on certain capital outlay projects such as technology and information systems hardware and software, and technology infrastructure. The ballot stated the measure was being imposed for "new schools, land, additions, renovations, equipment, and technology systems." A notebook issued by the board detailed eight curriculum/technology initiatives. One of these was to replace 30,563 obsolete workstations that would affect students and staff in all academic areas. The measure passed, but the board used $59 million of the $75 million technology portion of the tax proceeds for the purchase of a laptop computer for each middle and high school student in the district. A taxpayer sued the board in a state court, arguing the laptop purchase was an abuse of discretion.

The case reached the Supreme Court of Georgia, which noted the laptops were intended only for the district's middle and high school students. **State law limited the use of SPLOST proceeds for the exclusive purpose or purposes specified in the resolution or ordinance calling for the imposition of the measure.** In this case, the board resolution authorizing the SPLOST stated the funds would be used on designated capital outlay projects, such as "system-wide technology improvements." The resolution further described this as the acquisition and installation of instructional technology, information systems hardware and software and infrastructure at all schools and selected facilities. The board could not use SPLOST proceeds for a purpose entirely different from its reports. The board was bound by the specifically delineated projects in the notebook. The evidence authorized the trial court's finding that the school board did not comply with its legal duty by seeking to "re-budget" the original technology initiative and substituting the laptop initiative. As the board had abused its discretion, the court affirmed the judgment for the taxpayer. *Johnstone v. Thompson*, 631 S.E.2d 650 (Ga. 2006).

◆   A New York school board's proposed budget eliminated 18 positions and $786,000 in spending, but district voters twice voted it down. Even with the cuts, the proposals would have increased district spending by $1.1 million and increased district property taxes by 12.68%. The district adopted a contingency or "austerity" budget nearly $500,000 less than the one voters had rejected. About $350,000 was saved by eliminating all funding for field trips, interscholastic sports and extracurricular activities. The contingency budget still increased district spending by over $600,000 from the prior year, due to higher costs of employee health insurance premiums and retirement system contributions, special education costs and debt servicing. A taxpayer group filed an action in a state trial court, claiming Education Law Section 2023 required the funding of field trips, athletics and other extracurricular activities. The court found the board properly exercised discretion to eliminate field trips from the budget. However, the elimination of athletics and extracurricular activities was an abuse of discretion, and the court ordered the board to make a pro rata reduction of other budget items. The board appealed.

The New York Supreme Court, Appellate Division, noted many of the school district's budgeted expenses were imposed by law, and cost increases for others were outside the board's control. **The court held Section 2023 did not require school boards to fund interscholastic athletics, field trips and other extracurricular activities as part of a contingency budget.** The trial court's interpretation of the law was at odds with the discretion historically allowed to school boards in determining district budgetary priorities. The court reviewed the legislative history of Section 2023 and found no requirement for a board to fund every category of "ordinary contingent expenses" at the level proposed to voters or at any other particular level. Section 2023 did not show an intent to deprive a school board of its discretion to determine whether to fund (and at what level) an ordinary contingent expense. The ordinary contingent expenses categories created by state law were discretionary, not mandatory. To prohibit boards from eliminating categories of ordinary contingent expenses would create irreconcilable statutory obligations. The court held that prohibiting the district from eliminating the items it selected would force it to compromise its educational mission or violate the legal limit on contingency budget spending. **There was no requirement for a board of education to fund interscholastic athletics, field trips and other extracurricular activities as part of a budget submitted to voters of a district.** As the taxpayers' position would nullify actions by the voters and the board, the court reversed the judgment. *Polmanteer v. Bobo*, 794 N.Y.S.2d 171 (N.Y. App. Div. 2005).

◆   The New Jersey education department approved the Passaic School Board's early childhood budget of over $18 million for 2002-03 based on a projected enrollment of 1,917. A mid-year audit revealed actual enrollment of 1,038, and the department reduced state Preschool Expansion Aid (PSEA) using only a per-pupil calculation. Near the end of the school year, the board revised its preschool program plan. However, it required over $1.1 million for preschool demands for the rest of the school year. The board challenged the exclusive reliance on a per-pupil methodology in adjusting its PSEA award. The case reached the state supreme court, which considered it with *Board of Educ. of City of Millville v. New Jersey Dep't of Educ.*, summarized in Section I.A, above. In *Millville,* the court held the commissioner could require the board to reallocate undesignated general funds to cover preschool budget shortfalls.

The board argued the commissioner could not adjust its PSEA award solely on a per-pupil methodology. The court disagreed, stating a per-pupil amount for increases or decreases in the preschool budget over the course of a school year was fair and based on projected cost. The commissioner had reduced the board's funding near the end of a school year. **The board was entitled to a meaningful opportunity to present data on fixed costs that could not be reduced when adjusting for lower preschool enrollment. This would require the commissioner to consider the board's "actual need."** *Board of Educ. of City of Passaic v. New Jersey Dep't of Educ.*, 183 N.J. 281, 872 A.2d 1062 (N.J. 2005).

C. Federal Funding

◆   **The U.S. Supreme Court has held the Secretary of Education has the authority to demand a refund of misused funds granted to states under Title I of the Elementary and Secondary Education Act of 1965.** Title I provides funding for local educational agencies to prepare economically underprivileged children for school. Recipient states must provide assurances to the secretary that local educational agencies will spend the funds only on qualifying programs. After federal auditors determined the states of New Jersey and Pennsylvania had misapplied funds, the secretary ordered them to refund the amount of misapplied funds. Both states appealed to the U.S. Supreme Court, arguing the secretary exceeded his statutory authority in ordering the refunds. **The Supreme Court held Title I, as originally enacted, gave the federal government a right to demand repayment once liability was established.** The 1978 amendments to Title I were designed merely to clarify the secretary's legal authority and responsibility to audit recipient state programs and to specify the procedures to be used in the collection of any debts. *Bell v. New Jersey*, 461 U.S. 773, 103 S.Ct. 2187, 76 L.Ed.2d 312 (1983).

The Supreme Court also held that the 1978 amendments' new, relaxed standards concerning local schools' eligibility to receive Title I funds could not be applied retroactively. *Bennett v. New Jersey*, 470 U.S. 632, 105 S.Ct. 1555, 84 L.Ed.2d 572 (1985). In a companion case, the Court held that the state of Kentucky's lack of bad faith was irrelevant in assessing its liability to repay misused Title I funds. *Bennett v. Kentucky Dep't of Educ.*, 470 U.S. 656, 105 S.Ct. 1544, 84 L.Ed.2d 590 (1985).

◆   The Federal Impact Act Program provides funding to school districts whose financial conditions are adversely affected by a federal presence. States may not offset Federal Impact Aid by reducing aid to school districts, but may reduce funding to equalize per-pupil expenditures among districts. The Act instructed the Secretary to calculate a disparity in per-pupil expenditures among school districts in a state. When doing so, the Secretary disregarded districts with per-pupil expenditures above the 95th percentile or below the fifth percentile of such expenditures in the state. The Secretary then determined whether a state aid program satisfied the federal equalization requirement. The expenditures of the district with the highest per-pupil expenditures could not exceed those of the district with the smallest per-pupil expenditures by over 25 percent.

New Mexico excluded 23 of its 89 districts for determining the equalization formula under the Impact Aid Program. The exclusion of districts was based on per-pupil revenues, rather than per-pupil expenditures. Two school districts challenged the calculation, as they stood to lose state funding due to an offset of Federal Impact Aid. **The case reached the U.S. Supreme Court, which found strong indications that Congress intended to leave the Secretary free to decide whether a state aid program equalized expenditures.** The alternative urged by the districts would permit gross disparities in district expenditures. The Secretary's method complied with the Act by comparing the per-pupil expenditures made by the state's highest and lowest spending districts. The Court upheld the Secretary's reading of the statute as reasonable. *Zuni Public School Dist. No. 89 v. Dep't of Educ.*, 127 S.Ct. 1534 (U.S. 2007).

◆ The Perkins Vocational Education Act authorizes federal grants to the states to assist them with vocational education programs. The receipt of Perkins Act funding requires each state to maintain or increase its annual level of financial support for vocational education within the state. An audit conducted by the U.S. Department of Education determined that Pennsylvania failed to maintain appropriate funding levels for two fiscal years. The department demanded a refund of over $3 million, and the state appealed to the federal Office of Administrative Law Judges. An administrative law judge held for the department and denied the state's request for an evidentiary hearing.

The state appealed to the U.S. Court of Appeals, Third Circuit. The court agreed with the administrative determination that **the state was not entitled to an evidentiary hearing. There was sufficient evidence that the state had not complied with Perkins Act requirements**, and the written record was adequate to resolve all factual issues. The court also rejected the state's argument that compliance with Perkins Act requirements infringed upon its authority to interpret its own laws. The federal act, and not state law, defined what constituted vocational education under the act. This did not infringe upon the state's sovereign authority. The court affirmed the administrative decision. *State of Pennsylvania v. Riley*, 84 F.3d 125 (3d Cir. 1996).

D. School Expenditures and State Appropriations

◆ In January 2005, the Supreme Court of Kansas held the state's public school finance system violated Article 6, § 6 of the Kansas Constitution. The legislature enacted 2005 H.B. 2247, which increased school funding by $142 million for the 2005-06 school year and authorized a study to find the cost of delivering a K-12 curriculum and required programs. In June 2005, the supreme court held H.B. 2247 did not comply with Article 6, Section 6, because it was not based on actual cost considerations. The court also held H.B. 2247 exacerbated existing funding inequities. Under-funding by the state forced some districts to use their local option budgets to fund the state's constitutional obligation. A legislative division of post-audit (LPA) cost study was insufficient to determine the actual costs of providing a constitutionally suitable education.

The governor called a special legislative session, which resulted in the passage of S.B. 3. This authorized an additional $147 million for the 2005-06 school year. The court found S.B. 3 complied with its order and approved the finance formula for interim purposes. In January 2006, the legislature enacted S.B. 549, containing vast changes to the school finance formula. The case returned to the supreme court, which held S.B. 549 "materially and fundamentally changed the way K-12 is funded in this state." S.B. 549 created additional at-risk weightings for districts with high numbers of at-risk students and students who were not proficient in reading or math. More districts with lower assessed valuation per pupil would now receive supplemental aid on local option budgets, bringing them up to par with other districts. A cap on local option budgets was eliminated, and a provision limited the use of supplemental aid for meeting accreditation requirements and improving student performance. The three-year cumulative total of aid under H.B. 2247, S.B. 3 and S.B. 549 was $121.7 million greater than in January 2005. S.B. 549 required the application of supplemental state aide to meet basic educational requirements, essentially making local option budget state aid a part of the foundation level of funding. The court held the legislature had substantially responded to its concerns that the funding formula did not provide adequate funding for students in districts with high minority, at-risk and special education populations. S.B. 549 responded to concerns about the equitable distribution of funding. **Equity did not require equal funding for each student or district. What was required was an equitable and fair distribution of funding to provide an opportunity for every student to obtain a suitable education.** As the legislature's 2005 and 2006 actions substantially complied with prior court orders, the case was dismissed. *Montoy v. State of Kansas*, 138 P.3d 755 (Kan. 2006).

◆ The Headlee Amendment of 1978 prohibits the state of Michigan from reducing funding for the necessary costs of existing activities or services mandated by the legislature. It also obligates the state to fund the necessary costs of new or increased activities that the legislature mandates. A group of taxpayers and school districts sued the state in 1980 for violating the amendment. After years of litigation, the state supreme court held the legislature could not reduce its share of funding for special education and held for the districts in *Durant v. Michigan*, 456 Mich. 175, 566 N.W.2d 272 (Mich. 1997) ("*Durant I*"). The legislature then passed M.C.L. § 388.1611f, which gave relief to districts that were not plaintiffs in *Durant I*. To receive funds, districts had to waive any right or interest similar to that asserted in *Durant I*. Despite widespread acceptance of this waiver, a new group of taxpayers and districts sued the state in 1998, claiming continuing violations of the Headlee Amendment from 1997 to 2001. The court of appeals largely held in their favor in *Durant II*, but a third case, *Durant III*, resulted in a decision for state officials.

A new challenge was brought against state officials, asserting insufficient funding for new or increased levels of activity. At issue were 12 statutes, including legislation increasing the hours of pupil instruction, seven administrative rules mandating new special education activities and services, and an executive order mandating new services without increased funding.

The court of appeals held for the state, finding *Durant I* and the waiver and release provisions of M.C.L. § 388.1611f barred any new action involving these claims. All but one of the claims could have been raised in the earlier case. A single record-keeping claim did not violate the Headlee Amendment. On appeal, the state supreme court held that **except for the record-keeping claim, the taxpayers and districts could have brought their claims in *Durant I*. As the claims could have been asserted in the earlier case, they were barred.** The 382 districts that accepted the M.C.L. § 388.1611f waiver were also barred from raising similar claims. Only three claims were based on post-*Durant I* mandates, including the record-keeping claim. The court reversed the appellate decision on this claim, finding an executive order establishing the Center for Educational Performance and Information required districts to create and maintain student data. **If proven, this unfunded "off-loading of state funding responsibilities onto local units of government" would violate the Headlee Amendment.** *Adair v. State of Michigan*, 680 N.W.2d 386 (Mich. 2004).

On remand, the court of appeals held the school districts could not prove the statutory record-keeping requirement and executive order amounted to a shifting of state funding responsibility. The supreme court held the court of appeals misapplied its 2004 decision, and it vacated the appellate decision. *Adair v. State of Michigan*, No. 230858, 2006 WL 839246 (Mich. 2006).

◆   The California Constitution requires the state to reimburse local districts for the cost of new programs or higher levels of service mandated by the state. The San Diego Unified School District filed a test claim for reimbursement of the increased costs of hearings to expel students under two statutes. Education Code § 48915 compelled suspension with a recommendation for expulsion of students found in possession of a firearm at school or school activities. It permitted expulsions at the discretion of the principal for damaging or stealing property, receiving stolen property, selling or using illegal drugs, possessing tobacco or drug paraphernalia, and disruption. Section 48918 granted students a hearing and appeal rights if expulsion was recommended. The Commission on State Mandates found the mandatory firearms provision was a new program or higher level of service because most of the costs related to expulsion hearings exceeded the requirements of federal due process. However, hearing procedures that only complied with federal due process were not reimbursable.

The case reached the Supreme Court of California. It held the intent of Article XIII B, Section 6 of the state constitution was to require the state to reimburse local agencies for performing government functions, not expenses related to generally applicable laws. State laws increasing the cost to local government of providing services did not necessarily establish a new or higher level of services that had to be reimbursed by the state. **The court held the compelled expulsion provision of Section 48915 was a state mandate for which all hearing costs were fully reimbursable. However, the discretionary**

expulsion provision of Section 48915 was not a new program or higher level of services required by the state. Hearings for Section 48915 discretionary expulsions only implemented federal due process mandates. Neither Section 48918 nor federal law required an expulsion recommendation. This was true despite a No Child Left Behind Act requirement that schools expel students for firearms possession which resembled the requirements of Section 48915. The cost of these hearings was minimal and not reimbursable. *San Diego Unified School Dist. v. Comm'n on State Mandates*, 33 Cal.4th 859, 16 Cal.Rptr.3d 466, 94 P.3d 589 (Cal. 2004).

◆   The California Constitution severely limits the taxing authority of state and local government entities and requires the state to reimburse local governments for any increased cost of providing new state-mandated programs or higher levels of service. Two school districts and a county participated in state-funded educational programs requiring them to establish school councils and advisory committees. The districts and county claimed new legislatively-required notice and agenda mandates imposed higher service levels on them that required state reimbursement. The state Commission on State Mandates held the statutorily required meeting notices and agendas were reimbursable state mandates.

A state superior court affirmed the commission's decision, as did the state court of appeal. The Supreme Court of California **rejected the district's argument that participation in eight of the nine education programs at issue was legally compelled.** Each of the laws creating these programs required districts to adopt policies ensuring school site councils would be created and proper notices and agendas be posted. **There was no requirement that districts participate in the programs, and no state mandate existed.** The Chacon-Moscone Bilingual Bicultural Education Act of 1976 differed from the other eight programs, as the program it created had "sunsetted" in 1987. However, it was still funded by the state. The court stated district program participation was voluntary. While state law required advisory committees that existed as of 1979 to continue as a requirement to continued funding, the court held the cost of complying with the notice and agenda requirements was still not reimbursable. These costs were modest. Significantly, **nothing prevented districts from using part of the funds received from the programs to cover these costs.** The state education programs did not present districts with "certain and severe penalties" for non-participation. The court found that local governments might be entitled to state reimbursement for noncompulsory programs that required the expenditure of additional funds in some circumstances. As districts were free to decide whether to participate in each of the optional programs in this case, the districts and county were not entitled to reimbursement. *Dep't of Finance v. Comm'n on State Mandates*, 30 Cal.4th 727, 134 Cal.Rptr.2d 237, 68 P.3d 1203 (Cal. 2003).

◆   In 1994, the Arizona Supreme Court held the state's property-tax-based funding scheme resulted in significant disparities among districts that violated the state constitution. *Hull v. Albrecht*, 950 P.2d 1141 (Ariz. 1997). The legislature enacted new legislation, which the court struck down in 1997. The Students FIRST Act of 1998 created a capital finance program funded by dedicated revenue from a state transaction privilege tax. The supreme court upheld the act's minimum adequacy standards for capital facilities, but it disapproved of a provision allowing districts to opt out of state capital funding requirements through local funding. The legislature amended the act by establishing three mechanisms to fund school facilities, including the Building Renewal Fund (BRF). It disregarded the formula for the 1998-99 school year and simply increased BRF funding by 10% over the prior year. This resulted in $27 million less for the BRF than the formula required. While the formula for the 2001-2002 school year would have resulted in over $122 million to the BRF, the legislature allowed only $672,093 to reach schools. The BRF formula for 2002-2003 called for $128 million, but only $38 million went into the fund. The legislature suspended the BRF formula for 2003-2004.

A state court ordered the legislature to restore $90 million it had subtracted from the BRF. The Arizona Court of Appeals held the **state's constitutional obligation was to fund an "adequate" public school system. This included a minimum quality and quantity standard for buildings and sufficient funding for necessary facilities and equipment to enable students to master educational goals set by the legislature.** The Students FIRST Act reflected the supreme court's mandate to provide facilities necessary for student academic achievement and prioritized funding for district facilities "directly necessary for scholastic success." **The court found school districts had to first expend BRF funds for buildings identified in the BRF database.** BRF funds were unavailable for other district buildings until those in the database were repaired. Academic needs expressed by the districts would not likely be remedied by BRF funds, because that money was not used for new construction. **While the districts showed they had capital facilities requiring repairs and renovation, they did not link those needs to student scholastic performance.** The court held the failure to fund the BRF formula was not a constitutional violation. As there was no unequivocal evidence that the cuts had an impact on student academic achievement, the court reversed the judgment. *Roosevelt Elementary School Dist. No. 66 v. State of Arizona*, 74 P.3d 258 (Ariz. Ct. App. 2003). The Arizona Supreme Court decided not to review this decision in 2004.

◆ The Supreme Court of Missouri held the governor was entitled to order a part of the elementary and secondary school appropriation not be distributed. The governor ordered part of the budgetary appropriation not be distributed after learning that actual revenues were less than estimated. Fourteen school districts filed a petition in the state supreme court for an order compelling the governor to distribute the originally-appropriated amounts. **The court stated Article IV, Section 27 of the Missouri Constitution specifically authorized the governor's action.** The governor was authorized to control the rate at which any appropriation was expended during the period of appropriation.

The constitutional provision permitted the governor to reduce state expenditures below their appropriations whenever actual revenues were less than the revenue estimates upon which the appropriations were based. The districts did not contest the revenue shortfall but claimed other constitutional provisions exempted school funds from Article IV, Section 27. The court disagreed, noting that **Article IV, Section 26 limited the governor's**

powers of appropriation, not expenditures. Since Article IV, Section 27 broadly authorized the governor to control the rate of expenditure for any appropriation, and to balance the state budget by reducing expenditures, the court denied the petition of the districts. *State ex rel. Liberty School Dist. v. Holden*, 121 S.W.3d 232 (Mo. 2003).

◆ In 2000, Washington voters passed Initiative 732, which required the state to provide cost-of-living increases to help ensure the state attracted and retained the best teachers and school employees. The increase applied a cost-of-living index to any state-funded salary base in funding formulas for school employees. The initiative required the state to allocate for the increase and to fully fund the cost-of-living increase as part of the basic education requirements obligation of the state constitution. Taxpayers and school employees filed an action in a state superior court, seeking a declaration that the initiative required the state to fully fund the cost-of-living increases for all district employees. The court held for the state, ruling employees must be provided with annual increases but that the state was only required to fund increases for employees whose salaries were funded by the state as part of its constitutional duty to fund a "basic education."

On appeal, the Washington Supreme Court rejected the state's argument that the initiative did not mandate an annual cost-of-living increase for each school district employee. The initiative clearly stated that the increase was to be provided for all district employees. The court agreed with the state that **a provision in the initiative requiring it to fully fund the increase for all employees was unconstitutional. It expanded the meaning of a "basic education" under the state constitution to include impermissible consequences, such as tying basic education dollars to tax levies.** While voters intended that the state fully fund the cost of the salary increases for all school district employees, this intent could not be carried out by funding increases that disregarded the concept of a basic education. As the unconstitutional section of the initiative was severable, the court held the initiative should be deemed to have been enacted without it. The state had to fully fund the cost-of-living increases for all district employees mandated by the initiative. *McGowan v. State of Washington*, 60 P.3d 67 (Wash. 2002).

E. Student Fees and Tuition

1. Transportation Fees

◆ North Dakota statutes authorized thinly populated school districts to reorganize into larger districts for efficiency. Reorganized districts had to provide for student transportation to and from their homes. School districts choosing not to reorganize were authorized by statute to charge students a portion of their costs for transportation. The parents of a nine-year-old student refused to sign a transportation contract with the school district. The family was near or at the poverty level. Claiming inability to pay the fee, the family made private transportation arrangements that were more costly than the school's fee. The parents sued the school district in a North Dakota trial court for an order to prevent the district from collecting the fee on grounds that it violated the state constitution and the Equal Protection Clause. After losing at the trial court level, the parents appealed to the North Dakota Supreme Court. The court upheld the lower court decision on state and federal constitutional grounds.

On appeal to the U.S. Supreme Court, the parents claimed that the user fee for bus service unconstitutionally deprived poor persons of minimum access to education and placed an unconstitutional obstacle on education for poor students. The Court noted that the student had continued to attend school during the time she claimed she was denied access to the school bus. **The Equal Protection Clause does not require free transportation. Education is not a fundamental right under the U.S. Constitution. The Court upheld the statute, as it bore a reasonable relationship to the state's legitimate objective of encouraging school districts to provide bus service.** The statute did not directly impose a bus fee requirement. It did not discriminate against any class or interfere with any constitutional rights. *Kadrmas v. Dickinson Public Schools*, 487 U.S. 450, 108 S.Ct. 2481, 101 L.Ed.2d 399 (1988).

◆   A Kentucky school board furnished bus transportation and allowed students to attend schools that were outside their attendance area but within the same district. However, to limit class sizes, the board instituted a revised transportation policy that permitted students to attend schools within the district but outside their attendance areas only if they utilized private transportation. The parent of a student affected by the change filed a lawsuit in a Kentucky trial court, claiming that the transportation policy was arbitrary, capricious and unreasonable and violated his constitutional rights to due process.

The court granted summary judgment to the school board, and the parent appealed to the Kentucky Court of Appeals. The court affirmed the trial court's judgment, finding the board's decision was not arbitrary, capricious or unreasonable. The due process rights of students and parents had been protected by numerous public meetings held during the policy revision. Its impact on students already availing themselves of the policy was mitigated by the use of a grandfather clause. **Any change in school policies might have an adverse impact on some students, but some such impacts could not be avoided.** The court affirmed the trial court's decision. *Swift v. Breckinridge County Board of Educ.*, 878 S.W.2d 810 (Ky. Ct. App. 1994).

2. Tuition and Other Fees

◆   An Indiana school district charged each of its students a mandatory $20 fee to address a $2.3 million budget deficit for 2002 that was projected to increase to $5.5 million in 2003. The district deposited the fees in its general fund with state funds and local property tax receipts to help pay the salaries of nurses, media specialists, counselors and a student services coordinator. The district also used the fees to pay for alternative education, a police liaison program, and for athletic, drama and music programs. The parents of students who qualified for reduced or free school lunch and textbook programs filed a class action against the school district in a state court, asserting the fee violated the state and U.S. constitutions. The court held for the parents, finding the fee violated the Due Process Clause of the Fourteenth Amendment. The case reached the

Supreme Court of Indiana, which noted Article 8, Section 1 does not provide for a system of "free schools," as many state constitutions do. Instead, it provides for "a general and uniform system of Common Schools, wherein tuition shall be without charge, and equally open to all." The subtle distinction between "free schools" and tuition-free schools was significant in this case.

The court found the framers intended a uniform, statewide system of public schools that was supported by taxation, but not a completely subsidized education. The state General Assembly had made a policy decision regarding what qualified as part of a uniform system of public education. **Without a specific statutory authority, fees or charges could not be directly or indirectly assessed against students or parents for public education cost items. The court found only extracurricular activities could be considered as not a part of a publicly funded education.** However, the fee in this case was imposed on all students. The student fee was deposited into the district's general fund and used to offset the cost of non-instructional staff salaries, a police liaison program, alternative education program, and music and drama programs. The state board had already deemed these items as "part and parcel of a public school education." **The court held a mandatory fee, imposed generally on all students, was a "charge for attending a public school and obtaining a public education" in violation of Article 8, Section 1.** *Nagy v. Evansville-Vanderburgh School Corp.*, 844 N.E.2d 481 (Ind. 2006).

◆   A New Jersey family lived in Princeton until June 1998, when they moved to West Windsor. They then transferred their children into West Windsor schools. Five months later, the parents listed their West Windsor house for sale and contracted for a condominium in Princeton. The parents returned the children to school in Princeton and closed on their condominium. They were unable to sell the West Windsor house for over a year and spent time in each residence during this period. The Princeton district sent an attendance officer to observe the family. He found the family spent most of its time at the West Windsor residence. Princeton brought an administrative action against the parents to force them to pay tuition. An administrative law judge (ALJ) found Princeton was not the family domicile. The parents did not change addresses on their drivers' licenses and auto registrations and were unable to testify about the furnishings of the Princeton house or their social life there. The ALJ discounted the parents' evidence of tax bills, homeowner's insurance, association dues and utility bills. The family did not establish a permanent home in Princeton and did not intend to abandon the West Windsor house. The state board of education and commissioner ordered the parents to pay Princeton over $27,000 in tuition.

The parents appealed to the state appellate division. The court explained N.J.S.A. § 18A:38-1(a) states **any person domiciled in a district is entitled to a free education from that district. "Domicile" is "the place where a person has his or her true fixed, permanent home and principal establishment," and to which the person intends to return whenever absent.** A person may have several residences, but only one domicile at a time. The court stated **a student is domiciled in a district when he or she is living with a parent or guardian whose permanent home is located within the district.** The parents spent substantial time in both their houses. There was no evidence they intended to retain the West Windsor house or maintain a permanent residence there. The evidence indicated the family spent most of its time in Princeton. The parents' failure to get new drivers' licenses could not determine the outcome of the case. There was overwhelming evidence they intended to establish a permanent home in Princeton as of the date they closed on the residence there. The court reversed and remanded the case for a determination of the amount of tuition due Princeton, if any. *D.L. and Z.Y., on Behalf of T.L. and K.L. v. Board of Educ. of Princeton Regional School Dist.*, 840 A.2d 979 (N.J. Super. Ct. App. Div. 2004).

◆   As a result of increased enrollment, a Pennsylvania school board approved a program providing for a district-financed tuition scholarship for any student legally residing in the district for attendance at any private school or non-district public school. A group of resident taxpayers filed a declaratory judgment action against the district in the state court system challenging the program. The trial court agreed with the taxpayers and granted their motion for judgment on the pleadings, ruling that the district lacked authority to implement the plan.

The district and board appealed to the Commonwealth Court of Pennsylvania, which noted that **because school districts are created by legislation, they have no powers except those authorized by express statutory grant and necessary implication. The School Code did not expressly authorize reimbursement of tuition and fees.** The court rejected the argument that the broad grant of authority found in 24 P.S. § 5-501 created implied authority for the plan. **While the section authorized district expenditures for building, maintaining and equipping schools, it required too great a leap of logic to conclude that school districts should provide financial incentives not to attend public schools.** Where a district found its financing insufficient, its options were to either obtain a court order or follow procedures established by the secretary of education. The legislature did not authorize tuition payments to parents in the situation presented in this case, and there was no implied authority for the district plan. A statewide program resembling the plan was struck down by the U.S. Supreme Court in *Sloan v. Lemon*, 413 U.S. 825 (1973). The district had clearly acted outside the scope of its statutory authority, and the court affirmed the trial court order. *Giacomucci v. Southeast Delco School Dist.*, 742 A.2d 1165 (Pa. Commw. Ct. 1999).

◆   A 13-year-old U.S. citizen who was born in Texas resided with his parents in Mexico until he was sent to live with his aunt in Illinois. The aunt's school district of residence refused to recognize documents from his parents granting custody to the aunt, stating that only an American court could confer legal guardianship rights to the aunt. Because the parents were unable to enter the U.S., the district denied the student's application for tuition-free enrollment. The aunt obtained the assistance of a congressman, and the Illinois State Board of Education requested that the student be enrolled without tuition. The local board rejected the request and affirmed the denial of enrollment. The aunt obtained a temporary restraining order from an Illinois circuit court allowing the immediate enrollment of the student. The court then made the order permanent and the district appealed to the Appellate Court of Illinois.

The court observed that the Illinois Constitution confers the right to tuition-free education upon resident students. **A child presumptively resides in the school district where his parents reside; however, this presumption may be rebutted by circumstances** including the permanency of the student's residence, the extent to which the parents exercise care, custody and control over the student and the presence of noneducational reasons for living apart from the parents. There was evidence that the student was not applying for residence in the district solely for educational purposes, and contrary evidence that he had moved to Illinois to escape economic and social hardships in Mexico. Because there was sufficient evidence to support the circuit court decision, the court affirmed it. *Joel R. v. Board of Educ. of Mannheim School Dist. 83, Cook County, Illinois*, 686 N.E.2d 650 (Ill. App. Ct. 1997).

◆   North Carolina statutes permit local education boards to charge tuition to students who do not reside within the school's administrative unit or district. A school district determined that a student who resided in its administrative area was not properly domiciled within the territory and attempted to charge tuition to her parents. The district filed a lawsuit in a North Carolina trial court to recover tuition from her parents. The court held for the parents and the school district appealed to the Court of Appeals of North Carolina, which observed the distinction between residence and domicile. Residence was defined as an actual place of abode while domicile was a permanent, established home. It was possible for a student to reside in a place other than with his or her parents and therefore have different places of domicile and residence. In this case, **the student resided within the school's administrative unit and could not be assessed tuition charges**. The court remanded the case for the entry of judgment for the parents. *Chapel Hill-Carrboro City Schools System v. Chavioux*, 446 S.E.2d 612 (N.C. Ct. App. 1994).

F. Private Contractors

◆   A disappointed bidder claimed that a Georgia school board had to accept its bid because of an immaterial defect by the low bidder for a construction project. The invitation for bids disallowed changes without board approval, but reserved the board's right to reject bids and waive "technicalities and informalities" in its best interest. The low bidder did not initially provide a subcontractor list, as required by the project specifications. It provided the list within two hours of the opening of the bids, and the board voted to accept it. The contractor that submitted the next-lowest bid filed a state court petition to prevent the board from contracting with any other entity. It also sought a declaration that it was entitled to an award of the construction project. The court denied its request for relief, finding delay of the construction project would have consequences on the citizens of the county. The supreme court accepted the contractor's appeal.

The court held Section 36-91-21(b)(4) of the state code did not mean every statement in an invitation for bids had to be met precisely and without deviation. This would curtail the authority government entities are given and make the "responsive bidder" provision of Section 36-91-21 superfluous. The court also found reference to "material respects" in that section was to be honored. **The district retained statutory powers to waive technicalities. There was no law,** regulation or ordinance requiring all project subcontractors to be listed on public bids. **The trial court did not commit error by concluding the list of subcontractors was immaterial and could be waived.** The bid invitation did not suggest that a list of subcontractors was a material requirement. As the board had determined a list of subcontractors should be in all bids, the board could also find this was not a material requirement, but a technicality that could be waived. The trial court did not abuse its discretion in denying relief to the contractor, and the supreme court affirmed the judgment. *R.D. Brown Contractors v. Board of Educ. of Columbia County*, 626 S.E.2d 471 (Ga. 2006).

◆ **The Supreme Court of South Carolina permitted a contractor that bid on a school renovation project to increase its bid to reflect the amount of a subcontractor's services that had been inadvertently omitted from its bid.** The contractor bid $16.3 million on the project and was the low bidder by more than $1 million. After bids were opened, the contractor advised the district it had failed to include a roofing subcontractor's bid and asked to either add $613,500 to its bid or to withdraw the entire bid. The district allowed the adjustment, and the contractor's bid was still $461,500 less than the second-lowest bidder. The second-lowest bidder sued the district in a state court for an order preventing the district from accepting the contractor's bid. The court held the bid adjustment complied with the district's procurement code and regulations, and the second-lowest bidder appealed. On appeal, the state supreme court examined a provision of the procurement code that allowed the correction or withdrawal of an erroneous bid before or after award. The same provision allowed the cancellation of bid awards or contracts based on mistaken bids.

The code stated no change in bid prices could be made if this would be prejudicial to the interest of the school district or fair competition. The district's procurement code allowed a bidder to correct a mistaken bid after bid opening if it would cause the bidder to have the low bid, but only if the mistake was clearly evident from examining the bid document. The court found the correction did not cause a bidder to have the low bid. It was within the district's discretion to find correction of the contractor's mistaken bid was proper. The court found no violation of district rules. The mistake was clear, and the amount the contractor had intended to bid for the roof was evident from examining the subcontractor's bid, as this had been submitted to several general contractors. **The correction did not jeopardize the integrity of the sealed bidding process, and was not prejudicial to the interests of the district or fair competition. It would have been prejudicial to the district had it been bound to accept the second-lowest bidder's bid, which was $461,500 higher.** The court affirmed the judgment. *Martin Engineering v. Lexington County School Dist. One*, 365 S.C. 1, 615 S.E.2d 110 (S.C. 2005).

◆ An Arizona school district solicited bids for the construction of new classrooms. The low bidder was a contractor that had performed work for the district four years earlier. It had begun that project prematurely, prior to the completion of asbestos removal, and the district was fined for violations. The district required the contractor to acknowledge it would ensure this would not be repeated. The school board voted to accept the contractor's bid on the new project. The board's executive director signed a notice to proceed, and a meeting was scheduled to execute the contract. The night before the meeting, the contractor began work at the construction site. The district refused to sign the contract and cancelled the contractor's bid. The contractor denied it had been instructed not to begin work before signing the contract, and it claimed the district had no authority to cancel or modify the contract. The district re-bid the project. The contractor sued the district in a state court, arguing the signing of a contract and posting of a performance bond were "mere formalities" and were not a prerequisite to the formation of a contact. A jury returned a verdict for the contractor. The state court of appeals affirmed, and the district appealed.

The Supreme Court of Arizona held a public agency accepting a bid on a public project was not bound until a formal contract existed. The state code directed the award of a contract to the lowest responsible and responsive bidder whose bid conformed in all material respects with the invitation for bids. **The court found nothing in the code prohibited a public entity from withdrawing a bid after acceptance of the bid, but prior to the award of a contract.** Sections of the state code distinguished between the award of a bid and the execution of a final contact. A section of the state code required bid security to accompany certain bids. The purpose of bid security was to compel a contractor to enter into a contract according to the terms of its bid. Another code provision required bidders to post a performance bond upon the formal execution of a contract. Relevant code provisions anticipated an interval between the award of a bid and the execution of a public contract. This interval would allow the successful bidder to present the required bonds at the contract execution. The court remanded the case to the trial court with instructions to enter judgment for the district. *Ry-Tan Construction v. Washington Elementary School Dist. No. 6*, 111 P.3d 1019 (Ariz. 2005).

◆ A California contractor was the low bidder for a $6 million elementary school improvement project. The project was delayed by heavy rains, and the parties agreed to delay the completion date. The school district terminated the contract after the project remained unfinished for four more months. The district demanded completion of the project from the contractor's surety under its performance bond. The surety hired another party to complete the job. The contractor sued the district and one of its employees in a state superior court for a host of claims, including breach of contract. The contractor presented evidence that the district's action cut its bonding limit in half, resulting in over $3.1 million in lost profits on "unidentified projects." The jury returned a verdict for the contractor, awarding the lost profits claimed as the result of reduction or loss of bonding capacity. The district and employee appealed.

The case reached the Supreme Court of California, which explained that contractual damages are intended to approximate agreed-upon performance. **Damage awards cannot exceed what an injured party would have been paid had there been no breach.** "General damages" are those flowing directly from a breach of contract. By contrast, "special damages" are those based on particular circumstances of the contract or the parties. Special damages may be recovered only if the particular circumstances from which they arise are known to (or should be known by) the breaching party. The contractor's projected profit was limited by the contract price. **The contract did not include potential profits on future unidentified projects.** The court held termination of the contract did not directly cause the contractor to lose potential profits or future contacts. Any loss resulted from the limits on the contractor's bonding imposed by the surety. The court held the loss of profits was improperly awarded to the contractor as general damages. It was also improper to award them as special damages, as the contractor did not show the district reasonably contemplated a breach of contract would lead to reduction of its bonding capacity. Since the lower courts had erroneously awarded the contractor damages based on the imposition of bonding limits after the contract termination, the court reversed the judgment. *Lewis Jorge Construction Management v. Pomona Unified School Dist.*, 34 Cal.4th 960, 102 P.3d 257, 22 Cal.Rptr.3d 340 (Cal. 2004).

◆   A New Mexico school board invited bids on a project to re-roof five buildings. The board selected a contractor that submitted the low bid on several items but did not submit a complete bid for the project. A disappointed bidder sued the school board in a state court, seeking a declaration that it was the lowest responsive bidder and was entitled to the contract. The court agreed with the bidder and ordered the board to void the contract with the selected bidder. The selected bidder then sought payment for its expenses under the contract, plus a profit. When the board failed to pay this amount, the selected bidder sued the district in a state court, seeking payment. The court granted the district's summary judgment motion. The contractor appealed to the Court of Appeals of New Mexico, which considered the district's argument that state law required partial payments to a terminated contractor only where a local public body declares a contract illegal. **The court of appeals stated that because the trial court had instructed the school board to void the contract, it had been set aside by a local agency, satisfying statutory language requiring compensation of the selected bidder.** The court reversed and remanded the district court judgment. *Hamilton Roofing Co. of Carlsbad, Inc. v. Carlsbad Municipal Schools Board of Educ.*, 123 N.M. 434, 941 P.2d 515 (N.M. Ct. App. 1997).

G. Insurance Cases

◆   The Texas Political Subdivisions Property/Casualty Joint Self-Insurance Fund is a self-insurance risk pool and claim administrator for member districts and political subdivisions. A school district submitted a claim for extensive water and mold damage to some of its facilities. The fund denied the claim, stating the policy did not cover the damage. The district sued the fund in a state court, which denied the fund's claim to state law immunity. The Court of Appeals of Texas reversed the trial court's decision. The state legislature then enacted a limited waiver of immunity, which became Section 271.152 of the Texas Local Government Code. The Supreme Court of Texas agreed to hear the school district's appeal. The court found the fund was composed of members such as the school district, which were themselves entitled to immunity. The Texas Government Code provided that the establishment and maintenance of a self-insurance program by a governmental unit was not a waiver of immunity.

The fund was a combination of political subdivisions that enjoyed local government status under the Texas Interlocal Cooperation Act. However, the legislature was entitled to weigh the conflicting public policies associated with waiving immunity. **The court held the insurance contract between the fund and the district was governed by Texas Government Code Section 271.152. The section allowed the enforcement of contracts against local governmental entities by waiving their immunity.** Nothing indicated that the legislature intended to exclude self-insurance fund agreements from this waiver. The act's legislative history indicated the legislature "intended to loosen the immunity bar" from suits arising from contracts. As the fund did not have Section 271.152, immunity, the court reversed the judgment. *Ben Bolt-Palito Blanco Consolidated Independent School Dist. v. Texas Political Subdivisions Property/Casualty Joint Self-Insurance Fund*, 212 S.W.3d 320 (Tex. 2006).

◆ Louisiana school board employees sued the board for injury and illness from exposure to toxic substances, safety hazards and toxic mold. They claimed the board was negligent in the upkeep and repair of a high school. The board sought coverage from its general liability insurer. The insurer claimed coverage was barred by exclusions for employees and for expected or intended injury. A Louisiana trial court awarded summary judgment to the insurer, and the board appealed. The Court of Appeal of Louisiana found the policy's employers liability exclusion applied to bodily injury to an employee, arising out of and in the course of his or her employment. **The policy's expected or intended bodily injury exclusion applied to any intentional injury. The court found these provisions unambiguously excluded coverage for employees and for intentional conduct.** It rejected the employees' assertion that the policy did not bar coverage because they made their claims against "administrators" as well as the board. The judgment was affirmed. *Hemstad v. Jefferson Parish School Board*, 916 So.2d 1174 (La. Ct. App. 2005).

◆ A Maryland student sued a teacher in a federal court for abusing him when he was a pre-teen. The county code required the board's self-insurance program to cover employees for tort claims arising from acts within the scope of an employee's official duties. There was no coverage for actions "outside the scope of employment" or for "wanton or malicious" or intentional conduct. The teacher sought defense (legal counsel) from the board under its self-insurance program. The board found she was being sued for actions outside the scope of her employment and denied her requests for defense and indemnification. The teacher obtained defense from her own insurance, which was issued to her by the Maryland State Teachers Association (MSTA). A state court found the complaint raised the potential for coverage and held the board had a duty to defend her in the federal case. An intermediate state court of appeals affirmed a judgment of over $100,000 for the MSTA's insurer and the board appealed.

The Court of Appeals of Maryland explained that school boards may satisfy their state law obligation to carry comprehensive liability insurance through self-insurance programs. Such insurance must conform to terms and conditions of private liability insurance. **The state Education Article independently required boards to provide counsel for teachers who are sued for claims "in the performance of their duties, within the scope of employment, and**

without malice," and where a board determined the teacher acted within his or her official capacity. The county self-insurance program also provided for defending such claims against teachers. The court held liability insurers are obligated to defend actions against their insureds when there is a chance the claim could be covered. **The board's obligation to defend the teacher arose from Education Article requirements, and its own self-insurance program contained the same duty to defend as would exist under a standard policy.** The board had to defend the teacher "if there was any potentiality of coverage." The MSTA's insurer correctly argued the student had asserted contacts that went beyond the proper teacher/mentor role. As the student's complaint showed the potentiality of coverage, the board was required to defend the teacher. Because it did not, the MSTA's insurer was entitled to reimbursement, and the court affirmed the judgment. *Montgomery County Board of Educ. v. Horace Mann Insurance Co.*, 383 Md. 527, 860 A.2d 909 (Md. 2004).

◆   The family of an Illinois student with disabilities sue their school district for violating the Individuals with Disabilities Education Act (IDEA), Section 504 of the Rehabilitation Act, and the Americans with Disabilities Act (ADA). The district tendered defense of the lawsuit to its insurer. The insurer paid the district $50,000 under a supplementary payments provision of its policy that limited coverage for defense costs to $50,000 for non-monetary claims involving disputes in special education. The insurer denied responsibility for further defense costs, relying on a policy exclusion precluding coverage for relief "other than monetary damages." It asserted the family's suit was limited to the special education placement and did not seek damages. A federal district court and the Seventh Circuit Court of Appeals held for the district.

The family appealed the IDEA claims to the U.S. Supreme Court. The Court declined the case, but the appeal cost the district an additional $9,901 in legal costs and fees. The district filed a separate action against the insurer in a state court for additional defense costs. The court held that since monetary damages are available under the ADA and Section 504, the insurer had to defend those claims. The Appellate Court of Illinois noted the policy required the insurer to pay all sums the district "shall become legally obligated to pay as damages to which this insurance applies" by reason of wrongful acts. A policy exclusion declared the insurer would not make payment for or defend any suit "seeking relief or redress in any form other than monetary damages." The court noted the ADA, Section 504 and IDEA claims sought reimbursement for the cost of obtaining independent evaluations and services. The family would have been entitled to payment from the district had these claims succeeded. **The claims for reimbursement sought monetary damages as contemplated by the policy, and the insurer was required to defend the district.** The court affirmed the judgment for defense costs arising under the ADA and Section 504, and it reversed the judgment denying defense of the IDEA claims. The district was entitled to the additional costs of defending the Supreme Court appeal, as it involved an IDEA claim. *General Star Indemnity Co. v. Lake Bluff School Dist. No. 65*, 819 N.E.2d 784 (Ill. App. Ct. 2004).

II. DESEGREGATION

In Brown v. Board of Educ., *347 U.S. 483, 74 S.Ct. 686, 98 L.Ed. 873 (1954), the U.S. Supreme Court declared unconstitutional separate but equal systems of segregation in public schools. Fourteen years after its landmark decision in* Brown, *the Court responded to widespread resistance by school districts to federal court desegregation orders by ruling that segregation must be eliminated "root and branch."* Green v. County School Board of New Kent County, *391 U.S. 430, 88 S.Ct. 1689, 20 L.Ed.2d 716 (1968).*

By 1992, the Court declared that formerly segregated, dual school districts could be released from federal court supervision upon a demonstration of good-faith compliance with a desegregation decree, where the "vestiges of past discrimination have been eliminated to the extent practicable." Freeman v. Pitts, *503 U.S. 467, 112 S.Ct. 1430, 118 L.Ed.2d 108 (1992). Courts rely on the factors identified in* Green *to determine if a district should be declared unitary and released from federal court supervision. They also consider more recent cases such as* Freeman, Board of Educ. of Oklahoma City Public Schools v. Dowell, *498 U.S. 237, 111 S.Ct. 630, 112 L.Ed.2d 715 (1991), and* Missouri v. Jenkins, *495 U.S. 33, 110 S.Ct. 1651, 109 L.Ed.2d 31 (1990).*

The test from Freeman *and* Dowell *for releasing a school system from federal court supervision is whether there has been compliance with the decree, whether retention of the case by the court is necessary or practicable to achieve compliance with the decree, and whether the school district has demonstrated a good-faith commitment to the desegregation decree to the public and to minority parents and students. The* Freeman *decision is also important for approving the concept of the withdrawal of federal court supervision in stages as partial unitary status is achieved with respect to specific programs and areas including school facilities, faculty and staff assignments, extracurricular activities, transportation and student assignments.*

A. Release from Federal Court Supervision

◆   In 1969, a Georgia school system was enjoined by a federal district court from discriminating on the basis of race and was required to close all legally recognized black schools. The system complied, and the case remained inactive until the 1970s. In 1983, the plaintiff class returned to court contending that the school system improperly limited minority transfers to a predominantly white school and that the proposed expansion of a white high school would perpetuate segregation. The court ruled that the school system had achieved unitary status and did not have a discriminatory intent in deciding to expand the high school. The U.S. Court of Appeals, Eleventh Circuit, reversed, stating that the school system could not be declared unitary without a hearing, and that until it was declared unitary, its intent was immaterial. On remand, the district court held that the school system had not yet achieved unitary status. The school system would achieve unitary status when all schools possessed minority staffs within 15% of the system average. However, the court refused to impose additional duties on the school system in the areas of student assignment, transportation, and extracurricular activities. Both parties appealed the ruling.

The court of appeals stated that the system had not discharged its duty in the areas of student assignment, transportation, and extracurricular activities by closing all legally recognized black schools in response to the 1969 order. The court stated that the system would not achieve unitary status until it maintained at least three years of racial equality in the six categories set out in *Green*: student assignment, faculty, staff, transportation, extracurricular activities, and facilities. The court ordered the district court to require the system to file a plan in accordance with its opinion. The U.S. Supreme Court, however, held on appeal that the *Green* framework did not need to be applied as construed by the court of appeals. **Through relinquishing control in areas deemed to be unitary, a court and school district may more effectively concentrate on the areas in need of further attention. The Court held that the "incremental" approach was constitutional**, and that a court may declare that it will order no further remedy in any area that is found to be unitary. The order of the court of appeals was reversed, and the case was remanded to the district court. *Freeman v. Pitts,* 503 U.S. 467, 112 S.Ct. 1430, 118 L.Ed.2d 108 (1992).

On remand, the school district presented evidence that there was no greater than a 15% variation in minority staff rates among district schools and that district spending per student was also within an acceptable range. **The court rejected the complaining parties' evidence that the district continued to discriminate in its resource allocation and that an unacceptable gap persisted in student achievement that could not be explained by nonracial factors.** The court characterized the complaining parties' evidence as not demonstrating a pattern of discrimination or absence of good faith by the district. It therefore granted the district's motion to be released from federal court jurisdiction. *Mills v. Freeman*, 942 F.Supp. 1449 (N.D. Ga. 1996).

◆ In 1977, a federal district court found the Oklahoma City public school district had achieved unitary status and issued an order terminating the case. In 1984, the board adopted the Student Reassignment Plan (SRP). The SRP assigned students who were in grades K-4 to their neighborhood schools but continued busing for grades 5-12. The parents who had brought the original desegregation case filed a motion to reopen the case, claiming that the SRP was a return to segregation. The court refused to reopen the case and held that its 1977 finding that the district was unitary could not be relitigated. The parents appealed to the U.S. Court of Appeals, Tenth Circuit. The court held that the 1977 order was binding, but this did not mean an earlier injunction was terminated. The case was remanded to determine if the injunction should be lifted. On remand, the district court held the SRP was not designed with discriminatory intent and lifted the injunction. The appeals court reversed the decision, and the school board petitioned the U.S. Supreme Court for review. **The Supreme Court held the 1977 order did not dissolve the desegregation decree. The supervision of local school districts by the federal courts was meant as a temporary means to remedy past discrimination.** The Court remanded the case and instructed the district court to determine whether the school district had complied with constitutional requirements when it adopted the SRP. *Board of Educ. of Oklahoma City Public Schools v. Dowell,* 498 U.S. 237, 111 S.Ct. 630, 112 L.Ed.2d 715 (1991).

On remand, the district court reaffirmed its prior findings without a hearing.

It held the parties had received a full opportunity to present their evidence and adopted the school board's proposed order almost verbatim. The court of appeals affirmed the decision, ruling it did not violate the Supreme Court's remand instructions by failing to hold a new hearing and by adopting the board's proposed order. The board had complied with the desegregation decree and maintained a unitary school system. **Because the board met its burden of showing that the current racial imbalance at its schools was not traceable to prior violations, the court affirmed the decision.** *Dowell v. Board of Educ. of Oklahoma City Public Schools*, 8 F.3d 1501 (10th Cir. 1993).

◆ In 1963, a federal district court assumed supervision over a Florida school board after finding that it operated a racially segregated, *de jure* dual school system. The district began mandatory busing of students in 1971 to implement student reassignment, and the judgment was amended throughout the 1970s and 1980s. By 1989, only 18 of the board's 142 schools were identifiably black. The board and plaintiffs agreed to end mandatory busing in 1990 and sought a negotiated settlement. The parties agreed to a "corrected stipulation and agreement" (CSA) establishing desegregative goals, including the aggressive promotion of magnet programs to attract white students to racially unbalanced schools. The board agreed to commit $60 million to renovate or replace core city schools and meet target goals for racial equality in faculty and staff hiring, transportation, extracurricular activities, facilities and capital expenditures. The court approved the CSA and in 1996 the board moved for a declaration that the district met constitutional requirements for unitary status and had fulfilled its obligations under the CSA. The court found the board had acted in good faith by substantially achieving CSA goals and fulfilling its constitutional obligation to eliminate vestiges of *de jure* segregation "to the extent practicable." It declared the district unitary, vacated all prior orders and dismissed the case.

The NAACP appealed to the Eleventh Circuit, which explained that under Supreme Court precedents, school boards that formerly operated racially segregated dual school systems had a duty to take necessary steps to create unitary systems in which racial discrimination is eliminated. The board had the burden of showing that any current racial imbalance in its schools was not traceable to a prior constitutional violation. The Supreme Court has recognized that this burden may be overcome by proof of demographic shifts beyond a board's control. **If a board proves that external forces have substantially caused current racial imbalances, it overcomes any presumption of segregative intent and there is no constitutional violation.** The court stated that requiring every school in every community to reflect the racial composition of the whole school system would result in perpetual federal court supervision. The court approved of the district court's finding that the board had met five of the six factors outlined by the Supreme Court for achieving unitary status in *Green v. County School Board of New Kent County*. Although 26 district schools remained identifiably black, the board had eliminated the vestiges of *de jure* discrimination. **The current racial imbalance in some district schools was the result of "white flight" and other demographic factors beyond the board's control.** Since the continued existence of racially identifiable schools was not a vestige of prior *de jure* segregation, and the board acted in good faith to implement the CSA, the court affirmed the judgment. *NAACP, Jacksonville Branch v. Duval County School Board,* 273 F.3d 960 (11th Cir. 2001).

◆   Illinois citizens filed an action in 1989 on behalf of minority students who claimed intentional discrimination by the Rockford Board of Education that resulted in racially segregated schools. The city had been the subject of earlier desegregation litigation and had operated under a remedial decree as early as 1973. A federal court held the board engaged in intentional race discrimination. It fashioned a complex remedial decree that was vacated in large part by the Seventh Circuit due to its imposition of racial quotas on employees, classroom composition, student tracking and cheerleading squads. The board moved the district court to dissolve the decree, arguing it fully complied with the decree and that remaining inequalities in educational achievement could not be attributed to its own illegal conduct. A federal magistrate judge ruled that some of the provisions of the decree must remain in effect for at least six more years.

On appeal, the Seventh Circuit noted the decree had cost the district $238 million through 1999 and that the parties' legal fees alone were almost $20 million. **Rockford schools were now less segregated than those in any previous case in which a system was declared unitary.** The minority composition range established by the magistrate was tighter than that imposed in most desegregation cases. Although minority educational achievement lagged behind that of white students, **the court held the board had no legal duty to remove vestiges of societal discrimination for which it was not responsible**. Factors such as poverty, parents' education and employment, peer pressure, and ethnic culture might be created or exacerbated by discrimination, but the board had no federal constitutional duty to remedy them. There was no evidence of bad faith by the board. The court reversed and remanded the case. *People Who Care v. Rockford Board of Educ.*, 246 F.3d 1073 (7th Cir. 2001).

B. Compliance with Desegregation Orders

After a court finds a school district or agency liable for maintaining racially segregated facilities, the agency becomes subject to the jurisdiction of the court and court orders requiring remedial action. Many desegregation orders come in the form of a consent decree, which is a court-approved agreement of the parties to implement particular desegregation programs.

◆   Little Rock School District (LRSD) has been in desegregation litigation since 1956. A federal district court approved an inter-district settlement plan in 1989 permitting court supervision of remedial desegregation by LRSD and two neighboring districts. In 1998, the parties agreed that if LRSD substantially complied with a revised plan, the district would be declared unitary after the 2000-01 school year. The revised plan required the LRSD to assess certain academic programs each year to determine whether they improved achievement by African-American students. In 2002, the district court granted the LRSD "partial unitary status." LRSD complied with the revised plan, except for provisions governing academic programs for improving African-American student achievement. The court imposed a compliance remedy upon LRSD. In

2004, the U.S. Court of Appeals, Eighth Circuit, affirmed the finding of substantial compliance. LRSD then asked to be declared unitary. The district court held LRSD did not comply with the academic assessment provisions.

The case reached the Eighth Circuit again in 2006. The court found the impetus for the academic achievement section of the consent decree was the "achievement gap" between minority and white students in public schools. **No court had ever determined what portion, if any, of the racial achievement gap was causally linked as a vestige of *de jure* segregation.** A parent who intervened in the case failed to show any evidence that the achievement gap was attributable to *de jure* segregation. LRSD identified almost 100 programs to improve and remediate academic achievement among African-American students. **The purpose of the revised plan was to make sure the programs actually worked to improve the academic achievement of African-American students. Compliance with this provision was crucial.** The appeals court found it significant that LRSD had agreed to evaluate only a small subset of academic achievement assessment programs identified in the interim report as "key programs." The court held the revised plan was a contract between the parties that the district court was not free to embellish upon. The district court order contained a highly detailed compliance remedy that came close to "crossing the line" between proper judicial enforcement of a desegregation decree and improperly imposing new requirements upon the parties. The court decided not to reverse the decision, as it was not "clear error" for the district court to find LRSD had not substantially complied with the revised plan. *Little Rock School Dist. v. North Little Rock School Dist.*, 451 F.3d 528 (8th Cir. 2006).

◆ The Pasadena Unified School District (PUSD) operated under a federal consent decree to remedy *de jure* racial segregation in its schools from 1970 to 1979. It was then released from court oversight and implemented a series of voluntary integration plans. The school board approved an integration policy in 1998 that instituted a lottery system for assigning students to magnet schools. The policy gave priority assignment to students whose siblings were already enrolled at a school and then used a computerized lottery. The lottery formula considered factors such as race, gender, socioeconomic status and special education needs. However, the factors were considered only "when necessary to create an integrated setting." PUSD conducted lotteries for two magnet schools without using race, ethnicity or gender as a factor because the applicant pools were deemed representative of the district's overall student population.

A group of students sued the district in a federal district court, which agreed that the lottery violated their equal protection rights. PUSD appealed to the Ninth Circuit, which considered whether the students were in realistic danger of suffering a direct injury as a result of the use of the lottery provision. At the time PUSD conducted the lottery, they could not know whether the race or gender provisions would be applied and whether this would be a disadvantage. **The mere existence of a policy to which students objected did not create a real case or controversy.** Only two of the students remained eligible to apply for a PUSD magnet school in the future. Because the others were no longer eligible to attend a magnet school, their claims were moot. There was no genuine threat of adverse treatment due to enforcement of the lottery provision in future years. The district court had erroneously held PUSD's monitoring activities caused an actual injury. PUSD did not indicate it intended to apply a weighted factor in future lotteries. Even if it did so, the district superintendent stated this would only be done in "compelling circumstances." The district court had also committed error by allowing the case to proceed without requiring proof that the lottery policy was applied in any student's case or determining that there was a risk of this in the future. The court reversed the judgment and dismissed the case. *Scott v. Pasadena Unified School Dist.*, 306 F.3d 646 (9th Cir. 2002).

C. Liability Issues

Courts reviewing the actions of government officials in desegregation cases may find liability for civil rights violations where actions by the officials foreseeably perpetuate racial segregation in schools. Relief for constitutional violations may be apportioned among state and local school agencies.

1. Government Liability

◆   A group of African-American families and the National Association for the Advancement of Colored People sued the City of Thomasville (Georgia) School District in a federal district court, asserting the district did not dismantle its *de jure* racially segregated school system. The district had never been under court supervision, and it first attempted to desegregate its schools in 1965. During the late 1970s, district schools became racially imbalanced. The number of white students in the district declined substantially, while the number of African-American students remained stable. The court found racial imbalances in the schools were the result of the demographic changes and were not traceable to the prior *de jure* system. The district responded to the imbalances with an assignment process based on parent preferences. The court found classroom assignment of students was racially imbalanced due to the district's use of "ability grouping" or tracking of students. It attributed the imbalance to a disproportionate number of low-income students in low-ability groups. While most of these students were African-American, the court attributed the assignments to their low-income environment. Other areas of racial imbalance, such as staff and faculty assignment, student discipline, and gifted student and special education eligibility, could not be traced to *de jure* segregation.

The families appealed to the U.S. Court of Appeals, Eleventh Circuit, which found **the mandate of *Brown v. Board of Education* was limited to eliminating vestiges of *de jure* segregation "to the extent practicable," but not "to the maximum potential."** The district court did not commit error by failing to find the system was now "unitary." The system had never been under judicial supervision, and the term was not relevant here. **Under Eleventh Circuit case law, a district satisfied its constitutional duty by showing demographic shifts had substantially caused the current racial imbalances in the system.** The school district carried its burden of proving the racial imbalances in each area were not traceable to the prior system of segregated schools. Where there was no constitutional obligation, a school board was not under a duty to remedy racial imbalances. However, the district court did not apply Eleventh Circuit precedents on student ability groupings or tracking practices. It had found any imbalances were the result of district educational policy and were beyond court review. The Eleventh Circuit remanded the ability groupings question to the district court for reconsideration. **Ability groupings may be permissible in spite of segregative effects, if the assignment method is not based on the present results of past segregation or will remedy such results through better educational opportunities.** The court found that race was not a motivating factor in any of the other areas of district operations, including student discipline, assignment to gifted and special education programs, extracurricular activities and transportation. There was sound evidence that racial imbalances were due to demographic changes. *Holton v. City of Thomasville School Dist.*, 425 F.3d 1325 (11th Cir. 2005).

◆ California's Proposition 209 added Section 31 to Article I of the state constitution. It prevents the state from discriminating against, or granting preferential treatment to, any individual group on the basis of race, sex, color, ethnicity or national origin in the operation of public employment, education or contracting. A school district maintained an open transfer policy with a racial and ethnic balancing component, as required by California Education Code Section 35160.5. The component applied to the only high school in the district that was "ethnically isolated." The school's ethnic composition was 45% Asian, 30.5% Latino and 16% white, with other groups making up the difference. Section 35160.5 required school boards to establish open enrollment policies and to maintain appropriate racial and ethnic balances. The district's racial balancing provision barred white students residing in the school's attendance area from transferring out of the school unless another white student was willing to transfer in. A similar restriction applied to non-white students. A resident taxpayer challenged the transfer policy in state court, alleging it violated Article I, Section 31. The court held for the district.

On appeal, the Court of Appeal of California held **racial classifications by schools are presumptively invalid, unless there is an extraordinary justification for them. The goal of ensuring participation in government programs by a specified percentage because of race or gender was "discrimination for its own sake," in violation of the California Constitution.** The court rejected the district's argument that its transfer policy neither discriminated against nor created preferences for students based on their race. **The restrictions on students who sought to transfer into or out of the district's racially unbalanced high school were inconsistent with the "freedom of choice" that truly voluntary programs provide.** The policy created different transfer criteria solely on the basis of race. The court rejected the district's argument that the policy was required by the Equal Protection Clause. **While the Equal Protection Clause prohibits districts from acting to segregate schools, it does not require any "proactive program of integration."** Racial isolation or imbalance did not require a discriminatory plan of racial desegregation, unless this was necessary to correct the effects of racist government action. The court held the balancing component of Section 35160.5 violated the California Constitution, and it reversed the judgment.

Crawford v. Huntington Beach Union High School Dist., 121 Cal.Rptr.2d 96, 98 Cal.App.4th 1275 (Cal. Ct. App. 2002).

2. Inter-District Remedies

◆ In 1985, the Englewood Cliffs Board of Education petitioned the New Jersey state education commissioner to sever a longstanding agreement with the city of Englewood Board of Education, under which Englewood Cliffs students attended one of Englewood's high schools. Englewood opposed the petition, seeking to prevent further racial imbalance that would result from termination of the agreement. It also joined as a party to the action the Board of Education of Tenafly, a wealthy community that in 1982 began accepting nonresident students to Tenafly High School on a tuition-paying basis. An administrative law judge (ALJ) held the Tenafly policy enticed white and Asian students from Englewood, exacerbating Englewood's racial imbalance. The ALJ held state education officials had a constitutional and statutory responsibility to prevent segregation and ordered the Tenafly Board to stop accepting tuition-paying students from both Englewood and Englewood Cliffs. The state education commissioner adopted the ALJ's decision, and the state board affirmed it.

The case reached the state supreme court, which held the state board and commissioner had an affirmative duty to take action to remedy racial imbalances at the high school. The school had gone from 65.8% black and Hispanic in 1982-83 to 84% in 1987-88. **The first step in achieving a racial balance that would effectuate state policy was to enjoin all other districts, including Tenafly, from accepting Englewood and Englewood Cliffs students** into their schools. The state board had improperly and perhaps unintentionally allocated the responsibility for addressing racial imbalances to the Englewood Board. The court rejected compulsory regionalization, and the commissioner and state board retained ultimate responsibility for addressing racial imbalance at the school. *Board of Educ. of Borough of Englewood Cliffs v. Board of Educ. of City of Englewood*, 170 N.J. 323, 788 A.2d 729 (N.J. 2002).

◆ The U.S. Supreme Court affirmed an intra-district school desegregation plan that included busing in *Columbus Board of Educ. v. Penick*, 443 U.S. 449, 99 S.Ct. 2941, 61 L.Ed.2d 666 (1979). However, in the landmark Detroit school busing case, the Court rejected a plan that would have required multi-district, inter-district busing. It said there was no evidence that suburban districts outside Detroit which were included in the plan either operated segregated school systems or by their actions affected segregation in other districts. The Court held that **absent some inter-district constitutional violations with inter-district effects, racial segregation existing in one district could not be remedied by inter-district solutions**. *Milliken v. Bradley*, 418 U.S. 717, 94 S.Ct. 311, 41 L.Ed.2d 1069 (1974).

◆ In 1979, a federal district court required the inter-district busing of students between primarily black Indianapolis public schools and primarily white public schools in local suburban areas. The court found Indianapolis Public School District (IPSD) boundaries were deliberately maintained to preserve segregated schools and that the city's housing authority refused to build public housing that would encourage desegregation. Years later, the Indianapolis school board moved the court to lift the busing injunction, observing that the lawsuit was 30 years old and claiming that the district had achieved unitary status.

The court denied the motion and ordered all kindergarten students in designated sections of the city to participate in mandatory busing, rescinding an earlier order permitting parents to select busing at their option. IPSD appealed to the U.S. Court of Appeals, Seventh Circuit. **The court held that the school board should have received an opportunity to present evidence at a hearing to consider whether the order should be dissolved.** The district court had erroneously denied the board this opportunity. In addition, the district court had improperly modified the decree to include the compulsory busing of kindergartners. The court vacated and remanded the case, so that the district court could develop a record based upon an evidentiary hearing. *U.S. v. Board of School Commissioners of City of Indianapolis*, 128 F.3d 507 (7th Cir. 1997).

3. Budget Issues

◆ In 1971, a federal district court entered Order 5281, requiring the desegregation of Texas school districts that had taken no steps to comply with *Brown v. Board of Education*. Order 5281 prohibited the Texas Education Agency (TEA) from allowing student transfers that reduced or impeded desegregation, or that perpetuated discrimination. Hearne Independent School District (HISD) was not a party to Order 5281, but had been the defendant in another desegregation case. Its total student enrollment dropped from near 1,700 in 1991 to under 1,200 in 2004. Mumford Independent School District (MISD) grew from 57 students to over 400 during the same years, largely by receiving students from HISD of Hispanic or African-American descent. HISD and MISD remained "majority-minority" both before and after the transfers. The U.S. government and HISD claimed the transfers violated Order 5281 and sued the TEA and MISD in a federal district court to halt the transfers. The court prohibited further transfers of white students to MISD.

On appeal, the Fifth Circuit noted the racial composition of Texas public schools had changed drastically since 1971. It found **"recent litigation under Order 5281 has involved small rural school districts fighting over student population in contests rooted more in resource allocation than racial injustice."** Order 5281 required consideration for the racial balance of both HISD and MISD. This took into account Hispanic, white and African-American students. The district court "skewed its analysis" toward HISD alone and "arbitrarily excluded Hispanic students." The court noted that during the past decade, HISD had lost students of all races via transfers, dropouts and changes of residence. The TEA had a "liberal transfer policy" in which state funding followed students across district lines. The district court had rejected the TEA's balancing approach and ordered the TEA to cease all funding for the transfer of white students, including those who had attended MISD schools for their entire school careers. **Court-ordered relief must not exceed the scope of a constitutional violation. Small changes in the racial composition of a district due to student transfers did not justify mandatory inter-district**

desegregation remedies. The court found the TEA's funding of transfers had no significant net racial impact upon either district. The district court remedy grossly exceeded any possible violation of Order 5281. The battle between districts was for transfer dollars, not racial justice, and the district court order was vacated. *U.S. v. State of Texas*, 457 F.3d 472 (5th Cir. 2006).

◆   In 1977, the Kansas City, Missouri, School District (KCMSD), its school board and a group of resident students sued the state of Missouri and a number of suburban Kansas City school districts in a federal district court, claiming the state had caused and perpetuated racial segregation in Kansas City schools. The district court held that the state and KCMSD were liable for an intra-district constitutional violation. The defendants were ordered to eliminate all vestiges of state-imposed segregation. Because the district's student population was almost 70% African-American, the court ordered a wide range of quality education plans that converted every high school and middle school, and some elementary schools, into magnet schools to attract white students from adjoining suburbs. This action was based upon the court's finding that KCMSD student achievement levels still lagged behind national averages in some grades. The state contested its court-ordered responsibility to help fund capital improvements for KCMSD schools. It also contested orders requiring it to share in the cost of teacher salary increases and quality education plans.

Appealed reached the U.S. Supreme Court. The Court observed **the district court's remedial plan had been based on a budget that exceeded KCMSD's authority to tax**. There was a lack of evidence in the district court record to substantiate the theory that continuing lack of academic achievement in the district was the result of past segregation. **The Court determined that the district court had exceeded its authority by ordering the construction of a superior school system to attract white students from suburban and private schools.** Its mandate was to remove the racial identity of KCMSD schools, and the inter-district remedy went beyond the intra-district violation. **The magnet district concept of KCMSD schools could not be supported by the existence of white flight. The district court orders for state contribution to salary increases, quality education programs and capital improvements were reversed.** *Missouri v. Jenkins*, 115 S.Ct. 2038, 132 L.Ed.2d 63 (1995). In earlier stages of the litigation, the Court prevented the district court from imposing a property tax increase, ruling that relief should be directed against local authorities who could then impose the tax increase. *Missouri v. Jenkins*, 495 U.S. 33, 110 S.Ct. 1651, 109 L.Ed.2d 31 (1990).

The district court established a remedial plan and budget for the 1996–1997 school year and ordered the phase-out of a voluntary inter-district transfer program involving 13 students in a suburban district. The state of Missouri appealed to the Eighth Circuit, and the class representing African-American students cross-appealed an order prohibiting the use of desegregation funds to market magnet school programs to private school students. **The court approved of the marketing and recruiting efforts directed at non-minority private school students**, finding nothing in the Supreme Court's decision preventing it. **It also approved of the continued funding of the inter-district program while present enrollees continued their education.** The court approved the inclusion of an extended day program within the 1996–1997 budget. However, it remanded to the district court certain remedial and budgetary issues concerning the retention of permanent substitutes at district schools. *Jenkins by Jenkins v. State of Missouri*, 103 F.3d 731 (8th Cir. 1997).

The full Eighth Circuit reversed a district court finding that the district had achieved unitary status. The district court should have held a hearing to allow both sides to present evidence on the issue prior to issuing a ruling. *Jenkins by Jenkins v. State of Missouri*, 216 F.3d 720 (8th Cir. 2000).

◆　A group of African-American students sued a South Carolina school district in 1962, seeking an order to compel the desegregation of its schools. A federal district court entered an order in 1970 requiring the district to implement a desegregation plan. The U.S. intervened in the case in 1990, claiming that the district violated the 1970 order by maintaining segregated schools. The school district filed a motion to join the state of South Carolina, claiming that it was partly responsible for perpetuating segregated schools. The court rejected the state's claim for Eleventh Amendment immunity and approved a consent order resolving several remedial issues. It ordered the state to participate in desegregation remedies, fund necessary transportation services and pay 15% of the capital costs and operating expenses of implementing the desegregation order. The state appealed to the Fourth Circuit.

The court held that had the U.S. or the original plaintiffs filed the claim against the state, the district court could have apportioned relief between the district and state. However, **because only the school district had sought relief against the state, the district court could not order any relief against the state**. Because the U.S. and the original plaintiffs had failed to name the state as a defendant, there was no basis for the district's claim against the state for contribution. The court reversed the district court judgment pertaining to the imposition of liability on the state, but otherwise affirmed its judgment. *Stanley v. Darlington County School Dist.*, 84 F.3d 707 (4th Cir. 1996).

Prior to the release of the court of appeals' decision, the school district revised the selection and admission process for a new magnet school by eliminating a set-aside of seats from the school's attendance zone and the initial requirement for a 50/50 student racial composition. The U.S. objected to the revised selection and admission criteria, and the court held a hearing to consider the revisions. It determined that the school board had ignored research by the magnet school task force and disregarded expert opinions in imposing the revisions. **Evidence indicated that a 50/50 racial composition was important to prevent a racial identity in the community which might stigmatize the school.** It was also important for resident students to enjoy the benefits of the school to engage community support. Because the school board action removed all desegregation mechanisms from the selection and admission criteria, it jeopardized the success of the magnet school and the orderly desegregation of the district. The court found the district in default of its obligation to establish a magnet school and held that its prior interim order remained in effect. *Stanley v. Darlington County School Dist.*, 915 F.Supp. 764 (D.S.C. 1996).

III. SCHOOL DISTRICT OPERATIONS

School district powers are created by state laws, and actions exceeding statutory authority may be set aside by a reviewing court. If state law provides, school district territories may be altered by annexation and detachment where economics or demographics make such action necessary.

A. School Closing and District Dissolution Issues

◆ **Nebraska's supreme court held the state legislature did not violate voter civil rights by ordering the dissolution, attachment or detachment of certain school districts five months before the same issue would be presented to voters in a referendum election.** The legislature passed L.B. 126, an act to reorganize school districts so that each district offered education for grades K-12. A voter organization obtained over 87,000 signatures on a petition to refer L.B. 126 to a statewide voter referendum election. This represented 7.7% of all Nebraska voters and was sufficient to place the referendum on the November 2006 ballot. However, it was less than the 10% of registered voters that would be required to suspend the act's operation under the Nebraska Constitution. Several school districts and individual voters filed a class action lawsuit against the state committee and its members in the state court system, seeking relief from L.B. 126 prior to the November voter referendum.

A Nebraska district court found the act's deadline for dissolving and attaching Class I territories violated the state constitution. The committee appealed to the Supreme Court of Nebraska, which found no constitutional requirement for the legislature to delay the effective date of legislation until after a referendum election occurred. The complaining parties had obtained only 7.7% of the statewide electorate in their petition. This was sufficient to refer L.B. 126 to the voters at the next general election, but less than the 10% threshold required to suspend operation of an act specified in the Nebraska Constitution. The court held the complaining parties did not show entitlement to suspension of the act in the interim. The court found L.B. 126 did not violate the voting or speech rights of the complaining parties, and it reversed the judgment. *Pony Lake School Dist. 30 v. State Committee for Reorganization of School Districts*, 271 Neb. 173, 710 N.W.2d 609 (Neb. 2006).

◆ The Pittsburgh Board of Education announced plans to close 18 schools and held a public meeting to address its fiscal budget shortly thereafter. A newspaper advertisement publicizing the meeting did not mention the issue of school closure. Several parents and students claimed they did not receive adequate notice of the meeting under state law and that others who attended the meeting were able to prevent the closure of their schools. The group sued the district, its superintendent and board in federal district court, asserting constitutional rights violations under 42 U.S.C. § 1983. The court dismissed the case, and the group appealed to the U.S. Court of Appeals, Third Circuit.

The court noted that while the decision to close the schools may have occurred before the group received the notice it deserved under state law, this did not rise to the level of a constitutional violation. Section 1983 is a critical means of vindicating the denial of federally guaranteed rights, but it cannot be invoked each time local officials act contrary to state or local procedural law. The group's complaint was properly left to the Pennsylvania court system, not the federal courts. **The students had no constitutional property or liberty interest in attending their school of choice** and did not have a valid due process claim. The court affirmed the judgment for the district, superintendent and board. *Mullen v. Thompson*, 31 Fed.Appx. 77 (3d Cir. 2002).

◆   A New Jersey regional high school district served six municipalities. Five of the municipal education boards and governing bodies applied to the county school superintendent to dissolve the district under a state law allowing for such action where any constituent district suffers an excessive debt burden, an efficient school system cannot be maintained, insufficient students will be left in any constituent district, or for any other reason that the regional board may deem sufficient. The superintendent recommended against dissolution, but four of the constituent education boards and governing bodies obtained approval by the state education commissioner for permission to hold a referendum to dissolve the regional district. A district with a tax levy per student that was only half the average of the other districts objected to the commissioner's order.

A majority of regional voters elected to dissolve the regional district, and the objecting district appealed. The Superior Court of New Jersey, Appellate Division, held that none of the three enumerated statutory reasons for denying a referendum were satisfied here. **The objecting district failed to show dissolution was inconsistent with the state's obligation to assure the maintenance of a thorough and efficient school system.** The lack of a sufficient tax base by the objecting district was not a policy reflected in the statute, and the commissioner's decision was affirmed. The court also rejected the complaining district's argument that the action violated the state open public meetings act. *In re Dissolution of Union County Regional High School Dist. No. 1*, 298 N.J.Super. 1, 688 A.2d 1082 (N.J. Super. Ct. App. Div. 1997).

B. Redistricting and Zoning

◆   A New York school district provided special education services at private, religious schools to students with disabilities who were members of the Satmar Hasidic group. The group's religious beliefs include segregation of school-aged boys and girls and separation from mainstream society. A U.S. Supreme Court decision in 1985 prohibited the state from paying public school teachers for teaching on parochial school grounds. The state legislature passed a statute establishing a separate school district entirely within the Hasidic community to provide special education services. The New York Court of Appeals held the statute endorsed religion in violation of the Establishment Clause.

The U.S. Supreme Court agreed to review the case. It held that **a state may not delegate authority to a group chosen by religion**. Although the statute did not expressly identify the Hasidim as recipients of governmental authority, it had clearly been passed to benefit them. The result was a purposeful and forbidden fusion of governmental and religious functions. **The creation of a school district for the religious community violated the Establishment**

Clause. The legislation extended a special franchise to the Hasidim that violated the constitutional requirement of religious neutrality by the government. The statute crossed "the line from permissible accommodation to impermissible establishment." The Supreme Court affirmed the judgment of the court of appeals. *Board of Educ. of Kiryas Joel Village School Dist. v. Grumet*, 512 U.S. 687, 114 S.Ct. 2481, 129 L.Ed.2d 546 (1994).

The legislature passed new legislation allowing municipalities to establish their own school districts upon the satisfaction of several criteria. Noting these criteria had the effect of restoring the Hasidic school district, the taxpayers renewed their challenge. A state trial court upheld the act. The taxpayers appealed to the New York Supreme Court, Appellate Division, arguing the new legislative criteria created the same result as the prior unconstitutional law. The court agreed, observing that one of the criteria was apparently meaningless and had been included only to limit the applicability of the statute and afford special treatment to village residents. **The legislation had no educational purpose, was not generally applicable and was enacted as a subterfuge** to avoid the Supreme Court decision. The statute violated the Establishment Clause. *Grumet v. Cuomo*, 647 N.Y.S.2d 565 (N.Y. App. Div. 1996).

The state's highest court held that **despite the neutral criteria of the amendments, the Hasidic village was the only municipality that could ever avail itself of the amendments.** Because the law applied only to municipalities in existence as of the effective date of the amendments, no other municipality could become eligible for redistricting, and the legislation impermissibly favored the Satmar sect. Since the law could be perceived as being for the sole benefit of the sect, the court affirmed the judgment for the taxpayers. *Grumet v. Cuomo*, 90 N.Y.2d 57, 659 N.Y.S.2d 173, 681 N.E.2d 340 (N.Y. 1997).

The legislature amended the law again in 1997, in an attempt to conform with the court of appeals' decision. After a decision by the appellate division invalidating the amended statute, the case again reached the New York Court of Appeals. It held that despite the law's facial neutrality with respect to religion, it only benefited Kiryas Joel residents, and its potential benefit extended to only one other district in the state. **Since other religious groups would be unable to benefit from the law in the manner enjoyed by the Satmar sect of Kiryas Joel, the law was not neutral in effect** and violated the Establishment Clause. *Grumet v. Pataki*, 93 N.Y.2d 677, 720 N.E.2d 66 (N.Y. 1999).

◆ Wisconsin residents petitioned for the detachment of their property from the school district in which the property was located, seeking attachment to adjoining districts. The adjoining districts approved the petitions, but the residence district denied them. The residents appealed to the state school district boundary appeal board, which allowed the detachment of many property parcels even though they did not share a common boundary with the attaching school districts, creating "island parcels." The district that lost the property appealed to a Wisconsin circuit court, which affirmed the board's decision.

The Supreme Court of Wisconsin found that a 1981 amendment to Wisconsin law deleted a reference to boundary lines in school district property detachment cases. Although there was ambiguity in the amended statute, the court agreed with the board's interpretation, which permitted noncontiguous property annexation. While common borders were no longer an issue in detachment and annexation cases, the board was required by the legislation to consider the geographical characteristics of the affected school districts, travel time, student educational needs, potential adverse effects on curricular and extracurricular programs and the fiscal effects of proposed reorganizations. **Because the evidence indicated that the board's decision was within its discretion and jurisdiction, the court approved of the detachment of property.** *Stockbridge School Dist. v. Dep't of Public Instruction School Dist. Boundary Appeal Board,* 550 N.W.2d 96 (Wis. 1996).

◆   Thirteen Texas students attended school in a school district adjoining their district of residence without officially transferring. The Texas Education Agency had previously refused requests by other students residing in the same subdivision to transfer to the adjoining district as violative of a federal district court desegregation order. When the adjoining district discovered that the students were attending its schools without official transfers, it threatened to charge them tuition. Residents of the subdivision sought detachment of the subdivision from their district and annexation to the adjoining district. The state commissioner of education ordered detachment of the subdivision. The case reached the state court of appeals. It held that **although the action resulted in a 2.5% decrease in the white student population in the ceding district, and the annexing district had a higher rate of white attendance, the proposed boundary change did not violate the federal court order.** The proposed boundary change would not create, maintain, reinforce, renew or encourage a dual school system. Both systems were unitary. The court rejected the ceding district's argument that the detachment would lead to the defection of other white subdivisions to the annexing district. *Texas Educ. Agency v. Goodrich Independent School Dist.,* 898 S.W.2d 954 (Tex. Ct. App. 1995).

IV. SCHOOL BOARDS

A. Membership

1. Appointments, Elections, Residency and Recall

◆   A Washington school board voted to reschedule a school makeup day in violation of a collective bargaining provision. Many teachers did not report for work and those who did received no pay. The board found some substitutes, but it resorted to hiring jugglers and clowns to keep students occupied for the day. An arbitrator held the board violated the collective bargaining agreement by unilaterally changing the makeup day. The arbitrator found board members had "knowingly and willfully" violated contract rights by withholding pay. The incident cost the district almost $75,000. Three district residents filed recall petitions against two board members. A state superior court partially approved the petitions. It found the board members had knowingly violated employee contractual rights and caused the district to incur "significant unnecessary costs" and legal fees. The hiring of "entertainers" resulted in substandard instruction and supervision for students, and it violated the board members' oaths of office. The recall petitions could proceed to the signature-gathering phase.

The board members appealed. The Supreme Court of Washington stated the courts serve a "gateway function" in the recall process. Courts do not evaluate the truth of the charges in a petition, but only decide whether they are factually and legally sufficient. **To be legally sufficient, the petitions needed only "state with specificity substantial conduct clearly amounting to misfeasance, malfeasance or violation of the oath of office."** The court held "if an elective public officer knowingly and willingly breaks a collective bargaining agreement and thereby unnecessarily causes substantial financial harm, this may be considered an improper act and a violation of the oath." As the charges against the board members were legally sufficient, the petitioners could continue seeking a special election to recall the members from office. *In re Recall of Young*, 100 P.3d 307 (Wash. 2004).

◆   Texas is a covered jurisdiction under Section 5 of the Voting Rights Act of 1965. The Texas legislature enacted a comprehensive statutory scheme for holding local school boards accountable to the state for student achievement. The law contained 10 possible sanctions on districts for failing to meet legislative standards governing the assessment of academic skills, development of academic performance indicators, determination of accreditation status and the imposition of accreditation sanctions. The law's most drastic sanctions – appointment of a master or a management team to oversee district operations – required the exhaustion of the lesser sanctions first. In compliance with Section 5, Texas requested administrative pre-clearance for the amendments. The attorney general approved most of the sanctions as not affecting voting but found the appointment of a master or management team could result in a Section 5 violation.

Texas appealed to the U.S. District Court for the District of Columbia, which held that the claim was not ripe for adjudication. **The U.S. Supreme Court agreed to review the case, and it stated the general rule that a claim is not ripe for adjudication if it rests upon contingent future events that may not actually occur.** Texas had not identified any school district in the state that might become subject to the appointment of a master or management team and was not required to implement the sanctions until one of the remedies already approved by the attorney general had been exhausted. Because the issue presented was speculative and unfit for judicial review, the Court affirmed the judgment. *Texas v. U.S.*, 523 U.S. 296, 118 S.Ct. 1257, 140 L.Ed.2d 406 (1998).

◆   The Tennessee Constitution and the Tennessee Education Improvement Act mandate popularly elected school boards. Shelby County Tennessee, which encompasses the city of Memphis, has two school districts, one of which serves only Memphis residents. The county enacted an electoral plan calling for the election of county board members from seven single-member districts throughout the entire county. As a result, Memphis residents could vote in county education board elections, even though students from Memphis attended school in a different system. The county board of commissioners filed a federal district court action against state officials including the attorney general, seeking a declaration that the Education Improvement Act violated the Fourteenth Amendment rights of county voters who did not reside in Memphis. The court agreed with the commissioners, and the state officials appealed.

The U.S. Court of Appeals, Sixth Circuit, stated the courts have established a number of factors to determine whether non-district voters have a substantial interest in school board elections. These included the degree to which one district finances the other, the voting strength of district voters, the potential for crossover students and joint programs between districts. In this case, Memphis voters did not substantially finance the county school district, and they outnumbered county voters by three to one. There was very little crossover of students and a negligible number of joint programs between city and county districts. Applying these factors, **the court held the Education Improvement Act was unconstitutional as applied to county school board voters. It improperly diluted votes and placed the majority of votes in the hands of out-of-district voters.** The court affirmed the district court's judgment. *Board of County Commissioners of Shelby County, Tennessee v. Burson,* 121 F.3d 244 (6th Cir. 1997).

◆   Section Two of the federal Voting Rights Act of 1965 bars all states and their political subdivisions from maintaining discriminatory voting practices, standards or procedures. Section Five of the act is limited in scope to "covered jurisdictions." It prohibits the passing of new discriminatory laws as soon as old ones are struck down by freezing election procedures in covered jurisdictions unless the changes are nondiscriminatory. A Louisiana school board that was covered under Section 5 addressed population disparities revealed in the 1990 census by adopting a plan preserving a white majority in each of its 12 single-member districts. The board rejected a proposal by the local National Association for the Advancement of Colored People (NAACP) that would have created two districts with a majority of African-American voters. The board complied with Section 5 procedures by obtaining pre-clearance from the U.S. District Court for the District of Columbia. The U.S. Attorney General's office appealed to the U.S. Supreme Court, where it joined with the NAACP in arguing that a change in voting practices that violates Section 2 also constitutes an independent reason to deny pre-clearance under Section 5.

The Supreme Court held the sections addressed different voting policy concerns. Nothing in the statute justified presuming that a violation of Section 2 was sufficient for denying pre-clearance under Section 5. However, some of the evidence presented in support of a Section 2 claim might be relevant in a Section 5 proceeding. **Because the district court had failed to consider evidence of the dilutive impact of the board's redistricting plan, the Court vacated the judgment and remanded the case.** *Reno v. Bossier Parish School Board,* 520 U.S. 471, 117 S.Ct. 1491, 137 L.Ed.2d 73 (1997).

On remand, the district court again granted pre-clearance to the board, and the Attorney General obtained Supreme Court review. The Supreme Court held **Section Five does not prohibit pre-clearance of a redistricting plan enacted with a discriminatory but non-retrogressive purpose. Accordingly, the Court affirmed the judgment.** *Reno v. Bossier Parish School Board,* 528 U.S. 320, 120 S.Ct. 866, 145 L.Ed.2d 845 (2000).

2. Misconduct, Conflict of Interest and Nepotism

◆   After a Kansas teacher won a four-year term as a school board member, the board sought to disqualify her from service while she continued her teaching duties. It alternatively sought to prevent her from receiving her teaching salary while serving as a board member. A state district court held that although state law prohibited certain persons from school board membership, it did not specifically exclude teachers. The court also found that the board's policy prohibiting members from receiving compensation for employment by the district was void as an unlawful attempt to determine who was qualified to serve as a board member. The school board appealed to the Kansas Supreme Court.

According to the state supreme court, the district court had erroneously found the teacher was not subject to disqualification simply because teachers were not specifically listed among those excluded from serving as board members in Kan. Stat. Ann. § 72-8202. In the absence of legislative authority, the court analyzed the case under the common law doctrine of incompatibility of office, which considers whether the nature and duties of two offices render it improper as a matter of public policy for one person to retain both positions. The court concluded **the offices of teacher and board member are demonstrably incompatible with the common law rule**. Under the dual-service arrangement, the teacher occupied one position that was subordinate to the other. She was both employer and employee, and she sat on a policy-making body that negotiated with the employees' collective bargaining representative. This presented a clear conflict of interest. She was subject to discipline by the board and could be fired by it in certain circumstances. **Because the fulfillment of one office by the teacher was invariably at odds with the other, the offices were incompatible and the dual arrangement was prohibited.** Applying equitable principles, the court found that her employment as a teacher endured and disqualified her from serving on the board. *Unified School Dist. No. 501, Shawnee County, Kansas v. Baker*, 269 Kan. 239, 6 P.3d 848 (Kan. 2000).

◆   A Georgia citizen complained that three elected school board members had participated in decisions affecting the compensation and benefits of their spouses, who were employees of the school system. The individual also asserted that the board members' recent election of a new superintendent was improper because the new superintendent would "be beholden to the [board members] and would reciprocate by granting [their] spouses additional privileges, compensation or benefits." A Georgia trial court dismissed the complaint for failure to state a claim upon which relief could be granted, finding no enforceable duty among the board members to refrain from voting on matters that might affect the financial interests of their employee spouses.

The citizen appealed to the Georgia Supreme Court, which affirmed. The constitutional provision at issue stated that "[p]ublic officers are the trustees and servants of the people and at all times amenable to them." This broad language had been construed in other cases as prohibiting a public officer from financially benefiting as the result of performing official duties. In this case, the alleged benefit to the board members' spouses was speculative, and the language of the state constitution did not support the citizen's construction.

There was no precedent for the position that the familial relationship of locally elected school officials disqualified them from participating in school operations decisions. The ineligibility criteria of state law did not include familial relationships, and the trial court had properly dismissed the complaint. *Ianicelli v. McNeely*, 272 Ga. 234, 527 S.E.2d 189 (Ga. 2000).

◆ An Iowa school board member publicly denounced an assessment test given to all eleventh-grade students in the district. The district responded by copyrighting the test and ordering the dissenting board member to return her copies of it. She refused and requested test-scoring information. The district custodian of records denied the request under the confidentiality exception to the state public records act. The board passed a resolution vesting the superintendent with discretion to determine whether materials should be released to a board member. The dissenting board member filed an action in a state district court for release of the testing materials. The court held the materials were confidential records that were excluded from the public records act and enjoined the dissenting board member from copying, distributing or disseminating them. She appealed to the Supreme Court of Iowa.

The court held **the tests were confidential records even though they had already been released** to the board member and were available for public inspection as the result of the copyright action. **Records do not lose their confidential nature because of a limited release of information.** The custodian of records had exercised his discretion in a reasonable manner by withholding the further release of testing materials. However, **the board member was entitled to receive the information since she needed the information in her capacity as a board member.** The court held that the board's policy limiting her access to the information was improper and reversed the part of the district court order prohibiting disclosure. The court modified the decision by enjoining her from any further dissemination of confidential materials. *Gabrilson v. Flynn*, 554 N.W.2d 267 (Iowa 1996).

◆ The Kentucky General Assembly established school-based councils to oversee individual school operations while preserving the role of the school board as the authority over each school district in the state. The legislation contained an anti-nepotism clause prohibiting school district employees or their spouses from serving as parent members of school-based councils, which are composed of two parents, three teachers and the principal or administrator of each school. Two parent members of school-based councils gained election despite the fact that their spouses were employed at a district grade school.

They challenged their removal actions by the state department of education in a Kentucky circuit court, seeking a declaratory judgment and order prohibiting their removal. The court determined that the anti-nepotism provision was unconstitutional, and the state department of education appealed. The Supreme Court of Kentucky observed that the trial court had subjected the statute to an improper level of scrutiny. Parents were not a suspect class who enjoyed a constitutionally protected fundamental right to serve on school councils. **There was a clear indication in the amendment that the legislature intended to eradicate nepotism within school districts, and the amendment**

was not unconstitutional. The court reversed the circuit court decision. *Kentucky Dep't of Educ. v. Risner*, 913 S.W.2d 327 (Ky. 1996).

◆ A Virginia teacher worked for a county school board for six years. Following a 13-year absence from teaching, she reapplied to the board for employment. However, during her absence, her brother-in-law was elected chairman of the board. Because the Virginia Code prohibited a district from employing a person related to a board member, her employment application was denied. The teacher sued the board in a Virginia trial court, claiming she was entitled to an exception applicable "to any person within such relationship who has been (i) regularly employed ... by any school board prior to the taking of office of any member of such board." The court held for the school board, and the teacher appealed. The Supreme Court of Virginia noted the legislature had used the present perfect tense in the statute, indicating action beginning in the past and continuing to the present. This required an interpretation that **persons seeking to avail themselves of the exception be employed by the school board at the time the conflict of interest arose.** Because the teacher was not employed by the board at the time her brother-in-law was elected chairman, she could not avail herself of the exception, and the trial court had properly held for the board. *Williams v. Augusta County School Board,* 445 S.E.2d 118 (Va. 1994).

B. School Board Powers and Duties

◆ **The Supreme Court of Montana held a citizen's challenge to the continued use of Native American mascots by a school board had to be heard by the state human rights commission.** The superintendent had no jurisdiction over the challenge to the board's decision to retain mascots named "Chief" and "Maiden" by the district, which is located entirely within the Flathead Reservation. The court held the human rights commission was the appropriate agency for determining whether the mascots created a hostile environment under the state human rights act. A "mere disagreement" with the district did not entitle the citizen to a hearing before the superintendent. *Dupuis v. Board of Trustees, Ronan School Dist. No. 30,* 128 P.3d 1010 (Mont. 2006).

◆ Two Indiana home-schooled students sought to attend public schools on a part-time basis. The district superintendent denied their request under a district policy prohibiting non-public school students from enrolling in less than six credit-generating courses, unless they had an individualized education program. The students appealed. An administrative law judge held they should be allowed to attend classes part-time in district schools. The district appealed to an Indiana trial court and sought to stay the administrative order. The court granted the request for a stay and scheduled a "preliminary hearing." The state board asked for and received an extension to respond. Meanwhile, the hearing was held. The trial court invited the parties to submit additional briefs, but they declined. It then vacated the order of the administrative law judge as contrary to law.

The board appealed to the Court of Appeals of Indiana, which held the board had been denied due process. **Due process requires notice, an opportunity to be heard, and a chance to confront any witnesses. Notice** must be reasonably calculated to afford parties a chance to present their cases. The court found it unreasonable for the parties to expect a "preliminary hearing" would be their last and only chance to present their cases. The board received notice of the hearing only seven days in advance. This was not reasonable notice. Statements by the parties indicated the subject of the hearing was a stay of the administrative order, not a final review. The parties believed the purpose of the preliminary hearing was to consider a stay, and they clearly expected additional hearings. As the board was not put on notice of the finality of the hearing, it was denied due process. *Indiana State Board of Educ. v. Brownsburg Community School Corp.*, 842 N.E.2d 885 (Ind. Ct. App. 2006).

◆   A Montana citizen sued a school district in the state court system, asserting a right to participate in the selection of a new superintendent. She claimed the school board failed to notify her of votes and decisions leading to the hiring. A state district court dismissed the case, and the citizen appealed. The Supreme Court of Montana noted that the state constitution grants the right to a reasonable opportunity for citizen participation in the operation of government, and the right to examine documents or observe the deliberations of public bodies and agencies. **In order to satisfy the requirement of standing to bring suit, the citizen had to clearly allege a past, present or threatened injury to a property or civil right. She further had to claim an injury that was distinguishable from injury to the public at large.** The court rejected her claim that being an informed and interested citizen conferred standing. As there was no indication in the record that she had any personal stake or interest in the hiring of a new superintendent, the case had been properly dismissed. *Fleenor v. Darby School Dist.*, 331 Mont. 124, 128 P.3d 1048 (Mont. 2006).

◆   The Salt Lake City School Board considered school facilities usage, school boundaries and school closings for a period of over four years. It eventually closed two elementary schools in one part of the city and planned to build new schools in another area that it identified as underserved. Parents who objected to the actions claimed the board acted arbitrarily and failed to consider its own policy in closing the schools. A state trial court consolidated separate actions by parents and other opponents of the school closings. It held a trial, where the opponents claimed the board violated a 1973 policy requiring it to follow several factors in making school closing decisions. The factors included keeping neighborhood schools as close as possible to students and communities, student safety, minimizing student transportation, the placement of students in efficient and functional buildings, use of newer school buildings and replacement of older ones. The court found the opponents did not show the board ignored its closure policy, or act arbitrarily and capriciously in closing the schools. It found that even if the board did not have the policy before it, the factors enumerated in it were fully incorporated into new documents that guided the closing decisions. The opponents appealed to the Supreme Court of Utah.

The court accepted the trial court's determination that the board considered its policy when it acted. Meeting minutes, instructions to subcommittees and other documents were "replete with discussion of the factors" contained in the policy. **The trial court did not commit error by finding the board had thoroughly discussed the policy factors when it made the closure decisions. The factors themselves indicated the discretionary nature of the board action.** The court was reluctant to disturb the board's discretion in the absence of arbitrary action or a due process violation. The remedy for opponents of the closings was "in the voting booths," and the court affirmed the judgment. *Save Our Schools v. Board of Educ. of Salt Lake City*, 122 P.3d 611 (Utah 2005).

◆   **The Supreme Court of New Hampshire rejected a taxpayer challenge to a school district's decision to enter into a three-year contract with an adjoining district to provide education for high school students.** The Bedford School District (BSD) did not operate its own high school. For over 70 years, BSD contracted with the Manchester School District (MSD) to educate its high school students. In 2001, MSD notified BSD and several other districts it would terminate their 20-year tuition contracts at the end of the 2002-03 school year. Bedford voters did not approve a new 20-year tuition contract with MSD. BSD and MSD then negotiated a three-year tuition contract that included a per-pupil tuition payment. The payment had an operating expense component and a capital expense component. At BSD's annual meeting in 2004, BSD voters approved a $1.8 million deficit appropriation to fund the capital component of the tuition contract. Voters also approved a general budget to fund the entire tuition payment for the 2004-05 school year. This included a $4.4 million appropriation for the capital component. Two taxpayers sued BSD and MSD in a state court, challenging the validity of the three-year contract and the votes. They sought an order barring payment of the capital component of the tuition payment and restoration of amounts of capital expenses already paid.

The case reached the state supreme court. It held RSA Section 194:22 permitted school districts to make contracts and to raise and appropriate the money to effectuate them. Nothing in this statute required voter approval before a contract could be made. While Section 194:10 referred to a district's "voters," this meant voters at a district's annual meeting. The court found the taxpayers misapprehended the nature of school districts. **State law made districts "corporations," with powers to sue and be sued, hold and dispose of real and personal property, and the ability to make contracts. The authority to appropriate money rested with the school district meeting, as this was the district's legislative body.** The board had authority to make necessary contracts such as the tuition payment contract. BSD voters had been informed of the contract and its financial consequences before approving of the deficit appropriations. As voters had ratified the board's actions, and the taxpayers did not show fraud, the court affirmed the judgment. *Foote v. Manchester School Dist.*, 152 N.H. 599, 883 A.2d 283 (N.H. 2005).

◆   A Minnesota school district reassigned all its junior high school grades to a high school building. The building that housed both elementary and junior high school grades was divided into separate "schools." Grades seven and eight made up 53% of the student population for the building, and classes for these grades occupied about half its space. A district committee issued a report recommending that grades seven and eight be moved from the building and into the district's only high school. The board adopted the committee's recommendation at a meeting, and a citizens' group petitioned the Court of Appeals of Minnesota for an order setting aside the action.

The court noted the closing of a schoolhouse was a "quasi-judicial decision" under state law that could be reviewed by the court. The citizens argued that the reassignment was in effect a schoolhouse closing under Minn. Statutes Section 123B.51. The building's student population had declined from 313 to 143 as a result of the board's action. The building had previously been considered as made up of two schools. **The court held the building was a single "schoolhouse," even though the junior high and elementary grades had been considered separate "schools." The legislature intended the notice and hearing requirements of Section 123B.51 to apply only when a school shut its doors.** The statute did not apply when a school remained open with a different student body composition. For a "schoolhouse closing" to take place, a district had to totally suspend or cease all the operations of a facility. The court found the changed composition of the building irrelevant. While the reassignment action had greatly reduced the student population at the building, the district had not totally suspended or ceased all operations there. The court held the reassignment of grades was not a "schoolhouse closing" as defined by state law, and the board was not required to follow the procedures of the school closing statute. The case was not reviewable by writ of certiorari. The court discharged the petition. *Citizens Concerned for Kids v. Yellow Medicine East Independent School Dist. No. 2109,* 703 N.W.2d 582 (Minn. Ct. App. 2005).

◆   **An Ohio court held parents have no constitutional right to attend school activities or be present on school grounds. School authorities may exclude parents from school activities and property without a hearing.** The parent of a middle school student got into a "verbal altercation" with her daughter's volleyball coach at a neighboring school. School administrators banned her from school activities for three months. The district had no rule in place regarding non-student attendance at activities or on school grounds. The school board considered the arguments of the parent's attorney at a hearing. It voted to uphold the ban and deemed any failure to comply with it to be trespassing. The parent appealed to a state common pleas court, arguing school authorities could not ban her from school without a board rule adopted under Ohio R.C. § 3313.20. This law requires school boards to make necessary rules for governing employees, students and other persons entering upon school grounds or premises. The court stated the Ohio legislature vested school boards with almost unlimited reasonable authority to manage and control schools. Board decisions were presumed valid unless there was an abuse of discretion.

The court restated the rule that **"boards of education are the sole judges of policy regarding management and control of the schools."** The court did not act as a "super board of education" to second-guess the wisdom of a board's action. Unless the board abused its discretion, it could decide how to manage and control its schools. **Ohio school boards may govern school activities and property without adopting formal rules on all aspects of governance, subject to the "abuse of discretion standard."** There was no abuse of discretion in this case. The court held the right to a free public education belongs to students, not their parents. **Although parents have a liberty interest in the education and upbringing of their children, this did not create any constitutional right for them to attend school activities or be present on school property.** As the parent had no constitutional liberty interest in being on school grounds or attending school activities, the board could exclude her from them without a hearing. The court awarded judgment to the board. *Nichols v. Western Local Board of Educ.*, 805 N.E.2d 206 (Ohio Common Pleas 2003).

◆   A 29-year-old former student sued a Connecticut teacher for sexual assault and related claims arising from his conduct as a physical education instructor, teacher and coach 16 years earlier. The teacher filed a separate action in a state trial court against his school board, seeking to compel it to provide him with legal representation. He then admitted to substantially all the conduct of which he was accused. The court granted his motion for summary judgment and ordered the board to provide him with counsel to defend the action. The board appealed to the state appellate court, which transferred the case to the Supreme Court of Connecticut. It noted Section 10-235(a) of the state general statutes requires education boards to "protect and save harmless" any teacher from financial loss and expense from any claim or judgment resulting from alleged negligence that was not "wanton, reckless or malicious," in the course of his or her duties or within the scope of employment. The legislature intended the provision to indemnify teachers for losses resulting from personal injury claims.

Subsection (b) of the statute contained similar language, indicating **the legislature intended to impose a duty of indemnification upon school boards**. The court observed **Section 10-235(b) contained no specific language requiring boards to indemnify teachers**. Instead, the legislature intended that a teacher who is ultimately held liable for injuries resulting from willful, wanton or malicious conduct to reimburse a school board that voluntarily elects to provide a defense. The court held that a statutory duty to indemnify teachers for attorneys' fees could not coexist with a duty to defend, since it was impossible for a board to indemnify a teacher for fees if it had already provided the teacher with counsel. In this case, the student alleged negligent conduct, as well as willful, wanton or malicious conduct. **The board thus had a potential duty to indemnify the teacher for negligence occurring within the scope of his duties. Because of this potential exposure, it could elect to provide him with legal representation rather than indemnify him** after a judgment. If the board did so, it would be entitled to reimbursement from him for expenses incurred in providing defense for any willful, wanton or malicious conduct. The court reversed and remanded the case. *Vibert v. Board of Educ. of Regional School Dist. No. 10*, 793 A.2d 1076, 260 Conn. 167 (Conn. 2002).

◆   Section 2-3.25g of the Illinois School Code allows school districts to petition the state education board for waiver or modification of statutory requirements. **The Chicago Board of Education applied to the state board for a waiver exempting high school juniors and seniors from mandated daily physical education classes.** The state board approved the request, and the Illinois General Assembly took no action to disapprove the request, effectively granting it. A group of taxpayers, parents, teachers and the Chicago Teachers

Union sued the city board in a state court, seeking an order prohibiting the plan on grounds that it encroached upon legislative and executive powers in violation of the separation of powers doctrine. The court dismissed the Chicago Teachers Union and parents from the action, but held that two physical education teachers and two taxpayers had legal standing to mount the challenge. The city board appealed to the Illinois Supreme Court, which held the trial court had erroneously allowed the case to proceed. *Chicago Teachers Union, Local 1 v. Board of Educ. of City of Chicago*, 189 Ill.2d 200, 724 N.E.2d 914 (Ill. 2000).

◆ A Mississippi school district assigned a six-year-old student to a different elementary school than the one attended by his older sister. His parents alleged that if he was not allowed to transfer, each of their three children would attend different schools. Moreover, the six-year-old's assigned school was farther from home than his sister's school, and he would be required to walk home from his bus stop along a potentially hazardous route. The school board denied the transfer request, and the parents commenced a county circuit court action against the board. The court agreed with the school board that it did not act arbitrarily by denying the transfer. However, it found that denying the requested transfer when space became available would be arbitrary and capricious.

On appeal, the state supreme court reviewed Miss. Code Ann. § 37-15-15, which details a number of considerations for school boards when making student assignments. Included items were the educational needs and welfare of the child, the welfare and best interests of all students attending the school and the availability of school facilities. **The court agreed with the parents that the district failed to comply with Section 37-15-15, which requires school districts to make assignments on an individual basis by considering the listed factors.** The school superintendent admitted in his testimony that the district considered only its attendance zones when denying the transfer application. Contrary testimony of the district's director of student services indicated that the district had considered district policy when declining the transfer application. This supported the circuit court's finding that the board did not arbitrarily deny the transfer application at the time it was made. The court also agreed with the circuit court that the district would be acting arbitrarily and capriciously if it continued to deny the transfer when space became available in the school the parents wanted the student to attend. The court affirmed the circuit court decision for the family. *Pascagoula Municipal Separate School Dist. v. Barton*, 776 So.2d 683 (Miss. 2001).

◆ The Alabama Supreme Court held a school board exceeded its authority by contracting with a private company to manage its transportation services. The court noted that city education boards were vested with "all powers necessary or proper for the administration and management" of their schools. The board's decision to enter into the contract was consistent with the interest of students. The contract did not violate state budget acts by calling for payment of a set fee for transportation services. However, the contract violated state law by requiring the board to pay the salaries of personnel not under its own direct control and supervision. **The board's inability to pay its employees from legislatively allocated funds violated state law by denying the employees legal rights or**

benefits, including the procedures of the state Fair Dismissal Act. The board exceeded its statutory powers by entering into the contract. *Laidlaw Transit Inc. v. Alabama Educ. Ass'n*, 769 So.2d 872 (Ala. 2000).

◆   The Oklahoma School Code allows students to transfer to schools outside their residence districts upon the approval of the education boards in both the residence and receiving districts. Graduating seniors in counties having a population in excess of a specified number who are previously enrolled in the school district to which they wish to transfer are exempt from the requirement of approval by the receiving district. A student who attended a public school as a transfer student for 11 years applied again for attendance in the receiving school district for his senior year. However, the district denied his application for transfer, and the student's parents appealed to a county district court. The court found that the receiving district had no discretion to deny the transfer.

The receiving district appealed to the Supreme Court of Oklahoma, arguing that transfers were discretionary except for the limited circumstances listed in the statute. The court disagreed, finding that **where a previously transferred student seeks a transfer for a senior year and the requirements of law are otherwise met, a receiving district has no discretion to disapprove a transfer request.** Because the district was within a county that was in excess of the specified population level and had allowed the student to transfer into the district for 11 straight years, it had no discretion to disapprove the transfer request. The court affirmed the judgment for the student. *Hill v. Board of Educ., Dist. I–009, Jones, Oklahoma*, 1997 OK 111, 944 P.2d 930 (Okla. 1997).

C. Open Meeting Laws

◆   A Washington school board held a meeting for the public to evaluate candidates for an open board position. A citizen sought handouts provided by candidates at the meeting, an audiotape of the meeting and letters of interest from the candidates. The district made an audiotape and the letters available, but said it did not have any copies of the candidates' handouts. The citizen claimed the audiotape did not work in his car stereo and refused to listen to it on a district system. He sued the district in a state superior court for alleged violations of the state Public Disclosure Act (PDA). The court held for the district, and the citizen appealed to the Court of Appeals of Washington.

The court held the PDA did not require an agency to explain, conduct research on, or create documents that did not exist and were not in its possession. The citizen had no evidence to contradict statements by district employees disclaiming possession of the documents. The court held a document that is not possessed by an agency is not, by definition, a public document. While the PDA required an agency to give the fullest assistance to persons seeking to review public records, the law did not specify a format for audiotapes. The district had complied with the PDA by providing the citizen with the candidates' letters of interest and the tape, and by offering its equipment to listen to it. The court affirmed the judgment for the district. *Boss v. Peninsula School Dist.*, 125 Wash. 1024 (Wash. Ct. App. 2005).

◆   **An Ohio trial court ordered three school board members removed for retaining uncertified teachers and systematically violating the state Public Records and Open Meetings Acts.** The board members intentionally violated the Open Meetings Act by going into executive session without notice 10 times in 11 months. The board failed to approve minutes for public review and granted a single board member power to assume the board's full authority when it was not in session. The board members retained two unqualified and uncertified teachers. At the same time, they did not address "explosive issues," such as investigating sexual abuse charges against an employee. One member voted for the district to employ her husband and her daughter. The court held board members "owed a duty to provide their High School students with competent and certified teachers in a zone of safety." *In re: Removal of Kuehnle*, No. 2004 CV-08-214 (Ohio Common Pleas 2004).

◆   Some New York citizens appeared at a regular school board meeting with a video camera and attempted to videotape the meeting. The board instructed them to turn off the camera, and they complied. Two weeks later, the citizens came to another board meeting, which they again sought to videotape. When the board instructed them to discontinue the taping, they protested, and the board allowed them to record the proceedings. Later, the board adopted a new resolution that purported to reserve the right to allow or disallow videotaping of its meetings by the public. After the board denied further efforts by the citizens to videotape board meetings, they sued the district in the state court system to annul the amended resolution as a violation of the New York Open Meetings Law. The court dismissed the citizens' action, ruling the law did not give them the right to videotape board meetings.

The citizens appealed to the New York Supreme Court, Appellate Division, which reviewed the legislative intent of the Open Meetings Law. This declared it essential to the maintenance of a democratic society to perform public business in an open and public manner. It rejected the board's claim that videotaping meetings would make them "less open" by stifling shy citizens. **The court held that although the Open Meetings Law did not explicitly compel the board to allow videotaping of its meetings, a liberal interpretation of the law allowed the citizens the right to record them.** In doing so, the court relied on a state court case allowing the recording of public comment by hand-held tape recorders. It also cited a number of state court decisions allowing videotaping of board meetings. Because the board could not ban the tape recording of its meetings, the court reversed the judgment. *Csorny v. Shoreham-Wading River Cent. School Dist.*, 2003 N.Y. Slip. Op. 14079, 2002 WL 32092581 (N.Y. App. Div. 2003).

◆   California parents complained about an elementary school principal, and she received a negative performance evaluation. The district superintendent placed her on administrative leave for several incidents of unprofessional conduct. He then presented the board with written, verified charges of her unprofessional conduct and persistent violation of laws in a closed session. The board did not take any testimony, but it initiated termination proceedings. It served her with notice of its intent to dismiss her unless she requested a hearing.

The principal made such a request, but it was delivered to the wrong address. The board eventually received the principal's request but concluded the request was untimely and that she waived her right to a hearing. It voted to terminate her employment and reaffirmed its decision two months later in a closed session. The principal asserted the board violated the California Open Meetings Act by failing to give her notice of the two meetings. She sued the district in a state court, which ordered the board to set aside its decision.

The district appealed to a California Court of Appeal. It observed that **the open meetings act permitted school boards to conduct closed sessions to consider employee performance and disciplinary matters**. As a condition to holding a closed session, the board was required to give the employee written notice of the right to open the session. However, the law did not create a right to a hearing where one did not otherwise exist. It only required boards to give appropriate notices and nullified actions taken in unauthorized sessions. The court rejected the principal's assertion that the presentation of charges by the superintendent to the board was a "hearing" under the open meetings act. The board did not consider evidence on the charges. It considered whether the charges warranted the initiation of a disciplinary proceeding against the principal. **The superintendent's recommendation for termination and the grounds for it did not make the board session a "hearing," and the principal was not entitled to receive any advance notice.** The court reversed the judgment and remanded the case. *Proud v. San Pasqual Union School Dist. No. D037921,* 2002 WL 31174297 (Cal. Ct. App. 2002).

◆   A Washington administrative employee took on additional responsibilities as her school district's communications coordinator. The school board's newly elected president took office amid rumors that he had a "hit list" of employees for termination. The employee felt she was on the hit list and that the president exchanged e-mails with other board members before and after he and two other members took their oaths of office. After the board voted to remove the district superintendent, a rotating group of interim superintendents held the position. One of the interim superintendents reassigned the employee in an attempt to shield her from discharge. When the employee's contract expired, the district did not renew it. She sued the district, board and three board members in a Washington court for violations of the Open Public Meeting Act (OPMA).

The court awarded summary judgment to the employee on her OPMA violation claims and imposed a $200 statutory penalty on each board member. On appeal, the state court of appeals initially explained that the OPMA was modeled on similar open meetings laws in California and Florida. Courts in those states had disagreed on whether elected but unsworn officials were covered by open meeting laws. The court agreed with a California decision stating that in the absence of clear legislative direction, persons elected to office may not take official action until they assume authority. The court reversed the trial court's judgment on the individual board members' liability under OPMA. **The court held the OPMA applied not only to board meetings, but extended to deliberations, discussions, and other communications. Courts in other states have applied open meetings acts to telephonic communications, e-mails, individual meetings between superintendents** and board members, and serial electronic communications among a quorum of board members. **The court held e-mail exchanges could be "meetings" if certain statutory factors were present.** The OPMA would not be violated if less than a majority of board members was involved in the exchange of e-mails and the participants did not collectively intend to transact official business. Passive receipt of an e-mail did not qualify as a "meeting." There had to be "action," as defined by OPMA. Summary judgment had been improper, as there was evidence that the e-mails related to board business, some board members had knowledge that the OPMA might be implicated, and there was an active exchange of e-mails. The court remanded the OPMA claim. *Wood v. Battle Ground School Dist.*, 27 P.3d 1208 (Wash. Ct. App. 2001).

◆   Iowa school officials proposed suspending a student and placed a letter in an aide's personnel file for initiating an incident between the two. The aide then became fearful that her reputation might be harmed by the incident. The school board's attorney notified the family that the student's suspension hearing would be closed, and the board voted to close it pursuant to Iowa law. The suspension was stayed, and the family sued the school board in an Iowa district court for violations of the state open meetings act. The court held the board's closure action was void and enjoined the board from making future violations. It also awarded the family $3,000 in attorneys' fees. The board appealed to the Supreme Court of Iowa, which held that **the open meetings law required an open proceeding upon request by a student or parent**. Meetings may not be closed unless they are intended to evaluate the professional competency of an employee or to make employment actions such as hiring and discharge. Since no exception applied under the open meetings act, the court affirmed the district court judgment, including the award of attorneys' fees. *Schumacher v. Lisbon School Board*, 582 N.W.2d 183 (Iowa 1998).

◆   The Michigan Open Meetings Act contains an exception allowing closed sessions for strategy and negotiations related to a collective bargaining agreement. An education board considered a contract for its teachers at an open meeting, but it closed the session to discuss negotiations with the union. One of the board members stated that any vote in closed session violated the law and walked out of the room. He filed a complaint against the other board members in a Michigan trial court for violations of the open meetings act. The court granted summary judgment to the other board members. The dissenting member appealed to the Court of Appeals of Michigan, where he argued that any voting in closed session was forbidden by the act. **The court observed that the act specifically permitted the consideration of collective bargaining negotiations in closed sessions** and that a straw poll of board members did not constitute a vote or decision as defined by the law. The trial court had properly granted summary judgment to the other board members. *Moore v. Fennville Public Schools Board of Educ.*, 566 N.W.2d 31 (Mich. Ct. App. 1997).

CHAPTER TWELVE

Academic Practices

Page

I. REFORM LEGISLATION 487
   A. The No Child Left Behind Act of 2001 487
   B. State Reform Acts...493
   C. Charter Schools 496
      1. Legislation...496
      2. Applications...498
      3. Operations and Finance 500

II. CURRICULUM AND GRADING 505
    A. Curriculum..505
    B. Bilingual Education 507
    C. Grading 509

III. STUDENT RECORDS 513
     A. Student and Parental Rights.....................................513
     B. Media Requests 520
     C. Electronic and Video Records...................................523

IV. TESTING..526

V. EDUCATIONAL MALPRACTICE.......................................531

I. REFORM LEGISLATION

A. The No Child Left Behind Act of 2001

The No Child Left Behind (NCLB) Act of 2001 reauthorized the Elementary and Secondary Education Act (ESEA) of 1965. It requires the states to use academic assessments to annually review school progress and determine if "adequate yearly progress" (AYP) has been made under state standards. The AYP requirement is a condition for the receipt of Title I funds under the ESEA.

States were required to test students in grades three through eight in mathematics and reading by 2005-2006 to determine AYP. By 2013-14, all students must score in the proficient level. Students in each of four identified subgroups must score in the proficient level (see 20 U.S.C. § 6311(b)(2)(C)). The subgroups are: economically disadvantaged students, students from major racial and ethnic groups, students with disabilities and students with limited English proficiency.

Schools that fail to achieve AYP for two consecutive years are designated for "school improvement." If they remain in this designation for two years, "corrective action" and "restructuring" are required. NCLB Act notice and transfer provisions are triggered when schools are identified for improvement, corrective action or restructuring. Schools in the second year of designation for improvement must offer eligible students "supplemental educational services" such as tutoring (see 20 U.S.C. § 6311(b)(2)(B)).

◆ Instead of annual tests as required by the NCLB Act, Connecticut held formative testing several times each year to give "immediate, frequent feedback" to students, teachers and parents. It also allowed special education students the option of testing at their instructional level, rather than grade level. Connecticut administered tests in grades four, six, eight and 10, and used a short essay format in addition to multiple choice questions. Since 1986, the state administered its own assessments, and student scores were among the nation's highest. Connecticut permitted English language learner (ELL) students to study in the U.S. for three years before taking state assessments. By contrast, the NCLB Act required testing within one year of entering the country. Connecticut remained in compliance with NCLB Act requirements, but the U.S. Education Secretary denied three requests to modify testing requirements.

The state sought to continue its formative testing regimen, testing of ELL students and testing of special education students. It argued strict compliance with NCLB Act requirements would cost it more than double the federal funding provided for testing. The state sued the Secretary in a federal district court, arguing the NCLB Act's unfunded mandates provision required full federal funding for all the act's provisions. **The court stated that overall federal funding under the act had never fallen below the amount promised to relieve states of their testing obligations. It agreed with the Secretary that there could be no "pre-enforcement" challenge under the act.** The state's constitutional theories were based on the threat of penalties if it were found not compliant with the act. For this reason, a pre-enforcement challenge based on constitutional violations was also premature. The court disagreed with the state's claim that the denial of its waiver requests had been arbitrary and capricious. The Secretary correctly argued that waiver requests were committed to agency discretion and were non-reviewable by the courts. The court refused to dismiss the state's appeal from the denial of its plan amendments. However, the court would have to analyze the plan amendments in question to determine whether the state's Administrative Procedures Act violation claim had any validity. This required the creation of an administrative record. *Connecticut v. Spellings*, 453 F.Supp.2d 459 (D. Conn. 2006).

◆ **The No Child Left Behind Act requires each state to develop a definition of "persistently dangerous" schools. Local school systems must report criminal offenses at schools to the state education department.** The Court of Appeals of Georgia considered a student assault case in which the parents of the victimized student claimed the school had an official policy of discouraging accurate reporting of incidents of school violence to avoid a "persistently dangerous" designation. The court held official immunity protects public officials and employees from lawsuits in their personal capacities. However, a jury could find the intentional conduct of officials in this case defeated any claim for immunity. The court reversed and remanded the case to a state trial court. *Bajjani v. Gwinnett County School Dist.*, 278 Ga.App. 866, 630 S.E.2d 103 (Ga. Ct. App. 2006).

◆   The National Education Association (NEA) sued the U.S. Department of Education for unlawfully enforcing the NCLB Act. It filed a federal district court action on behalf of school districts in Michigan, Texas and Vermont and its affiliates in 10 states. The complaint stated the Secretary of the Department of Education (Secretary) violated the act's "unfunded mandates" provision and the Spending Clause of the U.S. Constitution by requiring states and districts to comply fully with the NCLB Act, but not providing the funds for full compliance.

The court stated the NCLB Act's "unfunded mandates" provision, Section 9527(a), requires any state accepting federal funding under Title I to revise state curriculum standards in core academic areas, develop and administer standardized tests, and measure the progress of public school students in meeting those standards. Based on the performance of all but a very small group of students, districts are required to determine whether schools and the districts themselves are making adequate yearly progress (AYP) in improving student performance on those tests. Schools or school districts not making AYP must then take specific actions for these schools and districts and ensure staff have certain qualifications. The court reviewed evidence that the costs of NCLB Act compliance "are enormous, and far exceed the limited increase in Title I funding that followed enactment of the NCLB."

The act could not be "construed to authorize an officer or employee of the Federal Government to mandate, direct, or control a State, local education agency, or school's curriculum, program of instruction, or allocation of State or local resources, or mandate a State [or state subdivision] to spend any funds or incur any costs not paid for under this Act." The court agreed with the Secretary that this sentence simply meant that no federal officer or employee could require states or school districts to spend funds or incur costs not paid for under the act. According to the court, it would make no sense for Congress to pass the elaborate act if states could avoid its requirements by simply claiming they had to spend some of their own funds to comply with it. The words "officer or employee" prevented a reading of the section that the federal government had to fully fund all NCLB Act requirements. The court held Congress meant only to prohibit federal officers from imposing additional, unfunded requirements beyond those specified in the act. As Section 9527(a) could not be interpreted as prohibiting Congress from conditioning federal funding on NCLB Act compliance, the court dismissed the case. *School Dist. of City of Pontiac v. Spellings*, No. Civ.A. 05-CV-71535-D, 2005 WL 3149545 (E.D. Mich. 2005).

◆   A group of California school districts, nonprofit organizations, students and parents sued the state, claiming an NCLB Act section requires that all children must receive a fair, equal, and significant opportunity to reach proficiency on challenging state academic achievement standards and state academic assessments. The section, 20 U.S.C. § 6311(b), states that "limited English proficient students shall be assessed in a valid and reliable manner and provided reasonable accommodations on assessments, including, to the extent practicable, assessments in the language and form most likely to yield accurate data on what such students know and can do," until these students have achieved English language proficiency. The complaint noted academic assessments are allowed in languages other than English. Fourteen other states utilize Spanish-language tests or modified-English tests that reduce linguistic complexity.

The school districts and other complaining parties requested a state court order requiring the state to implement valid and reliable testing of students with limited English proficiency and to halt "illegal expenditures of taxpayers' funds" in violation of California Code of Civil Procedure § 526. State education officials removed the case to a federal district court. The court explained that federal district courts have jurisdiction (the power to hear a controversy and to issue binding orders on the parties) when presented with a question of federal law. **The U.S. Supreme Court has held that if a federal law does not provide a private cause of action, a state law action based on violation of the federal law does not raise a substantial federal question. The court found the dispute arose under California law. It agreed with other federal courts which have held the NCLB Act does not create a private cause of action.** (See *Ass'n of Community Organizations for Reform Now v. New York City Dep't of Educ.*, 269 F.Supp.2d 338 (S.D.N.Y. 2003)). The complaining parties were not challenging the validity or construction of the NCLB Act itself. The court declined to substantively interpret the act, and it remanded the case to the state court system. *Coachella Valley Unified School Dist. v. State of California*, No. C 05-02657 WHA, 2005 WL 1869499 (N.D. Cal. 2005).

◆   **A federal district court dismissed an action asserting school district compliance with the NCLB Act required schools to disregard individual obligations to students under the Individuals with Disabilities Education Act (IDEA).** Two Illinois districts had schools in "school improvement" or "watch status," or were required to complete remediation activities solely due to achievement scores from their special education student populations. If not for the special education student scores, the districts would have made adequate yearly progress (AYP). The districts alleged the special education students were making meaningful and significant progress on specific individualized education program (IEP) goals and objectives prior to the failure of their schools to make AYP. As a result of the failure of the schools to make AYP, the districts claimed each of the students would need changes to their IEPs. The complaint asserted NCLB Act student subgroups, including the subgroup of special education students, did not allow for individual differences. The districts said they could not comply with NCLB requirements of "categorical and systemic change to the IEPs of students" while also complying with the IDEA. They sought a U.S. district court declaration that NCLB Act sections on state plans and academic assessment were invalid as in conflict with the IDEA.

The court explained that the districts did not demonstrate "injury in fact," a necessary element of legal standing. It found the districts' claim of injury in fact relied on the conclusory statement that they were "required to employ systemic remediation activities which require the modification of individual students' IEPs without regard to the student's disability." **The districts did not show the NCLB Act mandated specific actions. The act allowed districts discretion to**

implement "pedagogical questions." The U.S. government correctly argued that nothing in the NCLB Act prevented the districts from implementing changes that took student IEPs into account. The court stated the districts could make systemic changes that did not require modification of IEPs, such as "appointing an outside expert, decreasing managerial authority, or replacing ineffective staff." The districts did not explain how IEP modifications to improve student performance would cause harm. For a district to make AYP, the AYP of disabled students had to improve. Since the districts lacked standing, the court dismissed the case. *Board of Educ. of Ottawa Township High School Dist. No. 140 v. U.S. Dep't of Educ.*, No 5 C 655 (N.D. Ill. 2005).

◆ Pennsylvania's education secretary identified 13 schools in the Reading School District as failing to achieve AYP. The NCLB Act requires districts to report the test scores of four subgroups when the number of students in the subgroup exceeds a state-designated number. The secretary had established this "N" number at 40, based on several computer studies. The district claimed the secretary arbitrarily set the N number and did not provide adequate assistance. The district sued the secretary and the case reached the Commonwealth Court of Pennsylvania. It found no evidence to contradict the secretary's selection of the number 40 as appropriate. The court held the secretary provided the district with adequate technical assistance. NCLB Act language suggested an ongoing process of technical assistance. The department had already offered the district resources on a Web site with school improvement plan templates and training materials. **The state was not required to provide all the assistance specified in the NCLB Act at the moment a school was identified for improvement.** As the secretary did not abuse her discretion, the court affirmed her decision. *Reading School Dist. v. Dep't of Educ.*, 855 A.2d 166 (Pa. Commw. Ct. 2004).

The school district then sent the department its plans to bring six schools into compliance. It submitted a cost estimate for the plan in excess of $26 million for 2003-2004. The district estimated it would receive about $8 million in federal funding, and it asked the state education department for the shortfall. The department did not respond to the request for funds, but found six schools and the district as a whole failed to achieve AYP for 2003-2004 and would be placed on level-one or level-two sanctions for 2004-2005. The district appealed, asserting the department did not provide federal funds to implement the act, mandatory technical assistance to sanctioned schools, or Spanish language testing on a required statewide assessment. The state education secretary dismissed the district's appeal as a violation of a new department appeal policy.

The district appealed again to the commonwealth court, asserting due process violations. It argued the NCLB Act requires each state to develop plans to implement the act, and that failure to achieve AYP is a state, not a federal determination. **The court held school districts were due the same protections in agency actions as citizens received in other legal actions. The department policy was not consistent with the act.** The department violated the district's due process rights by limiting the grounds for appeal in its policy. As the policy was unconstitutional, the court vacated the secretary's order. *Reading School Dist. v. Dep't of Educ.*, 875 A.2d 1218 (Pa. Commw. Ct. 2005).

◆ The state of Ohio approved a private educational service as a provider of "supplemental educational services" (SES), as defined in the NCLB Act. The service claimed the Toledo Public Schools "misappropriated" NCLB funds by hiring other SES providers while excluding it from Toledo schools. The service sued the board in a federal district court for damages, an accounting of NCLB funds received by the district and an order allowing it to bid and contract for SES tutoring. The court explained the NCLB Act required local education agencies that did not make AYP for a specified time period to arrange for SES. Local agencies in this status had to provide notices to parents, identify approved SES providers, briefly describe their services and qualifications, and help parents choose a provider. After parents selected an SES provider, the board was required to contract with it.

The court held the NCLB Act provides no procedure for individual entities to enforce its provisions. The act's "penalties" section only recites the ability of the U.S. education secretary to withhold funds from states. When Congress enacts legislation under its spending power, the typical remedy for state noncompliance with federal conditions is termination of federal funding. Laws with an "aggregate" focus do not concern particular persons and generally demonstrate no intent to create individual, private rights. A centralized enforcement mechanism also indicates Congress did not intend to create individually enforceable rights. The court found no clear and unambiguous statement of intent by Congress to privately enforce the NCLB Act. It refused to recognize a direct, private right of action to enforce the NCLB Act, or an indirect private right of action to enforce it under 42 U.S.C. § 1983. The court found **Congress did not seek to enable particular services to provide SES; it sought instead to ensure SES was of an overall minimum, uniform quality.** The NCLB Act's central enforcement mechanism indicated Congress did not intend for piecemeal enforcement by individuals. As nothing in the act indicated a Congressional intent to create individual rights, the court dismissed the action. *Fresh Start Academy v. Toledo Board of Educ.*, 363 F.Supp.2d 910 (N.D. Ohio 2005).

◆ A group of New York parents and students sued state education officials, the New York City Department of Education and the Albany School District, claiming education officials failed to comply with NCLB Act parental notification requirements and provisions allowing the transfer of students to better schools. They also asserted the officials were liable for other untimely or unlawful conduct in violation of the NCLB Act, 42 U.S.C. § 1983 and the New York Constitution. The court considered a request for a preliminary injunction by the complaining parties, together with a dismissal motion by state and local education officials. It recited the history and purpose of the NCLB Act, which was enacted "to ensure that all children have a fair, equal and significant opportunity to obtain high-quality education," and reach minimum proficiency levels on state academic achievement standards and assessments. States that receive federal NCLB Act funds must comply with the act's provisions or face potential sanctions by the secretary of the U.S. Department of Education.

The NCLB Act establishes certain time frames for notices and provides some exceptions for its transfer requirements. The court noted **the act lacks any** procedure for parents or students to seek legal recourse for state and local noncompliance. The only remedy stated in the act's "penalties" section is the withholding of state funds by the U.S. Secretary of Education. The court held **Congress did not create "individually enforceable rights" when it enacted the NCLB Act**. The Supreme Court held in *Gonzaga Univ. v. Doe*, Section III, below, that Congress must "evince a clear and unambiguous intention" when it enacts legislation to create individual rights that form the basis for a private legal cause of action. The NCLB Act's notice, transfer and supplemental educational services (SES) provisions have no language indicating the creation of individual rights. **The act focuses on the regulation of state and local entities, not on conferring direct benefits to students and parents. Congress was concerned with improving the educational conditions of "children as a whole," not with ensuring individual student rights.** Because the act did not reflect a clear Congressional purpose to create individually enforceable rights, the education officials were entitled to dismissal of the action. *Ass'n of Community Organizations for Reform Now v. New York City Dep't of Educ.*, 269 F.Supp.2d 338 (S.D.N.Y. 2003).

B. State Reform Acts

Well before the No Child Left Behind Act of 2001, state legislatures were addressing public school accountability in reform legislation designed to improve student performance. Reform acts may place schools or districts under state control for continued failure to meet specified performance standards. The testing provisions of these acts are discussed in Section IV, this chapter.

◆ The Kentucky Education Reform Act (KERA) created site-based councils to provide greater accountability and decentralize school management. A KERA provision, KRS § 160.345(2)(h), required site-based councils to select principals from applicants recommended by the district superintendent. The provision required superintendents to provide councils with names of additional applicants upon request "when qualified applicants are available." A superintendent fired a high school principal for poor performance. He received nine applications for the resulting vacancy, including one from the former principal himself. The superintendent forwarded three applications to the site-based council. The council rejected them and asked the superintendent for the others. The superintendent refused and appointed one of his three candidates as interim principal. A state court granted the council's request for an order compelling the superintendent to forward all nine applications. The superintendent complied with the order, and the council recommended rehiring the former principal. The council obtained a court order requiring the superintendent to comply, and the state court of appeals affirmed the order.

The state supreme court consolidated the case with that of an assistant principal who claimed she was passed over for a vacant principalship because of her gender. It considered whether the superintendents in both cases had authority to limit the pool of "qualified applicants" under Section 160.345(2)(h). The court held the superintendents' interpretation of the section ran counter to the objectives of accountability and decentralization found in the KERA. The court stated the **site-based councils were created in direct response to widespread mismanagement caused by an overly centralized system of school governance**. The term "qualified" in Section 160.345(2)(h) meant "meeting statutory requirements." The superintendents were thus required to send their site-based councils the applications of all applicants who met state law requirements, including the assistant principal and the fired principal. A contrary reading of the law would run counter to KERA goals, allowing superintendents to avoid virtually all accountability by recommending only the applicants they wanted to hire. **The legislature intended the site-based councils to have the ultimate authority to select principals.** The court affirmed the judgments in both cases. *Young v. Hammond*, 139 S.W.3d 895 (Ky. 2004).

◆ In 1993, Maryland's state education board adopted school performance standards that mandated reporting requirements and improvement plans for each public school. Schools that did not meet the standards were place under the direct control of the local school board. If they failed to improve under local reconstitution, they were designated for "state reconstitution." By 2000, the state board had placed 97 Maryland schools under local reconstitution, 83 of which were in Baltimore. The state board reconstituted three low-performing Baltimore public schools, but their performance remained stagnant after three years. The state board hired a private education company to provide the schools with curriculum, curriculum development, instructional services, instructional and support personnel, teaching tools, special education and related services, educational services for limited and non-English proficient students and other necessary services. The company hired and managed the professional staff for the three schools. The collective bargaining agent (CBA) for school employees sued the state education board in a state court, arguing the board could not adopt regulations creating student performance standards and reconstitution. The court held the board was statutorily authorized to contract with the company.

The CBA appealed to the Court of Appeals of Maryland, the state's highest court. **The court rejected the CBA's argument that no state law authorized the state board's reconstitution regulations.** Even if it initially lacked such authority, the general assembly enacted legislation in 1997, 1999 and 2000 showing its awareness and approval for the board to contract with private vendors under the reconstitution regulations. **The 1997, 1999 and 2000 laws also recognized that under state reconstitution, public school teachers might be employed by private entities.** It could be inferred that the legislature approved of and ratified the reconstitution regulations. The court refused to consider an untimely argument by the CBA that the regulations violated the state constitution, and it affirmed the judgment. *Baltimore Teachers Union v. Maryland State Board of Educ.*, 379 Md. 192, 840 A.2d 728 (Md. 2004).

◆ The Pennsylvania Educational Empowerment Act (EEA) was enacted in 2000 to "fix broken school districts" in urban areas. It placed districts with a history of low test scores on a list maintained by the state education department. Listed districts appointed "empowerment teams" to develop improvement plans with specific methods and goals for improving under-performing schools. Local boards could replace personnel, establish charter or privately run schools, employ new staff and reallocate district resources. The state education department certified districts that did not improve enough to be removed from the empowerment list as "education empowerment districts" under a three-member board of control. Boards of control had powers previously exercised by the local board, plus the ability to close schools. The EEA created an "expedited recovery plan" that waived the empowerment designation of the Harrisburg School district and immediately certified it as an empowerment district. **The Pennsylvania Supreme Court struck down the EEA as special legislation in** *Harrisburg School Dist. v. Hickock*, 563 Pa. 391, 761 A.2d 1132 (Pa. 2000).

The legislature amended the EEA by expanding the class of cities for which placement on the empowerment district could be waived. The provision applied to four cities, including Harrisburg. The Harrisburg district and other interested parties then sought a state court order declaring the amended EEA unconstitutional. The Supreme Court of the Pennsylvania held the state constitutional prohibition on special legislation was intended to end favoritism. **The Constitution did not prohibit limited remedial legislation as part of a long-term strategy to fulfill state obligations.** Equal protection principles did not prevent the legislature from enacting laws promoting the public health, safety and welfare. The legislature had undertaken aggressive action to address the systematic failure of the Harrisburg School District. It was permitted to treat cities of various sizes differently to address the "seemingly intractable problems facing their school districts." **The legislature was entitled to find social issues including crime, poverty and tax bases were more severe in urban districts than in rural areas, "and sufficiently so to warrant special treatment under the EEA."** While Harrisburg was the only district automatically certified as an empowerment district under the EEA, it was possible others would come within the designation. The class had not been drawn through artificial or irrelevant distinctions and was reasonably related to the legislature's constitutional duty to provide for a thorough and efficient system of public education. *Harrisburg School Dist. v. Zogby*, 574 Pa. 121, 828 A.2d 1079 (Pa. 2003).

◆ The Michigan School Reform Act replaced the Detroit school district's elected board with an appointed one. The act was modeled on Illinois legislation that led to higher standardized test scores, better attendance and graduation rates, and lower dropout rates. Voting on the Michigan act was polarized, with Detroit legislators largely voting against it and out-of-city legislators voting for it. The act suspended the elected board's authority and prevented its members from serving on the reform board. Opponents of the act claimed that it disenfranchised and discriminated against Detroit voters. They sued the reform board and other officials in a federal district court. The case reached the Sixth Circuit. It noted that while Detroit was the only district currently affected by the act, the act would apply to any district that achieved a specified population.

The court held the legislature was entitled to treat Detroit differently than smaller districts. The law was not prohibited as a local act under the state constitution. The court held the Voting Rights Act applied only to elective systems, not to appointive ones. There is no fundamental right to elect administrative officers such as school board members. The court noted the act contained no racial classifications. **There was no evidence that the legislature** acted with any racial motive or had the goal of preventing African-Americans from electing school boards. The act did not apply to four smaller Michigan districts that were predominantly African-American, indicating the legislature sought to improve large districts, not disenfranchise voters. The reform act was rationally related to the legitimate government interest of addressing problems in the Detroit schools. The legislature was entitled to believe the act would address the problems unique to a district that was more than six times the size of any other in Michigan. **The Equal Protection Clause did not prevent the legislature from enacting experimental reforms where no suspect classification or fundamental right was involved.** The court affirmed the judgment for the reform board and other officials. *Moore v. Detroit School Reform Board,* 239 F.3d 352 (6th Cir. 2002).

C. Charter Schools

1. Legislation

Charter school laws were among the first of the educational reforms of the 1990s to be tested in the courts. They have survived numerous legal challenges asserting violations of state and federal constitutional provisions.

◆ A coalition including the Ohio Federation of Teachers, Ohio Congress of Parents and Teachers and the Ohio School Boards Association sued state officials in an Ohio trial court, challenging the state's program of community schools, which are known elsewhere as charter schools. The coalition sought a declaration that the community schools program violated the Ohio Constitution. They sought restoration of funds "diverted" from school districts because of allegedly unconstitutional payments to community schools. The court ruled for the state entities, finding many of their claims were barred by the Ohio Supreme Court's decision in *DeRolph v. State,* 97 Ohio St.3d 434, 780 N.E.2d 529 (Ohio 2002). The Court of Appeals of Ohio affirmed the trial court's decision in part and reversed it in part, and the Supreme Court of Ohio agreed to review certain constitutional claims. **The court explained that community schools are independently governed public schools funded from state revenues. Community schools are independent from school districts and must be formed as non-profit or public-benefit corporations. They cannot charge tuition, and must be non-sectarian.** Community schools must comply with state academic standards and are monitored by sponsors that are accountable to the Ohio Department of Education. Their contracts may be cancelled by the governing authority for failure to meet their objectives. The court held the General Assembly's authority to set educational standards and requirements for common schools allowed it to set different standards for community schools.

The General Assembly complied with the constitutional mandate by adding flexible, deregulated education opportunities to the traditional school system. Community schools had to administer the standardized tests given in traditional public schools and were monitored by the state education department. The court rejected the claim by community school opponents that the state's funding method diverted funds from school districts.

The General Assembly had exclusive authority to spend tax revenues to further a statewide system of schools. There was no violation of state constitutional provisions for local control of city school boards and local tax revenue. The General Assembly had the power to create and modify school districts and did not intrude upon local powers by creating additional schools that were not part of a school district. The court rejected the community school opponents' additional arguments, noting that educational policy matters were best left to the General Assembly. *Ohio Congress of Parents and Teachers v. State Board of Educ.*, 111 Ohio St.3d 568, 857 N.E.2d 1148 (Ohio 2006).

◆ An Oklahoma school district approved a charter school application pending completion of the application. It later denied the application on two occasions. After the board rejected a revised application, the applicants requested binding arbitration under the Charter Schools Act (CSA), which provides that an unsuccessful charter applicant "may proceed to mediation or binding arbitration or both" as provided in the state Dispute Resolution Act (DRA). The district refused to participate in arbitration, but offered to participate in non-binding mediation. The applicants refused and sued the district in a state court. The court awarded summary judgment to the school district. The applicants appealed to the Supreme Court of Oklahoma.

The court noted that the CSA provided for mediation or binding arbitration under the DRA. However, the DRA did not authorize binding arbitration, and the supreme court had never adopted rules for it. **The court upheld the trial court ruling that arbitration could not proceed in the absence of DRA rules. As the DRA authorized only mediation, compulsory binding arbitration under that act was legally impossible.** Since the trial court had correctly resolved the case under the DRA question, the supreme court did not consider the school district's arguments that the CSA was unconstitutional. *Pentagon Academy v. Independent School Dist. No. 1 of Tulsa County, Oklahoma*, No. 98,384, 2003 OK 98, 82 P.3d 587 (Okla. 2003).

◆ Three school boards claimed New Jersey's 1995 charter school legislation was unconstitutional. The case reached the state supreme court, which noted the legislative intent was to improve public learning, increase available educational choice, encourage innovation, establish a new form of accountability, require measured outcomes and provide for teacher improvement and opportunity. The act provided for charter school approval and funding at a level that could be determined by the commissioner but was presumed to be 90% of the local levy budget per pupil in a school district. **The court reasoned that the legislative choice to include charter schools in the range of educational options was permissible so long as it did not violate the thorough and efficient system of education required by the state constitution.**

The court found the act adequately provided for the maintenance of non-segregated public schools. The funding mechanism presumptively assigned to each charter school an amount equal to 90% of the local levy budget per pupil in the school district for each specific grade level. The commissioner could set the amount to be forwarded by the school district of residence to a charter school in a way that complied with the thorough and efficient mandate of the New Jersey

Constitution. The court also upheld state regulations arising under the charter schools act that established a two-step application and review procedure. The review process was a reasonable implementation of the statute and was efficient and practical. *In re Grant of Charter School Application of Englewood on Palisades Charter School*, 164 N.J. 316, 753 A.2d 687 (N.J. 2000).

2. Applications

◆ Illinois charter school applicants submitted a proposal for a school that would offer unemployed high school drop-outs opportunities to earn a diploma while acquiring vocational skills. Participants would divide time between school and work at low-income housing sites. The local district's board stated the school district could not take on more debt in view of its "dire financial situation." The charter school would target students already being served in the district's alternative school. A state appeal panel found the proposal complied with state law. The state board disagreed, noting the district had a $32.65 million deficit and faced additional budget cuts if it lost a pending voter referendum. The state board found the proposal was not economically sound for the district. A state circuit court affirmed the decision, as did the Appellate Court of Illinois. The applicants appealed to the Supreme Court of Illinois.

The court found the Charter Schools Law was intended to expand educational opportunities for "at-risk pupils." The law created 15 requirements for each charter school proposal, including evidence that the terms of the charter are economically sound for both the charter school and the school district. **The contract between a charter school and its local school board included agreement on funding and any services the district would provide the school, including per capita student tuition.** This was the amount of funding provided by the state. The applicants argued the state board could not deny a charter school proposal solely because of a school district's financial condition. They asserted their proposal met 14 of the 15 statutory requirements. Reducing the statutory inquiry into a single question of finance would defeat the purpose of the charter schools law, which was to create educational choice and competition. The supreme court disagreed, explaining the charter schools law made a district's finances a "legitimate concern." A key term in any charter school proposal was the funding the school expected from the local district. The applicants in this case had refused to accept anything but 100% per capita funding. **The court found the terms of a proposed charter, including funding issues, must permit both the school and the district to be financially secure.** It agreed with the state board's interpretation of the law as requiring proposals to meet all 15 statutory requirements. The Charter Schools Law "was not intended to drive fiscally challenged districts out of business." As the proposal was not in the best interests of students in the district, the court affirmed the board's decision. *Comprehensive Community Solutions v. Rockford School Dist. No. 205*, 216 Ill.2d 455, 297 Ill.Dec. 221, 837 N.E.2d 1 (Ill. 2005).

◆ A Florida school board denied a charter school application based on inadequate school funding. The application was made by United Cerebral Palsy of Central Florida (UPC), and it received 51.8 of 60 possible points on the board's rating system. However, the board held approval of the charter would dilute the capital funding of all new and existing charter schools in the district. The board denied the application, and the applicants appealed. The Florida Charter School Appeals Commission recommended approval of the application, and this decision was accepted by the State Board of Education. The school board appealed to the district court of appeal, which noted **the state code limits the denial of a charter application to "good cause."** However, the charter school law did not define "good cause." The state board had found the application met all the requirements of Fla. Statutes Section 1002.33(6).

The school board argued "good cause" may be based on factors other than those in the statute and the unique financial problems in the county gave it good cause to deny the application. The court disagreed, stating **inadequate school funding was a statewide problem and was not a ground to deny the application.** The creation of the new school would have no impact on the capital funding for existing charter schools in the county for at least three years. The local board was aware of this when it approved the application with a high score on its rating scale. The court noted Osceola County was the lowest-ranked school system in the state for receipt of state operational funding. Eight of 10 charter schools in the district operated with deficit balances. The court held the local board presented no evidence of harm if it approved the charter. It only showed the district was underfunded. State law provided for the indemnification of a local board from the private debts of a charter school. The court held the legislature intended the denial of a charter application to be based on more than financial projections. Otherwise, districts could block any charter school application by claiming financial hardship. *School Board of Osceola County v. UPC of Cent. Florida*, 905 So.2d 909 (Fla. Dist. Ct. App. 2005).

◆   A Pennsylvania school district denied an application for a charter school for mentally gifted students. After public meetings and a hearing, it found the application discriminated on the basis of intellectual ability, did not demonstrate sustainable community support, had insufficient site, staff and financial information, and failed to show it would provide opportunities not already available in the district. The State Charter School Appeal Board reversed the decision and granted the charter. The board appealed to the Commonwealth Court of Pennsylvania, which rejected the district's claim that the school discriminated against non-gifted students. The state Charter School Law (CSL) prohibited discrimination on the basis of intellectual ability in admissions policies or practices, but it allowed schools to limit admission by grade level, a targeted population group of at-risk students, or academic concentration.

The CSL permitted charter schools to establish reasonable student evaluation criteria. Although the school targeted mentally gifted students, it did not discriminate in admissions, and its policy did not violate the law. The school employed no screening devices and would accept any student, regardless of intellectual ability or mental aptitude. There was no discrimination in the school's enrollment policies, and it was prepared to address the needs of non-gifted students. **The application satisfied CSL requirements for community support, a financial plan and sufficient operating funds.** The CSL did not require the applicants to submit more than a description of the physical facility it planned to use, its address, the ownership of the facility and its lease arrangements. The board had found the applicants satisfied these application requirements and others concerning the school's site, faculty, professional development plan, criminal history records and clearance statements. The court agreed with the board's findings that the charter school would provide an innovative program for gifted students distinct from district programs, and it affirmed the board's decision. *Cent. Dauphin School Dist. v. Founding Coalition of Infinity Charter School*, 847 A.2d 195 (Pa. Commw. Ct. 2004).

◆   A South Carolina school board denied a charter school application based on the failure of the applicants to show the school's facilities would meet state health and safety requirements by the proposed start up time. The application failed to meet the civil rights requirements of state law because it did not comply with a 1970 desegregation agreement. The application also failed to satisfy state law provisions governing the racial composition of school districts. A state court upheld the school board's decision and the applicants appealed.

The South Carolina Supreme Court noted evidence that the charter school application did not meet state statutory requirements for showing that the proposed school will be economically sound. **Because the applicants relied on speculative revenue sources, the board had not rejected the application arbitrarily. The court upheld the charter denial on the additional ground that the application adversely affected other students in the district by failing to identify prospective students and creating a racially identifiable school.** The court affirmed the judgment, but remanded an appeal by the state attorney general challenging a charter schools act provision requiring that the racial composition of a charter school not deviate from that of the district by over 10%. *Beaufort County Board of Educ. v. Lighthouse Charter School Committee*, 335 S.C. 230, 516 S.E.2d 655 (S.C. 1999).

3. Operations and Finance

◆   The Individuals with Disabilities with Education Act (IDEA) and the Elementary and Secondary Education Act (ESEA) authorize state recipients of federal funds to distribute grant money to local educational agencies (LEAs). Public charter schools are within the definition of an LEA under both laws. An "elementary school" under the IDEA and ESEA is defined as a "nonprofit" day or residential school, "including a public elementary charter school, that provides elementary education." Similarly, a secondary school is defined as "including a public secondary charter school, that provides secondary education." A U.S. Department of Education audit of the Arizona Department of Education (ADE) concluded the ADE had improperly awarded ESEA and IDEA funds to for-profit entities that operated charter schools in the state. The Arizona State Board for Charter Schools and several for-profit charter school operators petitioned for review. A federal district court held the statutes expressed a congressional mandate that in order to receive federal funds, charter schools must be nonprofit. The state board and the schools appealed.

The U.S. Court of Appeals, Ninth Circuit, held that only nonprofit institutional day or residential schools are eligible for federal funding

under the ESEA and IDEA. The court held Congress clearly intended to "prohibit the funding of for-profit schools, charter or otherwise." Ensuring that only nonprofit charter schools received ESEA and IDEA funds would assist the nationwide expansion of charter schools. **Nearly half of the states with charter school laws either prohibited for-profit entities from applying for charters or prevented them from operating or managing charter schools.** The court rejected additional arguments of the state board and charter school operators. The district court's decision was consistent with the plain meaning of the statutes, their legislative history and the education department's interpretation, and the court affirmed the judgment. *Arizona State Board for Charter Schools v. U.S. Dep't of Educ.*, 464 F.3d 1003 (9th Cir. 2006).

◆ A Texas corporation operated three "distance learning" charter schools in California. According to the families of some students enrolled in the schools, the corporation collected over $20 million annually in state educational funds, based on average daily attendance (ADA) funding of $4,350 per student. They claimed the schools did not provide computers, instruction, assessment, review, curriculum, equipment, supplies and services, and "functioned only to collect [ADA]." The families asserted the corporation "aggressively recruits poor rural districts" to approve charter schools. They claimed districts then intentionally failed to perform their oversight duties. The families sued the corporation and the chartering districts in a state court for breach of contract, misrepresentation, state constitutional violations and misuse of taxpayer funds. They added a claim under the California False Claims Act (CFCA) for submission of fraudulent claims and an Unfair Competition Law (UCL) claim for unfair and deceptive business practices. The court dismissed the CFCA, UCL and breach of contract claims as unrecognizable private claims for "educational malfeasance."

On appeal, **the Supreme Court of California explained that charter schools must operate under the terms of their charters and comply with the state Charter Schools Act**. They are otherwise exempt from many laws governing school districts. **Charter schools were eligible for a share of state and local ADA funding.** The court stated the CFCA creates liability for those who defraud the state in the amount of three times the damage to the state. The court held school districts are not "persons" who may be sued under the CFCA. Exposing districts to CFCA liability would significantly harm their core public mission of providing free public education within their limited budgets. By contrast, **charter school operators were "persons" who could be held liable under the CFCA.** While charter schools were deemed part of the public school system for academics and state funding, nonprofit corporations which ran the schools were given substantial freedom. UCL purposes were served by subjecting the school operators to deceptive business practices claims. The families did not have to comply with state Tort Claims Act notice provisions prior to bringing a CFCA claim. Restrictions on independent study programs created by Education Code Section 51747.3 applied to charter schools, and they could not provide incentives to independent study pupils. The case was returned to a lower court for further proceedings. *Wells v. One2One Learning Foundation,* 39 Cal.4th 1164, 48 Cal.Rptr.3d 108, 141 P.2d 225 (Cal. 2006).

◆   The University of Wisconsin-Parkside established a charter school under Wisconsin Statutes Section 118.40(2r). The school was located within the Racine Unified School District, but operated entirely independent of the district. Wisconsin law treated independent charter schools differently than district-sponsored charter schools. School districts had to transport all resident public, private and parochial school students, if the school they attended was within their designated attendance area and was at least two miles away, or if students would encounter unusual hazards. The charter school requested transportation for its students who resided within Racine's boundaries. **The state department of public instruction determined school districts did not have to transport students attending independent charter schools.** The board then voted to deny the charter school's transportation request. The school sued the district in a federal district court, claiming violations of the Equal Protection Clause. The court granted summary judgment to the district, finding charter school students were not "similarly situated" to students attending district schools.

The school appealed to the U.S. Court of Appeals, Seventh Circuit. The court stated an Equal Protection Clause claim requires that the individuals being compared be identical in all relevant respects. The school was within the district's geographical boundaries, but was an "administrative island" that was not subsumed by the district. The charter school had its own board, faculty and staff, and was operated wholly independent of the district. The two had no legal relationship. The charter contract between the university regents and the charter school vested the school with authority to contract with "other school districts" or entities to transport its students. This suggested it was always contemplated that the school would contract for busing. **The court held the charter school was the functional equivalent of an independent school district and was responsible for its own busing.** Students in the school and the district were not similarly situated under the Equal Protection Clause. The school did not show intentional discrimination by the district, and the judgment was affirmed. *Racine Charter One v. Racine Unified School Dist.*, 424 F.3d 677 (7th Cir. 2005).

◆   A California charter school submitted a facilities request to a school district to serve 223 students in grades K-8. The district rejected the school's request to use a single site that was being used primarily for nonacademic purposes. The district's "final facilities offer" to the school included 9.5 classrooms at five different school sites a total of 65 miles apart. The school filed a state court action against the district, asserting violation of the state Charter Schools Act.

The Court of Appeal of California explained **Education Code Section 47614 required districts to allow charter schools to use any facility not currently used by a district**. Section 47614 further required districts to make facilities available to charter school students in a district "in conditions reasonably equivalent" to those students would enjoy if they were attending other public schools in the district. Section 47614 declared an intent that public facilities be shared fairly among all public school students, including those attending charter schools. **Charter school facilities had to be "contiguous," and state education department regulations required districts to minimize the number of sites and consider student safety.** The court noted "a faulty premise underlying the district's position: the notion that charter school students are not 'district' students," and the implication that their needs were secondary to students in district-operated schools. **The Education Code declared charter schools were a part of the state's public school system.** The court held a school district responding to a facilities request had to "give the same degree of consideration to the needs of charter school students as it does to the students in district-run schools." A charter school should be housed at a single site, if one with sufficient capacity exists. School site size was a factor to consider in determining if a site was "reasonably equivalent." The court held the district was obligated to provide the school with facilities that were both reasonably equivalent and contiguous. Providing five sites did not balance the needs of the charter school and district-run schools. The district's decision was reversed and remanded for an order requiring a new final offer of facilities. *Ridgecrest Charter School v. Sierra Sands Unified School Dist.*, 130 Cal.App.4th 986, 30 Cal.Rptr.3d 648 (Cal. Ct. App. 2005).

◆ A California charter school sought to use a school district's facilities, stating it projected over 80 in-district students would attend the school in each of the next three years. The district sought information including student names, dates of birth, grade levels, home addresses and parent names. The school stated the information was confidential and could not be released without parental consent. The district denied the facilities request for lack of documentation required by the California Code of Regulations, Title 5, Section 11969.9, subd. (c)(1)(C). The school sought a state court order to compel the district to process the request. The school later agreed to provide the student information, but the district again denied the facilities request. The court ordered the district to offer its facilities to the school for the current school year, and the district appealed.

The state court of appeal held California Education Code § 47614 required districts to make facilities sufficient for a charter school to accommodate all the school's in-district students in a manner similar to other district schools. Charter schools had to provide districts with a reasonable projection of average daily classroom attendance of their in-district students. Section 47614 allowed districts to deny facilities requests for projections of less than 80 students for a year. **Section 47614 did not require charter schools to "demonstrate arithmetical precision" in their projections.** The school had to submit reasonable projections for in-district students to the district by October 1 of the preceding fiscal year, but did not do so. This limited the district's ability to respond. The request was incomplete, as it lacked relevant documentation for its enrollment projections. There was a rational reason for denying the facilities request based on safety concerns, and the judgment was reversed. *Environmental Charter High School v. Centinela Valley Union High School Dist.*, 122 Cal.App. 4th 139, 18 Cal.Rptr.3d 417 (Cal. Ct. App. 2004).

◆ Pennsylvania residents tried to convince their district to renovate an elementary school instead of closing it. When this failed, the residents applied for a charter school in the same building. They entered into a management agreement with a for-profit management company to operate the charter school. The school board denied the charter application, but the state Charter Appeal Board (CAB) held the application complied with the state Charter School Law

(CSL) and directed the board to grant the application and sign the charter. The board appealed to the Commonwealth Court of Pennsylvania. It rejected the board's assertion that the CAB had improperly failed to defer to its factual findings and legal conclusions. The CSL specifically allowed the CAB to state its own reasons for agreeing or disagreeing with a local board's conclusions.

The court stated local school boards have a significant interest in whether a charter is granted. **The legislature recognized local biases against charter schools in the CSL. In order to assure the minimal requirements of due process by providing a neutral fact-finder, the CAB was empowered to make its own factual findings.** There was substantial evidence to support the CAB's decision. The CAB found broad community support for the charter school, including a petition signed by 554 individuals and donations or pledges of over $50,000. The management company selected to operate the school was a for-profit entity, but the CSL allowed this, so long as the school itself was not a for-profit entity, school trustees had real and substantial authority for school decisions, and teachers were charter school employees. The charter complied with the CSL, and the order directing its approval was affirmed. *Carbondale Area School Dist. v. Fell Charter School*, 829 A.2d 400 (Pa. Commw. Ct. 2003).

◆ The Mosaica Academy Charter School received a charter from the Bensalem Township School District under the Pennsylvania Charter School Law (CSL). The school determined that 60% of its student body resided in Philadelphia and sought tuition subsidies from the Philadelphia School District (PSD) under a CSL provision requiring the district of residence of each student enrolled in a charter school to pay a per-student amount. The school also asked the PSD to provide transportation for resident students who attended the school. The PSD denied the request, and the school petitioned the Pennsylvania Commonwealth Court for an order requiring the PSD to either provide the funding for resident students or to compel the state education department to pay them. The court granted motions for summary judgment by the school and state officials, holding the challenge to the school's charter was impermissible.

The state Supreme Court held **the PSD failed to comply with clear statutory mandates requiring it to pay tuition subsidies and provide transportation to resident students who attended the charter school.** In enacting the CSL, **the state legislature had gone to great lengths to keep charter schools independent from the existing school structure**. The state charter school appeal board was vested with the exclusive power to review appeals by charter school applicants. There was no appeal from a local board's decision to grant a charter, and the court affirmed the commonwealth court's decision that the PSD had no defense to the school's claim for tuition subsidies for Philadelphia residents. **The PSD could not bypass CSL procedures by bringing a commonwealth court action to invalidate a charter.** The CSL required the PSD to pay for the transportation of resident students attending the charter school on the same terms as it provided transportation to resident students attending private schools. The court affirmed the commonwealth court's rulings on tuition subsidies and transportation. *Mosaica Academy Charter School v. Comwlth. Dep't of Educ.*, 813 A.2d 813 (Pa. 2002).

◆   A North Carolina charter school received a per-pupil allocation from the Asheville School District's local expense fund for the first three years of the school's existence. When calculating the allocation, Asheville excluded revenue from supplemental school taxes, fines and forfeitures. The resulting per-pupil allocation for the school was about $1,000 less per student than it would have been had Asheville included supplemental school taxes, fines and forfeitures. The school obtained an advisory opinion from the state attorney general's office stating Asheville was required to include the disputed funds when calculating the allocation. When Asheville refused to recalculate the allocation, the school sued it in a state court for an order requiring Asheville to provide the disputed money and demanding recalculation of its allocation from 1997 to 1999. The court held for the school, and Asheville appealed.

The North Carolina Court of Appeals rejected Asheville's assertion that the terms "appropriation" and "fund" as used in the state school budget act and charter schools act referred to different expenses. Under Asheville's interpretation, "appropriation" in the charter schools act is a specific amount and does not include money from supplemental school taxes, fines and forfeitures. The court found the statutory terms "appropriation" and "fund" interchangeable. For this reason, **all money in the local current expense fund was subject to use when calculating the per-pupil allocation for charter schools**. The court noted that when the charter schools act was passed, the North Carolina legislature intended charter schools to be funded the same way as public schools. Since state law required the use of the local current expense fund for schools, charter schools were entitled to use the same sources of funding as public schools. The court upheld the trial court decision, requiring Asheville to recalculate the per-pupil allocation amount due the charter school from 1997 to 1999. *Francine Delany New School for Children Inc. v. Asheville City Board of Educ.*, 536 S.E.2d 92 (N.C. Ct. App. 2002).

II. CURRICULUM AND GRADING

Educators have considerable discretion in academic, curricular and grading matters. Courts do not subject official decisions in these areas to close judicial scrutiny. For religious challenges to curriculums, please see Chapter Two, Section I.B.1. Constitutional challenges on secular grounds appear in Chapter Three, Section IV.B. Testing is considered in Section IV of this chapter. For cases involving students with disabilities, see Chapter 13, Section VII.C.

A. Curriculum

◆   A Connecticut parent challenged the use of "the Responsive Classroom" model by a school her children had attended many years earlier. The Responsive Classroom paradigm was designed to improve cooperation and communication among students and faculty. It involved morning meetings at which students discussed their concerns and teachers mediated any arguments that might arise. The parent claimed the paradigm "encouraged, created and tolerated an atmosphere of chaos, disruptiveness and violence" at the school, interrupted the structure necessary for learning, and increased student tensions and confrontations. The parent waited until years after her children had left the school to sue school officials in the state court system. She did not claim any actual violence against her children, but claimed they witnessed bullying of other students. The court found no evidence that student perpetrators had victimized any of the parent's children. The most serious incident the parent identified involved an aide's accidental locking of her youngest child in a classroom after he returned to retrieve his lunch box. Another included the pulling down of a kindergartner's pants while he was standing in the lunch line.

The court found no evidence of a "culture of violence or chaos," as the parent alleged. While she testified of "nearly constant fearfulness on the part of her children," teachers and other staff "described only the usual sorts of school-based problems with none of the dramatic upheaval" she alleged. **The principal had handled disciplinary problems and tried to foster an atmosphere of communication and cooperation. The court dismissed the parent's claim based on "an inadequate education because of an emphasis on social cooperation and group problem-solving" at the expense of traditional academics.** The students suffered no emotional damage, and there was no extreme or outrageous conduct by school officials. Most of what the parent related in her testimony concerned her own emotional state, not that of her children. Despite her concerns, they were all successful students at the school. While bullying was a dangerous problem in schools, these children were not victimized by it. School officials responded appropriately to every incident they knew about. The court held the mother did not prove any part of her emotional distress claim against the school board and principal. *Bell v. West Haven Board of Educ.*, No. NNH-CV-970399597, 2005 WL 1971264 (Conn. Super. Ct. 2005).

◆   A Texas student was in first place in a race for school valedictorian. She claimed the school principal intentionally scheduled a Spanish III class at an inconvenient time for her that was calculated to assist a classmate's effort to become valedictorian. The student's parents demanded that Spanish III be deleted from the curriculum. When the principal refused, the parents were granted a hearing to discuss removing Spanish III from the curriculum, but they were not allowed to cross-examine witnesses or discuss additional grievances.

The parents sued the board in a federal district court for constitutional rights violations. The court held the parents were not entitled to cross-examine witnesses or discuss prior inconsistent decisions by the school administration. **The student had no constitutionally protected interest to attend a course of her choosing at a particular time.** For a person to have due process rights, there must be a liberty or property interest deserving of constitutional protection. **Although education is of "unquestioned importance," it has not been recognized as a fundamental right under either the U.S. or Texas Constitution. The student had no protected property interest in becoming class valedictorian. The property interest recognized in education cases such as *Goss v. Lopez*, 419 U.S. 565 (1975), is the right to participate in the overall educational process, not in a particular course or individual component of the process.** The court rejected the parents' claim based on their right to direct their daughter's upbringing. As they had no constitutional right to direct, control or determine what classes or curriculum the district would offer, the board was entitled to summary judgment. *Jeffrey v. Board of Trustees of Bells Independent School Dist.*, 261 F.Supp.2d 719 (E.D. Tex. 2003).

◆ A private driving school that charged students $379 for its program filed a lawsuit in a Georgia trial court against a school board after the board began offering its own extracurricular driver education program to students for only $195. The court awarded summary judgment to the board, and the driving school appealed to the state court of appeals, where it argued that the program exceeded the board's legal and constitutional authority. The court observed that the state Quality Basic Education (QBE) Act prohibited local boards from charging resident students tuition or fees as a condition of enrollment or full participation in any instructional program. The QBE Act did not limit schools to teaching core classes during the regular school year. The driver education program was authorized under the QBE Act as part of the emphasis for local boards to provide opportunities beyond the core curriculum. **The legislature did not intend to prohibit boards from offering driver education courses to students for a fee after regular school hours. The program did not violate any law and did not violate the state constitution,** because it only applied to supplementary instruction offered by a local board on a private basis during the summer or after school. The court affirmed the judgment. *Kristin National Inc. v. Board of Educ. of the City of Marietta*, 552 S.E.2d 475 (Ga. Ct. App. 2001).

B. Bilingual Education

◆ California voters approved Proposition 227 in 1998, which declared it the state's policy to teach literacy in the English language. As a result, the state's bilingual education programs, which taught limited English proficient (LEP) students in their native languages, were replaced by "structured English immersion." LEP students could participate in "sheltered English immersion" with other LEP students for one year, then transfer to English-language classes. They were also entitled to waivers from English immersion in certain circumstances. A group representing LEP students brought a federal district court action against state officials, asserting Proposition 227 violated the Equal Protection Clause. The court held a trial and found no constitutional violation.

On appeal, the Ninth Circuit found nothing in the record indicated Proposition 227 was race-motivated. **The state's bilingual education system did not operate to remedy identified patterns of racial discrimination but was instead intended to improve the educational system.** The reallocation of political authority represented by Proposition 227 addressed educational, not racial issues, and the fact that most of California's LEP student population was Latino did not create a viable equal protection claim. **Despite the obvious racial implications of bilingual education, the court found no evidence of discrimination or discriminatory motivation** behind Proposition 227, and it affirmed the judgment. *Valeria v. Davis*, 307 F.3d 1036 (9th Cir. 2002).

◆ New Mexico enacted the Bilingual Multicultural Education Act (BMEA) to insure equal educational opportunities for students by making local school districts eligible for bilingual instruction. To qualify for the program, districts had to provide for the educational needs of linguistically and culturally different students, including Native American students and others who wished to participate. The Albuquerque Public School District operated the Alternative Language Services (ALS) program pursuant to the BMEA, providing bilingual education for limited English proficient students. The U.S. Department of Education's Office for Civil Rights, which oversees local compliance with Title VI, reviewed the ALS program and entered into an agreement for corrective action with the district in 1995. The agreement established new procedures for identifying and serving limited English proficient students.

A group of Albuquerque students in the ALS program sued the district in a federal district court, asserting the BMEA and ALS were discriminatory, since the programs classified and created placements for students on the basis of race or national origin. A group of ALS supporters intervened in the action, and the court awarded summary judgment to the district. The objecting students appealed to the U.S. Court of Appeals, Tenth Circuit. The court found no reason to disturb the district court order. **The district court had properly found that the BMEA did not violate the Equal Protection Clause or Title VI.** There was no evidence that the district violated the 1995 agreement with the Office for Civil Rights by forcing students to participate in the ALS program without notice or consent. Moreover, the limited English proficient students were not "third party beneficiaries" of the agreement who were entitled to any kind of injunctive relief enforcing the agreement. The court concluded the ALS program and the BMEA did not violate the federal Equal Education Opportunity Act's mandate to take appropriate action to overcome language barriers that impede equal participation by its students. *Carbajal v. Albuquerque Public School Dist.*, 43 Fed.Appx. 306 (10th Cir. 2002).

◆ Limited English proficient students attending schools in a Chicago-area district asserted that district officials failed to comply with state requirements for the Illinois Transitional Education Program. They alleged that state officials refused to sanction the district, despite their power to cut district funding or place it on probation for noncompliance. The students and their parents sued state and local education officials, including the Illinois State Board of Education (ISBE), its members and state superintendent in a federal district court for violation of the federal Equal Education Opportunities Act (EEOA), which bars states from denying equal educational opportunities for individuals on account of race, color, sex or national origin. The EEOA addresses failure by a state educational agency "to take appropriate action to overcome the language barriers that impede equal participation by its students in its instructional programs." The state officials moved for dismissal of the case, arguing that there had been no violation of federal law, that the court lacked jurisdiction to compel it to adhere to state law, that the students and parents lacked legal standing to advance the claim, and that the action was barred by a 1988 class action settlement by a different group of students against the ISBE.

The court held the state officials had the power to impose sanctions on the district but had failed to do so. The court thus had the power to order relief that would redress the harm. The ISBE could be held liable under the EEOA for a local district's failure to take appropriate action. **The students and parents had thus stated valid claims for which relief could be granted concerning a state-level failure to properly supervise the district and the district's noncompliance with state and federal law requirements.** The court refused to impose a higher standard than the "appropriate action" referenced in the EEOA. It rejected the ISBE's argument that it was required to find "deliberate indifference" in order to impose any liability on the state. The court denied the motion to dismiss the action against the state officials. *Cortez v. Calumet Public School Dist. No. 132*, No. 01 C 8201, 2002 WL 31177378 (N.D. Ill. 2002).

C. Grading

In Regents of Univ. of Michigan v. Ewing, *474 U.S. 214 (1985), the U.S. Supreme Court held courts may not override academic decisions unless there is "such a substantial departure from accepted academic norms as to demonstrate that the person or committee responsible did not actually exercise professional judgment."*

◆ **The Supreme Court of Arkansas held two teachers and a middle school principal had discretion to deny reading credit to a student who claimed to have read four Harry Potter books in less than one week. No law entitled the student to the relief he sought in court.** The student participated in his school's accelerated reader program, in which students could win prizes or awards by reading books and taking tests based on them. He stated he read four of five books in the Harry Potter series because of the high points assigned to the books. After the student scored 100% on each of the tests, his reading teacher accused him of cheating, stating it was impossible to read the books in the required one-week period. The student's classroom teacher agreed and confronted him about cheating. The student's mother sought reinstatement of the scores. The school principal permitted only one to be reinstated, finding no obligation to reinstate the others under program incentive rules.

The student petitioned a state court for an order requiring the principal and teachers to reinstate the cancelled scores, apologize publicly and by letter, and prevent them from "further humiliating and using coercive tactics." The court dismissed the case and awarded the school district $1,500 in attorneys' fees. The student appealed to the state supreme court, which held he was not entitled to relief. **No law compelled school officials to reinstate scores in voluntary reading programs. The court found "a general policy against intervention by the courts in matters best left to school authorities." Reinstatement of test scores was left to the discretion of school officials.** As the student had no legal remedy available, the court affirmed the judgment, including the award of attorneys' fees. *T.J. v. Hargrove*, 362 Ark. 649, 210 S.W.3d 79 (Ark. 2005).

◆ A Michigan student ranked first in his class at the end of his junior year. He maintained dual enrollment in his high school during his senior year but took no classes there. The student worked as a paralegal in his mother's law office for an employer-based course taken through a county intermediate district. Although an "A" was the highest possible grade under the intermediate district policy, the student's high school district allowed A+ grades. The student's mother awarded him an A+ for the employer-based course. However, the report card issued by the high school district indicated an A for the course. The high school district refused the mother's request to change the grade to A+, and the student sued it in the state court system, asserting due process violations.

The court held for the district, and the student appealed to the state court of appeals. He argued a high school district policy allowing grades to be weighted or adjusted did not apply to intermediate district courses. **The court stated a district's board of education had authority to implement a grading system under Michigan law.** There was no merit to the student's arguments. The paralegal training course was administered by the intermediate school district, not the high school. The highest possible grade was an A. The high school district's policy prevented weighting or adjustment of the grade. **There was no due process violation, as no fundamental right was implicated.** Since the student had no vested property interest in an A+ and no legal right to a particular grade, the court affirmed the judgment. *Delekta v. Memphis Community Schools*, No. 249325, 2004 WL 2290462 (Mich. Ct. App. 2004).

◆   Kentucky Revised Stat. § 159.051 required school principals to notify the state transportation department whenever a 16- or 17-year-old student dropped out of school or became "academically deficient." The law applied only to students attending school or residing in a district that operated an alternative education program. A student with a learning disability was declared academically deficient and lost her driver's license under Section 159.051. She sued state officials in a Kentucky circuit court, which certified the case as a class action. She also filed a complaint with the U.S. Department of Education (DOE), asserting the law violated the Family Educational Rights and Privacy Act (FERPA). The DOE agreed with the student, and the state transportation department began using new consent forms with a parental release provision as part of its licensing procedure. The court held two statutory classifications infringed on fundamental educational rights: the distinction between 16- and 17-year-olds from 18-year-olds; and the geographical distinction between students residing or attending school in districts with alternative education programs and those living elsewhere. The law unlawfully discriminated against disabled students. The Court of Appeals of Kentucky reversed the circuit court decision, and the student appealed to the state supreme court.

The court held Section 159.051 did not infringe upon the fundamental right of students to pursue an adequate education. The law only attached adverse consequences to academic failure. **While the right to an education included the right to equal academic opportunity, it did not include a guarantee of success.** Since 18 was the age of majority, there was a rational basis for the law's age distinction. However, the geographic distinction between districts with alternative education programs and those without them had no rational basis. **The court found no indication that an alternative education program added anything to special education requirements.** Regardless of whether a district operated an alternative education program, it was required to provide for the needs of disabled students. There was no rational basis for using the existence of an alternative education program to classify which students were subject to the revocation or denial of a driver's license. The court reversed the appeals court decision, as Section 159.051 violated student equal protection rights. *D.F. v. Codell*, 127 S.W.3d 571 (Ky. 2003).

◆   **An Ohio school district did not violate a student's rights by suspending her for excessive tardiness under an attendance policy that assigned students failing grades for poor attendance.** An Ohio appeals court upheld the policy as a constitutional means of promoting good attendance. According to the appeals court, **under state law, school policies are generally left to the discretion of the school board.** The board policy in this case promoted attendance for academic performance and provided sanctions for excessive unexcused absences. It distinguished between excused and unexcused absences and was neither unreasonable nor unconstitutional. The court affirmed the judgment for the board. *Smith v. Revere Local School Dist. Board of Educ.*, No. 20275, 2001 WL 489980 (Ohio Ct. App. 2001).

◆   A California middle school music teacher assigned three students conduct grades of "needs improvement" or "unsatisfactory." Parents complained about the poor conduct grades, which made the students ineligible for honor society and field trips. The principal then changed the grades to "satisfactory" without consulting the teacher. The teacher filed a grievance that was denied at all three levels, culminating with the school board. The teacher and his collective bargaining association filed a state court action against the district and principal. The court ordered reinstatement of the grades, and the district appealed.

The California Court of Appeal noted **the state Education Code provides that a grade assigned by a classroom teacher is final and can be changed only in limited circumstances such as clerical or mechanical mistake, or where the assignment is characterized by bad faith or incompetency.** The court rejected the district's argument that the code section did not apply to citizenship grades. Performance in a secondary school has both academic and behavior components that are graded separately. Citizenship grades reflected a teacher's assessment of student performance for cooperation, attitude and effort, and there was no reason to believe the legislature meant to distinguish them from academic marks. **The court held that even if citizenship marks were not considered grades, the district had exceeded its authority in changing them.** Under the Education Code, parents can request the change of a school record for inaccuracy or if the record is based on an unsubstantiated personal conclusion or an inference outside the observer's area of competence. Since none of these circumstances was present, the district had exceeded its authority in changing the citizenship grades. *Las Virgenes Educators Ass'n v. Las Virgenes Unified School Dist.*, 102 Cal.Rptr.2d 901 (Cal. Ct. App. 2000).

◆   A Louisiana high school senior missed many history and algebra classes because of personal medical problems. Her progress reports indicated failure in both subjects. The history teacher refused to accept overdue assignments and assigned the student an F. Although the algebra teacher stated at one point during the semester that she had never failed a senior, she assigned the student an F for algebra and the student was not allowed to graduate with her class. She filed a lawsuit against the school board in a Louisiana district court, asserting outrageous behavior that caused her emotional distress, humiliation and embarrassment. The court granted summary judgment to the school board, and the student appealed to the Court of Appeal of Louisiana, First Circuit.

The student claimed she should have been allowed to demonstrate the intent of school district employees to cause her emotional distress. **The court found no evidence of extreme and outrageous conduct, which is required to recover damages for intentional infliction of emotional distress.** Evidence indicated that the student had been graded and evaluated on the same scale as other students in the district and that her progress reports indicated she was failing both classes. The negligent infliction of emotional distress claim also failed because the school district had no legal duty to allow the makeup of missed assignments and tests. The history teacher was permitted to insist upon the timely submission of work. The court affirmed the judgment for the school board. *Barrino v. East Baton Rouge Parish School Board,* 697 So.2d 27 (La. Ct. App. 1997).

◆ A Dallas high school math teacher alleged that his principal instructed him to give a student-athlete a passing grade in his class, even though the student was failing. After the teacher refused, the principal allowed the student to transfer out of the teacher's class. The Texas Education Agency (TEA) investigated the school's grading policies on the basis of an anonymous tip, and the school was disqualified from the state football playoffs. The school district then transferred the teacher to a middle school, placed him on probation for a year, froze his salary, assigned him an unsatisfactory performance rating and prohibited him from teaching math. An administrative panel upheld the school board's decision, but the TEA reversed it. Although prevailing in the TEA action, the teacher resigned from teaching and filed a Texas district court action against the school district and certain school officials, including the principal. The court granted judgment to the school district and officials.

The teacher appealed to the Court of Appeals of Texas, Dallas. The court held **the teacher had no constitutional right to refuse to assign a grade as instructed by his supervisor. This was not an example of academic freedom protected by the First Amendment**, because the assignment of a grade is not a teaching method. Accordingly, the district could not be held liable for maintaining a policy or custom of causing constitutional injuries and enjoyed immunity from the tort injuries alleged by the teacher under the Texas Tort Claims Act. The teacher also failed to allege that he had been subjected to intolerable working conditions that would support a constructive discharge claim. The court affirmed the judgment for the district and officials. *Bates v. Dallas Independent School Dist.,* 952 S.W.2d 543 (Tex. Ct. App. 1997).

◆ A North Carolina high school changed its method of selecting honor students when a newly appointed principal determined the existing method was in conflict with school board policy. The new method ranked students using a weighted semester grade average. As a result of the change in policy, one student dropped from first to fourth in her class standing and was not selected valedictorian of her graduating class. The student's parents appealed the decision to implement the semester average formula, but were advised by the superintendent of schools that the new system was fair and in compliance with school board policy. This decision was affirmed by the board of education. The student filed a lawsuit against the board in a North Carolina trial court for negligent infliction of emotional distress, with additional constitutional claims.

The case reached the Court of Appeals of North Carolina. The student presented evidence that an advisor had told her she was first in her class during the year of the change in policy and that the board had interfered with her "right to be valedictorian of her senior class." The court found **she did not allege the district's calculations were incorrect or different from any other student's computation. There had been no error by the trial court in dismissing the claim for negligent infliction of emotional distress.** *Townsend v. Board of Educ. of Robeson County,* 454 S.E.2d 817 (N.C. Ct. App. 1995).

III. STUDENT RECORDS

The Family Educational Rights and Privacy Act of 1974 (FERPA), 20 U.S.C. § 1232g, was enacted to grant parents access to their children's education records and to protect those records from access by unauthorized persons. FERPA denies federal funds to schools that release student education records to third parties without express written parental consent.

FERPA applies only to "education records," which are "records related to a student that are maintained by an educational agency or a party acting for the agency." Records that originate from a school, or are created by non-school entities, may become education records if they are "maintained" by a school.

Records that are excluded from FERPA definitions include notes used only as a personal memory aid and kept in the sole possession of the maker. These "desk drawer" notes cannot be revealed to any other person, except a temporary substitute for the maker of the record.

The Health Insurance Portability and Accountability Act (HIPAA) was enacted to ensure continued health insurance for persons changing jobs, and to address the problem of health information confidentiality. Under federal regulations, records covered by FERPA are exempt from HIPAA. However, since schools typically provide services deemed to be within HIPAA definitions, schools may be considered "covered entities" under HIPAA in some situations.

Several federal court decisions have held HIPAA does not create a private right of action for individuals to bring lawsuits. These include Dominic J. v. Wyoming Valley West High School, *362 F.Supp.2d 560 (M.D. Pa. 2005),* Runkle v. Gonzales, *391 F.Supp.2d 210 (D.D.C. 2005), and* Swift Lake Park High School Dist. 108, *No. 03 C 5003, 2003 WL 22388878 (N.D. Ill. 2003).*

A. Student and Parental Rights

◆ A Minnesota student told his mother two other students were showing papers with information about him to others at school and were calling him "dumb," "stupid," and "retarded." The mother recognized the papers as copies of his assessment summary report, which was used to determine special education eligibility. The students had found the report blowing around in the wind in a school parking lot. The papers had been in a garbage bag that was torn open. The student's mother sued the school district in a state court for violating the Minnesota Government Data Practices Act (MGDPA). The court denied the district's request for summary judgment, and a jury found the district violated its MGDPA duty to set appropriate safeguards for student records. The jury verdict awarded the family $60,000 in past damages for pain, embarrassment and emotional distress, plus $80,000 in future damages for embarrassment and emotional distress. The court denied the district's motion for a new trial and ordered it to pay over $47,000 of the parent's claim for attorneys' fees and costs.

On appeal, **the Court of Appeals of Minnesota held the MGDPA required each school district to establish appropriate security safeguards for all records containing data on individuals**. The MGDPA provided for civil damage awards, requiring a responsible authority to pay damages to a person who suffers injury as the result of a violation. **This created a duty to establish appropriate safeguards for all records containing student data.** District manuals lacked procedures for the destruction of documents, and employees were not trained how to destroy records. The court found evidence that the district did not establish appropriate MGDPA safeguards. There was also evidence that the incident would have a devastating effect on the student for a lifetime. As the evidence was sufficient to support the jury verdict, the court affirmed the judgment. *Scott v. Minneapolis Public Schools, Special Dist. No. 1*, No. A05-649, 2006 WL 997721 (Minn. Ct. App. 2006).

◆   A New York school district policy required staff members to report student pregnancies to a school social worker to encourage students to inform their parents. A teachers' association sued the school board and superintendent in a federal district court on behalf of female students attending district schools. The association claimed the policy violated due process, privacy and equal protection rights, New York Public Health Law Section 2504(3) and other laws. The court refused to grant a preliminary order to prevent enforcement of the policy. The court later considered a motion by school officials to dismiss the case. The court refused to apply abortion cases to "the unrecognized protections claimed by Plaintiffs to prevent the disclosure of a minor's pregnancy to her parents." No court had ever recognized such a right. **Parental notification of a student's pregnancy did not intrude upon any "right to ultimately seek an abortion or carry her fetus to term." The policy had exceptions and the principal and superintendent had discretion not to notify the parents.**

There was no due process or equal protection violation. The policy did not violate any state or federal confidentiality requirements. Contrary to the association's argument, 8 N.Y.C.R.R. § 136.3(a)(5) required schools to inform parents of conditions affecting the health, safety and welfare of their children. **Failure to inform the parents of a student's pregnancy would likely result in civil and possibly criminal liability.** The court held "federal law would also seem to require that a school disclose a student's pregnancy to her parents." **An "educational record" under FERPA "would seem to cover records evidencing the pregnancy of a student." The court dismissed the case, holding "it is the parent's – and not the school's – responsibility to make decisions in the best interests of their child."** *Port Washington Teachers' Ass'n*

v. Board of Educ. of Port Washington Union Free School Dist., No. 04-CV 1357
TCP WDW, 2006 WL 47447 (E.D.N.Y. 2006).

◆   New Jersey social service agencies assembled a community group to assess
local youth needs. The town education board agreed to survey its students for
the community group to understand youth needs, attitudes and behavior, and to
better use town programs and resources. The survey sought information about
drug and alcohol use, sexual activity, violence, suicide, racial attitudes and
parent-child relationships. Some parents expressed concern that explicit
questions about drug and alcohol use, sexual activity and suicide suggested
"such activity was within normal adolescent experience." Although the survey
was supposed to be voluntary and anonymous, some students believed it was
mandatory. Objecting students and parents sued the board and school officials
in a federal district court for violations of the FERPA and the U.S. Constitution.
The court held for the board.

   On appeal, the Third Circuit found evidence that all students in the district
had participated in the survey, indicating involuntariness. No consent forms
informed parents how they could avoid their child's participation. However, the
district court had correctly held the survey protected student anonymity. **The
constitutional right to prevent disclosure of intimate facts is not absolute
and is to be balanced against the public interest in health and safety.
Student privacy rights did not extend to the survey in this case.** Disclosure
of personal information occurred in the aggregate, and personal information
was safeguarded. The survey did not violate the parents' fundamental right to
make decisions concerning the care, custody and control of their children. The
board did not substantially interfere with their decision-making and did not
indoctrinate students. The court found no violation of student rights against
compelled speech. There was no evidence that students were punished or
threatened for failing to complete the survey. As the survey results did not
permit individualized student identification, the court held for the board. *C.N. v.
Ridgewood Board of Educ.*, 430 F.3d 159 (3d Cir. 2005).

◆   **A Pennsylvania school district did not violate the state Right to Know
Act by denying a citizen's request for copies of letters to and from the
district superintendent. The Commonwealth Court of Pennsylvania held
the letters were not "public records" under the act. Public agencies may
charge a reasonable fee when copying public records.** The 25 cents per copy
charged by the school district in this case was reasonable. The school district
was more like a college, county or government agency than a copy store,
making it unfair to use those businesses for cost comparison. *Weiss v.
Williamsport Area School Dist.*, 872 A.2d 269 (Pa. Commw. Ct. 2005).

◆   A Florida superintendent made an 8,000-page investigation report on a
school principal accused of misconduct. It referenced other faculty members
and included confidential student information. The superintendent notified the
principal and other faculty members they could receive copies of the report,
which had information that could be considered derogatory and could end up in
employee personnel files. A group of faculty members declined an offer by the

superintendent to sign confidentiality agreements covering student information found in the report, or to receive copies of the report with student information redacted (removed) to prevent disclosure of identifying material. The faculty members sued the superintendent in a state trial court to require the district to release the report with no restrictions on data. The court directed the board to provide the faculty members the report with all student identifying information redacted. The order required the board to notify students of their right to object to the redacted information. After this notice was provided, several students, parents and faculty members objected. The faculty members again sought copies of an unredacted report to better respond to it. The court held any report became public after it was turned over to a school board. It held the report only implicated the privacy rights of exceptional students.

The faculty members appealed to the Florida Court of Appeal, arguing they were unable to respond to the heavily redacted report. The court agreed with the superintendent that **all student identifying information should be concealed in the report, not just the information relating to exceptional students. Florida law required investigatory information from a complaint against school employees to remain confidential while the investigation was active.** When an investigation was no longer active, the complaint and all material became public. The report contained personally-identifying information about students. **Florida Statutes § 119.07(1) made all personally identifiable student records and reports confidential and exempt from disclosure.** The court reversed the judgment and instructed the district to redact all personally identifying information from the report. It held **although teachers were required to protect student confidentiality, "being a teacher does not grant access to confidential student information."** The rights of faculty members to respond to the report did not "trump" the right of students to keep the information confidential. If the report had derogatory material about teachers that was unrelated to disciplinary charges, that information was to be excluded from their files. *Johnson v. Deluz*, 875 So.2d 1 (Fla. Dist. Ct. App. 2004).

◆   **A Florida District Court of Appeal rejected a parent's argument that a test booklet and questions from the Florida Comprehensive Achievement Test (FCAT) are "student records" as defined by state law.** A parent sought to review the FCAT instrument after his daughter failed the test. The state education department denied the request, and he sued the department and state education officials, alleging the instrument was a "student record" under the Florida Student Records Law. A trial court held for the parent, and education officials appealed to the court of appeal. The court examined statutory language addressing tests. The statute included the "scores" of standardized achievement tests, intelligence tests, aptitude tests and psychological tests. However, the statute "conspicuously makes no mention of the test instruments themselves."

The trial court's decision was in conflict with provisions of the School Code. Although the lower court tried to harmonize these provisions by allowing the parent "meaningful access" to supervised review of the FCAT instrument, the student record provision did not authorize any limitation on access to student records. The education department interpreted the student record provision as excluding testing instruments. The trial court was required to give the department deference, as it was charged with enforcing the school code. The department's interpretation gave meaning to the term "scores" while allowing full effect to other statutory provisions. Because the department's interpretation of the law was reasonable, the court of appeal reversed the judgment. *Florida Dep't of Educ. v. Cooper*, 858 So.2d 394 (Fla. Dist. Ct. App. 2003).

◆   A divorced Vermont father had custody of a child and the right to make her educational decisions. The divorce decree gave the mother rights to "reasonable information" regarding the child's school progress. The father and child then moved into another school district, where an Individualized Education Program (IEP) team determined the child had an emotional behavioral disability. The mother was initially excluded from the IEP team, but later was allowed to join. When her request for an independent educational evaluation was denied, she sought a due process hearing. A hearing officer denied her request, finding the custody order deprived her of standing to request a hearing. The mother challenged the accuracy of the child's educational files and unsuccessfully sought to change them. She commenced a federal district court action under the Individuals with Disabilities Education Act (IDEA) and FERPA against two school districts, state and local education officials, the state education department and others. A federal magistrate judge held that as a non-custodial parent, the mother lacked standing to proceed.

The mother appealed to the Second Circuit, which found that her ability to proceed on her IDEA claim depended on whether she was considered a "parent" under the act. **The court held that a parent's IDEA rights are determined by state law. Because the Vermont family court had vested the father with the right to make the child's educational decisions, the mother had no standing to demand a due process hearing. She also lacked standing to pursue her records access claim under FERPA, which is enforced by educational agencies, not through private lawsuits.** Since there is no private right of action in a FERPA case, dismissal of this claim was proper. The mother's claimed right to amend the child's records was properly dismissed, as the father was given all legal rights over the child's education. The court agreed with the mother that her access to records was not revoked by the divorce decree, which gave her the right to "reasonable information" regarding the child's school progress. The hearing officer had properly denied her request for a hearing due to her lack of standing. **The district court should not have dismissed the IDEA action based on access to records, as it was conceivable that the information the mother sought was considered "reasonable information" she was entitled to receive.** *Taylor v. Vermont Dep't of Educ.*, 313 F.3d 768 (2d Cir. 2002).

◆   A Washington private school student intended to teach in the state's public school system after his graduation. At the time, the state required new teachers to obtain an affidavit of good moral character from the dean of their college or university. When the university's teacher certification specialist overheard a conversation implicating the student in sexual misconduct with a classmate, she commenced an investigation of the student and reported the allegations against him to the state teacher certification agency. She later informed the student that the university would not provide him with the affidavit of good moral character he needed for certification as a Washington teacher. The student sued the university and the specialist under state law and 42 U.S.C. § 1983 for violating FERPA. A jury awarded him over $1 million in damages. The case reached the U.S. Supreme Court, which held **FERPA creates no personal rights that can be enforced under Section 1983. Congress enacted FERPA to force schools to respect students' privacy with respect to education records. It did not confer enforceable rights upon students.** The Court reversed and remanded the case to a state court for further proceedings. *Gonzaga Univ. v. Doe*, 536 U.S. 273, 122 S.Ct. 2268, 153 L.Ed.2d 309 (2002).

◆ The parent of three Oklahoma students learned their teachers sometimes asked students to grade each other's assignments and then call out the results. She asserted the policy was embarrassing to her children and sued the school district and school administrators in a federal district court for violations of FERPA and the Due Process Clause. The court held that the policy did not violate any constitutional privacy rights and that the practice of calling out grades did not involve "education records" within the meaning of FERPA. The parent appealed to the Tenth Circuit, which reversed the district court judgment.

The U.S. Supreme Court accepted the district's petition to review the question of whether peer grading of papers violated FERPA. The Court observed that **an "education record" under FERPA is one that is "maintained by an educational agency or institution or by a person acting for such agency or institution."** According to the court, student papers are not "maintained" within the meaning of FERPA when students correct them or call out grades. **The word "maintain" suggested that FERPA records were kept in files or cabinets in a "records room at the school or on a permanent secure database."** The momentary handling of assignments by students did not conform to this definition. A contrary decision would drastically alter the existing balance of authority among state and federal governments. The appeals court committed error by deciding that a student acted for an educational institution under FERPA when assisting with grading. The term "acting for" connoted a teacher, administrator or other school employee. The court held FERPA should not be construed to prohibit techniques currently used by teachers. Congress would not have burdened teachers in this manner and would not extend any obligation to maintain records to students. **FERPA language implied that education records were "institutional records kept by a single central custodian, such as a registrar, not individual assignments handled by many student graders in their separate classrooms."** Because Congress did not intend to intervene in drastic fashion with traditional state functions by exercising minute control over teaching methods, the Court reversed and remanded the case. *Owasso Independent School Dist. No. I-011 v. Falvo*, 534 U.S. 426, 122 S.Ct. 934, 151 L.Ed.2d 896 (2002).

◆ A Massachusetts student disrupted his special education classroom and directed racial slurs at his teacher. School officials suspected him of writing racial graffiti on the blackboard in her room and photographed the graffiti. Several weeks later, the school was vandalized by obscene words and other marks on the hallways. A faculty member observed the student in the hallway near the time of the incident, and the graffiti was photographed. A school vice principal provided the police with written samples of the student's schoolwork to help determine whether it matched the writing on the walls and blackboard. A handwriting expert determined the student had likely written the graffiti. The commonwealth of Massachusetts commenced proceedings against the student for malicious destruction of property and violation of civil rights. A trial court held the handwriting samples had been obtained in violation of a state law requiring student or parental consent prior to the release of a "student record."

The Supreme Judicial Court of Massachusetts observed that state regulations permit private third parties to have access to student records upon written consent from the student or the student's parents. "Student record" was defined as the transcript and temporary record, including all information or any other materials concerning a student, organized on the basis of the student's name in such a way that the student could be individually identified. The regulations additionally required that the information be kept by the public schools. **The court rejected the student's argument that his handwriting samples were "student records" within the meaning of state law. Homework, tests and other assignments were not a part of a student's transcript and were not typically "kept" by schools.** The court declared that the inclusion of homework, written classroom work, tests and quizzes within the definition of "student record" would be inimical to ordinary teaching practices. The handwriting samples provided to the police were not student records and were not protected by state confidentiality requirements. The information was turned over to a governmental agency, not a private third party, and although the provision of samples to the police was a "search" under the Fourth Amendment, the action was reasonable in view of the reduced privacy expectation of students in school. The school had a clear obligation to use the student's papers only for educational purposes, but it also had an obligation to prevent racial harassment of a teacher and further property damage. The court vacated the judgment and remanded the case. *Comwlth. of Massachusetts v. Buccella*, 434 Mass. 473, 751 N.E.2d 373 (Mass. 2001).

◆ A Utah elementary school student was disciplined for verbally and physically abusing other students. The school district notified his parents of several victims and witnesses by sending memorandums to them. The district communications revealed the incidents had occurred and that the student was accused of verbally and physically abusing others. The district also reported that each child had been questioned about the incident, that each had reported abuse of some kind and that the student had been advised to cease his abusive behavior. The district suspended the student for 10 days, and his parents sued the district and school officials in a federal district court, asserting violations of the state and federal constitutions, Section 504, FERPA, and state law.

The court dismissed the complaint, and the parents appealed. The U.S. Court of Appeals, Tenth Circuit, held the parents' privacy claims failed because **the disclosure of information about their son to the parents of student victims and witnesses did not constitute prohibited disclosures of an "educational record" under FERPA.** The district memorandums did not violate FERPA because "**the contemporaneous disclosure to the parents of a** victimized child of the results of any investigation and resulting disciplinary actions taken against an alleged child perpetrator does not constitute release of an 'education record'" under FERPA. The court stated FERPA allowed the targeted, discrete disclosure of this information to the parents of victims. The district court had properly dismissed the case. *Jensen v. Reeves*, 3 Fed.Appx. 2001 (10th Cir. 2001).

B. Media Requests

◆ A California school district denied requests to disclose documents relating to student suspensions and expulsions during a certain time period. It asserted student privacy rights and offered the requestor some statistical information on school discipline instead. The requestor filed a state court action against the district, citing Education Code § 48918 and a state attorney general's opinion deeming student names and the reasons for expulsions "public information." The court agreed with the requestor, and the district appealed. The state court of appeal noted that while student records are generally unavailable to the public, the Education Code treated expulsion records differently. Even though students may opt for a private expulsion hearing, the formal action to expel a student must be public. Under state law, expulsion records were also public. On the other hand, the state Government Code provided that it did not require the disclosure of records that are exempt or prohibited from disclosure by state or federal law. FERPA provides for the privacy of student education records.

Under federal court precedents, student disciplinary records are protected from public disclosure as "education records" under FERPA. **Because FERPA conditions the receipt of federal funding on conformity with its provisions, the district risked the withdrawal of federal funds if it disclosed the requested student expulsion records, despite the state law provision allowing disclosure.** The court held it was impossible for the district to obey both laws, and that FERPA preempted Section 48918. It reversed the superior court order. *Rim of the World Unified School Dist. v. Superior Court*, 104 Cal.App.4th 1393, 129 Cal.Rptr.2d 11 (Cal. Ct. App. 2002).

◆ The Massachusetts Education Department administered the Massachusetts Comprehensive Assessment System (MCAS) to over 220,000 students in three grades. It contracted with Harcourt Educational Measurement to score the tests. A *Boston Globe* reporter made a written request from the department's commissioner for release of all 2000 MCAS scores, as soon as the department received them. Five days later, the department released statewide test results to the public, but did not include compiled test results for individual schools because it did not receive that information until the next day. After receiving individual school testing information, the department announced an additional one-week delay in releasing the results. This was to allow local school officials time to correct potential errors. Officials detected many errors, and Harcourt established an error reporting hotline that resulted in a 15-page log with over 100 error reports. The *Globe* sought a state trial court order requiring the department to immediately release the 2000 MCAS test results. The court denied the *Globe*'s motion and awarded summary judgment to the department.

The *Globe* appealed to the Massachusetts Supreme Judicial Court, which stated that the case involved the proper interpretation of Massachusetts G.L. c. 66, § 10, the state public records law. The court commented that while the law specifies that public records shall be released by their custodian "without unreasonable delay," it also allows the custodian 10 days to comply with a records request. The *Globe* asserted the law's 10-day period was a maximum, and that the department had unreasonably delayed releasing the MCAS results. The department asserted the release of public records within 10 days was presumptively reasonable and that it complied with the law by releasing the results in seven days. The court agreed with the department and affirmed the judgment. Public records were to be available for public examination at reasonable times and without unreasonable delay. **The release of public records within 10 days of a request was presumptively reasonable. As the department had an obligation to release accurate information, the court held it did not unreasonably delay releasing the MCAS scores by allowing local districts to review the raw scores for errors.** *Globe Newspaper Co. v. Commissioner of Educ.*, 439 Mass. 124, 786 N.E.2d 328 (Mass. 2003).

◆ A *Chicago Tribune* reporter submitted a request to the Chicago Board of Education for approximately 1.1 million records on current and former Chicago public school students. The request included personal data such as school, room number, active or inactive status, medical status, special education status, attendance data, race, transportation status, free or reduced-cost lunch status, class rank, grade average, bilingual education status, date of birth, and standardized test scores. The board denied the request as burdensome and as a high risk of disclosing personal information in violation of federal law and state laws including the Freedom of Information Act (FOIA) and Student Records Act. The *Tribune* sued the board. A state court held the information request was masked to hide student identities and would not allow for easy identification. The court awarded judgment to the *Tribune*.

On appeal, the Appellate Court of Illinois stated the FOIA required public bodies to comply with records requests unless one of its exemptions applied. An exemption applied to "files and personal information maintained with respect to students." The court stated **FOIA's student records exemption was a *per se* rule that did not require a court to engage in case-by-case balancing of the competing interests in public information and individual privacy**. The clear language of the FOIA created an exemption from disclosure for student files. Most of the data requested by the *Tribune* was considered private and confidential. This included information on student medical, guardian, special education and bilingual education status. Because the request was entitled to the *per se* exemption of state law, the board had properly denied it. The court reversed and remanded the judgment. *Chicago Tribune Co. v. Board of Educ. of City of Chicago*, 332 Ill.App.3d 60, 773 N.E.2d 674 (Ill. App. Ct. 2002).

◆ Arizona law required the state education board to develop and adopt the Arizona Instrument to Measure Standards (AIMS) and eventually make a passing score a high school graduation requirement. About 92% of the students who took the first AIMS administration in 1999 failed one or more of its three components. After the state released the scores, a newspaper publisher asked to inspect and copy "Form A," as the first AIMS administration was known. The state allowed limited inspection of the form but refused to allow note-taking or copying of it. The newspaper filed a special action in a state superior court, seeking an order allowing the inspection and copying of Form A. The court distinguished between "anchor questions" that would be repeated in future administrations of the exam, and questions that would not be repeated. It held the state education department was not required to disclose any of the anchor questions, but had to make all others available for public inspection.

The parties appealed unfavorable aspects of the decision to the state court of appeals, which observed that the AIMS Form A documents were subject to the state public records law. **State law created a presumption in favor of disclosure, but this could be overcome where the state showed that non-disclosure served the privacy or confidentiality interests of the state, or otherwise served the state's best interest.** To justify withholding public documents, the state interest in non-disclosure had to outweigh the general policy of open access. Because student graduation would depend on passing the AIMS, the state had a strong interest in assuring its fairness. It designed six forms of the examination and used them in rotation, repeating anchor questions in all forms. This procedure was intended to promote fairness and ensure equivalency among forms. **The court held the anchor questions from Form A should not be disclosed because they were to be repeated** in subsequent forms. Public release of the anchor questions would significantly increase test scores and threaten the equating function that enabled comparison of the various forms. **The superior court had correctly ordered the state to release non-anchor Form A questions for public inspection.** The public interest in disclosure of these questions was not as strong as for anchor questions and did not implicate substantial costs to the state. The high failure rate of the AIMS test implied that the test was inapt or that schools were failing. *Phoenix Newspapers Inc. v. Keegan*, 35 P.3d 105 (Ariz. Ct. App. 2001).

◆ A Kentucky news reporter made open records requests to inspect and copy a school district's student disciplinary hearing records for 1990 through 1996, seeking the school of origin and the reason for each disciplinary action. The superintendent of schools initially denied the request, but later provided the reporter with copies of board minutes concerning expulsion votes, with all other information redacted. The state attorney general concluded the Kentucky Open Records Act required disclosure without redacting the school name and category of offense. A state court held the requested information was excluded from the Open Records Act as an education record under FERPA and state law. The state appeals court reversed the decision, and the district appealed.

The Kentucky Supreme Court noted that FERPA defined "educational records" as materials containing information directly related to a student. **The definition of "personally identifiable information" included name, address and personal characteristics that made a student's identity easily traceable. Courts have held that records pertaining to a single student meet these criteria, but statistical compilations do not.** The information requested by the reporter did not directly relate to a particular student and was not an educational record under FERPA. Because the requested information did not meet the FERPA definition of educational record, it was not exempt from disclosure under the Open Records Act, which generally favors public disclosure of records. The act stated that no exemption existed for the "disclosure of statistical information not descriptive of any readily identifiable person." The court affirmed the appeals court decision, requiring the district to release the records of student disciplinary hearings without redacting the names of the schools and the offenses appearing in the records. *Hardin County Schools v. Foster*, 40 S.W.3d 865 (Ky. 2001).

C. Electronic and Video Records

◆   An Indiana student was suspected of participating in a drug deal. The assistant principal stated a security camera had videotaped the transaction, but he denied the mother's request to view it. The student was later suspended for 10 days, pending an expulsion hearing. He obtained negative results on a drug test. At the expulsion hearing, the assistant principal testified, using the unsigned statements of six student witnesses as evidence. He made several references to the videotape but did not present it as evidence. The school denied the student's request to cross-examine witnesses. At the hearing, the student denied lifting a chair to block the security camera. The assistant principal then produced a time- and date-stamped photo taken from the videotape that showed the student holding a chair in front of the camera. The expulsion examiner found the student was in possession of marijuana, and the student was expelled for the last four months of the school year. He sued the school district in a state court, which granted his request for a temporary restraining order to overturn the expulsion. The district removed the case to a federal district court. Meanwhile, a hearing review officer upheld the expulsion. In that proceeding, the names of witnesses, the security video, and the students' original statements were provided to the student and his mother.

The court found **"the clear weight of authority holds that a student facing an expulsion hearing does not have the right to cross-examine witnesses or even learn their identities."** The assistant principal was present at the hearing, under oath and in possession of the original statements. The federal rules of evidence do not apply in school discipline cases. **The tape was as much a matter of personal knowledge to the assistant principal as if he had been in the cafeteria.** The student received the opportunity to question the assistant principal. The district's procedures provided him notice of the charges and a full opportunity to be heard. **Allowing the student and his mother to see the videotape or to know the identities of witnesses would not have reduced the risk of a due process deprivation.** *D.L. v. Warsaw Community Schools*, No. 3:06-CV-229RM, 2006 WL 1195215 (N.D. Ind. 2006).

◆   Washington students were involved in a school bus fight that was recorded by a bus surveillance camera. The district allowed the parents of both students involved in the fight to view the videotape, but it refused to deliver a copy of the videotape for their lawyer's review. The district stated the tape was maintained for disciplinary purposes and was exempt from the state Public Disclosure Act

(PDA) and FERPA. The parents sued the district in a state court under the PDA. The court held the tape was exempt from public disclosure as it had information that would allow a viewer to identify other students. It denied the parents' demand for a tape with personally identifying student information blocked.

The parents appealed. **The Court of Appeals of Washington stated the PDA generally required public agencies to disclose requested public records. The court rejected the parents' claim that the PDA protected only information that would be found to violate a person's right to privacy. The act reflected the state legislature's heightened protection for students**. The tape contained personal information on students because it showed their identities. **The lower court had properly found the tape exempt from public disclosure. The district was not required to provide the parents with an edited version of the tape.** Even if this was feasible, editing would block out faces, bodies, voices and clothing, and no meaningful information would remain. The court affirmed the judgment, and it denied the parents' claims for attorneys' fees, costs, penalties and sanctions. *Lindeman v. Kelso School Dist.*, 111 P.3d 1235 (Wash. Ct. App. 2005).

◆   A New York student was videotaped fighting with a teacher during school. Other students were also recorded on videotape. School officials viewed the videotape and sent it to the local police department. The district held a disciplinary hearing for the student. The hearing officer did not view the videotape. After the hearing, the hearing officer recommended suspending the student for the rest of the school year, based on the testimony of a staff member and the student's own testimony that he hit the teacher. The student asked the school district to provide him with videotapes or audiotapes of the incident. The district refused, stating a need to protect the privacy rights of other students on the tape. The student petitioned a state court for an order requiring the district to provide him the recordings. The district argued it could not give the tape to the student because it was an "education record" under FERPA.

The court held the videotape was not an education record under FERPA. The district had voluntarily disclosed it to the police. Under FERPA, education records are "records, files, documents and other material which contain information directly related to a student." FERPA is intended to protect records relating to a student's performance and does not apply to a videotape recorded to maintain the school's security and safety. The court held the videotape was not an education record within the meaning of FERPA. The student's due process rights to appeal his suspension outweighed the district's interest in protecting the confidentiality of school records. While FERPA does not create a private right of action, the student was not suing the district. He was petitioning the court to have the videotape released so he could appeal the suspension. The court granted the student's request to release the videotape. *Rome City School Dist. Disciplinary Hearing v. Grifasi*, 10 Misc.3d 1034, 806 N.Y.S.2d 381 (N.Y. Sup. Ct. 2005).

◆   A group of Kentucky special education students complained their teacher mistreated them. The school installed cameras in her classroom to monitor her performance. The school principal denied the teacher's request to view class videotapes under the state open records act, stating they were "education records" under FERPA and its Kentucky counterpart, the KFERPA. The district superintendent claimed both FERPA and KFERPA prohibited the release of the videotapes to the teacher, and the state attorney general upheld this ruling.

A state circuit court held for the district, and the teacher appealed. The Court of Appeals of Kentucky found the circuit court did not consider a state Open Records Act exception permitting teachers to inspect "education records." **A FERPA exception exists for school officials, including teachers, who have "legitimate educational interests" in a student from whom consent would otherwise be required.** The court held the circuit court erroneously found the teacher did not qualify for FERPA and KFERPA exceptions for school officials with a legitimate educational interest in the requested record. The court agreed with the attorney general and circuit court that the videotapes were "education records" under FERPA and KFERPA, but rejected their finding that the teacher was only a "member of the public." Instead, her request had to be judged in view of her position as a teacher who was present in the classroom when the videotapes were recorded. The teacher was aware of the camera installation and the videotapes to monitor her performance. **Her presence in the classroom voided any confidentiality issue, as she would have obvious knowledge of her own students. The only way to prevent the teacher from viewing the videotapes under FERPA or KFERPA would be to find she lacked "a legitimate educational interest."** As the board did not show she lacked a legitimate educational interest in viewing the videotapes, the court reversed and remanded the case for a hearing. *Medley v. Board of Educ. of Shelby County*, No. 2003-CA-001515-MR, 2004 WL 2367229 (Ky. Ct. App. 2004).

◆ A Florida broadcasting company sought access to surveillance videotapes recorded on school buses to monitor student conduct. The company also requested incident reports concerning student misconduct on buses. The company limited its request to records with student identities redacted (blocked) to prevent personal identification of any student. The board and superintendent denied the request, and the company sued the board in a state trial court. The court held for the board and the company appealed. The Florida District Court of Appeal stated Art. I, § 24 of the Florida Constitution created a public right to inspect and copy public records, except for those deemed "confidential." **Florida Statutes § 228.093(3) made personally identifiable student information and any personal information in a student report or record both confidential and exempt from the state Public Records Act (PRA).** The same section defined "records and reports" to include official records, files and data directly related to a student that were created, maintained and used by public educational institutions. **Protected student records included identifying data, social security numbers, academic work, grades and standardized achievement test scores, scores on intelligence, aptitude or psychological tests, health, attendance and family data, teacher or counselor ratings and reports of serious or recurrent behavior patterns.** The court agreed with the board that even if the records were redacted, they were still "confidential" and exempt from disclosure under the PRA.

The court stated Section 228.093(3) recognized the strong privacy interest of students in their educational records. A 1995 decision held **videotapes of** students on school buses were "records and reports" under the school code. The court had previously used the definition of "personally identifiable information" from FERPA. However, FERPA calls for the deprivation of eligibility for federal funds only if an educational agency violates federal privacy requirements. **The Florida Code went beyond FERPA by protecting the privacy of students against the release of any personal information contained in records or reports permitting the personal identification of a student.** The court held the state code protected as confidential even those records or reports that were redacted of any personally identifying information. As the requested records were confidential and exempt from the PRA, the court affirmed the judgment for the board. *WFTV, Inc. v. School Board of Seminole,* 874 So.2d 48 (Fla. Dist. Ct. App. 2004).

IV. TESTING

State reform and accountability legislation has imposed new testing requirements on students that raise issues of privacy and fairness.

◆ In 2003, the California state board of education announced all public school students graduating in spring 2006 would have to pass both the language arts and mathematics parts of the California High School Exit Exam (CAHSEE) to receive a diploma. Each school district was required to notify parents about the CAHSEE diploma requirement beginning in the 2000-01 school year. Districts had to offer supplemental instruction to all students who did not demonstrate sufficient progress toward passing. The legislature appropriated $20 million in supplemental funding for districts with the highest percentage of students who had not yet passed the CAHSEE. The state superintendent of public instruction distributed supplemental funding only to districts in which 28% or more of the class of 2006 had yet to pass the CAHSEE. School districts in which no school had a CAHSEE failure rate of at least 28% received no supplemental funding. A lawsuit was filed in Alameda County Superior Court on behalf of 47,000 students who had satisfied other diploma requirements for spring 2006, but had yet to pass at least one part of the CAHSEE. The case alleged equal protection and due process violations.

The court found students in poor communities were not provided equal opportunities to learn the materials tested on the CAHSEE. Some schools had not fully aligned curriculums to the exam, and the lack of preparation disproportionately affected English language learners. The court issued an order preventing the state from requiring students in the class of 2006 to pass the CAHSEE as a condition of graduation. The Supreme Court of California found the superior court's remedy inappropriate, and sent the case to the state court of appeal. **The court of appeal held the superior court did not properly assess separation of powers principles. The superintendent had authority to give priority to the schools with the highest numbers of students who failed both parts of the CAHSEE.** The $20 million appropriated by the legislature was not nearly enough to provide $600 for each eligible student. The court found nothing arbitrary in the allocation of a limited sum of money to benefit school districts that appeared to have the greatest need. Students failing the CAHSEE had nine publicly funded options to continue their education and obtain diplomas. Awarding diplomas without passing the exam would stigmatize these students, deprive them of remedial instruction available to pass the CAHSEE, and debase the value of a diploma. The superior court order would force the "social promotion" of students. Cases holding that education is a fundamental right did not support the finding of a fundamental right to a diploma. The court vacated the superior court order. *O'Connell v. Superior Court of Alameda County,* 47 Cal.Rptr.3d 147 (Cal. Ct. App. 2006).

♦   In 2000, a federal district court held Arizona's English language learner (ELL) program did not satisfy the federal Equal Opportunity Act. The parties agreed to a consent order requiring the reassessment of ELL students and the court ordered a cost study with a deadline for compliance. The legislature increased funding for ELL students and authorized a further study. However, the study was never submitted. The court ordered the state to comply with its judgment by adequately funding ELL programs by the end of the legislative session. In December 2005, the court gave the legislature just over a month to comply with its funding order or face contempt fines of $500,000 per day for 30 days. **The district court further held that until the state adequately funded its ELL programs, ELL students would not have to pass the Arizona Instrument to Measure Standards (AIMS) to receive a diploma.**

By the time a funding agreement was reached, the fines had accumulated to $21 million. House Bill 2064 increased annual funding for each ELL student from about $358 to $432. The court ordered the $21 million in fines distributed to local school districts for ELL programs. The state appealed to the U.S. Court of Appeals, Ninth Circuit, which issued an order preventing the distribution of fines. The district court then issued an order which found House Bill 2064 was not based on research, and that the $432 allocated for each ELL student was $18 less than the amount suggested for such programming in a 1988 study. The court held the funding program would illegally divert federal funds to other uses. The Ninth Circuit consolidated several appeals from district court orders. It found the legal landscape of educational funding had changed significantly since the 2000 court order. The court vacated the orders holding the state in contempt and rejecting House Bill 2064, and it remanded the case to the district court for a hearing. *Flores v. Rzeslawski,* 204 Fed.Appx. 580 (9th Cir. 2006).

♦   A Maryland principal intern was accused of misconduct when taking a Praxis Series School Leaders Licensure Assessment Test. When she took the test, a site administrator submitted irregularity reports citing her for misconduct. The reports were based on alleged failure to stop writing in her test booklet when time was called. The intern challenged the reports in writing, stating that she had conformed completely to the test standards described to her. The Educational Testing Service (ETS) then cancelled her scores and returned her fee. The intern sued the ETS and the site administrator in a Maryland county court for breach of contract and other claims. The trial court judge awarded summary judgment to the ETS on the breach of contract claim and dismissed all of the intern's remaining claims. The intern appealed to the state court of special appeals, which noted the site administrator had worked for the ETS and other testing agencies for about 10 years. The Praxis registration bulletin stated the rules for the test and the consequences of breaking test rules. **The ETS reserved the right to cancel a test score for misconduct. Misconduct was defined as "a directly observable violation of the rules during a test administration," including working after time was called.** The court agreed with the intern that a jury should be allowed to determine if her test scores had been cancelled in bad faith. She correctly stated that all contracts have an implied covenant of good faith and fair dealing. The court reversed the judgment and remanded the case to the trial court. The intern would have to "surmount a gigantic hurdle" unless she could show the administrator had some motive to lie. *Hildebrant v. Educational Testing Service*, 171 Md.App. 23, 908 A.2d 657 (Md. Ct. Spec. App. 2006).

◆ **A Florida district court of appeal upheld an administrative ruling rejecting charges that a teacher provided inappropriate assistance to her students during the Florida Comprehensive Assessment Test.** The state education practices commission filed a complaint against the teacher for providing answers and other help to her students on the test. However, after a hearing, an administrative law judge found all of the commission's student witnesses not credible. The judge accepted the testimony of the lone student who testified for the teacher. The commission held another hearing and issued a final order suspending the teacher's certification. The court of appeal held the commission had improperly modified the judge's findings. As substantial evidence supported the judge's decision, the complaint was dismissed. *Stinson v. Winn*, 938 So.2d 554 (Fla. Dist. Ct. App. 2006).

◆ California Education Code Section 60856 required the state board of education to study alternatives to the California high school exit exam (CAHSEE) for highly proficient students who were unable to pass the exam. A 2003 report concluded the CAHSEE satisfied professional standards for a high school exit exam. However, the report "also expressed some concerns about the fairness of imposing the CAHSEE diploma requirement on students who could legitimately claim that the public school system had not adequately prepared them to pass the exam." In 2003, the legislature directed the superintendent of public instruction and state board to commission a study regarding alternatives to the CAHSEE for students with disabilities. However, no action was taken.

The board delayed implementing the CAHSEE diploma requirement until the graduating class of 2006. The independent consultant continued to issue reports regarding the CAHSEE's validity and impact. In 2005, it recommended that the diploma requirement be implemented as scheduled for 2006. A public interest law firm sued state education officials in the state court system, alleging violation of Section 60856. The lawsuit alleged the state did not conduct the study of alternatives to the CAHSEE specified in 60856 in time for the legislature to consider it before the exam became a diploma requirement. A state superior court denied the request for relief. **On appeal, the Court of Appeal of California found Section 60856 had no language requiring the completion of the study of alternatives at a specific time.** By contrast, three other sections of the CAHSEE legislation that required studies set specific deadlines. The court found no ambiguity in Section 60856 and refused to imply a deadline that was not there. The section could not be interpreted as requiring the completion of a study of CAHSEE alternatives by a particular time. *Californians For Justice Educ. Fund v. State Board of Educ.*, No. A114190, 2006 WL 2790463 (Cal. Ct. App. 2006).

◆   The Massachusetts Supreme Judicial Court held the state legislature had a duty to ensure all public school students received an education with specific training in *McDuffy v. Secretary of Executive Office of Educ.*, 415 Mass. 545, 615 N.E.2d 516 (Mass. 1993). The legislature responded with the Massachusetts Education Reform Act of 1993, intended to ensure safe public schools, a high quality education, a deliberate process for educational performance goals, and a mechanism for monitoring students and holding educators accountable for student achievement. The act specified a comprehensive diagnostic assessment of students in the fourth, eighth and tenth grades, with satisfaction of the tenth-grade examination a high school graduation requirement. The state education board adopted the Massachusetts Comprehensive Assessment System (MCAS) examination to carry out Reform Act requirements for academic standards, curriculum frameworks and objective annual assessments in core areas. Although student failure rates were as high as 53% in some core areas on the first MCAS administration in 1998, the board made the English, math, science and social studies parts of the exam a graduation requirement for students in the class of 2003. The board planned to phase other subjects into the graduation requirement and to raise the threshold scaled score over time. By 2003, about 90% of the state's seniors passed the tenth-grade MCAS and became eligible to graduate. Students who did not pass could receive remediation after grade 12 and further opportunities to take the exam.

A group of students from the class of 2003 sued the board in a state superior court, challenging the regulation requiring them to pass the MCAS exam as a graduation prerequisite. All but one of the students attended public schools, and some of them received special education. The court denied the students' request for an order prohibiting the board from enforcing the regulation. The students appealed to the Supreme Judicial Court, which held the board had considerable leeway to adopt the regulations interpreting the act. **The board could phase in the testing of core subjects in a reasonable manner and timetable. The court held the board had authority to gradually incorporate core areas in the MCAS examination, and to test students in English and math before doing so in other areas.** The regulation largely accomplished the Reform Act goal of holding educators accountable through required academic standards, curriculum frameworks and competency determinations. The legislature twice ratified the MCAS exam appropriating substantial funds for remediation programs. This indicated acceptance of the board's phase-in approach. The court affirmed the superior court decision. *Student No. 9 v. Board of Educ.*, 440 Mass. 752, 802 N.E.2d 105 (Mass. 2004).

◆   The Chicago Board of Education spent over $1 million on standardized tests to evaluate students as part of a three-year pilot program. It instructed teachers who administered the tests to refrain from copying them and to collect all test papers after administrations. The tests were "secure," so that results could be validated from year to year. In addition to instructing teachers not to copy the tests, the board applied for copyright protection. A teacher opposed using the tests and published six of them in a newsletter he edited for teachers. The board sued him in a federal district court for copyright infringement. A federal magistrate judge issued a permanent restraining order for the board and awarded it $500. The teacher appealed to the Seventh Circuit, which pointed out various deficiencies in the district court order that required the case to be vacated and remanded. In doing so, the court noted that copyright protection extends to "secret documents" such as standardized tests.

The court found the tests were expressive works, created at great expense to the board. Copyrights were available for unpublished works that an author never intended for public release. The teacher argued the copying and publication of the tests was a "fair use" allowed by the Copyright Act. **The court stated the fair use defense permitted individuals to criticize copyrighted works by quoting all or part of the work. The fact that the tests were to be secret did not exclude the possibility of a valid fair use defense.** The board correctly argued the teacher went beyond mere criticism of the test by publishing six of them in their entirety. **A fair use copier must copy no more than reasonably necessary to criticize the work.** The teacher did not present sufficient evidence to withstand summary judgment. Many teachers shared his negative views on standardized tests and the use of his tactics could lead to the board's abandonment of standardized testing. The court rejected the teacher's remaining argument based on the First Amendment. **Copyright law contained built-in First Amendment accommodations that had already been taken into consideration by the fair use analysis.** While the court agreed with the board on the substance of the appeal, the district court order failed the basic requirement of an injunction to be specific in its terms and reasonably describe what acts were prohibited. The court affirmed the judgment in part, vacated it in part and remanded the case. *Chicago Board of Educ. v. Substance, Inc.*, 354 F.3d 624 (7th Cir. 2003).

◆ A North Carolina school board adopted a student accountability policy calling for the retention of students in grades three through eight who failed a state-developed standardized test. The policy contained a waiver for students who achieved passing grades during the school year, as long as they obtained teacher and principal approval. Students and parents filed a federal district court action against school officials, challenging the constitutionality of the policy. The court rejected the group's assertion that students would suffer irreparable harm if they were retained in a grade for failing to pass the test.

The complaint was based on speculative injuries including low self-esteem, negative school attitudes and a reduced chance of succeeding in school. The students failed to present the court with cognizable constitutional claims, since **a student who was not promoted to the next grade would be given a remedial year to catch up on skills in which future performance could be enhanced.** Public policy discourages a federal court from substituting its judgment for that of publicly elected school board members. The policy employed rational means to further a legitimate academic purpose. The court denied a motion by the group for a preliminary order that would prohibit the use of the standardized test. *Erik V. by and through Catherine V. v. Causby*, 977 F.Supp. 384 (E.D.N.C. 1997).

V. EDUCATIONAL MALPRACTICE

Claims of educational malpractice have, for the most part, failed. Courts have been reluctant to interfere with a school's internal operations.

◆ A Florida family obtained an evaluation of their son after he experienced problems in school. He was found eligible for special education and provided with an individual education plan. The family then received information about the Celebration School. The family claimed a property developer and Osceola County School Board employees told them Celebration School provided "a quality education based upon a time-tested and successful curriculum known as 'best practices.'" After moving to the Town of Celebration, the family enrolled their children in Celebration School. The parents became disenchanted with the school and placed their children in private schools. They sued the developer, school board and several universities in a state court for misrepresentation, claiming the school did not live up to the representations they received. The court dismissed the action, and the parents appealed. A state district court of appeal reinstated their claim based on a special education appeal that had been voluntarily dismissed in a federal court.

The court found the claims for fraudulent inducement and negligent misrepresentation were not "educational malpractice claims," as the trial court had found. The trial court should have allowed the parents leave to amend their complaint to allege sufficient facts and attempt to prove each element of these claims. However, **the trial court had properly dismissed the family's claim under Article IX, section 1 of the Florida Constitution, which guarantees a high quality free public education. The provision was not self-executing and there was no benchmark for determining how to define a "high quality education."** As this determination was for the legislature to make, the claim was dismissed. The family would have to plead specific facts and state how the representations were false to avoid dismissal of the case. The complaint contained over 100 paragraphs describing fraud, without describing what was specifically meant by "best practices." The family would also have to assert they had suffered damages from alleged fraud. *Simon v. Celebration Co.*, 883 So.2d 826 (Fla. Dist. Ct. App. 2004).

◆ A group of parents sued the Denver Public Schools and its superintendent in a state court for failing to provide students with a quality education. The complaint asserted that the school system failed to provide course books, failed to impose adequate discipline on students, improperly used credit waivers to inflate graduation rates, maintained a pattern of poorly performing schools, and used "dumbed-down" standards for measuring school performance. It also alleged damages for intellectual and emotional harm, diminution of educational and career opportunities, discrimination, and asserted that parents were forced to send their children to private or alternative schools. The court dismissed the case on grounds that the constitutional and statutory claims were not justiciable. It agreed with the board that the contract claim failed because no contractual relationship existed between public schools and their students.

The state court of appeals agreed to review the contract claim and distinguished it from contract claims against private schools. Contract claims attacking the general quality of public education have been rejected because they are not truly based in contract but instead seek damages for educational malpractice. **Public school students, unlike those attending private schools, have not individually contracted with their school systems for specific educational services and cannot assert breach of contract claims.** There was no legally enforceable promise to provide a curriculum, books or other educational services in this case. The court held the matter was political in nature and not within the power of the courts to decide. **No court in the nation has recognized a breach of contract claim rooted in legislative policy.** The court affirmed the judgment for the board and superintendent. *Denver Parents Ass'n v. Denver Board of Educ.*, 10 P.3d 662 (Colo. Ct. App. 2000).

◆ A second-grade Michigan student hanged himself the night after viewing a film at school featuring the attempted suicide of a young disabled character who eventually learns to overcome his disability. The student's estate brought a state court action against the school district, superintendent, members of the board of education, principal, teacher, staff members and the distributor and producer of the film *Nobody's Useless.* The court held the distributor and producer had no duty to state the age-appropriateness of the film, and that the principal, teachers, and other school staff had no duty to refrain from showing the film to second-graders. However, the court denied a motion by the district, board and superintendent for summary disposition on the grounds of absolute governmental immunity. The case reached the Court of Appeals of Michigan.

The court of appeals held Michigan's governmental immunity statute applied to the board members, the superintendent and the district. The district was a governmental entity performing duties contemplated in the immunity statute. The board members and superintendent were also entitled to absolute governmental immunity. **The court affirmed the finding that there was no duty to refrain from showing the film to a second-grader. This theory was rooted in educational malpractice, a claim the court refused to recognize.** Any lawsuit based upon educational malpractice was impossible to prove and unreasonably burdensome to the educational system. The court also affirmed the finding that the film's producer and distributor were not liable. *Nalepa v. Plymouth-Canton Community School Dist.*, 525 N.W.2d 897 (Mich. Ct. App. 1994).

I.   THE IDEA 534
     A. IDEA Substantive Requirements 534
     B. Procedural Protections 536
        1. IEPs and Team Meetings 537
        2. Notice and Hearing Requirements 541

II. DISCIPLINE OF STUDENTS WITH DISABILITIES 545
     A. Discipline as a Change in Placement 545
     B. Manifestation Determinations 546
     C. Delinquency and Juvenile Justice...........................548

III. PLACEMENT OF STUDENTS WITH DISABILITIES 550
     A. Identification and Evaluation 550
     B. Child Find Obligation.......................................553
     C. Least Restrictive Environment 556
     D. Change in Placement and the 'Stay-Put' Provision..........559
     E. Other Placement Issues 562
        1. Behavior Problems 562
        2. Extended School Year Services 564
        3. Transfer Students 565

IV. RELATED SERVICES...567
     A. Medical Services...567
     B. Level or Location of Services 568
     C. Provision of Related Services at Private Schools...........571

V.   TUITION REIMBURSEMENT 572
     A. Private School Tuition Claims 572
     B. Parental Conduct 575

VI. TRANSITION AND GRADUATION 578
     A. Transition Plans...578
     B. Graduation 579
     C. Compensatory Education 582

VII. SECTION 504 AND THE ADA 584
     A. Section 504 Accommodation Plans 584
     B. Discrimination Claims 586
     C. Standardized Testing..590

I. THE IDEA

The IDEA provides federal funding to local educational agencies through grants to the states. To receive IDEA funds, states must demonstrate they maintain a policy assuring that all children with disabilities have access to a free appropriate public education (FAPE). FAPE is defined as special education and related services provided at public expense that meet state educational agency standards in conformity with an individualized education program (IEP).

Local educational agencies (LEAs) receiving IDEA funds must include satisfactory assurances that they are identifying and providing special education services to all students with disabilities residing within the local jurisdiction, regardless of the severity of the disability.

The Individuals with Disabilities Education Act (IDEA) was reauthorized in 2004 by H.R. 1350, and its key provisions are noted throughout this chapter.

A. IDEA Substantive Requirements

The IDEA's only qualitative standard for the provision of special education and related services is that they "meet the standards of the state educational agency." Courts have thus refrained from extensive review of contested IEPs, focusing instead on IDEA procedural rights. The U.S. Supreme Court held the IDEA establishes a basic floor of opportunity for students with disabilities, and imposes no requirement on schools to maximize their potential.

◆ A New York student with hearing impairments sought the provision of a sign-language interpreter from her school district. She had residual hearing and was an excellent lipreader, which allowed her to attain above average grades and to advance through school easily. The student's parents requested the services of a sign-language interpreter at school district expense, arguing that the IDEA required the district to maximize her potential. A U.S. district court held the disparity between the student's achievement and her potential to perform as she would if not for her disability deprived her of a free appropriate public education. This decision was affirmed by the U.S. Court of Appeals, Second Circuit, and the U.S. Supreme Court agreed to review the case.

The Court found no requirement in the IDEA that public schools maximize the potential of each student with a disability. The opportunities provided to each student by their school varied from student to student. The IDEA was primarily designed to guarantee access to students with disabilities to allow them to meaningfully benefit from public education. The IDEA protected the right to access education by means of its procedural protections, including the annual IEP meeting and review process. In IDEA cases, courts were to limit their inquiry to whether the district had complied with IDEA procedural protections, and **whether the IEP was reasonably calculated to enable the student to receive educational benefits**. If the district satisfied this two-part inquiry, the court's analysis was at an end and the district was entitled to judgment. *Board of Educ. v. Rowley*, 458 U.S. 176, 102 S.Ct. 3034, 73 L.Ed.2d 690 (1982).

◆   The parents of a New York student with disabilities sought private school tuition reimbursement. After winning at administrative and federal court levels, they sued to recover $29,350 in fees for assistance provided by an educational consultant throughout the process. A federal court awarded only $8,650 in fees, allowing only those charges accumulated between the hearing request and the administrative ruling. The Second Circuit affirmed that decision, but the U.S. Supreme Court reversed. It found that **nothing in the IDEA made clear to the states that accepting federal funds would make them responsible for reimbursing parents for expert witness fees**. Further, the expert witness fees could not be deemed costs so as to be reimbursable. *Arlington Cent. School Dist. Board of Educ. v. Murphy*, 126 S.Ct. 2455, 165 L.Ed.2d 526 (U.S. 2006).

◆   A Tennessee school board violated the rights of a student with autism by failing to consider Lovaas programming and improperly staffing his IEP team meetings. The U.S. Court of Appeals, Sixth Circuit, held **the IDEA's "meaningful educational benefit" requirement had to be gauged in relation to the student's potential**. The IDEA's legislative history supported exceeding the "meaningful educational benefits" standard where there was a "difference between self-sufficiency and a life of dependence" for a child. *Hamilton County Dep't of Educ. v. Deal*, 392 F.3d 840 (5th Cir. 2004).

◆   A Georgia student with a tracheotomy tube entered an early childhood center under an IEP. On his second day there, he collapsed on the playground. His teacher and paraprofessional attempted to resuscitate him and noticed that his tracheotomy tube was dislodged. Paramedics took him to an emergency room, where he died from asphyxiation. His mother sued the school district in federal court for wrongful death and IDEA violations. **The Eleventh Circuit held personal injury claims for tort-type damages are not available under the IDEA.** *Ortega v. Bibb County School Dist.*, 397 F.3d 1231 (11th Cir. 2005).

◆   **In 2002, Missouri amended its special education law to delete the requirement that special education programs maximize the capabilities of students with disabilities.** A disabled student and a public interest law center challenged the amendment as violative of the Missouri Constitution, and the case reached the state supreme court. The court held that the amendment did not violate the state constitution. It did not amend the law in a way that changed its original purpose. As a result, Missouri now uses the federal standard for determining the sufficiency of special education services. *McEuen v. Missouri State Board of Educ.*, 120 S.W.3d 207 (Mo. 2003).

◆   A Louisiana student with cerebral palsy, bladder incontinence and developmental delays used a wheelchair. When he was 18, his mother requested a due process hearing, asserting the district had denied him a FAPE. She alleged deficiencies in his IEPs and claimed his high school lacked accessible facilities. An administrative hearing officer and a state level review panel ruled against her, and the case reached the Fifth Circuit. The court found that **the student's IEP had been reasonably calculated to provide him with a FAPE**. He raised his grade point average in several areas. Although he did not improve in every area, his improvement in some areas showed that he received an educational benefit under his IEP. The board had provided aides to assist him in getting around the school and using the lavatory, so it had provided reasonable accommodations under the ADA and Section 504. *Pace v. Bogalusa City School Board,* 325 F.3d 609 (5th Cir. 2003).

◆   A Texas student struggled in his public school placement. He did not initially qualify for special education. His parents obtained an independent evaluation and learned the student had dyslexia and attention deficit disorder. They enrolled him in a private school. The student returned to the public school system and was eventually referred to an admission, review and dismissal (ARD) committee, which identified reading and language deficiencies. The ARD committee recommended 10 hours per week in a reading and language resource room with an hour of weekly speech therapy. The student continued to experience some difficulties and received extended-year services and 25 hours of compensatory speech therapy. His parents objected to the district's failure to implement certain IEP modifications. A hearing officer found that the district failed to consistently or appropriately implement the IEP. The parties then failed to agree upon an IEP for the seventh grade and the parents withdrew him from public school in favor of a private placement.

The district appealed to a federal district court, which granted it summary judgment. The court dismissed the parents' counterclaim for private school compensatory services reimbursement, and the parents appealed to the Fifth Circuit. The court discussed the free appropriate public education requirement described in *Board of Educ. v. Rowley*, 458 U.S. 176 (1982). **Under *Rowley*, an IEP need not maximize a student's educational potential**; it must only be designed to meet the student's unique needs and provide the student with a basic floor of opportunity to receive educational benefits.

The court also discussed the test for appropriateness of an IEP from *Cypress-Fairbanks Independent School Dist. v. Michael F.*, 118 F.3d 245 (5th Cir. 1997). This called for assessing whether education is provided in a coordinated and collaborative manner by key stakeholders and indicates that the student is receiving positive academic and nonacademic benefits. Here, any shortcomings in the implementation of the IEP were remedied by compensatory services. The student received educational benefits. **A student challenging the adequacy of an IEP must demonstrate that school authorities failed to implement substantial or significant IEP provisions.** The district court correctly relied on the student's increasing test scores during his public school education. It was unnecessary for him to improve in every academic area to receive educational benefit from his IEP. The claim for tuition reimbursement was properly rejected. *Houston Independent School Dist. v. Bobby R.*, 200 F.3d 341 (5th Cir. 2000).

B. Procedural Protections

The individualized education program (IEP) is the IDEA's most important procedural protection. The IDEA requires adequate notice to parents and opportunities for parental participation in the development of a student's IEP.

Students are entitled to an impartial "due process hearing" to review any issue related to identification, evaluation, placement or the provision of FAPE. Only after the administrative review process is complete may an aggrieved party in an IDEA action appeal to a state or federal court.

The 2004 IDEA reauthorization added new provisions on IEP requirements for transfer students. Schools are allowed to conduct an evaluation of any student who transfers from a school outside the state before becoming obligated to develop a new IEP. The reauthorized IDEA also specifies that when parents repeatedly refuse a school's efforts to conduct an individual evaluation of a child, the school is relieved of the obligation to convene an IEP meeting and is not considered in violation of IDEA requirements.

The reauthorized IDEA states that if the IEP team and parents agree, an IEP team member may be excused from an IEP meeting, if there is no discussion or modification of the team member's area of curriculum or related services. An excused team member must submit written input into the IEP prior to the meeting. LEAs are encouraged to consolidate reevaluation meetings.

1. IEPs and Team Meetings

◆   Ohio parents disagreed with the IEP prepared for their autistic son and placed him in a private school. They filed a due process hearing request but lost at two administrative levels. Without the assistance of an attorney, the parents appealed to a federal district court. The court held for the school district, and the U.S. Court of Appeals, Sixth Circuit, later held they could not pursue the case unless they hired an attorney. **The U.S. Supreme Court agreed to review the parents' appeal, and held that various IDEA provisions accorded them independent enforceable rights. The Court found it would be inconsistent with the statutory scheme to bar them from continuing to assert these enforceable rights in federal court.** There was no legal bar to finding an intent by Congress to grant parents a stake in IDEA entitlements. As the IDEA did not differentiate between the rights of disabled children and their parents, the Court reversed the judgment, permitting the parents to pursue their case. *Winkelman v. Parma City School Dist.*, No. 05-983, 2007 WL 1461151 (U.S. 2007).

◆   An Ohio student began experiencing disciplinary problems in sixth grade and his IEP was then changed twice. His mother rejected his seventh-grade IEP on the grounds that it had been predetermined by the IEP team. She eventually sued, and the case reached the Sixth Circuit. The court of appeals held that predetermination is not the same as preparation and that the **IEP team members could prepare reports and come to meetings with pre-formed opinions about the best course of action for a student.** Here, the parties had met 16 times over a two-year period and had daily communications about homework. The school district's preparation work prior to the IEP meeting did not violate the IDEA. *Nack v. Orange City School Dist.*, 454 F.3d 604 (6th Cir. 2006).

◆   An autistic student's mother signed his IEPs, but objected to their failure to include behavior interventions or a behavior intervention plan. The school board asserted that any inappropriate behaviors were being managed through instruction in a predictable, structured environment. The mother claimed the student's inappropriate, self-injurious and aggressive behavior was increasing, and she requested a due process hearing. The hearing officer found the student's most recent IEPs were improperly written and violated his right to a free appropriate public education. None of the IEPs prepared for the student had a behavior management component. The board never conducted a functional behavior assessment for him. The hearing officer sharply criticized the IEPs for lacking notations for mastery of benchmarks and for vague statements of the student's present levels of performance. This made it impossible for the student's parents and IEP team members to track his progress.

A federal court agreed with the hearing officer that the fact that the student's behaviors were directly related to autism did not excuse the board from providing behavior management techniques in his IEP or in a separate behavior intervention plan. The hearing officer had correctly rejected the board's "convoluted and demonstrably flawed rationale that no behavior plan was warranted." Without a clear statement of present levels of performance, the student's annual goals were "unmoored, untethered and meaningless." While technical perfection is not the objective of the statute, procedural defects may violate the IDEA if they cause a loss in educational opportunities or benefits, or if the parents are deprived of participation. The defects in the student's IEPs went to the suitability of his entire program. **Vague and unmeasurable goals could not confer educational benefit, and made it impossible to measure achievement.** *Escambia County Board of Educ. v. Benton*, 406 F.Supp.2d 1248 (S.D. Ala. 2005).

◆ A Washington student with autism and low cognitive ability attended kindergarten under an IEP that allowed for placement in an integrated class. His teacher was certified in both regular and special education. The student's mother attended class with him for most of the five days he was in school. She observed that he was teased on several occasions, and reported the teasing to the teacher, though she admitted that her son might not even have noticed one incident, and was happy during another. She also reported the teasing to the vice principal, then pulled the child from school after the fifth day. The district offered to place the student in a self-contained classroom in another school, but the parents rejected the proposal. They also refused to attend the IEP meeting, at which a self-contained classroom with mainstream opportunities was proposed. The parents requested a due process hearing, claiming that the absence of a regular education teacher at the meeting violated the IDEA.

The case reached the Ninth Circuit, which held that **the district violated the IDEA by failing to have the regular education teacher present at the IEP team meeting. It was not enough that she was on the IEP team; she had to attend the meeting**. However, this did not cause a loss of educational opportunity for the student because a self-contained classroom was the best placement for him, and the placement would not have changed had the regular education teacher been present at the meeting. Further, the district was deprived of the chance to end the teasing when the parents removed the student from school after only five days. The district's procedural violation of the IDEA did not result in the denial of a free appropriate public education. *M.L. v. Federal Way School Dist.*, 341 F.3d 1052 (9th Cir. 2003).

◆ A Tennessee student with ADHD had serious behavior problems and received special education under an IEP for a number of years. However, the school's team of evaluators eventually concluded that her behavioral problems were volitional and not the result of her disability. The IEP team met to consider the evaluation team's report and determined that the student was ineligible for services under both the IDEA and Section 504 of the Rehabilitation Act. The student's mother requested a due process hearing, where she complained that some of the IEP team members had met prior to the IEP team meeting and decided to find the student ineligible for services. An administrative law judge ruled against the mother, but a federal district court held the team denied her right to participate in the initial determination of eligibility. The Sixth Circuit reversed, noting that **experts and IEP team members can confer prior to an IEP team meeting. There is no substantive harm caused by pre-meeting discussions where a parent fully participates in IEP team meetings.** *N.L. v. Knox County Schools*, 315 F.3d 688 (6th Cir. 2003).

◆ An Ohio student with autism and pervasive disability disorder exhibited violent, disruptive behavior in kindergarten and first grade. His second-grade IEP placed him in regular classes with a full-time aide. Early in the year, the IEP team met and modified the student's IEP to include pull-out services and a behavior plan to address his increasingly violent and disruptive behavior. Days after the meeting, the student disrupted his class during a math test, flew into a rage and repeatedly struck his teacher. She took him to the hallway and restrained him, but when she released him, he kicked her in the face and neck. The teacher sued the student's parents and the school district in a state court for negligent and intentional conduct. The court found nothing in the student's behavioral history indicated he would cause injuries of the kind alleged by the teacher. It held for the parents and district.

The Court of Appeals of Ohio held parents may be held liable for failing to exercise reasonable control over a child, despite knowledge that injury to another person is a probable consequence. The student frequently hit and kicked students, teachers and aides. He lashed out when frustrated in his classes or when touched or bumped by classmates. The case was complicated by special education law purposes and procedures. **Merely advocating for the placement of the student in regular education settings could not make the parents liable.** While they were IEP team members, the placement decision was not theirs alone. There was evidence that the parents' "aggressive participation and pressure at the IEP meetings was a major factor in the IEP team's final decision." The court reversed the judgment for the parents. *Coolidge v. Riegle*, No. 5-02-59, 2004-Ohio-347, 2004 WL 170319 (Ohio Ct. App. 2004).

◆ An Arizona student attended a private school for students with deafness on a tuition-free basis as part of a study on children with cochlear implants. When the grant ended, her parents sought continued funding from the school district so she could remain at the private school. The district instead created a new program for students with hearing impairments and offered to place the student there. The parents rejected the offer and commenced a due process hearing against the district. When they were notified of an IEP team meeting, they asked to reschedule it, but the district refused to do so because two staff members would be unavailable later in the summer. The district held the meeting without the parents or a representative from the private school. The parents re-enrolled the student in the private school, then sought tuition reimbursement for what they asserted was the student's "stay-put" placement. The Ninth Circuit held that the district's procedural violation of the IDEA entitled the parents to tuition reimbursement. **A student's teacher must participate in the formation of an IEP.** The district made no attempt to include a representative from the private school, so the teachers who were most knowledgeable about the student did not attend the IEP meeting. *Shapiro v. Paradise Valley Unified School Dist. No. 69*, 317 F.3d 1072 (9th Cir. 2003).

◆   An Ohio student with obsessive compulsive disorder, Tourette Syndrome and Asperger's syndrome passed all his seventh- and eighth-grade classes and made progress in his socialization skills. However, his mother told school officials that other students victimized him and that his behavior at home made her life "a living hell." The school district proposed an IEP for the student's freshman year that had similar goals to the IEP of the previous year. The parents attended two IEP team meetings, at which a consultant's report was discussed, but they were not allowed to attend a "staff meeting." They requested a due process hearing to challenge their exclusion. After prevailing at administrative levels, a federal district court ruled against them. The Sixth Circuit held the district had offered their son an appropriate IEP. The district had revised the student's IEP after reviewing the consultant's report and noting the student's deteriorating behavior. **The parents were properly excluded from the staff meeting, which was an in-service to train teachers in accordance with the consultant's report and was not conducted to revise the student's IEP.** *Kings Local School Dist. v. Zelazny*, 325 F.3d 724 (6th Cir. 2003).

◆   A New York second-grader was tested and classified as a student with a learning disability. Her school district developed an IEP for her and began providing special education services during the last month of the school year. During the summer, her parents unilaterally placed her in a private school that used Orton-Gillingham methodology. For the next three years, the student remained at the private school. Her parents challenged the district's IEPs but lost at the administrative level. A federal court then held that the district failed to comply with IDEA procedures on all three challenged IEPs because of extensive delays in developing and reviewing the IEPs. The court also held that the district's "formulaic articulation of goals and strategies" evaluating the student's progress violated the IDEA as generic rather than individualized IEPs. The Second Circuit reversed, finding **the delays did not affect the student's education because the parents did not show that they would have changed her placement had there been more timely decisions on her IEPs.** The parents were not entitled to tuition reimbursement. *Grim v. Rhinebeck Cent. School Dist.*, 346 F.3d 377 (2d Cir. 2003).

◆   The parents of a Michigan student with disabilities unilaterally placed him in a private residential school based on a doctor's recommendation. They then sought tuition reimbursement. A due process hearing officer ruled for the parents, and a federal court held that the school district committed procedural and substantive violations of the IDEA by failing to timely advise the parents of their rights. The district also failed in its child find obligations, such that an IEP was not created for the student until seven months after he was placed in the residential facility. The court ordered reimbursement, but limited it to the seven months prior to the development of the IEP. The Sixth Circuit affirmed. The IEP that was eventually developed was adequate to provide the student with a free appropriate public education. Further, **the district's failure to include the student's doctor on the IEP team did not violate the IDEA because the district considered all relevant educational and medical information.** *Lakin v. Birmingham Public Schools*, 70 Fed.Appx. 295 (6th Cir. 2003).

◆   A Maryland student had difficulty in the use of phonic and structural analysis to decode words. The district IEP team altered his fourth-grade IEP and his parents approved it. Prior to the student's fifth-grade year, his parents had him tested by a speech/language pathologist, who recommended regular speech/language therapy sessions. The district accepted the test results and created new goals and objectives for the student. However, the parents removed the student from school and placed him in a private school. At due process, they claimed that the district failed to provide a FAPE. An administrative law judge ruled for the district, and a federal court upheld that ruling. **The parents were never denied the chance to participate as IEP team members, and the district did not violate the student's IDEA procedural rights.** As for his substantive rights, the court also found no IDEA violation. His failure to progress in the single area of phonics and decoding words was insufficient to show he was deprived of a FAPE, especially considering his IEP's overall success and his significant progress in other areas. *Alexis v. Board of Educ., Baltimore Public Schools*, 286 F.Supp.2d 551 (D. Md. 2003).

2. Notice and Hearing Requirements

Under the reauthorized IDEA, LEAs must provide parents with notices of their procedural rights once a year, and upon an initial referral or evaluation for special education and related services, the filing of a due process complaint, or other parental request. Schools and districts may place procedural safeguard notices on their Web sites. The reauthorized IDEA sets a two-year limitation period on the filing of IDEA complaints. A party appealing from an adverse due process hearing decision must appeal within 90 days from the date of the hearing officer's decision, unless the state has its own limitation period.

◆   **The U.S. Supreme Court held that parents who challenge their children's IEPs in special education due process hearings have the burden of proving the IEPs are inappropriate.** The case was filed by the parents of a Maryland student with learning disabilities and a speech impairment. After he attended private schools for years, the parents sought to place him through the

Montgomery County Public Schools. The district evaluated him and drafted an IEP that would have placed him in one of two district middle schools. The parents rejected the offer, seeking a smaller classroom setting with more intensive services for their son. They requested a hearing. An administrative law judge (ALJ) found the evidence was close, and held the parents had the burden of persuasion in the case. As a result of this allocation of the burden, the district prevailed. The parents appealed to a federal district court, which reversed the decision, finding the district should bear the burden of persuasion. The case reached the U.S. Court of Appeals, Fourth Circuit, which reversed the decision, finding no reason to depart from the normal rule which assigns the burden of proof to the party seeking relief.

The U.S. Supreme Court explained that a plaintiff, who seeks to change the state of affairs, should be expected to bear the burden of proof. This was the case, for example, in cases arising under Title VII of the Civil Rights Act of 1964 and the Americans with Disabilities Act. Congress has repeatedly amended the IDEA to reduce its administrative and litigation costs. The Court affirmed the judgment, holding the burden of proof in an administrative hearing to challenge an IEP is on the party seeking relief. *Schaffer v. Weast*, 546 U.S. 49, 126 S.Ct. 528, 163 L.Ed.2d 387 (2005).

◆   The parents of a 20-year-old student with Down syndrome sought to have him participate in the Virginia Alternate Assessment Program (VAAP) (used to assess students who have traditionally been exempt from other tests). They also requested sign-language services, but the IEP team was unable to agree on an IEP for the school year. At a due process hearing, the parents learned that their son had been promoted to grade 12, making him ineligible for the VAAP. The hearing officer held that the promotion violated the IDEA, and the Fourth Circuit ultimately agreed. **Promoting the student without notifying his parents was just an attempt to avoid placing him in the VAAP.** *County School Board of York County v. A.L.*, 194 Fed.Appx. 173 (4th Cir. 2006).

◆   After a New York student was diagnosed with a learning disability, her school district's committee on special education found she could progress in regular education classes with tutoring. After the tenth grade ended, the student's parents requested her grade-eleven IEP by August 20. They also asked for student profiles for their daughter's upcoming classes. The district failed to respond by the August 20, and the parents sought a due process hearing. Upon losing there, they appealed. The case reached the Second Circuit, which held that **IEPs do not have to be produced at the time parents demand them.** Also, the district did not have to provide student profiles for classes where enrollment had not yet been finalized. *Cerra v. Pawling Cent. School Dist.*, 427 F.3d 186 (2d Cir. 2005).

◆   While incarcerated, the father of a New York child with a disability attempted to challenge the school board's decision that the student did not need additional special instruction. The board denied his request to review assessment materials and obtain an impartial due process hearing because he had no custodial rights over the child. A federal district court held that **non-**

custodial status did not automatically divest the father of all parental rights. On appeal, the Second Circuit ruled that the lower court would have to decide whether the mother should be joined as a necessary party by examining state law and the divorce decree. *Fuentes v. Board of Educ. of City of New York*, 136 Fed.Appx. 448 (2d Cir. 2005).

◆   A federal district court held a New York school district violated state special education law by failing to give the non-custodial father of a disabled student notice of his IDEA due process hearing rights. **New York special education regulations require districts to inform parents of their state law procedural rights and safeguards.** Instead of referring the father to the administrative process, the district referred him to a private attorney and his ex-wife. This did not conform to state law, and the father could not be penalized for failing to exhaust his administrative remedies. The court granted the school district's motion to dismiss the case, but allowed the father, who was acting as his own attorney, to hire an attorney to pursue the action further. Non-attorney parents must be represented by counsel when bringing an IDEA action on behalf of a child. *Fauconier v. Committee on Special Educ.*, No. 02 CIV. 1050 RCC RLE, 2002 WL 31235786 (S.D.N.Y. 2002).

Instead of hiring an attorney, the father appealed to the Second Circuit, which held that his claims had been properly dismissed. **As a non-attorney parent, he had to be represented by counsel when suing on behalf of his child.** *Fauconier v. Committee on Special Educ., Dist. 3, New York City Board of Educ.*, 112 Fed.Appx. 85 (2d Cir. 2004).

◆   A family moved to North Carolina to take advantage of TEACCH programming for their autistic child. They were unable to agree with the district on an IEP for several years and obtained homebound Lovaas therapy for their son. The parents rejected the district's offer for extended school year or in-home services. They later signed an IEP calling for one and a half hours of direct special education and speech therapy but sent the child to a private preschool. A district reevaluation found the child no longer eligible for special education. The district declined the parents' request for reimbursement and they requested a due process hearing. The hearing officer refused to hear testimony by two experts who had never seen the child's IEPs or evaluations. The case was dismissed because the parents never challenged the IEPs and did not commence due process proceedings within the 60-day limitations period.

The Fourth Circuit later held that the parents were not bound by the 60-day period because the district never notified them about the time limitation. On remand, a federal district court held the parents were not entitled to reimbursement because they unilaterally arranged for private educational services without notifying the district of their dissatisfaction with the IEP. The parents could not counter the district's evidence of an appropriate IEP. The case returned to the Fourth Circuit, which held the case should have been remanded to a hearing officer to consider whether the IEP would provide the student a free appropriate public education. The district court should not have resolved that question without a final administrative ruling. *M.E. and P.E. v. Buncombe County Board of Educ.*, 72 Fed.Appx. 940 (4th Cir. 2003).

◆   A Nevada school district eligibility team found a preschool student eligible for special education based on her language, cognitive, self-help, social and emotional needs. The district denied a request by the student's mother for copies of her assessment reports, instead sending her a two-page summary. A psychologist found the student was "severely autistic," but this was not communicated to the parents. After the family moved to California, the student was diagnosed as autistic and began an in-home intervention program using discrete trial training. The parents obtained the child's records from Nevada. They learned of the earlier evaluation indicating severe autism. A Nevada hearing officer determined that the student was misidentified and denied a FAPE, but a state review officer reversed. A federal court affirmed the review officer's decision, and the parents appealed.

The Ninth Circuit observed that autism is a little-understood condition whose early diagnosis is critical. Research indicated that without early identification and diagnosis, children with autism are unable to benefit from educational services. **The IDEA guarantees parents a right to examine all records relating to a child and participate in meetings to identify, evaluate and place a child.** Districts are specifically required to give parents copies of their procedural safeguards, evaluation reports and documentation regarding a determination of eligibility. The district did not provide the parents with copies of reports indicating the possibility of autism or the need for further evaluation, resulting in a blatant violation of the IDEA. The information withheld from the parents could have changed the educational approach employed for the student by increasing individualized speech therapy and beginning discrete trial training much sooner. By failing to disclose the student's full records upon request, the district denied her a FAPE. The court reversed the judgment with instructions to reinstate the hearing officer's decision. *Amanda J. v. Clark County School Dist.*, 267 F.3d 877 (9th Cir. 2001).

◆   A Virginia school district concluded a preschool age child with autism was eligible for special education, but did not provide the parents with notice of their IDEA parental rights at that time. The parents did not attend his first IEP meeting. They signed an IEP and attested to the receipt of an "Advisement of Parental Rights" form. The district did not implement the IEP for three months. The next school year, the district formulated a new IEP that reduced the level of services for the student. The mother signed the IEP, but the parents unilaterally removed him from public schools and placed him in a private Lovaas program. Over a year later, they learned of their right to a due process hearing. The parents requested a hearing nearly two years after they made the placement. A hearing officer held the district did not notify them of their hearing rights and had a pattern and practice of failing to follow IDEA procedures. He awarded the parents almost $118,000 in educational expenses. A review officer affirmed the decision but held Virginia law barred reimbursement prior to the date of the request for a due process hearing. A federal district court held the parents were relieved of the limitations statute for much of the time for which they sought reimbursement, because the district kept them ignorant of their hearing rights.

The district appealed to the Fourth Circuit, which upheld the district court finding that the district's failure to inform the parents of their due process rights deprived them of the opportunity to seek a hearing. No statute of limitations applied until the date they first learned the district had a duty to inform them of their rights. The parents' claims were viable because they did not learn about these rights until at least a year after they removed their son from public schools. The Fourth Circuit agreed with the district court's finding that **repeated failure by school officials to provide the parents with notice of their hearing rights amounted to failure to provide the student with a free appropriate public education**. Even though the parents had signed a form acknowledging the receipt of notice of their IDEA hearing rights, they testified they had never received this notice. Their signatures on IEP documents did not demonstrate they received notice of their rights. The court affirmed the reimbursement award calculated by the district court, noting evidence that Lovaas therapy was appropriate and benefited the student. *Jaynes v. Newport News School Board*, 13 Fed.Appx. 166 (4th Cir. 2001).

II. DISCIPLINE OF STUDENTS WITH DISABILITIES

A. Discipline as a Change in Placement

Disciplinary removals of over 10 days, or a pattern of removals that exceeds 10 days in a school year, may constitute a "change in placement" under the IDEA. The reauthorized IDEA alters 20 U.S.C. § 1415(k), governing rules for the placement of disabled students in alternative settings. The provision will allow schools to "consider any unique circumstances on a case-by-case basis when determining whether to order a change in placement" for a student with disabilities who violates a student code of conduct. In 2004, a new sub-point (G) was added to 20 U.S.C. § 1415(k), which specifies the "special circumstances" in which schools may remove a student to an interim alternative educational setting for up to 45 days. The change will be allowed regardless of whether the behavior leading to discipline is a manifestation of a disability.

The "special circumstances" are: weapons possession, the sale, use or possession of drugs; or infliction of serious bodily injury while at school, on school grounds, or at a school event. A hearing officer reviewing a disciplinary removal may return the child to his or her placement, or order a change in placement to an appropriate interim alternative setting for not more than 45 school days. To do so, the hearing officer must find maintaining the current placement is "substantially likely to result in injury."

The reauthorized IDEA is intended to limit the procedural protections formerly available to students who were not found eligible for special education and related services. Section 1415(k), as before the reauthorization, allows the placement of students who violate a student code of conduct in an appropriate interim alternative setting for up to 10 days.

◆ Two emotionally disturbed children in California were each suspended for five days for misbehavior that included destroying school property and assaulting and making sexual comments to other students. Pursuant to state law, the suspensions were continued indefinitely during the pendency of expulsion proceedings. The students sued the school district in U.S. district court contesting the extended suspensions on the ground that they violated the "stay-put" provision of the IDEA, which provides that a student must be kept in his or her "then-current" educational placement during the pendency of proceedings which contemplate a change in placement. The district court issued an injunction preventing the expulsion, and the school district appealed.

The U.S. Court of Appeals, Ninth Circuit, determined that the indefinite suspensions constituted a prohibited "change in placement" without notice under the IDEA and that there was no "dangerousness" exception to the IDEA's "stay-put" provision. The California Superintendent of Public Instruction filed for a review by the U.S. Supreme Court.

The Supreme Court declared that the intended purpose of the "stay-put" provision was to prevent schools from changing a child's educational placement over his or her parents' objection until all review proceedings were completed. While the IDEA provided for interim placements where parents and school officials were able to agree on one, no emergency exception for dangerous students was included. **Where a disabled student poses an immediate threat to the safety of others, school officials may temporarily suspend him or her for up to 10 school days.** The Court affirmed the court of appeals' decision that indefinite suspensions violated the "stay-put" provision of the IDEA. It modified that court's decision on fixed suspensions by holding that suspensions up to 10 rather than up to 30 days do not constitute a change in placement. The Court also upheld the court of appeals' decision that states could be required to provide services directly to disabled students where a local school district fails to do so. *Honig v. Doe*, 484 U.S. 305, 108 S.Ct. 592, 98 L.Ed.2d 686 (1988).

B. Manifestation Determinations

*A manifestation determination review is required when a district wants to take a disciplinary action that would result in a disabled child's removal from school for over 10 days. The IEP team must perform the review. **If the team finds the child's behavior is not a manifestation of a disability, the disciplinary procedures applied to nondisabled children may be applied to the child.** If the team finds the misconduct is related to the child's disability, it may still seek the parents' agreement to change the placement. Language about manifestation determinations was changed in 2004, but still allows discipline in the same manner and duration as for nondisabled students, if the behavior leading to discipline is not a manifestation of the child's disability.*

A local education agency (LEA) that disciplines a student with disabilities must continue to provide the student with a free appropriate public education if a placement is changed. This is irrespective of whether the child's behavior is found to manifest a disability. Parents and IEP team members who review the information in a student file during a manifestation determination are to determine "if the conduct in question was caused by, or had a direct and substantial relationship, to the child's disability." If so, the team must determine if the conduct was a direct result of an LEA's failure to implement the IEP.

◆ A disabled New Jersey student was caught smoking marijuana after she had previously been suspended for refusing a drug test. She again refused to take a drug test and was suspended for 20 days. She requested an expedited due process hearing, which was adjourned because her mother refused to participate. An administrative law judge then ordered the student returned to class because the school had improperly suspended the student for more than 10 days without a manifestation hearing. A federal court reversed that ruling. **Under the IDEA, a student can be suspended for up to 45 days, without a manifestation determination, for drug or weapon possession.** *A.P. v. Pemberton Township Board of Educ.*, 2006 WL 1344788 (D.N.J. 2006).

◆ Classmates called a learning disabled New York student "faggot" and "PLC," which stood for "prescriptive learning class." A fight broke out between the student and a classmate, and the student was suspended for five days. The district notified him of a hearing to consider a longer suspension. The superintendent accepted the hearing officer's recommendation for another five-day suspension pending a manifestation hearing. The school's committee on special education found the student's behavior was not a manifestation of his disability, and the superintendent then planned to suspend the student for the rest of the year. The student sued the district in a federal district court, which ruled in his favor. The court found that **"PLC" was a reference to his learning disability, making the incident "related to" his disability**. Also, the district treated the manifestation determination "dismissively" and did not afford the student due process under the IDEA. *Coleman v. Newburgh Enlarged City School Dist.*, 319 F.Supp.2d 446 (S.D.N.Y. 2004).

◆ After a Massachusetts student transferred schools, her new school noticed that she took medication at home for ADD. Despite the fact that the student failed all of her ninth grade classes, she was not referred for a special needs evaluation. The following year, the student was suspended for giving or selling drugs to others. The student denied providing drugs to others, but the school expelled her after a hearing. The student sought a hearing with the state department of education's bureau of special education appeals, arguing that the school had knowledge of a qualifying disability when it expelled her, and that it violated the IDEA by failing to provide her with IDEA disciplinary procedures. A hearing officer ordered an evaluation.

A manifestation determination hearing resulting in a finding of no IDEA disability. Eventually, a lawsuit arose and a federal court explained that the IDEA requires a manifestation determination hearing whenever a school seeks to discipline a student with disabilities. **The goal of a manifestation hearing is to determine whether the behavior leading to discipline was a manifestation of the disability. If it is not, the school may discipline the student as it would any other student.** If it is, any discipline must comply with the IDEA. Students who have not yet been formally identified as disabled within the meaning of the IDEA are entitled to assert IDEA protections if the school is "deemed to have knowledge" of a disability in one of four circumstances. One of these occurs when "the behavior or performance of the child" demonstrates the need for special education and related services. If the school has knowledge of a possible disability, the student may invoke IDEA rights. The student stated the minimal factual basis for an IDEA claim by claiming that the school had knowledge of a disability at the time it initiated expulsion proceedings. *S.W. v. Holbrook Public Schools*, 221 F.Supp.2d 222 (D. Mass. 2002).

◆   An eighth-grade Maine student with a learning disability brought marijuana to school. After admitting his misconduct, he was suspended for 10 days. The school board expelled him for the rest of the school year at a hearing. The day after the hearing, the district attempted to schedule a manifestation review meeting. Attempts to schedule the meeting within 10 days were unsuccessful and the hearing was held 12 days later. During the period between the expulsion decision and the manifestation review meeting, the parents requested a due process hearing. At the manifestation review meeting, it was determined that the student's misconduct was not a manifestation of his disability. An IEP for the remainder of the student's expulsion called for two hours of in-home, one-to-one instruction in core subjects and two hours of weekly specialized reading instruction. The parents requested a second due process hearing, challenging the manifestation review meeting. A state hearing officer found the district did not need to hold the meeting prior to the expulsion and that the delay did not deny the student a FAPE. The hearing officer upheld the conclusion that the student's misconduct was not a manifestation of his disability.

On appeal, a federal court noted that 20 U.S.C. § 1415(k)(4)(A) requires a manifestation determination within 10 days of a change in placement, regardless of the nature of the disabled student's offense. However, the two-day delay here did not result in any harm. The IEP developed at the manifestation review meeting did not deny the student a FAPE. It allowed him to participate in and progress in the general curriculum during his expulsion, as required by Section 1415(k)(3)(B). Although the student was unable to participate in gym, art and computer classes during his expulsion, this did not violate the IDEA. These classes were not mandatory for graduation. The failure to conduct a timely functional behavioral assessment was also harmless, as it had no bearing on the proceedings and decisions that were made. The student was not entitled to remain in his pre-expulsion placement for the first 45 days of his expulsion while his parents appealed. **The district had the right to suspend him for 45 days under 20 U.S.C. § 1415(k)(1)(A)(ii).** The school district followed all applicable procedural requirements, and the student's behavior was not a manifestation of his disability. The district and parents were ordered to arrange for a functional behavioral assessment. *Farrin v. Maine School Administrative Dist. No. 59*, 165 F.Supp.2d 37 (D. Me. 2001).

C. Delinquency and Juvenile Justice

◆   An Illinois student who received special education and related services was charged with lighting fireworks and throwing them at others. A juvenile court adjudicated him delinquent and placed him on probation. When he violated probation, his probation officer recommended a residential placement. His mother moved to a new school district, which was notified that it should appear in juvenile court regarding its potential liability for funding the student's placement. The juvenile court agreed with the probation officer that the student should be residentially placed, and ordered the district to fund the placement. The district challenged the decision in a state court and won. **The Illinois Supreme Court held the student's placement was not made under the School Code, but under the Juvenile Court Act.** It was made to remedy a probation violation, not the student's educational needs. Also, the district was not given the opportunity to show that it could educate the student. The state had to fund the placement. *In re D.D.*, 819 N.E.2d 300 (Ill. 2004).

◆   A Pennsylvania student with multiple disabilities picked up a chair and moved toward his teacher, as if to strike him. The police were summoned and the student was arrested. The police placed him in a holding cell, where he allegedly remained for 21 hours without necessary medication. The student claimed that a few weeks later, a school police officer intentionally and maliciously hit him while he was standing in a school hallway. He filed a lawsuit against the district, its superintendent, the teacher, school police officer and an assistant principal in a state court, asserting false imprisonment, battery, infliction of emotional distress and constitutional rights violations.

The court stated that the school employees could not be held responsible for police conduct while he was in custody. The district was justified in removing the student from his class, regardless of his reason for picking up classroom furniture. The teacher was required to restore order and did so by taking him to the school office. School officials complied with school policy by summoning the police and allowing them to handle the matter. There was no merit to the student's claim that school officials acted in a manner that shocked the conscience. The court rejected the student's argument that the arrest violated his due process rights or the stay-put provision of the IDEA. The court explained that **the stay-put provision applies only to due process proceedings under the IDEA, and not to aversive techniques, such as arrest,** that may be required to remove a special education student from a current educational setting. The district was not liable for any of the violations alleged by the student, since he could not show he was injured by the district's policy of reporting violent incidents to the police. The court awarded judgment to the district on the student's constitutional claims. *Valentino C. v. School Dist. of Philadelphia*, 815 A.2d 666 (Pa. Commw. Ct. 2003).

◆   A New York principal initiated a family court proceeding to determine if a student was in need of supervision based on 16 unexcused absences from school during a two-month period. The family court ordered the school's committee on special education to conduct an evaluation. It found that the student was emotionally disturbed and had a disability. After the court placed the student on probation for a year, he appealed. The New York Supreme Court, Appellate Division, ruled that the **adjudication of the student as a child in need of supervision did not constitute a change in placement** under the IDEA. The student's placement was not changed. He was simply ordered to attend school and participate in his IEP. *Erich D. v. New Milford Board of Educ.*, 767 N.Y.S.2d 488 (N.Y. App. Div. 2003).

◆   An Illinois student was disruptive and frequently truant and became a serious disciplinary problem. A psychologist determined that he did not have a learning disability but suffered from depression, substance abuse and a conduct disorder. The student's mother objected to a proposal by the school district for the resumption of his placement in a therapeutic day school. Upon the student's release from jail, she unilaterally placed him in a Maine residential school and requested reimbursement. School officials refused the request, and the mother commenced an administrative proceeding. A state hearing officer ordered the district to pay for the residential placement, but a review officer reversed. A federal court reversed that decision and the district appealed.

The Seventh Circuit noted that the review officer had found no evidence that the Maine facility provided a superior educational placement to that of the therapeutic day school. The review officer had properly determined that the IDEA does not require a school district to pay for the confinement of a truant student. The Maine school did not provide the student with psychological services, and did not offer treatment for his depression or conduct disorder. It only provided confinement, and was "a jail substitute." The only difference between the therapeutic day school and the Maine school was its residential character. The student's problems were primarily the result of improper socialization, as he had the intelligence to perform well in school and had no cognitive defects or disorders. **Residential placement was improper where it was not a necessary predicate for learning or where medical, social or emotional problems were separate from the learning process.** Residential placement was appropriate only if confinement was a related service under the IDEA. Since it was obviously not, the district court erroneously reversed the review officer's decision. *Dale M. v. Board of Educ. of Bradley Bourbonnais High School Dist. No. 307*, 237 F.3d 813 (7th Cir. 2001).

III. PLACEMENT OF STUDENTS WITH DISABILITIES

The IDEA requires each local education agency to identify and evaluate students with disabilities in its jurisdiction. After a district identifies a student as disabled, it must develop and implement an individualized education program (IEP). The IEP must be reasonably calculated to provide educational benefits and where possible, to include the student with nondisabled students.

A. Identification and Evaluation

The 2004 IDEA reauthorization made several changes to IDEA eligibility provisions. Parents may request the initial evaluation of a child for special education and related services, as may the state or the local educational agency (LEA). An evaluation is to take place within 60 days of receiving parental consent, or within a time frame established by the state. LEAs are exempt from the 60-day requirement in transfer cases or if a parent "repeatedly fails or refuses to produce the child for the evaluation." LEAs may pursue an initial evaluation by using due process procedures if parents repeatedly refuse to allow an initial evaluation. Parents who have not allowed an evaluation of their children, or have refused special education and related services, will be barred from later asserting IDEA procedural protections in disciplinary cases.

A special rule for eligibility determinations states that lack of appropriate instruction in reading or math may not be used to make an IDEA eligibility determination. Lack of English proficiency is also specifically excluded from entering into eligibility determinations. When determining whether a child has a specific learning disability, LEAs may not consider a severe discrepancy between achievement and intellectual ability in oral expression, listening comprehension, written expression, basic reading skill, reading comprehension, mathematical calculation or mathematical reasoning.

◆   After a regular education student was suspended, his mother sought to have him evaluated for special education. A district assessment found that the student was not entitled to special education. His mother then sought an independent educational evaluation at district expense. Three weeks later, the district asserted that its assessment had been appropriate. Three months later, the district filed a due process hearing request. A hearing officer ruled that **the district had to pay for an independent evaluation because it failed to show that it conducted its assessment properly**. A California federal court agreed. The delays by the district meant that it waived its right to contest the request for an independent education evaluation. *Pajaro Valley Unified School Dist. v. J.S.*, 2006 WL 3734289 (N.D. Cal. 2006).

◆   The grandmother (and guardian) of a Texas student with a rare nervous system disorder participated in IEP team meetings and agreed to a mainstream placement. She accompanied the student to class each day the student attended and sat in the back of the classroom, but was disruptive in her care for the student. The teacher barred her from continuing to attend classes, and the student was then pulled from school. When the district later sought a reevaluation of the student, the grandmother refused, claiming it would seriously harm the student. The case reached the Fifth Circuit, which ruled that **the district had to be allowed to evaluate the student to complete the IEP**. The district needed more medical information to provide the special education the grandmother wanted. *Shelby S. v. Conroe Independent School Dist.*, 454 F.3d 450 (5th Cir. 2006).

◆   A Maine sixth-grade honors student attempted suicide after an argument with her mother. She was then diagnosed with Asperger's syndrome. Her parents sought special education, and her school district's pupil evaluation team (PET) determined she did not qualify for special education and related services. However, it found her eligible for a service plan under Section 504 and offered her 10 hours of weekly tutoring. Instead, the student's mother enrolled her in a private school and requested a due process hearing. A hearing officer held the district did not have to provide special education to address "a mental health issue." The Section 504 plan reasonably accommodated the student, who had seriously resisted returning to her public school.

The parents appealed to a federal court, seeking tuition reimbursement, compensatory education and other relief. A federal magistrate judge noted that

34 C.F.R. § 300.7(b)(7), an IDEA regulation, required the existence of an adverse effect on educational performance for a student to be IDEA-eligible. The student's evaluations indicated her short-term mental health crisis did not have a significant adverse effect on her education. She excelled academically, could complete homework, tests and projects, and was well-behaved. The Asperger's diagnosis alone did not qualify her for special education. The First Circuit has held that **the IDEA does not require a district to pay for a residential program to remedy a poor home setting** or make up for some other deficit not covered by the act. Here, the student's disabilities did not adversely affect her performance. At the time of her crisis, she deliberately tried to do poorly in school. The magistrate judge recommended affirming the decision to deny tuition reimbursement under the IDEA. The Section 504 claim was also dismissed. *Mr. and Mrs. I. v. Maine School Administrative Dist. No. 55*, No. Civ. 04-165-P-H, 2005 WL 1389135 (D. Me. 2005).

◆   A Minnesota student received special education and related services for Asperger's syndrome and a specific learning disability. He had an emotional/behavioral disorder that required an IEP. Several years later, a triennial evaluation found that the student was average in intelligence, achievement, reading, math and written language. An evaluator also determined that no behaviors set him apart. The school district concluded he no longer met state special education eligibility criteria but continued to implement his IEPs. Later, a hearing officer found that the district could terminate special education services for him. The Minnesota Court of Appeals agreed. **Evaluations and observations of the student revealed that his behavior did not set him apart from his classmates.** Nor was there a showing of severe underachievement or an information processing disorder. *In re Chisago Lakes School Dist.*, No. A04-1615, 2005 WL 1270947 (Minn. Ct. App. 2005).

◆   The mother of a Florida student attending regular classes under a Section 504 plan sought other accommodations for him. After his fourth-grade year, she requested a due process hearing. After consenting to a less-than-full evaluation of her son, she agreed to a full evaluation. However, a school psychologist conducted only intellectual and process tests, based on his supervisor's instructions. These tests found the student had normal intelligence and did not qualify as an exceptional student. An administrative law judge found that the board had done all that could be expected to define the student's needs. The Florida Court of Appeal held that **the district violated the IDEA and state law by making insufficient efforts to evaluate the student.** His IDEA rights were not "extinguished by his mother's failure immediately to accede to the School Board's every suggestion." The case was remanded with instructions to order the board to perform a complete evaluation of the student. *M.H. v. Nassau County School Board*, 918 So.2d 316 (Fla. Dist. Ct. App. 2005).

◆   The parents of a 10-year-old California student with autism placed him in a private school at their own expense, pending a special education evaluation by their school district. After conducting an assessment, the district declared the student eligible for special education. The parents rejected the district's proposal for a public school special day program, asked for an administrative hearing and sought to have their expert observe the special day program. The district refused to let the expert observe the program. When the parents sued, **the California Court of Appeal ruled that their expert should have been allowed to observe the program.** *Benjamin G. v. Special Educ. Hearing Office,* 131 Cal.App.4th 875, 32 Cal.Rptr.3d 366 (Cal. Ct. App. 2005).

◆ A Pennsylvania student with frequent behavior problems was diagnosed with ADHD, emotional disturbance and other health impairments during two different evaluations, and received special education under an IEP that included a behavior intervention plan. Later, the student was involved in a drug incident and placed in an alternative school. Testing and evaluations there revealed that the student's behavior problems were more related to social maladjustment than emotional disturbance. As a result, the IEP team found he had been improperly identified as eligible for special education. His mother requested a due process hearing, at which the hearing officer considered conflicting testimony. The hearing officer found that the school had performed a more thorough evaluation of the student than the parents' expert, and that the student was not eligible for special education. A review panel reversed, but the Commonwealth Court reinstated the hearing officer's decision. **The evidence supported a finding that the student was socially maladjusted, not emotionally disturbed.** *Mars Area School Dist. v. Laurie L.,* 827 A.2d 1249 (Pa. Commw. Ct. 2003).

◆ The father of a student who received special education under the IDEA submitted a written request to the District of Columbia Public Schools for a comprehensive reevaluation under 34 C.F.R. § 300.536(b). He later filed a request for a due process hearing. A hearing officer dismissed the complaint, ruling that the district did not have to complete new evaluations on request unless there was a showing that changed conditions clearly warranted a new evaluation. A federal court held that **the father was entitled to have his son reevaluated.** The "clearly warranted" standard applied by the hearing officer should not have been applied because the father was asking for the reevaluation. Instead, the standard was to be used where a person or agency other than a parent or teacher was requesting an evaluation. *Cartwright v. District of Columbia,* 267 F.Supp.2d 83 (D.D.C. 2003).

B. Child Find Obligation

The IDEA's "child find" obligation requires the states, through their local educational agencies (LEAs), to "identify, locate, and evaluate all children with disabilities residing within their boundaries." The child find obligation is triggered as an individualized duty to a child when an educational agency "has knowledge" that the child has a disability. As a result, students who were not identified as eligible for IDEA services frequently made successful claims for IDEA procedural protections when their schools sought to discipline them.

The 2004 IDEA Amendments addressed this situation in a provision now found at 20 U.S.C. § 1415(k)(5)(b). Effective July 1, 2005, the circumstances under which students who have not been declared eligible for special education and related services may claim IDEA procedural protections in disciplinary cases have been reduced to three. A school may still be deemed to have knowledge that a child is disabled if: (i) before the behavior leading to discipline, the child's parent "has expressed concern in writing" to a teacher or to supervisory or administrative personnel that the child is in need of special education or related services; (ii) the child's parent has requested an individual initial evaluation to determine if the child has a disability; or (iii) the child's teacher, or other school personnel, "has expressed specific concerns about a pattern of behavior demonstrated by the child, directly to the director of special education of such agency or to other supervisory personnel of the agency."

LEAs must "conduct a thorough and complete child find process" to determine the number of parentally placed students with disabilities attending private schools in the LEA. LEAs and private schools must have "timely and meaningful consultation" for that purpose. Schools must "undertake activities" for parentally placed private school students similar to activities for public school students. Services to parentally placed students may be provided at private schools, including religious schools, "to the extent consistent with law." The child find process must be designed to ensure the equitable participation of parentally placed private school children with disabilities.

The "child find" duty of each state now explicitly applies to children with disabilities who are homeless or wards of a state. States may not distribute funds to LEAs "on the basis of the type of setting in which the child is served."

◆ The mother of a District of Columbia second-grader attending regular education classes met with his teacher and principal to discuss his behavior, academic and attention problems. After considering holding him back a year, the school district promoted him to third grade. The student attended school in California the following year, but returned for grade four. At the end of that year, he was identified with ADHD and a learning disability, and an IEP was developed for him. By the end of the next school year, the district again sought to hold him back, and his mother filed a due process hearing request.

A hearing officer ruled that the district failed to identify the student as in need of special education for three years in violation of the IDEA child find obligation, and awarded him one hour of compensatory education for each day he was denied a free appropriate public education. The mother appealed, seeking more compensatory education for her son. A federal court upheld the hearing officer's decision. The court stated **the IDEA child find obligation is triggered whenever a school has reason to suspect a child has a disability and requires special education to address it**. The discussions about the student did not satisfy the IDEA's requirement of a written request for an evaluation. Oral expressions of concern by parents about the educational performance of their children do not trigger a school's child find duty. The student was only entitled to one hour of compensatory education for each day he was denied FAPE. There was no "day-for-day" compensation requirement. *Reid v. District of Columbia*, 310 F.Supp.2d 137 (D.D.C. 2004).

◆ A Tennessee student with learning disabilities and an emotional disturbance never attended public schools. His parents enrolled him in a private Connecticut school with a curriculum designed for students with learning disabilities. They did not contact the local school district before making the placement and did not request an evaluation. When they requested an evaluation over a year later, the district took more than six months to complete it. The evaluation was hampered by the student's absence from the district and by delays in obtaining information. During a meeting to discuss the student's educational program, his father expressed his intention to keep his son in the Connecticut facility for the rest of the school year and did not complain about the lengthy evaluation process. The district certified the student for special education services and proposed a public school placement. The parents commenced an IDEA action against the district, asserting they were entitled to reimbursement and claiming that the district had an insufficient child find plan.

A federal court noted that the district had a plan for the dissemination of information to all area private schools, day care centers, nursery schools, hospitals and other places where medical professionals were likely to encounter children with special education requirements. The district also made public service announcements in the local media and conducted an outreach program. It had made adequate child find efforts. The parents appealed to the Sixth Circuit, which observed that they had never contacted the district about their son's placement before seeking reimbursement. **The district's publicity campaign fulfilled its IDEA child find duties.** The child find obligation does not require districts to pursue the parents of private school students who do not act upon available information. Although the student's evaluation took six months to complete, the parents were not entitled to reimbursement on that basis. The court affirmed the judgment for the district. *Doe v. Metropolitan Nashville Public Schools*, 9 Fed.Appx. 453 (6th Cir. 2001).

◆ Near the end of a New York private school student's kindergarten year, her parents voiced concerns about a public school placement. The next year, they obtained an evaluation recommending placement in a different private school. They notified their school district of the evaluation and explained that they were interested in the private school placement. A district special education committee drafted an IEP but never completed it. The parents rejected the draft and requested transportation to the private school. The district agreed. The parents moved out of the district near the end of the school year and requested a due process hearing. A hearing officer held that the district violated its IDEA child find duty, failed to notify the parents of their due process rights and did not identify public school facilities available to the student. The district also did not evaluate the student or prepare a complete IEP. The hearing officer approved the private school placement and held that the district must reimburse the parents up to the time they moved. A review officer denied tuition reimbursement because the parents had no intention of enrolling their daughter in public schools.

A federal court stated that tuition reimbursement may be awarded where a district fails to provide a student with a FAPE and the placement selected by the parents is appropriate to the student's needs. There was ample evidence in this case that the district had failed to provide the student with a FAPE. The court focused on whether it was fair to award the parents tuition reimbursement in view of all the relevant factors. **While the parents had made statements indicating an interest in the private school placement, they should not be blamed for the district's failure to perform its child find obligation.** The district had never advised the parents of their due process rights or explained what public school facilities were available in the district. The review officer had improperly set aside the hearing officer's decision awarding them tuition reimbursement, as the district had failed to contact them and advise them of appropriate procedures. The district's conduct amounted to a gross violation of special education due process procedures. The court reinstated the award of tuition reimbursement. *Wolfe v. Taconic-Hills Cent. School Dist.,* 167 F.Supp.2d 530 (N.D.N.Y. 2001).

◆   A Wisconsin student experienced behavior problems while in grade 10 at a parochial school. A private counselor determined he had depression, but the parents did not allow school employees access to this information. After the student ran away from home, the family enrolled him in an out-of-state residential treatment program. Six months later, the family asked the district to evaluate the student. The district sought his private school records, but by the time the records were forwarded, he was over 18 and had withdrawn himself from school. A hearing officer held that the school had reason to know he was eligible for an evaluation and needed special education. The district was ordered to pay the student's educational costs and therapeutic expenses. A review officer reversed the decision, and the family appealed.

A federal court held that **the district had no reasonable cause to suspect the student had exceptional educational needs.** There was no violation of the IDEA's child find obligation and no evidence that district screening policies were deficient. The most serious problems experienced by the student, falling asleep in school and receiving lower grades, did not indicate a disability. He passed all but one of his classes and was receiving some educational benefit. District employees had no reasonable cause to suspect that the student was emotionally disabled or required special education. He was removed from district schools before the pre-referral screening process was complete, and the family resisted early screening efforts. The court found the family had a strictly financial motive and blocked the district's good faith efforts to evaluate the student. The district was entitled to summary judgment. *Hoffman v. East Troy Community School Dist.,* 38 F.Supp.2d 750 (E.D. Wis. 1999).

C. Least Restrictive Environment

The IDEA requires placing students with disabilities in the least restrictive possible setting, described as the least restrictive environment (LRE). Each IEP must explain the extent to which a child will not participate in regular education classes. In analyzing the LRE requirement, many courts rely on Oberti v. Board of Educ. of Borough of Clementon School Dist., *995 F.2d 1204 (3d Cir. 1993). The* Oberti *analysis evaluates whether the district made reasonable efforts to accommodate a student in regular classes, whether appropriate supplemental aids and services were made available, and the possible negative effects for other students if the student remains in regular education classes.*

◆   A New York student with autism-spectrum disorders began to withdraw from reality. Her mother removed her from the private day school placement specified by her IEP and placed her in an unapproved private school in Connecticut. The district reimbursed her for the amount of tuition that would have been charged by the New York private school. The following year, the district recommended a public school placement. The mother rejected the IEP and sought tuition reimbursement. A federal court overturned the hearing officer and review officer, and held that the IEP was inadequate. However, the Second Circuit reversed, finding considerable evidence to support the administrative decisions in favor of the district. **The student's recent social progress indicated she could make educational progress in an environment consistent with the IDEA's preference for mainstreaming.** *Cabouli v. Chappaqua Cent. School Dist.*, 202 Fed.Appx. 519 (2d Cir. 2006).

◆   A Kansas student with Down syndrome scored in the 0.1 percentile on the knowledge and skills portion of the Woodcock-Johnson achievement test. His district proposed placing him in a self-contained classroom. His parents objected, and a trial placement was made in a regular classroom. However, the student could not keep up with his classmates and became frustrated and disruptive. A hearing officer determined that **a self-contained classroom was his least restrictive environment**. A federal court and the Tenth Circuit agreed. The student would continue to have interaction with regular education students in nonacademic classes. *T.W. v. Unified School Dist. No. 259, Wichita, Kansas*, 136 Fed.Appx. 122 (10th Cir. 2005).

◆   A New Jersey school district proposed placing a disabled student in a resource room for social studies rather than a regular classroom even though he had earned a B the prior year. His parents objected. They also claimed the district violated the IDEA by changing the student's grading to pass-fail in science without notifying them because his IEP called for letter grades. An administrative law judge (ALJ) ruled for the district, but a federal court reversed, noting that **the ALJ did not take into account the least restrictive environment when finding the resource room placement acceptable**. Also, the district failed to show that the pass-fail change was necessary, and it should have provided notice before attempting to change the IEP. *D.E.R. v. Board of Educ. of Borough of Ramsey*, 2005 WL 1177944 (D.N.J. 2005).

◆   When Florida triplets with autism turned three, they "aged out" of the state's early intervention program and the responsibility for their special education needs passed from IDEA Part C to Part B. Their local school district became obligated to provide them with IEPs. Because their school district did not yet have their IEPs in place, their parents sought to use the stay-put provision to continue their individual family service plans. A federal court ruled against them. **Their Part C placements did not represent their current educational placements for stay-put purposes.** On the application for initial admission to public school, students must be placed in the public school until all proceedings are complete. *D.P. v. School Board of Broward County, Florida*, 360 F.Supp.2d 1294 (S.D. Fla. 2005).

◆   The IEP team for a Michigan student with Down syndrome felt that she needed a categorical classroom placement to meet her IEP goals. The only categorical classroom placement in the district was at a school 7.3 miles from her home. Her parents rejected that proposal and asked for a resource room placement. A due process hearing officer upheld the IEP team's proposal, focusing on the appropriateness of the classroom placement, and a state level review officer agreed. A federal district court held the IDEA's least restrictive environment requirement mandated the student's education at her neighborhood school. The Sixth Circuit reversed, noting that **an IDEA regulation requiring placement "as close as possible to the child's home" did not apply if a necessary program was unavailable at a neighborhood school**. Since the categorical classroom placement was appropriate, and unavailable at the neighborhood school, the proposed IEP complied with the IDEA. *McLaughlin v. Holt Public Schools Board of Educ.*, 320 F.3d 663 (6th Cir. 2003).

◆   An Illinois student had Rett syndrome, a neurological disorder that causes severe cognitive and physical disabilities. She attended regular classes in her neighborhood elementary school with a full-time, one-on-one aide. Her curriculum paralleled that of her non-disabled peers, but she had severe cognitive limitations and was nonverbal. School officials sought to place her in an educational life skills (ELS) program when her peers reached middle school. The student's parents objected and requested a due process hearing. A hearing officer upheld the school's placement decision, as did a federal court.

On appeal to the Seventh Circuit, the court noted that various experts estimated the student's cognitive ability at from 12-18 months old to four to six years old. Although she had attended regular classrooms for seven years, she was unable to fully participate in the curriculum. The ELS setting recommended by the district offered her many opportunities for mainstreaming. The court upheld the hearing officer's finding that the proposed district placement was appropriate. The district was not required to prove that the student received "no educational benefit" at her neighborhood school in order to change her placement. **Although the IDEA contains a strong preference for placement in the least restrictive environment (LRE), it does not suggest doing so when a regular classroom setting provides an unsatisfactory education.** The ELS setting satisfied the IDEA's FAPE and LRE requirements. The decision to remove the student from her neighborhood school did not violate the LRE requirement, as her academic progress there had been virtually non-existent and her developmental progress limited. The placement proposal did not violate the IDEA and the court affirmed the judgment. *Beth B. v. Van Clay*, 282 F.3d 493 (7th Cir. 2002).

◆   A California student with a language disorder began receiving special education at age three. Her parents and her school district were unable to agree on a placement for kindergarten, with her parents insisting on full inclusion and the district offering a half-day of special education and a half-day of regular kindergarten classes. The parents requested due process, but proceedings were not completed until near the end of the next school year. In a subsequent lawsuit, a federal district court found that for the year prior to kindergarten, the district failed to offer a free appropriate public education because it did not provide for any mainstreaming. However, for the student's kindergarten year, the proposed IEP complied with the IDEA. **The student would not receive an educational benefit from a full inclusion placement**. For this reason, the district had no obligation under the IDEA to "adequately discuss mainstreaming" with the parents at IEP team meetings. *Katherine G. v. Kentfield School Dist.*, 261 F.Supp.2d 1159 (N.D. Cal. 2003).

◆ A Pennsylvania student with leukemia endured a treatment regimen that left him with a fragile immune system. His doctor recommended that he stay home from school when the risk of infection increased. His parents requested the use of video teleconferencing (VTC) equipment to allow him to "virtually participate" in class at times when he was prevented from attending school. The district agreed to utilize the VTC equipment but did not incorporate its use into his IEP. Although the VTC link allowed the student to maintain relationships with his fellow students, he began to act as though he was on stage through the link, engaging in disruptive behavior. His parents later initiated a due process hearing, seeking to include the VTC link as part of his IEP. The hearing officer ruled for the parents, but a state appeals panel reversed. A federal court held that **the student's IEP was appropriate without the VTC link**. The disruption caused by the link prevented him from progressing on his social and behavioral goals. Declining to include the VTC equipment in the IEP did not violate the IDEA's least restrictive environment requirement. *Eric H. v. Methacton School Dist.*, 265 F.Supp.2d 513 (E.D. Pa. 2003).

D. Change in Placement and the 'Stay-Put' Provision

The IDEA requires school districts to provide parents of students with disabilities prior written notice of any proposed change in placement. If the parents wish to contest the change in placement, a hearing must be granted. The IDEA further requires that during the pendency of such review proceedings, the child is to remain in the "then-current" educational placement. This is known as the "stay-put" provision.

◆ An Ohio school district made addendums to a student's IEP in three consecutive months during his sixth-grade year. The third addendum sought to phase out a point reward system used to reinforce his behavior. The addendum also stated if the target behavior was not maintained, the original IEP would be reinstated. The parents did not learn that the addendum was being implemented until the district sent them a certified letter several days after the IEP meeting. A due process hearing officer found that the student's sixth-grade IEP included the third addendum, rendering it the student's "stay-put" placement pending the outcome of the due process hearing. The Court of Appeals of Ohio held that the district did not provide adequate notice that the final addendum would be implemented. The court remanded the case for a determination of **whether the addendum fundamentally changed the student's IEP, and whether the stay-put provision was implicated**. *Stancourt v. Worthington City School Dist. Board of Educ.*, 841 N.E.2d 812 (Ohio Ct. App. 2005).

◆   A Louisiana school district transferred a student with deafness from his neighborhood school to a cluster school located about four miles farther away from his home. His parents claimed the transfer was a change in placement under the IDEA that required the district to give them prior written notice. They requested a due process hearing. A federal court upheld the decision to transfer the student. The parents appealed. The U.S. Court of Appeals, Fifth Circuit, held that **the change in a school site at which an IEP is implemented is not a "change in placement" under the IDEA.** The few changes the student experienced as a result of the transfer to the new school did not amount to a change in placement. Riding a special bus for disabled students instead of a regular school bus and sharing a transliterator with another student instead of having his own were not fundamental changes to his IEP. *Veazey v. Ascension Parish School Board*, 121 Fed.Appx. 552 (5th Cir. 2005).

◆   A Virginia special education student with an emotional disability attended a gifted and talented program in an elementary school. He persuaded a classmate to place a threatening note in another student's computer file stating "death awaits you." The district assembled a manifestation determination review committee, which found no relationship between the student's disabilities and the threatening note. It recommended expelling the student, but the district instead transferred him to a gifted and talented program at a nearby school for the remainder of the year. His parents objected to the transfer decision and requested a due process hearing. The hearing officer ruled against the parents, and the Fourth Circuit affirmed, noting that **the student's transfer to a nearly identical program at a nearby school did not implicate the IDEA's stay put provision.** The court also held his IEP was appropriate. *A.W. v. Fairfax County School Board*, 372 F.3d 674 (4th Cir. 2004).

◆   A New Jersey school district placed a student with profound sensorineural hearing loss in a public school for deaf children outside the district. The next year, it proposed placing the student in a self-contained school for the deaf located in the neighborhood school the student would have attended if not for her special needs. It did not explain why it failed to propose that placement previously, or what had changed to make the new placement appropriate. The student's family challenged the placement, and an administrative law judge (ALJ) ruled in their favor. A federal district court held the ALJ "got it wrong" without explaining why the decision was incorrect. On appeal, the Third Circuit reversed the decision, **finding the district's emphasis on least restrictive environment misplaced.** The district had not shown that the new placement would provide meaningful educational benefit. The neighborhood school would offer only minimal mainstreaming opportunities. The district was not allowed to change the student's placement. *S.H. v. State-Operated School Dist. of City of Newark*, 336 F.3d 260 (3d Cir. 2003).

◆   The parents of a Michigan student with disabilities asserted the IEP offered by their school district was inappropriate, denying him a free appropriate public education. They requested a due process hearing, challenging the IEP, then withdrew their son from school and placed him in a private school. The hearing officer dismissed the case upon learning of the unilateral placement. A state-level review officer upheld that decision, as did a federal district court. The court noted that the school district did not violate the IDEA by failing to annually update the student's IEP. **Once an IDEA action has been commenced, the student's most recent IEP continues to operate under the stay-put provision until conclusion of the appeal or litigation.** *Kuszewski v. Chippewa Valley School Dist.*, 56 Fed.Appx. 655 (6th Cir. 2003).

◆   A New York middle school student ran out of classrooms and his school building without permission. This was a particular danger because the school was located near a heavily traveled expressway. The student also chased other students in his classroom, hit teachers and students with a folder or crumpled paper, and chewed on sharp objects while leaning back in his chair. The school sought to suspend him with homebound instruction pending a psychiatric evaluation and review by the district's committee on special education. The student and his parents petitioned for a court order preventing the proposed action. A state appellate division court noted that students must remain in their educational placement during the pendency of any special education proceeding. Even where a student presents a danger to himself or others, a district must not unilaterally change a placement from regular to homebound instruction while special education proceedings are pending. The court stated that school districts may seek injunctive relief under 20 U.S.C. § 1415(k)(2)(A), an IDEA section authorizing the extension of a suspension upon showing that maintaining a current placement is substantially likely to result in injury to the student or others. The evidence demonstrated that **allowing the student to return to the regular classroom was substantially likely to result in injury.** *Roslyn Union Free School Dist. v. Geoffrey W.*, 740 N.Y.S.2d 451 (N.Y. App. Div. 2002).

◆   A Missouri student with cerebral palsy underwent surgery to implant a pump in his abdomen to deliver medication to his spine. He received home instruction during his recovery and continued to receive it due to complications. The district believed the student's home was no longer an appropriate learning environment and notified the parents it would provide him the same services at school. The parents refused to bring him to school and he received no services until a federal district court issued a preliminary order 10 months later. A due process hearing panel held the district provided the student with a FAPE and did not violate the IDEA stay-put provision. However, the panel ordered the district to provide the student with extended school year services and other relief while phasing out his home schooling. A federal district court held the change from a home program to school setting violated the stay-put provision. The district appealed.

The Eighth Circuit noted the stay-put provision requires that a student remain in his or her "then-current educational placement" during the pendency of any IDEA action. **The transfer of a student to a different school building for fiscal reasons does not constitute a change of placement.** The district court findings were not clearly erroneous, and the remedy it ordered was well within its discretion. The court held there was no IDEA violation. *Hale v. Poplar Bluff R-I School Dist.*, 280 F.3d 831 (8th Cir. 2002).

E. Other Placement Issues

1. Behavior Problems

◆ In *Jones v. Indiana Area School Dist.*, 397 F.Supp.2d 628 (W.D. Pa. 2005), a federal court found that **a school district's removal of a behavior plan from a student's IEP was evidence of deliberate indifference to sexual harassment of a general education student**. The case is summarized in Chapter 4, Section V.A. of this volume. The court used the Title IX liability standard from *Vance v. Spencer County Public School Dist.*, 231 F.3d 253, 261 (6th Cir. 2000). In that case, the U.S. Court of Appeals, Sixth Circuit, held "where a school district has knowledge that its remedial action is inadequate and ineffective, it is required to take reasonable action in light of those circumstances to eliminate the behavior."

◆ A Minnesota student with a behavior disorder and other disabilities received special education and related services under the IDEA. When behavioral incidents occurred at school, paraprofessionals who were assigned to him escorted him to a separate room so he would have a place to calm down. His family contested his education and the parties agreed to develop an IEP that would address his needs as he transitioned to high school. The IEP called for a written behavior intervention plan (BIP), but none was created by the deadline. The family sued, and the case reached the Eighth Circuit. The court of appeals held that **nothing in state or federal law required a written BIP in a student's IEP**. The school had responded to the student's behavioral incidents using set procedures, and there was no substantive or procedural violation of the IDEA. *School Board of Independent School Dist. No. 11 v. Renollett*, 440 F.3d 1007 (8th Cir. 2006).

◆ An autistic student with a history of aggressive outbursts and violent tendencies attended a public school in California. His behavior included kicking, screaming, yelling, spitting, biting and throwing objects. The student's IEPs included a behavior intervention plan that permitted physical restraints when necessary to protect others. When his parents withdrew their consent to the use of restraints, serious behavior incidents resulted in the student's suspension and kept him outside the classroom with one or two aides most days. A settlement agreement with the parents called for a private organization to conduct behavior and academic assessments and to develop a new IEP. After the parents complained that the school district was not complying with the agreement, the district sought a state superior court order allowing the transfer of the student to a school for students with behavior difficulties. A federal district court found no evidence of discrimination or retaliation under the Rehabilitation Act.

The court held the school district did not have to respond to the parents' written request before resorting to a state court. In *Honig v. Doe*, 484 U.S. 305 (1988), the U.S. Supreme Court expressly allowed school districts to seek temporary relief when a student is considered dangerous in a current placement. The district's decision to seek state court relief did not violate the IDEA, and there was no evidence of discrimination or retaliation under Section 504. The court noted that **"state law explicitly allows school officials to physically restrain students when the student poses an immediate danger to himself or others."** See Cal. Code Regs., Title 5, Section 3052(I). As there was no evidence to overcome the district's legitimate, nondiscriminatory reasons for seeking state court relief, the court awarded the district summary judgment. *Alex G. v. Board of Trustees of Davis Unified School Dist.*, 387 F.Supp.2d 1119 (E.D. Cal. 2005).

◆   An Illinois student with a neurological disorder began exhibiting behavioral problems during grade two. A school psychologist conducted a functional behavioral assessment and prepared a functional behavioral analysis for him. Before a behavior intervention plan could be implemented, the student became increasingly violent, injuring teachers and fellow students in several attacks that resulted in suspensions. His IEP had to be revised several times. The student's mother then requested a due process hearing. A hearing officer held the district did not create an IEP that was reasonably calculated to provide the student with educational benefits. The Seventh Circuit disagreed. **Since the IDEA does not create specific substantive requirements for behavior intervention plans, the district's plan did not violate the IDEA.** Also, the district appropriately considered the student's disruptive impact on other students as a relevant consideration in determining the adequacy of his program. *Alex R. v. Forrestville Community Unit School Dist. #221*, 375 F.3d 603 (7th Cir. 2004).

◆   A Wisconsin student with autism could not function in social settings that were not highly structured. Various placements were tried, including a regular education placement with services, a residential placement and a special school, but his unmanageable behavior continued. His guardian rejected a proposal calling for a return to the residential placement, and sought to keep him in his regular school with a full-time aide. The district assigned him instead to a program of home instruction. The guardian requested a due process hearing, at which an administrative law judge (ALJ) held the district failed to diagnose the student as autistic. He held that the district should not have placed the student in a restrictive home setting without services for a full month while it determined an appropriate placement. Also, the district should have given more consideration to a regular school placement with a full-time aide.

The case reached the Seventh Circuit, which held that the ALJ wrongly substituted his own judgment for that of district administrators. Not even a full-time aide could have restrained this wild child when he started kicking and biting people, tearing his clothes, breaking furniture, and otherwise acting out. **District administrators did not unreasonably assign the student to a temporary homebound placement.** He had a "disastrous history" in regular school and did not function well in any setting except the residential facility. Here, the ALJ improperly focused on the district's failure to categorize the student as autistic. Labels were irrelevant in this case, as there was no evidence that a formal diagnosis of autism would show it was unreasonable to keep the student out of school. *School Dist. of Wisconsin Dells v. Z.S.*, 295 F.3d 671 (7th Cir. 2002).

◆ A Minnesota student with brain lesions and a long history of psychiatric illness had many disciplinary incidents in his public school setting, including the use of physical restraints. However, he showed academic progress there. His mother eventually agreed to a home instruction plan, but then placed him in a private school, where he continued to experience behavioral difficulties. She requested a due process hearing, seeking tuition reimbursement and alleging that the school district's lack of positive behavioral interventions, as well as the high number of physical restraints, prevented the student from receiving a free appropriate public education. The hearing officer ruled in favor of the student, but a state-level review officer reversed. A federal court and the Eighth Circuit Court of Appeals affirmed the review officer's decision. **Contrary to the mother's assertions, the student's academic progress was not irrelevant to the question of the adequacy of his IEP.** The fact that more behavioral interventions could have been made did not mean the school district had not acted in good faith in assisting the student with his educational goals. Tuition reimbursement was disallowed. *CJN v. Minneapolis Public Schools, Special School Dist. No. 1*, 323 F.3d 630 (8th Cir. 2003).

◆ A Missouri student with autism and a learning disability was prone to inappropriate behavior that prevented him from interacting with peers when unmanaged. His school district drafted an IEP that called for placement in a self-contained classroom and the use of a paraprofessional, but it did not include a behavior management plan. The student's behavior problems increased dramatically, but the school did not formulate a behavior management plan until near the end of the school year. At a due process hearing, the parents brought in an autism expert who testified that the student required a formal behavior management plan. A state administrative panel credited that testimony and ordered the district to craft an appropriate behavior management plan. A federal court upheld the panel's decision, and awarded the parents $16,000 in attorneys' fees. However, it refused to reimburse them for expert witness fees. The Eighth Circuit Court of Appeals affirmed. **The district's failure to create a cohesive behavior management plan prevented the student from achieving a meaningful educational benefit.** The student's minimal academic and social progress was offset by the behavior problems not addressed in the IEP. The parents were prevailing parties entitled to attorneys' fees, but not expert witness fees. *Neosho R-V School Dist. v. Clark*, 315 F.3d 1022 (8th Cir. 2003).

2. Extended School Year Services

◆ The IEPs for a Kentucky student with cerebral palsy and delayed cognitive development addressed his ongoing behavior issues. His parents believed he was regressing and sought direct occupational therapy for him as well as a summer placement. Ultimately, the district rejected extended school year (ESY) programming for the student's next school year. The parents unilaterally placed the student in a residential facility that offered summer programs and requested a due process hearing. A hearing officer ruled for the district, but an appeals board and a federal district court reversed his decision. On further appeal, **the Sixth Circuit reversed the lower court decision, holding ESY programming**

was the exception, not the rule. The parents would have to show that ESY was necessary to avoid something more than "adequately recoupable regression." *Kenton County School Dist. v. Hunt*, 384 F.3d 269 (6th Cir. 2004).

◆ A Virginia student with autism received ESY services prior to entering kindergarten. In kindergarten, he progressed in all but two of the 27 goals stated in his IEP. His parents sought to continue the one-on-one services he received during the summer, but were unable to agree with their school district on an IEP. A hearing officer and a federal court both ruled that the purpose of ESY services was to make reasonable progress on unmet goals. The court found that the district's IEP was adequate. The Fourth Circuit Court of Appeals held that **ESY services are necessary only when the regular school year benefits to a student will be significantly jeopardized in the absence of summer programming**. The court remanded the case to the hearing officer for a redetermination of the appropriateness of ESY services using the correct standard. *J.H. v. Henrico County School Board*, 326 F.3d 560 (4th Cir. 2003).

◆ A Minnesota student attended her neighborhood school during the school year, but her parents wanted her to attend an out-of-state ESY placement in the summer. A due process hearing officer held that the district could provide adequate ESY services locally. The following year, prior to another due process hearing, the parties attended mediation at which the district agreed to fund the educational component of the out-of-state ESY placement. When the parents' insurer later refused to fund the residential component of the placement, the parents sought the entire cost of the ESY placement from the district. A federal court ruled that **the district's agreement to fund a portion of the ESY placement did not make it the student's "then-current educational placement" under the stay-put provision** of the IDEA. An agreement to pay is not a placement. Accordingly, the court refused to order the student's placement at the out-of-state program. *Pachl v. School Board of Independent School Dist. No. 11*, 2003 WL 21406191 (D. Minn. 2003).

3. Transfer Students

◆ The mother of a Michigan special education student sought to enroll him in a neighboring school district, which had accepted 67 applications from nonresidents under the state's school choice law. However, because the process was less streamlined for special education students due to the higher costs, the two districts were unable to reach an agreement and the neighboring district rejected the student's application. His mother sued for discrimination and the case reached the Sixth Circuit. The court of appeals held that the school choice law did not violate equal protection. **There was a rational reason for the stricter transfer requirements for special education students.** *Clark v. Banks*, 193 Fed.Appx. 510 (6th Cir. 2006).

◆ When a student with autism moved to Rhode Island, his new school district assembled an IEP team and proposed an interim IEP within two weeks of the parents' first contact. The district wanted to place the student in a newly established self-contained classroom that used a modified version of the TEACCH method. The parents asserted that only DTT methodology was appropriate. They rejected the IEP and notified the district that they would be placing their son in a private school. They then rejected a second IEP developed by the district. A due process hearing officer ruled for the parents, but the First Circuit Court of Appeals ruled for the district, noting that **the IDEA did not require the best possible education for students with disabilities**. Here, the IEP was reasonably calculated to provide an appropriate education. The classroom was half the size of the student's previous placement, and the teachers had extensive experience and training with autistic children. Further, many of the elements of DTT would be available through the use of the TEACCH method, including considerable one-on-one instruction. *L.T. on Behalf of N.B. v. Warwick School Committee*, 361 F.3d 80 (1st Cir. 2004).

◆ A Seattle first-grade student with mild mental retardation and Down syndrome was assigned to a unique classroom combining special education and general education students. Just before the start of the next school year, her mother moved and sought a regular education placement for her daughter. The new district offered a temporary placement in a self-contained special education class until it could perform an evaluation. Two months into the school year, the student had yet to attend class, and the district offered a temporary placement of four hours of special education with at least an hour of regular education. It proposed increasing time in the regular education classroom as appropriate.

A due process hearing officer upheld the district's temporary placement as the closest approximation to the student's last IEP. A federal court and the Ninth Circuit agreed with the hearing officer that the district's placement was appropriate. **The temporary placement was not a "take it or leave it" proposition, but was rather designed to get as close to the student's previous unique placement as possible pending an evaluation.** The temporary IEP conferred educational benefits on the student. *Ms. S. and her Daughter G. v. Vashon Island School Dist.*, 337 F.3d 1115 (9th Cir. 2003).

◆ A California school district that became responsible for the education of a student with autism when he turned three years old did not have to replicate the individualized family service plan designed for him by the regional center that was formerly responsible for his education. The Ninth Circuit held that the status quo necessarily changed when responsibility for his education shifted to the district. According to the Ninth Circuit, the hearing officer and district court had properly analogized the case to that of an incoming transfer student. **When a student transfers from one public agency to another, the receiving agency is required only to provide a program that conforms with the last agreed-upon placement, not provide the exact same program.** The purpose of the IDEA stay-put provision is to strip schools of the unilateral authority they formerly had to exclude students from school, and to protect students from retaliatory action. The change in responsibility for the student's education necessarily changed the status quo. *Johnson v. Special Educ. Hearing Office*, 287 F.3d 1176 (9th Cir. 2002).

◆   A student attended a private special education school under an IEP formulated by the District of Columbia Public Schools. His family moved to Pennsylvania and his new school district proposed placing him in one of two district programs. The family instead unilaterally enrolled the student in a private school. He remained there for 41 days before the family moved to New Jersey. The student's parents sought tuition reimbursement. A hearing officer held that because state standards differ, the adoption of an IEP from another state would require the receiving state to approve of standards that would not necessarily be applicable. The parents appealed to a federal court, which agreed with the school district and hearing officer that the Pennsylvania district did not have to accept the District of Columbia IEP.

The family appealed to the Third Circuit, which observed that the stay-put provision does not specifically address student transfers between states. Under the IDEA, provision of a FAPE requires that special education and related services meet the standards of the state educational agency and that states have policies, procedures and programs consistent with their own standards. The court found it unlikely Congress intended the stay-put provision to require a state to implement an IEP from another state. Where a parent unilaterally removes a student from a placement determined under state procedures, the stay-put provision is inoperative until the parties reach a new agreement. Because the student was without a "then-current" educational placement in Pennsylvania, he was not entitled to stay-put protection. **When a student moves into a new state, the receiving state is not obligated to automatically effectuate a prior IEP from another state, and parents maintain the risk of unilateral private school placements.** *Michael C. v. Radnor Township School Dist.*, 202 F.3d 642 (3d Cir. 2000).

IV. RELATED SERVICES

Related services include the provision of sign language interpreters, transportation, speech pathology, psychological and counseling services, and physical and occupational therapy. The IDEA requires school districts to provide services that are necessary for students with disabilities to receive educational benefits, but excludes medical services from coverage except where required for evaluation or diagnostic purposes. See 20 U.S.C. § 1401(26).

A. Medical Services

◆   **The U.S. Supreme Court ruled that clean intermittent catheterization (CIC) is a related service not subject to the "medical service" exclusion of the IDEA.** The parents of an eight-year-old girl born with spina bifida brought suit against their local Texas school district after the district refused to provide CIC for the child while she attended school. The parents pursued administrative and judicial avenues to force the district to train staff to perform the simple procedure. After a U.S. district court held against the parents, they appealed to the U.S. Court of Appeals, Fifth Circuit, which reversed the district court ruling. The school district then appealed. The U.S. Supreme Court affirmed the court of appeals' ruling that CIC is a supportive related service, not a medical service excluded from the IDEA. *Irving Independent School Dist. v. Tatro*, 468 U.S. 883, 104 S.Ct. 3371, 82 L.Ed.2d 664 (1984).

◆ An Iowa student suffered a spinal cord injury that left him quadriplegic and ventilator dependent. For several years, his family provided him with personal attendant services at school. A family member or nurse performed catheterization, tracheostomy suctioning, repositioning and respiratory observation during the school day. When the student entered the fifth grade, his mother requested that the district provide him with continuous, one-on-one nursing services during the school day. The district refused, and the family filed a request for due process. An administrative law judge held the school district was obligated to reimburse the family for nursing costs incurred during the current school year and to provide the disputed services in the future.

The district appealed to a federal district court, which granted summary judgment to the family. The Eighth Circuit held the disputed services were related services which the district was obligated to provide under the IDEA. The district appealed to the U.S. Supreme Court. The Court agreed with the Eighth Circuit that the requested services were related services, not medical services. The court based its decision in the IDEA definition of related services, its previous holding in *Tatro,* and the IDEA purpose of making special education available to all disabled students. Adopting a bright-line, physician/non-physician standard, the Court held that **since the disputed services could be performed by someone other than a physician, the district was obligated to provide them**. *Cedar Rapids Community School Dist. v. Garret F. by Charlene F.,* 526 U.S. 66, 119 S.Ct. 992, 143 L.Ed.2d 154 (1999).

◆ **A Virginia school board did not have to reimburse a disabled student for hospitalization costs that were paid years earlier by his father's group health insurance**, even though the payments counted against the lifetime medical benefits limit of the policy. The father made several requests to recover the $200,000 cost of the hospitalization from the board, but he did not request a due process hearing for almost 10 years. The hearing officer held the action was barred by a one-year Virginia statute of limitations. A federal district court affirmed. The Fourth Circuit agreed that the action was untimely. Also, the student was now an adult and was no longer covered by his father's insurance policy. He had his own Medicaid coverage, and this insurance was not affected by the decrease in lifetime medical benefits to his father's plan. *Emery v. Roanoke City School Board*, 432 F.3d 294 (4th Cir. 2005).

B. Level or Location of Services

◆ A Georgia student with a disability complained that words became fuzzy or three dimensional when he tried to read. A behavioral optometrist diagnosed accommodative and convergence disorder and recommended visual therapy to reduce vision loss. The district refused to pay for such therapy on the grounds that the student was receiving a free appropriate public education. The parents paid for the therapy, then sought due process. An administrative hearing officer and a federal court found that the parents were entitled to reimbursement for the therapy as a related service. The Eleventh Circuit agreed. **Although the student's condition had not yet caused poor academic performance, it did prevent him from receiving a FAPE.** *DeKalb County School Dist. v. M.T.V.*, 164 Fed.Appx. 900 (11th Cir. 2006).

◆   The IEP of an Illinois third-grade student with Down syndrome called for 30 minutes weekly of direct occupational therapy (OT). The therapist who provided OT services to the student received her master's degree before the start of the school year, but did not obtain her license until near the end of the year. Using the results of the student's triennial evaluation, the district proposed an IEP for the student's fourth-grade year that called for 30 minutes of monthly OT consultation and less physical therapy than the parents desired. They rejected the IEP and obtained independent evaluations. A due process hearing officer agreed with the district's denial of reimbursement for the independent evaluations. Although she rejected the parents' claims of IEP deficiencies for 9 of the 11 areas they identified, she held that the district should provide 60 minutes weekly of direct OT services as compensatory services during the fourth grade because the occupational therapist was unlicensed and improperly supervised during the third grade. A federal court upheld the IEP, but ordered the district to provide the OT services the hearing officer required. It also awarded reimbursement for the independent evaluations and awarded attorney fees. The Seventh Circuit agreed that **60 minutes of direct OT services each week was appropriate given the failure of the district in the third grade year to properly supervise the unlicensed occupational therapist**. However, the parents were not entitled to reimbursement for the independent evaluations because the district's evaluations had been appropriate. The parents were prevailing parties and were entitled to attorneys' fees. *Evanston Community Consolidated School Dist. No. 65 v. Michael M.*, 356 F.3d 798 (7th Cir. 2004).

◆   A hearing-impaired Louisiana student attended a public school with the assistance of a cued speech transliterator to supplement spoken information in his classes. Although other hearing-impaired students in the district who used American Sign Language attended their neighborhood schools, the cued speech transliterator served only at a centralized location. The student achieved substantial academic benefit at the centralized school. However, his parents decided he should attend his neighborhood school for social reasons. The district denied their transfer request. A hearing officer upheld the decision, but a federal district court held the student was entitled to attend his neighborhood school with the transliterator. The Fifth Circuit reversed. The student's IEP satisfied the IDEA, and his parents were seeking the neighborhood placement for primarily social reasons. **They did not have veto power over the district's decision to provide the transliterator only at the central location.** *White v. Ascension Parish School Board,* 343 F.3d 373 (5th Cir. 2003).

◆   An Illinois student with autism attended a private Boston school under an IEP that called for the school district to pay for 12 round trips a year for the parents. Four years later, the district reduced the number of paid annual visits from 12 to six. The parents requested a due process hearing, at which the hearing officer noted that the parents had never made more than six trips a year and determined that six trips a year were appropriate. The parents appealed, and a federal court ruled for the district. During the 38-month period from the time of the due process hearing request to the court's decision, the parents took 12 trips to Boston in addition to the six specified in the IEP. When the district sought to be reimbursed for the extra 12 trips the parents had taken, the court refused to force them to repay the district the amount in question (over $13,000). Even though the parents seemingly took advantage of the stay-put provision by increasing their visits during litigation, IDEA policies justified allowing them to keep the money. *Aaron M. v. Yomtoob*, 2003 WL 22836308 (N.D. Ill. 2003). In a separate opinion, the court ruled that **travel for parental training can be a related service under the IDEA**, but that six trips per year were sufficient to meet the statute's requirements. *Aaron M. v. Yomtoob*, 2003 WL 223469 (N.D. Ill. 2003).

◆ A New Hampshire student with hearing impairments underwent surgery for a cochlear implant and later had 19 separate appointments with audiologists for the mapping of his speech processor. His parents sought reimbursement from their school district for their mileage to the appointments as well as reimbursement for the $10 office co-pays for each mapping appointment. The district refused to reimburse them and a hearing officer held the mapping services were necessary related services under the IDEA. A federal district court agreed. The student's IEP included a cochlear implant as his method of communication and confirmed that the educational methodology selected for him was a necessary part of a free appropriate public education. **Cochlear implant mapping was a related service under the IDEA.** *Stratham School Dist. v. Beth*, 2003 WL 260728 (D.N.H. 2003).

◆ Two autistic students resided in a New Jersey group home and attended special education programs located in other districts. Their parents resided in districts other than the one where the group home was located. The parents' districts asked the state education commissioner for an order requiring the group home district to pay for their transportation costs. The Superior Court of New Jersey, Appellate Division, held the parents' districts had to fund the transportation. Under state law, **the students were deemed to be residents of their parents' homes, making those districts liable for transportation costs**. *Board of Educ. of West Windsor-Plainsboro Regional School Dist. v. Board of Educ. of Township of Delran*, 825 A.2d 1215 (N.J. Super. Ct. App. Div. 2003).

◆ A South Dakota student who suffered epileptic seizures was provided transportation to and from school by her district as a related service under the IDEA. She was accompanied by a nurse during the ride. Although parents could designate different pick-up and drop-off sites within a specific school area boundary, students were not transported outside the boundary unless it was necessary to obtain an educational benefit under an IEP. The district denied a request by the student's mother to drop her off at a day care center outside the boundary. The state Office of Special Education ordered the district to pay for transportation to the day care center, but a hearing examiner ruled it was not necessary. A federal court agreed, and the Eighth Circuit affirmed the decision that **the district did not have to provide transportation to the day care center**. The request was for the mother's own convenience and was not necessary to provide the student with educational benefit. *Fick v. Sioux Falls School Dist. 49-5*, 337 F.3d 968 (8th Cir. 2003).

C. Provision of Related Services at Private Schools

◆   An Arizona student attended a school for the deaf from grades one through five and a public school from grades six through eight. During his public school attendance, a sign language interpreter was provided by the school district. The student's parents enrolled him in a parochial high school for ninth grade and asked the school district to continue providing a sign language interpreter. The school district refused, and the student's parents sued it in a U.S. District Court under the IDEA. The court held for the district and the Ninth Circuit affirmed, stating the placement of a public school employee in a parochial school would create the appearance of government sponsorship of the private school.

The U.S. Supreme Court held that the Establishment Clause did not completely prohibit religious institutions from participating in publicly sponsored benefits. If this were the case, religious groups would not even enjoy police and fire protection or have use of public roads and sidewalks. Government programs which neutrally provide benefits to broad classes of citizens are not subject to Establishment Clause prohibition simply because some religiously affiliated institutions receive an attenuated financial benefit. **Providing a sign language interpreter under the IDEA was part of a general program for distribution of benefits in a neutral manner to qualified students.** A sign language interpreter, unlike an instructor or counselor, was ethically bound to transmit everything said in exactly the same way as it was intended. The Court reversed the decision. *Zobrest v. Catalina Foothills School Dist.*, 509 U.S. 1, 113 S.Ct. 2462, 125 L.Ed.2d 1 (1993).

◆   A Pennsylvania school district determined that a student was not IDEA-eligible, but was eligible for occupational therapy under Section 504. The student's parents enrolled him in a private school, but also dually enrolled him in public schools so he would be able to get occupational therapy at a public school. **The district refused to provide the occupational therapy services, but a state court ordered it to do so.** The student was not seeking tuition reimbursement or even related services at the private school. He was merely seeking Section 504 services at a public facility, and was "enrolled" in the district. He did not have to actually attend a public school to be eligible for occupational therapy. *Lower Merion School Dist. v. Doe*, 878 A.2d 925 (Pa. Commw. Ct. 2005).

◆   A Rhode Island student with a disability attended a parochial school for the sixth grade and received on-site resource services from her local public school. The next year, her parents enrolled her in a parochial school located in another town. The school committee discontinued providing on-site resource services but made the services available at off-site locations. The committee asserted that it provided on-site resources for parochial school students only when their schools were within walking distance of a public school. The parents agreed to send their daughter to after-school sessions at a local public school. However, this became unacceptable and the student's parents filed a due process hearing request under the IDEA, arguing that the committee's unwritten walking distance rule was unfair because two other students received on-site services at parochial schools. The hearing officer agreed with the parents and ordered the committee to provide resource services to the student at her school, declaring the committee's walking distance rule inequitable, arbitrary and discriminatory.

The school committee appealed to a federal, which stated that an IDEA regulation, 34 C.F.R. Part 300.456, permits local education agencies to provide on-site services to private school students with disabilities, including those who attend religious schools. No court has ever interpreted this permissive language as a requirement to provide on-site services to students who are voluntarily enrolled at parochial schools. The hearing officer had applied an equity analysis, which was inappropriate. The court held **the IDEA and its regulations clearly gave the school committee power and discretion to provide on-site resource services at the parochial schools of its choosing**. Due to the student's change in schools, the committee was required to hold an IEP meeting so that her educational needs could be evaluated. If it had not already done so, the committee would have to evaluate the student's IEP. The committee would not be required to provide on-site services at the current school, but could do so it if chose. *Bristol Warren Regional School Committee v. Rhode Island Dep't of Educ.*, 253 F.Supp.2d 236 (D.R.I. 2003).

V. TUITION REIMBURSEMENT

If a school district is unable to provide special education services to a student with a disability in its own facilities, it must locate an appropriate program in another district, hospital or institution. When a private placement is required, the district becomes responsible for tuition and other costs.

A. Private School Tuition Claims

◆ A South Carolina ninth-grader with a learning disability attended special education classes. Her parents disagreed with the IEP devised by their school district. The IEP called for mainstreaming in regular education classes for most subjects. The parents requested a due process hearing and unilaterally placed the student in a private school. A hearing officer held that the IEP was adequate. After the student raised her reading comprehension three full grades in one year at the private school, the parents sued the district for tuition reimbursement. A U.S. district court held the educational program and achievement goals of the proposed IEP were "wholly inadequate" under the IDEA. Even though the private school was not approved by the state education department, it provided the student with an excellent education that complied with IDEA substantive requirements. The parents were entitled to tuition reimbursement. The U.S.

Court of Appeals, Fourth Circuit, affirmed, and the school district appealed to the U.S. Supreme Court, which held that **the failure of the school district to provide an appropriate placement entitled the parents to tuition reimbursement, even though the private school was not on any state list of approved schools**. This was because the district denied the student FAPE and the private education provided to her was found appropriate by the district court. South Carolina did not release a list of approved schools to the public. Under the IDEA, parents may unilaterally place children in private schools at their own risk. To recover tuition costs, parents must show that the placement proposed by the school district violates the IDEA, and that the private school placement is appropriate. The Supreme Court upheld the lower court decisions for the parents. *Florence County School Dist. Four v. Carter*, 510 U.S. 7, 114 S.Ct. 361, 126 L.Ed.2d 284 (1993).

◆ The U.S. Supreme Court held that the parents of a child with a disability did not waive their claim for reimbursement of the expenses involved in unilaterally placing their child in a private school during the pendency of proceedings to review the child's IEP. The case involved a learning disabled child who was placed in a public school special education program against the wishes of his parents. The parents requested a due process hearing and, prior to the resolution of their complaint, placed their child in a private residential school recommended by specialists. The parents then sought reimbursement for their expenses. The U.S. Court of Appeals, First Circuit, found the IDEA stay-put provision to be "directory" rather than "mandatory." It decided that this "status quo" provision did not bar claims for reimbursement.

The U.S. Supreme Court held that to bar reimbursement claims in cases of unilateral parent placement was contrary to the IDEA, which favors proper interim placements for disabled children. However, **parents who unilaterally change a child's placement during the pendency of proceedings do so at their own financial risk**. If the courts ultimately determine a child's IEP is appropriate, the parents are barred from obtaining reimbursement for any interim period in which the placement violated the IDEA. The Court affirmed the appellate court ruling. *Burlington School Committee v. Dep't of Educ.*, 471 U.S. 359, 105 S.Ct. 1996, 85 L.Ed.2d 385 (1985).

◆ The parents of a Maryland student with ADHD placed him in a private school after he began suffering academic and emotional problems. Their district agreed to fund the placement through 2001-02. When they sought to continue the placement through 2002-03, the district notified them that the school had not yet been approved as a fundable special education school for that year. The district recommended another private school, but the parents kept their son where he was. The school was approved for the 2003-04 year, and the parents then sought tuition reimbursement for the 2002-03 year. The case reached the Fourth Circuit, which **denied reimbursement because the district had offered a free appropriate public education at the other private school**, and the parents did not properly notify the district of their intent to reject the IEP. *Z.W. v. Smith*, 2006 WL 3797975 (4th Cir. 2006).

◆   When the parents of a multiply disabled student rejected a school district's IEP, they placed their son in a Quaker school and requested a due process hearing seeking tuition reimbursement. The hearing officer dismissed the action, holding that New Jersey law prohibited tuition reimbursement for unilateral sectarian school placements. A federal court overturned that decision. It noted that 34 C.F.R. § 403(c) specifies that **unilateral placements need not meet state standards; the placement must simply be appropriate, and the district must have denied a free appropriate public education to the student**. Also, paying religious school tuition did not violate the Establishment Clause because it was the parents who decided where the money was going, not the government. The court remanded the case for a determination of whether the district had provided FAPE to the student. If not, the hearing officer would have to determine whether the Quaker school placement was appropriate. *L.M. v. Evesham Township Board of Educ.*, 256 F.Supp.2d 290 (D.N.J. 2003).

◆   A learning disabled Indiana student received special education and regular education instruction, and generally achieved good grades. When his grades dropped off during the eighth grade, his mother became concerned and hired a private evaluator who recommended Orton-Gillingham (OG) programming and an extended school year. The district conducted its own evaluation and developed an IEP for the student's ninth-grade year that increased his special education assistance, but did not offer OG instruction or extended year services. The student's mother agreed to the IEP, but then unilaterally enrolled him in a private Connecticut school for disabled students. The next year, she requested tuition reimbursement for the private placement. When the district refused, she requested a due process hearing. A hearing officer held the district denied the student FAPE, and ordered the district to reimburse the mother for four years of private school tuition. A federal district court held for the district.

On appeal, the Seventh Circuit stated parents who unilaterally change the placement of a student with disabilities do so at their own financial risk. In tuition reimbursement cases, **parents must show their district has denied a student a FAPE as well as prove the private placement they selected is appropriate**. The attainment of passing grades and regular advancement from grade to grade are generally accepted indicators of satisfactory progress. While advancement from grade to grade does not by itself indicate IDEA requirements are satisfied, the student had earned his promotions through good classroom test scores. He also improved his standardized test scores, which were in the average range for reading and written language. The district had proposed increasing the level of special education services for the student and its proposed IEP for ninth grade contained detailed instructional methods that had worked well in the past. The proposed IEP was reasonably calculated to provide educational benefits, and the judgment was affirmed. There was no evidence the student would regress during the summer without extended year services. *Todd v. Duneland School Corp.*, 299 F.3d 899 (7th Cir. 2002).

◆   The First Circuit held **school officials may not seek reimbursement from parents for a school year covered by an administrative decision ordering reimbursement**. It was thus unnecessary to award any relief to a Maine parent seeking protection from such reimbursement claims as a result of the district court's reversal of an administrative decision requiring the school committee to fund her disabled child's residential placement. Even if the student's IEPs for the 1998-1999 and 1999-2000 school years were deemed adequate, the parent would not be required to reimburse the committee for amounts it paid. *Rome School Committee v. Mrs. B.*, 247 F.3d 29 (1st Cir. 2001).

B. Parental Conduct

The IDEA discourages unilateral conduct by school districts and parents alike. The IDEA allows for the reduction or denial of reimbursement to parentally placed private school students, if the parents fail to give at least 10 days notice of the intended placement, do not make the child available to designated school employees for an assessment and evaluation before the child's removal from public school, or if a judge so rules.

◆ The parents of a New York student home-schooled her until she was 14. They did not comply with state requirements to provide the school district with an individual home instruction plan, and did not begin reading instruction until the student was 8. They did not provide the district with the student's educational records and did not express any concerns about a possible learning disability. No evaluation for a disability was made. They unilaterally enrolled her in a private residential school for children with learning disabilities, and referred the student to the district for some evaluative testing to satisfy the private school's admissions process. The student was not referred to the district for a full evaluation by the district's Committee on Special Education (CSE). Eight months later, the parents moved to another school district. They did not notify the new district of the student's learning disability until less than a month before a new school year. They then submitted incomplete records to the district. The district's CSE was unable to act upon their request for services prior to the school year.

A federal court observed that the 1997 amendments to the IDEA clarified that reimbursement is available only if privately placed students had previously received special education services under the authority of a public education agency. The IDEA bars private school tuition reimbursement without the consent of, or referral by, a public agency. If a district made a FAPE available to the student, but the parents elected to place the student in a private facility, it does not have to pay for private school tuition. Such a policy deals with the problem created by referral of a student to a CSE for special education evaluation and services after the parents have already made a unilateral private placement. Parents may not receive tuition reimbursement without letting the district know special education is an issue before placing the student in a private school. The district must be given a chance evaluate the student and develop an appropriate IEP. **The parents never gave the previous district a meaningful opportunity to consider whether the student could receive a FAPE in district schools** before they re-enrolled her at the private school. Tuition reimbursement was unavailable. *Carmel Cent. School Dist. v. V.P.*, 373 F.Supp.2d 402 (S.D.N.Y. 2004).

◆   An Ohio student with profound hearing loss received speech and language therapy, and pre-tutoring of new vocabulary and concepts from a school district through grade four. His school performance dropped during that year, when he earned Ds and Fs in math. His IEP team recommended promoting him to grade five with resource room placement for part of the day. His parents agreed. However, two months later, they notified the district of their intent to place the student in a private school that did not offer special education. They then sought tuition reimbursement. A hearing officer denied reimbursement because the parents failed to properly notify the district of their placement decision. The Sixth Circuit agreed that **the parents had failed to inform the district of their objections to the IEP prior to removing the student from school**. Also, the private school placement was not appropriate because it did not provide the student with any of the special education services he required, including speech and language therapy, and the pre-tutoring services the parents had insisted upon from the district. *Berger v. Medina City School Dist.*, 348 F.3d 513 (6th Cir. 2003).

◆   A Georgia student attended regular education classes through sixth grade. He then attended a private school, and a psychologist diagnosed him with a nonverbal learning disability. Weeks before the end of the student's eighth-grade year, his mother informed the school district she wanted to enroll him in public school. The district formulated an interim IEP for the ninth grade, and the student began attending the public school. However, he remained there only five days. His mother then sent a letter rejecting the IEP and informing the district she intended to enroll the student in the private school. The parents sought tuition reimbursement. An administrative law judge held for the district, finding the parents did not provide sufficient notice and deprived the district of a reasonable chance to accommodate the student by removing him from school after five days. A district court granted summary judgment to the district, but the Eleventh Circuit vacated and remanded the judgment. The district court should have considered whether the district complied with IDEA procedures and provided a FAPE in addition to examining the parents' actions. **Even though the parents' failure to provide the requisite 10-day rejection notice might allow denying their reimbursement claim, a trial had to be held.** *Loren F. v. Atlanta Independent School System*, 349 F.3d 1309 (11th Cir. 2003).

◆   A Maryland student with multiple learning disabilities and sensory integration issues was placed in a public school for special education services. Midway through the school year, her parents began the application process for a private school. Near the end of the school year, they presented the district with the results of independent evaluations they had arranged. The parents did not sign the IEP proposed by the school district for the next school year, and later rejected the proposed IEP. They enrolled the student in a private school for the next school year. After the school year started, the parents finally disclosed to the district the results of an independent speech and language assessment. They requested a due process hearing, seeking reimbursement of their private school tuition costs. An administrative law judge denied the parents' request for tuition reimbursement, observing that they "demonstrated their lack of good faith."

A federal district court noted the parents had never intended to accept a public school placement. It would have been inequitable to award them tuition. There was no merit to the parents' allegations that the IEP was significantly deficient. While they disagreed with the proposed IEP, they raised no objection in the IEP meeting to its objectives or goals. The court adopted the ALJ's findings regarding the parents' failure to report back to the IEP team and the determination that none of the alleged IEP deficiencies denied the student educational opportunities. There was no substantive IDEA violation in the IEP proposal. The student was essentially performing at grade level. The court commented that while a finding that a school district had provided a FAPE to a student would normally resolve the question of tuition reimbursement, **parental non-cooperation can also create the possibility that a court could deny tuition reimbursement**. In order for parents to reject a school district's IEP proposal, they had to cooperate in good faith with the development of an IEP. As the parents had failed to demonstrate, good faith, the court affirmed the decision. *S.M. v. Weast*, 240 F.Supp.2d 426 (D. Md. 2003).

◆ A Nebraska student with spinal meningitis required constant medical care and received special educational services at home, pursuant to his IEP. His parents moved him to a licensed nursing facility located within the school district for noneducational reasons. The district discontinued the student's educational services and the parents filed an administrative complaint. A hearing officer held that the parents were not entitled to relief because they had placed the student at the nursing facility without consulting school officials. The parents appealed to a state trial court, and the school district removed the case to a federal district court. The court held that state law and the IDEA required the district to provide services at the nursing facility.

The district appealed to the Eighth Circuit, which noted that the school district remained willing to provide the student with a FAPE at school facilities or at his home. The parents had chosen the nursing facility for non-educational reasons and had acted unilaterally, without the consent or approval of the student's IEP team. Their arguments were foreclosed by the 1997 amendments to the IDEA, which clarified that **local education agencies are not required to pay for the cost of a private school education if they have offered a FAPE to the student and the parents nonetheless make a voluntary private school placement**. The court considered the parents' state law claim, which arose from a section of the Nebraska Special Education Act that requires school districts to provide visiting teachers for homebound students with disabilities. The section did not mandate the provision of on-site teaching services to homebound students. According to regulations published by the Nebraska Department of Education, school districts were not required to pay for the costs of educating a student with a disability at a nonpublic school or facility if the district made a FAPE available at the student's home and the parents made a unilateral choice to place the student in the private facility. Since the district offered the student a FAPE, the district complied with the IDEA and Nebraska special education laws and regulations. The circuit court reversed the district court judgment. *Jasa v. Millard Public School Dist. No. 17*, 206 F.3d 813 (8th Cir. 2000).

VI. TRANSITION AND GRADUATION

The IDEA and its regulations require a statement of a student's transition service needs for the IEP of each student with a disability no later than the age of 14, or earlier if appropriate. See 34 C.F.R. Part 300.347(b).

Introductory language in the 2004 IDEA Amendments declared an increased emphasis on the provision of effective transition services for disabled students, in view of their increasing graduation rates. Transition services are defined in part as "a results-oriented process, that is focused on improving the academic and functional achievement of the child with a disability ..."

A. Transition Plans

◆   The parents of a Pennsylvania student with dyslexia, memory disorder and ADHD agreed with their school district on a twelfth grade IEP that called for transition services in a college preparatory program in Maryland. The district did not provide the transition services, but at the end of the year, it recommended that the student be graduated. The parents objected, and the IEP team met without the parents to finalize an IEP for a thirteenth year of services that also did not include transition services. A due process hearing officer found that the student had received a free appropriate public education, but a state special education appeals panel reversed. The Commonwealth Court of Pennsylvania upheld the panel's decision. **The district had failed to provide agreed-upon transition services, then scheduled the student's graduation.** The court ordered the district to provide the student with a year of compensatory education in the college preparatory program. *Susquehanna Township School Dist. v. Frances J.*, 823 A.2d 249 (Pa. Commw. Ct. 2003).

◆   An Alabama student with learning disabilities had a traumatic event with her special education teacher at the start of her fifth-grade year and was withdrawn from her public school. At due process, the parties entered into a settlement agreement that required diagnostic testing, tutoring, consultation and more. When the parties could not agree on a new IEP, the student's mother made a second due process request, accusing the board of violating the settlement agreement. The hearing officer ruled that the board did not deny the student a FAPE. However, a federal court reversed. It noted that the board had performed some, but not all, of the diagnostic testing required by the agreement. This resulted in a denial of FAPE because of the lack of information on the student's areas of need. Also, **there was no plan to transition the student back to school and no IEP provision for educational services at home. This was a substantive violation of the IDEA** because the IEP omitted discussion of how the student would be educated if she could not return to school full time. The court ruled for the student but denied an award of money damages. *E.D. v. Enterprise City Board of Educ.*, 273 F.Supp.2d 1252 (M.D. Ala. 2003).

◆   The parents of a 20-year-old Pennsylvania student with disabilities requested a due process hearing to resolve a dispute with his school district over his diagnosis. The hearing resulted in an administrative order requiring the district to conduct an evaluation and devise a new IEP. The student's parents disputed the resulting IEP and arranged for independent evaluations. They did not participate in further IEP and multidisciplinary team meetings and requested a second hearing. A hearing officer held for the district, and the parents appealed. A state appeals panel affirmed the decision that the appropriate classification of the student was physically disabled and mentally retarded, and denied the parents' request for reimbursement for independent evaluations. The panel held that the IEPs for the student's three most recent school years were inadequate in the areas of transition planning and assistive technology. It awarded him over 600 hours of compensatory education.

The district appealed to a federal court, which stated that the IDEA requires a statement of transition services for students no later than age 16. In this case, the transitional evaluation prepared by the school multidisciplinary team was inadequate because the team did not include personnel who had evaluated the student's transition needs. The district also failed to include aspects of transition planning in his IEP. The court adopted the panel's decision, finding the IEP was not sufficiently tailored to meet the student's needs. The district improperly delayed providing him assistive technology. Applying the Third Circuit's standard for awarding compensatory education, the court held that **the district knew or should have known that the student's IEP lacked appropriate transitional planning and assistive technology provisions**. Accordingly, compensatory education was appropriate. The court modified the appeals panel decision by slightly decreasing the amount of compensatory education. *East Penn School Dist. v. Scott B.*, 1999 WL 178363 (E.D. Pa. 1999).

B. Graduation

The 2004 IDEA amendments relieved schools of any duty to seek an evaluation before terminating the eligibility of a student who has graduated with a regular diploma or become too old to be eligible for a FAPE. When an eligible child graduates or "ages out" of school, the school district must give the child a summary of his or her academic achievement and functional performance, with recommendations for assistance in meeting the child's postsecondary goals.

◆ A 19-year-old Florida student had Asperger's syndrome and was non-verbal. His senior-year IEP identified writing as a priority need. At an IEP meeting held three months before the end of the year, the district proposed eliminating goals requiring him to complete written work. It also advised the parents their son would graduate at the end of the year, if he received all of his academic credits. The parents rejected the proposal to graduate their son and to eliminate his written work. They requested a new IEP meeting or mediation and new evaluations. Less than two weeks before graduation, the board advised the parents it would hold an IEP meeting to discuss a diploma and review the IEP. It then informed them the graduation ceremony was the day before the IEP meeting. Although the student graduated with a 3.09 grade average and passed the Florida Comprehensive Assessment Test, the parents requested a due process hearing to preserve his placement. An administrative law judge denied the request, but a federal district court held the due process request before graduation triggered the stay-put provision. The board appealed to the Eleventh Circuit, arguing a mediation request did not trigger the stay-put provision.

The court noted IDEA and Florida special education regulations explaining the stay-put provision do not mention the mediation process. The Code of Federal Regulations, at 34 C.F.R. Part 300.514, states only that the filing of a due process hearing invokes a stay-put injunction. **The court rejected the district court's finding that the board had misled the parents by scheduling an IEP meeting the day after their son's graduation.** There was no evidence that the board did not intend to hold the meeting if the student failed to graduate. The district court should not have back-dated a stay-put injunction to return the student to high school. The court vacated the decision and remanded the case, with instructions to decide if a preliminary order should be issued. Unlike an "automatic" stay-put order, this involved balancing the relative harm to the parties if the court intervened. *Sammons v. Polk County School Board*, No. 05-14013, 2006 WL 222811 (11th Cir. 2006).

◆ A Washington student became pregnant when she was a high school senior. She failed a quiz near the end of the school year. Hours before graduation, the student and her mother met with a teacher and the school principal, who stated the class grading policy prevented raising the grade. The student was not allowed to participate in the ceremony. The district superintendent later met with the family and suggested a Section 504 plan could be used to increase the student's point total for the failed course. She drafted an agreement for a Section 504 plan. The resulting increase in points for the course allowed the student to graduate. The student and her family sued the district and school officials in a Washington superior court, alleging discrimination and due process violations. A jury found the district violated the student's due process rights and awarded her $5,000, with over $31,000 in attorneys' fees and costs. However, the jury found no discrimination against the student. The court denied post-trial motions by the district, which appealed to the Court of Appeals of Washington.

The court found little support for the student's claim that attending a graduation ceremony was a fundamental, constitutionally protected right. **No state or federal law created an entitlement for students to attend graduation ceremonies.** The court agreed with a Pennsylvania court's statement that "commencement ceremonies are only symbolic of the educational result, not an essential component of it." The student had received an opportunity to meet with the principal to resolve her grievance prior to the ceremony. State law did not create procedures for school administrators to follow before forbidding a student's participation in graduation ceremonies. As the student was not deprived of any interest protected by the Constitution, the superior court should have granted the district's post-trial motion. *Nieshe v. Concrete School Dist.*, 128 Wash.App. 1029 (Wash. Ct. App. 2005).

◆ A Minnesota student with chronic fatigue syndrome missed many classes due to his condition and was no longer on track to graduate with his peers. His school district expressed doubt about the validity of his condition, and contested his eligibility for special education. A hearing officer found the student eligible for special education under the IDEA. The district presented no medical evidence, and the hearing officer ordered it to "consider how [the student] may participate in the graduation ceremony with his class." She also held he was entitled to compensatory educational services. The district held an IEP team meeting a few days before graduation and rejected the student's request to participate in the commencement ceremony. The state education department interpreted the hearing officer's order as requiring his participation in the ceremony and found the district was out of compliance with the order.

The student petitioned a federal district court for an order to enforce the administrative decision. The court held the opportunity to graduate with peers was an important educational benefit that could not be repeated. Denial of the opportunity was irreparable injury to the student. The balance of harms and the public interest favored the student. Little or no harm would result to the school district if the court ordered relief. **The student was entitled to an order requiring his participation in graduation ceremonies**. The court recommended the parties implement the hearing officer's suggestion to allow him to simply walk with his class at the ceremony and receive a blank paper. *Olson v. Robbinsdale Area School Dist.*, 2004 WL 1212081 (D. Minn. 2004).

◆ A federal district court held that an Illinois school district improperly decided to graduate a high school student with multiple disabilities on the basis of his accumulation of required credits instead of his progress toward his individualized goals. Because the district committed several violations of the IDEA with respect to the student's educational program and IEPs, the district was required to reimburse his parents for private school costs and provide him with compensatory education at a private school until he reached the age of 22. The violations included designing IEPs with vague and immeasurable goals, not changing IEP goals from year to year despite the student's regression, and the failure to develop a timely transition plan. Contrary to the district's argument that its obligation to the student ended upon his graduation with a regular diploma, the court stated federal regulations require districts to provide a FAPE to students with qualifying disabilities until the age of 21. **In order to be eligible for graduation, the student had to meet general graduation requirements and make progress on IEP goals and objectives.** *Kevin T. v. Elmhurst Community School Dist. No. 205*, 2002 WL 433061 (N.D. Ill. 2002).

◆ A 20-year-old Pennsylvania student with Down syndrome received instruction in a learning support environment for two-thirds of the school day under an IEP. His parents requested that the school IEP team allow him to participate in graduation ceremonies at the end of the school year, even though he would not graduate at that time. The district refused the request, and the parents requested a due process hearing. A hearing officer upheld the district policy requiring students to complete all local and state graduation requirements, including IEPs, before participating in graduation ceremonies. A state appeals panel reversed.

The district appealed to the Pennsylvania Commonwealth Court, arguing that it was vested with discretion to develop its own criteria for participation in graduation ceremonies, and that its decision to exclude the student was a valid exercise of its discretion. The court agreed, observing that the state general assembly had vested local districts with the authority to establish graduation requirements and confer diplomas upon those who completed them. Any ceremony celebrating the completion of these requirements, and the decision to award a diploma, was within the local district's educational policy discretion. Both state and federal special education law mandated that the student receive instruction under his IEP and **it was appropriate that he complete requirements beyond those required of students without disabilities before becoming eligible to graduate and receive a diploma**. The district's policy did not violate the IDEA. The practical effect of the IDEA was to give students with disabilities the right to an IEP, not a right to graduate with their peers. The court reversed the appeals panel's decision. *Woodland Hills School Dist. v. S.F.*, 747 A.2d 433 (Pa. Commw. Ct. 2000).

C. Compensatory Education

Compensatory education is the belated provision of necessary educational or related services to a student to which the student was entitled, but which the education agency failed to provide. Compensatory education may be awarded to students who are over the statutory age of entitlement (usually 21) to prohibit education agencies from indefinitely delaying the provision of necessary services until the student is beyond school age.

◆   A Texas student with multiple disabilities had an IEP that included a goal to initiate communications about his need to go to the bathroom. The district used a voice-output device for him to communicate this need and gave a device to the parents for home use, explaining its proper use to his mother. The student regressed in his ability to use the device at home and in his extended school year program, and he wet the bed every morning. His parents challenged the IEP's schedule of in-home and parent training. A hearing officer noted that the district provided only four of ten scheduled training sessions, and ordered 150 minutes of compensatory training. However, a federal district court ruled that **the student's regression in toilet training was not a failure to implement a significant portion of the IEP**. The award of compensatory training was reversed. *Clear Creek Independent School Dist. v. J.K.*, 400 F.Supp.2d 991 (S.D. Tex. 2005).

◆   A District of Columbia student with multiple disabilities received special education. An evaluation team determined that he was making progress but that he required new evaluations. However, they were not performed. After six months, the student's mother requested a due process hearing. A hearing officer determined the district failed to provide the student with a FAPE, but limited compensatory education to the two-month period prior to the hearing request. The mother appealed. A federal court noted that **the district had failed to show it was providing the services required by the IEP and did not conduct a reevaluation required by the IDEA**. Accordingly, the student was entitled to compensatory education for the entire three-year period at issue. *Argueta v. Government of District of Columbia*, 355 F.Supp.2d 408 (D.D.C. 2005).

◆   The mother of a Nevada student with autism took her son to a childhood autism program ordered by a hearing officer as compensatory education. The district was required to pay "all out-of-pocket expenses" – nearly $65,000. When the mother sought an additional $26,515 to fully compensate her for wages and benefits she lost while transporting her son to the program, the Supreme Court of Nevada held that she was not entitled to them. **Out-of-pocket expenses did not include lost income.** *Gumm v. Nevada Dep't of Educ.*, 113 P.3d 853 (Nev. 2005).

◆   A 19-year-old Tennessee student with no hands, one foot and cerebral palsy was dropped while school district attendants were attempting to move him from his wheelchair. His parents sued for his injuries and received his complete academic record for the first time. They believed his IEPs had been inappropriate and requested a due process hearing. A hearing officer ruled for the school system, but a federal district court held the system violated the IDEA by failing to relay information from the student's previous assessments. The court also held, however, that the student received a FAPE, and it denied his request for compensatory education. After the student received a special education diploma, the Sixth Circuit reversed, ordering the district court to determine whether the case was moot in view of the issuance of a diploma. The district court then held that **the student's compensatory education claim was based on his assertion that the school system had denied him a FAPE at a time when he remained eligible for services.** Even though he was now 24 and had a special education diploma, his compensatory education request involved past violations and the case was not moot. *Barnett v. Memphis City School System*, 294 F.Supp.2d 924 (W.D. Tenn. 2003).

The case returned to the Sixth Circuit, which affirmed the ruling for the student. The case was not moot despite the special education diploma, and the failure to share evaluations with the parents was a procedural violation of the IDEA. Further, even after the student failed to reach his IEP goals, the district did not recommend any different instructional approaches for him. *Barnett v. Memphis City Schools*, 113 Fed.Appx. 124 (6th Cir. 2004).

◆   A Pennsylvania student with disabilities attended a private school for over a year until his parents became concerned with his physical safety and alleged noncompliance with his IEP. They requested an in-home placement with five months of compensatory education. The district agreed to remove the student from the school, but could not find a suitable one-to-one assistant or certified homebound teacher. Although the student turned 21 before the next school year began, the district's special education director acknowledged that he was still entitled to IDEA services. Over a year later, the district found a private placement with a one-to-one assistant. The student's mother rejected the placement. A due process hearing officer ordered the district to provide compensatory education equal to the number of days the student had missed school during the year. A state appeals panel affirmed the decision. The parents then sued the district under 42 U.S.C. § 1983, seeking money damages and three years of compensatory education. A federal court held that **the hearing officer had appropriately ordered compensatory education for the time the**

student missed school, rather than the three years requested by the parents. However, the parents could seek money damages for the district's IDEA violations under Section 1983. *Dombrowski v. Wissahickon School Dist.*, 2003 WL 22271654 (E.D. Pa. 2003).

◆ A California student was on a home/hospital instruction plan during a school year. His school district did not provide him with instruction from a teacher with a special education credential until late in the year. For the first three months of the year, it provided him with a regular education teacher, but for the next two months, it did not provide any teacher. The next school year, the district placed the student in a class for students with serious emotional disturbance, even though he was not seriously emotionally disturbed. A federal district court awarded the student compensatory education and held his parents should be reimbursed for certain expenses.

The district appealed to the Ninth Circuit, which observed that the IDEA requires educational agencies to provide eligible students with instruction in the least restrictive possible environment. Improper placement in the seriously emotionally disturbed classroom violated the IDEA's least restrictive environment requirement. **The district's failure to provide the student any special education services for a significant part of a school year meant that it did not provide services reasonably calculated to provide him with educational benefits.** The IDEA requires districts to provide qualified students with access to specialized instruction and related services. The district fell below the minimum "basic floor of opportunity" by failing to provide access to a special education teacher. Parents have an equitable right to reimbursement for compensatory education when a district fails to provide FAPE. Despite the parents' repeated requests for services, the student did not graduate with his class and did not perform at his grade level while in school. Although he had now left school, he was entitled to compensatory education. *Everett v. Santa Barbara High School Dist.*, 28 Fed.Appx. 683 (9th Cir. 2002).

VII. SECTION 504 AND THE ADA

The Americans with Disabilities Act (ADA), 42 U.S.C. § 12101, et seq., and Section 504 of the Rehabilitation Act of 1973, 29 U.S.C. § 794, are federal statutes that prohibit discrimination against persons with disabilities. Both statutes require schools and their employees to make reasonable accommodations for qualified individuals with disabilities, but no institution is required to lower its academic standards in order to do so.

A. Section 504 Accommodation Plans

◆ A Pennsylvania student had multiple sensitivities to chemicals, including pesticides. Her school district announced a plan to spray pesticides on all its school playing fields. The student's parents demonstrated at a school board meeting to oppose the spraying plan. The high school which she was to attend the next year was in a rural area. The district proposed a Section 504 service agreement granting her accommodations including adaptive physical education, a chair to sit on during indoor physical education, and 48-72 hour notice of any chemical spraying by the district. The district also offered to place the student in a high school located in an urban area with no adjacent farms or fields. The parents objected to the service agreement, as she would "look like an outcast" sitting in a chair and there was no guarantee balls used indoors would not have pesticides on them. The parents would not accept a plan allowing the school nurse to call 911 in an emergency, stating they did not use the local hospital.

The school district requested a due process hearing, and a special education hearing officer found the Section 504 plan appropriate. The plan allowed the student to attend a school in the district that was not surrounded by fields and farms where pesticides were used. The parents withdrew their daughter from school and sued the district in a federal district court for abusing its power and violating Section 504. **The court ruled for the district, finding no abuse of power in requesting a due process hearing or in any of the Section 504 procedures it used.** The hearing officer had upheld the plan as appropriate. Instead of appealing the decision, the parents withdrew their daughter from school, waited more than two years, then sued the district for damages. *Sutton v. West Chester Area School Dist.*, 2004 WL 999144 (E.D. Pa. 2004).

◆ A Minnesota student with schizophrenia attended school under a Section 504 plan that called for teachers to monitor him. The student's medication improved his behavior noticeably. During the school year, a paraprofessional revealed the student's schizophrenia to others at the school. The student then experienced extensive verbal and physical harassment. According to his family, the district did not take corrective action to reduce the harassment. Prior to the start of the next school year, the district offered to transfer the student to another school district. The parents accepted the offer, but then had to transport the student to his new school. After a due process hearing, the parents sued their son's former district under the IDEA and Section 504. The court granted pretrial judgment to the district, but the Eighth Circuit Court of Appeals reversed in part. Although the new district was responsible for the student's educational program under the IDEA, the former district could be liable for discrimination under Section 504. **The district may have acted in bad faith or with gross misconduct by failing to amend the student's Section 504 plan after the disclosure of his schizophrenia.** The court remanded the case. *M.P. v. Independent School Dist. No. 721*, 326 F.3d 975 (8th Cir. 2003).

◆ After attending a private kindergarten program, a student with severe asthma, motor difficulties and sensory sensitivity enrolled in a Pennsylvania public school. The district found her eligible under Section 504, and the parties met to discuss a Section 504 service agreement. The parents rejected a district proposal to provide the student 19 specific accommodations and enrolled her in a private school. When the district refused the parents' request for private school tuition reimbursement and independent evaluation fees, they requested a due process hearing. A hearing officer held the district provided the student with a FAPE, and denied tuition reimbursement. However, she ordered the district to meet with the parents to enhance the accommodations for the student.

The parents commenced a Section 504 action against the district. The court held that the substantive requirements of Section 504 in the education context are equivalent to those of the IDEA. As in IDEA cases, there is no firm rule in a Section 504 case to determine when a school district has provided an appropriate education. Here, each of the district's proposed accommodations were appropriate. The court approved of the service agreement's provision for a classroom aide during the student's classes and recess, agreeing with the district that the student required some supervision when she had difficulty with asthma or using playground equipment. It also approved the district's offer to provide her with preferential seating at lunch and on buses. As a general means of accommodating the student's hypersensitivity to sensory stimuli, the district proposed an opt-out feature so she could avoid negative sensory experiences. The court found the service agreement educationally appropriate. It was irrelevant whether the private school placement proposed by the parents was "better" than the district's proposal, as this consideration is made only if a district fails to provide an appropriate education. **The 19-part service agreement was a holistic approach to accommodating the student's disabilities** that provided significant learning opportunities and conferred meaningful benefit. The parents were not entitled to reimbursement. *Molly L. v. Lower Merion School Dist.*, 194 F.Supp.2d 422 (E.D. Pa. 2002).

B. Discrimination Claims

The standard of liability for Section 504 and ADA claims is much higher than in IDEA cases. To create liability under Section 504 or the ADA, there must be evidence of either bad faith or gross misjudgment by school officials.

◆ A New York student with pervasive development disorder and dyslexia claimed that he was harassed and bullied on numerous occasions over two years, alleging that he was body-slammed and beaten and had his books thrown in the trash at least five times. His mother also complained to school officials. Eventually, he was admitted to a hospital psychiatric emergency room. He was then sent to another school at the district's expense. His mother nevertheless sued the district and superintendent under the Rehabilitation Act and the ADA.

The court refused to dismiss the case, finding issues over the credibility of school employees who professed ignorance to the harassment and bullying despite numerous incident reports. The court held that *Davis v. Monroe County Board of Educ.*, 526 U.S. 629 (1999), put school officials on notice that disability harassment by peers is unlawful. In *Davis*, the U.S. Supreme Court held that school districts are liable for peer sexual harassment under Title IX, if officials are "deliberately indifferent" to harassment, their response is "clearly unreasonable," and the harassment is so severe that it deprives the victim of access to educational opportunities. *K.M. v. Hyde Park Cent. School Dist.*, 381 F.Supp.2d 343 (S.D.N.Y. 2005).

◆ A Virginia student received special education until he moved into a new district. The new district denied his mother's request for an evaluation. Two years later, the district finally conceded he was eligible for special education. The mother then sued the district for violations of the IDEA and Section 504.

She also sought money damages under 42 U.S.C. § 1983. The IDEA claim settled, and the other two claims reached the Fourth Circuit. The court held that **the student was not entitled to money damages under Section 1983**. The IDEA established a comprehensive remedial scheme and the student obtained all the relief he was due under it. However, the Section 504 claim could proceed. *Duck v. Isle of Wight County School Board*, 402 F.3d 468 (4th Cir. 2005).

◆ The parents of two Hawaii students with autism initiated due process, at which the hearing officer found significant problems in the delivery of services. The education department was ordered to ensure that the students received a free appropriate public education. The parents then sued for personal injury damages under the IDEA and Section 504. A federal court ruled against them. **They could not show the education department had demonstrated deliberate indifference to their children** so as to prove intentional discrimination. *Mark H. v. Lemahieu*, 372 F.Supp.2d 591 (D. Haw. 2005).

◆ A Louisiana student had a spinal condition known as spondylolisthesis. She missed a mandatory graduation practice session because a painkiller she took the night before caused her to sleep through her alarm. School staff made several unsuccessful attempts to contact her father and made a phone record of the attempts. The principal rejected a medical excuse supplied by the student and excluded her from graduation ceremonies under a mandatory attendance policy that was previously announced, printed and distributed to all graduating seniors. The student was not allowed to walk in the ceremony, but she received her diploma within a week. The student sued the school board and principal in a federal district court for violating Rehabilitation Act Section 504 and the ADA.

The court found that **the student's spinal condition was not so severe as to substantially limit her ability to perform major life activities**. At the time leading up to, during, and after the missed graduation practice, she was able to participate in many activities in which a healthy student would participate. She attended her classes, did volunteer work, held a job requiring her to stand for long hours and attended private graduation parties. The court noted medical evidence documenting the student's return to normal daily living activities shortly after a second corrective surgery. She did not frequently feel discomfort and had sporadic flare-ups. The court awarded summary judgment to the board and principal. *Soirez v. Vermilion Parish School Board*, No. 6:04 CV 00959, 2005 WL 2286951 (W.D. La. 2005).

◆ A Michigan high school student was diagnosed with developmental disabilities. The private psychologist who diagnosed the student recommended remedial instruction and accommodations under Section 504. The district declared the student eligible for Section 504 accommodations and assigned him to Project Read, a remedial program offered for students with literacy impairments. Although the parents' psychologist identified Project Read as similar in approach and effectiveness to Orton-Gillingham (OG) instruction, the parents placed the student in a private OG program. A hearing officer found the school's program was equivalent or superior to the OG program. He held the district did not discriminate against the student, and that selection of instructional methodology was the responsibility of the school, not a prerogative of parents and advocates. The parents appealed.

The Sixth Circuit held that to prevail in a claim under Section 504, there must be evidence that an individual with a disability is qualified to participate in a program but has been deliberately excluded from it on the basis of disability. A Section 504 claimant alleging discrimination by a school district must show failure to provide an education that was appropriate to his or her individual needs. Here, the student could prove a Section 504 violation only if the OG program was a reasonable accommodation, and that the Project Read placement was not. **Since the student failed to show that the Project Read course was not a reasonable accommodation, he could not show that the district denied him a FAPE.** *Campbell v. Board of Educ. of Centerline School Dist.*, 58 Fed.Appx. 162 (6th Cir. 2003).

◆   A Wyoming student with cerebral palsy attended school in a district that initially did not have accessible buildings. The district hired a full-time aide to assist her during the school day. During her entire school career, the student continued to have accessibility issues. The district did not make accessible seating in the school gym available, and locked her out of a school building because an accessible door was not working. Also, during her senior year, her aide frequently missed school due to a personal situation. When the student sued the district under Section 504 and the ADA, the district sought to have the case dismissed. The court refused to do so, noting that **the mere hiring of the full-time aide did not mean that the district had not intentionally discriminated against the student**. Not only was the aide absent at times during the school day, but she was also not present for extracurricular activities and events. A trial would have to be held. *Swenson v. Lincoln County School Dist.*, 260 F.Supp.2d 1136 (D. Wyo. 2003).

◆   A New Jersey student with disabilities had substantial fatigue that made her unable to attend school for a full day. Under her IEP, she attended morning classes and received home instruction from school staff during the afternoon. Despite her disability, she earned a weighted GPA of 4.6894 and scored 1570 out of 1600 possible points on the SAT. Although she was the highest ranked student in her class, the district superintendent sought to have district policy changed to allow for multiple valedictorians. The student sued under Section 504 and the ADA, asserting that the district's action discriminated against her on the basis of her disability. A federal court agreed. Her home placement put her at a disadvantage because she was unable to take some Advanced Placement courses that could have lifted her GPA even higher. The student's IEP did not give her an advantage; it merely leveled the playing field. **The district could not retroactively change its policy to allow for multiple valedictorians.** *Hornstine v. Township of Moorestown*, 263 F.Supp.2d 887 (D.N.J. 2003).

◆   A Virginia student with ADHD brought a pellet gun to school. District officials sought to expel him, and a manifestation committee determined that his behavior was unrelated to his disability, such that expulsion was proper. An impartial hearing officer reversed the finding of the manifestation committee but ruled that it did not commit procedural violations. Before a review officer could consider the case, the parents sued under Section 504, alleging that the board's policies and procedures were inadequate. They did not allege disability discrimination. A federal court dismissed the lawsuit, noting that **although Section 504 confers a private right of action to enforce discrimination claims, it does not provide a private right of action to assert procedural violations**. The case was remanded to the review officer. *Power v. School Board of City of Virginia Beach*, 276 F.Supp.2d 515 (E.D. Va. 2003).

◆ An Illinois student suffered from asthma symptoms only while at school. Away from school, she resolved her breathing problems with a single puff of her inhaler. She was placed on homebound status for much of her junior and senior years, and graduated despite being unable to receive homework assignments for some classes. She sued the school district for discriminating against her by refusing to adjust her grades for absences, and for preventing her from playing softball. A federal court ruled against her, noting that she did not qualify for protection under Section 504 of the Rehabilitation Act. **She was not substantially limited in her ability to breathe except at her school, and she could have attended another location.** *Block v. Rockford Public School Dist.*, 2002 WL 31856719 (N.D. Ill. 2002).

◆ A New York student became chronically ill during seventh grade, and her frequent absences from school prompted school officials to threaten filing negligence charges against her mother with a state child protection agency. After the student returned to school, she soon experienced severe abdominal pain. An immunologist diagnosed the student with chronic fatigue syndrome and fibromyalgia. The mother decided to home school her. She completed seventh grade, receiving only 20 days of home instruction from the district. She was medically able to return to school for eighth grade, but school officials initially refused to promote her. Her mother rejected the eighth-grade placement and home schooled her. They sued the district, board and education officials for disability discrimination and retaliation under Section 504, the ADA, the IDEA, and other laws. The court held the student did not have a learning disability, and failed to show her illness substantially limited her ability to learn. She also failed to show that she was a student with disabilities under the IDEA.

On appeal, the Second Circuit held that the lower court erroneously dismissed the Section 504 and ADA claims based on its finding that the student was not learning disabled. This was a fundamental misinterpretation of the disability inquiry under Section 504 and the ADA. The student was "disabled" under both acts. She was substantially disabled from major life activities such as walking, exerting herself and attending school. **The district failed to reasonably accommodate her by denying her any meaningful public education for much of her seventh-grade year.** The district court erroneously dismissed the retaliation claim, ignoring strong inferences of retaliation by school officials. The complaint contained many examples of threats to initiate child welfare investigations and abuse charges against the mother. The district's failure to notify the student and her mother of the availability of IDEA remedies was a deprivation of procedural rights and denied them an opportunity to take advantage of due process remedies. The student's complaint clearly alleged that her condition entitled her to IDEA coverage as having an "other health impairment," as defined by the IDEA and its regulations. The dismissal of the IDEA claim was reversed. Because the IDEA and other federal claims were valid, the Second Circuit reinstated the student's claim for damages. *Weixel v. Board of Educ. of City of New York*, 287 F.3d 138 (2d Cir. 2002).

◆   A fourth-grade Minnesota student received 25 disciplinary write-ups for harassment and making inappropriate comments on his school bus. His class participated in a geography program that involved a field trip to the Minnesota Vikings training facility. The student submitted a picture of a football player in Green Bay Packers colors in response to an assignment to color a player in Vikings colors. Due to this failure to follow instructions, his picture was left out of a class display. The school later excluded him from participating in a holiday parade for not wearing Vikings clothing, as requested. The school principal met with him shortly before the Vikings field trip, asserting he would not be allowed to go unless he discontinued his school bus misconduct. The student's behavior became increasingly disruptive, and staff decided to exclude him from the trip as a consequence. He sued the district and school officials in a federal court for speech rights violations and disability discrimination.

The case reached the Eighth Circuit, which held that the student showed no deprivation of constitutional rights. Even assuming a fourth-grader had a constitutional right to free expression at school, school officials did not violate it by requiring him to follow directions on school projects. The teacher's reasonable, curriculum-based decisions did not create district liability. There was no evidence that the school had disciplined the student for supporting the Packers. The district court had properly awarded judgment to the district on the student's state and federal disability discrimination claims. **In order to prevail in a disability discrimination claim under the ADA there must be a showing of bad faith or gross misjudgment by school officials.** The student could not show he was excluded from the Vikings field trip on the basis of his disability. The discipline was based on his documented misconduct. The court affirmed the judgment for the district. *Sonkowsky v. Board of Educ. for Independent School Dist. No. 721*, 327 F.3d 675 (8th Cir. 2003).

C. Standardized Testing

◆   The father of a California student with special needs requested copies of his son's test protocols prior to a scheduled IEP team meeting. The district refused to provide a copy of the copyrighted protocols for an achievement test because it believed that doing so would violate federal copyright law. A federal district court held that **the district had to provide the test protocols in accordance with state education law**. The father would only receive the part of the test identifiable with his son. This was a "fair use" under copyright law. *Newport-Mesa Unified School Dist. v. State of California Dep't of Educ.*, 371 F.Supp.2d 1170 (C.D. Cal. 2005).

◆ A federal district court denied a request by students with learning disabilities for a preliminary order preventing administration of the California High School Exit Exam (CAHSEE) in March 2002. The court held that in the absence of accommodations, the scheduled test administration was likely to violate the rights of students with individualized education programs or Section 504 education plans. The IDEA required districts to provide learning disabled students with accommodations when they took the exam. The state was ordered to provide students alternate assessments if they were unable to take the exam due to their learning disabilities.

The Ninth Circuit reversed the district court order requiring the state to develop an alternative assessment to the CAHSEE. **Federal courts could not bar the state from exercising its authority to set graduation requirements.** The appeals court left intact a provision of the district court order permitting students to use the accommodations described in their IEPs and Section 504 plans on March 2002 CAHSEE administrations. Their participation in the CAHSEE only had to be "meaningful" to comply with the IDEA. *Smiley v. California Dep't of Educ.*, 45 Fed.Appx. 780 (9th Cir. 2002).

◆ A class of Indiana students with disabilities challenged the Indiana graduation qualifying examination. One subclass of students asserted the state violated their due process rights by making the Graduation Qualifying Examination (GQE) a graduation requirement in 2000. The students were previously exempted from the examination and did not receive instruction in the tested material. A second subclass of students claimed denial of testing accommodations and adaptations in violation of the IDEA. They alleged that the state denied them permission to use the accommodations called for in their individualized education programs during the test.

The case reached the Indiana Court of Appeals. It held the students had a property interest in a diploma, if they met all their graduation requirements. The state had provided school districts with at least five years' notice about the GQE and the students learned of it at least three years in advance. This notice was adequate, in view of multiple opportunities provided to students for remediation and retaking the GQE, if necessary. The court found that the students received exposure to the curriculum tested on the GQE. The trial court properly found the remedy for failing to teach students the subjects tested on the GQE was remediation, not to award diplomas. The IDEA does not require such a result. **The state did not violate the IDEA by failing to honor accommodations specified in IEPs where they would affect the validity of GQE results.** It permitted accommodations such as sign language responses, use of Braille, special lighting and furniture, large type and individual or small group testing. The state was not required to provide all accommodations specified in IEPs during the GQE. The court affirmed the judgment for the state. *Rene v. Reed*, 751 N.E.2d 736 (Ind. Ct. App. 2001).

◆ The Texas Assessment of Academic Skills (TAAS) has been administered to all Texas students since 1990 to measure mastery of the state-mandated curriculum. Passing the tenth grade test is a requirement for graduation. Groups representing Texas minority students sued the Texas Education Agency (TEA), asserting the exit-level TAAS exam had a disparate impact on minority students in violation of the Due Process Clause and Title VI of the Civil Rights Act of 1964. The court dismissed many of the claims, then held a trial on the Due Process and Title VI claims. It reviewed evidence that minority failure rates on the TAAS exam were much higher than those for majority students. However, minority students were rapidly narrowing the passing-rate gap. The court held the TAAS exam did not disadvantage minority students. Students failing any part of the exam receive concentrated, targeted educational remediation. The court accepted the TEA's evidence that school accountability and mandated remediation helped to address the effects of prior discrimination in Texas. Cumulative pass rates did not demonstrate a severe disparate impact on minority students for the classes of 1996 through 1998.

The exam provided an objective way to assess student mastery of the skills and knowledge required for graduation. **The selection of a 70 percent exam passing score was not arbitrary and bore a relationship to the state's legitimate goals**, as was the use of the TAAS exam as a graduation requirement. The students failed to identify equally effective alternatives to the use of the TAAS exam for achieving the state's goals of holding students, teachers, and schools accountable for teaching, learning, and ensuring equal opportunity to learn. The exam did not violate student Due Process interests because it was not fundamentally unfair to minority students. The exam reliably measured what it purported to measure and met accepted standards for curricular validity. Students had adequate notice and opportunity to learn all covered subject matter and disparities in test scores did not result from flawed testing or administration. TAAS exit exam administrations addressed educational inequalities and did not violate Title VI regulations or the Due Process Clause. The court awarded judgment to the TEA. *GI Forum v. Texas Educ. Agency*, 87 F.Supp.2d 667 (W.D. Tex. 2000).

CHAPTER FOURTEEN

Private Schools

Page

I. PRIVATE SCHOOL EMPLOYMENT 593
   A. Employment Discrimination................................594
   B. Labor Relations...596
   C. Termination from Employment 598

II. STATE AND FEDERAL REGULATION 601
   A. Accreditation 601
   B. Sex Abuse and Mandatory Reporting..............602
   C. Taxation..604
      1. Federal Income Taxation..............................604
      2. State and Local Taxation 605

III. PRIVATE SCHOOL STUDENT RIGHTS....................609
   A. Admissions and Other School Policies 609
   B. Athletics and Extracurricular Activities 611
   C. Breach of Contract 612
      1. Educational Programs....................................612
      2. Tuition 614
   D. Discipline, Suspension, and Expulsion 615
   E. Students with Disabilities 618

IV. PUBLIC AND PRIVATE SCHOOL COOPERATION 622
   A. Dual Enrollment 622
   B Textbook Loans and Other Materials 623
   C. Transportation 625
   D. Personnel Sharing..627
   E. School Facilities and Property 628
   F. Release Time Programs 631

V. STUDENT FINANCIAL ASSISTANCE 632

I. PRIVATE SCHOOL EMPLOYMENT

Title VII of the Civil Rights Act of 1964 is a federal anti-discrimination law that applies to employers with at least 15 employees. Private religious organizations and their affiliated schools may be exempt from Title VII and state laws by demonstrating a bona fide reason for using discriminatory employment practices on the grounds of religion. See Chapter Seven for additional cases discussing employment discrimination in public schools.

A. Employment Discrimination

◆   A Minnesota Lutheran school teacher was also a pastor. He became chair of the school's theology department. His duties included student counseling, and he was responsible for ensuring students followed the beliefs and doctrines of the synod – an advisory body of Lutheran congregations and ministers. After 22 years at the school the teacher told his family he was gay. When a church bishop contacted the teacher, the teacher admitted he was gay, but said he was not in a homosexual relationship and had never lived a gay lifestyle. The bishop and the teacher met with the school principal. They decided the teacher should remain "closeted" and celibate. When the school found a replacement, the teacher resigned. He sued the school in a state court, alleging discrimination based on sexual orientation in violation of the Minnesota Human Rights Act, Minn. Stat. § 363A.08, subd. 2(b). **The act prohibits employers from discharging employees because of their sexual orientation.**

The trial court held that resolving the teacher's claim would violate the First Amendment, as it would result in excessive entanglement between church and state. On appeal, **the Court of Appeals of Minnesota explained that courts cannot inquire into or review the internal decision-making of a religious institution. If a dispute can be resolved according to neutral principles of law – rules that are applied without regard to religious institutions or doctrines – a court may address a claim against a church without excessive entanglement.** The teacher contended that although part of his job entailed pastoral duties, he was also a secular teacher, and the court could apply neutral principles of law. He also asserted he could continue teaching because he was celibate and did not speak openly about his sexual orientation. The court affirmed the judgment, because the lawfulness of a discharge based on sexual orientation would have required it to delve into church doctrine in violation of the Establishment Clause. There was no evidence showing the teacher's position could be split into secular and nonsecular parts. *Doe v. Lutheran High School of Greater Minneapolis*, 702 N.W.2d 322 (Minn. Ct. App. 2005).

◆   Employees of a Maryland Christian school filed separate actions against the school under Chapter 27 of the Montgomery County Code, claiming they were fired because they were not Baptist. Chapter 27 barred employers from discriminating against employees on grounds including religious creed. The statute included an exemption for religious organizations, allowing them to hire employees of a particular religion "to perform purely religious functions." The employees had performed secular duties for the school. They claimed the school could not fire them based on their religious creed because they did not perform purely religious functions. In the first suit, a jury found the school fired employees based on their religious affiliation and awarded them compensatory damages. In the second, a court granted summary judgment to a former teacher's aide and awarded her $31,000 in damages and attorneys' fees.

On appeal to the Court of Appeals of Maryland, the school claimed the exemption violated the Free Exercise and Establishment Clauses of the First Amendment, as well as the Maryland Declaration of Rights. It also claimed the exemption conflicted with state laws prohibiting employment discrimination.

Maryland exempts religious organizations from state laws prohibiting discrimination based on religion. **The court held the exemption violated the Free Exercise and Establishment Clauses, as well as the Maryland Declaration of Rights.** After the court deleted the portion of the exemption for employees who perform purely religious functions, **the statute allowed religious organizations to make employment decisions based on religion for any employee.** The school did not violate state law. *Montrose Christian School Corp. v. Walsh*, 363 Md. 565, 770 A.2d 111 (Md. 2001).

◆   A Montana school run by an association based on the beliefs of the Roman Catholic Church fired an assistant counselor. The school claimed the termination was the result of the elimination of the position. The counselor sued the school in a state court, claiming it violated Montana discrimination law by firing her because of her marital status or gender. **According to the counselor, she was terminated due to her supervisor's disapproval of her cohabitation with a man who was not her husband.** The counselor further contended that she was fired in retaliation for testifying in another discrimination suit brought against the school. The court entered summary judgment for the school, finding the counselor's claim interfered with the school's religious Free Exercise rights.

On appeal, the Montana Supreme Court held that even if the school's proffered reason for firing the counselor was a pretext, the case was not about marital status or gender – it was about the code of conduct she agreed to follow when she signed her employment agreement with the school. The counselor failed to present case law suggesting the state's anti-discrimination laws prohibited discrimination based on conduct. The court noted **the counselor did not demonstrate that her situation involved a right that surmounted the school's First Amendment right to freely exercise its religion through its employment practices.** The grant of summary judgment in favor of the school was affirmed. *Parker-Bigback v. St. Labre School,* 7 P.3d 361 (Mont. 2000).

◆   The U.S. Supreme Court held the Mormon Church could discriminate on the basis of religion in hiring for a nonreligious job. The case involved an employee who worked at a church-operated gymnasium for 16 years. After being discharged for failing to meet several religious requirements for employment, he sued the church in a U.S. district court alleging religious discrimination in violation of Title VII of the Civil Rights Act of 1964. The court denied a dismissal motion by the church. It agreed with the claim that if Section 702 allowed religious employers to discriminate on religious grounds in hiring for nonreligious jobs, it would violate the Establishment Clause.

The Supreme Court noted Section 702 provides that Title VII "shall not apply ... to a religious corporation, association [or] educational institution ... with respect to the employment of individuals of a particular religion to perform work connected with the carrying on by such [an organization] of its activities." **The Court reversed the district court decision and upheld the right of nonprofit religious employers to impose religious conditions for employment in nonreligious positions involving nonprofit activities.** *Corp. of the Presiding Bishop of the Church of Jesus Christ of Latter-Day Saints v. Amos,* 483 U.S. 327, 107 S.Ct. 2862, 97 L.Ed.2d 273 (1987).

B. Labor Relations

The courts have ruled that "pervasively religious" schools may be able to avoid any obligation to bargain with employees under the National Labor Relations Act (NLRA). This exception to the NLRA's coverage is based upon First Amendment religious freedom considerations. Managerial employees are not protected by the NLRA.

◆ The right of employees of a Catholic school system to form a collective bargaining unit was successfully challenged in a case decided by the U.S. Supreme Court. In this case, the unions were certified by the National Labor Relations Board (NLRB) as bargaining units but the diocese refused to bargain with them. The Court said that the religion clauses of the U.S. Constitution, which require religious organizations to finance their educational systems without governmental aid, also free the religious organizations of the inhibiting effect and impact of unionization of their teachers. **The Court agreed with the employers' contention that the threshold act of certification of the union would necessarily alter and infringe upon the religious character of parochial schools.** This would mean that the bishop would no longer be the sole repository of authority as required by church law. Instead, he would have to share some decisionmaking with the union. The Court held this violated the religion clauses of the U.S. Constitution. *NLRB v. Catholic Bishop of Chicago*, 440 U.S. 490, 99 S.Ct. 1313, 59 L.Ed.2d 533 (1979).

◆ A group of elementary schools operated by the Catholic Diocese of Camden, New Jersey employed a number of lay teachers. A union asserted that it was elected by a majority of the lay teachers. When it sought to have the schools recognize it as the collective bargaining representative of the lay teachers, a Board of Pastors, acting on behalf of the schools, informed the union that it would be recognized only if it signed a document that vested in the board complete and final authority to dictate the outcome of any dispute. It also prohibited the union from assessing dues or collecting agency fees from nonunion members. When the union refused to sign the document, the schools refused to recognize the union or to bargain collectively. The union sued to compel the schools to recognize it as the collective bargaining representative of the lay teachers. The court granted the schools' motion for summary judgment, and the case reached the Supreme Court of New Jersey.

The court examined the U.S. Supreme Court decision in *NLRB v. Catholic Bishop of Chicago* and found the case distinguishable. The regulatory scheme of the NLRA requires the NLRB to act as a monitor-referee and causes much more entanglement of government with religion than the New Jersey Constitution. **The court held that requiring the schools to bargain would not violate the religion clauses of the state or federal constitutions because the agreement between the diocese and representative for the lay teachers would preserve the bishop's exclusive right to structure the schools.** As long as the scope of collective bargaining was limited to secular issues such as wages and benefit plans, neutral criteria could be used to ensure that religion was neither advanced nor inhibited. **The schools could be required to bargain**

under New Jersey law because the state constitutional guarantee of the right to organize and bargain collectively for persons in private employment was neutral and of general application. The state had a compelling interest in allowing the lay employees to unionize and bargain collectively over secular terms and conditions of employment. The fact that this incidentally burdened the free exercise of religion did not violate the Free Exercise Clause. *South Jersey Catholic School Teachers Organization v. St. Teresa of the Infant Jesus Church Elementary School*, 150 N.J. 575, 696 A.2d 709 (N.J. 1997).

◆   A Roman Catholic secondary school in New York City employed lay and religiously affiliated faculty and taught both secular and religious subjects. After a union began representing the lay faculty, the school administration and the union met repeatedly to negotiate the terms of a collective bargaining agreement. When those efforts failed, the union staged a strike. The school discharged the striking workers and ended negotiations. **The state Employment Relations Board** cited the school for alleged violations of the state Labor Relations Act. It **charged the school with refusing to bargain in good faith and with improperly discharging and failing to reinstate striking employees.** The case came before the Court of Appeals of New York.

The court held the state Labor Relations Act governed labor relations between the school and its lay faculty. The act was a facially neutral, universally applicable and secular regulatory regimen. It did not implicate religious conduct or beliefs, and it did not restrict or impose any burdens on religious belief or activities. The court held that the Establishment Clause argument failed because the state board's supervision over collective bargaining with respect to secular terms and conditions of employment was neither comprehensive nor continuing and did not entangle the state with religion. Here, **the government was not forcing the parties to agree on specific terms but was ordering the employer to bargain in good faith on secular subjects.** *New York State Employment Relations Board v. Christ the King Regional High School*, 90 N.Y.2d 244, 660 N.Y.S.2d 359, 682 N.E.2d 960 (N.Y. 1997).

◆   Two teachers at a Pennsylvania Catholic elementary and secondary school attempted to organize a teachers union. Through an association of Catholic teachers, they petitioned the Pennsylvania Labor Relations Board (PLRB) to compel an election. The teachers were fired, and the association filed a second petition that was dismissed on the grounds that the school was not a public employer and the teachers were not public employees under the Public Employee Relations Act (PERA). The teachers appealed to a state trial court, which reversed the PLRB decision. The commonwealth court held Catholic teachers are excluded from coverage by the PERA, and the teachers appealed.

The Supreme Court of Pennsylvania noted the Supreme Court's decision in *NLRB v. Catholic Bishop of Chicago.* **The NLRA does not apply to lay teachers employed at church-operated schools.** However, the NLRA and the PERA do not have the same scope. The PERA defines a public employee as any individual employed by a public employer but excludes employees at church facilities "when utilized primarily for religious purposes." **As the school was**

operated primarily for religious purposes, the teachers were excluded under the PERA. The court noted that even if this interpretation was incorrect, the legislature did not affirmatively indicate its intention that teachers at religious schools be covered under the PERA. The court affirmed the judgment. *Ass'n of Catholic Teachers v. PLRB*, 692 A.2d 1039 (Pa. 1997).

◆ A religious order operated a parochial school in Albany, New York. The collective bargaining agreement between the school and the union representing the school's lay teachers expired, and formal negotiations toward a new agreement were begun. However, the school gave notice that it was withdrawing its recognition of the union and that it would no longer collectively bargain with it. The union filed an unfair labor practice charge against the school with the state Employment Relations Board, which held the school violated the state Labor Law by withdrawing its recognition of the union. The union then sued the school in a New York court to enforce the order. The court held for the union.

On appeal, a state appellate division court held the board's assertion of jurisdiction over the school did not violate its Free Exercise and Establishment Clause rights under the First Amendment. The state Labor Relations Act was a facially neutral, universally applicable and secular regulatory regimen that did not violate the Free Exercise Clause. It did not impose any express or implied restriction or burden on religious beliefs or activities. Nor did the act violate the Establishment Clause. There was no excessive entanglement in the board's relationship with religious schools over mandatory subjects of bargaining. **Even though lay faculty members were expected to instill Christian values in students, this did not serve "to make the terms and conditions of their employment matters of church administration and thus purely of ecclesiastical concern."** The U.S. Supreme Court's decision in *NLRB v. Catholic Bishop of Chicago* did not apply because the case involved a state agency exercising its jurisdiction over religiously affiliated schools. The court affirmed the judgment. *New York State Employment Relations Board v. Christian Brothers Academy*, 668 N.Y.S.2d 407 (N.Y. App. Div. 1998).

◆ In *NLRB v. Yeshiva Univ.,* the U.S. Supreme Court held that in certain circumstances, faculty members at private educational institutions could be considered managerial employees. The ruling was based on the conclusion that Yeshiva's faculty decided school curriculum, standards, tuition rates and admissions. The Court's decision applied only to schools that were "like Yeshiva" and not to schools where the faculty exercised less control. **Schools where faculty members do not exercise binding managerial discretion do not fall within the scope of the managerial employee exclusion.** *NLRB v. Yeshiva Univ.*, 444 U.S. 672, 100 S.Ct. 856, 63 L.Ed.2d 115 (1980).

C. Termination from Employment

◆ A Louisiana Christian School hired a principal for its elementary/pre-school division under a contract requiring the submission of all employment-related disputes to Bible-based mediation or arbitration by the Institute for Christian Conciliation (ICC). The school discharged the principal before the end of the school year and paid her salary and benefits through the end of the year. She sued the school in a federal district court, alleging breach of contract, gender discrimination, sexual harassment and retaliation. The court granted the school's motion to compel arbitration. According to ICC rules, arbitration was conducted under the Montana Uniform Arbitration Act. After a hearing, an arbitrator held the school breached its contract with the principal. The arbitrator found the school violated the law and Matthew 18, and awarded the principal over $150,000 in damages. However, the arbitrator found no evidence of gender discrimination, sexual harassment or retaliation.

The principal then filed a lawsuit in a Louisiana federal court, seeking confirmation of the award. The court affirmed the award, finding Montana law applied and that arbitration agreements applying a particular state's law will not be overturned unless they conflict with the Federal Arbitration Act (FAA). The school appealed to the Fifth Circuit. **The dispute was subject to the FAA in a broad sense, and was to be analyzed under case law interpreting the FAA. The FAA did not bar parties from structuring their contracts, or preempt state laws on arbitration. The district court improperly held the reference to Montana required application of that state's law to the case.** While Montana law applied to the arbitration, the contract itself was properly interpreted under Louisiana law. The district court incorrectly held the arbitration agreement expanded the scope of judicial review. The case could not be resolved on the face of the contract and required further factual development. The court vacated the judgment and remanded the case for further proceedings. *Prescott v. Northlake Christian School*, 369 F.3d 491 (5th Cir. 2004).

◆ A teacher contracted with a Nebraska Catholic high school for a school year. The contract reserved the school's right to terminate the contract "immediately without notice or hearing, in the event of overt conduct in violation of Catholic Church doctrine, or marriage in violation of Catholic Church doctrine, or any other conduct which reflects grave discredit upon the school." Three months later, the teacher sought to be released from his contract to obtain a public school teaching position. The school refused the teacher's request and informed him that unless he reaffirmed his commitment to the contract, the school would withhold $1,000 in pay and cancel his benefits. When the teacher did not reassert his commitment, the school withheld his pay and canceled his benefits. He petitioned a Nebraska trial court for a declaration that the school constructively terminated his contract. The school responded that the teacher's letter of resignation undermined that claim.

The teacher filed an amended complaint seeking a declaratory judgment that his contract was unconscionable and unenforceable. The school argued that the court lacked jurisdiction to review the terms of the contract because it would be an impermissible inquiry into church doctrine in violation of the First Amendment. The court agreed and the teacher appealed. The Nebraska Court of Appeals affirmed, focusing on the contract clause permitting the school to immediately terminate a teacher for violating a doctrine of the Roman Catholic Church. **The court held an analysis of whether or not the contract was unconscionable would require it to examine Roman Catholic doctrine. This is an impermissible inquiry under the First Amendment.** Courts in other jurisdictions have also decided not to review teaching contracts at religious institutions where the inquiry would eventually lead the court to assess the institution's religious doctrine. *Parizek v. Roncalli Catholic High School of Omaha*, 11 Neb. App. 482, 655 N.W.2d 404 (Neb. App. 2002).

◆   An Indiana Episcopal school hired a head teacher for its middle school. The one-year contract conferred the right of termination on the school "in its sole discretion that a reasonable cause exists to terminate the contract." Early in the school year, the headmaster informed the teacher she was inappropriately brusque with others. Although the headmaster documented the teacher as needing to show improvement in areas such as communication, he offered her a contract for a second year. The teacher was responsible for ensuring adequate supervision at the school's spring dance. However, she attended another school event and assigned four teenagers to serve as chaperones. The headmaster met with a school personnel policy committee after the dance, and the committee agreed with his decision to terminate the teacher's contract. He wrote a letter to parents advising them of five personnel changes for the upcoming school year. The letter stated, "it was in the best interest of the middle school program" that the teacher not return. The teacher sued the school, its board and the headmaster in an Indiana trial court for breach of contract and defamation, adding claims against several parents for interference with her contract. The court awarded summary judgment to the defendants, and the teacher appealed.

The Indiana Court of Appeals rejected the teacher's assertion that the headmaster had no contractual authority to discharge her. The school had explicitly delegated this authority to the headmaster in his employment contract. There was no merit to the teacher's argument that the school breached her contract by failing to provide her with any post-termination notice. **The school was under no contractual duty to provide any written notice, and this was not a condition precedent to discharging her.** Because the breach of contract claim failed, there could be no viable action against the parents for interference with the contract. **The letter to parents contained no defamatory imputation. When an employer does not say anything negative about an employee beyond a vague or neutral statement, a defamation claim should be dismissed.** There was no defamatory meaning in any of the headmaster's written comments. Even if they could be found defamatory, the statements were true and resulted in a complete defense to the defamation claim. The headmaster's statements were also protected by a qualified privilege of common interest. They were made in good faith on a subject that he had a duty to communicate to parents. They had a common interest in knowing about the status of school faculty members. The trial court decision was affirmed. *Gatto v. St. Richard School*, 774 N.E.2d 914 (Ind. Ct. App. 2002).

◆   Santa Fe Preparatory School offered a teacher a full-time teaching contract for a school year. The agreement allowed the school to "refuse to reemploy the teacher without cause, and this contract shall not give rise to any entitlement to or expectation of reemployment." The teacher signed the contract, but added an annotation stating her objection to the last provision. She wrote, "I deserve and expect just cause for [the] non-renewal of continuation of my teaching." The school claimed the teacher was uncooperative with regard to her performance evaluation and did not rehire her. She sued the school in a federal district court for violations of the federal Age Discrimination in Employment Act (ADEA) and state law. A magistrate judge found age was not an issue in the termination decision and dismissed the ADEA claim. In examining the breach of contract claim, the judge characterized the annotation as a counteroffer that was accepted through the school's silence. Consequently, the non-renewal of the teacher's contract could only be for just cause. Since the school did not show just cause, the termination violated state law. The teacher was awarded $60,000 in damages. Both parties appealed aspects of the decision to the Tenth Circuit.

The court affirmed the judgment, but reversed and remanded the award of damages. Under New Mexico law, acceptance of an offer must be unconditional. The court agreed with the determination that the annotation served as a counteroffer. New Mexico law also recognizes that acceptance can be accomplished through silence or performance. **Santa Fe's failure to respond to the addition to the contract and to proceed under the contract bound the school to the disputed provision.** The court held the magistrate judge did not err in this determination. The notation obligated Santa Fe to terminate the teacher for "just cause," and its failure to comply with it resulted in breach of contract. There was no explanation of how the evidence supported the $60,000 amount, and the question was remanded to the district court. *Shively v. Santa Fe Preparatory School*, 21 Fed.Appx. 875 (10th Cir. 2001).

II. STATE AND FEDERAL REGULATION

Private schools must meet state standards for accreditation and compulsory attendance. All teachers are mandatory child abuse reporters.

A. Accreditation

◆ The Ohio superintendent of public instruction registered Golden Christian Academy in the Ohio Pilot Project Scholarship Program. As a condition of registration in this voucher program, Golden signed an "assurance of compliance" stating the school would meet all applicable state minimum standards for nonpublic schools and that all employees who worked with voucher students would pass criminal background investigations. The superintendent informed the school that she intended to revoke its registration for failure to meet the assurance of compliance. A hearing officer ruled that, while Golden was out of compliance, the superintendent lacked the authority to revoke its registration. The state department of education objected to the decision, and the superintendent ultimately revoked Golden's registration. Ohio Rev. Code § 3313.976 deals with the superintendent's authority over and relationship to the scholarship program. Section 3313.976(A) lays out the various requirements a private school must meet in order to register for the voucher program. Section 3313.976(B) provides, "[t]he state superintendent shall revoke the registration of any school if, after a hearing, the superintendent determines that the school is in violation of any of the provisions of division (A) of this section." Golden appealed to an Ohio common pleas court, arguing the superintendent had no authority to revoke the school's registration. The court affirmed the superintendent's decision, and Golden appealed.

Golden argued it currently complied with the assurance of compliance. It claimed the lower court should have either ruled that the superintendent's decision was no longer relevant or remanded the issue for further proceedings. The court rejected this argument, as state law provides that a court is confined to using the evidence initially on the record or newly discovered evidence. The reports noting Golden's current conformance with the assurance of compliance were merely evidence of facts that occurred after the court proceedings began and not newly discovered evidence. Agreeing that Section 3313.976 is unclear about the superintendent's authority in this situation, the court examined the legislature's intent when passing the law. **The court found it would be illogical for the statute to grant the superintendent the power to register a school for the voucher program but not to revoke its registration.** In light of this and the fact that the voucher program's intent was to provide a safe and quality education that met minimal state standards, **the court held the superintendent could revoke Golden's registration.** *Golden Christian Academy v. Zelman,* 760 N.E.2d 889 (Ohio Ct. App. 2001).

B. Sex Abuse and Mandatory Reporting

◆   A Delaware student alleged a priest sexually molested him from the time he was eight years old until he was 17. The priest was a high school teacher who later became the school principal. The student filed a state court lawsuit in 2004, alleging the last incident of molestation occurred in 1985. He claimed that his parents reported the incident to church officials, who allegedly responded by threatening to draw out any litigation the family filed "to maximize the physical, emotional and psychological injury." The parents then entered into a contract with church officials in which they agreed not to file suit so long as the priest was denied the opportunity to be near minors, removed from the school and placed into psychotherapy. The suit against the school and other defendants alleged intentional misrepresentation, assault and battery, breach of contract and negligence. The church claimed the action was untimely under Delaware's two-year statute of limitations for personal injury claims, and the state's three-year limitation period for breach of contract claims. The student claimed his delay in filing his claims was excused because he suppressed any memory of the abuse until less than two years before he filed his lawsuit. He also claimed that the church actively concealed the breach of the contractual agreement.

The court noted that Delaware recognizes "the discovery rule exception" in cases involving child abuse. This exception delays the start of the limitations period based on suppressed memories of sexual abuse. In this case, the student presented expert testimony indicating he had suppressed memories of the abuse. Although he could not rely on the discovery rule exception with respect to the incident he reported to his parents in 1985, he could rely on the exception with respect to 900 other alleged incidents of sexual abuse. The court held that those claims were not barred by the statute of limitations. It also found enough evidence to create a factual issue as to whether the church breached the contract by affirmatively concealing alleged molestations. The court dismissed claims against a bishop who did not begin service to the diocese until 1996. He played no part in directing, ordering or otherwise authorizing the alleged molestations. *Eden v. Oblates of St. Francis de Sales*, No. 04C-01-069 CLS, 2006 WL 3512482 (Del. Super. Ct. 2006).

◆ An Ohio high school student received counseling from a psychologist at her private school for about one year. Sometime during the year, the psychologist made a report to the Cuyahoga County Department of Family Services that she believed the student's father had abused her. The report was investigated and the allegation of abuse deemed unsubstantiated. The father filed suit against the psychologist, claiming she was required to act in good faith when filing the report. An Ohio trial court granted summary judgment for the psychologist, and the father appealed. He also appealed the court's failure to allow him access to certain material relating to the report and investigation.

The court affirmed the judgment, holding **the psychologist was statutorily obligated to report suspected child abuse by virtue of her position as a psychologist, and was entitled to immunity from the father's claims**. Under state child abuse reporting law, if an individual is subject to the mandatory reporting statute, that individual is granted immunity from liability when making a report mandated under Ohio Rev. Code § 2151.421(G)(1). The court stated there is no statutory requirement that a report be made in good faith, despite the father's assertion to the contrary. As for his contention that he was denied investigation materials, the court held they were confidential and privileged. *Liedtke v. Carrington,* 763 N.E.2d 213 (Ohio Ct. App. 2001).

◆ In 1984, a 13-year-old New Jersey child told her mother that her father had sexually abused her. The mother took her to their parish pastor. The child did not disclose the abuse to the pastor, but when she was taken for counseling, she told her Catholic Social Services (CSS) case worker. In 1986, the child reported the abuse to a teacher at her Catholic school. The teacher sent her to the school principal, who allegedly told the child he could not help her because it was too late, and that "sometimes it's just best to leave things in the past." The child took this to mean she should stop talking about the abuse. In 1987, after an incident where her father molested her sister, the child described her own experience with abuse to a pastor. He allegedly told her that she could no longer work her weekend job at the rectory because of her reports of incest to several priests. She interpreted the termination as a directive to stay quiet. The abuse was finally reported to the police in 1991 and the father was sentenced to 10 years in prison. In 1994, the child filed a lawsuit against parties to whom she disclosed the abuse, including three priests, the CSS, the case worker, her parish and the diocese. She alleged their failure to report the abuse caused her mental anguish, that church officials were negligent in hiring the parties to whom she had disclosed abuse, and conspiracy to protect pedophiles and sexual predators.

The case was initially part of a class action suit by children claiming sexual assault by priests in New Jersey and Rhode Island. The court dismissed the case because it was filed over seven years after the child turned 18, when the statute of limitations began to run. She appealed to the Superior Court of New Jersey, objecting to the trial court's decision to exclude her experts' testimony. Her first expert, a priest, stated she suffered from "religious duress," which he explained as "a state of mind whereby a person feels internally compelled to do or not to do something because of a fear induced by a religious power or authority." Her other expert was a psychiatrist who maintained that she did not file her complaint until her father's incarceration because she feared he would hurt her. He added that the failure of the church and other defendants to help her enabled her father to continue abusing her and coercing her to stay quiet. The court held this testimony was opinion without factual basis. **Neither the child nor her experts made any link between her failure to file a complaint within the statute of limitations and the defendants' actions.** The court failed to see how her father's incarceration "freed her from her fear of excommunication or eternal damnation." It affirmed the dismissal of the case. *Smith v. Estate of Reverend P. Kelly*, 778 A.2d 1162 (N.J. Super. Ct. App. Div. 2001).

C. Taxation

1. Federal Income Taxation

◆   Section 501(c)(3) of the Internal Revenue Code provides that "corporations ... organized and operated exclusively for religious, charitable ... or educational purposes" are entitled to tax exempt status. The Internal Revenue Service (IRS) routinely granted tax exemptions under Section 501(c)(3) to private schools regardless of whether they had racially discriminatory admissions policies. In 1970, however, **the IRS concluded that it could no longer grant tax-exempt status to racially discriminatory private schools because such schools were not "charitable" within the meaning of Section 501(c)(3).** Two private colleges whose racial admissions policies were rooted in their interpretations of the Bible sued to prevent the IRS from interpreting the federal tax laws in this manner. The U.S. Supreme Court rejected the challenge and upheld the IRS's interpretation. The Court's ruling was based on what it perceived as the strong public policy against racial discrimination in education. Because the colleges were operating in violation of that public policy, the colleges could not be considered "charitable" under Section 501(c)(3). Thus, they were ineligible for tax exemptions. The Court held that the denial of an exemption did not impermissibly burden the colleges' alleged religious freedom interest in practicing racial discrimination. *Bob Jones Univ. v. U.S.*, 461 U.S. 574, 103 S.Ct. 2017, 76 L.Ed.2d 157 (1983).

◆   Parents of African-American public school children sought a federal court order requiring the IRS to adopt more stringent standards for determining whether private schools had racially discriminatory admissions policies. The parents claimed IRS standards were too lax and that certain private schools were practicing racial discrimination and were still obtaining tax exemptions. **The Supreme Court dismissed the parents' claims, ruling they had shown no injury to themselves as a result of the allegedly lax IRS standards.** None of their children had sought enrollment at the private schools involved, and the abstract stigma attached to living in a community with racially discriminatory private schools was also insufficient to show actual injury. Further, the parents' theory that denial of exempt status to such schools would result in greater white student enrollment in area public schools, and hence result in a greater degree of public school integration, was only speculation. *Allen v. Wright*, 468 U.S. 737, 104 S.Ct. 3315, 82 L.Ed.2d 556 (1984).

2. State and Local Taxation

◆   Arizona Rev. Stat. § 43-1089 allows taxpayers to deduct up to $500 from state income taxes each year for voluntary contributions to qualified "school tuition organizations" (STOs) that distribute grants to students attending private schools. Married couples filing joint returns may deduct up to $625 annually for these donations. The law does not prevent STOs from directing money to schools that provide religious instruction or have admissions preferences on the basis of religion or religious affiliation. Section 43-1089 survived a state court challenge in *Kotterman v. Killian*, 193 Ariz. 273, 972 P.2d 606 (Ariz. 1999).

Another group of taxpayers filed a federal court challenge against Arizona state officials, asserting Section 43-1089 violated the Establishment Clause. State officials opposed the action on grounds including the federal Tax Injunction Act (TIA). The court held the TIA required dismissal of the case, and the taxpayers appealed. The U.S. Court of Appeals, Ninth Circuit, held the act was intended to prevent federal courts from interfering with state efforts to assess, levy and collect taxes. The action did not adversely affect the state's ability to raise revenue and, if successful, would increase state tax revenues. The court reversed and remanded the district court's judgment.

State officials appealed to the U.S. Supreme Court. The Court analyzed TIA language preventing federal district courts from enjoining, suspending or restraining "the assessment, levy or collection of any tax under State law where a plain, speedy and efficient remedy may be had in the courts of such State." 28 U.S.C. § 1341. It found the meaning of the TIA term "assessment" was the crucial inquiry in this case. "Assessment" involved the recording of the amount a taxpayer owed the government. While closely tied to the collection of a tax, assessment was only the official recording of tax liability, not the entire plan or scheme for taxing. Otherwise, the words "levy" or "collection" would not be necessary in the TIA. The Court stated the TIA shields state tax collections from federal court restraints. Previous TIA decisions involved state taxpayers seeking federal court orders that would enable them to avoid state taxes. The Court had never interpreted the TIA as restraining state taxpayers from a federal constitutional challenge to tax benefits. A line of federal cases interpreting the TIA and the Anti-Injunction Act held **the TIA did not immunize from review all aspects of state tax administration. It only prevented federal courts from interfering with state tax collections. The Court held the "decades-long understanding" of courts was that the TIA did not bar a third-party constitutional challenge to tax benefits such as this action.** In a "procession of cases" indistinguishable from this one, no justice had ever raised a TIA objection requiring dismissal. The Court affirmed the judgment for the taxpayers. *Hibbs v. Winn*, 542 U.S. 88, 124 S.Ct. 2276, 159 L.E.2d 172 (2004).

◆   A Maine nonprofit corporation operated a summer camp for children of the Christian Science faith. Activities included supervised prayer, meditation and church services. Weekly tuition for the camp was roughly $400. A Maine statute exempted charitable institutions from real estate and personal property taxes. However, institutions operated primarily for the benefit of nonresidents were only entitled to a more limited tax benefit, and then only if the weekly charge for services did not exceed $30 per person. Because most of the campers were not Maine residents and weekly tuition was over $30, the corporation was ineligible for the state tax exemption. It petitioned the town for a refund of the taxes it had paid, arguing that the exemption violated the Commerce Clause of the U.S. Constitution. The case reached the U.S. Supreme Court.

The Court noted that the Commerce Clause was designed to override restrictive and conflicting state commercial regulations that fostered local interests and prejudiced nonresidents. It found that the camp was engaged in commerce not only as a purchaser, but also as a provider of goods and services. **The Court held a real estate tax, like any other tax, could impermissibly burden interstate commerce and noted that if the exemption applied to for-profit entities, there would be no question of a Commerce Clause violation.** It found no reason why an entity's nonprofit status should exclude it from Commerce Clause coverage and noted that nonprofit institutions are subject to other laws regulating commerce as well as federal antitrust laws. Finally, the Court found the town could not defend the statute by showing that it advanced a legitimate purpose that could not be obtained by reasonable, nondiscriminatory alternatives. *Camps Newfound/Owatonna, Inc. v. Town of Harrison, Maine*, 520 U.S. 564, 117 S.Ct. 1590, 137 L.Ed.2d 852 (1997).

◆   Burr and Burton Academy is a Vermont private high school operated by Burr and Burton Seminary, a nonprofit corporation. In 1996, Burr and Burton constructed "Head House" as a residence for the academy's headmaster. Traditionally, housing had been part of the headmaster's compensation package. In April 1997, the town of Manchester appraised Head House at $290,000 and decided it was subject to applicable property taxes. The next year, the town added a Burr and Burton student dormitory to the taxable property list. However, the dormitory property had been placed on the real estate market in 1994 and had been leased to various tenants until being sold in 1999. Burr and Burton challenged the appraisals, asserting the properties fell within a state property tax exemption for property owned by educational institutions.

A state court granted summary judgment to the town, finding neither property was involved in the running of the school. On appeal, the state supreme court held **Head House qualified for the property tax exemption because it served an educational purpose.** During the 1998-99 academic year, Head House held 11 school-related events. Case precedents in other jurisdictions have held that residences for headmasters and faculty serve an educational purpose. The fact that Head House was part of a compensation package did not prevent it from qualifying for the exemption. Head House was exempt from taxation under 32 Vt. Stat. Ann. § 3802(4). However, **the dormitory property was ineligible for the exemption. The court found that it had not been used for any educational purpose** since 1994. Burr and Burton's lease of the property violated the section of the statutory tax exemption provision requiring that the property not be used for "general commercial purposes." As the dormitory property had been used for commercial purposes, the academy was required to pay the assessed property taxes. The lower court's decision was reversed with respect to Head House and upheld regarding the dormitory property. *Burr and Burton Seminary v. Town of Manchester*, 782 A.2d 1149 (Vt. 2001).

◆ In a companion case to *Burr and Burton Seminary v. Town of Manchester*, the Berkshire School sought a tax exemption for a 212-acre parcel of land. The land had been donated to the school, which intended to use the property for a student mountain program and environmental science classes. The town of Reading appraised the undeveloped land at $250,000 and assessed taxes against Berkshire. Berkshire grieved the appraisal, asserting that under the language of 32 Vt. Stat. Ann. § 3802(4), mere ownership was sufficient for the exemption. A state court agreed and the town appealed to the Vermont Supreme Court.

The court reversed the judgment under its decision in *Burr and Burton Seminary*. It reiterated the holding that an educational use requirement was implicit in the statutory language. **Even though the land was not being used for any purpose, educational, commercial or otherwise, nonuse would not qualify for exemption** under the statute. If Berkshire used the land for educational purposes in the future, "the issue of exemption may be raised again at the next appraisal." *Berkshire School v. Town of Reading*, 781 A.2d 282 (Vt. 2001).

◆ Pennsylvania's Institutions of Purely Public Charity Act exempts qualifying entities from real estate taxes. A private school in Pottstown was founded as an all-boys school, but started admitting females in 1998. In 1996, the Pottstown School District and the local borough petitioned the county board of assessment appeals to remove the school's real estate tax exemption. They argued the school was barred from tax exemption because the statutory exemption states that it includes charities that benefit a "substantial and indefinite class of persons." The borough and school district claimed the school's policy of denying female students admission demonstrated it did not benefit a substantial and indefinite class of persons. The board affirmed the school's tax-exempt status, and the school district appealed to a state court. Meanwhile, the school amended its admittance policy to include females. The district successfully argued the school was discriminatory and should not be considered a public charity under the statute. The court initially held for the district but then vacated its order, finding the school's all-male admittance policy did not disqualify it under the Purely Public Charity Act.

The Pennsylvania Commonwealth Court explained that the case involved a state law claim to determine whether the school was a purely public charity. It applied a two-part test to determine if the exemption was authorized by the state constitution as an "institution of purely public charity," and if the Pennsylvania General Assembly enacted legislation to exempt the property. The state constitution provides that only "portion[s] of real property of such institution, which [are] actually and regularly used for the purposes of the institution" may be exempt from taxation. The court held the case turned on whether the school benefited a substantial and indefinite class of persons who were legitimate subjects of charity. **Based on state court precedents, the school's exclusion of females did not undermine its status as a purely public charity under the state constitution.** Once the court determined the Pennsylvania Constitution did not bar the disputed tax exemption, it examined whether the state legislature had statutorily exempted the property. The court found that application of the Purely Public Charity Act did not alter the school's tax-exempt status. Although the statute specifically excludes those schools that discriminate in violation of federal or state law, **Pennsylvania courts have long held that single-sex schools are considered purely public charities. The court stated if the legislature had intended to exclude this type of school from the statute, it would have done so.** The school was exempt from real estate taxation as a purely public charity under the Pennsylvania Constitution and the Charity Act during the disputed time period. *Pottstown School Dist. v. Hill School*, 786 A.2d 312 (Pa. Commw. Ct. 2001).

◆   The Illinois Education Association-NEA sued state officials in an Illinois court for a declaration that 35 ILCS 5/201(m) violated the state constitution. The law allowed taxpayers to take a $500 income tax credit equal to 25% of their "qualified education expenses" on behalf of a full-time K-12 student at a public or qualified nonpublic school. "Qualified education expense" was defined as an amount in excess of $250 for tuition, book fees and lab fees. The complaining parties alleged the credit supported private religious schools, since public schools did not charge tuition or book and lab fees in excess of $250 per year for any student. They asserted the credit reduced state revenue and was the equivalent of a legislative appropriation for private schools, the vast majority of which were sectarian. The court dismissed the case, holding that money accruing from the credit did not constitute "public funds."

The complaining parties appealed to the Illinois Appellate Court, which rejected their argument that the term "public fund" has a broad, expansive meaning that includes tax credits. The credit was not an "appropriation," as they argued. **The statute had the secular purpose of assisting parents with their educational costs and furthered the state interest of ensuring students were well educated. Private schools relieved taxpayers of the burden of educating students who would otherwise attend public schools.** The credit was available to parents of public and private school children alike, and funds became available to private schools only as the result of private choices by parents. **Any attenuated benefit to private schools was created by a neutral tax program that was part of a general government program that did not unconstitutionally advance religion.** The tax credit did not create religious entanglement with the government, since its administration involved only a determination of whether expenses claimed by taxpayers were "qualified." This was no different than any number of other tax deductions and credits allowed by state law. The court rejected the complaining parties' arguments that the tax credit discriminated against low-income families and was not for public purposes. It affirmed the judgment for the state revenue director and department of revenue. *Toney v. Bower*, 744 N.E.2d 351 (Ill. App. Ct. 2001).

III. PRIVATE SCHOOL STUDENT RIGHTS

Private school students do not enjoy the same level of constitutional protection as the courts have granted to public school students. Generally, courts have demonstrated a reluctance to interfere with private school academic and disciplinary policies. Federal discrimination and civil rights statutes also only provide limited protection. For example, civil rights cases attempting to assert private school liability under a constitutional theory or federal statutory right pursuant to 42 U.S.C. § 1983 require a determination that the school is a state actor. Although a private school may become a state actor based on performance of duties normally associated with government entities or close cooperation with the government, the U.S. Supreme Court in Rendell-Baker v. Kohn, 457 U.S. 830, 102 S.Ct. 2764, 73 L.Ed.2d 418 (1982), *limited the circumstances in which an ostensibly private institution can be found to be acting "under the color of state law."*

A. Admissions and Other School Policies

Although the U.S. Supreme Court has applied 42 U.S.C. § 1981 to private schools to prohibit race discrimination, the Court noted that its holding did not extend to religious schools that practiced racial exclusion on religious grounds. Similarly, Title VI of the Civil Rights Act of 1964 (42 U.S.C. § 2000d) prohibits discrimination on the basis of race, color, or national origin but only applies to "programs or activities" receiving federal financial assistance. In the context of sex discrimination, Title IX applies to recipients of federal funding but also provides a specific exclusion which allows private undergraduate institutions to discriminate on the basis of sex in admissions (20 U.S.C. § 1681(a)(1)).

◆ In *Runyon v. McCrary*, the U.S. Supreme Court relied on 42 U.S.C. § 1981 to declare that black students could not be excluded from all-white elementary schools. In this Virginia case, the parents of black students sought to enter into contractual relationships with private nonreligious schools for educational services advertised and offered to members of the general public. The students were denied admission because of their race. **The Supreme Court recognized that while parents have a First Amendment right to send their children to educational institutions that promote the belief that racial segregation is desirable, it does not follow that the practice of excluding racial minorities from such institutions is also protected by the same principle.** The school's argument that Section 1981 does not govern private acts of racial discrimination was rejected. However, the Court observed that its holding did not extend to religious schools that practiced racial exclusion on religious grounds. *Runyon v. McCrary*, 427 U.S. 160, 96 S.Ct. 2586, 49 L.E.2d 415 (1976).

◆ A non-native Hawaiian student unsuccessfully applied to the Kamehameha Schools, a private K-12 educational institution created via a charitable trust. The trust was established by the last direct descendant of the Hawaiian monarchy and was specifically dedicated to the education of native Hawaiians. The school admits non-native Hawaiians only if openings remain after all qualified applicants of Hawaiian ancestry have been accepted. The unsuccessful applicant had no Hawaiian ancestry but was deemed a "competitive applicant." The school conceded that he probably would have been admitted if he was of Hawaiian ancestry. The applicant claimed he was denied admission on the basis of his race, in violation of 42 U.S.C. § 1981. A federal district court upheld the schools' admissions policy, but a three-judge panel of the Ninth Circuit said it amounted to unlawful race discrimination. The full Ninth Circuit reconsidered the case. A majority of the full panel affirmed the district court's decision that the policy was legally permissible. After concluding it was proper to apply principles used to analyze Title VII claims of employment discrimination, the court determined that the applicant had made a preliminary showing of bias.

The school conceded that it considered the race of applicants when making admissions decisions. Because the school responded that the policy was nondiscriminatory and remedial, **the key question in the case was whether the policy constituted a valid affirmative action plan. The court held the policy responded to a significant imbalance in the educational achievement levels of native Hawaiians as compared to other ethnic groups.** "Native Hawaiian students," the court said, "are systemically disadvantaged in the classroom." The admissions preference did not "unnecessarily trammel" the rights of non-native Hawaiians. The record did not show that students of non-Hawaiian ancestry lacked adequate educational opportunities. Congress has repeatedly recognized that native Hawaiians have faced difficult challenges in the educational arena. The policy did no more than was necessary to correct the imbalance suffered by native Hawaiians. It admitted non-native Hawaiians when openings remained following the acceptance of all qualified Hawaiian applicants. The preference will be applied only until the effects of past discrimination are remedied, and the court held it was a valid affirmative action plan. *Doe v. Kamehameha Schools*, 470 F.3d 827 (9th Cir. 2006).

◆   An Ohio statute required that all public schools administer proficiency tests to their students. The statute was then amended to include testing of all students, both public and private. The tests were first given in the ninth grade, and each student had to pass by the end of the twelfth grade in order to graduate. The tests covered reading, writing, mathematics, science and citizenship. Failure to administer the tests would result in the loss of the school's charter. A group of private secondary schools and an association of private schools filed suit against the state in an Ohio federal district court, alleging that the testing requirement violated their rights under the First and Fourteenth Amendments. The court held for the state, and the private schools appealed to the Sixth Circuit.

The court considered the schools' argument that the statute infringed on Fourteenth Amendment rights of parents to direct, by choice of school, the education of their children. The statute, in effect, eradicated the distinction between public and private education and therefore the strict scrutiny standard should apply. The court instead applied the rational basis standard, finding the state need only show that the testing requirement was rationally related to a legitimate governmental interest. **Since the state had an interest in ensuring certain educational standards were met, the schools' rights were not compromised.** However, the court noted that a more intrusive testing requirement could displace a private school's discretion to design its own educational program. **The schools' First Amendment rights were not violated because the testing requirement did not restrict the teaching of any particular material.** The court affirmed the district court's decision. *Ohio Ass'n of Independent Schools v. Goff*, 92 F.3d 419 (6th Cir. 1996).

B. Athletics and Extracurricular Activities

◆ Tennessee Secondary School Athletic Association (TSSAA) recruiting rules were considered for the third time in recent years by the U.S. Court of Appeals, Sixth Circuit. The court held the TSSAA could not claim immunity against antitrust claims. Brentwood Academy, a TSSAA member, has had very successful interscholastic athletic programs, especially in football. In 1998, Brentwood's football coach wrote letters to eighth-grade boys who had enrolled at the academy, inviting them to practice with the team. He then made follow-up calls to their families. The coach also supplied two students with free tickets to Brentwood football games. Public high school coaches reported the coach's conduct, and the TSSAA investigated. It then fined Brentwood $3,000 for violating recruiting rules and excluded the school from football and basketball tournaments for one school year. Brentwood sued the TSSAA in a federal district court under 42 U.S.C. § 1983, a federal law that contains no substantive rights but provides a legal cause of action to vindicate rights created by other federal laws and the U.S. Constitution. The court held the TSSAA was a state actor that violated Brentwood's First Amendment rights. The TSSAA appealed to the Sixth Circuit, which reversed the judgment. The U.S. Supreme Court held the TSSAA had a public character and was a state actor for Section 1983 claims. *Brentwood Academy v. Tennessee Secondary School Athletic Ass'n*, 531 U.S. 288, 121 S.Ct. 924, 148 L.Ed.2d 807 (2001).

On remand, the Sixth Circuit found the TSSAA's recruiting rules, on their face, did not violate the First Amendment. Prohibiting coaches from contacting students was not a total ban on communication. The case was reversed and remanded to the district court to decide if the TSSAA unconstitutionally applied its rules to Brentwood. The district court held for the TSSAA on an antitrust claim by Brentwood, but otherwise held for the school. The parties appealed to the Sixth Circuit. **The court held the TSSAA's application of the recruiting rules to Brentwood based on the contacts between the coach and students violated the First Amendment.** While the TSSAA had a substantial interest in protecting students from exploitation, the TSSAA did not punish Brentwood in a way that would ensure student-athletes were not being exploited. TSSAA's use of its recruiting regulations to punish Brentwood seemed to "burden substantially more speech than is necessary." The court held the TSSAA's decision to punish the school for providing free football tickets to two students did not violate the school's due process rights. However, the district court had properly found due process violations in TSSAA hearings on the case. Despite the due process violations, the TSSAA's executive director was entitled to qualified immunity. The due process rights of a private school in a state athletic association action were not clearly established. The TSSAA was not immune from Brentwood's antitrust claims. Nothing indicated the state actively supervised the TSSAA. The judgment was reversed on that issue and the case was remanded for further activity. *Brentwood Academy v. Tennessee Secondary School Athletic Ass'n*, 442 F.3d 410 (6th Cir. 2006).

◆ Maine parents chose to home-school their children for religious reasons. Maine law Section 5021(5) permits home-schooled children to participate in athletic programs at public high schools located in their attendance areas. The Maine Principals Association (MPA) operates interscholastic athletics programs in the state. An MPA rule prohibited home-schooled students from participating in private school athletic programs, except on an exhibition basis. The MPA refused the parents' request to allow their children to fully participate on the track team of a Christian School. The family challenged the MPA's denial of the request in a federal district court on constitutional grounds. The claims alleged violations of parental due process rights to educational choice and the First Amendment right to religious freedom. The court refused to grant relief, finding the MPA rule did not violate any constitutional rights. In its analysis, **the court drew a distinction between the constitutional protections available regarding education and the lack of constitutional protection for individuals interested only in competing in interscholastic athletics**.

The Due Process Clause of the Fourteenth Amendment prohibits states from denying parents the option of sending their children to private schools. The court stated there is no constitutional right to participation in athletics. The fact that private school athletic programs were not fully open to home-schooled students did not establish that Maine burdened the right of parental educational choice. Since the court found that the family' right to educational choice was not burdened, it declined to address their related substantive due process claim. The court found the parents' free exercise claim untenable. **Since MPA rules were religiously neutral, they would generally be considered constitutional, even if they incidentally burdened a religious practice.** There was no showing that the MPA rule barring complete participation in athletics unduly burdened the family's free exercise of religion. *Pelletier v. Maine Principals' Ass'n*, 261 F.Supp.2d 10 (D. Me. 2003).

C. Breach of Contract

1. Educational Programs

◆ The mother of a student who attended a private Kentucky school became dissatisfied with his progress. A teacher recommended another school and more contact between the student and his estranged father. During a phone conversation with a parent volunteer, the mother said there could be trouble for the school if the student's father became involved. This was taken as a threat that the father could hurt the teacher or the school. The teacher was informed of the conversation and filed a criminal complaint alleging the mother had made terroristic threats. The complaint was eventually resolved, and the mother agreed to not have any inappropriate or unlawful contact with either the school or the teacher. The mother then sued the school, teacher and parent volunteer in a Kentucky court, alleging educational malpractice. She claimed the teacher and parent volunteer defamed her by initiating criminal proceedings and maliciously prosecuted the charges. The court awarded summary judgment to the school, teacher and volunteer, and the mother appealed.

The Kentucky Court of Appeals found no evidence to support the mother's claims. It held **Kentucky law does not recognize claims for educational malpractice** and upheld the summary judgment on this claim. **The court held the breach of contract and fraud claims against the school were also not viable. These claims were very similar to the educational malpractice claim, and the contract did not cover any aspect of the student's academic performance.** There was no fraud, since no school employee or representative ever promised the student would accomplish specific things. Turning to the defamation claim, the court said the trial court correctly concluded any defamatory statements were privileged. For a privileged statement to be defamatory, it must be made with actual malice. Since there was no evidence of actual malice, and the statements were privileged, summary judgment was proper. The court rejected the mother's assertion that the trial court erroneously granted summary judgment to the teacher and parent volunteer on her malicious prosecution claim. Because the resolution of the criminal charges was not favorable to the mother, she failed to meet one of the essential elements of a malicious prosecution claim. *McGurl v. Friends School Inc.*, No. 2002-CA-000115-MR, 2003 WL 1343248 (Ky. Ct. App. 2003).

◆ A high school senior had attended a private preparatory school in Georgia since kindergarten. She was taking a make-up math test in a study hall when a classmate showed her how to do a problem correctly. While the student was receiving the correct answer, a staff member and a math teacher caught both students cheating. The student was permanently expelled from school, even though she was within days of taking her final exams before graduation. In the Honor Council proceedings that led to her expulsion, the school justified its action by noting that during the prior year, the student had been found guilty of an honor code violation regarding an "intent to cheat." The student and her parents sued the school in a Georgia trial court for intentional infliction of emotional distress, breach of fundamental fairness and due process, and breach of contract. The court granted the school's motion for summary judgment, and the student appealed to the Court of Appeals of Georgia.

The court reviewed a Georgia Supreme Court case, *Woodruff v. Georgia State Univ.*, 304 S.E.2d 697 (Ga. 1983), which held **the court would not review a teacher's academic assessment of a student's work.** The court of appeals found that the case applied to this situation. **Cheating is a fundamental breach of trust by the student.** The student and her parents had contracted with the school to impliedly do four things essential to the student-school relationship: diligently seek to learn and perform as a good student; be honest and responsible; maintain reasonable discipline and self-discipline in the academic setting; and pay fees, tuition, and expenses. Failure to render any one at any time was such a fundamental breach of the contract as to result in termination of the student's relationship with the school. The court held there was a total failure of consideration, and breach of contract on the part of the student and her parents. **The expulsion was not arbitrary or capricious, but a reasonable**

exercise of administrative and academic discretion. There was no violation of fundamental fairness in the treatment of the student. The court affirmed the judgment for the school. *Blaine v. Savannah Country Day School*, 491 S.E.2d 446 (Ga. Ct. App. 1997).

2. Tuition

◆   A student attended a private Ohio college for two or three weeks in the fall of 2002 because he had a problem with his financial aid package. The college told him he could not continue to attend until he paid his tuition. He withdrew before a withdrawal deadline. The college sued the student in an Ohio court for $6,000 in tuition, interest and other expenses. The student testified he had not participated in the school's activities or used the technologies the school billed him for. The court held in his favor. On appeal, the Court of Appeals of Ohio stated the college needed to submit evidence of a binding agreement to prevail.

The court noted *Lake Ridge Academy v. Carney*, 613 N.E.2d 183 (Ohio 1993), which involved a parent's reservation for a student in a private elementary school. In that case, the Supreme Court of Ohio held when a parent is given the option to cancel the agreement before a certain date without incurring a penalty for the full tuition and does not do so, the parent may become liable for the full tuition if the contract allows it. **A parent's notification of cancellation, if given after the option date, is ineffective to discharge this liability. Subsequent failure to make scheduled tuition payments is a breach of contract.** The court of appeals held that without a contract, it could not determine if the student owed tuition. Accordingly, the judgment was affirmed. *Hiram College v. Courtad*, 834 N.E.2d 432 (Ohio Ct. App. 2005).

◆   A Georgia parent who removed her children from a private school based on concerns about their academic progress was still obligated to pay the balance of her tuition bill. The parent became dissatisfied with the academic progress of her children, who were both unable to read. She removed them from the school and enrolled them in a public school. The parent also hired a private learning center for the children. After she refused to pay the balance of her tuition bill, the private school sued her for breach of contract in a Georgia trial court. The parent filed a counterclaim, asserting the school breached its educational obligations and seeking reimbursement for her tuition payments and private learning center costs. The court held for the school, and the parent appealed.

The Georgia Court of Appeals explained it would not reverse the lower court's findings of fact as long as there was any evidence to support them. **The court found the private school had performed its obligations under the contract by providing the children with a school, teachers and facilities. Since the school performed its part of the contract, the parent was required to perform hers by paying tuition.** When she refused, she breached the contract. The court affirmed the judgment for the private school. *Fuller v. Lakeview Academy*, 261 Ga.App. 607, 583 S.E.2d 282 (Ga. Ct. App. 2003).

◆   A Connecticut private school filed a breach of contract and unjust enrichment action against a parent for his failure to pay his three sons' tuition.

A state court entered a default judgment against the parent when he continually failed to appear for a settlement conference. An attorney trial referee then conducted a hearing on damages and granted the school reimbursement for the deficient tuition payments plus interest totaling $68,819.66 as well as $26.11 per day if the parent failed to pay the tuition within two days of the judgment. The parent filed motions to open the default and object to the attorney referee's report. Both motions were denied, and the parent appealed.

The Appellate Court of Connecticut stated that a trial court can proceed with a case even if a defendant fails to appear in court. Although the parent had been diagnosed with hypertension, a letter explaining his poor health was not filed on record until the day the trial court entered judgment against him. **The court upheld the judgment against the parent. However, the amount of the judgment was improper.** The school's complaint sought recovery of tuition for one academic year, but the attorney trial referee granted tuition reimbursement for two years. The amount of interest had also been miscalculated. The case was remanded for a reconsideration of the amount of damages. *Brunswick School v. Hutter*, 730 A.2d 1206 (Conn. App. Ct. 1999).

D. Discipline, Suspension and Expulsion

◆ Four 14-year-old Alabama private school girls played strip poker at a party in a private home. After leaving, they communicated electronically with boys who had been at the party. A boy convinced the girls to photograph themselves in the nude and e-mail him the pictures. The boys promised the girls that they would delete the pictures after viewing them. Instead, they circulated the photos to others. Copies of the photos were distributed throughout the school and an explicit photo was set as the wallpaper on a computer in a sixth-grade computer lab, leading to a shutdown of the system. The school's headmaster expelled the girls and the boy who had taken responsibility for distributing the photos.

The girls sued the school, headmaster and the school board chair for breach of contract, negligence, invasion of privacy, outrage and related claims. In a separate suit, the girls sued two male classmates and the parent of a third male student for negligence, invasion of privacy, fraud and defamation. The two suits were consolidated, and an Alabama trial court granted summary judgment to the boys and the parent. On appeal, the Supreme Court of Alabama rejected claims that the school breached the enrollment contract by failing to provide them with due process during the investigation. **Although the headmaster did not meet with the students before dismissing them, he met with their parents, informed them of the situation, showed them the photos, and gave them a chance to respond. Each of the students and their parents signed a pledge in which they promised to abide by the student handbook and stated they were aware of its provisions.** The handbook expressly provided that "[o]ff-campus behavior which is illicit, immoral, illegal and/or which reflects adversely on [the school] subjects the student to immediate expulsion." The school did not breach the enrollment contract. The court also rejected the claims against one of the male students and the third student's parent. *S.B. v. St. James School*, No. 1031517, 2006 WL 3530651 (Ala. 2006).

◆   An evangelical Christian student attended a psychology program at a private Minnesota university. After he made anti-gay statements, an evaluation committee required him to address his "general lack of social awareness and sensitivity." The student failed to timely develop a written plan to address the committee's concerns. He then sued the university and three faculty members, saying they violated his constitutional rights to free speech, freedom of religion, due process, equal protection, and freedom of conscience. The student added state law and common law claims. He claimed the university should be subject to constitutional claims because it issued degrees that were a prerequisite to engaging in the state-licensed activity of practicing psychology. The court rejected the student's arguments. **While private institutions that exercise governmental power may be sued for constitutional violations, the university did not exercise any government authority.** As the private education of psychologists is not an exclusive state function, the university could not be considered a state actor and could not be sued for constitutional claims. The court rejected the student's other claims, including religious bias, breach of contract, and libel and slander. The university was entitled to summary judgment. *Schumacher v. Argosy Educ. Group*, No. 05-531 (DWF/AJB), 2006 WL 3511795 (D. Minn. 2006).

◆   A Maine student attended a private school under a tuition agreement with a school district. He entered a gym with a soft drink, in violation of school regulations. When a teacher removed the drink, the student responded with profanity, and then used profanity toward the dean and pushed aside a table. A 10-day suspension was immediately issued and the student was not permitted to return without documentation of a "safety evaluation" by a psychologist or psychiatrist. The school did not provide him with notice or an opportunity for a hearing. The student's parents were unable to schedule a psychiatric evaluation until after the expiration of the 10-day suspension. Eventually, a therapist met with school officials and the student was permitted to return to school. As a result of the delay, his 10-day suspension increased to 17 days. The student sued the private school, the school district and officials from both entities in a federal district court, alleging federal and state due process violations. The court granted summary judgment against the student on his federal law claims.

On appeal, the First Circuit stated that to prevail on a Section 1983 due process claim, the student had to establish the private school was a state actor. Several doctrines transform a private entity into a state actor, including the "public function" doctrine and the "entwinement" doctrine. Since neither doctrine applied in this case, the private school was not a state actor for Section 1983 purposes. The court found no indication the school disciplined students in an outrageous manner. Moreover, the student might have redress in state court under a contractual claim. While the district and its superintendent were state actors, **there was no due process violation when they failed to include procedures governing discipline in the tuition agreement**. The court held the district was not obligated to ensure that the private school provided the student with the same due process procedures the district would be required to provide. *Logiodice v. Trustees of Maine Cent. Institute*, 296 F.3d 22 (1st Cir. 2002).

◆   A New Mexico student was expelled from a college preparatory military high school for physically attacking his roommate. The student, who received a hearing before a board of school officials, admitted the attack was racially motivated. The school superintendent upheld the expulsion. The student then sued officials and the school, alleging he was denied his constitutional right to due process and equal protection. He claimed he was not given adequate notice of the charges against him before the hearing. A federal district court granted the school's summary judgment motion, and the student appealed.

The U.S. Court of Appeals, Tenth Circuit, cited the U.S. Supreme Court's ruling in *Goss v. Lopez*, 419 U.S. 565 (1975), which set the due process standard for short-term school suspensions. The *Goss* court determined that students are entitled to written or oral notice of the charges against them, an explanation of the evidence obtained by authorities and a chance to present their side of the story. **The student was well aware of the allegations against him since he had received verbal notice of the hearing regarding the assault.** His argument that he was not informed of the charge of racism against him failed. The record showed the student was expelled for the assault, not because he was a racist. He claimed other local schools would have given him written notice, and that the school violated his equal protection rights. The court agreed with the school that this difference in procedure was related to the school's military nature. "**The principle difference between a military school and other schools is the degree of discipline imposed on students... . This difference is a fundamental ingredient of a military education.**" The award of summary judgment was upheld. *Watson v. Beckel*, 242 F.3d 1237 (10th Cir. 2001).

◆   An eighth-grade Ohio parochial school student sold a broken BB gun to a classmate for $17 and a social studies outline. A few months later, the classmate brought the gun to school and sold it to a third student. The boy who purchased the gun later used it to threaten a classmate. The principal learned that the student had originally owned the gun. She interviewed him several times and met with his parents, the pastor and the school's attorney. The student eventually admitted selling the gun and turning in the social studies outline as his own. The principal notified his parents that he would have to withdraw from school within a week or be expelled under the school's "zero-tolerance" weapons policy. The parents sued the school in a state court, alleging the expulsion was a breach of contract and a violation of their son's due process rights. The court granted summary judgment to the school, and they appealed.

The Ohio Court of Appeals stated that **courts should only intervene in private school disciplinary decisions if the evidence demonstrates the school clearly violated the terms of the contract or clearly abused its discretion by applying its disciplinary standards in a way that breaches the contract.** The court held **the school did not abuse its discretion when it expelled the student, because it was well within the terms and purpose of the handbook's disciplinary policy.** His actions violated the behavioral norms set by the school in the handbook by initially lying about the gun sale and plagiarizing a social studies outline. In addition, he facilitated the classmate's misconduct. The trial court did not overlook testimony of the former principal who disputed the "zero-tolerance" weapons policy. The appeals court rejected the parents' defamation claim, since they could not show a letter sent to all parents contained false statements. The court affirmed the decision and awarded attorneys' fees to the school. *Riley v. St. Ann Catholic School*, No. 78129, 2000 WL 1902430 (Ohio Ct. App. 2000).

◆ Just before the start of his senior year, a New Jersey parochial school student and his parents were informed he was being placed on disciplinary probation for the first semester. During the fall semester, the student was suspended once. In February, the student was suspended again. Shortly thereafter, two classmates told the assistant principal that the student was using and selling steroids, and bragging about relieving himself in lockers. At a meeting between the student, his parents and the assistant principal, the student was informed that he was suspended indefinitely. The school's disciplinary committee determined the student should be dismissed from school and made that recommendation to the principal. When the student refused to withdraw, he was dismissed. The student then sued the school in state court, claiming his dismissal violated the Due Process Clauses of the U.S. and New Jersey Constitutions. The school unsuccessfully sought to dismiss the case.

On appeal, the Superior Court of New Jersey, Appellate Division held the school complied with due process requirements. Because the school was a private parochial school, it could not be considered a state actor (as required to establish a federal due process violation). This was so even though it received state aid. For the same reason, the court held that the due process provisions of the New Jersey Constitution were not implicated. No state court had addressed the procedural requirements applicable to private school expulsions. While the protections required when expelling a public school student or a college student were well established, those required for private high school students were uncertain. **The court developed a two-part test, which first required schools to follow their established procedures for dismissal and expulsion, and to ensure that those procedures were "fundamentally fair."** The court held the school followed its procedures before expelling the student. The second step was also met, as the school notified the student of the allegations against him, gave him an opportunity to defend himself, and allowed him to appeal his suspension and dismissal to the school director. Under these circumstances, the dismissal was fundamentally fair. *Hernandez v. Don Bosco Preparatory High School*, 322 N.J.Super. 1, 730 A.2d 365 (N.J. Super. Ct. App. Div. 1999).

E. Students with Disabilities

◆ A Pennsylvania student attended a private co-educational Catholic school. As a first-grader, he earned high grades but was defiant in the classroom. He often shouted out answers without being called on and mocked other students for their mistakes. He punched a student and threatened another with a pencil. Other students and their parents complained to the school about the student's behavior. The student's teacher spoke to his parents about his misbehavior. The principal suggested the student be evaluated by a private testing institution. The school sent the parents the paperwork required to perform an evaluation, but the parents did not return it and no evaluation was done. The school refused to readmit the student for the following school year. A psychologist diagnosed him with attention deficit hyperactivity disorder (ADHD). The family sued the school in a Pennsylvania trial court, alleging it violated the Americans with Disabilities Act (ADA). The case was removed to a federal district court.

The court stated that Title III of the ADA protects individuals with disabilities from discrimination in public accommodations. To be disabled within the meaning of the ADA, a person has to be physically or mentally impaired in a way that substantially limits one or more major life activities. Major life activities include thinking, learning and seeing. **The court found the student was not disabled, because his exceptional academic performance showed he was not substantially limited in these activities. Although private schools are considered "places of public accommodation" under Title III of the ADA, religious schools such as the one in this case are not. As the school was not a place of public accommodation, it was exempt from the requirements of Title III.** The court awarded summary judgment to the school. *Marshall v. Sisters of Holy Family of Nazareth*, 399 F.Supp.2d 597 (E.D. Pa. 2005).

◆ A New York student with learning disabilities attended a private school as a kindergartner. His parents contacted their school district to determine an appropriate placement for the next school year. After the district performed several evaluations, it recommended a public school placement in a modified instructional services program, with speech/language therapy and counseling. The parents rejected the placement offer and kept their child in the private school. They filed a due process hearing request, seeking tuition reimbursement from the district. An independent hearing officer agreed with the parents and ordered the district to reimburse them. A state review officer affirmed the hearing officer's decision, finding the school district's committee on special education was improperly constituted. While a special education teacher from the district had attended the committee meeting, the student's private school teacher had been unable to attend due to a hospitalization.

The school district appealed to a federal district court. **The court relied on 20 U.S.C. § 1412(a)(10)(C), an IDEA provision limiting private school tuition reimbursement to "parents of a child with a disability, who previously received special education and related services under the authority of a public agency." The court agreed with the school district. The clear language of the IDEA prohibited reimbursement in this case.** The court explained Section 1412(a)(10)(C) "ensures that a parent's rejection of a public school placement is not based on mere speculation." The court granted summary judgment to the school district. *Board of Educ. of City of New York v. Tom F.*, No. 01 Civ. 6845 (GBD), 2005 WL 17838 (W.D.N.Y. 2005).

◆ A private school student in Michigan had a brain tumor that was in remission. Because of his problems walking, his mother requested a physical therapy needs evaluation from the school district. The district found that he did not need additional physical therapy. The mother then asked for an individual education evaluation at the district's expense. When the district refused, a lawsuit resulted. **The Michigan Court of Appeals held that state law required special** education for "every handicapped person." **Further, nothing in state law limited individual education evaluations to public school students. The district had to pay for the evaluation.** *Michigan Dep't of Educ. v. Grosse Pointe Public Schools*, 701 N.W.2d 195 (Mich. Ct. App. 2005).

◆   A Pennsylvania student with learning disabilities in math, reading and written language attended a private school at the district's expense for three years until the district determined that he should attend a public school. His parents objected to the new individualized education program (IEP) offered by the district, but a hearing officer found that the IEP was reasonably calculated to provide the student with meaningful educational benefits. A federal court upheld that decision. **The district did not have to perform the full scope of testing required for an initial evaluation when it reevaluated the student for the transfer to public school. Nor did it have to create a separate behavior intervention plan or create a transition plan.** The IEP properly addressed the student's skills and needs and did not violate the IDEA. *Robert B. v. West Chester Area School Dist.*, No. Civ.A. 04-CV-2069, 2005 WL 2396968 (E.D. Pa. 2005).

◆   The parents of a Maryland student with multiple disabilities placed her in private schools for kindergarten and first grade. Soon after making the first-grade placement, they contacted the principal at a public elementary school about enrollment procedures. The elementary school staff lost a certified letter from the parents containing required information for enrollment and three evaluations of their daughter. As a result, the staff took no further action to develop an IEP. The parents requested a due process hearing over six months later. The school finally found the missing letter. An administrative law judge awarded tuition reimbursement for most of the student's first-grade year. However, a federal court reversed. **Even though the failure to develop an IEP denied the student a free appropriate public education, the IDEA allows reimbursement only where the disabled student was at one time receiving "special education and related services from a public agency." The parents were not eligible for tuition reimbursement.** *Baltimore City Board of School Commissioners v. Taylorch*, 395 F.Supp.2d 246 (D. Md. 2005).

◆   The parents of a New Hampshire student with disabilities placed him in a Catholic school, then met with a school district team to develop an IEP for him. The IEP called for transportation to and from a public school speech/language program for one hour per week. Later, the parents challenged the IEP, and **a hearing officer held they were not entitled to a due process hearing because they had voluntarily placed their son at the religious school. The First Circuit agreed. By placing their son in the private school, the parents had to accept the disadvantages as well as the benefits.** Congress had chosen not to provide the same benefits to private school students as it did to public school students. *Gary S. v. Manchester School Dist.*, 374 F.3d 15 (1st Cir. 2004).

◆   When a Pennsylvania private school student was having problems, his mother told the principal she believed he had a learning disability. She did not make a written request to the school district where they lived for an evaluation.

Years later, the parents made a written request for an evaluation. The district exceeded the 60-day time limit for completing the evaluation, then crafted an IEP near the end of the school year. The parents approved of the IEP but requested a due process hearing, alleging that the district violated the IDEA child-find obligation and claiming tuition reimbursement for the past six years. The hearing officer ruled against them. **A federal district court held the district did not fail in its child find obligations. Any delay in completing the evaluation and IEP was harmless because it was highly unlikely the parents would have removed their son from school for the last few weeks of the year.** *Alex K. v. Wissahickon School Dist.*, No. Civ. A. 03-854, 2004 WL 286871 (E.D. Pa. 2004).

◆ The parents of a private school student with emotional and academic problems asked their school district of residence to evaluate her. However, they rejected a proposed IEP and requested a due process hearing, keeping the student in the private school. The district failed to respond to the due process request, and the following year, the parents made another due process request. Fourteen months after the original request, a hearing officer determined that the district had offered the student a free appropriate public education. The parents appealed, and a federal court ruled for the district. **The parents had to show more than an IDEA procedural violation to receive tuition reimbursement, and they failed to prove that the district's IEP was inappropriate.** *Caitlin W. v. Rose Tree Media School Dist.*, 2004 WL 3009027 (E.D. Pa. 2004).

◆ An Ohio first grade student was enrolled in a private Catholic school. A doctor determined the student had a hearing impairment, and his parents decided to enroll him in a Montessori school for second grade. While attending the Montessori school, the student was diagnosed with a learning disability and provided with an individualized learning program. After attending the Montessori school through the sixth grade, the student returned to the parochial school. Despite his poor academic performance, he graduated.

The student's parents sued the school, alleging it breached a contract between the parties established by the school's student and parent handbook, fraudulently promised to comply with the handbook and violated the IDEA. The case reached the Sixth Circuit, which found no support for a breach of contract claim. **The section of the school handbook that the parents sought to enforce contained "indefinite and aspirational" language regarding the school's mission, not a promise to provide specific educational services.** There was no material representation of fact to support the fraud claim. The handbook did not promise specific educational services, nor could the parents demonstrate that school personnel promised the student would receive certain services. The lack of definiteness, a required element of a fraud claim, defeated the claim. The court held that the school could not be liable for the family's claims arising under the IDEA. The statute applies to state and local educational agencies, not private schools. **Since the school was private, it was not subject to the IDEA.** The court affirmed the grant of summary judgment for the school on all the claims. *Ullmo v. Gilmour Academy*, 273 F.3d 671 (6th Cir. 2001).

IV. PUBLIC AND PRIVATE SCHOOL COOPERATION

Cooperation between public and private schools must avoid the appearance of government approval of religion and must not constitute government aid to, or excessive entanglement with, religious organizations.

A. Dual Enrollment

◆ Many Indiana local educational agencies and private schools employed dual-enrollment agreements under which the agencies provided secular instruction to private school students at public schools. Public funds were also used to provide computer and internet services to private schools, including those with religious affiliations. A group of taxpayers opposed the dual-enrollment process as a public subsidy of religious schools. They sued state officials in a state trial court for violations of Article 1, Section 6 of the Indiana Constitution. The court held the taxpayers had no standing to advance their claims. The dual-enrollment process did not violate the state constitution.

The Court of Appeals of Indiana affirmed the decision on the grounds of standing, and the taxpayers appealed to the Supreme Court of Indiana. It held the taxpayers could proceed with the action because it was based on their shared public interest in the expense of public funds, not on a claim of private rights. The court considered Article 1, Section 6, which stated "No money shall be drawn from the treasury, for the benefit of any religious or theological institution." The provision was added to the state's constitution in 1851, and was patterned after provisions in the constitutions of Michigan and Wisconsin. There was evidence the prohibition did not apply to schools. The court explained **the determinative issue in the case was whether the dual-enrollment process conferred substantial benefits upon participating parochial schools or directly funded religious activity.** Decisions by Michigan and Wisconsin courts interpreting analogous constitutional provisions found **the receipt of incidental benefits by a religious entity did not invalidate an otherwise constitutional program for a public purpose.** These decisions were consistent with Indiana cases decided under Article 1, Section 6. The court held the dual-enrollment programs provided significant educational benefits, affording students educational resources and training they would not otherwise receive. Local education agencies providing services under these arrangements benefitted from increased funding. The dual-enrollment programs did not result in the payment of public funds directly to religious institutions, and any cost saving realized by parochial schools was relatively minor and incidental. Since the programs did not confer substantial benefits on religious institutions or directly fund religious activity, the court affirmed the judgment. *Embry v. O'Bannon*, 798 N.E.2d 157 (Ind. 2003).

◆ An Illinois student tested two grades above grade level at the end of his sixth-grade year in a private school. His mother asked the superintendent of their school district of residence for permission to enroll him in an Algebra I course in a public school on a part-time basis. The superintendent denied the request and the student took Algebra I as an independent study course at the private school. His quarterly grades included three Bs and one C. The parents sought to enroll the student in Algebra II or geometry in district schools as he entered grade eight. The private school principal made a request on behalf of the student to place him in a public school math class the next year. The superintendent contacted the principal and the independent study teacher, seeking the student's grades, homework, quizzes, tests and scores. The superintendent allowed the student to enroll in district schools on a part-time basis, but placed him in an Honors Algebra I class. The student instead enrolled in an Algebra II course at a local community college while remaining in eighth grade in his private school. The family sued the district and superintendent in a federal district court for due process and equal protection violations.

The court considered a motion for summary judgment by the district and superintendent. **An Illinois law, 735 ILCS 5/10-20.24, permitted private school students to attend public school part-time but required such requests to come from the private school principal before May 1 of the prior school year.** The request following the student's grade-six year had come from his mother, not the principal, and was untimely. The principal's request on behalf of the student prior to grade eight met statutory requirements, but the student could not prevail on his constitutional claims. The superintendent conferred with private school staff and reasonably determined the student's proper placement was in Honors Algebra I. There was no evidence other private school students had attempted to take a math course on a part-time basis in district schools but were assigned to a lower level than requested. Summary judgment was proper on the equal protection claim. State law did not create a protected property interest to attend a student's class of choice. As students have no property interest in public education, no reasonable jury could find a due process violation by the district and superintendent. **As courts may not interfere with the daily operations of a school system unless a conflict sharply implicates constitutional values**, the court held for the district and superintendent. *Hassberger v. Board of Educ., Cent. Community Unit School Dist. 301*, No. 00 C 7873, 2003 WL 22697481 (N.D. Ill. 2003).

B. Textbook Loans and Other Materials

The provision of textbooks by the state to private and parochial school students is permissible under the First Amendment. In Cochran v. Louisiana State Board of Educ., *281 U.S. 370, 50 S.Ct. 335, 74 L.Ed.2d 1929 (1930), the U.S. Supreme Court upheld a state law that authorized the purchasing and supplying of textbooks to all school children, including parochial school children, on the basis of what is now called the "child benefit" doctrine. The Court held that the textbook loan statute was constitutional because the legislature's purpose in enacting the statute was to benefit children and their parents, not religious schools.*

◆ A group of Louisiana citizens sued the Jefferson Parish School Board in 1985 for violating the First Amendment, alleging that the board improperly provided Chapter Two funds to parochial schools to acquire library materials and media equipment. The group asserted expenditures for books, computers, software and other audiovisual equipment violated the Establishment Clause. The district court agreed, granting summary judgment to the group because the funding failed the test from *Lemon v. Kurtzman*, 403 U.S. 602 (1971). The court held that the loan of materials to sectarian schools constituted direct government aid under *Meek v. Pittenger*, 421 U.S. 349 (1975) and *Wolman v. Walter*, 433 U.S. 229 (1977). Two years later, the district court reversed itself, citing the intervening *Zobrest v. Catalina Foothills School Dist.*, 509 U.S. 1 (1993) decision. The citizens appealed to the Fifth Circuit, which held the Chapter Two grants were unconstitutional under *Meek* and *Wolman*.

On review, **the U.S. Supreme Court stated that it has consistently applied the principle of neutrality in funding cases, upholding aid that is offered to a broad range of recipients without regard to religion. Where assistance was suitable for use in public schools, it was also suitable for private school use. The Court found less concern for attributing religious indoctrination to the government where its assistance lacked any specific content.** There was no basis for finding the board's use of Chapter Two funds advanced religion. Use of Chapter Two funds by private schools did not result in government indoctrination because eligibility was determined on a neutral basis and through private choices by parents. **Chapter Two had no impermissible content and did not define its recipients by reference to religion.** The distribution of Chapter Two funds did not create an improper incentive for parents to select religious schools. A broad array of schools was eligible for assistance without regard to religious affiliation. Students who attended schools receiving Chapter Two funds were the ultimate beneficiaries of the assistance. The Court upheld the board's use of Chapter Two funding and held that the parish did not need to exclude sectarian schools from its program. *Mitchell v. Helms*, 530 U.S. 793, 120 S.Ct. 2530, 147 L.Ed.2d 660 (2000).

◆ A 1997 Wisconsin law created the Technology for Education Achievement (TEACH) Board, which administered the Education Telecommunications Access program. The TEACH board approved access for data lines and video links under a heavily subsidized program in which both public and private schools participated. A taxpayer group objected to the program on constitutional grounds because $58,873 of the program's annual total of over $1.9 million was awarded to nine religiously affiliated Wisconsin schools and private colleges. The taxpayers filed a federal district court action against state education officials, including the TEACH board. The court held the program as a whole did not violate the Constitution, but found that unrestricted cash grants to private, sectarian schools violated the Establishment Clause's prohibition on state support of religion. The parties appealed to the Seventh Circuit.

The taxpayers dismissed their appeal concerning the constitutionality of the full program in view of the Supreme Court's intervening decision in *Mitchell v. Helms*, above. The Seventh Circuit proceeded to the question of grants to religious schools under the Wisconsin law, noting that the test for evaluating the constitutionality of private school funding remains the one devised by the Supreme Court in *Lemon v. Kurtzman*, as modified by *Agostini v. Felton*, 521 U.S. 203 (1997). The Seventh Circuit summarized the *Agostini* inquiry as asking whether the program or statute results in governmental indoctrination, defines its recipients by reference to religion or creates excessive entanglement between the government and religion. **The Wisconsin law violated the third** *Agostini* **criteria, because in the absence of any restriction on the expenditure of public funds by the schools, the expenditures had a primary effect that advanced religion.** The subsidies could easily be used for maintenance, chapels, religious instruction, or connection time to view religious Web sites. The law did not bar schools from using the grants for these and other constitutionally impermissible purposes. Because direct aid from the government to a sectarian institution in any form is invalid, the court affirmed the district court's finding that the provision of direct subsidies to religious schools was unconstitutional. *Freedom From Religion Foundation, Inc. v Bugher*, 249 F.3d 606 (7th Cir. 2001).

◆ The U.S. Supreme Court reaffirmed the validity of the child benefit doctrine in a case involving a New York textbook loan statute. This statute required local school districts to lend textbooks free of charge to all children in grades seven through twelve. Parochial school students were included. The Court observed that the textbooks loaned to parochial school children were the same nonreligious textbooks used in the public schools. **The loaning of textbooks was permissible because the parochial school students used them for secular study.** There was no state involvement in religious training. The state of New York was merely providing a secular benefit to all schoolchildren. *Board of Educ. v. Allen*, 392 U.S. 236, 88 S.Ct. 1923, 20 L.Ed.2d 1060 (1968).

◆ The Supreme Court held **private schools with racially discriminatory admissions policies may not benefit from textbook loan programs**. This ruling was based on the principle that the state may not give assistance to acts of racial discrimination. Textbooks were "a basic educational tool," said the Court, and to permit racially discriminatory private schools to benefit from state textbook loans would be to allow the state to accomplish indirectly what it could not accomplish directly: a state-funded racially segregated school system. *Norwood v. Harrison*, 413 U.S. 455, 93 S.Ct. 2804, 37 L.Ed.2d 723 (1973).

C. Transportation

The use of state funds to reimburse private schools for transportation for field trips was declared unconstitutional by the U.S. Supreme Court in Wolman *v.* Walter, *433 U.S. 229 (1977). There was no way public officials could monitor the field trips to assure that they had a secular purpose. Even if monitoring by the state was feasible, the monitoring would be so extensive that the state would become entangled in religion to an impermissible degree.*

◆ Transportation may be provided to parochial school students without violating the First Amendment under a 1947 U.S. Supreme Court case. The case involved a New Jersey law that allowed reimbursement to parents of children attending nonprofit religious schools for costs incurred by the children in using public transportation to travel to and from school. The law's purpose was to provide transportation expenses for all schoolchildren regardless of where they attended school, as long as the school was nonprofit. The Court analogized free transportation to other state benefits such as police and fire protection, connections for sewage disposal, and public roads and sidewalks, which also benefited parochial school children. **It was not the purpose of the First Amendment to cut off religious institutions from all government benefits. Rather, the state was only required to be neutral toward religion.** *Everson v. Board of Educ.*, 330 U.S. 1, 67 S.Ct. 504, 91 L.Ed.2d 711 (1947).

◆ Before the start of the 2000-01 school year, the Pittsburgh School District notified the Roman Catholic Diocese of Pittsburgh that it would no longer provide busing for half-day kindergarten programs for either public school students or private school students. The diocese challenged this decision, arguing that under Section 13-1361(1) of the Pennsylvania Public School Code, the district was obligated to provide midday bus service for kindergartners. Eventually, several students and their parents filed a lawsuit in state court, seeking injunctive relief. After two hearings, the court granted a preliminary injunction ordering the district to provide busing. The district appealed.

The Commonwealth Court of Pennsylvania explained the students were entitled to a preliminary injunction if a violation of the Public School Code occurred. The district had focused on the "identical provision" language of the statute, arguing its bus service to private schools only had to mirror the service provided to public school students. The diocese asserted the "regular school hours" provision required the district to provide busing for all kindergarten students who attended diocesan schools, regardless of which program they attended. The diocese did not establish "regular school hours" for its kindergarten classes and instead offered parents a variety of half-day options. This meant the district was providing multiple round trips to accommodate individual choices of schedules, which was "not identical to the transportation offered [to] the public school kindergartners." **The district was only required to offer the same transportation services to private school students it offered to public school students.** Under the circumstances, the private school students were eligible for a different, upgraded version of the transportation provided to district students. The court held the preliminary injunction issued by the trial court was too broad. It vacated the injunction and remanded the case. *Crowe v. School Dist. of Pittsburgh*, 805 A.2d 691 (Pa. Commw. Ct. 2002).

◆ Wisconsin law requires high school districts to provide private school students with transportation to and from their schools. Elementary districts may elect to provide the services instead of the high schools and may contract directly with parents to do so. The parents of students who attended Providence Catholic School contracted with elementary school districts to provide transportation. When the amount paid to the parents became less than the cost of transportation, Providence requested additional funding. The districts denied the request, and parents sought a state court order requiring the districts to provide transportation to the parochial school. The court denied relief. The state court of appeals **held the school districts were statutorily allowed to contract with the parents of private school students regarding transportation.** The parents' assertion that state law barred these contracts and required the provision of transportation services was rejected, as state law gave the districts assorted options for providing transportation to private school students. One of these options was contracting directly with the parents. *Providence Catholic School v. Bristol School Dist. No. 1,* 605 N.W.2d 238 (Wis. Ct. App. 1999).

◆ For six years, a West Virginia school board provided transportation for children residing within the county to a private, religious school in a nearby county. The school district then began to experience severe financial difficulties and eliminated a number of activities and jobs, including two bus driver positions. The district could no longer afford to transport students to the private school. **Thirty-two students were affected by this decision, and the father of two of them requested that the board either resume bus service to the private school or furnish a stipend** for their transportation costs. The board refused, and the father sought an order from the Supreme Court of Appeals of West Virginia to compel the board to provide transportation or a stipend. The father argued that because the board had transported the students for six years, it could not later withdraw the service without violating his equal protection and religious freedom rights. **The court held that the board had no legal duty to transport the students and had not acted arbitrarily or capriciously in terminating its discretionary bus service for private school students.** It had withdrawn the service as a response to extreme financial difficulties and had also been forced to cut many other services and job positions. Because the father had failed to present any evidence contradicting the board's financial difficulties, the court denied the requested order. *State of West Virginia v. Board of Educ. of Summers County,* 478 S.E.2d 341 (W. Va. 1996).

D. Personnel Sharing

◆ Title I of the Elementary and Secondary Education Act of 1965 provides federal funding through the states to local educational agencies for remedial education, guidance and job counseling to at-risk students and students residing in low-income areas. Title I requires that funding be made available for all eligible students, including those attending private schools. Local agencies retain control over Title I funds and materials. The New York City Board of Education attempted to implement Title I programs at parochial schools by allowing public employees to instruct students on private school grounds during school hours. The Supreme Court held this violated the Establishment Clause in *Aguilar v. Felton,* 473 U.S. 402, 105 S.Ct. 3232, 87 L.Ed.2d 290 (1985).

On remand, a federal district court ordered the city board to refrain from using Title I funds for any plan or program under which public school teachers and counselors appeared on sectarian school grounds. In response to *Aguilar,* local education boards modified their Title I programs by moving classes to remote sites including mobile instructional units parked near sectarian schools. However, a new group of parents and parochial school students filed motions seeking relief from the permanent order.

The case reached the U.S. Supreme Court, which agreed with the city board and students that recent Supreme Court decisions required a new ruling on the question of government aid to religious schools. For example, the provision of a sign language interpreter by a school district at a private school was upheld in *Zobrest v. Catalina Foothills School Dist.*, 509 U.S. 1 (1993). The Court held it would no longer presume that the presence of a public school teacher on parochial school grounds creates an unconstitutional symbolic union between church and state. The provision of Title I services at parochial schools resembled the provision of the sign language interpreter in *Zobrest* under the Individuals with Disabilities Education Act. **New York City's Title I program was constitutionally permissible because it did not result in government indoctrination, define funding recipients by reference to religion or create excessive entanglement between education officials and religious schools.** The Court reversed the lower court judgments. *Agostini v. Felton*, 521 U.S. 203, 117 S.Ct. 1997, 138 L.Ed.2d 391 (1997).

◆ In *Lemon v. Kurtzman*, the U.S. Supreme Court invalidated Rhode Island and Pennsylvania statutes that provided state money to finance the operation of parochial schools. It applied a three-part test, which remains in use by the courts today. **"First, the statute must have a secular legislative purpose; second, its principal or primary effect must be one that neither advances nor inhibits religion, ... finally, the statute must not foster an excessive government entanglement with religion." The programs excessively entangled the state with religion because of the highly religious nature of the Roman Catholic parochial schools that were its primary beneficiaries.** Consequently, **the programs were held to violate the First Amendment.** *Lemon v. Kurtzman*, 403 U.S. 602, 91 S.Ct. 2105, 29 L.Ed.2d 745 (1971).

E. School Facilities and Property

◆ **The Supreme Court of Georgia held an arms-length commercial lease between the Atlanta Independent School System and a Baptist church did not violate the Establishment Clause of the Georgia Constitution.** The school board authorized the lease of classroom space at the Buckhead Baptist Church to create a kindergarten annex. The lease required the school system to rent space from the church for over five years and pay for renovations and improvements on church property that would be credited against rent due. A citizen claimed the lease agreement violated the Establishment Clause of the Georgia Constitution and sued the school system in a state superior court to halt payments to the church. The court granted judgment to the school system.

On appeal, the supreme court explained the state constitution's Establishment Clause prevented the taking of money from the public treasury, directly or indirectly, to aid any church, sect, cult or religious denomination, or of any sectarian institution. The clause prevented the state and its political subdivisions from owning, controlling or giving monetary aid to a church or religious institution. While a state political subdivision could not give money to a religious institution to promote sectarian work, the court held this did not mean a subdivision could not "enter into an arms-length commercial agreement with a sectarian institution to accomplish a non-sectarian purpose. And that is what happened here." The court held the school system had simply leased space from the church to run a public kindergarten in a non-sectarian environment. **Lease payments did not foster the education of students in a sectarian school and was not state monetary aid to the church. As the lease agreement did not violate the Georgia Constitution, the court affirmed the judgment for the school system.** *Taetle v. Atlanta Independent School System,* 280 Ga. 137, 625 S.E.2d 770 (Ga. 2006).

◆   The Milwaukee Parental Choice Program was created by 1989 legislation to subsidize private education for underprivileged students in Milwaukee. A Catholic High School was located primarily in St. Francis, but 20% of its school grounds, including green space, a parking lot, driveway and track area were located in Milwaukee. The school petitioned the state superintendent of public instruction for an order declaring it eligible to participate in the choice program. This request was denied. In 2002, the school sought to have the portion of its property that was located in St. Francis annexed to the city of Milwaukee. Voters in St. Francis defeated a referendum that would have allowed it to detach its land. The governor did not include a provision modifying the program in a proposed budget bill for 2001-03. In 2003, the state assembly considered, but rejected, a bill that would have allowed schools located in Milwaukee County to participate in the choice program. The superintendent denied another petition by the school, finding its buildings had to be located in the city, and that program administrative rules required a certificate of occupancy issued by the city of Milwaukee. A state trial court affirmed the superintendent's ruling, and the school appealed.

　　The Court of Appeals of Wisconsin noted the school's unsuccessful attempts to participate in the choice program through voters, the governor and the legislature. The statute plainly indicated the school was not eligible to participate in the program. There was no conflict between state law and the administrative requirement for schools to obtain a certificate of occupancy from the city of Milwaukee. The court found other indicators suggesting the school's argument was incorrect. The title of the statute was "Milwaukee parental choice program." Had the legislature intended for schools with buildings not located in the city to participate in the program, it would not have required them to submit copies of their certificates of occupancy "issued by the city." Under the school's argument, "any school, anywhere can become a Choice school by buying a small plot in the City of Milwaukee." **Without the required certificate of occupancy from the city of Milwaukee, the school was ineligible for the program, and the court affirmed the trial court's decision.** *Thomas More High School v. Burmaster,* 704 N.W.2d 349 (Wis. Ct. App. 2005).

◆   An Iowa parochial school held a fundraiser for its baseball and softball teams. Individuals and businesses purchased 37 boosters signs that were hung from the outfield fences of school athletic fields. The Iowa Department of Transportation (IDOT) determined the signs violated a state law prohibiting billboard advertising within 660 feet of a state highway. The school challenged an IDOT directive to remove the signs, claiming they were not visible from the highway and that the IDOT was infringing on commercial speech in violation of the First Amendment. An administrative law judge agreed with the IDOT that the signs had to be removed, but an Iowa district court held they fell within an exception to the outdoor advertising statute. The court also found the statute violated the First Amendment by restricting commercial speech.

The IDOT appealed. The Iowa Supreme Court held the signs clearly violated the statute, as they were visible from the highway. It rejected the trial court's conclusion that the signs were permitted under the exception, because they did not relate to the activities of the school. **The court held the law was not an impermissible regulation of commercial speech. The statute regulated signs based on their location, not their content.** The court held the statute did not impermissibly restrict the school's speech rights. The IDOT had a compelling state interest in traffic safety and ensuring an aesthetic environment. The court noted the statute only prohibited the booster signs from being placed where they were visible from the highway. The school could still place them elsewhere on its property. *Immaculate Conception Corp. and Don Bosco High School v. Iowa Dep't of Transportation*, 656 N.W.2d 513 (Iowa 2003).

◆   **The U.S. Court of Appeals, Sixth Circuit, held the issuance of tax-exempt industrial development bonds to a Tennessee Christian university to fund a renovation project did not violate the Establishment Clause of the U.S. Constitution. The type of tax-exempt bonds issued by the board did not violate the Establishment Clause because public funds were not used to issue them, and the method for obtaining them did not implicate any public funds. The bonds were issued in a neutral manner and the issue had a secular objective.** The court found the effect of issuing the bonds neither advanced nor inhibited religion because the bonds were available to a variety of entities. There was no perception of impermissible government endorsement of religion. *Steele v. Industrial Development Board of Metropolitan Government of Nashville*, 301 F.3d 401 (6th Cir. 2002).

◆   Under a Montgomery County, Maryland zoning ordinance, all businesses and organizations must obtain a special exception in order to build a non-residential structure on land designated for residential use. The county appeals board will grant a petition for special exception only after determining, through a public hearing, that the new building will not disrupt the surrounding community. **The ordinance exempts lots owned or leased by religious organizations from having to obtain a special exception.** A federal district court examined the constitutionality of the exemption after residential neighbors of the Connelly School of the Holy Child, a parochial school, objected to the school's construction of a new building. The district court found the exemption unconstitutional because it favored religious schools over other nonprofit schools and constituted an excessive government entanglement with religion. The Connelly School appealed to the Fourth Circuit.

The court held **the exemption had the secular purpose of allowing the county to prevent government interference with the religious mission of various organizations** and avoided creating a forum during special exception hearings in which anti-religious views might be expressed. The exemption neither advanced nor inhibited religion. The county merely relieved religious schools from the burden of applying for a special exception. The court held any advancement of religion that followed would be the result of the religious schools' own acts in light of the exemption. Finally, the exemption did not foster an excessive entanglement with religion. As the ordinance did not violate the Establishment Clause, the district court decision was reversed. *Renzi v. Connelly School of the Holy Child Inc.*, 224 F.3d 283 (4th Cir. 2000).

F. Release Time Programs

◆ **An Illinois program allowed public school students to receive religious instruction in their public schools.** Although religious groups supplied the religious education teachers at no cost to school districts, the superintendent of schools exercised supervisory powers over them. A taxpayer sued a local school board, claiming the release time program violated the Establishment Clause. The U.S. Supreme Court agreed. "This is beyond all question a utilization of the tax-established and tax-supported public school system to aid religious groups," said the Court. "[T]he First Amendment has erected a wall between Church and State which must be kept high and impregnable." *McCollum v. Board of Educ.*, 333 U.S. 203, 68 S.Ct. 461, 92 L.Ed.2d 649 (1948).

◆ Four years later, the Supreme Court upheld a different kind of release time program. In this New York program, **students could be released from public school classes during the school day for a few hours to attend religious education classes.** Unlike the program in the *McCollum* case, students in the New York release time program received their religious instruction off the public school grounds. Church officials made out weekly attendance reports and sent the reports to public school officials, who then checked to assure that the released students had actually reported for their off-school-grounds religious instruction. **The Court approved the New York program largely because the religious instruction took place off school grounds. There was no religious indoctrination taking place in the public school buildings nor was there any expenditure of public funds on behalf of religious training.** Also, there was no evidence of any subtle or overt coercion exerted by any public school officials to induce students to attend the religious classes. The public schools were merely accommodating religion, not aiding it. The Court declined to invalidate the New York release time program, saying, "We cannot read into the Bill of Rights such a philosophy of hostility to religion." *Zorach v. Clauson*, 343 U.S. 306, 72 S.Ct. 679, 96 L.Ed.2d 954 (1952).

◆ The U.S. Court of Appeals, Second Circuit, revisited *Zorach v. Clauson.* Two former students claimed a New York district implemented a "released time" program in an unconstitutional way. They asserted the district released Catholic and Protestant students so they could attend nearby programs at designated times during the school day. Others remained in classrooms with nothing to do until the released students returned. The family sued the district in a federal district court, asserting the administration of the released time program violated the Establishment Clause. The court held for the district, ruling it did not implement the released time provision of New York Eduction Law § 3210(2)(b) in a way that advanced Christianity over other religions and non-religion. The family appealed to the Second Circuit.

The court noted the Supreme Court had upheld the program authorized by

Section 3210(2)(b) in *Zorach v. Clauson*, above. The family insisted the district's implementation of the program violated the Establishment Clause by favoring Christianity over other religions and non-religion. The court disagreed, finding nothing in this case suggested a different result than *Zorach*. The program used no public funds and involved no on-site religious instruction. As the Supreme Court held in *Zorach*, **the program called for schools to simply adjust their schedules to accommodate student religious needs. The court rejected the argument that the school's imprimatur was placed on a program of religious instruction and that churches used the schools in support of their religious missions.** Nothing in this case suggested the released time program was administered in a coercive manner. The family's arguments were indistinguishable from those made in *Zorach* 52 years earlier. As the district implemented the law consistently with *Zorach*, the judgment was affirmed. *Pierce v. Sullivan West Cent. School Dist.*, 379 F.3d 56 (2d Cir. 2004).

V. STUDENT FINANCIAL ASSISTANCE

To be constitutionally permissible, government financial assistance for religious school students must primarily benefit the students, not their schools. Federal funding of programs and activities requires compliance with federal statutes such as Title VI, Title IX, the Rehabilitation Act, the Americans with Disabilities Act and the Age Discrimination in Employment Act. Students receiving federal grants will be deemed to be receiving assistance for federal law purposes. For cases involving school voucher programs, please see Chapter Two, Section IV.

♦   **The U.S. Supreme Court held the U.S. Department of Education could intercept a 67-year-old disabled Washington man's Social Security benefits to offset a student loan that was outstanding for over 10 years.** The man failed to repay federally reinsured student loans he incurred between 1984 and 1989 under the Guaranteed Student Loan Program. The loans were reassigned to the Department of Education, which certified the debt to the U.S. Department of Treasury through the Treasury Offset Program. The U.S. government began withholding part of the man's Social Security benefits to offset his debt, part of which was more than 10 years overdue. He sued the U.S. in a federal district court, alleging the offset was barred by the 10-year statute of limitations of the Debt Collection Act of 1982. The court dismissed the case, and the U.S. Court of Appeals, Ninth Circuit, affirmed. The U.S. Supreme Court agreed to review the case. It noted the Debt Collection Act permits U.S. agency heads to collect an outstanding debt by "administrative offset." However, Section 407(a) of the Social Security Act limits the availability of benefits to offset a debt.

The Court explained that the Higher Education Technical Amendments of 1991 "sweepingly eliminated time limitations as to certain loans." This included the student loans in this case. The Debt Collection Improvement Act of 1996 clarified that, notwithstanding any other law, including Section 407, all payments due under the Social Security Act were subject to offset. The Court held the Debt Collection Improvement Act clearly made Social Security benefits subject to offset. Moreover, the Higher Education Technical Amendments removed the 10-year limit that would otherwise bar an offset of Social Security benefits. The Court held the Debt Collection Improvement Act gave the U.S. the authority to use Social Security benefits to offset debts. The retention of the 10-year limit on debt collection in the Higher Education Technical Amendments did not apply in all contexts, including this administrative offset. The Court affirmed the judgment for the U.S. government. *Lockhart v. U.S.*, 546 U.S. 142, 126 S.Ct. 699, 163 L.Ed.2d 557 (2005).

◆   **The U.S. Supreme Court held a state could exclude devotional theology candidates from a scholarship program.** Washington law created the Promise Scholarship Program, which made state funds available to qualified students for education-related costs. Scholarships were worth $1,542 for the 2000-2001 academic year. To be eligible, students had to graduate in the top 15% of their class or score well on a college entrance exam. Students had to enroll at least half-time in an eligible post-secondary institution in the state. The program was limited to families whose incomes were less than 135% of the state median. Despite the program's prohibition on scholarships for theology majors, students who attended religiously affiliated schools could still obtain Promise Scholarships so long as they did not major in theology and the institution was accredited. The law creating the program codified a Washington constitutional prohibition on funding for students to pursue degrees that were "devotional in nature or designed to induce religious faith." The institution, rather than the state, determined whether a student's major was devotional and thus ineligible for a scholarship. A student who received a Promise Scholarship enrolled as a double major in pastoral ministries and business at a private Christian college. The college director of financial aid advised him he could not use the scholarship to pursue a devotional theology degree and could receive program funds only by certifying he would not pursue a theology degree.

The student sued state officials including the governor in a federal district court, seeking an order to prohibit them from refusing to award a scholarship based on his decision to pursue a theology degree. He alleged violations of the Free Exercise, Establishment, Speech and Equal Protection Clauses. The court awarded summary judgment to the state, and the student appealed. The U.S. Court of Appeals, Ninth Circuit, reversed the decision, finding the state had no compelling interest in excluding theology majors from the program. The U.S. Supreme Court granted the state's petition for review. It observed the case involved the tension between the Establishment and Free Exercise Clauses of the First Amendment. According to the Court, **"there is room for play in the joints" between these clauses, as some state actions permitted by the Establishment Clause are not required by the Free Exercise Clause**. The Court acknowledged its decision less than two years earlier in *Zelman v. Simmons-Harris*, 536 U.S. 539 (2002), which found any link between government funds and religious training was "broken by the independent and private choices" of Ohio school voucher recipients. The U.S. Constitution permitted states to fund students pursuing devotional theology degrees. **There was no Free Exercise Clause violation, as the program did not require students to choose between their religious beliefs and the receipt of a**

government benefit. As there was no violation of the student's Free Exercise Clause rights, the Court applied the "rational basis" scrutiny to his Equal Protection Claim. The state met this standard, because **the training of ministers was essentially a religious endeavor that could be treated differently than training for other callings. There was no evidence of any state hostility toward religion.** The Court held "the Promise Scholarship Program goes a long way toward including religion in its benefits," by permitting recipients to attend pervasively religious schools that were accredited. Only students seeking a theology degree were denied scholarships. Nothing in the history or text of Article I, Section 11 of the Washington Constitution, or of the Promise Scholarship Program, suggested anti-religious bias. The state interest in denying funds to theology majors was substantial and placed only a minor burden on recipients. The Court reversed the judgment, noting "[i]f any room exists between the two Religion Clauses, it must be here." *Locke v. Davey*, 540 U.S. 712, 124 S.Ct. 1307, 158 L.Ed.2d 1 (2004).

◆ The parents of three Georgia students enrolled in nonsectarian private schools filed suit in state court against the state, the Board of Education and others for the enforcement of the state Tuition Grant Act. The act provided for direct grants of money, under specified conditions, to the parents of students attending grades K-12 in nonsectarian private schools. The parents alleged that they were denied these grants which, in turn, denied them the equal protection of the law since students in pre-kindergarten and post-twelfth grade programs at private schools had state funds available to them. The parents requested that the court order the defendants to implement and enforce the act. The defendants filed a dismissal motion, which the trial court granted.

The parents appealed to the Supreme Court of Georgia. **The court noted that to establish an equal protection claim, a plaintiff must show that he or she is similarly situated to members of the class who are treated differently.** Although the two groups in this case were treated differently with regard to educational funding, they were not similarly situated. Children in K-12 had a constitutional right to an education at state expense and were required to attend school. However, the group of children in pre-kindergarten and post-twelfth grade had no constitutional right to education and were not required to be enrolled in educational programs. Public education for the K-12 students was supported by taxation, but the funding for the other students resulted not only from taxation but also from lottery proceeds. **The court held that the disparate entitlements and obligations of the two groups prevented them from being similarly situated.** It refused to grant the writ and affirmed the trial court's decision. *Lowe v. State of Georgia*, 482 S.E.2d 344 (Ga. 1997).

◆ A private, not-for-profit technical school in Indiana participated in the Guaranteed Student Loan (GSL) program authorized by Title IV of the Higher Education Act. **The program required the school to make refunds to the lender if a student withdrew from school during a term.** If the school failed to refund loans to the lender, the student would be liable for the full amount of the loan. The treasurer of the school conferred with the school's owners and initiated a practice of not making GSL refunds. As a result, the school owed

$139,649 in refunds. After the school lost its accreditation, a federal grand jury indicted the treasurer for "knowingly and willfully misapplying" federally insured student loan funds in violation of 20 U.S.C. § 1097(a). A federal district court dismissed the indictment because it lacked an allegation that the treasurer intended to injure or defraud the United States. The U.S. Court of Appeals, Seventh Circuit, reinstated the prosecution, and the U.S. Supreme Court granted review. The Supreme Court held that Section 1097(a) did not require the specific intent to injure or defraud. **If the government can prove that the defendant misapplied Title IV funds knowingly and willfully, that is sufficient to show a violation of Section 1097(a).** The Court affirmed the court of appeals' decision to reinstate the prosecution against the treasurer. *Bates v. U.S.*, 522 U.S. 23, 118 S.Ct. 285, 139 L.Ed.2d 215 (1997).

◆ The U.S. Supreme Court unanimously held the First Amendment did not prevent the state of Washington from providing financial assistance directly to a disabled individual attending a Christian college. The plaintiff, a blind person, sought vocational rehabilitative services from the Washington Commission for the Blind pursuant to state law. The law provided that visually impaired persons were eligible for educational assistance. However, **because the student attended a Christian college intending to pursue a career of service in the church, the Commission for the Blind denied him assistance**. The Washington Supreme Court upheld this decision on the ground that the First Amendment to the U.S. Constitution prohibited state funding of a student's education at a religious college. The U.S. Supreme Court took a less restrictive view of the First Amendment and reversed the Washington court. **The operation of Washington's program was such that the Commission for the Blind paid money directly to students, who could then attend the schools of their choice.** The fact that the student in this case chose to attend a religious college did not constitute state support of religion because "the decision to support religious education is made by the individual, not the state." The First Amendment was therefore not offended. *Witters v. Washington Dep't of Services for the Blind*, 474 U.S. 481, 106 S.Ct. 748, 88 L.Ed.2d 846 (1986).

On remand, the Washington Supreme Court reconsidered the matter under the state constitution, which is far stricter in its prohibition on the expenditure of public funds for religious instruction than the U.S. Constitution. **Vocational assistance funds for the student's religious education violated the state constitution because public money would be used for religious instruction.** The commission's action was constitutional under the Free Exercise Clause because there was no infringement of the student's constitutional rights. The court reaffirmed its denial of state funding for the student's tuition. *Witters v. State Comm'n for the Blind*, 771 P.2d 1119 (Wash. 1989).

◆ In *Hunt v. McNair*, **the U.S. Supreme Court upheld a South Carolina plan that allowed both private and public colleges to use the state's authority to borrow money at low interest rates**. The case involved a Baptist college that used this money to finance the construction of a dining hall. The college had no religious test for either its faculty or students and the student body was only about 60% Baptist, the same percentage found in the surrounding community. The Court found that the college was not "pervaded by religion." Unlike the situation commonly found in K-12 parochial schools, religiously affiliated colleges and universities are often not dominated by a religious atmosphere. **The Court concluded that both the purpose and effect of the state's borrowing program was secular and thus constitutional.** The argument that aid to one (secular) portion of a religious institution makes it free to spend more money on religious pursuits was rejected as unpersuasive and irrelevant. If that were the case, the Court noted that police and fire protection for religious schools would have to be cut off as well. *Hunt v. McNair*, 413 U.S. 734, 93 S.Ct. 2868, 37 L.Ed.2d 923 (1973).

◆   In 1973, the U.S. Supreme Court invalidated a New York program that provided $50-$100 in direct money grants to low income parents with children in private schools, and authorized income tax credits of up to $1,000 for parents with children in private schools. **The program had the primary effect of advancing religion and thus was constitutionally invalid. The Court characterized the tax credits as akin to tuition grants** and observed that they were really cash giveaways by the state on behalf of religious schools. *Committee for Public Educ. & Religious Liberty v. Nyquist*, 413 U.S. 756, 93 S.Ct. 2955, 37 L.Ed.2d 948 (1973).

◆   **The Supreme Court upheld a Minnesota program that involved tax deductions (as opposed to tax credits) that were available to parents of public and private school children alike.** The program allowed state income tax deductions for tuition, nonreligious textbooks and transportation. In upholding the program, the Court held the state had a legitimate interest in assuring that all its citizens were well educated. Also, the tax deductions in question were only a few among many other deductions such as those for medical expenses or charitable contributions. Unlike the program in the *Nyquist* case, the Minnesota program was part of a bona fide income tax deduction system available to parents of all school children. The Court held that the First Amendment was not offended by the Minnesota tax deduction program. *Mueller v. Allen*, 463 U.S. 388, 103 S.Ct. 3062, 77 L.Ed.2d 721 (1983).

CHAPTER FIFTEEN

Interscholastic Athletics

		Page
I.	HIGH SCHOOL ATHLETICS	637
	A. Drug Testing	637
	B. Athletic and Extracurricular Suspensions	639
	C. Eligibility Rules and Restrictions	641
	1. Transfer Students	641
	2. Other Rules	644
II.	DISCRIMINATION AND EQUITY	647
	A. Gender Equity	647
	B. Race Discrimination	651
	1. Secondary Schools	651
	2. Intercollegiate Athletics	653
	C. Students with Disabilities	655
III.	ISSUES IN COACHING	659
	A. Employment	659
	B Defamation	662
	C. Liability	665
	D. Misconduct	668

I. HIGH SCHOOL ATHLETICS

Courts have upheld evenhanded rules holding student-athletes to a higher standard of conduct than the general student population due to the representative role they play and their reduced expectations of privacy.

A. Drug Testing

Drug testing by urinalysis constitutes a "search" under the Fourth Amendment to the U.S. Constitution. Testing limited to potential interscholastic sports participants has met with court approval where justified by a compelling school interest. For additional drug search cases involving broader sections of the student population, see Chapter Five, Section II.B.

◆ An Oregon school district responded to increased student drug use by instituting a random drug testing policy for all students wishing to participate in varsity athletics. Each student-athlete was to submit a consent form authorizing a test at the beginning of the season and weekly random testing thereafter. The policy provided for progressive discipline leading to suspension for the current and following athletic seasons. Students who refused testing were suspended from sports for the rest of the season. A seventh-grader who wanted to play football refused to sign the drug testing consent form and was suspended from sports for the season. His parents sued the district in a federal district court, arguing that the policy violated the Fourth Amendment and the Oregon Constitution. The court upheld the policy and the parents appealed to the Ninth Circuit, which held it violated both the U.S. and Oregon Constitutions.

On appeal, the U.S. Supreme Court stated the reasonableness of a student search under the Fourth Amendment is determined by balancing the interests between the government and individual. Prior decisions of the Court indicated **students have a lesser expectation of privacy than the general populace, and that student-athletes have an even lower expectation of privacy in the locker room.** The invasion of privacy in this case was no worse than what was typically encountered in public restrooms. Positive test results were disclosed to only a few school employees. **The insignificant invasion of student privacy was outweighed by the district's important interest in addressing drug use by students who risked physical harm while playing sports.** The Court vacated and remanded the decision of the court of appeals. *Vernonia School Dist. 47J v. Acton*, 515 U.S. 646, 115 S.Ct. 2386, 132 L.Ed.2d 564 (1995).

◆   **The Supreme Court expanded the reach of its *Vernonia* decision in** *Board of Educ. of Independent School Dist. 92 of Pottawatomie County v. Earls.* It held an Oklahoma district with no discernable drug problem could implement a program of testing for all students seeking to participate in extracurricular activities. **The Court found no reason to limit random drug testing to student-athletes, extending *Vernonia* to cover all extracurricular activities participants.** For a full summary of the case, please see Chapter Five, Section II.B. *Board of Educ. of Independent School Dist. 92 of Pottawatomie County v. Earls*, 536 U.S. 822, 122 S.Ct. 2559, 153 L.Ed.2d 735 (2002).

◆   A Pennsylvania coach suspected a student was taking drugs and required him to take a drug test. A drug treatment facility determined the student had no drug abuse problem, but he claimed the principal did not reinstate him to swim and water polo teams despite the evaluation results. He claimed the coach cut a lock off his locker, performed a search, and seized his property. The family brought a variety of state and federal claims against the coach, principal and school district in a federal district court. **The court held the complaint did not allege any constitutional violations resulting from a policy, practice or custom of the school district.** The coach's order to undergo drug screening was a "search" for purposes of a Fourth Amendment claim. While officials may not unreasonably encroach upon student Fourth Amendment rights, students have reduced privacy expectations when compared to the public. **The privacy expectations of student/athletes are even lower than that of the general student population. The coach suspected the student was using drugs because his behavior was unusual. There was an immediate concern for safety. Subjecting the student to drug screening was an effective means for determining if he was using drugs.** The drug screening was reasonable.

The student did not assert a valid Fourth Amendment claim against the coach based on the locker search. The student's First Amendment claim failed, as he was not prevented from associating with team members. Relationships of a purely social nature are not protected by the First Amendment. **The removal of a student from school athletic teams did not implicate any due process rights. Students do not have a due process property interest in any particular component of a public education, such as extracurricular activities participation.** There was also no due process violation based on the disclosure of medical information. The results of the drug testing were only revealed to the student's parents and his medical condition was not indicated. The court held for the district and school officials on all the claims. *Dominic J. v. Wyoming Valley West High School*, 362 F.Supp.2d 560 (M.D. Pa. 2005).

◆ A Washington school district implemented a policy that required student-athletes to consent to random drug testing as a condition of participating in sports. A group of parents sued the district on behalf of their children, alleging state and federal constitutional violations. The court denied their motion for a preliminary order halting the testing, and they appealed. Meanwhile, the district agreed to stop testing students pending trial. The state court of appeals held that even if the district continued testing, **there was no showing that the drug testing policy invaded any clear legal or equitable right**. The Washington Supreme Court and the U.S. Supreme Court have allowed suspicionless searches in certain circumstances under the "special needs" exception to the Fourth Amendment. This exception allows the government to conduct searches without a warrant or probable cause, if special needs beyond law enforcement exist that make constitutional probable cause requirements impracticable.

To determine whether the special needs exception applies, courts examine the nature of the privacy interest and the character and degree of the intrusion. **If a compelling state interest justifies the intrusion, and the intrusion is narrowly tailored, the search will be allowed.** The district had to justify the policy by showing a compelling state interest and devising a narrowly tailored means of serving this interest. Since the parents did not show the policy was unreasonable per se or demonstrate that it invaded a clear legal or equitable right, the court remanded the case and dismissed the appeal as moot. *York v. Wahkiakum School Dist. No. 200*, 40 P.3d 1198 (Wash. Ct. App. 2002).

B. Athletic and Extracurricular Suspensions

The courts have not recognized any constitutional right to participate in interscholastic athletics or other extracurricular activities. The possibility of obtaining a college athletic scholarship is also not protected.

◆ An Indiana student violated his school code of conduct as a high school freshman, and he was suspended for half a track season. As a senior, he violated the code again by allowing friends to bring beer and intoxicated persons to his house. The student's parents called police and told the school of the incident. The student was suspended from extracurricular activities based on his second violation of the code of conduct. The parents appealed, but two separate hearing panels affirmed the action. The parents sued the school district in a federal district court, asserting the district athletic director had appointed cronies to the hearing panels. They asserted the district maintained unconstitutional, arbitrary, capricious and fraudulent policies and procedures. The court rejected a motion to dismiss the case based on mootness. Although the student had graduated and was ineligible to participate in high school athletics, he sought money damages.

The court then considered the district's motion to dismiss the due process claims. The parents claimed district policies encouraged them to "communicate confidentially with school officials concerning substance abuse, and then sanction them for doing so." They stated the district appeals process promised relief but provided none because of the athletic director's influence. **The court held Indiana law does not recognize a constitutional right to participate in interscholastic athletics.** It refused to apply a Wisconsin case urged by the parents as requiring high school athletics to satisfy due process principles. **The possibility of obtaining a college athletic scholarship was not protected by the Due Process Clause.** The court dismissed the case, refusing to consider the parents' claim that the district policies and procedures violated the state constitution or contract law. *D.N. v. Penn Harris Madison School Corp.*, No. 3:05-CV-716RM, 2006 WL 2710596 (N.D. Ind. 2006).

◆ A Kentucky high school student admitted to the school principal that he had been drinking alcohol before coming to a school dance. The school board excluded him from playing basketball and all other extracurricular activities. He sued the board and principal in state court, asserting the discipline was arbitrary and capricious. He further alleged discrimination and due process violations. The court dismissed the complaint, and the student appealed. **The Court of Appeals of Kentucky first noted that students have no fundamental or vested property right to participate in interscholastic athletics. For that reason, the student's constitutional claims were not viable and had been properly dismissed.** The court stated a school board may suspend or expel a student for violating lawful school regulations. The courts could not interfere with school board discretion, unless a board acted arbitrarily or maliciously. The student claimed the board acted arbitrarily and capriciously in denying his opportunity to participate in interscholastic athletics. The court held he stated a viable claim for arbitrary and capricious action by the board and principal, and the trial court should not have dismissed it on the summary basis of the record. *Critchelow v. Breckinridge County Board of Educ.*, No. 2005-CA-001194-MR, 2006 WL 3456658 (Ky. Ct. App. 2006).

◆ Several parents reported to school officials that a Washington student-athlete and several other football team members were drinking alcohol at a dance. School officials investigated and learned from the coach of an opposing team that one player believed the student and some teammates had been under the influence of alcohol during the previous week's football game. A school security staff member saw a beer container in the student's car. A search of the car yielded an empty beer carton, cigars and tobacco residue. The school suspended the student for 10 days for violating a high school policy against drinking alcohol as a member of the football team. He appealed the discipline, and the athletic board suspended him from a football game and five wrestling matches. He had to forfeit his football letter and individual honors and was recommended for alcohol evaluation and treatment. The principal upheld both the academic and athletic sanctions pursuant to an informal conference, as did a district hearing officer and the school board. The student sued the school district in a state court for violating his due process rights. He also made claims for unlawful search and seizure and state law violations. The court held for the district, and the student appealed to the Court of Appeals of Washington.

The student argued he had a protected property interest in interscholastic sports participation and other extracurricular activities. He contended his property interest in athletics was heightened by his hopes for a college football scholarship. The district countered that athletic participation is a privilege, and that no state or federal court has ever held there is a fundamental right to engage in interscholastic sports. **The court agreed with the district, finding interscholastic sports participation is not required for graduation or by law and is a privilege, not a constitutionally protected property or liberty interest.** The school district provided the student with more process than required under the circumstances by applying the state law procedures for short-term academic suspensions. The district was not required to provide him with the kind of protections he would receive for an expulsion proceeding. The judgment for the district was affirmed. *Taylor v. Enumclaw School Dist. No. 216*, 133 P.3d 492 (Wash. Ct. App. 2006).

C. Eligibility Rules and Restrictions

State athletic association eligibility rules requiring a sit-out period for athletes transferring into a district from a neighboring school district, private school or from out of state, may be enforced if they are reasonably related to the prevention of recruiting student-athletes. Challenges by students with disabilities are considered in Section II C., below.

1. Transfer Students

◆ The U.S. Court of Appeals, Eleventh Circuit, affirmed a district court judgment against a Georgia high school football coach and former players who alleged harm when the state high school association forfeited their games for a season. The association found the school improperly included a non-resident player on the team. The lower court rejected student claims based on lost opportunities to receive college scholarships. **Students have no constitutional right to participate in athletics. As the coach was not discharged or demoted, his constitutional rights were also not violated.** *Stewart v. Bibb County Board of Educ.*, 195 Fed.Appx. 927 (11th Cir. 2006).

◆ A Louisiana student played interscholastic basketball for a high school in Livingston Parish. The family residence was on a tract of land with a barn and dog kennels. The parents decided to move to St. John the Baptist Parish to serve the special education needs of the student's brother, and they rented an apartment in that district. The family advertised their Livingston Parish real property for sale and changed their mailing address. They continued to use the property for dog breeding and left personal property there. The parents enrolled the student and her brother in a private school. The school principal believed the student was eligible to play varsity basketball under a Louisiana High School Athletic Association (LHSAA) transfer rule and a related rule on bona fide changes of residence. The LHSAA received a complaint about the school and hired a private investigator. The parents claimed two LHSAA officers demanded to search their house and threatened to immediately declare the student ineligible if they refused. They let the officers search the house.

The LHSAA commissioner ruled that the school violated its transfer and change of residence rules by letting the student play basketball. The LHSAA placed the school on probation, fined it, assessed it for the private investigator's services and made it forfeit the 15 games in which the student played. The LHSAA executive committee upheld the decision, and the student sued the LHSAA and its officers in a state court. The court dismissed the case, and the student appealed. The Court of Appeal of Louisiana noted she had graduated. Her claims for injunctive relief were moot, but she could still assert claims for monetary damages. The court found no merit to the claim for procedural and substantive due process violations. **The court found the student's claim to "an opportunity for an athletic scholarship to college" was a speculative and uncertain expectation, not a protected property interest. The student had no due process rights to participate in interscholastic sports.** The court found her equal protection claim did not specifically allege how she was treated differently from others. The student would be allowed to amend her complaint to specify equal protection violations. **The court held the LHSAA was not a state actor that could be held liable for an unlawful search of a private home. However, the complaint stated sufficient facts to support a claim for invasion of privacy under state law.** The court reversed that part of the judgment. *Johansen v. Louisiana High School Athletic Ass'n*, 916 So.2d 1081 (La. Ct. App. 2005).

◆ The parent of a Kansas high school freshman claimed a public high school athletic director recruited his son extensively. According to the parent, the director sent another student to their home to ensure his son would attend the school's summer football practices. The student attended the school for two half-days and then decided to transfer. He sent the athletic director a "limited eligibility transfer form" that would allow him to remain eligible for non-varsity sports after a transfer. The director refused to sign the eligibility form, asserting the transfer was athletically motivated. The state athletic association's executive director approved the denial, as did the association's executive and appeals boards. The boards relied on statements by school officials, who declared the parent considered his son's athletic opportunities when making the transfer decision. The parent claimed the transfer was not motivated by athletics, and he sued the association, school district and athletic director in a federal district court. He asserted due process and equal protection violations based on the transfer denial and association hearing procedures.

The court considered the parent's request for a preliminary injunction and noted the student would not suffer any irreparable harm if it failed to intervene. He would miss only 18 weeks of basketball eligibility and could still practice with the football team. The court held **association hearing processes did not**

violate any due process rights, as they included several levels of review. Contrary to the parent's argument, cross-examination rights are not a necessary component of due process in administrative hearings. The court held the board had a basis for denying the eligibility request and refused to overturn it. **As there is no recognized property interest in playing non-varsity sports, the court found no equal protection violation**. *Love v. Kansas State High School Activities Ass'n*, No. 04-1319-JTM, 2004 WL 2357879 (D. Kan. 2004).

◆ An Indiana public high school student transferred to a private school due to "mental and emotional stress." The Indiana High School Athletic Association (IHSAA) rejected her request to compete on the private school's varsity basketball team under its transfer rule. The IHSAA held the student was not entitled to a hardship exemption, but she obtained a preliminary order from a state trial court declaring her eligible to play varsity sports. The order did not mention enforcement of the IHSAA's restitution rule, which permits the association to require schools to forfeit victories and titles won with ineligible students. The private school decided not to allow the student to play on its varsity basketball team, fearing the risk of forfeitures under the restitution rule. The IHSAA appealed to the state court of appeals, and the student petitioned the trial court for a contempt order against the IHSAA. The court upheld the sanctions against the IHSAA, which appealed to the Indiana Supreme Court.

The court noted the trial court order restrained the IHSAA from attempting to enforce its transfer rule, but did not mention the restitution rule. Even if the IHSAA's appeal was an effort to enforce the restitution rule, the preliminary order was not sufficiently clear to permit a contempt finding. The student did not notify the IHSAA that her school was keeping her off the basketball team. The trial court lacked sufficient grounds to find the IHSAA had willfully and contemptuously disregarded its preliminary order. **In previous decisions, the supreme court upheld the validity of the restitution rule, finding it did not authorize interference with a court order. The student could not prevent enforcement of the restitution rule through a contempt action**, and the court reversed the contempt order. It also vacated a fine imposed on the IHSAA. *Indiana High School Athletic Ass'n v. Martin*, 765 N.E.2d 1238 (Ind. 2002).

◆ A student completed his twelfth-grade classes in Australia, where students are allowed to repeat subjects. He then sought to repeat courses in the U.S. so he could play intercollegiate sports. A California high school coach helped the student with immigration papers, and an assistant coach offered him lodging. The California Interscholastic Federation (CIF) declared the student ineligible under its eight-semester and transfer rules. After an unsuccessful CIF appeal, the student petitioned a state trial court for an order requiring the CIF to rescind its eligibility determination. The court found insufficient evidence his transfer request was motivated by athletic purposes. The CIF commissioner then found the high school and coach violated CIF rules by exercising undue influence on the student. After exhausting his CIF appeals, the student filed another state court action, seeking to vacate the undue influence ruling.

The court directed the CIF to vacate the undue influence ruling, declaring two CIF bylaws unconstitutional for failing to provide minimal

due process. The CIF appealed both rulings and an order awarding the student's attorney more than $92,000 in fees. The Court of Appeal of California held **interscholastic athletic participation is not a "property interest" protected by the state constitution. As there was no property interest at stake, the student had no due process right to play varsity sports.** The court rejected his attempt to expand the state constitutional right to a free public education into a broader right to participate in a particular component of a public education, such as interscholastic sports. The student had no viable claim for damage to his reputation from the undue influence charge, since it pertained to the coach. CIF bylaws provided a prompt decision-making process and the opportunity for full hearings. Because CIF procedures were valid and the student received all the process he was due, the court reversed the judgments. **Substantial evidence supported the CIF's finding of undue influence by the head coach, as he had improperly assisted the student.** *Ryan v. California Interscholastic Federation*, 114 Cal.Rptr.2d 787, 94 Cal.App.4th 1033 (Cal. Ct. App. 2001).

2.   Other Rules

◆   A West Virginia student who had been home-schooled sought to participate on a middle school wrestling team. The West Virginia Secondary School Activities Commission (WVSSAC) denied the request, as its rules limited inter-scholastic sports to full-time students in WVSSAC-participating schools. The student's parents sued the WVSSAC and state and local school officials in a West Virginia court, which issued a preliminary order finding the WVSSAC and the officials violated state constitutional and statutory requirements. It held the total ban on interscholastic sports participation by home-schooled students was unreasonable. WVSSAC and school officials appealed to the Supreme Court of Appeals, West Virginia's highest court. **The court found the most persuasive reasons for excluding home-schooled students from interscholastic sports were the state's interests in promoting academics over athletics, and protecting the economic interests of public schools.**

WVSSAC rules required students to maintain a 2.0 grade average to remain eligible for interscholastic sports. Students also had to do passing work in four subjects per week in which they could earn credit toward graduation. Home-schooled students were evaluated only once per year. The court stated school boards should not be required to spend funds to support home-schooled student participation in interscholastic sports. **The court recognized in prior decisions that participation in extracurricular activities did not rise to the level of a fundamental or constitutional right under the West Virginia Constitution.** Equal protection principles were not violated when public and non-public school students were treated differently with respect to allocation of state aid and education resources. **The court had no difficulty finding that excluding home-schooled students from interscholastic sports did not violate equal protection. Like the parents of private school students, the parents of home-schooled children voluntarily chose not to participate in the state's public school system.** In making this choice, these parents agreed to forego the privileges of a public school education, one of which was the opportunity to qualify for interscholastic sports. State law did not expressly require the

WVSSAC to allow home-schooled students to play sports. The state statute relied upon in the circuit court's decision did not even address interscholastic sports. The court held the WVSSAC did not exceed its authority in issuing the eligibility rules. As the rules were not arbitrary or capricious, and were reasonably related to legitimate state purposes, the court reversed the judgment. *Jones v. West Virginia State Board of Educ.*, 218 W.Va. 52, 622 S.E.2d 289 (W.Va. 2005).

♦   A New York student did not participate in any interscholastic sports during his freshman year, when he was home-schooled "under the supervision and/or assistance of the Kolbe Academy." He then attended a private school for grade 10, repeated grade 10 at a different private school, and attended grade 11 at still another school. New York State Public High School Athletic Association rules did not specifically address home-schooled students. One regulation stated each "pupil shall be eligible for senior high school athletic competition in a sport during each of four consecutive seasons of such sport commencing with the pupil's entry into grade nine and prior to graduation." The student returned to the school where he had repeated grade 10 for his senior year and sought to play varsity football. The school's athletic director found this was his fifth season of competition since grade nine, and he was not seeking an eligibility extension due to any of the reasons specified in the association's rule. The athletic director contacted the commissioner of the association, who advised him that the student was ineligible. The student's parents did not seek review by the commissioner or the appropriate Extended Eligibility Commission. Instead, they sued the association in a New York court, asserting he had been excluded from interscholastic participation based on their decision to home school him.

   The court observed that the school's athletic director had found the student ineligible for football because he was in his fifth season of competition since beginning grade nine. **He was not eligible for an extension because home schooling was not one of the circumstances listed in the commissioner's regulations. The court found no basis for an equal protection challenge, since a student's athletic eligibility began with entry into ninth grade, whether this was in a public or private school, or at home.** A request for a fifth year of eligibility must be made to the Extended Eligibility Committee, but no such application had been made in this case. As a result, there was no decision by the athletic association for the court to review. The court agreed with the commissioner that the parents' failure to seek administrative review barred the lawsuit. The petition also had to be dismissed because the student had already received his four years of high school athletic eligibility. *Guy v. New York State Public High School Athletic Ass'n*, 9 Misc.3d 1116(A), 808 N.Y.S.2d 917 (N.Y. Sup. Ct. 2005).

♦   A Florida student attended All Saints Academy, where he played varsity baseball. He asked the Florida High School Athletic Association (FHSAA) for a hardship waiver. The FHSAA denied the request. The student sued the FHSAA in a state court, asking for an injunction so he could play varsity baseball for another year. After a hearing, the court granted his request and the FHSAA appealed to the Court of Appeal of Florida. **The court held it could intervene only if the FHSAA's actions adversely affected "substantial**

property, contract or other economic rights" and FHSAA internal procedures were inadequate or unfair, or if the association acted maliciously or in bad faith. There was no evidence that the FHSAA improperly denied the student's request, or that its internal procedures were inadequate. The trial court did not have sufficient grounds to intervene in the case. The student did not show the decision adversely affected his substantial property, contract or other economic rights, or that the FHSAA acted maliciously or in bad faith. The court found no exceptional circumstances to support court intervention, and it reversed the judgment. *Florida High School Athletic Ass'n v. Marazzito*, 891 So.2d 653 (Fla. Dist. Ct. App. 2005).

◆   A Pennsylvania student was home-schooled for his seventh- and eighth-grade years. A school district allowed her to play interscholastic basketball both years. The student ended her home school program in grade nine and enrolled in a state-chartered and certified "cyber charter school." The school district let the student play on an interscholastic basketball team, but it later excluded her for failing to meet district requirements. The student's family sued the district in a federal district court. The case was voluntarily dismissed after the state legislature amended the state Charter School Law to specifically authorize cyber charter schools. The family's second action was dismissed.

The family appealed to the U.S. Court of Appeals, Third Circuit. It noted the district's interscholastic sports participation requirements included at least a ninth-grade academic level, a similar curriculum to that of the students enrolled in district schools, verifiable attendance documentation, passing grades and at least average citizenship grades. All of the student's attendance and class time was self-verified, under a curriculum provided by the University of Missouri. As her attendance was not verified by certified instructors and her curriculum was not approved by the state board of education, the school district could find her ineligible for interscholastic sports. **The decision denying the student's participation in interscholastic sports did not violate her constitutional rights of association. There is no right to education under the U.S. Constitution.** The district court had properly dismissed the due process claim. **There is no due process interest in extracurricular activities participation.** The equal protection claim was also properly dismissed. As the district's stated justifications for excluding the student met the court's minimal rational basis review, the court affirmed the judgment. *Angstadt v. Midd-West School Dist.*, 377 F.3d 338 (3d Cir. 2004).

◆   An Ohio student's custodial mother registered her to play basketball. The student tried out for the team and was selected for it. School policy required student-athletes to take school transportation to and from all athletic events. Another policy required them to attend all practices and games, including those held during school vacations. The student's non-custodial father sued the school board in a state court, seeking a declaration that its policies interfered with his court-ordered visitation rights. He also sought an order prohibiting the board from further "interfering" with these rights. The court awarded summary judgment to the board, and the father appealed. The Ohio Court of Appeals explained Ohio law vests each school board "with the authority to enact policies which are necessary to govern its schools and students." **Boards retain the discretion to decide what policies are necessary, and their decisions will be upheld in court, so long as they are reasonable and fairly calculated to ensure good government and promote education.** School policies are struck down only if they are unreasonable, an abuse of discretion or a violation of law. Courts evaluate policies according to standards of common sense, judicial experience and public policy considerations. The court affirmed the judgment, as the board's policies met these standards. *Kimball v. Keystone Local School Dist.*, No. 03CA008220, 2003 WL 22093257 (Ohio Ct. App. 2003).

II. DISCRIMINATION AND EQUITY

Federal civil rights laws forbid discrimination based on sex, race or disability in federally funded school athletic programs. All public school districts must also comply with the Equal Protection Clause.

A. Gender Equity

Title IX of the Education Amendments of 1972, 20 U.S.C. § 1681(a), prohibits sex discrimination and exclusion from participation in any educational program on the basis of sex by any program or activity receiving federal funding. Federal regulations at 34 C.F.R. Part 106.41 provide guidance on equal athletic opportunities for members of both sexes. In determining whether equal opportunities exist, the U.S. Department of Education's Office for Civil Rights (OCR) considers several factors including: (1) whether selection of sports and levels of competition accommodate both sexes; (2) the provision of equipment or supplies; (3) the scheduling of games and practices; (4) travel and per diem allowances; (5) coaching and tutoring opportunities; (6) coaching and tutoring assignments and compensation; (7) provision of locker rooms, practice and competitive facilities; (8) provision of medical and training facilities and services; and (10) publicity. See 34 C.F.R. Part 106.41(c).

◆ The Michigan High School Athletic Association (MHSAA) scheduled girls' basketball, volleyball and soccer seasons during non-traditional seasons throughout the state. Female student-athletes sued the MHSAA for violating the Equal Protection Clause, Title IX of the Education Amendments of 1972 and the state Civil Rights Act. A federal district court noted psychological harm was done to female athletes in the form of a message that they were subordinate to males. The scheduling created many disadvantages for girls, including lost scholarships and the inability to participate in "March Madness" events and tournaments. The court prohibited the MHSAA from continuing to schedule girls' sports in disadvantageous seasons. The MHSAA agreed to submit a compliance plan to the district court and appealed to the Sixth Circuit. The court reviewed the district court's findings of the many harms created by MHSAA scheduling practices. **Competition in non-traditional seasons harmed girls, particularly by sending them a message that they were "second class" or were less valued than boys.** The court did not review the Title IX and state law claims. The MHSAA appealed to the U.S. Supreme Court. In a memorandum known as a "grant/vacate/remand order" or "GVR," the Court vacated the decision and remanded the case to the Sixth Circuit to reconsider whether the MHSAA could be sued for constitutional rights violations under 42 U.S.C. § 1983 in light of its then-recent decision in *City of Rancho Palos Verdes v. Abrams*, 544 U.S 113 (2005).

The Sixth Circuit again affirmed the district court decision. This time, it not only found the MHSAA had violated the Equal Protection Clause, but had also violated Title IX. The court agreed with the female student-athletes that the *Rancho Palos Verdes* decision did not prevent them from pursuing a Section 1983 claim. The court stated the Supreme Court's GVR memorandum did not necessarily indicate the high court desired a different result. The Sixth Circuit agreed with the student-athletes that **Title IX did not preclude a recovery under Section 1983 for their equal protection claim. The Section 1983 claim was not an attempt to avoid Title IX procedures. The court upheld the district court's decision that the MHSAA was a state actor that could be held liable for constitutional violations.** The MHSAA's evidence did not establish that separate seasons for boys and girls maximized opportunities for their participation. Female athletes were always required to play in disadvantageous seasons. The scheduling differences were properly found to be discriminatory, as boys' and girls' schedules were separate and treated unequally. As the MHSAA could not justify its scheduling disparity, the court affirmed the judgment on the Equal Protection, Title IX and state civil rights act claims. *Communities for Equity v. Michigan High School Athletic Ass'n*, 459 F.3d 676 (6th Cir. 2006).

◆ A Wisconsin boy wanted to participate on the girls' gymnastics team at his high school. He filed a state court action against the Wisconsin Interscholastic Athletic Association (WIAA), alleging constitutional and Title IX claims. The student challenged a WIAA rule prohibiting all interscholastic activity involving boys and girls competing against each other, except as permitted by law and board of control interpretations. He added Wisconsin statutory and constitutional claims for injunctive relief. The court denied any relief, noting the WIAA is a private, voluntary association. As the WIAA was not a public entity, no equal protection suit could be brought against it. The WIAA received no federal funds and could not be sued under Title IX.

The student appealed to the Court of Appeals of Wisconsin. The court found that in order to sue the WIAA for constitutional rights violations, the student had to show the state was intertwined with WIAA management. However, the court found he failed to offer any evidence that the WIAA was engaged in action traditionally reserved to the state. **The trial court had properly dismissed his equal protection claims. The student also failed to show that the WIAA received federal funds. Without proof that it did so, the WIAA had no Title IX liability.** The student's state law claims consisted of one sentence. The court affirmed the judgment for the WIAA. *Bukowski v. Wisconsin Interscholastic Ass'n*, 726 N.W.2d 356 (Table) (Wis. Ct. App. 2006).

◆ New York state and regional championships for girls' soccer were held in the fall, and 649 of 714 schools offering soccer scheduled it accordingly. Some districts scheduled girls' soccer in the spring, stating this was done to avoid jeopardizing their girls' field hockey programs. Two districts scheduled their boys' soccer seasons for fall, and their boys' teams remained eligible for state and regional competition. Girls' soccer was the only sport held outside the state championship season in either district. The families of two students who sought to play girls' soccer for teams in the districts filed a federal district court action against the districts, asserting Title IX violations. The court heard evidence that playing high school soccer during spring presented significant disadvantages, such as loss of participation in tournaments, disadvantages for college recruitment, scheduling conflicts and increased risks of injury. The court held the scheduling of girls' soccer seasons in spring violated Title IX. The districts were ordered to devise a plan to offer soccer to both sexes in the same season.

The districts appealed to the Second Circuit, which noted **34 C.F.R. Part 106.41 requires federal funding recipients to provide equal athletic opportunities for members of both sexes according to 10 factors**. A Title IX policy interpretation addressing intercollegiate athletics could be used in high school cases. **The interpretation required equivalent treatment, benefits and opportunities, and the accommodation of interests and abilities of both sexes.** Under U.S. Department of Education compliance standards, institutions are deemed in compliance with Title IX if program components are "equal or equal in effect." Compliance was generally not measured by "sport-specific comparison," but instead by examining program-wide opportunities. **The scheduling of girls' soccer in spring created a disparity that had a negative impact on girls.** The districts did not identify any area in which girls received comparably better treatment than boys. They could not offset the disadvantage created for girls by scheduling their soccer seasons during spring. The disparity created by scheduling the girls soccer season in spring, while maintaining boys soccer in fall was substantial enough to deny girls equality of athletic opportunity. **The scheduling of girls' soccer in spring sent girls the message they were not expected to succeed and that the school did not value their athletic ability as much as it valued the ability of boys.** The districts were unable to justify the disparity in opportunities for equal athletic opportunity between the girls' and boys' soccer teams. There was no reason why soccer and field hockey could not be played in the same season. The court affirmed the judgment but remanded the case to modify the requirement for a compliance plan. The district court was to consider whether boys and girls received equal opportunities for post-season competition. *McCormick v. School Dist. of Mamaroneck*, 370 F.3d 275 (2d Cir. 2004).

◆ The Minnesota State High School League recognized girls hockey as a varsity sport in 1994, many years after it began sponsoring boys hockey. Boys hockey tournaments took place in professional sports arenas, including the Target and Xcel Energy Centers. The league selected Ridder Arena, home of the University of Minnesota women's hockey team, to be the site of the 2004 girls tournament. A group representing girls hockey team members and their parents sued the league in a federal district court for Title IX and state Human Rights

Act violations. The court considered a motion for a preliminary order to venue the girls tournament at the Xcel Energy Center, site of the 2004 boys tournament and home of the Minnesota Wild professional hockey team. It held **neither Title IX nor state law required the identical treatment of boys and girls athletics. Instead, the laws required "equivalent treatment and equal accommodation."** While Ridder's seating capacity was far less than Xcel's, the group did not show it was insufficient to host the girls tournament. The court found girls hockey was rapidly becoming more popular, creating the possibility that differences in seating capacity might cause illegal discrimination in the near future. As the group did not show it was entitled to an injunction, the court denied its request. *Mason v. Minnesota State High School League*, No. Civ. 036462 (PAM/RLE), 2003 WL 23109685 (D. Minn. 2003).

The court later considered the league's motion for summary judgment and noted not all the considerations that resulted in denial of the preliminary order remained at issue. There was now no concern for the immanency of the next tournament. The court noted Xcel Center was "one of the nation's finest hockey arenas" and was equipped with large color scoreboards, closed-circuit televisions and padded seating. Ridder lacked these features and had more modest locker facilities. The court stated **federal policy interpretations of Title IX required that "program components must be equal or equal in effect."** The Minnesota Supreme Court has held the state human rights act requires the treatment of "separate teams must be as nearly equal as possible."

The court held the girls demonstrated enough differences in the way the league handled the tournaments to avoid pretrial dismissal. They raised questions regarding whether the league treated them equally. The league did not show its gender classification was "exceedingly persuasive," that the arenas it used were "equal or equal in effect," or that the overall effect of the difference was negligible. The league scheduled other girls sports events at Xcel and a boys tournament there drew smaller or comparable crowds than girls events. **The girls raised the issue of what message the choice of venue sent to female hockey players and fans.** Since the evidence could lead a jury to find the league's scheduling policy violated Title IX, the court denied the league's motion and ordered a trial. Less than a month after the decision, the parties announced a settlement under which the girls tournament would be held at Xcel Center beginning in 2006. *Mason v. Minnesota State High School League*, No. Civ. 03-6462 (JRT/FLN), 2004 WL 1630968 (D. Minn. 2004).

◆ An eighth-grade Kansas student was the only girl on her junior high school wrestling team. Although she compiled a record of five wins and three losses for the junior high school team, **she was prohibited from joining the high school team as a freshman based on a decision by the superintendent** of schools. The superintendent anticipated parental objections, sexual harassment lawsuits, student safety problems and school disruption. He also noted that regulations under Title IX of the Education Amendments of 1972 classified wrestling as a contact sport and thus did not require her participation. The student filed a lawsuit against the school board, district and superintendent in the U.S. District Court for the District of Kansas, which considered her motion for a preliminary order allowing her participation.

The court agreed with the school officials that because wrestling is a contact sport under Title IX regulations, the Title IX claim would likely be dismissed at a trial. However, it rejected the officials' argument that Title IX established a comprehensive remedial scheme that precluded the student's constitutional claims. Sex-based discrimination by a government agency could be justified only where the discrimination was substantially related to important governmental objectives. In this case, school officials had identified no important governmental objective. **Parental objections and the inconvenience of providing separate locker room facilities were not important governmental objectives**, and there was no evidence that the student's participation was likely to result in great danger. The court granted her request for a preliminary order. *Adams v. Baker*, 919 F.Supp. 1496 (D. Kan. 1996).

◆ **A male Rhode Island high school student desired to compete as a member of his school's girls' field hockey team.** However, the regulations of the Rhode Island Interscholastic League forbade boys from participating on girls' athletic teams. A federal district court denied the student's request for an injunction based on the Fourteenth Amendment's Equal Protection Clause. The student then sued the league in a Rhode Island state court, seeking an injunction based on the state constitution's equal protection provisions. The trial court granted the request, noting that the state constitution required stricter scrutiny of gender classifications than the U.S. Constitution. It granted the injunction, and the league appealed to the Rhode Island Supreme Court. The state supreme court held the trial court had applied the wrong standard. **Gender classifications under the state constitution need only serve important governmental objectives and be substantially related to the achievement of those objectives. Safety concerns and physical differences between the sexes justified the rule.** The injunction was vacated and the action remanded. *Kleczek v. Rhode Island Interscholastic League*, 612 A.2d 734 (R.I. 1992).

◆ In *Williams v. School Dist. of Bethlehem*, 998 F.2d 168 (3d Cir. 1993), the U.S. Court of Appeals, Third Circuit, reversed and remanded a district court order allowing a Pennsylvania boy to compete on a girls' field hockey team.

B. Race Discrimination

1. Secondary Schools

As discussed in Chapter Four, Section IV of this Volume, Title VI of the Civil Rights Act of 1964 prohibits race discrimination in any program that receives federal funds. Title VI is based on the principles of the Equal Protection Clause, and many discrimination complaints allege violations of Title VI, the Equal Protection Clause, and analogous state law provisions. Liability in a Title VI action is limited to cases of intentional discrimination.

◆ Thirteen suburban Chicago school districts withdrew from the South Inter-Conference Association after over 30 years of membership. They formed two new athletic conferences, excluding two school districts in Thornton, Illinois that served mostly African-American students. The Thornton districts alleged a racially motivated conspiracy among the 13 districts, resulting in three racially segregated conferences. They joined several Thornton parents and students in a federal district court action against the 13 districts. Among the allegations was the claim that the 13 districts "revived racial segregation in public schools, separating the races," more than 50 years after *Brown v. Board of Education* outlawed segregation. The complaint stated the 13 districts had "gerrymandered themselves" via an "apartheid-like realignment" using public funds.

The Thornton parties claimed the "secession from the association by the defendants is white flight," and "the defendants have erected a racial Mason-Dixon line down I-57." They included a racially charged statement by a board member of one of the 13 districts accusing African-Americans of ruining neighborhoods in Chicago's south suburbs. The court explained that allegations in a complaint may be stricken if they are either prejudicial or unrelated to the controversy. The Thornton parties claimed that the reference to *Brown* stated the grounds of their lawsuit. While its relevancy was unclear at the early stages of the case, the court found the 13 districts did not show it was immaterial or prejudicial. As the Thornton parties claimed the reference to gerrymandering went to the heart of the case, the court found no reason to strike it. The court agreed with the 13 districts that references to apartheid, white flight and a racial Mason-Dixon line were "impertinent" and "inappropriate hyperbole." As there was no basis for any of them, the court struck them from the complaint. The lengthy statement by the board member was redundant and served no purpose but to scandalize the conduct of the 13 districts. His remarks might be inadmissible hearsay and had to be stricken. *Board of Educ. of Thornton Township High School Dist. 205 v. Board of Educ. of Argo Community High School Dist. 217*, No. CIV A. 06 C 2005, 2006 WL 1896068 (N.D. Ill. 2006).

◆   A Mississippi student's parent claimed the school's head football coach called her son "nigger" and "fat black ass" during team practices. She alleged a teammate repeated these epithets after hearing them from the coach. According to the parent, the teammate and another player hit her son's helmet with rocks during practice. She claimed the coach did nothing and that the principal took no action when she reported this. In a later practice, the teammate allegedly lunged at the student and gouged his eye, causing permanent injury. The principal investigated the incident, but no one admitted seeing an assault. The parent sued the district, coaching staff and school officials in a federal district court, alleging deprivation of her son's civil rights. The court dismissed the claims, and the parent appealed to the U.S. Court of Appeals, Fifth Circuit.

The court found the teammate was not a state actor and thus could not be liable for civil rights violations under 42 U.S.C. § 1983. There was no evidence of any conspiracy between the teammate and coaches to deprive the student of his civil rights. The Due Process Clause did not require the coaches to protect the student from the teammate. There was no "special relationship" between the coaches and student that would create an exception to the general rule of non-liability for acts of private violence. The parent's claim of lack of supervision rested on the wrongful idea that the state was a guarantor of a student safety. There was no evidence of active participation or "significant encouragement" of alleged racial bias by the coach. While the court found the conduct of school officials "morally reprehensible," the teammate's actions could not be attributed to them. **The court held the use of racial epithets, without evidence of harassment or other deprivation of established rights, does not constitute an equal protection violation. The school investigated the incident, and while its response may have been inadequate, it did not show inaction creating an equal protection violation.** Apart from the racial epithets, the parent produced no evidence of bias by school officials. The district court had properly declined jurisdiction over the state law claims, and the judgment was affirmed. *Priester v. Lowndes County*, 354 F.3d 414 (5th Cir. 2004).

The case returned to the district court, which found the student had alleged sufficient facts to avoid summary judgment on his race discrimination claims against the district. He claimed he was deprived of due process by being suspended from school and having his transfer revoked. The court would have to further consider if he had been punished more harshly than white students. Disputed issues of fact surrounded the student's expulsion, including whether he had shoved the coach and threatened to kill the teammates while disobeying instructions to avoid a confrontation with them. **The court found that if a jury agreed with the coach's account, the student would be unable to prove he was treated differently than the white teammates. As the school board had made the decision to expel the student, only it could have potential liability for his due process and equal protection claims.** These claims would proceed to further court activity. The court awarded summary judgment to the coaches and other school officials for the claims against them in their individual capacities. *Priester v. Starkville School Dist.*, No. 1:03CV90, 2005 WL 2347285 (N.D. Miss. 2005).

2. Intercollegiate Athletics

National Collegiate Athletic Association (NCAA) rules intended to improve college graduation rates have been the subject of major federal court litigation alleging race discrimination against African-American students seeking opportunities to compete in intercollegiate athletics.

◆ NCAA Proposition 16 increased the number of core high school courses in which students needed to have a minimum grade point average and determined eligibility for freshman student-athletes based on a formula that combined their GPAs and standardized test scores. A group of African-American students claimed the NCAA purposefully screened out from eligibility greater numbers of black students by adopting Proposition 16, in violation of Title VI of the Civil Rights Act and 42 U.S.C. § 1981. A federal district court in Pennsylvania dismissed the case and the students appealed to the Third Circuit.

The court held the class made a sufficient pretrial showing of intentional discrimination by the NCAA to avoid dismissing their claims under Title VI and Section 1981. However, one of the students, who had a learning disability, had no standing to pursue discrimination claims against the NCAA under the Americans with Disabilities Act and Section 504 of the Rehabilitation Act. The court noted the case closely resembled *Cureton v. NCAA*, below, but added new claims based on intentional and disability discrimination. **The court agreed with the students that the NCAA had expressly considered race when it adopted Proposition 16.** Although the NCAA may have adopted Proposition 16 for the laudable goal of increasing minority graduation rates, **the Supreme Court has clearly stated the consideration of race subjects a decision maker to liability for discrimination.** The court held the complaint alleged intentional discrimination and refused to dismiss the Section 1981 and Title VI claims prior to a trial. The case was remanded to the district court to determine whether the students' Title VI and Section 1981 claims for purposeful discrimination could be substantiated. *Pryor v. NCAA*, 288 F.3d 548 (3d Cir. 2002).

◆   Four African-American students filed a federal class action suit against the NCAA to challenge Proposition 16, which increased the number of required high school core courses from 11 to 13 and established an initial eligibility index regarding the standardized testing requirements for college freshmen seeking to participate in intercollegiate sports. The students claimed the requirements had a disproportionate effect on college-bound African-American students. A federal district court initially held the NCAA could be sued under Title VI, because the NCAA was an indirect recipient of federal funds. The court reviewed evidence that a statistically relevant number of college-bound African-American students failed to meet the Proposition 16 testing requirements. The NCAA argued Proposition 16 was designed to raise the graduation rates of African-American students and close the gap between the graduation rates of white and African-American students. The court rejected the NCAA's assertion, finding the students had successfully demonstrated racial discrimination. The NCAA was unable to overcome this showing with evidence that Proposition 16 was justified by educational necessity, and it did not show any particular test score was a valid predictor of graduation rates. While raising the graduation rate of student-athletes was a legitimate educational goal, the NCAA's attempt to redress the racial disparity in graduation rates was not. As there was no evidence this was the goal of Proposition 16, the court granted the students summary judgment. The NCAA appealed to the Third Circuit.

According to the court, the NCAA did not receive federal funds either directly or indirectly based on its relationship with member institutions. There was insufficient evidence to establish that the National Youth Sports Program, an NCAA affiliate that received federal funds, was the alter ego of the NCAA. Title VI regulations are program specific, and it was not alleged that NCAA programs and activities themselves had a disparate impact on African-Americans. The court also rejected the theory that the NCAA was a federal funding recipient based on its authority over member schools that received federal funds. The ultimate decision-making power for freshman athletic participation remained with member schools. The threat of NCAA sanctions, although undesirable to colleges, did not result in NCAA control. Because NCAA member institutions retained their authority, each of the students' arguments for Title VI liability failed. The court reversed the judgment for the students and remanded the case. *Cureton v. NCAA*, 198 F.3d 107 (3d Cir. 1999).

The students moved the district court to amend their complaint with a claim alleging intentional discrimination. The court denied the motion, finding they had waited too long to amend the complaint and that the amendment was futile and would result in impermissible prejudice to the NCAA. On appeal, the Third Circuit upheld the district court decision, agreeing that the amended complaint was filed too late. *Cureton v. NCAA*, 252 F.3d 267 (3d Cir. 2001).

C. Students with Disabilities

Although school districts and state high school athletic associations may adopt nondiscriminatory limits on varsity athletic competition, rules that prevent students from competing beyond a stated number of semesters or age have been found to violate state and federal anti-discrimination laws.

◆   A Colorado student was diagnosed with attention deficit disorder (ADD) at age eight. He received medication and attended a speech class for grade four. By middle school, the student's special education program ended, and he stopped taking medication for ADD. In high school, his academic modifications were limited to additional time for tests and homework, and the provision of class notes. The student missed several weeks of school in ninth grade due to a sinus infection and repeated grade nine. His parents divorced near this time. The student played varsity football during high school and was considered a team leader. When the student reached grade 12, state athletic association rules barred him from playing football again because he was in his ninth consecutive semester of high school attendance. The association denied his request for a hardship waiver. The student sued the association in a state court, seeking an order that the eight-semester rule violated the Colorado Anti-Discrimination Act (CADA). The court denied the student's request for preliminary relief, and he appealed to the Court of Appeals of Colorado.

The court stated that the CADA is interpreted like the Americans with Disabilities Act (ADA). There was substantial evidence that the student had repeated grade nine because of his parents' divorce, problems adjusting to a new school, and his sinus infection. The court stated "disability" was as an impairment that substantially limited one or more of a person's major life activities. **To be considered a "substantial limitation," an impairment must prevent or severely restrict an individual from performing a major life activity.** The court held the student was not disabled under the CADA. The term "substantial" suggested an impairment of ample or considerable amount, quantity or dimension. The impairment must also have permanent or long-term effects. **The court held the "mere diagnosis of a disability does not itself indicate that the disability substantially affected an individual's major life activities."** The student no longer received treatment or medication for ADD. His special education program was discontinued and he now received only minor accommodations. **The court held a single failed year of school was a temporary and short-term event that did not render the student "disabled" under the CADA or the ADA.** There was no evidence that the student had a developmental disability as defined by the CADA. The trial court had properly denied his request for temporary relief and the judgment was affirmed. *Tesmer v. Colorado High School Activities Ass'n*, 140 P.3d 249 (Colo. Ct. App. 2006).

◆   A Pennsylvania student with learning disabilities was classified as educable mentally retarded. **His individualized education program (IEP) required him to participate in extracurricular activities.** The student did not reach high school until he was 16 years old, when he attended school as a non-graded student with no numerical grade. Under the Individuals with Disabilities Education Act (IDEA), the student was entitled to attend high school at least until he turned age 21. The student turned 19 years old prior to the start of his fourth year of high school, 28 days before the date when a Pennsylvania Interscholastic Athletic Association (PIAA) bylaw would operate to exclude him from further interscholastic sports eligibility. The PIAA rejected his request for a waiver, and he commenced a federal district court action against it under the Americans with Disabilities Act (ADA), Section 504 of the Rehabilitation Act and the IDEA. The court denied his motion for a temporary order that would have allowed him to compete in football, wrestling and track.

The court found **the student had no competitive advantage in football or track when compared to younger students that might contravene the stated purposes of the age 19 bylaw. However, there was evidence that he excelled in wrestling and had a competitive advantage in that sport.** The court held the student did not exhaust his administrative remedies under the IDEA by requesting a due process hearing. The PIAA was not a recipient of federal funding, as required to create Section 504 liability. Since these factors were fatal to the claims, the court disposed of them in the PIAA's favor. The ADA claim involved a request for modification of a program and was considered under *PGA Tour, Inc. v. Martin*, 532 S.Ct. 661 (2001). In *Martin*, the U.S. Supreme Court held **the ADA requires an individualized inquiry to determine whether a requested modification is reasonable and necessary for the disabled individual, and whether the modification would fundamentally alter the nature of the competition.** The court found the student's participation in football and track programs would not fundamentally alter the nature of interscholastic competition. It issued a permanent order prohibiting the PIAA from enforcing its age bylaw, unless it did so under a waiver rule providing individual evaluation of each request. *Cruz v. Pennsylvania Interscholastic Athletic Ass'n*, 157 F.Supp.2d 485 (E.D. Pa. 2001).

◆   A New Jersey student with learning disabilities was recruited for football by several NCAA Division I schools. **The NCAA ruled that a number of his high school special education cases did not satisfy its core course requirement** and declared him ineligible for interscholastic sports during his freshman season. The student claimed the universities then stopped recruiting him and that the NCAA's core course requirement violated Section 504 of the Rehabilitation Act and the ADA. He filed a federal district court action against the NCAA, universities and the ACT/Clearinghouse, which administers college entrance examinations. The court found that because of an intervening change in NCAA rules, the student had the potential of regaining a year of eligibility. While the ADA and Section 504 claims against the NCAA were dismissed, he could proceed against the universities under the ADA and Section 504.

The court then considered summary judgment motions by the NCAA, ACT/Clearinghouse and universities concerning the student's claims under the

New Jersey Law Against Discrimination (LAD). **While the NCAA was potentially liable for LAD violations, there was no evidence that the ACT/Clearinghouse had engaged in any discriminatory behavior.** The court awarded the ACT/Clearinghouse's motion for summary judgment, but denied the NCAA's motion. *Bowers v. NCAA*, 151 F.Supp.2d 526 (D.N.J. 2001).

The student died, but his estate continued the litigation. The Third Circuit heard appeals by the University of Iowa concerning Eleventh Amendment immunity, and two universities concerning their potential liability to Iowa and other universities that were named as parties. The court held the history and structure of ADA Title II and Section 504 did not suggest a right to contribution. **The two third-party universities would not have to contribute to any judgment won by the student's estate against Iowa and the other universities named as parties.** *Bowers v. NCAA*, 346 F.3d 402 (3d Cir. 2003).

While the case was on appeal to the Third Circuit, the parties resumed pre-trial fact-finding activities, called "discovery." In 2004, the student's mother revealed to the NCAA and universities for the first time that the student had been in and out of drug treatment and mental health programs from fall 1998 until 2001. He was hospitalized in 1999 after attempting to commit suicide. The mother revealed that the student's death resulted from an apparent drug overdose. His medical records indicated his pre-existing drug condition, which had never been disclosed to the NCAA or the universities. The district court sanctioned the mother and her attorneys. It held the failure to disclose the information was willful and in bad faith. The case returned to the Third Circuit.

The court found the district court's ruling immunized the NCAA and universities from liability. The judgment was "fundamentally flawed" by failing to focus on the correct time frame. **The court held a determination of whether a person is a "qualified individual with a disability" under the ADA is not made from the time a lawsuit is filed, "but from the time at which the alleged discriminatory decision was made."** The discrimination being alleged took place during the 1995-96 school year, when the student was deemed ineligible for football under NCAA rules. The evidence of any substance abuse by the student in 1995-96 was minimal. His substance abuse was irrelevant for purposes of establishing liability. The district court's contrary ruling was reversed. The mother would not, however, be permitted to use posthumously revealed information to her own advantage. The court reversed a district court order sanctioning the mother's attorneys for failing to disclose the student's full medical history. The lower court did not provide them any notice that they were subject to sanctions and had to provide them an opportunity to be heard. The court held the University of Iowa was not entitled to Eleventh Amendment immunity under the Rehabilitation Act, based on its acceptance of federal funds. Congress had validly exercised its powers and overcame Eleventh Amendment immunity when enacting ADA Title II. The ADA's affirmative obligation to accommodate disabled persons was reasonable. **The court held ADA Title II was valid legislation as applied to public education.** While finding the action was "an ongoing saga," it returned the case to the district court for a determination of whether the NCAA and universities violated the ADA and Rehabilitation Act. *Bowers v. NCAA*, 475 F.3d 524 (3d Cir. 2007).

◆   A Kentucky school district had a no-cut policy for ninth-grade students on the junior varsity basketball team. A few days after practice began, a coach was advised to investigate medical records to see if it was appropriate for a student to play. The coach reviewed a physical form stating the student should not engage in activities that would put him at increased risk of physical injury and indicating he had hemophilia and hepatitis B. The school principal then instructed the coach to put the student's status on "hold" and seek further medical information. The coach, principal and others determined the student should remain on hold status until they received a statement from a physician concerning his participation. The physician faxed a letter to school officials, but the coach was dissatisfied with its vagueness. Within 10 days, the principal advised the coach to allow the student to practice and play with the team.

Before the principal's decision was communicated to the family, the student decided he no longer wanted to play for the team. The family commenced a federal district court action against the school district, board and school officials, asserting violations of Section 504 and the Americans with Disabilities Act (ADA). The court entered judgment for the school district and officials, and the family appealed to the U.S. Court of Appeals, Sixth Circuit. The court noted that **under either Section 504 or the ADA, a person with disabilities may be excluded from a program if participation presents a direct threat to the health and safety of others**. In this case, the school district was attempting to determine whether the student's participation on the junior varsity basketball team presented a serious health risk to others. Congress created a narrow exception to the broad prohibition against discrimination contained in the ADA in cases where an individual with disabilities presents a direct threat to the health and safety of others. **School officials had never removed the student from the team but had placed him on hold status while awaiting medical advice. The action was appropriate in view of the potential liability faced by the school if a competitor became infected as a result of his participation.** It appeared the student had chosen not to participate on the team of his own volition, and there was no violation of his rights under Section 504 or the ADA. *Doe v. Woodford County Board of Educ.*, 213 F.3d 921 (6th Cir. 2000).

◆   A learning disabled Tennessee student transferred from a Christian school to a metropolitan public school. The executive director of the Tennessee Secondary Schools Athletic Association (TSSAA) ruled the student ineligible for interscholastic sports for a period of 12 months. The TSSAA denied the student's request for hardship waiver and then denied his further appeals. The student's parents sued the TSSAA in a federal district court, claiming its actions deprived him of his rights under the Individuals with Disabilities Education Act. **The court held a student who transfers schools in order to receive special education cannot be excluded from extracurricular activities, since such a prohibition would amount to discrimination based on disability.** *Crocker v. Tennessee Secondary School Athletic Ass'n*, 735 F.Supp. 753 (N.D. Tenn. 1990). The Sixth Circuit affirmed the district court judgment in *Crocker v. Tennessee Secondary School Athletic Ass'n*, 908 F.2d 972 (6th Cir. 1990).

III. ISSUES IN COACHING

A. Employment

Coaches typically receive a salary supplement for their coaching duties under separate contracts. In these cases, their property interests in their coaching assignments are limited to the term of the supplemental contract and severable from teaching contracts. Under these circumstances, coaching duties do not have the same statutory protections as regular teaching assignments.

◆   An inner-city Alabama high school basketball coach was a tenured science teacher with 20 years of teaching experience. Before the start of the 2004-05 basketball season, he agreed with players to use a "one-minute drill" or "circle" as a form of discipline in practices. The "drill" consisted of the team encircling the rules violator, then hitting or kicking him for up to one minute. The coach looked on and timed the hitting with a stopwatch. The punishment was used 11 times in a six-week period. One player broke his hand after the coach told him to fight another player for being late to practice. The punishment was discontinued before the team's first home game, when a player announced he was quitting the team. After the media reported the player's injuries, the school district placed the coach on administrative leave. A hearing officer found the coach engaged in serious misconduct but did not recommend canceling his contract. Instead, the coach was barred from coaching for four years, suspended without pay for 30 days, and ordered to apologize to all players and parents.

After the state court of civil appeals reversed the decision, the case reached the Supreme Court of Alabama. It noted that the state Teacher Tenure Act gives hearing officers broad decision-making authority. Courts must affirm hearing officer decisions unless they are arbitrary and capricious. At his hearing, the coach acknowledged his mistake and promised it would never happen again. Players uniformly stated that he was a positive influence in their lives. **Section 16-24-10 of the Alabama Teacher Tenure Act permitted consideration of a teacher's employment history, including matters occurring in previous years.** The court found Section 16-24-10 let hearing officers determine if a contract should be cancelled, or if less serious punishment should be imposed. The coach had no prior disciplinary record, and parents and students expressed a strong and almost unanimous desire for him to remain. The hearing officer found the coach had been able to improve grades and make college a realistic goal for his players. The court found the hearing officer had attempted to balance a number of vital concerns. As the decision was not arbitrary, the court reinstated it. *Ex parte Dunn*, No. 1051387, 2007 WL 30071 (Ala. 2007).

◆   A teacher/coach and his wife worked for a Texas school district. He sued the district in 1999, claiming Title VII violations. The action was settled, but the district did not rehire him for 2000-01 based on complaints about his coaching abilities. The district did not fill his position. As a result, the girls' coaching staff was made up of the teacher/coach's wife and a male employee. The district later placed the male employee on administrative leave and brought in high school coaches to help coach the middle school girls' teams. When the male employee resigned, the district decided to delay hiring a replacement. The district did not post any job announcement, review applications or interview anyone for the male employee's position, but the teacher/coach submitted an application for it. The teacher/coach's wife complained to the district athletic director that another coach should be hired. The athletic director allegedly stated that he could not hire her husband because of his previous lawsuit.

The teacher/coach sued the school district in a federal district court, claiming retaliation based on his prior lawsuit. A jury agreed with the teacher/coach and found he should receive $5,400. On appeal, the U.S. Court of Appeals, Fifth Circuit, held the teacher/coach did not suffer "adverse employment action." The district did not fill the male employee's position. **The court held an employer does not discriminate or retaliate against an employee if there is no job vacancy.** The athletic director was not responsible for deciding if an available position existed at the time of his statements. The district had determined that teaching duties could be covered by a long-term substitute. The teacher/coach submitted an unsolicited application for full-time work. **The fact that a position had become vacant did not make it "available."** The jury verdict was unsupported, and the court reversed the decision. *Adams v. Groesbeck Independent School Dist.*, 475 F.3d 688 (5th Cir. 2007).

◆ **The U.S. Court of Appeals, Eleventh Circuit, held an untenured Alabama teacher had no constitutional right to continuing employment and did not engage in protected speech regarding her duties.** The teacher was the faculty sponsor for the junior varsity cheerleading squad. Parents complained about unfairness in cheerleading tryouts. The school principal investigated and gave the teacher a questionnaire. She responded to the questionnaire and raised her own questions about the tryouts. The principal decided not to renew the teacher's contract, and she sued the school board in a federal district court for speech and due process violations. The court awarded summary judgment to the board, and the teacher appealed. **The Eleventh Circuit held that a public employee who does not speak as a citizen on a matter of public concern has no First Amendment claim based on his or her employer's reaction to the speech. Public employees are not speaking as "citizens" when they speak about their own official duties.** The teacher's responses to the questionnaire were unprotected. **Under Alabama law, an untenured teacher has no right to reemployment**, whether "statutory or otherwise." The court affirmed the judgment for the school board. *Gilder-Lucas v. Elmore County Board of Educ.*, 186 Fed.Appx. 885 (11th Cir. 2006).

◆ During a job interview with an Indiana school board, a coach disclosed his criminal convictions, including one for conspiracy to distribute marijuana. He assured the board he had "turned his life around," and the board hired him. The coach was then offered additional positions teaching special education and coaching the girls' basketball team. He obtained a limited one-year teaching license to teach special education. Near the end of the coach's term, an interim district superintendent asked him for written documentation that he would have sufficient academic work to renew his limited license in time for the next school year. She then recommended not renewing his teaching contract due to the expiration of his limited teaching license. The non-renewal of the coach's contract was reported in the media. The board voted to immediately remove him as the girls' basketball coach. He resigned as football coach and sued the board in a federal district court for denial of his equal protection and due process rights, and violations of the Family and Medical Leave Act and state law.

The court awarded summary judgment to the board. The coach appealed to the Seventh Circuit, where his sole argument was that the board had singled him out by requiring him to take drug tests. He stated the district athletic director had been caught stealing from the school but was not required to submit to drug testing. **The court held the coach and athletic director were not "similarly situated" and could not be compared for purposes of an Equal Protection claim. The athletic director was never prosecuted for any crimes, while the coach had a felony drug conviction.** There was no evidence of defamation. The court affirmed the judgment, stating that the board could do as it chose after the coach's one-year contract expired. *Ott v. Edinburgh Community School Corp.*, 189 Fed.Appx. 507 (7th Cir. 2006).

◆ A Mississippi teacher's football coaching duties included summer work, but he refused to attend eight of 24 summer workouts. The school board voted not to renew his primary teaching contract for the next year as a result. After a state chancery court upheld the decision, the teacher appealed to the Court of Appeals of Mississippi. He argued his coaching rider did not permit the non-renewal of his teaching contract, and that the rider was not enforceable because it required him to work for no pay, in violation of state and federal wage laws.

The court held state law did not prohibit school boards from including riders or attachments in school employment contracts. Local school boards would unduly burdened if they were forced to receive state board approval for every contract attachment or rider. The court held the teacher's rider was valid, and that the trial court did not commit error by finding he failed to perform his duties by skipping the summer workouts. There was no merit to the teacher's argument that the extended time period specified in his coaching rider violated state and federal wage laws. Federal regulations published under the Fair Labor Standards Act exempt teachers and those with coaching duties from coverage. There was no merit to the teacher's claim that the rider applied only to cases of resignation or involuntary termination. The employment contract and rider both referred to the single position of teacher/coach. As the teacher had defiantly chosen not to attend the summer workouts, the court upheld the judgment for the school district. *Smith v. Petal School Dist.*, No. 2005-CC-01394-COA, 2006 WL 2672100 (Miss. Ct. App. 2006).

◆ After working for six years for his district, an Alabama teacher transferred to a high school to teach physical education and coach basketball. He discovered the girls' team did not receive the same funding or access to equipment and facilities as boys' teams. The teacher claimed his job was made difficult by lack of adequate funding, equipment and facilities, and he began complaining to supervisors. He stated the district did not respond to his complaints and gave him negative evaluations before removing him as girls' coach. The teacher sued the school board in a federal district court, claiming the loss of his supplemental coaching contracts constituted unlawful retaliation in violation of Title IX. The court dismissed the case, and its decision was affirmed by the Eleventh Circuit.

The U.S. Supreme Court stated Title IX prevents any education program that receives federal funding from excluding a person from the program, denying benefits to a person, or discriminating on the basis of sex. **The Court held Title IX covers retaliation against a person for complaining about sex discrimination. It found "[r]etaliation is, by definition an intentional act,"** and is a form of discrimination, since the person who complains is treated differently than others. **A program that retaliates against a person based on a sex discrimination complaint intentionally discriminates in violation of Title IX.** Without finding that actual discrimination had occurred, the Court held the teacher was entitled to bring his case before the district court and attempt to show the board was liable. A private right of action for retaliation was within the statute's prohibition of intentional sex discrimination. Title IX did not require the victim of retaliation to also be the victim of discrimination. The Court stated "if retaliation were not prohibited, Title IX's enforcement scheme would unravel." **Teachers and coaches were often in the best position to vindicate the rights of students by identifying discrimination and notifying administrators.** The text of Title IX itself gave the board sufficient notice that it could not retaliate against the teacher after he complained of discrimination. Title IX regulations have been on the books for nearly 30 years. The Court found a reasonable school board would realize it could not cover up violations of Title IX by retaliating against teachers. It reversed and remanded the case to allow the teacher to attempt to show the board retaliated against him. *Jackson v. Birmingham Board of Educ.*, 544 U.S. 167, 125 S.Ct. 1497 (U.S. 2005).

◆ The Supreme Court of Illinois denied review of a decision holding the Illinois High School Association (IHSA) could not claim state law immunity because it was not a "local public entity." The case involved a basketball coach charged with violating IHSA recruiting rules. The IHSA prohibited him from coaching for one year. The coach sued the IHSA in a state court for negligence. The court dismissed the case, finding the IHSA had immunity under a statute protecting local public entities from liability. **The state appellate court reversed the decision, noting the IHSA was more like a state agency than a local government.** The state supreme court then denied further review. *Hood v. Illinois High School Ass'n*, 217 Ill.2d 601, 844 N.E.2d 965 (Ill. 2006).

B. Defamation

◆ Michigan High School Athletic Association rules required transfer students to sit out of interscholastic athletic competition for two semesters if a transfer was "athletically motivated." A star student-athlete told his football coach and others he was considering a transfer because "the program was in disarray." The student's mother told the principal the transfer was academically motivated, but the principal filed a complaint with the state athletic association, asserting the transfer was athletically motivated. The association found insufficient evidence to support the complaint. Two newspapers interviewed school officials, then published articles speculating that the student's transfer was athletically motivated. The association's executive board denied the principal's appeal.

The student then sued the school district, principal, coach and the district athletic director in a state court for defamation and other claims. The court held for the district and officials and the student appealed. **The Court of Appeals of Michigan held the principal, coach and athletic director were entitled to speak to reporters who were already aware of the story. Talking to them was not "outrageous" conduct.** The trial court had properly dismissed the defamation and invasion of privacy claims based on governmental immunity. School districts are entitled to immunity from liability in tort cases if they are engaged in a government function. The statements to the association were limited to furthering the district's interest and were made in a proper manner. There was no evidence any statements were made with actual malice, defeating the student's defamation claims. The statements to the reporters were not defamation, as there was no evidence that they caused any special harm. **The student himself openly spoke about his transfer at school and the information disclosed did not concern his private life.** The court rejected additional arguments by the student and affirmed the judgment for the district and officials. *Cassise v. Walled Lake Consolidated Schools*, No. 257299, 2006 WL 445960 (Mich. Ct. App. 2006). The Supreme Court of Michigan denied further review. *Cassise v. Walled Lake Consolidated Schools*, 476 Mich. 866, 720 N.W.2d 311 (Mich. 2006).

◆ A Louisiana student and her mother were spectators at a game. She claimed a coach became physically and verbally threatening and called the police to have them removed from the gym. The student sued the school board and coach in a federal district court, claiming "threatening and abusive language is actionable" in actions for federal civil rights violations under 42 U.S.C. § 1983. The coach moved for dismissal, asserting there was no viable Section 1983 claim, and that she was also entitled to qualified immunity. The court agreed with the coach, stating **the Due Process Clause "does not transform every tort committed by a state actor into a constitutional violation."** Even in a state custodial situation, "the use of words, no matter how violent, does not comprise a Section 1983 violation." **The court rejected the student's claim alleging harm to her reputation. The conduct she alleged did not raise a valid constitutional claim. Any harm to reputation was not a deprivation of a constitutional liberty or property interest recognized by state or federal law.** The court declined jurisdiction over the student's assault and battery claim and granted the coach's dismissal motion. *Paige v. Tangipahoa Parish School Board*, No. Civ.A. 04-354, 2005 WL 943646 (E.D. La. 2005).

◆ A Minnesota school district decided not to rehire a varsity football head coach. A newspaper published articles quoting sources who said the coach was "known for his temper, inappropriate comments and foul language, which people claim he uses to intimidate players." Although the news accounts did not identify the source of these comments, it attributed one statement to a former assistant coach. The head coach sued the school district and four employees in a state court for defamation, breach of contract and other claims. Although he did not sue the reporter who obtained the quotes, he sought to compel him to identify the staff members who made them. The court twice denied motions by the coach to identify staff members who allegedly defamed him, then awarded partial summary judgment to the district and employees. Summary judgment was denied on the defamation claim and the court granted the coach's third motion to compel the reporter to identify his sources. The Court of Appeals of Minnesota reversed and remanded the case, and the district court again ordered the reporter to identify the employees who made statements. The case returned to the court of appeals, which held the reporter could not be compelled to reveal his sources as this would hamper his ability to gather news. The court held the coach did not show the statements were false or made with "actual malice."

The coach appealed to the state supreme court, which considered the case under the Minnesota Free Flow of Information Act (FFIA). The FFIA protected the media by creating a legal privilege not to reveal sources of information or disclose unpublished information. An exception to the FFIA required disclosure when the person seeking it could demonstrate the identity of the source would lead to relevant evidence on the issue of actual malice. **The court recited the elements for a defamation claim, which are: (1) a false and defamatory statement (2) in an unprivileged publication to a third party that (3) harmed the plaintiff's reputation in the community. Public officials must also demonstrate that the statement was made with "actual malice." In Minnesota, public school teachers and coaches are deemed public officials.** The coach met the FFIA exception by showing the identity of the source would lead to relevant evidence on the issue of actual malice. Since the identity of the speaker was anonymous, the court held the identity of the speaker would necessarily lead to relevant evidence on the issue of actual malice. The district court had found the statements, if false, were defamatory. If any school employee was the source of the statements, there was probable cause to believe the speaker had relevant information. As the coach satisfied each of the requirements for disclosure under the FFIA, the court reversed the decision. *Weinberger v. Maplewood Review*, 668 N.W.2d 667 (Minn. 2003).

◆ The Tennessee Secondary Schools Athletic Association (TSSAA) scrutinized a private school's highly successful athletic programs. The TSSAA's executive director wrote to the school principal about alleged recruiting violations by the school's head football coach. The director's letter described the coach's practice of treating potential transfer students as "enrolled" when they completed their applications, even if they never actually transferred. Twelve such students were invited to participate in a spring football practice. The practices were described as "aggressive contact with potential athletes" that went "beyond what is normal and is undue influence." The school challenged the TSSAA's recruiting bylaws in a case that reached the U.S. Supreme Court (see *Brentwood Academy v. Tennessee Secondary School Athletic Ass'n*, Chapter Fourteen, Section III.B). The coach commenced a separate action for defamation and invasion of privacy against the TSSAA, its director and a public school administrator who furnished information to the director. He claimed the administrator supplied information that was based on false rumors and that the director's letter implicated him in other violations.

The court awarded summary judgment to the TSSAA and officials, and the coach appealed to the Tennessee Court of Appeals on the invasion of privacy claim. The court stated the coach could prevail by showing he was publicized in a highly offensive manner, with reckless disregard for the falsity of the publication. The literal truth of a publication was no defense, and **it was necessary to show the publication was made with actual malice. The court found no evidence that would allow a jury to conclude the TSSAA, director or administrator knew or recklessly disregarded the possibility that they would portray the coach in a false light.** Although the coach claimed the letter "made him out as a liar, a cheat" these words were his "own invention." "Undue influence" was prohibited by TSSAA rules, and the coach admitted the conduct giving rise to this charge. Mentioning it in the charges against the coach could not create a false impression. Failure to investigate matters that are made public does not demonstrate actual malice, and the court affirmed the lower court decision. *Flatt v. Tennessee Secondary Schools Athletic Ass'n*, No. M2001-01817-COA-R3-CV, 2003 WL 61251 (Tenn. Ct. App. 2003).

C. Liability

Coaches typically avoid liability for student injuries, unless there is a showing of willful or wanton misconduct. For additional cases involving liability in the context of school athletics, see Chapter One, Section II.

◆   A Texas basketball coach and an athletic trainer were blamed for the death of a student who collapsed after completing a two-mile run with her team. About five minutes after the student completed the run on an August morning, the coach determined she required medical attention. The head trainer examined her and called 911 about 12 minutes later. The student's parents alleged the coach and trainer failed to perform CPR or give her other necessary medical attention and that their delays caused her death. They sued the district, coach and trainer in a federal district court, asserting constitutional rights violations and state tort claims against the district. **The court explained that to show a school employee has violated a constitutional interest in bodily integrity, there must be proof of deliberate indifference toward the victim.**

The family had alleged negligence, not deliberate indifference. The coach attended to the student about five minutes after she finished running, and the trainer saw her about 12 minutes later. As this was not "conscious disregard" for her health and safety, the employees had qualified immunity. The school district was entitled to immunity for the constitutional claims. There was no showing it had intentionally failed to adopt adequate medical procedures for heat-related illnesses. The district also had immunity on the state law claims, and the court awarded it summary judgment. *Livingston v. DeSoto Independent School Dist.*, 391 F.Supp.2d 463 (N.D. Tex. 2005).

◆   A 15-year-old Mississippi student became fatigued at a football practice held on a hot August day. He complained to the coach that he felt weak and needed a water break. The coach told the student he was "faking it" and refused the request for a break. After allegedly suffering a heatstroke, the student sued the district and coach in a state court for negligence. The court held a trial and found the student suffered damages of $350,000, including $68,000 in medical bills. However, the court found the coach and district were entitled to immunity under the Mississippi Torts Claims Act (MTCA) because their conduct was discretionary. The student appealed to the Supreme Court of Mississippi.

The court explained **government entities and their employees are entitled to MTCA immunity against all claims based on the exercise of discretionary duties**. According to the court, "**when an official is required to use his own judgment or discretion in performing a duty, that duty is discretionary**." *Prince v. Louisville Municipal School Dist.*, 741 So.2d 207 (Miss. 1999), established that **decisions and acts by high school coaches are considered discretionary**. In assessing whether the actions of the coach were discretionary, the court balanced the need to provide students a well-rounded education with the serious, negative repercussions that could occur if the discretionary choices of coaches were not exempt from liability under the MTCA. **The court held the coach was in the best position to know his team and had to motivate and discipline players. Imposing liability on the coach and district would result in their loss of control over high school football programs due to the risk of lawsuits.** Since the coach's actions were discretionary within the meaning of the MTCA, it was not necessary to discuss whether he exercised ordinary care. The supreme court affirmed the judgment for the district and coach. *Harris v. McCray*, 867 So.2d 188 (Miss. 2003).

◆ A 14-year-old California student joined her junior varsity swim team as a freshman. She told two coaches of her great fear of diving into shallow water. They allowed the student to swim the first leg of team relay races during the first meets of the season, which allowed her to start in the water. Minutes before the start of a meet, a coach informed the student she could not start the relay and would have to dive into the pool. She panicked and begged him to change the rotation to allow her to start from the water. The student claimed he refused and threatened to exclude her from the meet. She broke her neck on a practice dive. The student later sued the school district and coach in a state court. She presented evidence from a certified water safety instructor that the dive she tried was ultra-hazardous if done by an inadequately trained swimmer. The court awarded summary judgment to the district and coach, finding they could not be held liable under the doctrine of "primary assumption of risk." The Court of Appeal of California affirmed the judgment, and the student appealed.

The state supreme court explained the doctrine of primary assumption of risk barred negligence claims. **A school district generally has no duty to protect a student from the inherent risks in a sport.** However, **sports instructors and coaches have a duty not to increase the risks of sports participation beyond what is inherent in the sport.** Simply urging a student to strive for excellence or to reach a new level of competence did not increase the risk of inherent harm and did not create liability. **Coaches who challenged or pushed students to try new or more difficult maneuvers should not be subject to liability.** They had no duty to eliminate all risks of inexperience. The court held **there must be a showing of intentional conduct to impose liability on a coach for requiring a student to perform beyond his or her**

capacity without adequate instruction. A student could also prevail by showing the coach acted recklessly by conduct "totally outside the range of the ordinary activity involved in teaching or coaching the sport." The court rejected the lower court findings that the coach had only challenged the student. The courts failed to credit the student's expert and her statements concerning the lack of instruction, her fear of diving into shallow water, and her claim that the coach threatened her if she did not dive. On remand, the trial court was to determine if the coach acted recklessly and consider the nature of his promises and threats. It would also have to evaluate whether there had been a lack of training and whether the coach was aware of the student's fears. *Kahn v. East Side Union High School Dist.*, 31 Cal.4th 990, 4 Cal.Rptr.3d 103, 75 P.3d 30 (Cal. 2003).

◆ A Nebraska high school football player was injured in a game when he struck his head on the ground. He felt dizzy and disoriented, but stayed in the game a few plays before taking himself out. Coaches observed he was short of breath but attributed this to hyperventilation. Because the student made normal eye contact with an assistant coach and had normal speech and movement, no medical attention was sought. The student later asked to return to the game, and coaches allowed him to do so, as he seemed normal and did not complain of a headache. The student suffered a headache the entire weekend, but coaches denied he said anything about it the next week. They allowed him to practice with the team, and he suffered a closed-head traumatic brain injury.

The student sued the school district in a Nebraska trial court for personal injuries. The court dismissed the case, ruling the coaches were not negligent. The Nebraska Supreme Court held the trial court should not have discredited testimony by the student's expert witnesses, who were certified athletic trainers who taught state-required courses for coaching endorsements. They testified Nebraska **high school coaches should be aware that headache, dizziness and disorientation are symptomatic of a concussion**. The trial court improperly gave greater weight to the district's expert, believing community standards governed the conduct of coaches. **The standard of care for high school coaches did not vary among districts, but was instead that of a "reasonably prudent person holding a Nebraska teaching certificate with a coaching endorsement."** As the trainers were competent to testify on this standard, the supreme court remanded the case to the trial court. *Cerny v. Cedar Bluffs Junior/Senior Public School*, 262 Neb. 66, 628 N.E. 2d 697 (Neb. 2001).

The trial court held a new trial, and heard testimony by the student's experts and a retired Nebraska high school football coach who testified for the school. The coach stated that at the time of the incident, little training or literature was available to coaches about head injury. **The court found high school football coaches in Nebraska had to be familiar with the symptoms of concussion. They had to evaluate players with head injuries for symptoms at repeated intervals before allowing reentry into a game. Coaches had to evaluate the seriousness of an injury and whether it was appropriate to remove the player from all contact pending a medical examination.** The court held the coaching staff complied with the standard of care required of a reasonably prudent person with a state coaching endorsement. Finding no negligence, it dismissed the case. The student appealed, arguing the trial court applied an incorrect standard of care and made improper factual findings. The supreme court disagreed, ruling the trial court had authority to determine what weight to give the testimony of witnesses. As the record contained ample support for the trial court's findings, the court affirmed the judgment. *Cerny v. Cedar Bluffs Junior/Senior Public School*, 268 Neb. 958, 679 N.W.2d 198 (Neb. 2004).

◆ A 110-pound eighth-grade Louisiana student played for his elementary school football team. In a game played against another elementary school team, a 270-pound eighth-grade player from the opposing team tackled the student, causing a fracture of the student's leg. There was no penalty called on the play. The student and his parents sued the coaches of both football teams and the insurer of one of the coaches, claiming they were liable for the injury. It was claimed the accident was caused by allowing smaller elementary school students to scrimmage and play against larger students. The coaches and insurer filed a motion for summary judgment in a Louisiana trial court, claiming there was no duty by the coaches to prevent players from being injured in supervised, refereed inter-school football games and that the tackling was neither unexpected nor unsportsmanlike. The court granted the summary judgment motion and the student and his parents appealed to the Court of Appeal of Louisiana, First Circuit. **The court found there was no duty imposed upon coaches to protect players against the potential risk of injury from playing football games with players of different weights.** Even though the Louisiana Supreme Court had abolished the doctrine of assumption of risk several years previously, the absence of any duty to protect players precluded a finding of liability. The summary judgment decision of the trial court was affirmed. *Laiche v. Kohen*, 621 So.2d 1162 (La. Ct. App. 1993).

D. Misconduct

◆ A California student made her varsity softball team as a high school freshman. This achievement and her relationship with the team's head coach "stirred up some resentment among the other softball team members." The student claimed other students, parents and staff rumored she was having a lesbian relationship with the coach. The principal warned the coach to avoid favoritism, "maintain a proper professional distance" and avoid being alone with the student. The coach disobeyed the warning and a later written directive and was seen alone with the student. She also lost her temper several times, pushing one player out of her way, making an obscene gesture at another student, and blocking a parent's vehicle with her own in a school lot. The district put the coach on administrative leave and did not renew her probationary contract. The student claimed students continued calling her "homo" on and off campus and that teachers who witnessed the harassment did nothing to stop it. However, she reported only one incident to the school. A vice principal responded to the report by meeting with the student and a harasser. The coach attended a softball game as a spectator after the district's decision not to rehire her. The student then claimed school staff "interrogated" her about her continuing relationship with the coach. The team's new coach dismissed her from the team, stating she had been a "cancer on the team." The student sued the district, principal, vice principal and other staff in a state court.

The court found no pervasive sexual harassment and awarded summary judgment to the district and staff. The student appealed to the Court of Appeal of California, which found **the principal responded to the inappropriate relationship between the student and coach as soon as it came to his attention. He told the coach to keep a professional distance from the student, treat her the same as other players, and avoid seclusion with her.** The student had been rude and disrespectful to the new head coach, an assistant coach and her teammates. While she alleged others harassed her, she could not now recall the name of any student who stated she was gay or was having an inappropriate relationship with the coach. Only one potentially harassing remark was ever reported to the school, and the vice principal responded to it. The court found no evidence of pervasive harassment or discrimination on the basis of sex or perceived sexual orientation by district staff. **The student herself claimed her softball skill, not sexual harassment, was the reason for taunts and teasing.** For this reason, there could be no district or individual liability under Title IX, or other federal laws. The district took required steps to eliminate harassment. The student's conduct exacerbated the perceptions of favoritism or personal involvement. **The student sought damages for "school yard insults and name calling," most of which were never brought to the school's attention.** As she did not show harassment so severe, pervasive and objectively offensive that it denied her equal access to education under Title IX, the court affirmed the judgment. *Ashby v. Hesperia Union School Dist.*, No. E034905, 2004 WL 2699940 (Cal. Ct. App. 2004).

◆   A Pennsylvania coach suspected a member of the high school swim team was pregnant. He repeatedly asked her if this was true. She consistently denied it but eventually agreed to take a pregnancy test. The result was positive, and the coach asked an orthopedist whether it was permissible for a pregnant swimmer to compete. After learning that there was no medical reason to prevent the student from swimming competitively, the coach let her remain on the team. However, she continued to deny her pregnancy until a doctor determined she was six months pregnant. The student alleged that after her baby was born, the coach attempted to alienate her from her peers, refused to speak with her and retaliated against her by removing her from competition. She sued him in a federal district court for civil rights violations under 42 U.S.C. § 1983 and state law. The court held the coach was entitled to qualified immunity. The student appealed to the Third Circuit, which found the district court had improperly held the student had no clearly established right to be free of such testing. **A review of current federal cases revealed that requiring a student to submit to a pregnancy test, if proven, would be an unlawful search and seizure under the Fourth Amendment.**

The court found that a reasonable swim coach would not have forced a student to take a pregnancy test. Because the coach did not "justify his failure to respect the boundaries of reasonableness," he was not entitled to qualified immunity on the student's Fourth Amendment claim. This aspect of the district court's judgment was reversed and remanded. The court also reversed and remanded the student's claims based on violations of her constitutional privacy rights and state law. Her pregnancy was entitled to privacy protection under the Due Process Clause. The coach was not entitled to qualified immunity, since current law put him on notice that the compelled disclosure of personal information was not objectively reasonable. Because the student's claim based on the right to familial integrity and her parents' right to raise their children without undue state interference was not clearly established, the coach was entitled to immunity on this claim. *Gruenke v. Seip*, 225 F.3d 290 (3d Cir. 2000).

◆   A Georgia high school student was involved in a fight with another player and complained to his football coach. The coach allegedly told him "you need to learn how to handle your own business." The student returned to the other player and hit him in the head with a weight lock. **The coach then allegedly asked the student "what did you hit him with; if you hit him with it, I am going to hit you with it," then struck him with the weight lock.** The blow caused severe and permanent injury to the student's eye, and he sued the coach, principal, school board and district superintendent in a federal district court for civil rights violations. The court granted motions by the board, district, superintendent and principal for failure to state a claim under 42 U.S.C. § 1983. The district court held that while the coach's spontaneous action could have been an assault under state law, it was not corporal punishment.

The student appealed to the Eleventh Circuit, which held **corporal punishment may be defined as the application of physical force by a teacher to punish a student for some kind of school-related misconduct.** In this case, the coach was responding to an incident of misconduct on school grounds. He had not attempted to break up the fight, but had instead used force against the student to discipline him. The court examined the leading U.S. Supreme Court case on corporal punishment, *Ingraham v. Wright*, 430 U.S. 651 (1977), and the Fifth Circuit decision in the same case. The *Ingraham* decisions did not foreclose the claim for substantive due process violations alleged by the student. *Ingraham* was distinguishable because the corporal punishment administered in that case came under a school policy with sufficient constraints and restrictions to prevent arbitrary action by school employees. **In this case, the coach's action was not expressly authorized by the school board and he had arbitrarily punished the student through the use of intentional and obviously excessive force that presented a reasonably foreseeable risk of serious injury.** The student alleged that the corporal punishment was so brutal, demeaning and harmful as to shock the conscience, implicating his substantive due process rights. The court reversed and remanded the judgment. *Neal v. Fulton County Board of Educ.*, 229 F.3d 1069 (11th Cir. 2000).

APPENDIX A

United States Constitution

[Provisions of Interest to Educators]

ARTICLE I

Section 1. All legislative Powers herein granted shall be vested in a Congress of the United States, which shall consist of a Senate and House of Representatives.

* * *

Section 8. The Congress shall have Power To lay and collect Taxes, Duties, Imposts and Excises, to pay the Debts and provide for the common Defence and general Welfare of the United States; but all Duties, Imposts and Excises shall be uniform throughout the United States:

To borrow money on the credit of the United States;

To regulate Commerce with foreign Nations, and among the several States, and with the Indian Tribes;

To establish an uniform Rule of Naturalization, and uniform Laws on the subject of Bankruptcies throughout the United States;

* * *

To promote the Progress of Science and useful Arts, by securing for limited Times to Authors and Inventors the exclusive Right to their respective Writings and Discoveries;

* * *

To make all Laws which shall be necessary and proper for carrying into Execution for the foregoing Powers, and all other Powers vested by this Constitution in the Government of the United States, or in any Department or Office thereof.

* * *

Section 9. * * * No Bill of Attainder or ex post facto Law shall be passed.

Section 10. No State shall * * * pass any Bill of Attainder, ex post facto Law, or Law impairing the Obligation of Contracts, or grant any Title of Nobility.

* * *

ARTICLE II

Section 1. The executive Power shall be vested in a President of the United States of America.

* * *

ARTICLE III

Section 1. The judicial Power of the United States, shall be vested in one Supreme Court, and in such inferior Courts as the Congress may from time to time ordain and establish. The Judges, both of the supreme and inferior courts, shall hold their Offices during good Behaviour, and shall, at stated Times, receive for their Services a Compensation, which shall not be diminished during their Continuance in Office.

Section 2. The judicial Power shall extend to all Cases, in Law and Equity, arising under this Constitution, the Laws of the United States, and Treaties made, or which shall be made; under their Authority; to all Cases affecting Ambassadors, other public Ministers and Consuls; to all Cases of admiralty and maritime Jurisdiction, to Controversies to which the United States shall be a party to Controversies between two or more States; between a State and Citizens of another State; between Citizens of different States; between Citizens of the same State claiming Lands under the Grants of different States, and between a State, or the Citizens thereof, and foreign States, Citizens or Subjects.

* * *

ARTICLE IV

Section 1. Full Faith and Credit shall be given in each State to the public Acts, Records and judicial Proceedings of every other State.* * *

Section 2. The Citizens of each State shall be entitled to all Privileges and Immunities of Citizens in the several States.

* * *

Section 4. The United States shall guarantee to every State in this Union a Republican Form of Government, and shall protect each of them against Invasion; and on Application of the Legislature, or of the Executive (when the Legislature cannot be convened) against domestic Violence.

ARTICLE V

The Congress, whenever two thirds of both Houses shall deem it necessary, shall propose Amendments to this Constitution, or, on the Application of the Legislatures of two thirds of the several States, shall call a Convention for proposing Amendments, which, in either Case, shall be valid to all Intents and Purposes, as part of this Constitution, when ratified by the Legislatures of three fourths of the several States, or by Conventions in three fourths thereof, as the one or the other Mode of Ratification may be proposed by the Congress; Provided that no Amendment which may be made prior to the Year One thousand eight hundred and eight shall in any Manner affect the first and fourth Clauses in the Ninth Section of the first Article; and that no State, without its Consent, shall be deprived of its equal Suffrage in the Senate.

ARTICLE VI

* * *

This Constitution, and the Laws of the United States which shall be made in Pursuance thereof; and all Treaties made, or which shall be made, under the Authority of the United States, shall be the Supreme Law of the Land; and the Judges in every State shall be bound thereby, any Thing in the Constitution or Laws of any State to the Contrary notwithstanding.

The Senators and Representatives before mentioned, and the Members of the several State Legislatures, and all executive and judicial Officers, both of the United States and of the several States, shall be bound by Oath or Affirmation, to support this Constitution; but no religious Test shall ever be required as a Qualification to any Office or public Trust under the United States.

* * *

AMENDMENT I

Congress shall make no law respecting an establishment of religion, or prohibiting the free exercise thereof; or abridging the freedom of speech, or of the press; or the right of the people peaceably to assemble, and to petition the Government for a redress of grievances.

* * *

AMENDMENT IV

The right of the people to be secure in their persons, houses, papers, and effects, against unreasonable searches and seizures, shall not be violated, and no Warrants shall issue, but upon probable cause, supported by Oath or affirmation, and particularly describing the place to be searched, and the persons or things to be seized.

AMENDMENT V

No person shall be held to answer for a capital, or otherwise infamous crime, unless on a presentment or indictment of a Grand Jury, except in cases arising in the land or naval forces, or in the Militia, when in actual service in time of War or public danger; nor shall any person be subject for the same offence to be twice put in jeopardy of life or limb; nor shall be compelled in any criminal case to be a witness against himself, nor be deprived of life, liberty, or property, without due process of law; nor shall private property be taken for public use, without just compensation.

AMENDMENT VI

In all criminal prosecutions, the accused shall enjoy the right to a speedy and public trial, by an impartial jury of the State and district wherein the crime shall have been committed, which district shall have been previously ascertained by law, and to be informed of the nature and cause of the accusation; to be confronted with the witnesses against him; to have compulsory process for obtaining witnesses in his favor, and to have the Assistance of Counsel for his defense.

AMENDMENT VII

In Suits at common law, where the value in controversy shall exceed twenty dollars, the right of trial by jury shall be preserved, and no fact tried by jury, shall be otherwise re-examined in any Court of the United States, than according to the rules of the common law.

AMENDMENT VIII

Excessive bail shall not be required, nor excessive fines imposed, nor cruel and unusual punishments inflicted.

AMENDMENT IX

The enumeration in the Constitution, of certain rights, shall not be construed to deny or disparage others retained by the people.

AMENDMENT X

The powers not delegated to the United States by the Constitution, nor prohibited by it to the States, are reserved to the States respectively, or to the people.

AMENDMENT XI

The Judicial power of the United States shall not be construed to extend to any suit in law or equity, commenced or prosecuted against one of the United States by Citizens of another State, or by Citizens or Subjects of any Foreign State.

* * *

AMENDMENT XIII

Section 1. Neither slavery nor involuntary servitude, except as a punishment for crime whereof the party shall have been duly convicted, shall exist within the United States, or any place subject to their jurisdiction.

Section 2. Congress shall have power to enforce this article by appropriate legislation.

AMENDMENT XIV

Section 1. All persons born or naturalized in the United States, and subject to the jurisdiction thereof, are citizens of the United States and of the State wherein they reside. No State shall make or enforce any law which shall abridge the privileges or immunities of citizens of the United States; nor shall any State deprive any person of life, liberty, or property, without due process of law; nor deny to any person within its jurisdiction the equal protection of the laws.

* * *

Section 5. The Congress shall have power to enforce, by appropriate legislation, the provisions of this article.

APPENDIX B

Subject Matter Table of
Education Cases Decided by the
United States Supreme Court

Note: Please see the Table of Cases (located at the front of this volume) for Supreme Court cases reported in this Volume.

Academic Freedom

U.S. v. American Library Ass'n, Inc., 539 U.S. 194, 123 S.Ct. 2297, 156 L.Ed.2d 221 (2003).

Univ. of Pennsylvania v. EEOC, 493 U.S. 182, 110 S.Ct. 577, 107 L.Ed.2d 571 (1990).

Epperson v. Arkansas, 393 U.S. 97, 89 S.Ct. 266, 21 L.Ed.2d 228 (1968).

Meyer v. Nebraska, 262 U.S. 390, 43 S.Ct. 625, 67 L.Ed.2d 1042 (1923).

Aliens

Toll v. Moreno, 458 U.S. 1, 102 S.Ct. 2977, 73 L.Ed.2d 563 (1982).

Plyler v. Doe, 457 U.S. 202, 102 S.Ct. 2382, 72 L.Ed.2d 786 (1982).

Ambach v. Norwick, 441 U.S. 68, 99 S.Ct. 1589, 60 L.Ed.2d 49 (1979).

Vlandis v. Kline, 412 U.S. 441, 93 S.Ct. 2230, 37 L.Ed.2d 63 (1973).

Collective Bargaining

Chicago Teachers Union v. Hudson, 475 U.S. 292, 106 S.Ct. 1066, 89 L.Ed.2d 232 (1986).

Minnesota State Board for Community Colleges v. Knight, 465 U.S. 271, 104 S.Ct. 1058, 79 L.Ed.2d 299 (1984).

Perry Educ. Ass'n v. Perry Local Educators' Ass'n, 460 U.S. 37, 103 S.Ct. 948, 74 L.Ed.2d 794 (1983).

City of Madison Joint School Dist. v. WERC, 429 U.S. 167, 97 S.Ct. 421, 50 L.Ed.2d 376 (1976).

Compulsory Attendance

Wisconsin v. Yoder, 406 U.S. 205, 92 S.Ct. 526, 32 L.Ed.2d 15 (1972).

Pierce v. Society of Sisters, 268 U.S. 510, 45 S.Ct. 571, 69 L.Ed. 1070 (1925).

Continuing Education

Austin ISD v. U.S., 443 U.S. 915, 99 S.Ct. 3106, 61 L.Ed.2d 879 (1979).

Harrah ISD v. Martin, 440 U.S. 194, 99 S.Ct. 1062, 59 L.Ed.2d 248 (1979).

Corporal Punishment

Ingraham v. Wright, 430 U.S. 651, 97 S.Ct. 1401, 51 L.Ed.2d 711 (1977).

Desegregation

Missouri v. Jenkins, 515 U.S. 70, 115 S. Ct. 2038, 132 L.Ed.2d 63 (1995).

U.S. v. Fordice, 505 U.S. 717, 112 S.Ct. 2727, 120 L.Ed.2d 575 (1992).

Freeman v. Pitts, 503 U.S. 467, 112 S.Ct. 1430, 118 L.Ed.2d 108 (1992).

Board of Educ. of Oklahoma City Public Schools v. Dowell, 498 U.S. 237, 111 S.Ct. 630, 112 L.Ed.2d 715 (1991).

Missouri v. Jenkins, 495 U.S. 33, 110 S.Ct. 1651, 109 L.Ed.2d 31 (1990).

Crawford v. Board of Educ., 458 U.S. 527, 102 S.Ct. 3211, 73 L.Ed.2d 948 (1982).

Washington v. Seattle School Dist. No. 1, 458 U.S. 457, 102 S.Ct. 3187, 73 L.Ed.2d 896 (1982).

Board of Educ. v. Superior Court, 448 U.S. 1343, 101 S.Ct. 21, 65 L.Ed.2d 1166 (1980).

Columbus Board of Educ. v. Penick, 443 U.S. 449, 99 S.Ct. 2941, 61 L.Ed.2d 666 (1979).

Bustop v. Board of Educ., 439 U.S. 1380, 99 S.Ct. 40, 58 L.Ed.2d 88 (1978).

Vetterli v. U.S. Dist. Court, 435 U.S. 1304, 98 S.Ct. 1219, 55 L.Ed.2d 751 (1978).

Dayton Board of Educ. v. Brinkman, 433 U.S. 406, 97 S.Ct. 2766, 53 L.Ed.2d 851 (1977).

Milliken v. Bradley, 433 U.S. 267, 97 S.Ct. 2749, 53 L.Ed.2d 745 (1977).

Pasadena City Board of Educ. v. Spangler, 427 U.S. 424, 96 S.Ct. 2697, 49 L.Ed.2d 599 (1976).

Milliken v. Bradley, 418 U.S. 717, 94 S.Ct. 311, 41 L.Ed.2d 1069 (1974).

Bradley v. School Board of City of Richmond, 416 U.S. 696, 94 S.Ct. 2006, 40 L.Ed.2d 476 (1974).

Keyes v. School Dist. No. 1, 413 U.S. 189, 93 S.Ct. 2686, 37 L.Ed.2d 548 (1973).

Drummond v. Acree, 409 U.S. 1228, 93 S.Ct. 18, 34 L.Ed.2d 33 (1972).

U.S. v. Scotland Neck City Board of Educ., 407 U.S. 484, 92 S.Ct. 2214, 33 L.Ed.2d 75 (1972).

Wright v. Council of City of Emporia, 407 U.S. 451, 92 S.Ct. 2196, 33 L.Ed.2d 51 (1972).

Winston-Salem/Forsyth County Board of Educ. v. Scott, 404 U.S. 1221, 92 S.Ct. 1236, 31 L.Ed.2d 441 (1971).

Dandridge v. Jefferson Parish School Board, 404 U.S. 1219, 92 S.Ct. 18, 30 L.Ed.2d 23 (1971).

Guey Heung Lee v. Johnson, 404 U.S. 1215, 92 S.Ct. 14, 30 L.Ed.2d 19 (1971).

North Carolina State Board of Educ. v. Swann, 402 U.S. 43, 91 S.Ct. 1284, 28 L.Ed.2d 586 (1971).

McDaniel v. Barresi, 402 U.S. 39, 91 S.Ct. 1287, 28 L.Ed.2d 582 (1971).

Davis v. Board of School Commissioners, 402 U.S. 33, 91 S.Ct. 1289, 28 L.Ed.2d 577 (1971).

Swann v. Charlotte-Mecklenburg Board of Educ., 402 U.S. 1, 91 S.Ct. 1267, 28 L.Ed.2d 554 (1971).

Northcross v. Board of Educ., 397 U.S. 232, 90 S.Ct. 891, 25 L.Ed.2d 246 (1970).

Dowell v. Board of Educ., 396 U.S. 269, 90 S.Ct. 415, 24 L.Ed.2d 414 (1969).

Carter v. West Feliciena Parish School Board, 396 U.S. 290, 90 S.Ct. 608, 24 L.Ed.2d 477 (1970).

Alexander v. Holmes County Board of Educ., 396 U.S. 19, 90 S.Ct. 29, 24 L.Ed.2d 19 (1969).

U.S. v. Montgomery County Board of Educ., 395 U.S. 225, 89 S.Ct. 1670, 23 L.Ed.2d 263 (1969).

Monroe v. Board of Commissioners, 391 U.S. 450, 88 S.Ct. 1700, 20 L.Ed.2d 733 (1968).

Raney v. Board of Educ., 391 U.S. 443, 88 S.Ct. 1697, 20 L.Ed.2d 727 (1968).

Green v. New Kent County School Board, 391 U.S. 430, 88 S.Ct. 1689, 20 L.Ed.2d 716 (1968).

Rogers v. Paul, 382 U.S. 198, 86 S.Ct. 358, 15 L.Ed.2d 265 (1965).

Bradley v. School Board, 382 U.S. 103, 86 S.Ct. 224, 15 L.Ed.2d 187 (1965).

Griffin v. County School Board, 377 U.S. 218, 84 S.Ct. 1226, 12 L.Ed.2d 256 (1964).

Goss v. Board of Educ., 373 U.S. 683, 83 S.Ct. 1405, 10 L.Ed.2d 632 (1963).

U.S. v. State of Louisiana, 364 U.S. 500, 81 S.Ct. 260, 5 L.Ed.2d 245 (1960).

Cooper v. Aaron, 358 U.S. 1, 78 S.Ct. 1401, 3 L.Ed.2d 5 (1958).

Brown v. Board of Educ. (II), 349 U.S. 294, 75 S.Ct. 753, 99 L.Ed. 1083 (1955).

Bolling v. Sharpe, 347 U.S. 497, 74 S.Ct. 693, 98 L.Ed. 884 (1954).

Brown v. Board of Educ. (I), 347 U.S. 483, 74 S.Ct. 686, 98 L.Ed. 873 (1954).

Disabled Students

Winkleman v. Parma City School Dist., No. 05-983, 2007 WL 1461151 (U.S. 2007).

Arlington Cent. School Dist. Board of Educ. v. Murphy, 126 S.Ct. 2455, 165 L.Ed.2d 526 (U.S. 2006).

Schaffer v. Weast, 126 S.Ct. 528 (U.S. 2005).

Cedar Rapids Community School Dist. v. Garret F. by Charlene F., 526 U.S. 66, 119 S.Ct. 992, 143 L.Ed.2d 154 (1999).

Lane v. Pena, 518 U.S. 187, 116 S.Ct. 2092, 135 L.Ed.2d 486 (1996).

Florence County School Dist. v. Carter, 510 U.S. 7, 114 S.Ct. 361, 126 L.Ed.2d 284 (1993).

Zobrest v. Catalina Foothills School Dist., 509 U.S. 1, 113 S.Ct. 2462, 125 L.Ed.2d 1 (1993).

Dellmuth v. Muth, 491 U.S. 223, 109 S.Ct. 2397, 105 L.Ed.2d 181 (1989).

Honig v. Doe, 484 U.S. 305, 108 S.Ct. 592, 98 L.Ed.2d 686 (1988).

Honig v. Students of California School for the Blind, 471 U.S. 148, 105 S.Ct. 1820, 85 L.Ed.2d 114 (1985).

Burlington School Committee v. Dep't of Educ., 471 U.S. 359, 105 S.Ct. 1996, 85 L.Ed.2d 385 (1985).

Smith v. Robinson, 468 U.S. 992, 104 S.Ct. 3457, 82 L.Ed.2d 746 (1984).

Irving Independent School Dist. v. Tatro, 468 U.S. 883, 104 S.Ct. 3371, 82 L.Ed.2d 664 (1984).

Board of Educ. v. Rowley, 458 U.S. 176, 102 S.Ct. 3034, 73 L.Ed.2d 690 (1982).

Univ. of Texas v. Camenisch, 451 U.S. 390, 101 S.Ct. 1830, 68 L.Ed.2d 175 (1981).

Southeastern Community College v. Davis, 442 U.S. 397, 99 S.Ct. 2361, 60 L.Ed.2d 980 (1979).

Discrimination Generally

Smith v. City of Jackson, 544 U.S. 228, 125 S.Ct. 1536, 161 L.Ed.2d 410 (2005).

Lapides v. Board of Regents of Univ. System of Georgia, 535 U.S. 613, 122 S.Ct. 1640, 152 L.Ed.2d 806 (2002).

Toyota Motor Manufacturing, Ky., Inc. v. Williams, 534 U.S. 184, 122 S.Ct. 681, 151 L.Ed.2d 615 (2002).

Reeves v. Sanderson Plumbing Products, 530 U.S. 133, 120 S.Ct. 2097, 147 L.Ed.2d 15 (2000).

Kimel v. Florida Board of Regents, 528 U.S. 62, 120 S.Ct. 631, 145 L.Ed.2d 522 (2000).

Murphy v. United Parcel Service, Inc., 527 U.S. 516, 119 S.Ct. 2133, 144 L.Ed.2d 484 (1999).

Sutton v. United Airlines, Inc., 527 U.S. 471, 119 S.Ct. 2139, 144 L.Ed.2d 450 (1999).

Bragdon v. Abbott, 524 U.S. 624, 118 S.Ct. 2196, 141 L.Ed.2d 540 (1998).

U.S. v. Virginia, 518 U.S. 515, 116 S.Ct. 2264, 135 L.Ed.2d 735 (1996).

Jett v. Dallas Independent School Dist., 491 U.S. 701, 109 S.Ct. 2702, 105 L.Ed.2d 598 (1989).

Carnegie-Mellon Univ. v. Cohill, 484 U.S. 343, 108 S.Ct. 614, 98 L.Ed.2d 720 (1988).

School Board of Nassau County v. Arline, 480 U.S. 273, 107 S.Ct. 1123, 94 L.Ed.2d 307 (1987).

Hazelwood School Dist. v. U.S., 433 U.S. 299, 97 S.Ct. 2736, 53 L.Ed.2d 768 (1977).

DeFunis v. Odegaard, 416 U.S. 312, 94 S.Ct. 1704, 40 L.Ed.2d 164 (1974).

Monell v. Dep't of Social Services, 436 U.S. 658, 98 S.Ct. 2018, 56 L.Ed.2d 611 (1978).

Due Process

Gilbert v. Homar, 520 U.S. 924, 117 S.Ct. 1807, 138 L.Ed.2d 120 (1997).

Univ. of Tennessee v. Elliot, 478 U.S. 788, 106 S.Ct. 3220, 92 L.Ed.2d 635 (1986).

Memphis Community School Dist. v. Stachura, 477 U.S. 299, 106 S.Ct. 2537, 91 L.Ed.2d 249 (1986).

Cleveland Board of Educ. v. Loudermill, 470 U.S. 532, 105 S.Ct. 1487, 84 L.Ed.2d 494 (1985).

Perry v. Sindermann, 408 U.S. 593, 92 S.Ct. 2694, 33 L.Ed.2d 570 (1972).

Board of Regents v. Roth, 408 U.S. 564, 92 S.Ct. 2701, 33 L.Ed.2d 548 (1972).

Elections

Reno v. Bossier Parish School Board, 528 U.S. 320, 120 S.Ct. 866, 145 L.Ed.2d 845 (2000).

Texas v. U.S., 523 U.S. 296, 118 S.Ct. 1257, 140 L.Ed.2d 406 (1998).

Reno v. Bossier Parish School Board, 520 U.S. 471, 117 S.Ct. 1491, 137 L.Ed.2d 730 (1997).

Dougherty County Board of Educ. v. White, 439 U.S. 32, 99 S.Ct. 368, 58 L.Ed.2d 269 (1978).

Mayor of Philadelphia v. Educ. Equality League, 415 U.S. 605, 94 S.Ct. 1323, 39 L.Ed.2d 630 (1974).

Kramer v. Union Free School Dist. No. 15, 395 U.S. 621, 89 S.Ct. 1886, 23 L.Ed.2d 583 (1969).

Sailors v. Board of Educ., 387 U.S. 105, 87 S.Ct. 1549, 18 L.Ed.2d 650 (1967).

Federal Aid

Lockhart v. U.S., 126 S.Ct. 699 (U.S. 2005).

Traynor v. Turnage, 485 U.S. 535, 108 S.Ct. 1372, 99 L.Ed.2d 618 (1988).

Selective Service System v. MPIRG, 468 U.S. 841, 104 S.Ct. 3348, 82 L.Ed.2d 632 (1984).

Bell v. New Jersey and Pennsylvania, 461 U.S. 773, 103 S.Ct. 2187, 76 L.Ed.2d 312 (1984).

Valley Forge Christian College v. Americans United for Separation of Church and State, 454 U.S. 464, 102 S.Ct. 752, 70 L.Ed.2d 700 (1982).

Board of Educ. v. Harris, 444 U.S. 130, 100 S.Ct. 363, 62 L.Ed.2d 275 (1979).

Wheeler v. Barrera, 417 U.S. 402, 94 S.Ct. 2274, 41 L.Ed.2d 159 (1974).

Tilton v. Richardson, 403 U.S. 672, 91 S.Ct. 2091, 29 L.Ed.2d 790 (1971).

Financing

Hibbs v. Winn, 542 U.S. 88, 124 S.Ct. 2276, 159 L.Ed.2d 172 (2004).

Locke v. Davey, 540 U.S. 807, 124 S.Ct. 1307, 158 L.Ed.2d 1 (2004).

Camps Newfound/Owatonna, Inc. v. Town of Harrison, Me., 520 U.S. 564, 117 S.Ct. 1590, 137 L.Ed.2d 852 (1997).

Papasan v. Allain, 478 U.S. 265, 106 S.Ct. 2932, 92 L.Ed.2d 209 (1986).

Bennett v. New Jersey, 470 U.S. 632, 105 S.Ct. 1555, 84 L.Ed.2d 572 (1985).

Bennett v. Kentucky Dep't of Educ., 470 U.S. 656, 105 S.Ct. 1544, 84 L.Ed.2d 590 (1985).

Lawrence County v. Lead-Deadwood School Dist. No. 40-1, 469 U.S. 256, 105 S.Ct. 695, 83 L.Ed.2d 635 (1985).

Grove City College v. Bell, 465 U.S. 555, 104 S.Ct. 1211, 79 L.Ed.2d 516 (1984).

San Antonio v. Rodriguez, 411 U.S. 1, 93 S.Ct. 1278, 36 L.Ed.2d 16 (1973).

Freedom of Religion (see also Religious Activities)

Edwards v. Aguillard, 482 U.S. 578, 107 S.Ct. 2573, 96 L.Ed.2d 510 (1987).

Ansonia Board of Educ. v. Philbrook, 499 U.S. 60, 107 S.Ct. 367, 93 L.Ed.2d 305 (1986).

Freedom of Speech

Garcetti v. Ceballos, 126 S.Ct. 1951, 164 L.Ed.2d 689 (U.S. 2006).

Rumsfeld v. Forum for Academic and Institutional Rights, 547 U.S. 47 (2006).

Board of Regents of Univ. of Wisconsin System v. Southworth, 529 U.S. 217, 120 S.Ct. 1346, 146 L.Ed.2d 193 (2000).

Rosenberger v. Univ. of Virginia, 515 U.S. 819, 115 S.Ct. 2510, 132 L.Ed.2d 700 (1995).

Board of Educ. of Westside Community School v. Mergens, 496 U.S. 226, 110 S.Ct. 2356, 110 L.Ed.2d 191 (1990).

Board of Trustees of the State Univ. of New York v. Fox, 492 U.S. 469, 109 S.Ct. 3028, 106 L.Ed.2d 388 (1989).

Hazelwood School Dist. v. Kuhlmeier, 484 U.S. 261, 108 S.Ct. 562, 98 L.Ed.2d 592 (1988).

Bethel School Dist. v. Fraser, 478 U.S. 675, 106 S.Ct. 3159, 92 L.Ed.2d 549 (1986).

Board of Educ. v. Pico, 457 U.S. 853, 102 S.Ct. 2799, 73 L.Ed.2d 435 (1982).

Givhan v. Western Line Consolidated School Dist., 439 U.S. 410, 99 S.Ct. 693, 58 L.Ed.2d 619 (1979).

Mt. Healthy City School v. Doyle, 429 U.S. 274, 97 S.Ct. 568, 50 L.Ed.2d 471 (1977).

Papish v. Board of Curators, 410 U.S. 667, 93 S.Ct. 1197, 35 L.Ed.2d 618 (1973).

Grayned v. City of Rockford, 408 U.S. 104, 92 S.Ct. 2294, 33 L.Ed.2d 222 (1972).

Police Dep't v. Mosley, 408 U.S. 92, 92 S.Ct. 2286, 33 L.Ed.2d 212 (1972).

Tinker v. Des Moines, 393 U.S. 503, 89 S.Ct. 733, 21 L.Ed.2d 733 (1969).

Pickering v. Board of Educ., 391 U.S. 563, 88 S.Ct. 1731, 20 L.Ed.2d 811 (1968).

Keyishian v. Board of Regents, 385 U.S. 589, 87 S.Ct. 675, 17 L.Ed.2d 629 (1967).

Adler v. Board of Educ., 342 U.S. 485, 72 S.Ct. 380, 96 L.Ed. 517 (1952).

Labor Relations

Christensen v. Harris County, 529 U.S. 576, 120 S.Ct. 1655, 146 L.Ed.2d 621 (2000).

Central State Univ. v. American Ass'n of Univ. Professors, Cent. State Univ. Chapter, 526 U.S. 124, 119 S.Ct. 1162, 143 L.Ed.2d 227 (1999).

Lehnert v. Ferris Faculty Ass'n, 500 U.S. 507, 111 S.Ct. 1950, 114 L.Ed.2d 572 (1991).

Fort Stewart Schools v. Federal Labor Relations Authority, 495 U.S. 641, 110 S.Ct. 2043, 109 L.Ed.2d 659 (1990).

Minnesota State Board for Community Colleges v. Knight, 465 U.S. 271, 104 S.Ct. 1058, 79 L.Ed.2d 299 (1984).

NLRB v. Yeshiva Univ., 444 U.S. 672, 100 S.Ct. 856, 63 L.Ed.2d 115 (1980).

NLRB v. Catholic Bishop of Chicago, 440 U.S. 490, 99 S.Ct. 1313, 59 L.Ed.2d 533 (1979).

Abood v. Detroit Board of Educ., 431 U.S. 209, 97 S.Ct. 1782, 52 L.Ed.2d 261 (1977).

Loyalty Oaths

Connell v. Higgenbotham, 403 U.S. 207, 91 S.Ct. 1772, 29 L.Ed.2d 418 (1971).

Whitehill v. Elkins, 389 U.S. 54, 88 S.Ct. 184, 19 L.Ed.2d 228 (1967).

Elfbrandt v. Russell, 384 U.S. 11, 86 S.Ct. 1238, 16 L.Ed.2d 321 (1966).

Baggett v. Bullitt, 377 U.S. 360, 84 S.Ct. 1316, 12 L.Ed.2d 377 (1964).

Cramp v. Board of Educ., 368 U.S. 278, 82 S.Ct. 275, 7 L.Ed.2d 285 (1961).

Slochower v. Board of Higher Educ., 350 U.S. 551, 76 S.Ct. 637, 100 L.Ed. 692 (1956).

Maternity Leave

Richmond Unified School Dist. v. Berg, 434 U.S. 158, 98 S.Ct. 623, 54 L.Ed.2d 375 (1977).

Cleveland Board of Educ. v. La Fleur, 414 U.S. 632, 94 S.Ct. 791, 39 L.Ed.2d 52 (1974).

Cohen v. Chesterfield, 414 U.S. 632, 94 S.Ct. 791, 39 L.Ed.2d 52 (1974).

Private Schools

Zelman v. Simmons-Harris, 536 U.S. 639, 122 S.Ct. 2460, 153 L.Ed.2d 604 (2002).

Brentwood Academy v. Tennessee Secondary School Athletic Ass'n, 531 U.S. 288, 121 S.Ct. 924, 148 L.Ed.2d 807 (2001).

Mitchell v. Helms, 530 U.S. 793, 120 S.Ct. 2530, 147 L.Ed.2d 660 (2000).

Bates v. U.S., 522 U.S. 23, 118 S.Ct. 285, 139 L.Ed.2d 215 (1997).

Agostini v. Felton, 521 U.S. 203, 117 S.Ct. 1997, 138 L.Ed.2d 391 (1997).

Farrar v. Hobby, 506 U.S. 103, 113 S.Ct. 566, 121 L.Ed.2d 494 (1992).

Corporation of the Presiding Bishop of the Church of Jesus Christ of Latter-Day Saints v. Amos, 483 U.S. 327, 107 S.Ct. 2862, 97 L.Ed.2d 273 (1987).

St. Francis College v. Al-Khazraji, 481 U.S. 604, 107 S.Ct. 2022, 97 L.Ed.2d 749 (1987).

Witters v. Washington Dep't of Services for the Blind, 474 U.S. 481, 106 S.Ct. 748, 88 L.Ed.2d 846 (1986).

Aguilar v. Felton, 473 U.S. 402, 105 S.Ct. 3232, 87 L.Ed.2d 290 (1985).

Grand Rapids School Dist. v. Ball, 473 U.S. 373, 105 S.Ct. 3216, 87 L.Ed.2d 267 (1985).

Grove City College v. Bell, 465 U.S. 555, 104 S.Ct. 1211, 79 L.Ed.2d 516 (1984).

Mueller v. Allen, 463 U.S. 388, 103 S.Ct. 3062, 77 L.Ed.2d 721 (1983).

Bob Jones Univ. v. United States, 461 U.S. 574, 103 S. Ct. 2017, 76 L.Ed.2d 157 (1983).

Valley Forge Christian College v. Americans United for Separation of Church and State, 454 U.S. 464, 102 S.Ct. 752, 70 L.Ed.2d 700 (1982).

St. Martin Evangelical Lutheran Church v. South Dakota, 451 U.S. 772, 101 S.Ct. 2142, 68 L.Ed.2d 612 (1981).

Committee v. Regan, 444 U.S. 646, 100 S.Ct. 840, 63 L.Ed.2d 94 (1980).

NLRB v. Catholic Bishop of Chicago, 440 U.S. 490, 99 S.Ct. 1313, 59 L.Ed.2d 533 (1979).

New York v. Cathedral Academy, 434 U.S. 125, 98 S.Ct. 340, 54 L.Ed.2d 346 (1977).

Wolman v. Walter, 433 U.S. 229, 97 S.Ct. 2593, 53 L.Ed.2d 714 (1977).

Runyon v. McCrary, 427 U.S. 160, 96 S.Ct. 2586, 49 L.Ed.2d 415 (1976).

Roemer v. Board of Public Works, 426 U.S. 736, 96 S.Ct. 2337, 49 L.Ed.2d 179 (1976).

Meek v. Pittenger, 421 U.S. 349, 95 S.Ct. 1753, 44 L.Ed.2d 217 (1975).

Wheeler v. Barrera, 417 U.S. 402, 94 S.Ct. 2274, 41 L.Ed.2d 159 (1974).

Sloan v. Lemon, 413 U.S. 825, 93 S.Ct. 2982, 37 L.Ed.2d 939 (1973).

Committee for Public Educ. and Religious Liberty v. Nyquist, 413 U.S. 756, 93 S.Ct. 2955, 37 L.Ed.2d 948 (1973).

Hunt v. McNair, 413 U.S. 734, 93 S.Ct. 2868, 37 L.Ed.2d 923 (1973).

Levitt v. Committee for Public Educ. and Religious Liberty, 413 U.S. 472, 93 S.Ct. 2814, 37 L.Ed.2d 736 (1973).

Early v. Di Censo, 403 U.S. 602, 91 S.Ct. 2105, 29 L.Ed.2d 745 (1971).

Lemon v. Kurtzman, 403 U.S. 602, 91 S.Ct. 2105, 29 L.Ed.2d 745 (1971).

Board of Educ. v. Allen, 392 U.S. 236, 88 S.Ct. 1923, 20 L.Ed.2d 1060 (1968).

Flast v. Cohen, 392 U.S. 83, 88 S.Ct. 1942, 20 L.Ed.2d 947 (1968).

Zorach v. Clauson, 343 U.S. 306, 72 S.Ct. 679, 96 L.Ed. 954 (1952).

McCollum v. Board of Educ., 333 U.S. 203, 68 S.Ct. 461, 92 L.Ed. 649 (1948).

Everson v. Board of Educ., 330 U.S. 1, 67 S.Ct. 504, 91 L.Ed. 711 (1947).

Farrington v. Tokushige, 273 U.S. 284, 47 S.Ct. 406, 71 L.Ed. 646 (1927).

Racial Discrimination

Gratz v. Bollinger, 539 U.S. 244, 123 S.Ct. 2411, 156 L.Ed.2d 257 (2003).

Grutter v. Bollinger, 539 U.S. 306, 123 S.Ct. 2325, 156 L.Ed.2d 304 (2003).

Texas v. Lesage, 528 U.S. 18, 120 S.Ct.467, 145 L.Ed.2d (1999).

St. Francis College v. Al-Khazraji, 481 U.S. 604, 107 S.Ct. 2022, 97 L.Ed.2d 749 (1987).

Wygant v. Jackson Board of Educ., 476 U.S. 267, 106 S.Ct. 1842, 90 L.Ed.2d 260 (1986).

Runyon v. McCrary, 427 U.S. 160, 96 S.Ct. 2586, 49 L.Ed.2d 415 (1976).

Lau v. Nichols, 414 U.S. 563, 94 S.Ct. 786, 39 L.Ed.2d 1 (1974).

Norwood v. Harrison, 413 U.S. 455, 93 S.Ct. 2804, 37 L.Ed.2d 723 (1973).

Religious Activities in Public Schools

Elk Grove Unified School Dist. v. Newdow, 542 U.S. 961, 124 S.Ct. 2301, 159 L.Ed.2d 851 (2004).

Santa Fe Independent School Dist. v. Doe, 530 U.S. 290, 120 S.Ct. 2266, 147 L.Ed.2d 295 (2000).

Board of Educ. of Kiryas Joel Village v. Grumet, 512 U.S. 687, 114 S.Ct. 2481, 129 L.Ed.2d 546 (1994).

Lamb's Chapel v. Center Moriches Union Free School Dist., 508 U.S. 384, 113 S.Ct. 2141, 124 L.Ed.2d 352 (1993).

Lee v. Weisman, 505 U.S. 577, 112 S.Ct. 2649, 120 L.Ed.2d 467 (1992).

Karcher v. May, 484 U.S. 72, 108 S.Ct. 388, 98 L.Ed.2d 327 (1987).

Bender v. Williamsport Area School Dist., 475 U.S. 534, 106 S.Ct. 1326, 89 L.Ed.2d 501 (1986).

Wallace v. Jaffree, 472 U.S. 38, 105 S.Ct. 2479, 96 L.Ed.2d 29 (1985).

Widmar v. Vincent, 454 U.S. 263, 102 S.Ct. 269, 70 L.Ed.2d 400 (1981).

Stone v. Graham, 449 U.S. 39, 101 S.Ct. 192, 66 L.Ed.2d 199 (1980).

Epperson v. Arkansas, 393 U.S. 97, 89 S.Ct. 266, 21 L.Ed.2d 228 (1968).

Chamberlin v. Dade County Board of Public Instruction, 377 U.S. 402, 84 S.Ct. 1272, 12 L.Ed.2d 407 (1964).

Abington School Dist. v. Schempp, 374 U.S. 203, 83 S.Ct. 1560, 10 L.Ed.2d 844 (1963).

Engel v. Vitale, 370 U.S. 421, 82 S.Ct. 1261, 8 L.Ed.2d 601 (1962).

McCollum v. Board of Educ., 333 U.S. 203, 68 S.Ct. 461, 92 L.Ed. 649 (1948).

West Virginia Board of Educ. v. Barnette, 319 U.S. 624, 63 S.Ct. 1178, 87 L.Ed. 1628 (1943).

Residency

Martinez v. Bynum, 461 U.S. 321, 103 S.Ct. 1838, 75 L.Ed.2d 879 (1983).

Elgins v. Moreno, 435 U.S. 647, 98 S.Ct. 1338, 55 L.Ed.2d 614 (1978).

School Liability

Chavez v. Martinez, 538 U.S. 760, 123 S.Ct. 1994, 155 L.Ed.2d 984 (U.S. 2003).

Owasso Independent School Dist. No. I-011 v. Falvo, 534 U.S. 426, 122 S.Ct. 934, 151 L.Ed.2d 896 (2002).

Clark County School Dist. v. Breeden, 532 U.S. 268, 121 S.Ct. 1508, 149 L.Ed.2d 509 (2001).

Gebser v. Lago Vista Independent School Dist., 524 U.S. 274, 118 S.Ct. 1989, 141 L.Ed.2d 277 (1998).

Regents of Univ. of California v. Doe, 519 U.S. 337, 117 S.Ct. 900, 137 L.Ed.2d 55 (1997).

Bradford Area School Dist. v. Stoneking, 489 U.S. 1062, 109 S.Ct. 1333, 103 L.Ed.2d 804 (1989).

Smith v. Sowers, 490 U.S. 1002, 109 S.Ct. 1634, 104 L.Ed.2d 150 (1989).

Deshaney v. Winnebago County DSS, 489 U.S. 189, 109 S.Ct. 998, 103 L.Ed.2d 249 (1989).

Sex Discrimination

Burlington Northern & Santa Fe Railway Co. v. White, 126 S.Ct. 2405 (U.S. 2006).

Michigan High School Athletic Ass'n v. Communities for Equity, 544 U.S. 1012, 161 L.Ed.2d 845 (2005).

Davis v. Monroe County Board of Educ., 526 U.S. 629, 119 S.Ct. 1661, 143 L.Ed.2d 839 (1999).

National Collegiate Athletic Ass'n v. Smith, 525 U.S. 84, 119 S.Ct. 924, 142 L.Ed.2d 929 (1999).

Burlington Industries, Inc. v. Ellerth, 524 U.S. 742, 118 S.Ct. 2257, 141 L.Ed.2d 633 (1998).

Faragher v. City of Boca Raton, 524 U.S. 775, 118 S.Ct. 2275, 141 L.Ed.2d 662 (1998).

Oncale v. Sundowner Offshore Offshore Services, Inc., 523 U.S. 75, 118 S.Ct. 998, 140 L.Ed.2d 201 (1998).

Franklin v. Gwinnett County Public Schools, 503 U.S. 60, 112 S.Ct. 1028, 117 L.Ed.2d 208 (1992).

Ohio Civil Rights Comm'n v. Dayton Christian Schools, 477 U.S. 619, 106 S.Ct. 2718, 91 L.Ed.2d 512 (1986).

Mississippi Univ. for Women v. Hogan, 458 U.S. 718, 102 S.Ct. 3331, 73 L.Ed.2d 1090 (1982).

Rendell-Baker v. Kohn, 457 U.S. 830, 102 S.Ct. 2764, 73 L.Ed.2d 418 (1982).

Cannon v. Univ. of Chicago, 441 U.S. 677, 99 S.Ct. 1946, 60 L.Ed.2d 560 (1979).

Board of Trustees v. Sweeney, 439 U.S. 24, 99 S.Ct. 295, 58 L.Ed.2d 216 (1978).

Striking Teachers

Hortonville Joint School Dist. v. Hortonville Educ. Ass'n, 426 U.S. 482, 96 S.Ct. 2308, 49 L.Ed.2d 1 (1976).

Student Searches

Board of Educ. of Independent School Dist. 92 of Pottawatomie County v. Earls, 536 U.S. 822, 122 S.Ct. 2559, 153 L.Ed.2d 735 (2002).

Vernonia School Dist. 47J v. Acton, 515 U.S. 646, 115 S. Ct. 2386, 132 L.Ed.2d 564 (1995).

New Jersey v. T.L.O., 469 U.S. 325, 105 S.Ct. 733, 83 L.Ed.2d 720 (1985).

Student Suspensions

Regents v. Ewing, 474 U.S. 214, 106 S.Ct. 507, 88 L.Ed.2d 523 (1985).

Board of Educ. v. McCluskey, 458 U.S. 966, 103 S.Ct. 3469, 73 L.Ed.2d 1273 (1982).

Carey v. Piphus, 435 U.S. 247, 98 S.Ct. 1042, 55 L.Ed.2d 252 (1978).

Board of Curators v. Horowitz, 435 U.S. 78, 98 S.Ct. 948, 55 L.Ed.2d 124 (1978).

Wood v. Strickland, 420 U.S. 308, 95 S.Ct. 992, 43 L.Ed.2d 214 (1975).

Goss v. Lopez, 419 U.S. 565, 95 S.Ct. 729, 42 L.Ed.2d 725 (1975).

Teacher Termination

Patsy v. Board of Regents, 457 U.S. 496, 102 S.Ct. 2557, 73 L.Ed.2d 172 (1982).

Chardon v. Fernandez, 454 U.S. 6, 102 S.Ct. 28, 70 L.Ed.2d 6 (1981).

Delaware State College v. Ricks, 449 U.S. 250, 101 S.Ct. 498, 66 L.Ed.2d 431 (1980).

Beilan v. Board of Public Educ., 357 U.S. 399, 78 S.Ct. 1317, 2 L.Ed.2d 1414 (1958).

Textbooks

Norwood v. Harrison, 413 U.S. 455, 93 S.Ct. 2804, 37 L.Ed.2d 723 (1973).

Board of Educ. v. Allen, 392 U.S. 236, 88 S.Ct. 1923, 20 L.Ed.2d 1060 (1968).

Cochran v. Louisiana State Board of Educ., 281 U.S. 370, 50 S.Ct. 335, 74 L.Ed.2d 1929 (1930).

Transportation Fees

Kadrmas v. Dickinson Public Schools, 487 U.S. 450, 108 S.Ct. 2481, 101 L.Ed.2d 399 (1988).

Use of School Facilities

Good News Club v. Milford Cent. School, 533 U.S. 98, 121 S.Ct. 2093, 150 L.Ed.2d 151 (2000).

Ellis v. Dixon, 349 U.S. 458, 75 S.Ct. 859, 99 L.Ed. 1231 (1955).

Weapons Control

U.S. v. Lopez, 514 U.S. 549, 115 S. Ct. 1624, 131 L.Ed.2d 626 (1995).

THE JUDICIAL SYSTEM

In order to allow you to determine the relative importance of a judicial decision, the cases included in *2008 Deskbook Encyclopedia of American School Law* identify the particular court from which a decision has been issued. For example, a case decided by a state supreme court generally will be of greater significance than a state circuit court case. Hence a basic knowledge of the structure of our judicial system is important to an understanding of school law.

Almost all the reports in this volume are taken from appellate court decisions. Although most education law decisions occur at trial court and administrative levels, appellate court decisions have the effect of binding lower courts and administrators so that appellate court decisions have the effect of law within their court systems.

State and federal court systems generally function independently of each other. Each court system applies its own law according to statutes and the determinations of its highest court. However, judges at all levels often consider opinions from other court systems to settle issues which are new or arise under unique fact situations. Similarly, lawyers look at the opinions of many courts to locate authority which supports their clients' cases.

Once a lawsuit is filed in a particular court system, that system retains the matter until its conclusion. Unsuccessful parties at the administrative or trial court level generally have the right to appeal unfavorable determinations of law to appellate courts within the system. When federal law issues or constitutional grounds are present, lawsuits may be appropriately filed in the federal court system. In those cases, the lawsuit is filed initially in the federal district court for that area.

On rare occasions, the U.S. Supreme Court considers appeals from the highest courts of the states if a distinct federal question exists and at least four justices agree on the question's importance. The federal courts occasionally send cases to state courts for application of state law. These situations are infrequent and, in general, the state and federal court systems should be considered separate from each other.

The most common system, used by nearly all states and also the federal judiciary, is as follows: a legal action is commenced in district court (sometimes called trial court, county court, common pleas court or superior court) where a decision is initially reached. The case may then be appealed to the court of appeals (or appellate court), and in turn this decision may be appealed to the supreme court.

Several states, however, do not have a court of appeals; lower court decisions are appealed directly to the state's supreme court. Additionally, some states have labeled their courts in a nonstandard fashion.

In Maryland, the highest state court is called the Court of Appeals. In the state of New York, the trial court is called the Supreme Court. Decisions of this court may be appealed to the Supreme Court, Appellate Division. The highest court in New York is the Court of Appeals. Pennsylvania has perhaps the most complex court system. The lowest state court is the Court of Common Pleas. Depending on the circumstances of the case, appeals may be taken to either the Commonwealth Court or the Superior Court. In certain instances the Commonwealth Court functions as a trial court as well as an appellate court. The Superior Court, however, is strictly an intermediate appellate court. The highest court in Pennsylvania is the Supreme Court.

While supreme court decisions are generally regarded as the last word in legal matters, it is important to remember that trial and appeals court decisions also create important legal precedents. For the hierarchy of typical state and federal court systems, please see the diagram below.

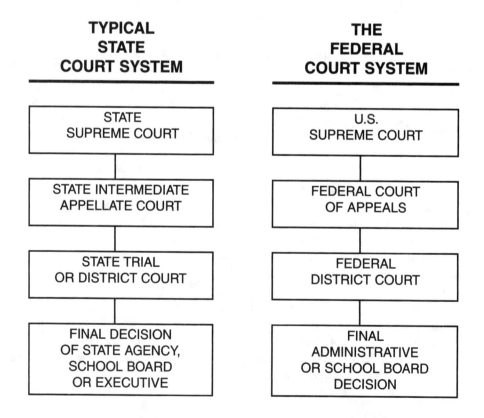

TYPICAL STATE COURT SYSTEM

STATE SUPREME COURT

STATE INTERMEDIATE APPELLATE COURT

STATE TRIAL OR DISTRICT COURT

FINAL DECISION OF STATE AGENCY, SCHOOL BOARD OR EXECUTIVE

THE FEDERAL COURT SYSTEM

U.S. SUPREME COURT

FEDERAL COURT OF APPEALS

FEDERAL DISTRICT COURT

FINAL ADMINISTRATIVE OR SCHOOL BOARD DECISION

Federal courts of appeals hear appeals from the district courts which are located in their circuits. Below is a list of states matched to the federal circuits in which they are located.

First Circuit	— Maine, Massachusetts, New Hampshire, Puerto Rico, Rhode Island
Second Circuit	— Connecticut, New York, Vermont
Third Circuit	— Delaware, New Jersey, Pennsylvania, Virgin Islands
Fourth Circuit	— Maryland, North Carolina, South Carolina, Virginia, West Virginia
Fifth Circuit	— Louisiana, Mississippi, Texas
Sixth Circuit	— Ohio, Kentucky, Michigan, Tennessee
Seventh Circuit	— Illinois, Indiana, Wisconsin
Eighth Circuit	— Arkansas, Iowa, Minnesota, Missouri, Nebraska, North Dakota, South Dakota
Ninth Circuit	— Alaska, Arizona, California, Guam, Hawaii, Idaho, Montana, Nevada, Northern Mariana Islands, Oregon, Washington
Tenth Circuit	— Colorado, Kansas, Oklahoma, New Mexico, Utah, Wyoming
Eleventh Circuit	— Alabama, Florida, Georgia
District of Columbia Circuit	— Hears cases from the U.S. District Court for the District of Columbia
Federal Circuit Appeals	— Sitting in Washington, D.C., the U.S. Court of Federal Circuit, hears patent and trade appeals and certain appeals on claims brought against the federal government and its agencies

HOW TO READ A CASE CITATION

Generally, court decisions can be located in case reporters at law school or governmental law libraries. Some cases can also be located on the Internet through legal Web sites or official court websites.

Each case summary contains the citation, or legal reference, to the full text of the case. The diagram below illustrates how to read a case citation.

case name (parties)　　case reporter name and series　　court location

Lee v. Pine Bluff School Dist.,　472　F.3d　1026　(8th Cir. 2007).

　　　　　　　　　volume number　　first page　year of decision

Some cases may have two or three reporter names such as U.S. Supreme Court cases and cases reported in regional case reporters as well as state case reporters. For example, a U.S. Supreme Court case usually contains three case reporter citations.

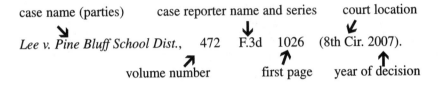

first reporter　　　　　　third reporter

Gratz v. Bollinger, 539 U.S. 244, 123 S.Ct. 2411, 156 L.Ed.2d 257 (2003).

second reporter

The citations are still read in the same manner as if only one citation has been listed.

Occasionally, a case may contain a citation which does not reference a case reporter. For example, a citation may contain a reference such as:

case name　　year of decision　first page　　year of decision

Saxon v. Chapman,　No. 266077,　2006　WL　1237036　(Mich. Ct. App. 2006).

　　court file number　　　　WESTLAW[1]　　　court location

The court file number indicates the specific number assigned to a case by the particular court system deciding the case. In our example, the Michigan Court of Appeals has assigned the case of *Saxon v. Chapman* the case number of

---

[1]WESTLAW® is a computerized database of court cases available for a fee.

"No. 266077" which will serve as the reference number for the case and any matter relating to the case. Locating a case on the Internet generally requires either the case name and date of the decision, and/or the court file number.

Below, we have listed the full names of the regional reporters. As mentioned previously, many states have individual state reporters. The names of those reporters may be obtained from a reference law librarian.

P.	**Pacific Reporter**	
	Alaska, Arizona, California, Colorado, Hawaii, Idaho, Kansas, Montana, Nevada, New Mexico, Oklahoma, Oregon, Utah, Washington, Wyoming	
A.	**Atlantic Reporter**	
	Connecticut, Delaware, District of Columbia, Maine, Maryland, New Hampshire, New Jersey, Pennsylvania, Rhode Island, Vermont	
N.E.	**Northeastern Reporter**	
	Illinois, Indiana, Massachusetts, New York, Ohio	
N.W.	**Northwestern Reporter**	
	Iowa, Michigan, Minnesota, Nebraska, North Dakota, South Dakota, Wisconsin	
So.	**Southern Reporter**	
	Alabama, Florida, Louisiana, Mississippi	
S.E.	**Southeastern Reporter**	
	Georgia, North Carolina, South Carolina, Virginia, West Virginia	
S.W.	**Southwestern Reporter**	
	Arkansas, Kentucky, Missouri, Tennessee, Texas	
F.	**Federal Reporter**	
	The thirteen federal judicial circuits courts of appeals decisions.	
F.Supp.	**Federal Supplement**	
	The thirteen federal judicial circuits district court decisions. *See, The Judicial System, p. 689* for specific state circuits.	
Fed.Appx.	**Federal Appendix**	
	Contains unpublished decisions of the U.S. Circuit Courts of Appeal.	
U.S.	**United States Reports**	
S.Ct.	**Supreme Court Reporter**	U.S. Supreme Court Decisions
L.Ed.	**Lawyers' Edition**	

GLOSSARY

Age Discrimination in Employment Act (ADEA) - The ADEA, 29 U.S.C. § 621 *et seq.*, is part of the Fair Labor Standards Act. It prohibits discrimination against persons who are at least 40 years old, and applies to employers that have 20 or more employees and that affect interstate commerce.

Americans with Disabilities Act (ADA) - The ADA, 42 U.S.C. § 12101 *et seq.*, went into effect on July 26, 1992. Among other things, it prohibits discrimination against a qualified individual with a disability because of that person's disability with respect to job application procedures, the hiring, advancement or discharge of employees, employee compensation, job training, and other terms, conditions and privileges of employment.

Bona fide - Latin term meaning "good faith." Generally used to note a party's lack of bad intent or fraudulent purpose.

Class Action Suit - Federal Rule of Civil Procedure 23 allows members of a class to sue as representatives on behalf of the whole class provided that the class is so large that joinder of all parties is impractical, there are questions of law or fact common to the class, the claims or defenses of the representatives are typical of the claims or defenses of the class, and the representative parties will adequately protect the interests of the class. In addition, there must be some danger of inconsistent verdicts or adjudications if the class action were prosecuted as separate actions. Most states also allow class actions under the same or similar circumstances.

Collateral Estoppel - Also known as issue preclusion. The idea that once an issue has been litigated, it may not be re-tried. Similar to the doctrine of *Res Judicata* (see below).

Due Process Clause - The clauses of the Fifth and Fourteenth Amendments to the Constitution which guarantee the citizens of the United States "due process of law" (see below). The Fifth Amendment's Due Process Clause applies to the federal government, and the Fourteenth Amendment's Due Process Clause applies to the states.

Due Process of Law - The idea of "fair play" in the government's application of law to its citizens, guaranteed by the Fifth and Fourteenth Amendments. Substantive due process is just plain *fairness*, and procedural due process is accorded when the government utilizes adequate procedural safeguards for the protection of an individual's liberty or property interests.

Education for All Handicapped Children Act (EAHCA) - [see Individuals with Disabilities Education Act (IDEA).]

Education of the Handicapped Act (EHA) - [see Individuals with Disabilities Education Act (IDEA).]

Employee Retirement Income Security Act (ERISA) - Federal legislation which sets uniform standards for employee pension benefit plans and employee welfare benefit plans. It is codified at 29 U.S.C. § 1001 *et seq.*

Enjoin - (see Injunction).

Equal Pay Act - Federal legislation which is part of the Fair Labor Standards Act. It applies to wage discrimination which is based on gender. For race discrimination, employees paid unequally must utilize Title VII or 42 U.S.C. § 1981. Unlike many labor statutes, there is no minimum number of employees necessary to invoke the act's protection.

Equal Protection Clause - The clause of the Fourteenth Amendment which prohibits a state from denying any person within its jurisdiction equal protection of its laws. Also, the Due Process Clause of the Fifth Amendment which pertains to the federal government. This has been interpreted by the Supreme Court to grant equal protection even though there is no explicit grant in the Constitution.

Establishment Clause - The clause of the First Amendment which prohibits Congress from making "any law respecting an establishment of religion." This clause has been interpreted as creating a "wall of separation" between church and state. The test frequently used to determine whether government action violates the Establishment Clause, referred to as the *Lemon* test, asks whether the action has a secular purpose, whether its primary effect promotes or inhibits religion, and whether it requires excessive entanglement between church and state.

Fair Labor Standards Act (FLSA) - Federal legislation which mandates the payment of minimum wages and overtime compensation to covered employees. The overtime provisions require employers to pay at least time-and-one-half to employees who work more than 40 hours per week.

Federal Tort Claims Act - Federal legislation which determines the circumstances under which the United States waives its sovereign immunity (see below) and agrees to be sued in court for money damages. The government retains its immunity in cases of intentional torts committed by its employees or agents, and where the tort is the result of a "discretionary function" of a federal employee or agency. Many states have similar acts.

42 U.S.C. §§ 1981, 1983 - Section 1983 of the federal Civil Rights Act prohibits any person acting under color of state law from depriving any other person of rights protected by the Constitution or by federal laws. A vast majority of lawsuits claiming constitutional violations are brought under § 1983. Section 1981 provides that all persons enjoy the same right to make and enforce contracts as "white citizens." Section 1981 applies to employment contracts. Further, unlike § 1983, § 1981 applies even to private actors. It is not limited to those acting under color of state law. These sections do not apply to the federal government, though the government may be sued directly under the Constitution for any violations.

Free Exercise Clause - The clause of the First Amendment which prohibits Congress from interfering with citizens' rights to the free exercise of their religion. Through the Fourteenth Amendment, it has also been made applicable to the states and their sub-entities. The Supreme Court has held that laws of general applicability which have an incidental effect on persons' free exercise rights are not violative of the Free Exercise Clause.

Handicapped Children's Protection Act (HPCA) - [see also Individuals with Disabilities Education Act (IDEA).] The HPCA, enacted as an amendment to the EHA, provides for the payment of attorneys' fees to a prevailing parent or guardian in a lawsuit brought under the EHA (and the IDEA).

Hearing Officer - Also known as an administrative law judge. The hearing officer decides disputes that arise *at the administrative level*, and has the power to administer oaths, take testimony, rule on evidentiary questions, and make determinations of fact.

Incorporation Doctrine - By its own terms, the Bill of Rights applies only to the federal government. The Incorporation Doctrine states that the Fourteenth Amendment makes the Bill of Rights applicable to the states.

Individualized Educational Program (IEP) - The IEP is designed to give children with disabilities a free, appropriate education. It is updated annually, with the participation of the child's parents or guardian.

Individuals with Disabilities Education Act (IDEA) - Also known as the Education of the Handicapped Act (EHA), the Education for All Handicapped Children Act (EAHCA), and the Handicapped Children's Protection Act (HPCA). Originally enacted as the EHA, the IDEA is the federal legislation which provides for the free, appropriate education of all children with disabilities.

Injunction - An equitable remedy (see Remedies) wherein a court orders a party to do or refrain from doing some particular action.

Jurisdiction - The power of a court to determine cases and controversies. The Supreme Court's jurisdiction extends to cases arising under the Constitution and under federal law. Federal courts have the power to hear cases where there is diversity of citizenship or where a federal question is involved.

Mainstreaming - Part of what is required for a free appropriate education is that each child with a disability be educated in the "least restrictive environment." To the extent that disabled children are educated with nondisabled children in regular education classes, those children are being mainstreamed.

National Labor Relations Act (NLRA) - Federal legislation which guarantees to employees the right to form and participate in labor organizations. It prohibits employers from interfering with employees in the exercise of their rights under the NLRA.

Negligence per se - Negligence on its face. Usually, the violation of an ordinance or statute will be treated as negligence per se because no careful person would have been guilty of it.

Occupational Safety and Health Act - Federal legislation which requires employers to provide a safe workplace. Employers have both general and specific duties under the act. The general duty is to provide a workplace which is free from recognized hazards that are likely to result in serious physical harm. The specific duty is to conform to the health and safety standards promulgated by the Secretary of Labor.

Overbroad - A government action is overbroad if, in an attempt to alleviate a specific evil, it impermissibly prohibits or chills a protected action. For example, attempting to deal with street litter by prohibiting the distribution of leaflets or handbills.

Placement - A special education student's placement must be appropriate (as well as responsive to the particular child's needs). Under the IDEA's "stay-put" provision, school officials may not remove a special education child from his or her "then current placement" over the parents' objections until the completion of administrative or judicial review proceedings.

Preemption Doctrine - Doctrine which states that when federal and state law attempt to regulate the same subject matter, federal law prevents the state law from operating. Based on the Supremacy Clause of Article VI, Clause 2, of the Constitution.

Prior Restraint - Restraining a publication before it is distributed. In general, constitutional law doctrine prohibits government from exercising prior restraint.

Rehabilitation Act - Section 504 of the Rehabilitation Act prohibits employers who receive federal financial assistance from discriminating against otherwise qualified individuals with handicaps solely becuase of their handicaps. An otherwise qualified individual is one who can perform the "essential functions" of the job with "reasonable accomodation."

Related Services - As part of the free, appropriate education due to children with disabilities, school districts may have to provide related services such as transportation, physical and occupational therapy, and medical services which are for diagnostic or evaluative purposes relating to education.

Remand - The act of an appellate court in returning a case to the court from which it came for further action.

Remedies - There are two general categories of remedies, or relief: legal remedies, which consist of money damages, and equitable remedies, which consist of a court mandate that a specific action be prohibited or required. For example, a claim for compensatory and punitive damages seeks a legal remedy; a claim for an injunction seeks an equitable remedy. Equitable remedies are generally unavailable unless legal remedies are inadequate to address the harm.

Res Judicata - The judicial notion that a claim or action may not be tried twice or re-litigated, or that all causes of action arising out of the same set of operative facts should be tried at one time. Also known as claim preclusion.

Section 1981 & Section 1983 - (see 42 U.S.C. §§ 1981, 1983).

Sovereign Immunity - The idea that the government cannot be sued without its consent. It stems from the English notion that the "King could do no wrong." This immunity from suit has been abrogated in most states and by the federal government through legislative acts known as "tort claims acts."

Standing - The judicial doctrine which states that in order to maintain a lawsuit a party must have some real interest at stake in the outcome of the trial.

Statute of Limitations - A statute of limitation provides the time period in which a specific cause of action may be brought.

Summary Judgment - Also referred to as pretrial judgment. Similar to a dismissal. Where there is no genuine issue as to any material fact and all that remains is a question of law, a judge can rule in favor of one party or the other. In general, summary judgment is used to dispose of claims which do not support a legally recognized claim.

Supremacy Clause - Clause in Article VI of the Constitution which states that federal legislation is the supreme law of the land. This clause is used to support the Preemption Doctrine (see above).

Title VII, Civil Rights Act of 1964 (Title VII) - Title VII prohibits discrimination in employment based upon race, color, sex, national origin, or religion. It applies to any employer having fifteen or more employees. Under Title VII, where an employer intentionally discriminates, employees may obtain money damages unless the claim is for race discrimination. For those claims, monetary relief is available under 42 U.S.C. § 1981.

U.S. Equal Employment Opportunity Commission (EEOC) - The EEOC is the government entity which is empowered to enforce Title VII (see above) through investigation and/or lawsuits. Private individuals alleging discrimination must pursue administrative remedies within the EEOC before they are allowed to file suit under Title VII.

Vacate - The act of annulling the judgment of a court either by an appellate court or by the court itself. The Supreme Court will generally vacate a lower court's judgment without deciding the case itself, and remand the case to the lower court for further consideration in light of some recent controlling decision.

Void-for-Vagueness Doctrine - A judicial doctrine based on the Fourteenth Amendment's Due Process Clause. In order for a law which regulates speech, or any criminal statute, to pass muster under the doctrine, the law must make clear what actions are prohibited or made criminal. Under the principles of the Due Process Clause, people of average intelligence should not have to guess at the meaning of a law.

Writ of Certiorari - The device used by the Supreme Court to transfer cases from the appellate court's docket to its own. Since the Supreme Court's appellate jurisdiction is largely discretionary, it need only issue such a writ when it desires to rule in the case.

INDEX

Abuse, mandatory reporting of, 275-278, 602-604
Academic freedom
      library materials, 134-136
      school productions, 137-138
      textbooks, 136-137
Academic practices
      bilingual education, 507-509
      charter schools, 496-505
      curriculum, 505-507
      educational malpractice, 531-532
      grading, 509-513
      reform legislation, 487-505
      testing, 526-531
Accidents, injuries and deaths generally, 1-54
Accreditation of private schools, 601-602
Admissions and attendance, 149-160
Affirmative action, 300-302
Age discrimination, 307-311
Agency fees, 404-407
Alcohol
      See Drugs and alcohol
Americans with Disabilities Act (ADA), 314-320, 584, 586, 587, 588,
      589-590, 618-619, 632
Arbitration and grievances, 419-428
Assault, 7-8, 37, 52, 670
Association, freedom of, 131-134
Assumption of risk and waiver, 12-13
      athletics injuries, 12-13
Athletics, 8-14
      discrimination, 647-658
      drug testing, 637-639
      eligibility rules and restrictions, 641-647
      extracurricular suspensions, 639-641
      gender equity, 647-651
      high school, 637-647
      injuries to participants, 8-13
      injuries to spectators, employees and parents, 13-14
      intercollegiate, 653-655
      students with disabilities, 655-658
      transfer students, 641-644

Bilingual education, 507-509
Bona fide occupational qualification, 280
Breach of contract and private schools, 612-615

Budget and finance
    educational finance and equal opportunity, 431-440
    federal funding, 442-443
    generally, 431-457
    insurance cases, 455-457
    private contractors, 452-455
    property taxes and other local funding issues, 440-442
    school expenditures and state appropriations, 443-448
    student fees and tuition, 448-452
Budgetary reductions and reductions in force, 325-328

Certification and licensure, 254-259
Charter schools, 496-505
    applications, 498-500
    legislation, 496-498
    operation, 500-505
Civil rights, students, 166-168
Coaches
    defamation, 662-665
    employment, 659-662
    liability, 665-668
    misconduct, 668-670
Collective bargaining agreements, 381-383, 407-419
Compensatory education, 582-584
Compensatory leave, 270-272
Compulsory attendance, 160-165
    attendance policies, 164-165
    home study programs, 162-164
    truancy, 160-162
Confederate flag, 108-111
Corporal punishment, 33, 165-172
Curriculum
    and religion in public schools, 60-64
    and speech rights, 141-143
    generally, 505-507

Defamation, 45-50
Desegregation
    budget issues, 466-468
    compliance with desegregation orders, 461-463
    inter-district remedies, 465-466
    liability issues, 463-468
    release from federal court supervision, 458-461
Disability discrimination, 311-322
Discrimination
    See Employment discrimination
Discrimination against veterans, 322-324

Dress codes
　　See also Speech, freedom of
　　students, 114-123
　　teachers, 130-131
Drug testing
　　employees, 240-241
　　students, 225-228, 637-639
Drugs and alcohol, 202-207, 215-219, 219-220, 221-222, 225-228, 232-234, 234-235, 237, 313-314, 637-639
Due process, employees
　　generally, 385-400
　　hearings, 393-400
　　notice, 390-393
　　property interest, 386-390
Due process, students, 187-200
　　alternative placements, 193-197
　　notice and procedural protections, 187-193
　　zero-tolerance policies, 197-200
Duty of care
　　athletics, 8-10
　　other supervised school activities, 21-23
　　physical education class injuries, 14-17
　　school bus accidents, 51-52
　　shop class injuries, 19-20
　　unsupervised accidents off school grounds, 26-28
　　unsupervised accidents on school grounds, 25-26

Educational malpractice, 531-532
Elementary and Secondary Education Act
　　See Title I
Employee examinations
　　generally, 243-244
Employee qualifications, 254-264
　　certification and licensure, 254-259
　　residency, anti-nepotism and patronage policies, 261-264
　　testing and reform legislation, 259-261
Employment discrimination
　　age discrimination, 307-311
　　disability discrimination, 311-322
　　discrimination against veterans, 322-324
　　private schools, 594-595
　　race and national origin discrimination, 294-302
　　religious discrimination, 302-307
　　sex discrimination, 280-293
Employment practices
　　employee qualifications, 254-264
　　employee search and seizure, 239-244
　　personnel records, 246-252

reassignments, transfers and suspensions, 272-275
reporting abuse and neglect, 275-278
voluntary employee leave, 264-272
Employment termination, resignation and retirement
budget reductions and reductions in force, 325-328
generally, 325-365
immorality and other misconduct, 328-338
incompetence, 341-346
insubordination and other good cause, 346-350
resignation and retirement, 350-358
unemployment benefits, 358-362
wrongful discharge, 362-365
Equal Access Act, 78-81
Expulsions and suspensions
academic, 213-215
due process, 187-200
generally, 187-212
misconduct, 200-213
private schools, 615-618

42 U.S.C. § 1981, 296, 297, 609-610, 653-654
42 U.S.C. § 1983, 3, 75-76, 81, 98, 101, 114, 123, 132, 167, 168, 183, 184,
186, 279, 293, 296, 322-323, 323-324, 492-493, 583-584, 586-587, 609,
611-612, 647-648, 652-653, 663, 669-670
Facilities, use of, 74-90
Fair Labor Standards Act, 307
Family and maternity leave, 264-270, 287
Family Educational Rights and Privacy Act (FERPA), 510-511, 517, 520,
522-523
Federal Labor Relations Authority, 411
Financial Assistance and Voucher Programs, 93-96
Freedom of Information Acts, 246-252

Gang affiliation and free speech, 122-123
Gender equity, 647-651
Governmental immunity
athletics, 10-12
employee misconduct, 32-34
other supervised school activities, 23-25
physical education class injuries, 17-19
school bus accidents, 52-54
shop class injuries, 20-21
student misconduct, 38-41
unsupervised accidents off school grounds, 28-29
unsupervised accidents on school grounds, 26
Grading, 509-513
Graduation ceremonies and religion, 65-67
Grievances and arbitration, 419-428

Hair length and appearance, 120-122
Hearing as due process requirement, 393-400
Home study programs, 162-164

Immorality and other misconduct
    criminal conduct, 333-336
    immoral conduct, 330-333
    misuse of technology, 338-341
    neglect of duty, 336-338
    sexual misconduct, 328-330
Immunization, 72-74
Incompetence, 341-345
    procedural problems, 344-345
    teaching deficiencies, 341-344
Individuals with Disabilities Education Act (IDEA)
    See also Students with disabilities
    generally, 534-545
    placement under, 550-567
    related services under, 567-572
Insubordination and other good cause, 346-350

Leaves of absence, 270-272
Library materials, 134-136

Misconduct
    cell phones and electronic devices, 212-213
    coaches, 668-670
    drugs, alcohol and weapons possession, 202-207
    employees, 29-34
    extracurricular and co-curricular events, 207-209
    fighting and violence, 209-212
    parents, 41-43
    sexual harassment, 200-202
    students, 34-41

National Labor Relations Act and private schools, 596-598
National origin discrimination, 297-300
Negligence, 2-8
    defenses, 3-8
    elements, 2-3
Nepotism, 475-476, 477
No Child Left Behind Act, 487-493
Non-school publications, 113-114
Notice as due process requirement, 390-393

Obscenity, 98-99
Open records, 246-252

Personal appearance
    See Speech, freedom of
Personnel records, 246-252
        disclosures to third parties, 250-252
        electronic communications, 253-254
        media access, 246-250
Police involvement: student searches, 228-237
        drug-sniffing dogs, 234-235
        liability, 235-237
        Miranda warnings, 229-232
        police-assisted searches, 232-234
Pregnancy discrimination, 285-287
Probationary employment
    See Tenure
Professional associations
        agency fees, 404-407
        collective bargaining agreements, 407-419
        grievances and arbitration, 419-428
        representation, 401-404
        strikes, 428-430
Property interest in employment, 386-390

Race and national origin discrimination, 172-176, 294-302
Rape
    See Sexual assault
Reductions in force, 376-380
Rehabilitation Act, 311-314, 539, 580, 584, 585-586, 632, 656-657
Reinstatement and recall of employees, 377-378
Related services, 567-572
Release time programs, 631-632
Religion
        commencement ceremonies, 65-67
        curriculum issues, 60-64
        employee religious activity, 90-93
        Equal Access Act, 78-81
        establishment of in public schools, 55-74
        financial assistance and voucher programs, 93-96
        limitations on employee religious activity, 90-93
        limitations on the free exercise of, 89-90
        literature and symbols in public schools, 85-90
        prayers and Bible readings, 56-60
        school policies and, 67-74
                immunizations, 72-74
                Pledge of Allegiance, 67-70
        student free exercise rights, 89-90
        student groups and, 75-78
        textbook, 64-65
        use of school facilities for, 74-90

Religious discrimination, 302-307
Religious establishment, 55-74
Residency requirements
    students, 154-160
    teachers, 261-264
Resignation, 350-353
Retirement, 353-355
Retirement benefits, 355-358

School boards
    appointments, elections, residency and recall, 472-474
    membership, 472-477
    nepotism, conflict of interest and misconduct, 475-477
    open meeting laws, 483-486
    powers and duties, 477-483
School bus accidents, 51-54
School closing and district dissolution issues, 469-470
School operations
    budget and finance, 431-455
    desegregation, 458-468
    generally, 431-486
    school boards, 472-486
School productions, 137-138
School reform legislation, 487-505
Search and seizure
    drug and alcohol testing, 225-228, 240-241
    drug searches, 215-225
    individualized suspicion, 215-225, 241-242
    locker searches, 222
    markers, 218-219
    off-campus searches, 220
    police involvement, 228-237
        drug-sniffing dogs, 234-235
        liability, 235-237
        Miranda warnings, 229-232
        police-assisted searches, 232-234
    strip searches, 222-225
Sex discrimination
    equal pay and gender, 287-290
    generally, 280-293
    pregnancy discrimination, 285-287
    sexual harassment, 290-292
    sexual orientation, 292-293
    students, 176-186
    Title VII, 280-285
Sexual assault, 31, 32, 201-202
Sexual harassment
    employment, 290-292

staff, 180-185
students, 176-180, 192
Sexual misconduct: employees, 328-330
Sick leave, 270-271, 272
Speech, freedom of
    academic freedom, 134-138
    curriculum, 141-143
    employee association rights, 131-134
    employee personal appearance and dress codes, 130-131
    employees, 123-134
    gang affiliation and, 122-123
    library materials, 134-136
    obscenity and, 98-99
    parents, 138-143
    protected employee speech, 124-130
    protected student speech, 98-111
            confederate flags, 108-111
            disciplinary cases, 98-101
            Internet cases, 106-108
            threats and bullying, 101-106
    school productions, 137-138
    student personal appearance and dress codes, 114-123
    student publications, 111-113
    students generally, 97-123
    textbooks, 136-137
    use of school facilities, 143-148
State Reform Acts, 493-496
Strikes, 272, 428-430
Student due process rights, 165-168
Student organizations and demonstrations, 143-146
Student records, 513-526
Student rights
    admissions and attendance, 149-160
    compulsory attendance, 160-165
    corporal punishment, 165-168
    due process rights, 165-168
    expulsions and suspensions, 187-212
    generally, 149-186
    searches and seizures, 215-237
    sex discrimination, 176-186
Students with disabilities
    change in placement, 545-546
    compensatory education, 582-584
    discipline, 545-550
    discrimination, 584, 585, 587-590
    generally, 534-590
    graduation, 579-582
    identification and evaluation of, 550-553

placement, 550-567
related services, 567-572
transition plans, 578-579
tuition reimbursement, 572-578
Suicide, 43-45, 312-313
Suspensions, students
    See Expulsions and suspensions
Suspensions, teachers, 274-275

Taxation and private schools, 604-608
Teacher liability protection, 168-172
Teachers
    resignation, 350-353
    retirement, 353-355
    speech rights, 124-130
    termination, 325-350
Tenure
    collective bargaining agreements, 381-383
    due process requirements, 385-400
    generally, 369-400
    reductions in force, 376-380
    state statutes, 369-385
    status, 369-376
Testing, 526-531, 590-592
Textbook selection, 64-65, 136-137
Title I, 442, 627-628
Title IX, 176-185, 562, 586, 647-651
Title VI, 364-365, 507-508, 609, 651, 653-655
Title VII, 280-285, 294-297, 593, 595, 609-610
Transfer, 274-275
Transportation fees, 448-449
Transportation to private schools, 625-627
Tuition and other fees, 449-452, 572-577

Unemployment benefits, 358-362
    eligibility requirements, 358-359
    misconduct, 360-362
Unions
    See Professional associations

Vacation leave, 271
Voting Rights Act, 474
Vouchers, 93-96

Weapons, 192-193, 196, 209, 219, 220-221, 222, 231-232
Workers' compensation, 366-368
Wrongful discharge, 362-366